PENGUIN BOOKS

BRITAIN'S BEST MUSEUMS AND GALLERIES

Ma
sin
Gal
Arc
(19

Mark Fisher

Britain's Best Museums and Galleries

PENGUIN BOOKS

PENGUIN BOOKS

Published by the Penguin Group
Penguin Books Ltd, 80 Strand, London WC2R 0RL, England
Penguin Group (USA) Inc., 375 Hudson Street, New York, New York 10014, USA
Penguin Group (Canada), 90 Eglinton Avenue East, Suite 700, Toronto, Ontario, Canada M4P 3YZ
(a division of Pearson Penguin Canada Inc.)
Penguin Ireland, 25 St Stephen's Green, Dublin 2, Ireland (a division of Penguin Books Ltd)
Penguin Group (Australia), 250 Camberwell Road,
Camberwell, Victoria 3124, Australia (a division of Pearson Australia Group Pty Ltd)
Penguin Books India Pvt Ltd, 11 Community Centre,
Panchsheel Park, New Delhi – 110 017, India
Penguin Group (NZ), cnr Airborne and Rosedale Roads, Albany,
Auckland 1310, New Zealand (a division of Pearson New Zealand Ltd)
Penguin Books (South Africa) (Pty) Ltd, 24 Sturdee Avenue,
Rosebank 2196, Johannesburg, South Africa

Penguin Books Ltd, Registered Offices: 80 Strand, London WC2R 0RL, England

www.penguin.com

First published by Allen Lane 2004
Published in Penguin Books 2005
1

FRONTISPIECE *Sir John Soane's Museum, London:
the Dome area with R. W. Sievier's bust of Sir Thomas Lawrence*

Typeset by Rowland Phototypesetting Ltd, Bury St Edmunds, Suffolk
Printed and bound by Hung Hing Off-set Printing Co., Ltd

To Candia

Contents

Charles Rennie Mackintosh furniture
at the Hunterian Art Gallery, Glasgow

Acknowledgements

This book would not have been attempted were it not for Andrew Rosenheim, who, when managing director of Penguin Press in 2001, commissioned me to write it and has continued to give practical encouragement and advice throughout the subsequent three and a half years. In those years I have incurred debts large and small, general and specific, to a host of people whose knowledge and love of museums have informed and shaped my own.

When I began the research for this book I received invaluable advice from the directors of the Area Museum Councils. I am particularly grateful to Sue Underwood (North-east), Ian Taylor (North-west), Chris Bailey (Northern Ireland), Sam Hunt (South-west), Kathy Gee (West Midlands) and Barbara Woroncow (Yorkshire) for their help.

Visiting the museums in this book, and many besides, I have met nothing but enthusiasm and help from directors, curators and attendants who have generously shared their knowledge of the collections in their care. I am particularly grateful to Frances Bailey, James A. Bennett, Tristram Besterman, Kevin Byrne, Richard Calvocoressi, Michael Clarke, Sir Timothy Clifford, Nicholas Dodd, Oliver Fairclough, David Fraser, Richard Green, Gareth Griffiths, Alun Gruffydd, Michael Harrison, Georgina Hobhouse, Brian Kennedy, Hélène La Rue, Sarah Levitt, Shan McAnena, James McGregor, Sarah McHugh, Brian Mackey, Andrew Moore, Michael O'Hanlon, Duncan Robinson, Julian Spalding, Liba Taub, Keith S. Thompson, Julian Treuherz, Clare van Loenen, Lisa White, Pamela Wood, Christopher Woodward and Pam Woolliscroft.

Among those working in national museums in London, Stephen Deucher, Mark Jones, Neil MacGregor, Charles Saumarez Smith, Rosalind Savill and Sir Nicholas Serota, and Sir Hugh Roberts at the Queen's Gallery, have been generous with their advice and comments. To Richard Verdi at the Barber Institute of Fine Arts I owe special thanks. His knowledge of regional collections, manifest in his work on the 1999 *Art Treasures of England* exhibition at the Royal Academy and the exhibition he curated at the Hayward Gallery in 2003 to celebrate the centenary of the National Art Collections Fund, *Saved!*, is wide and deep, and he has been a continual guide and inspiration.

I am indebted to the curators and directors of all the museums and galleries described here for their advice and for the way in which each has patiently read the draft entry pertaining to his or her own museum and corrected factual errors. It goes without saying that any errors that remain are my own.

Over the past six years I have learned a great deal from my colleagues on the Acceptance-in-Lieu Committee, in particular from David Barrie, Gerry McQuillan, Georgina Stonor, Lindsay Stainton, Lucy Wood and the committee's chairman Jonathan Scott, and from Alastair Laing, who has guided me through the National Trust collections for which he is responsible as curator of pictures and sculpture, despite my inability to include all the fifty-two National Trust collections that, in his view, could not and should not be excluded.

From my time on the Museums and Galleries Commission I learned much from James Joll, its then chairman, from Val Bott and from the late, and greatly missed, Richard Foster, Director of the National Museums and Galleries on Merseyside, 1986–2000. I am indebted too to Clive Aslet and Michael Hall, who commissioned a weekly column in *Country Life*, April 2002–October 2003, the research for which complemented work on this book. For his advice on collections of archaeology, and for bringing the museum at Kilmartin to my attention, I am grateful to Tim Schadla-Hall (of the Institute of Archaeology, University College London, and former director of museums for Leicestershire County Council).

Anyone attempting a book of this nature is conscious of an overall debt to the work of Nikolaus Pevsner and the many architectural historians who worked with him on *The Buildings of England*; to that of Francis Haskell; to Hugh Honour and John Fleming, particularly for their panoptic *Penguin Dictionary of Decorative Arts*; to that of Kenneth Hudson, to whose *Cambridge Guide* I pay tribute in the introduction; and for the contemporary criticism of David Sylvester, who was generous with his advice in the months before his death. I owe thanks, too, to the staff of the Bodleian and Sackler Libraries in Oxford upon whose fine arts and decorative arts collections I have relied.

In the process of turning a sprawling manuscript into a publishable book I am grateful to many at Penguin, in particular to the publishing director, Stuart Proffitt, who throughout has given me shrewd and invaluable advice; to my editor Helen Conford, for her enthusiasm and support; to Keith Taylor, who oversaw the copy-editing with such efficient despatch; to Anne Askwith, who copy-edited, with amazing good grace, a text that was still being amended and augmented as she worked; to Douglas Matthews, who compiled the two indexes; and to Richard Marston, who, in designing this book, has presented illustrations that admirably capture the beauty of these collections.

As I began this project Francesca Mitchell and India Fisher set about typing from my wearying zigzag handwriting, and I am much indebted to them. Without Crispin Hunt's unflagging energy, generosity and skill at deciphering, sometimes intuiting, what I had written, and his patience in organising its disparate parts, this book's transformation from my manuscript to typescript, and eventually to disc, would have been impossible. He has processed more than a million words, returning again and again to entries to amend them. At every turn he has offered invaluable Internet research and positive opinions. He undertook the additional tasks of picture research and coordination with persuasive skill. His curiosity and appetite have sustained me and, as I piled unreasonable quantities of work upon him, all to be completed to still-more-unreasonable deadlines, he never complained. Without him this book would have been completed a long time hence.

To Minoo Dinshaw, I offer my heartfelt gratitude. His weekends and holidays have been lived under the benign shadow of these museums and in visiting so many of those in this book he has contributed more than he knows, only once showing exhaustion (at the prospect of an eighth museum visit in the space of thirty hours). I only wish that my gratitude might have taken the tangible form of *The Nylghai* by George Stubbs (the Hunterian Art Gallery, Glasgow), to which lugubrious beast he formed a particular attachment.

To Minoo's mother, Candia McWilliam, I am more grateful than I can say. Since her early life was inhabited by her father, the late Colin McWilliam's, unsleeping work on *The Buildings of Scotland*, she knows the demands made on domestic, intellectual and emotional life by such volumes and it is chastening to reflect that, in her father's case, she knows the level of scholarship and artistry to which they may attain. For her resistance to alliteration, her proper pedantry and her patience, I offer her my thanks.

Introduction

When I was a small child in the late 1940s my father and I would walk at weekends to South Kensington to see the working models in the Science and Geological Museums and to wander in the cavernous galleries of the Victoria and Albert Museum. In my memory it is always winter, it is always cold, the pavements of the Old Brompton Road are always wet and gritty, it is always afternoon. In the V&A we would leave my favourite galleries, the Cast Courts, until last. Once there, we would have to pay our respects to the Michelangelos, the huge *David*[1] and the *Madonna and Child*,[2] and puzzle at the portico of Santiago Cathedral, which intrigued me by leading nowhere.[3] Only then could we turn to what was, for me, the real purpose of each visit: to gaze at the two mighty trunks of Trajan's Column with their frieze of soldiers that wound round and round, without beginning, without end.

Once home, my father would read to me from Macaulay's *The Lays of Ancient Rome* as we ate toast in front of the popping gas fire. On mine I would have dripping topped with a layer of black molasses, a combination that I had learned from my best friend at school who was what was then called Siamese. My father spread his with Gentleman's Relish.[4]

As he read, the solemn rhythms of Macaulay's phrases, 'Lars Porsena of Clusium' and 'the great house of Tarquin', would summon up the line of soldiers marching on and on up the column with their 'long array of helmets bright,/the long array of spears'. I did not know that the Dacian campaign and sieges carved on the column occurred centuries after Horatius hewed down the bridge and killed Astur, the great Lord of Luna, with so fierce a thrust that 'the good sword stood a handbreadth out/Behind the Tuscan's head'. For me Trajan's Column with its soldiers, and their breastplates and short swords, *was* Rome. I could hear the tramp of 'that great host, with measured tread' and the clash of 'gilded arms'. Column, poem and event became one.

I have loved museums ever since, turning to them to be educated, and to learn; to be provoked and amused; for solace and for stimulus. They have been both presiding preoccupation and occupation in my life. During the last twenty-five years I have been involved with local museums when I was a member of Staffordshire County Council;[5] I have visited museums all over the country as Shadow Minister for the Arts during ten long years in opposition; I have briefly been the minister, and I have, most happily, served on the Museums and Galleries Commission and on the Acceptance-in-Lieu Committee that advises the government whether objects offered in lieu of death duties should be accepted and, if so, to what museum or gallery they should be allocated. These experiences have served only to intensify my love for museums, and my deep belief in their importance.

This book is a celebration of Britain's museums but it is also precisely not an elegy. Three of the elements that make museums distinctive and valuable (the object; the past; scholarship itself) are in danger of being marginalised. I hope that this book will help to reassert their central importance.

Britain is well endowed, perhaps even over-endowed, with museums and galleries, having now more than 2,500 of them. With the exception of mid-Wales and the Highlands of Scotland, you are seldom more than twenty miles from a museum or gallery. Across these regional collections are strewn notable jewels and curiosities: a large Tintoretto in Gateshead;[6] treasures retrieved from the Spanish Armada galleass *Girona* in Belfast;[7] an Antony Gormley statue on top of a tree outside Wakefield;[8] a Salvador Dalí in Glasgow;[9] a piece of a meteorite 6,500 million years old in Manchester;[10] a tiny Anglo-Saxon sculpture of a man, sitting in thought, in Norwich, forming the lid of a funerary urn.[11] Of the thousands of surviving Anglo-Saxon urns and lids, this is the only one that shows a human being.

We have museums grand (Waddesdon Manor) and museums modest (Stromness); museums that contain millions of objects (the Natural History Museum) and one that comprises but a single object (the SS *Great Britain*); museums that are staffed by servants of the Queen (Windsor Castle) and by part-time volunteers (Tangmere Military Aviation Museum), that are in buildings ancient (the Tower of London, 11th century) and modern (Falmouth, 21st century), that have collections created by a connoisseur (Sir John Soane) or by an eccentric (Charles Paget Wade at Snowshill Manor); collections made by those who have great wealth (the Saatchi Gallery) and those who have none (the People's History Museum, Manchester). We have collections that contain the spoils of war (Apsley House) and the trophies of Empire (the Horniman, the V&A); collections that record innovations in agriculture (Acton Scott) and revolutions in industry (Ironbridge).

I have attempted to give a representative sample of the many different types of museum (agricultural, maritime, industrial, regimental) and of collections (carriages and clocks; boots and boats; newspapers and *netsuke*), spread geographically across the country, with the final choice being determined by my own, I hope transmitted, enjoyment.

I believe these 350 collections are the most interesting and enjoyable. Those I have chosen range from the splendours of the British Museum, encompassing the cultures of the world, to the charm of Flintham Museum, which encompasses the life of a single Nottinghamshire village shop. To do this I have visited museums from Orkney to Penzance, from the west coast of Fermanagh to the east coast of Suffolk. Together they form a portrait of Britain and its inhabitants. These collections provide the study for that portrait. Here is the evidence of what we value, what we have found and learned and made, what we consider beautiful or curious, what we love.

The choice of the first 200 was not difficult. For the final 150 it would have been possible to choose almost any of three or four hundred. Inevitably there are many delightful small museums that I regret not having been able to include. Nor have I been able to find space for more than a selection of the great collections in National Trust, and privately owned, properties open to the public. In the brief notes that introduce each region I have mentioned some of these museums and collections and their addresses are listed on pages 709–15.

Throughout I have followed the definition of a museum that ICOM[12] (the International Council of Museums) adopted in the early 1970s: an institution, open to the public, that 'conserves and displays, for purposes of study, education and enjoyment, collections of objects of cultural and scientific significance'.

Placing the emphasis on collections, rather than on buildings or ownership, has allowed the inclusion of a selection of the best collections in private houses (Chatsworth, Harewood, Wilton) and in National Trust or English Heritage properties, where paintings and sculptures, furniture, tapestries and ceramics may be seen in the domestic and architectural context for which they were made. It has also allowed the inclusion of collections of plants, in the botanic gardens at Kew and at Oxford, of sculpture parks, and of museums whose principal objects are in the landscape: Sutton Hoo, Avebury (the Alexander Keiller Museum) and Kilmartin House Museum, created in 1997 by David Clough and after the vision of Marion Campbell. There, cairns and barrows, forts and duns, crannogs and standing stones are scattered down Kilmartin Valley, bearing witness to the history and evolution of that landscape over the last 6,000 years.

Emboldened by how Kilmartin House envisages a new way forward for museums of pre-history and of the landscape, I have included one museum that does not exist. The islands of Colonsay and Oronsay off the west coast of Scotland are as rich in sites and artefacts, flora and fauna, history and association, as Kilmartin. From these dispersed sites and objects, and armed with an Ordnance Survey map, imaginative and energetic museum visitors have the opportunity to consider an entire island as a living museum.

I am not concerned with those aspects of museums that are liable to change: the quality of their cafés, their amenities and opening hours, their temporary exhibitions.[13] There are numerous excellent guides that provide that information. The Museums Association publishes a *Museums and Galleries Yearbook*, but the best, most reliable and most friendly, in my opinion, is the *Cambridge Guide to the Museums of Britain and Ireland* (1987) by that great man of museums, the late Kenneth Hudson, and Ann Nicholls. Their guide, with more than 2,000 entries, is comprehensive. Having a mere 350, this book can only attempt to be representative. Each *Cambridge Guide* entry of, typically, 100–150 words is factual and informative, with times of opening, facilities and the nearest means of public transport, compiled from a questionnaire sent to every museum in Britain. It also attempts to be objective: Hudson believed that 'it would be both impossible and unjust to try to indicate the quality of a museum.'[14] My book is discursive and opinionated, and necessarily subjective. This has allowed me to describe and discuss the collections at greater length.

I was fortunate to know Kenneth Hudson. No man knew or loved British, and European, museums better. In researching and writing this book I have referred often to his publications[15] and have engaged in a running interior dialogue with him, not least concerning his scepticism about ethnographical museums which, in his opinion, 'may collect widely, but ... do not dig deeply'.[16] In my view the British Museum, the Horniman Museum, the Pitt Rivers Museum and the Cambridge University Museum of Archaeology and Anthropology, at least, cast doubt on that judgement.

I have grouped my choices geographically, to give some impression of the way in which they reflect their surrounding geology and communities, but I was initially attracted to the idea of ranging them chronologically, starting with Hampton Court Palace and the Royal Collection (16th century), and the Ashmolean Museum (17th century), and ending with the National Maritime Museum at Falmouth (21st century): an order that would help describe the development of the museum in Britain.

The history of museums is the history of objects, of the people who loved and collected them and of the scholarship they established to understand and interpret the significance of those objects. Tracing that history tells us much about economic, political and social change: the rise of the merchant class and of democracy; the creation of markets in art and antiquities; the growth of universities; the emergence of such new academic disciplines as archaeology and anthropology. Who collects; what they collect; how, where and to whom collections are exhibited – all these change from generation to generation, reflecting event, knowledge, fashion, taste and politics.

Collecting is informed by a sensibility that is capable of attributing to an object value beyond its immediate use. In Britain before the 16th century, generally only the King and the Church collected. What has survived may be seen in the great cathedrals, in their chapter houses and treasuries; in the Royal Collection, the British Library and in one or two other libraries such as that of Duke Humfrey at the Bodleian in Oxford.

By the 17th century, rich and powerful men (among them Arundel and Buckingham) and learned men such as Sir Thomas Browne, conscious of the collections across Europe of the Medici, the Dukes of Burgundy and Berry, the Emperor Rudolf in Prague, were beginning to collect objects of artifice (medals, coins, antiquities, ceramics, jewellery) and of natural wonder (corals, crystals, shells, fossils and bezoars).[17] Francis Bacon was of the opinion that every learned gentleman should have 'a goodly, huge cabinet, wherein whatsoever the hand of man by exquisite act or engine has made rare in stuff, form or motion; whatsoever singularity, chance, and the shuffle of things hath produced; whatsoever nature has wrought in things that want life and may be kept; shall be sorted and included'.[18]

The John Tradescants, father and son, made 'Tradescants' Ark', their collection, famous throughout Europe. It was visited by any cultivated traveller who passed through London. One merchant captain, Peter Mundy, took a day 'in peruseings and that superficially' its 'Coines, shells, fethers etts.', its 'diverse Curiosities in Carvinge, painteinge, etts., as 80 faces carved on a Cherry stone', its 'Medals of Sondrey sorts', and 'a little garden with diverse outlandish herbes and flowers', – 'Soe that I am almost perswaded a Man might in one day behold and collect into one place more Curiosities than hee should see if hee spent all his life in Travel'.[19] When later offered to Oxford University by Elias Ashmole, the Tradescants' collection became the basis of what is now the Ashmolean Museum.

This aspiration, to bring together the world 'into one place', inspired many 17th- and 18th-century collectors, notably Sir Hans Sloane, who left his vast collection[20] to the Royal Society; from this the British Museum was born.

Sloane's was the last of the 'universal collections'. When Carl Linnaeus saw it, he was horrified by its 'complete disorder'. The rigorous classification and cataloguing that Linnaeus introduced captured the spirit of the Enlightenment that ran through late 18th-century museum collections, such as the mass of natural history specimens that Joseph Banks brought back from Captain Cook's first Pacific voyage, and that also passed to the British Museum. Such collections were driven by the determination that empirical knowledge should replace belief and superstition and that the resulting collections should be elucidating instruments of education and training. In 1813 Sir John Soane opened his private collection at his home, 12 and 13 Lincoln's Inn Fields, in order that 'Amateurs and Students in Painting, Architecture and Sculpture' and his own students at the Royal Academy, where he was professor of architecture, 'might have easy access to them'.[21]

In the 19th century this perception of museum collections as aids to teaching spread widely (v. the Marischal Museum at the University of Aberdeen and the museums founded by William and John Hunter at, respectively, the University of Glasgow's Hunterian Museum and the Royal College of Surgeons, London). The demand of the new middle class for entertainment led Sir Ashton Lever to open his house in Leicester Square to the public in 1774, to view, in the words of Fanny Burney's sister Susan, his 'birds of paradise', 'pelicans, flamingos, peacocks', 'bats, toads, frogs' and a monkey 'put in the attitude of Venus de Medicis [sic]' and 'scarce fit to be looked at'.[22] Visitors were charged for admission. Thirty-six years later, in 1810, William Bullock, the brother of the Liverpool designer and artist George Bullock, opened his Museum and Egyptian Hall at 22 Piccadilly. By 1816 his *Companion* guide had gone into a seventeenth edition.[23]

Museum collections became a means of expressing the glory of the state: the Louvre opened to the public in 1803 as the Musée Napoleon; Desenfans and Bourgeois put together, for the then King of Poland, the collection that is today at the Dulwich Picture Gallery. This idea of national prestige was part of what inspired John Wilkes, Sir George Beaumont and others to press for the founding of the National Gallery. Across the country, local literary and philosophical societies and natural history societies were being formed. Their members collected local antiquities, minerals, fossils, etc. When the 1845 Museums Act gave local councils the power to levy a rate and found museums, many of these collections were absorbed into new local museums and galleries (those at Leeds, Liverpool, Newcastle and Torquay provide examples here).

What is collected and exhibited in each generation holds up a mirror to contemporary society. The development of, and popular interest in, archaeology in the 19th century (at home by Augustus Lane Fox, later Lord Pitt

Rivers, and abroad by Layard, Petrie and others) led to the establishment of museum collections across the country. The ethnographic collections here have origins that are more complex and various: in discovery and Empire (the British Museum, the V&A); in trade (the Horniman Museum); in the work of missionaries and colonial administrators (the Royal Albert Memorial Museum, Exeter); in academic research (the University of Cambridge Museum of Archaeology and Anthropology).

The industrial towns and cities that boomed in the 19th century, particularly in Lancashire, Yorkshire and Scotland, benefited from the generosity of local magnates who built museums and bequeathed founding collections. In the 20th century Glasgow, Birkenhead and Coventry owed their collections and their museums to the civic pride and philanthropy of, respectively, Sir William Burrell, William Hesketh Lever, Lord Leverhulme and Sir Alfred Herbert. When John W. Blyth made a fortune in linoleum in Kirkcaldy he chose to build and endow a museum and art gallery, in part as a memorial to his son, who was killed in the First World War, in part to return something to the town in which he lived and to the people on whose work his fortune was founded, and in part to realise the liberal, democratic ideal expressed by Antonio Panizzi when addressing a Select Committee of Parliament in 1836 on the future of the British Museum's library: 'I want a poor student to have the same means of indulging his learned curiosity, of following his rational pursuits, of consulting the same authorities, of fathoming the most intimate inquiry as the richest man in the Kingdom ... and I contend that the Government is bound to give him the most liberal and unlimited assistance in this respect.'[24]

The 20th century has seen the forming of industrial museums (Ironbridge, Quarry Bank Mill), folk museums (St Fagan's, Cardiff; the Ulster Folk and Transport Museum) and museums of social history (Beamish, Linen Hall Library). Perhaps even more striking is the increase in the total number of museums in Britain from between 600 and 700 in the 1950s to over 2,500 today. Between 1950 and 1990 the number was growing by 10 per cent every five years, with more than two new museums opening every week during the 1980s: an expansion that reflected a number of social changes (increased prosperity and leisure time; the growth of tourism, which led to a demand for new visitor attractions) and was occasioned in part by the desire in many communities to find a use for buildings (factories, schools, churches) that were becoming redundant.

To have arranged the museums and galleries in this book along these chronological lines would have made good sense, but so too does organising entries by region, since the nature of museums' collections so often reflects local circumstances of geology or history, custom or industry. It also makes for ease of reference, and of visiting. On balance the claims of context seemed to me to outweigh those of chronology, so I have prefaced each regional section with a brief note of the character of museums and galleries in that region.

It is a British vanity and vice to describe such of our institutions as the BBC, the legal system or our great universities as 'the best in the world'; but some of our museums and galleries are indeed among the best: the British Museum, the British Library, the Natural History Museum, the V&A, the National Gallery, the Royal Collections, and, possibly, because they influenced so many others, the Ashmolean and the botanic gardens at Oxford and Kew.

We have not always led. The Musée Nationale des Techniques in Paris (1794) predated the Science Museum by fifty years, as the Skansen Museum of Folk Culture at Stockholm (1891) did its British equivalents, St Fagan's outside Cardiff, the Ulster Folk and Transport Museum and Beamish. The 17th-century Swedish warship, the *Vasa*, was raised and salvaged, in a remarkable feat of marine excavation and conservation, years before the *Mary Rose* in Portsmouth. Nevertheless few other countries can equal the number or general quality of our museums.

This book tries fairly to identify the weaknesses as well as the strengths of our museums. Although there are museums devoted to witchcraft,[25] to dog collars[26] and to objects made of Bakelite,[27] there are few that are concerned directly either with politics or religion. Simon Jenkins has made a persuasive case for parish churches being 'a dispersed gallery of vernacular art'[28] and many of our cathedrals now charge the public to enter, as if they were indeed museums, but there is no museum of Roman Catholicism, of Protestantism or of Methodism.[29] There is a museum of labour history[30] but not one of trade unionism. Parliament has superb archives and interesting art collections in Pugin's magnificent palace, but there is no museum or gallery of Parliament.

When I began to research this book I set out on a series of journeys across Britain. I anticipated that I would find many museums in a poor state of repair. Constraints on local government expenditure throughout the 1980s and early 1990s had led to some closures (the delightful Passmore Edwards Museum in Stratford East, London)[31] and many more had been unable to rehang or redesign their collections. In the same period the Heritage Lottery Fund spent £968 million on museums. Superb new museums have been built, in Salford, Oldham and Falmouth, and others renovated, in Liverpool, London, Manchester and Cambridge, although only a disproportionately small percentage of that investment has gone to non-metropolitan towns and cities (Falmouth, Walsall, Henley). Britain has not seen a museum programme to match this since the end of the 19th century.

But if capital investment is strong, at least for the fortunate few, revenue funding remains poor, undermining the quality of collections, when new acquisitions cannot be funded, and the overall quality of museums, particularly when curatorial posts have to be cut. If curators are not replaced, scholarship dies and knowledge, the lifeblood of objects, drains away. That attrition of scholarship and curatorial skills is being aggravated by those museum boards that are moving towards the market with more enthusiasm than thought. Museum professionals are being replaced by managers in the presumption that they will be more effective at dealing with financial problems. They may keep better accounts but they are not able to enhance the morale of staff or the reputation of a museum. To do that requires an understanding, and love, of a museum's collection. It is noticeable that, frequently, the best and most scholarly directors (Neil MacGregor at the British Museum, Timothy Clifford at the National Galleries of Scotland, Nicholas Serota at the Tate Galleries) run the most successful museums and consequently have least difficulty in attracting sponsorship, gifts and bequests. Benefactors do not want to entrust their beloved paintings or objects to commercial managers; nor do the public visit a museum because its shop arranges good promotional tie-ins with films or television programmes.

Even though curatorial posts are being lost, new curators of outstanding ability are emerging (Christopher Woodward at the Holburne Museum of Art in Bath, Matthew Rowe at the Towner Art Gallery and Museum in Eastbourne, Rhian Harris at the Foundling Museum in London), and the public continues to visit museums and galleries in huge numbers: one hundred million in 2003. Furthermore they are visiting museums and galleries that are showing everything from Titian to the Turner prize, medical apparatus to dinosaurs. If you stand in galleries and listen to those visitors, of all ages, it is clear that they are questioning, valuing and learning from the museums that they visit. This book celebrates the history and collections of these museums and galleries, and it also celebrates the habit of museum-visiting, without which they would not exist.

Now that I have taken this journey across the country, through these collections, what I have learned is that museums are the most social of universities, the most ecumenical of cathedrals. They stand in our towns and cities, monuments to civic pride and generosity, to discovery and learning, to the investment of our past in our future. They were established by confident communities and by people who wanted to share their love of objects, to open high the windows of their collections and cabinets and let in the light of curiosity and the balm of meaning, to furnish and deck the mind and clear the eye of anyone who opens himself to them.

Today there is a growing danger that those responsible for the governance of our public museums and galleries have become less concerned about objects and more concerned about the contribution that museums make to social policy. There are those, within and without the world of museums, who are content to see objects pushed aside by the more immediate drama of new technologies. For them the past is a place, at best of curiosity, at worst of mere theoretical, rather than instrumental, relevance; conservation and scholarship are seen to be of less importance than the single-minded, politically correct, pursuit of 'access'. That pursuit threatens to turn museums and galleries into instruments of social policy, valued for what is extrinsic, for what they can achieve, for the targets (of attendance and income) that they can hit, rather than for those qualities that are intrinsic and intangible, that can move us and can alter the ways in which we see, and understand, ourselves and our world.

Museums are valued by local and central government for their effect: for championing learning and education, for promoting access and inclusion, for turning their museums into beacons of excellence and agents of social change, even for combating loneliness and isolation, for affirming 'opportunities for identity, positive social roles and friendship with others who share our values'. They have been given to understand that they must modernise, reinvent themselves, become more relevant; that they must take their collections into pubs and shopping malls, follow the 'inexhaustible march of technology' and make 'a clean break with the past'. Such advice is oddly ignorant of history.

Public museums paid for by the tax- or rate-payer have always been driven by the desire to attract visitors and to inform, educate and entertain them. They were Reithian long before Reith. When Henry Cole and Richard Redgrave were appointed, respectively, head and superintendent for art in the new Department of Science and Art (subsequently the South Kensington Museum and eventually the Victoria and Albert Museum), their brief was to inspire and educate a new generation of artists and artisans who would recover the ground lost to Germany, among others, in the design and export of manufactured goods. They knew that the taste of the general public would need to be widened and developed if the work produced by those artisans was to find a market. To achieve this, Cole turned the museum into a place of popular entertainment, crowded at weekends, open free to the public three days and two evenings a week. He opened the first museum restaurant in 1866, designed by William Morris with stained glass and painted panels by Sir Edward Burne-Jones, and lobbied for public transport to bring visitors from central London to the suburbs of South Kensington. Cole even anticipated the idea of the museum as a key element of urban regeneration (to be returned to in the late 20th century in Glasgow, Liverpool, Salford, Bankside and elsewhere). He noted in his diary of 5 January 1852, when recording a meeting with Prince Albert to discuss the likely impact on Kensington of the new museum: 'I agreed that to bring there the out-flowings of the British Museum would aid all other proceedings in the neighbourhood.'

Attracting visitors, contributing to education, playing a part in urban regeneration are all worthy activities but they are criteria that identify only the extrinsic, social value of museums. The more vital, intrinsic importance of museums to us as individuals is in altering the ways in which we see and understand ourselves and our world. In their collections are the objects that past generations have valued, whether made or found (the classes of objects that the Tradescants' first catalogue identified as 'Artificiall' or 'Naturall').

We live in an age that is increasingly uncertain about its attitude to the past. Tradition and precedent are valued less than innovation, and the ties that link the one to the other are loosening. We exhibit a sentimental nostalgia for aspects of our heritage once they have been sanitised and dressed up. At the same time the media and the market demand new products, new ideas, novelty. Politicians respond. For them it can appear that the past is a shadow-land of past failures and outmoded thinking, the future a sunlit place of hope and possibility. Conveniently, too, the future never arrives.

Such a view of the relative merits of the past and the future is a travesty. There is no such dichotomy. We need both. The past is not dead. It is not even past. It is where imagination, so close to memory, grows from. If we do not value the ability of the past to help us place ourselves, to learn from past success and failure, we spoil our future at root.

Objects, messages from the past, whether paintings or ceramics, fossils or minerals, describe the diversity of the world in which we live and the genius of its peoples, in this country and across the globe. Museums are not the only institutions that can help us to such perspectives – universities and libraries have the same potential – but only museums do it through the medium of the physical, authentic object. In the words of Sir Neil Cossons, lately director of the Science Museum, 'There's only one quality that distinguishes a museum from all other types of entertainment, from scholarly, academic

and recreational activities, and that is that we hold collections of objects.'
In museums and galleries the object is King and the past his Queen.

The new technology of the Internet allows us to do things we have never
done before. We can conjure up on to our desk images from galleries around
the world. We can command every painting in the Getty Museum in Los
Angeles and zoom in on a single brushstroke. We are, virtually, Prospero.
However, such images do not, and never can, replace the objects themselves,
whose potency lies in their presence. In the Towneley Hall Art Gallery and
Museum at Burnley, it is the patient precision of the stitching on the Whalley
Abbey dalmatics that conveys the embroiderers' love of God. In the Cecil
Higgins Art Gallery, Bedford, J. M. W. Turner's working methods are brought
to life when you examine *A First Rate Taking in Stores* (1818) and can see
how 'he [Turner] tore, he scratched, he scrubbed at it in a kind of frenzy and
the whole thing was chaos – but gradually and as if by magic the lovely ship,
with all its exquisite minutiae, came into being', watched by Hawksworth
Fawkes, the fifteen-year-old son of his friend Walter Fawkes of Farnley.[32] It
is seeing the scratched sheet that puts you at Turner's shoulder and makes
the past present.

William Hazlitt described the wonder of entering the exhibition of paintings once owned by Philippe Égalité, Duc d'Orleans, at the Lyceum in 1798:
'I was staggered when I saw the works there collected and looked at them with
wondering and with longing eyes. A mist passed away from my sight: the
scales fell off. A new sense came upon me, a new heaven and a new earth
stood before me ... Time had unlocked his treasures, and Fame stood
portress at the door. We had heard the names of Titian, Raphael, Guido,
Domenichino, the Carracci – but to see them face to face, to be in the same
room as their deathless productions, was like breaking some mighty spell –
was almost an effect of necromancy.'

The epiphany of museums, captured by Hazlitt, comes from being in the
presence of an authentic object. To stand before Mantegna's *Triumphs of
Caesar* in the Orangery at Hampton Court Palace; to be within inches of the
speed and confidence of Bernini's carving of Thomas Baker's proud curls
in the V&A, the tumbling weight of the locks, the delicacy of the filigree lace
collar; to stare into the lustrous blue-grey glaze of a 13th-century Guan-ware
bottle vase in the Percival David Foundation of Chinese Art, is to feel the
charisma of these objects. It is a sensation hard to define but easy to identify,
and not a sensation merely. It cannot be conveyed at second-hand.

In these ways objects can transport us across continents and time and,
in doing so, place our contemporary concerns into a wider perspective and

encourage a measure of humility and tolerance. Colin St John Wilson, the architect of the New British Library, believed that 'the Library, and what it houses, embodies and protects the freedom and diversity of the human spirit in a way that borders on the sacred.'[33]

This is not an academic debate. The future shape and funding of museums depend on its outcome. If the primacy of the object is weakened, the role of scholars and curators to care for and interpret those objects is similarly weakened. If the past is relegated in importance, museums slide into the soft ground of entertainment and sensation. Visitors will be invited to look, be diverted, pass by, gaining little or nothing.

To animate this dialogue between the past and objects we need people, three groups who are the ever-present heroes of this book: the visitors, without whom these collections would have no audience; the benefactors without whose generosity these museums and galleries would not exist; and the curators, without whose scholarship these objects would remain inert.

The influence of some brilliant directors and curators runs like a refrain through these pages: in the 19th century, Cole and Robinson at the V&A; Madden and Franks at the British Museum; Eastlake and Burton at the National Gallery; at the Natural History Museum the remorseless ambition of Richard Owen and the genius of William Flower with his 'new museum idea'. In the 20th century the influences of Kenneth Clark, John Rothenstein and John Pope-Hennessy have been matched in recent years by those of Nicholas Serota and Neil MacGregor while, outside London, you can trace the impact of David Baxandall (National Museum and Gallery of Wales, National Galleries of Scotland), Timothy Clifford (Manchester Art Gallery and National Galleries of Scotland) and Julian Spalding (also Manchester Art Gallery, and Glasgow Museums); of Frank Atkinson (Beamish) and Neil Cossons (Ironbridge and the Science Museum); of Helen Kapp (Wakefield Art Gallery and Abbot Hall), Hans Hess (Leicester New Walk Gallery and Museum and York Art Gallery) and many others. While researching this book I met young curators who had had the benefit of being educated at the Courtauld, or by Richard Verdi at the University of Birmingham, and who carry forward the values they have learned there. It is they who must hold to a belief in the importance of the past, and to their love of objects, if these museums and galleries are to continue to serve those who visit them.

There is a danger that we are losing confidence in museums, even that some museums are losing confidence in the ability of their permanent collections to command attention. The word 'museum' is beginning to be seen as a deterrent rather than an attraction. New galleries and museums are beginning to eschew the word entirely: the Lowry Centre, the Eden Project, Jorvik, Tate Britain, Tate Modern. In jettisoning both 'the' and 'gallery', 'Tate' becomes a brand.

By not valuing the past, we lose and we are set loose, adrift without connections to the past or to one another. As individuals we carry the past with us. Our past, and our memory of that past, are what we are. By bringing our collective pasts together in these museums, we offer ourselves an opportunity to reflect on what Man has made, and found, and to recognise that the past lives on in us. Beset, as we are, by fearful schism and anathema (deriving considerably from ignorance), museums can help us to recognise that nothing human is alien, that we must understand one another or die. From museums we can learn tolerance, without which nothing.

These museums and their objects are not only places of education and inspiration. They can help us come to terms with the greatest of mysteries: life and death. Museums offer, in a time that is increasingly secular and increasingly fundamentalist, places in which, through the contemplation of a work of art or an object, a sense of spiritual response, connection or consolation may be felt. It is not a coincidence that, after 11 September 2001, many who were certain of their atheism or adrift in their agnosticism felt a need to visit museums and to be touched by and to receive what it is that such places hold.

In his 'Urne Buriall',[34] Thomas Browne observed that 'the long habit of living indisposeth us for dying.' Museums can assist us by being the mirror image of what Bernard Berenson apprehended to be Art's ability to reconcile us with life. The existence of an object in a museum affirms that the past, and what we have made of it and in it, does not die.

The Best of the Best

There are more than 2,500 museums and galleries in Britain. The 350 with individual entries in this book have, in my view, the best collections. Each of them merits a star-rating that confirms that it is 'worth a detour'. So great are the variations in the scale and nature of their collections that it is not easy to rank them more precisely. However, I offer the following as a guide:

*****   Collections of international reputation and significance
****   The best national collections
***   Collections of national importance
**   The best in the region
*   Good collections, well worth a detour

THE SOUTH-WEST

Four stars

Holburne Museum of Art

Three stars

Barbara Hepworth Museum and Sculpture
   Garden
Bristol City Museum and Art Gallery
Montacute House
National Maritime Museum, Cornwall
Plymouth City Museum and Art Gallery
Royal Albert Memorial Museum and Art
   Gallery
Tate St Ives
Wilton House

Two stars

American Museum in Britain
British Empire and Commonwealth Museum
Cheltenham Art Gallery and Museum
Corinium Museum
Museum of Costume

Royal Institution of Cornwall
Salisbury and South Wiltshire Museum
Stourhead
Torquay Museum
Victoria Art Gallery
Wiltshire Heritage Museum

THE SOUTH-EAST

Four stars

Hampton Court Palace
Pallant House Gallery
Petworth House
Windsor Castle

Three stars

Brighton Museum and Art Gallery
Fishbourne Roman Palace
Knole
Portsmouth Historic Dockyards
Royal Pavilion

Southampton City Art Gallery
Towner Art Gallery and Museum

Two stars

Booth Museum of Natural History
Portsmouth City Museum and Art Gallery
Powell-Cotton Museum
Sandham Memorial Chapel
Stanley Spencer Gallery
Tangmere Military Aviation Museum
Weald and Downland Open Air Museum

EAST ANGLIA

Five stars

Fitzwilliam Museum

Four stars

Kettle's Yard

Three stars

Colchester Castle Museum
Holkham Hall
Houghton Hall
Norwich Castle Museum
Sainsbury Centre for Visual Arts
Sedgwick Museum of Earth Sciences
Wolsey Art Gallery and Christchurch Mansion

Two stars

Cambridge University Museum of
   Archaeology and Anthropology
Dunwich Museum
Gainsborough's House
Southwold Museum
Sutton Hoo

THE EAST MIDLANDS

Four stars

Cecil Higgins Art Gallery
Chatsworth

Three stars

Derby Museum and Art Gallery
Leicester New Walk Gallery and Museum
Nottingham Castle Museum

Two stars

Calke Abbey
Kedleston Hall
Museum of St Albans
Northampton Museum and Art Gallery
Usher Gallery, Lincoln
Verulamium Museum

WEST MIDLANDS

Five stars

Ashmolean Museum
Barber Institute of Fine Arts

Four stars

Birmingham Museum and Art Gallery
Christ Church Picture Gallery
Waddesdon Manor: the Rothschild Collection

Three stars

Ascott Collection
Bate Collection
Blenheim Palace
Oxford University Museum of National
   History
Pitt Rivers Museum
Potteries Museum and Art Gallery
University of Oxford Botanic Garden

Two stars

Acton Scott Historic Working Museum
Ironbridge Gorge Museums
Museum of the History of Science
Snowshill Manor
Soho House
Upton House
Walter Rothschild Zoological Museum
Wolverhampton Museum and Art Gallery

THE NORTH-WEST

Five stars

Walker Art Gallery

Four stars

Lady Lever
Manchester Art Gallery
Whitworth Art Gallery
World Museum Liverpool

Three stars

Abbot Hall
John Rylands Library
Manchester Museum
Ruskin Library

Two stars

Blackburn Museum and Art Gallery
Bolton Museum and Art Gallery
Brantwood
Dove Cottage and the Wordsworth Museum
Gallery Oldham
Harris Museum and Art Gallery
Imperial War Museum North
Lowry Centre
Ruskin Museum
Tate Liverpool
Towneley Hall Art Gallery and Museum
Tullie House Museum and Art Gallery

THE NORTH-EAST

Four stars

Bowes Museum

Three stars

Laing Art Gallery
Shipley Art Gallery

Two stars

Arbeia, Roman Fort and Museum
Beamish: the North of England Open Air
    Museum
Hancock Museum
Hatton Gallery
Segedunum
Sunderland Museum and Art Gallery

YORKSHIRE AND HUMBERSIDE

Four stars

Harewood House
Temple Newsam

Three stars

Cartwright Hall Art Gallery
Castle Howard
Ferens Art Gallery
Graves Art Gallery
Leeds City Art Gallery
National Museum of Photography,
    Film and Television
National Railway Museum
Royal Armouries
York Art Gallery
Yorkshire Sculpture Park

Two stars

Beck Isle
Beningbrough Hall
Henry Moore Institute, Leeds, and the Centre
    for the Study of Sculpture
Leeds Museum

Lotherton Hall
Mappin Museum and Art Gallery
National Coal Mining Museum for England
Wakefield Art Gallery
Weston Park Museum and Art Gallery
Yorkshire Museum

SCOTLAND

Five stars

National Gallery of Scotland

Four stars

Aberdeen Art Gallery
Burrell Collection
Glasgow Museum and Art Gallery
Hunterian Art Gallery
Museum of Scotland
Scottish National Gallery of Modern Art
Scottish National Portrait Gallery

Three stars

Dean Gallery
Duff House Country Gallery
Hunterian Museum
Kilmartin House Museum
Kirkcaldy Gallery
McLean Art Gallery and Museum
Pier Art Centre
Pollok House
Stromness Museum

Two stars

Fergusson Gallery
GOMA (Gallery of Modern Art, Glasgow)
Inverness Museum
Laidhaye Croft Museum
Marischal
McManus Galleries and Museum
Paisley Museum and Art Gallery
Paxton House
Perth Museum and Art Gallery
Raymond Russell Collection of Early
    Keyboard Instruments
Talbot Rice Gallery
West Highland Museum

WALES

Five stars

National Museum and Gallery of Wales

Three stars

Glynn Vivian Art Gallery
National Library of Wales

Two stars

Aberystwyth School of Art Collection
Big Pit: National Mining Museum
Cardiff Castle
Ceramics Gallery
Erddig
Museum of Welsh Life
Newport Museum and Art Gallery
Penrhyn Castle
Roman Legionary Museum, Caerleon
Swansea Museum

NORTHERN IRELAND

Three stars

Linen Hall Library
Ulster Folk and Transport Museum
Ulster Museum

Two stars

Castle Coole
Florence Court
Irish Linen Centre and Lisburn Museum

LONDON

Five stars

British Library
British Museum
Dulwich Picture Gallery
National Gallery
Natural History Museum
Queen's Gallery
Royal Botanic Gardens, Kew
Tate Britain
Victoria and Albert Museum

Four stars

Courtauld Collection
Horniman Museum
National Maritime Museum
National Portrait Gallery
Percival David Foundation of Chinese Art
Sir John Soane's Museum
Wallace Collection

Three stars

Estorick Collection of Modern Italian Art
Geffrye Museum
Hunterian Museum
Imperial War Museum, London
Kenwood House
Museum of London
Ranger's House
Science Museum
Tate Modern

Two stars

Apsley House Wellington Museum
Bethnal Green Museum of Childhood
Design Museum
Freud Museum
Gilbert Collection
Guildhall Art Gallery
Houses of Parliament
Leighton House Museum
London Transport Museum
National Army Museum
National Museum of the Performing Arts
Old Operating Theatre Museum and Herb
    Garret

Petrie Museum of Egyptian Archaeology
Queen's House
Royal Academy
Royal Observatory, Greenwich
Saatchi Gallery
Westminster Abbey Chapter House, Pyx
    Chamber and Abbey Museum

The South-west

Geology and geography are powerful presences in the museums and galleries of the south-west. The long, exposed coastline winds around Portsmouth and Falmouth, Penzance and St Ives before ending up in the great port of Bristol. The light, reflected up from the sea, has drawn artists here: two generations of Newlyn painters to Penzance (Stanhope Forbes, Laura Knight, Dod Procter) and successive waves of artists to St Ives (Christopher Wood and Ben Nicholson, Barbara Hepworth, Naum Gabo, Patrick Heron, Roger Hilton, Terry Frost).

In the 18th and 19th centuries English painting was dominated by West Countrymen. Thomas Hudson was from Exeter. So too was his pupil Joshua Reynolds who, as a boy, had a 'florid complexion' and a voice 'tinctured with a Devonshire accent'. Francis Hayman, James Northcote, those fine water-colourists Samuel Prout and Francis Towne, all came from down here. Their paintings recur in the museums and galleries of the south-west.

The museums and galleries of the region are as loaded with geology as with art. The area, much of it on Devonian rock formations 350 million years old, is rich in minerals, as is clear from the collections at Torquay, Exeter and Truro. One of Cornwall's mottoes is 'Fish, tin and copper'; the Rashleigh Collection at Truro adds a treasury of minerals, including spun-glass gypsum and white pieces of calcite. China clay transformed the region's economy. The excavations of such early geologists and archaeologists as William Buckland and William Pengelly transformed more than the economy: what Pengelly found in Windmill Hill was irrefutable proof that Darwin was right, and that the Bible was wrong; that the world was not made by God in six days, 4,004 years before Christ. The collections in these museums reverberate with that evidence.

Into the ports of the south-west, notably Plymouth and Bristol, came early news of what was being discovered in distant continents, so it is not surprising that their museums have early, and excellent, ethnographic collections.

I regret that pressure on space has not allowed me to include several out-standing National Trust collections: Kingston Lacy; Cotehele; Saltram with its saloon and dining room by Robert Adam, plasterwork by Joseph Rose and

Devon

A30

Cornwall

A38

○ PLYMOUTH

○ ST AUSTELL

ST IVES   A30   ○ TRURO
○

○ FALMOUTH

○ PENZANCE

CHELTENHAM○

Gloucestershire

CIRENCESTER○

A429

A419

Gwent

SWINDON○

A429

M4

BRISTOL○ CHIPPENHAM○

AVEBURY○

Avon

○BATH

M5

DEVIZES○

A338

A350

Wiltshire

Somerset

STOURHEAD○

SALISBURY○

A303

TAUNTON○

○YEOVIL

A338

MONTACUTE○

M5

Dorset

A30

EXETER○

BOURNEMOUTH○

WEYMOUTH○

TORQUAY○

20 miles

ceiling paintings by Antonio Zucchi; and, my favourite, the beautiful, quiet Antony outside Plymouth.

Nor is it possible to include all the numerous museums in Bath: the Postal Museum, based on Rowland Hill's first postal service; Herschel House; and those that explain the architectural history of England's best and most elegantly planned city (No. 1 the Royal Crescent and the Building of Bath Museum).

Fine though the region's towns and cathedrals are, it is the sea and the light and the ancient, wild landscape of standing stones and henges that are the prime factors in the south-west. It is a pagan landscape of ritual and mystery. No wonder that it was to here that William Stukeley traced back his history of the Ancient Britons; no wonder that it maintains its spell in these museums and galleries.

ALEXANDER KEILLER MUSEUM ∗

High Street, Avebury, nr. Marlborough, Wiltshire SN8 1RF

Tel. 01672 539250

Standing stones and an ancient landscape in the middle of a village

You may drive your car across the middle of this great henge, cutting through the bank and ditch, within feet of the standing stones. You have no alternative. The main road from Devizes to Swindon bisects the site; the village of Avebury has developed around, over and beside this ancient place for over five centuries.

Yet it survives, the oldest and greatest Neolithic monument in Europe. It 'does as much exceed in greatness the so renowned Stonehenge, as a cathedral does a parish church,' wrote the antiquary John Aubrey in 1663, having come across it while hunting with friends. 'With awe and diffidence I enter the sacred precincts of this once hallowed sanctuary, the supposed parent of Stonehenge, the wonder of Britain,' confessed the early-19th-century connoisseur Sir Richard Colt Hoare, master of Stourhead.[1]

A huge misshapen circle is bounded by a ditch and a bank, twenty feet high. Within are ninety-eight sarsens and within them rather smaller standing stones that make two further circles, perfectly round, of equal size. All this is in a ceremonial landscape, whose main features are the West Kennet Long Barrow and Silbury Hill, a Neolithic earthwork 1,000 years older and even larger than Avebury, entirely man-made, an English pyramid.[2]

What was the purpose of these mighty edifices? What need drove those who constructed them? Were they temples to the gods? Were they places of ritual, symbolic of fertility or death? Antiquarians and archaeologists since Aubrey and William Stukeley have pondered these questions. There were excavations in the late 19th century, pursued by Harold St George Gray between 1908 and 1922, but there was no concentrated archaeological exploration until Alexander Keiller, the heir to the Keiller Dundee marmalade fortune, intervened in 1923. He did so initially to prevent the wireless company Marconi erecting a radio mast on Windmill Hill.

Keiller was an engineer, a skier,[3] a collector,[4] a driver of fast cars, a womaniser[5] and an amateur. He was interested in witchcraft and demonology,[6] and he was a very competent and methodical (self-taught) archaeologist. 'Archaeological excavation,' he wrote, 'can, and indeed must partake of the nature of an exact science. The excavator is the recorder of demonstrable fact . . . The technique of the methods which he employs must of necessity be scientific in the strictest sense of the term.'[7] Not only did he bring energy and money to the pursuit of Avebury's secrets: he also pioneered, with O. G. S. Crawford, the first Archaeological Officer of the Ordnance Survey, the archaeological use of aerial photography.

Between 1925 and 1939 he directed nine major exacavations and surveys in and around Avebury,[8] assisted by such outstanding young archaeologists as Stuart Piggott and W. E. V.

Young. The results can be seen in this museum, which he established in 1938. Here are the bones (animal and human), stone axes, mace heads, flint chippings, querns and fragments of clay pots that you might expect from a site that had soil conditions that were ideal for the preservation of bones and artefacts. Here too are chalk balls. Connected by sinew, were they weapons or toys? Keiller's scrupulous methods meant that he excavated and was able to reassemble whole skeletons of a dog and a goat.[9]

As at Kilmartin House Museum (q.v.), the museum can offer clues and help to make some sense of the context, but it is the site itself that is the heart of Avebury. Archaeologists estimate that there were originally a minimum of 247 stones within the henge.[10] Over the centuries many of them have been broken up for building stone, and many have fallen and become buried. In 1937 the great Swindon Stone at the west of the north entrance, the largest megalith at Avebury, had become 'encumbered by trees and overgrown with bracken'.[11] Keiller and Piggott transformed the appearance of the circles by uncovering and raising many stones. In the 1937 season alone eight stones were re-erected in the Great Circle.[12]

To sense the force that they exert, follow them away from the village, examine their varied shapes and feel their surfaces, pockmarked, worn, rough with lichen. Time has wrought personality upon these great stones. The questions they ask we still cannot answer.

AMERICAN MUSEUM IN BRITAIN **

Claverton Manor, Bath, Somerset BA2 7BD
Tel. 01225 460503, fax 01225 469160
e-mail: info@americanmuseum.org

American life of the 17th–19th centuries displayed in furnished rooms

At first sight Claverton Manor, an 1820 house designed by Sir Jeffry Wyatville[13] in Bath stone for Sir John Vivian, could not be a less suitable

setting for 'a museum of the decorative arts of American history illustrating domestic life in America from colonial times to the end of the 19th century'.[14] The setting is utterly English. The house looks east over the valley of the River Avon. To the south, from the top windows, you can see Stourhead against the skyline. Winston Churchill made the first speech of his political career here in 1897.[15] Yet its rooms are well suited, in scale and size, to display the furnished period interiors that are, and contain much of, the museum's core collection.

The museum was founded in 1961 by two Americans, Dallas Pratt and John Judkin. Pratt was a psychiatrist, Judkin an antiques dealer. Having secured Claverton Manor in 1958, they assembled the collection in two and a half years, thanks to some distinguished assistance from David Stockwell,[16] the American dealer and collector, and the sisters of the late Joseph Downs, the curator of the American wing of the Metropolitan Museum of Art in New York and the first curator of the Henry Francis du Pont Winterthur Museum, whose period rooms were the inspiration for this museum. Pratt and Judkin were invited to choose furniture from Downs's personal collection in Connecticut and Henry Francis du Pont gave them a handsome Philadelphia high chest (1760–75) for the opening of the museum.

The 17th- and 18th-century rooms make the point, at a glance, that until 1776 the American states were colonies of Britain and looked to England for fashions in design. The elaborate panelled fireplace wall (1769) in the Deming Parlour was based on designs in 18th-century English carpentry books; the Delft ware in the Lee Room was made in Lambeth, Bristol and Liverpool; the lantern clock in the 17th-century Keeping Room was made by Charles Banyard in Dereham, England, 1690–1700. Not until the 19th-century rooms (the Greek Revival Room, the New Orleans Bedroom) do English and American designs diverge, the heavily carved, mahogany half-tester bed in the New Orleans Bedroom being an adaptation of French (Louis XV) designs by Prudent

Mallard, who opened a factory in New Orleans in 1838, but they also reinforce Pratt and Judkin's contention that 'we [Americans], or at least our ancestors, had both taste and originality.'[17]

The embroidery of the samplers differs little from that worked by young ladies in England but the collection of quilts, particularly the seven made by the Amish with their strong, solid colours and straight-line geometric patterns, are wholly non-European, while the simplicity of the Shaker furniture anticipates the British Arts and Crafts furniture of the late 19th century, though few pieces by Voysey or Mackmurdo can match the poise and lightness of the Hancock rocking chair made by the Shaker community in Pittsfield, Massachusetts (c. 1820).

Room after room disabuses an English visitor of preconceptions and misconceptions, not least those about the American Indians gleaned from Hollywood movies. Here can be seen how discrete and different are the Indian cultures: the Plains Indians (Sioux), the Iroquois and Algonquins from the forests of the north-east, the Arctic Inuit and Alent, and the Navajo of the south-west. Their crafts, seldom seen in the ethnographic collections of British museums, are rooted in the ways in which these peoples view the natural world around them and in their beliefs in the spiritual and supernatural.

Most remarkable of all is Dallas Pratt's collection of maps of America and the world pre-1600: Abraham Ortelius's *Theatrum Orbis Terrarum*, published in Antwerp in 1570 with engravings modelled on the world map of Gerardus Mercator; the 1494 Basel edition of Christopher Columbus's letter describing his exploration of 1492.

This is a collection unlike any other in Britain, a corrective to any latent British snobbery about America. Jefferson resisted the claim of the 18th-century French historian and philosopher Abbé Reynal that 'America has not yet produced one good poet, one able mathematician, one man of genius in a single art' by insisting that 'this reproach is as unjust as it is unkind.' This collection demonstrates that in the domestic decorative arts America was, from its beginnings, producing work at least as elegant as anything made in England.

HOLBURNE MUSEUM OF ART ★★★★

Great Pulteney Street, Bath, Somerset
BA2 4DB
Tel. 01225 466669
www.bath.ac.uk/Holburne/

A triumph of connoisseurial taste: porcelain, silver, bronzes; and paintings by Ramsay, Gainsborough and Stubbs

Stand on the Pulteney Bridge and look down Great Pulteney Street. At the end, framed in terraced symmetry, is the former Sydney Hotel, now the Holburne Museum of Art. It was designed and built by Charles Harcourt Masters in 1795–6 as a speculative 'hotel' to provide tea rooms, card rooms, a concert room and ballroom to add to the enjoyment of Sydney Gardens. Jane Austen notes in her letters: 'There is a public breakfast in Sydney Gardens every morning, so we shall not be wholly starved.'

It changed use in 1913–16 when Sir Reginald Blomfield[18] added what Pevsner calls 'his indispensable touch of the French Dixhuitième'[19] when converting it into a museum to house the collections of Sir William Holburne. These collections, of coins, miniatures, silver, ceramics, glass, furniture and paintings, contain many pieces of beauty and curiosity which compose, too, an intact record of the taste and interests of a regional English collector in the first half of the 19th century.

For the earlier part of his life William Holburne was neither a connoisseur nor an expert. As a younger son, he had no expectations and went to sea instead of school and university, serving as a midshipman, aged twelve, on the *Orion* at the battle of Trafalgar. After his elder brother, who was in the Guards, died of his wounds in the last year of Wellington's Peninsular campaign in 1814, Holburne came

into a comfortable inheritance and a baronetcy on the death of his father in 1820.

He retired on half pay from the navy and set about educating himself by undertaking an extended Grand Tour, 1824–5, through France, the Low Countries, Germany, Austria and, particularly, Italy. The works he began to acquire were simply for his own enjoyment, to furnish his house in Bath. A miniature here by Charles Jagger (1827) shows Holburne as an open-faced, rather handsome man; he never married and lived for the rest of his life with his three sisters in a house directly opposite the present museum. The earliest, privately printed, catalogue of his collection records the rooms in which works were displayed, indicating his preferences: Romanelli's beautiful *Entombment* in the Drawing Room, two small Paninis in the Dining Room.

His tastes were catholic and did not conform to fashion. He liked the 17th-century Dutch Italianate landscape artists and bought a Jan Asselijn and a Cornelius van Poelenburgh, both of whom on returning from Rome transferred their delight in Italian skies and light to Dutch scenes. At the same time he had a sweet tooth for Dutch genre paintings: alehouse scenes by Brouwer and van Ostade.

He seems never to have bought extravagantly. At William Beckford's sale in Bath in 1845, when glamour and curiosity drove up prices, he came away with only a set of six gold spoons and some Meissen porcelain. However, at the sale of the Earl of Sussex's famous collection of silver in 1843, he bought decisively and well, most notably a large collection of sealtop spoons and a silver gilt Mannerist rosewater dish (1616), rich with repoussé foliate scrolls, formerly owned by Queen Charlotte and bearing her initials. For this he paid the substantial sum of £60. 4s. 9d.

The collection of silver is fine, and wide-ranging in its taste, including as well as the Mannerist dish a plain 16th-century Sussex plate, a 1613 bell salt, a porringer decorated with chinoiserie (c. 1680–89, possibly by

Rosamund Sargent by Allan Ramsay at the Holburne

John Jackson) and 18th-century rococo pieces.

That Holburne bought for enjoyment rather than for 'name' is made clear by his purchase of a beautiful small bronze which he described in his first catalogue as a 'Kneeling Venus, a fine Florentine bronze statuette'. Recent research has established that she was sculpted and cast by Antonio Susini from an original model made by his master, Giambologna, sculptor to the Medicis in Florence. She is likely to be the 'Kneeling Woman' by Susini in Cardinal Richelieu's collection (1642) and, from the number 35 incised on her shoulder, is the 'Crouching Venus' acquired by Louis XIV from the Hesselin sale and displayed at Versailles until the Revolution. Unaware of this provenance, Holburne loved her because she was beautiful. Her torso gently turns. Her raised left arm is curved behind her neck, which inclines. She is all calm, delicacy and poise.

Holburne wrote little and his catalogue gives no dates of acquisition, so it is difficult to know whether his tastes and interests changed or whether they remained wide, and often contradictory, throughout his life. His collection of ceramics includes a thoughtful selection of Wedgwood neoclassical Black Basalts and jasperware, alongside soft paste, Bow porcelain and some Italian maiolica which, while not comparable to that in the Wallace Collection, includes pieces from Castel Durante, Pesaro, Urbino and Derutà.

In the 20th century the museum has added glass, miniatures (many of Bath figures, including Nathaniel Hone's memorable likeness of an elderly, somewhat dissolute, 'Beau' Nash, Bath's Master of Ceremonies in its 18th-century heyday) and some fine Dutch and English 17th-century furniture, walnut veneered with decorative marquetry.

The most striking additions have been to Holburne's collection of paintings. He had a severe portrait of a burgomaster by Nicholaes Elias, known as *Pickenoy*, c. 1625, more flamboyant works by William Wissing of *William, Prince of Orange* and *Lawrence Hyde, Duke of Rochester*, and a debonair, early *Self-portrait* by Thomas Barker (c. 1794), painted at a time when a fine, possibly great, career seemed in prospect. He stands before his easel, palette and brushes in one hand, the other poised on his hip. He half turns to the viewer, handsome, a smile almost forming on his lips. He has just returned from Italy and on the canvas is an oil sketch of the Temple of Vesta at Tivoli. Bath was his and he was set to conquer London, but the brushwork here may, like his later work, be read two ways: swift and confident, or somewhat casual and cursory.

In the last fifty years two major bequests have brought some excellent paintings. The dispersal of Ernest Cook's collection in 1955 brought the museum a good Turner water-colour, *Pembroke Castle* (*c.*1829–30), from his *Picturesque Views in England and Wales* series; a delightful outdoor conversation piece by Stubbs, *Reverend Robert Carter Thelwall and his Family* (1776), as notable for the landscape and figures as for the two patient horses which await the Thelwalls' pleasure; and *Dr Rice Charleton* (*c.*1764), a portrait of Gains-borough's physician in Bath.

This portrait is a striking example of the development in Gainsborough's technique after he left Ipswich for Bath. Ozias Humphrey watched the portrait being completed and wrote that it 'absolutely seemed, upon first entering the room, like a living person'. This ability to capture likeness brought him new commissions in Bath but his handling of background landscape and studio foliage in a full-length such as this is equally striking.

The other major bequest was from Sir Orme Sargent, a Foreign Office grandee who retired to Bath, in 1962. This brought a portrait by Jonathan Richardson of *Garton Orme at the Spinet* (*c.*1707) and a pair of portraits by Allan Ramsay of *John Sargent* and his wife, *Rosamund* (1749).

Rosamund Sargent was the sister of Ephraim Chambers, the publisher of the first English encyclopaedia in 1728. Horace Walpole wrote in 1759 that Ramsay 'is all delicacy. Mr Reynolds seldom succeeds in women. Mr Ramsay is formed to paint them,' and this portrait, perhaps his finest work in an English public gallery, confirms that view. Ramsay

concentrates all the light on the white froth of her lace cap, the pink and cream of her flawless complexion, the gleam of her eye and her bright blue bow. The background palette of smoky pink (silk dress), black (lace) and deep brown (hair and field), all in an oval frame within a frame, sets off her pearly beauty.

In the same period the museum increased its collection of Gainsboroughs with the loan of *The Byam Family* (1765), whose composition anticipates *The Morning Walk* on a canvas that is unusually wide and allows Gainsborough to extend the landscape to the left, and *Robert Nugent* (*c.*1760). He exhibited this at the 1761 Society of Artists' Exhibition in London to great acclaim and it secured his reputation in Bath. Not only was Nugent the Member of Parliament and at the centre of Bath society but the bold, unusual pose, with Nugent sitting in profile, his thick calf and ankle crossed on his knee, made it clear that here was a talent with a difference.

This museum perpetuates the care, taste and sheer enjoyment that Holburne brought to his collection, virtues exemplified by a marble piece purchased more than 120 years after his death. Giuseppi Plura (*fl.*1749–56) was a young sculptor from Turin who came to Bath in 1749 in search of commissions. He married the daughter of the main building contractor to Bath's leading architect, John Wood, and carved this delicious *Diana and Endymion* to demonstrate his talents. He captured the beauty of both goddess and shepherd but died of a fever before his undoubted talent could be recognised.

This piece was acquired from Hugh Honour and John Fleming, art historians and connois-seurs *sans pareil* of the late 20th century – a fitting tribute to Sir William Holburne and to this museum.

MUSEUM OF COSTUME **

Assembly Rooms, Bennett Street, Bath,
Somerset BA1 2QH
Tel. 01225 477789
www.museumofcostume.co.uk

Fashions of past centuries brought to life in the Assembly Rooms

There can be no more appropriate setting for a museum of costume than the Assembly Rooms, Bath, designed by John Wood the Younger in 1771. The Corinthian columns, Vitruvian scrolls and glass chandeliers by William Parker have provided a setting for fashion and display ever since.

The building was financed by a £20,000 tontine and opened with a ridotto (a combined ball and concert) to which Thomas Gainsborough was sent three complimentary tickets, having donated a full-length portrait of Captain William Wade, the Master of Ceremonies. Captain Wade published rules for guests, 'it being absolutely necessary that a propriety of dress should be observed'.

Founded by the costume collector Doris Langley Moore[20] in 1963, the collection covers European costume and fashion, for men and women, from the late 16th century to the present day.

The earliest garments are a man's plain linen undershirt with fine black embroidery from 1580–90, a woman's jacket (*c.* 1620), embroidered with leaves, flowers and insects in silks and silver thread, fastened by a salmon-pink ribbon, and a formal dress of silver tissue trimmed with parchment lace (*c.* 1660).

As ornate as the silver tissue dress is simple are the mid-17th-century gloves in white goatskin or stiffened silk. One pair (*c.* 1630–50) has a gauntlet of white satin on which a forest scene with deer, rabbits and birds is embroidered.

Between the Restoration in 1660 and the mid 18th century men competed with women for attention (wigs, muffs, ribbons, lace, embroidery, breeches like petticoats), although with the exception of waistcoats, the materials of men's coats and breeches were simpler than the sparkling, brocaded silks of women's dresses, as a sack-back gown and petti-coat of cream, blue and silver (*c.* 1760–70) demonstrates.

In every period the collection is careful to relate the style and silhouette of the outer clothes to what was worn underneath. An embroidered stomacher, laced whalebone stays, and a portable pocket show how an 18th-century woman maintained the line of her dress.

The collection also charts the ways in which politics, war, the rise and fall of the economy and technology have shaped fashion. The French Revolution led women to abandon their elaborate clothes, hoop petticoats and panniers. Ostentation gave way to modest cottons, linens, muslins and lawns imported from the East; these softer textures suited a gentler silhouette. There was generally no need for corsets or petticoats; arms were bare, slippers low. Fashion has scarcely been simpler, scantier or more beautiful than a white evening dress, *c.* 1804.

Men's clothes too became simpler. Lace ruffles gave way to wrist bands, cravats to neck cloths. The demands of hunting were the key influences: there were knee breeches, riding boots, top hat (for protection) and tail coats cut back to the waist, although still no trousers, 'sans culottes' remaining a revolutionary term. When Arthur Wellesley, later Duke of Wellington, 'presented himself in 1814 at the fashionable Almack's in a pair of trousers',[21] he was refused admission.

The dresses in the collection from the early 19th century exhibit the increasing influence of the fashion magazine and the fashion plate. *The Gallery of Fashion*, first published by Nicklaus von Heideloff in 1794, and *The Lady's Monthly Museum* (1798), were soon rivalled by *Le Beau Monde* and *La Belle Assemblée*. Each featured fashion plates, their etching coloured by hand. Add to that the invention of the sewing machine in 1846 by Elias Howe, developments in printing technology, paper patterns, better dyes and the opening of department stores made accessible by the new

railways, and it is easy to see how the speed and the spread of fashion grew faster throughout the 19th century.

Dresses here chart the proliferation of petticoats in the 1840s until they became so cumbersome that they were supplanted by the crinoline in 1854 which, in turn, gave way to the 'dress improver' or bustle in 1870. By the mid 1870s the bustle had fallen from favour until it re-emerged, in an amended form, as the half crinoline or Thomson Crinolette in 1880, worn with a chemise, corset and drawers.

The way in which the Edwardian corset affected the shape of the beauties as painted by John Singer Sargent and others is also explained. The machine-woven corset did not just hold in the waist (to 21 inches, not the 18 inches of myth): it also tipped the torso forward and pushed the breasts up, creating a full bosom and an accentuated rear, the S bend.

In the 20th century two world wars, women's suffrage and women's employment accelerated changes in fashion. From the black suit of Christian Dior's New Look collection of 1947 (worn by Dame Margot Fonteyn) and the 1950s ball dresses of John Cavanagh and Norman Hartnell, to the architectural simplicities of Mary Quant, and the elaborations of Bill Gibb, Gina Fratini and Zandra Rhodes,[22] it has been a hectic journey for couture. On the streets the Teddy Boys of the 1950s, the Mods and Rockers of the 1960s, and the hippies and skinheads of the denim age have shadowed that journey. Both worlds plunder the fashions of the past 400 years collected in this museum.

Costumes at Bath: Yves Saint Laurent cocktail dress

ROMAN BATHS *

Pump Room, Stall Street, Bath, Somerset
BA1 1LZ
Tel. 01225 477774
www.romanbaths.co.uk

Astonishing Roman remains, mosaics and monuments around the sacred spring of Aquae Sulis

The hybrid name Aquae Sulis was what the Romans called this city. It combines the Latin for water with the name of the Celtic goddess of springs and rivers, Sulis, who was worshipped by the Dobunni. Sulis's attributes of healing, wisdom and military skill made it easy for the Romans to conflate her with Minerva, goddess of war and wisdom, most beloved child of Jupiter, produced from his brain without a mother, the mightiest of the gods after her father.[23] To the Dobunni and to the Romans the bubbling emergence of water from the earth, hot to the touch, staining the rocks red with iron salts, overhung with steam, was a wonder and it remains so to us today.

Around the sacred spring the Romans developed a reservoir, temple and baths, entered through a door opposite the main altar, around which sacrifices were made to the gods and auguries foretold. As the baths and temple were excavated piecemeal between the mid 18th century and the present day the history of the site was revealed. In the development of the centre of Bath in the 18th century, the gilded bronze head of Minerva was discovered (in 1727, under Stall Street) and the eastern end of the baths (1755) and the temple (1790) excavated.

More of the temple was uncovered in 1867 when the Grand Pump Room Hotel was built, but the major discoveries followed attempts by the city surveyor and architect, Major Charles Davis, to locate a leak in the King's Bath in 1878. His excavations revealed large parts of the Great Bath and many Roman artefacts – discoveries that have been added to in recent years by Professor Barry Cunliffe.[24]

The excavations of the temple have revealed

only fragments of the steps and columns and what is called the Gorgon's Head. This is surrounded by a most delicate carving of wreaths of leaves, and a tantalising fragment of the skirt and a foot of two winged victories. To call this startling head 'Gorgon' is confusing as this is indubitably a man, surrounded by beard and wild hair as if by the rays of the sun, rather than by serpents. It resembles more a water god, Oceanus or Neptune.

It is not easy today to read the shape of the Roman site beneath the Italianate scheme with which the architect J. M. Brydon[25] covered it but it is possible to gain some sense of the baths' history, Celtic, Roman, Saxon and medieval.

Although the architecture and engineering change through the ages, some things remain: the water and the gods. Of these it is Minerva who stands out. The life-sized gilded bronze head, stripped of its usual Corinthian helmet, confronts you with its level, implacable gaze. Her beauty is without end. It is no wonder that she was Jupiter's favourite nor that she could defy the desire and prayers and force of Vulcan.

Visitors to the shrine would seek to placate the goddess with gifts and coins, as their Celtic predecessors had done (witness the Dobunni coins dredged from the reservoir). A fine enamelled penannular brooch, made in Ireland in the 4th century, is among the haul of bowls, candlesticks, inkpots, jugs and over 12,000 coins that have been retrieved. Many are made of pewter, as are the tablets on which prayers to the goddess were written, calling for curses on miscreants. 'To Minerva . . . I have given the thief who has stolen my hooded cloak, whether slave or free, whether man or woman. He is not to buy back this gift unless with his own blood'; 'May he who has stolen VILBIA from me become as liquid as water'; 'Whoever has perjured himself there, you are to make him pay for it to the goddess Sulis with his own blood' are typical of the curses invoked.

Dedications on altars and tombstones tell

Bath's Roman baths

gentler stories. 'To the goddess Sulis, for the welfare and safety of Aufidius Maximus, centurion of the sixth Legion Victrix, Marcus Aufidius Lemnus, his freedman, willingly and deservedly fulfilled his vow' is the dedication on one altar. The parents of a dead child inscribed this on a tomb: 'To the spirits of the departed, to SUCCESSA PETRONIA, lived three years, four months, nine days, Vettius Romulus and Victoria Sabina set this up to their dearest daughter.'

Such examples of human fragility qualify the grandeur of the site but have their origins in faith, in the curative water and in the gods.

VICTORIA ART GALLERY **

By Pulteney Bridge, Bath, Somerset
BA2 4AT
Tel. 01225 477233
www.victoriagal.org.uk

Three hundred years of painting in and around Bath

Unmoved by the spread of galleries and museums across Britain that followed the 1853 Museums Act, Bath remained without a public gallery until the Victoria Art Gallery opened in May 1900.

It did so without the benefit of a major bequest and one of its first curators, Reginald Wright, who remained in post from 1919 to 1954, had to build its collection by stealth and shrewdness. The handsome 17th-century portrait of *James Scott, Duke of Monmouth*, attributed to John Riley, he bought for £10 in Bath market in 1953.

At first glance it is hard to see any coherence in the collection, whether of period, style or taste. Here is an excellent William Roberts, *The Dressmaker* (1943), in which the geometry of the four women creates a dance of arms and necks; a small, 17th-century Dutch *Interior of a Church* by Peter Neffs the Elder; indifferent examples of the work of William Etty, Richard Wilson and David Cox; Zoffany at his most informal and charming, depicting a somewhat anxious twelve-year-old French girl, with

John Nash's The Canal Bridge, Sydney Gardens, Bath *(Victoria Art Gallery)*

bitten fingernails, cradling a cat; paintings by Rex Whistler and Sandra Blow; an excellent small Kenneth Armitage sculpture, *People in the Wind* (1950), with its terracotta maquette. It appears to be a lucky dip.

On closer inspection the gallery does have a theme: Bath, its views and the painters who have lived and worked here. Gainsborough and Lawrence made their names here. Joseph Wright failed to do so. William Hoare and Thomas Barker thrived.

Benjamin West, president of the Royal Academy, reported that 'Drawing Masters at Bath make fortunes' after a visit in 1807 to drink the waters.[26] At the height of its Georgian popularity, visitors could have their silhouettes made for 1s. in five minutes, or be sketched in oils in one sitting. The great and good could have a face by Barker. In 1822 he charged £100 for three group portraits of the Elton family. A full-length by Gainsborough cost sixty guineas. It was a competitive market in which artists rented the most elegant house and studio they could afford (Gainsborough ended up in the Circus, Hoare in Edgar Buildings, where he lived, noted George Vertue, 'in a handsome, genteel manner').[27]

The gallery has portraits by Gainsborough, Beach and Lawrence (born in Bristol, moved to Bath in 1780), and by Leighton, of his sister, who lived and died here. There is also a large collection of the work of Thomas Barker, who admired Gainsborough and sought to emulate him. His best work here, the early *Thomas Barker with his Preceptor, Charles Spackman*

(1789), shows the young, handsome Barker, half turned to face inwards, as his patron, Spackman, looks on. It is the same informal, attractive pose[28] he chose for his self-portrait in the Holburne Museum (q.v.), 300 yards down Great Pulteney Street.

Spackman spotted Barker's talent, educated him, sent him to Rome, acted as his agent and set him up in London. When Spackman's finances collapsed, Barker struggled and finally returned to Bath, where he had great commercial success with paintings that were repetitive and conservative: a sad end to a talent that promised much.

A stronger talent was Gainsborough's friend William Hoare, who is represented here by oils of 'Beau' Nash and William Pitt, Earl of Chatham, but it is *The Drake Family of Fernhill, Berkshire* (displayed in the Assembly Rooms in Bath), that does him the justice that his best works, invariably in pastels, merit.[29]

Reginald Wright also put together a collection of Bath scenes by local artists, even the best of which, by Joseph Sheldon, have a mainly historical interest. In the 20th century John Nash and Walter Sickert visited the city and painted cityscapes: Sickert, Paradise Row and Beechen Cliff; Nash, Sydney Gardens, the canal and the suspension bridge. Pleasant though these are, they provoke the question, why has there been no Canaletto or Bellotto,[30] or even a Samuel Scott, of a city as beautiful as Bath? The block of over two hundred drawings by Samuel Poole, given by Alderman Cedric Chivers in 1929, does not answer.

All the paintings are exhibited in a good, top-lit gallery upstairs. Its frieze, a replica of the Parthenon marbles, was given by the gallery's architect, J. M. Brydon,[31] in 1900. Between the gallery and the stairs he made a rotunda, under which stands a cast of Hebe by Antonio Canova. A run of cabinets holds the gallery's ceramics collection. This, too, is a mixture, of Wedgwood, Jackfield ware, early Delft ware, and Derby, Chelsea and Worcester porcelain. Among this is a plate by William Billingsley after he left Derby, painted at some stage on his progress south via work in Worcester, Nantgarw (1813) and Swansea (1820).

A further curiosity is the mid-18th-century Lichfield clock.[32] It has a wood cabinet painted to resemble stone, a glass front and five tunes played on the horn, one of which is a minuet by Handel.

The charm and oddity of this piece captures one aspect of the gallery's personality. It is a place in which to rummage. If you do, you may chance on a rare, joint work by John Hoppner and the diarist Joseph Farington, *The Fishing Party*; a portrait attributed to Francis Bird of *Cloudesley Shovell* – Shovell's mistake wrecked a substantial part of the navy off the Scillies in 1707 and led to the Longitude Act of 1714 (v. the Royal Observatory); or a picture of real quality, *The Adoration of the Magi* by Hugo van der Goes.

It is this possibility of imminent surprise that gives the gallery its character and its charm.

RUSSELL-COTES ART GALLERY AND MUSEUM *

East Cliff, Bournemouth, Dorset BH1 3AA
Tel. 01202 451800

A collector with more ambition than knowledge and more money than taste

Was Sir Merton Russell-Cotes (1835–1921) a social-climbing poseur and a cheapskate, or was he, as his entry in *Who Was Who* describes him, 'an art collector and connoisseur' whose recreations were 'art, music, foreign travel, exploration'?[33] Is his collection, as the man of parts himself records, 'the most complete representative collection of British Art that they [the auction house Christie, Manson and Woods] had had through their hands'?[34] Or is it, in the main, meretricious, the hoard of a nouveau riche philistine[35] with more money (his wife's) than taste?

The gallery and museum that bear his name offer enough evidence for visitors to be able to make up their own minds.

When his wife Annie inherited her father's cotton-spinning fortune in 1877, Russell-Cotes was able to upgrade the Bournemouth hotel that they ran, the Bath, renaming it the Royal Bath Hotel,[36] and to travel around the world. He returned from nearly two years touring Australia, the Pacific Islands, Japan and India 'an explorer' and 'an art collector'. He published an article about his travels, and was accepted as a member of the Royal Geographical Society and as a founding member of the Japan Society. In Tokyo 'over a hundred cases were filled with the curios purchased by my wife and myself . . . [including] some very rare and antique specimens of Japanese art.'[37] The majority of this was tourist miscellania, new and old, bought from bazaars, shops and curio-dealers. It did include some good pieces: a gold and silver elephant 'in laid with various other metals' and 'precious stones' made by the great Japanese metal maker Komai of Kyoto, and a Buddhist shrine, the kakemona or 'Incarnation of Buddha' which had belonged to a mikado.

At the hotel he was already collecting genre works by such minor 19th- and early-20th-century Royal Academicians as Edward John Gregory and Henry Stacy Marks, T. Sydney Cooper's studies of cows in landscape and paintings of dogs by Walter Hunt and Briton Rivière.

To house these and his Japanese collection Russell-Cotes built an architectural extravaganza on Bournemouth's East Cliff, all verandah, bay windows and squat towers, designed by the architect John Frederick Fogerty, intended in Cotes's words to 'combine the renaissance with Italian and old Scottish Baronial styles'. Pevsner calls it 'thoroughly debased, i.e. not cognizant of any of the then respectable or enterprising trends'.[38] Russell-Cotes gave it to his wife, in 1901, and then together they gave it to Bournemouth Corporation as a museum and art gallery with the proviso that he might live there until he died.

The house is a pile-up of styles. The Drawing Room has a Tudor ceiling and an Elizabethan inglenook fireplace. There is naturally a Japanese Mikado's Room and a Moorish alcove based approximately upon designs from the Alhambra. In the Main Hall is a plaster rendition, on panels, of the Parthenon frieze[39]

which has been cut, pasted and bodged together,[40] turning it into a drunken comic strip in bas-relief.

Russell-Cotes intended house and collection as his great memorial but the more closely you look at them, the more doubts encroach upon you. The wall paintings by a local decorator, John Thomas, and his son Oliver, are inept. In Russell-Cotes's bedroom upstairs *Venus Rising*, painted opposite his bed by the same hands, is embarrassingly bad. The Drawing Room doors are from an 18th-century palazzo in Florence. Like the Parthenon frieze, they have been cut down to fit the available space.

Russell-Cotes built picture galleries to house the enormous canvases of his favourite artist Edwin Longsden Long, among which the fifteen-foot-wide *Anno Domini* or *The Flight into Egypt* (1883) is the centrepiece. He also greatly admired the work of Albert Joseph Moore, whose *Midsummer* (1886–7) is here.[41] The quality of his collection is at best uneven. There are poor works by some artists (G. F. Watts, Arthur Hughes), a terrible Etty, *The Dawn of Love* (1828), a heavy-handed Frederick Goddall, a small copy of Landseer's *Flood in the Highlands* (1864) and, among all this, an extremely interesting oil sketch of William Powell Frith's *Ramsgate Sands* (1905)[42] which shows how Frith built up his grand teeming panoramas and confirms Sickert's high opinion of him: 'Surprises lurk in [his paintings] like Easter eggs.'[43]

Russell-Cotes was an accumulator rather than a collector. He gave no provenance for any work; indeed he had no library, despite portraying himself to the *Art Journal* as someone for whom 'books, of course . . . are a necessity.'[44] This dearth makes it difficult to assess the collection, particularly its sculpture: a curious combination of neo-classical sentimentalism (Laurence Macdonald, Edward Bowring Stephens), powerful French bronzes (Louis-Ernest Barrias, *The First Funeral*, 1878) and a rare example in a British collection of the work of Ludwig Michael von Schwanthaler, a marble, *Melusine* (c.1841–5).[45]

There is no doubt that Russell-Cotes was a

vain man and no connoisseur. However this collection, and its setting, do reflect late-19th-century popular taste. Having toured the pictures around British cities in an act of sedulous philanthropy he secured a knighthood. Since his death the museum has strengthened the collection with some excellent Japanese pieces (a late-19th-century lacquer production set that is considered to be the best preserved and largest in Britain) and D. G. Rossetti's *Venus Verticordia* (1864–8); these give the collection something of the quality that Russell-Cotes desired but could not himself achieve.

BRISTOL CITY MUSEUM AND ART GALLERY ✳✳✳

Queen's Road, Bristol, Avon BS8 1RL
Tel. 0117 922 3571
www.bristol-city.gov.uk/museums

Rich maritime and mercantile haul

'Keep the collection British . . . The purchase of foreign pictures for a British gallery would only be logically advisable if the foreign pictures could teach the English school something,'[46] advised the painter and academic Hubert von Herkomer when he opened the Bristol Art Gallery, designed by Sir Frank Wills,[47] in 1905.

The museum had been founded by the Bristol Philosophical and Literary Society in 1823 and already had an exceptionally large collection of paintings by local artists, including 1,500 drawings and watercolours that recorded the city in the 1820s before its industrialisation, commissioned by the merchant and collector George Weare Breakenridge, and works by W. J. Müller, the son of the first curator of the Bristol City Museum.[48]

Francis Danby lived here in his twenties and there is an idyllic pastoral *View of Avon Gorge* (1822) and the more characteristic *Sunset at Sea after a Storm*, painted in 1824 just before his debts drove him to London. 'It was a work that made [his] reputation.'[49] A blood-red sun sets over the ominous ocean as, in the foreground, Géricault-like figures[50] huddle

together on a raft. It was bought by Lawrence and shows Danby at his best, as expansive as John Martin but less hysterical.

Others who passed through the city and painted it include Hogarth, Thomas Shotter Boys and, in the 20th century, Tristram Hillier and John Piper, who painted three of the city's churches bombed in the Second World War.

To this local collection have been added good 18th-century English paintings by Richard Wilson;[51] an early, bravura portrait by Lawrence aged twenty-three, of the *Third Duke of Portland* (1792);[52] and an unusual, small Reynolds, *The Out of Town Party* (1759–61). This conversation piece, commissioned by Horace Walpole, depicts George Selwyn, MP, Lord Mount-Edgecumbe, MP[53] and 'Gilly' Williams, who used to meet at Strawberry Hill every Christmas and Easter.

The gallery's small 19th-century collection avoids for the most part the Pre-Raphaelites (there is a late Millais, *The Bride of Lammermoor*, 1870, and two large Burne-Joneses) and the genre paintings acquired with such zeal by many public galleries, favouring instead pictures by William Etty, G. F. Watts (one of several versions of *Love and Death*)[54] and a seductive Leighton, *The Fisherman and the Siren* (1856–8), in which all the elements, the swirling waves, the writhing fishes, the siren's arms and hair and tail conspire to suck the fisherman down.[55]

This emphasis on local material is marked in the museum's decorative arts collections which have, not surprisingly, excellent examples of Bristol Blue glass (signed pieces by Isaac Jacobs) and 19th-century Nailsea glass; Bristol-made and hallmarked silver (17th–19th centuries); English Delft ware made in Bristol and at nearby Brislington (*c.*1640–*c.*1785); soft-paste porcelain from Benjamin Lund's factory (1748–51) and hard paste porcelain by Richard Champion and William Cookworthy (1770–78). In the 19th century Edward Raby, working at the Bristol Pottery, produced enamelled and gilded porcelain of splendid extravagance (the 'Raby' vase, *c.*1840).

The museum also inherited from the Literary and Philosophical Society strong collections of geology and mineralogy. In the limestone of the Avon Gorge and the nearby Mendips are to be found fossils from the Carboniferous and Triassic periods. Jurassic marine vertebrates swam in the seas over what is now Somerset and Wiltshire, as did reptilian sea dragons, plesiosaurs, pliosaurs and the 26-foot-long ichthyosaur recovered from the Lower Jurassic rocks at Charmouth on the Dorset coast. Such local minerals as celestine (strontium sulphate) were the raw materials on which local industries such as sugar-refining were developed.

Bristol has been a great port for 500 years. Through it has passed England's trade with, first, Europe, and then America, Africa, the East: tobacco, textiles, slaves, manufactures. It is inevitable, and proper, that the museum's collections should reflect those wider worlds. As you enter the building you are met by Ernest Board's painting of *Cabot Leaving* and a roll-call of 'some who have made Bristol famous': John and Sebastian Cabot, John Wesley, William Penn, Edmund Burke, Humphry Davy but, surprisingly, not Isambard Kingdom Brunel, whose SS *Great Britain* (q.v.) was built in the docks within sight of the museum.

Sailors, merchants, missionaries and explorers brought back the masks, weapons, tools and clothes that comprise the ethnographic collection, presided over by mounted wild animals from the natural history collection: a crested porcupine, an aardvark, a yellow mongoose, a zorilla,[56] a young adult giraffe and Alfred, the Western Lowland gorilla who lived in Bristol Zoo from 1927 to 1948.

The museum had already acquired three Assyrian reliefs (*c.* 860 BC), excavated by Sir Henry Layard in 1845, from the north-western palace of Ashurnasipal II at Nimrud, described by Layard as 'a sun-burnt yellow heap', and 163 drawings by Giovanni Battista Belzoni, the only record of the subsequently damaged tomb of the Pharaoh Sethos I in the Valley of the Kings.

Belzoni went to Egypt in 1813 looking for work. The British Consul-General, Sir Henry Salt, employed him to move the stone head of the young Memnon from Thebes to Alexandria, for shipment back to Britain. In doing so he discovered the temple of Abu-Simnel and seven tombs, including those of Rameses I and Sethos I. Howard Carter called Belzoni 'one of the most remarkable men in the entire history of archaeology'. These drawings, and the obelisk at Kingston Lacy, are the best memorials to him in Britain.[57]

Here too are pots, coffins and mummies from the Egypt Exploration Fund, co-founded by Amelia Edwards, the popular novelist, amateur archaeologist and patron of Flinders Petrie (v. the Petrie Museum).

Other bequests have added distinction to the museum. Ferdinand Schiller, Recorder of Bristol (1935–46), and his brother, Max, gave their 400-piece collection of Chinese ceramics, notable for its Song, Kuan and Hunan ware and for a very rare piece of Wa-Cha-P'ing ware (late Tang Dynasty, *c.* 907–60), one of only two examples outside China, the other being in the Boston (Massachusetts) Museum of Fine Arts. With the collection of Chinese glass (Manchu Qing Dynasty, 1644–1912) and 18th-century Japanese prints (including works by Harunobu), this comprises the strongest collection of Far Eastern art, outside the national collections, in Britain.

In 1978 James Bomford gave his collection of Roman, Egyptian and Syrian glass, blown and moulded, with pieces from 1500 BC to AD 500. Glowing quietly in cases their delicacy defies time. 'How could anything so fragile still be in existence after being buried under the earth for such a long time?' Bomford wondered.[58] Note a freeblown flask (4th–5th century AD), with a ringed neck and internal threads of pale transparent brown, and an Alexandrian (1st century BC–1st century AD) footed flask with composite swirls of brown and white.

It is fortunate that the art gallery viewed Herkomer's advice with some scepticism. Had it not done so we would have been deprived of a fine small collection of Old Masters that includes Giovanni Bellini's *Descent of Christ into Limbo*, possibly a copy of a lost Mantegna (his brother-in-law); a superb early Venetian capriccio by Bernardo Bellotto, Canaletto's nephew and pupil; and a glorious, immense extravaganza, *Noah's Ark* (*c.*1710), by the Dutch Jan Griffier. All these would grace a national collection, as would the *Crucifixion and Lamentation* (*c.*1335) by Giotto's pupil Taddeo Gaddi and a portrait of *Martin Luther* by Lucas Cranach, whose rippling silhouette of black cloth against a pale green ground provides a powerful setting for the head.

The Dutch collection is small but of good quality: a Jacob van Ruisdael, a William van der Velde the Younger, a Jan van der Heyden and the *Tavern Scene* by Adriaen Brouwer, which was once owned by Rubens.

The consistent quality of the various picture collections owes much to Hans Schubart, the gallery's German director from 1953 to 1968. He gained the confidence of the National Art Collections Fund and the Contemporary Art Society and significantly enhanced the collection of French paintings. Its strength is the mid 19th century (Corot, Delacroix, Courbet, the Le Nain brothers) but he also acquired works by Vuillard, and a beautiful, small sketch by Georges Seurat, a 'croqueton', *Sunset* (1881), painted at the start of his too brief, ten-year working life.

Typical of Schubart's taste are two purchases: a rare (in British galleries) portrait of the wife of a Genoese ship-owner *Madame Brugiere* (1796) by Baron Antoine-Jean Gros, pupil of David and tutor of Bonington and, more unusual still, *The Flight into Egypt* (*c.*1600–10) by the Milanese artist Giovanni Battista Crespi, called Il Cerano. The painting had no provenance and its artist was 'anonymous'.[59] Nevertheless Schubart recognised the beauty and intensity of this huge canvas. The figures (Joseph, a donkey, a putto) move in a circular, clockwise rhythm. The Virgin Mary and the Christ Child form a small counter rhythm above. Her arm also moves clockwise but her head and the Christ's arm are inclined anti-clockwise as the infant reaches down for an apple. Its palette comprises fawns and warm browns, at the centre of which is the rich, soft rose-pink of the dress. It is a work of tenderness and subtlety, public in scale, private in emotion.

Schubart was also largely responsible for the thoughtful, and full, collection of 20th-century English painting and sculpture here. Starting with Sickert, Gilman, Gore, William Nicholson and Gaudier-Brzeska, it maintains its quality throughout its overview of the century: Bomberg, William Roberts, Nevinson, Wadsworth, Augustus John, Gwen John, Christopher Wood between the wars; Hepworth, Ben Nicholson, Henry Moore, Ivon Hitchens in the 1940s and '50s; and more recently artists who are seen too seldom in public collections such as Ian Stephenson and David Nash, and finally the Bristol-born sculptor Richard Long, with a work made in local slate. It is a collection that establishes Schubart as one of the outstanding regional directors of the 1950s and '60s, able to stand beside Ellis Waterhouse at the Barber Institute of Fine Arts and Hans Hess at the York Art Gallery.

Bristol Art Gallery and Museum cannot match the Ashmolean Museum, the Fitzwilliam Museum or the Walker Art Gallery (all q.v.) but in one century, without exceptional investment or endowments, it has made itself a prince among regional museums.

SS GREAT BRITAIN *

Great Western Dock, Gas Ferry Road,
Bristol, Avon BS1 6TY
Tel. 0117 926 0680
www.ss-great-britain.com

Brunel's great ocean-going iron ship, from Queen of the seas to storage hulk and back again to harbour

The *United Service Gazette* (1843) declared: 'The *Great Britain* is the largest vessel that has been constructed since the days of Noah.'[60] Startling though her size was, it was not simply that but also her wrought-iron hull, her screw propeller, her watertight bulkhead that combined to make her design, by Isambard Kingdom Brunel, revolutionary.

She was the first modern ship, 'the great-grandmother of every modern ocean-going ship'.[61] Her design brought about a trans-formation in world trade, communications and travel; it led to the dominance of British shipbuilders and shipping for much of the 19th century, thus contributing to the expansion of the British Empire; it made possible the European diaspora to the United States. As Basil Greenhill, former director of the National Maritime Museum, wrote: 'It is impossible to imagine a more important survivor of our heritage in terms of her significance to the industrial, economic and social development of Britain.'[62]

Today she sits in a floating harbour in the docks that Brunel built to construct her sister ship the *Great Western* in 1836–7. Out of the water she bulges on each side, a designed feature by Brunel to maximise internal space. Above the waterline she is sleek and sheer with the thrusting bows of a clipper ship for speed. Her hull is 'clinker built', its vast black iron plates riveted to overlap horizontally. Above its deck rise five masts[63] and a single tall black funnel. She is all power and beauty.

Within, the Forecastle, the Engine Room, the Promenade Deck and Cabins, and the First Class Dining Room have been restored to their 1845 glory, carpeted, mirrored, glittering.

Between her glorious launch by Prince Albert on 19 July 1843, when 'every church has displayed its flags, the ships have been dressed out in a variety of colours; peals have rung, and cannon fired; indeed every demonstration has been made that loyalty and rejoicing could inspire,'[64] and her restored state today, the *Great Britain* has lived a saga.

She had a triumphant first voyage to New York; encountered technical and commercial setbacks; and ran aground on the coast of Northern Ireland in 1846. In 1850 she was sold for less than one fifth of her original cost and converted to ply a trade in emigrants (out) and gold and wool (return) to Australia. In the Crimean War and the Indian Mutiny she served as a supply and troopship. By 1876, having carried an estimated 250,000 emigrants from Britain to Australia, she was sold and reduced to the ignominy of carrying coal

round Cape Horn to San Francisco, returning with wheat – a voyage that took nearly a year. On her third such trip she foundered and sought refuge in the Falkland Islands, where she became a store ship, first for wool, then for coal. When even that modest role became uneconomic she was towed out into Sparrow Cove in 1937 and beached, with holes knocked in her stern to ensure that she would never float again.

But this is a romantic saga and in 1967 Dr Ewan Corlett[65] and others started a campaign to salvage her. Financed by Sir Jack Hayward,[66] they raised her and brought her 7,000 miles back to Britain on a pontoon, entering Bristol on 19 July, 127 years to the day after she was launched by Prince Albert.

To walk on or below the *Great Britain*'s decks is to summon up the spirit of her many lives: the luxury of the First Class Dining Room, served by twelve stewards, the toughness of life in steerage with food (salt beef and fish) and water rationed, and passengers sharing a water pump with the crew. On the way out to Australia passengers travelled in hope (adventurers, emigrants) or desperation (failures, remittance men). Above it all is the ship herself,[67] Brunel's wonderwork.

BRITISH EMPIRE AND COMMONWEALTH MUSEUM **

Clock Tower Yard, Temple Meads,
Bristol BS1 6QH
Tel. 0117 925 4980
www.empiremuseum.co.uk

Enormous collection of ethnographic and social archival effects of Empire, upon which the sun did set

The collections of the British Empire and Commonwealth Museum began with a single object, presented by one of its trustees, Sir Jack Hayward, on 25 September 2001. With it he gave money to convert Brunel's restored Old Station at Bristol Temple Meads on condition that the building work be completed within one year. The museum opened on 26 September 2002.

That one object was Roderick Mackenzie's monumental painting *The State Entry Procession at the 1903 Delhi Durbar* (1903). Here is the Empire at its zenith, in full fig and pomp. The Viceroy leads the procession, perched in a gilded howdah on a mighty elephant, followed by a train of Indian princes. On a video screen beside the painting plays newsreel film of the same procession, the grandeur flickering. Mahouts and elephants, their saddle cloths encrusted with silver-thread zardozi embroidery, roll past the silent cheering crowd.

The museum sets itself the challenge of providing an all-encompassing view of Empire and Commonwealth, a defiantly brave gesture that requires it to pick its way between jingoism and apology. It is not afraid to face the failings of the British; nor does it turn away from the achievements of creating and administering an Empire that in 1900 held subject one-fifth of the world's population and a Commonwealth of fifty-four nations that today has a population of 1.7 billion.

On entering, the first object you see is a large video screen. Others are positioned throughout the building. On them play continuously interviews from the museum's archive of over 3,500. Screens and interviews make a clear statement that the museum will tell its story through the detail of individual experience. This archive is a triumph, as impressive a use of video as in any British museum.

The idea of the museum came to John Letts, long-time board member of the Museums and Galleries Commission and founder of the Museum of the Year Award, while sitting in his garden in 1972. He reflected that many museums across the Commonwealth and in Britain had large and relevant collections (notably ethnographic) but that no single museum was concerned with the legacy of the Empire and Commonwealth. Initially the board and the first director, Gareth Griffiths, envisaged this as a museum with a rotating collection loaned from other museums, turning the potential problem of the lack of a founding collection into an asset. This approach received strong support from universities and scholars, but the Museums and Galleries Commission declined to recognise it as a museum because it had no permanent collection, thus making it ineligible for any support.

Fortunately some individual museums have been more positive and objects have been loaned which tell parts of the story: the origins of the Honourable East India Company (1600) which by 1780 effectively ruled over 20 million Indians; the less well-known Hudson's Bay Company (1668) whose founders were 'absolute lordes and proprietors' of all lands that drained into Hudson's Bay; the slave trade promoted by the Royal African Company (1698) which sold 4 million Africans into slavery between 1640 and 1807; the opening up of Africa, the development of her assets and the destruction of such civilisations as Benin; the first convict settlements in Australia (1788).

These galleries make it clear that it was trade and the appetite for new raw materials (sugar, tea, spices, gold, diamonds) that drove the expansion of the Empire, and military power that effected it. The weapons of the conquered are displayed beside those of the conquerors: a Fijian club, 'tido-ni-gata', on which are notched the club's fifteen victims (pre 1841); a bird-shaped Maori club, 'patu'; a Zulu assegai, 'isijula', from the battle of Ginginhloru (1879); a Sudanese Beja hide shield; British rifles. 'With your weapons you shoot from afar,' observed Chief Ndausi Kumalo, veteran of the Anglo-Ndebele wars of 1893–6, 'and do not know who you are killing: that is unmanly. We prefer to fight man to man. These weapons are too dreadful for us.'

One line of graphics records the wars and uprisings, twenty-six in the 19th century, from the Mysore Rising (1799) to the Red River Rebellion (1869), the Afghan wars (1878) to the Ashanti wars (1900), the Barbados Revolt of Slaves (1816) to the Boxer Rebellion (1898–1900), Aden (1839) to the Boer Wars (1800–99).

Jean Barbot, a 17th-century trader with Benin, observed in 1631: 'Oedo, the metropolis of Benin, is prodigious large ... no town in Guinea can compare to it for extent and beauty ... The inhabitants of this Great City are ... very civil and good natured people ... according to their ancient customs, and will not suffer them to be abolished.' In 1897 the great Edo civilisation was destroyed by British soldiers and 900 of their sacred Edo bronzes removed to Britain.[68]

In exchange for the trophies and natural wealth of these nations, the British offered religion, technology, know-how and order. 'It is the duty of Government to civilise and to maintain peace and good order, and this can only be done by the introduction of British concepts of wrongdoing,' reported the 1934 Royal Commission into Criminal Justice in East Africa.

With a subject of this size it is inevitable that some aspects receive less attention than they might. The contribution of the Scots in opening up these countries is noted but not fully explored. Nor is the role of (foreign-owned) mining companies. There could be more about cartography: how maps both reveal and subjugate new worlds. How did the British Empire differ from the other European Empires – French, Dutch, Spanish, German, Portuguese? More attention could be given to the transition from Empire to Common-wealth. Where is Gandhi, where India's struggle for independence? What connection can be made between British rule, British with-drawal and the rise of such rulers as Idi Amin and Robert Mugabe? As Linda Colley, Professor of History at the London School of Economics, has noted, 'we may be in a post-colonial world but we are not yet in a post-imperial world.'

Many of these questions are addressed implicitly in the archive of recorded interviews with people from every Commonwealth country and from many walks of life, public

The State Entry Procession at the 1903 Delhi Durbar *by Roderick Mackenzie (British Empire and Commonwealth Museum)*

and private: with Minoo Masani, who helped write the Indian constitution, and Dr Usha Mehta, who ran the underground radio for the Indian National Congress, both colleagues of Mahatma Gandhi; with B. C. Dutt, who took part in the Royal Indian Navy mutiny of 1946; with Pearl Connor, who came from Trinidad in 1938 to what she sees as a 'step-mother land', cold even in spring.

The historian Jan Morris has called the Empire 'the most thundering contribution these Islands ever made to history'. This enlightening museum records the scale of that contribution and the ambiguous rumble of that thunder.

CHELTENHAM ART GALLERY AND MUSEUM **

Clarence Street, Cheltenham, Gloucestershire GL50 3JT
Tel. 01242 237431
www.cheltenham.artgallery.museum

Nationally important Arts and Crafts furniture and Dutch paintings

Cheltenham has the finest collection of Arts and Crafts furniture and design in Britain, outside the Victoria and Albert Museum (q.v.), with works by all the major architects and craftsmen who contributed to that move-ment: C. R. Ashbee, C. F. A. Voysey, M. H. Baillie Scott, Ernest Gimson, and Ernest and Sidney Barnsley. The art gallery also contains decorative arts collections, notably of Chinese ceramics, and British and Dutch paintings of the 17th, 18th and 20th centuries.

In 1929 the Royal Academy mounted a great exhibition of 17th-century Dutch art. Four of the paintings had been in the collection that Baron de Ferrières gave Cheltenham in 1898: two Jan Steens, *The Lean Kitchen* and *The Fat Kitchen*; a Gerrit Dou self-portrait; and *A Man and a Woman at Wine* by Dou's pupil, Gabriel Metsu.

Another pupil of Dou, Godfried Schalcken, has a *Portrait of Rachel Ruysch*, an artist whose own painting, *Flowers in a Vase*, is also here,

beside works by Adriaen van Ostade, his pupil Cornelis Dusart, and Philips Wouwermans, and a large landscape by Jan Looten, which is marked by the influence of Hobbema.

It is a collection whose quality overshadows the 18th-century English works (portraits by Thomas Hudson and Francis Cotes) and the French (a landscape by Claude Joseph Vernet). Near by are two curiosities: a chalk drawing of the *Head of an Old Man*, *c.* 1550, by Giorgio Vasari, the architect, pupil of Michelangelo and author of *Lives of the Artists* (1550), and two large panoramic landscapes, primitive and anonymous, of Dixton Manor, Gloucestershire (*c.* 1715), its fields laid out like illustrated maps.

The 20th-century collection includes paintings by Henry Lamb, Vanessa Bell, David Bomberg, Stanley Spencer and Paul Nash; sculpture by Lynn Chadwick; and furniture including a chair, in birch, by Alvar Aalto (*c.* 1930s).

Galleries that continued to acquire contemporary work through the 1950s and '60s are comparatively rare. Here the acquisitions demonstrate that determination, but it is hard to discern in them a coherent taste with a characteristic other than 'English' and 'figurative'.

The Chinese ceramics reflect the interests of Berkeley Smith, who collected them mainly in India. In them we can see the tides of the Indo-Chinese trade. Between 1300 and 1433, and from 1500 to 1675, that trade was mainly by sea. Here is an early Ming (late 14th century) celadon charger, and a mid-14th-century Yuan charger in blue and white, decorated with egrets and lotus flowers. Here too are everyday objects, jars and wine flasks, from the 10th–11th-century Liao Dynasty, and funerary objects (a horse, a ram, a boat, a cockerel) from the late 14th century.

In the mid 18th century China's patrons in India were the new European ruling class. Their taste was for cobalt blue and white ware called Kraak after the Portuguese carrack

Silverware at Cheltenham Art Gallery and Museum

or galleon, but this market wanted Chinese designs on European shapes and Berkeley Smith's collection demonstrates the crosscurrents of influence: the glazes and colours that inspired Spode adapted to plates with flat edges and cups with handles; armorial services that an English family ordered from China; copies of Chinese subjects by Bow and Worcester.

In contrast, the Arts and Crafts collection has been put together with singular coherence and so provides an overview of the way in which the movement developed. Born in reaction to the Great Exhibition of 1851, which promoted industrial design and the glories of mass production, it was inspired by the writings of Ruskin and the work of William Morris. There is a fair representative sample of Morris's work here: a painted pine table (1856), made while he was living with Edward Burne-Jones in Red Lion Square, and later used in Kelmscott village hall; curtains, of Morris's 'Tulip and Rose' design, which remained in production from 1876 to 1928; some 'Blackthorn' wallpaper and an 1896 proof page from the Kelmscott Press's edition of *The Works of Geoffrey Chaucer* (1896), with wood engravings by Burne-Jones.

Given the diversity of his work it is not surprising that the influence of Morris on the next generation of designers was similarly diverse. Here is George Jack's display cabinet (*c.* 1902), whose simplicity of line goes back to Sheraton; C. F. A. Voysey's swan chair (1896) and cabinet (1899), made to house a copy of Morris's *Chaucer*; the strong, rectilinear lines of C. R. Ashbee's writing cabinet (1902).

All were trained as architects, conscious of line, of form and of the effect of what Philip Webb called 'the truth to materials': veneered ebony and holly (Ashbee's cabinet), walnut and Macassar ebony (Gimson's dining table) and oak (Baillie Scott's settle, Voysey's swan chair). Each piece is distinguished by the signature of the craftsmanship, seen most clearly in the work of the Cotswold workshop that Ernest Gimson set up with Sidney and Ernest Barnsley.

All were affected by the romantic socialism

of Morris and Ruskin, as described in *Unto This Last*, but the economics of their crafts-manship meant that only the rich could afford their work. Gimson's dining table in walnut and Macassar ebony took 688 hours to make, its matching sideboard a further 453 hours. It sold for £109. 6s. od. at a time when the aver-age annual income was £110. Walter Crane could urge that 'the true root and basis of all Art lies in the handicrafts' and that his mission was to 'turn our artists into craftsmen and our craftsmen into artists' but the economic reali-ties were against him, and against Gimson and the Barnsleys.

Ashbee came to recognise the inevitability of industrial design and manufacture. He was among the first to see the importance of Frank Lloyd Wright and by 1910 was of the opinion that 'modern civilisation rests on machinery, and no system for the encouragement or the endowment of the teaching of the arts can be sound that does not recognise this.'

Others took to teaching, W. R. Lethaby becoming the first principal of the Central School of Arts and Crafts in London, but the influence of the movement lived on: in Europe, in the work of the Bauhaus; in the United States in Frank Lloyd Wright and in groups such as the Craftsman Workshops, Eastwood, New York; and in Britain in individual designers such as Alan Peters, an apprentice of Sidney Barnsley's son Edwin. Their roots are here in the grain and the detail of these individual pieces.

FOX TALBOT MUSEUM *

Lacock, Chippenham, Wiltshire SN15 2LG
Tel. 01249 730459
www.r-cube.co.uk/fox-talbot/index.html

The haunting legacy of the inventor of the photographic process

The world's earliest authenticated surviving negative, 1⅜ inches by 1⅛ inches, the size of a postage stamp, photographed by William Henry Fox Talbot in August 1935, is of a latticed oriel window in the South Gallery of Lacock Abbey. Black light streams through; 'the squares of glass about 200 in number could be counted, with the help of a lens,' wrote Fox Talbot.

It is an inappropriately quiet image through which to convey a process that was about to change the world, but it reflects the tone that runs through this museum, which is housed in a 16th-century stone barn near the entrance to Fox Talbot's house, Lacock Abbey. As the museum describes the life and work of Fox Talbot, it is necessary to keep reminding yourself that you are witnessing the birth of a revolution.

'I think the year 1839 may fairly be con-sidered as the real date of the birth of the Photographic Art,' wrote Fox Talbot.[69] In 1839, as Charles Darwin was publishing *The Voyage of the Beagle* and J. M. W. Turner was painting *The Fighting Temeraire*, four men (Louis-Jacques Mandé Daguerre, Hippolyte Bayard, Niécephore Niépce and Henry Fox Talbot) were on the brink of finally fixing a photo-graphic image.

That such images could be made had been known for centuries. Roger Bacon, a Fran-ciscan friar, had used lenses and mirrors to produce 'visible pictures' in the 13th century. Leonardo da Vinci and the Neapolitan Battista Porta had described the camera obscura. Canaletto and numerous 18th-century painters had used its projections to help create precise and accurate paintings. But no one had been able to 'fix' those images.

Thomas Wedgwood, son of Josiah, and Humphry Davy had identified the role that silver nitrate could play when exposed to light, but a sure process remained elusive. On 6 January 1839 Daguerre announced his success. 'I have seized the light, I have arrested its flight,' he proclaimed. Fox Talbot res-ponded with a paper to the Royal Society on 31 January.[70] On 28 February the word photograph was coined by Sir John Herschel, the astronomer, whose understanding of sodium hyposulphate had helped Fox Talbot. Photography was born.

From the outset the dual nature of photog-raphy was apparent: were its roots in art or in science? Were the images produced a neutral record or a work of art?

Daguerre was a painter of theatrical backdrops. Fox Talbot was a classicist, a mathematician (elected as a Fellow of the Royal Society at the age of thirty-one) and a scientist, drawn to the problems inherent in photography by his experiments in chemistry, optics and the nature of light. Their processes reflected these differences. Daguerre's was a far superior image, a single opaque plate on which the image was reversed, but which could only yield a single reproduction. Fox Talbot's was a negative from which, in theory, unlimited copies could be made.

Exhibits in the museum trace the progress of Fox Talbot's experiments: the Chevalier microscope under which he examined specimens of tourmaline and Icelandic fluorspar to observe the crystalline structure of polarised light; the Nicol prism and solar microscope with which he pursued these investigations, making some of his first photographic experiments with the latter that explored the sensitivity of nitrate of silver to the action of light; and finally, the lattice window negative of 1835.

Here are some of the first calotypes (from the Greek καλός, meaning beautiful) he made in the 1840s – *Canterbury Cathedral from across the Water Meadows* (1845) – after he established a studio and printing works in Reading in 1844. It was here that he published *The Pencil of Light*, in six parts, each with between three and seven photographs, describing his invention of photography and demonstrating a variety of subjects, his *liber studiorum*.

The studies include porcelain objects, glassware, a manuscript, a shelf of books in his library, and photographic drawings of tree foliage and lace. The extent to which the public found it difficult to comprehend this new medium is illustrated by the advice in the text, intended to reassure anxious prospective sitters, that 'groups of figures take no longer time to obtain than single figures would require, since the camera depicts them all at once, however numerous they may be.' Despite such reassurances the *Athenaeum*

Review predicted that 'the effort required to take a photograph is too great for it to ever become a generally useful means of illustration.'

Among the plates in *The Pencil of Light* are three which show Fox Talbot's skills of composition: two still lifes, *The Haystack* (plate x) and the enigmatic *The Open Door* (plate vi), in which light falls through an open door on a diagonal that is parallel to a broom leaning against the door frame; and the first photograph to feature people, *The Ladder* (plate xiv).

The Reading studio lost money and although Fox Talbot patented his inventions he never derived much income from them. He continued to try to perfect techniques of photo-mechanical reproduction but he concentrated, for the last twenty-seven years of his life, on biblical and archaeological matters and on deciphering Assyrian cuneiform.

Fox Talbot's scientific intellect and aesthetic imagination enabled him to summon up and fix images out of light, demonstrating conclusively the truth of Novalis's assertion that 'All that is visible rests upon an invisible foundation.'[71]

CORINIUM MUSEUM **

Park Street, Cirencester, Gloucestershire
GL7 2BX
Tel. 01285 655611, fax 01285 643286
www.cotswold.gov.uk/museum

Mosaics and sculpture from Roman Cirencester

Here on the far north-western edge of the Roman Empire are mosaics that depict the fountains, peacocks, flowers and fabrics of the East, of Antioch and Byzantium, of Persia and Arabia. They were part of a river of thought and images that flowed through the Empire and lapped Britain briefly.

Corinium Dobunorum (now Cirencester) was, in size and population, the largest town in Roman Britain after London. Inscriptions on the Septimus stone establish that it was the capital of the province, Britannica Prima. This museum displays the wealth and importance of the town. There is no shortage of domestic objects of quality: jewellery, games, cosmetics and phials for them, coins, Samian ware and well-crafted tools. The highlights are six mosaics, of which four are outstanding.

An excavation in Dyer Street in 1849 by Buckman and Newmarsh uncovered two mosaics, the *Four Seasons* and *Hunting Dogs*, both largely intact, which establish Corinium as a major centre of mosaic production using local limestone and sandstone, with glass and tile fragments being used for contrast. The seasons, of which spring (*flora*), summer (*ceres*) and autumn (*pomona*) have survived, are in corner panels. In the centre are scenes of a bearded Silenus, preceptor of Bacchus, riding on a donkey and of Actaeon at the moment of being turned into a stag and attacked by his own dogs. In the *Hunting Dogs* mosaic the three central dogs are complemented by masks of Neptune and by dolphins and winged sea beasts.

A further mosaic from an excavation at Barton Farm is of Orpheus; in it fierce animals – a lion, a leopard and a tiger – prowl round the central medallion in which Orpheus is depicted with his lyre, surrounded by a spellbound aviary of peacocks, a pheasant and a duck.

Fine though these are, the museum's prize is the hare mosaic, found in Beeches Road, Cirencester, in 1971. In its largest panel a hare grazes, enclosed by interlaced squares of guilloche and surrounded by lozenges, squares and triangles. Unusually the guilloche has a treble strand, a technique employed frequently at Bignor, West Sussex, but on only one other mosaic here.

Much can be learned of, and from, the religious life of Corinium. As was not unusual in Roman Britain (v. the Roman Baths at Bath), local gods and cults coexisted or were fused with Roman gods. There are statuettes of Vulcan, Diana and Mercury, as well as a unique relief of three (a significant and magical Celtic number) mother goddesses, *deae matres*, dressed in tunics, with baskets, bread and fruit. The quality of the carving in the oolitic Cotswold limestone is fine. A small acrostic, scratched into plaster, tells of

someone who clung in secret to the Christian faith he had adopted.

Very little Roman public statuary survives in Britain. However, examples here include two column capitals (one carved with acanthus leaves; the other depicting gods and goddesses) and a head of Mercury. His heavy face and large features have led some to compare it unfavourably with contemporary Mediterranean classical statues, but it is not inexpertly made: rather, it is the product of a different aesthetic.

More evidence of this may be seen in the reliefs on tombstones. Among the headstones ('to the spirits of the departed [and] to Julia Casta, his wife [who] lived 33 years' and 'to . . . Aurelius Igennus, aged 6 years [less] six months, Aurelius Enticianus, his parent, placed this here') is a substantial one to a trooper in the Cavalry Regiment of Thracians, Sextus Valerius Genialis. He was a Frisian tribesman, aged forty, who had served for twenty years in the Roman Army and was buried here, hundreds of miles from home. His heir erected a stone statue, seven feet high, depicting Genialis on a fine horse, drawn sword in hand. There is nothing classical about either the pose or the modelling.

'What the Corinium Museum has to offer is a rich collection that demonstrates the interaction between a Roman provincial town and its countryside,' writes Professor Barry Cunliffe. The exposure of Britain to Roman culture in the first millennium was brief but its mark is here.

WILTSHIRE HERITAGE MUSEUM **

41 Long Street, Devizes, Wiltshire SN10 1NS
Tel. 01380 727369
www.wiltshireheritage.org.uk

Fine prehistoric collections from the cradle of British archaeology

'We speak from facts, not theory . . . I shall not seek amongst the fanciful regions of Romance on the origin of our Wiltshire Britons,' insists Sir Richard Colt Hoare in his introduction to

Ancient History of North and South Wiltshire.[72]

His work with William Cunnington made them 'the fathers of archaeological established excavation in England'[73] and laid the foundations upon which subsequent generations of archaeologists have been able to build an understanding of our Neolithic past. Colt Hoare came from the landed Wiltshire family that owned Hoare's bank. Cunnington was a wool merchant and draper from Northamptonshire who had come south to the Wiltshire downlands. In a series of summer excavation campaigns across Wiltshire between 1803 and 1810, planned, supervised and financed by Colt Hoare, and conducted by Cunnington, they undertook 'the accurate investigation of the numerous British and Saxon earthen works with which our country abounds'.[74]

At Windmill Hill, above the great temple at Avebury, Cunnington and Colt Hoare uncovered evidence of a large settlement of people who had crossed from the European mainland (*c.* 3500 BC) in search of fresh land on which to raise stock and cultivate crops. That they were sophisticated may be seen from the quality of the pottery found in the Windmill Hill causeways and barrows, now in this museum: a carinated bowl, with shallow channelling above the carination, and a bowl with fingernail impressions on the rim,[75] both from causewayed camps, both made from clay 'levigated with grits, and fine enough to allow quite thin walls and a well-smoothed, glossy surface'.[76]

Colt Hoare and Cunnington's excavations at Windmill Hill, Woodhenge, Normanton Down and West Kennet Long Barrow brought to a close 300 years of English antiquarianism. Henges and barrows had been inspected and speculated upon by Leland and Camden[77] in the 16th century, by John Aubrey in the 17th century and after the founding in 1718 of the Society of Antiquaries, with increased fervour by, among others, William Stukeley, the champion and populariser of the Druids, whose romantic theories were given rein by the absence of artefacts.

The objects that came from Colt Hoare and Cunnington's digs, and from the work of those who followed them, are here: flat-bottomed ware from West Kennet, decorated with grooves and incised and pointillé patterns; beakers from Roundway; stone axes from Woodhenge; later Bronze Age finds from warrior and royal graves at Winterbourne Stoke and Wilsford; the paraphernalia of a princely burial, *c.* 1750–1550 BC, at Normanton Down, complete with mace, axe, large decorated daggers and a diamond-shaped plaque for his chest; and, the centrepiece, the Marlborough bucket, excavated in 1807. Its staves of yew are bound by three iron hoops, alternating with friezes of thin embossed bronze sheets, showing heads (full face and in profile) and pairs of horses. Probably made in Northern Gaul, *c.* 150 BC–AD 50, it is one of the finest examples of Celtic la Tène metalwork.

Although their digs were crude by modern standards, Colt Hoare and Cunnington kept 'accurate and exhaustive account'.[78] Cunnington's, in the form of letters and memoranda, comprises thirteen books. At the time the understanding that could be gleaned from them was limited but, together with the fossils and objects in this collection, they have provided the raw materials from which others, notably Pitt Rivers in the 1880s, M. E. Cunnington in the 1930s and Stuart Piggott in the 1940s and '50s, have been able to recover these periods of British prehistory, establishing, from the techniques of metalwork and the sources of copper, tin, bronze and stone, that these people had strong cultural and economic connections with central Europe.

Cunnington kept many of these objects in the garden of his house at Heytesbury in a large summerhouse museum. After his death his collection of finds was purchased by Colt Hoare and displayed at Stourhead (q.v.), finally being acquired in 1878 by the Wiltshire Heritage Museum (q.v., then known as Devizes Museum). This progress, from display in private (often aristocratic) houses to public buildings, reflects the emergence of the 19th-century archaeological museum just as clearly as Colt Hoare and Cunnington's excavations mark the move from antiquarianism to archaeology.

Colt Hoare was anxious that his finds should

be replicated, as Greek and Roman antiquities had been, and he commissioned Josiah Wedgwood to produce a series in basalt and in jasperware, overriding Wedgwood's reservations. Up to six dozen copies of each pot were made, some of which are here.

But Wedgwood's commercial instinct was correct: there was no need for Wedgwood replicas. Colt Hoare and Cunnington's work is its own memorial. It has 'an international fame among archaeologists and prehistorians',[79] providing archives and material from which still more understanding can be elicited and which are, in the opinion of Professor Stuart Piggott, 'not only important but indispensable'.[80]

They help the layman to imagine the lives of the people who built these structures, the massive iconic monuments of early British civilisation.

ROYAL ALBERT MEMORIAL MUSEUM AND ART GALLERY ***

Queen Street, Exeter, Devon EX4 3RX
Tel. 01392 665858

Encyclopaedic use of stone in the construction of the museum; fine collections of natural history, ethnography and Devon artists

Its name does not lie. It honours the memory of Prince Albert, as do the Victoria and Albert and the Natural History Museums, all sustaining his belief that a museum should be both for education and for entertainment, and should be free.

As a regional natural history museum, this museum gives more than a nod to Waterhouse's Natural History Museum, even in its 1865–6 design by Exeter architect John Hayward: a long, confident Gothic facade, enlivened by a variety of red, buff and grey stones from Chudleigh, Bath and Aberdeen. Its collections too, of fine and decorative art, ethnography, geology, natural history and archaeology, echo the V&A and the Natural History Museum.

These early ambitions are most fully realised in the ethnography collections which, if they cannot compare with the scope and scholarship that Pitt Rivers and Reinhold Forster brought to the Pitt Rivers Museum in Oxford (q.v), are eloquent about the spread of Empire and the dedication and curiosity of British officials, missionaries, soldiers and traders as they encountered other cultures around the world.

Here are Edgar Dewdney and his wife, Blanche Elizabeth Plantagenet, living with the Blackfoot Indians of the North American plains and bringing back the headdress of deerskin, golden eagle feathers and buffalo horns that belonged to Crowfoot, the principal chief of the Blackfoot, 1865–90.

Here is Richard Dennett, who went to the Congo in 1879 to represent the Liverpool company Hatton and Cookson, and sent home a Bakongo priest's tribal costume of wood and hornbill feathers that would keep spirits away. Dennett founded the *Congo Mirror* newspaper and the Congo Reform Association, to campaign against Belgian excesses.

Here are Micronesian weapons and ritual ornaments collected by Lt. George Phillpotts, RN, killed by the Maoris, and the Yoruba collection of G. Townsend, shown at the Great Exhibition.

These collections tell of the respect that these colonialists, all Devon born, had for the skill and sophistication of other cultures: an 1869 Aleutian Island ceremonial parka/kamleika of airy beauty, its material of white sea mammal gut delicately woven at the seams with human hair, a flicker of red wool embroidery at neck, cuff and hem; a cloak (1845) from the Makah nation of North America made from beaten cedar bark.

The late-19th-century collections by Percy Sladen of sea urchins and starfish are of special interest. Be guided by the words which form a decorative frieze round this small gallery: 'Look in the frame of this wide universe and therein read the endless kinds of creature who

Tahitian mourner's costume (Royal Albert Memorial Museum and Art Gallery)

by name thou canst not count much less their natures, all which are made wondrous with respect and with admirable beauty deckt.' Displayed beneath this, in his mahogany cases and cabinets, are Sladen's library and his microscopes, the tools with which he explored the 'admirable beauty' and variety of these echinoderms.

There are solid collections of ceramics (notably the late-19th-century work of the four Martin brothers) and of Exeter silver (by the 11th-century smiths John Jones and Richard Hilliard, and the 18th-century John Elston). The furthest room of the museum houses a collection of clocks, gently passing the time: fine long cases by Thomas Tompion and Edward East, chief clock maker to Charles II; Nicholas Lambert's clock (c. 1750–60), whose chime plays a descending octave at each quarter, and the Exeter clock of Jacob Lovelace (c. 1730–40) combining calendar, automation and musical clock with decorative casework attributed to John Channon, over which is inscribed 'TEMPUS RERUM IMPERATOR'.

The strengths of these collections are augmented by some of William Pengelly's finds from Kent's Cavern in Torquay (v. Torquay Museum) and good rooms of local medieval building techniques, starring a life-sized polychrome oak sculpture, c. 1500, of St Peter trampling the devil. St Peter has a model church and keys in his right hand, a bible in his left; the devil writhes beneath his feet.

Regrettably the galleries for the above, excellent collections, leave little space for the museum's collections of fine art. Selections of work from the fine art collection are shown on a rolling programme. As in Plymouth, priority has been given to local painters of the 18th and early 19th centuries: the portraitist Thomas Hudson, Francis Towne, his pupil John White Abbott and Samuel Prout. The Romantic artist Benjamin Robert Haydon was also Exeter born and the museum has bound volumes of his drawings, as it has those of John Constable. In the 20th century collections were made of the artists of the Camden Town Group (Gilman, Gore, Bevan) and, more recently, of St Ives painters (Frost, Heron, Wells, Barbara Hepworth). But it is the Sladen Collection and the way in which the museum's recent Director Katherine Chant has made a living link between Devon and the ethnographic collections from around the world that capture the spirit of the Sladen frieze when it urges us to 'look in the frame of this wide universe'.

NATIONAL MARITIME MUSEUM, CORNWALL ***

Discovery Quay, Falmouth, Cornwall
TR11 3SA
Tel. 01326 313388
www.nmmc.co.uk

A museum of boats moored at the water's edge in a building of craft and beauty

The National Maritime Museum, Cornwall sits at the harbourside, its keel in the water. It is a museum of boats, built like a boat, to a design by M. J. Long of Long and Beamish.[81] Its walls are clinker-clad with planks of unvarnished green oak that overlap to withstand the salt and the weather. At the edge of the quay is a tall, lighthouse-like tower. From its height you look west to Trefusis Point, the village of Flushing and the Carrick Roads, an estuary with some of the best sailing in Britain. On a calm day the boats ride gently in the harbour, nudging each other, a forest of masts and stays. When the wind is from the east it blows straight into the harbour, whipping up the water to test itself against harbour, boats and museum.

This is a museum as much of sail as of small boats. There is not an engine in sight. At its core is a collection of rare and unusual boats which, lacking space at the National Maritime Museum in Greenwich (q.v.), had been languishing in a red-brick and concrete ex-Ministry of Works building in south-east London, shrouded in plastic and canvas.

When the Cornwall Maritime Museum found that it needed either to expand or to

Falmouth flotilla

close, the two museums came together to apply for Heritage Lottery Fund investment to commission this new building. Cornwall contributes two side galleries, on the peninsula's maritime history and traditions and on the 18th–19th-century Falmouth packet that delivered the Royal Mail first to Spain and Portugal in 1689 and then across the Atlantic to Barbados, Jamaica, Surinam, Rio de Janeiro and Buenos Aires, running the gauntlet of pirates and enemy ships. It was once attacked by a man-o'-war of His Majesty's navy when it misread the packet ship's signals.

With no village more than sixteen miles from the sea, Cornwall is inseparable from ships and boats, its coastline indented by coves and anchorages, harbours, warehouses and quays: St Mawes, St Ives, Portreath, St Agnes; Port Isaac, Fowey and Bude. 'The sea has played a greater part in the life of the Cornish people than the land on which they dwelt,' writes John Rowe in his history, *Cornwall in the Age of Industrial Revolution*. Falmouth was its most westerly deep-water harbour: the quay to the Atlantic. It was fishing, for mackerel, herring and pilchards,[82] that sustained the economy: bringing back the fish for men and packing them in barrels for women. There are fine photographs in the museum (lean men, strong women, on the quayside, staring straight at the camera), though no photographer of the quality of Frank Sutcliffe in Whitby, and sadly few artefacts.

It is the collection of small boats that makes the heart of this museum beat. In a darkened gallery, films projected on to nine large screens tell the stories of North Sea, Inuit and Newfoundland fishermen. The soundtracks of the films tell of the roar of storms, the crack of lightning; the still silence of calm, and the gulls. Below you, in the deep shadows of the gallery, lurk real boats. It is well done but it lacks the vision that renders memorable the main gallery, in which there is a changing selection of the National Maritime Museum's boats. M. J. Long has built a cathedral to the boat, soaring three storeys high. Within it are suspended craft. In air, not water, they do not

move but the grace of their solid geometry floats there before you.

Here are boats that have worked all their lives (a Thames wherry, c. 1865, an oak clinker-built Fenland punt); exotic boats (the ornate Maltese dghaisa, c. 1870; a jangada, c. 1970, a raft-like Brazilian fishing boat made of logs from the piúba tree, lashed together); boats that raced (the Monotype in which Peter Scott won a bronze medal at the 1936 Olympics; *Defiant*, the sailing canoe built by Uffa Fox in 1933); boats with stories (the Rob Roy canoe, c. 1868, in which John MacGregor, the father of modern canoeing, paddled the Middle East, taking with him up the River Jordan a Norfolk jacket, slippers and an umbrella).[83] Here are coracles and kayaks, dinghies and inflatables, and the *Monarch*, the 65-foot-long, ten-oared, clinker-built racing boat used at Eton College for 100 years in the school's annual Procession of Boats on the Fourth of June.

Having seen the naked elegance of the boats below the waterline, you can observe more closely how they are constructed in a workshop in a corner of this gallery. Students from Falmouth Marine College work every day stripping, re-caulking, replacing thwarts, strengthening transoms, shaping new keels. They use the same tools that shipwrights have used for generations, the same as those that belonged to the Ferris family, featured in the Cornwall Gallery, used for 150 years: adze, bevel, auger, mute; chisel, draw-knife, hand-brace, gouge.

Today boats are built from fibre-glass, thermoplastics or Kevlar (aramid fibre, seven times stronger than steel) but the physics of sailing a hull through water change as little as the physics of constructing this beautiful museum to withstand the attrition of the east wind.

MONTACUTE HOUSE ***

Montacute, Somerset T A15 6XP
Tel. 01935 823289
e-mail: montacute@ntrust.org.uk

Great yet delicate house, the new home of the National Portrait Gallery's proud Elizabethan courtiers' portraits

Honey-stoned Montacute is one of the happiest and most exuberant of the great early 17th-century houses, gentler and more human in scale than Hardwick or Woollaton. It makes an appropriate setting for a fine collection of the National Portrait Gallery's Tudor and Jacobean portraits but it is also home to Sir Malcolm Stewart's tapestries, furniture and works of art and to Dr Douglas Goodhart's samplers, both collections strong in the 17th century.

Among the tapestries three stand out: the millefleurs of *A Knight on a Caparisoned Horse*, woven in Tournai between 1477 and 1479 by the workshop of Guillaume Desremaulx; the Flemish *The Eleventh Labour of Hercules*, also late 15th century and with a millefleurs background; and the 18th-century panel *The Hunter*, from the set called *Les Nouvelles Indes*, designed by François Desportes and woven at the Gobelins factory under the entrepreneur James Neilson, a Scot and friend of Robert Adam.

To place Goodhart's domestic samplers with these mighty textiles is a risk, but samplers were an important way of recording and passing on stitches and the best of them – notably those by Mary Quelch (1609) on parchment and by Alice Jennings (1692) – are works of modesty and beauty.

In 16th- and 17th-century houses the top floor long gallery was usually a single room for exercise, games and masques or for displaying statuary. Here the Long Gallery, and the rooms off it, present the National Portrait Gallery portraits, images of power and personality, fashion and frailty. Elizabeth I (attributed to George Gower, *c.*1588) is surrounded, as in life, by handsome men: the vain Robert Dudley, Earl of Leicester, her favourite, hand on hip, gleam in eye; the extravagant rake Edward de Vere, Earl of Oxford, poet, patron and hereditary Lord Chancellor; the doomed figure of Sir Walter Raleigh.

The diplomat and scholar Sir Edward Hoby looks down, mouth pursed, cheeks sucked in, as if drawn by Ronald Searle. Sir John Harington, translator of Ariosto and inventor of the water closet, lets slip an amused, ironic smile, confirming Elizabeth's description of him as 'that saucy poet, my godson'. William Cecil, Lord Burghley and John Thornborough, Bishop of Worcester, show two faces of power. From rheumy-eyed Cecil, his white hands holding the slim rod of the Lord High Treasurer's office, there is sadness in the weary exercise of power. Thornborough, Elizabeth's chaplain, 'particularly active against Roman Catholics', blazes with bitterness and anger.

Around them images of Edward VI, James I, Charles I and his elder brother the brilliant Henry, Prince of Wales, all painted as boys, are pallid and poignant.

The Tudor and Jacobean periods were an age in which portraiture was poised between flatness and perspective, between symbolism and the portrayal of character. In the 16th century portraits frequently incorporated inscriptions, coats of arms, mottoes, medallions, the date of the work, the age of the sitter. Symbols (a half moon hovering behind Raleigh, burning boughs above Robert Sidney, 1st Earl of Leicester) augment the image.

What is striking is the quality of the painting: Sir Nathaniel Bacon's foxy-faced self-portrait; the miniaturist H's portrait of Raleigh, its grey, black and silver palette for the seed pearls glowing on his goffered shirt, relieved by his soft pink cheeks and lips; and two works by Marcus Gheeraerts the Younger. His portrait of Henry, Prince of Wales (*c.*1603) is all flat pattern. Twelve years later, in his portrait of Mary Throckmorton, Lady Scudamore, the background is still flat but her pose, quizzical half-smile and calm gaze at the viewer, predict the revolution about to transform portraiture.

As you look out of the Long Gallery's

windows into the yew-cushioned gardens, give thanks for the setting that they and the house provide and which so nearly was lost. After more than three hundred years of being lived in by the Phelips family, who built the house, Monacute was rented to Lord Curzon, former Viceroy of India, who lived here with his mistress, the novelist Elinor Glyn. In 1932 it was saved from demolition by Ernest Cook, grandson of Thomas Cook, the travel agent, when it was valued at £5,882 for building materials. The motto on Raleigh's portrait is 'AMOR ET VIRTUTE' ('by love and virtue').

PENLEE HOUSE GALLERY AND MUSEUM *

Morrab Road, Penzance, Cornwall
TR18 4HE
Tel. 01736 363625
www.penleehouse.org.uk

The Newlyn painters at home

'The plein air artists were then in the ascendant. Millet and Manet with their palettes of revolt, and Lepage ... with a very clear open-air eye.' So wrote Norman Garstin in his introduction to the Spring Exhibition of 1902 at the Whitechapel Art Gallery.

Garstin was one of a group of artists, including Stanhope Forbes and Walter Langley, who moved to Newlyn in the early 1880s to break free of the studio and the city, and to paint *en plein air*, as the Barbizon School had been doing in France since the 1860s. In Newlyn they sought out new subjects – fishing, harvesting, wet piers, anything so long as it was outdoors and caught what Forbes called 'the unflinching realism of the cult of Bastien-Lepage',[84] to 'study the life of our time and people in their natural environments'.[85]

Penlee House Gallery and Museum has the largest public collection of the work of these artists. They were serious, committed and hardworking. They were good-humoured and good-natured. They played the St Ives artists in an annual cricket match. They did their best to paint the way of life of this fishing

The Rain it Raineth Every Day by Norman Garstin (Penlee House)

community without too much sentimentality.

They had studied in Paris in the early 1880s. The first Impressionist Exhibition had been in 1874. Six more had followed by 1882. The work of Cézanne (twenty years older than they were), Pissarro and Seurat was there for them to see. Yet they fearlessly followed the Barbizon, eschewing the 'art for art's sake' approach of the Impressionists in favour of the 'rural-realist' style of their hero Bastien-Lepage.

The style of the Newlyners' work was a radical break with the English art establishment, but followed a different path from the aesthetic movement of Sickert and Whistler, for whom Forbes in particular expressed contempt. Forbes's reaction to the New English Art Club exhibition of 1888 was to declare that Sickert was 'tawdry, vulgar and [exhibited] the sentiment of the lowest music hall'.[86] Whistler he despised. 'Unless the Whistler influence is stamped out, the club will go to the bad.'[87]

The Newlyners were painterly and skilled. Both Forbes (in *A Fish Sale on a Cornish Beach*, 1885, Plymouth City Museum and Art Gallery, q.v.) and Garstin (in *The Rain it Raineth Every Day*, 1889, Penlee House) can make water slick on sand or pavement. The landscapes and scenes depicted by Walter Langley and Samuel John 'Lamorna' Birch show us the Cornwall of the late 19th century. Their paintings are well composed and attractive and it is therefore not surprising that they are popular with the general public but most of them are forgotten as soon as seen. Whistler, Sickert and George Moore were devastating in their criticism. Some will wonder why these artists have a gallery devoted to them, but, a century later, their paintings continue to draw the public.

Twenty years after the colony established itself, there was a second wave of artists in Newlyn, many of whom came to study at Stanhope and Elizabeth Forbes's School of Painting, established in 1899. Among these artists were Harold and Laura Knight, Ernest and Dod Procter, and Norman Garstin's daughter Alethea.

Unlike their predecessors, all were affected by the strong colours and shapes that exploded upon London in Roger Fry's 1910 exhibition *Manet and the Post-Impressionists*.

By the 1920s all five were finding new subjects: portraits, landscapes and interiors. Although less celebrated in her lifetime than Laura Knight, Dod Procter's work stands out today. The portraits of herself (1922) and of Eileen Mayo, both on long-term loan to Penlee House, have strength and a direct sexuality. In them the lines are clear, the bodies solid, the light held in blocks. Her work is worth seeking out, in Tate Britain, Manchester Art Gallery, Southampton City Art Gallery, Glynn Vivian Art Gallery (a rare townscape) and the Laing Art Gallery (all q.v.). Her finest work returned to the studio from which the *plein air* artists had fled years earlier, and, arguably, was the better for this confinement.

PLYMOUTH CITY MUSEUM AND ART GALLERY ***

Drake Circus, Plymouth, Devon PL4 8AJ
Tel. 01752 304774
www.plymouthmuseum.gov.uk

The Cottonian Collection, including works by Joshua Reynolds, local boy made good

At the heart of the Plymouth City Museum and Art Gallery is the Cottonian Collection, bequeathed by William Cotton III in 1848 'for the use of the inhabitants of Plymouth, Stonehouse and Devonport for their amusement and instruction'. William Cotton had two aims: 'to prevent the dispersal of the Charles Rogers collection of art, books, prints, bronzes etc., and to preserve some memorial to my family and my name'. The quality and title of the collection achieve both aims.

Charles Rogers was an outstanding late-18th-century connoisseur. He himself was bequeathed 'all my library and £1,000 sterling' in 1740 by his employer and patron, William

Towson, Chief Clerk of the Customs House. All trade, including fine art, passed through the Customs House, giving the chief clerk the opportunity to make a fortune and to cultivate the friendship of such artists as James Thornhill, Samuel Scott and Jonathan Richardson, whose works featured in Towson's collection.

Rogers *by Sir Joshua Reynolds at Plymouth*

To these Rogers added drawings (by Michelangelo, Rubens, Brueghel, Altdorfer, Guercino, Watteau), paintings (by Angelica Kauffmann, Willem van der Velde, Salomon van Ruysdael, Joshua Reynolds) and outstanding prints by the finest engravers (Francesco Bartolozzi, Johann Jacob Frey).

Unusually for a connoisseur in the age of the Grand Tour, Rogers never went abroad.

He bought through agents, with such determination that, at his death, he owned 12,000 prints, 1,800 drawings and a library of over 3,000 books. The scale is daunting but the quality compels. Everywhere there are works of great beauty: Francesco Colonna's *Hypnerotomachia Poliphili* (1499), printed in Venice by Aldus Manutius, whose paper, typefaces and delicate woodcuts ravish the eye; a startling mezzotint by W. Dickinson (1778) after a painting by W. Peters of the blind Sir John Fielding, Chair of the Quarter Sessions for the City of Westminster and brother of the novelist Henry Fielding, the face of implacable justice; Reynolds's tender portraits of his sister Fanny and other members of his family, which have the direct engagement and affection so often absent from the painter's bravura full-lengths.

Rogers had talent as well as taste. His *Collection of Prints in Imitation of Drawings* (1778, 2 vols.) is a great work in which the engravings of his friend Bartolozzi do justice to the drawings of Leonardo, Raphael, Titian and Rembrandt among others. His library is here displayed in the walnut-veneered bookcases he had made, a setting of elegance for a collection of distinction that carries you back into the 18th century.

There is more to Plymouth than the Cottonian. As at Exeter, artists who were born or who worked in Devon are featured – Prout, Towne, Haydon, Northcote, Eastlake; and there is a large holding of the Newlyn School in which Dod Procter stands out. The quintessential Newlyn work, Stanhope Forbes's *A Fish Sale on a Cornish Beach*, demonstrates the strengths of this school (low tide, a wet beach well done) and the weaknesses (formulaic background sea, poor detail, stiff groupings). It would be kinder to some (Charles Napier Hemy, Charles Walter Simpson, Herbert Truman) to retire them to the peace of the storeroom.

Having been extensively redeveloped since bomb damage in the Second World War, Plymouth has some interesting finds from rescue archaeology: a Saintonge jug (*c.* 1280–1330) from the Prysten House in Finewell Street, a tyg (drinking vessel) *c.* 1150–1250 from Kitto Street and Bronze Age urns.

To the museum's credit, pride of place is given on the main stairs to a large group portrait by Robert Lenkiewicz (1986–7) of the museum staff: curators, keepers, attendants, volunteers, cleaners, all with the tools of their roles, from busts to brooms.

SALISBURY AND SOUTH WILTSHIRE MUSEUM **✶✶**

The King's House, 65 The Close, Salisbury, Wiltshire SP1 2EN
Tel. 01722 332151
www.salisburymuseum.org.uk

Pitt Rivers's other collection, the birth of British archaeology and the henges explained

Salisbury is an excellent local museum, a series of cabinets in which you come across many curiosities and surprises. Here is a collection of 18th-century glass with virtuosi stems, single tear drop, air twist, knotted air twist and baluster; there, the Brixie Jarvis Wedgwood Collection which includes pieces from the Frog Service that Wedgwood made for Catherine the Great in 1773–4.

Among the unusual collection of objects collected from the city's drains are medieval keys, buckles, pilgrim badges, knives, the preserved skeletons of a cat and a rat, once immured, and the 13th-century head of a troubled young man carved in stone. There are also 14th-century walrus ivory chess pieces; 17th-century silver civic cups; the Salisbury giant, a pageant figure of the Guild of Tailors; a brass clock signed 'Nicholas Snowe at Salisburie fecit 1636', one of the few existing pre-Civil War clocks; Turner watercolours of Salisbury Cathedral; and stuffed great bustards extinct since the 19th century, extant on the crest of Wiltshire County Council. Wherever you dip you are lucky.

To this should be added a gallery which does a very reasonable job of explaining the hitherto inexplicable: the how and the why of Stonehenge, and an archaeological collection from the many Wessex digs, including objects from the Beaker burial at

Wedgwood's Frog Service at Salisbury

Shrewton, Roman objects from Grovely Ridge, and Saxon jewellery from Swallowcliffe Downs and Winterbourne Gunner.

But the most compelling reason to visit Salisbury is the Pitt Rivers Collection. Pitt Rivers is best known for the Oxford University museum that bears his name (q.v.) and holds his ethnographic collections, but Salisbury has the fruits of his archaeological work and the story of the museum he created at Farnham in Dorset. The former developed much of the methodology of modern archaeology. The latter was 100 years ahead of its time. Both are of national importance.

Lt. Gen. Augustus Henry Lane Fox Pitt Rivers was a professional soldier in the Grenadier Guards. Given the job of testing the army's rifles, he became interested in the ways in which this weapon had developed. In 1858 he published *On the Improvement of the Rifle as a Weapon for General Use*,[88] which charted the evolution of technology as surely as Darwin did that of zoology and botany in *The Origin of Species*,[89] published the next year.

In 1880 Pitt Rivers inherited family estates stretching from Cranborne Chase in Dorset to the sea. It included archaeological sites of great potential, which he set about excavating with soldierly efficiency, recording and classifying all he found. 'Progress is like a game of dominoes,' he wrote; 'all that we know is that the fundamental rule of the game is

sequence.'[90] He was well schooled in archaeology by Canon William Greenwell and
subscribed to Greenwell's precept that 'the
urn, the dagger and the arrowhead possess a
very trifling interest and give us comparatively
little information, unless we know the circumstances of their deposit and the objects
with which they were associated.'[91]

Pitt Rivers's excavations of a Bronze Age
barrow group[92] yielded treasures displayed
here with the contoured mahogany models
of each dig that he had made by his estate
carpenters. But it was his method that transformed archaeology. Fifty years later Professor
Christopher Hawkes and Stuart Piggott wrote
that Pitt Rivers 'recorded it so well, and preserved his finds so carefully, that this process
can really amount to a re-excavation of his
sites. One can pay no greater tribute to his
genius.'[93]

Pitt Rivers was a compulsive collector. In
the Nile Valley in 1881, on a Thomas Cook
holiday, he discovered Palaeolithic disc flint
implements in the stratified gravel, establishing the existence of primitive man in the valley
long before the Pharaohs' time. Aged seventy,
after his last dig, he began to collect Benin
bronzes.

To communicate his enthusiasms, he
created a museum on his estate, the Larmer
Grounds, in 1880. Since Farnham was thirteen
miles from the nearest railway station, he concluded that people would need to be offered a
real outing if they were to be persuaded to
travel such a distance. The museum was open
seven days a week; visitors were collected at
the station; admission was free; and crockery
and cutlery was provided for picnics. There
were 'German skittles, bowls and swings . . .
provided in the shrubbery'[94] and each Easter
a sports day was organised, with dancing on
the lawns in the evening, lit by thousands of
lamps. The Larmer Grounds drew over 40,000
visitors a year.

Against the grain of Victorian joy-killing,
Pitt Rivers linked these entertainments to
the purpose of the museum: to explain to
visitors what they were seeing and to get them
to ask questions. A 'Notice to all Visitors,

Professors, Pedlars, Politicians, Poultry keepers' demanded 'Why have you come here and
what do you expect to see? Please ask Yourself
These Questions (as all anthropologists have
asked themselves): What are you (by race, by
descent, by nationality)? Are you civilised?
Are you educated? What do you mean by
civilisation? What is the purpose of education?
Please think. We ask you to read the labels
and form your own opinion on the evidence
that you will see.'[95]

Even after his death his work inspired
innovation. His was the first collection of
objects to be accepted by the Treasury in lieu
of death duties because of its pre-eminent
historical importance.

As you leave, take care to look at the
museum's two final treasures. The Monkton
Deverill gold torc (Middle Bronze Age, 1300–
1000 BC) is in its simple beauty very sympathetic to contemporary taste. More remarkable
still is the Warminster jewel, found in a field
on Cley Hill in 1997. In the late 9th century
King Alfred sent to each diocese his translation
of Pope Gregory's *Pastoral Care*, and gave with
it an aestel, a rock crystal in a frame of gold
wire, used probably as a pointer when reading
manuscripts. Only four survive: the Alfred
and the Minster Lowell jewels (Ashmolean
Museum, q.v.), the Bowleaze Jewel (British
Museum, q.v.) and the Warminster jewel.
Alfred's aestels yoke together scholarship and
craftsmanship. There could be no happier
setting for this jewel than here, in the shadow
of Salisbury Cathedral.

WILTON HOUSE ✳✳✳

Wilton, Salisbury, Wiltshire SP2 0BJ
Tel. 01722 746720
www.wiltonhouse.co.uk/

*Dazzlingly realised, Inigo Jones-inspired great
house, flooded with light and splendid with
treasures within*

James Lees-Milne described Wilton House,
the home of the Earl of Pembroke, as 'one of
the most beautiful buildings in all England'.[96]

It was designed with the 'advice and appro-bation' of Inigo Jones.[97]

You arrive in front of Sir William Chambers's Triumphal Arch,[98] topped by an equestrian statue of Marcus Aurelius, and enter the North Forecourt, a rectangle of pleached limes that outline a parterre of clipped box.[99]

The north front and entrance, rebuilt by James Wyatt in 1801, do not convey the archi-tectural merits of the house, unlike the Inigo Jones/John Webb south front, which epitomises Jones's belief in the virtues of external restraint and internal flamboyance. 'Outwardly, every wise man carries a gravity,' he wrote, 'yet inwardly has his imagination set on fire and sometimes licentiously flies out.'

The range of superb state rooms along the south front culminates in the Double Cube Room, 60 by 30 by 30 feet. Within these geometrical constraints Jones and Webb created a part-classical, part-baroque extrava-ganza, decorated in gold and white, with swags of fruit and flowers and classical motifs. The room was designed to take the 4th Earl's collection of Van Dycks. It makes a fine con-text for Van Dyck's largest painting, *Philip, Fourth Earl of Pembroke and his Family*.

This is Van Dyck at his grandest and most stately. Two monumental pillars and a vast tapestry displaying the Pembroke arms create a powerful framework of verticals, before which the members of the family are depicted in poses of studied artifice: hands crooked, spread, raised, dropped; on chest, on hip; hand held. At the centre are the Earl and Countess, both in black. His right hand is open as if he is offering this scene to you; he indicates that the future rests with his daughter-in-law. The Countess crosses her arms calmly. Above them putti look down from a wisp of cloud and the light from the distant sky flickers in and out across the scene creating diagonals that play against the vertical pillars.

Next door the Single Cube Room (30 by 30 by 30 feet) is scarcely more restrained. Below the dado are twenty-six paintings by Emmanuel de Critz illustrating Sir Philip Sidney's *Arcadia*, written while staying at

Wilton with his sister Mary, wife of the 2nd Earl. The ceiling has a vertiginous depiction by Giuseppe Cesari of *Daedalus and Icarus*. Above the fireplace is Lely's portrait of *Henrietta de Keroualle*, wife of the 7th Earl and sister of Louise de Keroualle, mistress of Charles II. In the corner are two double portraits by Van Dyck, as gentle as that of the 4th Earl's family is grand, of the Earl and Countess of Bedford and of the Countess of Morton and Mrs Killigrew.

Throughout the house are further family paintings which span 250 years of British portraiture from Hans Eworth and John Greenhill, by way of Michael Dahl, Charles Jervas and Pompeo Batoni, to Sir Joshua Reynolds and Sir Thomas Lawrence.

The Herberts have lived here in an un-broken male line for more than four hundred and fifty years. Shakespeare dedicated his First Folio to the 3rd and 4th Earls for their patronage. The 8th Earl was a connoisseur who collected most of the paintings (two Lorenzo Lottos, an Andrea del Sarto, a Claude, a Rubens, and the Wilton Diptych, now in the National Gallery, q.v., since being sold in 1929). The 9th Earl, the 'Architect Earl', was a friend of Lord Burlington and William Kent, who commissioned the exquisite Palladian Bridge, designed by Roger Morris; he also commissioned the house's gilt furniture by Kent and the violin bookcase from Chippen-dale, notable for its cartouche of musical instruments.

More surprisingly he was responsible for one of the few commissions that Richard Wilson received, and completed, for six views of the house and grounds. Joseph Farington records that Wilson 'had little respect for what are called connoisseurs, and did not conciliate their regard by any flattery or attention'.[100]

That Wilton was, in the view of John Aubrey, 'an academie as well as a palace' is borne out by the Pembrokes' patronage of Shakespeare and Sidney, and by recent evi-dence that suggests that the 1st Earl's collection of nearly sixty paintings might have included *Christina of Denmark, Duchess of Milan*, by Hans Holbein the Younger (1538), now in the

National Gallery (q.v.).[101] In the 20th century the family has collected Fred Astaire's dancing shoes and the colours that General Dwight Eisenhower flew when Wilton was the headquarters of the US Southern Command during the preparations for D-Day in 1944. Despite this apparent declension the house's many beauties confirm the judgement of James Lees-Milne.

EDEN PROJECT *

Bodelva, St Austell, Cornwall PL24 2SG
Tel. 01726 811911
www.edenproject.com

Exactly what the name suggests: a re-creation of creation – under great lunar conservatory domes

The name invites hyperbole: 'earthly paradise' declared *Architecture Today*;[102] 'the living theatre of plants and people' is the Eden Project's more modest self-description.[103] The ambition and the scale of the enterprise are indeed massive.

Tim Smit, the originator of the project, came across the Bodelva quarry outside St Austell when it was about to become redundant. Kaolinised granite 'clay' had been extracted from it for over a hundred years, leaving a crater over 200 feet deep and a quarter of a mile wide, covering 454 acres. It was a moon crater, sans soil, sans drainage, sterile. Its sides were prone to slippage, the water table was 100 feet above the bottom of the crater and it contained no soil: it was a blasted Eden.

Working with the architects Nicholas Grimshaw and Partners[104] and the structural engineers Tony Hunt Associates,[105] Smit explored how life might be returned to this desert. The initial idea, a modern version of Joseph Paxton's Crystal Palace with huge curved trusses 'arching gracefully between the top of the pit and its base',[106] was abandoned as being too heavy. They turned to Buckminster Fuller's Manhattan geodesic dome, supported by triangular space-trusses and clad in ETFE

(ethyltetrafluoroethylene), a material that is transparent, strong, self-cleaning and many times lighter than glass.[107]

In these 'biomes' the project's landscape designer Dominic Cole of Land Use Consultants has created environments in which all varieties of plant can grow, given the right soil. It would have been impractical to truck soil into the site, so 85,000 tons of different soils have been manufactured on site. In them are growing more than 3,000 plants.

It is a mighty and Sisyphean achievement – all the more so because much of the soil was washed away in a storm just before the Project opened. Inside the biomes temperatures range from 15°C in the Warm Temperate Zone to 35°C, Humid Tropical. They squat, seven of them, giant bubble cushions reflecting the sky. They are curiously endearing, even if they lack the exaltation of Paxton's glasshouses.

As a museum of plants they are less happy. The plants thrive, indeed in this artificial environment many are growing at unprecedented rates, but the Warm Temperate Zone may fail to convince Europeans and Californians. A few vines and olive trees 'represent' the Mediterranean Basin. Beyond them are orange and lemon trees. You step along the 'Liquid Gold pathway',[108] its colour 'a celebration of the long tradition of olive oil as a symbol of light, life and divinity', directly from Greece to South Africa and the flora of the Cape: lilies, orchids, irises and exotic proteas, like huge scaly teasels. Around a bend in the Liquid Gold pathway lies California: blue ceanothus, followed by the white sage and buck bush of the chaparral.

In the Humid Tropical Zone there are lush, soaring banana trees, bamboos and palms of every kind: coconut, betel nut, a Bismarck palm from Madagascar. A torrent rushes through it. The sound, the heat, the luxuriant greenness, the way that the plants drip or overhang the path make rather less unrealistic the project's aim to evoke 'something of the majesty of the rainforest', though 'the scent of the Spice Islands' remains uninhaled.

The project reminds you continually that it cares about our environment and about conservation, that it wants to entertain and educate, that it believes that it, and you, can 'make a difference'. It tries to open the eyes of its visitors to the diversity of the natural world and the ways in which plants touch every part of our lives (medicine, transport, energy, technology) and in which 'we are part of nature, indivisible from it'. The Project is working with the Royal Botanic Gardens, Kew (q.v.), and other bodies, but it also feels a manifest need to amuse and interest.

The plantings outside the biomes are handsome, blocks of bushes, grasses and flowers that tumble down the steep inclines. In one of the many cafés and restaurants, surrounded by a banked amphitheatre, you eat watched by serried ranks of kohlrabi, cabbages, sea kale and chard. Sometimes the project tries too hard. Everywhere there are artists attempting to interpret and animate plants: plaiting willow, weaving sisal, processing flax. There is a monumental sculpture of a bee. 'Dancing maenads ... Mirror the twisting shapes of the vines'; 'Cornish automata makers craft the Crops and Cultivation arch, where cola pods, cocoa pods and chicle sap meet cola drinks, cupcakes and chewing gum.' There are poems on banners: 'Rubber Blubber/ Bounce flounce/Wind it/Stretch it/Throw it/ Sit on it.' Andy Goldsworthy, David Nash and Richard Long have shown that art and the natural world can interact in the hands and imaginations of powerful and coherent artists, but the artists here are less successful. The Eden Project has noble ambitions. It wants to promote 'ethical commerce' and 'social enterprise'. It also wants to 'solve problems apolitically'. But the scale of these global environmental problems makes apolitical solutions impossible. The countries of the world have been locked in disagreement at the summits at Kyoto and Cancun (2003). Consumers and producers clash over GM crops. Coca-Cola Inc. sells sugared water in cans in countries that endure malnutrition, where there is no work and often no clean water to drink.

Much of the world is determinedly blind and deaf to the environmental problems we are causing. If the Eden Project encourages people to ask questions, which it does, it is to be welcomed as a project, if not an Eden.

BARBARA HEPWORTH MUSEUM AND SCULPTURE GARDEN ***

Barnoon Hill, St Ives, Cornwall TR26 1AD
Tel. 01736 796226

As though the sculptor had just set her chisel down in her light-scoured studio and lush garden

'Finding Trewyn Studio was a sort of magic. For ten years I had passed by with my shopping bags not knowing what lay behind the twenty foot wall ... Here was a studio, a yard and a garden, where I could work in open air and space,'[109] wrote Barbara Hepworth about Trewyn Studio – now the Barbara Hepworth Museum and Sculpture Garden – where she lived and worked from 1949 until her death in 1975. The entrance is a modest doorway in a narrow street that gives on to a dark ground-floor room (formerly her kitchen, dining room and bathroom); then visitors go up to her living room, and out into her garden, studio and workshop, each space throwing more light on her thoughts and her work.

'Perhaps what one wants to say is formed in childhood and the rest of one's life is spent in trying to say it.'[110] Anyone wanting to explore what it was that Hepworth was saying and why she was such a fine sculptor, certainly the great landscape-inspired sculptor of the late 20th century, should start here. Tate Modern (q.v.) may hold more of her works but this collection, in the studio where most of them were made, is an essential starting point.

Downstairs is a rich archive: reviews (by Herbert Read, Paul Nash, Adrian Stokes): catalogues (by Arthur Tooth, Alex Reid and Lefevre); designs for sets (Tippett's opera *A*

Spring: garden as gallery at Barbara Hepworth's Trewyn Studio, St Ives

Midsummer Marriage; the Old Vic *Electra*, directed by Michel Saint Denis, with Peggy Ashcroft); a description of her first meeting with Piet Mondrian in 1931, at which her apprehension was melted by his 'thinking eyes and kindness in mouth and expression' and a copy of *Circle*, the magazine edited by Ben Nicholson, J. L. Martin and Naum Gabo, with contributions by Braque, Klee, Picasso, Léger and Kandinsky, which was crucial to the development and acceptance of modernism in Britain. Here is the world that shaped her work.

The room is low and dark and to climb up into her living room, now a gallery, is to burst into brilliant light, a fine setting for the sculptures.

Hepworth's sympathy with the texture and properties of wood and stone lives in each work as a dryad in a tree. Hoptonwood stone, white marble, blue marble, alabaster, walnut, broadleaf elm, lignum vitae, scented guarea wood (she got hold of seventeen tons of this African hardwood in the mid 1950s), each yields up its qualities to her.

Look at the early *Infant* (1929) in Burmese wood, an exclamation of clenched fists and solid chest and arms bursting out of the polished grain, or the silken alabaster texture of *Three Forms* (1934), its smooth planes sliding across each other.

As you regard these pictures describing her responses to form and weight and texture, conjugating abstraction, your eye is stopped by the table she had in this room, ornate Italian, with a marble top on which is a grey Venetian glass jug.

Outside, the garden, which she made with her friend Priaulx Rainier, is lush with semi-tropical trees and plants: palms, bamboos, agapanthus, white osteospermums, variegated hebes, tall arum lilies. All around are larger works of the 1950s and '60s: huge bronzes (*Figure for Landscape*, 1960, and *Four Square*, 1966), which you can walk through, and her last big bronze of 1973, *Conversation with Magic Stones*, its massy blocks surrounded by willowy bamboo, set in pale delicate stone chippings.

All the motifs and subjects that engaged her are here: closed and open forms, the standing figure and, above all, landscape. Throughout her life she was affected by landscape, in her childhood in the West Riding of Yorkshire, in Italy and here in 'the pagan landscape which lies between St Ives, Penzance and Land's End' of rocks and sea, Neolithic stones and hillsides in which the human figure stands proud. 'The sensation has never left me. I, the sculptor, AM the landscape.'[111] Although there are more than twenty works in this small garden, its paths, corners and concealed spaces mean that it doesn't feel crowded and you are able to walk around works, watch the light falling on surfaces, and savour the highly polished flowing sensuousness of *Coré* (1960s), a work from the period when the sculptor and craftsman Denis Mitchell was her assistant.

In the garden are her studio and workshop as she left them when she died in a fire here in 1975. They are a masonic nursery with hammers, mallets, files, steps, set squares, spheres of marble, cans of wax, her overalls, a tin ashtray, Players' Navy Cut, a jar of Maxwell House and a block of stone halted half-hewn. A skin of stonedust bleaches everything.

Birthplace or workplace museums seldom convey a sense of person. This one does. That may be because the work has been stopped *in situ*, in mid flow; or because of surprising details: succulent cacti in the greenhouse, a hybrid tea rose amid the exotics, a bed in the summerhouse, a bronze of her hand (1943–5, but cast from the plaster original in 1967) lying casually on a table in the gallery; or because the garden she planted lives.

Her sculptures are all over St Ives, as well as in the Tate, but it is here that her works continue to say what she was trying to say.

TATE ST IVES ✳✳✳

Porthmeor Beach, St Ives, Cornwall
TR26 1TG
Tel. 01736 796226
www.tate.org.uk

Seems to generate its own salt light and shed it on the post-war works within

'The Tate Gallery St Ives . . . allows the visitor to see the works of art in the area in which they were conceived and close to the landscape and sea which influenced them,' explains Sir Richard Carew Pole,[112] chairman of the Tate Gallery St Ives Steering Group. It realises 'the idea of a permanent home in the region' writes Nicholas Serota, director of the Tate Gallery, 'for the distinctive modern art of St Ives [that] has long been cherished by many who live in or visit the area'.[113]

Thanks to the acquisitions made by its directors, Sir Norman Reid and Sir Alan Bowness,[114] the Tate had the paintings and sculptures to realise those ambitions, from the primitive paintings of the fisherman Alfred Wallis, and the early modernism of Ben Nicholson, Christopher Wood and John Wells in the late 1920s and early 1930s, through the war years when Nicholson and his second wife Barbara Hepworth had studios in the town, as did Naum Gabo, Adrian Stokes, Margaret Mellis and Wilhelmina Barns-Graham, to the younger artists who worked there in the late 1940s, '50s and '60s – Bryan Wynter, Roger Hilton, Peter Lanyon, Patrick Heron and Terry Frost.

By 1993 the Tate had a site, on the old gasworks overlooking Porthmeor Beach, and a new gallery designed by David Shalev and Eldred Evans.[115] Shalev said that he wanted to make a building that was 'in dialogue with the landscape and seascape of the place'.[116] It is true that the gallery sits comfortably on the edge of St Ives, overlooking the beach, and that from its upper floors you can look across the roofs of the town to the harbour beyond, but Shalev and Evans achieved more than that. Their gallery picks up the light that is reflected back between sea and sky throughout St Ives and borrows the shape of the sail lofts that have been turned into artists' studios, and works these elements together into a gallery of grace and magic.

On a constrained site they have fitted in a Loggia, a Rotunda which takes the eye spiralling round and up through the building, and five galleries of different heights, sizes and shapes which continually surprise with glimpses of the sea and the town. There are views inward to the stairwell and to other galleries, a terrace that feels like the bridge of a ship and a curved gallery, Gallery 2, that picks up on similar semi-circular galleries at the National Museum and Gallery of Wales and the Guggenheim in New York, and wraps around you a curved wall of glass, unmarred by a single mullion, that looks over the sea.

This is a seaside building, friendly, ungrand. Its galleries are modest in size, designed for paintings that, with the exception of some produced by Patrick Heron in the last years of his life, are domestic in scale.

In achieving their intended dialogue with sea and land and, above all, light, Evans and Shalev have designed ideal spaces in which to see the works of St Ives artists. There are other places where some or all of them can be seen: Kettle's Yard (particularly strong on Alfred Wallis, Christopher Wood, early Ben Nicholson) and the Pier Art Centre (more than a dozen small Hepworths and abstract Nicholsons from the 1930s and '40s, and works by Margaret Mellis, Lanyon, Hilton and others) (both q.v.). The Pier Art Centre is even closer to the sea and has similarly pervasive and intense light, if somewhat colder and more northern. But St Ives is a place to which artists have been coming since Whistler and the young Sickert painted here in the winter of 1883–4.[117] They come for the reflected light, and for those aspects of this wild coast that are sublime: the sea rolling in from the Atlantic and the ancient landscape with its headlands, outcrops, standing stones and quoins.

The harbour and the sea are depicted here directly in the paintings of Alfred Wallis and his successor and fellow naïf Bryan Pearce,

in Patrick Heron's *Harbour Window with Two Figures, St Ives July 1950*[118] and views of St Ives made by Ben Nicholson in the 1940s, and in Terry Frost's *Green, Black and White Movement* (1952) in which curved geometric forms, pitched at angles, evoke the rocking movements of small boats at anchor.

Peter Lanyon was born and brought up on the Penwith peninsular, and taught by Borlase Smart. His landscapes – the brooding *Headland* (1948) and *Porthleven* (1951), commissioned for the Festival of Britain, depicting the town pitching down its valley to the harbour and sea – convey the idiosyncrasies of the Cornish land. Terry Frost recalled in an interview with Lanyon, 'You didn't draw a tree by just looking at it. You felt the tree, the bark, you felt the angles, you leant against the wind. The whole thing was a totally different experience,'[119] a visceral response echoed by Bryan Wynter: 'The landscape I live among is bare of houses, trees, people; it is dominated by winds, by swift changes of weather, by the moods of the sea; sometimes it is devastated and blackened by fire. These elemental forces enter the paintings and lend their qualities without becoming motifs.'[120]

The works here are thoroughly British. Even when abstract, they are sensual and dense in colour and shape, their response to atmosphere and place romantic. They deserve this gallery that so well reflects their world. However, despite Nicholas Serota's promise of 'a permanent home' for their work, Tate St Ives, since the departure of its first curator Michael Tooby in 2000, has exhibited its permanent collection of St Ives artists less than wholeheartedly. In the summer months temporary exhibitions, invariably of high quality featuring such contemporary artists as Antony Gormley (2001), occupy the galleries, with St Ives artists squeezed into one small space.

The explosion of colour and light that pours through Patrick Heron's *Window for St Ives* (1992) continues to be the first work of art that

Patrick Heron's Window for St Ives
(Tate St Ives)

every visitor sees, with its spaces of deep pink, blue, sea-green, carrying you up into the air and plunging deep into water,[121] but it no longer heralds a celebration of the work of St Ives artists throughout the building designed for them. Their work spanned at least sixty years and they were never a coherent group or school, but they would benefit from being shown more consistently in context and together, 'close to the landscape and sea which influenced them'.

STOURHEAD **

Stourton, Warminster, Wiltshire BA12 6QD
Tel. 01747 841152
www.nationaltrust.org.uk

Banking family's fine Regency library, paintings and garden of edenic repose

Sir Richard Colt Hoare (1758–1838), classicist, antiquarian, art collector and amateur artist, inherited Stourhead from his grandfather Henry Hoare II (or 'Magnificent') in 1785 and with it a fine collection of mainly Italian paintings.

Colt Hoare was a major early patron of Turner but all his Turners and much of his outstanding library were sold at the Stourhead heirlooms sale in 1883.[122] Nevertheless what remains in the house provides an unusual view of the taste of two generations of Grand Tour collectors. Henry Hoare II bought through dealers in Paris and Rome and through Sir Horace Mann, the British Resident in Florence (1740–86). His grandson, Colt Hoare, also benefited from Mann's advice and introductions when living in Italy between 1785 and 1791.[123]

Both collections benefit from their setting, the house designed by Colen Campbell for Henry Hoare I in 1721–4,[124] based on Palladio's Villa Fanzola (1560s).[125] Although modest in size (the wings that flank the portico were added by Colt Hoare in 1792 to create a library and a picture gallery), it is a model of Palladian beauty, a 'correspondence of all parts arranged in their proper place'.[126] A fire in 1902 gutted the original, central part of the house, which was rebuilt first by Doran Webb and then by Sir Aston Webb (no relation), a work of Edwardian vandalism, particularly in the Saloon, where Doran Webb destroyed the proportions by lowering the ceiling and extending the room to create a passageway and more bedrooms above.

Nevertheless, within and without, Stourhead contains many treats. Henry Hoare II's pictures include landscapes by Richard Wilson and Gaspard Dughet; family portraits in pastel by William Hoare of Bath and Francis Cotes; major works by Nicolas Poussin, Cigoli, Carlo Maratta[127] and Anton Raphael Mengs; and, in the Entrance Hall, a huge equestrian portrait of Henry Hoare II, the figure of Hoare by Michael Dahl, the horse by John Wootton, facing Samuel Woodforde's portrait of *Sir Richard Colt Hoare Being Recalled to England by his Son* (1795–6), over the chimneypiece. There is also a gleaming gilt-bronze bust of Charles I by Hubert le Sueur, originally in the Palace of Whitehall; and a remarkable collection of terracotta *modelli* by J. M. Rysbrack.

Elegant though the Entrance Hall is, the contribution of Richard Colt Hoare is yet more distinguished. The Library he built for his collection of books of topography and archaeology is austere and elegant, one of the finest Regency rooms in the country. With the exception of the chimneypiece and overmantel (containing the model for Pierre Legros's marble relief of *Tobit Lending Money to Gabael* in the chapel of the Monte di Pietà in Rome), it is as he designed it, complete with furniture in the Egyptian style by Thomas Chippendale the Younger, a carpet woven to resemble a Roman pavement and two marble busts in niches by Rysbrack, of Milton in youth and in old age. In this room Colt Hoare wrote his *Ancient History of North and South Wiltshire*, in two volumes, recording the excavations he conducted with William Cunnington between 1803 and 1810, finds from which can be seen in the Wiltshire Heritage Museum (q.v.).

In the library anteroom are the works of his earlier passion, painting: his own efforts are competent if tentative, beside those of his painting tutor, John 'Warwick' Smith, and two watercolours by J. R. Cozens.

In the Column Room is what remains of Colt Hoare's collection of watercolours, small in number but great in interest, particularly the thirteen large paintings of Italian scenes by the Swiss artist Abraham-Louis Ducros. Ducros takes the familiar Grand Tour views of the Tivoli, the Villa of Maecenas,[128] the Arch of Constantine and the Colosseum, and renders them majestic, sublime and picturesque, by the scale on which he works and the intensity of his watercolours, strengthened by gouache.

In his *History of Modern Wiltshire* (1822) Colt Hoare, with a degree of self-congratulation, claims that 'the advancement from drawing to painting in watercolours did not take place till after the introduction into England of the drawing of Louis du Cros.' Certainly he introduced Turner to Ducros's works at Stourhead in 1795, and Lindsay Stainton notes that this 'exactly coincided with Turner's developing a taste for sublime subjects'.[129]

Colt Hoare's taste in oil painting was more conventional. In *Modern Wiltshire* he calls his collection 'a pleasing selection of fancy pictures, by modern Artists of the British School' but they are a limp lot: Henry Thomson's[130] *A Girl Deploring the Death of a Pheasant*; Samuel Woodforde's *A Shepherdess with a Lamb in a Storm*. An exception is *The Adoration of the Magi* (1605) by Cigoli (Ludovico Cardi), purchased in Florence with the help of Sir Horace Mann from the Albizzi chapel, when San Pietro Maggiore was demolished in 1790. It is the centrepiece of the Picture Gallery in a spectacular gilded frame, topped by a ram's head, by Chippendale the Younger.

Colt Hoare's commissions from Chippendale over twenty-five years (1795–1820) are the final glory of Stourhead.[131] Although many pieces were lost in the fire, this collection remains, with that at Harewood House (q.v.), the best and most complete expression of the younger Chippendale's craftsmanship, much of it a considerable distance from his father's *Gentleman and Cabinet-Maker's Director*

(1754). Beside the Library pieces there are sofa seats (1802) in the Library ante-room; bergère chairs in the Music Room; a mahogany dining table and sideboard with leopard's heads and lion's-paw feet (1802); French-style satinwood and ivory chairs; and purely neo-classical chairs in the Picture Gallery. Originally he designed four settees (now lost) to fill this imposing space but his unusual white jardinières that resemble sarcophagi more than suffice today.

STEAM – THE MUSEUM OF THE GREAT WESTERN RAILWAY *

Kemble Drive, Swindon, Wiltshire
SN2 2TA
Tel. 01793 466646
www.steam-museum.org.uk

Brunel's Great Western Railway steams from London to Bristol

The track of Brunel's Great Western Railway (GWR) left its mark across England as clearly as the Romans' roads. It lengthened the infant steps of 19th-century engineering into giant strides, and launched the age of mass transport. A museum that lauds 'God's Wonderful Railway', Isambard Kingdom Brunel and the Age of Steam has at its disposal heroic material, but Steam fails to find the required bravura.

The setting is fine. The museum, opened in 2000, is in the building of the GWR's Swindon workshops, great sheds that housed the machine shops, boiler shop, blacksmith's shops and locomotive works. 'A' shed, the erecting shop, was the size of three football pitches and employed 1,000 people to produce three completed engines every week.

The engines are majestic, dwarfing the visitor. Even at rest they exude irresistible power. *Caerphilly Castle*, designed in 1923 by C. B. Collett, has driving wheels that are 6 feet 8½ inches high. Its polished, gleaming chimney towers above you. Between London and Bristol its firebox would burn three tons of coal. *King George V* and *The Bristolian* are

similarly grand. But these giants do not run; nor do they breathe fire. When 'A' shed was a test plant, static locomotives would be fired at 80 mph. Here they are asleep.

Consequently there is no noise, no smell, no heat, no steam. Graphics in the recreated boiler shop inform you that the noise of the mechanical hammers, at a time when there was no ear protection, left most workers deaf by the age of thirty. The machinery is all here – lathes and drills, mechanical hacksaws and slotters (to cut or enlarge holes in metal components) – but they are as still as the tableaux in the recreated offices and stores where mannequins are caught forever unawares.

The building of the line is conveyed in statistics – six years, 118 miles – and a survey of all the alternative routes that Brunel, first on horseback, then in 'The Flying Hearse'[132] conducted in three months. His theodolite, tripod, drawing board and T-square are here, but there is nothing to convey the unremitting manual labour of the navvies (sixteen-hour shifts, shovelling four hundredweight of spoil every day) as they made a track that was so flat it was known as Brunel's billiard table.

There is ready nostalgia here – the platform ticket machine, the livery, the old carriages, the advertisements for the expresses to the 'Cornish Riviera' – but the romance of the GWR's long bends which unwound through the Thames Valley, of the level miles across the Vale of the White Horse, of the swoop into Bath through the Box Hill tunnel and of the swing along the coasts of Devon and Cornwall are all left to memory and imagination.

SWINDON ART GALLERY *

Bath Road, Swindon, Wiltshire SN1 4BA
Tel. 01793 466556

Formed with the advice of the Tate and others, a civic collection of 20th-century British painting: unique, admirable and good

'They take Art seriously in Swindon. They are good people. I have a great admiration for them,' was the view of Sir Kenneth Clark when chairman of the Arts Council. Building on the gift of 1946 by a local collector, H. J. P. Bomford, of twenty-one modern British paintings, Swindon has shown what a small local authority can achieve with limited resources.

Bomford's gift included works by Henry Moore, Paul Nash, L. S. Lowry, Kenneth Martin and Graham Sutherland, and a superb Ben Nicholson painting from 1933, a year crucial in his development. In *Composition in Black and White* the shift towards pure abstraction, influenced by Miró, is apparent. Nicholson had begun to paint on gesso, scraping and incising its smooth ground to create texture.

The following year the Contemporary Art Society (CAS) gave a Wilson Steer, followed by a powerful Michael Ayrton of Roman backstreet life (1952) and a John Nash (1954), but it was only after the decision in 1963 to appoint an independent adviser on acquisitions that the collection really developed.

Sir Laurence Gowing, two of whose paintings had been in Bomford's original gift, was the first adviser until he gave way in 1966 to Richard Morphet, a young curator at the Tate Gallery. Morphet's judgement, supported by a remarkably wise and knowledgeable director of arts and recreation, Denys Hodson,[133] gave the collection its essential shape and characteristics.[134]

Over the next twenty-five years Morphet bought forty-five works on a budget that seldom exceeded £1,000 a year. He was determined that contemporary artists should be supported and so bought Bernard Cohen, Howard Hodgkin, Mark Lancaster, Tom Phillips, Richard Long, Michael Craig-Martin and Christopher Le Brun when they were in their twenties or early thirties.

He was convinced that this tiny budget could also fill some of the gaps in the early 20th-century collection and acquired works by Roger Fry, Robert Bevan, Mark Gertler, Edward Wadsworth, Alfred Wallis and Christopher Wood in the 1960s and Vanessa Bell, Sylvia Gosse and Julian Trevelyan in the 1970s. Not surprisingly the collection became a regular beneficiary of CAS gifts, which

included works by Terry Frost, Roger Hilton, John Hoyland, John McLean and Richard Hamilton.

Although the collection represents many of the main tendencies and groupings of 20th-century art in Britain (more precisely, in England, since the collection contains few Scottish or Welsh artists), such as the Seven and Five Society (Henry Moore, Ben Nicholson, David Jones, Christopher Wood), the neo-Romantics (Paul Nash, John Piper, Graham Sutherland) and post-war St Ives (Terry Frost, Roger Hilton), it is inevitable that a collection of this size can give only a partial view.

The collection shows how surprisingly self-contained were many 20th-century British artists. With obvious exceptions (Nicholson, Wood, Richard Hamilton) the influence of France or Italy or the United States is conspicuous by its absence.

What the works have in common is a love of mark-making and of painting. Artists here as diverse as Vanessa Bell, Gillian Ayres, Howard Hodgkin, John McLean and Christopher Le Brun exhibit a relish for the physical qualities of paint that is a hallmark of the collection.

In recent years, with the growing pressure on local authority budgets, the growth of the collection has been less spectacular. There are, however, plans for a new gallery to replace the present rather spartan rooms. Such a gallery would justify and consolidate Kenneth Clark's trust that they take art seriously in Swindon.

SOMERSET COUNTY MUSEUM *

Taunton Castle, Castle Green, Taunton, Somerset TA1 4AA
Tel. 01823 320200/320201, fax 01823 320229
e-mail: county-museums@somerset.gov.uk

Taunton Castle (partly 12th century) holds especially fine East Coker mosaics; also military history

Important 19th-century archaeological excavations form a seam through the south-west: Pitt Rivers's at Cranborne Chase, Alexander

The story of Dido and Aeneas in the Somerset County Museum

Keiller's at Avebury, Pengelly's at Exeter and Arthur Bullie's at Glastonbury Lake Village.

The Somerset Archaeological and Natural History Society was formed in Taunton in 1849 in the wake of the 1818 excavation of a Roman villa with a 4th-century mosaic at East Coker, but Taunton is unusual in that its most exciting finds have been in the mid and late 20th century.

Its collections form the basis of this museum: the bones of animals that roamed the Mendip Hills 10,000–200,000 years ago; Iron Age finds from Meare Lake Village and from Cadbury Castle; worked timber from Neolithic and Bronze Age trackways preserved for 6,000 years in the waterlogged Somerset Levels.

In 1980 a hoard of silver coins was discovered on a building site in East Street, Taunton. The coins were buried in an earthenware pot at the time of one of the devastating sieges of the town in 1644 and 1645.

In 1998 two cousins, Martin and Kevin Elliott, took their metal detector to a site at Shapwick, a parish that had yielded two small finds of 4th-century silver in the 1930s. They located 9,238 silver denarii, the largest hoard of denarii ever found in Britain and very large by the standards of the area of the Roman Empire as a whole. The coins span 250 years, from those with which Mark Antony paid his legions during his doomed struggle with Octavian for control of the Roman Empire (32–31 BC) to those minted in Rome for Severus Alexander (AD 193–224). Many are in immaculate condition.

Equally pristine, and perhaps even more affecting, is the mosaic (c. AD 350) revealed when the Roman villa at Low Ham was excavated in 1944–5. It depicts the story of Dido and Aeneas in scenes from the *Aeneid*. The characters are introduced; Aeneas arrives at Carthage; Dido falls in love, observed by a sulky Cupid; the relationship is consummated during a lion hunt: Aeneas departs and Dido kills herself, two cupids indicating their fortunes with torches, one raised, one lowered. The ship's oars, the arched necks of the horses, Dido's dapper little boots, the generous size of her bottom on the stallion – such details make the story immediate and personal.

These finds maintained the spirit of the Archaeological Society which bought Taunton Castle to house its collections in 1873. It is an appropriate setting for Somerset's military collections, which recount the history of the Somerset Light Infantry. The 1846 regimental colours are here, faded and torn from service in the Afghan Wars and the Indian Mutiny. The regiment was among those forced to withdraw from Kabul in January 1842. Only one man out of 16,000, Dr William Brydon, survived. Lady Butler works her customary heroics in *The Remnants of an Army* (1879), which shows him struggling into the safety of Jellalabad.

The regiment served in the Crimea and in the Second World War. There is a diorama of the battle of Kambula, 1879, when Commander Evelyn Wood reversed the humiliation of Isandhlwana, one of the disasters of British imperial history.

The museum has some fine individual objects: a late 14th-century stone reredos from St John the Baptist's Church, Wellington, defaced during the Reformation, laid as a floor but still intact; the Ilchester mace, whose latten head (late 13th–early 14th century) depicts three kings and an angel; an 1865 beam engine with cast iron classical columns; and the Taunton cabinet, made by Stevens of Taunton for the 1851 Great Exhibition, where its flamboyant swags of carved flowers and fruit were said to be 'one of the gems' of the exhibition.

Upstairs is a curiosity: a collection made by Miss Primrose Peacock of 19th- and 20th-century buttons: buttons made of glass, shell, enamel, steel, corozo, black horn; oriental buttons, art nouveau buttons, buttons commemorating coronations; and buttons from Berlin in the 1920s and '30s brought to England by a refugee, Adolph Gans.

TORQUAY MUSEUM **

529 Babbacombe Road, Torquay, Devon
TQ1 1HG
Tel. 01803 293975
www.torquaymuseum.org

Where William Pengelly began to prove, at Windmill Hill, that the world was not made in six days and Agatha Christie solves mysteries too

Many 19th-century museums were initiated by local philosophical or natural history societies. Torquay is one of the few with which the original society is still involved, holding weekly meetings throughout the winter and maintaining a fine society library. Among the founding members in 1844 was William Pengelly, a local geologist and mathematician. It is his collection that makes this museum exceptional. In 1858, the year before the publication of Darwin's *The Origin of Species*, Pengelly's excavation at Windmill Hill in

Brixham uncovered the remains of extinct animals, together with evidence of human tools, thus indicating that man was far older than the 4,004 years the leading biblical scholars claimed.

Over the next twenty years Pengelly continued to excavate Brixham and Kent's Cavern, putting together a sequence of fossil fauna and human artefacts that was unrivalled in Britain, including Lower Palaeolithic hand axes (350,000 years old), Mousterian artefacts of Neanderthal origin from the Middle Palaeolithic and a Late Upper Palaeolithic bone needle (15,000 years).

Significant as these finds are, it is the methods and recording techniques that Pengelly employed – methods of 'scientific excavation' that anticipated by twenty years much of Pitt Rivers's work at Cranborne Chase – which are commonly considered to have established the foundations of modern archaeology.

Pengelly worked in 'yards', 3 feet by 1 foot by 1 foot. Each yard, and each object within each yard, was numbered, allowing him to observe and record everything in its natural stratigraphy with a precision and rigour that have enabled his work to be re-examined and developed.

The object at the centre of this collection, the object from which all its magic glows, is a piece of human jawbone, no more than 1½ inches long, with three teeth, ground down, excavated in Kent's Cavern in 1927. It is over 30,000 years old, one of the oldest known fossils of modern (that is, not Neanderthal) man in Britain: the oldest human fossil in the world to be carbon-dated.

The importance of Pengelly's finds was equalled by his courage. The significance of the evidence coming from these caves between the 1820s and the 1860s was disputed by two leading geologists, the Revd Dr William Buckland of Christ Church, Oxford, and Adam Sedgwick,[135] of Trinity College, Cambridge. Both were sceptical and hostile. Yet Pengelly was determined.

He wrote to his wife in 1861, 'My heart ached to think of the thousand thousand questions which forced themselves before me, and which

I felt sure I shall never live to answer, and my mental eyes ached looking so far into the abyss of antiquity.' His findings, and his methods, went some way to fill that abyss.

The museum has other collections of interest: William Pengelly's daughter, Hester Forbes-Julian, bequeathed a collection of letters and autographs whose authors include Keats, Jane Austen, Verdi, Abraham Lincoln, Charles Darwin and Dr David Livingstone; and Dr W. S. Holden his 20th-century collection concerned with the geology and natural history of Devon.

Since Torquay was the birthplace of Agatha Christie, the museum has a Christie Gallery, but it is the work of Pengelly, as quiet and modest as Pitt Rivers was charismatic, which commends this museum.

ROYAL CORNWALL MUSEUM **

River Street, Truro, Cornwall TR1 2SJ
Tel. 01872 272205

Archaeology and history of Cornwall; fine mineral collection; De Pass Old Master drawings

Banks and museums store treasures but the Royal Cornwall Museum is that rarity, a museum in a former bank, by local 19th-century architect Philip Sambell Jnr.[136]

The Royal Cornwall Museum sets itself the task of maintaining a comprehensive county museum, telling the story of Cornwall: its archaeology and geology, and its natural, social and artistic history. If this is hard for a national museum (such as the National Museum and Gallery of Wales and the Museum of Scotland), it is daunting for a county, and the Royal Cornwall Museum is successful only in part.

There is no shortage of material with which to create a Cornish cabinet of curiosities. Kneller's portrait of Anthony Payne, the Cornish giant (1680), is matched by an anonymous[137] portrait of Black John of Tetcott, a dwarf jester who lived by the kennels of his master's hounds, which he followed on foot. Here is the White Witch of Helston, Tamsin Blight, and a bust of John Wesley, who crusaded for Methodism through the county between 1743 and 1789. The Trewinnard coach, reputedly the first four-wheeler in the south-west (1789), is beside a model of Richard Trevithick's steam-driven locomotive of 1804, which inspired George Stephenson and Timothy Hackworth to engineer the first goods and passenger locomotives. But these flashes do not convey the quiddity of Cornwall. For that you must dig: into the sea for fish, the soil for clay, into buried time for minerals.

Cornwall has been inhabited along its coasts since the Mesolithic period. From about 2300 BC there are signs of influence from the Continent in the technology and sophistication of bronze weapons, tools and jewellery, notably, in this museum, collars of beaten gold with decorated edging found at Harlyn Bay, near Padstow, and St Juliot, near Tintagel, and a penannular bracelet found on the foreshore of St Martin's in the Scilly Isles. As important are Bronze Age axes and moulds, pottery funerary urns and an Iron Age bronze bowl from Warbstow, made of beaten metal, its rim finished on a lathe.

Here is a world as skilled and aesthetically polished as the Roman and Christian societies that succeeded it, and it is illustrated here by a Saxon silver hoard found at Trewhiddle, near St Austell and a unique 12th-century pewter crucifix from Ludgvan Church.

Relics of Cornwall's coastal life and fishing traditions are thin here but the basis of its copper industry is fully explored in the centrepiece of the museum, the Rashleigh Collection.

Philip Rashleigh (1729–1811) of Menabilly was a landowner whose estates included the Gwennap, Fowey Consols and other great mines. A true amateur, rather than a scholar, Rashleigh built up a collection of mineral specimens, a description of which he published in 1797 in three volumes entitled *Specimens of British Minerals*. The first volume was illustrated by the local artist Henry Bone, who later became the official enamel painter to George III, George IV and William IV. In this, Rashleigh first described chalcophylite, chinoclase, bayldonite, scorodite and bournonite.

His collection dazzles: the glitter of tetrahedrite; the glow of yellow fluorite; the lurking green of olivenite; the turquoise glint of linoconite; the crystalline crust of brilliant blue langite; the coffee sugar of dolomite sprinkled on dark quartz. Here too is the false glitter of spangly iron pyrites; the white crust of allophane, the dull black gleam of chalcocite, the smooth polish of blister copper and the botroidal mass of haematite, the 'kidney ore'. Rashleigh was no James Sowerby, whose five-volume *British Mineralogy* (1804–17) was the definitive work, and he was severely criticised by the *Edinburgh Review* and others, but in this collection he offers the mineral beauties on which the history of Cornwall is based and gives the non-geologist a glimpse of the mineral museum that is beneath Cornish moors and valleys, laid down over thousand-fold millennia.

The Royal Cornwall Museum has one further surprise and delight: the Alfred de Pass Collection. De Pass (1861–1953) made his money in sugar in South Africa. Between 1888 and 1905 he built a collection of fine art. His bequests to Bristol City Museum and Art Gallery, the Tate, the Fitzwilliam Museum, the Ashmolean Museum, the National Portrait Gallery and the British Museum demonstrate his taste and generosity. To Truro he gave watercolours, Old Master drawings and prints. Here are works by Constable and Turner, by Cotman and Prout. More surprisingly, there are drawings by Claude (iron gall ink over chalk on paper creating the soft, warm tones he needed for this scene of a peaceful natural harbour with shipping) and by Piranesi. To his credit de Pass trusted his eye rather than reputations and found a delicious study of trees by Giovanni Francesco Grimaldi, the architect of the Villa Doria Pamphili, and works by Francesco Zuccarelli, Francesco Guardi and Frederico Zuccaro. A portrait of de Pass in profile (1899), by Augustus John, features his clear eye and confident moustache.

Hawker Hunter and Concorde at the
Fleet Air Arm Museum

FLEET AIR ARM MUSEUM *

Royal Naval Air Station, Yeovilton, Nr. Yeovil,
Somerset BA22 8HT
Tel. 01935 840565
www.fleetairarm.com

More than fifty aircraft including Concorde;
affecting displays on aerial war

Until 1903 man was rooted to the earth,
capable of winged flight in imagination only.
To fly was to escape, to be free, to seek the
heavens. He could only aspire to the soar and
glide of a bird, hanging motionless, swooping,
off a curve or a bowbend.

Within months of the Wright brothers' first
flight, there were men who were anticipating
the military potential of their planes (v. Royal
Air Force Museum, Hendon). At once questions arose: if flight was possible from land,
why not from sea? If from the sea, why not
from a ship?

In this museum, set in hangars on an
operational naval airfield, the development
of the Fleet Air Arm (of the Royal Navy) is
recorded. The first planes have a poignant
fragility, with their fuselages of wood, their
wings of canvas. They seem light enough
to take flight but too slight to survive the
buffeting of the upper air.

The imperative of war drove the development of the aeroplane. The first seaplane, the
Sopwith Baby, with wooden floats no bigger
than canoes, flew in 1915. The next year the
Sopwith Pup, 'the perfect flying machine',
was introduced and the Short 184 operated
from HMS *Engadine* at the battle of Jutland.
Lt. Col. H. R. Busted was catapulted into the
air off HMS *Slinger* in June 1918.

Squadron Commander E. H. Dunning made
the first landing on a moving ship, HMS
Furious, in a Pup on 2 August 1917, though he
died five days later when his plane went over
the side of *Furious* in another attempt. Flt.
Sub. Lt. Reginald A. J. Warneford destroyed a
Zeppelin LZ39, winning the first Naval Air
Service VC. The explosion when he dropped
his bombs turned his own aircraft over. He
survived but was killed ten days later, testing a

new aeroplane near Paris. The headline in the *Daily Express* was 'Mother's Grief and Pride'.

The novelty and pioneering danger of flying fostered a sense of fraternity between nations. Among the Sopwiths at this museum is a replica of a German Fokke DR1, the triplane of the Red Baron, von Richthofen.

Between the wars it was sport and commerce that maintained technical progress: the rivalry of seaplanes competing for the Schneider Trophy (1913–31) and the opening of commercial routes, the first of which, from London to Paris (1919), took two and a half hours and cost £21. A display of equipment shows flight deck calculators of 1920 which resemble astrolabes, and leather flying goggles of 1930.

The naming of planes moved from the earthbound Baby and Pup to creatures of the sea and sky: the Blackburn Skua (the first naval monoplane 1938–42); the Fulmar and Firefly, made by Fairey (1940–43); the Supermarine Sea Spitfire (1942–54), the naval version of Reginald Mitchell's Spitfire (v. RAF Museum Hendon), all with wings that folded back to allow storage below decks on an aircraft carrier.

The collection includes American and German planes of the Second World War, and a small gallery telling the story of the Kamikaze or Shimpu (Divine Wind). There are extracts from the diaries and letters home from young pilots awaiting their opportunity to fly, and to die – 'I think of springtime in Japan while soaring to dash against the enemy.' Here are their white Hachimaki headdresses, once blithe: 'Cherry blossoms glisten as they open and fall', a son tells his loved ones.

In a separate hangar, standing apart from the effective, densely engineered Blackburn Buccaneer and De Havilland Sea Vixen of the Cold War years, is the Concorde 002, aloof in its beauty. It is not a Fleet Air Arm plane but it is here because to look up from beneath the spread of its wings is to be reminded of the wonder of flight. Its design returns to the bird: all wing, slight body, a heron's legs.

Two images stay in the mind: the immensity of the aircraft carrier flight deck as you descend from your 'helicopter flight' and a scale model of Concorde – you could hold it in your outstretched arms – which, to put imagination to the test, was dropped from an aircraft and allowed to glide to earth.

The South-east

As London sprawls across southern England it seems to suck the discrete identities out of the Home Counties, creating one subtopia.

The south-east's museums and galleries, conversely, continue to convey a sharp sense of the region's diverse character, stretched out along the south coast from Portsmouth to the Isle of Thanet, and the Thames valley (Cookham, Windsor Castle, Hampton Court Palace): a royal progress towards London and royal coastal retreats at the Royal Pavilion, Brighton, and Osborne House on the Isle of Wight (for which, regrettably, there is insufficient space). Queen Victoria called Osborne 'a place of one's own, quiet and retired', when Prince Albert and the master builder Thomas Cubitt built this mansion and filled it with paintings by Winterhalter, Tuxen and Landseer.

If the region is light on Old Master collections, with the exceptions of Petworth House and Knole, it has public art galleries (at Southampton, Chichester, Brighton and Eastbourne) that concentrate on 20th-century and contemporary art. None had a major founding bequest, nor an industrial magnate – a Burrell (Glasgow) or a Walker (Liverpool); but each has created an excellent collection.

I am sorry not to have been able to include the new Turner Gallery at Thanet (not properly open as I write) or Wakehurst Place, the outstation of Kew, its 40,000 different plants drawn from every part of the world.

Royal Holloway has a fine collection of 19th-century British paintings and Canterbury Museum drawings by Tiepolo and Guardi – and the most comprehensive collection of T. S. Cooper's cowscapes. Cooper exhibited his paintings of cows at the Royal Academy every year from 1831 until just before his death in 1902.

Several outstanding National Trust collections are not included: the Vyne; Uppark, gutted by fire but miraculously restored; and the beautiful Polesden Lacey.

But the three museums whose omission I most regret are those at Winchester, whose Roman mosaics are possibly the best preserved in Britain; Hastings, with its North American Indian collections (tomahawks, pipes of peace, two scalps given by Chief Crazy Crow) and the warbonnet made for

the American Indian impostor Grey Owl, whose real name was Archibald Stansfeld Belaney; and Seaford, the only museum in the world housed in a Martello tower. Its glorious collections, pre- and post-Second World War, of wirelesses and gramophones, typewriters and sewing machines, are stacked on shelves from the floor to the ceiling: the technology of an age so recent and so distant.

POWELL-COTTON MUSEUM

**

Quex House and Gardens, Quex Park,
Birchington, Kent CT7 0BH
Tel. 01843 842168
e-mail: powell-cotton.museum@virgin.net

*Fantabulous array of African and Asian big
game and dioramas*

A lion is locked in battle to the death with a
buffalo bull in one of the finest examples of
19th-century taxidermy in Britain. This is the
same lion that, in the Congo in 1906, savaged
Major Percy Horace Gordon Powell-Cotton.
As you enter the museum, there, beneath a
portrait of the major, is the lacerated clothing
that he was wearing when the lion attacked.

The drama is the thing, played out through
the museum in dioramas. These splendid
tableaux of animals and habitats are showpieces for the skills of Rowland Ward, whose
family firm took taxidermy to new heights.
But within the heroics and the trophies is the
collection of a serious naturalist.

As a young man, heir to Quex House, the
surrounding estate and property in London,
Powell-Cotton chose to go round the world
rather than undertake a Grand Tour. He
travelled widely in India and the Himalayas
(1889–98) and began to collect mammal specimens for the museum that he founded here,
beside Quex House, in 1896.

His first diorama, of Himalayan sheep, goats
and wolves at dawn on the 18,000-feet-high
Baltoro glacier, shows his attention to detail.
He camped for three months in the Himalayas
during winter specifically to collect animals in
their winter pellage. A smaller diorama recreates an Indian forest at night in moonlight.
Each set piece tells a story. On the glacier a
wolf chases a goat over the cliff edge; in the
forest a leopard has killed an antelope and
dragged the carcass into a tree to keep it from
the tiger who prowls below.

In the late 1890s Powell-Cotton turned to
sub-Saharan Africa, with which he remained
preoccupied for the rest of his life, making

more than twenty expeditions in the next forty
years, to the Congo, Angola, Nigeria, Uganda,
Somalia and the Cameroons. These are recorded in dioramas of an African savannah,
with giraffe and zebra; a swamp with black and
white rhinoceros, a Kudu bull and a group of
giraffe; and a waterhole at dusk where ibex and
buffalo drink, watched by a pair of lions and a
massive bull elephant, 11 feet 6½ inches tall,
whose front leg breaks out of the diorama into
the gallery.

The way in which Rowland Ward restores
apparent animation to lifeless skins explains
his company's worldwide reputation: the lions
menace; the giraffe fold their front legs into
isosceles triangles in order to stoop to graze;
monkeys foregather in the branches of a tree;
antelope and gazelle sip tentatively, alert to
the approach of predators. Rowland Ward's
father, Henry, who travelled and worked with
John James Audubon in America, started
the company in 1829. His aunt emigrated to
Australia, where she was the first woman taxidermist, and his elder brother Edwin became a
taxidermist in California and wrote *Sportsmen
on the Field* (1872). Rowland Ward plagiarised
it for his own *Sportsman's Handbook*, which
became, in its many editions, the standard
text. The company's London premises were
the Jungle, 167 Piccadilly, with a telegraphic
address of 'Jungle, London'. Examples of their
work can still be seen in the Walter Rothschild Zoological Museum, the Royal Albert
Memorial Museum and Art Gallery,[1] and the
Royal Cornwall Museum (all q.v.).

Powell-Cotton was a demanding client.
Archived correspondence shows that he would
argue with Ward over three-eighths of an
inch of a specimen's position, and it is this
degree of attention to detail that gives his
collection its continued scientific importance.
He recorded in his diaries the circumstances,
map reference, altitude and time of day at
which each specimen was killed. Because he
dried his skins and refused to tan them in
formic acid, their DNA can still be identified,
making the collection a valuable scientific
resource.

Powell-Cotton extended this interest in the

African diorama at Powell-Cotton Museum

context of each kill to the way of life and culture of the tribes among whom he lived and he built up a useful, if almost incidental, ethnographic collection of 20,000 objects: weaving from the Cameroons, brass from Benin, elaborate reliquary brass boxes known as kuduo from Ghana and five carved and painted heads from the Kuyu River in the French Congo. Each has white teeth sharpened into points, a ritually scarified face and elaborate, traditional coiffure on which has been carved an animal. The fetish heads were part of the Kébé Kébé dance that honoured the snake ancestor, when life-sized puppets were carried by men hidden beneath cloaks.

Only the Horniman Museum and the Pitt Rivers Museum have more, or better, African ethnographic material and the African mammal specimens here are matched only by the Walter Rothschild Zoological Museum. Indeed the museum has almost ten times as many chimpanzee and gorilla specimens[2] with full provenance as does the Natural History Museum.

BRIGHTON MUSEUM AND ART GALLERY ✱✱✱

Royal Pavilion Gardens, Brighton,
East Sussex BN1 1EE
Tel. 01273 290900
www.brighton.virtualmuseum.info

Exemplarily displayed unconventional museum with notable furniture

Brighton is an exhilaratingly marginal place set between sea and downs; licence, minor criminality and bourgeois morality; pleasing datedness and edgy fashionability; holy day and holiday.

It was the town chosen by the Prince Regent in which to escape royal responsibilities, where he transformed Holland's pavilion into the minaretted fantasy of the Royal Pavilion; the town chosen by couples for snatched weekends of romance or adultery, actual or as demanded

by the old divorce laws; by families for sea breezes and piers of pleasure; by Mods and Rockers in the 1960s as a neutral promenade and a battleground; by gays as their kind of town. A suburb of Greeneland, its margins have always been on the move.

The museum and art gallery capture something of this invigorating, contradictory spirit. The entrance is approached through the Mughal North Gate and looks across Englishly planted flower beds to the extravagance of the Royal Pavilion. The museum was designed by the borough surveyor, Philip Lockwood (1871–3), on the site of Queen Adelaide's Stables and renovated at a cost of £10 million in 2002. Its frosted-glass windows, edged with Moorish patterns and topped with a star, are engraved with the town's coat of arms, fishes rampant, and its motto, 'IN DEO FIDEMUS', nicely covering confidence and desperation.

Inside, the museum treads the line between entertainment and scholarship with style. In its galleries, objects are pushed almost as close together as the goods in the antique shops in the nearby Lanes, yet never so as to prevent their breathing.

The museum has three main collections: fine art, ethnography (here described as World Art) and decorative art and design from Aestheticism and the Arts and Crafts movement of the 1870s to the present day.

In a single gallery at the centre of the building you are swept backwards from Philippe Starck's WW[3] stool and Ron Arad's narrow papardelle in bronzed steel (1994), past Salvador Dalí's sofa of Mae West's lips (*c.*1938)[4] and Marcel Breuwer's long chair (*c.*1936) made of bent laminated ply, to pieces by Mackintosh, E. A. Taylor, C. R. Ashbee and C. F. A. Voysey, by way of Art Nouveau and Art Deco.

Particular attention is paid to the changes in the design of chairs, with examples here by Charles Eames, Arne Jacobsen, Lord Snowdon and Frank Gehry. There are several outstanding pieces: a table by René Lalique in etched glass; a table and chair made by Charles Rennie Mackintosh for his Northampton patron W. J. Bassett-Lowke; the interior of a lift designed by Edgar Brandt for Selfridges store in Regent

Street (1927–8), an explosion of sun rays from roundels of nesting storks made from wrought iron and beaten tin; and a day bed, screen and chandelier made by Armand-Albert Rameau for his own apartment in Paris. The screen's shimmer (water-gilding and oil-gilding with silver leaf) is teasingly at odds with the neat chasteness of the narrow single bed and the frozen-water teasel of glass that is the chandelier above.

The gallery has an exuberant playfulness, kept on a leash by the quality of each object, and by the precise context created by the well-integrated period ceramics, glass and paintings. This spirit of real enjoyment animates the whole museum.

The fine art galleries are somewhat less successful. The collection of over two thousand paintings includes some interesting landscapes: a very early example by Gainsborough;[5] a small Richard Wilson; and *Cumberland Farm* (1930) by Ben Nicholson, one of a group of paintings[6] whose flat paint textures prepared the way for his move into abstraction.

The collection is strengthened by the quality of the gift, in 1903, of a local brewer and collector, Henry Willett,[7] which included two small Lucas Cranachs,[8] works by Jan Lievens, Aert de Gelder, Nicolaes Maes, Willem van Aelst and Aert van der Neer, and an early George Stubbs, *Shooting* (1761), painted before he came to London.

The impact of these works is somewhat reduced by their being dispersed through the museum. To find the Lievens, *The Raising of Lazarus* (1631), once owned by Rembrandt, in the corridor on the way to the toilets in the basement, or to pass the *Still Life with Carnations* by van Aelst on the stairs, a position not conducive to studied concentration, is disconcerting, if demonstrative of a certain diverting confidence.

The museum's redesign, financed by the Heritage Lottery Fund in 2002, has provided a purpose-built room for the strong collection of watercolours, which includes examples of all the major artists of the golden age (1750–1850) (Sandby, J. R. Cozens, J. S. Cotman, Girtin, De

Wint, Turner, Constable and Samuel Palmer) and many from the 20th century (John and Paul Nash, Edward Bawden, Eric Ravilious, Muirhead Bone, David Jones, John Piper, John Minton, Graham Sutherland), alongside a collection of 19th-century Sussex watercolour landscapes by local artists.[9]

Brighton was the first, indeed the only, public art gallery to buy work by Robert Bevan in his lifetime and that work, *The Cabyard at Night* (*c.* 1910), has been joined by a landscape of real charm. The gallery also has one of the best collections of work by Glyn Philpot, thanks to gifts made by the artist's family. Philpot was a fashionable and successful portrait painter who, towards the end of his life, broke with the constraints of society portraits. Here is a sexy portrait of *Gwen Cleaver* (1933) and the lightly massive *Acrobats Waiting to Rehearse* (1935), in which a heavy blue stage curtain has been pulled back to invite you to intrude on two acrobats whose crossed arms and set jaws defy you to come any closer.

In the late 1990s local government reorganisation led to the merger of Hove's and Brighton's galleries, so bringing here Hove's strong collection of 20th-century British art including a late (1929) Malcolm Drummond, *The Stag Tavern*; a Frances Hodgkins still life, *Eggs, Tomatoes and Mushrooms*; and a Henry Lamb portrait of *The Behrend Family* (1927).[10]

Apparently unrelated to any other works is a collection of American paintings that includes three different works by Frank Stella and pieces by Alexander Calder, Larry Poons and, incongruously, two small sculptures by Anthony Caro. They were a gift, in 1997, from Professor Paul Heyer, an erstwhile student at Brighton College of Art.

The display of the museum's collection of 20th-century costume, despite the curator's flair with the decorative art gallery, demonstrates that Brighton is as baffled as every other museum by the problems of exhibiting costume designs off the living body.

In contrast, the galleries devoted to the non-fine art collections of Henry Willett and to the ethnography/World Art collections of

F. W. Lucas and Melton Prior embody what is most attractive about this museum. Shaped by gifts and bequests received, the ethnography collections provide a glimpse of the people who have pioneered the study of other ways of life than our own over the past century: who they were, what they studied and collected, why and how.

The ethnological collection of a local solicitor, Frederick W. Lucas, demonstrates what could be acquired from English sale rooms. Lucas never travelled abroad but amassed a large collection of vertebrate skeletons (now in the Booth Museum of Natural History, q.v.) and ethnographic material that reflected his fascination with how other cultures used animal produce. The tools of animal husbandry he collected are utilitarian but they are also beautiful and have labels that he wrote by hand. Melton Prior was a war artist for the *Illustrated London News* covering the Zulu wars of the 1870s and '80s. Collector and imperialist, they had motives and experiences that were distinct from those of Thomas Joshua Alldridge and James Green[11] or of Mary Clare Adam, who lived with tribes in the Sepik region of Papua New Guinea.

Willett was an inveterate collector. He started with local fossils and went on to archaeology, iron firebacks and miscellaneous curiosities. Here is a fossil fish (90–100 million years old), casts of dodo pouts and a stuffed pangolin. Here too is his huge collection of ceramics, organised according to his own system into twenty-three separate categories: military heroes (Wellington, Cornwallis and Sir John Moore, the hero of Corunna); religion; drama; statesmen; conviviality and teetotalism; domestic incidents; and crime. The last features revealing and witty plaster models, made by the illustrator and cartoonist Randolph Caldecott, of the Queen's Bench and counsels in the trial of the Tichborne claimant (30 September 1873), the participants being portrayed satirically as birds (an owl, an eagle, a cockerel) and a tortoise.

You can leave the museum and find objects in the Lanes which are as heterogeneous as those that delighted Willett. What you can-not find is the value that can be added to objects only by considered juxtapositions and comprehensible interpretation rooted in the professionalism and scholarship of museum curators of the quality found at this museum.

BOOTH MUSEUM OF NATURAL HISTORY **

194 Dyke Road, Brighton, East Sussex
BN1 5AA
Tel. 01273 292777
www.booth.virtualmuseum.info

Comprehensive flight of stuffed and mounted British birds; also butterflies and local iguanodon

In an age in which political correctness hangs over museums and galleries, the Booth Museum of Natural History breaks all the rules triumphantly. It is a temple of taxidermy. Around its walls, tiers of cabinets display Edward Thomas Booth's collection of over three hundred species of British birds, floor to ceiling. Its labels are typed on card. There is scarcely a computer or video screen in sight: only birds, butterflies, insects, skeletons, shells, fossils and minerals.

The museum brings together Booth's three passions: birds, shooting and taxidermy. Having built the museum in the grounds of his Brighton home, Bleak House, for the enjoyment of himself and his friends, he determined to fill it with at least one example of every species of British bird, having shot or trapped each exhibit himself. As a man of independent means he could devote himself to this pleasingly circular life's work.

He had been taught taxidermy as a boy by Kent, the St Leonard's barber and bird stuffer, but for his collection he employed George Savile, full-time, at the reported rate of £25 a week. Later he used Brighton taxidermists: Brazenor Brothers, Swaysland and Sons, and Pratt and Sons.

Booth was an amateur watercolourist and designed the backdrops of each diorama, which he intended would show, accurately,

the habitat of each bird. These dioramas transformed the exhibition of natural history. Before Booth, stuffed animals were displayed on stands. His dioramas and their environmental settings based on observation and fact were copied all over the world and perfected in the United States at the American Museum of Natural History, New York, and the Smithsonian Institute in Washington, DC.

Here are three immature golden eagles, in snow (case 1). One is eating a rabbit, which it holds down with its claw. Here is a whooper swan (case 303), its wings spread to reveal their huge span. Here too are the dioramas (cases 153 and 154) of gannets, in which Booth was particularly interested. One shows nestlings at various stages of development; the other has adult and juvenile birds. These models cannot convey the beauty of flight or flock but they give the opportunity to gaze at the details of texture, scale and articulation of rare species such as the Temminck's stint (case 294) that Booth found on the Breydon mudflats in 1872, the great grey shrike (1911) or the group of six small bramblings, again in snow.

As you walk round the gallery, the cabinets provide a register of birds: a red-throated diver, a stately Bewick gull, a grey skua, a pink-footed goose, a grey phalarope, a roseate tern. Tits (bearded, willow, coal and blue), larks (black, calandra and short-toe); gadwall, ptarmigan and shag; a pair of great auks, with an egg, from St Kilda.

The museum also has over 400,000 specimens of insect and butterfly and a particularly strong collection of skeletons put together by F. W. Lucas, the Brighton solicitor whose ethnographic collection is now in the Brighton Museum and Art Gallery (q.v.), alongside the Henry Willett collection of ceramics. One Lucas skeleton is of a wolfhound, once the Lucas family pet.

Here in the Booth is Willett's collection of chalk fossils, which started him collecting. In 1871 he reflected that 'if the inspection of this collection should help one young man to find

Raggi's bird of paradise roller at the
Booth Museum of Natural History

his pleasure, and to spend his spare time in this direction, rather than to waste it in billiards or idleness, it will not have been formed or presented in vain.'

ROYAL PAVILION ✱✱✱

4–5 Pavilion Buildings, Brighton,
East Sussex BN1 1EE
Tel. 01273 290900
www.royalpavilion.org.uk

Nash's Mughal confection, touched with chinoiserie, built for the Regent

In 1786 George, Prince of Wales, aged twenty-four, instructed his Clerk of the Kitchens and Cellars, Louis Weltje, to find him a 'respectable farmhouse' in Brighton. He had secretly (and illegally) married the beautiful Mrs Fitzherbert, a Roman Catholic, and needed a quiet residence away from London and the court.

The Prince employed the elegant, restrained, neo-classical architect Henry Holland[12] to convert the farmhouse into a marine pavilion, with two wings, shallow bow windows and a low central rotunda. From this modest beginning sprang one of the most extravagant (and exotic) architectural follies in Britain: an example of royal patronage, the decorative arts in the early 19th century and, subsequently, scholarship and restoration as the pavilion has been restored, and re-restored, throughout the 20th century.

The marine pavilion came to be overshadowed by the huge Mughal dome of the Royal Stables, built beside it by William Porden, and in 1805 Humphry Repton was commissioned to make drawings for the adaptation of the pavilion in a similar Indian style,[13] although the plan was abandoned because of the shakiness of the Prince's finances.

In 1815, his finances restored, the Prince commissioned his by then favourite architect, John Nash, who 'threw his fancy dress over'[14] Holland's pavilion with a wondrous mixture of Islamic minarets and scalloped arches: Gothic windows and 'friezes of cusped lozenges, a motif familiar from Perp parapets';[15] and

Indian pinnacles, columns, domes and yet more breasting domes by the side of the English sea.

Indoors, China replaces India. Dragons abound. Crimson and gold predominate. The interiors are stages on which the designers, Frederick Crace and Robert Jones,[16] could compete. In 1817 the Prince of Wales, now Prince Regent, met them to determine whose talents would be used where. Crace was given the Music Room, the Saloon, the Entrance Hall and the three Galleries; Jones the Banqueting Room, the Red Drawing Room, the King's new private apartments and the redesign, in 1823, of the Saloon.

From the large domed ceiling of the Banqueting Room, Jones suspended a huge chandelier, thirty feet long, a ton in weight. It is held in the claws of a silvered dragon, its wings sheltering its element. Below it, lotus shades of frosted glass arise out of the mouths of six sub-ordinate dragons. Yet more busily employed dragons support the sideboard and the eight lampstands, each twelve feet tall, made of deep blue Spode porcelain and ormolu.

The table is laid for the dessert course of a banquet with Coalport porcelain plates and the silver from the Londonderry and Ormonde collections, chiefly by Paul Storr for the royal goldsmiths, Rundell, Bridge and Rundell (v. the Gilbert Collection). The table blazes with the work of the finest craftsmen: Benjamin and George Smith, Digby Scott, Christopher Haines, John Bridge. The sideboard cupboard is by Thomas Hope. The splendour is dazzling, and is overseen by an all-seeing eye, in a tri-angle, within a circle, the Masonic symbol for 'knowing and seeing all', set in the canopies at the end of the room, amid symbols of the moon and the planets. The Prince Regent was the Grand Master of the Prince of Wales Lodge.

Crace's design for the Music Room is equally spectacular. The domed ceiling, decorated with gilded cockleshells, reflects the light from nine lotus-shaped chandeliers. The walls are deco-

Frederick Crace's Music Room at the Royal Pavilion, Brighton

rated with huge canvases, painted by Crace and his assistant, Lamberlet, with Chinese scenes taken from William Alexander's *Views of China* in crimson and gold. Golden dragons hold up these canvases; others still serve to draw aside the swagged and tasselled curtains. Its exuber-ance is beyond vulgarity: a place of frivolity, for entertainment and display, not for daily life. It resists anything but itself; the Prince, the most distinguished royal collector of paintings since Charles I, did not attempt to hang any in the pavilion. As George IV, after 1827, he never returned to Brighton.

Although it was used by William IV and by Queen Victoria, the pavilion was sold to Brighton in 1850 after she and Prince Albert built Osborne House on the Isle of Wight – a transition in the recreational taste of the bour-geoisie that would repay study. The interior was stripped. Damage from accidents, fires and general neglect have led it almost con-tinuously to be under restoration, keeping alive the decorative and craft skills that make this a pavilion of royal fantasy.

NATIONAL MOTOR MUSEUM *

Beaulieu, Brockenhurst, Hampshire
SO42 7ZN
Tel. 01590 612345
www.beaulieu.co.uk

The great motor museum: over a century of vehicular dreams

The National Motor Museum conducts a romance with the motor car: its beauty, its speed, its glamour.

The first vehicle you see on entering is an 1898, 12 h.p. Daimler, number plate AA16, which belonged to the 2nd Baron Montagu, whose belief in and passion for motoring inspired his son, the 3rd Baron, to form this collection. With bodywork of the deepest moss green, wooden wheelspokes and wax candles in its carriage lamps, it was the first car to be driven into the gates of the Houses of Parlia-ment and the first British entry in the Paris to

Ostende race.[17] In a 1906 article Lord Montagu asked, 'What is the future of automobilism?' He was confident that 'it will replace nearly every other kind of traction upon the surface of the earth' and foresaw the effect it was likely to have on cities, agriculture, even internationalism. 'Europe in a few years' time will become for the motorist one vast holiday area.'[18]

When his son, the 3rd Baron, opened Beaulieu to the public in 1952, he exhibited a handful of cars in the front hall (an 1895 Leon Bollée Tricar, an 1898 Benz). The collection grew; outgrew sheds in the garden; and opened as the Montagu Motor Museum in 1959 and as the National Motor Museum in 1972.

The oldest car here is the first petrol-driven vehicle built by Henry Knight of Farnham in 1895. It has tiller steering, a wooden chassis and a top speed of 8 mph. When he took to the highway, Knight was fined 5s. for driving without a traction engine licence and never built another car. British opposition to motoring ensured that for the next twenty years innovation and development took place in France, Germany and the United States.

Here are vehicles made by all the pioneers: Gottlieb Daimler's 1898 12 h.p. as well as Carl Benz's 3 h.p.;[19] an 1899 Voiturette made by Louis, Marcel and Fernand Renault; a 1903 Model Q by Count de Dion and George Bouton with red leather upholstery; and a utilitarian 1914 Model T of Henry Ford, 'any colour you like as long as it is black'. The motor car had gone from handmade curiosity to international mass production in twenty years.

Herbert Austin's Austin Seven (1923) and William Morris's snub-nosed Cowley (1924) competed with Ford for the British family market between the wars but it was not until the 1948 Motor Show that motoring finally broke through the class barrier in Britain. A line of cars here records this (the Morris Minor, the Jowett Javelin, the Ford Anglia) and recalls my childhood to me. In 1948 my parents were about to divorce. My mother bought an upright Anglia, my father a Jowett Javelin with its aerodynamic nose and sleek tail. The Standard Vanguard, the Hillman Imp and the Mini (like the Morris Minor designed by Alec Issigonis) are here, as is the 'people car', the Volkswagen 'Beetle' designed by Ferdinand Porsche, offered to British manufacturers as part of Germany's post-war reparations and turned down because it was considered to be too ugly to sell. It became the best-selling car of all time.

Beside these modest cars painted in modest colours the glamour cars gleam back through the century: a 1993 Jaguar XJ220 whose price (£403,565) killed its sales, only 350 being made; a 1974 Ferrari Dino, scarlet testosterone; a 1956 Austin Healey 100N, open topped, with a leather belt holding down the power under its bonnet; in the style of pre-war America, a white 1935 Auburn 851 Speedster with white-walled tyres; and, displaying Edwardian elegance, a 1912 Hispano Suiza and a 1909 Rolls Royce Silver Ghost. Most luxurious of all is a 1913 Argyll with seats of button-upholstered beige velour, railway carriage windows, netting for top hats and opera glasses, and an ear trumpet to communicate with the chauffeur up front.

The museum is as strong on speed as it is on glamour. Here are the generations of Bluebirds in which Sir Malcolm Campbell and his son Donald pushed up the land speed record from 150 mph in 1923 to 300 mph in 1935 (father) and 403 mph in 1964 (son) before the rocket engine and jet power of Thrust SSC (763.035 mph in 1997) made the Bluebird a projectile and severed any connection it had with the motor car.

Beside these prodigies of speed is parked a 1933 Morris Commercial van, a mobile shop that would trundle from village to village selling anything and everything: eggs, tea, cider, dried milk, patches with which to repair saucepans. Here are the sedate pleasures of Fuller and Swatland Empire Tea, Yarmouth Bloaters, Star Line Fruit Fancies, Peek Frean Teddy Bear biscuits. Also from the 1930s the museum has combined the machinery, tools and stocks of two businesses[20] and recreated a rural garage of the time in which the mechanic was still the village blacksmith, wheelwright and repairer of bicycles as well as being the master of the new arts of sparking plugs and big ends.

Outside the museum's wooden barn doors are hand pumps to dispense National Benzole Mixture and Shell Mex (1s. 7d. a gallon), as advertised in the Shell Art Collection, whose archive is here with its posters and advertisements from the 1920s to the 1960s by such artists as Paul Nash, Eric Ravilious, Ben Nicholson, John Piper and Graham Sutherland. They capture the romance of motoring and of Britain, the open road of Mr Toad, the speed, the freedom before the grip of road building and the seizure of gridlock.

In his 1906 article Montagu was right that 'automobilism' would transform the 20th century. The variety of forms of that transformation, and the inherent tensions between craftsmanship and cost, safety and speed, are here to be seen. Montagu saw too that the simple principle of the motor car (a mechanical source of power to drive wheels) created movement through air: aerodynamics. Montagu had the sculptor Charles Sykes design *The Spirit of Ecstasy*, modelled on his personal assistant Eleanor Thornton, her hair and dress streaming out behind her, and placed it on the bonnet of his Rolls Royce. The company has used it as the mascot of its marque ever since.

FISHBOURNE ROMAN PALACE ***

Salthill Road, Fishbourne, Chichester, West Sussex PO19 2QR
Tel. (general information) 01243 785859
www.sussexpast.co.uk

The finest collection in Britain of in situ *Roman mosaics*

Neat south-coast suburbia, next door to a primary school and bordered by the A259, is an incongruous setting for the largest collection of *in situ* Roman mosaics in north-west Europe.

The excavation of the Fishbourne site by Professor Barry Cunliffe, begun in 1961, uncovered much about the Roman invasion of Britain by Roman legions in AD 43 at the order of the Emperor Claudius: the creation of a harbour from two creeks; the establishment of a base from which the legions could be supplied as they pushed into south-west Britain; the building of a large granary and the metalled roads that were needed to distribute equipment and goods.

When the supply depot had served its purpose, a house of wattle and daub was built. This was then replaced by one of masonry around AD 60. The latter was finally incorporated into a massive four-winged palatial building between AD 75 and 80. The remains of the north wing (the footings of walls, mosaic floors) are presented here in what was, in the 1960s, a wholly original way: left *in situ*, and protected by a cover building, to make the site a museum around which you proceed on raised walkways.

The site's museum offers glimpses of domestic Roman life: seal boxes, a stylus; mortice locks and a key; a brooch, melon beads and an onyx intaglio; lead weights and hooks for fishing; the head of a marble statue of a child with a succulent Cupid's mouth. Glass from Egypt, Samian pottery from Gaul and Germany, wine and oil vessels from Spain and Italy all illustrate the scale and sway of the Roman Empire, as do the origins of the ballast dumped by trading ships: sheared porphyrite from Jersey, grandiorite from Cornwall, Arkosite sandstone from Alderney; and marbles imported from Turkey, Italy and the Pyrenees.

It is the mosaics that transform interest into wonder. There are more than thirty mosaic floors here, ranging from simple, 1st-century black-and-white geometrics, through the coloured 2nd-century Medusa head to the superb late-2nd-century *Cupid on a Dolphin* surrounded by fabulous sea beasts, two sea horses and two sea panthers. Around them a tendril grows out of four vases as a border. In the corner a small bird perches, perhaps the signature of the mosaicist.

Alongside the *in situ* mosaics are two from elsewhere. One is from a 4th-century town house in Chichester and the other, excavated by Alex Down in 1963, is from nearby Chilgrove. The latter is an example of the

4th-century Central Southern Group of mos-aicists identified by the motifs of that work-shop: a floral cup, an interlaced square, a lotus bud and a spiked knot.

It is not possible to establish who lived in this palace but its scale, the splendour of the mosaics and the quality of the remains of wall paintings suggest that it was a man of great wealth and position, possibly a native British tribal king. Professor Cunliffe has suggested that the palace could have been that of Tiberius Claudius Togidubnus, King of the Atrebates. More importantly, he was also a 'Great King in Britain', if an inscription from nearby Chichester has been correctly inter-preted. The palace might have been built in recognition of Togidubnus's loyal support for Rome during the troubles of AD 60–61.

In the past, finds of this quality were transferred to the British Museum for safety, convenience and scholarly investigation. One of the benefits of retaining them *in situ* is that they can be seen in full context which, in this case, means formal gardens. Remarkably, the original bedding trenches, containing marled loam and tree pits, had survived centuries of ploughing. These were discovered during the 1960s excavations. They have now been re-planted with what might have been grown there; box, apple and Italian cypress. These trenches have been enhanced by a new garden area, where many different flowers, vegetables, herbs and soft fruit are grown in a re-established Roman setting with raised beds, arbours, pergolas and triclinium.

What Fishbourne gives us is a glimpse into the logical, orderly Roman mind: harbour, depot, roads; site, drainage, building, plumb-ing, heating; garden for relaxation, food and medicinal herbs. Fishbourne also teaches us about contemporary archaeology. There have been frequent rescue and research excavations in and around the palace site since Professor Cunliffe's pioneering work in 1961, which have revealed the *Cupid on a Dolphin*, further mosaics from the west wing, a previously un-suspected masonry building and evidence of pre-conquest activity. A signet ring, inscribed 'TI CLAVDI CATVARI', the seal of Tiberius

Claudius Catuarus, a possible relation of Togidubnus, was also found near by.

There will always be much that will remain unknown. Why was this massive palatial building constructed here? Was it really for a client king? If so, was it King Togidubnus? Why did the palace burn down, leaving an unfinished hypocaust system? Was it a careless workman or the result of arson?

Nevertheless, Fishbourne gives us insights into Romano-British life that are available nowhere else.

PALLANT HOUSE GALLERY
★★★★

9 North Pallant, Chichester, West Sussex
PO19 1TJ
Tel. 01243 774557
www.pallanthousegallery.com

18th-century town house, 20th-century paintings

In 1980 Chichester District Council converted Pallant House into an art gallery to display Walter Hussey's collection of 20th-century paintings and sculptures.

Pallant House was built in 1712 by a young Chichester merchant, Henry Peckham, and his wife Elizabeth. It is an elegant, red-brick Queen Anne town house that might be seen as an incongruous setting in which to display a contemporary collection, but it is a sur-prisingly happy choice. It is a confident piece of architecture[21] that was bold, even startling, in its time: its ground floor is raised ten steps above street level and the house is given the appearance of additional height by the upper storey sash windows being significantly taller than those on the ground floor. Its well-lit rooms have proportions that are strong and clean. In them the paintings by Graham Sutherland, John Piper, Ceri Richards and others that Walter Hussey collected look well beside 18th-century furniture (the Askew cabinet (*c.* 1730), built in the form of a Palladian villa) and Geoffrey Freeman's 300-piece col-lection of Bow porcelain.

Hussey was an Anglican priest, first at

Richard Hamilton's Swingeing London,
at Pallant House Gallery

St Matthew's, Northampton (1937–57), and then at Chichester Cathedral, where he was Dean from 1957 until his retirement in 1977. In both posts he commissioned some of the finest religious works of modern British art, from Henry Moore[22] and Graham Sutherland at Northampton, and from Sutherland,[23] Ceri Richards[24] and John Piper at Chichester, while collecting works by them, and others, for himself. His 1985 bequest of his collection to Pallant House Gallery inspired Charles Kearley, a developer and builder, to leave his collection to the gallery four years later. In the 1990s the architect of the British Library, Colin St John Wilson, made a loan, part temporary, part permanent, of the collection that he and his wife, the architect M. J. Long,[25] had created. These three collections give Pallant House one of the strongest and most interesting holdings of 20th-century art in Britain.

Hussey and Kearley belonged to the same generation, born before the First World War, and there is some overlap in the artists they collected (Henry Moore,[26] John Piper and Graham Sutherland). Hussey bought direct from artists he knew and relied on his own judgement and an open mind. He described the quality most needed by a collector as the willingness 'to understand the artist's point of view, always expressing his thoughts honestly, but at the same time willing to learn and to trust the artist'.

This absence of preconception led him to collect 18th-century watercolours (by J. R. Cozens and John Varley), drawings by Giulio

Romano and Jean Antoine Watteau, theatre designs by Bakst and ceramics by Lucie Rie and Hans Coper.

Kearley's collecting began with architecture: the need to buy paintings for the walls of an aggressively modern penthouse in Ladbroke Grove[27] and later for a house designed for him by John Lomax on the Goodwood estate near Chichester.[28] Kearley lacked Hussey's steady eye but was more adventurous. He bought Ben Nicholson's 1946 *Still Life (Cerulean)* the year it was painted, and Sam Francis's *Composition* (1956) in 1958, years before any British gallery took an interest in him. His Sutherland (*Devastation 1941 – City Panorama*, 1941) and Severini's *Danseuse No. 5* (1913) (bought in 1971 when nobody in Britain but Eric Estorick[29] was collecting the work of Italian Futurists) are two of the finest pictures in the gallery. These two collections are linked to each other, and to that of Colin St John Wilson, by two curiosities, a miniature model art gallery that Sydney Burney created in 1934 and its Millennium equivalent, assembled by the Pallant House Gallery director Stefan van Raay in 2000. Both are scale models of a gallery of modern art filled with original works, in miniature: Barbara Hepworth, Henry Moore, Ben Nicholson, Edward Wadsworth and Ivon Hitchens in the 1934 model; Frank Auerbach, Eduardo Paolozzi, Antony Gormley, Howard Hodgkin, Antony Caro, Tom Phillips and Patrick Caulfield in its successor.

The Hussey and Kearley Collections are more than matched by that of Colin St John Wilson and M. J. Long. As was the case with Hussey, most of the artists they have collected are their friends. In the tradition of Rembrandt, Rubens, Lely and Lawrence, Wilson is an artist/collector. 'Only the fellow addict can understand the catch in the breath and the thumping of the heart of love-at-first-sight that signals the next ("absolute must") acquisition,' he writes.[30] There are works here that stand out (Michael Andrews's *The Colony Room*, 1962, Howard Hodgkin's *Grantchester Road*, 1975, David Bomberg's last self-portrait) but as striking is the catholic range of his collecting: pop art (Peter Blake, Richard Hamilton, R. B.

Kitaj), sculpture (Dhruva Mistry, Eduardo Paolozzi, Claes Oldenburg), Sickert, Piranesi and Bonnard.

Wilson is particularly interested in process and his archive here records the thirty studies that Patrick Caulfield made in developing *The Portrait of Juan Gris* (1963) and the ninety-six and eighty sittings that Michael Andrews and William Coldstream, respectively, took to paint portraits of Wilson himself.

Unusually, Wilson values prints. He quotes William Morris's challenge to the exclusivity of the unique object, 'What is the use of art if it is not Art for All?'[31] and collects here examples, screenprints by 'the undisputed master of that innovation',[32] Chris Prater, who printed the work of Paolozzi, Hamilton and Kitaj, whose work often required dozens of separate screen processes.

With the addition of the Wilson/Long Collection, the gallery needed more space and in 2004 it opened a unique extension, galleries designed[33] by Wilson to house his own collection. The facade of the new wing complements the 1712 facade in symmetry, scale, texture and tone. The old and the new stand shoulder to shoulder here.

SCULPTURE AT GOODWOOD *

Goodwood, Chichester, West Sussex
PO18 0QP
Tel. 01243 538449
www.sculpture.org.uk

Contemporary sculpture in a wooded landscape (for show and for sale)

The sculptures displayed here are not the core collection. They represent the core collection. They are for sale. On some days some will already be sold. They are then removed. Yet this is not a commercial gallery. Behind these transitory sculptures is a core collection of drawings and models by contemporary sculptors that aims to change and improve the commissioning of sculpture in Britain.

Wilfred and Jeannette Cass founded Sculpture at Goodwood in 1994. To do so they sold their own collection of sculpture (Henry Moore, Elisabeth Frink) and bought Hat Hill Copse, twenty acres of Sussex woodland, in the middle of the Goodwood estate with views across arable farmland to Chichester seven miles away. In the wood they have cut rides, avenues, clearings and corners in which to site more than fifty large sculptures that they have commissioned. The artists are required to deposit drawings and models of their pieces. The full-scale works (and often editions of the maquettes) are for sale. The process is as ruthless, clear-headed and unsentimental as the way in which the Casses sold their own collection. Once a work is sold it goes and is replaced. Only new work by living artists is shown.

Since 1994 more than a hundred sculptors have been commissioned: Eduardo Paolozzi, Anthony Caro, Lynn Chadwick, Philip King; Tony Cragg, Richard Deacon, William Turnbull; Antony Gormley, Rachel Whiteread, Richard Long, Andy Goldsworthy; Marc Quinn, Dhruva Mistry, amongst others.

You approach Hat Hill Copse along a side road that runs between open fields. Around the wood runs a high flint wall in which is a circular gate, *Gate* (2001), in aluminium, by the jeweller Wendy Ramshaw: one of the foundation's aims is to enable artists to extend the range of their work. Fifty yards to your left, Andy Goldsworthy's *Striding Arch* (2001), in sandstone, leaps over the wall.

Inside, before you reach the wood, there are sculptures by the drive, in the car park, around the house. Between the trees you glimpse Paolozzi's *London to Paris* (2000); along the track from the house to the gallery are lined Gormley's *Bollards* (2001).

The gallery, designed by Craig Downey, is half in, half out of the wood, its deck flooring continuing beyond the windows. Inside is a continually changing display of maquettes in banks of perspex display units – Qubes.[34]

The trees in the wood, mature beech, ash, oak, rowan, sycamore, lime, copper beech, are as various as the sculptures. Some of these you come across as shadow in a corner; others

stand centre stage at the end of an avenue. Marc Quinn's *The Overwhelming World of Desire* (2003) is a steel orchid (*Paphiopedilum* Winston Churchill Hybrid), thirty-four feet high, staring down the nearby trees. On the edge of the wood David Annesley's *Mandala Eighty* (2003), a delicate dance of wires touching fingertips, disappears and reappears against the backdrops of the landscape as the shadows move.

The sculptures are in a variety of materials: stainless steel, bronze, cast iron, copper, leather, glass; the woods provide as sympathetic a setting for these as for those in granite, marble or limestone. Even a mirror and video screens sit here as easily as in a city-centre square. Few works defy the movement of the trees. George Cutt's *Reflexions* (1998), two sinuous columns in stainless steel, eleven feet high, dance slowly with each other.

Maquettes and drawings of many of these sculptures are at a new gallery that the Casses have opened in London at Percy Street.[35] The maquettes are sculptures prior to being scaled up, some of which are satisfactory in small, others not. The drawings are less predictable. Some (*The Heads*, 1997, by John Davies) are illustrations, literal and precise. Some are impressions (Peter Burke's *Host*, 1996). Shirazeh Houshiary's *The Extended Shadow* (1994) is a technical drawing with specifications. Anthony Caro's *Figure* (1986) is a romantic charcoal drawing, its forms and outlines blurred, that could scarcely be further removed from his welded, bolted, abstract metal sculptures.

Through all these works the foundation is attempting to provoke artists and those commissioning sculpture to dare. The Casses were both on the committee that originally commissioned sculpture for the western plinth in Trafalgar Square which has lain empty since the 1840s. Two of those who have had works temporarily occupying the plinth since 2001 have shown works at Goodwood: Bill Woodrow and Rachel Whiteread. Whiteread noted, 'After spending some time in Trafalgar Square observing the people, traffic, pigeons, architecture, sky and fountains, I became acutely aware of the general chaos of Central London life. I decided that the most appropriate sculpture for the plinth would be to make a "pause": a quiet moment for the space.'[36] Her *Inverted Plinth* (1999), a one-tenth scale maquette, has been sold. The Bill Woodrow is at Goodwood. Until, that is, it too is purchased.

STANLEY SPENCER GALLERY **

High Street, Cookham-on-Thames, Berkshire SL6 9SJ
Tel. 01628 471885
www.stanleyspencer.org

The home village of this quintessential British religious artist

'At last I can say my say about my pictures,'[37] wrote Stanley Spencer in the introduction to the catalogue of a retrospective exhibition of his work at the Tate in 1955. In this collection he has his say about much, if not all, of his life and his talents.

There is a strong autobiographical vein through his work which is brought out in this gallery. The gallery is in the chapel he attended every Sunday as a child; in the village where he lived all his life, with a few, mainly enforced, breaks, in a house, Fernlea, built by his grandfather.

The gallery, consisting of one room, is a modest conversion of the chapel and retains a sense of village. The Cookham in which he was born in 1891 was a village of red-brick cottages on the bank of the Thames. It had a church, marshy meadows, boathouses, a bridge and swans. 'There were hidden bits of Cookham as remote as the Milky Way,'[38] wrote his brother, Gilbert. For Spencer the village was a 'holy suburb of Heaven'. When he stopped commuting to the Slade School of Art in 1912 and was able to be in Cookham all day, every day, he felt as if he had returned to 'a kind of earthly paradise. Everything seemed fresh and to belong to the morning.'[39]

Throughout his life his paintings were steeped in the images, views and villagers of Cookham. In *Sarah Tubb and the Heavenly Visitors* (1933), based on a true incident, Granny Tubb is kneeling by her gate in the High Street, convinced that the brilliant sunset caused by the tail of Halley's Comet is the end of the world. She is comforted by 'heavenly visitors' in white, angels, who offer her pictures of flowers and a rack of postcards of Cookham.

The discovery of the extraordinary in the ordinary, of the visionary in the concrete, of the imagined in the observed, marks almost all Spencer's work. *The Betrayal of Christ* (1914) takes place in the back garden of Fernlea. In the background are the oasthouses Spencer could see as a child from his beddroom window. Christ approaches his crucifixion while village life goes on.

In *Christ Preaching at Cookham Regatta: Listening from Punts* (1954) and his last (and unfinished) major work, *Christ Preaching at Cookham Regatta* (1953–9),[40] many of the figures, in white flannels, boaters and bathing dresses, are based on local people, all of them listening to Christ as part of a holiday, in punts, in wicker chairs, hands on hips, hands in pockets, picnicking, feeding the swans.

In *The Last Supper* (1920) a religious subject is treated directly. Christ and the disciples are in white shifts, surrounded by brick walls. The humour, provided by the disciples' bare feet in two lines under the table, relates this moment, the first Eucharist, to any mealtime.

Although this is the largest collection of Spencer's work there are several important themes and subjects to which he returned throughout his life that are absent. The paintings and drawings that arose out of his experiences in the two world wars, in Macedonia (1915–18) and in the Glasgow shipyards (1940–46) are not here.[41] Nor are any of the series of nude portraits of his second wife Patricia Preece (some on her own, some double portraits with him), one of which the Royal Academy refused to exhibit in 1935, which led Sir Alfred Munnings to threaten a private prosecution against Spencer in 1950. There is only one self portrait (1923) of the many that he painted.

There are examples of the pen-and-ink drawings commissioned by Chatto and Windus for an almanac, two drawings for each month, published in 1926. They record scenes of spring-cleaning, dressmaking and gardening, remembered from his childhood. One oil, *Neighbours* (1936), was developed from the April illustration of two women awkwardly exchanging a bunch of tulips over a wide, unruly hedge. In the background the shapes of the bare pale branches of an apple tree and the dark thin branches of a yew mimic their outstretched arms.

There is invariably something exposed and often disturbing about Spencer's paintings. He deals with great themes – copulation and birth, death and resurrection, the humanity of Christ – in images that are ostensibly direct and concrete. Yet, tucked away, in detail, in corners, behind figures, are images that run against the nap.

In *The Beatitudes of Love: Contemplation* (1937) a couple gaze at each other 'as though they will never stop looking', according to Spencer.[42] They are overseen and overheard (a large ear abuts her profile): in the distance another couple gaze into each other's eyes in imitation. He appears amazed, horrified, held up by her left hand. Her right hand rests on her thigh, 'a hideous chicken claw'.[43] It is one of a series of ten paintings, *The Chapel of Love*, which Spencer wanted to install in the Church House, a secular version of the Sandham Memorial Chapel at Burghclere, in which, between 1927 and 1932, he painted frescoes that depicted his war experiences in Macedonia. He considered *The Beatitudes* to be 'more genuine than any religious painting I have ever done', adding, 'I can do without all my pictures except these.'[44] The figures are ugly and distorted, but for Spencer the ugly is redeemable. In *Sermons by Artists* he writes, 'Distortion arrives from the effort to see something in a way that will enable him to love it.'

Unlike at Burghclere, where Mr and Mrs Behrend commissioned the series and built the Sandham Memorial Chapel (q.v.) to house it, the Chapel of Love was never realised. Nevertheless series or cycles of paintings were of central importance to him: *The Passion* (1920–23), *Domestic Scenes* (1936), *Christ in the Wilderness* (1939), *Port Glasgow Shipbuilding* (1940–45), *The Resurrection* (1945), *The Marriage at Cana* (1953) and *Christ Preaching at Cookham Regatta* (1953–9).

Those canvases that are unfinished show the way in which his paintings were built up from the meticulous foundations of his fine draughtsmanship, drilled into him at the Slade by Professor Henry Tonks and evident in the drawings that are here at Cookham.

It is not difficult to recognise his greatness. It is less easy to see how he fits into the canon of the great English artists. The visionary line from William Blake to Samuel Palmer to Spencer is clear. His debts to Giotto and the Italian Primitives, particularly in his early work, are obvious. His sexuality; the violence, sometimes latent, sometimes explicit; the tenderness; the sense of danger; the wrestling with ideas; the exaltation and the despair; and the tensions between these go to the centre of Spencer's work.

The last say should be his. 'Do you know what good art is?' he once asked his friend, the director of the Tate Gallery, John Rothenstein. 'It's just saying "ta" to God.'[45]

HAMPTON COURT PALACE
★★★★

East Molesey, Surrey KT8 9AU
Tel. 0870 752 7777
www.hrp.org.uk/webcode/hampton_home.asp

Half a thousand years of British monarchy

The red-brick battlements and chimneys of the West Front of Hampton Court Palace look down on a moat whose bridge is flanked by heraldic beasts, griffins, dragons, unicorns and lions. In its walls are terracotta roundels of the heads of Roman emperors, Tiberius and Nero. It is the face that Hampton Court turns to the world, the basilisk stare of Henry VIII and of royal power. But all is not what it seems. The Trophy Gate was built not for Henry VIII but for William III and it is only in the next courtyard that you find the original 16th-century

West Front. The palace is a lamination. Behind the Tudor facade are additions by Christopher Wren in the 17th century[46] and William Kent in the 18th century.[47] This is a museum of the public and private faces of monarchy.

It is these wings that are open to the public and that house major parts of the Royal Collection, particularly those paintings commissioned and collected by Henry VIII, Charles I and Charles II, by Daniel Mytens, Marcus Gheeraerts the Younger, Kneller and Lely.

All that remains of Henry VIII's palace are Wolsey's apartments, the Great Hall and the terrifyingly named Great Watching Chamber, but their echoing proportions, decorated ceilings and tapestries summon up the Tudor court.

The Great Hall has a superb hammer-beam roof by the King's Master Craftsman, James Nedeham, and both rooms are hung with 16th-century Flemish tapestries: *The Story of Abraham*, commissioned by Henry VIII from the Brussels weaver William Kempaneer, in the Great Hall, and *The Triumphs of Petrarch*, woven for Wolsey, in the Great Watching Chamber.

More surprising are the four paintings commissioned by Wolsey to create for the young Henry VIII an image of a chivalrous, spectacular and victorious monarch, before whom the world would bow: *Henry at the Field of the Cloth of Gold*, *The Embarkation of Henry at Dover*, *The Meeting of Henry and the Emperor Maximilian I*, and the painting that is the pick of them, *The Battle of the Spurs* (1513).

Against blue hills and an empty landscape, the unknown painter has placed a pugnacious mêlée at the centre of which is the young Henry in gilt armour, his helmet topped by red, white and gold plumes, his visor thrown back to reveal his handsome face. In the scene he accepts the tribute of the defeated. This is sublime propaganda. The battle of the Spurs was an insignificant skirmish at which Henry might not even have been present.

Sir Christopher Wren's Chapel Royal at Hampton Court Palace

One of the most spectacular survivors from Henry VIII's palace is the Chapel Royal. The fan-vaulted ceiling, dripping carved and gilded pendants, dates from 1535–6; the stained glass, copied from the Tudor original, from 1894. Everything else, apart from the position of the Royal Pew, is from 1690–1710. Queen Anne had the pew panelled and the *trompe l'œil* window and the pew ceiling, with its putti playing with crown and orb, painted by Thornhill, who added swagged curtains above the pew, drawn apart by more putti, making the monarch the actor rather than the spectator. Opposite is Grinling Gibbons's great reredos of latticed marquetry flanked by Corinthian columns. After Belton this is his finest work.

Behind Wren's glittering baroque facade, Gibbons, appointed Master Carver to the Crown in 1693, was given full rein by Wren to make the frames, overmantels and cornices for the public and private rooms of the King's and Queen's Apartments. So too was Antonio Verrio, who was given similar licence to paint the ceilings and walls of the Queen's Drawing Room and of the staircase to the King's Apartments. Here Hercules soars upwards on a billowing, if solid, cloud in an explosion of angels, sightlines and activity, held together by the vertical strength of the pillars which frame the three screens.

As you walk from room to room, through the State Apartments, you catch continual glimpses of gardens which, like the palace itself, tell the story of changing taste and fashion, expressed by royal gardeners from John Tradescant (to Charles II) to Lancelot 'Capability' Brown (to George III).

Among the pictures are two sets of royal beauties: the Windsor beauties from Charles II's court, by Sir Peter Lely c.1662–5, and the Hampton beauties painted by Sir Godfrey Kneller for Mary II thirty years later. Both artists make their subjects' appearances conform to the accepted aesthetics of the day with little attempt to represent personality, the beauties being differentiated by Lely with symbolic accessories (apples and peaches; roses; a spear), by Kneller with the sumptuous handling of textiles.

Among all these public and private glories, the greatest beauty is tucked away outside in the Lower Orangery, Andrea Mantegna's *The Triumphs of Caesar*, a sequence of nine paintings described by Vasari as 'the best work he ever did': 'to express it in a word this entire project could not be more beautiful or any better executed.'[48] Charles I bought this splendid sequence from the Gonzaga Collection in 1629 after prolonged negotiations by his agent, David Nys. They have been at Hampton Court ever since. Even Cromwell, when selling off Charles's collection in 1649, held them back, recognising their importance.

Working from descriptions in Livy, Plutarch and Suetonius, Mantegna painted triumphant cavalcades processing from right to left. The upper half of each panel is crowded with pikes, flambards, cartouches, pennants, helmets, horns and palms, all set against the sky. The lower half is a press of dogs, swords, elephant trunks, a cripple, a dwarf and horses' legs. The nine are held together by a shared palette of colours (coral, yellow, blue and red), by being seen from below and by sharing a light source that comes from the left beyond the frame, an impression solidified by the rhythmic energy of the whole. In this consummately theatrical composition Mantegna deploys his figures across a shallow stage, foreshortening bodies and achieving a sense of continual movement by having figures enter right and exit left in mid step. Mantegna's victoriously achieved parade is perhaps the greatest expression of the Renaissance in Britain and constitutes a fitting triumph for this Tudor palace.

TOWNER ART GALLERY AND MUSEUM ✳✳✳

High Street, Old Town, Eastbourne, East Sussex BN20 8BB
Tel. 01323 417961
www.eastbourne.org/entertainment/towner_art_gallery.htm

A British art collection in which Eric Ravilious is especially happily shown

'I give and bequeath to the Corporation of the County Borough of Eastbourne Twenty of my Oil or Water Colour Paintings ... to be chosen ... by Major Harold Parminter Molineux,' with £6,000 'to be applied towards the building of an Art Gallery', wrote Alderman John Towner. It was hard enough in the 19th century to start a gallery with aldermanic enthusiasm, some capital and a handful of pictures, as the Walker Art Gallery (Liverpool), the Ferens Art Gallery (Hull) and the Harris Museum and Art Gallery (Preston) found. But this was 1920.

Major Molineux chose well from John Towner's collection: Victorian genre paintings by Henry Dawson (*The Bird Trap*), John Frederick Herring Snr (*The Blacksmith's*), George Smith (*The Launch*); early works by Frederick Goodall and his friend Thomas Sydney Cooper (inevitably of *Cattle* and *Sheep*, the subjects he painted and repainted during the fifty-seven consecutive years he exhibited at the Royal Academy); an *Italian Interior* by Lorenzo Cecconi; and two landscapes by James Orrock. Orrock is better known as the dealer who advised and bought for Lord Lever (v. Lady Lever); his love of Constable, apparent in *The Old Bridge Near Milford, Surrey*, led him to buy several Constables for Lord Lever. By 1923 the collection had found a curator, Mr Reeve Fowkes, an artist and the director of art at the Eastbourne School of Art; and a building, the handsome 18th-century Manor House, set in civic gardens. Reeve Fowkes concentrated on arranging temporary exhibitions and purchasing depictions of the Sussex countryside, one of which in 1936 was *The Downs in*

Winter by the young Eric Ravilious, who had trained at the Eastbourne College of Art.

Under the next two curators, John Lake and the Scottish abstract artist William Gear, the gallery began to attract several major bequests of 20th-century paintings, notably from Walter Richard Sickert from his personal collection; and further bequests, from Sickert's wife, Thérèse Lessore; from his friend Sylvia Gosse; and an unusual *Negro Head* by Alma-Tadema.

Gear secured funding from the Gulbenkian Foundation and in the early 1960s acquired abstract paintings by Alan Davie, Patrick Heron, Roger Hilton, Peter Lanyon, Ceri Richards and Gear himself. *The Observer* newspaper in 1962 called the Towner 'the most go-ahead municipal gallery of its size in the country'.

Such a reputation gives confidence to benefactors. Irene Law bequeathed a group of 16th–18th-century works by Henri met de Bles, Joseph Wright of Derby, Geeraert van Haautem and Joseph van Aken, the 'laceman' whose brilliance with costume was employed by Thomas Hudson in the 1750s, represented here by a rare conversation piece of his own. If *The Observer*'s claim was overenthusiastic in 1962, the Lucy Carrington Wertheim bequest (1971), bringing the gallery paintings by Christopher Wood and Alfred Wallis, and the deposit on long-term loan by his family of important works by Eric Ravilious,[49] have secured the gallery's reputation. There are seven works by David Bomberg, presented in his memory by the Bomberg family.

Christopher Wood left only a small body of work at his death, almost certainly by suicide, in 1930 aged twenty-nine. After Tate Britain, the Graves Art Gallery and Kettle's Yard, whose founder, Jim Ede, was a close friend of Wood, (all q.v.), no English gallery has a better selection of his work.

Wood was self-taught. He was open to the work of Cocteau and Picasso and to what was happening in Paris in a way no other English painter of the time was. *Girl on a Chair* and *Fair at Neuilly* (1922) are early works in which he struggles to find what and how he wanted

to paint. In *Treboul, French Crab Boat* (1930), finished just before his death, that struggle has been resolved. Around the crab boat at the centre of the canvas Wood places the picture's other elements: the sea wall, bottom left, and the town and church spire, top right, hold the boat in a bracket; the clear, skimmed sky, so light, lies above the weight of the ominous sea, painted with short, dark, choppy strokes. The scene is watched by three women while a fourth, perhaps a nun, turns away. It is hard not to read in it the encroaching shadow.

Eric Ravilious also died prematurely, at thirty-nine, accompanying an air-sea rescue over Iceland as a war artist in 1942. His family's loan is a comprehensive range of his work, always simultaneously entertaining and poignant: pre-war landscapes, ceramics for Wedgwood, book illustrations for J. M. Richards's *High Street*,[50] wood-cut illustrations for Nonesuch Press's 1937 edition of Gilbert White's *Natural History of Selborne*, and a disturbing interior scene, *The Bedstead* (*c.*1938). In this, a room, containing only an iron bedstead, some bright, flowered wallpaper and a small, patterned rug, leads through an open door to a second room that is even more bare and sterile.

Almost all his pre-war work (landscapes, townscapes, interiors) lack figures. His work as a war artist appears to have ended this restraint. In the remarkable *Submarine Series* here (1940), he creates a collage world of submarines, seascapes, floating waves of vibrant blue and submariners going about their duty. His facility of line and design is employed to create a world of silent, ghostly activity.

With the museum's collection being of such quality, it is not surprising that the Contemporary Art Society is engaged in a partnership to help the Towner purchase contemporary work. Since the mid 1970s the CAS's Special Collection Scheme has allowed the gallery to acquire Callum Innes's *Exposed Painting, Cadmium Orange* (1996), a site-specific sculpture by David Nash, *Eighteen Thousand Tides* (1996), and works by, among others, Julian Opie and Wolfgang Tillmans.

ROYAL NAVAL SUBMARINE MUSEUM *

Haslar Jetty Road, Gosport, Hampshire
PO12 2AS
Tel. 02392 510354
www.rnsubmus.co.uk

The world of war waged in the depths

You can reach the Royal Naval Submarine Museum by land or sea. If you take the water-bus from Portsmouth, on landing you walk up the Creek, a cobbled road along which sick or wounded sailors were taken in the 18th and 19th centuries to the Naval Hospital at Haslar – hence the expression 'up the creek'.

Only in the past century has man set himself free from the surface of the earth, up into the sky or down into the oceans. People had been designing submarine machines since the 17th century (De Son's submersible catamaran 1653, Papin's 1692). But none was successful until the 19th century, when the Irish American John Philip Holland designed a 'Wrecking Boat', a proper submarine, for the use of the Fenians against the British fleet in the Irish Sea. When the Fenians abandoned the plan the United States government purchased Holland's improved designs in 1900 and, the following year, the Royal Navy followed suit, building five Holland submarines under licence.

Holland 1 is here, resting in a glass-walled gallery, her black encrusted hull-plating, riveted, seven-sixteenths of an inch thick. Inside there is nothing except an engine, the propeller shaft, a torpedo tube, a periscope and wooden planks to walk on.

Traditionalists didn't like it. Many Admirals subscribed to the view Lord St Vincent expressed when Robert Fulton tried to interest William Pitt's government in the idea of a submarine in 1805 that it was 'a mode of warfare which they who command the sea did not want, but which if successful would deprive them of it'. Submarines were considered to be 'underwater, unfair, and damned un-English' and enemy submariners, if cap-tured in wartime, should, in the view of the Controller of the Navy in 1900, be hanged as pirates. Indeed to serve in submarines (known in the Royal Navy as being in 'the Trade') is to be in a caste apart. The danger and close confinement of life underwater breaks down barriers of class and rank in a way that life on board ship does not. When submarines return to port after a successful tour they demonstrate this faintly anarchic and piratical side by flying the skull and crossbones of a Jolly Roger.

Moored across from *Holland 1* is HMS *Alliance*, built by Vickers at Barrow-in-Furness in 1945, streamlined and modernised in 1960. Beside *Holland 1* with its crew of nine and its length of one cricket pitch, HMS *Alliance* is a shark-like monster; 1,385 tons, it was manned by a crew of sixty-eight. The void inside *Holland 1* has been filled by racks of torpedoes, loading hatches, batteries, engine rooms, heads, a galley, control room, motor room and bunks that spread out of the messes into the passageways. Everywhere there is the smell of diesel fuel and, when the submarine is moving on the surface, the thundering of the engines. No museum can capture the myster-ies of life deep under water (the silences, the waiting, the echoes) but even standing in the confinement of HMS *Alliance* you can feel your throat tightening.

In the museum's galleries are photographs and memorabilia that tell of submarine heroes, heroics and disasters, such as the sinking of HMS *Thetis* in Liverpool Bay in 1939. All but four of the crew died.

HMS *Alliance* was decommissioned in 1973 and came to the museum five years later, just as nuclear submarines were being intro-duced. In the display of weapons, beside the motorised torpedo, 'the Devil's Device', introduced by Robert Whitehead in 1866, lies a Polaris missile, painted white, slim and potent. Outside, the Creek is lined by weapons from simpler times, gently rusting beside an old conning tower, and the glass house of *Holland 1*.

WATTS GALLERY *

Down Lane, Compton, nr. Guildford,
Surrey GU3 1DQ
Tel. 01483 810235

Studio collection of grand old man of Victorian painting, George Frederick Watts

Compton is a village beneath the Hog's Back, only two miles from Guildford, folded deep in the Surrey countryside, a landscape of dips and hollows, trees and small hills. G. F. Watts (1817–1904) and his second wife, Mary Fraser Tytler, came here in 1890 for his health, to escape the fog and smog of London and 'to try how the climate in Surrey would suit them'.[51] The following year they bought some land and built a house, Limnerslease (limner meaning painter, lease to glean), designed for them by Sir Ernest George: large, clumsy, half-timbered, as if by Norman Shaw on an off day. Opposite they built this gallery (1903–4), to designs by Christopher Turnor, a protégé of Sir Edwin Lutyens. Its Arts and Crafts vernacular is altogether more successful and attractive than the house.

The gallery houses Watts's studio collection, and pictures by his friends and contemporaries from the collection of Percy French: Albert Moore, Arthur Hughes, Charles Hazelwood Shannon.

Watts's own paintings span his career, from a portrait of his father, a maker of musical instruments, begun when he was sixteen, and a self-portrait[52] made the following year, to the several works left unfinished at his death including the study for a monumental portrait sculpture of Tennyson for Lincoln.

Watts is best known for his portraits, thirty-six of which are in the National Portrait Gallery (q.v.),[53] the *Hall of Fame* series of eminent Victorians (D. G. Rossetti, W. E. Gladstone, Sir John Herschel, Robert Browning) that he began in 1850. Portrait subjects here include Garibaldi; two mistresses of Edward VII (*Mrs Lily Langtry*, 1879, and *Mrs Rachel Gurney, Countess Dudley*, 1885); his friend *Henry Thoby Prinsep* and Prinsep's

sister-in-law *Virginia, Lady Somers*, the most beautiful of the seven daughters of James Pattle of the East India Company. Here too are a study of his wife (1887) and a romantic portrait of *Lady Holland*, the wife of his early patron, whom he paints curled up on a sofa, her cheek on two pillows in a froth of muslin and lace.[54]

Personally modest, even diffident (he twice refused Gladstone's offer of a baronetcy, in 1885 and 1894), he was ambitious in his work. 'I would have liked to do for modern thought what Michelangelo did for theological thought.'[55] For years he cherished the dream of a project he called *The House of Life*, to produce a great sequence of paintings that illustrated the evolution of the world. Watts never succeeded in getting this commissioned but *The Creation of Eve* (a sketch) and *The Curse of Cain* (both parts of trilogies) indicate its scope, much as the original gessoes here hint of his enormous figure of *Physical Energy*, now in the Lancaster Walk of Kensington Gardens.

This striving for the great universal themes is reflected in the allegory and symbolism that permeate his work, as in *Love Triumphant*; *Time, Death and Judgement*; and *Destiny*. It is particularly clear in the two major works here, *Paolo and Francesca* (c. 1872–84) and the late *Sower of the Systems* (1902). He returned to the story of Paolo Malatesta and Francesca di Rimini, in the second circle from hell from Canto V of Dante's *Inferno*, throughout his life: a small fresco in 1843–7 and several drawings, variations on this design, in the Manchester Art Gallery (q.v.). This is his fourth and last attempt, 1872–4. He shows the lovers like corpses, their clothes as winding sheets: an allegorical image of their eternal fate.

The Sower of the Systems is Watts's attempt to depict God. 'There is only one great mystery – the Creator,' he said. 'If I were ever to make a symbol of the Deity, it would be as a great gesture into which everything that exists is woven.'[56] Here it is a gesture that slides into abstraction.

'Allegory is much out of favour now,' he wrote towards the end of his life, 'and by most

people condemned forgetting that ... ideas can only be expressed by similes, and that words themselves are but symbols ... Only by these I wish to be remembered.' He died the year after this gallery was completed.

Watts's reputation is currently over-shadowed by those of D. G. Rossetti and the Pre-Raphaelites.[57] The works here give an opportunity to judge the validity of Douglas Cooper's contention that, compared with Rossetti, Watts was 'an incomparably more interesting painter'.[58]

RIVER AND ROWING MUSEUM *

Mill Meadows, Henley-on-Thames, Oxfordshire RG9 1BF
Tel. 01491 415600
www.rrm.co.uk

A boat-shaped museum for a museum of rowing boats, from triremes to the Sydney Coxless Four

This is a museum that has been written. That is not to say that it is lacking in visual flair: the elegance of its building, the variety of its objects, the design of its galleries and its position on the bank of the Thames all please the eye. At the same time they make manifest a brief of three: the river, rowing and Henley, three answers to a question, 'What isn't there a museum of . . .?'

It is a reasonable question. But this is a construct, held together by its building. Its architect, David Chipperfield, has raised it on columns beside a line of poplars along the riverbank. It is clad in green oak and the roofs of its galleries are hulls turned keel up. He has employed reassuring textures and materials to set these collections within his sculpture.

Men have always been 'messing about in boats',[59] across streams, down rivers, out beyond the horizons of the sea. When there was no wind, they rowed. Here are rowing boats in which to recline (a Venetian gondola, 1200–1500), to hunt (an Arctic whaleboat,

Paolo and Francesca *by G. F. Watts*

1750–1850), to pilot (a fast 18th–19th-century gig from Cornwall and the Isles of Scilly), to taxi (a Thames wherry, rowed by liveried oarsmen) and to rescue (a coastal lifeboat built by William Plenty for the Appledore station in 1829).

The catalogue of such boats may be traced back to the trireme, recreated here in a life-sized model, a cross-section of *Olympias*, built by the classicist John Morrison and the naval architect John Coates in 1983, working from the dimensions described in Athenian naval inventories and evidence from pottery and reliefs. This is the boat with which the Athenian fleet won the battle of Salamis and so became the masters of the Mediterranean world. Here too is the craft that won the first boat race at Henley in 1829, built by Stephen Davies and Isaac King of Oxford to a design resembling a cutter: clinker-built of spruce, its timbers of oak, its ribs of ash, the ponderous parent of modern monocoque shells.

Above it, suspended upside down, the length of the ceiling, are the conjugated products of 200 years of boat design, culminating in the boat in which Stephen Redgrave and Matthew Pinsent won the 1996 Olympic coxless pairs in Atlanta, a slither of carbon fibre, Nomex honeycomb, Kevlar and epoxy resin.

A Hall of Fame identifies British rowing heroes of the 20th century back to the Olympic eight of 1908 and to Ted Phelps, world professional sculling champion in 1930 and the entire Phelps family, six of them winners of the Doggett's Badge, photographed in their red Doggett's Watermen's livery, unaltered since the 17th century.

The course from the Phelpses to Redgrave takes you from the romance of rowing to its science. George Pocock, the Seattle boat-builder, is quoted here, 'It's a great art, is rowing. It's the finest art there is. It's a symphony in motion.' To play it demands not only touch and lightness and strength but ergonomic training and technology. Here are photographs of Eadward Muybridge's 'stroke cycle' (1887), Kern's Patent Single Scull Rowing Machine (1901), a Concept II Model C Ergometer (1993), all seeking to drive through the water boats made of thinner and lighter materials, plywood giving way to veneer, to aluminium and now to carbon fibre.

The Rowing Gallery is rich in objects, displayed under clear, bright lights. In the River Gallery the light is watery and subdued, with plashy, soft, river sound effects. Objects give way to graphics, evidence to atmosphere.

The river is the Thames, 'the King of Island Rivers',[60] mapped from its source outside the village of Kemble near Cirencester, along its 220-mile journey to the sea by Cruikdale, Stanton Harcourt, Oxford; Wallingford, Henley and Cookham; Windsor, Hampton, Hammersmith and Fulham; Westminster, the Tower, Rotherhithe, Greenwich, Woolwich, Gravesend – England's history written on water. The gallery helps us to see what is the river: its water, banks, habitats, wildlife. It notes the familiar (the fritillary, the willowherb; the willow, the alder; the grey heron and mute swan; the trout, pike, gudgeon and dace), the rare (the white-clawed crayfish, the dragonfly, the Loddon lily, the otter, returning as eels are restocked) and the imported invaders (the Mandarin duck, the North American signal crayfish, the cormorant – decimator of fish stocks – and the mink, the greatest threat to the water vole). Through them the gallery draws you into the geology of the Thames and its history through Ice Ages and tropical times, to the more recent relationship with man (Bronze Age weapons, a Saxon long boat c. AD 405–530).

A bridge links the ends of the building and takes you to the Henley Gallery, regrettably the least successful of the three.

The town is history rich. Settled since 1170, it was bitterly contested in the Civil War. Its industries have included Ravenscroft glass in the 17th century (utilising the local black flint), W. H. Brakspear's brewery since 1779, boat building and engineering. The recusant Stonors of Stonor Park established a brickworks and Frederick, Prince of Wales, lived here at Park Place (1738–57), whose next owner, General Conway, built the graceful five-arch bridge, commissioning his daughter, the sculptor Ann Seymour Damer, to decorate

the consoles of the central arch with masks of Thamesis and Isis. A cast of Thamesis, complete with small fishes in his beard, is in the museum. In spite of everything, and despite the Henley Regatta, the Henley Gallery lacks splash.

David Chipperfield's building ensures that the museum does not. Nevertheless it is a museum that is stronger on 'messing about in boats' than on the river as 'a strong brown god'.[61] Ratty has its measure: 'Simply messing . . . in boats, or with boats, in or out of 'em, it doesn't matter . . . Whether you arrive at your destination or whether you reach somewhere else, or whether you never get anywhere at all . . . there's always something else to do, and you can do it if you like, but you'd much better not.'[62]

CHARLESTON *

Charleston, nr. Firle, Lewes, East Sussex
BN8 6LL
Tel. 01323 811626
www.charleston.org.uk

The creative hive of the Bloomsbury Group, aglow with colour and clutter

'I do not know whether pilgrimages to the shrines of famous men (and women) ought not to be condemned as sentimental journeys,' wrote Virginia Woolf in her essay on the Bröntes' Haworth. Later in the same essay she decides that such visits are 'legitimate' when they add 'something to our understanding',[63] but whether the journey is, or is not, sentimental is only one of a series of problems that arise when such shrine-houses are preserved as museums. Can their rooms avoid the appearance of stage sets? Should they be arranged as if the famous men and women had just stepped out of them? What period should be recreated? Is 'calculated informality' possible? To what extent, and how, should there be interpretation? Charleston deals with all these questions with intelligence and the impression of ease.

Charleston became the rural centre of 'Bloomsbury' after Vanessa Bell, Woolf's sister, and her family made it their (and her lover Duncan Grant's) home in 1916.[64] It is beside a working farm, at the end of a farm track, over cattle grids. There are cows, there is mud. The wind comes off the Downs. The views over the Sussex countryside have changed not at all. In Charleston's garden, laid out in the 1920s by Roger Fry, are the plants chosen by Bell and Grant, often for their intense colours: astrantia, dianthus, marguerites, red-hot pokers, geraniums. All this helps prevent a sense that the clocks have been wrested into stopping, but Charleston's greatest inspiriting asset is the way in which the Bells and Duncan Grant lived and worked here, continually decorating and redecorating every surface. The colours, shapes, images in the studio canvases overflowed on to walls, doors and furniture, in every room.

Roger Fry wrote to Vanessa Bell, 'You have a genius in your life as well as in your art.'[65] Certainly her style saturates Charleston: the subtle green and yellow colour scheme of her husband Clive Bell's bedroom, painted by Vanessa Bell in 1917 when it was her studio; the stippled grey pilasters on the lavender walls of the spare bedroom, painted with her daughter, Angelica, in 1936. 'We intend to introduce a fantastic note,' Vanessa wrote. She painted the circular table in the dining room, the fireplace decorations in Clive Bell's study, the doors either side of the fireplace in Duncan Grant's bedroom with large vases of bright, impressionistic flowers, and the cupboard in her own bedroom with circle motifs. Most striking, and elaborate, is the panel of wall beside the bed in Clive Bell's bedroom, part wallpapered, part painted, pattern set against pattern, frames set within frames, at its centre an incongruous, amateurish portrait, of two late-18th-century children, in a gilded frame.

The *Cockerel* and the *Dog*,[66] above and below the window in the library, are by Duncan Grant, as is the corner cupboard in Clive Bell's bedroom, the figures on the library door panels, and the log box and the two kneeling figures decorating the overmantel in the garden room.

Sometimes their works become a co-operative collage. In Vanessa Bell's bedroom she decorated the washstand (1917); her daughter Angelica painted the cupboard (1936) and Grant the bath panel (1945). The geometric, stencilled wallpaper in the dining room was painted jointly by Grant, Angelica and Quentin Bell, Vanessa's son, in 1939.

Almost every room has paintings by either Vanessa Bell or Duncan Grant, of which the most striking are Grant's portraits of *Lytton Strachey*, his cousin (1913),[67] and of *Vanessa Bell* (1942),[68] his *Self-portrait with Turban* (*c.*1909)[69] and Vanessa Bell's late *Self-portrait* (1958),[70] when she was seventy-nine.

There are paintings here by their friends: *Flowers* (*c.*1925–6) by Matthew Smith,[71] a portrait of *Clive Bell* (1908) by Henry Lamb,[72] *Floods near Guildford* (1911) by Roger Fry,[73] as well as works by Walter Sickert and Frederick Etchells and a small pencil *Study for a Frieze* by Delacroix,[74] bought by Maynard Keynes in 1918 at the sale of the contents of Degas's studio.

Maynard Keynes had his own bedroom here until he married[75] in 1935 and moved to nearby Tilton Manor.[76] He wrote *The Economic Consequences of the Peace*[77] at Charleston after resigning from the Paris Peace talks in 1919, and the *Treatise on Probability*[78] in 1920.

Roger Fry visited frequently (and the house is full of furniture and ceramics produced by the Omega Workshop, which he founded) as did T. S. Eliot, E. M. Forster, Lytton Strachey, Desmond MacCarthy and, later, Benjamin Britten and Peter Pears. Virginia Woolf lived near by, at Rodmell.

With such varied friends and relations it is surprising that the books on the shelves are those that any decently educated family of the period might have had: Macaulay, Gibbon, Carlyle; Scott, Thackeray, Meredith; Byron and Swift; Voltaire, Balzac and Flaubert. In Clive Bell's bedroom there are volumes of *Punch* beside those of Victor Gollancz's Left Book Club, and there is a collection of paperbacks in French (Maurois, Guitry, de Montherlant).

Although neither Vanessa Bell nor Duncan Grant was a great artist, this is a house that captures the charm and rhythmic fluency of their work, which continues to animate every room with a sense of felt life. Vanessa Bell wrote to Roger Fry while moving in to Charleston in the autumn of 1916, 'I wish you could come and see it all. It would be such fun to show it to you.' That sense of enjoyment ensures that a visit to Charleston is not merely a sentimental journey.

MAIDSTONE MUSEUM AND BENTLIF ART GALLERY *

St Faith's Street, Maidstone, Kent ME14 1LH
Tel. 01622 602838
www.museum.maidstone.gov.uk

Japanese art, Roman remains, pilgrims' tokens and natural history

Natural history and archaeology are staples of local museums. The Medway Estuary and the way in which this land between the English Channel and the estuary has been fought over by Romans, Anglo-Saxons and Normans give Maidstone rich resources.

Wildlife has not changed on the estuary for centuries; oystercatchers, shovelers, moorhens, dunlins, terns, assorted gulls, the great crested grebe and the tufted duck abound on the mud-flats and in the reedbeds. Excellent taxidermy allows them all to assemble here in handsome cases beside roach and rudd, carp and chub, perch and dace which swim in suspension, motionless, thanks to the skills of J. Cooper and Son (1900–30).

Maidstone's distant history lies buried. Four Roman legions under Aulus Plautius landed near by at Richborough in AD 43 and fought a decisive battle at the River Medway. The area became one of the most prosperous in Roman Britain and Mount Villa (AD 150–400) was only one of several grand houses locally (Hartlip, Lullingstone, East Malling). Although now under the Chatham approach road it was excavated in 1843 and 1944, and yielded Samian ware, amphorae, coins, funerary glass, a Dragonesque brooch and a bronze statue of Minerva (from Plaxtol).

There are few objects here left by the Jutes, the Angles or the Saxons, who filled the vacuum left by the Romans, but an Anglo-Saxon claw beaker of pale cloudy glass (late 6th–7th century) from a cemetery at Faversham is of Germanic manufacture and evidence of the links with the Merovingian Franks. The Merovingian princess Bertha married King Aethelbert of Kent in 597. She converted him to Christianity and opened the way for Augustine's mission.

The museum is set back from the road in Chillington Manor House, which was built in 1561, probably by Nicholas Bareham, a lawyer and one of the town's first Members of Parliament. It is an architectural patchwork, heavily restored in 1875. You enter through the original Elizabethan oak screen into the Great Hall, but this 16th-century core is pushed back by two Victorian wings designed by Hubert Bensted in the 1890s. The back of the building is an even more complicated mixture of 17th-, 19th- and 20th-century additions, and the wing of the 15th-century, half-timbered Court Lodge from East Farleigh, re-erected here in 1811–15. The resulting rooms make indifferent galleries, although they suit the museum's strong medieval collection.

Maidstone is on the Pilgrim's Way to Canterbury. Here is the jetsam of pilgrimage: badges, seals, rings, buckles. Here too is a group of 13th-century squat Baluster jugs made at the Tyler Hill pottery near Canterbury, decorated with geometric patterns in imitation of Roman pottery, and manuscripts: a 13th-century *Book of English Sermons* in which are also collected verses, letters, financial accounts and a poem, 'Death's Wither-clench', which has musical notation and is one of the earliest pieces of written music in Britain. A tiny 15th-century book of hours was illustrated by the Flemish master Guillebert de Mets (1425–50) and volume two of the Lambeth Bible[79] was made for Liessies Abbey, Hainault, in 1146, the high summer of English Romanesque decoration. Here too is a collection of acoustic jars (*c.* 15th century), glass vessels that were embedded in church walls to amplify the singing and chanting.

The museum has had a disparate mixture of benefactors. Julius Brenchley was a Victorian traveller who collected art, ethnography and natural history with more enthusiasm than judgement.[80] His paintings comprise the core of the art collection, an assortment of pictures 'influenced by', 'after' and, optimistically, 'attributed to' Jan Brueghel the Elder, Jan Steen, Gerrit Dou and Aert van der Neer, relieved only by two Panini capriccios, a Frans Snyders, a portrait by Hoppner of *Mrs Fox* (the wife of Charles James Fox), and a self-portrait (1802)[81] by the essayist William Hazlitt, who wrote of his attempts to paint, 'I could never satisfy myself with what I did, yet the pain of failure had not yet stiffened into anguish.'

Doreen, Lady Brabourne, sister of Earl Mountbatten of Burma and killed with him by the IRA in 1979, lived near by and left the museum her wardrobe from the 1950s and '60s: clasp bags, linen costumes, tweed suits, beach dresses, a beaded jacket and a tiara: post-war chic.

Two other erstwhile local residents, Henry Marsham and Walter Samuel, Lord Bearsted, provide the greatest surprise in this lucky dip of a museum: a gallery of Japanese decorative art from the Edo period, 1600–1868. Marsham collected non-porcelain pottery and Samuel armour, lacquer, inro, netsuke, kimonos, obis, swords, prints and landscape paintings by Ando Hiroshige and Katshuishika Hokusai, a collection greatly superior to that of Russell-Cotes.[82] Walter Samuel gave his collection, and the money to build a new wing in which to display it, when he moved to Upton House in 1924.

TYRWHITT-DRAKE MUSEUM OF CARRIAGES *

Archbishop's Stables, Mill Street, Maidstone, Kent ME15 6YE
Tel. 01622 685471

Carried away by carriages, horse-drawn and horseless

Landau, phaeton; bier, barouche; cart, droitzchka; brougham or gig: the names of the carriages here are as various as their shapes and sizes. What they have in common is that they convey people, for pleasure, work or ceremony.

The state landau built by Holmes & Co. of London and Derby for Queen Victoria's third son, the Duke of Connaught, towers above the pedestrian, its carriage lamps emblazoned with crowns. It was given to the museum in 1954 by Maidstone's then MP, Sir Alfred Bossom, of whose name Churchill remarked, 'Neither one thing nor the other.'

Near by is a funeral bier made at the same time: four wheels and a slab of wood to carry the impecunious deceased for the Hildenborough Parish Burial Board. Its only decoration is the hope painted on its side, 'Lord of Life and Love We Pray/Grant Us Mercy in That Day'.

The idea of collecting carriages came to Sir Hugh Garrard Tyrwhitt-Drake when he noticed that the horse-drawn vehicles of his childhood were being superseded by the motor car. He also had a private travelling circus and a zoo. The carriages are displayed in the simplest manner, drawn up in ranks, as if waiting patiently for horses, on the two floors of a 14th-century barn that used to be the stables for the Archbishop's Palace in which his Grace would break his progress from London to Canterbury.

Most of the vehicles are from the 19th century. The oldest is an Italian sediola (*c.*1675), consisting of a single seat raised up high, supported by carved figures, dragons with long tails and female centaurs; the most recent is an ice cream cart, a tub on two wheels

that Mr Di Marco pushed through the streets of Maidstone in the 1940s and '50s.

Between these are vehicles humble and quotidian (a wagonette omnibus of 1898, a prim governess cart) and vehicles stylish (a ladies' phaeton for elegant park driving, an American gig designed by Henry Studebaker, who built carriages, and anything on wheels, decades before his first motor cars).

Some are for play (an 18th-century Continental sleigh in the shape of a nautilus shell, supported by putti, its prow a carved phoenix, with wings unfurled, on a nest of foliage), some for display (Queen Victoria's state landau, carved and gilded, built by George Norgate Hooper of Hooper & Co., St James's Street – one of the few royal landaus outside the Royal Mews).

Some have stories to tell: a dress chariot built by F. Stolken of Halkin Street, Belgravia, for Count Walewski, the son of Napoleon I, when he was appointed French Ambassador to the Court of St James in 1854, or an 1830 coach built for John, 12th Earl of Moray, and never used. Lord Moray intended that it should sweep him and his bride, the daughter of the Earl of Elgin, away from their wedding, behind slatted windows. Instead the wedding was abandoned, the carriage was never used and the horses were shot.

These vehicles tell something of the story of horse-drawn transport (which itself determined something of the pace of history) and something more about social hierarchy: those upfront, or behind; within, or without; driving, or driven. All are here. Only the horses are absent.

Sediola chair at the Tyrwhitt-Drake Museum of Carriages

SANDHAM MEMORIAL CHAPEL **

Harts Lane, Burghclere, nr. Newbury,
Berkshire RG20 9JT
Tel. 01635 278394
e-mail: sandham@ntrust.org.uk
www.nationaltrust.org.uk

Stanley Spencer's Giotto-inspired murals in a specially built chapel

'What ho, Giotto!' was Stanley Spencer's response to the commission offered by Mr and Mrs J. L. Behrend. In a purpose-built chapel, an English version of Giotto's Arena Chapel in Padua, Spencer would be able to produce the scheme of paintings that had preoccupied him for five years. His love of Giotto's frescoes would redeem the memories of war, his wartime experiences as a medical orderly in Bristol and Macedonia.

The site could not be less like Padua, a narrow grassy plot behind a clipped thorn hedge in the middle of this Berkshire village. The architect, Lionel Pearson, set the chapel well back from the road, so you approach it through a small apple orchard up a brick-paved path. There is the smell of box and lavender.

Inside, the chapel is small. The paintings, floor to ceiling on three walls, are close-up: intimate and immediate. The side walls each have four large arched 'lunettes', below which are small, rectangular predellas. Spencer soon abandoned the idea of fresco and painted them on canvas, which was fixed in place.

Each painting depicts an incident from Spencer's wartime experiences, at the Beaufort Hospital or at the front in Macedonia. Some are grim: a shell-shocked man scrubbing the floor, a soldier's wounds being painted with iodine. Some are mundane: sorting laundry, filling water-bottles, inspecting kit. Above these, two scenes stretch to the chapel's ceiling, showing soldiers in camp at Karasuli and Todorovo, occupying themselves with cooking, collecting litter and playing housey-housey while awaiting their fate. These scenes

are, in Spencer's words, a mixture of 'real and spiritual fact'.[83]

There are no officers, bar one. There is no violence. This is not Guernica but it is ruthlessly observed. The critic R. H. Wilenski wrote, 'we smell the flesh of the herded soldiers, we feel the texture of their clothes and towels, the exact consistency of every object they handle.'[84]

This is anything but cosy or reassuring. Although these soldiers may appear to be living out the example of St Augustine's God in his *Confessions* ('ever busy yet ever at rest, gathering yet never needing, bearing; filling; guarding; creating; nourishing; perfecting')[85] they are demonstrating, as Fiona MacCarthy observes, that, however men are treated, the human spirit can overcome the worst it can undergo.[86] As Spencer wrote in 1932, 'I have avoided any too unpleasant scene . . . because in the scheme, as in all my paintings, I wish to stress my own redemption from all that I have been made to suffer.'

Spencer worked on the Burghclere scheme between 1927 and 1932. He never spoke directly of its meaning, but preferred, as his brother Gilbert noted, 'winks, asides, smiles, gestures and points . . . His whole concentration now would be centred on describing the incident and what a lovely thing it was to paint.'[87]

The climax of the scheme is the altar wall, *The Resurrection of the Soldiers*, in which the soldiers rise up, live again, pile up their crosses or hand them in to the diminutive figure of Christ. Here, as in all Spencer's paintings, there is a wonderful sense of shape. In the side paintings there are repeated passages of white (sheets, tents, mosquito nets, slings, capes suggesting angels' wings). At the centre of the *Resurrection* are the bodies of two mules, white as unicorns; hands (touching, feeling, caressing a tortoise, opening a letter, stretching out to other hands); and, everywhere, crosses. 'The truth that the Cross is supposed to symbolise in this picture', wrote Stanley Spencer, 'is that nothing is lost when a sacrifice

Stanley Spencer's The Resurrection of the Soldiers *in the Sandham Memorial Chapel*

has been the result of perfect understanding.'

There is nothing else like this in Britain. In an age that is shy of matters spiritual Spencer's work looks without flinching into the dark of war and extracts from it the strength of the human spirit.

PETWORTH HOUSE ✶✶✶✶

Petworth, West Sussex GU28 0AE
Tel. 01798 342207
www.nationaltrust.org.uk/places/petworth

Connoisseurial Grand Tour collection, ravishing paintings by Turner

Few houses or museums can trump Petworth's Carved Room, restored in 2002 to allow the four landscapes that J. M. W. Turner painted for this room to be seen as the 3rd Earl of Egremont wanted, against a background of the carvings of Grinling Gibbons and John Selden (both c. 1690).

So fine and limpid are Turner's landscapes, such a miracle of intricacy is Gibbons's carving, that, if Petworth contained nothing else, these would be treat enough; but more rooms, more paintings, more sculptures vie for your attention here. The Chapel contains an intriguing amalgam of a baroque conceit (a magnificent wooden painted festoon curtain above the galleried family pew, transforming it into a box at the opera) and the Gothic windows and marble colonnettes of the original chapel built by Harry, Lord Percy, in the 14th century.

The Sculpture Court (the North Gallery) matches that at Holkham Hall (q.v.)[88] which, like this one, was designed by Matthew Brettingham the Elder. The 2nd Earl commissioned his son, Matthew Brettingham the Younger, to assemble a collection of Greek and Roman classical sculpture. Assisted, in Rome, by the painter Gavin Hamilton, he did so. There are a beautiful 4th century BC head attributed to Praxiteles, now entitled the *Leconfield Aphrodite*; an *Amazon* (mid 5th century BC), copied from an original by Pheidias; and an *Athlete*, a Roman copy of a Polykleitos bronze, c. 440–400 BC. The Roman portraits are as impressive and include a bust of *Septimus Severus* (AD 193–211), the Emperor who attempted to conquer Scotland.[89]

To this his son, the 3rd Earl, added the North Bay to exhibit the neoclassical sculpture that he commissioned from John Flaxman, Sir Richard Westmacott, and Westmacott's former assistant John Edward Carew, so mixing classical and neoclassical sculpture, as at Chatsworth (q.v.) and Woburn; what was unusual was that paintings were also hung on the walls. Unlike the commissions for those galleries by the Dukes of Devonshire and Bedford, which were of heroic or mythological subjects, many of Egremont's commissions were for subjects that were related to Britain, and by sculptors working in Britain: Flaxman's *St Michael Overcoming Satan* (1826), taken from Milton's *Paradise Lost*, or *A British Athlete* by John Charles Felix Rossi, whose monuments can be seen in St Paul's Cathedral. Here too are three marble busts of the 3rd Earl: by Joseph Nollekens (1815), by Sir Francis Chantrey (1830) and by Carew (1831).

Flaxman took ten years to complete his *Pastoral Apollo* (1825), for which he charged the Earl 900 guineas. At the same time, between 1824 and 1831, Egremont bought or commissioned five major marble sculptures from Carew, at a cost of over £21,000.

Both the 3rd Earl and his father, the 2nd Earl, were collectors and the house is rich with paintings. Constable called it 'that House of Art'. The Somerset Room has landscapes by Claude,[90] Cuyp, Ruysdael and Hobbema. Here and elsewhere there are paintings by Hieronymus Bosch, Adam Elsheimer,[91] Paul Bril, Bernardo Bellotto, Michael Dahl, Richard Wilson, Guercino, Bronzino and Titian. There is furniture by Chippendale and silver by Paul Storr and David Willaume. The diarist Thomas Creevey noted in 1828, 'the immensity of pictures on the ground floor of the house and, as I was informed, all the floors above are full. Then they are all mixed up together, good and bad . . . and he [the 3rd Earl] is perpetually changing their places'.[92]

It is no wonder that the house inspired Turner. After the 3rd Earl commissioned the four landscapes for the Carved Room, Turner stayed at Petworth at least six, possibly eight, times, in the ten years up to the Earl's death in 1837.[93] With his great friend and patron Walter Fawkes dying in 1825, Petworth became Turner's familiar and favoured retreat from London. He responded by painting (for himself) a series of watercolours and gouaches that recorded views of, and rooms in, the house.[94]

There are no less than twenty paintings in oil by Turner at Petworth (but bizarrely, the Treasury transferred ownership of them in 1984 to the Tate rather than the National Trust). The 3rd Earl first acquired a painting by Turner in 1802 (*The Egremont Seapiece*, in the North Gallery), and commissioned the landscape *Petworth, Dewy Morning* in 1809, flooded with Claude-like light but mocked by critics because of its whiteness. After 1812, when he painted *Teignmouth* and *Hulks on the Tamar*, Turner did no further paintings for Petworth until the two *Petworth Sunset* paintings (*A Stag Drinking* and *Fighting Bucks*, both 1828–30), and their companions *The Chain Pier, Brighton* and *Chichester Canal*, in both of which projects the Earl had a financial interest.

Gibbons's carvings, 'a mixture of fruit, flowers, fish, cherubs' heads, musical instruments, an amphora, and a fiasco . . . done in the round with a miraculously lively touch',[95] which were gathered together into the Carved Room by the 3rd Earl, dominate the room and would appear to defeat any painting hung near them, apart from the monumental full-lengths after Van Dyck.[96]

However the Earl commissioned Jonathon Ritson to make less flamboyant carvings to surround Turner's paintings that were 'given their final touches *in situ* in the Carved Room',[97] as was his practice before Royal Academy exhibitions, so that 'the glory of the sun is supreme'.[98] Turner, Gibbons and Ritson crown a house that shows 18th-century Grand Tour collecting and early 19th-century art patronage at their brilliant best.

PORTSMOUTH CITY MUSEUM AND ART GALLERY **

Museum Road, Old Portsmouth,
Portsmouth, Hampshire PO1 2LJ
Tel. 023 9282 7261
www.portsmouthmuseums.co.uk

Destroyed by the Blitz in 1941, Portsmouth is here recalled to life with local objects, local artists and excellent decorative arts

Portsmouth has had a public museum since the late 19th century, housed in the Old Town Hall. On the night of 10 January 1941 the city and docks were blitzed and the Old Town Hall and the museum's entire collection were destroyed. After the war Portsmouth put out a national and local appeal for material with which to re-establish the museum. So remarkable was the response to the appeal, locally and nationally, that it would not occur to the visitor today that the collections were not the result of at least a hundred years of diligent acquisition.

The social history of Portsmouth, as a town and as a port, is illustrated by every sort of artefact (manuscripts and books; prints and paintings; photographs and drawings; ceramics, furniture, domestic equipment and, it being the city in which he was born, much material associated with Charles Dickens).

Many artists have depicted Portsmouth's topography and its maritime life. There are views of the harbour here by Thomas Rowlandson and Dominic Serres and of *Gosport, the Entrance to Portsmouth Harbour* by J. M. W. Turner; a seascape by Clarkson Stanfield and paintings of the surrounding Hampshire countryside in the 19th and early 20th centuries by three generations of the local Cole family, George Cole, George Vicat Cole and Reginald Rex Vicat Cole.

The most substantial donation was from the Sickert Trust which gave, in 1947 and 1954, a number of Old Masters and early prints (Stefano della Bella and Mantegna; Gillray and Paul Sandby) that Sickert had owned, fifteen of his own etchings and a curiosity: three watercolours and a painting in oils by his grandfather, J. Sickert. The trust also gave paintings by artist friends of Sickert: Sylvia Gosse, Robert Bevan and Charles Ginner. In 1973 the museum acquired an oil by Sickert, *The Belgian Cocottes* (1906), which has the more dense design and thicker application of paint he adopted in his Camden Town years, 1905–14.

In rebuilding the collection the curators placed particular emphasis on acquiring the work of local artists and on the decorative and fine art of the 20th century. There is a strong group of work by artists associated with St Ives (Patrick Heron, Bryan Wynter, Terry Frost, Peter Lanyon, William Scott and Wilhelmina Barns-Graham), plus lithographs and a bronze, *Figure in a Landscape (Zennor)* (1940), by Barbara Hepworth. Unusually, the work of those studio potters influenced by Bernard Leach's work in St Ives is also represented here: Michael Cardew, Alan Caiger-Smith and, of course, David and Janet Leach. The collection also includes pieces by Gordon Baldwin, Glenys Barton, Ewen Henderson, Hans Coper and Lucie Rie.

Compared with many museums the fine and decorative arts collection here, although quite small, has a large proportion of work by women painters (Frances Hodgkins, Winifred Nicholson, Prunella Clough), potters (Alison Britton, Katherine Pleydell-Bouverie, Mary Rogers, Janice Tchalenko; pieces designed by Clarice Cliff and Susie Cooper) and designers (a screen by Vanessa Bell, an HMV cabinet gramophone painted by Dora Carrington and a textile by Tracey Emin, *Be Faithful to your Dreams*, 1999).

The furniture collection has work from 1450 to the present day, including a William Kent wardrobe (*c.* 1760), a table (*c.* 1849) by A. W. N. Pugin, pieces by Philip Webb, A. H. Mackmurdo, Ernest Barnsley and Frank Lloyd Wright, and a chair by Christopher Dresser, whose beautiful *Electroplated Teapot* (1880), with a Japanese-inspired ebonised wooden handle, is also here, commissioned from him by James Dixon and Sons (v. Millennium Galleries: Metalwork Galley).[99]

The former barracks building, a complex of relatively small rooms on three floors, serves the local history collection well but it is not ideal for fine or decorative art. However that is a quibble when set against the extraordinary achievement of creating new collections of such quality and interest from the rubble of 1941.

PORTSMOUTH HISTORIC DOCKYARDS ✱✱✱

Incorporating THE ROYAL NAVAL MUSEUM, THE MARY ROSE MUSEUM, HMS VICTORY and HMS WARRIOR

HM Naval Base (P66), Portsmouth, Hampshire PO1 3NH
Tel. 023 9286 1533

The Warrior, *the* Mary Rose, *the* Victory *and the Royal Naval Museum, Portsmouth's long naval pride*

There have been dockyards in Portsmouth since the end of the 15th century when Henry VII commissioned Sir Reginald Bray,[100] in 1495, to build a new shipbuilding dock on the site where HMS *Victory* now is. In these yards were built the *Mary Rose*, the *Peter Pomegranate* and the other ships that made up the fleets with which Henry VIII fought the First and Second French Wars (1512–14 and 1522–5) and which escorted him across the Channel to Calais to meet Francis I on the Field of the Cloth of Gold in 1520.

Portsmouth played its part in defeating the Armada and in the sea adventures of the Elizabethan Age but it was not until Samuel Pepys became Clerk of the Acts (1660), and then Secretary to the Admiralty (1684–9), that the Great Stone Dock was planned, and five years later constructed, making Portsmouth the chief naval base in the kingdom where ships were built, repaired and equipped from huge storehouses.

The dockyards that we see today date from the late 18th century when Sir Samuel Bentham,[101] Inspector General of Naval Works, built the (former) Pay Office (1790), immedi-ately on the right as you enter; all the docks to the north of, and including, HMS *Victory* (1797–1802); and the Block Mills (1800), in which the block-making machinery designed by Marc Isambard Brunel[102] was housed. The three great storehouses, in which is housed the Royal Naval Museum, were built between 1760 and 1800.

You enter the main gate with its imposing piers of Portland stone, past the Porter's Lodge, the oldest (1708) building in the dockyards. To your left is HMS *Warrior*, the first metal-clad warship; to your right, the Mary Rose Museum and, before you, the Royal Naval Museum, HMS *Victory* and the hall in which the *Mary Rose* is maintained in a state of suspended saturation.

Between them these four museums illustrate the development of the Royal Navy from 1511 (the *Mary Rose*) to 1860 (HMS *Warrior*) in dockyards that have at least as strong a claim to be a World Heritage Site as Chatham. It would make perfect sense for the visitor if they became four parts of one National Museum of the Royal Navy.

The *Mary Rose* has the most poignant history. She sank a mile off Portsmouth on 19 June 1545 when, engaging the French fleet, 'the wind caught her sails so strongly as to heel her over, and plunge her open gunports beneath the water, which flooded and sank her'[103] with the loss of all lives on board.[104]

She lay in forty feet of water, stuck fast on the sea bed, for over four hundred years until she was raised in 1982 in a remarkable feat of marine archaeology and engineering. You can enter No. 3 Dock (1799) and watch, from behind a wall of glass in a gallery, the starboard cross-section of the skeletal hull, four decks and the hold deep, through the mist of a constant spray of chilled fresh water which prevents her drying out and bacteria and fungi forming.

In the Mary Rose Museum is what was salvaged: the ropes, planes, augers, lead weights and steering compasses; the 2,000 arrows and 168 longbows made of yew; the iron shot, stone shot and lead shot; the cannons and culverins; the shoes, flasks, combs;

the jugs and mugs. With them were an oak backgammon board, a shawm and tabor pipes; rosaries and beads; a book bound in leather on which is inscribed, in Latin, 'the Word of the Lord Endureth for Eternity'.

At the heart of the dockyards is HMS *Victory*, a shrine to England's hero, Admiral Lord Nelson, and a memorial to the Royal Navy in the Napoleonic Wars. Painted in black and yellow and red, 'Nelson's Chequerboard' (each admiral and captain was allowed to paint his ship as he wished), she towers above you, her mainmast rising 205 feet above the quay.

You may go on board and walk the quarter-deck on which Nelson fell, and descend to the gun decks below, so low that you have to bend double, and the orlop deck where the junior officers lived and which, in battle, became the operating theatre where limbs were amputated, without anaesthetic, by the light of a candle.

You will be awed by the size of the anchors and the girth of the capstan (260 men were needed to weigh the anchor); you will wonder how 820 men lived, ate and worked here, each allowed fourteen inches of headroom for his hammock, slung between the guns on the lower decks, or how the three suits of sail (four acres of canvas each) were stowed.

In the Royal Naval Museum Nelson continues to dominate. There is a collection of ships' figureheads, startlingly gaudy and crude, presented by Mark Prescott Frost, one time Secretary to the Port Admiral, who founded the Dockyard Museum in 1911. There are portraits of naval heroes; material that illustrates the history and culture of the old sailing navy; and an oral history collection that records people's memories of the conflicts, and the social history of the Royal Navy, in the 20th century. But it is Nelson and Trafalgar to which the museum returns in the Nelson relics collected by the widow of his last surviving great-grandson, Mrs Suckling Ward (shoe buckles, watch bracelets, hair), and the Nelson memorabilia collected obsessively by the American Lily Lambert McCarthy.

The memory of Nelson has been a cult and an industry for 200 years and Mrs McCarthy is its acolyte and guide. Whatever the surface on to which the image of the hero of Trafalgar can be placed, etched, sketched, engraved or embroidered, she has tracked it down and bought it: plates, bowls, cups, mugs; badges, lockets, medals; glass, wood, enamel and metal; earthenware and porcelain; all are here, as is the portrait of Nelson by Heinrich Friedrich Füger that Mrs McCarthy saw when she was twelve and started her on this quest.

Those who lack Mrs McCarthy's steely ardour can turn to the Victory Gallery, where every detail of the battle of Trafalgar is pored over and where the monumental panorama of the battle painted by W. L. Wyllie, 42 feet by 12 feet, is displayed in its own gallery. When the foundation stone to this annexe was laid in 1929 Mr Wyllie said, 'This, the wish of my life, has come to pass. I lay this stone as a tribute to the memory of Nelson and his old sailing Navy': a painter after Mrs McCarthy's heart. He began work on it at the age of seventy-eight and died two years later shortly after its completion.

As you leave the dockyards on your right is HMS *Warrior*, in 1860 the largest, fastest, most formidable warship in the world, protected by an iron hull: a glimpse forward to the battle-ships of the 20th century, steam driven, armour plated. It is at rest here five hundred years after Sir Reginald Bray built the original dock.

Postscript

To have four naval museums on one historic site, and the Royal Naval Submarine Museum (q.v.) a five-minute ferry ride across the water at Gosport, each with its own board of trustees, director, staff, administration and policy is, for the visitor, inconvenient and incoherent. For the museums it wastes resources and reduces their potential impact. In 2000 Sir Alan Borg, former director of the Victoria and Albert Museum and of the Imperial War Museum, was commissioned to write a report. He proposed the merging of the museums to form one National Museum of the Royal Navy, bringing the senior service in line with the other armed services' National Army Museum and Royal Air Force Museum (both q.v.). In 2002 the five museums joined the three local authorities to publish a *Review of Strategy for the Future Development of Portsmouth Historic Dockyard.*

The review's ten-year development plan, implicitly, and the Borg Report more trenchantly, recognise that for the museums to continue operating separately is inefficient, hampers their ability to attract capital investment and minimizes their impact on the public. Work is now under way to bring them together under one company to realise the potential of what should be a World Heritage Site.

MUSEUM OF READING *

Town Hall, Blagrave Street, Reading,
Berkshire RG1 1QH
Tel. 0118 939 9800
www.readingmuseum.org.uk

Roman treasures, the other Bayeux Tapestry and the work of a forgotten watercolourist

Miss Elizabeth Wardle and thirty-five members of the Leek Embroidery Society of Staffordshire spent the year 1885 making a full-sized replica of the Bayeux Tapestry. The finished work toured England, America and Germany. It was finally bought for £300 by the Mayor of Reading for the town's new museum, where it now has a circular gallery to itself.

Miss Wardle's father was Thomas Wardle, an industrial dyer who had already engaged Burne-Jones as colour consultant at his Leek dye-works. The original Bayeux Tapestry[105] has threads of only eight colours which Wardle reproduced faithfully: three greens, two blues, two yellow, and terracotta red, all flat but never dull.

The drama is in the detail of the fifty-six panels: the primly arched necks of the horses throughout; Harold's fine moustache as he boards the ship for Normandy, his eager hawk on his hand; Harold's arms outstretched, the tips of his fingers touching two reliquary shrines as he swears the crucial oath of fealty to William; William inclining his head confidentially, charmingly, in conversation with his brothers; the frenzy of the battle, horses charging, stumbling, pitching forward, slain; William turning in his saddle, pushing back his helmet to show his face and rally his men; Harold killed twice, shot with an arrow and hacked down by a Norman knight.

Calligraphic surtitles pick their way through each panel – 'ISTI MIRANT STELLA; HIC WILLELM DUX IUSSIT NAVES EDIFICARE' – while above and below the panels borders run with figures: heraldic beasts, animals, birds, plants, rural scenes, erotic incidents. The meaning of these is not clear. Are they commentary, allegory, symbol or simply decoration? The style of drawing, sometimes flat, sometimes solid, can be traced back to the 9th-century Utrecht psalter and forward to 11th- and 12th-century religious manuscripts. Stem stitch is used for the outlines and letters, laid and couched work to fill areas of colour.[106] The story flows fast from panel to panel, punctuated only by occasional trees and buildings to set the scene. This is the masterpiece of Anglo-Saxon, and of Norman, art, triumphant and mysterious.

The museum's other collection of note comprises objects from the excavation of Calleva Atrebatum, Silchester, midway between Reading and Basingstoke. Silchester did not have the importance of the Roman sites near Colchester, Cirencester or St Albans but since its remains date from the height of Roman occupation in the reign of Constantine, (AD 306–337), the first Christian emperor, it has the only Roman church excavated in Britain. Its other remains are limited by having been built in local flint rather than in stone.

With Wroxeter and Hengistbury Head, Silchester was a centre for Roman silver refining and it is rich in everyday objects, metallic and non-metallic, including the Silchester eagle (now wingless, once probably part of an imperial group statue) and the Silchester bronze horse (*c.* 1st century AD). There are no gimmicks here. The jewellery, tools, coins, tesserae, Samian ware bowls and amber glass jars from Gaul are presented simply and clearly.

The museum is less successful in exhibiting its small but interesting collection of 20th-century paintings (Augustus John, Duncan Grant, John Bratby, John Minton, Carel Weight, Gilbert Spencer and a self-portrait by Stanley Spencer) which are not permanently displayed. There is also a sturdy collection of bronze and marble statuettes and maquettes that includes work by Epstein, Ayrton, Rodin and his friend and pupil John Tweed, alongside 12th-century Romanesque sculptures from Reading Abbey in the Window Gallery.

Here too is the largest collection of watercolours by William Havell, whose reputation today is regrettably modest. A friend of the Varleys, Joshua Cristall and J. S. Cotman, he was the youngest founding member of the Society of Painters in Watercolour and was one of the stars of their first exhibition in 1804.

He was a follower of Turner and had a talent that was widely acknowledged, albeit grudgingly, by the Royal Academy establishment. In the opinion of Sir George Beaumont, writing to William Wordsworth, he was 'an ingenious young man ... if you can inspire him with a little humility, you will be of great service to him and facilitate his progress.'[107] However he was unskilled in, or unsuited to, the politics of the art world. He did not submit himself for election to the Royal Academy and when his masterwork was rejected and failed to sell he took a post in China, remaining in the East for ten years, painting portraits in watercolours. When he returned the world had moved on. This collection of his oils and his watercolours from 1802 to 1851 demonstrates his facility and range.

KNOLE ***

Sevenoaks, Kent TN15 0RP
Tel. 01732 422100/450608
www.nationaltrust.org.uk

The house in England most immemorially grand, with as many rooms as a year has days

Knole 'has a deep inward gaiety of some very old woman who has always been beautiful, who has had many lovers and seen many generations come and go,' wrote Vita Sackville-West in *Knole and the Sackvilles*.[108] Built by Thomas Bourchier, Archbishop of Canterbury, in the mid 15th century, it has been owned by one family, the Sackvilles, since 1602, when Thomas Sackville acquired it from the Crown. That continuity provides a setting in which to see the family's collections of fine and decorative art *in situ*: portraits with plasterwork, tapestries with furniture, silver with ceramics.

During the following 200 years, the family, and the house, had three periods of greatness. Thomas Sackville, after he became 1st Earl of Dorset, used the great wealth he had acquired while serving his monarch as Lord Treasurer responsible for collecting all customs duties, to extend the house into a small Renaissance palace, employing master craftsmen from the King's Works Department: Richard Dungan (plasterwork), William Portington (wood carving) and Cornelius Cure (stonemasonry).

Their work can be seen as you proceed through the house – the Great Hall, in which master and servants ate; the three long galleries which were among the first picture galleries in the country; the bedrooms, dressing rooms and closets off them; the Rooms of State. It is in the decoration of the latter, and on the Great Staircase, that Jacobean craftsmanship is at its height.

Dungan's geometrically patterned ceilings are lightened by delicate bunches of flowers and foliage whose designs are taken from a herbal. In the Great Hall, Portington's carving is fierce with grotesque, Germanic ornament. In the Ballroom, the panelling and pilasters

The Venetian Ambassador's bed at Knole by Niccolò Molino

are decorated by strapwork, with winged horses bursting out of the capitals, and topped by a rich frieze of mermen, mermaids and hippocamps. The chimney piece in black, white and grey marbles, attributed to Cornelius Cure, dances with acanthus scrolls, musical instruments, fruit vases, garlands of flowers and ribbons.

The Great Staircase surpasses this. Other Elizabethan houses have stairs of bare stone and rely on scale to create a sense of occasion. Here Portington made the stair sweep round an open well, beneath another Dungan ceiling. Every inch of the well was painted by Paul Isaacson with cartouches, strapwork, and *trompe l'œil* of the Sackville heraldic leopards, coats of arms and grotesques.

At the foot of the staircase, from a later generation, is the nude plaster figure of Giovanna Baccelli, the mistress of the 3rd Duke, reclining.[109]

The early 17th century at Knole is marked by portraits which demonstrate the growing sophistication of English portraiture during those years. The portraits of the 1st Earl attributed to John de Critz, and those of the 3rd Earl and the wife of the 4th Earl, attributed to William Larkin, are stiff and formal, the faces and poses having little more life than is in the beautiful detail of muff, cuff and embroidery. The best of several by Daniel Mytens, of Lionel Cranfield, 1st Earl of Middlesex, (*c.* 1620), is powerful, with Cranfield's hooded eyes and dangerous smile hidden within his beard, caught by Mytens with confidence.

The contrast between these and the portrait of Cranfield's daughter, Frances, Countess of

Dorset, by Van Dyck (1637), is startling. Here is a Van Dyck of a beautiful woman to put beside his most majestic men (the Lords Bernard and William Stuart in Tate Britain, William Killigrew in the National Portrait Gallery, both q.v.). Van Dyck delights in the sheen of her ivory silk dress, the dash of turquoise, the delicacy of her dark eyes, her pearl necklace, the drift of the stole touched by her long fingers. All this is held as she half turns to glance at you, while behind, unusually for Van Dyck, is an interesting study of two trees.

Knole's collection of late-17th-century furniture is unrivalled. The 6th Earl was Lord Chamberlain to the Household of William III, 1689–97. One of the perquisites of this position was the right to dispose of any unwanted or surplus furniture in the royal palaces. Dorset was assiduous in fulfilling these duties. The royal state bed, made by Louis XIV's upholsterer to celebrate the marriage of the future James II to Mary of Modena; the Venetian Ambassador's bed, shimmering with gold and green with its suite of armchairs and stools; the Brussels tapestries woven by Hendrik Reydams; the X-framed chairs in the Brown Gallery; the Knole settee, ancestor of the modern sofa – all came from the palaces at Whitehall or Hampton Court, while the gilt table and candlesticks in the Cartoon Gallery were given to the 6th Earl by Louis XIV when he was Ambassador to Paris, 1669–70.

The third great period for Knole came a century later when the 3rd Duke embarked on a Grand Tour of Italy. Assisted by Thomas Jenkins in Rome and Count Vitturi in Venice, he bought numerous paintings, including Garofalo's *Judith with the Head of Holofernes* and Salvator Rosa's *Landscape with Bandits*, as well as many less distinguished works.

Back in England, he collected beautiful mistresses, including the Countess of Derby, the courtesan Nancy Parsons, Giovanna Baccelli and, reputedly, Marie Antoinette. Georgiana, Duchess of Devonshire, considered him 'the most dangerous of men ... for with that beauty of his he is so unaffected ... that makes one account very easily for the number of women he has had in love with him.' He also became a patron of contemporary painters, most particularly of Joshua Reynolds, ten of whose canvases hang in the Chinese Drawing Room or Reynolds Room. They are not perhaps Reynolds's most distinguished works but they include powerful portraits of Johnson, Garrick and Goldsmith, a self-portrait, one of his most ambitious history paintings, *Ugolino and his Children in the Dungeon* (1773) and an unusual portrait of the 3rd Duke's Chinese page, *Wang-y-tong*.

Tudor political magnate, Stuart royal functionary, 18th-century Grand Tourist: the Sackvilles acquired paintings and great furniture to embellish the house that Thomas Sackville gained for them.

Few such houses, when their ownership passed in the 20th century to the National Trust, had their guide book written by a descendant, as Knole had by Vita Sackville-West, who described it as 'the greatest relation of those small manor houses that hide themselves away so innumerably among the counties'.[110] It combines modesty and magnificence, display and discretion, in a manner quintessentially, elusively and absolutely English.

WEALD AND DOWNLAND OPEN AIR MUSEUM **

Singleton, Chichester, West Sussex
PO18 0EU
Tel. 01243 811348
www.wealddown.co.uk

Rescued vernacular buildings demonstrate local building from medieval times

The objects here are buildings but this, as its name declares, is a museum that is concerned with land (the Weald and the surrounding downs) and geology (the sandstone of the High Weald, the clay of the Low Weald, the chalk of the downs and the coastal plain).

These have yielded the materials for construction, and determined the nature of farming hereabouts, for centuries. The oak of the Weald was used for timber-framed dwellings and for roofs; cleft timber for wattle staves, laths, tile and thatch battens, and fencing, coopering and clapboarding. Farm buildings were sometimes made from less durable elm; walls with flints (nodular from the Downlands, cobble or pebble from the sea shore).

On this site of forty acres of fields and woodland in the Lavant Valley are more than forty buildings that between them show how people in this south-east corner of England have lived since the 16th century. A conference in 1965[111] identified the need for a museum that would rescue traditional buildings that were at risk and re-erect them here. The museum opened in 1971.

Overlooking the site, part shrouded by woodland, is a museum building designed in 2000 by the architect Ted Cullinan, a discreet and subtle building into which light is let as simply as it falls through trees. Below, re-erected farmhouses, cottages and barns are scattered along the bottom of the valley, while the 15th-century shop, the 17th-century market hall and the medieval hall-house cluster together, as in a village. In the distance is West Dean House, designed by James Wyatt in 1804 and altered in 1891 by Sir Ernest George and Harold Peto. Its owner in the late 1960s, Edward James, facilitated the founding of the museum by providing the site on a long lease at a peppercorn rent.

Comparison between Bayleaf Farmstead (early 15th century) and the nearby early-17th-century Pendean shows how patterns of living altered and, with them, buildings. Bayleaf has an open hall, heated by an open fire: the central feature of a 15th-century house. The skill and knowledge needed to build a chimney existed but the medieval pattern of life persisted. At Pendean the open hall has been replaced by a room heated by a huge central chimney. Bayleaf itself mirrored this change when a chimney stack was inserted into the hall, but it is reconstructed at the museum in its original form. In a house of the same period, North Cray, the evolution from open fire to chimney was by way of a 'smoke bay' in which was incorporated an upper floored area for the smoking of meat.

The superior status of Bayleaf is reflected in its having the luxury of a 'garderobe' (the Frenchified euphemism for a privy) as an adjunct to the upper chamber.

With the exception of the barn belonging to Bayleaf Farmstead, which dates from 1536,[112] the other farm buildings at the museum (the Kirdford Cattle Shed, the Wiston Wagon Shed, the Watersfield Stable) date from the 18th century because earlier examples were not built well enough to survive. Granaries too (West Ashling on five saddle stones, Littlehampton spectacularly poised on sixteen) date from the 18th century because valuable grain was kept within the house in medieval times.

The museum has examples of buildings associated with several trades and crafts: a smithy, a saw-pit shed, a carpenter's shop, a brick-drying shed. It also maintains local breeds of livestock: Sussex cattle, Dorking and Light Sussex hens, shortwool Downland sheep and longwool Romney Marsh or 'Kent' sheep. Charcoal is made on site, from coppiced underwood, the museum's charcoal camp having been built in the early 1970s by two retired charcoal burners from Horsham, Mr and Mrs Langridge. Mrs Langridge, whose family had been charcoal burners for generations, was born and brought up on a charcoal camp until the age of sixteen.

Along the hillside the museum has brought a hazel coppice back into rotation, providing wood for thatching spars and wattle fencing. Beside Bayleaf Farmstead, as part of the museum's project to recreate the surroundings of this 16th-century house with a typical garden and orchard, the shaws that were in the original location in Kent have been replanted. Shaws were small woodlands in the Weald that ran beside field border and homesteads, providing shelter for stock and a source of timber and underwood. Shaws have been consistently cut down since the 18th century and little is known about them. This project will allow them to be studied.

As you walk down the valley you hear distant hammering, the bleating of sheep. You smell smoke and muck. A chirking pheasant gets up. This is a museum that is exploring the life of the Wealds and downland for the benefit of both the visitor and the social historian.

SOUTHAMPTON CITY ART GALLERY ✳✳✳

Civic Centre, Commercial Road,
Southampton, Hampshire SO14 7LP
Tel. 023 808 32277
www.southampton.gov.uk/art

20th-century paintings and studio ceramics

The year 1939 was not an auspicious one in which to open a new regional art gallery.[113] Within months this infant institution had received a direct hit in an air raid. Several students were killed. The building was closed for the rest of the war.

Southampton City Art Gallery had two early benefactors: Councillor Robert Chipperfield, a pharmacist, and Councillor Frederick William Smith, a timber merchant. Chipperfield attached an interesting and helpful stipulation to his bequest: that the director of the National Gallery should be consulted on all acquisitions. The director in the late 1920s and early 1930s (Sir Charles Holmes) did not over-exert himself and decisions were made by a Council Committee, but in 1934, aged thirty-two, Kenneth Clark became Director of the National Gallery.

That Southampton has, seventy years later, one of the country's most interesting regional collections, is a tribute to him and to successive curators, who have assembled an unusual group of Old Masters, and collections that are particularly strong in early-20th-century English painting (the Camden Town Group and the New English Art Club) and in contemporary painting and sculpture.

At the National Gallery Kenneth Clark was under pressure from a forceful and opinionated board of trustees.[114] In advising Southampton he could breathe a little more freely; he began with the acquisition of Jacob Jordaens's *The Holy Family* in 1935. The following year he recommended that Sofonisba

Anguissola's restrained and intense *Portrait of the Artist's Sister Disguised as a Nun* should be bought. This High Renaissance picture came from the collection of the Earls of Yarborough and confirms Anguissola as one of the finest woman painters of her time. The foundations of a French 19th-century collection were also laid on Clark's advice with paintings by Lepine, Forain, Sisley and Pissarro.

His advice on what paintings should be added to the English and the 20th-century collections was more predictable but sound: de Wint, Thomas Barker, David Cox; Utrillo, Sickert, Duncan Grant.

Of greater significance than individual purchases was the policy he established, based on quality and the merits of individual works rather than on the celebrity of artists. He wrote to the gallery's first curator, G. L. Conran (1940–50), 'It is essential that the Southampton Gallery should contain several pictures of European reputation ... and it would be disastrous if it were laid down as a principle that only pictures of moderate cost could be bought, for in that way the greater part of the gallery would be filled with bargains and mediocre works.'[115]

G. L. Conran did not need convincing, particularly with regard to the importance of a good group of Old Masters which, he believed, was 'essential in providing a touchstone by which to judge later movements, and in building up a body of knowledge on which sure taste can be founded'. In the five years he had at the gallery after he returned from military service in 1945 and before he left to be director of Manchester Art Gallery, Conran bought a small Corot, a Richard Wilson and, from the dealer Arthur Jeffress, *The Martyrdom of St Catherine of Alexandria* by François de Nome (early 17th century), a bizarre and violent painting.

He was succeeded by Maurice Palmer, who remained as curator until 1970. It is his taste and judgement, initially reinforced by advice from Sir Philip Hendy at the National Gallery and working through Agnew's and Colnaghi's, that defines Southampton's collection. His first major purchase, the triptych of *The*

Coronation of the Virgin by Allegretto Nuzi (*c.* 1315–73/4), was typically confident. Nuzi may not have the reputation of such predecessors as Simone Martini, or such successors as Fra Angelico, but he merits this his only appearance in a British collection. The other two parts of this triptych are in the Museum of Fine Arts in Houston, Texas.

Palmer followed this with two uncharacteristically quiet Van Dycks (bought cheaply because their subjects, a man and his wife, are unidentified) and two outstanding paintings, by the 16th-century Milanese, Cesare de Sesto, and by the Netherlandish Goswijn van der Weyden. With them, and with, in the 1960s, the acquisitions of paintings by Salvator Rosa, Jan Baptist Weenix, Jacob van Ruisdael and Paul Bril, Palmer created a 'nucleus of Old Masters', the lack of which he had identified in 1957, in a letter to Hendy, as 'one of the problems that is most pressing here'.

He was as active in adding 20th-century British paintings to the collection, and as catholic in his taste, acquiring works by Ben Nicholson, William Gear, J. D. Fergusson, Euan Uglow and William Scott; and others by Sickert, Gore, Ginner, Gertler and Bevan.

During Palmer's time as curator the most significant additions to the collections were the bequest of his friend Arthur Jeffress, and one half[16] of the finest studio pottery collection in Britain, given by the Very Reverend Eric Milner-White. This contains pieces by Bernard Leach, Shoji Hamada, William Staite Murray and their pupils Katherine Pleydell-Bouverie and Sam Haile.

Jeffress[117] left ninety-nine paintings which included works by Bonnard, Vuillard and Douanier Rousseau, and several by John Piper and Graham Sutherland, who was Jeffress's favourite contemporary artist and who painted a full-length portrait of the dealer. Jeffress had been driven to commit suicide by public revelations about his homosexuality and it is ironic that the same public intolerance led to Palmer's resignation in 1970. By that time the quality and tone of the collection itself however was secure.

By now prices were rising fast and Claude Monet's *The Church at Vetheuil* (1880), purchased in 1975, cost more than the rest of the collection put together. The only Old Master acquisition since then, Giovanni Bellini's somewhat damaged *Madonna and Child*, was financed under the government's scheme for acceptance in lieu of capital transfer tax.

In the 1970s and '80s, new curators turned their attention to contemporary painting and sculpture and have made a collection unequalled in Britain outside Tate Modern (q.v.): Terry Frost, Roger Hilton, Patrick Heron; Howard Hodgkin, David Hockney, Frank Auerbach; and sculptures by Richard Long, Antony Gormley, Rachel Whiteread, Richard Deacon, David Nash, Bill Woodrow and the French artist Daniel Buren, whose painted installation *With Arcades, Three Colours* (work *in situ*, 1994), spans the vault of the main gallery.

Kenneth Clark's fears that the gallery would succumb, or be driven by inadequate resources, to collecting only 'bargains and mediocre works' have been triumphantly dispelled. Southampton stands alongside Aberdeen Art Gallery, Leicester New Walk Gallery and Museum and the Ferens Art Gallery as one of the outstanding local-authority collections.

MUSEUM OF ST ALBANS **

Hatfield Road, St Albans, Hertfordshire
AL1 3RR
Tel. 01727 819340
www.stalbansmuseums.org.uk

The tools of every country trade – sawyer, joiner, wheelwright, cooper; beauty in precision and a job well done

Ash, oak and elm are the timbers of England. Sawyer, turner, hooper and wainwright are the tradesmen who for hundreds of years turned these timbers into objects by splitting, splicing and hammering them with awls, adzes and mallets.

These woods, and the trades and tools associated with them, comprise the Salaman Collection here, the largest such collection in a public museum in Britain.[118] Arranged by trade[119] in one large room that has the clean, dry smell of seasoned timber, they are the embodiment of Raphael Salaman's definitive *Dictionary of Tools*[120] (1975): the smaller tools in cabinets, the larger in quasi-armorial displays on the walls.

Salaman's collection and the museum have the same aim: to 'describe every tool used in the woodworking trades from about 1700 to the present time, and to explain its purpose; to give ... some idea of the graceful shapes imparted to the tools by the men who designed and made them.'

Salaman was the youngest son of Jewish intellectual parents who moved to the Hertfordshire village of Barley just before Raphael Salaman was born in 1906. At that time there were more than thirty tradesmen working in and around the village: a farrier, a hurdle maker, a shoe maker (who was also the village barber) and a wheelwright who employed several sawyers. When Salaman returned after the Second World War he found that the Depression and modern machinery had eliminated these trades. Coming across a pair of 19th-century Lancashire pattern dividers[121] carved in one piece, whose dancing beauty, 'shaped forging and graceful *chamfers*' he described later, he began to collect tools, trade catalogues and information about how they were made and used.[122] Salaman tracked down the tools of a legendary itinerant smith from south Wales, 'Pincher Jack', a man 'of almost magical skills'[123] (born *c.*1860 near Crickhowell, died 1926), a pair of whose farrier's pincers is here, forged hot by hand from high-carbon steel for a Yorkshire blacksmith in about 1905.[124]

Displays in the museum demonstrate different trades. Pitsawing, a trade that was not finally superseded by mechanised, steam-powered sawmills until the 1870s, required two men to work in the sawpit 'with long and graceful saws'[125] that weighed fifteen pounds. To make such a saw required the tool maker to tapergrind it to one thousandth of an inch, by eye. During sharpening 'the saw emitted a melodious purr, purr, purr, purr'.[126]

It was arduous work. 'I do not remember seeing a sawyer laugh,' wrote George Sturt in his *Journals*, 1890–1927.

Near it is a display of wheelwrighting, showing the different woods that are required for different parts of a wheel: elm for the hub because its grain resists splitting; seasoned oak for the rim for its elasticity. Beech was not used because it rots easily, walnut because it was too valuable. Using techniques and tools that go back to the Romans, the wheel's felloes (curved rim sections cut to a pattern), six to a wheel, were pulled together in a samson (a vice). No glue was used.

Unlike Pitt Rivers,[127] Salaman was not primarily interested in the evolution of trades and tools. His hero and mentor was the archaeologist Sir Flinders Petrie, a friend of his father, whose book *Tools and Weapons* inspired Salaman's *Dictionary*. Through the useful beauty of the tools he wished to convey the skills of the tradesmen, as he did for the leather trades in his *Dictionary of Leatherworking Tools* (1986). And they do live on here in the museum and in their etymology. A cooper's tools included a croze, a brace, a buzz, a swift, a jigger or chiv and a chiming adze. The words are as clean as the wood, as direct as the tools. The epitaph for these trades is here on a stone tablet engraved by Eric Gill, which he kept in his workshop: 'BAD WORKMEN QUARREL WITH THEIR TOOLS BECAUSE GOOD WORKMEN DO NOT USE BAD TOOLS.'

TANGMERE MILITARY AVIATION MUSEUM **

Tangmere, Chichester, West Sussex
PO20 6ES
Tel. 01243 775223
www.tangmere-museum.org.uk

Battle of Britain airfield, hangars and control tower convey the courage of the few

Tangmere is a windswept aerodrome on the Sussex coast. From here in the Second World War squadrons of Hurricanes and Spitfires

Uplifting gallantry at Tangmere

took off, in the Battle of Britain, in daily efforts to intercept enemy aircraft and, in 1944, to support the D-Day landings. Lysanders based at Tangmere dropped Special Operations Executive (SOE) and Special Intelligence Service (SIE) agents at night into occupied France.

Today there are no aircraft and the only buildings that remain are the H-shaped control tower and part of the NAAFI. The only noise is of the cords clicking against the eleven flagpoles, one for each of the nations whose pilots flew with the RAF in the Second World War.

In November 1916 Eric Robins, flying an Avro 504, lost his way in fog and made a safe landing on a field known as Bayley's Farm. He reported that it would make a good aerodrome. The War Office acquired it and started to fly Sopwith Camels from here in 1918. On 4 September 1939, the first day of the war, the ten Whitley bombers that dropped leaflets over the Ruhr landed here at 4 a.m., short of fuel.

From then on Tangmere was in the thick of the war until after D-Day, when the successful invasion eventually allowed Allied aircraft to operate from French soil.

The story of those years, and Tangmere's brief involvement in the First World War, is told by the aircraft maintained lovingly and exhibited in the Merston Hall: a replica Hawker Hurricane Mk 1, destroyer of the greatest number of German bombers; a full-scale replica of the prototype of Reginald Mitchell's Spitfire K5054 (v. the Potteries Museum and Art Gallery), painted its original duck-egg blue.

Beautiful though these planes are, even when out of their element, tamed and tethered inside a building, the real stories are of the men and women who maintained, armed and flew them from Tangmere: Billy Fiske, the only American pilot to fight in the RAF during the Battle of Britain, killed on 17 August 1940; Wing Commander Douglas Bader, famously shot down while leading the Tangmere wing on 9 August 1941; Pilot Officer Johnnie Johnson, Bader's number two in 616 Squadron;

Flight Officer Sir Hugh 'Cocky' Dundas, who survived the war to become the Chairman of Thames Television; and Sergeant Dennis Noble who, aged twenty, crashed his Hurricane into the front garden of a house, severing the main water-pipe in the middle of Hove in August 1940. He and the remains of his plane were retrieved, almost intact, from beneath the streets of Hove in 1996. His plane is here, a somewhat macabre exhibit.

The exploits of the SOE and SIS are told through the example of Lieut. Violette Szabo, GC, who was dropped into France, captured and executed at Ravensbruck concentration camp in January 1945. Here is the agent's simple toolkit: a silk escape map; a wireless receiver, an attaché case containing one SOE transmitter, and a pack of playing cards that, when split, could be made into a map. Here too is the pistol taken from the Commander of Ravensbruck concentration camp by Odette Churchill.

After the war, Tangmere continued as the base for the RAF's High Speed flight. The 1946 world speed record of 616 mph was set from here by Group Captain 'Teddy' Donaldson in a Meteor. Seven years later Squadron Leader Neville Duke reset the record at 727 mph in a red prototype Hawker Hunter[128] above the Sussex coast between Bognor and Angmering.

Wherever you look there are mementoes: uniforms, medals, models, engines, logbooks, press cuttings, letters home. There are affectingly awkward tableaux with mannequins in uniforms receiving their orders in a recreated dispersal hut or relaxing between missions, feet up, in canvas chairs.

There are advertisements, one from 1941 for a dance with music by Ken Johnson's dance band from the Café de Paris, entrance 3s., HM Forces 2s. Everywhere there are photographs, pinned on boards, behind cellophane, inexpertly mounted, some curling at the edges, of improbably young men and women, invariably smiling. Over the tannoy there are the sounds of the 1940s: the siren to scramble, engines spluttering into life, aircraft flying overhead[129] and the music of Glenn Miller or Vera Lynn.

The museum is staffed by volunteers, many of whom were in the RAF, who are wholly involved in the life and achievements of Tangmere's pilots and planes. Any question to them unleashes a flood of anecdote and reminiscence. Their commitment banishes any threat of sentimentality that might lurk here. In Larry McHale's 1995 poem 'Tangmere, in Silent Tribute', 'Tangmere sleeps Her squadrons gone/Her pride intact Her duty done' or in Leo Marks's, in memory of Violette Szabo, 'The life that I have is all that I have/And the life that I have is yours . . .', there is deep feeling.

Outside rest several aircraft, in a state of loving restoration; the hulk of a US Lockheed T33 Advanced Training aircraft and a Royal Navy helicopter, gently rusting, fragile. The far side of the airfield now has commercial glasshouses on it. The tarmac of the perimeter track is clogged with weeds, the wind blows and the cords click against the flagpoles.

WINDSOR CASTLE ★★★★

Windsor, Berkshire SL4 1NJ
Tel. 020 7766 7304
www.royal.gov.uk/output/Page557.asp

The most royal of collections: Van Dycks, and supreme drawings by Leonardo, Michelangelo and more; Queen Mary's Doll's House, a palace within a palace

Because Windsor Castle is a major tourist attraction, visited by millions, depicted on tea towels and biscuit tins, postcards and souvenirs, some may not take it seriously either as a castle or as a museum. They would be wrong.

Windsor is a real castle, with motte, bailey and keep, built by William the Conqueror *c.*1080 on a naturally defensive site 100 feet above the Thames. It has been a royal residence for every monarch since Henry I in 1110, except when captured by Parliamentary forces during the Civil War when it was, briefly, a prison.

On his Restoration in 1660, Charles II commissioned the architect Hugh May (1673) to create the grandest baroque apartments in

England. The ceilings were painted by Antonio Verrio. Grinling Gibbons and his assistant, Henry Phillips, festooned their cornices and lintels with carvings, delicate loops and ribbons of wood.[130]

May's rooms make fine galleries for the castle's 17th-century paintings: Rubens's landscapes *Summer* and *Winter* (1620–30), and the magnificent Rembrandt *An Old Woman*[131] (c.1629), in which the artist's mother looks down, eyes narrowed, lips pursed. Here too are portraits by Dürer, Holbein the Younger, van Honthorst and Memling.

In most collections great paintings are typically hung in the grandest state rooms. Only the Royal Collection is so rich in masterpieces that it can place two of Gainsborough's finest portraits, of *John Hayes St Leger*[132] (1782) and the artist's friend, the musician *Johann Christian Fischer* (c.1780), in the King's Bed Chamber, albeit a room that was splendidly redecorated for the state visit of the Emperor Napoleon III, with a bed carved by the French cabinet maker Georges Jacob, its corona topped by ostrich feathers. Here too are six of the Canaletto views of Venice that Joseph Smith, the British Consul in Venice, sold to George III in 1762.

At the same time the King bought Smith's collection of drawings (and that of Cardinal Alessandro Albani in Rome): a dazzling library of sheets by Carracci, Domenichino, Poussin, Raphael and Bernini. With the drawings by Leonardo and Michelangelo that had been inherited, it is assumed, from Charles II,[133] this became one of the greatest print rooms in Europe.[134] The seemingly effortless control in Michelangelo's *The Fall of Phaeton* (1533) or *The Virgin, Child and St John* (c.1532) illustrate what he said to Francisco de Hollanda about drawing, that it 'is the fount and body of painting and sculpture and architecture and every other kind of painting and the root of all sciences'[135] and all emotions.

The remaining collections in the castle are about kingship. You enter up the Grand Staircase, its wall hung with armour and trophies. Wherever you look there are the trappings of royal power and the images of kings,

by van Somer, Mytens, Dobson, Riley, and principally, and most gloriously, by Van Dyck. Here, in the King's Dressing Room and the Queen's Ballroom, are the defining images of Charles I and his family: *The Five Royal Children* (1637) with the seven-year-old future Charles II in the middle, surrounded by his sisters, his hand confidently subduing a giant mastiff whose monumental head comes up to his chest; *Henrietta Maria*, coral in her hair, a coral pink ribbon at her waist, setting off a gown of the palest grey; and the great *Charles I in Three Positions* (c.1635–6), sent to Rome so that Bernini, whose principal patron Pope Urban VIII would not let him travel abroad, could carve his sculpture in marble, guided by Van Dyck's images. Bernini rose to Van Dyck's implicit challenge by making a sculpture that Charles declared a wonder 'as soon as the first plank of the case was raised', rewarding Bernini with a diamond worth £1,000. In this painting of calm, impassive authority, Van Dyck confirms the belief that Charles's father, James I, had impressed upon him: 'You are a little GOD to sit on his throne and rule over other men', a belief he held up to the death it led him to.

Kingship in the late 18th century is depicted with rather less subtlety by Sir Thomas Lawrence in the Waterloo Chamber. Here, under the eye of a huge portrait of the Duke of Wellington, are the twenty-seven portraits that George IV commissioned from Lawrence to record the Allied monarchs, statesmen and commanders who contributed to the victory at Waterloo. Field Marshall Gebhardt von Blücher, the true saviour hero of the day, is on Wellington's left.[136] Elsewhere images of kingship run the gamut from the literal (a line of busts of monarchs by Roubiliac, Nollekens, Sheemakers, Chantrey and others) to the banal (portraits that decline in quality as the 19th century gives way to the 20th – by Archer Shee, Winterhalter, Tuxen, Gerald Kelly, James Gunn). Overhead are less direct images by Verrio in the King's Dining Room: a banquet of the gods (complete with lobster) to which sovereigns could aspire.

That it is the pleasure and privilege of kings to try to order the world as they would wish it to be is demonstrated here by the Doll's House given to Queen Mary in 1924. It was designed by the Edwardian architect Sir Edwin Lutyens, a house in epitome, on a scale of one to twelve. Everything works: the plumbing, the electricity, the lifts, even the gramophone. The bottles in its cellar contain vintage French wines; the paintings and books are by contemporary artists and writers (Kipling, Hardy, Barrie). It lacks only a bottle marked 'DRINK ME' for it to be the ultimate museum within a museum, life within life.

East Anglia

The Broads, the Fens and the cold North Sea; the swept grey skies and the winds from the Urals: these widen further Noël Coward's 'very flat, Norfolk'.

Prey to invaders (Beaker People, Iron Age Celts, Romans, Vikings, Anglo-Saxons), East Anglia became, in every sense, Puritan country, Nonconformist, radical; set apart from the rest of Britain.

The rule of the Iceni, and their revolt against Roman occupation in which they burned Colchester to the ground, has left buried treasures for archae-ologists to find and museums to display. Colchester's collection of Roman remains is the largest in Britain from a single site. Today's metal detectors are continuing to uncover hoards, as one did recently at Oatlands Park, near Chelmsford: twenty-three gold coins stamped with Cunobelin's name and 'CAMU', Camulodunum/Colchester. It is now in the Chelmsford Museum (not included here).

Later centuries laid up other treasures: in the great university collections at Cambridge; at the grand houses of great landowners, Holkham and Houghton. Not included, sadly, are Lord Fairhaven's collection of clocks, tapestries and Claudes at Anglesey Abbey; eccentric Ickworth House, its curved corridors embracing its central rotunda, its rooms glorying in Titian, Gainsborough and Velásquez; or rose-bricked Blicking Hall, with the tiers of its Repton clock tower and its supreme Jacobean plasterwork ceilings in the book-lined long gallery rich with ornament: 'heraldic achievements, symbols, emblems and heroical devices'.[1]

Being set apart from London, and so from fashion, might have contributed to the coherence of the Norwich School of painters (Norwich Castle Museum) and so to the less formal group of Suffolk painters who prospered, locally, around the edges of Gainsborough's and Constable's great talents (Wolsey Art Gallery and Christchurch Mansion).

The pressure on space here from East Anglian museums may be less acute than in some other regions but that makes the omissions more painful: Cambridge's Zoology Museum is of national importance; Great Yarmouth Museum is not, but is as delightful a local museum as its neighbour Lowestoft Museum.

WELLS-NEXT-THE-SEA

A148

A140

Norfolk

NORWICH

A146

LOWESTOFT

A12

SOUTHWOLD

DUNWICH

BURY ST EDMUNDS

A14

Suffolk

A12

WOODBRIDGE

IPSWICH

SUDBURY

A12

COLCHESTER

20 miles

The local museum whose omission I regret most is the truly, deeply local Wisbech and Fenland Museum with its registers from twenty-seven parishes, its vestry minutes, Turnpike Acts and manorial land records. It is a museum worthy of the attention of W.G. Sebald had he allowed *The Rings of Saturn* to extend further across the expanses of Suffolk: one more reason to regret the too early death of that museum-loving writer and adopted East Anglian.

MANOR HOUSE MUSEUM *

Honey Hill, Bury St Edmunds, Suffolk
IP33 1HF
Tel. 01284 757076
www.stedmundsbury.gov.uk/manorhse.htm

Orreries, clocks and all manner of timepieces,
plus 17th-century portraits by Mary Beale

There are few clock collections in Britain.
Outside the British Museum (q.v.), which has
one of the greatest and most comprehensive
horological collections in the world, this is the
best in Britain.[2]

Its setting befits the most elegant of long-
case clocks, being an 18th-century town house,
designed by the antiquary and amateur architect Sir James Burrough (1736–8), for Elizabeth
Hervey, the second wife of John Hervey, 1st
Earl of Bristol. Having been acquired by the
county council in 1947 for offices, it opened as
a museum in 1993.

The house is alive with clocks, the steady
counterpoint of ticking broken by intermittent
chimes that tell the quarter, half and hour, in a
variety of voices and octaves. The collection,
bequeathed to the council in 1953, comprises
every type of mechanism for keeping the time
and recording the passing of the hours and the
movements of the planets: astrolabes, orreries,
sundials, diptychs, clocks and watches.

A Time Gallery describes the history of
timekeeping from a model of an 11th-century
Chinese water clock to the sundials whose
spike or gnomon measured true solar time
once the gnomon corresponded with the angle
of latitude (52° for Bury St Edmunds), and so
to the pendulum clocks of the 1650s and the
escapement that turns the pendulum's swing
into a clock's rotary movement.

Here are examples of clocks from Augsburg,
the centre of European clockmaking in the
early 17th century; a simple horizontal table
clock (*c.*1600); the elaborate showpieces that
an Augsburg clockmaker had to produce to be
accepted into the ranks of master craftsmen
(a gilt tabernacle clock by A. Mayer, 1600); a
lion clock whose eyes move with the ticking

and whose mouth opens and shuts as the hour
strikes; and a crucifix clock, at the base of
whose cross is a skull whose teeth chatter on
the striking of the hour.

In the Thirty Years War Augsburg was
besieged and sacked. Its clock industry never
recovered, and London replaced it as Europe's
clockmaking centre. There are clocks here by
all the leading 18th-century English makers,
including Thomas Tompion and his pupil, and
subsequently partner, George Graham.[3] There
are early, small long-case clocks, by Clement,
and clocks with elaborate marquetry by Windmill, by Lyons and by Johnson. There is a
lantern clock (1695) by Benjamin Stribling
of nearby Stowmarket and a fine Bury St
Edmunds clock by Mark Hawkins senior.

These craftsmen dominated clockmaking
until the start of the 19th century, when increased demand, particularly in America,
transformed the craft into an industry. Eli
Terry's water-powered machinery at his factory in Bristol, Connecticut, could make more
than a thousand wooden long-case movements a year. A gallery of handsome clocks by
Luman Watson of Cincinnati, and by Brewster
and Son, and Brewster and Ingrahams, shows
why, when they began to export to Europe,
they swept English clockmaking aside.

The walls of the house are hung with family
portraits of the Herveys/Bristols (including
a Reynolds of the *3rd Earl of Bristol*), of the
Cullums who lived at nearby Hawstead (portraits of *Sir Thomas Cullum and his wife Dudley*
by Sir Peter Lely, *c.*1660, and of the Revd Sir
John Cullum by Angelica Kauffmann) and of
their descendant *Sydney Milner-Gibson* (1872)
by James Tissot.

Downstairs there is one further collection,
as unusual as that of clocks: the work of a
17th-century woman artist, Mary Beale. Mary
Beale was the daughter and granddaughter
of Puritan clerics from Barrow, outside Bury
St Edmunds, who had, according to the 18th-
century art historian George Vertue, 'some
instructions ... in drawing and painting'
from Robert Walker, the painter favoured by
Cromwell and Parliamentarians, as Dobson
was by Royalists. When her husband lost his

Mary Beale's portrait of herself as a shepherdess
(Manor House Museum)

position in the Patents Office, Mary Beale set up in business as a painter of portraits, encouraged by Sir Peter Lely, who gave her work making copies of his portraits, for which there was a ready market. His influence is clear; poses, compositions, even props are borrowed from Lely. Her sitters are lit from the side, against a dark background, the right arm positioned across the chest.

Beale lacks the energy, sensuality and delight in flesh of Lely at his best, but the richness of her colours, the delicate handling of the hair and her quiet penetration of character compensate for some lack of animation. In Vertue's generous opinion 'she was little inferior to any of her contemporaries, either in Colouring, Strength, Force or Life.'

CAMBRIDGE UNIVERSITY MUSEUM OF ARCHAEOLOGY AND ANTHROPOLOGY **

Downing Street, Cambridge,
Cambridgeshire CB2 3DZ
Tel. 01223 333516
museum-server.archanth.cam.ac.uk/

World prehistory, local archaeology and Winchester's Inigo Jones screen

The study of archaeology and anthropology at Cambridge has roots in the Cambridge Antiquarian Society, founded in 1839. That this is so late, centuries after the enquiries of such antiquarians as William Stukeley and William Camden, generations after the Pacific expeditions of Captain Cook, is evidence of the grip that religious orthodoxy had over universities. Until Darwin, man's prehistory was subject to a biblical timescale.

In 1883 the society offered its collections of local antiquities to the university, just as Sir Sidney Colvin, the Director of the Fitzwilliam Museum, was acquiring land in Little St Mary's Lane in order to exhibit the university's cast collection separately. The university secured two galleries there for local antiquities and Baron Anatole von Hügel was appointed

curator, not least because he was acquainted with the president of the society and 'was a person of independent means'[4] and so was able to accept a reduction in his salary from £150 a year to £100. 'His strong point was ethnological studies.'[5]

In the same year two Cambridge graduates, Alfred Maudslay and Sir Arthur Gordon, the first governor of Fiji, deposited their collection of South Seas artefacts with the university, having known von Hügel in Fiji. 'There was some difference of opinion as to where they should be placed; some said they were purely antiquarian, others said they were part of the Natural History of man and therefore should be placed in the New Museums, with the large collection of crania.'[6] Eventually it was decided that they should remain with the society's local antiquities to form a new Museum of General and Local Archaeology, which incorporated some of the collections of individual colleges. Artefacts both from Captain Cook's first voyage[7] and from Sir Robert Cotton and John Camden's 17th-century collection of finds from Hadrian's Wall came from Trinity College.

Cambridge's position on a river and in good arable country meant that the area had been inhabited and cultivated for over 3,000 years, evidenced by a Beaker site (c. 2500 BC) at Little Downham, a settlement site (2,000 BC) at Shippea Hill and a barrow yielding bronze palstaves and a beautiful twisted gold torc (mid 2nd millennium) at Grunty Fen, Stretham. The Celts had hill forts and farmsteads (c. 600 BC), the Romans a town and river crossing, the Anglo-Saxons a 5th-century settlement whose cemeteries were on what is now St John's College Cricket Field. From these have come delicate Roman glass vessels and pewter jugs, Anglo-Saxon brooches, wrist clasps and an elegant blue-green glass beaker.

Despite not having a Flinders Petrie or an Arthur Evans to bring back treasures from celebrated excavations, the museum has attracted a good collection that illustrates world prehistory, and is strong on central Europe (Hungary, the Ukraine, Switzerland).

It also has artefacts from a unique 8th-millennium BC site, Star Carr in Yorkshire, which provides one of the most vivid pictures of how post-glacial hunters lived about a thousand years before Britain separated from the Continent. Preserved by waterlogged conditions are tools of all kinds, most of them hafted for handling use; a canoe paddle; and twenty red deer skulls complete with antlers that have been trimmed and shaped to be worn as headdresses. The American archaeology collection is probably even more noteworthy than the European.

Von Hügel's interest in ethnology and the Maudslay/Gordon gift were transformed by the work of Alfred Cort Haddon, a zoologist who, despite having no full-time post until 1901, led expeditions to the Torres Straights in 1888–9 and 1898–9, encouraged by the doyen of anthropologists J. G. Frazer, which laid the foundations of modern anthropology in Britain and produced the Oceanic collection that remains the pride of the museum.

From these expeditions, and Haddon's teaching, came anthropologists of stature: W. H. R. Rivers, C. G. Seligman, Gregory Bateson (who married the great and controversial American anthropologist Margaret Mead) and L. C. G. Clarke, who succeeded von Hügel as curator.

By the start of the 20th century the collection had outgrown Little St Mary's Lane and moved to the new buildings that Sir T. G. Jackson had designed along Downing Street, a tall facade with a high gable in the corner of the courtyard.

The museum has some spectacular artefacts (a bark cloth mask – Haddon; a Solomon Islands canoe prow ornament – Rivers; a Zuni Kachina doll – Clarke; a Sepik mask – Bateson); a 50-foot totem pole from Queen Charlotte's Island, British Columbia, from 1926 and, incongruously, on the second floor, the rood screen from Winchester Cathedral designed by Inigo Jones, 1634–8, dismantled at Winchester in 1820 as being a classical intrusion in a Gothic building.

Anthropology has been subject to continual shifts in academic theory in the 20th century, with the emphasis moving from social systems, to kinships, to customs and beliefs, to communication, from the descriptive to the theoretical. Although subject to interpretation and reinterpretation, the artefacts have remained here, still recognised as inextricably intertwined with social institutions.

CAMBRIDGE AND COUNTY FOLK MUSEUM *

2–3 Castle Street, Cambridge, Cambridgeshire CB3 0AQ
Tel. 01223 355159
www.folkmuseum.org.uk

Former inn crammed with illuminating human clutter from tools to dolls

As a site for a folk museum recording the daily life of a community, its customs and ceremonies, at work and at home, few buildings could be more appropriate than a former inn. The White Horse Inn on Castle Street, a pub for nearly three hundred years until 1934, is on a Roman road beside a 12th-century church, close to where the River Cam is crossed by Magdalene Bridge. Its warren of small, low-ceilinged rooms (bar, snug, staircases, corridors, bedrooms, kitchens) is a metaphor for the museum's collections, clusters of objects on every flat surface, wedged in every corner. They nudge at each other, jostle for your attention, hugger-mugger: tools and toys; shoes and spades; pipes and pots; photographs and drawings; the clobber of everyday life.

The museum opened in 1936 following an exhibition two years before of folk items by the Women's Institute. Its founding members included Florence Ada Keynes, Cambridge's first woman town councillor, mother of the economist and Bursar of King's College John Maynard Keynes.

Folk museums are not glamorous. To start and to survive they demand dedication and determination. Endowments and bequests are rare. Here every object has been donated. When Reginald Lambeth, the first curator, saw a complete Georgian shopfront on a demolition site and was refused permission to take it, he returned after dark on his bicycle for several nights, removed it a section at a time and rebuilt it at the museum, in whose yard it still is, sixty years later.

Reginald Lambeth was succeeded by Enid Porter, who remained as curator for twenty-nine years and determined the shape and character of the museum. She was a historian, writing on Victorian life in Cambridge (as described in the diaries of Josiah Chater) and the definitive, 400-page survey *Cambridgeshire Customs and Folklore*.

The museum has a collection of records that arise from this research by Enid Porter and relate to fenland history, acquired from an old fenman; an archive of stories and memories set down by W. H. Barrett; and a set of the tools needed for life in the fens: turf barrow, sedge pick, wooden spade, an eel gleve and an eel grig, or trap.

Life in the town is similarly well recorded by the tools of trades that are no longer practised there: those of a nail maker, and a brick and mould maker; and a hat maker's workbench and tools including a brim gauge, variable moulds, brushes and an iron.

A collection of traps for flies, beetles and mice gives a sideways glimpse of domestic life and a quiet obsession with mice, for whom a variety of traps were devised: Dead-fall; Spring-Noose Snapshot; and German Patent. Professor Okey, who began life as a basket maker, designed a wickerwork bedbug trap in 1925.

Here are shoes built into new houses in the 17th century to ward off evil; and a cutting from a local newspaper that tells of the attempt by a Mr Frost to build a 'Steam Aerial Machine' in 1877. It had four large spoked wheels, ostrich feather wings that flapped and an engine heated by coal. It failed to fly.

Appropriately for the former White Horse Inn, the museum has a collection of pub signs painted by a local artist, Richard Hopkins Leach, and a photograph of the pub's last landlord, Willoughby Dudley Hay.

Enid Porter retired in 1976. Since then people working here have included Nick Mansfield, director of the People's History Museum, and Cameron Hawke-Smith, curator from 1999. New technology, in the form of an interactive computer, is being used to record the stories of a roadsweeper, a farm-worker, a publican, a tourist guide and a college bedmaker: Cambridge folk at the start of the 21st century.

FITZWILLIAM MUSEUM
*****

Trumpington Street, Cambridge,
Cambridgeshire CB2 1RB
Tel. 01223 332900
www.fitzmuseum.cam.ac.uk

Rich connoisseurial collection with very fine antiquities, newly reopened

Richard, 7th Viscount Fitzwilliam of Merrion (1745–1816), having failed to buy the collection of the Duc d'Orleans (Philippe Egalité), did acquire in 1798 three of its Venetian masterpieces: Palma Vecchio's *Venus and Cupid*, Veronese's *Hermes, Herse and Aglauros* and Titian's *Venus, Cupid and the Lute Player*. Theirs was a gilded provenance. All three had been in the brilliant but ill-fated collection of the Habsburg Emperor Rudolf II at the Hradschin Castle in Prague before passing into the ownership of Queen Christina of Sweden when Prague fell to the Swedish army in 1648 at the end of the Thirty Years War.[8]

Fitzwilliam already had a good collection of Dutch paintings inherited from his mother's father, Sir Matthew Decker, and had built up a library of books; manuscripts; musical scores (including autograph sheets by Scarlatti, Purcell, Handel and Johann Christian Bach,[9] and the *Fitzwilliam Virginal Book*);[10] albums containing more than 40,000 prints; and one of the finest collections of Rembrandt etchings in Britain. He bequeathed all these to the University of Cambridge, together with £100,000 in South Sea annuities, to be used to house them, in order to further 'the Increase of Learning and other Great Objects of that

Noble Foundation'. No museum could have received a more propitious start. From the outset the museum bore the connoisseurial stamp that has characterised it ever since.

It is not therefore surprising that the museum attracted bequests and gifts of quality: from the Revd John Romney, 164 drawings by his father, the painter George Romney (1817); Daniel Mesman's collection of 300 Dutch paintings and drawings (1834); John Disney's collection of Roman sculpture (1850); and Ruskin's gift of twenty-five watercolours by J. M. W. Turner (1871).

An open architectural competition for a building for the museum was held in 1834 and won by George Basevi with a neo-Greek design that could not resist leaning towards the grand gestures of Victorian baroque. Basevi fell to his death from scaffolding on the West Tower of Ely Cathedral in 1845 and the building was completed by C. R. Cockerell,[11] with final additions by Sir Charles Barry's son, E. M. Barry, 1870–75.

To enter the Fitzwilliam by its main entrance you mount wide stone steps to a portico of eight giant columns. Inside, the staircase hall, which owes something to all three designers, is of black and pink marble 'and much gold ... crowned by an ornate dome with lantern carried by caryatids'.[12] The basic design and barrel vaults are by Basevi, the dome and ceiling decorations by Cockerell and the lantern by Barry.

The museum has been as well served by its directors as by its benefactors. The most flamboyant, Sydney Cockerell (1908–37), maintained that 'I found it a pig-stye; I turned it into a palace.'[13] This was less than fair to his predecessor, the self-effacing M. R. James,[14] who was responsible for establishing the quality of the early Italian collection by purchasing the three-panelled altarpiece of *Saints Geminianus, Michael and Augustine, with Angels Above*, by the foremost Sienese painter of the 14th century, Simone Martini, and for securing important collections of coins

Fitzwilliam Museum: Hermes, Herse and Aglauros *by Veronese*

and manuscripts from Frank McClean.[15] James also had a hand in securing the first gifts (of nineteen manuscripts, in 1904) made by Charles Fairfax Murray. From then until his death in 1918 Fairfax Murray gave 'an astonishing array of fine art which included more than a dozen Constables and as many Wilkie watercolours, five early Gainsborough portraits, a hoard of Pre-Raphaelite paintings, drawings, sketches and painted books, a Corot and, most spectacular of all, the superb Titian *Tarquin and Lucretia*'.[16] It is likely that he would have given the Fitzwilliam his portrait collection (forty-six paintings by Van Dyck, Hogarth, Lely, Gainsborough, etc.) if only Cambridge had been able to match Dulwich Picture Gallery's offer to build a separate gallery for them.[17]

Cockerell could be avid and overbearing. He offended Fairfax Murray bitterly by claiming that Murray's loan of a bronze *David* by Donatello gave the museum the right to acquire it, but the same brass-necked aggression did secure the collection of his friend Charles Brinsley Marlay, which included one of Cima's last, and finest, paintings, *St Lanfranc Enthroned Between St John the Baptist and St Luberns* (c.1516).[18] Cockerell proceeded to ask Marlay, successfully, for £50,000 to build a gallery to house his collection,[19] for a further £30,000 to staff it and for the lease on Marlay's house, later sold for another £10,000.

Notable collections secured by Cockerell after the First World War included F. Leverton Harris's Italian maiolica (1926), J. W. Glaisher's English and Continental pottery and porcelain (1928) and, in Cockerell's final year, an outstanding collection assembled by the artists and aesthetes Charles Shannon and Charles Ricketts. This collection included antiquities, drawings (Titian's *Couple in Embrace*; Rubens's delicate *Path Bordered by Trees*) and Van Dyck's portrait of *Archbishop Laud* (1635), which they 'bought at Christie's (all London having seen it), at the price of a good frame'.

The quality of these bequests makes the Fitzwilliam one of the outstanding art collections in the country. To study the ambition of the Renaissance in Tintoretto's *The*

Adoration of the Shepherds or Titian's *Tarquin and Lucretia*; to compare the 17th-century classical landscapes of Poussin, Claude and Domenichino with the northern light captured by Cuyp in *Sunset after Rain* or by Ruisdael in *Landscape with Waterfall*; to place Canaletto's view of *The Grand Canal* beside the identical view as seen by his nephew Bernardo Bellotto; to contrast Courbet's *The Charente at Port-Bertaud* with the landscapes of Cézanne or Monet is to enter into the bloodstream of European art history. The brilliant works by less celebrated artists are as impressive: G. A. Berckheyde's panel paintings of Amsterdam and Haarlem; Gerrit Dou's *Schoolmaster and Boys*; or Joos van Cleve's tender *Virgin and Child*.

Inevitably there are weaknesses. The museum's representation of the Spanish and German Schools is limited, as is that of French painting before the 19th century. Bequests by Frank Hindley Smith and Captain F. W. Sykes brought to the museum paintings by Degas, Renoir, Cézanne and Seurat but Picasso's *Cubist Head* (1910) does somewhat draw attention to the absence of Cubism.

In recent years the museum's directors have bought well. The Claude *Pastoral Landscape with Lake Albano and Castel Gandolfo*, painted for Pope Urban VIII, was in the Barberini Collection until acquired by Carl Winter[20] in 1963. In the 1970s Michael Jaffé[21] saved Stubbs's *Gimcrack* and Van Dyck's *Virgin and Child* from export. Today, the museum pursues an active acquisitions policy in all areas of the collections.

Bequests have continued, albeit at a slower rate; G. St G. M. Gompertz's Korean ceramics; Major R. G. Gayer-Anderson's Egyptian antiquities, which he was only able to bring out of Egypt in return for leaving behind his Islamic collection;[22] and paintings by Whistler, Courbet, Gauguin and Camille Pissarro given by the Revd Eric Milner-White, Chaplain and Dean of King's College. When Milner-White offered his collection of studio pottery and English stoneware, it was refused and was ultimately given to Southampton City Art Gallery and York Art Gallery (both q.v.).

Most striking is the collection of small Renaissance bronzes put together by Lt. Col. the Hon. Mildmay Thomas Boscawen and bequeathed by him in 1997. This celebrated traveller and explorer, whose journeys through India, Tibet, Arabia and Turkestan are comparable to those of St John Philby, Peter Fleming or Freya Stark, assembled (with the help of dealers, since his home was in a remote area of Tanganyika, now Tanzania) bronzes of outstanding quality by such 16th-century masters as Giovanni Francesco Rustici, Massimiliano Soldam-Benzi, Pietro Tacca and the French sculptor Barthelmy Prieur.

The connoisseur collectors here are variously embodied: the soldier and explorer (Boscawen), the aesthete (Shannon and Ricketts), the artist (Sir Frank Brangwyn), the academic (Dr Glaisher, Michael Jaffé), the amateur (Frank McClean), the financier (Sir Nicholas Goodison, who is presently giving contemporary furniture and ceramics), the Grand Tourist (Fitzwilliam). Their tastes sit together in a museum collection of beauty, quality and rarity that fulfils Fitzwilliam's founding intention to increase learning and give delight in 'a good substantial Museum Repository'.

MUSEUM OF CLASSICAL ARCHAEOLOGY **

Sidgwick Avenue, Cambridge, Cambridgeshire CB3 9DA
Tel. 01223 335153
www.classics.cam.ac.uk/ark.html

A collection that casts the great Greek and Roman sculptures in one gallery

This is a collection of plaster casts moulded directly from original Greek and Roman sculptures. It grew out of the enthusiasms of Sidney Colvin, Slade Professor of Art in the 1870s and the first director of the Fitzwilliam Museum (q.v.).

At the Fitzwilliam Colvin inherited three casts given by Mr P. B. Duncan in 1849–50 and thirty-five presented the next year by Mr John

Kirkpatrick.[23] They included casts of some of the most celebrated classical sculptures: the *Apollo Belvedere*, the *Townley Venus*, the *Farnese Hercules*, the *Barberini Faun*, the *Venus de Milo*.

Colvin valued the casts as a means of illustrating his lectures[24] and expanded the collection with casts from important contemporary excavations. From the 1875–6 excavation at Olympia he acquired the *Nike* of Paionios; from the 1877–8 dig the *Hermes* of Praxiteles. At the same time (1879) the university was altering the Classical Tripos by adding a Part II in which there was a new option, Classical Archaeology. The need for a museum separate from the Fitzwilliam became urgent and it opened, with more than six hundred casts, in Little St Mary's Lane, in 1884, on a 99-year lease from Peterhouse College.

From the first there was uncertainty as to whether the primary purpose of the cast collection was archaeological or artistic, for teaching or inspiration. This was reflected in the guest list and inaugural speeches at the museum's opening. Alongside Professor Richard Jebb, Regius Professor of Greek, and the luminaries of the Cambridge Classics Department, were Sir Frederic Leighton, President of the Royal Academy, Sir Lawrence Alma-Tadema and Sir Frederick Burton, Director of the National Gallery.

Leighton rejoiced 'as an artist to see art in her noblest form taking up her abode within your venerable walls'; Charles Newton, the British Museum's Keeper of Greek and Roman Antiquities, insisted that trying to teach archaeology without a cast museum was 'like trying to teach chemistry without a laboratory', while Lord Houghton, a trustee of the British Museum, believed that the cast collection could help end the mass export of original statues that was despoiling Greece 'by fraud, by force'.[25]

These arguments were not resolved. In 1982 the Peterhouse lease expired and the museum was reunited with the Classics Faculty in a new building.[26] Within is a cool, top-lit gallery, painted white, which has the space to exhibit the casts chronologically in ten bays, charting the development of classical statuary from the Archaic style of the 6th and 7th centuries BC, through the classical styles of the 4th and 5th centuries to the Hellenistic styles of the 1st, 2nd and 3rd centuries and their influence on Roman sculptors of the first two centuries AD.

The originals are scattered across Europe in museums in Athens, Rome, London, Berlin, Madrid, Munich, Florence and Copenhagen. The casts here taken from those originals allow the visitor in one gallery to compare and contrast, and to see how the rigid frontal and profile views of the Archaic style (in the Corfu pediment, *c.* 550–540 BC) gave way to twisting poses and then to movement (the *Wounded Soldier* from the Temple of Aphaia at Aegina, *c.* 490 BC) and the *Artemision Figure* (of Zeus or Poseidon) hurling a now-lost thunderbolt or trident, *c.* 460 BC (Athens); how Pheidias and Polykleitos blended nature and artifice to create an idealised view of the human body in the Parthenon friezes (Pheidias, 438–432 BC), the *Nike* of Paionios (425–420 BC) or the Farnese *Hera* (Polykleitos original 460 BC); how Praxiteles (the *Aphrodite* of Knidos, *c.* 350 BC) evolved into what the great art historian Johann Joachim Winckelmann called 'the Beautiful Style'; how that shifted towards baroque, theatrical poses (the *Dying Gaul*, Villa Ludovici, *c.* 200 BC; the *Barberini Faun* from the Mausoleum of Hadrian, Rome; or the *Nike* of Samothrace, *c.* 200 BC) and finally how the Romans took these skills and applied them to statuary and portraiture in the 1st and 2nd centuries AD.

Here are the roots of Western European art in which 'man [is] the measure of all things'. These are the works that inspired the Renaissance and that remain aesthetic ideals today.

What is baffling is that the 20th century turned away from casts. In an age of mass reproduction it is bizarre, even perverse, that the pursuit of signature and authenticity should reduce the value placed on casts, ignoring the fact that many of these great works (the Medici *Aphrodite*, the *Aphrodite* of

Capua, the *Aphrodite* of Knidos, the *Apollo Belvedere*, the Farnese *Hermes*) are themselves Roman copies of Greek originals. In Hugh Honour and John Fleming's paraphrase of Plato, 'perceptible objects are imperfect copies approximating to imperceptible ideas ... and hence all visual images are no more than copies of copies.'[27]

Despite their beauty, their significance remains a matter of contention. Mary Beard argues that 'the casts now have no educational function ... They are no "laboratory" for any Classicist; rarely (let's be honest) looked at; never studied.'[28] If this is so, we are the poorer for it. This is a collection that remains a metaphor for the ideal to which it aspires.

SEDGWICK MUSEUM OF EARTH SCIENCES ***

Downing Street, Cambridge,
Cambridgeshire CB2 3EQ
Tel. 01223 333456
www.sedgwickmuseum.org

A lode of fossils arranged according to age in a wittily carved and decorated setting

'I cannot promise to teach you all geology, I can only fire your imaginations,' wrote Adam Sedgwick to his students in 1835. For the fifty-five years that Sedgwick held the Woodwardian Professorship he redeemed that promise. Something of the flavour of the museum founded in his name is caught by the notice he pinned up in 1835: 'The Woodwardian Professor invites his class to meet him on horseback at the Barnwell Gravel Pits, on Tuesday, April 7th, precisely at Ten o'clock.' Among those who benefited from his field trips was Charles Darwin, whose two weeks spent in Wales with Sedgwick in 1831 comprised the only scientific training (besides reading Lyell's *Principles of Geology*) he had before joining HMS *Beagle*.[29]

Among Britain's geological museum collections, only the Ashmolean's (q.v.) is older.[30] The entrance is tucked into a corner of the courtyard that P. G. Jackson designed in 1891 to house Cambridge's growing science departments.

This museum remains part of the Department of Earth Sciences and the lack of glossification, and the way in which the specimens and heavy handsome cases are laid out, convey the museum's care and respect for these working collections. The cabinets gleam with 100 years of polishing and proper pride.

Between 1688 and 1724 John Woodward made a collection of 'fossils'[31] (roughly half minerals and rocks, half organic fossils) that was unusual in not being 'a miscellaneous assemblage of the rare and the curious'.[32] Rather it was a 'scientific' collection of around 9,400 specimens from Guam, China, India and Barbados as well as from England and Wales, for classifying and cataloguing. It is here in its four original burred-walnut specimen cabinets, beside Woodward's instruments and books. His aim, described in his book *An Attempt Towards the Natural History of the Fossils of England*, was 'to get as compleat and satisfactory information of the whole Mineral Kingdom as I could possibly obtain'.

Sedgwick also had available to him the mineral collection of the Revd William Whewell[33] who held the Chair of Mineralogy from 1828 to 1834.[34] These specimens glint and wink on glass shelves: jade and calcite; phosphates and fluorides; the silver and white porcupine prisms of the zeolite mesolite; and the smoky pink of the ring silicate rose beryl. Whewell was succeeded by W. H. Miller, who developed a notation of crystal faces, the Miller Indices, which render precisely diamond's most densely populated planes of carbon atoms as {111} and graphite, the most dispersed and softest, as {0001}.[35]

Sedgwick had little or no experience of geology when elected Woodwardian Professor. From mapping north Wales he identified the Cambrian as a distinct period of geological time and then collaborated with his friend and rival Sir Roderick Impey Murchison on the Devonian. Although he wrote no *magnum opus* he was a charismatic lecturer (born in the dales of the north-east, he once lectured to 3,000 miners on a beach in Northumbria) and a tireless advocate for Cambridge science, being a friend of Lord Palmerston and secretary to Prince Albert when he was Chancellor of the University. His legacy to his successors was a collection of over half a million specimens.

His immediate successor, Tom McKenney Hughes, concentrated on raising the money for, and building, the present museum, so it was left to A. G. ('Bertie') Brighton, the museum's first curator, to catalogue Sedgwick's collections. In thirty-one years (1937–68) Brighton catalogued 375,000 specimens. His neat handwriting can still be seen on labels and index cards.

These are collections that tell you much about the history of science in England (particularly about the Victorian golden age of geology) and specimens that tell you about the geological history of our island, tracing a timeline from the explosion of life in the Cambrian period 544 million years ago to the present day.

The museum's original specimen cases have been elegantly refurbished by the design company Blue,[36] with fibre optic lighting and new interpretative labels, models and illustrations. Each case offers a glimpse of millions of years of evolution: spiny hallucigenia and worm-like wiwaxia of the Cambrian era; Silurian brachiopods and crinoids on Wenlock Reef over 400 million years before A. E. Housman's poem; jawless agnathan fish of the Devonian age when ferns first grew and fish with legs struggled to land; cephalopods, ancestors of the octopus, squid and cuttlefish, and carnivorous spiders with a twenty-inch leg span; the extinction of nine out of ten paleozoic species by the beginning of the Triassic era, a mere 200 million years ago, when the waters receded and the land merged into a single massive continent, Pangaea.

After the challenge presented to our imaginations by these extinct species, Sedgwick's cast of the skull of a deinotherium from the valley of the Rhine, an iguanodon, an ichthyosaur or the skeleton of a giant deer, a mere 11,000 years old, that he bought in 1835 for £140, seem to embody normality itself.

This is a museum of science that captivates the non-scientist and fulfils Sedgwick's promise to 'fire your imaginations'.

WHIPPLE MUSEUM OF THE HISTORY OF SCIENCE *

Free School Lane, Cambridge, Cambridgeshire CB2 3RH
Tel. 01223 330906
www.hps.cam.ac.uk/Whipple.html

Scientific instruments from the 16th century to the present: the tools of the university's great scientific tradition

'I little thought when I bought an old telescope, for the sum of 10 francs from an antique shop in Tours in 1913, that I was embarking on the slippery slope of collecting.' So wrote Robert Stewart Whipple (1871–1953) about his collection of antique scientific instruments, with which this museum was founded in 1944.

Whipple's collecting arose directly from his work for the Cambridge Scientific Instrument Company. He began as assistant to the co-founder Sir Horace Darwin, eventually becoming managing director and chairman. That does not, however, account for the diversity or excellence of his collection. Until the early 20th century scientific instruments in Britain had, in the main, been valued by connoisseurs and virtuosi for their aesthetic qualities, by scientists for their utility. Only in Whipple's lifetime had it begun to be recognised that for the previous 400 years Western Europe's military, economic and cultural dominance was led by science. In that context the significance of the instruments that made these developments possible became compelling: instruments for observing (telescopes and microscopes; spectroscopes and stereoscopes), for navigating (quadrants, sextants, octants, plotting scales and artificial horizons), for measuring (callipers and slide rules; sundials and nocturnals; thermometers, barometers, galvanometers and whalebone hygrometers), for sweeping the heavens (astrolabes, orreries) and for weighing the earth

(scales and balances, precision, chemical or hydrostatic).

These collections are displayed here in a modest setting, behind a plain facade, a few doors down from the old Cavendish Laboratories in Free School Lane. A plaque notes that the building contains Cambridge's earliest school, the Perse Free School, completed in 1628. This is a working museum. Its exhibition areas (rooms rather than galleries) are upstairs above the university department of which it is a part.

There are historic objects here: Herschel's 10-foot telescope; the grand orrery made by George Adams at Tycho Brahe's Head in Fleet Street in 1750; and Castlemaine's globe, designed by Roger Palmer, made by one of the greatest of all English instrument makers, Joseph Moxon. Controversy raged about Castlemaine's globe, as it did about his life. A Roman Catholic, married to the beautiful Barbara Villiers, mistress of Charles II, Castlemaine was an MP, made an earl at the Restoration, twice denounced by Titus Oates (in the Popish Plot of 1673 and the Mealtub Plot of 1679), tried, imprisoned, acquitted and imprisoned again under James II.

Here are the rare (a Florentine thermometer, blown by Iacobo Marianni, *c.*1660, for the Accademia del Cimento in Florence, given in 1834 to Charles Babbage)[37] and the everyday (19th-century wooden models of crystals and geometrical solids that resemble children's building blocks).

Whipple's collections have been augmented by those of several Cambridge University colleges. St John's College has loaned 18th-century sextants made by Edward Nairne. Trinity College's loan includes a telescope in its original oak tube mounted on a four-foot stand, made by George Hearne of London. It came from Trinity's observatory, established by Richard Bentley who, having 'found the College filled . . . with ignorant, drunken, lewd Fellows and scholars' when he became master in 1700, determined to create a major observa-

Orrery at the Whipple Museum of the History of Science

tory. He achieved this despite his colleagues and in the teeth of opposition from the Astronomer Royal, John Flamsteed.

The virtuosi and connoisseurs were right. Almost every instrument here is pleasing. Some are satisfyingly elegant (the wave machines of Thomas Young, 1773–5); some exotic (Dr W. A. R. Dillon Weston's glass models of fungi, 1936–53); some exquisite (J. H. Cardin's 19th-century 'Grotto of Minerals', fragments of minerals – calcite, hematite, galena, malachite – that you examine through an alabaster mineral viewer); some (sundials and oriental astrolabes) simply beautiful.

Each has been in its time in the vanguard of scientific discovery. Each can impart its lesson to the layman. Each embodies the spirit of science that John Aubrey expressed more than three hundred years ago: 'It was Edmund Gunther who, with his Book of the Quadrant, Sector and Cross-Staffe, did open men's understanding, and made young men in love with that Studie. Before, the Mathematical Sciences were lock't up in the Greeke and Latin tongues and there lay untoucht, kept safe in some libraries. After Mr Gunther published his Book, these sciences sprang up again, more and more to that height it is at now.'[38]

KETTLE'S YARD ★★★★

Castle Street, Cambridge, Cambridgeshire
CB3 0AQ
Tel. 01223 352124
www.kettlesyard.co.uk

One of the country's most intimate and spellbinding museums, the collection of one man and his unerring eye; restorative, homely yet life-changing

Kettle's Yard offers a practical vision unlike that of any other gallery, of one aspect of mid-20th-century English and European art: the modernism, explored by Ben Nicholson and others, that led to abstraction. Here it is seen through the life, and the eye, of Jim Ede.

In 1921 H. S. 'Jim' Ede (1894–1990) was

appointed as an assistant to the director of the Tate Gallery, Charles Aitken. He had fought and been wounded in the First World War, studied at the Slade and worked at the National Gallery. He was steeped in the early Italians, Giotto, Monaco and Piero della Francesca, who inspired him to aspire to a dedication to clarity of form and line that was shared by his friends Ben and Winifred Nicholson.

Through them, and through friendships with Picasso, Miró and Brancusi, whom he met in Paris on Tate business, Ede developed a passionate interest in contemporary European art. He began to buy works by Nicholson[39] and, through him, Christopher Wood, Alfred Wallis (discovered by Nicholson and Wood in St Ives) and David Jones. At the Tate he came across the work of Henri Gaudier-Brzeska.

All these artists are represented here, but this is more than simply a collection of works. Here the setting and atmosphere, the (non) decoration of rooms, the placing of objects on surfaces express as much about Jim Ede's eye as does his selection of individual paintings and sculptures.

Ede bought Kettle's Yard in 1957 to be a home and as a place 'where young people could be at home unhampered by the greater austerity of the museum or public art gallery'. The four condemned cottages were converted by the architect Roland Aldridge[40] and Kettle's Yard became an 'open house' to which waves of undergraduates – of whom between 1963 and 1966 I was fortunate to be one – came to be given a cup of tea and to be introduced to contemporary art.

In the foreword to the 7th Exhibition of the Seven and Five Society in 1927, Ede wrote, 'everyday objects are apt to be nothing to us but mere objects, instead of having the living fluid movement seen by the artist, with whom it lies to help us also to perceive reality in this active manner' and 'We are still slaves to the insulting habit of comparing the depicted object with the object depicted.'

The rooms reflect Ede's strong views on what constitutes a good living space: scrubbed floors, whitewashed walls, the minimum of furniture:[41] the simplest setting for objects in which the smallest flash of colour startles. In 1941 he described how he would create his ideal space, 'clearing it of everything, and furnishing it with the light and air which were its nature'.[42] It makes a good setting for paintings and sculptures and for objects, man-made and natural.

Ede's eye favoured simple shapes and clean lines: an amphora, an 18th-century goblet, a Cretan bowl, a plate decorated by William 'Quaker' Pegg (v. Derby Museum and Art Gallery). He invited you to enjoy form and texture, whether of objects found (a fisherman's green glass buoy, a broom head that has lost its bristles)[43] or natural (a fossil, a stone, a seedhead, a pebble). Pebbles are everywhere, singly, in pairs, in circles, in bowls. Ian Hamilton Finlay has called Kettle's Yard 'the Louvre of the pebble'.

Here objects and art are of a piece: pebbles and stones; Brancusi's surfaces and Gaudier-Brzeska's ability to draw shape out of marble (the Rodin-like *Mermaid, c.*1913). The ceramics of Lucie Rie and William Staite Murray have been lifted out of Nicholson paintings of goblets and jugs. The textures of Nicholson's reliefs of the late 1930s and early 1940s are all around. A huge wooden screw from a 16th-century Norman cider press resembles a continuous spiral by Brancusi.

These correspondences are not forced: the materials (wood, stone, cotton) are sturdy, the textures practical, the eye steady.

Besides these objects are the paintings and sculptures. This is a rare collection because almost no one else in Britain in the 1920s, '30s and '40s was collecting these artists. The Tate (q.v.) and Margaret Gardner (v. Pier Art Centre, Stromness) started later; such galleries as Swindon Art Gallery and the Towner Art Gallery and Museum (both q.v.) much later.

The paintings and reliefs here by Ben Nicholson offer the most complete view of his career, from the early 1920s (landscapes of Cornwall and Cumbria; still lifes of goblets, mugs, jugs and pears), the 1930s (including two works from that crucial year, 1933, *Guitar* and *Musical Instruments*, painted just before he

Kettle's Yard: 'the Louvre of the pebble'

turned to abstraction; and *Relief Design* and *Abstract Design*, from 1934), the 1940s (a return to representation with *Boats in St Ives Harbour*, c. 1945, and *Pears*, 1948), through to the 1950s and '60s (*Argos*, 1962).

The same complete view is offered of Christopher Wood. A drawing of Jean Bourgoint, one of the protagonists of Cocteau's *Les Enfants Terribles*, in *Boy with Cat*, shows Wood still uncertain, his drawing of the feet and the left arm being clumsy, the chair unconvincing, but the uneasy presence of the cat and the stillness of the boy's eyes and head make clear his talent. The progress from that to the assurance of two of his finest paintings, *Le Phare* and *Building the Boat, Tréboul* (both 1930), made just before he died, is startling. In both these last the turmoil that led to his suicide threatens, in the coming storm and the Tarot cards in *Le Phare*, and in the coffin-like skeleton of the half-built boat.

Nicholson and Wood met the St Ives fisherman Alfred Wallis in 1928 and recognised his ability, evident not least in his instinctive,

confident rejection of one-point perspective. It is interesting to see Wood's work, often characterised as faux naïf, beside such true naïfs as Wallis and Bryan Pearce, whose work Ede promoted in the late 1950s and the 1960s.

Kettle's Yard has good examples of the solid yet airy paintings of Nicholson's first wife, Winifred Nicholson, and shows the full range of David Jones's talents: calligrapher, engraver, printer, poet, watercolourist.

Upstairs, the Attic is a room devoted to Gaudier-Brzeska's drawings, the remains of the collection of his life's work that Ede bought from his partner[44] and estate in 1926.[45] The linear precision of his drawings contrasts with the power and solidity of *Caritas* (1914) and the constant flowing movement of *Dancer* (1913), which is downstairs.

Gaudier-Brzeska's work, beside work by Brancusi, Miró and Ernst, is a reminder that Nicholson, Wood, Barbara Hepworth, Henry Moore and the other participants in *Unit One* and *Circle* were connecting British art with the work of Picasso, Braque and Miró in France and, from that nourishment, producing works of great beauty. Ede recognised this when others at the Tate did not,[46] J. R. Manson calling Brancusi's work 'idiotic' and 'not art', and turning down the opportunity to buy Severini, Moholy-Nagy and Matisse's *Red Studio* (v. Tate Modern).

Kettle's Yard was Jim and Helen Ede's home from 1957 to 1973, when they moved to Edinburgh; it remains as they left it. The books on the shelves are eloquent of a certain modest deep cultivation: Dante, Keats, Mallory, Milton, Browning; Hopkins, Whitman, Pound, T. S. Eliot. But for once we do not need such clues, for his essential biography is in the air of each room, and in the sculpture *Head* (1928), which Henry Moore gave him, and of which he wrote, 'In this small head the equilibrium of sculpture is reached, its life contained within its own nature; it is hard to think of it being made – it just is.'[47]

COLCHESTER CASTLE MUSEUM ***

Castle Park, Colchester, Essex CO1 1TJ
Tel. 01206 282939
www.colchestermuseums.org.uk

Great stone castle containing Roman treasures and tokens of daily life

Colchester Castle has the largest Norman keep in Britain. William I built it in 1076 on the foundations of the Romans' Temple of Claudius, making use of Roman bricks and stone. Both materials and site are appropriate to the present museum, which contains the most significant Roman collection outside London.

The Norman facing of stone, tile and ashlar has been worn away to reveal the rubble core of the walls, giving it a rusticated, almost Mediterranean, feel reinforced by the red pantiled roof put on by its 18th-century owner, Charles Gray, MP for Colchester from 1747, in the mistaken belief that the castle was Roman.

On the north bank of the Thames estuary, Colchester has always been of strategic, defensive importance, so it is not surprising that the museum's archaeological collections go back to the Neolithic period: a smooth polished flint axe (*c.* 4000 BC), found near Lawford; a pottery bowl of Grimstone ware from Layer-de-la-Haye (*c.* 4000–3000 BC), one of the earliest known pieces of pottery; the Dagenham idol, a pine wooden figure, eighteen inches high, preserved by the marshes in which it was found. With no arms, one eye socket and a fragment of nose, it stands defiant, the second oldest representation of a human being in Britain. From the Bronze Age is a cauldron (*c.* 1100 BC), found at Sheepen in remarkable condition, and funerary urns, 1500–1000 BC.

The golden age of Colchester archaeology begins in the last century before the Roman invasion. Cunobelin, king of both the Trinovantes and the Catuvellauni, had established his tribal capital, Camulodunum, here by AD 25. Unlike at Verulamium Museum (q.v.) archaeological evidence here of his rule is slight (some gold coins stamped with his mark; a running horse; some elegant 'fire dogs', *c.* AD 25). Only after Cunobelin's death did the Emperor Claudius feel confident enough to invade Britain in AD 43. He defeated Cunobelin's sons and established a Roman city here. Little survives of this first Roman settlement, burnt to the ground by Boudicca's Iceni in the AD 60 rebellion: some Samian ware,[48] a child's grave (AD 50–60) and the grave of the Stanway warrior (AD 43–60), complete with amber glass, a bronze brooch and a gaming board, displayed with glass counters laid out as if a game was in progress.

The rebuilt city, from which the Romans administered eastern Britain for 350 years, has yielded a wealth of objects (glass flasks and bottles, green as the sea; lead-glazed flagons from Gaul; the Colchester vase, *c.* AD 175, decorated with the figures of four gladiators)[49] and more than fifty tessellated and mosaic pavements. Among the finest are the Berryfield mosaic (*c.* AD 150), fragments of the Lion's Walk (*c.* 325 AD), and the Middlesbrough mosaic, whose lion and stag motif resembles a mosaic at Verulamium. This has more elaborate borders, an 'inhabited Scroll', in which are depicted a variety of birds. Two cupids wrestle in the centre panel. A 2nd-century mosaic from North Hill comprises geometric patterns: lozenges, swastikas, guilloche knots and L-shaped guilloche border panels.

Tombstones and coins give us detailed knowledge of the past and the museum is rich in both. The tombstone of a centurion of the Twentieth Legion, Marcus Favonius Facilis of the Pollian tribe in north Italy, was erected by his freedmen Novicius and Verecundus. That of a cavalry officer, Longinus Sdapeze, who died AD 43–9, records that he was a Thracian, from Sardica in modern Bulgaria. Below his horse's feet a naked man crouches; above are two lions with human faces either side of a sphinx.

There are coins here from every generation of Roman occupation (Tiberius, AD 14–37; Nero, AD 54–68; Galba, AD 68–9; Hadrian, AD 117–38; Marcus Aurelius, AD 161–80; Diocletian, AD 284–306) and then they stop and the Romans leave. The coins remained buried for 1,500 years, as did one of the finest Roman statues in Britain, a small, near perfectly preserved bronze of Mercury, a fitting emblem of this rich Roman collection, which is one of the finest in the country.

The cavernous interior of the keep should make a proud setting for such treasures, but it is broken up by hardboard pillars, pediments and display boards.

The small medieval collection is better treated. Thirteenth-century seals and a stone head from St Botolph's Priory; a 15th-century ivory, *Christ Crucified*; polychrome alabaster fragments; delicately painted stained glass; and the Colchester antiphonary (a choir book), illuminated for a Franciscan friary in Italy *c.*1260, bear witness to the city's importance and wealth, from the cloth trade, a proper continuation of Colchester's early history.

DUNWICH MUSEUM **

St James' Street, Dunwich, Suffolk
IP17 3EA
Tel. 01728 648796

Small rewarding museum with pleasingly melancholy displays of sunken Dunwich, rotten boroughs, smugglers and wildlife

Dunwich is disappearing. Every year the sea cuts away at its sandy cliffs. Roman settlement, Saxon city, medieval port – all have been eroded and erased. Today all that remains are shingle, reed beds and dunlin; about a hundred and twenty people, one church, one pub and a museum.

The museum, in a row of cottages rebuilt in the 1860s, tables the tides of the village's fortunes. Evidence of that past has been swept up on the shore: shards of Roman pottery, 2nd- and 3rd-century coins, tweezers and an enamelled disc brooch from Dunwich's days as a Roman port; medieval tokens and jewellery.[50] Growth in the 11th century is recorded in the Domesday Book: 'And 24 Frenchmen [Franci] with 40 acres of land, and they render all customs to this manor. And then 120 burgesses, and now 236. And 178 poor men.' The bronze seal of Aethilwald,[51] the last (9th-century) recorded bishop, indicates its importance as a religious centre. It was a free borough able to provide the king with eighty ships in 1241, its own seal (here) and, in 1297, represented by two Members of Parliament.

Repeatedly the sea has changed the coastline, leaving much under water, buried in mud and silt.[52] These changes, the silting up of the harbour, the diverting of the River Blyth, are shown here in graphics, as is the history of Dunwich's descent into a pocket borough and then a rotten borough in the 18th century, when Sir George Downing[53] and Mr Edward Vernon were returned to Parliament with thirty votes to ten, forgoing rent from tenants and paying 'election money' to secure victory.

No graphics are needed to appreciate the wildlife and natural history of Dunwich. Here, in cases, are stuffed specimens of local birds (spoonbill, gadwell, ruff, heron and two large, handsome bitterns) and displays of shells from the beach (cockle, whelk, winkle; mactra, razor, oyster, slipper limpets). Upstairs the museum looks across the marshes and reedbeds. In each window hangs a pair of binoculars so that you may study the collection living. The view across the reeds and the spit of shingle that faces the flat expanse of the North Sea convey better than any graphics how this exposed beach on an exposed coast has been battered continually by storms.

The stories of the great storms are told here: 1286, when 'the old port was left almost useless'; 1328, when 'the greater part of the town and upwards of four hundred houses . . . were devoured by the sea'; 1740, when 'the sea raged with such fury' that 'a great deal of their cliffs were washed away with the last remains of St Nicholas's church yard';[54] 1953, when many lives along the coast were lost and 'large pieces at the edge of the cliff disappeared before one's eyes';[55] and 1990, when part of the remaining portion of All Saints Church graveyard was lost and 'the debris at the foot of the cliffs yielded skulls and bones to those inclined to search for such reminders of man's mortality'.[56] The material in Dunwich for a museum is rich and the local people, who formed the museum in 1935 and have sustained and developed it since, have been unusually fortunate in having the services of Katherine Chant, one of the most distinguished British museum curators of recent years, who has a holiday home locally. She wrote *The History of Dunwich* in 1974 and was later director of the Royal Albert Memorial Museum and Art Gallery. She visits Dunwich frequently and is the museum's curatorial advisor. Few museums have volunteers of such ability but Dunwich deserves such good fortune. As Henry James wrote, 'I defy anyone, at desolate Dunwich, to be disappointed in anything.'

IMPERIAL WAR MUSEUM: DUXFORD *

Duxford, Cambridge, Cambridgeshire
CB2 4QR
Tel. 01223 835000
www.iwm.org.uk/duxford/index.htm

Comprehensive display of civil aircraft as well as machines of war, the might of the US Air Force

The wind blows across the flat Cambridge land: more a skyscape than a landscape, ideal for an aerodrome. Duxford has been an airfield since 1917, the year before the Royal Flying Corps and the Royal Naval Air Service merged to form the Royal Air Force.

Its history has followed the fortunes of the RAF. It was a training camp, then a bi-plane bomber base in the First World War, and the home of Cambridge University's Air Squadron between the wars. Key squadrons flew from here in the Battle of Britain before it was allocated to the US 8th Air Force in 1943; finally British jet fighters were here in the 1950s, before it became surplus to RAF requirements (too far south, too far inland) and it became first a depot for, and then a branch of, the Imperial War Museum.

This history is illustrated in the buildings that are dotted around the perimeter of the airfield: the 1930s Officers' Mess, breeze-block offices, a prefab bungalow, vast modern corrugated iron hangars and Norman Foster's[57] 1997 silver chrysalis which is the American Air Museum, its foundations sunk in a grassy mound, the sweep of its stretched metal dome blazing in the sun.

The museum is dispersed across seven hangars, hundreds of yards apart. Each evokes a different aspect of war in the air. Hangar 1, British aircraft, is dominated by huge machines, the Short Sunderland Mark V Flying Boat (1933–7) and the Avro Vulcan B2 bomber. Clustering under their wings, chicks to a hen, are the tiny De Havilland DH82 Tiger Moth and a Supermarine Spitfire F24 (the final version of Reginald Mitchell's design, dwarfed in this company). Under the Avro, the long-range bomber flown in the Falklands War, is a pallet on wheels carrying two small objects, WE177 nuclear bombs, just 16½ inches in diameter. Near by is a chunky Hawker Siddley Harrier GR Mk 3, its engines bulging like muscles, its short wings pinned back like ears, the first fighter (again in the Falklands) to be able to take off and land vertically. Incongruous in this hall of British flying machines is that elegant white bird, a Concorde.[58]

The American Air Museum demonstrates the same disparities of scale. The Boeing B-52D Stratofortress, the main strategic bomber of the Cold War, has a wing span of 185 feet and is 156 feet long. It fits in Foster's hangar with inches to spare. The other planes are squeezed round, beneath and (suspended) above it. On either side of it are a McDonnell Douglas F-4J Phantom and a General Dynamics F-111E. Hovering above are a SPAD S-13 and a Boeing Stearman PT-17, mere flies. Even the square-nosed Consolidated Liberator B-24 M bomber, hero of Second World War films, and the Boeing B-17G Flying Fortress, its beaten silver panels riveted like armour, fit under the Stratofortress wings, as does the Boeing B-29A, the Superfortress that dropped the A-Bomb on Hiroshima, and the beautiful, sinister Lockheed SR71A, the Blackbird, holder of the world speed record of Mach 3.31. You tread carefully, voice hushed, as you walk around and beneath these machines.

There are less awe-inspiring machines in Hangar 2. Here the planes are stripped down for repair and maintenance. There is a smell of oil. Parts lie boned out on the ground, engines, propellers, pieces of fuselage looking like picked-over fish. You are backstage. The principals are without carapace or prop, reduced to what they are made of, grounded.

Even when reassembled, in the hangars the planes are asleep. Their element is air.

WOLSEY ART GALLERY AND CHRISTCHURCH MANSION ***

Christchurch Park, Soane Street, Ipswich, Suffolk IP4 2BE
Tel. 01473 433554
www.ipswich.gov.uk

Tudor mansion with porcelain and plate; a panelled 17th-century oratory; and paintings by Gainsborough and Constable

Thomas Gainsborough and John Constable were Suffolk born and spent their early years here, so it is not surprising that they should be well represented at Christchurch, although, as a setting for their 18th-century work, it is unusual.

Christchurch is a Tudor manor house (1548–50) with a red-brick diamond-patterned frontage. Few objects associated with the original house remain but there are fine interiors, incorporating architectural features and furniture from other Ipswich timber-framed houses, so providing settings for the museum's ceramics (Lowestoft porcelain, creamware, salt-glazed stoneware and tin-glazed earthenware) and for an interesting collection of 17th-century portraits of Suffolk dignitaries including a Daniel Mytens of John Cotton.

The furniture collection is particularly strong, with 16th-century oak chests, cupboards and a bed with carved tester and headboard; late 17th-century pieces of walnut, walnut veneer and marquetry; and 18th-century long-case clocks, flock wallpapers and rococo plasterwork. A Tudor hall has been reconstructed to house the elaborately carved Wingfield panelling.

Of the interiors the outstanding curiosity is a tiny room lined with sixty painted panels which originally came from Hawstead Place near Bury St Edmunds, the home of Sir Robert and Lady Drury. This was Lady Drury's closet oratory in which she prayed and meditated. The panels were painted, either by her or at her direction, in 1610, the year in which her only child, the sixteen-year-old Elizabeth, died. The

QVOD SIS ESSE VELIS, NIHILQVE MALIS,
SVMAM NEC METVAS DIEM, NEC OPTES.

NVNQVAM MINVS SOLA.

Drurys commissioned John Donne to write an elegy to her, 'The Anniversaries': the first poem he published.

The images on the panels are drawn from emblematic books that Puritans such as the Drurys used in their devotions. Sir Francis Bacon called the emblem a 'narrow compass' which 'reduceth conceits intellectual to images sensible' and which, read in conjunction with the mottoes, takes the one who prays right into the heart of meditation, and whose tone is one of stern self-abnegation: 'FRUSTRA NISI DOMINUS' (in vain unless the Lord), 'DESCENDO ADIMPLEOR' (descending, I am filled), 'CUM MELLE ACULEUS' (with the honey, a sting).

This panelled room, unique in England, allows us a glimpse into a 17th-century world solidly bedded in ancient lore, largely untouched by science and increasingly hard for us to imagine or comprehend, when art was assuredly not for its own sake but had practical, evangelical meaning in a world of faith, prayer and solid consolation.

In 1932 the museum added a purpose-built art gallery, the Wolsey Art Gallery, to show its collection of the work of Suffolk artists. This is strong in seascapes (John Moore, Edward Thomas Smythe and, at the end of the 19th century, the Hon. Duff Tollemache and Philip Wilson Steer) and in landscapes (Thomas Churchyard, George James Rowe and the underestimated Henry Bright, who was a pupil of John Berney Crome and John Sell Cotman, and a friend of J. M. W. Turner).

Although the number of works here by Constable is small they are all of great interest. There are two early paintings: a *Landscape* (1800) and a portrait of his handsome younger brother, *Abram* (1806), which catches him in half-profile, uncertain, his dark curls and sideburns set off by his white cravat. The rest are from that crucial period 1813–16, when he was drawing and painting round East Bergholt, Flatford and Denham, learning to look at the landscape.

He notes in his 1813 sketchbook, 'I amused my leisure walks picking up little scraps, trees, plants, ferns, distances etc etc.' The oil sketch *The Mill Stream* (1814), in Tate Britain (q.v.), prepares the ground for *The Mill Stream* here. Its being behind glass makes viewing it frustrating but the handling of the pallid light on the stream, troubled by the turning of the inner millwheel, and of the sky above the poplars, is masterly.

The subjects of the two 1815 landscapes *Golding Constable's Flower Garden* and *Kitchen Garden* were of particular significance, both being the scene of his childhood and his long courtship of Maria, later to be his wife. He wrote to her on 18 September 1814, 'I can hardly tell you what I feel at the sight from the meadow where I am now writing of the fields in which we have so often walked . . . where some of the happiest hours of my life were passed.'

There are two fine late Gainsborough landscapes, *Cottage Door with Girl and Pigs* (1786) and *Country Cart Crossing a Ford* (1782–4) and an interesting early work, *View near the Coast* (1750–55), painted when he was living in Ipswich, an artificial landscape with rustic figures, cows, clouds and a church spire, Dutch in feeling, with something of Cuyp.

The portraits here are not those cool, rather stiff works of the early 1750s. Here is a portrait, more a competent likeness, of *Rev. Richard Canning* (c.1757) and a key one, probably done in 1758–9 as he was leaving for Bath, of *William Woolaston*, in which suddenly the composition and the brushwork are flooded with confidence. Woolaston is seated, leaning back, a flute in his hands. The gold braid, the long velvet waistcoat and the fall of his open coat are a bravura tumble of rococo shapes.

These are glimpses of Constable's and Gainsborough's early careers that add to the enjoyment of the later glorious work in the Tate, the National Gallery and the Victoria and Albert Museum (all q.v.).

The 17th-century Hawstead panels (Wolsey Art Gallery and Christchurch Mansion)

HOUGHTON HALL ***

King's Lynn, Norfolk PE31 6UE
Tel. 01485 528569
www.houghtonhall.com

Palladian palace built for 'Prime Minister' Walpole; chimney pieces and panels by Rysbrack

On the double staircase that rises from ground level to the *piano nobile* on the west front is a Latin inscription that, translated, reads: 'These stairs that were built by Robert Walpole and removed by his grandson were rebuilt in 1973 to their original design.' Their restoration brings full circle the fortunes of this magnificent house. Sir Robert Walpole, the Prime Minister under George I and II, commissioned a new house in 1720–21. Who designed it has been a matter of controversy. James Gibbs drew undated elevations complete with corner domes. By 1723 he was supplanted by Colen Campbell, who replaced the domes with towers, as at Wilton House (q.v.), publishing his designs in the third volume of *Vitruvius Britannicus* (1725). Walpole chose 'to build Gibbs's domes, not Campbell's towers'.[59]

The result is a Palladian facade with a difference, grand and graceful. It stands against its background of trees, golden cream in colour from the Aislaby stone that Thomas Ripley, who supervised the building operations, brought down from Yorkshire.[60]

Inside, Houghton is an anthem of praise to William Kent. The ceiling paintings in all the main rooms, with the exception of the Stone Hall, are his, as are the grisaille paintings on the staircase walls that tell the story of Meleager and Atalanta, and the furniture and pier glasses throughout.

The chairs and sofas, with scrolled feet and arms, in gilt, are covered in Utrecht wool velvet. Each one is magnificent, but all are outdone in the Green Velvet Bedchamber, by the state bed, embellished with needlework, above whose pedimented headboard a giant, gilded cockleshell rises to the ceiling.

The grandeur of Kent's contribution is – just – kept in place by the scale and classical proportions of the rooms. The Stone Hall is a splendid cube (40 by 40 by 40 feet), the exact measurements of the hall that Inigo Jones designed for the Queen's House at Greenwich (q.v.) a century before. Only here is Kent kept at arm's length, the ceiling painting being by the Venetian Giuseppe Artari and the chimney piece, pedimented doors and wall panel by John Michael Rysbrack, as are the statues of Britannia and Neptune on the east front and the bust of Sir Robert Walpole.

All this should be a splendid setting for a collection that George Vertue described in 1739 as 'the most considerable in England', with paintings by Van Dyck, Kneller, Hogarth, Poussin and Maratta. Twenty-five years of collecting left Walpole in debt and Houghton mortgaged. Parts of the collection were sold in 1748 and 1751 but when the nation declined to buy, about two hundred of the remaining pictures were bought by Catherine the Great in 1779. Many of these now hang in the Hermitage in St Petersburg. Sir Robert's son, the collector Horace Walpole, wrote to his friend Sir Horace Mann, 'You and I have lived long enough to see Houghton and England emerge, the one from a county gentleman's house to a palace, the other from an island to an empire, and to behold both stripped of their acquisitions and lamentable in their ruins.'

Horace Walpole eventually inherited Houghton in 1791 but by then he was in his seventies and too old to attempt to revive the hall with Strawberry Hill flair. Despite that, the contributions of Colen Campbell, James Gibbs, John Michael Rysbrack and William Kent are a rich enough feast.

LOWESTOFT MARITIME MUSEUM *

Whapload Road, Lowestoft, Suffolk
NR32 1XG
Tel. 01502 561963
www.aboutnorfolksuffolk.co.uk/lowestoft_
maritime.htm

*Cottage crammed with fishing history and
salty lore*

Lowestoft features just once in English history,
on 3 June 1665, when a naval battle took
place here. Dryden describes it in his *Essay of
Dramatik Poesie*: 'It was a memorable day, in
the first summer of the late War, when our
navy engag'd the Dutch: a day wherein the two
most mighty and best appointed Fleets which
any age had ever seen, disputed the command
of the greater half of the Globe, the commerce
of Nations, and the riches of the Universe.'
Pepys notes in his diary that the roll of gun-
fire could be heard in London. Since then
Lowestoft has proceeded with its business of

sending boats out into the North Sea in search
of herring, and the expeditious processing,
selling and exporting of fish.

This museum, in a flint-built cottage below
the lighthouse, conveys the quieter, more
detailed dramas of wresting a living from the
North Sea. The extension behind the cottage is
a chandler's yard of maritime history in which
you must rummage for Lowestoft's stories
between lifebelts and buoys, photographs and
medals, model boats and ships' bells, octants,
sextants and quadrants.

Here is a case of knots (bowline, catspaw,
carrick bend, sheet bend, and timber, half
and clove hitches) and here one of shipwrights' tools (axe, slice, socket chisel, mawl
weight, draw knife, steel drill ratchet). With
photographs and text, tales of heroism are told
of lifeboatmen and coastguards, in peace
and war, while a small wall plaque, dated 29
December 1881, tells of 'William Papper, aged
14, who was cruelly murdered on board the
Fishing Smack, *Rising Sun*, and his body

Shipshape at Lowestoft Maritime Museum

thrown into the sea. No parting, no funeral, no kind words of love, To cheer his last movements, or point him above.'

The heart of the museum, as of the town, is fishing. There are occasional moments of drama and glamour: a photograph, of 20 October 1925, of a royal sturgeon caught by Skipper Halsey, 11 feet 8 inches in length and weighing 5 hundredweight, 18 pounds, the faces of men crowding round the sea monster with pride and awe; the Prunier trophy, given annually (1936–66) by Madame Prunier, of the now defunct but once splendid St James's restaurant, to the skipper who made the largest single night's catch of autumn herring out of Lowestoft or Great Yarmouth. More typically there is the continual battle with the elements, the competition and the markets.

Photographs capture the port's glory days and its decline. In 1913 there were 1,163 herring drifters operating out of Lowestoft and Great Yarmouth. More than 1¼ million crans of herring were landed, 1,100 herring to a cran, each cran weighing 28 stone, worth £1. They capture too the lines of women on the quay packing vats of herring in brine or ice for export to Germany and Russia.

Today the shimmer of herring has all but disappeared, leaving only a roll-call of the fishermen who worked here: Cod's Eyes Robinson, Bethel Smith, Salter Freeman, Windy Beamish, Neeves, Stalks, Bush, Phinket and the Days – Chucker, Wiggy and Jogo.

NORWICH CASTLE MUSEUM ***

Norwich Castle, Norwich, Norfolk NR1 3JU
Tel. 01603 493625
www.norfolk.gov.uk/tourism/museums/
museums.htm

Crome, Cotman and the Norwich School of painters; Anglo-Saxon and Roman archaeology; the best teapots

Norwich Castle has looked down on its city for 900 years. Built by the Normans as a royal palace, it was the county gaol from the 13th

Silver Birches by John Sell Cotman (Norwich Castle Museum)

century until 1894, when the city's museum collections were moved here.

The Norfolk and Norwich Museum, run by the Literary Institution since 1824, had had rooms in which to exhibit its collections of archaeology, natural history specimens and ornithological books. Its curator from 1851 to 1910 was James Reeve. He collected sea- and freshwater shells, was a competent amateur artist and was one of the first to appreciate and collect the paintings of John Crome, John Sell Cotman and the Norwich School.

Edward Boardman was the Norwich architect chosen to convert the castle into a museum. Of the many influences on the design of museums, prisons and castles might be modestly low on any list, but they are not inappropriate. Boardman retained the features of the castle keep, transforming the prison cell blocks of the adjacent gaol complex into galleries. When the museum was further developed in 1969, by the then city architect David Percival, it was around a central rotunda, with the galleries now radiating from it. This reinterprets Boardman's design and makes it easy for the visitor to read the layout of the museum: the galleries that house the key collections (natural history, archaeology, fine and decorative arts) lead off the central hub.

The development of the museum has been shaped by outstanding benefactors and curators. Its first president, John Henry Gurney, collected birds of prey and left the museum nearly 5,000 mounted and unmounted specimens.[61] Further gifts have included a great auk (acquired in 1873) and a unique group of great bustards, now extinct in Britain. Around this have been gathered important collections of butterflies[62] and other insects, birds' eggs and W. J. O. Holmes's collection of 12,000 British molluscs.

The natural history collections reflect the nature of Norfolk, flatlands of marsh and reeds bordered by a coast of shingle, grassy sand dunes and low cliffs eroded by the sea. That erosion periodically reveals fossil teeth and

bones from the forest bed. The West Runton elephant was excavated (1992–5) from beneath a cliff, a mammoth (*Mammuthus trogontherii*) that died some 700,000–100,000 years ago along the coast.

In the Bronze and Iron Ages Norfolk was a major metalworking area and excavations have uncovered caches of gold torcs and bracelets and, notably, the Snettisham Treasure (1948), the biggest Celtic hoard ever discovered in Britain. It consists of votive material, intentionally buried by the Iceni a few years before the Boudiccan rebellion in AD 60–61. Over the past fifty years a series of excavations has brought to light more than seventy-five more-or-less complete torcs, together with fragments of 100 more. The great torc from Snettisham is in the British Museum (q.v.) but those here demonstrate the variety and sophistication of Icenian designs and techniques: 'butt-end' and 'cotton-reel' terminals; hoops that are hollow, or of various thicknesses of twisted gold wire.

With its coast facing Continental Europe, Norfolk was disputed land. The museum has strong Roman and Viking collections and the largest group of Anglo-Saxon burial urns (*c.* AD 600). The Anglo-Saxon cemetery at Spong Hill yielded more than 2,500 urns and lids including *Spong Man*, the only three-dimensional, representational Anglo-Saxon pot lid ever found.

In the decorative arts, Norwich, which had an assay office from 1565 to 1697, has one of the finest collections of civic silver (15th–18th century) in Britain, the Reade salt (1568) made by the Norwich silversmith William Cobbold being the outstanding piece. In ceramics there is here the conjoined Bulwer and Miller Collection of teapots of every size and shape. The collection demonstrates the ingenuity of the pottery industry over the past 250 years in designing and marketing novelties to respond to every fashion from 18th-century neoclassicism to 1960s pop art and beyond.

It is however for the Norwich School of painters, for John Crome, John Sell Cotman and their followers, that the museum is best known. James Reeve, the first curator, sold his collection of their drawings to the British Museum (q.v.). He had already advised Jeremiah John Colman, chairman of the mustard manufacturers Reckitt & Colman, in collecting their paintings, and it was Colman's bequest of these to the museum in 1898, followed by that of his son Russell Colman, that formed the basis of its art collection.

The reputation of Crome and Cotman overshadows the small but good collections of 20th-century and contemporary paintings: Walter Sickert, Gwen John, Wyndham Lewis, David Bomberg. In recent years the works of John Wonnacott and Ana Maria Pacheco, who have both taught at Norwich School of Art, have been acquired.

The Norwich School is put into context by an interesting group of English 18th-century paintings: Hogarth, Gainsborough, Zoffany and his underrated pupil Henry Walton. Zoffany is represented by an unusual joint portrait composition, with the landscape by John Farington and the horses and dogs by Sawrey Gilpin. There are also Dutch landscapes by van Goyen and Hobbema. Hobbema was idolised by Crome, whose last words are reputed to have been, 'Oh Hobbema! My dear Hobbema, how I have loved you.'

Despite that admiration, Crome's finest works here (*Norwich River, Afternoon*; *Postwick Grove*) show little of the influence of Hobbema. Cotman is represented by forty oil paintings including *The Baggage Wagon* (*c.* 1824–8) and *Silver Birches* (*c.* 1824) – landscapes that make it hard to understand why he was not more successful in oils in his lifetime – and by over eight hundred drawings and watercolours, amongst which are those painted at the height of his powers, during his visits to Yorkshire (1803–5), *Greta Bridge*[63] (1805) and *Devil's Elbow, Rokeby Park* (*c.* 1806–7). These demonstrate how in flattening his palette and his field and by defining shape not by line but by layers of translucent wash, he greatly influenced subsequent British watercolour painting.

The Norwich School is the only 'named' school that British painting[64] has produced, its members being joined by ties of friendship and family (Miles Edmund and John Joseph Cotman, and John Berney and William Henry Crome being the sons of John Sell Cotman and John Crome). Those they influenced (the watercolourist John Thirtle by Cotman; George Vincent and James Stark by Crome) are well represented here, as are Joseph Stannard, Henry Bright, John Middleton and Frederick Sandys, whose works merit greater attention.

This is a museum whose roots are all local: collections, curators, benefactors. Norfolk is a county of individuality and idiosyncrasy: of old Catholicism and nonconformity; of liberalism and the great houses of Holkham and Houghton; trading with Europe while being remote from the rest of England. It is scarcely surprising that its museum is so rich and various.

SAINSBURY CENTRE FOR VISUAL ARTS ✶✶✶

University of East Anglia, Norwich, Norfolk NR4 7TJ
Tel. 01603 593199
www.uea.ac.uk/scva/

Subtle building by Foster Associates houses coherent and authoratively free-thinking collection

Sir Robert Sainsbury described himself as follows: 'I have never regarded myself as a collector . . . [but] jointly with my wife, I have, for over forty years, been a "passionate acquirer" . . . my personal reaction to any work of art is mainly sensual, intuition mainly taking the place of intellect.'[65] Here are the roots of what has been described as 'one of the last century's most remarkable, strikingly individual collections'.[66]

The Sainsbury Centre for Visual Arts (neither gallery nor museum) holds three discrete collections: a small University of East Anglia Collection of 'constructive art movements of this century and the related fields of Architecture and Design'[67] (the English Vorticists, Russian Constructivists, German

Bauhaus); the Anderson Collection of Art Nouveau[68] (Lalique, Gallé); and the Robert and Lisa Sainsbury Collection.

To house their collection Robert and Lisa Sainsbury commissioned Norman Foster. Foster was thirty-eight; his two best-known public buildings (both featuring sleekly black glass) were the Willis Faber Dumas offices in Ipswich, and the Olsen building at Millwall Docks. He and the Sainsburys worked together on the design in 'a relationship so far removed from the normal realm of client and patronage'.[69] The design is rooted in the collection which, in Foster's view, 'appeared unique in its consistency which seemed to bypass fashion, style, artist periods and origins'[70] and is a mixture of European 20th-century paintings, sculpture and drawing, and objects from Asia, Africa, Australasia and America that span the last 6,000 years.

To house these Foster designed an apparently simple rectangular 'welded tubular steel box',[71] top-lit, that offered the maximum space and flexibility within, and merged public and private spaces. Glazed end walls give views on to the lake and wood outside. People can meet, eat, work and look at paintings and sculptures in one single space that is far removed from the museum as monument.

There are no internal walls on or against which to exhibit. As a consequence objects and paintings are placed in relation to each other, and to the visitor, in ways that are unlike those found in any other gallery. As you wend your way round screens, from object to object, there are always other works that enter the edges of your vision.

From the start of the collection, Robert Sainsbury trusted his eye and his intuition. His first two acquisitions, in 1932, were Henry Moore's *Mother and Child* and Jacob Epstein's *Baby Asleep* (1902–4). For someone with no training in art history, who had never bought a work of art before, they were surprising and courageous choices. Epstein's 1925 *Hudson Memorial* in Hyde Park was regularly denounced in the popular press and his relief sculpture of *Rima* was tarred. Moore, aged thirty-two, had had his first one-man

exhibition the previous year at the Leicester Galleries, which was well reviewed by Herbert Read, but his work was far from generally accepted. The director of the Tate Gallery, J. B. Manson, turned down the gift of two sculptures by Moore[72] and told Sainsbury, 'Over my dead body will Henry Moore enter the Tate.'[73]

By 1937, when the Sainsburys married, it was becoming clear that the works they were acquiring shared certain characteristics. Each was bought for the private pleasure that it gave them, not for public exhibition. Each was necessarily small in scale, to fit into their London home. Almost all of them were sculptures or, if drawings or paintings, sculptural. Almost all were representational, of human or animal forms. Most are monochrome. The Sainsburys set themselves an annual financial limit, their 'Art Account', initially of £1,000.[74] This forced them to be selective, to follow the dictum of their friend, the collector George Eumorfopoulos: 'Only buy *must haves*.'

They relied considerably on the advice and help of certain dealers (Bill Curtis at Wildenstein's and Erica Bransen at the Hanover Gallery for paintings and drawings; Pierre Loeb in Paris and William Ohly at the Berkeley Gallery in London for Indian, African and Asian art) and artists (Moore, Francis Bacon and, after 1949, Alberto Giacometti). In 1949 they also met a young dealer, John Hewett, who did more than anyone else to create the primitive, ethnographic parts of the collection. However, there is not a piece in the collection that did not pass what they described as Jacob Epstein's visceral 'stomach reaction'[75] of personal approval.

Just inside the entrance, the centre offers an introduction to Robert Sainsbury's eye: a display of some of the tiny objects that he kept in a cabinet in his bedroom, his 'Toy Department'. They are a heterogeneous mix, including a frog, a king, an urn, a horse; made of ivory, alabaster, stone, faience; from Egypt, Peru, the Arctic, Polynesia – Lilliputian artworks.

Degas: Little Dancer, Aged Fourteen
(Sainsbury Centre for Visual Arts)

The collection is not displayed chronologically or geographically. As you walk through the gentle chicanes of screens and cabinets you pass Giacometti's *Standing Woman*, knife thin (1958–9); a Mexican terracotta seated dwarf (*c.*1200–900 BC); a mid-18th-century Benin amulet; Degas's *Little Dancer, Aged Fourteen* (1880–81), chin up, shoulders back, feet in the third position; a Byzantine reliquary (AD 500–600); a Picasso drawing, *Female Nude*; three T'ang dancing girls, the first non-modern pieces they bought, in 1953; disparate works, juxtaposed, setting up odd dialogues.

Certain pieces stand out: the *Guro Mask* and the *Gabon Fang* reliquary head (both bought in 1953 from the Paris dealer Paul Guillaume); the Benin head of an oba that had been in the Pitt Rivers Museum at Farnham in the 1880s; the Khmer torso for which they outbid both Kenneth Clark and the Barber Institute of Fine Arts when George Eumorphopoulos's second collection was put up for auction at Sotheby's in 1940. 'If I was asked to name the greatest piece in the collection, I think I would probably say that the torso is very near the top,' said Robert Sainsbury, 'I can't think of any greater piece.'[76] These archetypes look across time to Giacometti's *Head of Isabel II* (1938–9),[77] Moore's *Mother and Child* (1932) and Francis Bacon's resigned and defiant *Study for a Portrait of P. L. No. 2* (1957).

What these have in common was described by Roger Fry in his *Last Lectures* as 'the vital essence of man, that energy of the inner life which manifests itself in certain forms and rhythms'[78] and by Henry Moore as 'a vitality of its own. I do not mean a reflection of the vitality of life, of movement, of physical action ... but that a work can have in it pent-up energy, an intense life of its own, independent of the object it may represent'.[79] Fry identified the vitality and the connection through an understanding of art history and theory. The Sainsburys did so through an eye, innocence and intuition that echoed August Macke's contribution to *Der Blaue Reiter*, the manifesto of German Expressionism (1912): 'Are not children creators who create directly out of the mystery of their emotions ... are not the savages artists who have their own forms, powerful like the sound of thunder.'[80]

It is perhaps inevitable that the University of East Anglia Collection should take second place to the Sainsbury Collection. It has some fine works: Victor Pasmore's *Transparent Relief Construction in Blue, White and Ochre* (1956–7); Charles Eames's *DKR Chair* (1953); five Sol LeWitt colour prints; and Tess Jaray's *Encounter Suite* prints (1972). But, separated on a mezzanine, their cool abstraction sits strangely with the passion and humanity of the Sainsbury choices. So strong and palpable is this tone that it survives even in the Reserve Collection, racked on screens on the lower floor. Beside it abstraction and passion are reconciled in the collection of studio pottery by Lucie Rie and Hans Coper that the Sainsburys put together in the 1980s. This is one of the half dozen best collections of studio pottery in Britain, made distinct by being assembled with the help of, and advice from, Rie and Coper.

Robert and Lisa Sainsbury were true amateurs. They bought only what they loved, what ravished their eyes, what inspired that 'stomach reaction'. Such a personal collection is quite unlike those found in public galleries. Although not formed as a teaching collection, it has much to teach us, about art and about collecting.

SOUTHWOLD MUSEUM **

9–11 Victoria Street, Southwold, Suffolk
IP18 6HZ
Tel. 01502 722437
www.southwoldmuseum.org/

A perfect local museum, down to the changing nature table

Many museums, local and regional, trace their origins back to a natural history society. Southwold is one of a small number that continues to be run and staffed exclusively by Southwold Archaeological and Natural History Society volunteers. Wild flowers are gathered every week and exhibited in an assortment of glasses, jars and bottles. In June you may find wild campion, sea sandwort, wild sage, tree lupin, viper's bugloss or green alkanet.

When the building, a late 17th-century cottage with a Dutch-style gable end, was condemned in 1931, the owner, Mrs Goddard, offered it to the society as a gift. It opened as a museum in 1933.

Southwold is a town that faces the sea that has been its life and its living and may yet, by erosion, bring its demise. This constant has shaped each of its main collections.

In the Middle Ages Southwold was bounded to the north by Easton Ness, a promontory extending well out to sea. As the Ness was eroded the cliffs slipped into the sea, revealing the geology and prehistory of Easton Bavents. It provided a complete stratigraphic profile of the coast, showing the effect of successive glaciations. In the museum there are the bones of the great southern elephant, whose territory this was for hundreds of years from about 1.5 million years ago to 750,000 years.[81]

Closer in time to us are objects that have been found washed up or abandoned on local beaches: 14th–15th-century brooches; a book clasp and a silver-gilt crucifix from the 16th century; a 17th-century iron key and pendant; pilgrim flasks and lead tokens sold at the shrines of saints and buttoned on to the hats or coats of pilgrims.

In this intimate museum displays jostle each other. A cabinet of pots (a 13th-century jar, a 19th-century spittoon, a 17th-century Bellarmine jar which would be buried under the front doorstep as a protection against spells cast by witches) is beside a table on which lies an assortment of pipes: clay, cherrywood, Dutch glazed; a bowl in the form of a plaster head of Napoleon III; a helmeted knight; a pipe commemorating Thomas Sayer's bare knuckle fight with Heenan over thirty-seven rounds, ending in a draw.[82]

There is a model of a three-masted barque and of a cross-section of Southwold lighthouse. There are cases of stuffed animals: a shy bittern, a heron, an otter, a whitetailed sea eagle, a buzzard and a pair of Dartford warblers. There are Coronation and Jubilee mugs going back to 1837, and there is a glass case, covered by baize, beneath which is a world, on parade, of butterflies and hawk moths of every size and character: convolvulus, privet, pine, elephant, hummingbird and death's head.

And wherever you look there is the sea, in photographs and pictures, engravings and models. For hundreds of years men launched longboats from the foreshore and fished for herring in yawls, clinker-built double-ended craft. The faces of Southwold fishermen that look down from photographs, creased as tarpaulin, defy erosion by the sea or the weather: Wally Upcraft, Worky Upcraft, Frank Upcraft; Forty Watson, Bushy Watson; Mopp Smith, Bill Smith, Little Fie Smith and Winna Smith, who insisted, 'You will never drown in a bowler hat.'

In the 20th century the town sought a future that was less fierce. With a pier, for pleasure, and (for a brief fifty years, 1879–1929) a railway, it could try on the summer clothes of holiday. Here are postcards of the pier, crested china from the sea-front hotels, advertisements that portray the shingle shore as a playground rather than ground scoured by fish and salt, battered down by the North Sea.

This is a town with its back to the land and its face to the sea. Its museum captures its position and its spirit.

GAINSBOROUGH'S HOUSE **

46 Gainsborough Street, Sudbury,
Suffolk CO10 2EU
Tel. 01787 372958
www.gainsborough.org

The artist's birthplace, housing his own works and others' that shed light upon him. Replete with domestic and artistic achievement

'If ever this nation should produce genius sufficient to acquire us the honourable distinction of an English School, the name of Gainsborough will be transmitted to posterity, in the history of the Art, among the very first of that rising name.'[83] This generous tribute to Gainsborough was offered by Reynolds in his 14th Discourse to the Royal Academy. Of the four 18th-century artists who could have formed that English school[84] – Hogarth, Gainsborough, Wilson and Reynolds himself – only Gainsborough has a gallery devoted exclusively to his work. His parental home here in Sudbury offers an opportunity to test Reynolds's claim.

Gainsborough's father, John, bought the house, a former inn, and had it altered and refaced in 1723. Four years later Gainsborough was born, the youngest of nine children. It is, in Pevsner's opinion, 'the only memorable house in the street'.[85]

Gainsborough lived here until he was thirteen, when his father sent him to London to train as an artist under the French draughtsman Hubert François Gravelot, a former pupil of Boucher. He returned to Sudbury between 1748 and 1752 before moving to Ipswich, and subsequently to Bath, in search of more and richer clients. However the influence of his family was strong. His mother was an amateur painter and a member of the Church of England. His father, a Nonconformist, had a cloth-selling business that failed. He became the town's postmaster. The decline in family fortunes meant that Gainsborough was always conscious of having to make money, at least until he began to achieve success in Bath in the 1760s.

The house contains objects that belonged to Gainsborough (a fob watch, a swordstick, a lock of his hair) but the interest of the collection lies in what it conveys of his influences, his working methods and his development as an artist.

The early chapters of the biographies of the great are invariably intriguing. So it is with Gainsborough's early works. Portraits of *Mr and Mrs John Vere* (c.1752), and of *An Unknown Girl and Boy* (c.1744–6), confirm his talent. The poses and torsos are stiff but the brushwork is already confident.

That is even more true of the early

landscapes (*Wooded Landscape with Figures*, 1741, and *Wooded Landscape with Peasants Resting, c.*1747), which is hardly surprising in view of the maturity of the Sudbury landscape of the same period, *Cornard Wood* (1748), in the National Gallery (q.v.). Already the debt to Wijnants and Ruisdael is apparent in the handling of light and shade, through, and on, trees.

The collection here contains portraits and landscapes from all stages of his working life. In *Mrs Nathaniel Acton* (*c.*1757), painted just before he left Ipswich, his depiction of her defiant glance is already bolder than of the rather blank faces in earlier portraits.[86] Only the portrait of *Harriet Tracy* (1763) marks the sudden leap forward that he made as soon as he moved to Bath and was able to study the work of Rubens and Van Dyck at such nearby houses as Wilton and Corsham Court. From his later Royal Academy years there are portraits of *Abel Moysey* (1771) and *Viscount Chetwynd* (1783). Indeed the only works that are not represented here are his 'fancy pictures' of shepherds, beggar boys and pig girls from an ideal Arcadia.[87]

Without doubt the finest late work here is *Wooded Landscape with Cattle by a Pool* (1782). Here is Gainsborough, the master of light. Every nuance of shadow is deployed: density, opaqueness; glow, gleam; reflection, diffusion. Light is revealed, melts, is extinguished. The sunset is worthy of Claude, the trees and shadows of Ruisdael or the whole of the *Landscape by Moonlight* by Rubens in the Courtauld Collection (q.v.). The evening appears to hold its breath but, for Gainsborough, light is never static: clouds build, shadows move, the light on the water slips away as, in the words of his friend the Revd Sir Henry Bate-Dudley, he 'paints to the heart'.

Although there are here none of the painted glasses used in the 'peep-show-box' experiments[88] with light that helped him with landscapes such as this one, there is a glimpse of some of his other working methods: the clay maquette he made in the 1760s of a carthorse, later owned and treasured by Constable, the equine equivalent of the dolls he used in order to work out the staffage in his pictures.

As revealing of his technical skills and his genius are the drawings here. Although he exhibited his *Book of Drawings* at the Royal Academy in 1770, he never sold a drawing in his lifetime. They were for study or for use in later paintings. The collection here is amongst the finest in existence and includes such gems as the *Study for Diana and Actaeon* (*c.*1784–6) in black chalk with grey and grey-black washes. This is a study for the oil *Diana and Actaeon*, in the Royal Collection.[89]

The sum of these rooms, these works, these objects is a sense of the man. The period drawing of his father[90] and the oil sketch of his wife, Margaret, painted on her wedding anniversary (as he made it a custom always to do) in 1785, are the works of a tender son and husband. He wrote of himself that 'they must take me altogether liberal, thoughtless and dissipated' but his letters,[91] particularly those to his great friend the composer William Jackson, are those of a subtle man of high intelligence.

The letters are free in form, fast, informal, tactless, light-hearted, not unlike the Sterne of *Tristram Shandy*. They lack the weight, the classical reference, the learning of Reynolds's writings. They move lightly like music, which he loved, but in his painting he was ever serious. Constable caught him in his lecture on landscape in 1836: 'the landscape of Gainsborough [and we might add his portraits too] is soothing, tender and affecting . . . his object was to deliver a fine sentiment, the depths of twilight, and the dews and pearls of the morning, are all to be found on the canvasses of this most benevolent and kind-hearted man. On looking at them, we find tears in our eyes, and know not what brings them.' The collection at Gainsborough's House refreshes and confirms that summation.

HOLKHAM HALL ✳✳✳

Wells-next-the-Sea, Norfolk NR23 1AB
www.holkham.co.uk

*Crowning Palladian masterpiece hung with
great landscapes, portraits, tapestries in
parkland idyll*

Holkham is a vast Palladian palace, the greatest
architectural expression of the 18th-century
Grand Tour, the epitome of the new style
that the 'committee of three' – the Earl
of Burlington, William Kent and Thomas
Coke, later Earl of Leicester – had developed,
inspired by Palladio.

It is set on an unpromising stretch of
Norfolk coast, protected from the cold North
Sea only by the trees that Coke planted. It
is a monument, in pale yellow/grey brick that
appears to be stone, to all that the three
had learned from their time in Italy, from the
Villa Ludovisi, the Palazzo Farnese and the
Palladian palaces of Vicenza.

On his tour, which lasted from August 1712
to May 1718, Coke began to buy marbles, the
best of which are now in Holkham's Statue
Gallery,[92] the heart of the collections if not of
the house. The bust of Thucydides is considered by many to be the earliest true portrait
in Greek art. The statue of Diana, reputed
to have been owned by Cicero, almost led to
Coke's imprisonment when he exported it
from the Papal States. In the central alcove is
the beautiful figure of Marsyas, bought, like
the faun crowned with vine leaves, from
Cardinal Albani in 1754.[93] These pieces look
down on Kent's gilt sofas and armchairs,
recovered in blue leather as described in the
1763 inventory.

If the Statue Gallery is the classical heart of
Coke's collections, the Marble Hall is the
showpiece of the house, its eighteen fluted
Ionic columns[94] carved by Joseph Pickford
from variegated Derbyshire alabaster, whose
colour ranges from blood red to vivid green.
They tower up from the basement through
the *piano nobile* to the coved and coffered ceiling. It is a mighty space, 'two thirds of the
width, one third of the length of the centre
block'.[95]

Only an interior as outrageously confident
as the Marble Hall could distract you from the
sequence of rooms on the south side (South
Dining Room, Drawing Room, split by the
Saloon) in which Kent was set free to create
his masterworks and on whose walls are
Coke's paintings by Claude, Poussin, Rubens
and Van Dyck.

In the South Drawing Room is Poussin's
Storm Scene, bought as a companion picture to
Claude's landscape, *Apollo Flaying Marsyas.*
Above the fireplace hangs a *Madonna in Gloria*
by Pietro de Pietri, a pupil of Carlo Maratta,
whose portrait of Coke's daughter is next door
in the Saloon.

There, above Kent's marble fireplace carved
by Thomas Carter, is Gainsborough's full-
length portrait of the 1st Earl of the second creation, his dogs circling his legs, which may
have been Gainsborough's last major commission; and, the pride of Holkham, Rubens's
huge *Return of the Holy Family.*

Next to that in precedence, and curiosity,
must be the contemporary copy by Bastiano
de Sangallo of Michelangelo's cartoon for his
mural in the Council Chamber in Florence.[96]
This, oddly, is tucked away in the Brown State
Dressing Room, which faces east.

Kent is rampant in the Dining Room and in
the Saloon. His gilded furniture is as ornate as
the marble fireplaces and the explosive ceiling
in the Saloon where, above a foliage frieze
adapted from Palladio, is a coving of octagonal
panels of rosettes taken from Desgodetz's
Temple of Peace. In an otherwise restrained
North Dining Room, whose walls, devoid of
pictures, are painted white, Kent has designed
stucco folds and tassels that are held up by the
claws of a gilded eagle and which frame a
recessed bust of the Emperor Lucius Verus.

It is almost a relief to reach the calm of the
Landscape Room and the peaceful light of
Claude's landscape, which Coke bought from
Cardinal Albani's bedroom in 1750: a moonlit
seascape of Perseus on the shore and two
shepherds with, behind them, an endless view
of the campagna.

Coke's influence was pervasive. *De Etruria Regali*, the 17th-century book by Thomas Dempster that Coke rediscovered and published at his own expense in Florence in 1723, launched the passion for Etruscan design that informed Adam's 'Antique Style' and on which Josiah Wedgwood built the success of his Etruria works at Stoke-on-Trent.

SUTTON HOO **

Sutton Hoo, Woodbridge, Suffolk IP12 3DJ
Tel. 01394 389700, fax 01394 389702
www.nationaltrust.org.uk

Well thought out display of the first page of English history in brand-new museum on heart-stopping site

Sutton Hoo is on flat, empty heathland above the estuary of the River Deben. It has no stone circle, no monumental walls, no ruins to whet the imagination: grassy mounds alone mark the passing of a great king. Yet Sutton Hoo offers the richest and most powerful insight into the Anglo-Saxon world we have.

In his *History of the English Church and People*[97] (731) Bede describes the men who had raided and then settled the east coast of Britain: 'These newcomers were from the three most formidable races of Germany, the Saxons, Angles and Jutes.' They were warriors, and pagan, and their kings, Wehha and Wuffa, Tyttla and Raedwald, ruled East Anglia in the middle centuries of the first millennium AD. One of them, probably Raedwald, King of East Anglia 599?–625,[98] who, Bede says, 'held sway over all the provinces south of the Humber',[99] is buried here with ceremony, surrounded by the weapons, silver, coins and jewellery that befitted his position.

These treasures came from Byzantium and Syria, from France, Germany and Sweden, indicative of the sophistication and reach of the Anglo-Saxon world. Most of them are now in the British Museum (q.v.), where you can marvel at the excellence of Saxon craftsman-

The Marble Hall at Holkham Hall

ship. But if you seek a glimpse of the world in which they were made, you must visit Sutton Hoo.

This is a cemetery and a place of ghosts. Indeed it might have been the talk of shadowy, ghostly figures being seen around the mound after dusk that prompted the 1930s owner of the site, Mrs Edith May Pretty, to contact Ipswich Museum in 1938 with a view to starting excavations.

You can see the route up to Sutton Hoo from the estuary, following the route that the Anglo-Saxons who buried their king must have taken as they dragged his ship on rollers up the headland before burying it with all that a king might need in the afterlife.[100]

Anglo-Saxon mound burials can be traced back to reports of the burial of Childeric, the Frankish king who was interred at Tournai *c.* 428. Fourteen horses were sacrificed and buried with him. In Britain we know only of the burial mounds at Snape and at Sutton Hoo.

What Mrs Pretty and those working on the 1939 excavation could not have been prepared for were the contents of mound 1, the abundance of objects with which this king was honoured. Here at Sutton Hoo, in the museum designed by van Heyningen and Haward in 2001, is a selection of the British Museum's treasures, some original, some in replica: a bronze hanging bowl, its central medallion delicately incised; a cloisonné sword belt, studded with garnet, blue glass and ivory; coins from Frankish mints;[101] silver spoons; burrwood bottles, a mailcoat and a bronze bucket depicting excited dogs hunting lions and an inscription that reads, in Greek, 'Use this in good health, master count, for many happy years.'

The Anglo-Saxons who made these were straddling several worlds: Byzantine, Germanic and Nordic. They could look back to residues and fragments of Greece and Rome. They were pagan but the intricate designs of their polychrome jewellery would be adapted within a century in the designs of illuminated letters in the Lindisfarne Gospels.[102]

The excavations of 1938–9, 1965–71 and 1983–93, in sifting and interpreting this

The Sutton Hoo helmet

evidence of the Anglo-Saxon world, provide a parallel narrative of the development of mid-20th-century British archaeology from the work of local amateurs to academic profession.

Mrs Pretty, having consulted Ipswich Museum, entrusted the initial work to a local self-taught archaeologist and amateur astronomer, Basil Brown, whose 'pointed features gave him the, not inappropriate, appearance of a ferret and were invariably topped with a rather disreputable trilby hat . . . His method was to locate a feature and then pursue wherever it led, in doing so becoming just like a terrier after a rat. He would trowel furiously, scraping the soil between his legs, and at intervals he would stand back to view progress and tread in what he had just loosened.'[103] Mrs Pretty paid him '30 shillings a week, accommodation in an upper room of the chauffeur's cottage and the help of two labourers from the Sutton Hoo estate'.[104]

When excavation recommenced in 1939 and rivets, from a ship, were found, Brown recorded in his diary, 'It is evident . . . that we are now up against a far larger thing than anyone expected.' Expert help was sought from Charles Phillips, Fellow of Selwyn College, Cambridge, and Christopher Hawkes of the British Museum.

Phillips was put in charge of the dig, assisted by people who were to become the giants of post-war British archaeology: Stuart Piggott, later Professor of Archaeology at Edinburgh University and the excavator of Avebury; his wife Peggy, later Curator of Wiltshire Heritage Museum (q.v.); O. G. S. Crawford, founder of the magazine *Antiquity* and Chief Archaeologist of Ordnance Survey, and W. F. Grimes, later director of the Institute of Archaeology.[105] All worked in the knowledge that war with Germany was imminent, Brown writing to his wife on 3 September, 'I hope you are alright in all this bother of war being declared.' The 1965 dig was led by Rupert Bruce-Mitford of the British Museum[106] and that of 1983 by Martin Carver.[107]

The National Trust's museum centre at Sutton Hoo tells these stories simply and strikingly well, without the intrusion of music or sound effects, but it is the mounds themselves that evoke the Anglo-Saxon world. Beyond them is a disc of landscape whose horizon is marked by a low line of trees and hedges. Its elements are sky and wind. Curlews, gulls, blackcaps and mistle thrushes wheel over the grass and out to the estuary away from this burial ground of one of the last pagan Saxon kings.

The East Midlands

There is little coherence, geographically or culturally, in this region, which extends from Derbyshire and Lincolnshire in the north down to Bedfordshire and Hertfordshire in the south.

Of its three principal cities, Nottingham, Leicester and Derby, each has two museums here. Elsewhere, there are good examples of several different types of collection: industrial (Royal Crown Derby Museum, Derby, and Coor's Visitor Centre, Burton upon Trent); Romano-British (Jewry Wall Museum, Leicester, and Verulamium Museum, St Albans); decorative arts, notably ceramics (Usher Gallery, Lincoln, and Cecil Higgins Art Gallery, Bedford), oddities (Flintham Museum of the village shop, and sleeping Calke Abbey) and the great houses (Chatsworth and Kedleston Hall).

To these last I could, indeed should, have added Burghley House with all the pomp and patronage of generations of Cecils (the Heaven Room is Verrio's masterpiece, the Bow Room Laguerre's); Hardwick Hall; and Belton House, Wren in spirit if not by his (documented) hand. The carvings in the main rooms of the Chapel Gallery are Grinling Gibbons at his greatest: ears of corn and garlands of flowers dropping effortlessly on panels. There are paintings by Rembrandt, Canaletto and Van Dyck and, on the stairs, Leighton's portrait of Adelaide Countess Brownlow, as described by her cousin, Constance Sitwell, in which he depicts 'her proud beauty, her self-lessness and her deep and tender goodness'.

Newstead Abbey, the Augustinian Priory that was Byron's family home, wants restoration and a fuller collection; association with *Childe Harold* cannot alone sustain it. That is true, too, of the various D. H. Lawrence museums around Nottingham.

This is an area of great geological and archaeological interest. The exploitation of mining (coal measures, lead seams) sustained Nottingham as the medieval centre for the production of alabaster carving; Blue John (fluorspar) from Derbyshire was a staple material for Matthew Boulton in the 18th century.

The stone circles and Beaker sites (Arbor Low, Nine Stones at Wheston) that mark the passing of civilisations in the Derbyshire moorlands are evident

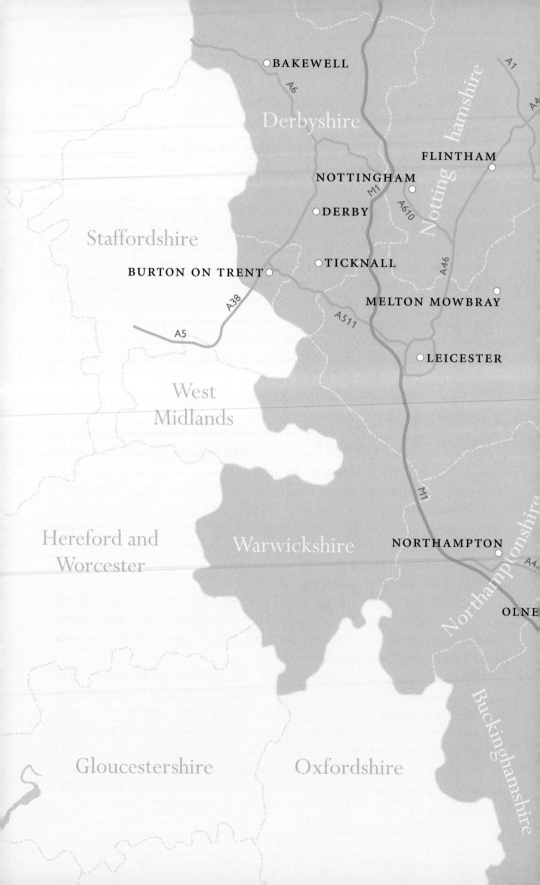

LINCOLN

Lincolnshire

A1

A1(M)

Norfolk

Cambridgeshire

BEDFORD

Bedfordshire

M1

Hertfordshire

Essex

ST ALBANS

20 miles

in Weston Park Museum and Art Gallery, Sheffield. In this region, Grantham, Newark and Scunthorpe have archaeological collections.

Near these sites in the Derbyshire moorlands is the 17th-century plague village of Eyam, whose new museum illustrates a contemporary problem: the collection-free museum. The story of the plague is interesting and affecting and the museum won awards and praise in 1998–9 as soon as it opened. However, its collection is minimal and the story of the plague is told in wall panels of (good) graphics, but graphics are a book writ large. They are no substitute for objects.

Those museums whose omission I regret most are the Boston Guildhall Museum in the building in which the Pilgrim Fathers were imprisoned in 1607, and Watford Museum, opened in 1981, with its collection of paintings by Sir Hubert von Herkomer, who lived near by at Lululand, Bushey, and works from the art academy, also at Bushey, founded by Dr Thomas Monro, for whom 'Girtin drew in outlines and Turner washed in the effects', as described by Joseph Farington.

CHATSWORTH ✱✱✱✱

Bakewell, Derbyshire DE45 1PP
Tel. 01246 565300
www.chatsworth.org

Palace and home and working house

Chatsworth is not a museum. It is a family house, but one that has been open to the public since it was rebuilt between 1685 and 1705.[1]

William Talman designed the south and east fronts before he and the 1st Duke of Devonshire (1640–1707) fell out and he was dismissed. The famous nine-bay west facade, its only facade to be brought together by a pediment, may have been designed by Thomas Archer,[2] with the active assistance of the 1st Duke. Or vice versa.

This mixture of hands (Sir Jeffry Wyatville added the North Wing, 1818–33) may deny Chatsworth the unity of great architecture but the house is at once grand, handsome and human, set in its parks and gardens and in gentle Derbyshire hillsides.

Within, there are collections of paintings (Rembrandt, Ricci, Veronese, Giordano, Hals) and furniture (William Kent, Vile and Cobb, a Tompion clock, a Schudi and Broadwood piano, a Gumley glass), sculpture and decorative arts that would grace any museum and to which each generation has added.

The 2nd Duke of Devonshire bought coins and gems. The 3rd Duke bought Rembrandt's *King Uzziah Stricken by Leprosy* (1639?) and a Van Dyck portrait of Arthur Goodwin (*c.* 1639). The 4th Duke married Lady Charlotte Boyle, the only surviving daughter of the 3rd Earl of Burlington. She inherited his houses, including Burlington House and Chiswick, and their contents, which included his library of architectural drawings, the finest collection in the country at the time. In it were Inigo Jones's designs for his court masques *The Barriers* (1610) and *Oberon* (1611). The 5th Duke commissioned Reynolds and Gainsborough to paint his famous wife, Georgiana, and Lady Elisabeth Foster, his mistress and his wife's best friend.

The hero of Chatsworth is the 6th Duke, the 'Bachelor Duke', whose hand is everywhere. He commissioned Wyatville to rebuild the North Wing and, with his gardener Joseph Paxton, created the Emperor Fountain, a feat of engineering as vehement as the beauty of its jet. He bought 'a number of contemporary' paintings and two complete libraries, and, driven by his love of stone[3] and sculpture, created the Sculpture Hall, a rare example of a 19th-century sculpture gallery. The Duke greatly admired the contemporary revival in classical sculpture that was taking place in Rome, led by Antonio Canova and Bertel Thorvaldsen and their followers John Gibson, Thomas Campbell and Ludwig Michael von Schwanthaler.

Here are reliefs by Thorvaldsen; *Mars and Cupid* by Gibson; and excellent copies of Canova's two *Lions* from the Rezzonico Monument in St Peter's, Rome: one (asleep) by Rinaldo Rinaldi, the other (crouching, watchful) by Francesco Benaglia. The pieces by Canova himself were the Duke's most prized: a bust of *Napoleon*, a seated portrait of *Napoleon's Mother*, a standing *Hebe* and *The Sleeping Endymion and his Dog* in which Endymion's lifeless body is transformed into the softest, most melting marble.

What makes Chatsworth exceptional is that here one may find paintings, sculpture and furniture of the highest quality in domestic rooms that have evolved over more than three centuries.

Many of these rooms are theatrical set pieces, baroque extravaganzas with ceilings by Louis Laguerre (and his assistant Ricard) and by Antonio Verrio, all three king's men fresh from their work for Charles II at Windsor Castle and Hampton Court Palace (both q.v.). These ceilings depict epic mythological or classical scenes (*Phaeton and Apollo* in the State Music Room; *Aurora and Diana* in the State Bedroom) but it is the covings that make them exceptional with their continual play of shadows and perspectives.

The double-height Chapel, unaltered since it was built (1688–93), is the pick of the interiors, dominated by a towering alabaster

reredos designed by Caius Gabriel Cibber, carved by Samuel Watson, his masterpiece.[4] Flanked only by four black marble columns,[5] it rises above the altar to a broken pediment, gathers itself and soars past two Cibber-carved figures[6] to frame Verrio's painting of *Doubting Thomas*. The 'feigned sculpture'[7] wall paintings, by Ricard, and the limewood carvings of the panelling are of comparable quality. These have been ascribed to Grinling Gibbons but are believed to be by Samuel Watson.[8]

Wherever you look there are surprises that delight: the *trompe l'œil* suspended violin by Jan van der Vaart in the State Music Room; the gilt ironwork by the French smith Jean Tijou (1689) and his local assistant John Gardom; the Mortlake tapestries woven (*c.* 1635) to the designs by Raphael now in the Victoria and Albert Museum (q.v.); the silver by Paul Storr, the family portraits from Van Dyck to Lucian Freud, and Tai-Shan Schierenberg's 1997 portrait of the Marquess of Hartington.

It is not surprising that the 6th Duke, in his *Handbook to Chatsworth and Hardwick* (1845), wrote, 'I enjoy being here before all earthly things ... I adore it ... I am drunk with Chatsworth'; nor that the present Duchess has commented on the *Handbook*, 'It reveals the mixture of grandeur and humility in his character, of pride of ownership and the extreme liberalism in his wish to share the enjoyment of his possessions with anyone who might be passing.'

CECIL HIGGINS ART GALLERY ★★★★

Castle Lane, Bedford, Bedfordshire
MK40 3RP
Tel. 01234 211222
www.cecilhigginsartgallery.org

Porcelain, glass, watercolours and furniture in the English taste and genius; Turner supreme

When Cecil Higgins died in 1941 he bequeathed his collection of glass, ceramics, miniatures

The Sculpture Gallery at Chatsworth

and jewellery to trustees with instructions that everything should be offered to the Bedford Corporation, together with an endowment for future acquisitions, provided that the Corporation would house and maintain it. This, after some hesitation, it did, in Castle Close, the house in which Cecil Higgins was born and died.

The will was shrewdly worded. All acquisitions would have to be approved by a 'recognised artistic authority such as ... the Victoria and Albert Museum'.[9] In 1951 Sir Leigh Ashton, the then director of the V&A, nominated Graham Reynolds,[10] the Deputy Keeper of Engraving, Illustration and Design, to oversee the trustees' decision, taken earlier that year, to collect English watercolours. Reynolds stepped down in 1955 and was succeeded by Edward Croft-Murray of the British Museum and Ronald Alley of the Tate Gallery. This novel arrangement stood guarantor of quality and is one of the reasons why the gallery's watercolours and drawings comprise one of the finest small public collections in the country.

Cecil Higgins came from an old Bedford brewing family whose fortunes he revived when he returned to the town in his fifties. In his seventies he began to collect, with the expressed intention of founding a museum 'for the benefit, interest and education of the inhabitants of ... Bedford'.[11] His love was for the 18th century, particularly its glass and porcelain. Taking expert advice, principally from James Kiddell of Sotheby's, and operating in a market whose prices were depressed by the state of the 1920s and '30s economy, he bought well.

His collection of glass is notable for its examples of lead crystal by George Ravenscroft. A jug and a dish (1676–78), both sealed with Ravenscroft's mark, a raven's head, are rare pieces[12] dating from the brief seven-year period during which he enjoyed a patent to make 'a particular sort of Christaline Glasse resembling Rock Cristall'.[13] The collection also contains fine Venetian (or façon-de-Venise) and Dutch glass.

His greater love was ceramics and his collection is strong on 16th- and 17th-century

J. M. W. Turner: A First Rate Taking in Stores
(Cecil Higgins Art Gallery)

earthenware and on 18th-century porcelain. The earthenware is mainly English but it includes such European examples as *The Four Seasons*, tin-glazed earthenware modelled by Karl Vogelmann in Wiesbaden *c.*1770 and aspiring to the appearance of soft-paste porcelain.

The porcelain focuses on the ware produced by the Meissen factory between 1733 and 1775, when Johann Joachim Kaendler was its chief modeller, and that of the Chelsea factory in its brief 'red-anchor period' (1752–6), when the factory was managed by Nicholas Sprimont and the chief modeller was Joseph Willems from Tournai.

The museum has good examples of most of Meissen's lines: figures from mythology, country life, street life (the *Drunken Fisherman*, Kaendler, *c.*1740) and Italian comedy (*Harlequin and his Family*, Kaendler, *c.*1740). Its prize piece is the portrait of Augustus II, Elector of Saxony, King of Poland, who is portrayed by Kaendler (*c.*1740) as a handsome, light-hearted freemason.[14] Kaendler took over responsibility for the Meissen factories founded by the Elector's father, Augustus the Strong,[15] in 1733 and oversaw their most glorious years, through which he (and his assistants, Johann Freidrich Eberlein from 1735, Peter Reinicke from 1743 and Friedrich Elias Meyer from 1748) mastered, apparently effortlessly, the transition from the baroque to the rococo.

Beautiful though the Meissen is, the museum is best-known for Cecil Higgins's collection of 'red-anchor' Chelsea bird tureens (the *Hen Protecting her Chicks*; the *Pair of Pigeons* – Higgins's favourite – and the life-sized *Swan Tureen*). The white feathers of the birds show off Chelsea's soft-paste porcelain with its opaque, cool white glaze, smooth as icing, apparently soft as down. The figures are based on contemporary engravings by Francis Barlow and by George Edwards but the idea of bird tureens originated at Meissen.

An unusual insight into the technical

problems of soft-paste porcelain is provided by the museum's figure of *The Girl with Flowers* (c.1740)[16] beside its original terracotta model, made about a year earlier. Such models were usually destroyed once a figure was in production but this one survives and shows how models were adapted to the demands of the kiln.

In the early years of the museum these collections (and Higgins's jewellery, his thirty-nine miniatures and the Thomas Lester Collection of Bedfordshire lace) were shown in Higgins's house, Castle Close. By the early 1970s the growth of the watercolour collection and the purchase of over two hundred items from the estate of Charles Handley-Read (glass by Émile Gallé and by Louis Comfort Tiffany; 19th-century ceramics by William De Morgan, Henry Cole and the Martin Brothers; and many pieces of furniture and silver by William Burges) made the building of a new wing essential. This released much of the house to be redesigned[17] as a series of Victorian show rooms in which there are some fine pieces: a mahogany armchair by C. F. A. Voysey (c.1905); and a fireplace by Norman Shaw (c.1881) in the Smoking Room; a huge carved mahogany cabinet by Alfred Waterhouse (c.1872) and a bronze bust of Sir Isaac Newton by John Michael Rysbrack (c.1740) in the Library; a long-case clock (c.1700) by Thomas Tompion, and a rosewood cabinet inlaid with ivory and mother of pearl made by Gillow & Co. (c.1890) in the White Room.

Most startling is the recreated Burges Room. The prize room has no connection with the house. It is a recreation of the bedroom of William Burges, the Victorian architect and designer. Charles Handley-Read and his wife put together the outstanding collection of Burgesiana in the 1950s and '60s when his medievalism was quite out of fashion. From this the gallery acquired pieces designed by Burges for his own use:[18] his bed, like the room, blood-red, with its bedhead panel painted by his friend Henry Holiday; the bed's companion dressing table; and later acquisitions which include a washstand, once given by John Betjeman to Evelyn Waugh, who

featured it haunting his alter ego Pinfold in *The Ordeal of Gilbert Pinfold*; a bookcase made by Morris & Co. (1862–3); and a decanter inlaid with rock crystal, malachite, mother of pearl, intaglios and Greek and Roman coins, its handle the hilt of an Assyrian dagger.[19]

Burges's designs pile colour on colour, motif on motif. They are the meeting of Augustus Pugin and oriental fantasy.[20] It is strange that they have come here, given that Burges hated 'the dark ages of Georgian furniture', the period that Cecil Higgins loved. Nevertheless this is the only gallery in England where his work can be seen in context.[21]

Despite this room and the excellent collections of glass and ceramics, the outstanding feature of this gallery is its collection of English watercolours, which has examples of every major watercolour painter (and many minor ones) from the 18th century to the present day.

It is a tribute to the quality of advice that the gallery has received from Graham Reynolds, Edward Croft-Murray and Ronald Alley, and from such dealers as Evelyn Joll of Agnew's, that the works are of the highest quality. Here are paintings by Paul Sandby and Alexander Cozens. His son, J. R. Cozens, has a ravishing landscape, *The Coast of Vietri and Salerno*, 'executed with uncommon spirit, very fine'.[22] Girtin's *Jedburgh Abbey from the River* is here, as is J. M. W. Turner's majestic *The Great Falls of the Reichenbach* (1804).

John Sell Cotman has several paintings here, thanks to the bequest of the Cotman collector and scholar Sydney Kitson; and John Constable has a fine drawing, *Firtrees at Hampstead* (c.1833), as do several artists who are out of fashion. There is a delicious Frederick Sandys, *Penelope* (1878). His control of tone and texture is altogether richer and more subtle than the study of *Fanny Cornforth* (1861), also in chalk, by Sandys's friend and mentor D. G. Rossetti.

Alan Reynolds, collected and praised by Sir Kenneth Clark in the 1950s, has a *Moonlight* landscape (1957) in the mood of Samuel Palmer. There is an actual Palmer, *The Bellman* from *Il Penseroso* (1881), and a fake

Palmer, *A Barn at Shoreham* (*c.*1965), expertly forged by Tom Keating (1917–84).[23]

Unusually the later 19th century (J. F. Lewis, David Cox, the Pre-Raphaelites) and the 20th century (Frederick Etchells, John Nash, Edward Burra; Ben Nicholson and Henry Moore; Alan Davie and Bridget Riley) have also been well collected.

Several paintings are of considerable significance. One example must suffice: J. M. W. Turner's *A First Rate Taking in Stores* (1818). The painting of it is unusually well documented as, also unusually, Turner allowed himself to be watched – by Hawksworth Fawkes, the fifteen-year-old son of his friend and patron, Walter Fawkes, who had challenged Turner over breakfast to 'make me a drawing of the ordinary dimensions that will give some idea of the size of a man of war'.

The boy sat and watched Turner all morning. 'He began by pouring wet paint on to the paper until it was saturated, he tore, he scratched, he scrabbled at it in a kind of frenzy and the whole thing was chaos – but gradually and as if by magic the lovely ship . . . came into being and by luncheon time the drawing was taken down in triumph.'

Evelyn Joll,[24] the great Turner expert of his generation, helped the gallery acquire it when a young dealer at Agnew's. Before he died in 2001 he wrote the catalogue of the gallery's watercolour collection and was able to include *The Loss of an East Indiaman* (*c.*1818), believed to be a pendant to *A First Rate Taking in Stores*,[25] sold by Agnew's to the gallery in 1997.

Such acquisitions have gone beyond the letter of the instructions in Cecil Higgins's will but they more than fulfil the spirit of his intentions: to found one of the finest small galleries in England.

COOR'S VISITOR CENTRE (FORMERLY BASS MUSEUM) *

Horninglow Street, Burton upon Trent, Staffordshire DE14 1YQ
Tel. 0845 6000 598
e-mail: enquiries@bass-museum.com

Brewing and beer and all (good) effects; shire horses too

Commercial companies establish museums out of both a sense of social responsibility and an enlightened self-interest, specifically shrewd marketing.

What was the Bass Museum presents a history of brewing in Burton upon Trent and a celebration of Bass & Co. In 2003 the American Coor's Brewery bought Bass and renamed the museum the Coor's Visitor Centre, while investing £500,000 in it.

The process of brewing is told with clear graphics, rich in detail (67,000 acres, the size of Greater London, were needed to grow one year's supply of malting barley for Bass in 1900; 85,000 are needed today) and in objects (bowls of hops and of barley through which you can run your hands; and a mighty pneumatic malting machine 'Retournem Mechanique', *c.*1900, made by J. Saladin, Brevete S. G. D. G., Nancy, driven by a belt from a Nander & Nander of Wantage engine, boxed solidly in wood).

Burton became a town whose economy depended on brewing because of the hardness of its water from wells that percolated through gypsum beds, ideal for the light, sparkling India Pale Ale on which Bass's fortunes were founded, and on account of its position at the heart of the network of canals in the 18th century, and of railways in the 19th century.

Brewing brought together many skills and trades which are extant here, on site. The cooperage is no longer making barrels, but all the tools are here: a chir, for smoothing the best oak from which casks were made; an auger for boring holes; an adze for cutting; and a swift for shaving and planing.

Next door four heroically named shire horses are stabled: Wellington, Ambassador, Majestic and Masterpiece. These nobles pull a five-ton dray, as powerful, gleaming and beautiful as they. The drays, with their scarlet wheels and polished shafts, are themselves as immaculate as their liveried stablemen. Together they undertake more than a hundred and fifty engagements a year: County Shows, competitions, promotions and the funerals of local farmers.

On the wall beside the shires' stalls are family photographs: *Field Marshal*, Champion Stallion, exhibited by H M King George V at the London Show of 1920; *Blaisdon Jupiter*, champion in 1915, exhibited by Lord Rothschild; *Starlight*, champion mare in 1892, exhibited by Mr Fred Crisp.

Almost as heroic as these luminaries are the engines, of which the most impressive is that built by Robey of Lincolnshire in 1905 to power eight Bass malthouses in Sleaford. Nikolaus Pevsner said of these maltings that 'For sheer impressiveness little English industrial architecture can equal the scale of this building',[26] a description that could apply to the status of the Robey in relation to industrial engineering. The Robey engine is run every Sunday. At other times it rests, in its livery of dark green paint and polished copper, smelling of oil and rags, sighing steam, biding its time.

Bass & Co. are not shy to tug your sleeve. There are pub signs and pub interiors (Edwardian: a polyphon, till, pumps, bar games; the 1960s: formica surfaces, a Bass cuckoo clock). There is Bass memorabilia: trays, mats, jugs, cards, dominoes, a motorist's touring map, all stamped with the name. There are Bass advertisements, including television commercials from the 1950s and '60s promoting 'the taste that satisfies'.

A huge table-top model of the brewery and surrounding streets in the 1920s, complete with goods yards, trains, cars, carts, backgardens, shows how Bass has saturated the town (physically).

Burton's employment and economy have benefited from Bass for over two hundred and fifty years. The town's health legacy balances a higher than average incidence of cirrhosis of the liver with a lower than average suicide rate.

There is little that tells of the lives of the men who worked here, besides a photograph of the Annual Summer Picnic at the Sleaford Maltings in 1914, showing twenty-eight employees, the manager, cricket bats, stumps and balls. Everyone wears a three-piece suit and tie. All but four have moustaches. The manager has a pale grey fedora, the men have flat caps, save five in bowlers and just one with a jaunty boater.

Nevertheless the museum is not short on animation and on triggers to the memory of Bass & Co.: the smells of horse and tack, machines and oil, and everywhere the sweet smell of hops, that continue to be at the heart of brewing whether here or in Coor's brewery in Golden, Colorado.

DERBY MUSEUM AND ART GALLERY ***

The Strand, Derby, Derbyshire DE1 1BS
Tel. 01332 716659
www.derby.gov.uk/museums

Joseph Wright; Blue John, Derby porcelain and local history

In the mid 18th century Derby was a crucible in which the Enlightenment met the Industrial Revolution. The energy released crackled through the intellectual, commercial and artistic life of the town.

Jedediah Strutt was Richard Arkwright's partner at Cromford and mechanised the hosiery industry. His son William was a Fellow of the Royal Society, as was John Whitehurst, clock maker, geologist and member of the Lunar Society. He supplied Matthew Boulton's Soho works (v. Soho House) with clock movements, helped Boulton develop Blue John for his vases and advised Boulton and James Watt on the double-acting engine (1782). His *An Inquiry into the Original State and Formation of the Earth* laid the foundations of modern geology.

Another (and founder) member of the

Lunar Society was Erasmus Darwin, physician, friend of Boulton, Wedgwood, Priestley and Watt. Around these titans were 'lesser' figures: William Hayley, friend of Cowper, Flaxman, Gibbon and Blake; Joseph Pickford, the architect who worked on the building of Kedleston Hall (q.v.); André Planché and William Duesbury, whose Derby porcelain factory established in about 1748 was the foundation of the Derby ceramics industry.

This museum charts the expression of this period in two ways: by means of its collection of the porcelain ware made by Planché and Duesbury's Derby porcelain factory and its successors between 1748 and 1848; and through the paintings and drawings of Joseph Wright of Derby, whose portraits depict many of those mentioned above and whose paintings chronicle the contemporary explosion of scientific knowledge.

This is the largest collection of Joseph Wright's work in Britain, and the best,[27] covering all periods and aspects of his career.

In 1751 he went to London to train with the portraitist Thomas Hudson, whose previous pupils had included Joshua Reynolds. By the 1750s Hudson's dominance of society portraiture was on the wane, his conventional and repetitive poses appearing stale beside Allan Ramsay's psychological penetration and Joshua Reynolds's classical allusions. Nevertheless Hudson provided more than a sound training. He himself had been taught by his father-in-law, Jonathan Richardson, and like him was a collector as well as an artist, owning more than eighty paintings and sculptures and eight hundred prints and drawings, including works by Rubens, Van Dyck and Lely,[28] which his pupils could study and copy.

Hudson's studio assistants included Joseph van Aken, known as 'The Tailor' because of the brilliance of his drapery, and Wright learnt well, as may be seen by comparing his early, rather stiff *Self-portrait* (1753–5), notable only for its handling of the red silk cloak and lace

The Alchemist Discovering Phosphorus
*by Joseph Wright (Derby Museum and
Art Gallery)*

collar, with the portraits he made of *Mrs Sarah Carver* and her daughter (1767) in which to the superb handling of costume has been added an understanding of the sitter.

The later portraits here, of *Richard Arkwright* (1790), *Rev D'Ewes Coke and his Wife Hannah, with Daniel Parker Coke MP* (1781–2) and *Jedediah Strutt* (1790), make you wonder how he could have failed so ignominiously as a portraitist in Bath in 1774–7.

Surprisingly, his portraits demonstrate little of the fascination with light that is a dominant feature of his landscapes, of his scenes of scientific discovery and even of his less successful attempts at historical and literary subjects.

The early Derbyshire landscape *The Earthstopper on the Banks of the Derwent* (1773) contrasts two sources of light, one from a moon partially obscured by cloud and by a tree, the other from the lamp by which the earthstopper works. The influences here are all Dutch, Aert van der Neer, and in *The Philosopher Lecturing on the Orrery* (1766), van Honthorst, Schalcken and Terbruggen. Two years in Italy (1773–5) opened his eyes to, in his words, the 'amazing and stupendous remains of antiquity' and to the work of Claude, Elsheimer and Poussin, which he saw in Rome.

In a letter to his sister he wrote 'the artist finds here whatever may facilitate and improve his studies.' That it did so is demonstrated in *A Grotto in the Gulf of Salerno, Moonlight* (1780s) in which the quality of the moonlight on the coast and on the water is intensified by the blackness of the grotto that frames the scene, and the fissure in its rocks through which the scene seems to crack on to the eye. It is evident too in later English Derbyshire landscape scenes that, as he wrote to his brother Robert, 'are to the eye what Handel's Choruses are to the ear . . . to have done these tremendous scenes any justice, I should have visited them twenty years ago.' He is too severe on himself: the handling of the rocks, roots and foliage, and the cool clear brown water through which pebbles may be seen in the foreground, is masterly.

It is his paintings, *The Philosopher Lecturing on the Orrery, A Hermit Studying Anatomy*

(1769) and *The Alchemist Discovering Phosphorus* (1771) that capture the revelations of science and of the age. Scientific discoveries were transforming the world. Such men as Boulton, Wedgwood and Strutt were industrial alchemists turning base matter into great wealth.

Wright captured the way in which the darkness of ignorance was being illuminated by magnesium flashes of intuition and knowledge. In the *Orrery* the children's faces are placed at the centre; their eyes gleam, while the light flickers on surrounding surfaces: skin, paper, pearls, materials. In the *Alchemist* the mystery of moonlight, through the window, is contrasted with the light from the Bunsen burner picking out the apprentice's face and the bluish glow of the phosphorus in the retort illuminating the elderly scientist's features.

James Keir, another member of the Lunar Society and discoverer of an alloy called eldorado (v. Soho House), had translated Macquer's *Dictionnaire de Chimie*, in which the making of phosphorus is described. Wright has turned those descriptions of experiments into enduring images.

The museum's ceramics collections cover Derby's ceramics industry from the mid 18th century to the present day but it is the work of the first Derby porcelain factory of Planché and Duesbury that is of particular interest. One of the earliest pieces is Planché's exuberant *Chinaman*.

The Chinaman demonstrates the improvements both in the factory's paste and in the confidence of the modelling. A little boy with arm raised looks up from the base, part of the swirling rhythms of the piece, twisting up as the Chinaman's long coat, legs and eyes fly out in all directions until they are resolved in the balance of the outstretched arms and the steady poise of the head and the neat beard: a triumph of ecstatic rococo.

After 1756 the company produced a succession of brilliant pieces such as this and went on to establish a reputation for producing the best flower decoration on plates. The origins of these skills can be seen here in the Prentice plate, the template from which

all apprentices were taught. It was painted in about 1790 by William Billingsley, the most celebrated of Derby's flower painters. Although battered by fifty years in the decorators' shop, being copied and handled, its border of pink roses, each distinct, each in a different position, retains its freshness. The petals are yielding and plump, each stem turns gracefully, each bloom has a depth and solidity created by Billingsley's technique of lifting out the highlights with a dry brush.

There were other decorators and modellers who worked for Duesbury, notably William 'Quaker' Pegg, Fidele Duvivier, 'Jockey' Hill, Zachariah Boreman and the modeller J.J. Spängler. But the 'Bloor-Derby' period (1811–48) saw a decline and the flair and invention that marked the early Planché and Duesbury years, and which charged the whole town in the previous generation, were dampened. For fifty years Derby had caught fire and the evidence is here.

KEDLESTON HALL **

Quarndon, Derby, Derbyshire DE22 5JH
Tel. 01332 842191
www.nationaltrust.org

Robert Adam's Roman home for the Curzons

Even before it was finished, Kedleston was open to the public, who came to marvel at what the 18th-century travel writer Sir Richard Sullivan described as its 'grandeur and magnificence'. 'In one word,' he continued, 'the whole strikes you as if it were designed for a more than mortal residence ... the hand of taste is evident in every part of it.'

He was right. Kedleston is the supreme early work of one of Britain's great artists, Robert Adam. It demonstrates how swiftly the classical taste and eye, acquired on the Grand Tour, captured England and how swiftly too, in the hands of Adam, it evolved. Here he is, at the start of his career, so much the master of the Palladian style that he could widen its

The Saloon at Kedleston Hall

classical vocabulary with a baroque energy and express it in the landscaping of the park, in the facade of the house, in the detail of plaster-work and furniture, and above all in the Marble Hall and the Saloon.

There are fine paintings in the house, which was the home of the Curzons: Curzon family portraits by Dahl, Kneller, Jonathan Richardson and Arthur Devis, and a Nathaniel Hone of *Sir Nathaniel Curzon, 1st Lord Scarsdale and his wife Caroline*, a full-length landscape studio portrait whose composition is not unlike Gainsborough's *Morning Walk*. Scarsdale's collection of paintings[29] includes Cuyp's ravishing *Ideal Landscape at Dusk* (one of the first Cuyps to come to England) and paintings by Luca Giordano, Ludovico Carracci, Benedetto Luti and Bernardo Strozzi. In the Indian Museum are the treasures brought back by Lord Curzon from his reign as Viceroy of India (1899–1905), none more dazzling than the peacock dress his first wife wore at the evening ball that followed the Coronation Durbar in Delhi in 1903. Made of cloth of gold with a pattern of overlapping peacock feathers in gold and silver thread, its train is trimmed with embroidered roses. This shimmering dress, bequeathed to Kedleston by his last surviving daughter in lieu of tax, speaks of the wealth, power and privilege of Imperial India and anticipates the inevitability of independence in 1947.[30]

Despite these attractions Kedleston is about Adam. You enter the park through the North Lodge (1760–62), whose design was based by Adam on the Arch of Octavia in Rome. He added wrought-iron gates by Benjamin Yates of Derby. The drive winds through the deer park to Adam's elegant three-arched bridge which crosses the lake where the Upper Lake falls down a cascade (1770–71) into the Middle and Lower Lakes.[31] From here you look across to the north facade of the house.

Sir Nathaniel had inherited Kedleston in 1758 and at once commissioned Matthew Brettingham, the executive architect of Lord Coke's Holkham Hall (q.v.) under Burlington and Kent, to design a new house. Adam was employed only on the designs of the gardens and their associated temples and lodges.[32] The ambitious Adam saw the possibilities and wrote to his brother James in December 1758, that he had 'got the entire Manadgement of his [Curzon's] grounds put into my hands with full powers as to Temples, Bridges, Seats and Cascades . . . you may guess the play of Genius & the Scope for Invention. A noble piece of water, a man resolved to spare no Expense, with £10,000 a Year, Good Temper'd & having taste himself for the Arts and little for Game.'

At the same time Sir Nathaniel consulted Adam about Brettingham's designs and within eighteen months Adam had supplanted not only Brettingham but his short-lived successor, James Paine.

Adam retained Brettingham's and Paine's original plan for the central block of the house, flanked by pavilions, but he made the north and south facades his own. The north, seen from the bridge, has a raised portico and six commanding Corinthian columns, as proposed by Paine.[33] On the south facade Adam substituted his own design (and carved an ambiguous 'AMICIS ET SIBI') with, at its centre, above a curved double staircase, a triumphal arch based on the Arch of Constantine in Rome.

Better than any other of his buildings, it exemplifies what Adam called 'movement' in architecture: 'The rise and fall, the advance and recess with other diversity of form, in different parts of a building, so as to add greatly to the picturesque of the composition . . . That is they serve to produce an agreeable and diversified contour, that groups and contrasts like a picture, and creates a variety of light and shade, which gives a great spirit, beauty, and effect to the composition.' Adam is painting in stone.

The promise of the facade is fully redeemed inside, particularly in the two great rooms, the Marble Hall and the Saloon. Throughout Adam employed his familiar team of artists and craftsmen: his chief draughtsman, George Richardson; Joseph Rose for the plasterwork; and Antonio Zucchi, William Hamilton, Morland and Zuccarelli for ceilings and panels.[34]

The Hall has twenty fluted columns of pink-and green-veined Nottinghamshire alabaster[35] whose Corinthian capitals are based on those Adam had seen in the Temple of Jupiter Stator near the Forum in Rome. The floor, of local Hopton Wood stone inlaid with white Carrara marble, has a design as sensuous as the columns are severe.

The softly pink and green ceiling is by Rose; the fireplaces are by Moneypenny; the fire baskets by Adam[36] and the roundels after Gravelot and Domenichino. In the niches are casts of antique Italian statues (the *Medici Apollo, Medici Venus, Apollo Belvedere, Vatican Meleager,* etc.) Twelve painted benches (1788) by John Linnell, to Adam's design, based on those on the Tomb of Agrippa in Rome, are the only furniture.

The grandeur of the whole makes this as stunning an entrance to a house as exists in Britain. It is matched by the Saloon that flanks it, beneath its huge rotunda, whose form Adam borrowed from the Pantheon in Rome. To the dome he added gilded rosettes and octagonal compartments inspired by the Basilica of Maxentius and the Temple of Venus in the Roman Forum. Above the doors are paintings of Roman ruins by William Hamilton; above the niches, brown monochrome panels of scenes from British history by Biagio Rebecca. The wooden floor was sprung for dancing but it was at first carpeted, to an Adam design that echoed the ceiling.

The Saloon is the vestibulum to the Marble Hall's atrium,[37] a room the Romans considered sacred to the gods and one that Adam intended would fill the mind 'with extensive thoughts' and stamp upon its visitors 'the solemn, the great and the majestic' that he found lacking in contemporary buildings.

Kedleston is full of other Adam-related pleasures: Rose's chaste white plasterwork in the Library; the four huge sofas carved by Linnell in the Drawing Room with their gilded mermaids and sea gods, inspired by Bernini; the mirrors (and an organ case in the Music Room) carved by Gravenor to Adam's design; the excess of the State Bed (also by Gravenor) with its palm tree bedposts topped by wild fronds. These stupendous props lie beneath Rose's most simple and plain neo-classical ceiling. Were these taken from their context and exhibited they would be the glories of any museum. Here they are integral to Adam's grand design.

Despite all these it is the facades and the two main rooms that are Adam's masterworks and that embody the Grand Tour design ideas of the mid 18th century and by which, as Sullivan wrote, 'the senses become astonished'.

ROYAL CROWN DERBY MUSEUM *

194 Osmaston Road, Derby DE28 8JZ
Tel. 01332 712800
www.royal-crown-derby.co.uk

More than two centuries of princely ware and master craftsmen at work

Royal Crown Derby is about decoration. The figures and ware produced since *c.*1750 by the manufactories that eventually became Royal Crown Derby are distinguished by the brilliance of their painters: 'Jockey' Hill, Zachariah Boreman, William Billingsley and William 'Quaker' Pegg in the 18th century; in the 19th century, first George Robertson, John Haslem, William Corden and Robert Brewer; then James Rouse Snr, Moses Webster and Désiré Leroy; in the 20th century Albert Gregory, William Mosley and John McLaughlin. No other pottery can demonstrate a succession of such quality.

Like Wedgwood, Spode and Minton, Royal Crown Derby has retained its pattern books and examples of its ware. Like Spode, but unlike Wedgwood and Minton,[38] Royal Crown Derby has a museum on the site of its factory, on the first floor of its visitor centre in a nondescript 1950s building. Its appearance, carpeted, anonymous, owes more to the showroom than the gallery, but the cabinets, arranged chronologically, are well lit and the quality of the ware shines through and overcomes the flat atmosphere.

Being able to view pieces close up allows you

to appreciate not only the skill of the painters but the qualities of the bodies: the soft-paste porcelain recipe that André Planché brought with him[39] from London in 1748, so suited to modelling; the later addition of calcinated animal bone, which gave Derby a surface so sympathetic to decoration;[40] the white, marble-like Parian ware.

The chronological display reveals no observable period of uncertainty in either the modelling or painting. The design skills of André Planché, the Huguenot designer who joined Duesbury, were absorbed at once. Here is the figure of a small charging bull, head down to the ground, a hoof raised, its eye and tail and the flower-strewn ground painted with precision and delicacy. Standard European subjects (*commedia dell'arte* figures, Chinese and mythological subjects) were refreshed by a vitality and humour that rivalled the Continental porcelain makers Sèvres and Meissen.

William Duesbury I, who went into partnership with Planché in 1756, was always keenly aware of competition. He bought the Vauxhall, Kentish Town, Bow and Chelsea works, closing them all by 1784 and bringing the best of their craftsmen to Derby to remodel existing figures. The effect of this can be seen in the Kedleston vase, made for Lord Scarsdale in 1790, its snake handles modelled by J. J. Spängler, its panels painted by Zachariah Boreman and James Banford, its swags of roses by Billingsley.

Derby had a succession of shrewd and imaginative owner/managers. Duesbury and his son, William Duesbury II, along with business partner Michael Kean, were succeeded by their clerk, Robert Bloor. When Bloor died the Nottingham Road factory closed in 1748 but the best of the potters and painters transferred to a new factory in King Street (1848–1935). The old shapes and patterns were retained and the quality of the ware maintained.

Important though this continuity of management, models and skills was, what distinguished Derby was the quality of the decoration and particularly the brilliance of William Billingsley and William 'Quaker' Pegg.

Billingsley was apprenticed to William Duesbury I in 1774, aged sixteen. He clearly learnt much from other Derby painters, Zachariah Boreman and Edward Withers. By his early twenties he had transformed the painting of highlights on flowers. Traditionally this was achieved by letting the white unpainted glaze be the highlight. Billingsley painted through and then brushed out in order to include further colours that added a new richness and subtlety to the exquisite delicacy of his mixed arrangements of flowers.

Examples of Billingsley's work can be seen in Cardiff, Swansea and Lincoln as, dogged by his successive failures in business, he moved from factory to factory. In contrast this museum offers a rare opportunity to appreciate Pegg's work, since he worked only in Derby, apart from a period of twelve years (1801–13) when he worked in a stocking factory. He joined the Society of Friends in 1800 and, enjoined by the prohibition in George Fox's *Book of Doctrinals* that 'Thou shalt not make any graven image, or the similitude of any figure ... by the express command of God', burnt his drawings and books.[41]

When he returned, for only seven years, the richness of his colours and his understanding of flowers (his father had been a gardener at Etwall Hall near Derby) matched that of Billingsley. Plates that depict a gentian (*c.* 1813) and a moss rose within a trailing ivy border (1820) have an immediacy that comes from painting from life, in contrast to the work of other decorators who relied on such works of botanical illustration as *Curtis's Botanical Magazine*. Pegg's 1813 *Sketchbook* of 112 watercolours and drawings demonstrates the delicacy of his skills.

The influence of Billingsley and Pegg can be seen in subsequent Derby painters, the Hancocks, John Whitaker, Moses Webster, Désiré Leroy and Albert Gregory. Those later

Italian commedia dell'arte figure, after a Meissen original (Royal Crown Derby Museum)

generations are well represented in the collection of 135 pieces that Ronald William Raven gave the museum in 1987, which sum up the sustained brilliance of Royal Crown Derby decoration.

FLINTHAM MUSEUM *

The Reading Room, Inholms Road,
Flintham, Nottinghamshire NG23 5LF
Tel. 01636 525111
www.flintham-museum.org.uk

One village shop through the 20th century

Founding bequests come in many shapes and sizes. Flintham's was singular, in both senses: the accumulated stock of a Nottinghamshire village shop, from 1911 to 1970, given by Miss Muriel White. It provides an unusual, even unique, view of a village community and of how people lived in rural England in the 20th century.

Miss White's father Fred opened the shop, White's Stores, in Main Street, in 1911. His aim was to supply anything and everything:

A century of stock at the Flintham Museum

groceries and tobacco; confectionery and stationery; toys, bicycles, musical instruments and medicines. He was the village milliner and the village photographer.

When Mr and Mrs Trevor Clayton, two of the museum's founding committee, first explored Miss White's '100 years of accumulated stock', they found over six hundred photographs taken by Mr White between 1895 and 1915: wedding groups, the building of a hayrick, badger baiting, a missionary's travelling caravan, the celebrations for Queen Victoria's Diamond Jubilee in Louth and dozens of photographs of Flintham. Some were half-plate glass negatives and one was a 15-inch by 12-inch plate of the *Plough Play*, a traditional folk drama of 'Birth, Death and Regeneration' performed annually in the village on Plough Monday, the first Monday in January, and featuring Beelzebub, St George, the Doctor, the Recruiting Officer, the Horseman, and Tom Fool and his love. The play was last performed in 1915.

Mr White kept a record of the weather, every day from 1912 to 1962. The museum has maintained this record and turned it into a display, changing daily, charting the weather across the decades. On 13 June 1912 there were showers; on that day in 1922 there was steady rain all day; 1932, fine and bright; 1942, heavy rain; 1952, dull and rainy; 1962, fine and warm.

Fred White was also the village's special constable and the Liberal Party Agent. He was in the Home Guard and kept the records of the village school from 1890 to 1940.

He never reduced prices, never had a clearance sale and never disposed of unsold stock, so here are packets of gramophone needles and of seeds (asters, lupins, mignonettes, candytuft); books and sheet music; bars of Peerless Erasmic soap and bottles of Carter's bath salt (the same firm, with the same logo, as that which sells seeds today).

Fred White dispensed Bland's pills (iron), liver pills, nerve powder, bile beans, influenza powder, children's worm powders, senna pods, syrup of rhubarb, Dr Maclean's stomach tablets and 'Mau Zau for Piles'.

From 1939 to 1953 he was responsible for not only the ration books but also the Ministry of Food licences. To run his shop he needed fifty-one separate licences. He had a sign to hang on the shop window, 'Register Here for Onions', from 1941 to 1942 when a poor crop led to onions being rationed.

From the first, in 1913, he offered ladies' woollen underwear: ladies' combinations, slender, 17s. 11d., outsize, 20s. 5d.; and ladies' bodices and spencers, 12s. 5d. and 14s. 5d. When popular music gained a hold, promoted by wireless programmes, he stocked sheet music and records: Rolando and his Blue Salon Orchestra; the Paramount Rhythm Boys with 'It Must be True' and 'When I Take my Sugar to Tea'.

All this is crammed into a two-roomed cottage which has its own history. It was a charity school in 1779, the village reading room in 1874, a clinic in the Second World War and used by the Scouts in the 1980s and '90s. As you scan its walls the years pass in a domestic elegy of brand names: Lokdine, Iodine socks, Victory Roll toilet paper, Wills's Sea King Plug, Mazawattee tea, Rinso, Nuttall's Mintoes, Parrish's Chemical Food and Ju-Vis, 'the Extract with the Full, Rich Flavour'.

From the first, Fred White found that making a living from a village shop was a struggle. In 1913 he printed and circulated a leaflet that asked, 'Why should I trade in my own village?' and offered four reasons, the last of which was, 'I can select what I require and see what I am purchasing, instead of buying "a pig in a bag".'

Today the committee of volunteers who maintain this collection ensures that it is a living museum. The weather continues to be charted daily, photographs taken and Flintham recorded.

JEWRY WALL MUSEUM *

St Nicholas Circle, Leicester, Leicestershire
LE1 4LB
Tel. 0116 225 4971
www.leicester.gov.uk/museums

Prehistoric, Roman and medieval artefacts; dramatic recreations of street scenes

What is now Leicester was at the dead centre of Roman Britain. Within four years of the invasion the Roman army had conquered the local tribe, the Corieltauvi, and built a regional capital, Ratae Corieltauvorum, served by a network of straight Roman roads, of which the Fosse Way is the longest and straightest.

As you drive into Leicester from the south you arrive at a huge roundabout on the inner ring road. Below, to the left, at Roman level, is the Jewry Wall Museum. On top of the museum, at street level, is the Institute for Lifelong Learning, the Adult Education Department of the University of Leicester.[42] Opposite the museum rises the massive Jewry Wall.

The museum's front on to the enclosed rectangular site is a glass wall, 'scarcely a barrier between the site and the related material inside'[43] in the opinion of Pevsner, allowing you to stand poised between modern and Roman Leicester.

Excavations in 1936–9 exposed the footings of Roman baths, arranged symmetrically, the cold baths flanked by larger hot rooms and changing rooms. In front of the glass wall are the furnaces that heated the water. Reduced to their foundations, the baths invite you into the minds of the men who designed and built them, with the orderly arrangement of space, the drains, the building techniques alternating thin bricks and stone, a rational mapping.

Inside the museum is the rich detritus of a Roman city: storage jars, Spanish amphorae, flagons, mortaria (mixing bowls); beakers, bowls and cups of red Samian ware; bronze spoons, glass cups. There are penannular brooches, silver rings, pins of bone and bronze, jewellery of jet; coins, dice, counters, a bronze lampstand, funerary jars and the (very rare) base of a Roman wooden coffin. A small child, wandering into the drying yard, has left his footprint on a roof tile before it was fired. A fragment of pottery is inscribed as a love token between Verecunda, an actress, and Lucius, a gladiator.

Ratae Corieltauvorum was the centre of the Western School of Romano-British mosaics, characterised by borders of overlapping shield patterns and miniature scroll work, which surround the 2nd-century Blackfriars mosaic here, excavated in 1830, one of the best examples of Roman craftsmanship in Britain.[44]

The *Peacock Mosaic* (c. AD 140–45) has, astride its central panel, a peacock whose feathers are highlighted by tesserae of blue glass. Faustina, the wife of the Emperor Antonius Pius, had died in AD 141. Her followers had adopted the peacock as her symbol, associating her with Juno, Jupiter's sister and wife, the Queen of the Gods, to whom peacocks were sacred.

The museum has wall paintings of the same period, c. AD 150–200, more elaborate than those at Verulamium Museum (q.v.). Their lower panels are painted to imitate marble veneer; the larger rectangular panels above are decorated with painted garlands. Excavated at Norfolk Street,[45] they have been restored by Dr Theodore Sturge, who also excavated the Blackfriars pavement.[46]

The Jewry Wall, its back to the Church of St Nicholas, presents its appropriate face composed of gritstone, Leicestershire granite and thin Roman brick.

LEICESTER NEW WALK GALLERY AND MUSEUM ✳✳✳

53 New Walk, Leicester, Leicestershire LE1 7EA
Tel. 0116 225 4900

The only German Expressionist collection in Britain. Natural history as good as its excellent paintings, ceramics and glass

Dr E. E. Lowe, director of Leicester Museum and Art Gallery after the First World War and president of the Museums Association, said in his 1922 Presidential Address: 'I feel more and more strongly as time passes that the chief aims of provincial museums and art galleries ... should be inspirational.'[47] For Richard and David Attenborough, children in Leicester between the wars, his museum was an inspiration: for one to become an actor and film director, the other a natural scientist.

With its collections of paintings, porcelain, insects, stuffed animals and birds, Leicester was in Lowe's time no more than a typical provincial museum, though typical of the best.

When in 1845 an Act of Parliament allowed local councils to levy a halfpenny rate to establish museums for the 'Instruction and Amusement of the Inhabitants', Leicester was among the first towns to take advantage of the opportunity, opening this museum on 19 June 1849 in the former Proprietary School on New Walk when the Leicester Literary and Philosophical Society transferred its collection to the town council. The museum is good-looking, a pedimented Greek Revival building designed by Joseph Hansom. It was filled from the first with 'foreign Curiosities, Indian Dresses ... Locomotive Machines' and an Egyptian mummy. A bequest in 1869 of 648 birds and animals under the will of Henry Bickley of Melton Mowbray ensured that the museum always had a strong natural history collection. Today it has an outstanding collection of bird skins and mounts, and, to its credit, has kept faith with its taxidermy.

The museum's curator in the 1880s and '90s, Montagu Browne, was a skilled taxidermist renowned for his *Two Tigers Fighting over an Elephant*, although this example has not survived. His work takes its place in a collection that includes most of the great 19th- and 20th-century taxidermists: Thomas Gunn of Norwich, one of whose representative specimens is a pink-footed goose; William Farrer of Cambridge, a chunky woodcock; the brothers Joseph and John Cullingford of Durham, a red-footed falcon on a bare branch, typical of their plain settings; also Peter Spicer, a barn owl in the act of catching a mouse with a delicately painted wooded background; and the great taxidermy firm Rowland Ward of London, who specialised in big game trophies, make their presence felt with notables such as leopard, polar bear, zebra, gorilla and orangutan. There is a tradition here of curator/taxidermists: Ted Williams worked in the museum until 1971 and later a splendidly muscular tiger that died in a local zoo was prepared by John Metcalf. The tradition continues today with Nigel Killips's poised kestrel.

The museum was relatively slow to collect fine art. A picture gallery was added in 1885 and advice sought on acquisitions from John Ruskin, who, somewhat surprisingly, replied: 'What use is there in me telling you what to do? The mob won't let you do it. It is fatally true that no one nowadays can appreciate pictures by the old masters, and that every one can understand Frith's *Derby Day*.' A committee of six 'gentlemen of the town' bought works by Frith, Ibbetson, Morland and Faed, Wilkie and the predictable Cooper cows during the period 1885–1908. In 1937, *The Meeting of Jacob and Rachel* by the Nazarene William Dyce was acquired. Ruskin was right to the degree that William Small's sentimental *Good Samaritan* was for many years the most popular painting.

Quietly, a good watercolours and drawings collection has been built up, as strong in 20th-century works as in those of the 18th and 19th centuries; 20th-century prints are well represented, including works by Hockney, Blake, Paolozzi and Lichtenstein. The English ceramics collection from the late 17th century to the present day is as wide-ranging as any other bar that in the Potteries Museum

and Art Gallery in Stoke-on-Trent (q.v.), the only significant omissions being Swansea and Nantgarw ware.

Among the Old Masters in the museum's collection are a mysterious, dark altarpiece of *The Holy Family* (c. 1530) by the Sienese Domenico Beccafumi, a delightful small portrait of a girl (1655–60) by Michael Sweerts, its gentle palette and soft shifts of light recalling Vermeer. The outstanding acquisition has been a little predella panel, *St John the Baptist Entering the Wilderness*. It was bought with help from the National Art Collections Fund in 1959 as attributed to Andrea di Bartoli but is now accepted as being by Lorenzo Monaco, the foremost artist in Florence in the early 15th century.[48]

English 20th-century paintings have been bought (Stanley Spencer, Mark Gertler, Matthew Smith, more recently Ivon Hitchens, Francis Bacon and Peter Doig) but what sets Leicester apart is its unique – for Britain – collection of German Expressionists.

In 1940 Trevor Thomas succeeded Dr Lowe as director and appointed as his assistant Hans Hess, a German refugee. With considerable courage Trevor Thomas mounted an exhibition of sixty-two German Expressionist paintings under the title *Mid-European Art*. Thomas persuaded the museum to buy works by Franz Marc (*Rote Frau*, 1912), Lyonel Feininger (*Behind the Church*, 1916) and Emil Nolde's seminal Die Brucke watercolour *Head With Red-Black Hair* (c. 1910), its primitive, mask-like face lit startlingly from below.[49]

In 1955, Thomas's courage was rewarded when twenty-four works on paper by Karl Schmidt-Rottluff were received from the estate of Dr Rosa Schapire. With further gifts and purchases the collection now includes works by the other Die Brucke artists, Ernst Ludwig Kirchner, Max Pechstein, Otto Mueller and Erich Heckel; and those who exhibited with Die Neue Sezession in 1910: Ernst Barlach, Max Beckmann, Käthe Kollwitz, as well as Oscar Kokoschka and Lovis Corinth. It is a collection whose quality and depth is equivalent to that of Tate Modern (q.v.). Hess went on to be director of the York Art Gallery (q.v.). Thomas had his contract terminated as a result of a court case relating to his homosexuality.

In the almanac *Der Blaue Reiter* (1910) Franz Marc wrote that all young artists should seek 'to create in their work symbols for their age, which will go on the altars of the coming spiritual religion'. Marc was killed at Verdun in 1916. His *Rote Frau* continues to remind us what was lost and what verve has repeatedly since been betrayed.

USHER GALLERY, LINCOLN **

Lindum Road, Lincoln, Lincolnshire
LN2 1NN
Tel. 01522 527980
www.lincolnshire.gov.uk/Usher.htm

Coins, miniatures, enamels and the largest Peter De Wint collection; Tennysoniana

James Ward Usher (1845–1921) was a jeweller and the son of a jeweller/watchmaker. It is not perhaps surprising that throughout his life he should have collected clocks and watches, coins and silver, enamels, miniatures and ceramics. After thirty years of collecting he published, in 1916, 'an illustrated record of it [his collection], historical and descriptive in character . . . I can safely say that all my leisure time . . . has been devoted to it. I have indeed been wedded to it.'[50] He bequeathed it to the city of Lincoln, along with a capital sum sufficient to build a gallery,[51] in the hope that 'it might form the nucleus of an art gallery and museum worthy of the City' and would demonstrate that 'my life has not been in vain, and that I have left Lincoln a little bit better than I found it.'[52]

Sir Reginald Blomfield, architect of the Menin Gate at Ypres, who had recently converted the Sydney Hotel in Bath (1913–16) into the Holburne Museum of Art (q.v.), built the gallery on a site just below the cathedral. It is a solid, rather dull building described by Pevsner as 'mostly French dixhuitième . . . [with] lots of swagged bucrania in a pseudo-frieze'.[53] The galleries are well proportioned,

arranged on two floors around a handsome stone staircase and central areas which allow the display of the gallery's collections of neo-classical sculpture (Nollekens, John Gibson, John Bacon), from the Earl of Yarborough's Collection[54] at nearby Brocklesby, and of long-case clocks by Robert Sutton, which includes the only two known clocks with wooden movements after the style of John Harrison.[55]

Usher collected with care and discrimination. His Roman coins number only forty-four but include aurei of each reign from Augustus in 27 BC to Domitian in 96 AD. They have been added to subsequently by Celtic coins: the Scartho hoard,[56] the Bargate hoard[57] and coins issued by the local Celtic tribe, the Coritani.

His watches, English and French, 17th–19th centuries, were chosen for their decorative qualities rather than for any technical innovations. They glitter in gilt brass or gold cases studded with foiled rubies, rose diamonds, garnets, pearls and smoky, colourless jargoons.

His collection of porcelain (Meissen, Sèvres, Chelsea, Derby, Worcester) was of sufficient quality to encourage other bequests, including that from the G. R. G. Exley Loan Collection, which gave the Usher the largest collection in the country of the work of William Billingsley.

Billingsley was the finest ceramics painter of his generation, and known as 'the rose man'. After he left Derby (Derby Museum and Art Gallery) in 1795 he made several attempts to manufacture on his own account. All these failed, forcing him to change his name to Beeley and decamp to Worcester in 1808, and then to Nantgarw and Swansea in 1813. However subtle his change of name, his style of decoration remained the same, his roses persisting lush and soft, his technique of removing highlights his own. The beauty of the pieces here shows that his failures were commercial, not artistic.

The Pinxton flower pot (*c.* 1802), with its wide band of roses running around the middle, the service for Dr Henry Boot on De la Courtille porcelain (also 1802) and the Sharpe jug (1805) confirm his qualities. The Durham ox, or Benjamin Wilmot jug (*c.* 1807), based on a painting by John Boultbee, bears comparison with the work of George Stubbs for Josiah Wedgwood twenty years earlier.

Usher did not collect paintings but over the past seventy-five years a series of bequests has ensured that the gallery has a varied and interesting collection.

The Contemporary Art Society founded by Roger Fry, Lady Ottoline Morrell and D. S. MacColl, Director of the Tate Gallery in 1909, has given paintings by Sickert and Lowry, and by Terry Frost and Bryan Wynter.

The Dora M. Bond Bequest, made in 1985, is the collection made by John Stuart Bond, a Lincolnshire man, who was a housemaster and teacher of mathematics at Cheltenham School. The collection made by him and his first wife, also called Dora, expresses no singular taste, simply an enjoyment of paint and paintings, with notable works by Ivon Hitchens, Mary Potter and Anne Redpath. The Bonds were not rich. Theirs is a collection that shows what can be achieved with modest means.

In contrast the J. R. Hesham Trust, established in 1963 by a successful Lincoln-born businessman, James Reginald Hesham, was well endowed with a substantial area of building land that was sold and invested. The proceeds have helped the gallery purchase a Turner watercolour of *Stamford, Lincolnshire* (c. 1828),[58] John Ferneley's *The Burton Hunt* (December 1830) and Benjamin West's *Portrait of Sir Joseph Banks* (1771). Banks, aged twenty-eight, had just returned from the 'discovery' of Australia and New Zealand on the *Endeavour*, captained by James Cook, on which Banks was a botanist. He is wrapped in a Maori cloak of flax and surrounded by Polynesian trophies, a headdress, a canoe paddle, a fighting staff. To his left is a classical column and swagged curtain that remind us he was the book-learned heir to a country seat at Revesby, near Lincoln. At his feet is his notebook in which he recorded the flora of Australia which were subsequently named after him. His collections are among the most important in the Natural History Museum (q.v.).

The trust has also given works by Duncan Grant, Sir Alfred Munnings and John Piper, and several paintings, in watercolour and in oils, by Peter De Wint, to add to the collection of his work, which was already the largest in the country.

De Wint was born in 1784, the youngest of that remarkable generation of English water-colourists which started with Turner and Girtin (both born in 1775) and continued with Constable (1776), Varley (1778), J. S. Cotman (1782) and ended with Prout and David Cox (both 1783) and De Wint. The Usher collection confirms that De Wint can stand comparison with any of them. However his handling of light and colour is distinctly his own. His light tends to be flat, his shadows deep, but he could find rich varieties of tone in those shadows. He limited his palette to ten pigments in hard cake, never in moist colours.[59] He used only two brushes, both large, and favoured thickish paper, such as Old Cresswick or Whatman, over whose roughness he could drag his brush against the grain, floating in second colours to achieve a rich bloom and a transparent inward luminosity.

His subjects are the English countryside, rivers, cottages, churches, and the buildings and streets of Lincoln. He went abroad, to Normandy, only once, but his description of the familiar landscapes is always fresh. John Clare wrote in his *Essay on Landscape*, 'the only artist that produces real English scenery in which British landscapes are seen and felt upon paper with all their poetry and exillerating [sic] expression of beauty about them is De Wint.'

His oil paintings have been less widely appreciated. In his lifetime he found them almost impossible to sell and on his death they were found stacked in the attic of his house. The Usher has fourteen of his oil paintings, including the magnificent *Lincoln from the River at Sunset* and both the oil sketch on millboard and the finished version on canvas of *Lincoln from the South* (c. 1824).[60] In oils his light became warmer and his colours richer as he worked back into the gradations of shadow in a hedgerow or river bank, making it plain to see why, notwithstanding his fluency in watercolours, he preferred to work in oils.

This is a gallery rich in works of interest but the De Wints and the work of William Billingsley particularly and signally realise James Ward Usher's hope to leave Lincoln 'a little better than I found it'.

MELTON CARNEGIE MUSEUM *

Thorpe End, Melton Mowbray,
Leicestershire LE13 1RB
Tel. 01664 569946
www.leics.gov.uk/museums

The museum of hunting and the Melton Mowbray pie

If, like a river, hunting has a locatable source, it is here in Melton Mowbray, where the Belvoir meets the Quorn meets the Cottesmore. The fields are grass-rich, open and flat, the hedges thick and wide. It is country that invites man and horse to fly fences; country over which in the 1700s Hugo Meynell, then master of the Quorn, developed the modern faster fox-hunting, the 'scurry'.

In the 19th century the popularity of hunting transformed Melton Mowbray. Hunts needed stables[61] and farriers; those who hunted needed inns and lodging houses. For the rich sportsman there were such exclusive establishments as the Old Club, of which 'Nimrod' wrote, 'There is something highly respectable in everything connected with the Melton Old Club. Not only is some of the best society in England to be met with in their circle, but . . . [there are] no ostentatious displays at the table, though everything is as good of its kind, as a first rate cook can produce.'[62] For those who followed the hunt there were tap rooms and bars.

Hunts created a demand in the town for saddlers and boot makers. Displayed here are the tools of the trade of Gibson's, saddlers, and Rowell's, 'bespoke boot and shoe makers, hand-made throughout, riding boots a speciality', in the words of their advertisement.

This museum was opened in a former Carnegie Library in 1977 and was subsequently refurbished and reopened in 2002 as a museum of local life and of hunting. The late-19th-century red-brick building is small, with exhibition spaces that might be seen as either cosy or cramped. At the centre of its corner gallery on hunting are the 1930s pink coat and breeches of Major Guy Paget, author, and master of the Fernie. His *Melton Mowbray of John Ferneley* (1931) and *Sporting Pictures of England* (1945) are standard texts. He died in a hunting accident in 1952. In the next case are examples of the uniform of the hunt saboteur: T-shirt, anorak, jeans, horn and poster.

Here are the accoutrements of fox hunting: whips, horns and bowler hats. Here too are the memorabilia and trivia: biscuit tins and boxes of matches; plates and mugs; tea cosies and coasters; cigarette boxes, ashtrays and playing cards – all decorated with brightly coloured pictures of huntsmen and hounds.

The museum nods at Melton's past: an Anglo-Saxon bronze brooch and a pot; a helmet and cannon balls from the Civil War; a 19th-century 'Table of Tolls' from Melton market ('2d. a stall', 'every hamper of butter, eggs or lard, 2d.', 'live goose or turkey, 1d.; dead, 1s. 2d.', 'a cage of ferrets, pigeons or other birds, 2d.'); local cheese making (Leicestershire is one of only three counties, with Derbyshire and Nottinghamshire, licensed to make Stilton); the whey that is a by-product of cheese making is used to fatten pigs – hence Melton Mowbray's proud reputation for superb pork pies. Here is an advertisement for those made by Evans & Hills (1877): 'the meat is fresh and good; the flour is fine and sweet.'

Few sports have been depicted as thoroughly as foxhunting, from the paintings of James Seymour and Sawrey Gilpin in the mid 18th century; through those of John Boultbee (a Meltonian, a pupil of Reynolds and Stubbs) and Ben Marshall at the turn of the century; to John Ferneley Snr and Henry Alken in the 1830s and '40s and Sir Francis Grant, a passionate rider to hounds, and a sporting artist before he was elected to the Royal Academy in 1851 and concentrated on portrait painting. The paintings and etchings here are few but good: some watercolours by Henry Alken; drawings

A calf at the Melton Carnegie Museum

attributed to Grant; and half a dozen oils by Ferneley, another Melton man: *The Quorn at Quenby*; *the Ferneley Family Pew in Melton Mowbray Parish Church*; and the hunting conversation piece *John, Henry and Francis Grant at Melton*, in which Grant and his brothers are splendidly mounted.

Since the museum opened in 2002 hunting, in its turn, has become the quarry, being pursued by legislation that would run it to ground. The Melton Carnegie fleshes out hunting people's assertion that it is not just a sport but a way of life.

NORTHAMPTON MUSEUM AND ART GALLERY **

Guildhall Road, Northampton,
Northamptonshire NN1 1DP
Tel. 01604 238548
www.northampton.gov.uk/museums

Cromwellian boots to Queen Victoria's wedding shoes – the world's last word on shoes and shoe making; and an unusual collection of 16th–18th-century Venetian paintings

Tall boots, small boots, boots that march, boots that kick, boots for princes, boots for pilgrims; slippers, shoes, clogs, mules, pumps, galoshes, even a gambadoe (worn over riding boots, patented 1823): Northampton has them all.

The collection began in 1873 and now has more than 12,000 pairs exhibited here, in the manner to be found in shops, as single shoes (invariably the right). If that is to deter thieves, there cannot be many who could get into the tiny prize jockey boots with exquisite stitching (c.1800) or would want the awkward heavy shoes worn by the poet John Clare in St Andrew's Hospital 1841–64.

Northampton has been a boot and shoe town since the 13th century, the water of its rivers, the Nene and the Ouse, being ideal for tanning. This collection traces the development of cordwaining, which derives from Cordoba, the medieval source of fine Spanish leather, not from cobbling, which is merely the mending.

There are shoes of every period and every shape: jackboots, and slap-soled shoes with toes like tongues from the 17th century; indoor shoes in delicate morocco leathers from the 18th century; brocade shoes from the 1890s with 6½-inch heels and Queen Victoria's wedding slippers made in white satin by William Grundy and Sons of London, Royal Shoemakers from 1830 to 1900.

Here are shoes in Genoese velvet and patent leather; in white buckskin and black glacé kid; shoes made from crocodile and from the Karung snake; shoes that are braided, embroidered, decorated, painted.

Here are clogs from Africa, Armenia, Turkey, Japan, Spain and Holland; lasts of maple, beech, metal and plastic; machines for welting, moulding, blocking, patching, pegging and upper skiving. There's a two-row slugger, a standard pounder, a double lip turner and a commonsense splitter.

There are electrically heated boots made for the RAF and a pair of boots for an elephant, the safely named Jumbo, who led the 1959 British Alpine Hannibal Expedition retracing the Carthaginian army's crossing of the Alps in 218 BC.

There are modern designer shoes here by Jimmy Choo and Manolo Blahnik. Vivienne Westwood is represented by a pair of clogs, but there is no work by Ferragamo, Fratelli Rossetti, Kurt Geiger, Cleverly or J. P. Todd.

That aside, for foot fetishists, this is soul food.

Upstairs, above the boots, are jugs and mugs: a ceramics collection that starts with a 3rd-century, colour-coated earthenware jug, made in Caistor and excavated in 1878, and comes, by way of 17th-century slipware mugs and stoneware Bellarmine jugs, to hard and soft paste English porcelain of the 18th century, before arriving at a 1953 coronation mug, designed by Eric Ravilious for Wedgwood: more than 2,500 pieces, all of them everyday objects whose collective story, spanning the centuries, is modest and domestic, drinks taken, drinks shared.

These mugs and boots do not prepare you for Northampton's fine art, an unusual collection of 16th–18th-century Italian paintings. In 1865 the Revd F. G. Watkins gave the gallery *Jacob and Rachel* by the Genoese artist Giovanni Benedetto Castiglione but it was not until the 1950s that the gallery began to put together, with the help of the Victoria and Albert Purchase Grant Fund and the National Art Collections Fund, a collection that concentrates on the School of Venice, starting in its 16th-century days of imperial glory.

Not having the resources to acquire works by the Venetian masters of the 16th century (Lorenzo Lotto, Palma Vecchio, Sebastiano del Piombo, let alone Titian, Tintoretto or Veronese), the gallery chose the work of a little master, Francesco Bassano, to add to the (rare) tondo by Cima da Conegliano that it had been given in 1913. The Bassano (*The Return of the Prodigal Son*, 1570–80) has all the characteristic Venetian qualities of drama and glowing colour.

In the 17th century Titian's and Tintoretto's heirs were found not in Venice itself but in Rome (Poussin, Annibale Carracci), Madrid (Velásquez) and northern Europe (Van Dyck, Rubens, Rembrandt). Northampton's 17th-century Venetian paintings reflect that falling off but the works here by Antonio Bellucci, Antonio Molinari and Antonio Zanchi have style and confidence, and those of the 18th-century Francesco Fontebasso and Giovanni Raggi are not only impressive (Raggi's *Apelles and Campaspe* in particular) but rare in British collections. Beside them the view of the *Piazza San Marco* by Francesco Guardi is predictable, if pleasant.

To this thoughtful collection the gallery adds two further surprises, a Sienese carved and gilded cassone (*c.*1470) by Francesco Di Giorgio and Neroccio De Landi, probably bought by the 9th Earl of Carlisle in 1864, and a Spanish Royal Papeleiro cabinet (1653) designed by Diego de Medina, depicting, on eighteen small panels, scenes from Cervantes's *Don Quixote*, all set in a facade of ebony inlaid with tortoiseshell and ivory, a glorious exotic in this stalwart museum of boots and shoes.

NOTTINGHAM CASTLE MUSEUM ***

Lenton Road, off Friar Lane, Nottingham
NG1 6EL
Tel. 0115 915 3700

Sandby, Bonington, alabaster carvings, campaign relics and ancient oriental art

From a lofty site on a spur above the River Trent, Nottingham Castle Museum offers views of city, countryside and skies. This is an historic site: here William the Conqueror built a fortress in 1068; Henry VII proclaimed himself king after the battle of Bosworth in 1486; and Charles I raised his standard outside the castle walls in 1642 at the start of the Civil War.

Between 1674 and 1679 William Cavendish, 1st Duke of Newcastle, built a magnificent Italianate palace (a central feature, gleaming in sunlight, of Jan Siberechts's[63] *View of Nottingham from the East, c.*1700). This was gutted by fire in 1831 when Reform Bill rioters became incensed by the then Duke of Newcastle's opposition to Parliamentary reform.[64] Eventually Nottingham Corporation had the shell of the palace restored by local architect Thomas Chambers Hine as a public museum and art gallery. It was opened in 1878 and was the first municipal art museum outside London.

One of the major attractions of the opening was the Felix Joseph Collection of 18th-century Wedgwood jasperware, more than one thousand four hundred pieces,[65] now the finest collection of Wedgwood outside the Victoria and Albert Museum, the Lady Lever (both q.v.) and the Wedgwood Museum.[66] The Wedgwood Borghese vase in black jasperware, an apparently unique blue jasperware medallion with reliefs of *Venus and Cupid* (*c.*1776),[67] and a first edition of the Portland vase (*c.*1790)[68] were among its prize pieces.

The museum holds the most important collection of medieval alabaster carvings outside the V&A. Nottingham was one of three cities (York and Lincoln being the others) where the carving of alabaster into monumental sculpture, statues and reliefs became a substantial industry in the 14th and 15th centuries, the alabaster being quarried near by in Staffordshire and Derbyshire. Nottingham alabaster effigies can be found today in churches across Europe.

At the Reformation when such images were being destroyed, three alabaster figures, about three feet high, of the Virgin, a bishop and St Peter with a priestly donor at his foot, were buried beneath the floorboards of the chapel at Flawford near Nottingham. They came to light, by chance, in the 19th century and are now here in the museum.[69] Any lack of subtlety in the carving is more than compensated for by the delicate luminous quality of the stone.

Other bequests and gifts followed, of 17th-century Dutch and 19th-century British paintings, ceramics (including 18th-century Nottingham salt-glazed stoneware), glass and metalwork, all good, none outstanding. In 1968 a major collection of English Georgian domestic silver (the Richard Wagstaff Gibbs Collection) was presented to the castle. It is one of the finest collections of English silver ever presented to an English provincial museum, including work by the leading silversmiths of the period: a butter dish by Paul Storr (1817–18) designed as a coronet; tea canisters in a walnut tea chest (1739–40) by Paul de Lamerie.

Unusually what sets Nottingham apart is its collection on paper, particularly of the

Nottingham-born artists Paul Sandby and Richard Parkes Bonington.

Sandby is sometimes, erroneously, styled 'the father of 18th-century English watercolour'. The boldness of Alexander Cozens's[70] 'blot' watercolours should give him a prior claim to any such title, but the large Sandby portfolio here shows the range of his technical skills (pen and wash, body colour, transparent colour, drawings, aquatints) and of the way in which, through landscape portraiture, he raised the status of watercolour painting, being a founder member of the Royal Academy and one of the few to exhibit watercolours there in the Academy's early years.[71] Subsequent generations of watercolourists owe much to Sandby's mastery of an even lay of washes.

Although Bonington died at the age of twenty-five, he left a large body of work. Nottingham's holding is only matched in Britain by the Wallace Collection (q.v.), which has more oil paintings but fewer watercolours and drawings, and in the US by the Paul Mellon Centre. His fluency helps explain Constable's complaint that 'It is not right in a young man to assume great dash – great completion – without study or pains.'[72]

The museum did not begin to collect Bonington's work until the early 20th century, so its holding of both watercolours and of oils is limited, but it includes some gems: a landscape, *Figure in a Cornfield* (1826), whose diagonals whisk the eye through the scene; *The Castelbarco Tomb, Verona* (1827); and two fine coastal scenes, *Fisherfolk on the Normandy Coast* and the magnificent *The Undercliff* (1828), on the back of which his mother wrote, 'August 6th and 7th, 1828. The last drawing made by our dear son about prior to his fatal dissolution. Never to be parted with, E. Bonington.' *The Undercliff* took him, unusually, two days, as he was weakened by consumption, but it still has the freshness and vivacity of his finest work.

Providing a context for Bonington, Nottingham has paintings by his master François Louis Thomas Francia, *Landscape and Viaduct*

Nottingham Castle Museum's Portland vase

with Figures (1828), with shafts of sunlight filtered through trees; by his pupil Thomas Shotter Boys; by those he influenced – James Holland and William Callow; and by Eugene Delacroix, who was his friend (*Tam O'Shanter*, 1831).

Beside these the 19th-century collection sits stolidly: John Martin, Francis Danby, William Dyce, John Brett, William Quiller Orchardson, leavened by an Italian landscape by Richard Wilson, a fine Crome, *The Willow Tree*, and a complete set of all seventy-one published plates of J. M. W. Turner's *Liber Studiorum*.[73]

In the 20th century acquisition has been primarily by purchase and although some good paintings have been bought (Ivon Hitchens, Robert MacBryde, Edward Burra, Matthew Smith) there has been no clear guiding curatorial hand. There are a number of works by Nottingham-born Dame Laura Knight, and by her husband Harold, and a surprising group by William Nicholson. Nottingham has one of his elegant portraits, *The Viceroy's Orderly*, but it is the quality of his small landscapes here that is a revelation. Their monochrome restraint justifies John Rothenstein's description of Nicholson as a 'little classical master'[74] and looks forward to the small and similarly spare landscapes that his son, Ben Nicholson, painted in the 1920s (such as *Cumberland Farm* at Brighton Art Gallery, q.v.).

In recent years the museum has acquired contemporary textiles and photography through the Contemporary Art Society Special Collection Scheme. High-profile figures include Zarina Bhimji, Wolfgang Tillmans, Grayson Perry and Shelly Goldsmith. The museum has also developed its collection of studio pottery. The Rollo and Marion Ballantyne Collection of 20th-century British Studio ceramics features the solid, powerful pots of Michael Cardew (represented here by a huge stool the size and weight of an elephant's foot) and works by Ray Finch, David Leach and Richard Batterham, alongside the miniaturist delicacy of bowls by Gwynn Hannsen, small boxes by John Maltby and the fragile pods of Geoffrey Swindell. To these have been added the Derbyshire County

Council Loan Collection, with pots by Bernard and Janet Leach, Lucie Rie, Hans Coper and Katherine Pleydell-Bouverie, making it an exceptional 20th-century collection that few museums, with the exception of the Yorkshire Museum and the York Art Gallery, the Sainsbury Centre for Visual Arts and the Potteries Museum and Art Gallery (all q.v.), can match.

If Nottingham lacks heart-stopping paintings or objects there is much to find for anyone prepared to look. In 1833 the *Magazine of the Fine Arts* complained that, lacking the annual exhibition of fine art that York, Lancaster, Norwich and other county towns had, 'Nottinghamshire is still a barren and desert waste in all that is intellectual.'[75] The collection here today decisively refutes that charge.

GALLERIES OF JUSTICE *

Shire Hall, High Pavement, Lace Market,
Nottingham, Nottinghamshire NG1 1HN
Tel. 0115 952 0555
www.galleriesofjustice.org.uk

The process of justice from court room to cell, and to the gallows

There has been a court on this site since 1375 and a prison since 1445. The present building was designed, by James Gandon in 1770, as the Shire Hall, with imposing Doric columns in red sandstone. On its steps public executions were conducted until 1864. There could be no more appropriate place for the Galleries of Justice, the only museum of law, crime and punishment in the country.

The building, on High Pavement, Nottingham's main thoroughfare in the 18th century, appears to be two storeys high but it is pitched on the edge of a cliff that drops 100 feet sheer to Narrow Marsh, one of the city's poorest districts into which its sewers drained.

The visitor starts in the 19th-century Court Room at street level and descends to the cells below, the prison below them, and the dungeon caves, the Pits, on which the city is built and into which were cast 18th- and 19th-century prisoners who could not afford to pay for food and lodging.

You are given a ticket with the name and number of an authentic 19th-century prisoner. You follow that prisoner's journey through the courts and the prison system until he or she was hanged or transported to Australia. All are guilty; none rises again to the street and freedom.

George Beck was a twenty-year-old accused of 'riotously and tumultuously assembling' on 11 October 1831 in the Reform Bill Riots, during which Nottingham Castle was burnt down. Thirty-seven men and two women were charged. George Beck and two others were hanged on the Shire Hall steps. Seven were in fact sentenced to death, but four had their sentences commuted to transportation for life. Other cases involve William Doyle, aged seventeen, sentenced to six years in 1863 for stealing a sack of wheat; Lucy Ellis, condemned to death for murdering her baby in 1876, her sentence finally commuted to life imprisonment; and William Dear, sentenced to seven years' penal servitude, followed by seven years' police supervision, for stealing a piece of elmwood in 1875.

The museum has a number of collections from the police, the courts and the national prison service: the Ross Simms Collection of police uniforms and equipment; the Bramshill Collection of truncheons and tipstaves; judges' robes; legal documents and seals; police vehicles, including a 1939 bicycle; and a chilling collection of restraints that consists of display cabinets of handcuffs, speedcuffs, thumbcuffs, wrist crackers, scissor grips, claw grips, chain grips and darbies, whose design has scarcely changed since the 18th century.

Here too are the legal archives of some of the 20th century's great barristers (F. E. Smith, Sir Norman Birkett, Edward Marshall Hall) and, on a thin discoloured piece of paper, a typed list of the sentences given at the Nuremberg trial on 18 October 1945: of the 22 accused, 12 were sentenced to 'death by hanging' (including 'Hermann Wilhelm Goring' [sic], Joachim von Ribbentrop, Wilhelm Keitel, Martin Bormann); Rudolf Hess was imprisoned for life and three were not convicted (Hjalmar Schach, Franz von Papen and Hans Fritsche). Beside this page is a memo from the Russian judge dissenting and maintaining that none should have been acquitted.

But it is the theatre of crime and punishment that is the thing. When a member of the museum staff puts on the wig and fig of a judge in the 19th century Court Room, and sits raised up, under a canopy, the centre point of a huge carved wall, he becomes at once a figure removed, inspiring anxiety and fear.

You leave his court and go down to the cells (*c.* 1700), narrow and low, shared with three others; to the Prison Bath, complete with the pungent smell of carbolic soap; down to the Exercise Yard, on whose walls generations of prisoners have made their mark and to where executions were moved after 1864:[76] down further to the Condemned Cell; and, finally, to the Pits and the Dark Cells, the punishment cells devoid of light.

In a dark room a final piece of theatre consists of a glass wall that is suddenly illuminated to show a 20th-century prison hanging. The condemned man, hands strapped behind his back, ankles belted together, a white hood over his head, its corners pricked up like ears, stands facing away from you. A tape has the voice of the public hangman taking you through the moments that lead to the light being snapped off. It is a scene that might have been designed by Magritte. It is animated by the devil.

The museum has a clear didactic purpose, aimed at teenagers and young offenders, in a city that has a high level of youth crime and the highest level of gun crimes and murder in the country.

On the walls outside the cells, before you rise to street level and the world outside, are written the words 'None but those who have been immured for months in a gloomy prison cell can ever know the ecstasy of freedom' (Susan Willis Fletcher, 1884) and 'I don't want to leave. I dread what I shall have to face if I am discharged ... What can I do but starve or steal, and what will be my fate? I dread it' (a Dartmoor prisoner, 1920).

COWPER AND NEWTON MUSEUM *

Orchard Side, Market Place, Olney,
Buckinghamshire MK46 4AJ
Tel. 01234 711516
www.mkheritage.co.uk/cnm

*A house of friendship and 'Amazing Grace';
holes in the walls for Cowper's hares*

You cannot enter William Cowper's house by the front door. He kept it locked at all times for fear that his pet hares, who lived in his hall, would escape. Instead, you go in through the museum shop, next door.

It is a quiet entry into the house where Cowper lived between 1768 and 1786. During those years he and John Newton wrote evengelical hymns that have been sung throughout the world for the past 200 years. Their *Olney Hymns*, published in 1776, contains 'Amazing Grace', 'Glorious things of thee are spoken' and 'How sweet the name of Jesus sounds' by Newton. Cowper's smaller contribution (67 to Newton's 280) includes 'God moves in a mysterious way' and 'O for a closer walk with God'.[77]

With the exception of the celebratory 'Glorious things of thee are spoken', all their hymns express the unworthiness of man who is saved only by the grace of God. Cowper found God after a mental breakdown, during which he tried three times to commit suicide, once by drinking laudanum (he threw it out of the window, revolted by the taste), then by drowning himself in the Thames (he 'turned back at the sight of a porter waiting on the bank')[78] and finally by attempting to hang himself with a garter (it broke). Newton's conversion came during an Atlantic storm on 10 March 1748 when he remained at the wheel of the *Greyhound* for twenty-six hours.

For each of them, Olney, a small market town that traded in straw plait and pillow lace, was a sanctuary. Their homes (Newton, the curate for Olney, in the Vicarage; Cowper and Mrs Unwin, a widow who kept house for him and was his life's companion, in Orchard Side) were separated only by a paddock to whose owner they paid a guinea a year for the right to cross between their two gardens.

It is not easy for a museum to convey a man's mental torment or his religious zeal but the modesty of the house, which is furnished and decorated much as it was when Cowper and Mrs Unwin lived here, captures something of such a man and his eccentricities. The porthole in the wall between the kitchen and the hall allowed his hares to come and go. In a letter dated 28 May 1784 Cowper describes how 'Immediately commencing carpentry, I built them houses to sleep in; each had a separate apartment ... In the daytime they had the range of the hall, and at night retired to his own bed, never intruding into that of another.'

The house contains much memorabilia (the Pembroke oak fly-leafed table at which he wrote; Mrs Unwin's work box, a cribbage board, a family Bible, a drawing of Cowper said to be by his friend Sir Thomas Lawrence and exhibited at the Royal Academy in 1795)[79] but it is the quiet simplicity of the house that conveys this poignant and endearing man. In a 1783 letter to Mrs Unwin's son, Cowper explains why a friend of theirs, the Roman Catholic Sir John Throckmorton of Weston Hall, visited only rarely, 'though he is one of the most agreeable men I ever saw ... neither our house, furniture, servants or income being such as qualifies us to make entertainments.'

Cowper was an assiduous writer of letters and his letters cabinet here has false leather book spines, behind which are separate pigeonholes for each of his correspondents: the artist Henry Fuseli; William Wilberforce; Lawrence; his publisher Joseph Johnson; his cousin Lady Hesketh and his patron Lord Dartmouth.[80] Here too are first editions of his translation of the *Iliad*,[81] as plain and prosaic as Pope's translation, of which he disapproved, was ornate;[82] of his best-selling poem 'John Gilpin'; and of his poems 'The Truth' (1780–81) and 'The Task' (1784) with its tender, playful love of nature.

A separate room is reserved for John Newton and in particular for his campaigning with William Wilberforce (v. the Wilberforce House Museum) for the abolition of slavery. At Wilberforce's request Newton gave evidence to the Privy Council in 1788 and to a House of Commons Committee in 1790. His several years as a slave trader ('business at which my heart now shudders') gave particular force to his view that 'with equal advantages they [Africans] will be equal to ourselves in point of capacity. I have met many instances of real and decided natural capacity amongst them' and led to his paper, *Thoughts upon the Slave Trade*, in which he wrote, 'I am bound in conscience to take shame to myself by a public confession, which, however sincere, comes too late to prevent or repair the misery ... to which I have, formerly, been accessory.' Newton's campaigning had the same thunder and 'intense conviction of sin'[83] as his sermons but his personal relations showed an 'almost womanly tenderness'.

A sense of Cowper's gentleness can be caught in the garden behind the house, which has been recultivated with plants grown in Britain before 1800. Cowper was a keen gardener. In a letter to Mrs King (1788) he maintained that 'Gardening was of all employments, that in which I succeeded best ... I began with lettuces and cauliflowers: from them I proceeded to cucumbers; next to melons. I then purchased an orange-tree, to which ... I added two or three myrtles.'

Cowper would retreat to a summerhouse in the garden to write (his 'verse manufactory', he called it). It became, after his death in 1800, a literary shrine, with visitors inscribing their names inside on its plaster walls. Admiration for his poetry was shared by Jane Austen, Tennyson and John Constable, who wrote, 'He is an author I prefer to almost any other, and when with him I always feel the better for it'.[84] The hymns that he and Newton wrote live on in churches every Sunday; the memory of these zealous and gentle men in their biographies[85] and by the porthole into their lives provided by this museum.

VERULAMIUM MUSEUM **

St Michaels, St Albans, Hertfordshire
AL3 4SW
Tel. 01727 751810
www.stalbansmuseums.org.uk

*Supreme Roman collection; mosaics and the
Verulamium Venus*

'Nothing remains but ruins of walls, chequered pavements and Roman coins now and then digg'd up there,' reported the Tudor antiquary William Camden in 1586 of Verulamium, for 400 years from AD 50 one of the three largest towns, with Cirencester and London, in Roman Britain.

Boudicca and the Iceni burnt all three towns in their revolt of AD 60–61 and it is these remains that have told us so much of what we know about Roman Britain. Verulamium's contribution has been to our understanding

Apsidal shell mosaic at Verulamium Museum

of domestic life. In London we may see the grandeur of the Temple of Mithras and of Haddon Baths. In Colchester it is the remains of the great Forum where the population loyal to Rome made their desperate last stand. Here, at Verulamium, we can recover the everyday.

Dr Mortimer Wheeler and his first wife Tessa began excavating here in 1930. He had worked on earlier excavations at Colchester (1917 and 1920), Carnarvon (1921–23), Brecon (1924–5) and Caerleon[86] (1926–7) but St Albans's proximity to the London media made this the first modern excavation that caught the public's imagination with the display and interpretation of the objects on site. In 1939 the St Albans City Council, encouraged by the Wheelers, and in particular by Tessa Wheeler, opened this museum.

It is on the edge of the modern city, an unpromising site facing its own car park on scrubby municipal land. Immediately beyond are the River Ver and flat arable fields, buried beneath which are the shops and houses of Verulamium.

The Wheelers' work was continued, first by Kathleen Kenyon (the Basilica and Theatre in 1934) and then by Professor Sheppard Frere (1955–61) (the Belgic Mint and the wall paintings). What was recovered is here in this single-storey museum, whose modest exterior resembling many 1950s branch public libraries gives no hint of the treasures within.

Here is the familiar jetsam of archaeological trove: coins and brooches; pins and rings; beads of jet; tiles and shards; funerary urns and monuments. What is unusual is that these are all from the 200-year lifespan of a well defined and relatively undisturbed urban site.

The pre-Roman coins, bearing the letters VER, VERO and VERL for Verulamium, tell us of the rule over the Catevellauni of Tasciovanus (25–5 BC) and of his successor Cunobelin (the model for Shakespeare's Cymbeline) before he moved his capital to Camulodunum (Colchester).

Significant burials provide evidence of various stages of Roman occupation: the pit and funeral pyre of a local client king cremated in AD 43–55 (excavated 1992), the cemetery in which Mortimer Wheeler excavated 140 cremations and the lead coffin (excavated 1989) in which a middle-aged man had been buried c. AD 200. The coffin is decorated with carved scallop shells, symbols of life after death and representing the oceans across which the dead had to travel.

It is the personal objects handled every day that allow us to imagine most readily the life of these Roman citizens in Britain, and to relate their experience and routines to our own lives. The spoons and knives are too familiar to effect such recognition but the tweezers, mirrors and nail cleaners used by smoothly groomed Roman women can do so, as can the unusually complete set of carpentry tools: the iron axe, saw blade, chisel, nails, drill bit, all identical in design and function to their equivalents today. If the Design Museum (q.v.) seeks an illustration of their adage 'Form follows function', it is here. The decorator's oyster shells, used for mixing paint, and his bone for combing patterns on to tiles or pottery are equally recognisable.

Excavations at Verulamium have yielded a number of large town houses burnt in the fire that destroyed much of the town in AD 155. In their ruins were fine wall paintings and mosaics. Until the Wheelers began to restore these, very little was known about Roman-British wall painting. Samuel Lyons had excavated a villa at Combe End in Gloucestershire in the 1790s and Pitt Rivers's work at Iwerne Minster, Dorset, had uncovered another in 1897,[87] but neither of these sites had been preserved. Lt. Col. G. W. Meates and C. D. P. Nicholson had further success at Lullingstone in Kent.[88] Here, first the Wheelers, and in 1955 Sheppard Frere, were able to save and recreate wall paintings that made clear the Romans' fresco technique and showed how their paintings imitated marble veneers, columns and cornices to give an impression of wealth and luxury. These paintings were brilliantly restored by Dr Norman Davey, who worked both with the Wheelers and with Frere.[89]

The best of the mosaics are from the late 2nd century. Some are of patterns and plants: a superb apsidal mosaic (c. AD 150), its wave crescent pattern a fan-tail of grey and white; a chequerboard mosaic (c. AD 300), whose crudity is evidence of a decline either in technique or in wealth. Some are of figures: the Lion and Stag Mosaic (AD 175–80) in Antonine polychrome, whose lion, stag's head in mouth, prowls with feline power; the Oceanus (AD 160–90), also polychrome, heavily muscled, with lobster claws in his hair. All are from the same school as those at Colchester. Most are bordered by tightly executed chain guilloche patterns.

These twenty-four mosaics are riches but the prize find is a bronze figure, eleven inches in height, a Venus, holding a golden apple. She stands naked except for a cloak or skirt knotted on her hips. Her arms are open wide in invitation. She is demonstrably a goddess of love and beauty, desire and seduction.

She, and the figure of Mercury discovered here twelve years later in 1971, were made by the 'cire perdue' method in which a clay mould is built around a wax model that is then melted and replaced by molten bronze. The

Touched-untouched Calke Abbey: Sir Vauncey Harpur Crewe's bedroom

cooled casting is finished by being polished with fine sand. Their sophistication matches their beauty.

Mortimer Wheeler was more than a show-man, the first of the modern media archaeologists. Here at Verulamium he opened the doors to Roman Britain through which such eminent successors as Professor Barry Cunliffe followed to show us our Roman past.

CALKE ABBEY **

Ticknall, Derbyshire DE73 1LE
Tel. 01332 863822
www.nationaltrust.org.uk

A sleeping beauty, woken, and put back carefully to tended sleep

The architecture of Calke Abbey defeated Pevsner: 'A large stone mansion dated 1703, all but unknown to architectural history'.[90] It is a stern judgement on a house whose Greek Revival portico was built to designs by William Wilkins (1806–10), but it is just in that there is little exceptional here: it is simply a solid, handsome house, deep in a Derbyshire valley.

Only inside does it become apparent that this is a house in which time has stood still. Little has changed since the death of Sir Vauncey Harpur Crewe,[91] 10th Baronet, in 1924, and nothing since 1985 when Henry Harpur-Crewe (1921–91) gave up the struggle to maintain the house and estate in the face of £8 million death duties, and transferred it to the National Trust.

For that last hundred years the house lay entirely still in time: there was no electricity until 1962; much was collected; nothing thrown away. The house is an epitaph to the rise, fall and eccentricity of the English country house.

The National Trust, having taken every stuffed owl, broken hatstand and chipped bowl and catalogued them, has replaced each as it was found. At first glance the main rooms are decorated conventionally with mahogany furniture, family portraits and paintings of horses and cattle. On closer inspection the trophy heads in the Entrance Hall are not big game but are the prize cattle of Sir John, 9th Baronet. The Saloon, with a good portrait of *Lady Frances Harpur and her Son Henry* (*c.*1766) by Tilly Kettle over the fireplace, doubled as the family chapel, and contained a billiard table that was overlooked by serried cases of stuffed birds and foxes, an alligator skull and 'a collection of Egyptian Curiosities' brought home from Egypt and Nubia by Sir Vauncey in 1870.

Upstairs there is a Bird Lobby stacked with more cases of stuffed birds, and corridors of rooms filled with broken chairs, abandoned lamps, picture frames and antlers.

The eight generations of Harpurs and Crewes who lived here were enthusiasts for horses and for natural history. There are several good paintings of horses by John Ferneley, John Nost Sartorius and Sawrey Gilpin. Stuffed birds, birds' eggs and minerals are in boxes with their original labels and straw packing.

Sir Henry Crewe, 7th Baronet, the boy in the Tilly Kettle, known as 'the isolated Baronet', redecorated the Breakfast Room as a Music Room, which he hung thickly with paintings of variable quality,[92] the best being a set of views of Naples by Gabriele Ricciardelli (1747); characteristically they were said to have been 'bought out of an inn at Leicester'. He commissioned Haydn to compose *The Derbyshire Marches*, but this 'sad shy creature' lived in seclusion. The artist and diarist Joseph Farington wrote in 1812 that 'He is shy of communication to such an excess that he sometimes delivers his orders to his servants by letter.'

His grandparents, Sir Henry and Lady Caroline Harpur, were more modestly eccentric. Having been given a magnificent bed as a wedding present by Princess Anne, the daughter of George III, to whom Lady Caroline was a maid in honour, they left it in its original boxes where it was found 250 years later in 1984 by the historian Sir Howard Colvin, its brilliant Chinese silk hangings, embroidered with flowers and peacocks and pagodas, untouched.

This house of sleep is a curiosity, a monument to a form of Englishness, unshowy, self-contained. Generations of Harpur Crewes did their duty to the estate and to the county (as high sheriffs) but they remained unconcerned with the world and its fashions, preferring their own, particular, known world.

The West Midlands

The Industrial Revolution has stamped itself on the landscape of the West Midlands, from the urban sprawl of Birmingham as it merges into Wolverhampton, Dudley and Walsall, to Stoke-on-Trent in the north.

Steel and heavy engineering, ceramics and textiles, motor and aircraft manufacturing, above all coal mining, have left their scars. Most of these industries have now closed or are in decline, leaving museums that mark their high days, and a network of canals. Birmingham has more miles of canal within its boundaries than Venice.

The region's museums reflect that history. The birthplace of the Industrial Revolution, Abraham Derby's Ironbridge, is remembered by Telford's soaring bridge and a series of linked museum sites forged by (now Sir) Neil Cossons in 1977. Matthew Boulton's Soho House overlooked his foundry and was the meeting place of the Lunar Society, which counted the titans of the Enlightenment, Josiah Wedgwood, Joseph Priestley, Erasmus Darwin, James Watt and Boulton, among its members.

The Spode Museum is on the site of the original (and still working) Spode potbank. Sadly, the Wedgwood Museum, as complete a record of the 18th-century manufactory as that at Spode, closed, but the collection is intact, in packing cases, and there are hopes that the museum may reopen. The Black Country Museum at Dudley (not included) gives an 'experience' of the local industries. By contrast, the Cheddleston Flint Mill offers a low-tech look at one aspect of one industry, the grinding of flints for the Potteries.

The region may not have many art galleries but the collections at Birmingham and Stoke-on-Trent are strong and those at the Barber and the Ashmolean glorious. It would have been good to have found the space to include the excellent collection of 20th-century art the University of Warwick has created at the Mead Gallery.

It was sad, too, not to include the National Trust's Chastleton House, near Moreton-in-the-Marsh, but Upton House and the two Rothschild properties, Ascott and Waddesdon, are outstanding and the Trust's Snowshill Manor is unlike any other collection, a treasure house of eccentricity.

Shugborough Hall's collection is not as distinguished as the building and

park, and is not included, but its 18th-century farm contrasts well with the humbler Acton Scott (19th to early 20th centuries), a few miles further west in Shropshire.

Sadly Peter Moores's redesigning of Compton Verney as what is likely to be a major art gallery is taking place just too late for inclusion.

ACTON SCOTT HISTORIC WORKING MUSEUM *

Wenlock Lodge, Acton Scott, Church Stretton, Shropshire sy6 6qn
Tel. 01694 781306
www.shropshireonline.gov.uk/museums.nsf

Nineteenth-century working farm: shire horses and Shropshire sheep

Deep in the Shropshire hills, Acton Scott is a twenty-three-acre farm recreated, and worked as it would have been between 1875 and 1920.

You park in a field and walk up past medieval fishponds to the Hall, built in 1580, and the 19th-century farmyard and buildings. These are rich farming lands, owned by the Actons and the Burnells since the 15th century, as the names of the surrounding villages witness: Acton Burnell, Acton Reynald, Acton Round, Acton Scott. Robert Burnell was Chaplain and Secretary to Edward I, later becoming Lord Chancellor and Bishop of Bath and Wells.

In the fields are short- and long-horn cows, Shropshire sheep and shire horses. By the ponds are Aylesbury ducks, Brecon Buff geese and Dorking hens with five toes. But thoughts of an agricultural idyll have little place here. Farming in the 1870s was hard and uncertain. Imported cereals from North America and Argentina and refrigerated mutton from New Zealand were driving down prices. Wheat halved in price between 1870 and 1900. A million sheep carcasses were being imported each year; 2½ million arable acres were lost and, despite the efforts of Joseph Arch and the first agricultural trade union, wages were less than 14s. for a six-day week, twelve hours a day. In this Great Depression, aggravated by the wet harvest of the 1870s and the droughts of the 1890s, up to half a million farm labourers moved to the industrial cities or emigrated. Acton Scott survived, working a four-crop rotation of winter corn, ley (grass or clover), spring corn and roots or forage, the ley and roots (mangolds) feeding the livestock, the corn providing the income.

Although the main draught force was the shire horse, the farming economy was becoming increasingly mechanised. Robert Ransome had designed a plough in 1808 that could be taken apart and adapted to different functions. By the 1840s Ransome, Sims and Jeffries of Ipswich had made eighty-six attachments: ploughs for ridging, for double furrows, for lifting potatoes; a thistle cutter, a potato spinner, a single row root gapper, a horse hoe/scuffle. All are here, alongside a threshing machine made by Edward Humphries & Co. at their Atlas works in Pershore in 1884, a Cumbrian mower by Powell Brothers and Whittaker and a 1920s Albion potato planter by Harrison and McGregor of Leigh, still made to be powered by a single horse.

Acton Scott has machines for every task: a potato riddle for grading, a kibbler to bruise corn, an oilcake breaker, a chaff cutter, a root pulper, an 'Unchokeable' made by Bentall Heybridge of Maldon, Essex and a double horse gin to drive the farmyard machinery. These were an agricultural arsenal, seen off by the tractor.

Here, under the power of the shire horse, is relived a calendar of work: sowing, weeding, mowing, haymaking, threshing; lambing and shearing; farrowing, fattening, sticking and salting. Every day at 7.30 a.m. and 4 p.m. the cows are milked by hand, their milk to be made into cheese and butter.

There is a working dairy; a granary; cowhouses, barns, stables; and a tack room in which, among saddles and harnesses, are instruments for treating horses: mouth gags for administering pills; a drenching horn for liquid medicines; castrating irons. There is the sweet leathery smell of horse and tack and saddlesoap.

The farm is full of smells and sounds: sacking, straw, hay and muck; the irregular chat of hens and ducks, the blarting of distant sheep, the occasional cry of a donkey, the squeals of curly-tailed piglets and the grunts of their mother, a Tamworth sow who stands on her pointed trotters, her hind legs primly together.

Around the yard are the workshops of

craftsmen: blacksmith, wheelwright, saddler and cooper. A farmworker's cottage is furnished with a sewing machine and small organ, a dolley tub and mangle, a bread oven and a copy of the *Daily Express* of 24 April 1900, whose headline is 'The Queen Wins Ireland's Love. Erin's Bright Hope.'

As you walk back down the lane you pass the fishponds in whose dark waters lurk rudd, tench, carp and perch: another, hidden, crop.

UPTON HOUSE ✶✶

Banbury, Warwickshire OX15 6HT
Tel. 01295 670266, information 0870 609 5390
www.nationaltrust.org.uk
email: uptonhouse@ntrust.org.uk

The Bearsted Collection: Stubbs, Gainsborough, El Greco; English porcelain

Marcus Samuel, 1st Viscount Bearsted, made several fortunes in the late 19th century in shipping and in trading with the Far East, culminating in the forming of the Shell Transport and Trading Company in 1897.[1] In 1895 he bought the Mote at Bearsted, outside Maidstone, from Lord Romney and with it a collection of English portraits. When he died, his son Walter, 2nd Viscount Bearsted, sold the Mote and bought Upton House for the excellence of the hunting in the surrounding Warwickshire countryside, and to house his father's portraits and his own fast-growing collections of paintings and porcelain.

He had already put together an important collection[2] of Japanese decorative and applied art, which he gave to Maidstone Museum (q.v.) in 1924. Now, in a post-First World War market that favoured collectors, he turned to London and Continental dealers and the London auction rooms. His tastes were as catholic in paintings (Stubbs and Hogarth, Jan Steen and Pieter Saenredam, El Greco and Canaletto, Giovanni di Paolo and Rogier van der Weyden) as they were specific in porcelain (Chelsea Red Anchor and Gold Anchor, and Sèvres).

You approach the house, on foot, up an avenue of holly and firs. It is low, wide and plain, built of local Hornton stone. In the Entrance Hall are five large tapestries, 17th-century reworkings of the set of 16th-century *Hunts* (of the Emperor Maximilian I) from designs by Bernard van Orley.[3] The next two rooms, a Lobby and the Dining Room, contain 18th- and early 19th-century hunting pictures (Francis Sartorius, John Herring Snr, John Ferneley and a large Ben Marshall) and Stubbs's three great farming paintings: *Labourers* (1779), *Haymakers* (1783) and *Reapers* (1783),[4] their friezes of foreground figures set against huge skies made endlessly deep by contrast with the dark trees and shadows.

Bearsted bought for his own enjoyment, and when he bequeathed the house and the collection to the National Trust in 1948, he expressed a wish that the house should be kept alive by his family continuing to live in it, which they did until 1988. That spirit is maintained: the lighting is domestic, not gallery quality; there are no barriers in front of pictures; there are vases and bowls of flowers in every room. You can step up close to Pieter Jansz Saenredam's *The Interior of the Church of St Catherine, Utrecht* to scrutinise the precision of its geometry; you can step back to get the full effect of Romney's full-length of *William Beckford*, skied in the Picture Room. This is an atypically swaggering Romney. It was painted on Beckford's return from his first Grand Tour and just before his coming-of-age party at Fonthill: 'a tumult of balls, concerts and illuminations', he told Lady Hamilton. Here he is, the richest young man in Europe, looking forward to an apparently untroubled life of collecting and writing. Romney flatters him by giving him endlessly long legs and surrounding him with a plinth, statuary and deer: an English park rather than the Italian campagna. There is no hint of nemesis, although a grieving figure (of Lear or Job) is depicted on the plinth.

There can be no doubting Bearsted's love of Stubbs (he also owned a charming painting of *A Lady Reading in a Park* that has remained in the possession of his family), and of English sporting and narrative painting, and conversation pieces. But he was also an accumulator. He adapted the house to accommodate more pictures, turning the squash court into the Picture Gallery. Even so paintings 'were stacked against the wall ... while new purchases were hidden from his less enthusiastic wife under the bed in his dressing room. By the end of his life the storerooms in the basement were crammed with pictures, porcelain, glass and books.'[5]

He accumulated well. El Greco's *El Espolio*, although one of several smaller versions of the altarpiece in the sacristy of Toledo Cathedral (1577–9) is so forceful, its tones so vivid, as to persuade many that it is the model, rather than a copy. Delácroix, who owned it, believed so. It also has the stamp on the back of the earlier great collector Don Gaspar de Haro y Guzman, Marquès del Carpio y de Heliche.

Here are two small portraits, both entitled *An Unknown Man*, both probably the right halves of diptychs, by Hans Memling and his master Rogier van der Weyden, whose quality is quietly underlined by the delicacy with which the hands are painted.[6] Bearsted favoured 15th-century Flemish painters (Pieter Brueghel the Elder, Jan Provoost) but there are fewer works from the early Italian Renaissance. *The Presentation of the Virgin* by Giovanni di Paolo (with Sassetta and Domenico di Bartolo, the leading painter in early 15th-century Siena) reconciles here the flattened figures of the 14th century with the new understanding of architectural perspective and composition: observe the two attendant women on the left,[7] and the recession of the steps up to the tiny figure of the Virgin.

There are some surprises: a masterly drawing by Guardi, *A Study for a Crowd Seen From Behind*, and a pair of small paintings by Hogarth (*Morning* and *Night*, both 1737) of considerable significance. These form two parts of his series *The Four Times of the Day*, which marks the beginning of his move from morality to aesthetics. He advertised subscriptions for the four in the same edition of the *St James's Evening Post* (7–9 June 1737) in which he published an essay, signed 'Britophil', on

the lack of interest in native art among dealers, critics and connoisseurs (or 'quacks'), which culminated in his aesthetic treatise *The Analysis of Beauty* (1753).[8]

The porcelain is outstanding. Bearsted was fortunate that some excellent collections, held by Sir Samuel Scott, Baroness Burdett-Coutts and R. M. Wood, came on to the market after the First World War. He bought well and deeply. Here are some rare pieces of Chelsea from the Red Anchor period, 1752–8, notably *Matrimony* (*c.*1755), a young man and woman with a caged bird, the symbol of marriage, and some unrivalled Gold Anchor pieces: *Hercules and the Hydra* (*c.*1765) from the *Labours of Hercules* set, and *The Music Lesson* (1765), modelled after a painting by Boucher, a rococo extravaganza of lovers, lambs, a dog and a flute in a bower of flowers. The humour of these pieces, as gentle as the soft-paste modelling, contrasts with the hauteur of the Sèvres, some from the Grand Service made for Louis XVI's dining room at Versailles and some from the service made for Catherine the Great.[9] Upton's porcelain is not comparable with that at Waddesdon but the rarity of several of the Chelsea and Sèvres pieces distinguishes it.

At a time, the 1920s and '30s, when many regional public collections were marking time, Bearsted showed (as did William Burrell, Cecil Higgins[10] and Anthony de Rothschild) what could be achieved by the determined and discriminating collector, even though he never bought from Duveen, whose costliest items therefore all went to his American 'squillionaires'.

ASCOTT COLLECTION ✱✱✱

Wing, Leighton Buzzard, Bedfordshire
LU7 0PR
Tel. 01296 6688242

Rothschild treasures: Chinese ceramics; English, Italian and Dutch paintings; a very great Cuyp

Ascott was a Victorian hunting box. It was bought in 1874 from Baron Mayer de Rothschild by his nephew Leopold de Rothschild,

View of Dordrecht on the Maas *by*
Aelbert Cuyp (Ascott Collection)

whose own grandson Sir Evelyn de Rothschild
lives here today.[11] Ascott is like no other hunting box in having superb collections of Dutch,
Italian and English paintings, Chinese porcelain, and tapestries and furniture.[12]

The approach is low key. At the end of a
short, pleasant drive through tree-lined lawns,
you turn a corner and there is a low, undistinguished mock-Jacobean house. Pevsner finds it
'picturesque and irregular'.[13] He is generous.
The house incorporates a Jacobean farmhouse
(*c.* 1606), but extensions and alterations by
George Devey swamp the original. The facade
threatens low and dark rooms, an unpromising setting for pictures or porcelain.

Nothing could be more mistaken. Inside,
the rooms are elegantly decorated, their
proportions well suited to the outstanding
collection of Dutch paintings. At its centre is
one of the finest Cuyps in the world, *View
of Dordrecht on the Maas*, as good as any in
the National Gallery (q.v.). Around it, in the
Dining Room, are landscapes by Nicolaes

Berchem, Philips Wouwermans and Jan
Hackaert, genre scenes by Jan Steen and by
Adriaen and Isaak van Ostade, and a second,
smaller Cuyp, *A Landscape with a Horseman on
the Road*. In other rooms there are paintings by
Frans Snyders, Jan van der Heyden, Jan
Wijnants, Meindert Hobbema and Nicolaes
Maes. With the exception of Vermeer, de
Hooch, Saenredam and Metsu, almost the
whole of the golden generation of Dutch
painting in the mid 17th century is here.

Even in this company it is the *View of
Dordrecht on the Maas* that compels: its modulations of light and shade, the poise of its
proportions of town and river to sky, beneath
which the boats on the sheer surface of the
water appear to hold their breath. The canvas
had been cut in two (*Evening*, left, and *Morning*, right) when sold in 1841, but the parts
were reunited by the London dealer Thomas
Brown. Agnew's bought it for Anthony de
Rothschild from the sale of Sir George
Holford's collection in 1928.

The Italian collection is smaller but also of
high quality: a Florentine 16th-century *Portrait
of a Young Man* attributed to Salviati;[14] a

Tiepolo sketch for the vault of the Church of the Fratta at Friuli, which was reputedly gambled away by the artist's widow; a portrait of *A Prelate* by Lorenzo Lotto,[15] whose attribution (and even period) has been questioned, but which is a painting of quiet, serious beauty; and an outstanding *Madonna and Child with St John* by Andrea del Sarto,[16] whose gentle architecture of arms, drapery and haloes leads the eye to the quiet heart of the painting.

Ascott's hunting box origins[17] are here in paintings by John Wootton (*Racing on Newmarket Heath*, 1730), and by Sir Francis Grant (*Four Brothers of the Rothschild Family with Hounds*) and an outstanding conversation piece, *Five Mares* (*c.* 1770s), by George Stubbs, its lyrical, idealised landscape offset by the clarity and affection of Stubbs's observation of the mares and the balanced rhythm of the composition.

The remainder of the English collection, which includes paintings by Reynolds, Hogarth, Romney, Lawrence and Hoppner, is not exceptional, apart from Reynolds's *Miss Mayer as Hebe* and Gainsborough's portrait, wrongly called *Lady Mary Bruce, Duchess of Richmond*, a late, London portrait that shows the mastery of the landscaped studio portrait that Gainsborough had acquired by the 1770s.

The collection of Chinese ceramics that Anthony de Rothschild gave to the National Trust in 1949 is comprehensive, tracing the development of glazes from the Han Dynasty (206 BC–AD 220) to the Qing Dynasty (1644–1911). Within it, the 'fa-hua' stoneware is outstanding, as are the san ts'ai (three-colour) vessels and figures, the early Ching *famille verte* and the 17th-century K'ang Hsi baluster vases with trumpet mouths. The collection stands with the best in the British Museum, the Ashmolean Museum, the Bowes Museum and the Percival David (all q.v.). Curiously the dense beauty of the Mortlake tapestry proves to be an excellent complement to the ceramic chastity.

Ascott is a family house, designed and decorated to be lived in, but its furniture includes some outstanding pieces, mainly French: a black and gold lacquer secretaire by Joseph Baumhauer[18] (Paris, *c.* 1745) and Bernard van Risenburgh; a cylinder writing table by Jean-Henri Riesener from the late

1770s/early 1780s, when he worked extensively for the court of Louis XVI, and pieces by M. G. Garner, C. C. Saunier and Phillipe-Claude Montigny.

There is no dominant decorative style but the overall appearance is never bland. There are flashes of boldness (the black and red armchair with a shocking pink cushion in the Library), but the relaxed comfort of the decor, the *trompe l'œil* tiling on the walls of the Dining Room, painted blue and white in the 17th-century style by Renzo Mongiardino, allows this remarkable mixture of ceramics, paintings and furniture to blend. This is the home of successive generations of a family. In it books, objects and furniture have accreted to make a rich comfort that breathes culture and intelligence.

This is the extra ingredient of Ascott. These works have been brought together slowly, not for show, but for enjoyment, with discrimination and love. Without feeling an intruder or voyeur, you are able to walk among them, linger, retrace your steps, look again. So many pieces demand slow, measured consideration: the opalescent glaze, lavender shading to brown at the lip, of a small Sung bowl; the rhythms of the del Sarto; the transparent layers with which Gainsborough conveys the Duchess of Richmond's rustling dress in contrast to the flicking brushstrokes he employs to effect the foliage of the trees behind her. To take your time and to be able to stand and look in close detail are rare pleasures that go to the heart of looking at, and learning from, works of art.

Outside are thirty acres of gardens created by Leopold de Rothschild and Sir Henry Veitch in the 1880s. They occupy a superb, sloping site that looks across the Vale of Aylesbury to the Chilterns, but they are curiously uneven in design. Parts are beautiful: the Lily Pond at the end of the Serpentine Walk, the Madeira Walk with its palette of pinks, lilacs, mauves and blues (old roses, ceanothus, aquilegias, phlox, delphinium);

Edgar Degas's Jockeys Before the Race
(Barber Institute of Fine Arts)

some are crude to a post-Sissinghurst taste (the Dutch garden with its 19th-century beds of coleus, the style taken up and unrelinquished by municipal gardeners ever since); some bizarre: the topiary sundial that spells out a public declaration ('Light and shade by turn but love always') from Leopold de Rothschild to his wife, and the melodrama of Thomas Waldo Story's fountains.[19]

It is strange and happy that this unevenly designed but always humanly demonstrative garden and house provide such an appropriate setting for the superb collections within.[20]

BARBER INSTITUTE OF FINE ARTS *****

The University of Birmingham, Edgbaston, Birmingham, West Midlands B15 2TS
Tel. 0121 414 7333
www.barber.org.uk

One of the finest small picture galleries in the country

Lady Barber specified, in the 1932 trust deed that established the institute bearing her and her husband's name, that its collection should consist of 'works of art or beauty of exceptional and outstanding merit', and that it 'shall belong to and be used by the University for the study and encouragement of art and music'. She made two further stipulations: the trustees were not to accept any gifts other than her own and were not to acquire any 'pottery or china' or any pictures painted after 1899. They should be of 'that standard of quality required by the National Gallery and the Wallace Collection'.

Four months later she died, leaving the considerable fortune she had inherited from her husband, Sir Henry Barber, a Birmingham solicitor and property developer, to the Barber Institute of Fine Arts, part of the University of Birmingham. Robert Atkinson was the architect chosen to design a building and Professor Thomas Bodkin, the former director of the National Gallery of Ireland, was appointed as the institute's director.

The choice of Professor Bodkin was inspired. He began building the collection with speed and address, with paintings by Lancret, Tintoretto (*Portrait of a Youth*, 1554) and a ravishing landscape by Richard Wilson, *The River Dee, near Paton Hall, c.*1759–60. Within two years, 1937–9, he bought a Simone Martini, *St John the Evangelist* (1320); *The Crucifixion* (*c.*1490) by Cima; a magnificent Poussin, *Tancred and Erminia* (*c.*1634), more intense and beautiful than Poussin's version of this in the Hermitage; and a delicious James McNeill Whistler, *Symphony in White No. III* (1867), the first of his pictures to have a musical title.

Bodkin's decisiveness, and the quality of his choices, are not surprising. He had thought long about how a collection should be formed. In his book *The Approach to Painting* (1927)[21] he had rejected the advice of the former director of the National Gallery, Sir Charles Holmes, that 'all collectors . . . should collect one class of picture and stick to it'.[22] In Bodkin's opinion there was 'no more certain way of cramping the power of appreciation . . . [The collector] should think of himself as an explorer advancing into an illimitable country whose boundaries have not been and never will be charted, and he should strike from landmark to landmark, resisting as far as possible the temptation to wander down byways . . . The choicest collections are those made by men who have sought and found a sense of that elusive harmony which binds together in a common purpose the most divergent schools.'[23] Bodkin's early landmarks included the Italian paintings above; a fine, sombre Frans Hals, *Portrait of a Man Holding a Skull* (*c.*1610–14), acquired in 1938; an unusual biblical Jan Steen, *The Wrath of Ahasuerus* (*c.*1671–3), acquired in 1939; paintings by Turner and Ruisdael; and a Rubens, *Landscape in Flanders* (*c.*1636), painted in the happiest decade of his life, when he had set aside the politics of the court and retired to his estate, Het Steen. In it, Rubens persuades the sky, clouds, trees and river to sway and bend together.

The Second World War put a rein on the European art market but Bodkin took opportunities to acquire a monumental head from Thebes depicting Amenhotep III, Pharaoh of Egypt between *c.*1390 and 1352 BC, an Irish gold torc, 1000–700 BC, and a marble torso of Aphrodite, a Roman 1st-century BC/AD copy of a sculpture by Praxiteles. He also bought two outstanding portraits (by Reynolds, of *Dr Richard Robinson*; and by Gainsborough, of his friend the singer Giusto Ferdinando Tenducci).

After 1945, Bodkin's collecting regathered pace with the purchase of works by Bellini, Signorelli, Mabuse, Murillo and de Gelder, a very rare complete page of Rembrandt ink, wash and chalk drawings (*A Sheet of Studies, c.*1636) and, an enduring highlight of the collection, Gainsborough's *The Harvest Wagon*, of which he is reported to have said, 'I think this is one of my best compositions.'[24]

Bodkin gave as much thought to how a gallery should exhibit paintings as he did to what should be acquired. He believed that, too often in great galleries, pictures were 'necessarily hung in close proximity to each other; and it is quite impossible for any director to arrange them so that each gets a fair showing'.[25] The intensity of the light, the direction of the shadows, an incompatibility with nearby pictures, all meant that often it was hard to achieve that 'fair showing'. As for the visitor, 'when we crave to light a pipe and sit at ease before a picture, brooding upon it, we are compelled to keep moving in a queue before a barrier, glancing and speculating while we long to stare and ponder.'[26] Atkinson designed a gallery for him that consisted of a series of discrete, recessed bays, each holding about eight paintings. They may not have the wondrous proportions of Soane's galleries at the Dulwich Picture Gallery (q.v.) but there are no better galleries in Britain in which to look at, and enjoy, paintings.

The design of the exterior of the gallery is a solid, restrained but dull example of art deco architecture, the base of its Derby Dale stone topped by variegated brick, with a monumental portico set at one end of the facade, flanked by large coats of arms. This rather pompous entrance leads into a marble-lined concourse, at the end of which are stairs that lead you up to the exemplary galleries.

Professor Bodkin, and subsequent directors, responded to these, and to Lady Barber's brief, by usually limiting themselves to one example of the work of any painter. Invariably the examples they chose were good, being purchased for their qualities, not merely for the name of their artist. There is scarcely a wasted painting. There are some slight weaknesses: perhaps the Cuyp is not of the first rank, or the Veronese. In common with many, even most, British public collections, Spanish painting is not well represented, although the one Murillo, *The Marriage at Cana*, is outstanding: complex and subtle in composition and in the drift of light. French and Italian 18th-century work is not as strong here as English (three outstanding portraits by Gainsborough and Reynolds, and a very fine terracotta bust of *Alexander Pope* by Roubiliac)[27] but these minor weaknesses are mere quibbles beside the general excellence of Bodkin's acquisitions.

The Barber shows what can be achieved on acquisition budgets that, although generous by current standards, did not allow for the pursuit of Titians or Raphaels. It shows too the vital importance of scholarship. Bodkin's successor, Professor Ellis Waterhouse, the great Gainsborough scholar of his generation, maintained the quality of acquisitions with Van Dyck's *Ecce Homo*, Claude's *Pastoral Landscape* and the Symbolist Pierre Puvis de Chavannes's surprising *The Beheading of John the Baptist*.

Between them Bodkin and Waterhouse created a superb teaching collection for the university, a collection that had fine examples of almost all the main European schools: Sienese (the Simone Martini, one of only three in British collections; another trecentro panel by Ugolino; and a *Madonna with Sts John the Baptist and Michael* by Matteo Giovanni); Florentine (works by Signorelli and Botticelli) and Venetian (two delightful Bellinis, and the Cima *Crucifixion*). The Dutch and Flemish schools are also strongly represented.

In 1967 the trust deed was varied to allow 20th-century work to be acquired, so permit-

ting the next director, Professor Hamish Miles, to buy Odilon Redon's *Crucifixion*, a Léger still life and an outstanding Magritte, *The Flavour of Tears*, in which giant tobacco leaves become a mournful bird to be devoured by a caterpillar.

Rising prices in the last quarter of the 20th century have put most contemporary art out of reach of galleries such as the Barber without the help of the National Art Collections Fund or the Heritage Lottery Fund. With their assistance the current director, Professor Richard Verdi, bought the *Portrait of Bartolomeo Savona* by André Derain in 1997 and Johan Christian Dahl's haunting *Mother and Child by the Sea* (1840), only the second painting by Dahl in a major public collection in Britain.[28]

However, works on paper remain affordable and to the Fra Bartolommeo, Van Dyck, Rembrandt, Gainsborough, Ingres and Degas drawings acquired by Bodkin, Professor Verdi has added a strong collection of early 20th-century German drawings and etchings by, for example, Egon Schiele, Otto Dix, Max Beckmann and Emil Nolde. The latter's woodcut, *Prophet*, remains one of the bleakest, most desperate images of the 20th century. The Christ's hollow eyes, gouged from the wood's grain, look out at the horror of the wars and genocides to come.

The Barber is a superb teaching collection. Many of the Birmingham students who have benefited from it, and from the generous scholarship of Professor Verdi, have been appointed to curatorial posts in regional galleries described in this book. It is also a collection that exudes a constant love for the ability of paintings and drawings, in Thomas Bodkin's words, 'to kindle in our own spirit a . . . radiance'.

The Barber has one of the most satisfactory collections in the country and is certainly one of the finest small galleries, alongside Dulwich Picture Gallery and Christ Church Picture Gallery (both q.v.). The conditions in Lady Barber's trust deed expressed an ideal. Bodkin, Waterhouse, Miles and Verdi have realised it triumphantly.

BIRMINGHAM MUSEUM AND ART GALLERY ★★★★

Chamberlain Square, Birmingham,
West Midlands B3 3DH
Tel. 0121 303 2834
www.bmag.org.uk

Pre-Raphaelites supreme at the heart of great mercantile city

The establishment of the Birmingham Museum and Art Gallery was motivated by a desire to see, in the words of Thomas Collier Barnes, one of its first benefactors,[29] 'a great Industrial Museum ... centrally situated in the town of Birmingham': to achieve in the Midlands what the Victoria and Albert Museum (q.v.) was trying to achieve nationally.

'It is all very well for cities to exclaim against Birmingham manufacturers and artisans because of their inferiority to their foreign competitors in the matter of design and manufacture,' wrote Richard Tangye, Birmingham engineer and another of the museum's founding benefactors,[30] 'but what chance have they of improving in these respects? South Kensington is practically as far away as Paris or Munich, while our competitors on the continent, in almost every manufacturing town, have access to collections containing the finest examples of art, furnishing an endless variety of style and design.'

Tangye offered the city £10,000 to begin an art collection and a new building was designed by H. Yeoville Thomason. The links with the V&A were strengthened by the appointment of Whitworth Wallis as the first curator. Wallis was a South Kensington man, protégé of John Charles Robinson, Superintendent of Art Collections at the V&A and later Surveyor of the Queen's Pictures, who insisted, 'If it should be asked what use Italian sculptures, marble saints and madonnas ... are likely to be to Birmingham and its working thousands, my answer is that I entirely refuse to admit that art culture in the provinces should be a different thing, or pitched at a lower level than in London.'

This ambition was reflected in Thomason's building at the heart of the city centre, in a group of confident civic buildings: the Free Library, J. A. Hanson's classical Town Hall (1832–50), the 'rather flashy Renaissance Revival hulk'[31] of the Council House (1874–9) and Chamberlain and Martin's Municipal School of Art (1881–5), one of the loveliest of Gothic Revival buildings.

The museum had the backing of the city's commercial and industrial leaders, notably John Feeney,[32] proprietor of the *Birmingham Post*, and T. Clarkson Osler[33] of the glass-making company F. & C. Osler. Unusually their generosity was matched by that of Osler's principal glass-blowers, Thomas Collier Barnes and his brother Elijah. T. C. Barnes was the Secretary of the glass makers' union, the Flint Glass Makers Friendly Society. When he and Elijah won first prize for their glass at the 1870 International Workmen's Exhibition they presented half their glass to the Corporation and persuaded the City to buy the rest, thus establishing the museum's fine collection of English and Venetian glass.[34]

The heart of the museum, on the first floor, is the Round Room, a large top-lit rotunda hung floor to ceiling with Victorian paintings (Edward Poynter, Lawrence Alma-Tadema, Albert Moore's *Dreamers*, 1882, Lord Leighton's *Condittiere*, 1872, and several oils by David Cox including the expansive *Rhyl Sands*, 1854–5).

The Round Room led to the other galleries and to the 100-foot-long Industrial Hall, which Wallis began to fill with jewellery, ceramics, glass and furniture. The first piece to be accessioned, in 1864, was the 6th–7th-century *Sultanganj Buddha* from Bihar, over seven feet tall, the largest-known complete Indian sculpture in metal (copper). There followed acquisitions from all over the world (Egypt, Greece, the Middle East) and outstanding metalwork from South Asia and the Far East.

In 1891 a decision was made to collect the work of the Pre-Raphaelite Brotherhood and its followers with a particular emphasis on Edward Burne-Jones, who was born in Birmingham and from whom the city had already commissioned, in 1887, the vast *Star of*

Edward Burne-Jones's The Star of Bethlehem
(Birmingham Museum and Art Gallery)

Bethlehem, at 8 feet by 36 feet probably the largest watercolour in the world. By the end of the century the museum had paintings by Holman Hunt, Rossetti, Millais (*The Blind Girl*) and Ford Madox Brown (*The Last of England*).

This strong Pre-Raphaelite collection was transformed into one of outstanding importance when Wallis succeeded in buying from the artist and collector Charles Fairfax Murray, at well below market prices, 260 Rossetti and 226 Burne-Jones drawings (1903), 35 Burne-Jones stained-glass cartoons (1904) and 300 drawings by Millais, Madox Brown and Frederick Sandys (1907). Fairfax Murray had lived and worked at the heart of the Pre-Raphaelite Brotherhood since being taken on by Burne-Jones in 1866 to assist him in designing and making stained glass.

One of those who helped finance these purchases was a local solicitor, J. R. Holliday, who bequeathed his own collection of watercolours and drawings to several public galleries,[35] Birmingham among them. Holliday's collection of Burne-Jones's drawings was outstanding, as was a significant group of Morris & Co. stained glass. His generosity was dwarfed by that of J. Leslie Wright, who, in 1953, left over four hundred watercolours to the museum: by Gainsborough, J. R. Cozens, De Wint, Bonington.

The museum had always purchased Old Masters: a panel by Cima da Conegliano; Petrus Christus's tiny intense *Christ as the Man of Sorrows* (*c.* 1450); Adrien Isenbrandt's *Triptych* (*c.* 1510–12); and a glorious Claude, *Pastoral Landscape with the Ponte Molle* (1645) in which Claude is at his most magical, the light coming from impossibly far beyond the Ponte Molle, from, it seems, beyond the rim of the world.

After the Second World War the museum had for the first time a purchase grant and, in a market whose prices were low, the new director, Trenchard Cox (and subsequently his successor, Anna Woodall), bought well: Lely's portrait of *Oliver Cromwell* and Gentileschi's *Rest on the Flight into Egypt* (both 1949) which strengthened the museum's collection of 17th-century Italian baroque paintings by Guercino, Orazio Gentileschi, Bernardo Strozzi, Guido Reni, Carlo Carlone, Guiseppi Maria Crespi and Luca Giordano, some considerable time before Sir Denis Mahon's pioneering scholarship re-established their importance. It is appropriate therefore that Birmingham is one of the small number of galleries to whom Sir Denis has offered Italian 17th-century paintings[36] on long-term loan. The gallery's Old Masters collection is not comparable to that of the Barber Institute of Fine Arts (q.v.) but it includes paintings by Simone Martini, Giovanni Bellini and a Canaletto of *Warwick Castle* commissioned by Lord Brooke in 1748/9.

In the late 20th century the principal collections of material from archaeology and world cultures were received by gift and bequest between the wars, and with the receipt of material from the Wellcome Foundation from the 1950s onwards. These developed fine collections of Oceanian, Cypriot, Near Eastern and Pre-Columbian material – while at the same time building those collections that celebrate the achievements of Birmingham: the ormolu and metalwork of Matthew Boulton and John Fothergill; 18th-century steel buckles and buttons; the work of Birmingham designers (John Hardman, Bernard Cuzner).

The museum already had a solid collection of early-20th-century English painting (Sickert, Wilson Steer, Gilman; Matthew Smith, Stanley Spencer, Ivon Hitchens). It now set about collecting across a range of contemporary applied arts with key works by Alison Britton, Carol McNicoll, Grayson Perry, Edmund de Waal et al. In addition to ceramics (Lucie Rie, Hans Coper, Gordon Baldwin), in the field of fine metalwork the museum has perhaps the pre-eminent collection in Europe, and, when the adjacent Waterhall[37] was converted into a new gallery, contemporary art was collected with an energy that few other museums even attempt to match.

To the work of those artists you might expect to find in late-20th-century collections (Francis Bacon, Henry Moore, William Gear, Ben Nicholson, Patrick Heron, Bridget Riley, Howard Hodgkin, Eduardo Paolozzi) Birmingham is adding Callum Innes, Fiona Rae, Tony Bevan, Sean Scully, Maggi Hambling.

To have reached the art of today from your starting point among the 19th-century oil paintings of the Round Room, you will have picked your way through galleries of Egyptology, World Cultures and Birmingham History; fine and decorative arts from the 15th century, on the second floor; through galleries of glass, metalwork, jewellery and ceramics. If the museum is most celebrated, justly, for its collections of Pre-Raphaelites and of English watercolours, if it became deflected from its original ambition to be a great industrial museum, it has fulfilled the spirit of Thomas Collier Barnes's original ambition to be a proud museum in the centre of a proud city.

SOHO HOUSE **

Soho Avenue, Handsworth, Birmingham, West Midlands B18 5LB
Tel. 0121 554 9122
www.bmag.org.uk/soho_house

Matthew Boulton's house, that once overlooked his foundry, where he produced ormolu and metalwork for the world

Around the dining-room table in Soho House met some of the 18th century's most remarkable men: Joseph Priestley, the discoverer of oxygen; James Watt, who developed the steam engine; Josiah Wedgwood, potter; William Small, doctor and mathematician, Professor of Natural History at Williamsburg University, Virginia, and tutor to Thomas Jefferson;

A pair of ormolu and Blue John ewers by Matthew Boulton and John Fothergill (Soho House)

Erasmus Darwin, doctor and uncle of Charles Darwin; and Matthew Boulton, industrialist and entrepreneur, whose house it was. All were radicals, as concerned with the abolition of slavery and political developments in France and America as they were with the sciences and their relevance to the new manufacturing industries that were exploding around them as Birmingham, Stoke and Derby grew from villages into cities in their lifetimes. The Lunar Society,[38] as they called themselves, met once a month on the Monday nearest the full moon, with members coming from Birmingham and the wider Midlands area. Josiah Wedgwood rode the fifty miles from Stoke.

Soho House tells us about Boulton – his interests and tastes, how he redesigned and rebuilt his house incorporating the latest inventions – and gives us a glimpse of the buttons, buckles and boxes, the coins, the silver, silver plate and ormolu he produced at his Soho Manufactory and Mint, overlooked by Soho House.

Boulton commissioned first James Wyatt and then his brother, Samuel, to redesign and extend the small farmhouse on the site. As he had done at Shugborough, Samuel Wyatt clad the exterior with slate. Inside Boulton had several examples of the latest technology: a hot-air central heating system; a steam-heated bath, eight feet long, which took two empty-ings of the well to fill and one and a half hours to heat; and a Joseph Bramah patent flushing water closet (1787), whose twin is in Sir John Soane's Museum (q.v.).

Boulton's friend James Keir (another member of the Lunar Society) had patented a new alloy called 'eldorado' on account of its golden sheen. Boulton used eldorado to make the glazing bars of the sash windows in the Dining Room and the fanlight above the door of his daughter Anne's Sitting Room upstairs.

Since Boulton's son, Matthew Robinson Boulton, left the house to live in Great Tew in 1850, it has been a girl's school, a hotel, a vicarage for the newly built St Michael's Church, a hostel for GEC and, until recently, a hostel for young policemen. In spite of this it retains most of its original features: cornices,

columns, pilasters, chimney pieces, the glazed entrance doors, double mahogany doors (by Samuel Wyatt), glass handles and fingerplates, the original glass in many windows, even the mirrored glass set into the lower half of the shutters in some upstairs rooms.

Some of the furniture, too, is original, notably the Lunar Society's dining table, a Klismos chair, and several pieces by James Newton, a leading 18th-century cabinet maker, including a fine rosewood side cabinet in the Breakfast Room and japanned chairs there and in Anne Boulton's Bedroom.

The rest of the furniture is of the period but was not owned by Boulton. It includes a magnificent convex mirror, c. 1800, attributed to Thomas Fentham, in the Dining Room.

Many of the furnishings have been recreated to represent the originals, including wall-papers and '3 pair of french window curtains' and '55 yards of Brussells Carpet with a narrow border made up to plan' originally supplied by Newton for the Breakfast Room. The pillars and the curtains in the Dining Room have been repainted to the original Cornelius Dixon designs. But the outstanding re-creation is the 'painted canvas oylcloth' on the floor of the Entrance Hall, 'a work of more consequence than has ever been done in floorcloth'. It was the forerunner of linoleum and this example with its geometric pattern of yellow, blue and red could have come from a late-20th-century design company.

Upstairs there is a small, all too small, display of the work produced by the Manu-factory: candlesticks, salvers, spoons and forks in silver and in plate. Some early pieces are in a rococo style that was ceasing to be fashionable in the 1760s but most are designed on classical lines as if they were pieces of Wedgwood in metal.

Notable among these is a pair of ormolu mounted Blue John ewers (1772) and a wire-work bread basket (1785–90). More of the Manufactory's work can be seen at the Bir-mingham Assay Office and the Victoria and Albert Museum (q.v.).

Soho House describes Boulton's taste, eye and curiosity but it cannot capture the energy and daring with which he, and Watt, transformed 18th-century manufacturing, not just with steam power but with an ingenuity and imagination that transformed base metal. As Keir said in his 1809 memoir of Boulton, 'whatever he did or attempted, his success or failure were all on a large scale'. To see this in action visit the Science Museum (q.v.) where there are two majestic, working Boulton & Watt engines. But Soho House is a fine introduction to an entrepreneur and industrialist who merits a greater reputation.

HERBERT ART GALLERY AND MUSEUM *

Jordan Well, Coventry, West Midlands
CV1 5QP
Tel. 024 7683 2386
www.coventrymuseum.org.uk

Lady Godiva plus medieval treasures, silk ribbons, metalwork, paintings – and aero engines

The Herbert Art Gallery and Museum is well named. It was founded with a gift from Sir Albert Herbert, a local machine tool manufacturer; the foundation stone was laid by Sir Alfred; the gallery was designed by Anthony Herbert, Sir Alfred's nephew, built by the consanguineous Messrs Alfred Herbert & Sons,[39] and opened by Sir Alfred in 1960.

The collections are less Herbiferous. They comprise the history of the city's industries; Georgian silver; watercolours; 19th-century ribbons; 20th-century British sculpture and painting; motorbikes and engines; and Lady Godiva.

Coventry was an important Saxon and Norman city at the centre of the kingdom; fiercely contested in the Wars of the Roses and the Civil War (the city was Parliamentarian and its Royalist prisoners were not spoken to – hence 'sending to Coventry'); a medieval religious shrine to St Osburg, attracting a Benedictine priory, houses of the Greyfriars and the Whitefriars and a Charterhouse. Its cathedral was destroyed in the Reformation

and again in 1940 by German bombing, to rise again beside the museum, the new cathedral designed by Basil Spence with a triumphant tapestry by Graham Sutherland.

Alfred Herbert started work on his museum in 1939. After the war he recommenced building on a larger, adjacent site, conveniently cleared by the bombing. It opened in 1960, a flat undistinguished example of post-war municipal architecture on which Pevsner declines to comment.[40] Any admirers it has might describe its juxtaposed rectangular blocks as a homage to Mondrian in red brick and plate glass.

As you enter there is that rarity, a plaque in memory of the museum's first Director (1960–74), the Irish poet John Hewitt. Inside, the ground-floor galleries contain objects through which the city's history is told: the 6th-century Saxon Baginton bowl, excavated in 1934; misericords, dark with age and use, from the 14th-century Carmelite Whitefriars; the Coventry sallet, a medieval helmet; a 15th-century polychromed wooden sculpture of St George killing the dragon, from St George's Chapel by Gosford Gate; a knave's whipping post (1679) whose worn narrowness speaks of pain and humiliation; and a long-case clock (1691) by Samuel Watson, Coventry's master clockmaker and Mathematician in Ordinary to Charles II.

The 20th century is here in the form of a 1922 Triumph Ricardo motorbike, 'The Riccy'; the TE/20 'Little Grey Fergie' tractor of which Massey Fergusson sold half a million; and a gleaming 1949 Armstrong Siddeley Viper aero engine.

Two displays stand out. The first, on the city's 19th-century ribbon industry, has at its centre a jacquard loom[41] that is typical of the machines in Coventry in the mid 19th century when the ribbon industry was booming. Companies such as that owned by John and Joseph Cash (Cash's name tapes) produced silk ribbons of every colour, width and design. Here are their archives and catalogues, pages of snipped material, variations on every design, streamers of ribbons with which to trick up a bonnet, brighten a shawl or from which to hang a medal. The Cashes were Quakers, serious-minded Liberal employers, but other manufacturers were not and in 1831 weavers had burnt down the first steam factory of Josiah Beck, an outbreak of radical, Luddite anger by 'first hand weavers' marooned between the poverty and freedom of being semi-unemployed artisans and the captive security of the factory.[42]

The second display is of the metalwork of the Coventry craftsman Francis Skidmore, a silversmith who embodied the aesthetic of the Gothic Revival, which was led by A.W.N. Pugin, Sir George Gilbert Scott and others. The chalice here that Skidmore exhibited at the 1851 Great Exhibition gave him a national reputation and he proceeded to design and make the decorated arched roof of Deane and Woodward's Oxford University Museum of Natural History (1857) (q.v.) and the choir screen for Hereford Cathedral (1862), now in the Victoria and Albert Museum (q.v.). A trophy tankard made for the Warwickshire Rifle Volunteers (1862) and a missal cover (c.1864) show the intricacy of his work, as elaborate as that of William Burges,[43] if less eccentric.

Upstairs the art collection shows the influence of John Hewitt and of the museum's art committees. The museum opened with only a miscellaneous handful of paintings: a portrait of George III by Sir Thomas Lawrence (1792); works by Luca Giordano, George Morland, Paul Nash and John Piper, and two watercolours by J.M.W. Turner. A painting by Sir Augustus Wall Calcott was presented by Lord Kenilworth in 1955. Calcott was a landscape rival of Constable and was one of those who delayed Constable's election to the Royal Academy. The sunset in his Cow Boys (1807) here demonstrates his skill but also shows why Constable considered him 'artificial'.

To build a collection of 20th-century paintings, sculptures, watercolours and drawings, an art committee was established, advised by Hewitt.[44] Together in the 1960s they acquired paintings by Stanley Spencer, Ben Nicholson, John Bratby and Charles Nevinson,

a late Anne Redpath, A Mexican Figure (1962), and an unusual, and unusually large, oil by L.S. Lowry, Ebbw Vale; drawings by Mark Gertler, Henri Gaudier-Brzeska and Christopher Wood; sculptures by Barbara Hepworth and Jacob Epstein; and ceramics by Bernard Leach and Lucie Rie. They also bought six 19th-century watercolours by David Cox and, most exceptionally, an oil painting and ten drawings including an oil on paper by David Bomberg, considered by the art critic David Sylvester to be 'the forgotten man of British painting'.[45] Bomberg wrote of his own work, 'Drawing ... reveals the unknown things ... Style is ephemeral – Form is eternal.'[46] These drawings demonstrate that discovery, as they do Leon Kossoff's observation of Bomberg working: 'Once I watched him draw over a student's drawing. I saw the flow of form, I saw the likeness to the sitter appear. It seemed an encounter with what was already there . . .'[47]

Hewitt retired and the momentum of acquisitions slowed but in recent years the museum has bought drawings by Edward Burra, David Jones, Richard Hamilton and Joseph Beuys. The most significant post-Hewitt acquisition was, in 1974, the 155 sketches that Graham Sutherland made in preparation for the cathedral tapestry from 1952 to 1958. Here are drawings for the eagle of St John, the calf of St Luke, the lion of St Mark and the winged man. Here is the lion, sleeping, yawning, in the sun; here is Christ seated; in glory; blessing; with outstretched arms; on the Cross. Seldom can the process of designing a tapestry have been so thoroughly and so movingly documented.

Consistently the museum has acquired paintings of Lady Godiva, the wife of Leofric Earl of Mercia who founded the Benedictine Priory here in 1043. There are paintings of her by Landseer, Collier and Woolmer. None of these can resist depicting her nudity, suitably concealed by flowing hair. It is likely that the nakedness of the tale refers to her head being uncovered, without wimple or veil, sufficiently modest and self-abrogating for an 11th-century public protest against taxation.

UNIVERSITY OF OXFORD BOTANIC GARDEN ***

Rose Lane, Oxford, Oxfordshire OX1 4AZ
Tel. 01865 286690
botanic-garden.ox.ac.uk
e.mail: postmaster@botanic-garden.ox.ac.uk

A bravura royal entrance to Britain's first botanic garden, a museum of plants

For 'the glorification of the works of God and for the furtherance of learning' are the reasons that Henry Danvers, 1st Earl of Danby, gave £5,000 in 1621 to set up Britain's first botanic garden, originally a physic garden of medicinal plants.

Land was rented from Magdalen College,[48] levelled and enriched with '4,000 loads of mucke and dunge' from the college cesspits. Stone was brought from Headington Quarry and a triumphal arch, the Danby Arch (1633), designed by Neklaus Stone: the entrance to the garden.

You enter the original walled garden. At its centre is an ornamental pond, around which are eight rectangular lawns with beds of hardy plants laid out on a grid, separated by paths. Straight ahead are euphorbia; to the left are paeonies, poppies and violas; to the right are gentians, primulas, amaryllis and lilies; ahead are daisies. Elsewhere are plants that are grown for a commerical purpose: for food; for fibre (the stinging nettle, *Urtica dioica*, from which fabric finer than linen was made in the 17th century); for medicine (the poisonous but seductive-looking thorn apple, *Datura stramonium*,[49] currently being tested as a treatment for Parkinson's disease); for dye; for oil (the iris that is the source of the world's most expensive essential oil, orris). There are beds of variegated plants and, in every shade of velvety purple, maroon and yellow, the bearded irises so beloved of the Victorians. Against the creamy walls, shaded and dry, are beds of ferns, hardy Japanese orchids and Chinese winter-flowering shrubs.

This living museum repays continual visits. Come in autumn as the leaves of the vines are turning pink and the roses are swollen into dark hips. There is a heavy scent of wintersweet (*Lonicera fragrantissima*). The iris and aster are cut down, the last tissuey hollyhock rosette is holding on. People moor their punts and the sun is soft through the gingko. The garden settles itself, the beds go to sleep in families: *Tradescantia virginia*; *Allium cernuum*, *A. elatum*, *A. ramosum*.

Three months later the beds are stripped neat and clean. At the far end near the Bog Garden dahlias are safe under wicker cloches packed with fern, the leaves on the sweet gum are translucent. The ponds are frozen, plates of dark ice over the discs and flex of nymphaea. Only yellow *Hamamelis mollis* is in flower. In the glass houses visitors without scarves seek respite and find condensation; their spectacles steam up. There is the sweet promise of cardamom, coffee, vanilla.

By spring the neatly self-stowed ferns are uncurling, the evergreens producing bright growth in surprising tufts. You pass a blast of philadelphus; the first *Paeonia officinalis* is a deep red.

In June you are welcomed by a giant magnolia on the right and by beds of bee-friendly salvia and of old roses: 'Maiden's Blush' (pre 15th century), *Rosa × alba* (pre 16th century), common moss (*R. × centifolia* 'Muscosa') (pre 17th century), 'Comte de Chambord' (1860), the heady scent of deep purple 'Roseraie de L'Häy' (1901). The rock garden is bleached in the sun and people linger beside the shaded lily pond.

Sit in that shade and consider the four centuries of work that have made this garden, tended by superintendents, overseen by Sherardian Professors of Botany. The first Superintendent, Jacob Bobart, favoured yew hedges and trees. One of his yews, planted in 1650 outside the South Gate, is still there, the oldest plant in the garden. Followed everywhere by his pet goat, he compiled *An English Catalogue of the Trees and Plants in the Physicke Garden of the Universitye of Oxford*, 'with the Latine names added thereunto' in 1648. It listed the 1,600 species growing in the garden. They are remembered in the 1648 bed[50] by the glasshouses to the right of the herbaceous border: the delicate pale white-pink star flower of black masterwort (*Astrantia major*), 1596; the purple *Tradescantia virginia*;[51] the timeless severe ornamental foliage of *Acanthus mollis*.

Bobart's son, also Jacob, who succeeded him, circulated seeds to gardens around the world. When germinating the seed of an occidental plane tree sent him from Montpelier he saw that it was a hybrid, part occidental, part oriental. He grew it on: the original plane tree, the staple of city streets everywhere. His successor, Jacob Dillenius, propagated a Sicilian seed with less happy results: the Oxford ragwort, the blight of every railway siding and derelict site.

In 360 years there have been only thirteen superintendents,[52] one of the most influential of whom was George Robinson (1942–63). In 1945 he moved the garden outside Neklaus Stone's wall. Christ Church College had been using this large triangle of land as allotments during the war. For 6d. a year the garden took it on and Robinson created the Big Herbaceous Border, its classical proportions (137 feet long, 17 feet deep) the perfect backdrop for geraniums and delphiniums in April, globe artichokes in bursting summer flower, asters and seed-heads of *Echinops giganteus* in the autumn. Beside the new pond was created the Rockery and, at the far end, the Bog Garden, to make the Botanic Garden of today.

This is one of the earliest university museums and, like those that followed in its wake, the academic functions of research and reference lie behind the exhibited trees and flowers. Whether the visitor comes here to wonder at the 'black' flowers of the glasshouse border, or the ebullience of the early crocus; to admire the quiet beauty of the *Jeffersonia diphylla* or the medieval fruit of the medlar; to wander or to study, this garden fulfils Henry Danvers's purpose.

BATE COLLECTION ***

Faculty of Music, St Aldate's, Oxford, Oxfordshire OX1 1DB
Tel. 01865 276139
www.ashmol.ox.ac.uk/BCMIPage.html

A celestial collection of musical instruments

In appearance the Bressan recorder (*c.* 1720), boxwood and ivory, is like the other early 18th-century recorders on display at the Bate Collection. It is set apart as the father of recorders by the beauty of its rich, liquid sound which originates in the way it was made by Pierre Bressan (né 'Jaillard of Bresse': the English could play his instruments but found his name too difficult to pronounce). Bressan gave the windway a slight curve, and smoothed the internal gradients of the bore and the edges of the finger holes to create its tonal quality and tuning. It is only one of many original instruments here whose characteristics must be studied and understood if we are to appreciate the music that they made. They are to modern music what 'type specimens' are to natural history.

Philip Bate (1909–99) began collecting as a twelve-year-old child in Edinburgh, buying instruments from barrows or junkshops for threepence or sixpence each for the joy of playing them. After a career as a musical director for the BBC, he wanted a home for his collection of 300 woodwind instruments that would not only allow them to be played and enjoyed but would provide the scholarly context necessary to underpin the growing interest in original instruments, particularly of the baroque period. Here in Oxford, as part of the Faculty of Music, he found both.

With Anthony Baines and ten like-minded friends, Bate had formed the Galpin Society[53] to further the study of musical instruments and the Bate became the physical expression of the work of the society and its journal.[54] Anthony Baines was appointed the first lecturer/curator of the Bate on its opening in

Bows at the Bate Collection

1970, bringing with him his own collection of brass instruments.[55] To this were added, by gift and bequest, Reginald Morley-Pegge's collection of horns and the harpsichords collected by Michael Thomas.

The setting for the museum is modest. It is entered through a small side door in the Faculty of Music which is positioned between Christ Church college and the River Cherwell. Inside is a paradise of instruments: a corridor of cabinets of recorders; a wall of clarinets and saxophones; another of horns; a fourth of trumpets. Between these are harpsichords and clavichords with just enough room for the visitor to move between them. Timpani (a loan collection from Jeremy Montague, the curator who succeeded Anthony Baines, 1981–95) are squeezed into any gap.

Here are crumhorns and cornets; shawms, sackbuts and serpents; bagpipes and bassoons; cors anglais that arch their backs; horns that sweetly curl, left handed and right handed; trumpets and bugles; viols and violas (da gamba, between the knees, da braccio, on the shoulder – the violin); lutes, rebecs, mandolins and harps; virginals, spinets, clavichords and harpsichords; and a pipe and tabor as played by Will Kemp[56] on his progress from Norwich to London. This is Psalm 150 in the life: 'Praise him with the sound of the trumpet; praise him with the psaltery and harp./Praise him with the timbral and dance: praise him with the stringed instruments and organs./Praise him upon the loud cymbals: praise him upon the high sounding cymbals./Let everything that hath breath praise the Lord.'[57]

This flow of music making, loans to orchestras and students, demonstrations and research, is the core collection, which contains instruments of rarity and curiosity: the oldest English oboe (c. 1680) and its successor by the great Dutch maker Hendrick Richters (c. 1700); a beautifully incised trumpet by Simon Beale,[58] made in London in 1667 when Purcell was a boy; two horns by Hofmaster, with blood-red painted bells, owned by Granville Sharp and his family, depicted in the portrait of the Sharps by Zoffany.

Here too is an early (1859) example of the saxophone invented by Adolphe Sax in 1840. The saxophone combined a single reed mouthpiece with an ophicléide which itself superseded the serpent, represented here by at least seven fine examples from the Morley-Pegge Gift, including one made by Thomas Key 'before 1815' and played by Drummer Richard Bentwick of the 23rd Regiment of Foot at the battle of Waterloo.[59]

Among the keyboard instruments is a harpsichord (1700) made by Joseph Tisseran and a 1743 clavichord by Hieronymous Albrecht Hass in Hamburg. Beside it is the clavichord that Arnold Dolmetsch made in 1894 based on, and as a tribute to, the great Hass. Most remarkable and delightful is a harpsichord made by William Smith, c. 1720. It is almost certainly the instrument on which Handel is leaning in his portrait by Philippe Mercier,[60] identified by its idiosyncratic 'skunktail sharps' (sharps made of chevrons of alternate ebony and ivory).

The Bate offers us an understanding of how these instruments might have sounded, how they developed one from another and how they influenced composers: how Schubert was able in the 'Unfinished' Symphony and the great C Major Symphony to exploit the new chromatic possibilities of the trombone's slide in ways denied to Beethoven; how Beethoven turned the timpani into a tuned instrument in its own right, adding to its tonic and dominant other pitches, the tritone in *Fidelio*, the octave in the Eighth and Ninth Symphonies.

Upstairs, tucked at the back, are two cases which allow us to marvel at the craftsmanship of those who made instruments such as these. One is a case of bows by the great English bowmakers Edward Dodd, the Toutes, *père et deux fils* (Xavier and Francois), Arthur Bultitude and William Retford, trained by Bultitude in the workshop of W. E. Hill and Sons. The second case is a shrine to Retford, the greatest contemporary bow maker. In it are all his tools; his wire-framed spectacles, folded; and the last bow he made, for a cello.

OXFORD UNIVERSITY MUSEUM OF NATURAL HISTORY ***

Parks Road, Oxford, Oxfordshire OX1 3PW
Tel. 01865 272950
www.oum.ox.ac.uk

Ruskin-inspired architecture matched by superb collections

In this cathedral of glass and iron, science, religion and architecture come together as in no other museum in the land, with the exception of its younger cousin the Natural History Museum (q.v.). The beauty of its design, the technology of its construction, the detail of its decoration are all metaphors for its collections of natural history (fossils, insects, shells, minerals, rocks) and the significance that our society attaches to them.

The museum stands alone[61] beyond an expanse of grass that separates it from South Parks Road and Keble College. Its design was by the Dublin firm of Deane & Woodward, appointed after an architectural competition whose shortlist of two (the other being E. M. Barry)[62] was voted on by Convocation. You can read its facade in one good glance. At first sight its proportions are strange. The hipped roof of the central tower is a little too steep, the lower storey a little too elevated. The entrance is carved from a grey stone that contrasts with the honey sandstone of the facade. Its style is a form of Gothic, as desired by its aesthetic godfather John Ruskin,[63] but it owes rather more to medieval Belgian cloth halls[64] than to the Italian, specifically Venetian, Gothic that Ruskin had in mind.[65]

You enter through a second portal into a large hall flooded with light surrounded by an ambulatory and a gallery. The roof is what Dr Henry Wentworth Acland, Reader in Anatomy and the driving force behind the museum, described as being made from 'these railway materials – iron and glass' (the iron is both cast and wrought).

This is a building as forest. The supporting pillars and spandrels soar up to the steep glass roof, studded by rivets, decorated with stencilled plant forms. *Building News* deplored its 'Crystal Palace architecture Gothecised' and declared it a 'pernicious heresy ... to copy nature in structural steelwork'. The capitals of the columns are delicate branches in wrought iron, the whole by Francis Skidmore of Coventry.[66]

The carved stonework on the facade is as magnificent. The carving is by the Irish stonemasons James O'Shea, from Ballyhooly, County Cork, his brother and their nephew Edward Whellan. Within, each column is carved from a different British rock,[67] inscribed with the name of its stone and its source: the liquid grey of Devonian limestone from Torquay; the mottled purple of carboniferous limestone from County Limerick; the speckled brown of quartziferous porphyry from Trenice in Cornwall. The O'Sheas carved each capital exquisitely into plants that represented all the botanical orders, from specimens brought daily from the Oxford Botanic Gardens. James O'Shea wrote to Acland in 1859, 'If I were to doo [sic] all the upper windows I would carve every jamb for nothing for the sake of art alone'[68] and later, to Acland and Ruskin, 'I have never carved anything in my life that I will be so proud of if I do these'.[69] A myth has grown up that the O'Sheas were dismissed before their work was completed, perhaps because the building was over budget, perhaps because of insubordination.[70] However the museum's accounts show that they were working as late as 1879[71] on the building, whose beauty and brilliance was assured even though Woodward died in 1861 and the building was never completed.

No apology is offered for the space devoted to this building because it is, by some way, the most remarkable, satisfactory and integrated museum building in Britain, a work of art in its own right and the expression of its collections.

Acland was determined to have this museum because science in the university in the 1840s was at a low ebb. 'The Science studies of the University were from various causes almost extinct,' he wrote. 'The intellect of the

University was wholly given to ecclesiastical and theological questions.' This intellectual conservatism required every undergraduate to sign the Thirty-Nine Articles of Religion on entering the university.

The university had remarkable scientific collections (the Tradescants' zoological specimens, including a dodo; William Buckland's geological collection, which included a 25-foot-long *Megalosaurus bucklandii*, the first dinosaur to be named and scientifically described in 1824; the Revd Frederick William Hope's insect collection, presented in 1849) but the teaching was confined to what was already known. Acland wanted a 'great Museum' that would be a 'Book of Nature' to inspire the university's science departments.

The exhibits in the Main Hall demonstrate the extent to which he succeeded. It is a stage crowded with players: Buckland's dinosaur, his 'terrible lizard'; John Phillips's cetiosaurus;[72] a flight of suspended whales (white, bottle-nosed and killer) over the floorbound leather-back turtle, the giant tortoise. Sitting patiently in a cabinet is an albatross ('the snow white ghost of the haunted Capes of Hope and Horn' – Herman Melville) sharing a case with a tiny storm petrel, its pink beak seeming to suggest a smile. A twenty-nine-pound pike, found dead in Ewhurst Lake, Hampshire, with fury on his face, had swallowed a nine-pound pike. Anthropomorphism is hard to resist for the layman, even at the risk of Dr Acland's displeasure. Here is a black stuffed African crocodile with a watchful glass eye and the skeleton of a Nile crocodile, bleached white, grinning in the bone.

These specimens you gaze upon with delight. The marbles and decorated stones from the Faustino Corsi Collection (antique breccias of violet, red and white – breccia di Sette Basi, pietra del Vesuvio, striated greys) you need to look at under a microscope. One is provided for you to appreciate the sparkling greens and blues of hunks of malachite and azurite.

A Skidmore spandrel at the Oxford University Museum of Natural History

The museum opened in 1860, the year in which Charles Darwin published *The Origin of Species*. The museum hosted a meeting of the British Association at which Thomas Henry Huxley defended Darwinism against the 'argumentative, rhetorical, amusing' attacks of Samuel Wilberforce, Bishop of Oxford, in which the Bishop said he would feel some 'disquietude' were he to be descended from a 'venerable ape'. Huxley rose, white with anger. 'I should be sorry to demolish so eminent a prelate, but for myself I would rather be descended from an ape than from a divine who employs authority to stifle truth.'[73] One of Acland's purposes, to awaken the university's science departments, was achieved.

His wider aim was to display the diversity of God's creation and to reconcile science and the divine. For all but the most determined life-denier, the museum is true to this spirit.

ASHMOLEAN MUSEUM
★★★★★

Beaumont Street, Oxford, Oxfordshire
OX1 2PH
Tel. 01865 278000
www.ashmol.ox.ac.uk

The first public museum in Britain and one of the greatest

The collections of what is now the Ashmolean Museum start not with Elias Ashmole (1617–92) but with John Tradescant the Elder (*c.* 1570–1638) (gardener to the Duke of Buckingham and, after his death, to Charles I and Queen Henrietta Maria) and his son, John Tradescant the Younger (1608–62).[74]

In the course of their travels to find new plant species (the Elder to Flanders, France, Algiers and Russia; the Younger three times to America) from which they introduced to Britain lilac, acacia, the occidental plane and, from Algeria, the apricot, they collected such 'Rarities and Curiosities'[75] as 'Utensills, Householdstuffe, Habits, Instruments of Warre' as well as birds, beasts, shells and insects. All were housed at the Tradescant house in Lambeth, where their nursery and market garden were.

Private collections, whether Wunderkammern (of curiosities), Schatzkammern (of jewels and precious metals) or Kunstkammern (of fine and decorative art), had existed since the 15th and 16th centuries, but the Tradescants' 'Closet of Rarities' was one of the first to be opened to the public, the level of payment for each visit being determined by the time spent. A catalogue of their plants had been published in 1656, while the museum catalogue, divided between 'the Naturall' (animals and 'Outlandish-Fruits') and 'Artificialls' ('Carvings, Turnings, Sowings and Paintings'), appeared in 1656.

If public museums and galleries in Britain can be said to have a point of origin it is here in the Tradescants' 'Closet of Rarities', its catalogue prefiguring the separation of museums of the sciences from those of the arts. Indeed the present familiar use of the word 'museum' has its origins here with, prior to this, collections being more usually called repositories.[76]

Ashmole, lawyer, antiquarian, freemason and Windsor Herald to Charles II, helped Tradescant prepare the 1656 catalogue and after Tradescant's death, Ashmole inherited the museum.[77] In 1677 he drew up an agreement to give it to Oxford University where, in a new building on Broad Street, it was opened in 1683 by James, Duke of York, later James II. The museum of curiosities and 'Artificialls . . . Carvings and Paintings' was on the upper floor; natural philosophy was studied on the floor below and a laboratory occupied the basement.

By the 1830s the decision was made to build new University Galleries on Beaumont Street designed by C.R. Cockerell, a friend and pupil of Sir Robert Smirke, the architect of the British Museum (q.v.). The building is a powerful and original dichromic example of Greek Revival: the facade in honey-coloured Bath stone; four huge Ionic columns and the pediment, topped by a statue of Apollo, in white Portland stone.[78] In the view of the 19th-century architectural historian James

Fergusson 'there is perhaps no building in England on which the refined student of Architecture can dwell with so much pleasure'.[79] The collections of the old Ashmolean Museum were moved to premises here in the 1890s and the two institutions were merged to form the Ashmolean Museum of Art and Archaeology in 1908.

By gift, bequest, purchase and the scholarship of a succession of brilliant curators and directors, the Tradescants' rarities have been transformed into a dazzling assembly of collections: Egyptian, Greek and Roman antiquities; Western European paintings, drawings and sculpture of the past 500 years; Eastern arts including ceramics, paintings and prints of China, Japan and India, and of Islam; coins and medals; silver and glass; tapestries and furniture. It is a British Museum, National Gallery and Victoria and Albert Museum in epitome, in a single building.

Its Tradescant origins are not forgotten. At the top of Cockerell's elegant staircase is the Founders' Room, hung with portraits of the Tradescants, probably by Thomas de Critz, and two of Ashmole by John Riley, one in a glorious gilt frame that may have been carved by Grinling Gibbons. Ashmole, bewigged, grand and self-satisfied, is hung about with gold chains and medals.[80] The Tradescants, wigless, are modestly dressed. Hester Tradescant wears a steeple hat; her husband John the Younger, shirt open at the neck, shirt sleeves pulled back from the wrist, stands in his garden, hand on spade.

In the next room is what remains of the Tradescant collection: a model ship; a Russian abacus; 13th-century chessmen carved from walrus ivory; wooden tomahawks and Powhatan's cloak from Virginia; and a small 'landskip' by Sir Nathaniel Bacon, considered to be the earliest English landscape painting.

Although the museum's collections embrace the cultures of the whole world, from an Assyrian marble relief of the 9th century BC to a contemporary Chinese painting by Dong

Don Giovanni de' Medici *by Bronzino (Ashmolean Museum)*

Shouping, its roots are determinedly classical. As you enter, on your left, a gallery filled with the Arundel marbles declares the beauty and complication of that heritage. Thomas Howard, 2nd Earl of Arundel,[81] had his agents, Sir Thomas Roe and the Revd William Petty, scour the Mediterranean region for statuary. Some are Roman – a fine *Apollo* of the mid 2nd century AD; some are Roman copies of Greek originals – the *Sappho*, a copy of a Greek 5th-century-BC statue, used by G. F. Watts as the model for *The Wife of Pygmalion* (1868); some are 18th-century restorations/re-creations – notably a pair of late-2nd-century Roman marble candelabra excavated at Hadrian's Villa (*c.* 1724) at Tivoli and reworked by Giovanni Battista Piranesi.

Upstairs, through a maze of galleries large and small, you can pick your way through thousands of years of art history, from a Neolithic human skull (*c.* 7500–3000 BC), plastered and painted, with cowrie shells for eyes, excavated by Kathleen Kenyon in 1953 at Jericho, to Cretan clay tablets, before you reach what E. H. Gombrich called the Great Awakening of the 5th century BC and the precise glories of the Athenian red-figure painted vases, wine jugs and drinking cups collected by the great scholar Sir John Beazley, and the Etruscan statuettes, with stick-insect limbs as if cast by Giacometti. You follow the waxing and waning of the great British archaeologists – Sir Henry Layard in Mesopotamia and Egypt, Dame Kathleen Kenyon at Jericho in the 1950s – and the collections of Sir John Evans from across Europe, and the treasures recovered by his son, Sir Arthur, in Crete and Cyprus. Sir Arthur was appointed keeper here at the age of thirty-three, in 1884, and in twenty-four years transformed the museum's departments of antiquities and instituted the consolidation of the archaeological collections along with those of Western art in Cockerell's University Galleries.

Before 1840 the fine art collection had been small: the founders' portraits, a Pompeo Batoni of a young, confident *David Garrick*, who sat to him in Rome in 1764, a Robert Walker self-portrait. But in 1846 the museum received a fabulous collection of drawings by Michelangelo and Raphael that had belonged to a former president of the Royal Academy, the portraitist Sir Thomas Lawrence. After his death in 1830 he had wanted the collection to go to the British Museum which, incomprehensibly, declined to purchase it, even at a price far below its value. Lawrence's dealer, Samuel Woodburn, wished the Raphaels and Michelangelos to come to Oxford and the Earl of Eldon gave £4,000 to secure what is perhaps the finest group of Raphael drawings in the world.

In 1853 the Earl of Ellesmere gave sixty-eight drawings by the Carracci that had originally been in Lawrence's collection, and other bequests by Chambers Hall (1855) and Francis Douce (1863) meant that, in the space of twenty years, the Ashmolean had achieved a collection of drawings rivalled only by the monarch and the British Museum (q.v.), as strong in German and Dutch drawings (Dürer, Altdorfer, Grünewald, Holbein, Rembrandt, Van Dyck, van Ostade) as in Italian (Leonardo, Botticelli, Correggio, Pisanello, Procaccini, Peruzzi).

The collection was further enhanced by Ruskin's gift in 1861 of his drawings and watercolours, which included twenty-five sheets of J. M. W. Turner's drawings and twenty-three connected with Turner's *Rivers of France* engravings. In 1941 the then keeper of fine art, Karl (later Sir Karl) Parker[82] bought a series of the drawings, watercolours and etchings by Samuel Palmer, among which stand out the steady gaze of the youthful *Self-portrait* (*c.* 1824–5) and a unique set of six sepia drawings of 1825, the 'visionary landscapes'.

At about the same time, 1850, Fox-Strangways gave the museum that part of his collection of early Italian Primitive paintings that he had not presented to Christ Church twenty years earlier. Like William Roscoe in Liverpool, Fox-Strangways was at odds with prevailing taste. Neither the severe beauty of Barna da Siena's *Crucifixion and Lamentation* nor the delicacy of Fra Filippo's *Visitation* suited Victorian taste, though it is hard to see how any age could fail to respond to Paolo

Uccello's magical *Hunt in a Forest* in which, under a slivered moon, a hunt is caught in freeze-frame, every horse but one stationary, all about to be sucked into a perspective that is disappearing into the dark heart of the forest.

There are fine paintings here: Giovanni Bellini's *St Jerome in the Wilderness*, Giorgione's *Madonna*, de Koninck's *View over Flat Country*, all sky, and, best of all, Claude's *Ascanius Shooting the Stag*, painted in the last year of his life, 1682, aged eighty-two, for Prince Lorenzo Onofrio Colonna.

There are Italian and Welsh landscapes by Richard Wilson that draw the eye even from those here by J. M. W. Turner; and a delightful Gainsborough of his daughter, *Miss Gainsborough Gleaning* (c. 1758–9). There is an arresting portrait of *Don Giovanni de' Medici* by Bronzino, in which Don Giovanni stands, handsome, at ease, confident of the future. Like all Bronzino's best work it is 'finished with a delicacy that left nothing to desire', in the words of Vasari. Here too is a painting whose popularity rivals that of the Uccello, Piero di Cosimo's *A Forest Fire*, in which the near-human faces of its startled animals give it the quality of fable.

Despite these, the paintings are outshone by the drawings, even though there are strong collections of Dutch still lifes; Pre-Raphaelites; good French paintings from Corot to Braque; a wide selection of the work of the Camden Town Group; in 2003, a bequest from Morton and Ethel Sands of ten Sickerts including the unusual, near-abstract *Gaité Montparnasse: Dernière Galerie de Gauche* (1907); and recent acquisitions of paintings by Picasso, Kandinsky and Lucian Freud.

When Arthur Evans brought everything on to one compact site[83] he made it possible for the visitor to make correspondences between objects and across collections: antiquities and fine art; fine art and decorative art; antiquities and archaeology; and to consider the Roman bronzes (a plump *Cupid*, Cirencester, 2nd century AD; a *Dancing Lar*, 1st century AD) with their Renaissance successors, *Pan Listening to Echo* by Andrea Riccio, from the Fortnum Collection; a marble bust of *Lucius Verus* (AD 161–9) with Edward Pierce's baroque bust of Christopher Wren c. 1670); a Roman tetradrachm bearing the head of Alexander the Great with 15th-century medals by Pisanello. Such links form a living, whispering thread through the galleries.

Almost emblematic of the museum is an indicatorium, probably a pointer, the Alfred Jewel, perhaps the museum's most celebrated object. The inscription ('AELFRED MEC HEHT GEWYRCAN': Alfred caused me to be made), its function (to follow words on a page) and the existence of other, similar pointers (v. Salisbury and South Wiltshire Museum) suggest that the jewels might be equated with the jewels that Alfred sent to his bishops with copies of the Bible that he had caused to be translated into English. His preface to Pope Gregory's *Pastoral Care* says, 'I turned it into English, and to every bishopric in my kingdom will I send one; and in each there is an aestel which is worth 50 mancuses, and in God's name I command that no man remove the aestel from the book.'[84]

This aestel was found at Athelnay, Somerset, in the marshes where Alfred hid after his army was destroyed by the Viking king, Guthrun, in AD 878.[85]

In common with many other artefacts in the museum it is an object of beauty with a rich history. Notwithstanding those attributes, the objects that seem to me to embody the essential life of the museum are some of the smallest here, the coins and medals in the Heberden Coin Room, Greek, Roman, Celtic, Byzantine, Italian, English. These small reliefs tell us much about the rise and fall of nations and their rulers, the lives of their citizens, the skill of their artists and craftsmen. Their currencies paid for the making of most of the objects here. Passed from treasury to treasury, hand to hand, they have endured, to educate and move us today. Numismatics was Elias Ashmole's special interest. According to the diarist John Evelyn[86] he 'put in Order and Methodiz'd the Royal Collection after the Restoration'.[87] It was Ashmole's hope, expressed on his black marble gravestone in St Mary's, Lambeth, '*durante Musaeo Ashmoleano Oxon. nunquam moriturus*', that his name will never die as long as the Ashmolean Museum survives. It will survive, in his coins and in his gift, but so too will that of the Tradescants, memorialised on a tombstone in the graveyard outside the church in these words:

These famous Antiquarians that had been
Both Gardiners to the Rose and Lily Queen
Transplanted now themselves, sleep here: and
    when
Angels shall with their trumpets waken men,
And fire shall purge the world, these three shall
    rise
And change this Garden after them for
    Paradise.[88]

CHRIST CHURCH PICTURE GALLERY ****

Christ Church, Oxford, Oxfordshire
OX1 1DP
Tel. 01865 276172
www.chch.ox.ac.uk

Brilliant small, mainly Italian, collection of paintings and drawings in an illuminating sunken gallery

Christ Church Picture Gallery is small but it casts a brilliant light on Italian painting and drawing of the 14th to 17th centuries.

It comprises four separate bequests: that of General Sir John Guise (1682/3–1765), about two hundred 16th- and 17th-century paintings and over two thousand drawings; those of the Hon. William Fox-Strangways (1795–1865) and of the writer Walter Savage Landor (1775–1864), both of whom separately were collecting 14th- and 15th-century Tuscan/Florentine paintings in the 1820s; and the collection of more than two and a half thousand Italian, French and English drawings and prints acquired by Henry Aldrich (1648–1710), Dean of Christ Church. Together they form one of the finest small public collections of Italian Old Masters and give an insight into English collecting in the 17th, 18th and early 19th centuries.

Until the 1960s, they were exhibited on the ground floor of the college's Library in two large rooms on either side of the entrance hall. The Library's[89] facade of broad bays and 'grand unfluted Corinthian columns starting right off the ground'[90] with, inside, ornate stucco ceilings by Thomas Roberts, made it a splendidly grand setting for these collections, but not one that was entirely sympathetic.

In 1964 a gift by Sir Charles Forte enabled a commission to be offered to the architects Powell and Moya to design a new gallery. It is a quiet, subtle building, faced with a mixture of Portland stone and concrete, its galleries top-lit. Partly sunken, entered down steps, it holds itself apart from the rest of Christ Church as if its existence were private knowledge to be discreetly shared.

General Guise was described by Horace Walpole as 'a very brave officer, but apt to romance, and a great connoisseur of pictures'. His taste was consistent with mid-18th-century fashion, formed by a generation of Grand Tourism. He favoured Venetian painters of the 16th century, Tintoretto and Veronese, Lorenzo Lotto, Bassano and Strozzi. In drawings his tastes were more Catholic: Bellini, Michelangelo, Leonardo, Pontormo, Raphael; Rubens, Dürer and Hugo van der Goes.

Sixty years later Fox-Strangways and Landor were drawn to the 'primitives', the artists of the 14th and 15th centuries. They were both probably aware of the collecting and writing of William Roscoe, benefactor of the Liverpool Institution,[91] his biography of Lorenzo di Medici having been published in 1795. Even so they were in advance of popular British taste. The Arundel Society, whose object was to promote early Italian paintings so that 'the greater familiarity with the severer and purer styles of earlier Art would divert the public taste from works that were meretricious and puerile', was not formed by Prince Albert, Ruskin and Lord Lindsay until 1848 and the National Gallery (q.v.) did not acquire works by such artists as Duccio, Agnolo Gaddi or Filippino Lippi until

Filippino Lippi's The Wounded Centaur *(Christ Church Picture Gallery)*

1857, when Sir Charles Eastlake, the Director, secured the right to have the final say on acquisitions.[92]

Fox-Strangways, a diplomat, Secretary to the British Legation in Florence and subsequently Naples, was only in his thirties when he was collecting what he described as 'the simplicity and serenity of the early Florentines'. He was drawn to the calm beauties of Gherardo di Jacopo Starmina's *Virgin and Child*; the altarpiece panel, *St John the Baptist Enthroned*; and the enigmatic magic of Filippino Lippi's *The Wounded Centaur*.

Landor's taste was less secure but the Tuscan *Nine Scenes from the Lives of Hermits*[93] (*c*.1440–50) is a delightful piece of cartoon-like narrative, crammed with details of devils, lions and angels, and Giovanni di Paolo's *Calvary* is set against a stylised, decorative landscape whose formality is broken by the prancing stallions of the two mounted centurions at the base of the cross.

These works take you back to the austere, meditative roots of a Western Christianity that was closer to the East, to a time of stylites and eremites, before the worship of the Madonna as mediatrix, back to the days when Christianity was emotional but not exclamatory.

Powell and Moya tailored the design of the gallery to the collections: the larger for the Guise, the smaller for the Fox-Strangways and Landor, and a separate gallery for the prints and drawings. The large gallery is dominated by two works: Annibale Carracci's *The Butcher's Shop* (Guise) and Van Dyck's *The Continence of Scipio*.

Annibale Carracci's *The Butcher's Shop* was unusual, though not unique, in 16th-century Italy when most painters were depicting religious, historical or mythological themes. However its acuteness of observation (the lamb under the table; the old woman in the background; the cold white fat on the carcasses; the hand scales) raise it above the level of a genre painting, as does its distinguished provenance as one of the paintings that Charles I acquired from the Gonzaga Collection in Mantua in 1627.

The Continence of Scipio is an early work by Van Dyck, painted on his first visit to England when he was only twenty or twenty-one. It has the bravura, bold modelling and colouring that he had learned from Rubens but he had not yet acquired the confidence to combine fine passages of paintings (Scipio's coat, the two servants to the right) in a satisfactory whole. Its youthful 17th-century dash may appear to sit uneasily beside the masterly Tintoretto and Veronese but the gallery has several such non-Italian paintings of note: John Riley's portrait of *A Scullion of Christ Church*, Frans Hals's *Portrait of a Woman* and Reynolds's severe portrait of *Guise* in old age.

Visitors may come for the Carracci, the Filippino Lippi and the delicacy of the *Virgin and Child* (school of Piero della Francesca) but they come back for the gallery's drawings. Some works stand out: the beauty of the gently inclined *Head of a Young Woman* by Verrocchio, the penetration of the *Portrait of a Man* (attributed to Giovanni Bellini or to his brother-in-law, Andrea Mantegna), the grotesque head of da Vinci, Rubens's foreshortened *Head of the Emperor Galba* or the flowing lines of Pontormo. So rich is the collection that it can offer overviews of the influence of Raphael on his pupils (Giovanni Francesco Penni, Perino del Vaga, Polidoro del Caravaggio and Giulio Romano, later the court artist to the Gonzaga) and of those who were trained at the Carracci Academy (Guido Reni, Domenichino, Francesco Albani).

When so many galleries fail to do justice to their collections of prints, drawings or watercolours, blaming the technical difficulties of lighting works on paper, it is a pleasure here to see how it can, and should, be achieved. Powell and Moya's Print Room, with a chest-high bar on which to lean, is a model and influenced the redesign of the British Museum's Print Room. Throughout the gallery their design is discreet and intelligent, drawing together the collections, as does Atkinson's at the Barber Institute (q.v.). It gives a fine collection coherence and makes visiting and revisiting a continual pleasure.

MUSEUM OF THE HISTORY OF SCIENCE **

Broad Street, Oxford, Oxfordshire OX1 3AZ
Tel. 01865 277280
www.mhs.ox.ac.uk

Historic scientific instruments in the original Ashmolean building

When this museum opened in 1925 it had just two assets: Lewis Evans's great collection of historic scientific instruments, notable for comprising the world's largest collection of astrolabes and of sundials;[94] and a fine historic building, the original Ashmolean Museum (q.v.) building, the first (1678) public museum in Britain. This hallowed museum site was the home of the Tradescants' and Ashmole's collections until they were moved to C. R. Cockerell's new building in Beaumont Street.

The museum owes its existence to the persistence of Robert T. Gunther, a fellow of Magdalen College and author of *Early Science in Oxford*. Gunther was a more passionate antiquarian than scientist. He was determined that Oxford should have a museum of science, at whose centre would be the 17th-century science collections of the Tradescants and of Elias Ashmole. Gunther was no diplomat and managed to alienate much of academic Oxford, including the director of the Ashmolean Museum, Dr D. G. Hogarth. However he was tenacious and he persuaded Lewis Evans that his collection deserved to be seen in a dedicated museum rather than in the single room that the Ashmolean was offering.[95]

The museum is set back from Broad Street, a plain handsome stone building whose facade has 'five bays . . . with close-set cross-windows',[96] designed probably by a local master-mason Thomas Wood, as restrained and sober as Wren's Sheldonian Theatre beside it is showy, classical and referential.

The visitor enters up stone steps into the first-floor gallery through whose tall leaded windows the light pours pale grey. This is a place of quiet, of measure, of observation. In each corner of the gallery is a selection from

one of the museum's four core collections: Evans's; those of the Royal Astronomical Society and of the Royal Microscopical Society; and Christ Church's orrery collection. All comprise instruments with, through and by which we attempt with exactitude to identify the world around us. Astrolabes chart the heavens and the hours; orreries represent the motions of the planets about the sun by means of clockwork; microscopes examine the minutiae of the natural and man-made worlds. Here are Robert Hooke's 17th-century engravings, which compare the magnified edge of a fine razor, with its pitted imperfections, with such perfect natural forms as the wings of an insect.

For all the clarity and harmony of the instruments here it would be wrong to see this simply as a neo-classical collection in which science is at the centre of an ordered, enlightened world. Rather it reflects the many ways in which science has engaged with the world, so there is a 16th-century crystal ball, an Indian bhûgola or earth-ball (1493) and an early version of the alchemist Dr John Dee's holy table, by means of which the medium Edward Kelly put Dr Dee in touch with an angel, Uriel, who was to convey to him 'all original knowledge'.

Lewis Evans was not a professional scientist.[97] His interest in instruments was that of a connoisseur, delighted by the beauty or quality of an instrument as much as by its scientific use. His bequest established some of the priorities of the museum, whose collection of 150 astrolabes includes one made for Queen Elizabeth I by Thomas Gemini (1559), another for Archbishop Laud. Among his sundials, more than eight hundred in number, is a polyhedral dial made for Cardinal Wolsey by Nicholas Kratzer between 1518 and 1530 and an ivory sundial (*c.* 1600) incorporating a circular map of England.[98]

There are extravagances here that convey more about status than science: a microscope made in solid silver by George Adams for George III, whose utility is set around with classical pillars, urns and putti, or the earliest example of an orrery, the beautiful mechanism named in acknowledgement of the enlightened patronage of James Boyle, 4th Earl of Orrery.

There are such miscellaneous curiosities as the great lodestone given to the Ashmolean Museum in 1756 by Mary, Countess of Westmorland. It sits in state under an elaborate scarlet coronet, encased, its magnetism long since irrelevant. Here too is Isambard Kingdom Brunel's pocket sextant and the photographic equipment used by Charles Dodgson, aka Lewis Carroll.

There are objects here that changed our perception of the world (the blackboard on which, on 16 May 1931, Albert Einstein wrote the formula for establishing an equation for 'D', the measure of expansion in the universe)[99] and those that did not (Aristide Janvier's ten-hour clock, Paris 1798, a product of revolutionary France's desire to decimalise time).

As you walk up the wide, polished wooden stairs, from the first floor to the second, you pass huge original instruments from the Radcliffe Camera, a mural quadrant and a zenith sector, scientific toys for giants. Beside them is John Russell's ravishing pastel drawing of *The Face of the Moon* (1795). Russell was given a telescope by the Astronomer Royal Herschel, discoverer of Uranus, and made 'a Drawing in some measure corresponding to the Feelings I had upon the first sight of the gibbous moon through a Telescope'.[100]

This museum, with its astrolabes and sundials, clocks and watches, is about time. When the building was renovated in the 1990s, beneath the floorboards was the everyday detritus of over three hundred years: cherry stones, grape stalks, nut shells, coins, letters, a penknife and scraps of romantic verse by Mr Richard Parker, who worked here from 1761 to 1763.

PITT RIVERS MUSEUM ***

South Parks Road, Oxford, Oxfordshire
OX1 3PP
Tel. 01865 270927
www.prm.ox.ac.uk

The material cultures of the world given order by the father of ethnography: spears and skulls, masks and canoes – a store of wonders

The Pitt Rivers Museum was built in 1884 as an extension to the back wall of the Oxford University Museum of Natural History (q.v.), through which you must enter. You step out of its open, airy nave, flooded with light, the skeletons of whales and dinosaurs floating, suspended, overhead, into its opposite, the closed, low-lit, dense, flotsam-packed world of the Pitt Rivers.

As your eyes adjust to the light the plethora of objects, at first sight, is overwhelming, case upon case, each crammed with artefacts, ranked closely together: a case of necklaces and earplugs, carved from the bones of whales; a case of toys and games; a case of pipes; a case of drums and trumpets; a case of exotic charms and masks; a case of simple cord and string, woven into nets; a case of currency in all its guises: copper ingots, salt bars, the jaw of a dolphin, a brick of compressed tea; a case of the trophies of headhunters, a skull pierced by a bamboo spear, the skull of Yaukai, a renowned Naga warrior, lesser skulls, their jaws set in grins for good and all.

Every inch of space is used. Kayaks, canoes, an Indian catamaran and an Arctic dog sledge are slung from the ceiling. The profusion thrills, and daunts, and is misleading. This is not chaos, nor jumble. This is precise, deliberate order, in a museum whose deepest roots are in the idea of sequence.

Augustus Henry Lane Fox (later Pitt Rivers) (1827–1900) was sent to the Royal Military Academy, Sandhurst, aged fourteen, commissioned into the Grenadier Guards at eighteen, and fought in the Crimean War. The army was anxious to improve its rifles and Pitt Rivers, seconded to the School of Musketry at Hythe, was sent to write the standard manual on rifle training. He observed the ways in which the technology of firearms developed, from 14th-century hand cannons to 18th-century match-locks (oriental) and flintlocks (European) to 19th-century percussion guns. He began to collect guns, which he placed in sequence; and then other weapons; and then tools. Inspired by the *Origin of Species* (1859) of Darwin, and by T. H. Huxley, both of whom became his friends, he formulated his own theory of the evolution of culture,[101] 'to trace out, by means of the only evidence available (that is, artefacts), the sequence of ideas by which mankind has advanced from the condition of lower animals . . . and by this means to provide really reliable materials for the philosophy of progress'.[102]

He collected voraciously, invariably through field collectors and fellow members of the Anthropological Institute (such as E. H. Man, John Petherick, Sir Richard Burton) or through dealers and auctioneers (Boban of Paris, Christie's in London). He wanted objects not for their beauty or rarity but for 'the light they throw on prehistoric times . . . enabling us to trace out the origin of many of those customs which have been handed down to us by past generations'.[103]

He prized the everyday object. 'The value of relics, viewed as evidence, may be said to be in an inverse ratio to their intrinsic value,' he wrote.[104] He then placed them in order. 'Progress is like a game of dominoes . . . all that we know is that the fundamental riddle of the game is sequence'[105] – hence the displays here of spears, and swords, and fish hooks that were originally intended to chart the variations and improvements on each technology.

His purpose was education. He saw education as an essential ingredient of con-servatism in maintaining the Victorian social order: only through knowledge and under-standing of the past would 'the masses' be able to resist the 'scatter brained revolutionary sug-gestions' of 'demagogues and agitators, who strive to make them break with the past'.[106]

The collection, now with over 20,000 objects, outgrew the private museum he

established at his home and he loaned it to the Bethnal Green Museum in East London (now the Bethnal Green Museum of Childhood), satellite to the South Kensington Museum (later the Victoria and Albert Museum). Sub-sequently, the collection was displayed in the South Kensington Museum itself, but Pitt Rivers fell out with the museum authorities, who declined his offer to donate the collection. Finally in 1882 Oxford University accepted the collection and appointed the first lecturer in anthropology in Britain, Edward Burnett Tylor.

Two years before, Pitt Rivers had inherited a family estate of 8,500 acres at Cranborne Chase in Dorset and his driving enthusiasm was transferred to uncovering the Neolithic and Bronze Age treasures that lay beneath the Chase;[107] 'it almost seemed to me,' he wrote, 'as if some unseen hand had trained me up to be the possessor of such a property'.[108]

The Pitt Rivers Museum consists of a large court, overlooked by two levels of gallery, but from the start it was too small and the layout at Bethnal Green was replicated, the cabinets fill-ing the centre of the room in rows as well as lining the walls, so that the visitor is guided to a proper sequence: in weapons, for instance, 'throwing sticks and parrying shields . . . head-dresses . . . boomerangs and clubs . . . display of blowguns, darts and arrows, crossbows, flails, canoe paddles, and finally halberd spikes, swords, daggers and bayonets'.[109] Because this density in the display of objects has been retained, along with the old museum cases, today's visitor might think, mistakenly, that nothing has changed since the 1880s. That is not so. Almost at once the first curator of the museum, Henry Balfour, started to rearrange Pitt Rivers's series to incorporate new objects, and in the light of developments in anthropo-logical scholarship.[110]

Objects from Pitt Rivers's founding col-lection are still on show, and can be identified by their original handwritten labels. With one or two exceptions the collection continues to be displayed typologically, that is by classes of object rather than by geography or culture.[111]

The main collection grows and evolves. It

now comprises over 270,000 artefacts, along with a major photograph and manuscript collection, including gifts from such travellers and explorers as Wilfred Thesiger, T. E. Lawrence and Mary Kingsley. The outstanding addition has been material given to Oxford University by Johann Reinhold Foster, the official scientist on Captain James Cook's second expedition to the South Pacific in 1772–5, and his assistant (and illustrator), his seventeen-year-old son George. The collection comprises fewer than 200 objects and the handwritten *Catalogue of Curiosities sent to Oxford*, but it is the richest single source of 18th-century Pacific material, raising questions about the peoples of the Pacific and their history that remain apposite today. The collection and catalogue arrived in Oxford in 1776. The catalogue then disappeared and was rediscovered by Dr Adrienne Kaeppler in 1969.

Pitt Rivers feared for the future. In his 1876 presidential address to the Anthropological Institute he said, 'Aborigines are dying out, or fast changing their customs, and even in civilised countries landmarks are being removed so rapidly that in a few years' time the opportunity for collecting information will be lost.' He admired 'men of science' and had no time for 'political men who are merely wire-pullers and self-interested partisans'. A hundred and twenty-five years later his collection, and the ways in which it is taught and interpreted by men of science, continues to have relevance and to offer wisdom. As the Klickitat basket makers observed, 'you can stitch your thoughts into baskets'.

As we shrink our world with mobile phones, the Internet and jumbo jets, we need to be reminded of what makes us distinct, we need to know about where we have come from, we need to stop and contemplate. Here at the Pitt Rivers, as the poet James Fenton writes, 'You have come upon the fabled lands where myths/Go when they die.'

The Pitt Rivers, the parent of so many ethnographic museums, helps us to stretch out that understanding. While it does so its research is helping us to re-imagine the concept of an ethnographic museum.

SNOWSHILL MANOR **

Broadway, Worcestershire WR12 7JU
Tel. 01386 852 410
www.nationaltrust.org

The collector's dream house: a museum of the Platonic attic; the ranked armies of objects have conquered

Snowshill is the lumber room of our dreams. As you rummage through room after room you will find cabinets and chests, cribs and cards, quills and shells, bicycles and boneshakers, ships in cases, bobbins in boxes, planets in their place, a planetarium.

The world here shrinks as a Russian doll: model villages, model shops, model ships, model soldiers, model windmills, model wagons, a model stage coach.

There are objects on every table, chair, chimney piece, sill, stair: a weather prognosticator (1831); a perpetual almanac (1801); the side of a coach with the arms of Countess Cowper; a Buddhist shrine; an Egyptian aragonite alabaster unguent pot (*c.* 4000–3500 BC); a Bath chair; an Indian state palanquin (model); Cromwellian armour; an Armada chest; a horse measuring stick; a Spanish antiphonal (*c.* 1686); a drum said to have been beaten at Waterloo. Each object sets you off, into childhood, memories, fantasies, distant lands, half-remembered stories.

Everything was collected, between 1900 and 1951, by Charles Paget Wade. He was born in 1883 in Yoxford, Suffolk, surrounded by woodlands, cornfields, copses and spinneys. He had an innocent, solitary childhood of, as he recalled, 'a kingdom beyond the ken of grown-ups . . . [in a] happy realm of under the table and round the skirtings. How intimate one was with the legs of furniture, textures and patterns of carpets.'[112] At seven he was sent to live with his grandmother in Great Yarmouth where he encountered the sea, and boats, and her Chinese cabinet. 'Only on Sundays were the doors allowed to be set open and as they opened out came the fragrance of camphor, then the interior of this Enchanted Golden

Palace was revealed, a Palace fit for the greatest Mandarin.'[113]

On leaving school he trained as an architect and joined the firm of Parker and Unwin, the architects of Hampstead Garden Suburb, who were two of the leaders of the Arts and Crafts Movement. In the firm was M. H. Baillie Scott, who later helped him create the garden at Snowshill. In 1919 he bought Snowshill and began to rebuild it. He had inherited his family's sugar estates in St Kitts. The income gave him the means and the time to collect.

With his friend Commander Fred Hart as his Sancho Panza, he set out on 'hunting trips' to rescue abandoned objects from the barns, alleys and attics of the Cotswolds.

Entering a Cheltenham ironmonger's to buy a tap washer he saw the model of a life-sized Samurai in full armour. The ironmonger sold it on condition that they took away the six others he had in a shed. Here they are, with the twenty that Wade subsequently collected, in the Green Room, dramatically lit, poised to attack.

So diverse is Wade's collection that he might appear to have been a jackdaw returning to Snowshill with random trophies. Yet the collections are coherent and through them runs a cord of craftsmanship. Every object is well made; most are hand-made.

The collections of chests and cabinets include an Italian walnut cabinet (c. 1660), a 1560 German marquetry cabinet, one made in ebony and inlaid marble in Italy, and a 17th-century Spanish papileira. In the Music Room are cornopeans, two key bugles, a bass ophicléide, two bowed zithers, three hurdy-gurdies and four harplutes.

There are clocks of every type: lantern; Japanese pillar; Flemish bracket; a turret clock of 1803, common in churches, which strikes the hour but has no hands; a two-foliot escapement. There are machines: spinning wheels; hand looms; a box mangle; warping mills; skein winders; spinning chairs; fly shuttles; two clockmakers' lathes and a machine for rolling lead window cases.

All these are arranged in rooms, separately named: Meridian; Seraphim; Hundred Wheels; Seventh Heaven; Top Royal; Top Gallant; Zenith; Nadir.

Wade was an obsessive but it was a condition informed by love. He had no interest in value, only in utility, function and delight. In every room of Snowshill there is a sense of mischief, a glint of enjoyment.

It is tempting to seek the Rosebud of the collections, the object in a corner or a cupboard that was the *fons et origo*. Was it the model of an armed ketch? Or a doll's house he made, complete with 19th-century furniture, inhabited by Lord Mex and family? Or was it the model shop within the doll's house, complete with counter, tins and stock overseen by its proprietor Robert?

Clues are hard to find in the cottage across the yard, called the Priest's House, where Wade lived. These rooms make those in the manor look empty. Every inch of every surface is covered by bottles, bells, knives, shoe lasts, rings, jugs, yokes, jokes, pipes, skewers, string, sieves, cages, jars and bunches of lavender. Baskets, hats, lamps, lights are slung, hung and suspended from the ceiling. By his favourite porter's chair are copies of Dickens and Farnol.

Upstairs is his bedroom, the final room, a place at last of calm. Here is a panelled bed, a tall straw hat, a primus stove, a crucifix and a box with 'WADE' on it. His motto was 'Let nothing perish'. Outside on the bell are the words 'EVOCO CUSTODEM'.

SPODE MUSEUM *

Spode Works, Church Street,
Stoke-on-Trent, Staffordshire ST4 1BX
Tel. 01782 744011
www.spode.co.uk

The ware and designs of these great Staffordshire potters: far more than just 'Willow' pattern and blue and white pots

In his will of 1797, Josiah Spode I left 'all my works with meadow adjoining and the mill thereon erected, together with my dwelling

1291

1292

1602

1603

1606

1607

1604

1605

1608

house'[114] to his son, Josiah Spode II. The works are still there today, and still producing Spode china. The meadow has gone, remembered as part of the factory which is still called the Meadow; the site is encircled by Stoke's one-way traffic system and a ring of kebab houses, pubs and video rental shops.

Stoke has changed, as has Spode, which today develops its designs with a mixture of computers and traditional hand-drawn and engraving techniques, and fires its wares not in coal-fired bottle ovens but in gas-fired kilns. Yet the 18th-century fundamentals of making pottery persist: the buildings, techniques, recipes, shapes and many of the original Spode patterns.

The museum was set up in 1925[115] in the middle of the Spode works to record the history and manufacture of the company's wares. Its galleries were created in the factory buildings, making it feel more like a working showroom than a museum. As well as the museum there is also the Blue Room devoted to blue printed wares displaying pieces laid out on antique furniture, open by appointment only.

For many, Spode is synonymous with blue and white Staffordshire pottery. In the mid 18th century every potbank, whether in Stoke, Worcester or London, made blue and white ware in an attempt to compete with Chinese porcelain imports. It was not until Josiah Spode I 'introduced blue printing into Stoke in 1784' that anyone perfected, or exploited, it successfully.

Transfer printing on to porous earthenware was more difficult than on to porcelain. It was harder still to make it profitable. Spode was helped by a cut in the import tax on tea from 119 per cent to 12.5 per cent.[116] Demand for his blue and white tableware boomed. At the same time imports of ware from China were squeezed by the war with France and by a massive new import duty on chinaware of £109. 8s. 6d. per £100 of goods. Spode, with his copies of blue and white Chinese patterns, filled the gap.

Spode patterns

The museum shows how in the early years Spode, like all other 18th-century Staffordshire pottery manufactures, produced every sort of design. So too did Josiah Wedgwood who, like Spode himself, worked for and was trained by the first of the great Staffordshire potters, Thomas Whieldon.

In these years Spode made green-glazed 'greenware' (pieces in the shape of leaves), cane-coloured 'pastryware', neo-classical designs and black basalt pieces that could be mistaken for Wedgwood, for whom he even made 'blanks'.

He made 'exquisites': a tiny custard cup in blue jasper with a white lattice overlay (1808), an Egyptian-style pyramid incense burner (1805). The blue and white 'Willow' pattern that he devised in about 1790,[117] with its fence, tree, bridge, three people and pavilion on the left, was one of several Chinese patterns – 'Peacock' (pattern 2118), 'Willis' (2147), 'Ship' (3067) and 'Frog' (3248). 'Willow' is still in production.

Spode made richly coloured and gilded Japanese designs ('Imari' style)[118] and, as he perfected transfer printing, topographical images: scenes from Merigot's *Views and Ruins in Rome and its Vicinity* (1797–8);[119] scenes from Samuel Howitt's *Wild Sports of the East* in its 'Indian Sporting' pattern; mythological subjects derived from Sir William Hamilton's collection of Greek vases and the 'Caramania' pattern, and scenes from etchings by Luigi Mayer.[120]

The success of blue and white ware was based not only on catering for a wide range of customers' tastes and interests with images that could be revealed spoonful by spoonful as a meal progressed but on the quality of the ware and the elegance of the shapes (Spode's 'Bute' shape of teacup, 1806, became a standard). A crucial, and unsung, contribution to the latter was made by Henry Daniel, who was responsible for the decorating of other Spode wares from *c.*1805 to 1822, running a separate business on site. Some of the designs were startling. Pattern 822 (1806), a design of geometric shapes in platinum and gold, could be mistaken for a piece of Art Deco.

Spode knew how to exploit the quality of his ware and, like Wedgwood, understood the importance of creating a market in London. In 1794 he sent his son, Josiah Spode II, to open a London showroom. By 1806 he had been appointed Potter and English Porcelain Manufacturer to His Royal Highness, the Prince of Wales, having shown the Prince and his brother the Duke of Clarence round the Stoke works when they stayed with the Marquis of Stafford at Trentham Hall.[121]

These early cabinets contain pieces that illustrate the speed at which Spode developed and prospered. There are more ideas here for designs, shapes and types of porcelain than most companies could produce in a generation. The pattern books showed 5,191 separate designs when, in 1833, the company came under the proprietorship of William Taylor Copeland and Thomas Garrett, who retained the Spode brand name.

Under Copeland and his descendants, the company, while continuing to make a wide range of established patterns, developed in new directions. A new matte white porcelain-ware, Parian, was ideal for small pieces of statuary. The neo-classical sculptor John Gibson described it as 'the best material next to marble' and the company attracted leading sculptors (William Theed, Mary Thornycroft, R. J. Wyatt, Raffaele Monti) to create sculptures and portrait busts. Copeland became Lord Mayor of London and was a leading organiser of the 1851 Great Exhibition, following which major Spode pieces were exhibited regularly at International Exhibitions in Paris, Vienna and London.

In 1860 Spode's attracted one of Sèvres' top designers, C. F. Hurten, to come to Stoke, where he worked until 1896. His rich flower designs influenced Spode decorators, notably Samuel Alcock, whose two-handed vase here won first prize at the 1889 Exposition Internationale in Paris.

In recent years the museum has retrieved many rare blue and white patterns and shapes,[122] thanks to a bequest of Robert Alexander, an academic at Bradford University, who collected intensely in the early 1970s. It

has added some curiosities: the 'Feathers' pattern, on an Everest-shaped service, designed by Princess Margaret in 1957, its Prince of Wales feathers fanning outwards round the edge of each plate.

Unlike Josiah Wedgwood, Spode and his successors did not keep records of all the trials and bodies or firings, but the pattern books here are complete and the collection comprises a rare history of an English manufacturing company that has been successful for more than two hundred years and remains so.

GLADSTONE POTTERY MUSEUM *

Uttoxeter Road, Longton, Stoke-on-Trent, Staffordshire ST3 1PQ
Tel. 01782 319232
www.stoke.gov.uk/gladstone

The Staffordshire pottery industry as it was in the 19th century, complete with bottle ovens; and the history of sanitaryware

The buildings are the collection: five giant bottle ovens, in the centre of which are a cobbled yard and surrounding workshops.

Until the Clean Air Act of 1956 there were hundreds of such bottle ovens and yards through the length of Stoke-on-Trent. They followed the River Trent and the Trent and Mersey Canal as they wound thirteen miles down the valley. Potbanks and canal were following the seam of coal that lay beneath the valley and provided the source of steady, even-burning heat needed to fire pottery. The coal is the reason why the Staffordshire Potteries are here, not the local clay, which is of no more than average quality.

The banning of coal firing by the 1956 Act is why the museum is here. A group of local pottery manufacturers led by Robert Copeland of Spode and Derek Johnson of H. & R. Johnson Ltd watched with dismay the closure and destruction of the old bottle ovens in the 1960s as potbanks converted to gas firing.

Copeland and Johnson, and the Pottery Industry Preservation Trust that they formed, saved this site in September 1971 not because it was extraordinary but because it was ordinary: a small potbank that had been worked by family potters ever since Michael Shelley took a lease on it in 1774.[123] It was thus an appropriate site for a museum that would show the utilitarian side of the pottery industry. The beautiful decorative ware made by the Greatbachs, Wedgwoods and Spodes was displayed in the Potteries Museum and Art Gallery (q.v.). This museum would be concerned with everyday ceramics, particularly tableware, tiles and sanitaryware, and how they were made.

Starting in the yard with its setts, its piles of coal and straw, and its carts, the visitor follows the process from raw materials to finished product, as clay, bone, salt, lead and water are transformed into ware with the help of coal and muscle.

You begin in the Engine Room with its warm smell of oil and grease and steam, and the steady repetitive hiss and clank of its single-crank tandem compound steam engine[124] which drives all the machines at the potbank. You proceed to the Slip Room, where the clay is prepared in pugmills whose wheels, pulleys and gears click and grumble.

The jobs in a potbank were/are legion: there were jiggers and jollyers;[125] throwers and turners; casters, fetlers and spongers; dippers, gilders; mouldmakers and saggar makers[126] and the saggar maker's bottom-knocker.

The jobs were hard. Plumbism (lead poisoning from the glazes) and silicosis (lung disease caused by silica in the clay) were rife. Few who worked on potbanks lived beyond the age of forty until the health and safety legislation of the early 20th century began gradually to have an effect. Every surface, every object was thick with clay dust. The only colour was in the glazes and metallic oxides: green from chrome and copper; white from tin; blue from cobalt; violet and red from iron; black and brown from manganese; orange from antimony; silver from platinum; yellow from uranium. The Colour Sample Room, with its walls

of great pots, tureens and cases of more than nine hundred colours and gradations of colour (30 pinks, 40 blues, 80 greens) was an exotic treasure store amidst the pervasive dust.

Outside, all is dominated by the bottle ovens, large, squat, solid, their brick walls held together by the embrace of bonts, metal bands that held the kilns as the bricks expanded and contracted with firing and cooling.

Indoors, the Gladstone has a strong collection of tiles: the encaustic floor tiles of north Staffordshire's 13th- and 14th-century monasteries and abbeys; tin-glazed wall tiles imported from Spain and Italy in the 17th century; 18th-century painted Delft ware tiles; transfer-printed tiles introduced into England by John Sadler of Liverpool in 1756, and the rediscovery of the medieval encaustic[127] tiles as part of the 19th-century Gothic Revival. Tile making had never been a speciality of Staffordshire potters but Augustus Pugin's friendship with Herbert Minton led to the commissioning of Minton to provide all the encaustic tiles for the new Houses of Parliament.[128] This one contract transformed Minton & Co. into a major company. The Capitol Building in Washington, DC and parliaments, museums, libraries, embassies and universities throughout the British Empire followed Parliament's lead.[129]

The work of other 19th-century tile designers is here: John Moyr Smith, Henry Stacy Marks and Joseph François Leon Arnoux, for Minton & Co.; and W. J. Neatby's art nouveau tiles for Harrods Food Hall in 1902, made by Doulton & Co.[130]

Upstairs the Sanitaryware Gallery ends the popular myth that Thomas Crapper designed the modern flush lavatory and presents a more accurate, if more complicated, history. A London watch maker, Alexander Cummings, took out the first patent for a toilet, from which Joseph Bramah developed a popular, if expensive, version in 1778. Thomas Twyford, and others such as Wedgwood, made ceramic bowls for Bramah's toilets. With Twyford's 'Unitas', and the 'Beaufort', the bowl made by Frederick Humpherson, at last began the marketing of toilets that could be afforded by those on average earnings.

Thomas Crapper was an entrepreneur and retailer who popularised this work. Here are examples of every stage of toilet design from the Revd Henry Moule's first composting earth closet through Bramah's Rolls Royce of valve closets, triumphant with mahogany and brass, the 'Beaufort', to the avocado bathroom suite of the 1960s.

Downstairs, as you leave there is a small black curved tile in a glass vase, the tile of the future and very probably the future of the ceramics industry: a tile from the nose cone of the NASA Shuttle spacecraft of 1981 capable of withstanding re-entry temperatures of 1,357°C, fired earth fired from earth.

POTTERIES MUSEUM AND ART GALLERY ***

Bethesda Street, Hanley, Stoke-on-Trent, Staffordshire ST1 3DW
Tel. 01782 232323
www.stoke.gov.uk/museums/pmag

The greatest collection of Staffordshire pottery in the world

Up in the ceramics gallery is one of the six vases that Josiah Wedgwood made on 13 June 1769 to celebrate the opening of his new Etruria works. It is of black basalt, his own innovation, with red neo-classical decoration.

Although Wedgwood's skills as a potter and a manufacturer were outstanding, this museum demonstrates clearly that the reputation of the Staffordshire ceramics industry was not dependent solely on him.

An encaustic tile from the Augustinian priory at Trentham and a jug found at Audlem show that pottery had been made here at least since the 13th or 14th centuries using the local clay which, rich in iron oxide, fired to red or orange.[131] By the 17th century Thomas Toft and others were producing slipware: earthenware, whether thrown or moulded, decorated with a liquid clay or slip that was trailed (or slipped) over the ware, under the lead glaze.

It was not until the early 18th century that the industry began to expand in north Staffordshire, more because of the availability of good, cheap coal than for the local clay. Here is the heart of the collection, the golden age of British ceramics when Stoke and Staffordshire became a radiant focus. In that expansion the great potters Josiah Wedgwood, Thomas Whieldon his master, Josiah Spode and William Greatbach are placed here in a wider context.[132]

As historians Simeon Shaw[133] in the 19th century, and David Barker recently, have made clear, there were many skilled potters in mid-18th-century Stoke all chasing the same innovations and adopting and adapting each other's ideas, initially in search of an earthenware that would fire white and so compete with imported porcelain. Adding calcinated flint to a white-firing pipe clay (both of which had to be imported from Devon) produced a tolerable, off-white ware. Firing twice, and using a liquid glaze, produced further improvements. A piece by Enoch Booth of Tunstall, inscribed 'W. G. 1743',[134] may be the earliest piece of creamware here.[135]

By 1759 Josiah Wedgwood was bemoaning his perception that 'our Manufacture was in a very unimprov'd state, & the demand for it decreasing ... Something new was wanted to give a little spirit to the business.'[136] In 1765 he took an order that no other potter wanted, from Queen Charlotte for 'a service of Staffordshire ware'.[137] In supplying the order he gave her 'two setts of cream coloured Vases, engine turned and printed'.[138] In appreciation she appointed him 'potter to Her Majesty'.[139] Wedgwood renamed creamware Queens ware; in 1773 the Russian empress, Catherine the Great, ordered the huge Frog Service; and the reputations of Wedgwood, and of Staffordshire, were secured.

The collection shows clearly the width and strength of the Staffordshire industry. There are pieces here by William Greatbach (a creamware teapot, 1775–82); by John and William Turner (jasperware, 1780–1800); Edmund John Birch (black basalt, 1796) and numerous pieces by the Wood family, master modellers throughout the century,[140] but it is appropriate that a piece of Wedgwood should stand out, a huge neo-classical bowl, three feet in diameter, that he made to celebrate the Peace of Amiens in 1701, so demonstrating the flair for publicity that made him and his partner Thomas Bentley rich and successful.

This ceramics collection describes the 18th-century industry in its width and diversity. The slightness of the Wedgwood and Spode material here, a consequence of both manufactories having their own collections and museums,[141] is turned from a potential weakness into a strength. It allows such outstanding potters as Thomas Whieldon, Wedgwood's employer[142] and, later, partner (1754–9), and William Greatbach, the greater visibility their work merits.

The museum lays out the raw materials (ball clay, china clay, china stone, calcinated flint, bone ash, metallic oxides to provide colour) and distinguishes between bone china and soft-paste and hard-paste porcelains, stoneware and earthenware; between glazes, and how and when they are applied. It explains the importance of the 'right coal', a 'long flame' variety that lies under the Trent Valley on which Stoke is built; the role of moulds and models; decorating and transfer printing, overglaze and underglaze, throwing and pressing and what, precisely, are a 'saggar maker'[143] or a 'saggar maker's bottom-knocker'.

Only with this information can the bursting inventiveness of Booth, Whieldon, Greatbach and the rest be appreciated. They tumbled over each other, starting companies, cribbing designs, poaching craftsmen, making fortunes, going bankrupt, so as to improve bodies and glazes, moulds and modelling, and to keep ahead of fashion and the market.

The pressure to innovate continued in the 19th century: bone china (c. 1800), ironstone china (patented 1813), parian porcelain (1840s) maiolica glazes (c. 1850), colour printing (various, from the 1840s to '90s), tunnel kilns and gas firing; such curiosities as Staffordshire figures and toby jugs were popular, as were 'exotics' (Minton's maiolica glazed *Peacock*, 1873, and *Stork*, 1875) and cow creamers. The

collection of these cow-shaped cream jugs given by Gabrielle Keiller[144] in the 1950s forms a herd that numbers over six hundred, each with her name and provenance kept by Mrs Keiller in a Herd Book. The collection was given to the museum on condition that two-thirds would be displayed at any given time. They form a wall of soft-eyed, open-mouthed cows, spotted, mottled, chintzy, lustred.

In the 20th century the gift of two collections of studio pottery by Robert T. Pinchen and Dr Henry Bergen placed the museum alongside the other major public collections at York, Nottingham, Aberystwyth and Norwich,[145] with good examples of all the major potters: Leach, Hamada; the Vyses, Staite Murray; Rie and Coper; Cardew, Ray Finch, Ewen Henderson and others. The museum has the largest collection of studio pottery in the country.

It is perhaps inevitable that in this museum ceramics should hold the centre of the stage but there are other attractions of substance: natural history, geology, archaeology (all local), fine art and, an oddity, a Spitfire XVI, the source of much pride, as its designer, Reginald Mitchell, was a Stoke man.

The geology of the Trent Valley and the Staffordshire Moorlands, which rise ten miles to the east, is at the core of the ceramics industry, not simply for its red clay but for its minerals: coal, limestone, ironstone, gypsum, sand and copper. These are old lands of history and myth, pocked with Neolithic caves and burial places and close to the supposed setting of *Gawain and the Green Knight*. In 1995 Tony Rhodes, a metal detectorist, found a Bronze Age sword that was 2,800 years old. In more recent times the Augustinians and Cistercians established abbeys here, as evidenced by a log boat in Abbey Hulton and by 13th-century ceramic floor tiles at St Mary's and St Bertelin's, Stafford.

The links between the ceramics industry and fine art have always been strong. Josiah Wedgwood employed Joshua Reynolds and George Stubbs among others. In the 20th century the company commissioned designs from Eric Ravilious, John Minton and Edward

Bawden,[146] while John Currie worked as a decorator at Minton's (c. 1897–1903) before going to the Royal College in 1905.[147]

The Burslem School of Art produced a succession of decorators and modellers for the industry but it also produced artists. Arthur Berry's paintings of north Staffordshire, landscapes and people, still lifes of flowers fighting through overlays of coal dust and grime, are direct and moving, as evocative of Stoke as the paintings of L. S. Lowry are of Salford.

The lost talent is that of John Currie. Having gone to the Royal College in 1905 he fell in with Mark Gertler, Edward Wadsworth and C. R. W. Nevinson, and was taken up by Sir Edward Marsh, the collector and connoisseur, who bought his work and called him and Gertler 'decidedly two of the most interesting of "les jeunes".'[148] Currie committed suicide in 1914, having murdered his lover and model Dolly Henry, but the canvases he left suggest that he is an artist waiting to be rediscovered.[149]

The collection concentrates on the 20th century with only a handful of exceptions (drawings of nearby Trentham Hall by Constable and by its architect, Charles Barry; watercolours by David Cox and by Peter de Wint, born in Hanley). The Camden Town Group feature (Bevan, Ginner, Gertler), and there is a fine, restrained Wyndham Lewis portrait of *Stephen Spender* (1938), but it is in the relative byways of the 20th century that a collection such as this scores: works by Eileen Agar, Dod Procter and Meredith Frampton, who are only occasionally in evidence in other galleries, and a good collection of modern prints (Matisse, Picasso, Gill, Sutherland, Ayrton).

I have loved this museum and art gallery for more than thirty-five years and it never palls. Museum and city are rooted in one another, to the benefit of both.

Mrs Keiller's herd of creamers at the Potteries Museum and Art Gallery

IRONBRIDGE GORGE MUSEUMS **

Ironbridge, Telford, Shropshire TF8 7AW
Tel. 01952 432166
www.ironbridge.org.uk

Abraham Darby, the Iron Bridge and the birthplace of the Industrial Revolution

There are few more solidly satisfying sights than a single-span bridge, its arch described through the air with perfect balance. The Iron Bridge at Coalbrookdale was a symbol of a new age of engineering, of manufacture, of wealth. Its five iron ribs rise up from the river until they touch those from the far bank at the precise apex.

For Abraham Darby III and his company, the Iron Bridge was at once a commercial venture and a demonstration of what could be achieved with the cast iron that he, his father and grandfather had been making in the valley for sixty years, and of how it could transform the world.

These museums, ten of them, spread over six square miles down this thickly wooded gorge, together comprise 'Ironbridge'. It has a good claim to be called the birthplace of the British Industrial Revolution.

Abraham Darby I (1678–1717) chose to move to Coalbrookdale from Bristol, where he had a brassworks, because of the valley's ready supply of low-sulphur coal, the energy source that he and his apprentice John Thomas had discovered would make the coke needed to smelt iron successfully. He took out a patent in 1707 for 'a new way of casting iron bellied pots, & other iron bellied ware in sand only, without loam or clay'.

It is the great furnace where they achieved this in 1709 that is the heart of the museum site. To reach it, where it is enthroned and encased in a shell of bricks and rubble seven feet thick, you climb up simple open iron steps. From a railed platform you look down into the heart of the furnace as if into a volcano. Its roar by day and burning light by night dominated the valley.[150] Hannah, the eight-year-old granddaughter of Abraham Darby I, described it in a letter to her aunt in 1853, 'Methinks how delightful it would be to walk with thee into fields and woods, then to go into the Dale to view the works, the stupendous Bellows whose alternate Roars like the foaming Billows is awful to hear, the mighty cylinders, the wheels that carry on so many different Branches of the work is curious to observe.'

From this furnace all else flowed. Abraham Darby I and his successors, and other ironmasters in the valley such as John Wilkinson,[151] bored the first iron cylinders (1722),[152] made the first iron railway wheels (1729)[153] and rails (1767), built the first cast-iron bridge (1779) and the first iron boat (1787),[154] constructed the first iron aqueduct (1795–6)[155] and erected the first cast-iron-framed building (1796).[156] The achievements of these ironmasters and their fluctuating fortunes in developing their industry are illustrated in the Museum of Iron, a few yards from the Furnace, while other sites further down the valley (the Broseley Pipeworks, the Jackfield Tile Museum and the Coalport China Museum) show the associated industries that developed here. At Rosehill, Blists Hill and the Quaker Burial Ground, it can be seen how masters and workers lived.

The slump in the iron trade caused by the end of the Napoleonic Wars in 1815 forced the Darbys to diversify and Francis Darby, son of Abraham III, stopped smelting iron and transformed his works into one producing specialist fine art castings.

National and international exhibitions provided ideal showcases for parading the versatility of cast and wrought iron, and the skills of the artists whom Darby commissioned. At the 1851 Great Exhibition the statue of *Andromeda*[157] by John Bell caused a stir, as did his fountain of *Boy and Swan,* and the large iron *Setter and Greyhound* by the French sculptor Christophe Fratin.

Throughout the late 18th and 19th centuries the Iron Bridge attracted tourists to the valley. In 1784 the consortium that had built the bridge opened the Tontine Hotel to cater for visitors and 100 years later Ironbridge

was being advertised as 'the Brighton of the Midlands'. Bridge and valley were much painted: by François Vivares (1758), William Williams (1777 and 1780), Michael Angelo Rooker (1782), and Joseph Farington (1789); and the limekiln by J. M. W. Turner *c.* 1796.

After some years of comparative neglect in the 20th century a trust was formed in 1967 and the museum opened. Neil Cossons[158] was appointed Director in 1971. He defined his task as making 'on-site preservation more realistic in consumer terms'.[159] By 1986 the gorge had been declared a World Heritage Site by UNESCO.[160]

However remarkable the site, it is the Iron Bridge that remains the focus. It is not entirely clear who designed it. Pevsner maintains 'it was designed by Darby' and elaborates in a footnote, 'the attribution of the design to the Shrewsbury architect Thomas Farnolls Pritchard is not justified. The designs he submitted in 1775 were for a bridge of stone, brick and timber.'[161] Since then scholarly opinion has swung behind Pritchard.[162] Certainly Pritchard's were the designs, for a single arch bridge, for which an Act of Parliament was passed in 1776 and shares issued to finance its construction. When John Wilkinson transferred his shares to Darby, the latter altered the materials to iron and modified the design, but as late as 1779 Darby was paying Pritchard's brother (Pritchard having died) £40 for his 'late brothers drawing and models'. What is certain is that the bridge is one of the wonders of the 18th century.

WALTER ROTHSCHILD ZOOLOGICAL MUSEUM **

Akeman Street, Tring, Hertfordshire
HP23 6AP
Tel. 020 7942 6171
www.nhm.ac.uk/museum/tring/

An outstation of the Natural History Museum, a triumph of taxidermy: comprehending zebras and cassowaries

At a time when so many museums are retiring their stuffed animals to store, in order to replace them with videos and interactive screens, the Walter Rothschild Zoological Museum glories in taxidermy.

You enter the 1892 red-brick Arts and Crafts building[163] designed by the local architect William Huckvale in a quiet side street of Tring, to be confronted by canyons of floor-to-ceiling glass cases. In six galleries they contain more than 4,000 animals, mammals, fishes, birds, insects, vertebrates and invertebrates, from species flourishing and species extinct.

In the first case are a polar bear and a brown bear; in the second a spectacled bear; from the next, lions and leopards stare at you. There are dogs (racoon, red or dhole), jackals, hyenas and foxes (red, silver, sand and Blandford's). There are birds exotic (humming, of paradise, Lady Amherst's pheasant) and not (eider ducks, smew, harlequin ducks; scoters, surprised red-crested pochards). There are vultures, buzzards, kestrels, red-footed falcons and peregrines. Anxious lemurs peer, as does the gentle aye-aye from the forests of Malaysia with its bat ears and long fingers. Monkeys of every size and hue (brown capuchin, red uakari from Brazil) are separated from gorillas (the *Gorilla gorilla gorilla* from the Mountains of the Moon, the *Gorilla gorilla beringei* from south-west Uganda) and from a Sumatran orang-utan hanging by one arm.

In Gallery 2, thought to be Lord Rothschild's office and furnished as such, are cases of cassowaries from New Guinea, bred here in Tring Park; also a giant tortoise from the Galapagos given to Rothschild in 1915 by the Queen of the Sandwich Islands. Much photographed, it did not thrive and died two years later.

Lionel Walter Rothschild (1868–1937) was the eldest son of Nathan Mayer, 1st Baron Rothschild, the founder of the merchant bank that bears his name. At the age of seven Walter Rothschild announced, 'Mama, Papa, I am going to make a museum,' and started to collect insects, stuffed animals and butterflies, which he displayed in a garden shed. His father was benignly dismissive: 'Natural History is an interesting hobby like shire horses and the cultivation of orchids but not serious work.' Nevertheless, for his son's twenty-first birthday in 1889, he gave him some land on the edge of Tring Park and erected buildings to house the growing collections of specimens and books. In 1892 the museum was opened to the public.

As the collections grew, zoologists Ernst Hartert (an expert on vertebrates), Karl Heinrich Jordan[164] (butterflies, moths and beetles) and Arthur Goodson (insects) were employed. Their research and catalogues and the museum's own scientific journal, *Novitates Zoologicae* (first edition 1894), which they edited, gave the collection a worldwide scientific reputation. Over the following forty-five years they published more than 1,700 books and papers and described more than 5,000 new species. Before his death in 1937 Walter, now Lord, Rothschild gave the museum and its collections to the trustees of the British Museum, on condition that it remained a centre for zoological research.[165] Lord Rothschild's historical library collection is also in Tring, part of the combined ornithological library of 80,000 volumes, which is one of the finest collections in the world and includes illustrated books by John Gould and Edward Lear. The national ornithological collection, adjacent to the museum at Tring, contains 750,000 bird skin specimens including Darwin's finches, over 17,000 skeletons, 1 million eggs and 2,000 nests. Ironically it does not contain Lord Rothschild's ornithology collection as he sold it to the American Museum of Natural History in 1932.

In the park beside the museum Lord Rothschild kept a collection of rare livestock, giant tortoises, cassowaries and zebras which roamed free. There are more unusual specimens indoors: the quagga, okapi, bongo, puku; the kob from Zambia and the lechwe from the Sudan; the kudu and the nyala; a capybara and a giant moa; a fierce Komodo dragon, opposite dwarf kangaroos; a stern, serious, elderly eland and a shy aardvark with big eyes and a long nose.

Here lies the danger of taxidermy, that it tempts us to inappropriate and misleading anthropomorphism. Rowland Ward & Co., the great 19th-century taxidermists who prepared these specimens, had a very different view of natural history from that held today. The polar bear, a fearsome hunter in the Arctic, smiles benevolently. The gorillas, reclusive herbivores, are made ferocious. Despite this, stuffed specimens provide the public with an opportunity to get close to animals to study the detail of their fur, skin, claws, teeth, scale. Film can capture movement or flight but only the specimen allows you to stand rapt, to consider and reconsider.

Where else can you confirm that, indeed, the striped skins of zebras are, like human fingerprints, unique? Where else can you approach a cassowary, feared in New Guinea as capable of disembowelling a person with a single kick? Here you can wonder at the height (over five feet) of this cursorial bird, its useless wings, furnished with stiff featherless quills, like spines.

To its credit the museum retains its original Victorian fittings, ignoring political correctness and, while continuing scientific research, giving the public a kingdom of pleasure.

The Walter Rothschild Collection at Tring

WADDESDON MANOR: THE ROTHSCHILD COLLECTION ****

Waddesdon, nr. Aylesbury, Buckinghamshire HP18 0JH
Tel: 01296 653226
www.waddesdon.org.uk

Rothschild treasures in superhyperabundance in a French chateau overlooking the Vale of Aylesbury

Waddesdon is a French chateau set on a hill overlooking the Vale of Aylesbury. Baron Ferdinand de Rothschild, with no irony apparent, wrote, in his account of its building, *The Red Book*, 'The French sixteenth century style, on which I have long set my heart, was particularly suitable to the surroundings of the site.'[166]

He purchased that site and 2,700 acres from the Duke of Marlborough in 1874, levelled the top of the hill, planted hundreds of mature trees and commissioned Gabriel-Hippolyte-Alexandre Destailleur as his architect. Destailleur was an architect rooted in the past. He had recently rebuilt the Château de Mouchy near Beauvais. Baron Ferdinand disliked both Napoleonic modernism and the excesses of the Second Empire. Destailleur gave him at Waddesdon a building comprising outstanding features from the great chateaux: the paired spiral staircase of Blois, the steep roofs of Azay-le-Rideau, the dormer windows of Chenonceaux, the domed towers of Maritenou,[167] borrowings from the Louvre.

As with his taste in architecture, Baron Ferdinand's collecting looked to the past: the contemporary was of no interest to him. Here at Waddesdon and in his London house he assembled one of the greatest collections of French 18th-century decorative art in the world, surpassed only by the Louvre, the Wallace Collection (q.v.) and the Metropolitan Museum of Art in New York.

To create a setting for the French furniture and the Sèvres porcelain that are amongst the main glories of Waddesdon he imported genuine 18th-century boiseries (panelling)

taken from French *hôtels*,[168] laid Savonnerie[169] and Aubusson carpets and hung tapestries made at the Gobelins and Beauvais factories, the latter to designs by François Boucher.[170] He also added magnificent English 18th-century portraits and the finest 19th-century curtains and wall silks (painstakingly copied from 18th-century patterns) in a sumptuous, eclectic creation which became known worldwide as '*le gout* Rothschild'.

There are pieces here by all the principal French cabinet makers of the mid 18th century: Pierre Roussel, Jean-Louis Grandjean, Roger Vandercruse Lacroix and Martin Carlin, and a magnificent chest of drawers with gilt-bronze cupids and oak leaves by Charles Cressent, in the Grey Drawing Room.

Elegant though these are, they are overshadowed by the eleven pieces by Jean-Henri Riesener, several made for Louis XVI at Versailles. One, an exquisite marquetry dropfront secretaire, was ordered by Marie-Antoinette in 1777 for Louis's own use in the Petit Trianon. She then ordered a delightful small writing table for her own apartments in 1782. Another masterpiece is a huge cylinder-top desk in the Baron's Room, made between 1777 and 1781, traditionally believed to have belonged to Beaumarchais, the author of *The Marriage of Figaro* and *The Barber of Seville*.

Beaumarchais was Horloger du Roi, music master to Louis XV's daughters, pamphleteer and spy. Appropriately, the desk has secret compartments operated through elaborate mechanical devices, which have led to suggestions that the craftsman was Jean-François Leleu.

Almost every table, commode or secretaire has on it pieces of Sèvres porcelain: clocks, night lamps (*veilleuses*); trays; candelabras; pot-pourri vases, some signed by Charles Nicolas Dodin, some from designs by Boucher, one decorated with flowers and medallions in grisaille, painted by the head of the painters' workshop at Sèvres, Jean-Baptiste-Etienne Genest.[171] Baron Ferdinand's first major pur-

Mrs John Douglas by Thomas Gainsborough (Waddesdon Manor)

chase, when he was only twenty-two, was a stunning turquoise pot-pourri vase in the shape of a ship (only ten of this design survive) for which he retained a special affection.

These individual pieces are but *amuse-gueules* to whet your appetite for the Sèvres Rooms in the West Wing. Here are the 300-piece dinner and dessert service presented by Louis XV to the Austrian ambassador, Prince Starhemberg, in 1766 in recognition of his part in negotiating the 1756 Treaty between France and Austria (cemented later by the marriage between the Dauphin, later Louis XVI, and the Princess Marie-Antoinette) and the dessert service bought by Count Kiryl Razumovsky the following year.

The plates of the Starhemberg service, painted by Sèvres' best (Rosset, Méraud jeune, Parpette) are displayed not on a table but as decorative trophies on the walls, accompanying the massed array of tureens and dishes illustrating the stages of an 18th-century banquet; the Razumovsky service, with its ground of pulsating turquoise (*bleu celeste*), is in cabinets so that you can see the precise exotic brilliance of the birds copied from engravings by the English natural historian George Edwards.[172] These two services would be banquet enough but there are, in the Sèvres rooms, ice-cream coolers from the famous service made for the Prince de Rohan[173] and many pieces from a 235-piece dinner and dessert service ordered by Marie-Antoinette in 1781.

French furniture and porcelain are complemented by French drawings (Fragonard,[174] Carmontelle) and French paintings (Jean-Baptiste Greuze, Nicolas Lancret, Elizabeth Vigée-Lebrun, a portrait of *Madame de Pompadour*, surprised, by Boucher). Enamoured though the Rothschilds were with 18th-century France they also collected 17th-century Dutch and Flemish paintings. On the walls of the Morning Room, furnished with more pieces by Riesener and Dubois, Benneman and Kemp, are landscapes by Aelbert Cuyp, Philips Wouwermans and Jacob van Ruisdael, and paintings by Gerrit Dou, Gerard ter Borch, Gabriel Metsu and Pieter de Hooch. The room is dominated by the Reynolds over the fire-place, one of his most vacuous exercises in faux-classicism, a portrait of *Emily Potts as Thais*. Incongruous though this may seem, Baron Ferdinand was surely well aware of the impact of a portrait of a prostitute urging Alexander the Great to burn the great library at Persepolis as the centrepiece of a room containing his outstanding collection of rare books and bindings. There are also three Gainsboroughs, including his fancy portrait of Master Nichols, *The Pink Boy* (1782).

The best of the Reynolds and Gains-boroughs (and Romneys) are in the Baron's Room: Reynolds's *Mrs Sheridan as St Cecilia*[175] (1774–5), as sublime as Miss Potts is vapid, described by Reynolds as 'the best portrait I have ever painted'; his full-length of the coquettish *Duchess of Cumberland* (1772–3), who was described by Horace Walpole as having 'the most amorous eyes in the world, and eyelashes a yard long'; two Gains-boroughs, painted in his last years but at the height of his powers, *Mrs Sheffield* (1785) and *Mrs John Douglas* (1784). Upstairs in the Red Anteroom is another Reynolds in the theatrical vein, a superb portrait of *Garrick Between Tragedy and Comedy* (1761), the great actor torn in different directions.

There is the intriguing opportunity to compare these supreme portraitists in their paintings, in the same year (1781–2), of the same woman, the actress Mrs Robinson. Reynolds depicts her in a swaggering, feathery hat; Gainsborough hatless, simple, thoughtful. Waddesdon also offers the opportunity to see two more portraits by Romney of Emma Hart (later Lady Hamilton), as Circe and as Calypso.

Outside in gardens that are more English than French, Baron Ferdinand built an aviary (1889) whose delicate rococo trelliswork (in cast iron) looks back to 18th-century pavilions at Versailles and Chantilly and in front of which the original bedding scheme was recreated in 2003–4.

Waddesdon is a spectacular essay in French 18th-century taste. For some it is too rich. Mary Gladstone, the daughter of the Prime Minister, visiting in 1885, 'felt much oppressed with the extreme gorgeousness and luxury' and noted, unjustly, that 'there is not a book in the house save twenty improper French novels.' Poor Miss Gladstone! Her failure to enjoy Waddesdon was her loss. Lord Haldane, on the other hand, was moved to declare 'I love luxury' after an invitation to one of Baron Ferdinand's famous house parties in 1898.

In his habits Ferdinand was ascetic; a teeto-taller, he would drink water and eat dry toast as his guests dined, all his love of luxury being expressed in the artefacts with which he surrounded himself. His wife, Evelina, died in childbirth in 1866 (as did their baby) when he was twenty-six, and he never remarried. His undoubted melancholy streak was offset by friends, politics, travel and philanthropy. His last wish was: 'May the day be yet distant when the weeds will spread over the garden, the terraces crumble into dust, the pictures and cabinets cross the Atlantic, and the melancholy cry of the nightjar sound from the deserted towers.'

NEW ART GALLERY *

Gallery Square, Walsall, West Midlands
WS2 8LG
Tel. 01922 654400
www.artatwalsall.org.uk

The collection of Epstein's widow Kathleen Garman and Sally Ryan in a new gallery

The New Art Gallery, five storeys and 100 feet high, looks out across an historic industrial landscape in which towns merge: Walsall, Wednesbury, Wolverhampton. From without the gallery is neither beautiful nor elegant, its facades of pale grey tiles broken only by assymetrical small windows. It says 'mill' or 'silo', not 'art gallery'. Its head is high, it marks its place by the canal, but it is no more inviting than the empty space around it (Gallery Square, designed by the sculptor Richard Wentworth), too bleak to be called a piazza.

Even inside there are few indications that this is an art gallery. No paintings or sculptures

disturb the ground floor. The architects Peter St John and Adam Caruso have designed a building (2000) that reveals its virtues very slowly, but they do exist and they are detailed and thoughtful: handrails on the stairs tight bound by a skin of soft leather; pre-cast concrete that bears the faint marks of wooden shuttering; panelling and flooring cut from Douglas firs, almost pink; galleries that vary in size and shape, tailored to suit the objects displayed. The windows from within are placed at cunning and surprising heights and angles, each revealing a view: the canal, the town, the landscape beyond. Beside one window, whose view is the sky, is hung a Constable oil sketch, *Landscape with Clouds* (*c.* 1821–2).

Nominally the gallery houses the Garman Ryan Collection but in practice it is a homage to Jacob Epstein. Kathleen Garman was Epstein's lover from 1921 to 1955 when, his wife having died in 1947, he and Garman married. Sally Ryan was an American sculptor[176] who met Epstein in 1935 and became his disciple. Garman and Ryan began collecting in the early 1960s and their acquisitions comprise the greater part of the works that are here; but it is Epstein's eye that runs through these rooms, so it is appropriate that the first works of art that the visitor is invited (at last) to see are the pieces that remain from his private collection of 'primitive' art from Africa, Asia, South America and the Pacific Islands, and a collection[177] of his portrait busts.

Commissioned portrait busts provided Epstein with an income but they do not show him at his best. There are eleven here, among them portraits of T. S. Eliot, Rabindranath Tagore, David Lloyd George and Sally Ryan, and *First Portrait of Kathleen* (1921), which he is said to have modelled the morning after he and Garman first slept together. They demonstrate his energy, his modelling, his ability to gouge, smooth and squeeze so that the finished bronze is as plastic as the clay from which it was cast, but they take no risks, offer no surprises. They are about features, not forms.

His best work (the sculptures for the outside of the British Medical Association building[178] on the Strand, London, 1907; the sculpted memorial to *Oscar Wilde*,[179] 1909–11, in Père Lachaise Cemetery, Paris; the *Rock Drill*,[180] 1916, Tate Britain, q.v.);[181] all are carvings that have an elemental, mythic quality whose roots can be seen in this cabinet collection of small primitive pieces.

European artists had known about primitive art since 1848, when Rodolphe Toepffer, in his *Reflexions et menus propus d'un pientre genevois*, lauded the colossal stone heads from Easter Island as being the equal of Michelangelo's *Moses*, but it was only when collections of ethnography were exhibited in Europe that such works could be studied. Epstein visited the Trocadero Museum in Paris in 1903, as did Vlaminck, Derain and Picasso. The plastic rhythms and power of these masks, spirit heads, fetish heads and carvings had an immediate effect on his work and he began to put together what became one of the largest private collections of primitive art in the world.

When Epstein died, Garman sold his collection[182] in accordance with his will, retaining only a few dozen objects that were of particular significance to her and her husband: the poised Egyptian mask believed to be of Queen Nefertiti, 18th Dynasty, 1350–1300 BC, which may possibly be a copy but which Epstein gave her; the *Head of a Mourning Woman* (Roman, 1st century AD); the beautiful drawing *Caryatid* (*c.* 1913–14), which Modigliani gave to Epstein.

The remaining pieces are all small and are almost all representational. They reflect the width of his enthusiasms: a Greek terracotta cockerel (4th century BC); a bronze Etruscan *Figure of a Youth* (7th–5th centuries BC); a wooden royal stool from the Cameroons (*c.* 1920–30s); a pre-Columbian obsidian *Figurine of a Man* (*c.* 1000–1200). He collected for formal, sculptural qualities that combine balance and simplicity: an acknowledgment across the centuries from one artist to another.

After Epstein's death Kathleen Garman started to collect. It is unclear whether she did so for financial reasons or because of a simple love of objects. Nor is it clear when, why and

how she and Sally Ryan began to collect together, but by 1968 it was referred to, by Garman, as the Garman-Ryan Collection.

What is clear is its character: figurative; domestic in scale; including a very high proportion of works on paper; and catholic in its range and taste, from three woodcuts by Albrecht Dürer to watercolours by the children's author Kate Greenaway. There are works that reveal little-known sides of well-known artists (an oil sketch *Study of Wayside Plants*, 1866, by Edwin Landseer; a watercolour of a *Hollyhock* by Eugene Delacroix; van Gogh's only known nude drawing, *Sorrow*, 1882).

There are some excellent works (a Samuel Palmer etching, *The Early Ploughman*, c.1861; a Corot etching, *The Outskirts of Rome*, c.1865–6, and Robert Delaunay's *Portrait of Stravinsky*, 1918); some of indifferent quality (a disappointingly weak early – c.1797 – watercolour by J.M.W. Turner; unusually indecisive drawings by Matisse; and that rarity, a rank bad drawing by D.G. Rossetti of his wife, Elizabeth Siddal); and a curiosity (a self-portrait by William Makepeace Thackeray). It is a collection through which it is interesting to rummage but too many works appear to have been acquired for the artist's name.

More questionable is the decision to include the work of family members. Lucian Freud was for several years married to Garman's daughter Kitty, and has here a good early (1948–9) portrait of her, in profile, but Theodore Garman, Epstein and Garman's son, is a painter whose work might have been more happily retained within the family.

Epstein was a more considerable artist than his work here suggests. More clearly and directly than anyone else in England in the early 20th century he sought nourishment in tribal and primitive art, as did Derain, Picasso, Modigliani, Kirchner, Franz Marc and the *Blaue Reiter* group. This collection gives you a glimpse of how that arose and, in one maquette for the *Cavendish Square Madonna and Child* (1950), how he grafted those discoveries on to a Christian European tradition. For more than a glimpse you will have to see him elsewhere: the Strand, London; Père Lachaise Cemetery, Paris; the Metropolitan Museum of Modern Art, New York; or Tate Britain (q.v.), where his *Jacob and the Angel* shows the full pomp of his powers.

WOLVERHAMPTON MUSEUM AND ART GALLERY **

Lichfield Street, Wolverhampton, West Midlands WV1 1DU
Tel. 01902 552055
www.wolverhamptonart.org.uk

Victorian paintings and British and American pop art

This is a gallery of contradictions: in it is mid-Victorian genre painting by the Cranbrook Colony painters, and one of the four collections of British and American pop art; the cool stiffness of early-18th-century portraiture (Arthur Devis and Joseph Highmore) beside the history paintings of Francis Danby and Henry Fuseli; collections of 18th- and 19th-century glass and ceramics that have been mothballed in response to budget cuts; and a collection of contemporary figurative painting that has been added to annually for the past thirty years.

The origins of the museum were straightforward. Exhibitions of art and industry at the Mechanics' Institute in 1839 and 1869 were followed, without undue haste, by a gift of £500 to buy works of 'Art Manufacture' on condition that a place was provided for them to be exhibited. A local builder and alderman, Philip Horsman, offered to pay for, and build, a museum if two other councillors joined him in giving bequests. The Birmingham architect Julius Chatwin was commissioned and designed a building that Pevsner describes as 'original and functional. Italianate with several frontispieces with columns, the principal holding the porch of pairs of pink granite columns.'[183] Within it space was found for an art school. Relief sculptures on the facade by Bolton of Cheltenham represent the arts, architecture and astronomy, a public statement

Adonis in Y-fronts *by Richard Hamilton*
(Wolverhampton Museum and Art Gallery)

of the councillors' belief in the synergy of art, manufacturing and education that Henry Cole was developing in South Kensington. Following his lead, the museum made an early purchase of plaster casts for students to copy.

Founding bequests of contemporary paintings were made by Horsman and Councillor Sidney Cartwright, a manufacturer of tin toys. Both men collected genre work by the then popular Cranbrook Colony, a group of artists led by Frederick Hardy and George Bernard O'Neill, who took advantage of the new railway lines to the Kentish Weald to escape the metropolis. The titles describe the work: *Baby's Birthday, A Prayer for Those at Sea,*

The Chimney Sweep, Washday (Hardy); *Not Forgotten, The Nestlings, Expectation, Early Teaching* (O'Neill) – all hymns to the virtues of childhood innocence, thrift and duty.

The Victorian collection includes one or two striking pictures: Francis Danby's *The Shipwreck* (1859), in which a ship in a wild sea plunges off rocks like a whale as the tiny figures of its crew cling to rigging or ropes and a rainbow ironically finds its end on shore; E. J. Neimann has a small *Landscape with a View of Lincolnshire in the Distance* that competently borrows from Cuyp.

Elsewhere there are the solid mediocrities of the time: the Faeds; cows by Sydney Cooper; a lifeless Landseer of Queen Victoria in Windsor Home Park. It is hard to make claims for any of them. They chart the plodding decline of

the Royal Academy in the mid 19th century, resolutely insular. These are paintings that tell you what they are about. No subtext, no ambiguity, no surprise. No staying power.

Acquisitions continued to be made in the early 20th century (John Nash, Sir Alfred Munnings, a William Strang portrait of his wife, Kit, given by Sir Edward Marsh) until, after the Second World War, a decision was made to balance the 19th-century collection with 18th-century works: two Gainsborough full-lengths, portraits by Joseph Wright of Derby and Raeburn, an over-the-top Zoffany of *David Garrick as Sir John Brute* in Vanbrugh's *The Provok'd Wife*, a strange Richard Wilson of Niagara Falls (a failure, not painted from life: a subject wholly inappropriate to his quiet, subtle talents) and Fuseli at his most ecstatic, *The Apotheosis of Penelope Boothby* (1791), a child aged six being swept up into paradise in the arms of an angel, leaving behind a butterfly and a broken jug.

The outstanding feature of the 18th-century collection is a group of paintings by Joseph Highmore, pupil of Kneller, rival of Thomas Hudson, led by a large conversation piece, *The Family of Edward Lancelot Lee* (1736). The Lees of Coton Hall, Bridgnorth, could trace their ancestors back to the Norman Conquest and Highmore has assembled Mr Lee's widow and ten children in the drawing room while he, deceased, looks down from a painting on the wall and a daughter who died in infancy floats above, a cherub.

Highmore's dresses are more animated than his faces (all in half profile, featuring the prominent family nose) or his poses, although, unlike Hudson, he did not enjoy the services of a master of lace and drapery such as van Aken. Two further portraits, twenty and thirty years later, show Mr Lee's widow and eldest daughter ageing more than Highmore's style.

The late 1960s saw a further development in acquisitions policy. First Unit One works were purchased, then Surrealist paintings (Paul Nash, Edward Wadsworth and Roland Penrose), followed by the Twentyman Collection of works by John Piper and Graham Sutherland, and painters from St Ives (Alfred Wallis,

Ben Nicholson, Patrick Heron, Wilhelmina Barns-Graham).

The appointment of David Rodgers as director in 1969[184] led to the gallery starting to build a collection of British and American pop art that covers all aspects of that movement: art that responded to comics, advertisements, popular culture (Joe Tilson, James Rosenquist, Jim Dine); to consumerism (Peter Blake); to current affairs (Andy Warhol, Larry Rivers); but which also showed the painterly qualities of many pop artists: Roy Lichtenstein, Richard Hamilton, Patrick Caulfield.

After Rodgers's departure, the purchase of contemporary work was maintained on a broader basis with some emphasis on Scottish artists (John Bellany, Jock McFadyen, David Mach, Peter Howson) and some acquisitions in depth (the work of Ana Maria Pacheco, artist in residence at the National Gallery in 1997).

These works are a far stretch from the art and industry exhibitions of the mid 19th century or the sentimentalities of the Cranbrook Colony but they distinguish Wolverhampton as one of the few galleries, along with Southampton Art Gallery, the Towner Art Gallery and Museum, the Ferens Art Gallery, and the Aberdeen Art Gallery (all q.v.), that is consistently and imaginatively collecting the painting of today.

WIGHTWICK MANOR *

Wightwick Bank, Wolverhampton, West Midlands wv6 8ee
Tel. 01902 761400
www.nationaltrust.org.uk

The Pre-Raphaelites in a house decorated by Morris and Co.

When Morris, Marshall, Faulkner & Co. was launched on 11 April 1861 its prospectus declared: 'The growth of Decorative Art in this country . . . has now reached a point at which it seems desirable that artists of reputation should devote their time to it.'[185] Wightwick exemplifies this merging of decorative and fine

art, its Pre-Raphaelite art collection (Millais, Ford Madox Brown, D. G. Rossetti, Burne-Jones) being exhibited in a house decorated by Morris & Co. and by the craftsmen associated with 'The Firm' (Charles Kempe, William De Morgan and W. A. S. Benson).[186]

The conjunction is somewhat artificial, as the paintings and drawings did not begin to be collected by Sir Geoffrey and Lady Mander until 1937, while the house was built by the former's father, Theodore Mander, to designs by Edward Ould, between 1887 and 1901. Nevertheless they complement one another.

Ould's design is in an 'Old English' style: half-timbered, leaded windows, a battlemented tower. When Mander extended the house in 1893, Ould recreated a pastiche of a late-medieval manor house with a great hall, styled here the Great Parlour, while incorporating electric light, central heating and a Turkish bath.

Every room has Morris papers or fabrics on the walls: 'Larkspur', 'Willow Bough', 'Pimpernel', the rare and complex 'Acanthus' whose painting needs twenty-two wooden blocks, and 'Dove and Rose' silk and wool wall hangings. All the metalwork – gasoliers, chandeliers, firegrates – is by W. A. S. Benson, the disciple of Webb and Morris who eventually became a director of Morris & Co. There is stained glass throughout by Charles Kempe who also supervised the decoration of the Great Parlour, to which he contributed a coloured plaster frieze of the story of Orpheus and Eurydice.

There are pieces of furniture throughout the house by Morris (his black-stained, rush-seated Sussex chairs) and D. G. Rossetti; tiles (and lustreware) by William De Morgan; and some curiosities: mirrors, a cupboard with folding bed and a large cabinet, each panel painted with Rossetti designs,[187] which had belonged to Algernon Charles Swinburne and Theodore Watts-Dunton at No. 2, The Pines, Putney.

The stained glass, oak panelling, Flemish tapestries and embroidery create a dense, rich atmosphere: a connoisseur's sanctum created by Morris & Co. In fact Morris never visited

Wightwick and Theodore Mander bought everything from stock, with the exception of the Kempe glass.

Nevertheless its coherence and quality led W. G. Constable, the Slade Professor of Fine Art at Cambridge, to urge the Manders to offer Wightwick to the National Trust in 1937. It was the first property to be acquired under the Trust's newly established Country Houses Scheme. At once the Manders set out to acquire Pre-Raphaelite paintings, starting with the *Portrait of Jane Morris* in the Drawing Room, begun (1870s) by D. G. Rossetti and completed (1893) by Ford Madox Brown. It is a striking head, but curiously Madox Brown has painted Janey Morris's thick, black gypsy hair bright orange and has done so with crude brushstrokes, probably the consequence of the stroke he suffered in 1893.

The Pre-Raphaelites were not widely admired in the 1930s and '40s so the Manders and the National Trust were able to purchase two small paintings by Millais (of *Effie Ruskin*, painted the summer in which they fell in love while on holiday with Ruskin, 1853, and a self-portrait, 1878) and a fine G. F. Watts of *Jane Nassau Senior*[188] (1858), whilst Burne-Jones's *Love Among the Ruins* (1894) was transferred in 1948 by the National Trust from the Bearsted Collection at Upton House (q.v.). This is an elegy to Burne-Jones's agonised love for the beautiful Greek Maria Zambaco.[189] Burne-Jones's wife Georgiana observed that he was affected acutely by 'beauty and misfortune and far would he go to serve either'.[190]

The collection is particularly strong in drawings in chalks by Burne-Jones and D. G. Rossetti; in the work of painters (particularly women artists) who were on the periphery of the Pre-Raphaelites (Maria Spartali Stillman, Lucy Madox Brown, Elizabeth Siddal, Evelyn De Morgan, Emma Sandys); and in the sketches, cartoons and caricatures that the Pre-Raphaelites produced in profusion. In particular there are fifty-two early Rossetti drawings, from the 1840s, when he shared a studio with the sculptor Alexander Munro,[191] and a glorious cartoon of his sister, *Christina Rossetti in a Temper Tantrum*. She is shown wild-eyed, leaping with fury, both feet off the ground, a hatchet raised above her head. Her brother has quoted from the review of her poetry in *The Times* which was the cause of this: 'Miss Rossetti can point to work that cannot easily be mended.'

BLENHEIM PALACE ***

Woodstock, Oxfordshire OX20 1PX
Tel. 08700 602080
www.blenheimpalace.com

Vanbrugh's 'piece of magnificence' filled with condign paintings, furniture and tapestries

From the Column of Victory you look across Capability Brown's landscaped park, over Vanbrugh's Grand Bridge, to the mighty facade of Blenheim Palace. Is Blenheim, as Vanbrugh hoped, a monument of 'Beauty, Magnificence and Duration'[192] that led George III to declare, 'We have nothing like it' or is it, as Lord Shaftesbury maintained, 'a false and counterfeit piece of magnificence'?[193]

Its origin is written on a scrap of paper, displayed in the First State Room: a note sent by Marlborough to his wife, scribbled on the back of a bill as dusk fell on his victory over Louis XIV's army at the village of Blenheim on 13 August 1704. 'I have not time to say more, but to beg you will give my duty to the Queen, and let her know her army has had a glorious victory.'[194] To reward Marlborough for destroying the French and Bavarian armies, Queen Anne promised to build him a great house, a monument to the victory from a grateful Queen and nation.

From the first Blenheim was contentious. Marlborough chose as his architect Sir John Vanbrugh, the playwright who was in the middle of designing Castle Howard. He and Vanbrugh wanted 'a Royall and a National Monument',[195] symbolic and aesthetic. Marlborough's wife, the formidable Sarah, confidante of the Queen, did not. 'I mortally hate all gardens and architecture.' Her ideal was 'a clean sweet house and garden be it ever so small'[196] and her chosen architect was Sir Christopher Wren. The 'clean sweet house' Wren later built for her was Marlborough House in London.

The Duchess fought Vanbrugh ('as soon as I knew him and saw the maddnesse of the whole design I opposed it all that it was possible for me to do'[197]) and fell out with the Queen. The notional original cost of £100,000 doubled. In 1712 all building ceased and the Marlboroughs, now in the political wilderness under a Tory government, went into 'a sort of exile', leaving large debts on the unfinished building. They returned when the Queen died and building recommenced but this time financed not by royal grants but at Marlborough's own expense. Blenheim is a baroque masterpiece conceived in glory but finished, with numerous compromises, in exhaustion twenty years later.

The Duke and Duchess were neither collectors nor connoisseurs and so it has been with their descendants. Every painting here, with the exception of *Lady Killigrew and the Countess of Morton* and a portrait of the vanquished Louis XIV by Rigard, has been commissioned and features a member of the family. Closterman painted a large full-length of the 1st Duke and his family and a half-length of the Duke alone. There is a charming picture by Michael Wright of the Duke's brother and sister and two Knellers of the Duchess.[198]

The 4th Duke, for whom Capability Brown landscaped the park, is depicted, full length, in Garter robes, by Romney. He was a loyal patron of Reynolds, who painted him (in the Green Drawing Room), a family group (the Red Drawing Room) and the Duchess with her baby on her knee.

The 9th Duke married Consuelo Vanderbilt, or, to be precise, was married to her by her mother. A celebrated beauty with black hair and ivory skin, she was painted by Duran, by McEvoy, by Helleu and by John Singer Sargent, and she and her husband were sculpted by Waldo Story.[199]

What sets Blenheim apart, as a museum of baroque decorative art, is the work of the craftsmen who were employed by Vanbrugh

The Willis organ at Blenheim Palace

In
MEMORY
of
HAPPY DAYS
&
AS A TRIBUTE TO
THIS GLORIOUS HOME
WE LEAVE THY VOICE TO SPEAK
WITHIN THESE WALLS
IN YEARS TO COME
WHEN OURS ARE

and his assistant Nicholas Hawksmoor. Sir James Thornhill painted the Duke victorious at Blenheim on the ceiling of the Entrance Hall, and would have continued to the Long Library and the Saloon, had not the Duchess found his rates of 25s. a yard too expensive and employed Louis Laguerre to paint the frescoes and *trompe l'œil* ceiling of the Saloon[200] (*The Apotheosis of the Duke of Marlborough*).

Nicholas Hawksmoor did several other ceilings. In the Long Library the 'sumptuous plasterwork is by Isaac Mansfield and the marble door vases were carved by William Townesend and Bartholomew Peisley'[201] of Oxford.[202]

There are elegant pier mirrors by James Moore, designed when he was employed by the Duchess to replace Vanbrugh and Hawksmoor in 1716. The monument to the Duke in the Chapel is designed by William Kent and executed by John Michael Rysbrack, who also sculpted the portrait of Queen Anne in the Long Library, a gesture of posthumous reconciliation by the Duchess, commissioned twenty years after the Queen's death. The monument aspires to the flamboyance and brio of Bernini but falls short in its heroic but heavy English manner, Rysbrack being altogether more confident with subjects that do not move.

This roll-call of early 18th-century baroque craftsmen would not be complete without Grinling Gibbons. Vanbrugh and Hawksmoor gave him £4,000 worth of employment as mason at Blenheim: he contributed urns, lions, colonnades, coats of arms, fireplaces, the 'stone enrichments' in the Great Hall 'cutt Extraordinary rich and sunk very deep' and one marble doorcase in the Saloon but, remarkably, no wood carving. Vanbrugh's stately style appears to have restrained his characteristic flourishes. When work resumed in 1716 the terms he was offered to complete the Saloon doorcases were half the earlier 'Royal rates' and he declined to continue.

Of the varied ways in which Marlborough's victory at Blenheim is celebrated, perhaps the best artistically is the series of seven Flemish tapestries designed from cartoons by Judocus de Vos and woven in Brussels under the direction of Lambert de Hodt. The tapestries record the battle and campaign in well-chosen detail (faces and uniforms from life, a yapping dog, a nervous stallion) and place them against backgrounds that are given depth by the technique of embroidering the foreground figure in silk, which takes stronger and brighter dyes than the wool used for the backgrounds.

These heroics are brought forward into the 20th century in two rooms that are devoted to the life of Winston Churchill, who was born here in 1874, proposed marriage to Clementine Hosier here in the Temple of Diana and was buried near by in Bladon village churchyard in 1965. Letters record his famously undistinguished youth; his paintings depict views of the palace and park against a background of the tapes of the wartime speeches that inspired the country to resist Hitler as the orator's ancestor had resisted the French. He was a biographer of the 1st Duke and the cadences of their lives and histories run here together, in this 'piece of magnificence' that is anything but counterfeit.

ELGAR BIRTHPLACE MUSEUM *

Crown East Lane, Lower Broadheath, Worcestershire WR2 6RH
Tel. 01905 333224
www.elgarmuseum.org

Enigmatic clues to Elgar

Edward Elgar (1857–1934) was born in a small cottage in a small village in the Worcestershire countryside outside Malvern. His father was a piano tuner who ran a music shop in Worcester in which Elgar worked until he was thirty-two, as he struggled to gain recognition for his composing. Here is a copy of his earliest surviving manuscript, from 1872, *The Language of Flowers*, marked optimistically 'Not For Publication' (the original is in the British Library, q.v.).

Here too is the programme of the Worcester

Manuscript from the Elgar Birthplace Museum

CARLISLE

A595

Cumbria

A591

GRASMERE

CONISTON

BOWNESS-ON-WINDERMERE

A595

AMBLESIDE

BRANTWOOD

20 miles

Merseyside

LIVERPOOL

PORT SUNLIGHT

M53

ELLESMERE PORT

Clwyd

The North-west

Between 1850 and 1930 twenty-four public art galleries opened in the north-west. No other region made such dramatic use of the opportunities to found local galleries and museums that were offered by the 1845 Museums Act and the 1919 Public Libraries Act.

Manchester and Liverpool more than doubled in size and in such towns as Bury, Bolton, Oldham and Accrington fortunes were made in the booming textile industry. These new industrial magnates were invariably Nonconformist in religion and radical in politics, with a passion for education and a deep sense of civic pride, which came together and were expressed in the foundation of local museums and libraries.

William Henry Lever in Port Sunlight, Thomas Wrigley in Bury and the Grundy brothers in Blackpool are rare examples of enthusiastic collectors. For Edmund Robert Harris in Preston, A. B. Walker in Liverpool, E. R. Longworthy in Salford and Joseph Whitworth in Manchester, philanthropy, rather than a love of art, fired their generosity. Lacking strong founding collections, many galleries relied on the advice of dealers (principally Agnew and Zanetti, in Manchester) when purchasing paintings, and the influence of William Agnew is exhibited on the walls of the galleries at Salford, Bury, Bolton and more. Agnew's favourite artists (Poynter, Leader, Faed, Pettie, T. S. Cooper and Edwin Long) are everywhere to be seen.

That there were more than twenty museums and galleries founded within a twenty-five mile radius of the centre of Manchester is a consequence of local government legislation that fragmented conurbations into small, distinct communities. Even after the First World War brought the first signs of economic decline to the region, eleven of the thirty-five English cities (outside London) with a population of over 100,000 were in south Lancashire and north Cheshire.

To the north, in the Lake District, the increase in the number of museums, in response to the growth in tourism, did not occur until later. Abbot Hall Gallery (Kendal) did not open until 1957, the Wordsworth Museum at Dove Cottage until 1981.

There are good university museums in this region, in Manchester and

Music Festival of 1893 in which he wrote, 'I played first violin for the sake of the fee as I could gain no recognition as a composer,' and the programme of the premiere of his cantata *King Olaf*, on 30 October 1896 in the Victoria Hall, Hanley, Stoke-on-Trent, alongside the solid brown ceramic jug given to him to mark the occasion.

There followed the Enigma Variations (1899), *The Dream of Gerontius* (1900), *Cockaigne* (1901) and the *Pomp and Circumstance Marches* (1901–7).[203] They brought him fame and with it a doctorate at Cambridge University (1900), a knighthood (1904) and the Order of Merit (1911), the honours of international celebrity displayed in a cabinet.

A new building houses an archive of almost all his papers that are not in the British Library, notably the full scores of the Second Symphony, the early (1896) *Lux Christi* and the String Quartet, and twenty volumes of press cuttings.

A bank of headphones allows you to listen to different recordings of the Enigma Variations and to compare the 1916 recording of the second movement of the Violin Concerto, played by Marie Hall and the Symphony Orchestra, with that of Yehudi Menuhin and the London Symphony Orchestra in 1932, both conducted by Elgar.

Down at the cottage in which he was brought up are all the memorabilia you might expect of the composer of that great hymn to England and to Empire, 'Land of Hope and Glory', the possessions of a thoroughly English man: tobacco jar and pipes; cigarette and cigar cases; golf clubs; well-used passport; framed photographs of Henry Wood, Richard Strauss and Menuhin; scores of Haydn's and Mozart's quartets; Stanier's *A Treatise on Harmony*, Coward's *Choral Technique and Interpretation*; and a library including P. G. Wodehouse, Edgar Wallace, Walter Scott, O. Henry, R. D.

Blackmore, Somerville and Ross, Hilaire Belloc; Homer and Shakespeare are here too, alongside books of crossword puzzles.

But where are signs of the Elgar who, at the heart of the apparent directness of the Enigma Variations, describing his friends and finally, himself, set a theme that is never played? Where is the composer who headed the score of his Violin Concerto, 'Herein is enshrined the soul of . . . . .', the five dots (perhaps) representing Alice Stuart Wortley? Where is the Elgar whose Piano Quintet is pervaded by what Alice Elgar called the 'reminiscence of sinister trees' and whose radiant melody for viola in the Adagio is redolent with longing? Where is the passionate, romantic Elgar of the theme in the Third Symphony that describes his love, aged seventy-four, for the young violinist Vera Hockman? Where the Roman Catholic Elgar, whose oratorio *The Dream of Gerontius*, set to a poem by Cardinal Newman, describes the death of Gerontius and the journey of his soul towards the Judgement Seat of God?

Alongside Wodehouse and Belloc are books on religion, *The Apocrypha*, *The Acts of the Apostles* by R. B. Rackman, *The Antichrist Legend* by W. Bousset and A. H. Keane. When he died he was working on *The Last Judgement*, the final part of a religious trilogy started thirty years earlier with *The Apostles* and *The Kingdom*. In a letter to his friend the Revd W. E. Torr, he describes it 'beginning with the Strife [Antichrist], ending with Judgement and the Heavenly Kingdom'.

Towards the end of *The Dream of Gerontius* the Judgement theme rises to a mighty crescendo. 'For "one moment" must every instrument exert its fullest force,' Elgar writes in the score. 'Take me away, and in the lowest deep there let me be,' cries the Soul as it embarks peacefully at last, after torment, upon its cleansing.

SYMPHONY - 2.

"Rarely, rarely, comest thou
Spirit of Delight!"

Northumberland

Durham

North Yorkshire

○ KENDAL

M6

LANCASTER

Lancashire

M6

PRESTON ○   M65   ○ BURNLEY
        ○
        BLACKBURN
                ○

West Yorkshire

M61

BOLTON   BURY
        ○   ○

Greater   M60   ○ OLDHAM   A635   A635
Manchester   ○ STALYBRIDGE

SALFORD   ○
        ○   MANCHESTER

162

56

M60

○ STYAL

Cheshire

M6   Derbyshire

Liverpool, and in Lancaster, where in recent years the university has taken responsibility for the Ruskin archive (and commissioned a beautifully designed building to house it). Lancaster has also established its own collections of ceramics (the John Chambers Collection of Pilkington tile- and potteryware) and fine art (Professor Irene Manton's collections of prints, from Dürer to Hockney), exhibited on a rolling, temporary basis at the Peter Scott Gallery on the university campus.

The large number of civic museums and galleries in the north-west has prevented the inclusion in this book of fine collections at two grand Cheshire houses, Tatton Park (Van Dyck, Canaletto, Gaspard Dughet, J. S. Chardin) and Tabley House (Sir John Leicester's collection of portraits by Reynolds, Gainsborough and Romney); some more good local authority galleries at Rochdale (the Staithes School); Birkenhead's Williamson Art Gallery, with the best collection in Britain of the work of Philip Wilson Steer; and the Grosvenor Museum at Chester (good natural history and, unsurprisingly, archaeology).

Given the industrial heritage of south Lancashire and north Cheshire the region is relatively light on industrial museums. Apart from the Manchester Museum of Science and Industry and Quarry Bank Mill at Styal, there are St Helens's World of Glass and museums at Macclesfield (silk) and Nantwich, where salt has been mined since the Roman occupation and where recently a 'ship' for storing salt, carved out of a single oak tree 700 years ago, was excavated by York Archaeology Trust – a reminder that here, as in other regions, the past is still waiting to be reclaimed, and that museums are never settled nor completed.

ARMITT MUSEUM AND LIBRARY *

Rydal Road, Ambleside, Cumbria LA22 9BL
Tel. 015394 31212, fax 015394 31313
e-mail: info@armitt.com

Beatrix Potter watercolours and Kurt Schwitters portraits

The Armitt at Ambleside surprises. This quiet Lakeland town houses paintings by Kurt Schwitters and the collections of six Victorian women: the educationalist Charlotte Mason, who founded the Parents' National Educational Union and one of the first teacher training colleges; the writer and social reformer Harriet Martineau; Beatrix Potter; and the three Armitt sisters after whom the museum is named. The common ground is the place itself.

Schwitters came here at the end of the Second World War. In Germany in the 1930s his collages and assemblages were compared with those of Picasso, Tatlin and Duchamp, his stream-of-consciousness writing as marked as that of Joyce, Ferlinghetti and Kerouac. The Nazis designated him a 'degenerate artist'.

He escaped to Norway and then, in 1940, to Scotland and internment. At Elterwater outside Ambleside, with a $1,000 grant from the Museum of Modern Art in New York and the loan of a barn from local farmer Harry Pierce, he began his last great work, the *Merzbarn*, a three-dimensional collage of plaster, stones, wood and slate from the local landscape, with relief panels of wire, string and canes, incorporating whatever came to hand: part of a cartwheel, a rubber ball, a child's watering can, a metal window (v. Hatton Gallery). It has been called 'one of the key works of 20th century art . . . the Dada equivalent of Durham Cathedral'.[1]

Kurt Schwitters's portrait of Dr George Ainslie
Johnson *(Armitt Museum and Library)*

At the same time he was painting the figurative, conventional portraits and landscapes which comprise the collection here: a portrait of the local GP, *Dr George Ainslie Johnson* (1946), playing chess, and portraits of several others, on long-term loan, including three members of the Pierce family. The portrait of *Harry Pierce* (1947), in particular, is tenderly observed. Pierce was a farming organic horticulturist. Behind him, Schwitters depicts a narrow landscape of plants. 'He is a genius,' wrote Schwitters; 'he lets the weeds grow, yet by means of slight touches he transforms them into a composition as I create art out of rubbish.'

It is not easy to relate these gentle, closely observed paintings to the violent yoking of images in the *Merzbarn*, the paper collages[2] or his compositions such as *Die Sonate in Urlauten* (Sonata in Primeval Sounds), 1943. Yet Schwitters had always worked parallel veins.[3] 'No man can create from his fantasy alone,' he believed. 'Sooner or later it will run dry on him and only by the constant study of nature will he be able to replenish it and keep it fresh.'[4] In all these works his love of Ambleside is clear.[5]

If Ambleside was an unlikely home for Schwitters, so was it for Charlotte Mason, Harriet Martineau and the Armitt sisters, who lived there from the 1880s. Sophia, Anna Maria and Mary Louisa Armitt had run a school for young ladies in Eccles until, with the help of a legacy, they were able to retire to the Lake District and devote themselves to botany (Sophia), history, music and ornithology (Mary) and writing (Anna Maria). Their published works and private papers were the basis of the Armitt Library, founded in 1913, which incorporated the Ambleside Book Club (founded in 1828; William Wordsworth was among its members) and the Ambleside Ruskin Libraries.

The Museum's most striking feature is a collection of over two hundred and fifty botanical drawings of fungi by Beatrix Potter. They combine scientific accuracy with beauty of composition and convey the texture and delicacy of these mysterious plants whose names warn of magic, maybe of poison: ink cap fungus, velvet shank, dung mottle gill, old man of the woods, the blusher.

Her paper 'On the Germination of the Spores of *Agaricineae*' was read at the Linnaean Society in London on 1 April 1897 but never published. Three years later she wrote and illustrated *The Tale of Peter Rabbit*.

BLACKBURN MUSEUM AND ART GALLERY **

Museum Street, Blackburn,
Lancashire BB1 7AJ
Tel. 01254 667130

Three thousand years of coins plus illuminated manuscripts and fine editions

'Mildly Gothic with touches in the direction of Arts and Crafts'[6] is how Pevsner describes the Blackburn Museum and Art Gallery, designed by Woodgate and Collcutt (1872–4).

Its modest entrance is decorated by unusual sculptural relief panels by G.W. Searle[7] but what makes Blackburn notable is the bequest of Robert Edward Hart (1876–1946): a hoard of coins, icons, manuscripts and books unequalled by any regional museum.

Hart inherited a fortune from the family rope manufacturing business. He was educated at Rugby and then read Classics at Cambridge. He never married.

There are two groups of coins. The first describes the fortunes of Persia before Islam. The rule of the Zoroastrian Achaemenid kings (550–333 BC) is marked by a tiny silver siglos showing a king holding two arrows.

When Alexander defeated the Achaemenids in 333 BC he issued silver coins (the head of Heracles on the obverse, Zeus on the reverse) and gold coins (Athene, Victory). Greek coins continued to be issued by the Seleucids (312–123 BC) and the Parthians (171 BC–AD 226) who defeated them.

In Rome's wars against the Parthians the coins issued in Nero's (AD 54–68) reign stand out. When Rome was at war, coins depicted the gates of the Temple of Janus as being open.

Nero's coins, in his brief period of universal peace, show them as closed. His successors, Trajan (AD 98–117), Marcus Aurelius (AD 161–80) and Lucius Verus (AD 161–9) who reigned jointly, and Caracalla (AD 198–217), stamped images of victory on their coins, with all except Trajan calling themselves Parthicus, Conqueror of the Parthians.

In AD 226 coins show the world coming full circle. The Sassanians from southern Persia overthrew the Parthians and restored the old Zoroastrian traditions of Achaemenid times, with the fire altar of Zoroaster on the obverse of coins. Their coin technology improved and they could strike thin coins from sheet silver, a technique the Arabs adopted after their conquest of Persia in AD 640 and passed on to us, with 'hammered silver coins' becoming the standard currency of medieval Europe.

The second group is of English and Welsh coins since the 13th century, all stamped with the lion and the lys until, under Henry VIII, the Tudor coat of arms supplanted the English lion and the Welsh dragon.

The lion is ubiquitous on coins. A 1569 ryal of James VI of Scotland has a Stuart red lion rampant, the Scottish lion, the same lion that was to be found on the £1 coin in the 1990s. Other coins here from Venice, Spain, Ethiopia and India show the lions of St Mark, Leon, Judah and Ashoka respectively.

Of the manuscripts, a Roman missal of 1400 and a Flemish Book of Hours stand out. The first, written by Johannes de Berlandia in the Carthusian monastery of St Bartholomew of Trisulte in Alatri, is richly gilded. The sequence of devotions addressed to the Blessed Virgin Mary in the Book of Hours is written in beautiful script.

The collection of books makes up a history of printing. There is a single leaf from the Gutenberg Bible printed in Mainz in 1455, the first book to be printed using moveable metal type, a revolution embodied. Here is Thomas Aquinas's *De Veritate Catholicae Fidei*, printed with superb clarity and sharpness by Nicholas Jenson at Venice in 1480, and William Caxton's printing the following year of Vincent de Beauvais's *The Myrror of the World*, a popular medieval encyclopaedia. Here too is a copy of a *biblia pauperum*, a block book printed in Germany in the mid 15th century and coloured in afterwards by hand, an early cartoon.

Hart was not interested solely in the printing of books. His collection includes two medieval travel books: *The Travels of Sir John Mandeville*, translated into German by Otto van Derrieringen and printed at Strasbourg by J. Knoblauch in 1507, and Bernhard de Breydenbach's *Peregrinationes in Terram Sanctam*, printed by Peter Drach at Speier in 1490. It describes a pilgrimage to the Holy Land and has woodcut illustrations by Edward Renwich, who travelled with de Breydenbach.

Finally there are books from the 18th and 19th centuries which are themselves works of art. The edition of Lodovico Ariosto's *Orlando Furioso*, printed at Birmingham by John Baskerville in 1773, shows the wonder of that master's type. An edition of Jean de la Fontaine's *Fables Choisies* (Paris, 1775–9) has illustrations by Jean-Baptiste Oudry (v. the Wallace Collection) and Thomas Rowlandson illustrated William Combe's *The Tour of Dr Syntax in Search of the Picturesque* (sixth edition, printed in London by R. Ackerman in 1815).

Books illustrated by Edward Burne-Jones, Charles Ricketts and Charles Shannon, and C. R. Ashbee, and editions printed by contemporary printers, World's End Press and the Whittington Press, show that high-quality printing, even if it is not improving, is attempting to maintain the standards set by the masters of the past.

BOLTON MUSEUM AND ART GALLERY **

Le Mans Crescent, Bolton, Lancashire BL1 1SE
Tel. 01204 332211
www.boltonmuseums.org.uk

Botany and zoology; Egyptian antiquities and Lancashire machinery; and the American landscapes of Thomas Moran, Bolton boy made very good in the Wild West

Built in 1939, in the middle of a handsome crescent, Bolton Museum and Art Gallery has a classical portico, Ionic columns, an ornamental pediment and an Art Deco interior. It was designed by architects Bradshaw, Grass and Hope, a firm that specialised in Lancashire cotton mills and civic buildings. It is an appropriate building and setting for the diverse collections inside.

Bolton already had collections of taxidermy and Egyptology, of furniture and of cotton machinery from its previous museums at Mere Hall, a neo-classical house a mile north of the town centre, opened in 1890, and Hall-i-th'-Wood, a 16th-century house in which Samuel Crompton invented his spinning-mule in 1779. W. H. Lever, who later as Lord Leverhulme founded the Lady Lever, bought Hall-i-th'-Wood in 1899 and gave it to the Corporation of Bolton, where he was born, as a folk and furniture museum of the 17th century. To these had been added collections of taxidermy (birds, a leopard, a woolly opossum, a black-faced lemur, a three-toed sloth and others), of skulls animal and human (casts of Peking man, Cro-Magnon man and *Homo sapiens*, and a reconstruction of *H. neanderthalensis*) and of Egyptian artefacts from the Abydos royal tombs, c. 3100 BC (three green-glazed faience baboons, sacred to Thoth, the god of wisdom and writing, and an ivory lion used as a gaming piece) and scarabs, amulets, bracelets and rings from Dynasty XXV, c. 700–650 BC. Here too are Greek papyri of the 2nd, 3rd and 4th centuries AD: a 2nd-century fragment of Book XIII of the *Iliad*, private letters and a 4th-century account for food supplied (dried fish, beans, dates, cabbages, cakes, cheeses and honey).

In 2004 the museum was given a 3,300-year-old Egyptian statuette[8] carved in translucent alabaster. Sans head, sans arms, sans lower legs, she is still a figure of great grace and beauty, the ribbing of her dress clinging across her body that dips and sways.

The chief curiosities of the pre-Second World War collections are two paintings by Thomas Moran: *Sunset, Pueblo de Walpe, Arizona* (1880) and *The Coast of Florida* (1882), given by W. H. Lever and his nephew J. Lever Tillotson in 1911 and 1936, respectively. Moran was born in Bolton in 1837. His family emigrated seven years later and Moran became one of the leading painters of the American West and its sublime, empty landscapes.

The new, 1939, museum and the Second World War provided the opportunity for a fresh start. In 1940 a Bolton cotton manufacturer, Frank Hindley Smith, bequeathed forty paintings, drawings and sculptures. Hindley Smith had been a friend of Roger Fry and, with Maynard Keynes and Samuel Courtauld, had supported young modernist artists in the 1920s through the London Artists' Association. His bequest was a strange mixture of paintings by Duncan Grant, Vanessa Bell and William Roberts, and 19th-century northern regional painters, Edward Stott of Rochdale and F. W. Jackson.[9]

On this new base the museum began to buy contemporary British art: a collection of bronzes by Jacob Epstein (notably the 1941 *Study for the Slave Hold*[10] and the 1955 maquette for the TUC War Memorial), Eduardo Paolozzi and Henry Moore (*Helmet Head No. 5*, 1966 and *Mother and Child*, 1959); paintings by Roland Penrose, Ivon Hitchens and Edward Wadsworth; and a small group of studio ceramics (Bernard Leach, Janice Tchalenko, Takeshi Yasuda).

These purchasing policies were encouraged and sustained by the leader of the Bolton Council, Harry Lucas. Lucas worked all his life at the Locomotion Works outside Bolton. He was a staunch trade unionist and a collector of watercolours, which he bequeathed to the museum. These form the core of a strong and diverse collection (J. R. Cozens, Rowlandson, Lear, De Wint, Nicholson, Auerbach and Hepworth). There is a fine watercolour here, *The Avenue*, which J. M. W. Turner painted for his friend Walter Fawkes at Farnley Hall (*c.* 1815–19), described by John Ruskin as 'a quite magnificent sketch'. Beside it are a considerable number of works by Albert Goodwin, a follower of Turner, who was a particular favourite of Harry Lucas.

In 1998 the National Art Collections Fund and a Heritage Lottery Fund grant[11] helped Bolton acquire its largest and most splendid Moran, *Nearing Camp, Evening on the Upper Colorado River* (1882), confirming the gallery's position as the leading collector of Moran's work in Europe. Two studies of related *Green River Scenes* (also 1882), one watercolour, one pencil, confirm the good sense of Ruskin's advice to him, 'I do wish with my whole heart you could give up for a while all that flashing and splashing and roaring business – and paint, not etch – some quiet things like that little true landscape absolutely from nature.'[12]

BLACKWELL ∗

Bowness-on-Windermere, Cumbria LA23 3JR
Tel. 015394 46139
www.blackwell.org.uk

Baillie Scott's Arts and Crafts house displays, in its own fabric, intricate wood, iron, stone and decorative plasterwork

Blackwell offers a rare opportunity to see Arts and Crafts furniture, metalware and ceramics by some of the best craftsmen (Ernest Gimson, Sidney and Edwin Barnsley, Omar Ramsden) in one of the finest examples of domestic Arts and Crafts architecture by M. H. Baillie Scott.

The site for which the Manchester brewer Sir Edward Holt invited Baillie Scott to design a house is on a hillside above Windermere. Curiously Sir Edward chose to set the house facing south with its shoulder end-on to the view.

Sir Edward lived in, and was twice Lord Mayor of, Manchester. He wanted a Lakeland holiday home, partly to escape from the city, partly to be near the major reservoirs at Thirlmere and Haweswater, which the Manchester Water Works Committee were developing in order to bring fresh water to Manchester. Baillie Scott, thirty-three years old and newly married, came directly from his first commissions in the Isle of Man and from decorating the Grand Duke of Hesse's Palace at Darmstadt. Blackwell offered him a showpiece for his talents in England.

For the past sixty years the house has been a girls' boarding school (1941–76), a health club (complete with jacuzzi) and the regional offices of English Nature. Remarkably the fixtures and fittings (panelling, ceilings, fireplaces, windows) remained unscathed.

Here are all the elements you would expect in an Arts and Crafts house: an attention to materials (oak, Ancaster stone and Broughton slate); fine detail (delicate door handles shaped like leaves, carved panelling, motifs of rowan, ash, bluebells, daisies) and fine craftsmanship.

Baillie Scott employed local craftsmen, Simpson's of Kendal, for the elaborate wainscoting in the Hall with an intricate frieze of intertwined leaves and rowan berries. Stanley Davies made a chest of drawers and an elegant artist's chair of oak and leather.

Furniture has been introduced that was not designed for the house but that is of the period: a brass and iron trivet by C. F. A. Voysey; a 'Rossetti Chair' by William Morris; a pair of silver-gilt candlesticks by Omar Ramsden; a dresser and cabinet by the Barnsleys; and several pieces by Ernest Gimson (a chest of drawers, a single bed, a dressing table, the dining-room table and a delicate box inlaid with ivory). Beside them are local pieces by the Keswick School of Industrial Art. There is a small copper kettle by Christopher Dresser which is not Arts and Crafts – indeed was designed to be manufactured not hand-crafted – but is of such elegance and quality that it seems at ease here.

Baillie Scott's own work matches them

Stained-glass tulips at Blackwell

all with the everyday (a pair of fire dogs), the unusual (a Broadwood piano) or the outstanding (a wooden armchair, c. 1898, in ash, a simple throne of a chair with a high back, widely spaced arms and carved legs that swell and turn gently). It looks forward to modernism and is as poised as a sculpture by Henry Moore.

In almost every room Baillie Scott has designed stained glass within the windows, delicate roses and leaves in pinks, blues and greens, and finished them with wrought-iron latches. In the Dining Room his original hessian wall coverings have survived, although no longer the deep denim blue that he intended.

Baillie Scott designed with human understanding. He wrote, in *The Studio*, 'It is at the fireside that the interest of the room is focused, and in our inconsistent climate we may be driven, at almost any season of the year, to seek there that brightness and warmth which we fail to find in the outside world.'[13] The fireplaces are indeed a focus of each room: Delft tiles topped by a chimney piece of interlocking slabs of stone and slate in the Hall; De Morgan tiles in startling, refreshing lime green in one bedroom; and an elaborate inglenook fireplace in the White Drawing Room, the best of them all (ceramic tiles; carved capitals of leaves and berries, painted white; a double mantel; a marble inlaid hearth in black, grey and white around a pale rose centre; over all of which a pair of iron and enamelled firedogs stand guard).

Baillie Scott provides views through the breadth of the house, into the White Drawing Room and out over the lake. The calm beauty of the scene, a steamer gently moving up the lake, is what the house deserves.

BRANTWOOD **

Coniston, Cumbria LA21 8AD
Tel. 015394 41396
www.brantwood.org.uk/

Ruskin's final home overlooking Coniston Water, filled with his paintings and drawings and his serious intent

Different aspects of the life and work of John Ruskin can be seen in at least three museums in the north-west: the Ruskin Library (q.v.) at the University of Lancaster has the main archive of his manuscripts, books and drawings; the Ruskin Museum (q.v.) at Coniston places him in the context of the Lake District; and his house, Brantwood, tells the story of the last twenty-eight years of his life.

Architecturally Brantwood is not exceptional but its position at the north-east end of Coniston gives it unequalled views down the lake and across to the Old Man. When Ruskin moved here in 1872 he was only fifty-three but many of his achievements were already established: as art critic (*Modern Painters*, 1843 onwards), social and architectural historian (*The Stones of Venice*, 1851, and *The Seven Lamps of Architecture*, 1849), champion of the Pre-Raphaelites in the 1850s; and, increasingly, crusader against the social and economic conditions of industrial Britain (*Unto This Last*, 1860).

In the same year that he purchased Brantwood he founded the Guild of St George, through which he hoped that the ideas explored in *Unto This Last* and *Fors Clavigera* would change the face of England by establishing new communities living by his ideals, 'that there are no taxes to pay; that everybody had clothes enough; . . . that everybody had as many books and pictures as they could read or look at, with quantities of the highest quality in easily accessible libraries and galleries.'

Throughout the 1870s Ruskin launched from his study here what Carlyle called 'those fierce lightning-bolts Ruskin is copiously and desperately pouring into the black world of anarchy all around him. No other man in

England that I meet has in him the divine rage against iniquity, falsity and baseness that Ruskin has, and that every man ought to have.'

At the same time he was extending the Brantwood estate, constructing a harbour, an ice house and a garden, and showing visitors round the collection of treasures with which he filled the house: medieval manuscripts, paintings by Gainsborough, Turner and the Pre-Raphaelites: a cabinet of curiosities that epitomised his aesthetic. Although much of this was sold after his death by his cousin and heir, Joan Severn, and her husband the artist Arthur Severn, a substantial part (and ultimately the house itself) was bought back by Ruskin's great admirer, the Liberal MP John Howard Whitehouse.

The house today contains a good representative sample of his collections: a wall cabinet of his shells, fossils and rocks; his Roman coins; the large drawings he used to illustrate his lectures;[14] and watercolours and drawings by him and by his disciples such as John Wharton Bunney, Thomas Matthew Rooke and his secretary in the 1880s, Laurence Hilliard.

Here is a small selection of his books (Gaisford's *Poetae Minores Græci* and Roscoe's two-volume life of *Lorenzo de Medici*),[15] several pieces of the mahogany furniture that he designed for Brantwood, the wallpaper in his study – whose central motif he adapted from the embroidered cape of the rabbi in Marco Marziale's *The Circumcision of Christ*[16] – and a panel, over the fireplace in the Study, of *The Virgin and Child* by della Robbia.

More revealing is a room of drawings in which may be the seeds of his talents as a draughtsman and as an art historian. Ruskin's copy of Samuel Rogers's collection of poems, illustrated by J. M. W. Turner, is accompanied by a passage from his autobiography *Praeterita*: 'on my 13th birthday, 8th February 1832, my father's partner, Mr Henry Telford, gave me Rogers's *Italy*, and determined the main tenor of my life'[17] – that is, his love of Turner's work. Close by is one of the three small cabinets that held Ruskin's set of proofs of the Turner

vignettes of the book. Here is the source of Ruskin's life.

Ruskin was taught to draw by Samuel Prout; Prout's *Domo d'Ossola* (*c.*1824) and *Ratisbonne*, and Ruskin's *Merton College* (1838), *Richmond, Yorkshire* (1838) and *Cologne* (1841), show how closely the pupil studied the detail and clarity of his teacher's architectural drawings.

Ruskin bought Brantwood, without ever having seen it, for its views, and he proceeded to enhance them, designing a new dining room with seven magnificent lancet windows that bring a blaze of Venetian Gothic into the house; he designed too a turret to his first-floor bedroom, which is at the heart of the house. This turret is a wooden capsule suspended in space, large enough for one person to sit in, with views down and across the lake. It was the perfect place from which to contemplate the glories of nature and the sun setting behind the Old Man, so it is poignant that it was in this much-loved room, filled with watercolours by Turner, that Ruskin suffered his most severe mental breakdown in 1878. He saw demons dancing on his bedpost and he never slept there again.

The shadows in his mind were drawing in as he observed the changes in the weather that rolled up the lake in the 1880s. Too often the sun looked like 'a bad half-crown at the bottom of a basin of soap suds'. In a lecture to the London Institution in 1884 he warned of 'blanched sun ... blighted grass ... blinded man'. 'Manchester has become the funnel of a volcano, which, not content in vomiting pestilence, gorges the whole rain of heaven, that falls over a district as distant as the ancient Scottish border.' Yet, as he struggled to complete *Praeterita*, even these clouds of pollution could not destroy the beauty of Coniston, seen from Brantwood, that he had described in 1877: 'I raise my eyes to these Coniston Fells, and see them, at this moment imaged in their lake, in quietly reversed and perfect similitude, the sky cloudless beneath, and two level lines of blue vapour drawn across their sunlighted and russet moorlands, like an azure fesse across a golden shield.'

Ruskin was, in Tolstoy's view, 'one of those rare men who think with their hearts'. Brantwood evidences this high verdict. For all his passion and anger with the failings of the world, 'there is', he wrote in *Unto This Last*, 'no wealth but life. Life, including all its powers of love, of joy and of admiration.'[18]

TOWNELEY HALL ART GALLERY AND MUSEUM **

Towneley Park, Burnley, Lancashire BB11 3RQ
Tel. 01282 424213
www.burnley.gov.uk/towneley/index.htm

Townley's marbles are in the British Museum but there's plenty here: paintings, sculpture and the Whalley Abbey vestments, a triumph of opus anglicanum

Zoffany's *Charles Towneley's* (sic) *Library at 7 Park Street, Westminster* (1781–3) depicts Townley (*sic*) with three friends surrounded by the best marbles of his collection including the *Discobolos*[19] from Hadrian's Villa in Rome. Being a Catholic and therefore denied any role in public life, Charles Townley devoted himself to his estates and to his collection, most of which was bought through his agent in Rome, Thomas Jenkins.[20] After he died all his antiquities were bought by the British Museum,[21] leaving Towneley Hall, his family home, with none of the booty from his three Grand Tours[22] apart from a bust of Townley by Nollekens.

The Towneleys (*sic*) were a family who remained faithful to Roman Catholicism after the Reformation. The consequences of that pervade the house and much of the collection, though they are expressed in a way quite different from the home of the Throckmortons at Coughton Court, Warwickshire.

The building dates from the mid 14th century with major alterations made in the 17th century, in the 18th century by John Carr of York and in the 19th century by Jeffry Wyatville. An unknown architect rebuilt the south facade and hall in 1729, doubling the height of both. For the sculptural plasterwork he employed Francesco Vassalli, who worked for James Gibbs at Ditchley, and his assistant Martino Quadri, to create a 'grand and sumptuous' entrance with 'coupled pilasters and two splendid chimney pieces with big scrolls and two pieces of antique statuary against a stucco baldacchino'.[23] It stands comparison with the plasterwork at Temple Newsam (q.v.), designed by Carr, who employed a local plasterer, the brilliant Joseph Rose.

Beyond the wall is a Jacobean staircase leading to the 15th-century chapel which, until the 19th century, was the only remaining Catholic place of worship in this part of Lancashire. It contains the Towneley altarpiece, carved in Antwerp (1510–20), showing scenes from the life of Christ. The tableaux in the altar, which is late 18th century, have larger carvings of the Passion with figures compressed into each panel's dramatic action.

In 1536, at the time of the dissolution of the monasteries, Abbot Paslew is said to have sent Whalley Abbey's vestments to Sir John Towneley for safekeeping. The chasuble and dalmatics are rare examples of a style of 15th-century embroidery, opus anglicanum, worked with silk, silver and silver-gilt threads. Few such vestments survived the Reformation.[24]

The dalmatics (worn by deacons) tell the story of the betrothal of the Virgin Mary's parents, Joachim and Anne; the chasuble (worn by priests) the story of the events leading up to Christ's birth (the Suspicion of Joseph, the Visitation) to the Miracle of the Palm Tree, the Massacre of the Innocents and the Flight into Egypt. The ophreys set these scenes against diagonal gold stripes, decorated with stitched pink thistles. The vestments are displayed in a dark room, glinting and gleaming behind spotlights.

The hall was sold to Burnley Corporation in 1902 and became a museum, with the servants' bedrooms on the top floor making a fine barrel-ceilinged picture gallery.

In the 1920s the museum acquired 18th- and 19th-century English watercolours (Cotman, Dayes, Gainsborough, Girtin, Holland, Towne,

Varley, Cox), principally through Agnew's in Manchester. In the 1940s a small collection of 19th-century French paintings and water-colours (Daubigny, Harpignies, Lepine, Fantin-Latour, Troyon) was added to the standard body of Victorian paintings (Landseer, Dicksee, Linnell, Alma-Tadema, Poynter and the mandatory Thomas Sydney Cooper pastoral study of cattle). For most of these the dealer was Richard Haworth of Blackburn, who curiously also sold the museum an Andrea del Sarto.

The unlikely star of the collection, apart from the Zoffany, is John William Water-house's *Destiny*, painted for the Boer War Artists' War Fund. It is composed of three planes: a girl, her face reflected in a mirror, and the sea and distant landscapes reflected beyond her face. There is also a large David Cox oil painting, *A Vale of Clwyd*, which he painted in 1846 with uncharacteristically large, heavy brushstrokes as his sight began to fail.

Throughout the house there is oak furniture and some walnut floral marquetry pieces, all 17th-century. In the Regency rooms created by Wyatville is a square piano by Adam Beyer (1774) and work by Moral and Hughes, who also made furniture for Wyatville at Windsor Castle: a bergère chair in aburra wood with gilding, and a set of chairs for Northumberland House (1823).

These rooms contain portraits by Lely, Beechey and Thomas Hudson and two by John Partridge of notably flaccid and florid senti-mentality, along with a Venus by Antonio Canova, for which the model is believed to be Napoleon's sister Pauline Borghese.

It is impossible not to feel a twist of regret that there is not more of Charles Townley's great collection here. There are sixty water-colours and drawings of Towneley Hall and nearby Mitton Hall, which he commissioned from the 24-year-old Turner in 1798,[25] a marble bust of *Clytie*, and one of Townley himself, both by Joseph Nollekens; Richard Cosway's painting *A Group of Connoisseurs*, and the Zoffany: a tantalising glimpse of this remarkable collector, 'whose judgement in art', said his friend and fellow connoisseur

Richard Payne Knight, a little over-generously, 'was nearly as infallible as human judgement can be'.

It is a small memorial to a great connoisseur.

BURY ART GALLERY AND MUSEUM **

Moss Street, Bury, Lancashire BL9 0DR
Tel. 0161 253 5878
www.bury.gov.uk/culture.htm

A complete Liber Studiorum *by J. M. W. Turner and much more*

To buy paintings from Thomas Agnew's gallery in the 19th century was not necessarily to subsume your own taste to his. Certainly Thomas Wrigley's collection, built up between 1840 and 1880, which forms the founding core of the Bury Art Gallery, reflects his own conservative taste. He respected the Royal Academy, had no time for the Pre-Raphaelites and believed that good paintings should tell a story, preferably an improving one.

Wrigley, a successful manufacturer of paper, bought paintings for diversion and for investment. Seventeen years after his death in 1880, his three children offered the collection to the town on condition that the Corporation commission a suitable building to house it.

Designed by Woodhouse and Willoughby of Manchester, the result must have suited the aldermen well. It stands full-chested with civic pomp, 'two frontispieces left and right with columns in three orders and a three bay centre with an arched screen. The columns are Ionic above Doric.'[26]

Wrigley's love of narrative runs deep in these paintings, expressed in scenes from history that would have inspired G. E. Marshall (E. M. Ward's *The Fall of Clarendon* and Frederick Goodall's wholly unironic *An Episode in the Happier Days of Charles I*). Nor are literary subjects neglected. These draw on a catholic range of sources: Euripides (Briton Rivière's *Apollo*), Sir Walter Scott (Landseer's *The Random Shot*), Goethe (Maclise's *The Student*). None is more bizarre than Sir Joseph Noel

An Episode in the Happier Days of Charles I *by Frederick Goodall (Bury Art Gallery and Museum)*

Paton's *Dante Meditating* in which Dante, lost in thought, appears oblivious of the vaporous wraiths of the two swooning and naked lovers floating into the heavens above him, watched by a single guiding star.

Wrigley's taste in landscapes was considerably happier. Here are paintings by Turner, Crome, Constable and David Cox, a John Linnell that owes much to Gainsborough and through him to Hobbema, and a seascape by Clarkson Stanfield. Attractive though this work is, it is curious to think that in the 1820s and '30s, the artist was compared to Turner. Indeed his watercolours of Vesuvius in the Oppé Collection (Tate Britain, q.v.) were, until the 1970s, attributed to Turner. Here too is a landscape by the underestimated Patrick Nasmyth (*Cramond near Edinburgh*) and a cowscape by the ubiquitous Thomas Sydney Cooper.

Good though many of these works are, it is the Wrigley collection of watercolours that marks Bury out. Among the artists he favoured are Peter De Wint, David Cox, David Roberts, Copley Fielding, Clarkson Stanfield and Myles Birket Foster.

The pick of the four Turners is the *Ehrenbreitstein* of 1832. The fortress is described by Byron in *Childe Harold* as 'Ehrenbreitstein, with her shattered wall/Black with the miner's blast'. Here is Turner's watercolour of its destruction (1819–20), painted in part from sketches made on his visit to the Rhine in 1817 and in part from imagination.

For Wrigley, and for any visitor, the cream of his collection must be the complete set of seventy-one mezzotint engravings that make up Turner's *Liber Studiorum*. Turner wanted his work to be judged alongside that of Claude, whom he revered, so he set himself a project in imitation of Claude's *Liber Veritatis*, published thirty years before.

Turner began in 1807 to issue parts. In 1819 all had to be abandoned because of poor sales. Eleven engravers were used, including

J. C. Easling, who contributed a wonderful frontispiece (1812). The main printing colour was 'a fine, rich bistre' around which he worked the gamut of nuances and contrasts. In *Twickenham – Pope's Villa* (1819) the trees retreat in deep burnt shadows and the reflection in the water drifts away to the distant sky. The drama of *The Fifth Plague of Egypt* (1819) is expressed by the dark masses of the river (bottom left) and sky (top right) forced apart by a crevasse of white lightning.

Only the British Library, the Whitworth Art Gallery and Tate Britain (all q.v.) have complete *Liber Studiorum*s. This one makes Bury worth any detour.

TULLIE HOUSE MUSEUM AND ART GALLERY **

Castle Street, Carlisle, Cumbria CA3 8TP
Tel. 01228 534781
www.tulliehouse.co.uk/index2.htm

The museum of Cumbria and the Borders, which draws on local loyalty and love

The 'Debatable Lands', between Scotland and England, were fought over for 350 years in medieval times by rievers (raiders) from such families as the Armstrongs, the Maxwells and the Elliotts. Such feuding is recorded in this museum in the form of dramatic, large-scale audio-visual presentations. Of the others who contested this land in earlier periods only those who made their mark in stone are here. The Roman legions who marched north left a conquest stone *c.* AD 72 and numerous altars to their gods – Astarte, Jupiter, Dolichenus, Fortuna and many more. The Ninth Legion, lost in the mists, left only a tile stamped with their insignia.

Those lands were so deep in Celtic country that it is no surprise to see altars erected jointly to Roman and local gods. Soldiers of the Second Legion built an altar to Mars and to Cocidius, the Celtic god of war and hunting. There is an altar, inscribed in poor Roman lettering, to Belatucadrus, the warrior god of the local Brigantes tribe. On the tombstone

of a Roman citizen who died towards the end of the occupation is written 'ANIMAM REVOCAVIT', the soul recalled being a Christian concept.

This wild landscape, only slowly tamed by man, is old, marked centuries before Celtic shrines by Neolithic stone circles, *c.* 3000–1500 BC, at Long Meg, Castlerigg, Edenhall and Swinside. The Pennine Hills and Lakeland Fells retain their austere grandeur despite the impact of hill farming. The Solway Firth remains a vital resting and wintering area for birds migrating along the eastern Atlantic seaboard, its sands and salt marshes supporting wild geese and ducks, and waders such as oystercatchers, curlews, godwits and grey plovers: all represented in the museum's strong natural history collections.

With roots in the Carlisle Literary and Philosophical Society and the local Academy of Arts, the museum opened in 1893 in Tullie House, which was converted and much extended by the architect C. J. Ferguson. Then as now, it was a truly local museum, with photographs, costume, stuffed birds, archaeology and local-history material – including reminders of Carlisle's glory days as a railway town.

From the Carlisle Academy of Arts, dominated by Matthew Ellis Nutter and his son William Henry Nutter, there grew a strong local school of artists. The two most talented were William James Blacklock and Sam Bough, who both attended art classes under the largely self-taught Matthew Ellis Nutter. Blacklock's landscapes are polite and precise, Bough's stronger. He was prolific and painted fast. His handling of light and the shifts in weather in *Borrowdale* (1846) and *Baggage Wagons Approaching Carlisle* (1849), and in the watercolour *Cadzow Burn* (1856), is assured and dramatic. He left for Scotland and was elected to the Scottish Academy.

Wanting works other than those by local artists, the gallery initiated an imaginative purchase scheme in 1933. William Rothenstein, artist and principal of the Royal College of Art, was invited to advise on buying pictures, and given a budget of £100 a year.[27] He did this for nine years, receiving no remuneration, and was succeeded by Edward Le Bas (1948–57), Carel Weight (1953–62) and Roger de Grey (1963–75). Their purchases show what a small regional gallery, with a very limited budget, can achieve. Rothenstein bought the work of friends (Gilbert and Stanley Spencer; Wyndham Lewis;[28] studies by Augustus John) and gave works of his own, including a self-portrait.[29] Of Spencer's *Red Magnolia* (1938), Rothenstein wrote to the gallery, 'I am pleased you approve . . . I thought it a beautiful thing, such a *grand* piece of flower painting.' In 1954 the gallery received a bequest from Spencer's early patron Sir Edward Marsh, one of his first landscapes, painted when he was only twenty-three, *Cookham* (1914), the village of which Spencer said, 'Everything seems fresh and to belong to the morning.'[30]

Weight and de Grey chose oils by William Gillies, Sandra Blow, Sheila Fell and Elizabeth Blackadder, and drawings by William Roberts, L. S. Lowry and John Bratby: a thoughtful collection of real quality that turns a very good local museum and gallery into one of regional, even national, significance.

In 1949 a Lancashire poet, Gordon Bottomley, bequeathed his collection of more than six hundred paintings and drawings. A man of quiet modesty, Bottomley had a circle of friends that included much of literary and artistic London in the first half of the 20th century. There are drawings and water-colours here, given to him by his friends: Isaac Rosenberg,[31] James Guthrie, Stanley and Gilbert Spencer, Charles Ricketts and Charles Shannon, William Rothenstein and, perhaps his closest friend, Paul Nash, who designed the stage sets and costumes for Bottomley's play *King Lear's Wife* (1915).[32]

Bottomley once wrote, 'I have no biography, there is nothing that ever happened to me,' but he collected when he could afford to do so, favouring D. G. Rossetti and those influenced by the Pre-Raphaelite Brotherhood (Arthur Hughes, Ford Madox Brown and Simeon Solomon). Here too are a rare, awkward drawing by Elizabeth Siddal, Rossetti's model and muse,[33] and paintings and drawings by

Edward Burne-Jones, who, coincidentally, was a friend of the artist George Howard, 9th Earl of Carlisle,[34] for whom he carried out several commissions in local churches and at nearby Brampton.[35]

The museum contains one further surprise: an impressive collection of 18th- and early 19th-century English porcelain made by Robert Hardy Williamson, who had a shipbuilding yard in Workington. He and his wife collected porcelain at a time, 1910–30, when its popularity was in decline and prices were low. The 800 pieces here are from all the major factories: Chelsea, Bow, Derby, Worcester, Spode.

It is easy to see why Bottomley, Williamson, Rothenstein and Weight all held this museum in such high esteem. It inspires affection and loyalty. Through it runs a love of Cumbria and the history and landscape of these Debatable Lands.

RUSKIN MUSEUM **

Yewdale Road, Coniston, Cumbria LA21 8DU
Tel. 01539 441164
www.ruskinmuseum.com

Ruskin and his circle, their works, philosophies, achievements and effects

It is not surprising that the Ruskin Museum should have fine Ruskin memorabilia, displayed in cases of elegant design. Here are his pocket Horace, his (very small) box of water-colours, two walking sticks, maps and a letter that he wrote to his father in which, aged nine, he thought of making him 'a small model of any easily done thing', such as an orrery, but instead wrote a poem.[36]

Here is a delightful watercolour by his devoted friend and admirer W. G. Collingwood that depicts Ruskin, in his slippers, in his study at Brantwood. He is surrounded by bookcases and specimens, portfolios of drawings, his Bible, a globe. On the wall is a drawing, by J. M. W. Turner, of Florence. Ruskin's cat,

John Ruskin's Waterfall and Silver Birches *at the Ruskin Museum*

Tootles, is asleep on a chair and beyond him, through the window, the Old Man of Coniston can be seen across the lake.

Charming and intriguing though this collection is, it conveys little sense of Ruskin and even less of what he wanted us to see in the world around us. However this museum does so, in two ways.

Conventionally it shows you scenes through the eyes of the young Ruskin: his architectural sketches of Nancy and Newark; his view of his rooms at Christ Church, Oxford, all done before he was twenty. Less conventionally it helps you look afresh at the Lake District he loved, in particular at its geology and the troves of mineral treasures that lie beneath its surface: malachite or deep green brochantite, pale yellow pyrite, rose-pink erythrite.

Geology was Ruskin's first passion. His childood ambition was to be president of the Geological Society. In *Deucallion*, his collection of geological studies, he observed that 'no subsequent passion has had so much influence on my life.' He held precious the day in 1837 when, aged eighteen, he met Charles Darwin at the Oxford Geological Society.

The rocks of the Lake District are Silurian and Ordovician, forged by volcanoes more than 400 million years ago when they were part of a continent that lay south of the equator beneath deep ocean. Its landscape was sculpted by glaciers in the last 2 million years. It is this history that has given it andesite, glassy rhyolite, striated layers of volcanic sandstone, honeycombed limestone and the dark grey, even grain of siltstone whose dry tones and colours break through on every hillside.

In all his writings Ruskin is seeking ways to help us to see: 'To see clearly is poetry, prophecy, and religion – all in one'[37] and, again, 'the greatest thing a human soul does in this world is to see something and tell what it saw in a plain way.'[38] Of course he saw how picturesque were the Lakes and the fells: 'I noted it [Coniston] as more beautiful than anything I had ever seen to my remembrance in gladness and infinitude of light.' But he wanted us to see beneath that surface in order to understand how its beauty became.

Only then can the Old Man be seen not as a fine shape, a canvas for light and for cloud patterns, but as a piece of nature; only then can the colours of the Lake District be seen not as a palette of greys and greens and blues that is pretty and pleasing but as colours that are pressed at the core of these hills and valleys of slate.

This museum helps you to that understanding with modest authority. But it does more. The landscape is there in the design and materials of its buildings. The museum site is bounded by a wall, built by Andrew Loudon using both local drystone walling techniques: riven or dressed stone, and beck cobbles. The building was designed by local architect Ian Gibson (1999),[39] the galleries are of stone and wood with floors of slate by the design company Janus. Building and gallery form a Ruskinian metaphor.

Others have loved these lakes and peaks for different reasons and two such are remembered here: Arthur Ransome, who came to the Lake District in 1925, having been the *Daily Telegraph* correspondent in Moscow at the time of the Russian Revolution, and who wrote *Swallows and Amazons* here in 1929; and the Campbells (Sir Malcolm and his son Donald). Sir Malcolm set the world speed record in *Bluebird* on Coniston in 1939 and Donald came here to push forward that record every year from 1956 to 1959 until, in seeking his target of 300 mph, he died in the somersaulting *Bluebird* in 1967.

As if anticipating the incongruity, Ruskin had defined 'the right function of every MUSEUM' as being the manifestation 'of what is lovely in the life of Nature, and heroic in the life of Men'.[40]

BOAT MUSEUM *

South Pier Road, Ellesmere Port,
Cheshire CH65 4FW
Tel: 0151 355 5017
www.boatmuseum.org.uk

*Narrow boats at the mouth of Thomas Telford's
pioneering canal*

The *Starvationer*, or mine boat, is a wooden
boat reputedly so named because its ribs can
be seen. It was built at the command of the
Duke of Bridgewater and is the mother of all
the boats here. His boats were legged, or pulled
from hooked rings in the roof, through underground canals (built 1760–1820s) to his mines
at Worsley. On the return, the boats were then
washed out by the flow of water.

From the 1760s canals cut their way through
the English countryside. Along their towpaths,
past meadows of indifferent cows, back and to
between ports and the new manufacturing
cities, horses pulled barges heavy with flint and
clay, coal and timber, tar, creosote and crude
oil, hemp and cotton, pots and tiles – anything
that could be exported or imported at a profit.

Here at Ellesmere Port is a fine site for
Britain's premier canal museum where the
Shropshire Union Canal descends to link the
Manchester Ship Canal and the River Mersey,
and connects with the Trent and Mersey Canal
and, finally, with the Birmingham and Liverpool Junction Canal. In the distance you can
see many of the landmarks of the industrial
north-west: the cooling towers of Stanlow;
ICI's plant at Weston Point; Runcorn Bridge;
the skyline of Liverpool across the Mersey
broken by its two cathedrals.

The museum lauds the engineers William
Jessup and his assistant Cubitt, who built these
canals and the docks, locks, warehouses,
wharves and slipways that are clustered around
the basins. In many of these buildings, exhibitions or videos explain their function (the
Pattern Shop, the Stables, the Island Warehouse). In the Pump House are steam-driven
engines once used to power the hydraulic
cranes and capstans. Documents in the Toll
House record the cargoes and tolls: maize
from the Manchester Docks to Kellogg's
factory at Trafford Park, lime juice from the
West Indies for Rose's works at Boxmoor,
delicate china for export from Josiah Wedgwood's potbank at Etruria, African sugar for
Tate and Lyle's refinery, Middlewich salt in
calico bags for the return journey to Africa.

The museum's lode is in its boats, narrow
and broad on the canals, broad on estuaries
and rivers. Their development is traced from
the *Starvationer* to the *Mossdale* (1863), a
Mersey flat, the only survivor of hundreds;
the *Scorpio* (1890), a Liverpool sider or long
boat, which carried coal until 1971; *Shad* (1936)
and *Mendip* (1948), both Josher narrow boats
named after Joshua Fellows of the Birmingham
company Fellows, Morton and Clayton,
whose boat design remained fundamentally
unchanged from 1880 to the 1940s; *Cuddington*
(1948), a weaver packet, high out of the water,
which carried soda ash for ICI; and the
elephantine FCB 18, defying logic and sense
by being made of ferro-concrete in the Second
World War when wood and steel were at a
premium.

On many of these boats people were born
and raised, then worked and died, a family
sharing one cabin, 6 feet by 8 feet. The *Ilkeston*
(1912) has a side bed 3 feet 6 inches to 4 feet
long and a cupboard door that folded out to
make a double bed. The *Ferret* (1926, Fellows,
Morton and Clayton) was motorised and
pulled a butty boat allowing its family a coal
stove and a small oven. Even so the cupboard
door was needed to make a double bed.

Some of those who worked at the basin had
cottages on site. A row of twelve (Porters
Row) is conserved here with their communal
gardens and outdoor toilets. In 1863 coal/gas
lighting was provided; the 1900 cottage has gas
lights and cold running water in the scullery.
The cottages are decorated and furnished with
careful detail: a Bible on the table; a copy of the
Illustrated Mail (price 1d., the weekly edition of
the *Daily Mail*) of 26 January 1901, its headline
announcing 'DEATH OF QUEEN VICTORIA:
THE EMPIRE MOURNS ITS LOSS'; a 'Lakeside'
organ in the front parlour; tins of ointment

(Parkinson's Vapour, carbolic, mustard); gentian violet jelly; the ceiling distempered; the wallpaper secured with flour and water; an aspidistra; an antimacassar; a lit fire in the hearth; a ticking clock. A housekeeper sits in No. 10 tending to her baking in the oven of the huge black-leaded range that dominates the kitchen.

The 1930s cottage has electricity, a piano, a wireless, a gas stove; the 1950s home a three-piece suite, a GEC cooker and a radiogram, with shellac 78 rpm records. There is a television and a flight of ducks across the wall.

DOVE COTTAGE AND THE WORDSWORTH MUSEUM **

Town End, Grasmere, Cumbria LA22 9SH
Tel. 015394 35544
www.wordsworth.org.uk

The books and paintings of William and Dorothy Wordsworth, with a little help from Coleridge and the Lakes

In these pages are museums created from Edward Elgar's birthplace and from the house in which Sir John Soane lived and worked. Neither has interpreted its role as widely and boldly as has Dove Cottage in spawning first the Wordsworth Museum, to place the lives and work of William and Dorothy Wordsworth in the context of their contemporaries and then, wider still, the Centre for British Romanticism, in order to place them in the main tide of Romanticism, its ideas and ideals, its politics, its science and the ways in which it influenced and was influenced by the visual arts. It is a mighty undertaking, undertaken well.

At its centre is Dove Cottage, where William and his sister Dorothy Wordsworth lived from 1799 to 1808. These were years when Wordsworth wrote the manifesto of Romanticism, the preface to *Lyrical Ballads* (1800), and poems such as 'Michael', 'Resolution', 'Independence', 'I wandered lonely as a cloud', 'Ode: Intimations of Immortality' and, above all, the first version of his autobiographical poem *The Prelude*, arguably the greatest poem of the period, though not published until after Wordsworth's death in 1850. He was urged on by Coleridge, who wrote in 1799: 'I wish you would write a poem in blank verse, addressed to those, who, in consequence of the complete failure of the French Revolution, have thrown up all hopes of the amelioration of mankind, now sinking into an almost Epicurean selfishness, disguising the same under the soft titles of domestic attachment and contempt for visionary philosophies.' In *The Prelude* Wordsworth, tired of the dominance of reason that had led to the 'Reign of Terror', turned to a belief in the imagination.

Dove Cottage had been, since the early 17th century, a public house, the Dove and Olive, well positioned on the main road that ran through Grasmere from Whitehaven to the south. Today's main road runs parallel, closer to the lake's edge, leaving Dove Cottage, its climbing roses and its cottage garden, in a quiet narrow lane.

Inside, the cottage retains much of the atmosphere we may imagine it had 200 years ago. The rooms are dark, with slate floors downstairs and bare wooden boards upstairs. There is Wordsworth memorabilia (his spectacles, his ice skates, his shaving case, a pair of Italian ceramic candlesticks) but the rooms offer a hem that even when touched does little more than fill out the images created in readers' minds when reading Dorothy's journals. De Quincey's scales for measuring his opium, and a bottle of the opiate Lancaster blackdrop remind one that De Quincey lived in the house for twenty-five years, 1809–35.

The museum is more ambitious. Its building lacks resonance but its collection more than compensates. The facts of the Wordsworths' lives are quickly and simply told, with some help from manuscripts (his first published poem, 'An Evening Walk', 1793); a letter from Annette Vallon, the mother of his daughter, 20 March 1793). Their friends are depicted here in contemporary portraits: Coleridge by George Dance, Thomas Phillips and James Northcote; his son, Hartley Coleridge, by David Wilkie;

Southey by Thomas Phillips; William Hazlitt by William Bewick; Wordsworth's patron, Lady Beaumont, by Joshua Reynolds; and a startling drawing of Wordsworth, all nose and eyes, by Benjamin Robert Haydon, described by Hazlitt as 'the most like his drooping weight of thought and expression'.[41]

The museum proceeds to consider in greater detail key periods in Wordsworth's life, such as his time with Coleridge in the West Country. The 'theft' of the rowing boat on Ullswater when the cliff, Place Fell, 'upreared its head' to admonish him[42] is linked here to two paintings, by Thomas Walmsley in 1792 and by Joseph Wright of Derby, c. 1794–5, both showing the cliff-like face of Place Fell. Wright's image, in evening light, is particularly lovely and is one of his last paintings.

The museum's collection of watercolours and drawings allows it to explore the way in which the Lake District helped to create, and be created by, English Romanticism. Almost every contemporary artist came to draw and paint the lakes and fells. There are works here by Edward Dayes, Francis Towne, Thomas Hearne, Sir George Beaumont, Joseph Faring-ton, Thomas Gainsborough and Thomas Girtin, who worked at second hand from a drawing of Borrowdale by Beaumont, altering it for the sake of drama.

The Wordsworth Trust, through the Centre for British Romanticism, has used the collection to explore some of the great underlying themes of the period: revolution, the imagination, the discovery of nature. The inspiration for this wider scholarship at the Centre has come in recent years from the director, Dr Robert Woof, and his wife, Pamela Woof, who have between them produced a series of special exhibitions and publications. Under their dedicated tutelage Dove Cottage and the Wordsworth Museum bring together poetry, painting and scholarship in a way that illuminates past and present, and returns the visitor to the poems of Wordsworth, Coleridge and their contemporaries.

ABBOT HALL ✳✳✳

Kirkland, Kendal, Cumbria LA9 5AL
Tel. 01539 722464
www.abbothall.org.uk

A great Romney set piece and handsome local furniture in a dignified house, perhaps by Carr of York; surprising and dazzling 20th-century holdings

In 1757 Edmund Burke, in *A Philosophical Enquiry into the Origin of our Ideas of the Sublime and the Beautiful*, changed the way that landscape was seen. Hitherto what was mountainous was ugly; now it might inspire awe and exaltation. Instead of seeing the Lake District as Daniel Defoe did in 1724, as a place 'locked between the hills on one side as high as clouds . . . and the sea on the other [that] seemed desolate and wild', the landscape was, to Burke and to the poet Thomas Gray, romantic and sublime.

The Lake District began to attract artists and writers. Joseph Farington moved to Keswick in 1775 and submitted landscapes of the prospects he saw to the Royal Academy. He was followed by Thomas Hearne, Joseph Wright of Derby and Francis Towne.

Over the next fifty years artists, from Constable, Cotman, Varley, Julius Caesar Ibbetson and De Wint in the early 1800s to Turner and Ruskin, came to wonder and to work. All are represented in Abbot Hall's collection of drawings and watercolours.

In Hearne's *Derwent Water from Skiddaw* (1777) the two figures in the foreground are not staffage but are, almost certainly, Sir George Beaumont and Joseph Farington, who was touring with him. Joseph Wright of Derby, while dismissing watercolours as 'better adapted to the amusement of ladies than the pursuit of an artist',[43] painted *The Bowder Stone, Borrowdale* (1786) in monochrome greys. This would have pleased Reynolds, who himself advocated achieving 'grandeur of effect . . . by reducing . . . colours to little more than chiaro oscuro'.[44]

Not all the works here are of local subjects.

George Romney's The Leveson-Gower Children *(Abbot Hall)*

In his consummate *The Passage of Mount St Gothard* (1803–4), Turner handles the water, spray and rocks in a manner that is almost foreshadowing Vorticism, while many works in the sizeable collection of Ruskin watercolours are from his visits to the Alps.

The gallery is in a fine, severe, yet inviting and superbly maintained house[45] on the edge of Kendal with wide views across the River Kent.[46] With the exception of the watercolour gallery, the downstairs rooms are hospitable, decorated and furnished in period with good 18th-century pieces by Gillows of Lancaster, a secretaire in satinwood and mahogany, a Troue Madame games table and a satinwood table inlaid with roses, all of which composes a happy setting for a collection of portraits by George Romney and other local artists.

Romney lived and worked in Kendal until 1762, when he was twenty-eight, apprenticed to a local painter of portraits, Christopher Steele. Comparison between Steele's stiff and awkward work exhibited here and Romney's small study of his brother James holding a candle (1761), or his full-length portrait of *Captain Robert Banks* (1760), shows that he had little to learn from Steele.

Apart from a study for *The Death of Wolfe* (1762–3), Abbot Hall has few works from Romney's early years in London until his beguiling *The Leveson-Gower Children* (1776–7), which is perhaps his most ambitious painting. He did not have the classical training Reynolds and Ramsay acquired in Rome, nor did he have Reynolds's monumental quality, but he responded to personality and if his handling of the Leveson-Gower children does not match Gainsborough's portraits of his daughters (in the National Gallery and the Ashmolean Museum, both q.v.), it is still a fluent, dancing work.

Of his sequence of portraits of Lady Hamilton, Abbot Hall has only one, a small head, dated 1785–6, when she was still Emma Hart. Romney's colour tones – auburn hair, pink cheek, white neck – make it clear why he persuaded her to sit for him on more than three hundred occasions.

Abbot Hall's first director, appointed in 1962, was Helen Kapp, who came here from Wakefield Art Gallery (q.v.), where her pioneering exhibitions of the work of contemporary British artists established her reputation. She wanted Abbot Hall to 'give much delight to the eye, but also [to be] a stimulating and vibrating place – a place where clashes of ideas and feeling will reverberate'.[47]

Not surprisingly Kapp acquired work by several of the artists she favoured at Wakefield: Ben Nicholson (and his first wife, the Cumbrian painter Winifred Nicholson), Barbara Hepworth (Nicholson's second wife),[48] Patrick Heron, Keith Vaughan. Her successors as director, Mary Burkett, Vicky Slowe and Edward King, have maintained this purchasing policy and Abbot Hall now has an outstanding collection of mid-20th-century British painting and sculpture: John Piper, Ivon Hitchens, Stanley Spencer, Frank Auerbach, two Bridget Rileys, Paula Rego, a Lucian Freud etching, a particularly strong group of Scottish painters (S. J. Peploe, William Gillies, Joan Eardley,

Anne Redpath, Elizabeth Blackadder) and excellent ceramics by Bernard Leach, Lucie Rie, Hans Coper and Alan Caiger-Smith.

What sets this 20th-century collection apart is the collection of the work of Kurt Schwitters, who lived at Ambleside for the last three years of his life. To make a living he painted conventional, figurative portraits of friends and neighbours. Several are here: a drawing of *Francis O'Neill*, and an oil of *Mr Routledge* (1945) painted on a tea chest. In contrast to Armitt Museum (q.v.), which has similar portraits by Schwitters, Abbot Hall has paintings of his that relate to his *Merz* work.[49] *Flight* (1945), *Mier Bitte* (c. 1945–7), *YMCA Flag* and *Ambleside* (1947) are all *Merz* collages (the first, a construction; the others, collages on paper and board). All were given to the gallery by Edith Thomas, with whom Schwitters lived for the last seven years of his life.

Throughout this gallery, which is flooded with light, there is a careful attention to detail, a thread of quality which holds together these disparate collections.

RUSKIN LIBRARY ***

University of Lancaster, Lancaster LA1 4YH
Tel. 01524 593587, fax 01524 593580
e-mail: ruskin.library@lancaster.ac.uk

Beautiful new building holds largest collection of Ruskinalia

As you enter the campus of the University of Lancaster, the Ruskin Library is ahead of you, a lozenge, end on, raised on a knoll as if on an island floating on a lagoon of meadow grass, a reflection of Ruskin's Venice.

Of the generation of new museum and gallery buildings and extensions to which the Heritage Lottery Fund and the Millennium Fund have given birth, this is the most beautiful and subtle. Designed in 1995 by Richard MacCormac[50] 'as a symbolic gateway or propylaeum to the University',[51] it is built with white concrete blocks of a sparkly marble aggregate. These are separated by thin bands of dark green polished pre-cast concrete and split at the far end by bronze-clad aluminium double doors, at the front by a window that rises to the full height of the building, allowing you to glimpse the huge glass panel within, guarded by shutters as if it were a medieval diptych. Designed by Alexander Beleschenko, this panel is etched with an image of the north-west portal of St Mark's, Venice, taken from a Ruskin daguerreotype.[52]

The interior is as rich as the exterior is simple. At its centre is the treasury, a 'sar-cophagus, casket or ark',[53] encased in an oak frame with panels of Venetian red plaster. Throughout there are reflections, as if in water, and the warm smells of oak and leather.

The designers and the Ruskin Foundation, in relocating the collection from the Isle of Wight,[54] have heeded the word of Ruskin in *Modern Painters*, 'When public taste seems plunging deeper and deeper into degradation every day . . . it becomes the imperative duty of all who have any perception of what is really great in art . . . To declare and demonstrate wherever they exist, the essence and the authority of the Beautiful and the True.'[55] They have created an environment that is sympathetic to the study of Ruskin, 'deliberately church-like, with the entrance, archive and reading room standing for narthex, choir and sanctuary'.[56] The chairs and tables, in oak and walnut, are designed by Richard MacCormac and made by Jeremy Hall,[57] and beside them are some of the cabinets which used to hold pictures presented by Ruskin to Oxford University when he was Slade Professor of Art (from 1870).

The collection was founded by John Howard Whitehouse, the former MP and educationalist who sustained Ruskin's reputation as interest in him declined in the early 20th century. It comprises diaries, letters and other manuscripts, as well as the largest single collection of Ruskin's drawings and daguerreotypes.[58]

These illustrate the influences that shaped him: the watercolour by his father John James Ruskin of *Conway Castle* (c. 1795–1800) that Ruskin identified in a letter in *Fors Clavigera*[59] (Letter 54, June 1875) as having been crucial in

the development of his imagination; another by Samuel Prout, who was a family friend; the sketchbooks he had between the ages of ten and sixteen, which he criticised ruthlessly in *Praeterita*: 'I never saw any boy's work in my life showing so little original faculty, or grasp of memory. I could literally draw nothing [out of my head] . . . and there was, luckily, at present no idea . . . of teaching me to draw out of other people's heads.'[60]

He taught himself to look and to draw from life (*Hampton Court*, 1833–4, which he did aged fourteen, under the instruction of Charles Runciman) and to copy from Old Masters (*Zipporah*, 1874, after Botticelli). 'When I can paint a life size figure to my own tolerable satisfaction in 14 days, I am quite sure I ought to go on doing them,' he wrote to his cousin Joan Severn on Whit Sunday, 1874.

Here are numerous examples of his love of architecture and architectural detail, and of Venice (a glorious pencil and wash of *Capital 36 of the Ducal Palace, Venice*, 1849–52, described in *The Stones of Venice*: 'which, being at a height of little more than eight feet above the eye, might be read, like the pages of a book').[61]

There is only one drawing here by J. M. W. Turner: *Stirling Castle* (1801), given by Ruskin to Charles Eliot Norton in the late 1870s and bought by Whitehouse at Sir Michael Sadler's sale in October 1946, but it can be compared with Ruskin's own drawing of the castle, of which he wrote, 'what really was common to us both – intense love of form, as the basis of all subject'.[62]

Just as Turner helped Ruskin to see the world through his eyes, so Ruskin has helped us to see nature and architecture through his. The Ruskin of political anger is only glancingly to be seen but the spirit who exhorted us to seek 'the essence and the authority of the Beautiful and the True' floods through this collection and this building.

MERSEYSIDE MARITIME MUSEUM *

Albert Dock, Liverpool, Merseyside L3 4AQ
Tel. 0151 478 4499
www.merseysidemaritimemuseum.org.uk

Dockside museum of ships, piloting the 7 million emigrants who left Liverpool for new lives

The Americas made Liverpool a great port. As trade expanded to North America and the West Indies in the early 18th century, so, too, grew Liverpool. The importing of cotton, tobacco, sugar and rum made Liverpool merchants rich, as did the slave trade. Liverpool traders sailed to West Africa, sold goods, bought slaves, sold them in the Americas and returned to Liverpool with raw materials to be made into goods in the industrial cities of the north – a circle of trade dependent on slavery. 'Almost every man in Liverpool is a merchant,' wrote J. Wallace in his *History of Liverpool* (1795); 'The attractive African meteor has so dazzled their ideas, that almost every order of people is interested in a Guinea cargo. Many of the small vessels are fitted out by attornies, drapers, ropers, grocers, tallow-chandlers, barbers, taylors etc.'[63]

Historians do not agree on the scale of this trade in slaves: estimates vary between 12 and 20 million. Whatever the exact figure, considering the scale, the evidence in this museum is scant:[64] trade tokens, brass and copper manacles, shackles, a 19th-century carving of an African in a punishment collar and the incriminating ships' logs that record the human cargoes and their fate.

More poignant are the objects which bear witness to the nature of the communities from which they were taken: 16th- and 17th-century Benin bronze reliefs, an 18th-century Asante brass weight in the form of a man with a gun, an Asante gold pectoral disc. Many of the peoples swept up in this African diaspora, who were subject to a prolonged holocaust, were civilised and sophisticated. The calm elegance of *The Interesting Narrative of the Life of Olaudah Equiano or Gustavus Vassa the African*, written in 1789 by Olaudah Equiano and published in 1793, although not typical, confirms this.

Following abolition in 1807, illegal trading continued for more than half a century, but for Liverpool the traffic in voluntary emigration to the United States after 1830 grew to fill any shortfall in passengers.

Emigration[65] was voluntary in that it was not coerced but it was driven by poverty and persecution as much as by ambition. Photographs of emigrants on the Liverpool docks from Russia, Poland, Scandinavia and Germany show desperate souls.

In the absence of artefacts, both stories, of slavery and emigration, are told in reconstructions and tableaux. The darkness below decks on a slave ship's middle passage; a dockside street; low lights, barrels and cobbles do nothing to stimulate emotions or imagination.

Models and graphics are better at conveying the engineering brilliance, the scale and the luxury of the great Atlantic liners of the late 19th/early 20th centuries. The names tell something of their status: the *Olympic*, the *Oceanic*, the *Aquitania*, the *Berengaria*, the *Mauretania*, the *Lusitania* and the *Titanic*. The latter's fate and hubris feature prominently.

As Liverpool's maritime history approaches the present day, film (still and moving) is available. One film shows the part that Royal Navy ships played in the battle for the Atlantic. Shot from the bridge of a destroyer in a heavy Atlantic sea in 1944, it confronts you with the scale of the ocean, the heaving wall of water, the wind, the spray. All are hypnotic and convey for the first time in the museum the power and danger of the sea, and something of its romance.

That romance is also communicated by a collection of model ships and of paintings of ships and the sea. Few artists can convey the weight of the sea or the speed and triumph of a ship but the work here of Samuel Walters struggles nobly with the challenge, without resolving the question why the majority of ships are shown in profile, sails billowing, travelling from right to left.

Perhaps it is in the making of models that

people can most safely enjoy ships and the sea: ships on plinths, in bottles, in cases, in frames; ships that are fifteen feet long, and ships of three inches. There is a navy of ships made by French prisoners in the Napoleonic Wars, made of scrap wood, bone and sawdust, and using hair for rigging: a maritime world of dreams in a museum which has turned Liverpool's 19th-century Albert Dock into a tourist venue.

WORLD MUSEUM LIVERPOOL ★★★★

William Brown Street, Liverpool,
Merseyside L3 8EN
Tel. 0151 478 4399
www.liverpoolmuseum.org.uk

Wonderful collections, newly displayed

Liverpool was in the van of the British economy in the 18th century. Trade in cotton, tobacco and timber (in) and coal, ceramics and manufacture (out) was facilitated by the Bridgewater Canal. The city's first docks were built by Thomas Steers, with more docks added almost every decade, culminating in Jesse Hartley's gargantuan granite constructions, the Albert, Stanley and Nelson Docks (1824–60). Pevsner called them 'architecture for giants'.[66]

Liverpool was a key point in the triangular transatlantic slave trade (v. Merseyside Maritime Museum). The world, its peoples, its trade and its ideas poured through the city. It is not surprising that by the end of the 18th century Liverpool was a centre for radical politics (against the slave trade) and new thinking in the sciences and the arts.

The city bred such men as William Roscoe, historian, connoisseur, botanist, politician and banker; Sir James Edward Smith, the founder of the Linnaean Society; the abolitionist Earl of Derby; the designer George Bullock; Henry Blundell, collector and connoisseur; and the brewer William Lassell, who, in 1846, discovered Neptune's moon Triton.

Botanic gardens were opened in 1801, with

gifts of herbaria;[67] the Royal Institution in 1810; the Liverpool Academy in 1814. In such a climate, it is surprising it was not until 1852 that Liverpool Town Council passed its Liverpool Library and Museum Act, allowing it to set up and maintain such institutions with free public access. It is not surprising that the museum's core collections should have been presented by the 13th Earl of Derby (zoology) and the businessman Joseph Mayer (archaeology, ethnology and antiquities); nor that T. J. Moore, formerly on Lord Derby's staff at Knowsley, should be appointed its first curator.

The museum had no permanent home until William Brown, a Liverpool banker and MP for South Lancashire, put up the money for a dedicated building designed by Thomas Allom and completed by the council's architect John Weightman. It is opposite Harvey Lonsdale Elmes's St George's Hall, the most glorious Greek Revival building in England. Weightman might have intended his bays and Corinthian portico to be his homage to Elmes who had died, very young, ten years before. If so he was mistaken: it is not homage enough, though his building is civic and serious.

The visitor is met by two huge black marble statues of Sekhmet, the Egyptian lion goddess of doctors, who had the power of both causing and curing epidemics. They are from Mayer's collection; within, the Mayer treasures still dominate the Antiquities Department. He was an indefatigable collector: Mesolithic flints; Greek pottery and sculpture; Etruscan metalwork; Bronze Age and Anglo-Saxon urns; medieval ceramics and superb ivories (notably the *Nativity*, a delicate relief in which the Virgin lies on a bed angled and foreshortened); even American ethnology (the Codex Féjérváry-Mayer). In many other cities Mayer's collections would merit a dedicated museum.

Lord Derby's collection of 15–20,000 bird and mammal specimens from his private museum, and 200 more at Knowsley Park, remain at the heart of the Zoology Department after 150 years. They include rare type

Benin Head of Queen Mother *at World Museum Liverpool*

specimens. The Lord Howe Island gallinule (*Porphyrio stanleyi*)[68] is one of only two known; the type specimen of the opossum (*Caluromys derbianus*) is similarly rare.

To these were added the Ince Blundell classical sculptures, divided between the museum and the Walker Art Gallery (q.v.);[69] a collection of agates bequeathed in 1893 by Lord Derby's grandson, the 15th Earl, described as 'the most beautiful collection of agates and allied materials ever made'; the mosses, sponges and lichens of the Revd H. H. Higgins, a founder of the Museums Association; and outstanding botanical drawings (mainly from Lord Derby's collections) – the *Deliciae Botanicae* by Georg D. Ehret, volumes of Chinese and Indian[70] drawings, and sheets by Audubon and Gould.

Mayer's collections were enhanced in 1865 by the British coins and tokens collected by Robert Jackson; by surges of ethnological material from Mexico, the Amazon, the Arctic, North America, Japan and China; and, especially, by the collections of the Liverpool shipping engineer Arnold Ridyard, who worked on the west coast of Africa in the 1890s and collected masks, textiles, ceramics and figures from Gabon, Ghana, Nigeria, Sierra Leone and the Congo, and a 16th-century Benin bronze head of a queen mother, impassive in its dignity.

By the end of the century the Weightman building was too small and the new director, Henry Ugg Forbes, an ethnologist and zoologist, won the case for a major extension to the museum designed by E.W. Mountford, opened in 1906. Its convex bowed end, thrusting on to Byrom Street, contains on its upper floors superb horseshoe-shaped galleries, the upper with a barrel ceiling that wraps around the extension.

One hundred years later the pressure from new collections, particularly in the field of archaeology (excavations by the museum's director, J. H. Iliffe, in Cyprus in the 1950s; by the museum in Merseyside, the Wirral and the Falkland Islands since the 1970s)[71] and acquisitions (the Philip Nelson Collection of classical and medieval antiquities in 1953)

had become intense. That pressure was forcibly relieved in 1941 when a German air raid severely damaged the museum. Some collections had been removed but others suffered substantial losses, particularly the museum's fossils, shells and invertebrates.

A major redesign (2005) will transform the museum, allowing access to the full glories of the collections, some of which have been hidden in recent years even from the curators. A cabinet transferred from Bootle Museum proved to contain a collection made in the 1850s by Frederic Chevrier of Geneva, of 20,000 specimens of European beetles (varying in size from a pinprick to beetles four inches in length). With it was a catalogue in his own hand, an historic discovery. Other gems include pieces of timber brought back from the West Indies by Sir Hans Sloane in 1689 and the collections of 'stowaways' (grasshoppers, crickets, etc.) that came to Liverpool docks in ships.

There are sufficient collections of quality here to fill several museums, but Liverpool makes a positive case for keeping them under one roof, with the enlarged building providing a metaphor for their breadth, going from an aquarium in the basement to astronomy under the roof, sheltering what may be seen as truly the whole world and the sky.

WALKER ART GALLERY (NATIONAL MUSEUMS, LIVERPOOL) *****

William Brown Street, Liverpool, Merseyside L3 8EL
Tel. 0151 478 4199
www.liverpoolmuseums.org.uk/walker/index.asp

Rembrandt and Rubens; Reynolds and Romney; and Poussin's most moving painting. Masterpieces in every room, as well as And When Did You Last See Your Father?

The slave trade made 18th-century Liverpool a boom city, a violent mix of new capitalism, sugar and blood. Ranged against these dark

The Sculpture Gallery at the Walker

volatilities were philanthropy, connoisseurship and enlightenment, embodied by such men as William Roscoe (1753–1831) and those others of like mind with whom he helped found Liverpool's Academy, Botanical Garden, Royal Institution and Athenaeum.

Roscoe was a lawyer, collector, poet,[72] historian; a unitarian radical who, for one Parliament, was the city's MP (1806–7), elected on an anti-slavery ticket. He taught himself Italian and Latin; wrote the first and, for a century, the definitive biography of Lorenzo de Medici;[73] and collected 14th- and 15th-century Italian and Flemish books, paintings and drawings.

When Roscoe's own bank failed and he was declared bankrupt, his friends bought his collections and presented them to the Royal Institution which, in turn, loaned them to the city and, when it opened, to the Walker Art Gallery.[74]

Pressure from the academy and the institution for a permanent art gallery had been growing throughout the 19th century. Eventually, in 1874, the new mayor, local brewer and alderman Andrew Barclay Walker, provided the capital, architects Cornelius Sherlock and Henry Hill Vale were commissioned and the new gallery opened. Next door to the World Museum Liverpool and opposite St George's Hall, it is a monument to civic pride. A flight of steps, flanked by statues of Michelangelo and Raphael,[75] leads up to a portico with Corinthian columns.

Initially the gallery (dubbed 'the Academy of the North') lacked a permanent collection and so housed the annual autumn exhibitions that the city had inherited from the Academy in 1871.[76] Inspired by Burlington House, the exhibitions ran from September to December, and made a large profit each year from commission on sales. With this the Walker began to acquire contemporary paintings from the exhibitions.

The collection expanded rapidly, if somewhat erratically. The chairman of the Arts Committee was a local collector, Philip Henry Rathbone, who co-opted friends, such as James McNeill Whistler and the Glasgow artist Arthur Melville, on to the Hanging Committees. Despite their advice and Rathbone's preference for more challenging work, the committee invariably bought undemanding 19th-century narrative paintings, of which W. F. Yeames's sentimental *And When Did You Last See Your Father?* was much the most popular, and remained so for years. So the Walker entered the 20th century with a curiously lopsided collection: many Victorian genre and narrative paintings of indifferent quality; some excellent Pre-Raphaelites, thanks to Rathbone (J. E. Millais's *Isabella*, 1848–9, painted in the first year of the Brotherhood when Millais was only nineteen; D.G. Rossetti's *Dante's Dream*, 1871; and Holman Hunt's *The Triumph of the Innocents*, 1876–7); paintings by the Newlyn School; paintings by Leighton and von Herkomer; a rare painting by L. J. M. Daguerre, the early photographer;[77] and, incongruously, Roscoe's outstanding collection of Italian and Flemish Primitives, acquired a full generation before Prince Albert promoted their virtues in London. The most celebrated of these is Simone Martini's *Christ Discovered in the Temple* (1342), his last known work, a masterpiece of colour and line, of grace and charm, by this great pupil of Duccio.[78] Roscoe's eye was true. Paintings by Bartolommeo di Giovanni, the Dutch master of the *Virgo inter Virgines*, and by Ercole de' Robertí would grace any national gallery.

Rathbone died in 1895 and there were few significant additions to the collection until, in 1923, a local wine merchant, James Smith, bequeathed thirty paintings by G. F. Watts, six sculptures by Rodin, etchings by Samuel Palmer and Whistler, and a group of Liverpool Pre-Raphaelites (principally D. A. Williamson and W. L. Windus).

In 1903 a new Director, Frank Lambert, began to transform the collection with the help, for the first time, of a regular annual purchase grant from the city council. He plunged into the 20th century, buying good Camden Town pictures (by W. R. Sickert, Harold Gilman and others) as well as a sublime Richard Wilson (*Snowdon from Llyn Nantlle, c.*1765) and one of Zoffany's finest conversation pieces, *The Family of Sir William Young, c.*1770.

After the Second World War Lambert and his successor, Hugh Strutton, began to correct the exclusively British bias of the collection by acquiring Murillo's *The Virgin and Child in Glory* (1673); a lovely riverscape by Salomon van Ruysdael; by gift, an early (1630) Rembrandt self-portrait; and, in the 1960s, the collection's first Impressionist and Post-Impressionist paintings by Degas, Seurat and Monet, and an early Cézanne, *The Murder*, which has the painful black violence of a Goya.

Now the quality of the collection secured the enthusiastic support of the National Art Collections Fund, whose help made possible a succession of remarkable acquisitions: a Rubens, a Courbet, a Joos van Cleve, Hogarth's depiction of *David Garrick as Richard III* (1745), in which Garrick's body is stretched across the canvas in an illustration of Hogarth's 'Line of Beauty',[79] and the finest Poussin landscape in Britain, *Landscape with the Ashes of Phocion* (1648).[80] The latter was acquired under the directorship of Timothy Stevens.

Since 1957 the gallery has profited from returning to its roots and holding an annual (contemporary) exhibition, thanks to the sponsorship of Sir John Moores. As in the late 19th century, purchases from the exhibition are made each year and, in this way, works by David Hockney, R. B. Kitaj, John Hoyland, Lisa Milroy and Peter Davies have entered the collection. Besides works from the Moores exhibitions, there is an active contemporary acquisitions programme and recent additions have included works by Gilbert and George, and Bill Viola.

The collection has come full circle in other

ways: in 1959 Liverpool was given by Sir Joseph Weld the sculpture collection of his ancestor Henry Blundell of Ince, a collection of classical sculpture second only to Charles Townley's in the British Museum (q.v.). (The collection is now divided between the World Museum Liverpool (q.v.) and the Walker.) The mixture of antique pieces, acquired from sales at the Villa Mattei and the Villa d'Este; of excellent copies (*Artemis* by Bartolomeo Cavaceppi; a *Head of Jupiter* by Cavaceppi's pupil Giuseppe Angelini); of restorations (a vase by G. B. Piranesi); and of forgeries (a *Head of Lucius Verus*; a bust of *Otho*), make it a collection of particular fascination. In 1992 the Walker acquired two drawings from Holkham Hall (Guercino, Ribera) that William Roscoe catalogued in 1820 'for his friend, Mr Coke'[81] following his bankruptcy, and in 1995 the Walker succeeded in securing for Liverpool the Weld-Blundell Collection of European drawings, including masterworks by Mantegna, Domenichino, Reni and Rubens. Of some 300 drawings in this collection, over 160 were formerly owned by William Roscoe.

The gallery also has one of the largest collections[82] of the work of the neo-classical sculptor John Gibson, who lived in Liverpool from 1799 and was the protégé of Blundell and of Roscoe, whom he would visit weekly. Gibson later observed, 'If they [British sculptors] had followed such advice as I received from Mr Roscoe their work would have acquired a higher character and aim.' Gibson's relief portrait of Roscoe (1813) is here, as is his *Tinted Venus* (1851–6), Gibson's experiment in recreating original Greek polychrome sculpture, described by the *Sculptor's Journal* in the 1860s as 'one of the most beautiful and elaborate figures undertaken in modern times' and by *The Athenaeum* as a 'naked, impudent English woman' with 'enough vulgarity in it to destroy all alluring power, and every sign of the goddess'.

The Walker's curious history makes it impossible for this to be a collection that is simply representative or coherent. Out of it blaze some supreme works: the Simone Martini, the Poussin landscape, Lucas Cranach the Elder's enigmatic and seductive *The Nymph of the Fountain* (1534) and Adam Elsheimer's *Apollo and Coronis* (*c.*1607–9), perhaps the most beautiful Elsheimer in Britain. Supporting and contextualising these stellar paintings are drawings that enrich the byways of the collection: huge sheets by Romney; one of *The Death of Cardinal Beaufort* (1772) by Roscoe's friend John Henry Fuseli; Francesco Primaticcio's *Ulysses Shooting Through the Rings* (1555–9), owned first by Reynolds and then by Roscoe. It was sold with his collection in 1817 and reacquired for the Walker with the help of the National Art Collections Fund in 1998.

It is this rich, uneven brilliance, sustained by the scholarship of such curators as Julian Treuhertz, that sets the Walker apart from other collections.

SUDLEY HOUSE *

Mossley Hill Road, Aigburth, Liverpool, Merseyside L18 8BX
Tel. 0151 724 3245
www.sudleyhouse.org.uk

Liverpool shipowner's collection of 18th- and 19th-century British artists

Sudley is a heavy, square neoclassical house built in red sandstone in the south Liverpool suburb of Mossley Hill, with views down the Mersey estuary to the sea. It was built[83] in the first decade of the 19th century for Nicholas Robinson,[84] a corn merchant, whose son sold it to George Holt in 1884.

Holt's father, George Holt Snr (1790–1861), made a fortune as a cotton broker. His sons were in shipping: George traded with India, South Africa and South America through his own company, Lamport & Holt; his brother Alfred founded the Blue Funnel Line. They were very Liverpool merchants, philanthropic and Liberal. A third brother, Robert, was leader of the local Liberal Party, a councillor and Lord Mayor, and friend of W. E. Gladstone and the Earl of Derby.

George Snr was not a connoisseur but he left George Jnr some pictures when he died in

One of a pair of cabinets by George Bullock
(Sudley House)

1861, including an exotic John Philip[85] that he had commissioned in 1854 and a large Thomas Creswick landscape, *Evening*. It is not easy to see how George Jnr's taste developed but his love of Creswick's work (he owned eighteen paintings) was constant. Creswick was a Suffolk artist, influenced unsurprisingly by Constable and Henry Bright. *The Windmill*, here, owes much to Bright's *Windmill at Sheringham* in Norwich Castle Museum (q.v.). Like Holt's other favourite, Keeley Halswele, of whose works he owned five, Creswick

represents Victorian landscape painting at its modest best: well crafted and composed, faithful to its subject, picturesque, unambitious but not inconsiderable.

Indeed that could apply to many of the paintings that Holt bought between 1860 and 1884, by Sir Edwin Landseer, David Wilkie, William Mulready, William Collins, T. S. Cooper, W. P. Frith, E. M. Ward. Most are good examples of Victorian genre painting. Wilkie's *The Jew's Harp* is raised above that by his brilliant observation of the musician's hands and eyes, the tilt of his head. The four Landseers (two large Highland set-pieces, a *Lake Scene* sketch and the sentimental *Dog with a Slipper*) were among the flood of unsold, often unfinished, works that were released on to the market after the artist's death in 1873.

The tone of the collection changed when Holt moved to Sudley in 1884 and he began to buy for the house. Some artists recurred (Bonheur, Leighton, Corot, Turner) but he now chose better, more considered and more expensive examples, and developed an interest in the Pre-Raphaelites. He already had a painting, *Gethsemane*, by William Dyce, who was a considerable influence on the young Pre-Raphaelites. Now he acquired pictures by William Holman Hunt, John Everett Millais and Dante Gabriel Rossetti, all painted in the early years (1848–60) of the Brotherhood.

Holman Hunt's *Finding of the Saviour in the Temple* is a classic Pre-Raphaelite work, intensely coloured, intensely recorded. Rossetti's *Two Mothers* is a rare oil painting from his early years, a cut-down fragment from a much larger composition. Holt also developed a liking for the work of John Melhuish Strudwick, a studio assistant and follower of Burne-Jones, whose paintings here have all the outward signs of his master (medievalism; sad, yearning faces; rich texture and detail) but none of his intensity. George Bernard Shaw maintained that 'You sometimes remember a Strudwick better than you remember even a Burne-Jones of the same year', but Shaw was a better critic of music than of painting.

New, too, was Holt's interest in Georgian portraiture. Here are works by Reynolds, Romney, Raeburn and Lawrence. The Romney (*Mrs Sargent*, 1778) and the Raeburn (*Girl Sketching*) are outstanding examples of portraits that cut through the conventions of neo-classicism (Romney) and Romanticism (Raeburn) and reach into the sitter with, in both cases, a quiet but powerful sexual charge.

In these later years Holt's collecting became yet more discriminating and ambitious. Here is a ravishing late oil painting by Richard Parkes Bonington, *Fishing Boats in a Calm*, in which the air holds its breath, the ships' sails hang asleep and the sea is as smooth as glass. Here also are two major late Turners: *Schloss Rosenau* (1841) and the *Wreck Buoy* (1849),

both of which have fine provenances, unlike the two indifferent, even questionable, Turners of Margate subjects[86] that Holt already owned.

The *Schloss Rosenau* (1841) had been in the collection of Joseph Gillott,[87] the steel-pen magnate and important collector of Turner's works. Turner might have hoped that this painting of Prince Albert's birthplace would be bought by Queen Victoria. It was not, and its reception was mixed. *The Spectator* of 8 May 1841 praised it as 'luminously splendid in colour'. *The Athenaeum* of 5 June damned it as the 'fruits of a diseased eye and a reckless hand'. Ruskin answered this criticism with extravagant praise in the first volume of *Modern Painters*.

Wreck Buoy (1807 and 1849) had been owned by Turner's Scottish friend, the collector and amateur artist H. A. J. Munro of Novar. Turner borrowed it back from him in 1849 to repaint it prior to a London exhibition and added the two buoys, green and red, and the rainbows. Ruskin considered it 'the last oil picture that he painted, before his noble hand forgot its cunning'. The *Literary Review* of 12 May 1849 thought it 'a wonderful specimen of his power in colours . . . carried to an extent for which the eye hardly dares to vouch' but *The Spectator*, also of 12 May, was less generous, complaining that the rainbow's arc was 'shaped no better than the vault of an ill-built wine cellar'.

Holt's last acquisition, and his most expensive at 3,000 guineas, was Gainsborough's portrait of *Elizabeth, Viscountess Folkestone* (1776). In 1776 he was preparing to re-exhibit at the Royal Academy and so challenge Reynolds's position as London's leading portraitist with a sweep of portraits that included *Lady Graham* (National Gallery of Scotland, q.v.) and *Carl Friedrich Abel* (Huntington Art Gallery, San Marino). In 1776 he painted *Lady Brisco* (Kenwood House, q.v.), *Johann Christian Bach* and his quiet, poignant portrait of the elderly Lady Folkestone, the skin on her face as fragile and stretched as her silk dress drawn up to her neck, her left hand holding on to her shawl. She emerges from the darkness behind her, drained of colour, full of dignity, a moving example of Gainsborough's featherlight technique capturing not glamour but shadow and stillness.

The Turners and this Gainsborough say much about Holt's collection: serious, thoughtful, acquired not for public show or renown but to hang on his walls and give quiet pleasure. Holt was no Roscoe, no connoisseur. He wanted no Old Masters, simply paintings of quality. It is to their credit that National Museums, Liverpool have kept his collection at Sudley House separate from the riches of the Walker Art Gallery, where they would have been diluted, even lost. Sudley provides a modest, domestic setting in which to appreciate the taste of this intelligent mid-Victorian merchant collector.

In recent years the collection at Sudley House has been augmented, most notably by furniture designed by George Bullock. A pair of ebony veneer cabinets give a clear indication of what a talent was lost when Bullock died in 1818 at the age of thirty-five.[88] Bullock made these cabinets for his friend William Roscoe, the antiquarian and connoisseur who was the founding treasurer of the Liverpool Academy in 1810, of which Bullock was the president. They were designed to hold Roscoe's collection of medals, botanical drawings and prints.

At about this time Bullock was briefly in partnership with J. M. Gandy, the architect and architectural artist, who was closely associated with Sir John Soane.[89] Gandy and Bullock fell out when Gandy refused to join Bullock and Roscoe in the Liverpool Academy, the conditions of Gandy's membership of the Royal Academy (he was elected ARA in 1803) precluding membership of any rival society.

Examples of Bullock's furniture designs are in the Victoria and Albert Museum and Cheltenham Art Gallery and Museum (both q.v.). A chimney piece in Mona marble, from the Anglesey quarry which he owned, is in the rooms designed by Sir Jeffry Wyatville at the Towneley Hall Art Gallery (q.v.). Pieces from his last commission, for Matthew Robinson Boulton of Tew Park, Great Tew, Oxfordshire, are in the Birmingham Museum and Art Gallery (q.v.).

Bullock was also a sculptor and his busts of William Roscoe, Henry Blundell and Sir James Edward Smith, founder of the Linnaean Society, are in the Walker Art Gallery (q.v.).

TATE LIVERPOOL **

Albert Dock, Liverpool, Merseyside L3 4BB
Tel. 0151 702 7400
www.tate.org.uk/liverpool/

The Tate in the north looks out across Jesse Hartley's mighty docks

To build Liverpool's docks Jesse Hartley chose to use mighty granite, its rough blocks cemented together by 'a hydraulic lime with a consistency as hard as the granite itself'.[90] He built them not in the city, nor in the sea, but in the Mersey, on piles that rise and fall with the tide. On them he constructed five-storey warehouses borne on the shoulders of squat Tuscan pillars of cast iron: mighty architecture and engineering. Their grand simplicity made them a strong candidate when, in the 1970s, the Tate Gallery of London was looking for a city and a site in which to locate a regional outstation.

Such a move had been first proposed at a meeting of the trustees on 19 December 1968 by Stewart Mason,[91] the great educationalist and director of Leicestershire Education Authority. The then Director, Norman Reid, and his successor, Alan Bowness, were both enthusiastic and with investment made available by the Merseyside Development Corporation,[92] James Stirling, the architect of the new Clore Gallery wing at the Tate Gallery at Millbank,[93] was commissioned to design the conversion.

Stirling and his engineers[94] made few alterations to Hartley's building other than to insert at the entrance under the colonnade a post-modern screen of bright blue panels and orange lettering. Within, two blue balconies sweep out over the entrance hall.

The gallery's remit is to rotate, fairly slowly, parts of the permanent collection while also giving space to temporary exhibitions, often mounted in conjunction with other, international, galleries to show the work of artists from Japan, Australia, Spain, Africa and America.

Both types of exhibition benefit from the proportions of the galleries that Stirling created within the warehouse: long runs of walls, relatively low ceilings, their clean spaces interrupted only by cast-iron beams and, on the two lower floors, the occasional cast-iron pillar. Almost all forms of contemporary art look good in these strong, simple galleries. They are as sympathetic to paintings (Francis Bacon, Lucian Freud, Malcolm Morley, Stanley Spencer, even Walter Sickert) as to installations by Mark Dion, Matt Mullican or Catherine Yass.

Tate Liverpool allows curators to bring forward artists from the permanent collection for whom space cannot regularly be found at the two London galleries (Tate Britain and Tate Modern): Edward Wadsworth and Ithell Colquhoun; David Bomberg and Jacob Kramer; John Piper and John Craxton; Euan Uglow and Prunella Clough; John Bratby, Jack Smith and Michael Andrews. In particular these spaces provide an excellent setting for the Tate's collection of 20th-century sculpture. Richard Long (1991), Antony Gormley (1993), Barbara Hepworth (1994) and Rachel Whiteread (1996) have all had one-person shows here, but the depth of the collection extends back to the Geometry of Fear sculptors of the early 1950s (Armitage, Chadwick, Butler and Paolozzi) and to those who dominated British sculpture between the two world wars – Jacob Epstein, F. E. McWilliam, Frank Dobson – and to Henri Gaudier-Brzeska, twenty-five of whose pieces came to the Tate in 1926 when his partner, Sophie Brzeska, died intestate.

Stewart Mason envisaged not simply 'an outstation for the permanent collection' but the opportunity for 'those who lived so far from London'[95] to see such world-class works as Mark Rothko's *Seagram Murals*, which formed one of the first major shows here in 1988. Rothko was commissioned to make the series for the restaurant in Mies van der Rohe's Seagram Building in New York, but he refused to deliver them to such an exclusive venue.

Rothko killed himself in 1970. He had been due to donate them to the Tate. This setting in Liverpool makes a fine harbour for his monumental panels of colour, which echo the rise and fall of the granite docks.

MANCHESTER ART GALLERY ✶✶✶✶

Mosley Street, Manchester,
Greater Manchester M2 3JL
Tel. 0161 235 8888
www.manchestergalleries.org

Pre-Raphaelite and High Victorian paintings of special note in building by Barry

Timothy Clifford, Director of the Manchester Art Gallery 1978–84, predicted that 'One day the Galleries will have an extension, something they have been waiting for since 1897. When that happens the stored collections, like a wrinkled brown chrysalis, will undergo a metamorphosis into that magnificent and brightly coloured butterfly which at present lies dormant.'[96] Now that Charles Barry's two buildings, the Grecian-style Royal Manchester Institution (1824–34) and the Italian palazzo-style Athenaeum (1836–9), have been joined together by Sir Michael Hopkins and Partners' extension, which incorporates new galleries and a glass-walled atrium (2002), those hopes can be tested.

Manchester has very considerable strengths: one of the finest Pre-Raphaelite collections in Britain; an outstanding 17th-century collection of Dutch and Flemish paintings; applied art, particularly silver, ceramics and industrial design; and British art of the 18th, 19th and 20th centuries.

A collection of late-17th- and early-18th-century silver given by Mr and Mrs Edgar Assheton-Bennett (1979) contains examples of all the leading craftsmen; a chocolate pot by Pierre Platel (1705–6); a teapot by David Willaume (1706–7); an inkstand and candlestick by Augustin Courtauld (1720–21) and pieces by Paul de Lamerie that illustrate his career, from a teapot of 1716–17 to a plate

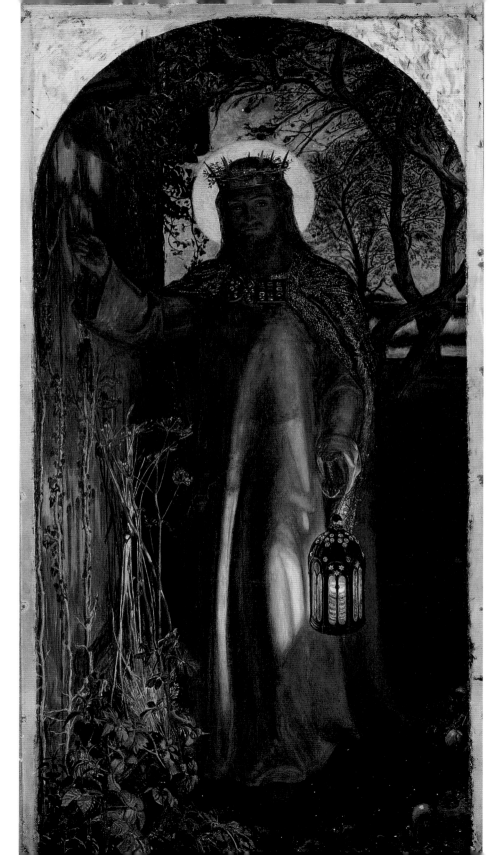

(1739–40) and a pair of escallop shells (1748). Here too is a spice box (1728–9) by Anne Tanqueray, that 18th-century rarity, a woman silversmith. Thomas Greg's collection of English earthenware (1923) is wide-ranging: a 16th-century pitcher, a 17th-century salt-glaze mug by John Dwight of Fulham, 18th-century tin-glaze ware from Bristol, Liverpool and Lambeth, a cauliflower teapot (1760s) by William Greatbach and a slip-trailed Royalist charger (c. 1670) by Thomas Toft (d. 1670) that depicts Charles II's head peering out of an oak tree, flanked by an heraldic lion and unicorn: one of the supreme achievements of 17th century English pottery.

The Assheton-Bennetts also bequeathed paintings by Dutch artists (Gerhard Terborch, Gerrit Dou, Pieter de Hooch) and Flemish artists (Adriaen Brouwer, David Teniers the Younger). Almost every 17th-century Dutch or Flemish artist of note has work here: Jan van de Cappelle, Jacob Ruisdael, Aert van der Neer, Jan Wijnants and more.

The gallery's collection of English portraits is similarly extensive, from George Gower and John Souch to Francis Bacon, Lucian Freud and David Hockney. Michael Wright, Lely, Reynolds, Gainsborough, Romney are all represented, and there is a curious group of paintings of eighteen eminent writers (including Homer, Shakespeare, Spenser and Voltaire) by William Blake commissioned by his patron, William Hayley.

The most striking portraits are those by Gower (of *Mary Cornwallis*, c. 1580–85, a study in silver and black, her billowing sleeves covered in stiff, transparent net) and by Souch, who was apprenticed in 1607 to Randle Holme, the Chester herald painter who taught him to write and paint genealogical rolls, funeral hatchments, pedigrees and wooden memorial tablets. In *Sir Thomas Aston at the Deathbed of his Wife* (1635), Sir Thomas, his son and his first (dead) and second wives are surrounded by images of life and death: skull, cross, navigational staff and globe. Souch's composition is

William Holman Hunt's The Light at the End of the World *(Manchester Art Gallery)*

rich in symbolic reference. In the dead centre he places a skull resting on the cot of the dead child; below is the Aston hatchment, surrounded by a laurel wreath, behind which is a vanitas, a richly embroidered cloth depicting scenes of worldly pleasure, of love and hunting.

Such a catalogue may give the (false) impression that the development of the gallery's collection was easy and smooth. The RMI started to collect as early as 1827, when it purchased James Northcote's handsome *Othello, the Moor of Venice* (1826) for thirty guineas from the first of its annual exhibitions, but when in 1882 the RMI gave its collections to the city council it comprised no more than fifty paintings (including a dramatic William Etty, *The Storm*, 1829–30, and G. F. Watts's gift of his own *The Good Samaritan*).

Electing to collect contemporary art, the city allocated £4,000 a year for the next twenty years for acquisitions. This led to moments of heated over-excitement (in 1889 £4,000 was paid for Leighton's huge *Captive Andromache* to make certain of outbidding Birmingham and Liverpool), but overall this budget was well spent.

In the 1880s and '90s the foundations of the Pre-Raphaelite collection were laid with the purchase of three paintings by Millais; D. G. Rossetti's *Astarte Syriaca* (1877), his last painting of Jane Morris, sexual and aloof;[97] and three of Holman Hunt's greatest works (*The Light at the End of the World*, *The Hireling Shepherd* and *The Scapegoat*), which built on the gift, by Thomas and William Agnew, of *The Shadow of Death*, and the purchase in 1885 of Ford Madox Brown's *Work* (1852–65).

The collection is as important for the context in which it places the central figures of the original Pre-Raphaelite Brotherhood as it is for these major works. Artists associated with the Brotherhood, such as Charles Alston Collins, Arthur Hughes, James Archer and John Brett are all represented. Collins's *The Pedlar* (1850) shows most clearly the rejection of Raphael,[98] while Brett's *Seascape* (1881) illustrates the Brotherhood's aim, expressed by William Michael Rossetti, 'to study Nature attentively', in line with Ruskin's advice to young artists in

Modern Painters, vol. 1 (1843) to 'go to Nature in all singleness of heart . . . rejecting nothing, selecting nothing and scorning nothing, . . . rejoicing always in the truth'.

These paintings, and those by second-generation Pre-Raphaelites, V. C. Prinsep, John Melhuish Strudwick, John William Waterhouse and Simeon Solomon and, above all, Edward Burne-Jones, trace the influence of the Brotherhood on half a century of British painting, from Millais's tiny *The Death of Romeo and Juliet*, painted in 1848 (the year that he, Holman Hunt and Rossetti came together),[99] to James Archer's *Thomas de Quincey*, painted in 1903.

The gallery did not ignore other late Victorian painters. Apart from the Leighton, J. W. Waterhouse's *Hylas and the Nymphs* (1896) was acquired, as were paintings by Landseer (*The Desert*, 1849, featuring a huge lion;[100] a replica of *Derby Day* that W. P. Frith considered to be better than the original) and the darkly beautiful *Sappho*,[101] (1887) by Charles Mengin.

In the early 20th century the purchase grant was reduced and the gallery had to depend increasingly on bequests and gifts, chief among which were those by the brothers James Thomas and George Beatson Blair (in 1917 and 1940), which included a majestic late Turner watercolour, *Heidelberg: Sunset* (*c.*1840–42) and landscapes by Constable, David Cox and B. W. Leader, and, in 1925, by Charles Rutherston of some eight hundred paintings and drawings by, among others, W. R. Sickert, Wyndham Lewis, C. R. W. Nevinson and Gwen John. Rutherston was the brother of the artist William Rothenstein and uncle of Sir John Rothenstein whose book *Modern English Painters* records the lives of many of these artists.

In the 1930s and '40s the gallery began once again to purchase contemporary work: Henry Moore's *Mother and Child* (1925) and Ben Nicholson's *Au Chat Botté* (1932), in which his manipulation of the several planes, reflected and actual, anticipates his later reliefs.[102]

Successive directors have bought with great skill: the exquisite *Virgin and Child and*

Goldfish by a follower of Daddi was purchased in 1959 and Stubbs's *Cheetah and Stag and Two Indians* (1765) was bought with the help of the National Art Collection Fund in 1970. Timothy Clifford acquired a superb *Cruxifixion* by a follower of Duccio, Claude's *Adoration of the Golden Calf* (1660) and two of Bernardo Bellotto's views of *The Courtyard of the Castle of Königstein* (*c.*1756–8), as remarkable a group of major paintings as any purchased by a regional gallery in the late 1970s and early 1980s.

This rich mixture of classic and contemporary has been extended in the past twenty years by an association with the Contemporary Arts Society's Special Collection scheme through which the work of Richard Deacon has been acquired and by the introduction of the work of such international artists as Juan Munoz and Tatsuo Miyajima.

Nevertheless this gallery remains conscious of its Mancunian, industrial roots. Space is dedicated to depicting the city through the eyes of its applied and fine artists: a bronze head (1926) by Jacob Epstein of C. P. Scott, editor of the *Manchester Guardian*; paintings by L. S. Lowry and by Adolphe Valette, who taught Lowry at the Manchester School of Art; Ancoats pressed glass by Molineaux Webb and Co., produced in the late 1880s; and animated films by Cosgrove Hall Films Ltd, produced a century later. Here too is craft silver commissioned in 1995 from Shannon O'Neill, a former student at Manchester Metropolitan University.

At last, with the Hopkins extension, Timothy Clifford's hopes for these 'magnificent and brightly coloured' collections can begin to take their flight.

MUSEUM OF SCIENCE AND INDUSTRY IN MANCHESTER *

Liverpool Road, Castlefield, Manchester,
Greater Manchester M3 4PP
Tel. 0161 832 2244
www.msim.org.uk

*Manchester's industries remembered in mighty
19th-century warehouses and market hall*

In October 1829 a competition was held at
Rainhill, outside Liverpool, to determine
whether the locomotives that were to haul
goods on a track between Liverpool and Manchester should be powered by horse, human or
steam power. The challenge for each locomotive was to pull three times its own weight,
seventy miles in less than ten hours. The
Rocket, designed by George Stevenson, won,
and within a year, on 15 September 1830, the
railway between Liverpool docks and Manchester was opened, giving the docks faster
access to new markets and providing Manchester with the raw materials it needed
to make it the largest, and fastest growing,
industrial city in Britain in the 19th century.

The line's terminus in Manchester was the
world's first purpose-built passenger and
goods railway station and is one of the five
historic industrial buildings that form the
Museum of Science and Industry that opened
in 1983. The others are the Railway Warehouse
(1830), believed to have been designed by
Thomas Haigh, built by David Bellhouse and
Company; the Transit Shed (1855); the Lower
Campfield Market Hall (1877); and an 1880
warehouse that is now the museum's main
entrance.

The buildings are as exciting as the collections and are in effect the museum's largest
exhibits. In particular the Lower Campfield
Market Hall and the 1830 warehouse are evidence of how industrial development was
driven by men such as David Bellhouse. The
Bellhouse family owned its own brickworks, a
foundry and a sawmill that processed the timber which they imported. It is not surprising

that his company was able to build the 1830
warehouse (apparently modified from designs
that Haigh had drawn up for warehouses in
the Gloucester Docks that had not been built)
in only four and a half months.

The visitor enters the 1880 warehouse, which
now holds the textile industry collection in the
Fibres, Fashion and Fabrics Gallery. The noise
of the machinery (Platt Brothers of Oldham) is
thunderous. Fibre is woven into fabric; fabric
is printed for dresses; dresses are sold from
a merchant's shop: cottonopolis in embryo.

The Power Hall (1855), once the transit
shed in which goods were transferred from rail
wagons to lorries for distribution, now holds
the Beyer-Garratt articulated steam locomotive, made in 1930 in Beyer, Peacock's Gorton
factory and run on the South African railways
until 1972. Beside it is a replica of *Novelty*,
which was defeated by *Rocket* in the Rainhill
trials, although it was liked best by those
watching. Also here are electric locomotives
and a variety of motor cars: a 1905 Rolls Royce
hand built in Hulme; a Ford Model T van
made at Henry Ford's Trafford Park factory
where Ford introduced British workers to the
disciplines of assembly-line production in 1911.

The museum does not attempt to represent
all the industries that have operated in Manchester over the past 200 years. There is no
hatting, no glass making, but the printing and
scientific instrument industries are here, as is
aerospace, in the elegant, airy space of the
Lower Campfield Market Hall, the cast-iron
frame of which was made at E. T. Bellhouse's
Eagle Foundry to designs by Mangnall and
Littlewood (1876).

The museum manages to convey the majestic power of 19th-century manufacturing industry and something of its detail. The majesty
is in the Power Hall machinery: the hot air and
diesel engines, the 1907 McNaught engine
from Firgrove Mill, the looming thirty-tonne
hydraulic accumulator. The detail is in the new
Manchester Science Gallery (2004), in which it
is possible to grasp something of the science
that has underpinned industry in Manchester
since the time of John Dalton, the father of
modern chemistry.

JOHN RYLANDS LIBRARY
***

150 Deansgate, Manchester, Greater
Manchester M13 9PP
Tel. 0161 834 5343
www.rylibweb.man.ac.uk

*One of Europe's finest neo-Gothic buildings,
housing remarkable rare manuscripts and
printed books*

As you enter the John Rylands Library, there
before you, in a Gothic 'forest of pillars and
vaulting shafts',[103] is a wall statue of three
figures by John Cassidy entitled *Theology
Directing the Labours of Science and Art*. Above
it is the inscription 'NIHIL MIHI LABORE EX
TERRA I CEM'. In it the sculptor embodies
the strengths of the library. It was built to
house the book collections acquired by Mrs
Enriqueta Rylands, principally the Althorp
Library of the 2nd Earl Spencer, rich in early
printed books, and the Earls of Crawford's
Bibliotheca Lindesiana, famous for its manuscripts.

The manuscripts include Greek papyri of
the 3rd century BC and the St John fragment
(2nd century AD), the earliest known piece of
New Testament manuscript. There are manuscripts in some forty languages, on linen,
parchment, palm leaf and bamboo, and even
one on clay, whose inscription commemorates
Nebuchadnezzar's rebuilding of the temple
of the god Shamash 605–562 BC. Among
the Arabic manuscripts are more than fifty
Korans, including 9th- and 10th-century texts
in Kufic and the Golden Koran (*c.* AD 1000).

The collection of printed books contains
more than 12,500 English books printed before
1641 and 34,000 foreign texts of before 1601.
Caxton's amended second edition (1484) (the
first had many textual errors) of Chaucer's
Canterbury Tales is one of sixty Caxtons. There
are examples of the work of such other early
printers as Richard Pynson (London) and
Christopher Valdarfer (Venice: his 1471 printing of Boccaccio's *II Decamerone*), and a 1476
Latin Bible printed by Nicolaus Jenson, also in

Venice, on vellum, richly illuminated, encrusted with gold, showing God seated on a
globe on a dark blue mound, behind which is
an infinite pale blue space.

In the modern ecclesiastical holdings,
Nonconformity, particularly Methodism, is
strongly represented. They include the manuscript collection of Charles Wesley's hymns in
his own handwriting.

Not surprisingly there is a fine archive of
deeds and documents from eminent Lancashire and Cheshire families, in particular
from the Bromley-Davenports and the
Cornwall-Leghs, including a papal bull, dated
14 May 1469, giving a dispensation of marriage
to Peter Warburton of Warburton Abbey
and Ellen Savage of Clifton, who were related
in the third degree.

The book as aesthetic object is not ignored.
Here is John Baskerville's *Virgil* (1757), with
the clear beauty of his typeface in mint condition; a 1906 edition of Christina Rossetti's
Verses printed on vellum at the Eragny Press
by Lucien Pissarro (son of Camille), who did
the woodcuts and decorations and designed
his own typeface, Brook, cut for him by E. P.
Prince.

The first Kelmscott Press book is here,
The Recuyell of the Historyes of Troyue (two
volumes, 1892), translated by William Caxton.
Kelmscott printed it in its Troy (a readable
Gothic) and Chaucer (a smaller Troy) faces.
William Morris designed the initials, orna-
ments and intricate foliage. Here too is
Kelmscott's 1896 edition of Chaucer, edited
by F. S. Ellis, on linen-based handmade paper,
set in a face based on those created in the 15th
century by Nicholas Jenson and Gunther
Zainer.

The Tregaskis Collection is remarkable.
James and Mary Tregaskis, booksellers, sent
seventy-six copies of a Kelmscott Press book,
The Tale of King Florus and the Fair Jehane
(1893), to bookbinders around the world.
Seventy-three were returned, duly bound, and
were exhibited in London. The cynosure was
by Kishun Chand of Delhi, bound in orange
satin embroidered with floral sprays whose
flowers are clusters of pearls.

Spectacular though those books are, it is likely that it will be the building that will make the greatest impression on the visitor. Designed in 1890 by the architect Basil Champneys, it stands comparison with Woodward's Oxford University Museum of Natural History (q.v.), not least in the quality of craftsmanship. The woodwork, in Polish oak, is intricately carved; the Arts and Crafts metalwork, early art nouveau in style, for the radiator grilles and light fittings, is worked in bronze; the Penrith sandstone for the exterior is surpassed by the stone used inside. This is swark, which ranges in colour from the softest grey buff to rose pink. When lit, the interior glows.

At each end of the Reading Room are large stained-glass windows by Charles Eames Kempe, in which are depicted sages and divines: Socrates, Plato, Aeschylus, St Thomas Aquinas, Erasmus, Kant and Hegel. Before them are statues of Homer, Shakespeare, Wesley and John Rainolds, who initiated the translation of the King James Bible.

This, one of the best secular buildings in the perpendicular neo-Gothic style, is a cathedral raised to the book and to learning.

MANCHESTER MUSEUM ✳✳✳

University of Manchester, Oxford Road, Manchester, Greater Manchester M13 9PL
Tel. 0161 275 2634
www.man.ac.uk/museum

University museum of fossils, anthropology, archery and antiquities: a fabulous, serious haul

The Manchester Museum opened in 1888, seven years after the Natural History Museum (NHM) in London (q.v.). Both were designed by Alfred Waterhouse, a scion of Manchester. The Manchester Museum is smaller, plainer, more church than cathedral, not simply because Owens College (the predecessor of the University of Manchester) was less rich than the Natural History Museum but because, from the outset, it was a post-Darwinian museum with a clear, scientific view of what

natural history was and of the relative roles of God and Man in the Universe.

Most crucial to the early history of the museum was the great biologist Thomas Henry Huxley (1825–95), friend and disciple of Charles Darwin. In 1867 Huxley was invited by Owens College to assess the suitability for the college of the collections of the increasingly insolvent Manchester Society of Natural History and of the Manchester Geological Society, until then housed in a handsome classical museum in Peter Street. On his advice, Owens College took responsibility for the collections as a unique teaching aid for the college's students and for the instruction of the public. Huxley wrote a detailed report recommending methods of display and curation and even provided sketches to show how the 'public' and 'private' spaces in the college's museum should be configured. The college commissioned Waterhouse, who was already engaged on the Natural History Museum, to design a natural history museum for Manchester.

Huxley's views on an appropriate design for the Natural History Museum, though forcefully expressed to the trustees, to Parliament and to the press, were ignored. Sir Richard Owen, the first Superintendent of the NHM and passionate opponent of Darwin's theories, wanted a huge museum in which the whole of God's creation would be displayed, to the glory of Britain and of God. Huxley wanted a museum that was selective, in which the public would be offered a coherent view of natural history through a careful selection of objects and specimens. Here, in Manchester, Huxley's philosophy became a reality, though his sketch layout was not followed in detail.

From the start, the museum had exceptional collections. Its oldest specimens were beetles collected by William Kirby; its most celebrated, those brought back by Charles Darwin from his voyage on HMS *Beagle*, and by Franklin while searching for the North West Passage; material collected by Carl Linnaeus, the father of modern botanical classification; and the Manchester moth (1829), of which only two other specimens are known.[104]

The subsequent expansion of the collections

The splendid leaf frog Agalychnis calcarifer, *live in the vivarium at Manchester Museum*

was accelerated by the addition of archaeology and ethnology. The work of Sir William Flinders Petrie and the British School of Archaeology in Egypt had been strongly supported, and financed, by the Manchester textile manufacturer Jesse Haworth, and in return the museum received part of Petrie's annual division of antiquities, most of the remainder going to the Petrie Museum of Egyptian Archaeology (q.v.). The material from Kahun, the town where the workmen who built the pyramids lived, from Tell-el-Amarna, city of the heretic Pharaoh Akhenaten, and from Rifeh, is particularly important. The contents of a tomb at Rifeh, excavated in 1907, included the mummies of two brothers, unwrapped the following year by the museum's first Curator of Egyptology, Dr Margaret Murray. In doing so she transformed forensic archaeology.

To accommodate those developments the building was extended north along the Oxford Road in 1912, by Waterhouse's son, and in 1927 by his grandson. Between 1999 and 2003 a further extension and series of careful interventions of contemporary design in the older buildings by Manchester-based Ian Simpson Architects created elegant new spaces on an historic site adjoining the old Schuster Physical Laboratory, in which the nuclear age was born: here Rutherford articulated his nuclear model of the atom in 1911–13 and split the atom for the first time when he disintegrated the nitrogen nucleus in 1917.[105]

Inside the museum the layout of galleries is logical and orderly. In the original Waterhouse building is a time line that takes the lay visitor from the universe of billions of galaxies to the galaxy nearest to us (Andromeda, 2.2 million light years away), to our sun (one of 100 billion stars in our galaxy), to meteorites formed 4.6 billion years ago, the oldest known objects on our planet, some having grains of matter that are older than our solar system. In that context the oldest fossil in the collection, the Apex Chert, a flint-like rock from western Australia, is a mere 3,500 million years old.

You are led through the evolution of this planet as clearly as in any museum in Britain, from the fossil of the earliest Precambrian multicellular animal, the *Dickinsonia costata* from Ediacava, South Australia (620 million years ago), emerging tentatively out of the rock, through perfectly etched trilobites, to the first (jawless) fish, the vertebrates that clambered out of the sea leaving footprints 385 million years ago, the first tree-like plants, reptiles, coalfields and dinosaurs (Owen's 'terrible lizards'), and finally, yesterday, to the Ice Age, the birth of man and the cave bones discovered by William Boyd Dawkins, who was the first keeper of the Manchester Museum (1870–89) and professor of geology at Owens College from 1879.

You proceed to zoology, given its own place in a reduced version of Waterhouse's wrought-iron gallery at the NHM. Here, observed by the suspended skeleton of a sperm whale, are stuffed mammals: the familiar (beaver, sloth, horse), the less familiar (viscacha, agouti, hutia) and Mister Potter's cow (the original, white British breed, stuffed by Timothy Harrop in 1837). From taxidermy you proceed to a vivarium, containing dramatically lit glass rooms of living plants and animals inhabiting naturalistic environments from desert to tropical rainforest. Here you can admire the panther chameleon, green tree pythons and a golden poison dart frog from Colombia, tiny, inoffensive, still, waiting, with poison enough to kill ten humans. And so to archaeology and anthropology to see what *Homo sapiens* has made of this inheritance: pots, tools, weapons, charm figures and sacred objects. The collections teem with life, demanding and receiving continuing research. Edward O. Wilson observed in 1972 that 'we dwell on a largely unexplored planet.' Two hundred and fifty years, and the identification of approximately 1.7 million species later, we may still have discovered only about one tenth of all species.

WHITWORTH ART GALLERY ★★★★

University of Manchester, Oxford Road, Manchester, Greater Manchester M15 6ER
Tel. 0161 275 7450
www.whitworth.man.ac.uk

One of the world's great collections of English watercolours; also historic wallpapers and textiles

The Whitworth Art Gallery is an exception. While other art galleries hide away their collection of watercolours in drawers and boxes, deterred by the real, but surmountable, problems of exposing the works on paper to daylight, the Whitworth glories in its paintings by Sandby and Cozens, Turner and Girtin, Cotman and Cox. This is the finest collection of watercolours, outside the Victoria and Albert Museum or the British Museum (both q.v.).

The founding committee of the Whitworth Institute in 1889 was determined to establish 'a permanent influence of the highest character in the directions of Commercial and Technical Instruction and the cultivation of taste and knowledge of the Fine Arts of Painting, Sculpture and Architecture'.[106]

Sir Joseph Whitworth, whose bequest made this possible, was described by Mrs Carlyle as 'the inventor of . . . many wonderful machines, has a face not unlike a baboon; speaks the broadest Lancashire; could not invent an epigram to save his life; but . . . one feels that one is talking with a real live man, to my mind worth any number of the wits that go about.' He established his reputation and his fortune by designing an internationally recognised standard for screw threads. He had no known interest in fine art. His will demonstrated this, assigning almost half his fortune to establish engineering scholarships and a considerably smaller sum to found schools of technology and art, integrated with an art gallery. Nevertheless his friend and executor Robert Dukinfield Darbishire did have such an interest and appointed Sir William Agnew,

Peter Blake's Got a Girl *(Whitworth Art Gallery)*

chairman of Agnew's, as president of the gallery's council. Agnew secured £40,000 for the institute from the profits of the 1887 Manchester International Exhibition, £20,000 of which was for the purchase of works of art.

Agnew purchased well, from the sale of the great watercolour collection of Dr John Percy at Christie's, and the institute was given its pick of the fine watercolours belonging to John Edward Taylor, the proprietor of the *Manchester Guardian.* In fewer than five years the Whitworth had the core of a distinguished collection, covering the development of the golden age of watercolour painting, 1750–1850.

The Taylor gift included Paul Sandby's *Ludlow Castle,* J. R. Cozens's *Lake Nemi Looking Towards Genzano,* Constable's *Feering Church and Parsonage* and one of William Blake's great watercolours, *The Ancient of Days,* painted just before he died in 1824. Blake depicts Urizen, the Creator, kneeling within

the circumference of the sun, bringing the Universe into existence by setting 'a compass upon the face of the deep'.[107] Crowning the Taylor gift was a large group of watercolours by Turner and Girtin.

This included Girtin's ravishing *Durham Castle and Bridge from the River Wear* (1799) in which he sets the massive Framwellgate Bridge to straddle the picture, above it the cathedral and castle on the high rock, below it the smooth, clear water of the river. Turner's works include excellent examples from every phase of his career, from the early topographical *St Anselm's Chapel, Canterbury Cathedral* (c.1794) to the late, atmospheric *Moonlight on Lake Lucerne with the Righi Beyond* (c.1841–4).

Steady, consistent purchasing, and a succession of bequests, have turned that fine foundation into a great collection, topped in recent years by the acquisition of the only known surviving sketchbook of Thomas Girtin, and the seven sketchbooks in which J. R. Cozens recorded landscape views on his visit to Italy with William Beckford in 1782–3. The gallery also owns eight of the watercolours that Cozens completed from these sketches.

The drawings collection is particularly strong in 18th- and 19th-century landscapes. There are some fine Richard Wilsons and a drawing by Gainsborough, aged eighteen, a large copy in chalks of Ruisdael's *La Fôret*, done at a time when he was struggling in London and learning from the landscapes of the Dutch masters.

The print collection is one of the largest outside London: 12,000 single-sheet prints and 500 illustrated books,[108] from the 15th century to the present day. Major gifts, by the collector George Thomas Clough in 1921 and 1929, of Italian and Northern Renaissance works, and by William Sharp Ogden (a bequest) in 1926 of later Old Master prints, augmented the teaching collection of the original Whitworth Institute, which included a complete set of Turner's *Liber Studiorum*, and of the University of Manchester's History of Art Department, transferred to the Whitworth in 1960. The highlights of the Old Master Print Collection are a group of seventy engravings and woodcuts by Dürer and prints by Rembrandt, van Ostade, Mantegna, Piranesi and Goya.

The collection includes examples of the print making of most of the major 19th- and 20th-century British and European artists, and some American, notably 17 etchings and 13 lithographs by J. McN. Whistler. Prints by Eduardo Paolozzi, Richard Hamilton, Patrick Caulfield, Howard Hodgkin, Damien Hirst, Marc Quinn, Rachel Whiteread and Gillian Wearing are among those by contemporary artists.

More unusually there is a fine collection of late 19th- and 20th-century British wood engravings[109] and a group of more than 500 Japanese colour woodcuts (17th–19th centuries) in which Hokusai, Tamara and Hiroshige are well represented.

A parallel journey through successive generations of print technology is traced by the wallpaper collection from the block printing and stencilling on single sheets of the 17th and 18th centuries to the continuous rolls and mechanisation of the 19th and 20th centuries, from the craft of A. W. N. Pugin and William Morris to the industrial products of Crown Wallcoverings Ltd.

It is the largest collection of historic and modern wallpapers outside London.[110] Every type of wall covering is here: French and Flemish embossed leather wall hangings; 18th-century wallpaper borders printed on unused sheets of a French publication (*c.* 1780); arabesque panels by Jean-Baptiste Réveillon and hand-block printed and flocked *trompe l'œil* drapery wallpapers by Dufour[111] and Leroy (*c.* 1825); the papers of William Morris and those of Walter Crane; the machine-produced papers, post 1840, of Jeffrey and Co., William Sanderson, William Shand Kydd and Crown and other wallpaper companies.

This remarkable spread was further enhanced by the acquisition of some seminal collections, chief among which was that of Wall Paper Manufacturers Ltd (who by the early 20th century had a virtual monopoly of UK wallpaper manufacturing)[112] and of items from the French Follot[113] Collection.[114]

The collection's diversity demonstrates the claim of A.V. Sugden and J. L. Edmondson in their definitive *A History of English Wallpaper 1509–1914*[115] that 'wallpaper, beyond question, is the most universal, as it is the most democratic, of the applied arts ... It can be produced cheaply, and at the same time artistically ... But democratic though wallpaper is in the widest sense of the term, its lineage is both high and ancient.'[116]

The textiles collection, which retains something of the founding governors' intentions to 'influence ... Commercial and Technical Instruction', was formed to inspire the textile industries of Manchester and Lancashire. The opening exhibition in 1890 was of textiles from the great collection of Sir Charles Robinson, the first superintendent of collections at the South Kensington Museum (later the Victoria and Albert Museum).

The Whitworth bought much of the Robinson Collection:[117] its wealth of 16th–18th-century European ecclesiastical material, vestments, altar hangings, copes; medieval damasks, velvets and brocatelles; and, later, the Coptic textiles associated with the archaeologist Flinders Petrie, later Sir Flinders (v. Petrie Museum). One of the finest Robinson acquisitions is a 15th-century tapestry-woven altar frontal from the Cologne region representing the Tree of Jesse. The ancestors of Christ, the twelve kings of Israel, grow like flowers from formalised sepals on a slender stalk which comes out of the chest of the centrally seated figure of Jesse. It depicts the prophecy of Isaiah: 'And there shall come forth a rod out of the stem of Jesse, and a Branch shall grow out of his roots.'[118]

The collection includes three of the earlier tapestries woven on the looms of William Morris's Merton Abbey workshops (*Flora, Pomona* and *Fox and Pheasants, c.*1885). However, early English embroidery is less well represented, an exception being the 17th-century casket embroidered by Hannah Smith, aged twelve, using a remarkable battery of stitches: fine tent and rococo on canvas, laid satin, long and short stitches, and raised work.

This is a gallery in which to see and apprehend the golden age of English watercolour when landscape was described again through soft light, the colour floating across the surface of paper and subject; a place where they are aglow, upon walls, not asleep in drawers. It is also a gallery in which its founding committee's desire to establish 'a permanent influence . . . in the directions of Commercial and Technical Instruction and the cultivation of taste and knowledge of the Fine Arts' is fully realised, most fully of all in the archive of Walter Crane, acquired in 2002 by the gallery, jointly with the John Rylands Library (q.v.).[119]

Crane was the dominant figure of the Arts and Crafts movement: a founder member of the Art Workers' Guild, president of the Arts and Crafts Exhibition Society and, appropriately, director of Design and Art at the Manchester School of Art. He worked in every medium with which the Whitworth is concerned: textiles, wallpapers, paintings, prints, drawings. In doing so, through his work, he permeated the visual consciousness of anyone born in Britain in the first half of the 20th century.

Only after responsibility for the gallery was transferred to Manchester University in 1958, and new galleries added by John Bickerdike to the originals by J.W. & J. Beaumont, did the collection of 20th-century oil paintings and sculpture gather pace.

The gallery already had drawings by van Gogh, Picasso, Matisse, Degas, Munch, Klee and an oil by de Chirico. It now concentrated on 20th-century English artists: the Camden Town Group, the Vorticists, the St Ives School (although not the Bloomsbury Group). There is a notably strong representation of British pop art from the 1960s: Peter Blake, Richard Hamilton, R. B. Kitaj, Derek Boshier.

Recent acquisitions have included Jacob Epstein's *Genesis* (1929–31), a fine example of his 'direct carving' in which, without a detailed maquette, the form of the work emerges through the process of working in stone, in this case a creamy mass of Sezavezza marble.

There are two portraits of Lucian Freud: by his friend Francis Bacon (1951) and a self-portrait of 1973. The Bacon is an uneasy, elusive image. Freud leans against a column or doorpost. Behind is a void. Before him, on the ground, are two shadows, one pale, one dark. The self-portrait, seen from below, is wary, perhaps defiant. Freud's right arm, thrust on a diagonal, against his cheek bone, skews the pyramid of his face, the paint is applied wet, thick, with a hog's hair brush, moulding the flesh as if it were clay. He outstares himself, and us.

Freud's self-image shows how far the gallery has moved from the schools of technology and art that Whitworth himself envisaged but as, in Mrs Carlyle's words, 'a real live man' and, in Robert Darbishire's opinion, someone with an infallible determination to think and do only what appeared to him to be right, he might have approved of the present gallery's collections.

GALLERY OF COSTUME *

Platt Hall, Rusholme, Manchester, Greater
Manchester M14 5LL
Tel. 0161 224 5217

Serious collection of clothes and costume

'We have to remove from period costumes the
appearance – almost the stigma – of being
"fancy dress",'[120] wrote Dr C. Willet Cunnington, with whose collection this gallery was
founded.

Cunnington and his wife, Dr Phillis Cunnington, were seeking, in the collection that
together they built up in the 1930s, to change
attitudes. The true value of costumes lay not in
their aesthetic, or the skill with which they
were made, or even with who wore them and
when. The Cunningtons were determined to
establish a 'scientific approach' that viewed
costume 'much as the archaeologist regards
fragments of pottery'.[121] In doing so they ran
counter to the collections in the Victoria and
Albert Museum (q.v.) 'displayed as art objects,
museum-worthy because of their beauty and
fine craftsmanship'[122] and in the Museum of
London (q.v.), whose clothes belonged to the
famous. What the Cunningtons collected were
19th- and 20th-century women's clothes that
were ordinary, that were worn everyday: the
clothes of domestic servants as well as of their
employers, of nurses, barmaids, circus per-
formers and policewomen. They collected very
few men's clothes.

To try to collect the clothes of 19th-century
working women is a vain quest. Such clothes
habitually wore out and were discarded.
Uniforms were seldom valued enough to be
kept.

We find Willet Cunnington corresponding
anxiously with the gallery's first curator, Anne
Buck, in 1948: 'Have you secured a police-
woman's uniform yet?'[123] When clothes could
not be found they collected photographs of
women who worked in mills, or on farms, or
who gutted fish. There is a fine photograph
here, *c.*1865, of two women workers at the
Tredegar Iron Works in south Wales. Both
wear boots and hats clamped over scarves.
Their sleeves are clinched tight halfway up to
the elbow, the better to work. They stare,
uncertain but proud, at the camera.

For such a collection Platt Hall is not an
entirely appropriate setting. It is an elegant,
red-brick Palladian house built for John Lees
in 1762–4 by Timothy Lightoler, from original
plans by John Carr of York.[124] Inside, the
staircase starts in one flight, sweeps back in
two under a Venetian window and leads to
the Dining Room. This retains its original
rococo stucco decoration. Over the fireplace is
a breathless landscape by Richard Wilson, *A
Summer Evening (on the Arno)* (1764). Platt
Hall is a building better suited, perhaps, for
exhibiting paintings from Manchester Art
Gallery's collection, which was its function
from 1925 until 1947 when the City Council
acquired the Cunnington costumes.

Since then the collection has been
augmented by clothes that belonged to the
Carill-Worsley family, descendants of John
Lees. Others take the collections back into the
17th century and forward from the 1940s to
the present day. In total, the collections of
clothes, accessories of all kinds, and textiles
now number around 22,000 items.

Despite the stern intent of the Cunningtons,
the costumes here cannot but be attractive: the
textiles alone delight. Arkwright's water frame
enabled cotton to be produced on a large scale,
affordable to a large public. Here are British
cottons printed by woodblock, from the 1720s,
which became popular when imported Indian
chintz was banned in 1701, and roller-printed
from engraved copper plates by 1800.
Embroidered materials were fashionable in the
mid 18th century before giving way to simpler
shapes and materials. Here is a plain shift in
white Indian muslin, *c.*1783, a *chemise à la
Reine* – a style introduced to the French court
by Marie-Antoinette, and a unique survival.

Display and surface decoration were prized
in the 17th century. A woman's cap here
(*c.*1600) is embellished with embroidered
flowers, pea pods, leaves, birds, butterflies
and caterpillars, a bodice (Italian, 1660–80),
with a scrolling leaf design. A man's cap

(1600–10) sports silver thread and coloured silks, with which are embroidered acorns, oak leaves and a phoenix. Fawn leather gloves, soft and stretched, have separate gauntlets decorated with birds, flowers, shells and a pelican in her piety. It would be an unyielding Cunningtonian who could turn away from such sport.

The Cunningtons attached particular importance to undergarments (night dresses, chemises, petticoats, bustles), arguing rightly that they explain much about dress and manners. The layers of undergarments worn by a typical middle-class woman in the mid 19th century made servants (or sisters) a necessity and ensured that such a woman had to live a sedentary, leisured and passive life.

Given the sociological approach of the Cunningtons it seems surprising that none of their costumes here has a documented provenance. Willet Cunnington argued, with blithe disregard for any scientific methodology, 'I was never particularly interested in the personal aspect and I found family histories about specimens were so unreliable as to be worthless.'[125]

Fortunately this anathema did not apply to documents and the Cunningtons collected a vast archive of fashion journals, costume and pattern books, illustrations, caricatures and etiquette books.[126] These were the basis of Willet Cunnington's seminal works, *English Fashion Clothing in the Nineteenth Century* (1937) and *Feminine Attitudes in the Nineteenth Century* (1935) and a series of costume handbooks for each century (1952–59).

The extensive 20th-century collection here includes much Cunningtonian, everyday material: uniforms from both world wars (including those worn by the Women's Land Army and the Red Cross and VAD nurses), suffragette sashes, a siren suit. It also has a post-Second-World-War fashion collection from high-street shops (Wallis, Mary Quant) and from designers (Oscar de la Renta, Courrèges, Jean Muir, Zandra Rhodes).

In 1933 the keeper of the costume collection at the Museum of London, R. E. M. Wheeler, wrote: 'A scientific treatise on the evolution of fashion is indeed long overdue. It is not extravagant to ask that this almost universal phenomenon, clothes, may some day receive a little of the reasoned, analytical and constructive study which in the past has been lavished upon earthworms, pigeons and even potsherds.'[127] Here something of such a study is provided, initiated by Willet and Phillis Cunnington.

IMPERIAL WAR MUSEUM NORTH **

The Quays, Trafford Wharf Road,
Trafford Park, Manchester, Greater
Manchester M17 1TZ
Tel. 0161 836 4000
www.iwm.org.uk/north/index.htm

Libeskind's building dominates: the world broken by war into three shards

The Imperial War Museum in London is object-heavy: there are guns, tanks and planes wherever you look. The Imperial War Museum North is object-light. Those it contains are well chosen and tellingly displayed but take second place to the building, which is itself a metaphor for the museum and its subject.

In designing it, the architect Daniel Libeskind wrote in 1997, 'I have imagined the world broken into fragments and taken to pieces to form a building, three shards that together represent conflict on land, in the air and on water.' On an open site in the Salford Quays opposite the Lowry Centre, the building's central element, the Air Shard, sweeps 158 feet into the air, silver and sheer, above the curve of the main exhibition hall, the Earth Shard, the first and last heroic gesture.

You enter through a small, skewed opening at the base of the shard, so small and low that you almost duck. Inside, in relation to the tower, the shard is hollow, a casing around a tower of scaffolding. If you anticipate some elemental insight into war and air, you will be disappointed, as you may also be by the Water Shard, the museum's restaurant. Thrust out over the water of the Quays it is a handsome site but it is not the Water Shard of a shattered maritime world.

These are quibbles, and they are silenced by the third element, the Earth Shard, the exhibition hall. You step into its low-lit, cavernous space and at once are thrown off balance. Is the floor slipping away to the left? Are the walls straight? Everything is judged to make you ill at ease. Nothing reassures. The walls tower over you. A Harrier jet is suspended in the air just above you. It is a relief to find something familiar: cabinets, set into the walls, lit internally, displaying objects that you would expect to see in a museum that was telling the story of the First World War. Moreover in this stylish cavern some of the objects are brightly coloured and richly textured: the plume of an Austrian Kaiserjaeger, the cockade of the Royal Horse Artillery. This is the world of established custom and ceremony that was swept away.

Further cabinets display rifles, shells, revolvers, entrenching tools. Films on screens show soldiers smiling to the camera as they file along trenches and fix bayonets before going over the top.

Contemporary quotations punctuate films and displays. 'Out of the darkness a great moan came' (Captain Harry Dillon, Oxford-shire and Buckinghamshire Light Infantry, 1914); 'Waiting, watching, suspense, mourning – will there never be anything else in life?' (Vera Brittain, VAD nurse, 1917); 'We live in a world where everyone is living solely to kill his brother man' (Lieut. William St Leger, 2nd Battalion, Coldstream Guards, 1917); 'I sat down in the mud and cried' (Private Jack Sweeney, 1st Battalion, Lincolnshire Regiment, 1916).

Around the walls you can follow the time line of the century: war, peace, war, Cold War, the present. Free-standing silos display exhibitions that explore aspects of war; Science, Technology and War; Women and War; the Legacy of War. In one silo ranks of identical filing cabinets are piled fifty feet high, the bureaucracy of loss and death in which each cabinet records one person's experience. Abraham Silver was a *News of the World*

journalist who became a corporal in the Royal Norfolk Regiment and was taken prisoner when Singapore fell in 1941. Here is his type-writer, which he kept throughout his captivity. William Harrison, a pacifist, joined the No-Conscription Fellowship and was arrested and court-martialled in 1917 when he refused to be called up. He was sentenced to hard labour in Wormwood Scrubs and Newcastle Prison until April 1919.

The museum's time line does not flinch from the complexity or the nihilism of these issues. 'We are all of us made by war, twisted and warped by war, but we seem to forget it. A war does not end with the Armistice,' Doris Lessing wrote in 1994. 'Close your hearts to pity. Act brutally,' was the demand of Adolf Hitler in August 1939.

In the open spaces between silos are free-standing objects, all huge: a Soviet T-34/85 tank from the Second World War, a Rolls Royce Olympus 101 jet engine; a British nuclear bomb, a 'practice bomb', the last one to be dismantled in 1998. It is slim, slight, ten feet long, two feet wide, painted dark khaki green. Its effect was designed to be twenty times that of the bomb that the United States dropped on Nagasaki in 1945. This advanced creation was capable of killing 90 per cent of all life within a two-mile radius of its blast.

Every hour the lights in the hall are turned off and the silos and walls become screens, on which are projected films (*Why War?*; *Weapons of War*; *Children and War*), the scale of whose images immerses you in realised memory, just still transmittable from those few who survive and more than ever essential to recall.

The sound and scale dwarf you. Your eye is pulled from the straight or predictable. You are not ever safe. Everything is at odds. It is a metaphor that is as simple and direct as the vain words expressed by Private Arthur Wrench of the Seaforth Highlanders in 1918: 'Surely this is the last war that will ever be fought between civilised nations.'

PEOPLE'S HISTORY MUSEUM *

The Pump House, Bridge Street, Manchester,
Greater Manchester M3 3ER
Tel. 0161 839 6061
www.peopleshistorymuseum.org.uk

*The museum of Labour history: banners of
protest, banners of trade unions, the blood
of Peterloo*

E. P. Thompson admitted in the first line of its
preface that *The Making of the English Working
Class*[128] had 'a clumsy title, but it is the one that
meets its purpose'.[129] This museum opened in
1975 in London as the National Museum of
Labour History. It adopted its present name
in 1994 when it moved to Manchester's last
surviving hydraulic pumping station on the
bank of the River Irwell.[130] Its original name, if
clumsy, met its purpose.[131]

The galleries, windowless, on two levels, feel
like a shelter or a burrow. On their walls are
banners from the Labour Party and the trade
unions. Banners have always been important
in crusades and campaigns. They raise spirits.
You can rally to them and march under them.

Here are banners old (the 1821 Liverpool
Tinplate Workers Society)[132] and banners new
(the 'March for Jobs' banner of 1986, at 60 feet
the largest banner in the collection); banners
simple ('Arms for Spain')[133] and elaborate (the
magnificent silken banner of the Amalgamated
Stevedores' Labour Protection League, made
for the Great Dock Strike of 1889);[134] banners
homemade (the docks' shop stewards' banner,
made by Diana Cameron, the wife of a seaman,
for £20) and banners professionally designed
(for example, by Walter Crane);[135] banners
verbose (the National Union of Railwaymen's
banner of 1920 with fifteen separate slogans)
and banners cryptic ('Educate, Agitate, Organise', the Central Labour College, 1922).[136]

They look down on the Labour Movement's
iconic objects and relics: a copy of Tom Paine's
The Rights of Man, Part Two (1792), which sold
200,000 copies within a year; his death mask;
the sabre of Captain Robert Hindley, wielded

by him in the attack by Manchester Yeomanry
at Peterloo in which twelve were killed.[137]

Here too are the memorabilia: the emblems
and badges, the certificates and the membership cards that helped bind people together in
a disparate movement. And here are their
heroes: Keir Hardie, William Morris, Joseph
Arch (who formed the National Agricultural
Labourers' Union in 1872 and was elected a
Liberal MP), Clement Attlee, Nye Bevan and
Ben Tillett (whose oratory held together the
dockers in the 1889 strike).

Without support from the national press
for most of its history, there came to be a
premium on communication for the Labour
Movement. The archive here contains pamphlets and leaflets from every major campaign
and election. However it was the image that
was all important and Labour was fortunate to
have the services of Walter Crane, who joined
the Social Democratic Federation in 1884
following the example of his friend and
mentor William Morris. His paintings and
illustrations are elegant but his utopian images
were straightforward: capitalism was a serpent
or a wolf; socialism bore a torch; Crane's
'Angel of Freedom' cheered up many drab
committee rooms.

More forceful and direct are the 20th-
century posters: the pair that Gerald Spencer
Pryce painted for the two 1910 General
Election Campaigns, 'WORKLESS' and 'JOB-
LESS';[138] 'GREET THE DAWN: GIVE LABOUR
ITS CHANCE' by A. S. Meredith for the 1924
general election;[139] and the classic 1945 election
poster designed by John Armstrong, 'AND
NOW WIN THE PEACE, VOTE LABOUR'.[140]

The cartoons here record important
political battles with wit and force: about
freedom of speech (Thomas Rowlandson's
1810 cartoon against the libel laws used to
silence William Cobbett's radical newspaper
The Political Register) and corruption (George
Cruickshank's 1832 support for Lord John
Russell's First Reform Bill sweeping away
rotten boroughs).

While warming itself with the record of past
battles and victories, the museum does not
lose sight of the dark side of these struggles.

The Tolpuddle Martyrs, six Dorset farm workers, were convicted of the crime of forming a branch of Robert Owen's Grand National Union to try to raise their wages of six shillings a week. They were tried and transported to Australia. Their crime was to take an oath of allegiance to the union,[141] the seriousness of which is dramatised here by a tableau that records the initiation oath sworn by James Hogarth when he joined the Tinplate Workers' Society[142] in Liverpool on 4 August 1821: 'I . . . being in the awful presence of Almighty God, do voluntarily declare that I will . . . support a brotherhood known as the Tinplate Workers' Society and . . . if I reveal any of this solemn obligation, may . . . what is now before me[143] plunge my soul into the everlasting pit of misery.'

GALLERY OLDHAM **

Greaves Street, Oldham, Greater Manchester
OL1 1AL
Tel. 0161 911 4653
www.galleryoldham.org.uk

New space-pod gallery on high shows contemporary paintings and fine 18th-century watercolours

Oldham has never been flashy. The new art gallery it built in 2002, designed by architects Pringle Richards Sharratt, won an award in the RIBA North of England category but got little national publicity. This says more about the reluctance of the architectural and art critics of the national media in London to travel north than about the quality of Ian Sharratt's design, a long curved tube of ovoid steel, raised three storeys high.

The city fathers who pushed through the building of the original gallery 120 years before, led by Dr James Yates and Samuel Buckley, had also employed a local architect, Thomas Mitchell. Yates kept faith with the building, even though it cost £26,748, rather than the original estimate of £8,000, and became known as 'Yates's Folly'. The same dogged confidence led the Oldham Corporation to allocate to the gallery an acquisitions budget of £500 a year and to keep spending it for nearly fifty years. Initially most purchases[144] were made from the annual Oldham spring exhibitions, including major works by William Orpen, Alfred Munnings and William Rothenstein. Ernest Normand's Orientalist *Vashti Deposed* (1890) and Samuel Colman's narrative *Belshazzar's Feast* entered the collection by this route, as did the Hon. John Collier's huge *The Death of Cleopatra* (1890), described by the *Manchester Courier* on 6 October 1894 as 'in size as in execution one of the most beautiful productions in any northern corporate collection'; but the gallery was prepared to look elsewhere and purchased Henry Herbert La Thangue's *The Last Furrow* (1893) from an exhibition in Bradford.

Local artists were favoured: Edward Stott of Rochdale, the Oldham landscape artist Charles Potter and, notably, William Stott of Oldham. Stott was the son of an Oldham mill owner, trained in Manchester and at the Beaux-Arts in Paris under Léon Bonnar and J. L. Gerome in 1879, well before La Thangue, Stanhope Forbes and the Newlyn painters ventured to France. Initially Stott's paintings were naturalistic, influenced by Bastien-Lepage, and he won medals at the Paris Salon in 1882. *A Freshet* (c. 1885) is a good example, painted in the open air, capturing the effect of a rush of water, after heavy rain or melting snow, with thin translucent paint. Later he turned to Symbolism: the circular *Venus Born of the Sea Foam*, featuring Whistler's mistress, Maud Franklin, as the goddess, the shore and waves reduced to rhythmic, geometric shapes.

Oldham's distinction comes from the collection of English 18th- and 19th-century watercolours left to the gallery in 1888 by Charles Lees. Lees was the third generation of a successful Oldham manufacturing family, Nonconformist, liberal reformers whose fortune came first from iron and subsequently from cotton. He was educated in Paris and Hanover, and as he began to collect works of art he was introduced to William and George Agnew, the Manchester art dealers, by his father Eli in the early 1870s. His first purchase

from Agnew's was a De Wint landscape in 1870 and in the next five years he bought an early topographical Turner and works by David Cox, John Varley and Miles Cotman, the son of John Sell Cotman. From 1883 the pace of Lees's collecting seems to have quickened and his choices reflect a more conscious effort to put together a collection that represents the golden age of watercolours. Between 1883 and 1885 he bought eight watercolours and drawings by Samuel Prout (six from Prout's visits to France and Italy between 1819 and 1827). Then in the year before he gave the gallery eighty works from his collection, Lees bought two superb late watercolours by J. M. W. Turner (*A Swiss Alpine Valley, c.* 1843 and *Bellinzona – the Bridge over the Ticino, c.* 1842), a complete (seventy-one sheets) set of Turner's *Liber Studiorum*,[145] an early Bonington, and six drawings and two water-colours by John Constable.[146]

This collection has some curious omissions (there are no works by John Sell Cotman) and is relatively weak on the mid 18th century (one Paul Sandby, one Thomas Hearne, no Thomas Gainsborough) but it has two stormy water-colours painted on the one day that John Robert Cozens spent at Paestum, 7 November 1782, on his ill-fated tour with William Beckford. Two other watercolours are of particular interest, copies of paintings by J. R. Cozens. They are attributed to the joint hands of J. M. W. Turner and Thomas Girtin from the time they spent, in 1789–90, at the 'school' of Dr Munro, copying and colouring.

Having given Oldham a substantial part of his watercolour collection, Lees seems to have turned to collecting oil paintings, by G. F. Watts (*Aurora*), J. E. Millais (*The Departure of the Crusaders*) and I. H. J. T. Fantin-Latour (*Roses II*), a rare purchase of the work of a foreign artist. Some paintings he bought dir-ect from the artist: *Phyllis* (1880) by George Clausen and *Circe Offering the Cup to Ulysses* (1891) by John William Waterhouse. These oil paintings and a watercolour by D. G. Rossetti,

Circe Offering the Cup to Ulysses by J. W. Waterhouse (Gallery Oldham)

Horatio Discovering the Madness of Ophelia, were given to the gallery after Lees's death by his daughter Marjory, as was a portrait, by John Pettie, of Lees, the resolute Victorian paterfamilias, luxuriant beard, clear eye fixed on the middle distance. In March 2004 the National Art Collections Fund added signifi-cantly to the collection of works on paper with the gift of fifty-five works including examples by Millais, Lord Leighton and Landseer.

Since the Second World War, the gallery has continued to buy contemporary paintings, often from the John Moores exhibitions in Liverpool (David Hockney's *Myself and My Heroes*, 1961, R. B. Kitaj's *Go and Get Killed Comrades*, 1966). More recently, the Contem-porary Art Society has built on its gifts of work by Howard Hodgkin and Mark Gertler, and pre-war studio pottery, with excellent pieces by Yasumasa Morimura and the British artist Laura Ford. The work of younger artists who are outside the London gallery loop has been added: Iftikhar Dadi, Nudrat Afza and Aneila Majid, and a significant collection of paintings by Bangladeshi artists, exhibiting, as in 1883, the gallery's confidence and lack of side.

HARRIS MUSEUM AND ART GALLERY **

Market Square, Preston, Lancashire PR1 2PP
Tel. 01772 258248
www.visitpreston.com/harris

Grand building, grand collections; Arthur Devis to the fore

There is no regional museum and gallery that has a more splendid setting than the Harris Museum and Art Gallery. The building was designed by the 'widely unknown'[147] architect and alderman James Hibbert, following a £300,000 bequest by Edward Robert Harris, a local lawyer. It is a magnificent mixture of German neo-classical certainty (fluted Ionic columns, sculptured pediment, giant pila-sters) and elegant French vainglory (a central rotunda and lantern, influenced by Les Invalides in Paris).

On the pediment over the entrance is the dedication 'TO LITERATURE, ARTS AND SCIENCE' and the promise that 'the mental riches you may here acquire abide with you always.'

Inside there is a plaster cast, by Bertel Thorvaldsen, of the *Alexander Frieze*, made to celebrate Napoleon's entry into Rome in 1812, comparing Napoleon with Alexander. When Napoleon failed to enter Rome it was kept in the Palazzo Quirinale and later two marble friezes were made from it, of which only one survives. The cast here was made for the International Exhibition in London in 1862, from where it went to the Victoria and Albert Museum and, in 1987, to the Harris, as a gift.

In case the visitor misses these hints about the importance of the building, beneath the central rotunda are *The Gates of Paradise*, a copy of the monumental doors to the Baptistry of the Duomo in Florence, made by Lorenzo Ghiberti in the 15th century. So elaborate are they that Ghiberti took fifty-two years to complete them, having been commissioned at the age of twenty-two. It was Michelangelo who named them. The originals are in bronze; the Harris's are in plaster, gilded, but the beauty and power of this Renaissance masterwork remain and make a bold statement about the seriousness and ambition of this museum.

The declamatory statement made by the building invites the expectation of collections of equal grandeur. The Harris does have good collections of fine and decorative arts (18th- and 19th-century English watercolours; portraits by Preston-born Arthur Devis and his family; some bronzes; scent bottles; coloured English glass; contemporary photography) but they are in a quieter mode.

Although between 1740 and 1760 Arthur Devis had one of the most successful portrait practices in London, he never succeeded in freeing himself from the limitations of the conversation pieces for which he is best known. He was so eclipsed by the rising reputations of his near-contemporaries Reynolds, Gainsborough and Zoffany that he died in obscurity in 1787 and remained largely forgotten for 150 years until his work was reappraised in the 1930s by the then curator of the Harris, Sidney Pavière.

A subsequent keeper of fine art, Stephen Sartin, curated a major Devis exhibition with the National Portrait Gallery (q.v.) in 1983–84 and his work here demonstrates his talents.[148]

Devis's conversation pieces showing figures in idealised landscapes or interiors were posed works of artifice. They existed in a doll's house world. Indeed Devis habitually used lay figures in constructing his compositions and as substitutes for the sitters. One of these lay figures or dolls, about thirty inches in height, with its own wardrobe of clothes, including a petticoat, shoes and socks, is in the museum's collection.

Inevitably Devis's figures have a manikin stiffness, not unlike early Gainsboroughs such as *Mr and Mrs Andrews* (c. 1750),[149] *Heneage Lloyd and his Sister* (c. 1750)[150] or the *Byam Children*,[151] but Devis lacks Gainsborough's or Reynolds's mastery of light and their psychological penetration.

The early portraits of his wife, *Elizabeth Faulkner* (c. 1742), and of *John Orlebar, of Hinwick House, Bedfordshire* (c. 1740) demonstrate his skill in depicting costume and fabrics, while the portraits of *Rev William Farington of Leigh* (c. 1741–2) and of *Nicholas Fazackerley, MP, Recorder of Preston* (1763), stern Lancastrians of substance, show that he was not solely a painter of fêtes galantes and polite tableaux. In the 1740s and '50s Preston was a Jacobite town, dominated by its town council, of which Devis's father was a member. This may account for his lack of critical reputation in Hanoverian London. Neither Horace Walpole nor Joseph Farington mentions him, despite his painting the latter's father; nor was he invited to donate work to Thomas Coram's Foundling Hospital, unlike Hogarth, Hayman, Hudson, Highmore and the young Gainsborough.

The Harris has works by Joseph Highmore and Jonathan Richardson, which place Devis in context. There are landscapes by his brother, Anthony Devis, and portraits by his son, Arthur William Devis, whose most famous work, *The Death of Nelson*, is at the National Maritime Museum (q.v.). Here he is represented by portraits he made in India. Their conventional likenesses are redeemed by the way he captures the wet brown light of India.

A founding benefactor of the museum, Richard Newsham, bequeathed his collection of British paintings in 1883. His taste was uneven. A strong Frank Dicksee and a confident David Roberts hang beside less distinguished work by Augustus Leopold Egg, E. M. Ward and Frederick Goodall, to which have been added paintings by Lord Leighton, a huge biblical Francis Danby, and many oils and watercolours by David Cox, including an excellent landscape, *Lancaster Sands*.

In the 20th-century collection there are paintings by Walter Sickert, Charles Ginner and Spencer Gore; by Augustus John and Roger Fry; and by Stanley Spencer and, unusually, by Spencer's first wife, Hilda Carline. Even less predictably there are portraits by Gerald Brockhurst (*Dorette*) and Sir James Gunn (*Pauline in the Yellow Dress*, 1944) which show how stylish and underrated these society portraitists were and are.

The Harris has a strong collection of bronzes (Gilbert Bayes, Hamo Thornycroft, Thomas Brock, Alfred Gilbert, Jacob Epstein), and collections of costume and of ceramics. Its glass collections include the Laura Seddon Collection of 18th- and 19th-century coloured English glass, one of the most important outside the Victoria and Albert Museum (q.v.), and the largest collection of scent bottles in the country, the Mrs Idonea French Collection of 2,700 mainly 19th-century pieces.

The Seddon Collection contains glasses, jugs and bowls from a range of factories: Bristol, Nailsea, Wrockwardine, Newent and Stourbridge; 18th-century wine glasses of sea green, emerald green and sapphire blue, some gadrooned and collared, some with waisted stems and knops; and cream jugs with reticulated moulding, or wrythen-moulded. A jug and bowl of blue and white latticino (*c.*1800) and a green jug, splashed red with white flecks, made in Shropshire (*c.*1820), catch the eye.

The Harris is that comparative rarity, a gallery with confidence in its works on paper. In 1925 the Revd John Park Haslam bequeathed fifty-five watercolours including two early Turners (*Southwell Minster from the North West c.*1795, and *West Front of Salisbury Cathedral, c.*1799) and *Kidwelly Castle, Carmarthenshire* (1833), in which the castle emerges out of a haze of light and colour, scratchings and rubbings. He also gave a sentimental, visionary late Samuel Palmer (*The Dawn of Life, c.*1865) and a beautiful 13th-century illuminated psalter once owned by John Ruskin.

Individually these collections may not be in the major key announced by Hibbert's building but they more than fulfil the inscripted promise to offer 'mental riches' that may 'abide with you always'.

LOWRY CENTRE **

Pier 8, Salford Quays, Lancashire M50 3AZ
Tel. 0870 111 2000
www.thelowry.com

Quayside spread commemorates one of Britain's most characteristically loved and characteristic artists

You will find a painting by L. S. Lowry in almost every city art gallery from Aberdeen to Southampton, from Norwich to Kirkcaldy, from Belfast to Bedford. More than forty galleries have examples of his work but only the Manchester Art Gallery (nineteen), the Tate (eight) and the Whitworth Art Gallery (all q.v.) have more than two or three. If you want to take a good look at Lowry, you must go to Salford, to the Lowry Centre, designed by Michael Wilford. The collection that the Salford Art Gallery and Museum has built, of over three hundred and fifty paintings and drawings, was moved in 2000 to the Lowry, where it is now displayed thematically in changing exhibitions.

Only here will you be able to see the range of his painting and have a chance to question the received ideas about his work: that he is limited, naïf, primitive: that he could not draw; that his work is repetitive, undemanding painting for people who do not like paintings.

It is true that his paintings of industrial

L. S. Lowry's Seascape *(Lowry Centre)*

scenes are familiar, reproductions of them having been displayed in classrooms for the past fifty years. He is reproduced widely because he reproduces well. The contrast between his figures and their white backgrounds is sharp. His colours, burnt sienna, umber, dark green, white and black, are clear, though reproductions do not do justice to his brushwork or to his cautious handling of paint. His drawings are rarely reproduced.

The Lowry's collection, which spans his working life from 1906 to 1973, allows you to see his development, his strengths and his weaknesses. Far from being a self-taught primitive, an Alfred Wallis of the industrial

north, he spent twelve laborious years at art school and took the best part of twenty years to discover his own style.

Lowry's first teacher was William Fitz, a German painter working in Manchester. His drawings in 1906 and a still life in oils show a painstaking student. When he enrolled at the Manchester School of Art and attended the classes of Adolphe Valette, he began to absorb some elements of Impressionism, as may be seen in two landscapes, *Country Lane* (1914) and *Landscape* (1912), while his drawings (*Figure Studies*, 1920, *Pages for Anatomical Sketchbook*, 1919) were vital to him throughout his life, and grew in confidence and competence.

The collection does not quite identify the

moment in 1916 when Lowry came out of Pendlebury station, saw looming at the end of the street the hulk of the Acme Spinning Company's mill and knew that this was the world he wanted to paint, but *Coming From the Mill* (*c.*1917–18) comes close to doing so, while a comparison between that and the 1930 picture of the same title tells you much about his development in the 1920s. He paints the same set of buildings from the same spot with the same pony and trap and the same handcart in the same positions, with the same strip of grimy grass and railings in the foreground holding the viewer back from the scene. By 1930 he had taken the advice of Bernard D. Taylor, one of his tutors at Salford School of Art and the art critic of the *Manchester Guardian*, who persuaded him to paint his figures against a white background. He had introduced colour (red, green, umber) and, most important of all, he had filled his street with people, not upright as in 1917, but bent, thin-legged bodies, caught in movement, the adults (though not the children) with their heads down, silent.

He developed these figures in these settings through the 1920s. He made numerous drawings from the windows of Salford School of Art of people below in Peel Park; these culminated in *Bandstand, Peel Park, Salford* (1928) and *Street Scene* (1925). At the same time he was drawing seascapes, landscapes, churches and other buildings.

The collection now charts a desperate period. In 1932 his father died and his mother, who was the centre of his life, took to her bed. He nursed her every evening when he returned from his work as a rent collector, and virtually stopped painting. Of work produced between 1906 and 1932, the Lowry has 170 drawings and paintings. Between then and 1939, there are only eight.

However he exhibited on eight occasions in London at the Royal Academy and the New English Art Club, in Edinburgh at the Scottish Royal Academy, in Salford and in Paris. In 1939 his work was seen by Alexander Reid of the Lefevre Gallery, who gave him a one-man show. The Tate, having acquired *Coming Out of School* in 1927 for its loan collection, at last bought a work, *Dwellings, Ordsall Lane, Salford* (1927) for the main gallery. Other public galleries followed suit and by 1950 there were thirty-seven Lowrys in public collections. Most are industrial northern scenes, with figures.

Despite these purchases, and contributions to twenty exhibitions, the 1940s were a fallow period for his painting. As he produced more in the 1950s his range of subjects widened: more landscapes, seascapes, churches and, for the first time, studies of single figures. As the spinning mills and terraced streets of Manchester were demolished he ceased to produce 'typical' street scenes.

When he did, they lack architectural backgrounds and as in *The Cripples* (1949) faces and bodies are distorted, becoming more clown-like, humours rather than individuals. Lowry is often accused of lacking emotion. In *The Cripples, The Funeral Party* (1953) and in individual studies (*Gentleman Looking at Something*, 1960) he views people with attention and curiosity rather than compassion. In a letter of 13 September 1948 he wrote: '*The Cripples* picture is progressing – I have operated on one of the gentlemen in the far distance and given him a wooden leg – . . . I still laugh heartily at the hook on the arm of the gentleman . . . that suggestion of yours was a master stroke.'[152]

The emotions in these works may be restrained but they are intense. The landscapes are of hills stripped of people or trees but those hills are weighted with feeling. *Seascape* (1952) has not a pebble, not a boat, not even a cloud, just flat sea and sky, from both of which colour has been withdrawn equally. It was not a popular success. Lowry commented, 'It took me 18 months to paint and I think it is one of the best things I've done.'[153] Only in two heads did he allow the viewer to be confronted by direct emotions: *Head of a Man* (1938) and *A Young Man* (1955) in Tate Britain. In both the eyes stare straight ahead, the pupils distended, locked in parallel, the head four-square, breath held. He painted *Head of a Man* after the death of his mother. It is an imaginary portrait or a portrait of his imagination, an inward scream. 'It was just a way of letting off steam, I suppose,' he remarked to a friend.[154]

This collection gives the lie to charges that Lowry was technically naïf or incompetent. The variety of his brushstrokes, his use of the palette knife, his pencil line, his scratching of the surface all demonstrate his proficiency. Few artists can have worked white ground with such patient determination or produced so many tones: look at the loaded brushstrokes in the street and sky in *Winter in Pendlebury* (1943) or the enamelled calm of sea and sky in *The Estuary* (1956).

Much of his inner life is kept out of his paintings: his love of opera, especially Bellini, learnt from his mother; his passion for Rossetti (of whose works he owned twelve), the eccentric single luxury he allowed himself in the 1950s and '60s as he became richer. Those few aspects of the world around him in which he was interested he looked at with quiet sustained attention; the resultant paintings and drawings repay similar concentration.

SALFORD MUSEUM AND ART GALLERY *

Peel Park, The Crescent, Salford, Lancashire
M5 4WU
Tel. 0161 736 2649
www.salfordmuseum.org/

Any early L. S. Lowry not at his new centre: another Victorian collection formed by Agnew's

For fifty years L. S. Lowry provided the reason to visit Salford Museum and Art Gallery. It was the perfect place for his collection. He had attended Salford College of Art, on the same site, from 1923 to 1938 and had a strong allegiance to both college and town. As you look out of the gallery's windows you see the views of Peel Park that he drew again and again. But with the opening of the Lowry Centre in 2000 (q.v.) his work was moved to Salford Quays, tearing the heart out of the gallery – or so you would have thought. It did reduce the collection and exposed how few works had been purchased or bequeathed in

the 20th century; but it revealed a Victorian collection that, although not distinguished, has some interesting aspects.

A considerable number of these pictures had been purchased either from the Manchester art dealers Agnew and Zanetti or on their advice.

All the popular Victorian genres are here: biblical paintings (Frederick Goodall, *The Sheep Shearing (Egypt)*, 1892, G. F. Watts, *The Meeting of Esau and Jacob*); seascapes (C. Napier Henry, *St Ives Harbour*, 1896, Alfred Montague's huge and dramatic *Ship on Fire*, 1856); historical (two monumental E. M. Wards, *The Last Sleep of the Earl of Argyll* and *The Execution of the Marquis of Montrose*, G. E. Marshall's *Our Island Story* in pictorial form).

Heavy, over-coloured, innocent, they tell the story of the Royal Academy in the mid 19th century. In this company a Crome, a Constable and a Nasmyth stand out, as does a small collection of good watercolours by Paul Sandby, George Barret Jnr, Samuel Prout and Frances Oliver Finch.

Agnew's cemented their relationship with the gallery with gifts: *The Bay of Tangier* by Edward Cooke, *Ptarmigan* by R. Ansell and two portraits by Lawrence of Antonio Canova and of John Philip Kemble.

Salford has one curiosity, hanging at the top of the main staircase: a panoramic portrait of *The Fancy Dress Ball* at the 1828 Manchester music festival, painted by Arthur Percival. Percival had turned his hand to most genres – Shakespearean, biblical, historical – and failed at them all. With 3,500 people attending the ball, including Robert Peel, the Home Secretary, he has seemingly shoehorned all of them on to his canvas (costumes provided by Nathans of London). Percival's colour is crude and his composition rudimentary. The several pentimenti emphasise regret.

This massive mess was exhibited for eight weeks at Agnew and Zanetti's gallery. When it failed to find a buyer it was raffled. Percival thereafter devoted his career to miniatures.

Although the Lowry Collection has moved, Salford is not without some examples of his work. The student sketches of Peel Park remain, views of the terrace, the steps, the bandstand and of what he could see from the art school windows. In conversation with the critic Maurice Collis in 1951, Lowry said, 'From the start I have been fond of this view and have put it into many of my paintings. You know that I never paint on the spot but look for a long time, make drawings and think.'

ASTLEY CHEETHAM ART GALLERY *

Trinity Street, Stalybridge, Lancashire
SK15 2BN
Tel. 0161 338 6767
www.tameside.gov.uk

Small but glittering; Italian paintings of the 14th and 15th centuries

John Frederick Cheetham's great-grandfather, George Cheetham, came to Stalybridge from the Isle of Man in the 1780s when 'Stalybridge was little more than a bridge, when the river which flows through it was a babbling brook of pure crystal water.'[155] He brought with him an innovative carding machine and set up in business.

The Cheethams did well. John Frederick (1835–1916) and his father John (1802–86) became Liberal Members of Parliament and both collected pictures, the father sitting on the general council[156] of the Exhibition of Art Treasures in Manchester.

It is not clear from family records who bought what, when,[157] but on John Frederick Cheetham's death in 1916 their collection, much of it acquired with the help and advice of Agnew's in Manchester and from William Graham's 1886 sale, included pictures by David Cox, Edward Burne-Jones, G. F. Watts, Clarkson Stanfield, Richard Parkes Bonington and Samuel Prout. In this it was not dissimilar from other contemporary collections – Charles Lees of Oldham (Gallery Oldham, q.v.) and Thomas Wrigley of Bury (Bury Art Gallery and Museum, q.v.) who also bought through

Agnew's. What sets the collection apart is the Cheethams' taste for late-14th-century Florentine artists: Masaccio, Luini, Cimabue, Giotto. The 'Cimabue' has since been reattributed to Jacopo di Cione,[158] the brother of Andrea Orcagna, and the 'Giotto' to the Master of the Straus Madonna,[159] but both are masterworks chosen by someone with taste and confidence.

Di Cione's *Virgin and Child with Two Adoring Angels* (c.1380) is the central panel of an altarpiece. At the Virgin's feet are two adoring, supplicant angels; around the Christ child's neck is a coral necklace; behind them is a richly patterned background. The angels, the Virgin's hooded eyes and her long fingers are consistent with the twelve 'Style of Orcagna' works in the National Gallery (q.v.).[160] In the *Virgin and Child Enthroned with Angels and Saints* by the Master of the Straus Madonna (c.1410), from a small altarpiece, the Virgin and Child are flanked by two angels and four saints. At the Virgin's feet lies Eve holding a tiny Tree of Knowledge, with one pear-like apple, and wearing a diaphanous dress. As with the earlier di Cione, the background is richly gilded and patterned.[161]

John Frederick Cheetham left these, a third Florentine triptych and 27 other oils, 16 watercolours and 17 engravings[162] to the Astley Cheetham Gallery, which he and his wife had built as a public library, designed by J. Medland Taylor, in 1901.

The use of the library to exhibit paintings was formalised in 1932, when the art gallery was established. Since then a number of 20th-century drawings and paintings have been acquired: a late (1943), delicate Wyndham Lewis drawing of a *Head of a Boy*, a world away from *Blast*; a Thomas Monnington given by the Contemporary Art Society in 1956; a Mark Gertler oil, *Daffodils* (1914); a Cedric Morris, *The Heron* (1941), rare in an English regional collection and, recently, some prints by David Jones. However it is the Florentine altarpieces that bring distinction to this small collection.[163]

QUARRY BANK MILL *

Styal, nr. Wilmslow, Cheshire sk9 4la
Tel. 01625 527468
www.quarrybankmill.org.uk

*Georgian textile mill in wooded valley, powered
by a giant wheel and the rushing might of water*

Until James Watt harnessed Newcomen's
engine to produce steam, the power demanded
by the Industrial Revolution came from rivers.
At Quarry Bank the River Bollin has a natural
fall of fifteen feet. When forced by a headrace
through a narrow channel its flow provided
all the power that Samuel Greg needed for the
cotton mill he built here in 1784.

Greg chose a dramatic spot in a narrow,
deep valley, heavily wooded with beech, oak
and pine. To reach the mill/museum you
descend by a steep path, glimpsing between the
trees the roofs of the five-storey mill buildings
below, hearing the rush of the river over the
weir that Greg made when he needed the
greater power required for weaving.

Five generations of the Greg family lived
here and ran the mill until ownership was
transferred to the National Trust in 1939. The
mill ceased production in 1959 and opened as
a museum in 1978, one of the first 'working
museums', directed initially by David Sekers,
who had created the Gladstone Pottery
Museum (q.v.) in 1974.

Quarry Bank shows how the cotton industry
developed and prospered in the late 18th
century as a rural manufacturing industry,
how cotton was prepared and processed,
and how mill workers, adults and children,
lived.

Samuel Greg chose the right moment.
Arkwright had developed his water frame,
the first cotton-spinning machine, only fifteen
years before, in 1769, and Greg caught the
resulting wave of expansion in demand and
technology.[164] When he died in 1834 he was
worth £314,000 (approximately £13 million in

Di Cione's Madonna and Child with Angels
(Astley Cheetham Art Gallery)

today's money) and at their flush of wealth
the Greg family owned five mills employing
2,000 people.

Inside the mill the architecture is largely
unchanged: open-plan floors allowed the
workers to be supervised and the maximum
number of machines to be accommodated.
The processes of turning cotton into cloth
(drawing, carding, spinning and weaving)
have not changed significantly; nor have the
machines, intact and in place: the 1880 bobbin
winding machine worked here well into the
20th century. Gone are the noise and the heat
and the air thick with fibres that caught in
the throats of all who worked here. These you
must imagine for yourself. The noises of the
mill are the same, in tone if not in volume: the
chatter of the smaller machines (plaiting,
drawing in), clacking, clicking; the throstle
of the spinning frame, a high-pitched singing;
the mumbling bass of the great wheel and the
incessant snaredrum of the rushing water. This
industrial orchestra played at deafening pitch
ceaselessly for sixteen hours a day.

Quarry Bank conveys the family nature of
18th- and 19th-century manufacturing that
shaped the lives of owners as it did of operatives. Here is a huge portrait of the family in
Belfast from which Samuel Greg came, and
here are the Greg family Bible (1800), family
letters and Samuel Greg's will of 1833. Here too
are the papers binding an eleven-year-old boy,
Thomas Podmore, to be apprenticed until the
age of twenty-one, signed over by his father.
The five generations of Gregs working here are
matched by six generations of the Venables
family, all mill-hands, from Robert Venables,
born 1745, to Alice Venables, born 1898.

The museum's archives document the wages
and rents (for tied property) and the truck
system that linked shop and mill, both owned
by the Gregs, in a closed cycle of labour, wages,
food and goods. The cost of all food and
goods was deducted from the wages. Working
conditions, fines, punishments and accidents
are also recorded as 19th-century legislation
began to exert some minimal regulation on
manufacturing.

Wherever you are in the mill you are

conscious of the power that flows under and through the building, of water and the great wheel. This replaced the original wheel in 1818, designed by the leading designer Walter Fairbairn. It was augmented by a steam-powered Boulton & Watt beam engine in the 1830s and finally in 1905 by two turbine engines. In the darkness underground you can stand close by and watch the slow beauty of the gears, horizontal and vertical, large and small. You look down into the heart of the wheel, the lumber of gears and the endless rush of water.

The Great Wheel at Quarry Bank Mill

LADY LEVER (NATIONAL MUSEUMS, LIVERPOOL) ★★★★

Lower Road, Port Sunlight Village, Wirral, Cheshire CH62 5EQ
Tel. 0151 478 4136
www.ladyleverartgallery.org.uk

Soap magnate's Port Sunlight model gallery: Pre-Raphaelites, Leighton, Alma-Tadema, period rooms, statuary, the lot

Few museums or galleries reflect or express the taste of one person. The Wallace Collection covers three generations of the Hertford family. The Courtauld Collection has been augmented by many subsequent collections. The gallery that William Hesketh Lever, 1st Lord Leverhulme, built in memory of his wife, is an exception.

His interests were wide: 18th- and 19th-century English paintings, sculpture, furniture and ceramics; Roman and Greek marbles; Chinese ceramics and Gobelins tapestries.

The origins of his collecting were crudely commercial. He wanted paintings that would advertise the delights of his prize product, Lever Brothers' Sunlight Soap. His acquisition in 1889 of W. P. Frith's *The New Frock* produced a fierce public argument with the artist. Frith's title for this painting of a pretty little girl holding up her spotless apron was 'Vanity of vanities, all is vanity'. Lever scrubbed away the irony and turned this on its head. It was the first of a series of sentimental pictures that he bought and was followed by John Collier's *The Water Baby*.

These, together with his purchase of a large manor house, started his collecting. In 1896 he met James Orrock, a dentist who had become a self-taught artist, connoisseur and dealer. Orrock's advice could be flawed. He acquired for Lever several pastiches or misattributions of 'Constable', 'Crome', 'Gainsborough' (probably a Thomas Barker landscape), 'Raeburn', 'Romney' and 'Ramsay'. But at a time when scholarship and attributions were often insecure, much of Orrock's advice was good.

Lever struck off on his own when he fell in love with the work of Frederic Leighton and, later, J. E. Millais. His four Leightons, two from the 1870s (*Psamathe* and *The Daphnephoria*) and two late works (*Fatidica* and *The Garden of the Hesperides*) make a stronger grouping than in any other gallery in Britain (including Tate Britain, the Fitzwilliam Museum and Manchester Art Gallery, all q.v.).

He bought *Psamathe* and *Fatidica*, both strong single classical figures, in 1893 and 1894. The others he acquired as part of the George McCulloch Collection sale in 1913. *The Daphnephoria*, in a prime position on the end wall of the Main Hall, shows Leighton's undoubted skill at grand composition (unmatched by any of his British contemporaries). Despite its ambition and organisation, though, it fails to come to life. The heavily symbolist *Garden of the Hesperides* (snake, mammary oranges, white birds) subverts its roundel with the three sisters forming a triangle around

which writhes the serpent. Together they show the great skills and lurking weaknesses of Leighton.

Orrock's influence is clear in Lever's collection of British portraits and landscapes from the period 1750–1850. There is a glorious late (*c.* 1840) Turner, *The Falls of Clyde*,[165] related to a large 1802 watercolour now in the Walker Art Gallery (q.v.), an excellent Crome, and Constable's *Cottage at East Bergholt*.

Apart from one classical landscape by Richard Wilson, the 18th-century works are all portraits, including unusually good examples by Romney, of *Sarah Rodbard*, and Hoppner, of *Lady Elizabeth Howard*. The Reynoldses are uneven. *Mrs Paine and her Daughters* (1767), *Mrs Fortescue* (*c.* 1750) and *Mrs Seaforth and Child* (1787) are all unsatisfactory, awkward works, but *Elizabeth Gunning* (1760) and *Mrs Peter Beckford* (1782) show Reynolds at his grand academic best, both being graced with impossibly elongated legs and complemented by classical allusions (doves, sculptures, a libation of Hygeia.)

Much of the outstanding collection of furniture is arranged in five 'period rooms', Tudor and Stuart, William and Mary, early 18th century, Adam and the Napoleon Room. It includes an exceptional collection of Palladian-style pieces (1720–40s) influenced by William Kent: chairs by Thomas Moore (1734), a side table from Stowe (1730) with powerful claw feet, gilded satyrs and a mask of Diana with a crescent moon in her hair; a mahogany cabinet from Kirtlington Park, Oxfordshire, with a bold design of acanthus scrolls on either side of a central scallop, showing that William Hallett's carving was as clear as his design. The collection's greatest strength is in its tracing of the development of the late 18th-century commode; these were Lever's favourite pieces. Here we can see the influence of the Paris-trained Swedish cabinet maker, Christopher Fuhrlohg, delicate marquetry surrounding a medallion after Angelica Kauffmann. He was employed briefly by John Linnell, whose piece here has a sumptuous marquetry palette of maple, purplewood, rosewood, holly, sycamore and walnut.

There are more fine commodes by Thomas Chippendale (1760), related to the Diana and Minerva commode he made for Harewood House (q.v.) (c.1767); by John Cobb; and by John Mayhew and William Ince, whose numerous pieces here range from the austere box-like shape of a commode for Lord Douglas (1773) to the elaborate work he did for Derby House (1775–80) to go in Robert Adam's Etruscan interior. It is an exceedingly fine collection, celebrating the heights of English cabinet making in the late 18th century.

It is perhaps strange that the most dramatic piece is anonymous: a cabinet-on-stand (c.1820–30), a collector's cabinet, made probably to hold specimens, each drawer veneered in a different wood, amboyna, padouk, pollard oak, etc. Inspired by Chippendale's designs for 'China Cases' in *The Gentleman and Cabinet-maker's Director*, it stands there, opens its unornamented doors and demands applause.

From the turn of the century Lever began to collect in a still more determined way with the aim of creating a public museum. Increasingly he bought existing collections, in whole or in part. Lord Tweedmouth's ceramics collection (acquired 1905) brought him a trove of Wedgwood, equalled only by the Wedgwood Museum,[166] strong on all types of jasperware (blue, green, lilac, yellow, pink). It included a 'first edition' copy of the Portland vase, John Flaxman plaques, black basalt vases (including a pair of the British Museum's *The Apotheosis of Homer*, also by Flaxman), and the Wedgwood enamel plaques on which George Stubbs painted a self-portrait and his *Haymaking* series.

There followed the Bennett Collection of Chinese ceramics (1911 and 1916); his acquisition of Greek and Roman antiquities from the dealer Moss Harris and from the 1917 sale of Thomas Hope's 18th-century collection; the

Gobelins (1915) and Mortlake (1918) tapestries of Sir James Matheson and Sir John Cowen, respectively; and the armour of Herbert Graystone (1923). This last, he believed, would be 'an attraction for those at the Gallery who . . . do not particularly admire pictures, statuary etc. I have to cater for all tastes at the Gallery.'

That calculation did not inform his purchase of the collection he liked most, that of Australian sheep magnate George McCulloch in 1913, with which he gained a significant number of the Pre-Raphaelites he loved. On occasion this love led astray his judgement. There are good examples here of Rossetti and Burne-Jones but there is also Holman Hunt's execrable *The Scapegoat* and indifferent works by Millais and Ford Madox Brown.

In the same year as the McCulloch sale he drew up the first plans for the gallery. A month later his wife died. The building, in an unmagical quasi-classical style, designed by William and Segar Owen, is sited impressively at the end of a wide, tree-lined avenue. It fails to rise to the setting and is surrounded by the Arts and Crafts estate that Lever built for his workers at Port Sunlight. Beneath the Portland stone cladding, the construction is of reinforced concrete.

Inside, the design works well, the top-lit Main Hall being flanked by smaller galleries. That hall, dominated by Leighton, the Pre-Raphaelites and very much lesser Victorians such as William Orchardson, Samuel Fildes, Edward Gregory and George Mason, gives a false impression of the collection as a whole. Lever had an aesthetic sweet tooth: he was drawn to classical nudes of monumental beauty (Maurice Ferrary, Edward Onslow Ford). He was not a connoisseur, but he was serious. His passion runs through this remarkable collection.

The Lady Lever art gallery

The North-east

Hadrian's Wall marked the northern limits of the Roman Empire. Since it was garrisoned for more than two hundred years it is not surprising that signs of Roman occupation are everywhere in the area. Two museums, Arbeia and Segedunum, on either bank of the River Tyne, are included in this book, but there are further museums inland along the wall, at Corbridge (English Heritage), Vindolanda at Hexham, and at Chesters (also English Heritage), where the excavations of the 19th-century antiquary John Clayton are exhibited in a small museum, designed by Richard Norman Shaw in 1895 and largely unchanged. Further south the Roman fort at Binchester, near Bishop Auckland, was one of a series of forts that guarded the Roman army's supply lines.

The region's industries (coal mining, ship building, glass) are represented at the Discovery Museum in Newcastle, at Beamish and in the Sunderland Museum and Art Gallery. The Hartlepool Maritime Museum (not included here) celebrates the decades in the mid 19th century when this was the third busiest port in Britain, with coal from the collieries inland coming by rail to the sea.

This is not a region with a large number of great houses, but Alnwick Castle and Wallington (neither of them included here) would stand out anywhere. Within Alnwick's forbidding castle walls are interiors by Robert Adam (Gothicised Georgian) and Anthony Salvin (Victorian), in which are paintings by Titian, Palma Vecchio, Van Dyck, Lely, Canaletto and Turner. So many are there that Raphael's *Madonna of the Pinks* hung unsung in an upstairs corridor, before being 'rediscovered', loaned to, and, in 2004, sold to the National Gallery.

Wallington is in border rievers' country. It was the home first of the coal-magnate Blacketts (who employed a local boy, Lancelot 'Capability' Brown, to landscape the grounds and who imported Italian plasterers, who lived in the village and modelled the magnificent ceilings), and then of the radical Trevelyans, who enclosed the central courtyard and commissioned William Scott Bell to decorate it with improving murals (*The Triumph of Iron and Coal*). Around the house are portraits by Reynolds, Gainsborough and

Northumberland

NEWCASTLE-UPON-TYNE ○

WALLSEND ○

A1058

River Tyn

A695

Tyne and Wear

STOCKSFIELD ○

GATESHEAD ○

A167

A1(M)

A6

DURHAM ○

Durham

A688

A688

A67

A1(M)

A67

BARNARD CASTLE ○

A67

10 miles

SOUTH SHIELDS

SUNDERLAND

A1018

A19

A19

Cleveland

MIDDLESBROUGH

A66

Romney, and a superb collection of porcelain that includes every great mark (Chinese, Japanese, Italian maiolica, Bow, Chelsea, Wedgwood, Sèvres and Meissen – *The Continents*, modelled by Johann Joachim Kændler). Wallington also has a great library and the desks at which Lord Macaulay, a Trevelyan relation, wrote his *History of England* and Sir George Otto Trevelyan wrote *The American Revolutions.*

Of the local museums I regret that I have not found room for Redcar, which has the oldest lifeboat in the world, the oak-built *Zetland*, in service from 1800 to 1878, nor for Berwick, which, within Britain's first purpose-built army barracks, houses a chamber version of the collection that Sir William Burrell, who lived at nearby Hutton, gave to Glasgow (v. the Burrell Collection): Impressionist paintings, medieval chalices and woodwork, Roman and Venetian glass and Imari pottery.

BOWES MUSEUM ****

Newgate, Barnard Castle, Durham DL12 8NP
Tel. 01833 690606
www.bowesmuseum.org.uk

French chateau in the moors, Spanish paintings in the chateau

The English have never much liked or understood El Greco.[1] He is held to be too morbid, too hysterical. Spanish painting in general is cordially ignored. Only the immaculate surfaces of Velásquez and the raw passion of Goya manage to avoid this blindness. So it is incongruous that in a high, remote stretch of the Durham countryside there should be one of the best collections of Spanish paintings outside the National Gallery[2] and the National Gallery of Scotland (both q.v.), and that at its heart should be El Greco's *The Tears of St Peter* (*c.* late 1580s/early 1590s).

It is here almost by accident. John Bowes bought it in 1869 with considerable reluctance for 200 francs as part of the collection of the exiled Condé de Quinto.[3] Bowes's agent, Benjamin Gogué, advised him, 'Although these two [El Greco and Goya] do not appeal to you as masters, I think you might well take one of each of them for your collection.'

So they are here, in the monumental French chateau that Bowes's French architect Jules Pellechet built, not as a residence, but as a museum. John Bowes already had a small collection of 15th-century paintings, bought in the 1840s: a predella panel sold to him as by Fra Angelico that is now considered to be by Sassetta; the *Crucifixion* by the Master of the Virgo inter Virgines. To fill their museum Bowes and his French wife Josephine[4] assembled, in just twelve years, a vast collection of paintings and sculptures; ceramics, glass and metalwork; tapestries and manuscripts; woodwork and ivories; objets d'art and *objets de vertu*.

The Bowes family, the Earls of Strathmore, were an old Teesdale family with estates across the north of England and their seat outside Barnard Castle at Streatlam Castle. John Bowes was the only son of the 10th Earl. His father had married his mother hours before he died, passing to his son his fortune, but not his title. After the end of the Napoleonic Wars, John Bowes went to Eton and Cambridge, became an MP and bred four Derby winners but threw it all up when, at the age of forty-one, he went to live in France and married his mistress, the actress Benoîte-Joséphine Coffin-Chevallier, to whom he gave, as a wedding present, the Château Du Barry at Louveciennes.[5]

After ten years they sold the chateau, bought twenty acres on the edge of Barnard Castle on which to build this museum, and began to acquire. Their aim was educational. Over the next fourteen years (1862–76)[6] they assembled a collection that ranges across the decorative and fine arts, from the 15th to the 19th century, including all European countries.

Although the Bowes fortune was substantial, it could not compare with that of the Hertfords (the Wallace Collection, q.v.) or the Rothschilds (Waddesdon Manor, q.v.). The Boweses acquired through agents, principally Gogué, and to a budget. This precluded the purchase of any masterpiece that came on to the market. Instead they bought works that were, at the time, unfashionable (Tiepolo, Giordano; German faience; Sèvres of the 1820s with its strongly coloured glazes and key patterns; clocks) or that were positively disliked (French works of the Revolution and Napoleonic Empire). They bought many works unseen. Rogiers, the dealer in Ghent who bought tapestries for them, wrote to them on 12 October 1869, 'I have been offered a tapestry of three square metres in the same state as the one from Bruges ... at a price of 60 francs (it won't stay there long).' They acquired soft-paste French porcelain before Lady Charlotte Schreiber started to collect but could not afford either the complete services that Rothschild bought or the star pieces that Wallace sought out.

Some of these constraints proved advantageous (there was little competition for Derutà maiolica). They also made some inspired purchases. The Warwick cabinet, attributed to Mayhew and Ince, was built

(c. 1780) to show a marquetry panel of stunning virtuosity, probably by André-Charles Boulle. The household furniture that the Boweses bought from Louveciennes and from their Paris house in the rue de Berlin was made by Monbro *fils aîné*, and is the finest group of French Second Empire furniture in Britain.

Josephine Bowes was an amateur artist and they brought into the collection several dozen of her paintings. They are attractive and, mostly, conventional. But in her collection of about 150 works by contemporary French artists, she bought works by such artists as Courbet and Boudin.

Delays with the building meant that the museum did not open until 1892, seven years after John Bowes's death. The trustees have continued to collect, while taking 1885 as an end date. In 1920 they made a decision to become the principal archaeological repository for County Durham, which is rich in Roman and Anglo-Saxon sites. In 1939 Sir William Burrell gave a collection of glass and embroidery, and the ceramics collections have been greatly strengthened by the acquisition of the collection of John Bowes's niece, Susan Davidson, and by Enid Goldblatt's porcelain, given in 1988, in which she sought, in a 'collection of rarities', to include a piece from every 18th-century factory in Europe.

A series of English period rooms from the 16th to the 19th centuries were also purchased in the 1950s and '60s, of which the Palladian Long Gallery from Gilling Castle (Matthew Ward, c. 1748) and the French rococo room from Chesterfield House, c. 1750 (from designs by Nicolas Pineau) stand out.

The diversity of the Bowes collection can distract. What is certain to stay in the memories of many visitors is the silver swan, a musical automaton, mechanism by John Joseph Merlin, that Josephine Bowes bought from a Paris jeweller. Once a day it is set in motion for ten seconds to preen its silver plumage, incline its neck and pick a silver fish from the silvery water. A sparkling illusion is maintained by the application of intricate design to a guiding principle.

TREASURES OF SAINT CUTHBERT, DURHAM CATHEDRAL *

The College, Durham DH1 3EH
Tel. 0191 386 4266

Medieval plate and episcopal vestments

Cuthbert was born in 635. He became a monk at Melrose Abbey in 651, the prior at Lindisfarne in 664, and died at Farne in 687. It was to mark his shrine that the priory and the cathedral of Durham were built.

This museum is in a single room off the cathedral cloister.[7] For the preservation of the ancient vestments and manuscripts, vulnerable to light, a near darkness, to which your eyes must adapt, is maintained. You are confronted immediately by the sanctuary knocker (c. 1140),[8] a large lion's head in bronze, its mane radiating in tendrils round its disturbingly human face. Beyond it are the treasures associated with St Cuthbert and with the cathedral. Together they embody much of the history of the Church in England over the past 1,300 years.

The foundation of the collection is the coffin of St Cuthbert, made of oak, and decorated with incised figures and symbols. At one end are the Virgin and Child, shown in their earliest English representation. At the other are the archangels Michael and Gabriel. One long side shows the other archangels and the other depicts the twelve apostles. On the lid Christ is surrounded by the symbols of the Evangelists: the lion of St Mark, the eagle of St John, the calf of St Luke and the angel of St Matthew, all in fine, incised line drawings. The coffin was kept in the shrine behind the cathedral's high altar until the Reformation, when it was buried under the feretory[9] floor.

Associated with St Cuthbert are a 7th-century portable oak altar that was said to have been used by him, and a pectoral cross (c. 640–70) buried in his grave in 687. The stole, maniple and girdle presented to the shrine of St Cuthbert by King Athelstan in 934 are important for being firmly dated to the

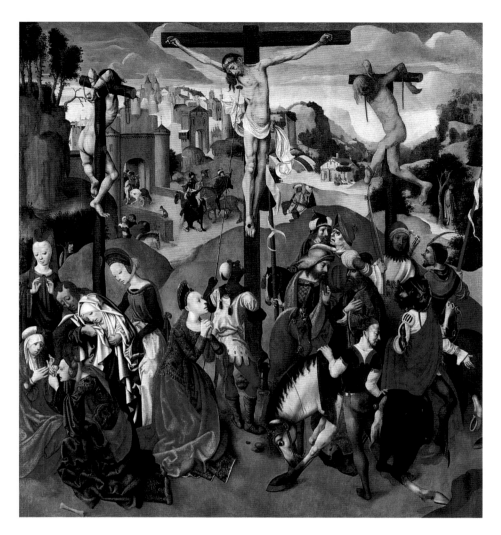

Crucifixion *by The Master of the Virgin Inter Virgines (Bowes Museum)*

10th century by the inscriptions on the reverse of the end panels. They are very fine examples of opus anglicanum, worked in gold thread and coloured silks, and are notable for being the only extant Anglo-Saxon embroideries depicting human figures. These vestments were preserved in St Cuthbert's coffin, the innermost of three that were excavated by James Raine in 1827.

There is a collection of seals here, impressed on documents from monarchs on ecclesiastical business and from bishops on the affairs of the Church and its estates, that extends from Henry I, on whose seal are the legends in Latin 'HENRY BY THE GRACE OF GOD DUKE OF THE NORMANS' (reverse) and 'KING OF THE ENGLISH' (obverse), through the great seals of Richard I, depicted mounted, in armour (1191); those of Henry IV, V and VI,[10] each of whose arms are quartered with the fleur-de-lys of France; to the seal (1547) used by Henry VIII and Edward VI, which shows the Holy Spirit in the form of a dove descending on the king, flanked by clerics. Its legend reads 'after God Supreme Head of the English Church'.

The rupture caused by the Reformation and its initially tenuous nature are illustrated in the statutes issued in 1555 (a 1600 copy of which is here) by 'King Philip and Queen Mary' establishing the constitution of Durham Cathedral as authorised by Act of Parliament.

The diocesan seals and documents relate to such various matters as indulgences (1275); a Letter of Confraternity (1517) granting the monks of Durham a share in the spiritual benefits of the works of devotion observed by the Bridgettine Abbey of Syon, near London; an obit-roll (1416) requesting prayers for the deceased; and account rolls of the priory's builder (1400–02) and its cellarer, William of Hexham (1314), who provided food and drink for the visit of Edward II on his way north to Scotland. He was defeated by the Scots at Bannockburn a month later on 24 June 1314.

Prayer books and Bibles provide a different prism through which to see the evolutions and revolutions experienced by the Church: an 8th-century commentary on the Psalms by Cassiodorus Senator;[11] an illustrated Bible (c.1089–91);[12] a Book of Hours (c.1511), printed in Paris by Antoine Verard, simultaneously a notable example of early printing and one of the last generation of English Books of Hours before the Reformation; and an English Bible (1535) translated by Miles Coverdale,[13] the first English Bible to be printed.

In the 17th century the Church's uneven fortunes under the King, Parliament, Commonwealth and Restoration are reflected at Durham in the career of John Cosin, first canon of the cathedral (1624), then in exile with Charles I and finally Bishop of Durham from the Restoration in 1660 till his death. Here is his Book of Sermons (1621–51), which he wrote by hand, in ink, and his Book of Common Prayer (1619)[14] with his annotations, the first draft of his revision to the prayer book that he presented to the Committee of Revisers in 1661. Here too is the fine chalice and cover (1651) given to Cosin by the Earl of Clarendon while in exile in Paris and the magnificent cope (c.1630), embroidered with silver and silver-gilt threads, worn, it is believed, by Cosin and by all Bishops of Durham until

copes were abandoned in the late 18th century.

In the calmer water of that century the then Dean commissioned the Chapter plate[15] (1766–7) (alms dish, candlesticks, flagons, chalices, patens, spoons, grace cups) engraved with Bishop Cosin's arms a century after his death, to sit beside the Auckland Castle plate that Cosin had commissioned from the Zurich silversmith Wolfgang Howzer in 1659–62 to celebrate the Restoration.

The alarms and excursions that have swirled round St Cuthbert's shrine at Durham are in contrast to the man who for much of his life was a contemplative on Inner Farne. Here in the near-darkness of the cathedral treasury is a fair place to stop to consider the history and beliefs that shaped, and cost, so many lives.

ORIENTAL MUSEUM *

Elvet Hill, Durham DH1 3TH
Tel. 0191 334 5694
www.dur.ac.uk/oriental.museum

Oriental ceramics and objects bring the calm of Buddhism to medieval Durham

The Oriental Museum is on the campus of the University of Durham, about a mile outside the city centre. It is built on a steep slope shaded by pine trees above what was known, prophetically, as Rising Sun Field before it was tarmacked over by university car parks. Beside the museum is the School of Oriental Studies, housed incongruously in what was a largish country house designed in about 1820 by Ignatius Bonomi.[16] Although purpose-built, the museum, unlike its excellent collections, is unprepossessing, tucked away in the elbow of the school, its small entrance enlivened only by the figures of the two guardian lions who flank it: Shishi and Koma-inn, who traditionally guard the doors to Buddhist sanctuaries and Shinto shrines.

Inside, the galleries are terraced in response

Basalt statuette of Senwosret, Middle Kingdom, 12th Dynasty (Oriental Museum)

to the contours of the land outside, each terrace showing a different aspect of the collection: Egyptian antiquities; Chinese jades, ceramics and paintings; Japanese porcelains, costumes and armour; decorative arts of India and South East Asia.

The museum's core is the collection of objects from ancient Egypt made by the 4th Duke of Northumberland[17] in the nineteenth century. Although he visited all the major antiquarian sites excavated in Egypt in the 1820s (Saqqara, Qasr Ibrim, Buhen), he acquired most of his collection from sales, in 1935 of Henry Salt's collection[18] and of James Burton's the following year.

After the Second World War the museum acquired Northumberland's collection despite competition from the British Museum (q.v.) and the Brooklyn Museum of Art in New York, as the then Duke wanted it to remain, if possible, in the north-east. The collection contains pieces from all dynasties but is particularly strong on those from the Eighteenth Dynasty of the New Kingdom (1550–1300 BC). A sphinx of Tuthmosis IV[19] and a small boxwood statue from the tomb of Meryptah, chancellor and chief priest of Amru under Amenophis III, stand out.

To this have been added objects from the collection of Sir Henry Wellcome; some pieces from Sir Leonard Woolley's excavations at Ur; two pieces of relief from Kuyunjik, the site of the Assyrian capital of Nineveh,[20] and a panel of calligraphy by the 17th-century artist Abd al-Rahman al-Hilmi. In the thuluth script he has written the phrase 'BISMALLAH' ('In the name of Allah, the Compassionate, the Merciful'), the phrase that is placed at the head of each chapter of the Koran and said by Muslims at the start of any enterprise. Below it, in nakshi characters, are the Prophet's directions about how it should be written.

In the late 1940s the university was given Sir Charles Hardinge's collection of Chinese jades and hardstone carvings and, twenty years later, 400 pieces of Chinese porcelain, mainly from the Song Dynasty, collected by the Rt. Hon. Malcolm MacDonald, son of the Prime Minister Ramsey MacDonald and a distin-

guished colonial diplomat.[21] There are fine examples of Jun and of Henan ware and an unusual flower vase with a bold design of paeonies and leaf scrolls in thick purple.

Professor H. N. Spalding, who had provided half of the money to buy the Northumberland Collection,[22] gave his collection of 19th-century Japanese ivories and a set of eight paintings, *Seasons*, by Gong Xian, one of the eight Masters of Yanking, depicting mountains in different moods. This is one of the highlights of a collection of Chinese painting of the past 600 years, from Pieu Wen Chin's delicate drawing *Three Quails* to the *Landscape with Waterfall* of Huang Bin Hong.

The wisdom of Northumberland's desire to ensure that oriental works of this quality were retained in the north-east was confirmed when a Northumbrian farmer discovered an 18th-century Burmese sutra chest[23] being used as a corn bin on his farm and the museum was able to provide an appropriate context for it.

BEAMISH: THE NORTH OF ENGLAND OPEN AIR MUSEUM **

Beamish, Durham DH9 ORG
Tel. 0191 370 4000
www.beamish.org.uk

The north-east in the 19th century come alive: pit terraces, steam engines, village shops

The creator and first director of Beamish, Frank Atkinson, explained the concept ten years before the museum opened. Beamish 'serves to illustrate the way of life, the institutions, customs and material equipment of the ordinary people. It is an attempt to make the history of a region live.'[24] More simply it was to show 'the northern way of life'.[25] By 1970 that was a way of life that was slipping away. The industries that had made the north-east great (shipbuilding, chemicals, iron and steel making, coal mining) were all in near-terminal decline.

Atkinson was aware of Skansen near Stockholm (1891), the Netherlands Open-

Air Museum at Arnhem (1912) and St Fagan's outside Cardiff (1949), but these were folk museums, in that the way of life that was being preserved in each of them was rural and agricultural: crafts, traditions and vernacular architecture. Atkinson wanted to use the same approach of preserving complete environments to interpret 19th-century industrial life. What he was proposing was a museum of social history that conveyed understanding through experience, education through entertainment, history through theatre, and that placed the visitor among the objects. It was a vision of what a museum could be and do as radical as was Sir Henry Flower's 'new museum idea' for natural history museums in 1884.[26]

In creating this new type of museum Atkinson faced considerable difficulties. He had no money and no collection with which to realise his idea, and he had just been appointed (1958) director of the Bowes Museum (q.v.)[27] at Barnard Castle, a museum devoted to 18th- and 19th-century European fine and decorative arts.

Eventually he found the ideal site, a 300-acre estate in a secluded, bowl-shaped valley outside Chester-le-Street in the heart of the Durham coal field. The Beamish estate had a farm and farmhouse, Pockerley Manor, a medieval defensive strong-house whose origins went back to the border rievers of the early 15th century; its own drift mine, which had only succumbed to closure in 1962;[28] and Beamish Hall, a manor house from the 11th century that had latterly been the home of the Eden and Shafto families.

The museum presents two distinct periods: c. 1825, when the nearby Stockton and Darlington railway (the world's first public steam-hauled railway to carry passengers) was opened, and 1913, the peak year of production of coal in the Great Northern Coalfield.

Atkinson invited the north-east to participate in the creation of the collections and promised that nothing would be refused. 'It is essential,' he said, 'that collecting be carried out as quickly and on as big a scale as possible. It is now almost too late.'[29] Lorryloads of objects started to arrive, first at the Bowes Museum, then at a disused army camp at Brancepeth and finally, in 1970, at Beamish. The key elements, in addition to those already on the site, were a north-eastern railway station, moved from nearby Rowley, and a row of pit cottages from Hetton-le-Hole. To them were added large objects (the Annfield Plain co-operative store, 1880s; a Victorian bandstand from Saltwell Park in Gateshead) and small items including a mangle, an 1842 mug commemorating the Northumberland heroine Grace Darling, and a miner's 'cracket'[30] found in a seam at the Ravensworth Park Drift.

The museum's stores now hold thousands of objects on shelves that rise to the ceiling of the 18-foot warehouse, a cathedral of reference: the tools, machines and catalogues of all trades (engineers, hatters, cobblers, opticians); trade union banners, train timetables and programmes of agricultural shows. There are 'hooky' or 'proggy' mats made from lengths of rag woven into a sack backing, and pub 'enamels' advertising Rajah cigars (2d. each, seven for 1s.) and Alpine cream teas ('Hard to Beat'). There are certificates presented by the UK Society of Amalgamated Smiths and Strikers (1911) and the Royal Antediluvian Order of Buffaloes Grand Lodge of England with its motto 'In things essential, UNITY; In things doubtful, LIBERTY; and in all things, CHARITY'. Near by is an engraving, 'LORD LONSDALE'S DRIVING MATCH AGAINST TIME, May 11th 1891', celebrating his lordship's driving 20 miles in 56 minutes 55 ⅘ seconds changing from buggy, to phaeton, to wagonette, to charabanc, to phaeton.

The museum has continued to develop since Atkinson retired in 1987. Latest additions include a bank, motor and cycle works and carriage house in the town, and a school and chapel in the colliery village. Pockerley Manor has been rebuilt and restored to represent the lifestyle of a squire and his family in 1825. In the valley bottom run full-scale working replicas of early 1800 steam locomotives. The visitor can walk round the site or take a period tram or replica bus.

The Carriage House at Beamish

All buildings are decorated and furnished. The pit cottages face the headframe and pulley wheels of the pit itself. Inside, tin baths hang on the wall, canaries are in cages, fires are kept lit. Outside, leeks are grown in the back gardens and hens peck. The town terrace houses a solicitor's (files, deeds, ledgers, book press, the formality of ink and leather) and a dentist's with a foot-driven drill (15s. a filling, 4s. for an injection of cocaine). The iron-monger's stocks linoleum in rolls, gas fires, dolly tubs, enamel bread bins and bicycles (Singer and Co., 'Only 10 guineas'), as well as familiar brands (Robin starch, Sunlight soap,[31] Brasso, Zebo grate polish). Some have even retained their original design. The museum makes, on the premises, rum balls, sugar mice, coltsfoot rock, sherbet pyramids and peaches-and-cream boiled sweets, sold alongside Cadbury's Empire Chocolate and Black Bullet Strong Mints, 'for miners'.

Atkinson recognised, as had Pitt Rivers one hundred years before at Larmer Grounds,[32]

that if people were to be persuaded to travel into the countryside and stay for at least half a day, museums must be entertaining and enjoyable. Beamish is both, but it avoids sliding into nostalgia or kitsch by the quality and detail of its scholarship and the authenticity of every object. Its photographic and tape archive is a social history resource that ensures the accuracy of Beamish's work in depicting the northern way of life.

SHIPLEY ART GALLERY
★★★

Prince Consort Road, Gateshead, Tyne and Wear NE8 4JB
Tel. 0191 477 1495
www.twmuseums.org.uk

A Tintoretto in Gateshead, Blaydon Races and fine contemporary studio pottery

This heavy, four-square building by local architect Arthur Stockwell (1917), is an un-likely setting for one of the best collections of contemporary crafts (particularly of studio ceramics) in the country.

The will of Joseph Shipley, a Newcastle and Gateshead solicitor, bequeathed his collection of Victorian, Dutch and Flemish pictures to the public, and £30,000 for the building of a gallery. His executors initially approached Newcastle but, with the Laing Art Gallery having opened there in 1915, they settled on a site in Gateshead near Saltwell Park where Shipley had lived. Shipley's collection of 504 paintings was undistinguished. *Ruth* by Charles Lavelle is typical: a romantic portrait of a beautiful model displaying a glimpse of breast, dignified by its biblical title.

Over the following fifty years paintings were purchased (a John Crome, *View near Norwich*; a landscape by Thomas Sydney Cooper painted when he was ninety-eight; works by David Wilkie, John Linnell and Richard Redgrave) but the collection betrays no legible sign of an acquisition policy beyond a predilection for the local: a landscape (*The Fire, Edinburgh*) attributed to John Martin, who was born across the moors at Hexham, overpraised in his lifetime,[33] unjustly deprecated since; a huge, carved sideboard by Gerrard Robinson,[34] the Shakespeare sideboard (1862), shown at the 1862 International Exhibition in London; and, recently, *Blaydon Races* (1903) by William C. Irving. This is W. P. Frith, but on a dionysian holiday. Irving depicts the fair that accompanied the races. Bookies, card sharks, pickpockets, jugglers, acrobats, thieving children, soldiers, lurchers jostle one another. Among them are real people: Cushey Butterfield of Blaydon; Nanny, the Master of Scotswood, Tommy Diddle the Tipster, George the Plunger, Mac the Welsher.

More remarkable in this company is Tintoretto's huge *Christ Washing the Disciples' Feet* (*c.*1547), commissioned for the Church of S. Marcuola in Venice. A version of it was, until recently, still in the church; another is in the Prado in Madrid, but the great Tintoretto scholar Pallucchini[35] argues that these are copies, the S. Marcuola painting having been substituted for the original in

the 17th century and the Prado version, also autographed, having been painted in 1546 or '48. This painting was presented to the Cathedral of St Nicholas, Newcastle-upon-Tyne, by Sir Matthew White Ridley in 1818, loaned to the gallery in 1980 and finally purchased in 1986.[36]

The gallery began to acquire studio ceramics in the late 1970s when John Millard, now at the Walker Art Gallery, was curator. The first piece to enter the collection was by Gordon Baldwin.[37] The gallery's interest attracted loans and eventually gifts, anonymously from one collector. Now titled the Eagle Collection, it numbers over three hundred pieces and is of a quality comparable with that in the Sainsbury Centre for Visual Arts and the Milner-White bequest at York Art Gallery (both q.v.). Indeed it features many of the same artists: Lucie Rie, Hans Coper and their disciples; and Bernard Leach and Shoji Hamada and their followers. The gallery has fine porcelain pieces by Rie from 1960 and 1983 and stoneware pieces by Coper from 1952 to 1974, as well as Leach's *The Pilgrim Plate* (1966–7), stoneware with tenmoku glaze.

In the last twelve years the gallery's keeper of contemporary crafts, Helen Joseph, has been purchasing a wide range of crafts, glass, textiles, ceramics and, particularly, metalwork: a silver butterfly vase, *Atrophaneura*, by Ndidi Ekubia, and *Propagation Project 202*, a piece in mild forged steel that resembles a black sea urchin, by Japanese artist Junko Mori. The Dutch designer Eric De Graaf has made display cabinets in which they gleam and glitter within the massy spaces of Stockwell's galleries.

DORMAN MUSEUM *

Linthorpe Road, Middlesbrough,
Cleveland TS5 5DL
Tel. 01642 813781/358113
www.dormanmuseum.co.uk

*Molluscs, mammals, minerals and Victorian
birds' eggs in Victorian cabinets; Christopher
Dresser's foray into industrial ceramic design*

Past the sad straggle of cut-price shops and discouraged take-aways that is Linthorpe Road, set to one side at the entrance to Albert Park, is the Dorman Museum, designed by local architects J. Mitchell Bottomley & Son and Welburn in red brick with terracotta dressing, topped by a copper domed tower.

It opened in 1904 as a memorial to Sir Arthur Dorman's son, who died in South Africa during the Boer War. The *North Eastern Daily Gazette* noted that 'Middlesbrough has set out to be a great town. It can achieve its purpose only by considering no real human interest as foreign to it, by becoming a home for the arts and sciences and fostering the highest ideals of culture.'

The museum was fortunate in being given a number of collections of shells and birds by members of local societies and of rocks, fossils and minerals by Dr William Young Veitch, a leading figure on the founding committee and the museum's first honorary curator. To these was added in 1901 a collection of African and Indian birds given by Sir Alfred Pease, the trophies of shooting expeditions to the Sahara, Abyssinia, Somalia and India: sunbirds, orioles, parakeets, pagoda starlings, Indian cuckoos and paradise flycatchers with streaming tail feathers; and material from archaeological digs conducted by the museum's first assistant curator, Frank Elgee.[38]

This bias towards natural history was strengthened by the bequest from Thomas Hudson Nelson of his collection of 435 birds and 2,700 birds' eggs from 253 species. Nelson made ornithology his life's study, publishing *The Birds of Yorkshire* in two volumes in 1907. Here that work is manifest in three tiers

of original glass cases that rise to the ceiling. Few of the specimens are rare but this orderly parliament of fowls is impressive: plovers, godwits; muffs and reeves; oystercatchers and scoters; geese (brent and barnacle), tiny dunlins, a small hoopoe, a creamy-chested goosander and gulls, guillemots, greeves and every coastal bird. They look down from their cases on more cases filled with their eggs, mottled (brent goose) and speckled (curlew); large (whooper swan) and small (swallow); brown (nightingale), porcelain blue (whinchat), green (rhea), black (emu); and a fossilised dinosaur egg from Xixia province in China with a patchwork of a shell, estimated to be 75 million years old.

The Dorman also has collections, contemporary and historic, of local social history, including a large painting, the *Lordship of Acklam* (1716), which lists and depicts the estates outside Middlesbrough owned by Sir William Hustler. In part a working tool of estate management, in part an iconic statement of power, it names numbered enclosures – Thornton's Garth, Milburn's Fell, Tyth Croft, North Broom Moor; identifies roads and bridleways; locates such landmarks as the windmill at Billingham.

Upstairs are galleries of Egyptian and Roman artefacts; of the geological and biological process that shaped the earth; one of the largest fossil ichthyosaur skulls ever found in the UK; and a gallery about industrial Middlesbrough. This tells the brief rise, and fall, of the nearby Linthorpe Pottery. This was launched in 1879 by the London designer Christopher Dresser, Charles Holme of Bradford and local entrepreneur John Harrison, owner of the Sun Brickworks. Dresser had visited the town and been appalled by 'the misery prevailing in the district through the temporary slackness of the iron trade'. It is not easy to identify what Dresser's motives were, whether philanthropic or opportunistic. Decorators and throwers were recruited, some from South Kensington Art School. The designer Henry Tooth was employed as pottery manager and Dresser supplied a stream of designs from London. The ware was to be inexpensive and produced on a large scale. Much of it showed the influence of Japan, where Dresser had been in 1877, but the body shapes also reflect classical, Celtic, even pre-Columbian motifs, as well as the clear geometric designs that distinguish Dresser's work from that of other late-19th-century designers: a jug of hemispherical form, a funnel-shaped vase with incised geometric decoration, a spherical vessel. The glazes are similarly various: streaked toffee, mottled yellow, pea green, flowing pink, speckled brown and gold as well as some of classical simplicity, plain ochre, cream, terracotta.

It is not easy to identify what went wrong. The failings were not the workforce's; the ware is excellent. It would appear that Dresser was, not for the first time, overextended. At the same time as he was launching Linthorpe he was forming the Art Furnishers' Alliance (1880) to supply 'all kinds of artistic house furnishing material, including furniture, carpets, wall-decorations, hangings, pottery, table-glass, silversmiths' wares, hardware and whatever is necessary to our household requirements';[39] he was appointed art editor of the *Furniture Gazette*; he designed the interior and furniture of Bushloe House, Wigston Magna, Leicestershire, for his solicitor, Hiram B. Owston; he was writing his book *Japan* (published in 1882); and he was producing metalwork designs for Hukin & Heath (Birmingham) and for James Dixon & Co. (Sheffield). In 1882 his partnership with Holme and Harrison ended and in 1883 the Art Furnishers' Alliance went into liquidation. Linthorpe continued to produce ware but without Dresser.

An article in *The Studio* (November 1899), referring to the demise of the Art Furnishers' Alliance, observes that their work was 'very good, and that the enterprise did not continue is perhaps owing to the fact that it was before its time'.

HATTON GALLERY **

The Quadrangle, University of Newcastle-upon-Tyne, Newcastle-upon-Tyne, Tyne and Wear NE1 7RU
Tel. 0191 222 6057
www.ncl.ac.uk/hatton

Fine art from Thomas Bewick to Kurt Schwitters, and African sculpture

The Hatton Gallery was transformed in the early 1950s, when Lawrence Gowing was director and the staff of the University of Newcastle's Fine Art Department, to which the gallery is attached, included Richard Hamilton, Victor Pasmore, Kenneth Rowntree and the art historian Ralph Holland.

Until then it had been a decorous, unexceptional institution housed in university buildings that gave it a good top-lit main gallery in which to show its founding 1926 bequest by R. G. Hatton (Professor of Fine Art at Newcastle) of maiolica, Indian miniatures and 19th-century design studies, and its small collection of Old Masters, which included paintings by Domenichino, Salvator Rosa, Camillo Procaccini and Govert Flinck, the overlooked contemporary and rival of Rembrandt.

Gowing discovered a £2,000 fund that had lain untouched and uninvested since 1919. He and his colleagues began to acquire. Holland found a Palma Giovane, *St Mark*. A student spotted a drawing by Charles Ginner, *Seated Figures*, at auction and bought it on Gowing's behalf for £14. Works by Keith Vaughan and Eduardo Paolozzi entered the collection, as did others by Hamilton and Rowntree, and reliefs by Pasmore.

With help from the Contemporary Art Society the gallery has more recently bought paintings by Francis Bacon (*Study for Portrait*, No. VI, 1956), Prunella Clough, William Roberts, Tom Phillips, John Bellany and Joe Tilson, and lithographs by Antoni Tàpies.

It has also been bequeathed, by J. P. Hall, the original woodblock of *The Chillingham Bull* (1789) by Thomas Bewick. Bewick completed

Schwitters's Merzbarn *at the Hatton Gallery*

the block on a Saturday and immediately took twelve impressions from it. It was left on the window ledge in the sunlight and by the following Monday it had cracked into three pieces, horizontally and vertically. Clamped together, its subsequent impressions have proved to be among Bewick's best-known images, but the rectangular format does not suit the lightness and delicacy of his engraving as well as the small oval frames within which he illustrated *Aesop's Fables* (1818); nor does the bulk of the bull suit his powers of observation and feel for anatomy as well as the birds in *The History of British Birds*, the first volume of which had appeared in 1787.

The outstanding work in the collection is Kurt Schwitters's *Merzbarn* (1947), which has the side wall of one gallery all to itself. For Schwitters Merz was an all-encompassing approach to art and to life. George Melly described Merz work as 'poetic collages created from the world's detritus'. Schwitters declared that 'Merz means creating relationships, preferably between all things in the world' (1924).[40] He applied it in every medium –

painting, drawing, graphics and sculpture – but it was the Merzbarn, the Merz building, that became his life's work. He made only three Merzbau: one in Hanover (1927 onwards),[41] where it had eight rooms and forty grottoes in which he placed found objects and personal refuse, each grotto being dedicated to an artist (Arp, Goethe, van der Rohe) or an idea (love, murder); another in Lysaker, Norway (1937–40), whose rural setting was expressed by grasses and flower heads in amongst newspaper and other material;[42] and his Merzbarn made in a barn in a field in Elterwater, Cumbria, in 1947 (v. Armitt Museum and Library).

Schwitters, a Jew, had fled Hanover in 1937 for Norway when his work, specifically his Merzbau, was banned by the National Socialists as 'degenerate'. When Norway fell to the Nazis in 1940 he and his son Ernst managed to secure places on the last ship for Britain. On arrival he was interned for a year on the Isle of Man, where a mix of academics and artists made it 'one of the best Universities in Europe', he claimed. Penniless, he went to live at Ambleside in the Lake District, where he painted 'potboiler' portraits to pay for food and lodging, and began his final Merzbarn, in a barn owned by a local farmer, Henry Pierce.

The inner wall of the barn was made of green slate constructed in the manner of a dry stone wall. Using quantities of plaster applied with a spatula, a spoon, a carving knife and his bare hands, he began 'a Merzbarn. In Elterwater. The greatest sculpture of my life',[43] approximately 15 feet by 10 feet, incorporating whatever was to hand: the rim of a cartwheel, the rose of a child's watering can, twigs, a china egg, a rubber ball, stones from Langdale Beck, a small metal window frame. He died before it was finished, on 8 January 1948, and it remained untouched in the barn for sixteen years.

There were retrospective exhibitions of Schwitters's work in London (1958) and at the Abbot Hall art gallery, Kendal (q.v.) (1964). The Tate Gallery thought about moving the Merzbarn[44] and abandoned the idea as too expensive. The following year Richard Hamilton and Rita Donagh took three students (Mark Lancaster, David Wise and Fred Brookes) to recce it and, with help from Laings, the engineers, and the removal firm Pickfords, the whole wall was lifted out of the barn, transported to Newcastle and slotted by a large crane into a purpose-built alcove cantilevered out of the side of the Hatton. Here, in this narrow space, the Merzbarn is lit, from the left, to allow shadows to fall on its projecting surfaces. As Naum Gabo said, 'It needs a poet like Schwitters to show us that unobserved elements of beauty are strewn and spread all around us.'

Interned with Schwitters on the Isle of Man was a lawyer and collector, Fred Uhlman. Seeking asylum first in Paris and then in London, he founded the Anti-Nazi Free German League of Culture. At the same time he and his wife Dorothy began, in Paris, to collect West African carvings and their collection is here: figures from the Baule and Alanga tribes of the Ivory Coast; masks from the Ibo, the Ogoni and the Ibibio; tall, thin Kurumba antelope headdresses from the Bobo in Mali, the animal faces as serious and dignified as the human.

Although the gallery became independent of the Department of Fine Art in 1998 this remains a working building, an art school. To reach the gallery's toilets in the basement you pass students' lockers, canvases, sculptures. Work is in progress, its clutter the spirit of Merz.

DISCOVERY MUSEUM *

Blandford Square, Newcastle-upon-Tyne, Tyne and Wear NE1 4JA
Tel. 0191 232 6789

Industrial museum in an industrial building; and HMS Turbinia, *the fastest in the fleet*

Where better to house a collection that displays the products of the industrial and engineering genius of Newcastle-upon-Tyne than the massive red-brick former headquarters building of the North East Cooperative Wholesale Society? Designed in the 1890s by local architects Oliver, Leeson and Wood to combine warehouses, offices and a great hall on the top floor, it is big and stout enough to display great pieces of machinery, indeed a turbine boat, while its original role as a headquarters is indicated by its corner turrets and their pale blue copper roofs.

Newcastle-upon-Tyne's manufacturing reputation for the last 150 years has been based on shipbuilding and engineering, of several sorts. Both feature strongly here. Indeed it was the North East Coast Institution of Engineers and Shipbuilders that founded the museum in 1934, in partnership with the local authority.

The first curator, Captain Ernest Swan, OBE, was honorary and voluntary and had no museum experience of any sort, and no collection. With the advice and assistance of the Science Museum in London (q.v.), Swan charmed and badgered local companies so successfully that hundreds of accessions were made every year. The collections now comprise between 20,000 and 30,000 separate artefacts. Electrical and marine engineering are particular strengths.

For the benefit of the non-scientist and

the non-engineer the highlights of these collections are displayed at the top of the building in a Science Maze. Here a penny-farthing (no gears, no chain) is next to a Rolls Royce Conway RCO 42–520 engine; the spotlight from the Sunderland Empire Theatre (1904–74) beside a 35 hp triple-expansion steam engine made in the 1930s by A. G. Mumford of Colchester; the chassis of a 1922 Austin 7 opposite an operating horizontal gas engine of Crossley Brothers, Manchester (1951) that emits a slow tick.

Inevitably it is the people behind the machines who fascinate: William Armstrong, whose large Wimshurst electrical discharge machine is here, that demonstrated the power of hydraulics and the phenomenon of static electricity to an audience of several hundred at the nearby Literary and Philosophical Society of Newcastle-upon-Tyne in the 1880s; George Stephenson demonstrated his miner's lamp; Joseph Swan illuminated the room with his first successful incandescent-filament electric lamp.

Particularly fascinating is Sir Charles Algernon Parsons, whose experiments on propeller cavitation resulted in HMS *Turbinia*, the world's first steam-turbine-driven vessel, the North Sea Greyhound, the Wonder of Spithead, at 34.5 knots (equal to nearly 40 land miles per hour) the fastest ship in the world in 1897, which is complete here in the museum.

One of six sons of the 3rd Earl Rosse, engineer and astronomer, Parsons was never sent to school. He spent time in his father's workshops and was tutored at home by a scientist, Sir Robert Ball. After Trinity College, Dublin, and St John's College, Cambridge (where he read mathematics as there was no engineering course), he joined the Newcastle shipbuilders W. G. Armstrong & Co. as a 'premium apprentice', for which privilege he paid £500 a year.

By 1893 he had designed *Turbinia*, long and sleek,[45] its slim deck stripped of everything except one funnel, her bow knife-clean. Her turbine engine was power itself but 'cavitation' (the formation of 'vacuous cavities' behind the propeller) slowed her down. Parsons solved this by installing three turbine engines, driving three shafts, each shaft having three propellers.

Parsons took *Turbinia* to Spithead, where the Prince of Wales, representing Queen Victoria, was conducting the Diamond Jubilee Review of the Fleet on 26 June 1897. *Turbinia* powered through the entire fleet at over thirty knots, leaving furious Royal Navy vessels chasing her, far astern. *The Times* reported: 'At the cost of a deliberate disregard of authority, she [*Turbinia*] continued to give herself an effective advertisement by steaming at astonishing speed between the lines A and B shortly after the Royal procession had passed.'

Turbinia's technology was adapted by the Cunard Line to power the 31,000-ton *Mauretania*; Parsons was knighted; *Turbinia* lies at sleek rest here.

Elsewhere in the museum, one makes the somewhat surprising discovery of the collections of the 15th–19th King's Royal Hussars and the Northumberland Hussars.

LAING ART GALLERY ***

New Bridge Street, Newcastle-upon-Tyne, Tyne and Wear NE1 8AG
Tel. 0191 232 7734
www.twmuseums.org.uk/laing/

Fine and decorative arts; the largest collection of John Martin's apocalyptic visions and of Beilby enamelled glass

The boat almost did not come in for the Laing Art Gallery. Newcastle's boom years[46] in the 1880s and '90s, when the Hancock Museum had benefited from the vast shipbuilding fortunes of men such as Armstrong, had begun to fade when Alexander Laing (1820–1905), a local wine and spirit merchant, offered £20,000 to build a new art gallery.

The architects chosen were James Thorburn Clackett and Robert Burns Dick, whose art nouveau/baroque buildings were already becoming a feature of the city centre.[47] The location was less happy, the main entrance beneath an ornate tower being in a narrow lane, Higham Place. Inside, Clackett and Burns

Dick provided a splendid staircase, expansive galleries, fossil-rich black Frosterley marble on the floor, and art nouveau detailing and door furniture.

Initially there was no permanent collection, but temporary exhibitions attracted public attention and the gifts and bequests began, the original intention being to create a comprehensive collection of fine and decorative British art, a Victoria and Albert Museum of the north-east. The Laing is not that, but it does have good collections of the decorative arts of the north-east: the 18th-century glass made by William Beilby (working 1762–7);[48] Sowerby pressed glass (19th century); local silver from the 18th century, when Newcastle had an Assay office;[49] and ceramics by C. T. Maling and Sons, who produced pottery on Tyneside from 1762 to 1963.

As the guardian of local talent, the gallery has oils and watercolours by the late-19th-century artist Ralph Hedley and the work of the Cullercoats artists (Robert and Isa Jobling, A. H. Marsh, members of an artists' colony that had much in common with Staithes or Newlyn in the 1890s). The area has always produced artists: the artist and wood engraver Thomas Bewick; Myles Birket Foster; the Richardsons; Thomas Miles Snr and Jnr; the sculptor John Graham Lough; and John Martin. Martin's huge canvases here of biblical, often apocalyptic, subjects (*The Destruction of Sodom and Gomorrah*, 1852, and *The Bard*, exhibited 1817) led to his being overpraised in his lifetime and deprecated since. David Wilkie, writing to Sir George Beaumont, called his work 'a phenomenon'. Later generations found him bombastic and mechanical but both he and his contemporary Francis Danby can now be seen as forceful and original, if flawed, artists.

The gallery has a strong holding of 18th-century portraits (Hudson, Reynolds, Ramsay, Raeburn, Batoni, Lawrence); landscapes by Richard Wilson and Thomas Gainsborough; a small but high-quality collection of Pre-Raphaelites that includes William Holman Hunt's *Isabella and the Pot of Basil* (1867) and Burne-Jones's masterpiece, *Laus Veneris* (1873–5), in which he rises above the decorative. Also here is a collection of English watercolours that includes Turner's painting of the fortress town of *Dinant-sur-Meuse* on his 1839 tour of the Meuse and Mosel and *Morpeth Bridge, Northumberland* (1802), one of Girtin's last paintings before his death at the age of twenty-seven. Its powerful storm-clouds press the brilliance of the reflected water under and through the two spans of the bridge in a way that anticipates Cotman's painting of *Greta Bridge* three years later.

Most strikingly, the Laing continued to buy contemporary paintings throughout the 20th century. For seventy-two years (1904–76) it was directed first by C. Bernard Stevenson and then by his son B. Collingham Stevenson. Both had a wide appreciation of good painting. The result is a collection that gives a good account of painting in Britain through those years: Newlyn, the Glasgow Boys, the Camden Town Group, Bloomsbury, the abstraction of the Seven and Five Society, through to the 1980s.

The outstanding painters are here (Sickert, Spencer, Nicholson, Auerbach) but so too are Mark Gertler, Dod Procter, Laura Knight, Christopher Wood, C. R. W. Nevinson, Keith Vaughan and Anne Redpath. It is a remarkable achievement. John Rothenstein's assertion in the introduction to the first volume of his *Modern English Painters*[50] that 'It is unlikely, it is hardly indeed imaginable, that the twentieth century will be accounted one of the great periods of painting', certainly in Britain, might prove to be true. The Laing's collection shows how impervious painting in Britain has been to foreign influences. You have to look carefully to see reflected here the great changes that swept through Paris or Berlin or Italy between the two world wars or those that turned painting on its head in New York in the 1940s and '50s. Yet if 20th-century painting in Britain did not shake the earth this collection shows that it was never less than interesting.

HANCOCK MUSEUM **

Barras Bridge, Newcastle-upon-Tyne,
Tyne and Wear NE2 4PT
Tel. 0191 222 6765
www.ncl.ac.uk/~nhancock/

*Plants, minerals and fossils, and Abel's ark of
African stuffed animals*

The motto above the door of the 1791 museum
that was to become the Hancock[51] reads 'QUID
HIC? INTUERI NATURAM.' (What is it? The
answer lies in nature).

A Natural History Society[52] has been active
in Newcastle since 1829. John and Albany
Hancock inspired the building of the present
museum to house its growing collections,
notably of ornithology. Today the Hancock
has one of only two collections of 18th-century
bird mounts in Britain.[53] The museum also has
a fine set of Thomas Bewick engravings and
the first wombat in Britain, donated by James
Hunter, Governor of New South Wales in
the 1790s. This is the wombat described by
Bewick in his *General History of Quadrupeds*
(1790).

The museum is on a raised site beside the
university. In brown sandstone with steps
leading up to an imposing portico, it conveys
the late-Victorian solemnity of its purpose.
Albany Hancock was a geologist, with a special
interest in molluscs, his brother John an orni-
thologist and a competent taxidermist. Their
purpose was the public good.

Their collections have attracted others.
Abel Chapman, born into a Sunderland wine-
importing family, spent thirty-two years from
1897 on big-game expeditions throughout
Africa and Europe. Here are his trophies: a
bison and a bush-baby; a coati with a pointed
nose, and a mournful aardvark; a greater kudu
with fierce twisted horns and a small, delicate,
Isabella gazelle.

Unconnected to Chapman is a miscellaneous ethnographic collection that includes a
feather helmet and cloak from the Sandwich
Islands (1820) and a coat of painted moose
hide made by a Cree woman called Sehwahta-

how and given by her to the surgeon Alfred
Robinson at the Hudson Bay Company's
York Fort in 1786. The Cree coat is exhibited
on the balconies above the Bird Galleries that
are the focus of the Hancock.

In low gentle light are lined up serried cases
of British birds: waders and skuas; shrikes and
dippers; flycatchers and waxwings; accentors,
summer visitors from north-west Africa, and
golden orioles from Europe. There is a strong
collection of owls: snowy, great grey, scops,
long-eared, Tengmalm's, hawk and barn, all
staring, some surprised, some disapproving.
There is an alpine lammergeyer, caught by
John Hancock in 1851, and a young great auk,
the only specimen in the world.

John Hancock's obituary in *The English
Illustrated Magazine of Ornithology* said,
'Hancock taught how to combine scientific
accuracy with artistic feeling and his name was
a password throughout England wherever
taxidermy was mentioned.' At a time when
some museums are losing confidence in taxidermy and either not displaying examples or,
in a misconceived fit of political correctness,
disposing of their collections, the Hancock
demonstrates their value and redeems its
motto, 'INTUERI NATURAM'.

MUSEUM OF ANTIQUITIES OF THE UNIVERSITY AND SOCIETY OF ANTIQUARIES OF NEWCASTLE-UPON-TYNE *

University of Newcastle, Newcastle-upon-
Tyne, Tyne and Wear NE1 7RU
Tel. 0191 222 7846
www.museums.ncl.ac.uk

Roman antiquities from Hadrian's Wall

Who were the Romans who built Hadrian's
Wall and garrisoned its forts? How did they
live? With what did they build the wall? In

*Hancock in his Studio by Henry Hetherington
Emmerson (Hancock Museum)*

what did they believe? Some of the answers are here, most directly in inscriptions on altars, coffins and tombstones and in the tools, jewellery, coins and fragments that they left here when they withdrew from the wall in the 4th century.

Although the Romans left no written record of Hadrian's Wall in official reports, diaries, speeches or poems, there are carved inscriptions here that identify when the wall was built, by whom and at whose command. One reads simply: 'This work of the Emperor Caesar Trajan Hadrian Augustus [was built by] the Second Legion Augusta under Aulus Platorius Nepos, propraetorian legate.'[54] It is this inscription that proves conclusively that the Roman wall was built on the orders of Hadrian in AD 122–4 (the dates between which Nepos was governor).[55]

Much of the wall was built by the Second Legion Augusta,[56] and other inscriptions witness how the wall was garrisoned by soldiers from every part of the Roman Empire: Phrygians, Asturians, Dacians, Lingonians, Tungrians and Hamian archers.

Here, at the northernmost extremity of the empire, they continued to worship familiar Roman gods – Jupiter, 'Best and Greatest', Mars and Minerva – and some less well known, such as Antenociticus.[57] Mithras, the Persian god of light and truth introduced into the Roman Empire during the reign of the Emperor Nero, was also worshipped in three temples on the wall[58] and inevitably Celtic gods were venerated. An altar here, found in 1835 south of the wall at Bettingham, is inscribed 'To the goddess Sattada, the assembly of Textoverdi willingly and deservedly fulfilled the vow'[59] while an inscription on a rough altar found at the fort at Benwell in 1751 says simply 'to the three witches'.[60]

Personal inscriptions bring the lives of individual Roman soldiers and their families into focus: 'To the spirits of the departed: Flavinius, trooper of the Cavalry Squadron Petriana, standard-bearer . . . aged 25, of 7 years' service, lies buried here'; 'Aurelia S . . . [set this up] to her very dear sister [who] lived 15 years, 4 months'; 'To the spirits of the

departed Lucius Novellius Lanuccus, Roman Citizen, aged 70', the oldest person recorded on a tombstone on the wall[61] and, poignantly, '[To the soul of] Satrus Honoratus who lived 5 years, 8 months' in the 3rd century at an outpost port at Risingham.

An array of tools from the 3rd and 4th centuries gives an indication of what was used to build and maintain the wall: chisels, axe heads, an iron adze with a claw, rock wedges, a blacksmith's tongs and a mason's pick and trowel. Their design remains unchanged 2,000 years later.

There are personal possessions here: an ivory clasp-knife; a bronze pen; a 1st-century bronze saucepan from Campania, Italy; figurines of Mercury, Hercules and Fortuna; and a fragment of a finely sculpted finger, from a larger-than-life-sized public statue.

The Aesica Hoard (c. AD 80), discovered in 1956, shows the sophistication and wealth of those serving at this far outpost of the empire: a huge silver brooch (c. AD 140–60), an enamelled bronze brooch of the trumpet type (c. 2nd century), an agate cameo and a finger ring, around which is the motto, in openwork, 'Aemilia, May You Live' (late 2nd century–4th century), which may be the earliest Christian artefact found in Britain.

The Romans bridged the Tyne at what is now Newcastle with the Pons Aelius. In 1928 a coin, a sestertius (c. AD 132–4), was excavated on the line of the bridge, presumably having been thrown from it into the river by a Roman making a wish, an offering to the god of the river. The head of Hadrian, the founder of the wall, is on the obverse. On the reverse he sits in a galley between military standards. The coin is inscribed, 'For the Good Fortune of the Emperor, Thrice Consul, Father of his Country, [issued] by resolution of the Senate', the founder of the wall.

ARBEIA, ROMAN FORT AND MUSEUM **

Baring Street, South Shields,
Tyne and Wear NE33 2BB
Tel. 0191 456 1369
www.twmuseums.org.uk/arbeia

*Roman fort overlooking the Tyne and the
North Sea, the limit of the Roman Empire*

This fort was built, probably in AD 60, on a low headland overlooking the mouth of the River Tyne. To the east is the North Sea, to the west the river and four miles away on the opposite north bank Segedunum (q.v.), the last fort of Hadrian's Wall at Wallsend.

Arbeia was originally garrisoned to protect a port that is presumed to have been on the estuary below it,[62] from which the mileposts and forts of Hadrian's Wall were supplied. It is a large, open site surrounded today by streets of 19th-century terraced housing, the outskirts of South Shields, through which the visitor winds to reach what is the most thorough excavation of any stone-built Roman supply base in Europe, complete with barracks, granaries, wells, latrines, strongrooms for holding pay and a tile kiln. The surrounding terraces of houses are oddly juxtaposed to this archaeological site but the visitor has only to close his or her eyes and the sound of the sea and the cold wind on this exposed headland, and the smell of the low box hedges, are what a Roman auxiliary would have heard and smelt 1,800 years ago.

In 1875 the South Shields Corporation bought some of the headland for development from the Dean and Chapter of Durham. Excavations revealed, among other things, a Roman column, jewellery, decorated metalwork and coins, and the Corporation agreed to preserve an acre of the site as a People's Roman Remains Park. Other excavations in the area led to the discovery of two beautifully carved tombstones. One is in memory of Regina, the British wife of Barathes, a trader from Palmyra, in Syria. He had bought her as a Catuvellunian slave, freed her and married

her. She died aged thirty and her tombstone, carved in the Palmyrene style, shows her sitting in a basketwork chair, a ball of wool in her lap, her jewel box open beside her. The inscription is in Latin and in Aramaic, the language of the sculptor and of Barathes. The second, carved in finer-grained stone, was erected by Numerianus, a cavalryman in the First Cavalry Regiment of Asturians (northern Spain), in memory of Victor, a Moorish freedman, aged twenty, who is depicted reclining, dining. Behind him is the Tree of Life.

These, among the finest Roman tombstones in Britain, are here in the museum beside that rarity, a complete inscribed tablet,[63] which commemorates the construction of an aqueduct by the Fifth Cohort of Gauls in AD 222 under the Legate of Lower Britain, Marius Valerianus. The calligraphy, set within an incised border, is superb, marred only by the chiselled deletion of the names and titles of the Emperor Severus Alexander, whose memory was condemned after his death.

In a second gallery are smaller objects from the site: a spur; arrowheads; an iron sword; a scabbard chape;[64] beads, bracelets and hairpins carved from Whitby jet; and rare imperial lead seals for securing official packages.[65] Objects and inscriptions demonstrate how pervasive and sophisticated was the culture of Rome even here at the northernmost point of Europe, where almost the entire occupying force came not from Italy but from the other conquering provinces in Gaul, Germany, Spain and the Middle East.

The human detail provided by objects can convey something of the lives of soldiers stationed here, but only from the foundations of the buildings on the site can we learn about the history of the fort itself. In 1949–50 Dr Ian Richmond uncovered evidence of thirteen large granaries – evidence that the fort was used as a supply base for the armies of the Emperor Septimus Severus in his campaigns to conquer Scotland AD 208–10. Seven more granaries were added after AD 222 so that Arbeia could meet the needs for grain to make bread and beer for all the garrisons along the wall.[66]

Richmond's discoveries led to the founding of this museum in 1953. Small-scale excavations were carried out in the 1960s under John Gillam of the University of Newcastle-upon-Tyne. Excavations have been continuous since 1977 under Roger Miket, Paul Bidwell and Nick Hodgson.[67]

It is probable that the name of the fort, Arbeia, derives from the Latin version of an Aramaic word meaning 'The Place of the Arabs', Aramaic being the native language of the Tigris bargemen, the legion having been raised in the Tigris area. John Leland, the 16th-century antiquarian, records the name of the fort as Caer Urfa, a likely corruption of Arbeia, the 'u' in Urfa being substituted for 'a' and the 'f' for 'b'.

For the past twenty years the museum has sought to interpret the foundations of these buildings by reconstruction. In 1984 English Heritage challenged the reconstruction of the West Gate. After a fiercely argued four-day inquiry, the reconstruction was allowed to proceed, since when a 3rd-century Barrack Block and Commanding Officer's House have been reconstructed, the latter being a building in the Mediterranean style with a courtyard, wall paintings and a hypocaust, an underfloor system of central heating. These reconstructions, particularly of the West Gate (1986), a mighty slab rising out of the flat, open site, convey the scale and solidity of Roman architecture and how awe-inspiring it must have appeared to the local population.

Within the Gatehouse a ten-foot long table-top model of the fort shows the order and discipline of a Roman garrison, with granaries lined up on a grid and two streets crossing at right angles. Outside remain the wind and the sea and the smell of box hedge at this final outpost of Rome's empire.

CHERRYBURN *

Station Bank, Mickley, nr. Stocksfield,
Northumberland NE43 7DD
Tel. 01661 843276
www.nationaltrust.org.uk

Thomas Bewick's birthplace, engravings, tools and a printing press; a farmyard complete with hens and a donkey

Stand in the farmyard at Cherryburn and look down the bank to the River Tyne below. Thomas Bewick, the finest engraver of the 18th century, was born here in 1753, the son of a tenant farmer who also worked a small coal mine. The prospect has scarcely changed in 250 years. There are sheep and donkeys in the fields; doves croon; oak, copper-beech and willow trees shade the river. This is the landscape of which Bewick never tired and to which he returned in his engravings throughout his life. 'From the little window at my bed head,' he wrote in his *Memoir*,[68] 'I noticed all the varying seasons of the year, and when the Spring put in ... the chief business imposed on me as a task ... was in my being set to scale the pastures and meadows, that is spreading the Molehills over the surface of the ground.'

The low rooms of the farmhouse make an appropriate setting in which to show Bewick's wood engravings, which seldom measure more than 2 inches by 3 inches. His story is well told, without gimmicks or fuss.

He was apprenticed in 1768 to a jobbing engraver, William Beilby, producing trade cards, bookplates, ball tickets, labels, invitations, bank notes, pamphlets, sermons and advertisements, all of which required decoration or illustration. Beilby did not enjoy wood engraving and within five weeks Bewick was cutting wood blocks for a mathematical text book, Charles Hutton's *A Treatise on Mensuration* (1768), whose title page is exhibited here. The publisher was Thomas Saint of Newcastle and over the next twenty years Bewick cut illustrations for at least thirty-five children's books for Saint.

Thomas Bewick at Cherryburn

The poor quality of the illustrations in most children's textbooks emboldened Bewick, and in 1781 he and Beilby resolved to publish *A General History of Quadrupeds* (1790), 'a concise account of every animal of that kind hitherto known or described'.[69] It was an enormous success, in Britain and in America (published in New York in 1804), and was followed by *A History of British Birds*[70] (1798 and 1804) and *The Fables of Aesop* (1818).[71] A poem by George Byles in the *Newcastle Advertiser* urges Bewick: 'Go on great Artist in thy pleasing way,/And learn us Nature as the rising day: . . ./Thy charming pencil claims our warm applause,/And leads us on to study Nature's laws.' The blocks and engravings here confirm the justice of Byles's verse.

The illustrations capture the characteristics of animals as well as their appearance, and set them in habitats that are accurately and beautifully observed. The museum's concise labels point out the incidents that are depicted in the backgrounds so very small that they might otherwise be overlooked: a milkmaid with a pail on her head behind *The Cow*; a distant horse-race glimpsed between *The Horse*'s legs; the tiny child behind *The Vicious Colt*'s rear legs (Bewick's younger brother suffered this mishap).

They are set in every sort of weather, season and time of day; against woods, meadows, cottages, stiles, reedbanks and, especially, rivers and streams, which are shown being crossed in at least eight different ways (stilts, stepping stones, fallen boughs, holding on to a cow's tail, etc).

Bewick's virtuosity is a delight. He can do every kind of plumage from the dazzling jewellery of a peacock's train to the smooth slickness of a duck's tail. He can convey scale, weight and speed, humour, fear and pathos, all with a line of ease, delicacy and precision. Even the best of his metropolitan contemporaries, Bartolozzi and Cipriani, who engraved for Reynolds and Gainsborough, are confounded.

His toolbox is here for the technically minded, who may study the ways in which he manipulated the hard-grained boxwood blocks; how he conditioned paper; how he lowered those areas of his designs that had to be printed more softly. The non-technical can consider the quality of his writing. Here is his mole: 'This animal, destined to seek its food and provide for its sustenance under the surface of the earth, is wonderfully adapted, by the all-wise Author of Nature, to its peculiar mode of living.'[72]

Apart from one brief period in London[73] in 1776, he lived in Newcastle and died in Gateshead. One of his last engravings was of his own funeral. His coffin is being carried down the hillside to the Tyne where Charon waits to help him cross this last river.

SUNDERLAND MUSEUM AND ART GALLERY **

Burdon Road, Sunderland,
Tyne and Wear SR1 1PP
Tel. 0191 553 2323
www.twmuseums.org.uk/sunderland/
index.html

Natural history, a vivarium and Sunderland glass, pressed and cut

On the day the Sunderland Art Gallery opened, 6 November 1879, Alphonse Legros did an oil sketch, in public, in about one hour, of one of the gallery's most vociferous advocates, Thomas Dixon. It is a profile of an Old Testament prophet, with high forehead, powerful nose, a penetrating eye.

Thomas Dixon was a cork cutter. Self-educated, he entered into correspondence with Thomas Carlyle, Charles Dickens, Dante Gabriel Rossetti and John Ruskin. Ruskin's book *Time and Tide* consists of the letters that he wrote to Dixon 'during the agitation for reform in the spring of the present year'[74] (1867) about the 'honesty of work, and honesty of exchange' and 'the share which a labouring nation may attain in the skill, and the treasures, of the higher arts'.[75] So it is no surprise that Dixon, a member of the museum committee, was one of the foremost voices in favour of adding an art gallery to the museum that had been opened in 1846.

Sunderland Corporation had been the first local authority to avail itself of the new powers in the Museums Act of 1845 to raise a rate and run a museum.[76] The collections of the Sunderland Natural History and Antiquarian Society were taken over (specimens, minerals, fossils, antiquities and curiosities, including the boots of Colonel John Lilburne, the 17th-century radical pamphleteer and parliamentarian) but the growth and development of the museum and art gallery were slow.

Dante Gabriel Rossetti had been persuaded by Dixon to present two chalk drawings, *Studies of a Head*,[77] and Ruskin offered watercolour sketches of a colour scheme for the gallery (red walls with an olive-green dado) which was never implemented, but there were no major founding bequests. Progress was faltering and the quality of the art collection led the *Daily Post* to call in 1905 for 'the overhaul of the collection with a view to the exclusion of worthless examples and palpable forgeries'.

In 1907 Edward Backhouse followed the donations he made in his lifetime by bequeathing the museum his large collection of natural history and archaeology in 1907. The following year John Dickinson, a local engineer, left thirty-one paintings to the gallery including works by Thomas Francis Dicksee and Joseph Clark's sentimental genre painting *The Sick Boy*.

Only after the Second World War[78] did the museum begin to collect work from two of Sunderland's great industries, ceramics and glassmaking. The Rowland Burdon Collection (acquired in 1945), when put beside the ware that came to the museum on the closure of Scott's Pottery in 1897, shows the range and quality of the Sunderland industry from 1720 (Newbottle) to its demise in 1957, not least in the production of copper and pink lustreware by Garrison/Sunderland between 1799 and 1865.

The introduction of a technique called pressing in the early 19th century made glass widely affordable but the factories making bottles, window glass and cheap tableware distracted attention from the excellence of such specialists as the Wear Flint Glass Co. (White and Young), who produced rummers, armorial goblets and the remarkable 160-piece Londonderry glass service (1819–24) for the 3rd Marquess of Londonderry, at a price of 2,000 guineas. The service was finally acquired by the museum in 1986.

In 1960 a new director, Tom Shaw, introduced a new art acquisitions policy advised by Dennis Farr of the Tate Gallery. Works by Edward Burra and Ian Stephenson were bought and an outstanding painting by Michael Ayrton, *Slow Dance for the Nativity* (1958).

In 1966 the Arts Council mounted a retrospective exhibition here of the work of L. S. Lowry, who had close links with the north-east and spent much time here. 'I like Sunderland because of the shipping and shipbuilding and the countryside at the back ... I like the sea. I sometimes escape to Sunderland. I get away from art and artists.'[79] The gallery began to buy his works and now has one of the largest collections outside London, including two examples, on long-term loan, of the rare, enigmatic *Self-portraits* from the mid-1960s, paintings not of his likeness but of lighthouses standing isolated in silhouette against a grey sea. 'I think one day I'll paint a self-portrait. I've an idea. A tall straight pillar standing up in the middle of the sea, waiting for the sea of life to finish it off.'

A new extension to the original Public Library and Museum by J. and T. Tillman was opened in 1964 and more than doubled the available display space. In 2001, as part of a Heritage Lottery Fund development scheme, a further extension was made. This gave the museum, described by Pevsner as 'hardly one of the ornaments of the Victorian age',[80] a contemporary Winter Gardens (designed by Napper Architects) under a huge glass rotunda, with exotic plants climbing round a thirty-foot steel water sculpture by William Pye. The scheme also included the creation of

Sunderland's pressed glass

a new entrance and new galleries for the museum's wide-ranging collections. The new galleries, designed by Redman Design, provide a fine setting for the collections that cover the natural and human world. The North Pennine minerals (galena, calcite, barite and several different fluorites) stand out on a glittering stage. Notable too is the 17th-century Anglo-Saxon glass from St Peter's Monastery, Monk-wearmouth, where the Venerable Bede was educated, 'delivered by the hands of my friends and kinsfolk, to be brought up by the most reverend Abbot Benet'.

Thomas Dixon and John Ruskin might have approved.

SEGEDUNUM **

Buddle Street, Wallsend, Tyne and Wear
NE28 6HR
Tel. 0191 236 9347
www.twmuseums.org.uk/segedunum/

Roman fort on Hadrian's Wall, Wallsend, next to Swan Hunter shipyard

On the north bank of the River Tyne at Wallsend the giant cranes of the Swan Hunter shipyard extend and dip their necks. In their shadow is Segedunum, the Roman fort that marks the eastern end of Hadrian's Wall. It is one of the most extensively excavated Roman fort sites in the Roman Empire.

The crane drivers, barely discernible in the cab eyries 120 feet above the ground, look down on the excavated footprint, the ground plan, of a Roman fort, laid out below them: gateways at each point of the compass, walls, the commanding officer's house, the head-quarters building, a hospital, a granary, bar-racks for infantry and cavalry. Across the north of the site cuts a present-day road, Buddle Street, by which visitors reach the museum.

This museum, opened in 2000, comprises galleries and an award-winning tower designed by North Tyneside Council Building Design Agency. It is topped by a semi-circular glass viewing gallery that local taxi drivers claim was modelled on the design of a Roman helmet but which the architects insist was inspired by the cabs on the cranes.

From the tower the orderly, squared-up layout of the Roman fort can be studied. The first excavations here were in the 1880s. In 1929 work by F. G. Simpson identified the line of Hadrian's Wall where it meets the fort and the exact position of the fort itself. At that time housing on the site prevented more exten-sive excavation but by 1975–6 that housing had been demolished and Charles Daniels of the University of Newcastle-upon-Tyne carried out a series of excavations that provided greater insight into the layout of the fort.

More work in 1979–99 brought to light pits probably covered by stone slabs in two barrack blocks consistent with the stabling of cavalry horses, the purpose of the pits being the collection of horses' urine. The cavalrymen slept in the same building as their horses, separated by a partition wall. Assuming three men to a room, it was possible to confirm that a cavalry turma comprised about thirty men led by a decurion.

A Roman baths building has been recon-structed, based on the remains at Chesters, a Roman fort further west on Hadrian's Wall. The reconstruction allows visitors to walk through the different rooms, some of which are decorated with frescoes. The Romans would have kept the rooms at different tem-peratures using a hypocaust system heated from a furnace – a system replicated in the reconstruction.

The museum next to the viewing tower consists of a number of themed rooms and cabinets holding authentic objects found during excavations. Artefacts include the only stone toilet seat from Roman Britain, original ringmail, an intact lattice-worked portable shrine, a die and gaming counters, and a unique set of cooking pots. There are good, atmospheric sound effects, including a taped recording of a briefing by the commanding officer in Latin.

An animated film in the viewing tower fast-forwards the landscape you can see below through the past 2,000 years, showing the native arable farming on the site before the

Roman fort, the decline and abandonment of the fort after the Romans withdrew in the 5th century, the re-use of the stone for other buildings, the return of agriculture, the mining of coal in the 18th century and the development of the shipyards in the 19th. In the Industry Gallery, the main film theatre and an exhibition further develop these post-Roman themes.

This is ground upon which each generation has left its spoor. Here, today, are a Roman fort, a shipyard and a museum.

Yorkshire and Humberside

The same combination of industry, money and booming 19th-century cities that led to the founding of so many museums and galleries in south Lancashire and north Cheshire is evident in south Yorkshire.

Here the industries were coal, iron, steel and wool (and on the coast, fishing and whaling) but the profits were as great as in the north-west, and the museums and galleries of Sheffield, Rotherham, Bradford, Leeds and Wakefield were the result.

In Yorkshire these grew in a county whose cultural roots were deep and strong. Two of the earliest museums in England were the Musaeum Thoresbyanum in Leeds (founded *c.*1680 by Ralph Thoresby, fellow of the Royal Society and friend of John Evelyn, Edward Lhwyd, Sir Hans Sloane and Sir Christopher Wren) and the Kirkleatham Museum in Redcar, founded by Cholmley Turner, with its coins and medals, and 'Bustos and Images' by John Cheere (now in York Art Gallery).[1]

The region was well served by literary and philosophical societies, from whose activities modern museums have evolved in Halifax, Barnsley, Keighley, York and Hull. In Leeds one of the three founding members of the local society in the early 1770s was the scientist Joseph Priestley.

The region has benefited from the work of great curators: Professor Louis Compton Miall at Leeds Museum, described by a colleague as being 'as clear, as honest, as cold as some mountain stream', and Tom Sheppard, curator and director of Hull's museums from 1901 to 1941, as warm as Miall was cold; and from such benefactors as Benjamin and William Gott, whose generosity founded Leeds Museum and whose portrait busts are in Leeds City Art Gallery.

The rural and folk collections of Dr John L. Kirk, a GP in Pickering, led to the founding of the York Castle Museum in 1930 and inspired the Beck Isle Museum thirty years later, as it did the Ryedale Folk Museum.

Rural Yorkshire is not short of great houses containing fine collections

20 miles

WHITBY

171

A171

A170

CKERING

A64

A64

A165

A165

Humberside

A1079

A165

M62

A63

HULL

Lincolnshire

(Beningbrough Hall, Harewood House, Castle Howard). I regret not being able to include Robert Adam's beautiful interiors at Nostell Priory, designed for Sir Rowland Winn and epitomised in Nostell's doll's house, a showpiece of Adam's genius and of the furniture of Thomas Chippendale.

The region's art collections have remarkable breadth: contemporary sculpture (Yorkshire Sculpture Park); 20th-century painting (Wakefield Art Gallery, Huddersfield Art Gallery, Leeds City Art Gallery, Graves Art Gallery, the Ferens Art Gallery and the University of Hull Art Collection – the last four being particularly strong on the work of the Camden Town Group); 20th-century studio pottery (York Art Gallery and the Yorkshire Museum); 19th-century painting (Cartwright Hall Art Gallery, Leeds City Art Gallery, York Art Gallery) and Old Masters at Harewood House, Castle Howard, York Art Gallery and Temple Newsam. The last two have outstanding collections whose reputations deserve to be noised abroad.

The quality of all these collections owes as much to a succession of curators and directors (Sir John Rothenstein at Leeds and Sheffield; Sir Philip Hendy at Leeds; Ernest Musgrave at Leeds and Wakefield; Hans Hess at York; Helen Kapp at Wakefield) as do the museums to Sheppard and Miall.

For all its great houses and fine collections, Yorkshire, certainly south Yorkshire, is rooted in its industries. All are celebrated in museums: coal at the National Coal Mining Museum for England; wool at Armley Mills, Leeds; whaling at Hull Maritime Museum; steel at Kelham Island, Sheffield, and at Magna, Rotherham; and fishing at the Fisheries Museum, Great Grimsby. I regret that I have not been able to find room for all these, as I have not for one of the most beautiful and original museum buildings in Britain, the Rotunda at Scarborough, designed by John Barry in 1837–8. Its walls are lined by its unusual cases, in which are 'a highly interesting series of geological curiosities arranged in the most instructive and pleasing manner'.

It is a tribute to the region that the Science Museum has moved two of its collections here (railways to the National Railway Museum, York, and photography to the National Museum of Photography, Bradford), the National Portrait Gallery some of its 18th-century collection to Beningbrough Hall, and the Royal Armouries its collection to Leeds. They sit well within the region's diverse collection of museums and galleries.

LOTHERTON HALL **

Lotherton Lane, Aberford, Leeds,
West Yorkshire LS25 3EB
Tel. 0113 281 3259
www.leeds.gov.uk.

High Edwardian style and taste

The Gascoigne family settled in Yorkshire in
the Middle Ages and became rich and powerful. Lotherton Hall was bought by Richard
Oliver Gascoigne in 1825, although it was
not until the time of his grandson, Colonel
F.R.T. Gascoigne, that the family lived here
permanently. Now one of Leeds Museums and
Galleries, Lotherton retains the decoration and
atmosphere of the Gascoigne family home
with books, music, magazines, newspapers and
letters left untidied-away.

There are numerous family portraits,
including a few star items. Sir Thomas
Gascoigne, the 8th and last baronet, is shown
resplendent in his red coat and breeches and
embroidered waistcoat in one of Pompeo
Batoni's grandest pictures, painted in Rome
in 1779 while Sir Thomas was on the Grand
Tour. In his hand is a snuff box with a portrait
of the French queen, Marie-Antoinette, which
is still in the collection. Thomas Banks's relief
of *Alcyone Discovering the Dead Body of her
Husband Ceyx*, carved in Rome *c.*1775, was
won in a raffle by Sir Thomas's friend and travelling companion Henry Swinburn, who gave
it to him. A bronze bust of Henry, modelled
by Christopher Hewetson and cast by Luigi
Valadier (*c.*1778), is also present, together with
a companion bust of Henry's wife Martha and
one of Sir Thomas himself.

There are some good pieces of furniture:
a pair of console tables and pier glasses by
William Vile and John Cobb (1761) at the start
of their three-year partnership in service to
the King; a stool and a pair of chairs designed
by A.W.N. Pugin, and made by Morel and
Seddon for Windsor Castle (1827–8); and a
grand piano and bedroom suite made by the
progressive Leeds firm of Marsh and Jones
in the 1860s for Sir Titus Salt Jnr, the second

son of the famous Sir Titus Salt of Saltaire.
There is also a mahogany zograscope (1821),
a French optical machine for magnifying
prints, and a collection of silver-gilt cups
won by the Gascoignes' race horses, including
the Doncaster Gold Cup for 1828, made by
the London smiths Rebecca Emes and Edward
Barnardi. This was modelled on an engraving
by G.B. Piranesi of a marble vase excavated by
Gavin Hamilton at Hadrian's Villa in 1769.

The 18th-century Gascoignes do not seem
to have been great art collectors, although
they were certainly discriminating patrons.
The collections at Lotherton, however, were
greatly enhanced at the end of the century
on the death of Sir Douglas Galton, Florence
Nightingale's cousin by marriage and long-
time collaborator. His daughter, Laura
Gwendolen, married Colonel Gascoigne, and
pictures from his house, Hadzor Park in
Worcestershire, can be seen in the Drawing
Room and the Boudoir. Notable amongst
them is *Peasants Dancing Outside an Inn* by
David Teniers the Younger, the Dutch 17th-
century artist, much revered by the Victorians.

Lotherton was given to the city of Leeds
by Sir Alvary and Lady Gascoigne in 1968. The
city was keen to accept, not only because of
the quality of the house and its contents, but
because the building provided suitable display
space for art collections that the city already
owned but had nowhere to display. Chief
among these were the costume collections,
now shown upstairs in the costume galleries,
and a collection of early Chinese ceramics,
most of which had been bequeathed by Frank
Savery in 1966. The pottery and porcelain
fit well with the Gascoigne gift, which included a Chinese armorial dinner service and
a tea and coffee service ordered from China
between 1770 and 1780, and a Tang Dynasty
figure of a camel, which was presented to Sir
Alvary by the staff of the British Embassy in
Tokyo when he left his post as ambassador
in 1951.

Frank Savery was also in the Foreign Office.
He was not rich but he put together a collection that goes from the Neolithic period to
the mid Ming Dynasty in the 15th century.

It contains no masterpieces and was bought mainly from dealers, but it has a strong personal character. Among the 350 pieces he bequeathed to Leeds, some stand out: Han and Tang jars and bowls (2nd–8th centuries AD), a Tang camel tomb figure, a buff stoneware jar from the late Chou Dynasty (3rd century BC) and two earthenware jars from the period of the Warring States (475–221 BC).

BENINGBROUGH HALL **

Beningbrough Hall, Beningbrough, York,
North Yorkshire YO30 1DD
Tel. 01904 470666
www.nationaltrust.org.uk

Handsome Georgian house of 18th-century treasures; the National Portrait Gallery's outpost in the north

Out of the flat, monotonous flood plain of the River Ouse, north of York, rises Beningbrough Hall, as handsome a baroque country house as there is in North Yorkshire.

Its design and building (1710–16) were supervised by William Thornton,[2] a carpenter and joiner who worked on the interiors of Castle Howard (q.v.). Here he created a simple facade in red brick, its elegant proportions embellished only by a fine Italianate central sash window[3] above a front door whose surrounds, intricately carved cartouche and segmental pediment are in stone.

As an outstation for the National Portrait Gallery (NPG) (q.v.), housing its collection of paintings from c.1688 to 1760,[4] it is well chosen. Within, the plasterwork in the Hall,[5] Thornton's carved friezes and overmantels in the Drawing Room,[6] and the wide, noble staircase[7] add distinction to the setting.

There are two small collections of portraits that come from previous owners of Beningbrough. Twelve are from John and Mary Bourchier, including family portraits by Jonathan Richardson, and five from the 10th Earl of Chesterfield, who lived here in the early 20th century (portraits of the 4th Earl – v. Rangers House – by William Hoare and Allan Ramsay,

and of the 10th Earl and his wife by the society portrait painter Ellis Roberts, though Roberts is no English Boldini and Lady Chesterfield, though handsome, is not Lady Colin Campbell).[8]

The NPG's portraits, hung throughout the house, provide an illuminating commentary on the development of English portraiture from Kneller to Gainsborough; from John Greenhill, John Closterman and Charles Jervas to Joseph Highmore, Thomas Hudson and Allan Ramsay, and so to Joshua Reynolds, William Hoare and Julian Opie; from the days when most portrait painters struggled to make a living out of likenesses, up to the early years of the Royal Academy and Reynolds's knighthood.

The NPG's outstations are doubly welcome. They allow portraits to be shown in rooms that are architecturally, proportionally and historically suitable, and they provide opportunities to explore the byways of the collection. In London, proud place must be given to the great images of those who bestrode the nation's stage, kings and queens, men of war and power. Here at Beningbrough there are space and time for the sitters and the artists whose names may reverberate more lightly but whose lives are as much a part of our national story.

Here is a very early portrait by Kneller of *James Vernon*, courtier and the artist's first patron, painted three years after he arrived in London. Here too is a Closterman, beautifully composed, of *The Children of John Taylor* (1696), and a portrait of *John Montagu, 4th Earl of Sandwich* in which Highmore casts off his besetting sin of stiffness and captures the serpentine weakness of Sandwich.

There is a moving, anonymous portrait in her sickbed of the actress *Margaret ('Peg') Woffington* (c.1758) who played opposite, and was the lover of, David Garrick.

The best-known portraits are those of the members of the Kit-Cat Club,[9] by Kneller. Twenty are here; the other twenty are in the National Portrait Gallery in London (q.v.). Less known, but the outstanding portrait here, is that of the philosopher the *3rd Earl of*

Shaftesbury and his brother *Anthony Ashley Cooper*, who are painted by Closterman against a studio neo-classical backdrop of a temple with Ionic pillars and a moist, mysterious grove that anticipates, in 1701–2, the classicism that would dominate the century.

On the top floor, in attic rooms, are NPG portraits of artists, connoisseurs and architects: self-portraits of Angelica Kauffmann and Antonio Verrio, and a moving, sober portrait by Reynolds of *James McArdell*, the mezzotinter who engraved many plates after portraits by Reynolds. This is early Reynolds at his very best, attentive, thoughtful, affectionate.

Finally there is a fine order of architects here: *Sir John Vanbrugh*; *James Gibbs*; *Richard Boyle, 3rd Earl of Burlington*; *John Carr of York*; and *Sir William Chambers*.[10] They could have no more comfortable billet than in this elegant house.

NATIONAL MUSEUM OF PHOTOGRAPHY, FILM AND TELEVISION ***

Pictureville, Bradford, West Yorkshire
BD1 1NQ
Tel. 01274 202030
www.nmpft.org.uk

What it says: the biggest and best collection of photography, now boosted by that of the Royal Photographic Society

The National Museum of Photography, Film and Television was opened in 1983 as an outstation of the Science Museum, which was designed in the mid 1960s as a theatre by Sir Richard Siefert. Nearly 150 years after William Henry Fox Talbot exposed the first photograph, *Latticed Window*,[11] at Lacock Abbey (v. Fox Talbot Museum) in 1835, a museum was engaging directly with the medium that had dominated and, with its offspring, film and television, transformed the 20th century.

The importance of photography was quickly understood. In 1857 Lady Eastlake, the wife of the Director of the National Gallery and President of the Royal Academy, Sir Charles Eastlake, was noting that 'Photography has become a household word and a household want; is used alike by art and science, by love, business and justice.'[12] In the same year the Victoria and Albert Museum (q.v.) started its collection of photographs at South Kensington. Acquisitions there were primarily for technical and documentary reasons. Fine art galleries in Britain, national and regional, public and private, ignored the new medium and continued to do so until the 1990s. The V&A now has a fine collection and in Mark Haworth-Booth an excellent, knowledgeable curator, yet successive directors gave photographs no priority. So entrenched, until recently, was the Tate Gallery's indifference to photography, that its authoritative official history in 1998 by Frances Spalding makes no mention of it.

That has changed at Tate Modern (q.v.) whose *Handbook*[13] declares loftily that, 'in the final decades of the 20th century', artists 'adopted the media of film, video and still photography as a means of making permanent these ephemera [performance art]. This led in turn to the creative use of these media to originate the work,' as if photographers had not been making remarkable images for 150 years.

In that climate of neglect, ignorance and artistic snobbery displayed by museums and galleries, and by most critics, the new museum was faced with the problem of defining and creating a collection. Within a year, the collection of Kodak, the camera company founded by the American George Eastman, came to Bradford from the company's museum in Harrow, north London. With it came commercial cameras going back to the 1880s, when Eastman advertised 'the smallest, lightest and simplest of all Detective cameras' with the slogan 'You press the button, we do the rest', price five guineas, or five weeks' average wages. By 1900 Kodak's Brownie was a quarter of that cost.

The Kodak Collection took the new museum in two directions: one with an emphasis on popular, practical photography;

La Madonna Riposata *by Julia Margaret
Cameron (National Museum of Photography,
Film and Television)*

the other with an emphasis on equipment and technology, from Fox Talbot's early wooden box cameras and the elegant pine and mahogany camera (c. 1839)[14] of Louis Daguerre through the Thornton-Pickard half-plate stand camera (1910–40) and Leica's early 35 mm cameras to the American Polaroid Model 95 (1963) and the digital cameras of today. A parallel collection of cine cameras focuses on moving pictures: Eastman's paper-based rollfilm of 1885, Edison's first kinetoscope machine (1894), which gave a show lasting twenty seconds, and the Lumières' cheaper combined camera and projector (1895). The collection fast-forwards to Logie Baird's first Model B television (1928), the Cossor Model 1210 television (1939) and the Bush 22 television receiver (1950), one of which my mother, like many other people, bought in 1953 in order to watch the Coronation, its thick screen tightly boxed in Bakelite.

There is a limit to how much technology a visitor can take in. The joys of this museum are in its images. Its collection was strong on the 19th century, having Fox Talbot's photographs, Alexander John Ellis's daguerreotypes of Italy and Julia Margaret Cameron's album of ninety-four albumen images of her eminent friends on the Isle of Wight: Charles Darwin; Robert Browning; Alfred, Lord Tennyson; and with white wild hair, his eyes to the heavens, the great astronomer Sir John Herschel (1867), who worked with Fox Talbot on the experiments that led to his first photographs and who passed on that knowledge to Cameron thirty years later.

The collection has always been diverse but for twenty years it has existed somewhat in the shade of the greatest British collection, that of the Royal Photographic Society (RPS) exhibited in a small building in the middle of Bath in which few of its great photographs could be shown. In 2003 the two collections came together in Bradford, making this conclusively the National Gallery of Photography.

Since 1853, the RPS had been collecting a record of the work of the society's members and of the development of photography. John Dudley Johnston, a very competent photographer who was the society's president and then curator,[15] reorganised and extended the collection beyond the great Victorians (Fox Talbot; Octavius Hill and Robert Adamson;[16] Roger Fenton, the photographer of the Crimean War who here has landscapes and still lifes of equal quality; and Francis Frith, the finest commercial photographer in the 19th century) to the topographical work of Linnaeus Tripe and Frederick Henry Evans, friend of William Morris and George Bernard Shaw. His photograph of Aubrey Beardsley in profile remains the finest image of that endomorphic exotic, taken shortly before his death from tuberculosis, all white bone, vulture-nose and tendril fingers.

Here too are photographs by Frank Meadow Sutcliffe of life in Whitby[17] and by Peter Henry Emerson, whose scenes of rural Norfolk could be by Bastien-Lepage.

The combined collection includes the finest American photographers (Alfred Stieglitz, Edward J. Steichen, Edward Weston) and extends to the present day with the war photographs of Larry Burrows and of Don McCullin, the documentary portraits of Tony Ray-Jones and of Richard Billingham and a record of our age, the archive of the Daily Herald newspaper, 2½ million prints that are a daily photographic diary of Britain from the 1930s to the 1960s.

With the addition of the RPS's collection the museum is strongest in still photography. With the closure of the Museum of the Moving Image in London, there is a powerful case to be made for a museum dedicated to film and television that combines the collection of the British Film Institute with that of Bradford.

CARTWRIGHT HALL ART GALLERY ***

Lister Park, Bradford, West Yorkshire
BD9 4NS
Tel. 01274 751212
www.bradford.gov.uk/tourism/museums/

English paintings of the past 200 years plus a growing contemporary collection of Indian art by Indians, at home and abroad

You approach the museum through Lister Park with its municipal flower beds of well-behaved begonias and geraniums. Cartwright Hall is a monument to the certainties of Edwardian prosperity and civic confidence. Enter, and the first piece you see, under a top-lit rotunda, is Anish Kapoor's *Turning the World Inside Out* (1997), a large, almost ovoid sculpture of highly polished stainless steel that in its glossy simplicity is at once modernist and ancient, Western and Eastern: a declaration that here, in a city that is home to over 80,000 people originating from Pakistan, India and Bangladesh, is the largest collection in Britain of contemporary Asian decorative and fine art outside London.

The gallery was opened in 1904 with money and a site[18] given by the local textile magnate Samuel Cunliffe-Lister, 1st Baron Masham, and named in memory of Edward Cartwright, the inventor of the power-loom that, when modernised and improved in the 1860s, made Cunliffe-Lister's fortune.[19]

Designed by Sir John William Simpson, who had recently finished Glasgow Museum and Art Gallery (q.v.), the gallery has a monumental Edwardian baroque facade, its portico topped by a central tower over an open arcade. It promises splendid galleries in which to display the 'honest, healthy English art'[20] that the *Bradford Observer* approved of in 1879 and it delivers: big canvases that all tell a story, whether Arthurian (John Collier), mythological (Wright Barker) or Egyptian (Edwin Long). Next door is a collection of Newlyn artists (Stanhope Forbes, Frederick Hall and Henry Tuke) and of the New English Art Club

(George Clausen, James Charles and Henry La Thangue). La Thangue worked in Bradford in the 1880s and was commissioned and collected by men of manufacturing substance who were members of the city's Arcadian Art Club, which was part of the impetus for the Cartwright. In *The Connoisseur* (1807) La Thangue has painted Abraham Mitchell, owner of a worsted spinning firm specialising in mohair, and his son Tom, surrounded by his picture collection. Adventurous spirits such as Walter Dunlop and John Aldam Heaton commissioned Rossetti, Burne-Jones and Ford Madox Brown.

The gallery has a small collection of rare Victorian and Edwardian bronzes (Francis Derwent Wood, William Reid Dick, Sir Alfred Drury), a handful of Old Masters (a Guido Reni, a Corrado Giaquinto and Giorgio Vasari's *The Holy Family with St John*) and a somewhat miscellaneous collection of English portraiture (early, immature portraits by Romney and Gainsborough, Reynolds's *Master Thomas Lister* ('The Brown Boy'), a lovely Raeburn and 20th century portraits by John Singer Sargent and Ambrose McEvoy, and by Nina Hamnett of the Russian sculptor *Ossip Zadkine*).

Between the wars the gallery received gifts from the Contemporary Art Society of a drawing by David Bomberg and oils by William Roberts (*Jockeys/The Paddock*) and Christopher Wood of his lover, Frosca Munster, *The Manicure*, painted the year before he committed suicide.

This attractive but slightly shapeless collection has been given new purpose by a sequence of directors since the 1950s. Peter Bird (1958–68) started to acquire work by Bradford-born David Hockney (since developed into a strong collection, with all his best-known series of prints[21] and several single works). In 1968 his successor John Morley initiated the Bradford International Print Biennale, held on eleven subsequent occasions, out of which has grown an unusual collection of prints by Czech, Polish, Turkish, Namibian and Japanese artists, beside work by British artists (Howard Hodgkin, Peter Blake, Peter

Howson, Patrick Caulfield), while in the 1960s John Morley had acquired etchings by Dürer, van Leyden, Guido Reni, Salvator Rosa, Tiepolo, Goya and William Blake.

It is, however, what the gallery calls its Transcultural Collection that distinguishes the Cartwright from other regional galleries. With no model to guide it, the gallery has felt its way carefully, holding temporary exhibitions of textiles, jewellery and contemporary art, and making acquisitions in the light of the public response. What was seen initially as a South Asian collection has widened to include Islamic calligraphy, costume and glass, all of them contemporary since the cultural policies of the governments of India and Pakistan forbid the exports of artefacts that are over 100 years old. This apparent restriction has proved to be a strength, with baghs and phulkaris from the Punjab, saris from Orissa, textiles from Rajasthan, a Tamil Nadu temple chariot-horse in painted wood all demonstrating the superlative quality of contemporary craftsmanship. The cross-reference between Britain and the subcontinent is already developing with the work of such artists as Laila Rahman, born in 1966 and trained in Lahore and at the Slade, and Sutapa Biswas, born in West Bengal in 1962 and trained at the Royal College of Art, as was Saleem Arif, born in 1949 in Hyderabad.

Most regional galleries offer the opportunity to see their city through the eyes of local artists. Here Bertram Priestman looks down on a Bradford of factories, smoking chimneys, churches and railway bridges; Edward Wadsworth in *Bradford: View of a Town* (1914) sees the same grey roofs and chimneys as a Vorticist grid; while Lubna Chowdhary views *Bradford City* as a series of architectural landscapes which she models in glazed stoneware: Lister's Mill, the Alhambra, the City Hall, the Wool Exchange with its roof askew and Cartwright Hall Art Gallery transformed from Simpson's baroque into an Indian palace, raised on delicate pointed feet, its windows and pediments transformed as if carved from ivory.

Sarbjit Natt's Mughal *at Cartwright Hall Art Gallery*

In the late 1980s the Victoria and Albert Museum spent several years pondering whether to move its Indian Collections to Bradford, to Lister's Mill. The Cartwright is exploring other, contemporary, ways in which East and West can meet.

BRONTË PARSONAGE MUSEUM *

Church Street, Haworth, Keighley, West Yorkshire BD22 8DR
Tel. 01535 642323
www.bronte.org.uk

As written by the Brontë sisters (and their brother); books and manuscripts and drawings from their created worlds

After the wild and bleak moorland landscapes described in Emily Brontë's *Wuthering Heights* and Anne Brontë's *The Tenant of Wildfell Hall*, the polite, almost genteel village of Haworth may be a surprise.

At the summit of the village beside the church, reached by a very cobbled street of cottages, teashops and gift shops, is the Parsonage, built of dark local stone in 1778, to which the Revd Patrick Brontë brought his wife and their six young children in 1820. Within a few years Mrs Brontë and the two eldest daughters were dead.

It is not easy to relate the outer orderliness of the house to the inner imaginations of the Brontës, whether expressed through the novels, the 'little books' they made as children (displayed here) or the maps of the imagined lands of Angria or Gondal into which they retreated in play.

Each room tells a part of their story: Mr Brontë's Study with its books of psalms, his pipe, stick, tobacco jar and the huge magnifying glass he needed as he became increasingly blind; the Drawing Room where Emily died in 1848, having been nursed through her last days on the sofa; the room at the back, originally a peat store where geese were kept, converted by Charlotte into a study for her husband, the Revd Arthur Bell Nicholls,

The Brontës' Parsonage at Haworth

following their marriage in 1854, decorated with green sprigged wallpaper and curtains; Mr Brontë's Bedroom overlooking the church and its graveyard, shared in his last years with Branwell; and Charlotte's Bedroom, in which Mrs Gaskell slept when she visited Charlotte in 1853 and in which Charlotte died in 1855.

All these could be rooms in the home of any parson of the period. To seek something of the Brontës you have to turn to such details as Charlotte's startlingly small shoes and kid gloves. Mrs Gaskell observed in her *Life of Charlotte Brontë* (1857) that 'her hands and feet were the smallest I ever saw, when one of the former was placed in mine it was like the soft touch of a bird in the middle of my palm.' Charlotte's handwriting, sewing and knitting

were all exceptionally neat and minute, but still nothing prepares you for the length and slightness of the little empty pods that are the fingers of her gloves.

Branwell Brontë's portraits here of friends and local worthies are plain and competent likenesses but the self-portrait of himself summoned from sleep by death is an image from beyond dreams. By contrast Charlotte's drawings (scalings-up of Raphael's *Madonna of the Fish* from an engraving by Louis Schalz or a *Classical Head* 'in the style of Raphael') are the conventionally accurate exercises of a well-educated young woman. More surprising is the portrait of Mr Brontë as a young curate newly arrived from Ireland, dramatically dark and handsome.

As so often it is the detail of the specific voice that leaps time. Here is the whisper of the eight-year-old Anne through her choice of scriptural text embroidered with care on her sampler: 'Let me die the death of the righteous, and let my last end be like his'[22] and Charlotte's, aged six, 'My humility and the fear of the Lord are riches, honour and life' contrasted with the full throat of the 37-year-old Charlotte in a letter to Mrs Gaskell of 31 August 1853, 'Come as soon as you can: the heather is in bloom now – I have waited and watched for its purple signal as a forerunner of your coming.'

Here too, among the lifeless cabinets of bonnets and bags, as surprising in its way as the little gloves, is the unlikely present of a pair of beaded moccasins given to Charlotte by the niece of the owner of the guest house in Scarborough where she stayed during Anne's last illness in 1849.

When the Parsonage was opened as a museum in 1928, the Brontë Society intended that it would be a shrine, and the gift by the American bibliophile Henry Houston Bonnell of his vast collection of Brontëana ensures that there is archive enough to fill two exhibition rooms. The present curators do well by placing it in the context of the Haworth in which the Brontës lived. An official survey, the Benjamin Hershel Babbage Report of 1850, found that 41.6 per cent of those living in the village died before the age of six and that the average age of death was 25 years 8 months – statistics not unrelated to the lack of sewerage and the absence of a supply of pure water. Photographs here will disabuse the visitor of any sense of the romance of mid-19th-century rural life. Those of Brandy Row, the poorest street in Haworth, show it to be as grim as any street in Manchester or Leeds. The Row was not demolished until 1960.

The Babbage Report and the graveyard connect you to the world in which the Brontës lived and died. To summon their spirit, re-read the novels or look at the eyes in Branwell's portrait of his sisters in the National Portrait Gallery (q.v.), and the way in which he has attempted to paint out his own image.[23]

HUDDERSFIELD ART GALLERY *

Princess Alexandra Walk, Huddersfield, West Yorkshire HD1 2SU
Tel. 01484 221964
www.kirkleesmc.gov.uk/art

Twentieth-century British painting

The advice that smaller public galleries seek on acquisitions is crucial. The obligation placed on the Cecil Higgins Art Gallery by their founder's will to have all acquisitions approved by 'a recognised authority such as . . . the Victoria and Albert Museum'[24] and the gallery's subsequent good fortune in being advised by Graham Reynolds (1951–5), Edward Croft-Murray and Ronald Alley (from 1957), ensured the quality of its collection of British watercolours. Swindon Art Gallery benefited greatly from its relationship first with Sir Lawrence Gowing (1963–6) and then with Richard Morphet of the Tate Gallery since 1966. In 1957 Huddersfield Art Gallery's newly appointed chief librarian and curator, Ken Aldridge, had the good sense to appoint Philip James, then Director of art at the Arts Council of Great Britain, as the gallery's adviser. In twelve years, with only a small budget, it acquired works by such contemporary artists as Henry Moore, Ivon Hitchens, Ceri Richards, Keith Vaughan and Ben Nicholson, and dragged the gallery's collection into the mid 20th century.

Before this appointment the collection had dozed, if not slept. The town had built a new City Library and Art Gallery in 1936 to designs by E. H. Ashburner, remarkably similar to, if smaller than, the Graves Art Gallery in Sheffield that he had designed two years before, but in Huddersfield there was no benefactor and no founding collection, beyond a handful of Victorian and Edwardian landscapes by Thomas F. M. Sheard, H. W. Adams, B. W. Leader and Walter J. Shaw, all of justly modest repute. Only a single oil painting by G. F. Watts, a drawing by W. Holman Hunt and an etching by J. McN. Whistler raise an eyebrow. In 1949 the council had established a fund of £300 a year, later raised to £500, for the purchase of works of art, backed by a special reserve fund of £10,000, but for seven years neither was called upon.

In 1958 Philip James plunged in by recommending the purchase of a major sculpture by Henry Moore, *Falling Warrior*, casts of which were already in Toronto and Antwerp. An exchange of letters between Moore, James and Aldridge makes clear the extreme nervousness of the Huddersfield councillors before the committee finally voted to approve the acquisition,[25] the clinching argument appearing to be that, as a Yorkshire artist, Moore was prepared to reduce the price for a Yorkshire public gallery.

Emboldened (and encouraged), James successfully recommended that works by Ivon Hitchens, John Piper and Michael Ayrton be bought and, in 1959, more by Ben Nicholson, Keith Vaughan, William Roberts and Terry Frost, and a sculpture by Frank Dobson.

From his time at the Arts Council James knew London artists and dealers and, in the next few years, bought widely and shrewdly from the Leicester Galleries, Gimpel Fils, the Redfern, the Beaux Arts and the New London Galleries for prices that ranged between 50 and 150 guineas.

With two exceptions, a painting by Terry Frost and one by Michael Kidner, all James's recommendations were figurative, but not all were contemporary. Paintings by members of the New English Art Club were acquired – Walter Sickert, Robert Bevan, Charles Ginner and Harold Gilman – as were works by Matthew Smith and Sickert's pupil, Sylvia Gosse; and in 1966 L. S. Lowry was commissioned to paint a townscape of *Chapel Hill in Huddersfield*. The result is more Salford than Huddersfield, hard streets and buildings without the sense of the surrounding hills that is ever present in Huddersfield.[26]

The flurry of acquisitions attracted bequests. D. R. H. Williams, who had written the introduction to the 1946 exhibition *Two Hundred Years of British Art*, opened by Sir Kenneth Clark, left at his death in 1963 his personal collection, which included paintings by Wilson Steer, Gilbert Spencer and D. Y. Cameron, and thirty Japanese prints by Hiroshige, Hokusai, Utamaro and others. Three years later a Dr Pye-Smith bequeathed a sum for four local artists, to be selected by Sir Philip Hendy, then Director of the National Gallery, to paint 'oil or water colour pictures of the Huddersfield district that people may realise the beauty in which their town is situated'. Sheila Fell, Carel Weight, Alan Lowndes and Peter Brook were selected.

Ken Aldridge resigned in 1967. The relationship with Philip James ceased and the policy on acquisitions reverted to one of buying spasmodically. When local government was reorganised in 1974 Francis Bacon's magnificent *Figure Study II* entered the combined collection of the Kirklees authority. With help from the Contemporary Arts Society and others, the 20th-century collection has been strengthened (Edward Wadsworth, Robert Colquhoun) and works by contemporary artists acquired (Frank Auerbach, Alan Davie, an Elizabeth Blackadder watercolour, a Nicola Hicks drawing).

FERENS ART GALLERY ✳✳✳

Queen Victoria Square, Hull,
Humberside HU1 3RA
Tel. 01482 613902
www.hullcc.gov.uk/museums

Enlightened gallery in the heart of Hull: Old Masters and new discoveries: the Camden Town Group in town

Hull's Philosophical Society was one of the first wave of such societies founded in Yorkshire[27] between 1818 and 1834 in the apparently secure and relatively prosperous years following the Napoleonic Wars. Unlike those in Leeds, Sheffield and York, the society in Hull failed to take root and no art gallery was established until 1900.

By 1903 the gallery's collection comprised four paintings and it was only in 1905 that the first purchase was made.[28] At this point the local industrialist and MP Thomas Robinson Ferens made the first of several donations,[29] which provided the capital with which to build a new gallery in 1927 and an endowment for purchasing works.

The building, designed by London architects S. N. Cooke and E. C. Davies, has a plain, neoclassical facade in Portland stone with powerful bronze entrance doors flanked by two Corinthian columns. Inside, the top-lit galleries are arranged symmetrically round a columned central rotunda with a first-floor balcony. The building is at the hub of the city, with the Hull Maritime Museum on the other side of Queen Victoria Square. Behind it is the Humber Estuary, beside it quays which today form a marina.

Ferens wanted the gallery 'to resist any temptations to buy any work that is not likely to be enduring in influence'. In the last fifty years the gallery has achieved that by concentrating on 20th-century British art, but initially directors interpreted this brief by acquiring 17th- and 18th-century Italian and Dutch paintings, 17th–19th-century English works and marine subjects, both local and Continental.

Their choice was well judged: a good, early (*c.* 1728) Canaletto, *A View on the Grand Canal*; a dramatic *Annunciation* (1657–60) by the Venetian Francesco Maffei; and a pair of polychrome rococo sculptures (carved wood and gesso) of *Hercules* and *Meleager* (*c.* 1700), by the Venetian Antonio Maragliano. Their curves and spiralling poses make playful the serious stories of Meleager's death and Hercules's labours.

The Dutch paintings include a *vanitas* still life (1644) by Cornelius Gysbrechts, a small and unusually bright landscape by Jacob van Ruisdael (*c.* 1685) and Frans Hals's *Portrait of a Young Woman* (1665–60), her wistful half-smile gently and affectionately observed by Hals.

In the English collection are landscapes by Richard Wilson and Julius Caesar Ibbetson, two good Leightons and one Constable, unsigned and of uncertain provenance.

A quiet strength of all three collections is the opportunity they offer to see works by less celebrated artists. The 17th-century church interiors of Daniel de Blieck and Pieter Neefs Snr stand comparison with those by Saenredam, De Witte or Houckgeest. The dramatic lighting in Volmarijn's *Supper at Emmaus* echoes the supreme skills of Caravaggio and van Honthorst, as portraits by de Keyser and van der Helst do the genius of Rembrandt. These are works that would be unlikely to feature in national collections but whose qualities merit attention.

It is appropriate, too, that the art gallery of an historic port, such as Hull, should have a strong marine collection with paintings by Willem van der Velde and Richard Parkes Bonington, and by local artists Francis Hustwick, Francis Holman and John Ward.

It is in the 20th-century English collection that the Ferens's ambitious policy of acquisitions is most happily realised. The work of the New English Art Club and the Camden Town Group are well represented by respectively Sickert, Wilson Steer, and Clausen; Gwen John, Gilman and Gore. There is room for interesting grace notes: a confident self-portrait in his last year at the Slade by the seventeen-year-old Albert Rutherston, the younger brother of William Rothenstein, and the dark black and red *Interior of a Cinema* (*c.* 1913–14) by Malcolm Drummond, painted when he was seeking out public subjects.[30]

An outstanding self-portrait by Wyndham Lewis, *Mr Wyndham Lewis as a Tyro* (1920–21) conveys the shock and excitement generated by Vorticism, with Lewis's dark features and gleaming, demonic eyes under an arched eyebrow, set against a burning yellow ground. Beside it, as context, are 1920s paintings by Jacob Kramer, David Bomberg and William Roberts.

There are two Stanley Spencer portraits: a gentle one of *Major E. O. Kay* (1943), red-faced in tweeds and waistcoat, monocled,[31] and the violently sexual portrait of his second wife, Patricia Preece (*c.* 1936–7). It is all flesh and face. With wide eyes, pendulous breasts, huge nipples and flesh hung from bones like a carcass, she confronts and challenges the artist and the viewer.

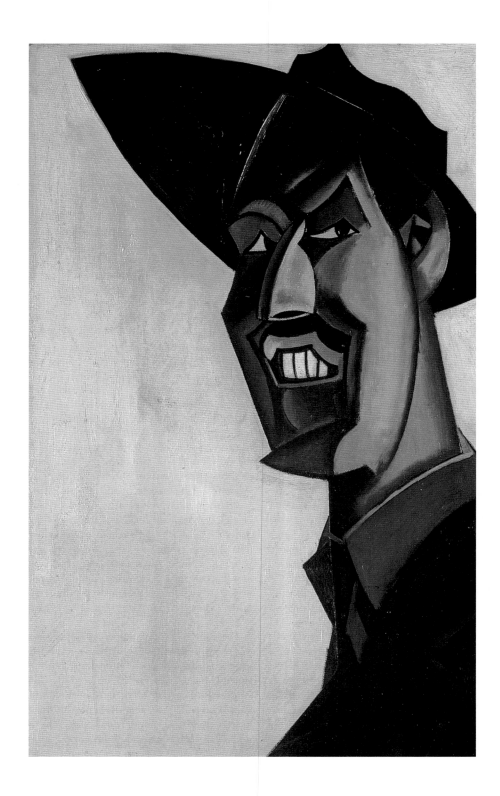

Around these are portraits by his brother, Gilbert; by Nina Hamnett (of *Madame Dolores Courtney*, who, like Hamnett, was associated with Roger Fry's Omega Workshop); and by Dod Procter.

Demonstrating how catholic and judicious has been the taste of successive directors are a small landscape by Ben Nicholson (*Winter Landscape, Cornwall*), painted in 1931, the year he moved with Barbara Hepworth to St Ives, a landscape on the turn towards abstraction though still retaining flashes of colour and figurative detail; and *A Game of Patience*, by Meredith Frampton, which although only painted two years earlier might have come from a different world of precise record and apparent realism, and fronts a raft of symbols. The model (Margaret Austin-Jones, who features in his earlier full-length portrait in the Tate collection, q.v.) sits at a card table, cool and still. Her skin is ivory. Before her on the table are cards, face down except for the king of spades; two apples; an ear of corn and a red poppy in foreskinned bud. Her breasts swell against the grey, puritan dress, at whose neck are ecclesiastical bands. She is framed by a background of architectural mouldings, to the right of which is visible a clear, toy-like rural landscape.

As other galleries faltered in purchasing new works in the late 20th century, the Ferens maintained its steady eye with paintings by Victor Pasmore, Leon Kossoff, Keith Vaughan, Patrick Heron, Terry Frost, Frank Auerbach, David Hockney and Bridget Riley, and sculptures by Epstein, Hepworth, Moore, Glyn Philpot and Lynn Chadwick. The gallery turned financial constraints to good effect by acquiring a collection of contemporary prints (Roger Hilton, Anish Kapoor, Eduardo Paolozzi, Maggi Hambling, Bruce McLean) to stand beside its strong holding of 19th-century etchings (Richard Dadd, Holman Hunt, Samuel Palmer), which contains one outstanding curiosity, the series of twelve mezzotints by Sir Frank Short after Turner's *Liber Studiorum*.

Mr Wyndham Lewis as a Tyro by Wyndham Lewis (Ferens Art Gallery)

Every part of each of this gallery's collections is considered and thought-provoking. The Ferens demonstrates that it is not only masterpieces that make a gallery's influence endure.

HULL AND EAST RIDING MUSEUM *

36 High Street, Hull, Humberside HU1 1PS
Tel. 01482 613902
www.hullcc.gov.uk/museums

The archaeology of Yorkshire

In July 1984 a large oak logboat, forty feet long and five feet wide, was discovered in a field near Hasholme Hall close to the River Foulness in the East Riding of Yorkshire. While drains were being dug there emerged from the mud a large fragment of wood that had been preserved by water, silt and clay for nearly 2,500 years.

A feat of engineering was needed to shift her and a feat of archaeology, led by Martin Millett and Sean McGrail, to preserve her. Only twenty[32] or so logboats have ever been found in northern Europe; from this one complete boat it has been possible to enrich our understanding of many aspects of life and of the changing environment of the area in the millennia either side of Anno Domini: the tree from which it was made, felled between 322 and 277 BC; the method of construction; its cargo (carcasses of butchered meat); the types of pollen, water beetle and mussels (fresh and salt water); the use of moss to caulk the boat.[33]

It was fortunate that the boat became the responsibility of Hull City Museums, which have had a strong archaeology department for several decades. Built around the core of the spectacular Mortimer Collection, the department was formed by Tom Sheppard, Director of Hull City Museums from 1900 to 1944. Sheppard was one of the great museum directors of the early 20th century. After leaving school at fifteen to become a railway clerk he joined the Hull Geographical Society in 1893; started to write papers that secured his election to the Royal Geological Society in 1900, aged twenty-four; and was appointed the first curator of the Hull Municipal Museum the following year. He believed not in cabinets of curiosities but in museums that had objects of scholarly importance, which preferably told a strong story about the community. He opened nine new museums in Hull including Wilberforce House Museum (q.v.) (1906), and the first maritime museum in the UK[34] (1912).

Sheppard and the East Riding made a good fit; this is an area that provides rich material for a geologist. Ice Age glaciers carved a new coastline as the ice ground its way down from the moors into the Plain of Holderness and Lake Humbert and Lake Pickering, leaving detritus to be found millennia later: the molar of a woolly mammoth, the antlers and teeth of deer, the bones of a woolly rhino at Kelsey Hill.[35]

The beauty of the late Neolithic objects here (a polished stone ovoid macehead, a stone ball, a slice of polished flint knife, the delicate lozenge of a razor-sharp flint spearhead) catches your breath.

Less than two years after Sheppard became Director, a farm labourer employed by Lord Middleton found a grave at North Grimston that when excavated proved to be that of an Iron Age warrior, surrounded by iron swords, rings of bronze and jet, and thin bronze sheets.

New Roman galleries were opened in 2002 that feature a reconstructed street scene and bath house. With the Old Roman Road following the western slopes of the Wolds before turning to York and Malton, it is not surprising that the sites of Roman villas have been uncovered ever since one was found at North Horkstow in north Lincolnshire in 1797. In this century Professor Sir Ian Richmond excavated the villa at Rudston in 1933 and there have been excavations at Brantingham (1941 and 1962), Harpham and again, in 1971–2, at Rudston. All of them uncovered mosaics, of which the three here that Richmond found at Rudston are the most spectacular. The Venus mosaic depicts the goddess naked with a mass of wild hair, a mirror in one hand, an apple in the other, her face half in deep shadow, half in blazing white light. The lines are crude (the central circle is drawn freehand) but the work is extraordinarily bold, as are the colours, red, black, grey, ochre, brown and green. In a panel to the right of the goddess is a 'crescent on a stick', the weapon of the Telegenii, famous animal-fighters in the African amphitheatres, all of which tends to confirm that these mosaics, by some means, derive from the mosaics of North Africa, even though they are crude when compared with the paving of the frigidarium in the Acholla thermae (2nd century) or the Acholla *Four Seasons* mosaic (3rd century) in the Bardo Museum, Carthage.

The East Riding continued to yield archaeological finds of importance, of which the most spectacular was the chariot burial found at Garton Slack ('a dry valley') in 1971 and excavated by T. C. M. Brewster. For the first time in Britain, a Celtic chariot burial was revealed with all its trappings: bridle bits, terrets (rein rings), hub hoops, soil stains and imprints of the spokes of the wheels. Even the felloes and the pole shaft were intact. Between the two iron tyres was the skeleton of the charioteer, a man of about thirty, whose left leg was shorter than his right. Beside him were the remains of his whip, the wooden handle impregnated by the copper sulphate from the pommel. His skeleton lies there, stretched out before the thin circles of the tyres, relaxed, as if asleep.

HULL MARITIME MUSEUM
*

Queen Victoria Square, Hull, Humberside
HU1 2AA
Tel. 01482 610610
www.hullcc.gov.uk/museums/maritime/
index.php

Sea-going history, whaling, scrimshaw

Beyond Hull there is only the North Sea. Its grey, unceasing waves, its changing moods and its salt air have determined the city. It has given work and fortune with one tide and left empty nets and death with another.

It is proper that, in the city centre, in Queen Victoria Square, by the quayside, there is the Hull Maritime Museum, in the former Dock Office, a grandly civic building. Inside, the original interiors have been retained, their solid Baltic pine[36] giving a sense of landlubberly security for those with no sea legs. The Court Room of the Dock Board, upstairs, is magisterial, with marble Corinthian columns, gilded.

Hull has long had a triple life, as a port for inshore fishing, as a whaling port from which ships set sail to cross the world in search of these leviathans, and as a port for trade with the Baltic and the Hanseatic ports.[37]

The North Sea fishing is recognised here by models of fishing boats: models large (of a smack with full sails, 1883, scale 1:16) and small (a clinker-built Yorkshire coble, 2 inches to 1 foot). There are models of steam trawlers (the *Lord Nelson*, killed off when the Cod War imposed a 200-mile limit in 1981) and motor trawlers (the *Arctic Corsair*, built in 1960 with a sidewinder on the starboard side only). There are ketches, brigs and brigantines for coasting and for the short sea-trade; topsail schooners; and a 1913 sloop.

But it is to whaling that this museum is in thrall: to the men who pursued the great beasts across the oceans, and to the equipment with which they killed them and turned their carcasses into cash. Here are the walrus harpoon, and lances, and the bomb lance that is shot from a gun and explodes within the whale. Here is a short stocky shotgun for sealing. Here are flensing knives and blubber knives. Here, a pair of spurs for keeping purchase when walking on the slippery skin of the whale during flensing. Here, a flensing spade for separating the plates of baleen, a Krening hook to remove fat and muscle from blubber, a closh to impale blubber, a pricker for pushing it into storage casks, and a blubber pot in which the blubber is rendered.

Only the teeth remain, to be carved as scrimshaw during long evenings. There is more scrimshaw here than you will ever have seen: the collection of Kathleen Eleanor Tizard. The origins of scrimshaw, even of the word

itself, are obscure. Scrimshaw typically comes from the Yankee whalers who voyaged to the Antarctic, the shorter passages to Greenland offering less time in which to do such work. Here ships and scenes of the whale hunt predominate as subjects and provide a visual history of whaling, as do paintings by John Ward, Thomas Binks and Thomas Fletcher.

And at the end, after the death and the division of skin from flesh, and flesh from blubber, and blubber from baleen, there is here the skeleton of a two-year-old southern right whale from Greenland, a type now almost extinct. And, with less dignity, a seat has been made from whalebone, its frame from two whale vertebrae, its back from whale ribs.

This is a museum not only to the whale but to the men who lived their lives in pursuit of this mighty beast: Captain (later Sir) Samuel Standidge who ran a fleet of whalers and became mayor of Hull; William Scoresby Snr who, in fifteen voyages in his ship *The Resolution*, regularly returned with more than ten whales;[38] William Scoresby Jnr, whaling captain, explorer, naturalist; and, finally, the Vicar of Bradford whose *History of the Arctic Regions* is still the standard reference work.[39]

The men live on in this museum and its galleries echo to the sounds of the sea and the ghostly songs of whales.

UNIVERSITY OF HULL ART COLLECTION *

The University, Cottingham Road, Kingston-upon-Hull, Humberside HU6 7RX
Tel. 01482 465035

Small and select choice of 20th-century British art and comprehensive Chinese ceramics

Only the foolhardy, the brave or the divinely inspired would try to create a serious collection of early-20th-century English art with an endowment of £300 a year. But the University of Hull has done it.

In 1963 Dr Malcolm Easton, the university's lecturer in the history of art, persuaded the university that it should use the small endowment left by the local industrialist and MP Thomas Robinson Ferens[40] for 'the encouragement of the Fine Arts' not only to fund lectures but also to buy works of art. He further convinced them that the collection should confine itself to the period 1890–1940.

Easton's choice of period was crucial. It spanned two world wars and the end of empire, and it took painting and sculpture from what he called 'the despotism of sentiment and story'[41] of Alma-Tadema, Leighton and Etty to the threshold of modernism with Nicholson, Hepworth and Moore. Within five years the range and quality of the collection were established. Dr Easton purchased works by Sickert, Augustus John and Lucien Pissarro; by Harold Gilman and Spencer Gore; by Duncan Grant and Vanessa Bell; by Jacob Epstein, Stanley Spencer and Ben Nicholson.

Such purchases inspired the executors and relatives of other artists to make gifts: of works by Roger Fry (given by his daughter); Ginner (given by his sister); and Epstein and Malcolm Drummond (given by their widows).[42] Since then sculpture by Henri Gaudier-Brzeska, Eric Gill, Henry Moore and Frank Dobson, and paintings by Matthew Smith, C. R. W. Nevinson and S. J. Peploe have been acquired.

Dr Easton's taste and knowledge have turned the small size of the collection to advantage by exhibiting the works of artists on the edges of the Camden Town and London Groups who are too often ignored by larger galleries or confined to their storerooms. Here is an opportunity to see works by Henry Tonks, who taught Stanley Spencer at the Slade; by Epstein's friend Earnshaw Greenwood, who taught at the Central School of Arts and Crafts; by J. D. Innes; and by Stanislava de Karlowska, the Polish artist married to Robert Bevan, whose painting here, At Church Staunton (c.1916), uses the same palette of deep blues and greens as Bevan and the same cloisonné-like technique of giving solidity to shapes by marking them with strong outlines.

The collection has works by Malcolm Drummond, a founder member of both the Camden Town and London Groups, who was alone among them in turning to public subjects after the First World War: the interior of cinemas,[43] the Hammersmith Palais de Danse, Chelsea Public Library and, here, an Old Bailey trial, Court Scene (1920). The drawings and etchings in the collection include Drummond's studies of this, and two etchings of it, as well as work by Aubrey Beardsley, George Clausen, Edward Gordon Craig, Mark Gertler, James Pryde and Ambrose McEvoy, and an archive of letters and papers documenting the groups.

Other works plumb, in portraits, the undertow of the London art world in this period. C. R. W. Nevinson used Henry Moat, the bull-headed, close-shaven butler of Osbert Sitwell,[44] as a model for an arms dealer in his anti-war He Made a Fortune but He Gave a Son (1918). Augustus John painted Dorelia,[45] his model and his mistress in a ménage à trois with his then wife Ida Nettleship. Following Nettleship's death in 1906, Dorelia became his wife. Vanessa Bell's Conversation Piece (1912) depicts her husband Clive Bell, Leonard Woolf and Adrian Stephens in Virginia Woolf's Asheham House near Firle in Sussex.

These are combined with curiosities such as Charles Ginner's palette, encrusted with neat columns of paint, some more than an inch high; Frank Dobson's Cornucopia (1925–7) in Ham Hill stone (the Fitzwilliam Museum, q.v., has it in bronze); and Eric Gill's A Roland for an Oliver (1910), the companion to his Crucifixion in Tate Britain (q.v.). Thus a collection of riches has come into being: one that, together with the York Art Gallery, Leeds City Art Gallery and the Ferens (all q.v.), makes Yorkshire an exceptional place to consider English art of this period. It is thus all the more regrettable that the university does not show its collections to better effect, burying them in two plain rooms in the basement of Middleton Hall, an undistinguished 1960s building, without benefit of signage.

The university's other collection, of Chinese ceramics, is displayed in wall cabinets in the corridor outside the two galleries. This collection, built up by Dr and Mrs Peter Thompson over the past forty years, offers two unusual perspectives. Their first collection, made in the

1970s, concentrates on the products of the two most important kiln complexes of the 17th century, Dehua in Fujian and Jingdezhen in North Jaingxi. In the second, the Thompsons have tried to acquire representative pieces from each period since the Tang Dynasty, so providing, in 121 pieces, an overview of Chinese ceramics in epitome.

The first collection focuses on the Transitional Period, 1620–83, which saw the decline and fall of the Ming Dynasty and the rise of the Manchu Qing. The Ming imperial patronage that Jingdezhen had enjoyed for 300 years ended with the death of Emperor Wanli in 1619 and Jingdezhen was forced to innovate and experiment with new shapes and designs for new markets, domestic and foreign, particularly in Japan and the Netherlands. The techniques of underglazing which made supreme the blue and white ware from these kilns was retained, as was the flowing quality of painting; but a new style of landscapes and figure subjects was adapted to new shapes such as tall vases and short cylindrical brushpots.

Dehua had never had imperial commissions but its white, vitreous, blanc de chine ware (mainly moulded or modelled rather than thrown) also had to adapt to the demand for foreign subjects.

In the second collection each piece is not only typical but of quality. Pieces from the Song Dynasty (a large lilac-blue Junyao bowl and a Dingya dish glazed white with a metal-bound rim) and from the Qing (Kangxi) Dynasty (a flared bowl with purple glaze and a translucent turquoise bowl) stand out.

The university is fortunate to have collections of this quality. They deserve to be better known.

WILBERFORCE HOUSE MUSEUM *

25 High Street, Hull, Humberside HU1 1NQ
Tel. 01482 613902

The birthplace of the great abolitionist of slavery remembers his campaign

The High Street is the oldest street in Hull. Set back from it, behind a high wall and a garden, is the house that is the birthplace of William Wilberforce. Its unique 17th-century, red-brick facade has a faintly Dutch appearance, modestly elegant. Since 1906 it has been a museum dedicated to Wilberforce and his Parliamentary battles to secure the abolition of slavery.

Inside, the rooms, oak-panelled and of Georgian proportion, contain objects and documents that tell something of those struggles, which occupied over forty-five years of Wilberforce's life, between 1787 and 1833, and of the history of the triangular slave trade in the 18th and 19th centuries.

Here is the 1764 log book of a slave trader itemising the trade in human beings as if they were livestock. Here is an iron with which slaves were branded and the iron ankle fetter and ring and staple that bound them. On the wall are hung gang-chains.

There is an inventory from the Valley Plantation, St John, Jamaica (1787), valuing its slaves (57 men, 25 women) at £5,690. 2s. 6d. In case you should forget that these are human beings, they are named: Jimmy, 'a carpenter in his prime', valued at £330; Zwan, an elderly half-breed cook, £20; Luis, 'a good carter', £125.

Ledgers record punishments of between 10 and 25 lashes. Near them are the leather whips, ropes, thongs and canes with which these were administered. In one six-month period on the Sarah Plantation in British Guiana (1828), 32 slaves received 499 lashes.

Wilberforce used information like this to help make his case. In front of one Parliamentary Committee he produced a model of the slave ship *Brookes*, exhibited here, to demonstrate conditions during the typical two months that a 'middle passage' from Africa to America took.

The campaign to abolish the slave trade and slavery itself extended over five decades and produced many items of anti-slavery memorabilia to support the cause: Wedgwood jasper medallions (1787 and 1790), fob signets, tobacco boxes from the Coalbrookdale Ironworks (Ironbridge Gorge Museums, q.v.); alabaster wall plaques; a handsome Coalport anti-slavery vase; and medallions struck in 1807 to celebrate (prematurely) abolition when the Bill finally received Royal Assent on 25 March. A bill to register slaves in the West Indies was introduced in 1812, unsuccessfully, across Europe and the campaign had to be prosecuted even more vigorously against the French, the Russians and the Dutch, at the Congress of Aix-la-Chapelle and not least with Christophe, Emperor of Haiti.

In the aftermath of Britain making the trade in slaves a felony, the conditions for slaves in the middle passage became worse as other countries took up the contracts, on which profits of over 120 per cent could be made. Lighter, faster craft were employed, into which chained slaves were packed ever more closely on decks that were reduced to two feet in height.

Although, by arguing the case for abolition so tenaciously in the House of Commons, Wilberforce was the main mouthpiece of the struggle to abolish slavery, the campaign pre-dated his involvement and involved many others. The copy of a poem by William Cowper, 'The Negro's Complaint' (1788), is an oblique reminder of the part played by John Newton, the former slave trader and composer of hymns who lived with Cowper at Olney (v. the Cowper and Newton Museum), as are two portraits of Thomas Clarkson, whose campaigning pre-dated that of Wilberforce.

It is proper that Hull should honour its great son in this museum, which opened in 1906. His struggle, into which he poured himself and his fortune, was heroic, the more since he was widely acknowledged as being a man of great sweetness, kindliness and simplicity. As the pamphlet published by the museum in 1906 on the dedication of his birthplace to the public declared, 'He was a poor man, living on the wreck of his fortune, but the sunshine was in his heart.'[46]

CLIFFE CASTLE MUSEUM *

Spring Gardens Lane, Keighley,
West Yorkshire BD20 6LH
Tel. 01535 618230

Victorian home displays rocks, crystals and fossils

Cliffe Castle is an unlikely building in which to house an important natural history collection. Halfway up a long hill out of Keighley, along which are strung the houses of the town's richest 19th-century families, it is a Gothic folly that appears to have accreted gable ends, chimney pots and conservatories with neither care nor attention. When Henry Isaac Butterfield (1819–1910) inherited Old Cliffe Hall, along with a fortune from the family's three worsted mills, he set about remodelling it (1875–83) with the help of George Smith, a local architect, who added towers, a *porte cochère* and more conservatories. On Smith's death, Butterfield employed another local architect, Wilson Bailey, to design battlements, a ballroom, a billiard room and a glass dome on the main conservatory. It looks a mess. Within, Butterfield demonstrated a taste for French boudoirs, cramming room after room with ornate furniture and heavy fabrics.

Sir Bracewell Smith, former Dulwich MP and a former Lord Mayor of London, bought it in 1950 and gave it to the town as a museum, somewhat slimmed down and simplified by yet another architect, Sir Albert Richardson. It opened in 1959.

Butterfield's ballroom, with its original carved ceiling and oak floor, now houses some of the museum's 19th-century collection of birds, the first few of which were mounted by the Derby taxidermist A. S. Hutchinson.[47] It is extensive but not exceptional, although it is strong on birds of prey from the surrounding moors: a red-footed falcon, a hen-harrier, one of the first English-born golden eagles and a Yorkshire red kite, common in the 19th century, almost extinct in the 20th and now returning.

The museum's strengths are its botanical and geological collections, as good as any in the region. The herbarium of Dr Arnold F. Lees[48] contains some European and North American material but its jewel is the collection of 20,000 specimens of British phanerogam material (flowering plants) and some 3,400 of British cryptogenic material (liverworts, mosses and lichens), which is complemented by the collection of Thomas Hebden.[49] Most of the lichens are stored in packets. Lee's work was continued by Dr W. A. Sledge, another nationally known botanist, and his herbarium was acquired in 1982.

More visually exciting are the fossils and minerals in the geological collection.[50] Many of the fossils are from Bradford Philosophical Society's collections and includes material from Cresswell Crags, Derbyshire, collected when L. C. Miall[51] was curator of the society in the 1860s. He found the large holotype fossil amphibian *Pholiderpeton scutigerum* Huxley[52] in the local Toftshaw colliery in 1868 and sent it to Thomas Henry Huxley, who declared it a genus and species new to science and named it as a holotype.

The mineral collection on display includes that purchased from Mr G. Hindcliffe in 1984 and from the estate of the chemist and geologist the Revd Joseph Dawson in 1865. Spot-lit in a darkened gallery, the minerals dazzle: a cut slab of ruby corundum in green zoisite; green malachite encrusted with blue azurite; a pale grey-blue agate surrounded by quartz; the blue-green sheen reflecting off labradorite feldspar of larvikite syenite.[53] It is more jewellery in the raw than science, as Hindcliffe's collection is not well documented and the lack of evidence of where specimens were found and in what context limits their scientific value.

By contrast Dawson's specimens, a few of which are exhibited here beside Hindcliffe's, are of considerable historical scientific interest, being documented meticulously in 1810 in

his 'firm, neat hand'.[54] His catalogue, like his cabinets, drawn up 'according to Dr Thompson's system of mineralogy',[55] is one of a very small number of contemporary records. Scientist and Nonconformist minister, Dawson owned and managed the Low Moor Ironworks, the largest in Yorkshire. Some of his specimens here are from his own mines. Their chemical properties gave them a practical as well as scientific interest.

For Dawson chemistry was the fundamental science,[56] but at his funeral Thomas Jervis in his oration identified why he so enjoyed mineralogy: 'It afforded an agreeable variety in the objects of inquiry, and a refreshing relaxation and relief to the mind, after the tedium ... of many other pursuits.'[57]

LEEDS CITY ART GALLERY
***

The Headrow, Leeds, West Yorkshire LS1 3AA
Tel. 0113 247 8248
www.leeds.gov.uk/tourism-museums+
galleries

Fine academic and Pre-Raphaelite painting; wide collection of modern art

Although he was curator at Leeds for only eleven years (1934–45), Philip Hendy left his imprint here even more clearly than he did on the National Gallery (q.v.), his next and final appointment.

He inherited responsibility for a collection that had, on the admission of his two predecessors, Frank Lambert and John Rothenstein, a considerably richer collection of watercolours than of oil paintings. He left it with one of the best collections of mid-20th-century British paintings, particularly strong on the work of the New English Art Club and the Camden Town Group (Sickert, Ginner, Gilman, Gore) and of those who took their lead from Wyndham Lewis and from *Blast*[58] and Vorticism.[59]

In view of the succession of talented curators who had directed the gallery, the weakness of the collections was surprising. It had opened in

The Day of Atonement *by Jacob Kramer*
(Leeds City Art Gallery)

1888 in a new building designed by W. H. Thorp with Victorian paintings typical of the period: large works of unmistakable moral and historical purpose by Daniel Maclise, Edward Armitage, George Bernard O'Neill and Frank Holl. Although the first curator (1888–1911), George Birkett, was a former London art dealer and friend of Ruskin, Rossetti and Burne-Jones, there is, surprisingly, only one Pre-Raphaelite painting here, William Holman Hunt's *The Shadow of Death* (1870–73), a gift. There are, however, some interesting works: Frederick Leighton's *The Return of Persephone* (1891), J. W. Waterhouse's *The Lady of Shalott*

(1894), an attractive J. J. Tissot, *The Bridesmaid* (1883–5), and one curiosity, a huge Barbizon landscape by Léon Richet, *Le Dortoir de Moret* (1890), presented to the gallery by a local collector, Charles Roberts.

When Birkett died, Frank Rutter, a young art critic on *The Sunday Times*, was appointed, despite never having worked in a gallery. He set himself the task of helping Leeds into the 20th century and organised a Post-Impressionist exhibition, which included works by Cézanne, Gauguin, Matisse and Kandinsky.

With Sir Michael Sadler, the vice-chancellor of the university, Rutter founded a 'Friend of the Gallery' scheme whose subscriptions formed a Leeds Art Collection Fund (1912) for acquiring new work, but neither Rutter nor

Sadler could persuade the Friends to buy the Post-Impressionists, even at affordable prices. Frustrated, Rutter resigned in 1917 with little to show for his time here apart from a bequest by Alfred Bilborough (1915) which laid the foundations of the watercolour collection, starting with a John Sell Cotman, *A Ploughed Field* (*c.* 1808), described by Cotman's biographer, the architect Sydney Kitson, as 'one of the loveliest glimpses of an imaginative landscape ever created by Cotman's mind and hand'.

Throughout the 1920s and early 1930s the watercolour collection grew with bequests, purchases and gifts by Sadler, Kitson and his brother, Robert Hawthorn Kitson, making this one of the finest collections of the golden age of British watercolours, second only to the Whitworth Art Gallery (q.v.). The oil painting collection was becalmed, apart from a bequest by local cloth manufacturer Sam Wilson, who, advised by the painter Mark Senior, had a large group of paintings by Sir George Clausen that included early works indebted to Monet and Corot rather than his later, ponderous homages to Millet, Bastien-Lepage and rural nostalgia.

Philip Hendy had previously worked at the Wallace Collection (q.v.) and the Museum of Fine Art, Boston, Massachusetts. At Leeds he threw open the windows, reviving the Collections Fund and persuading the council for the first time to vote money for acquisitions from the rates. Works by Augustus John, Stanley Spencer and Matthew Smith, by Ivon Hitchens, John Nash and C. R. W. Nevinson all entered the collection, as did a fine Edward Wadsworth (a friend of Hendy) and a lovely, melting Gertler, *The Pond at Garsington* (1916).

The paintings invariably were very good examples of each artist's work and some were outstanding: Jacob Kramer's *The Day of Atonement* (1919); Christopher Wood's *Tréboul Church, Brittany* (1930), painted weeks before his death. Wyndham Lewis's *Praxitella* (1921) is one of his finest portraits.[60] Only his *Self-portrait* in the Ferens Art Gallery (q.v.) is stronger.

Charles Roberts died and left the gallery his collection of paintings by the Barbizon School, whose jewel was a Courbet, *Les Demoiselles de Village*,[61] which hung well beside the Daubigny, Crome and De Wint that Hendy bought.

During the war the collection was moved for safe keeping to Temple Newsam, the former home of Lord Halifax, which the Leeds Corporation had bought more for its parkland than for the house. Hendy maintained that it 'can never be a suitable place for the exhibition of modern art in any quantity'. Nevertheless he mounted a series of exhibitions, of Jacob Epstein and Matthew Smith; of Paul Nash and Barbara Hepworth; of Gaudier-Brzeska; of Ben Nicholson; and, jointly, of Henry Moore, John Piper and Graham Sutherland, hailed by Kenneth Clark as 'a very great landmark in the history of British art'.

Hendy's predecessor, John Rothenstein, called the early 20th century not 'one of the greatest periods of painting [in Britain]' but 'of surpassing interest'.[62] Hendy's collection at Leeds regularly surpasses mere 'interest' or competence.

Leeds continued to appoint curators of distinction. Ernest Musgrave (1946–57) was killed in a car crash, too young; Robert Rowe (1958–83) and Christopher Gilbert (1983–95) were distinguished experts in, respectively, silver and furniture who transformed Temple Newsam (q.v.) but who also continued to acquire works for the gallery (Francis Bacon, Frank Auerbach, Bridget Riley, the St Ives School) that sustain the quality of the Hendy years. Problems with the gallery building that have dogged every curator since Rutter persist but the quality of the collections rises above such inhibitions.

HENRY MOORE INSTITUTE AND THE CENTRE FOR THE STUDY OF SCULPTURE **

74 The Headrow, Leeds, West Yorkshire
LS1 3AH
Tel. 0113 234 3158
www.henry-moore-fdn.co.uk

Centre for the study of sculpture

The statuary brought back from the Continent by British aristocrats on the Grand Tour inspired dedicated private sculpture galleries at Petworth House, Chatsworth, Kedleston Hall, Holkham Hall (all q.v.) and Arundel House, but few of the public museums of the 19th century collected or exhibited sculpture with any great enthusiasm.

The collection of sculpture here is among the largest and most comprehensive outside the Tate. Pieces from the 18th and 19th centuries are exhibited at Temple Newsam and Lotherton Hall (both q.v.). Those from the 20th century are held in the Leeds City Art Gallery (q.v.) and administered by the Henry Moore Institute (joined to the City Art Gallery by a covered bridge), which also houses an excellent archive and library.

The 17th-century collection consists of a single bequest by Mrs Dorothy McGrigor-Phillips of Italian marble busts of emperors (Claudius, Nero, Caligula, Lucius Verius, etc.). The 18th and early 19th centuries include works by John Cheere,[63] Christopher Hewetson, John Flaxman and Joseph Nollekens[64] and the first of Louis-François Roubiliac's series of busts of Alexander Pope,[65] his masterpiece, on which is inscribed a line from Horace's *Ars Poetica*: 'QUI NIL MOLITOR INEPTE' (he who never exerts himself foolishly). There are also works here by the Leeds-born sculptor Joseph Gott,[66] a plaster version of a relief by Berthel Thorvaldsen and Antonio Canova's *Venus*, based on the statue in the Uffizi in Florence, which was bought from Canova by the architect, designer and collector Thomas Hope.

The outstanding strength and breadth of the collection dates from the establishment of the Leeds City Art Gallery in 1888. Successive directors, most notably Philip Hendy (1934–45) and Robert Rowe (1958–83), have acquired works with determination and imagination. As a result it is possible to trace, through the collection, the development of, and lines of influence on, British sculpture: the line from Rome, through Thorvaldsen and Gibson, Gott, William Theed the Younger and Henry Weekes, to the Thornycrofts and so to the New Sculpture of Thomas Brock, Sir Frederick Leighton and Sir Alfred Gilbert; the line from Paris, from Rodin, through Henri Gaudier-Brzeska and on to Epstein, Gill, Moore and Hepworth. The influence of Rodin is manifest in the excellent cast (1907) of *The Age of Bronze* which Rodin personally supervised for his friend and patron Sir Gervase Beckett, and which was given to the collection by his son, the architect Sir Martyn Beckett.

The collection contains notable curiosities: a huge chimney piece that was commissioned from Sir Alfred Gilbert by the Leeds textile magnate, Sam Wilson;[67] the Adam and Eve garden roller (*c.*1933) that Eric Gill designed for Sir Hugh Lane and which was used to roll the tennis court at Eric Gill's house, Piggot's, in Buckinghamshire;[68] a bronze of *Queen Victoria* (1887) by her daughter, Princess Louise, Duchess of Argyll, who was a pupil of the Sculptor-in-Ordinary, Sir Joseph Boehm; and the strange, disturbing *Veiled Venus* (1900) by Kuhne Beveridge and her mother, Ella von Wrede.

Here also is a piece in alabaster by Gaudier-Brzeska (1912), originally coloured brown, red and yellow, the last of his painted sculptures, and an early work in Hopton Wood stone by Epstein, *Maternity* (1910), in which the figure arises from, yet is locked into, the unworked stone.

Appropriately, there are sculptures from every phase of Henry Moore's career, from the pieces (an enamelled plate, a plaster relief and a delicate, balanced *Seated Nude Man*, 1919–20) he made as a student at Leeds College of Art, to works made in the 1920s in which he explores shapes and themes and materials which he used for the rest of his career.[69] Some of these culminated in his first *Reclining Figure* (1929) and, ultimately, in the *Reclining Woman* (1981) in bronze, which is in front of Leeds City Art Gallery,[70] both of which owe much to the Tolmec-Maya carving *Chacmool*, whose reproduction he saw in the British Museum (q.v.).[71]

The size and breadth of the collection allows the qualities of sculptors whose work may, at present, have slipped out of fashion to be appreciated: the Thornycrofts, father, mother and, particularly, son, William Hamo Thornycroft; Leon Underwood, F. E. McWilliam, Reg Butler, Hubert Dalwood, Mary Martin and Bernard Meadows.

The sculptors who bestrode the post-war years are all represented: Anthony Caro, Elisabeth Frink, Lynn Chadwick, Kenneth Armitage, Philip King and Eduardo Paolozzi; as are the younger generation of Barry Flanagan, Richard Long, Tony Cragg, Anish Kapoor, Andy Goldsworthy and Antony Gormley.

Despite the inclusion of two or three works by Claes Oldenburg and Alexander Calder, the emphasis is on British sculpture. It is both a public collection and a study collection, and demonstrates that the two roles can co-exist and strengthen each other.

The study role is reinforced by the archive, a distinguished mausoleum of files in which the careers of Jacob Epstein, Frank Dobson, the Thornycrofts and Austin Wright are particularly fully documented and which contains such gems as the manuscript and the first edition of H. S. Ede's *A Life of Gaudier-Brzeska*.[72]

Here in notes, drawings, photographs and maquettes[73] are the constituents that articulate this medium as it draws form from air and matter.

LEEDS MUSEUM **

Town Hall, The Headrow, Leeds, West Yorkshire LS1 3AD
Tel. 0113 247 7241
www.leeds.gov.uk.

Natural history in all its forms in a building to be returned to life

There have been museums[74] in Leeds since Ralph Thoresby, a local cloth merchant, opened his Musaeum Thoresbyanum, *c.*1680. Thoresby, a fellow of the Royal Society and friend of Sir Hans Sloane, John Evelyn and Sir Christopher Wren, was inspired by visits to the Anatomy Theatre at Leiden and the Bibliotheca at Edinburgh and by his father's bequest of coins and medals, previously owned by Cromwell's Parliamentary general Thomas, Lord Fairfax. The museum was in the tradition of 17th-century cabinets of curiosities, its collections including seals, amulets, incunabula and Bibles; birds' eggs, fossils, corals; and 'the actual hand and arm of the Marquis of Montrose'.[75]

In the early 19th century commercial museums were opened by John Calvert, a gunmaker and taxidermist (the Old Leeds Museum, strong in ornithology and ethnography), and by a coal merchant Robert Cundall, whose Victoria Museum specialised in natural history. 'Natural History is no work for one that loves his chair or his bed,' wrote Cundall; 'Speculation may be pursued on a soft couch, but Nature must be observed in the open air.'[76]

Although a few objects from these collections have found their way into the present museum, its true roots are in the Leeds Philosophical Society, whose museum in the Philosophical Hall was designed by Richard Dennis Chantrell.[77]

Like many such museums, it underestimated its rate of expansion. A series of excellent curators – Henry Denny (1825–71), Professor Louis Compton Miall (1871–91) – proved to be so successful that, in 1860, it was forced to commission an extension by local architects Dobson and Chorley, doubling the museum's size and turning Chantrell's restrained Greek Revival Italianate.

Denny was the consummate professional curator: fieldworker, anatomist, researcher, lithographer. An entomologist whose specialism was lice, his modest and gentle enthusiasm was widely admired: Darwin gave him specimens from the *Beagle*, Livingstone from Central Africa. By his death in 1871 the national reputation of the museum was established. His successor, Miall, was scarcely less distinguished despite a personality that was 'as cold as some mountain stream'.

The geological collections are predominantly local, mapping the fossil-rich beds of the coal measures and the extensive mineral deposits. Donations were attracted from Dr William Buckland of Christ Church, Oxford, later president of the British Association, following his excavations in the hyena caves of Kirkdale, 1822–3, which laid down one of the first challenges to those who still believed that the world was created in six days. Buckland's protégée Miss Bennett also donated fossil finds from Wiltshire, and part of Sir Alexander Crichton's collection of Russian minerals was acquired. He had formed it while physician to Tsar Alexander I, its literal jewel a lengthened piece of prismatic black tourmaline on a large prism of dark brown quartz with cleavlandite.

The natural history and ethnography collections are equally exotic, drawn from all over the world: a Bengal tiger shot by Sir Charles Reid in the Himalayas, exhibited in the Indian Court at the London International Exhibition of 1862 and mounted by Rowland Ward; a great Tibetan yak shot in 1869 on the shores of the sacred lake of Manarsovar by Captain Edward Smyth, disguised as a Buddhist monk to circumvent the government ban on entering Tibet.

Here too among the museum's extensive oceanic collection is the Calvert cap, made of 160 cowrie shells on plaits of fibre. John Calvert described it in the 1829 catalogue of his museum as being worn by 'a Taheitan Chief' when pronouncing sentence of death on criminals but A.W. Franks of the British Museum maintained in 1870 that it was from New Guinea.[78]

The archaeology collections are as rich, containing Roman (the 4th-century wolf and twins mosaic from Isurium Brigantium – Aldborough near Boroughbridge), Saxon (10th-century Leeds crosses, featuring Weland the Smith strapped into a flying machine), and medieval objects (a Giggleswick tarn logboat, *c.* 1335, carved from a single ash; a Nottingham alabaster of the Assumption of the Virgin that retains almost all of its original polychrome painting, once the property of Sir Thomas More), beside antiquities of great interest. Petrie gave the museum vases from his Egyptian excavations and there are items from the Jericho digs of Professor Garstang (1930s) and Kathleen Kenyon (1950s). Both groups are overshadowed by the torsi from a group of nine life-sized equestrian statues in marble excavated by Sir John Savile Lumley at Lanuvium, twenty-five miles south of Rome. They were erected to commemorate the victories of the general Lucullus in the Second Mithridatic War (65–62 BC). Savile Lumley conducted his excavations while British Ambassador to Rome and divided the material between the British Museum (q.v.) and Leeds.

At the time of writing these remarkable collections have no home, having outgrown successive lodgings, most recently the municipal buildings next door to the City Art Gallery where they resided, unsatisfactorily, on the first floor from 1966 to 2000. They deserve better than their present billet in a 'resource centre', albeit publicly accessible, while they await their new museum, promised for 2007.

ROYAL ARMOURIES ✱✱✱

Armouries Drive, Leeds, West Yorkshire
LS10 1LT
Tel. 08700 344344
e-mail: webmaster@armouries.org.uk

The grandest armour as men dress for war

When Henry VIII died the contents of the several royal armouries were brought to the Tower of London and became, in effect, a museum to the glory of the king, to which privileged visitors were admitted. After the Restoration in 1660, Charles II opened the armouries to the paying public in a move whose symbolism was clear: the splendour of the English monarchy and the might of

Konrad Seusenhofer's helmet
(Royal Armouries)

English arms. As that might extended across the globe the oriental armoury was added, in part the 18th-century plunder of the East India Company, in part by acquisition from the 1851 Great Exhibition.

This is not simply a museum to what Winston Churchill called 'horrible war, amazing medley of the glorious and the squalid, the pitiful and sublime', the ugly practicalities of human butchery. It also celebrates the artistry and craftsmanship of armourers.

Here are helms and basinets, mail shirts, habergeon and aventail, visors and gauntlets from the Hundred Years War.[79] They plunge you into the vocabulary of battle: crossbows and halberds; bodkin heads and Jedburgh staves; spears, bills and brigandines; ahlspeiss and corseque; sallet and pavise; shield and breastplate; hammer and mace.

It is a vocabulary – common currency in armies – understood in every tongue and time. The museum has Corinthian helmets, campaign bronze armour, and a Greek spearhead from the 5th century BC. It has axes and spears made by the Franks in the 9th century AD and by the Vikings in the 10th century.

From the Wollaston burial site in the Nene Valley a 7th–8th-century Anglo-Saxon 'pioneer helmet' with a boar crest, representing the god Freyr,[80] was excavated in 1997.

The museum demonstrates but does not explain the lurches that have occurred in weapon technology. There was little development in weapons or armour until the introduction of gunpowder and the gun in the 15th century, and then little more until the late 19th century. Since then we have moved, in the space of 100 years, from the earliest repeating magazine rifles of the 1870s to the nuclear weapons of today, from a range of 500 yards for the Enfield rifled musket (1853) to guided missiles with a range of thousands of miles.

Until the late 19th century wars were personal, with men killing each other in hand-to-hand combat. Their weapons were personal too: those of the poor, rudimentary; those of the rich, of great beauty.

The medieval and Renaissance tournament brought the personal and the decorative together in ceremonies that were political and social, the international summit meetings of their day. The museum's collections, strong in Renaissance weapons and armour, illustrate the golden age of the tournament in the 15th and 16th centuries.

At the Field of the Cloth of Gold in 1520 Henry VIII and Francis I of France brought the tournament to its zenith. Here is Henry's foot-combat armour, uncompleted; built for this event, it was abandoned when the French changed the rules. Its replacement, a toilet armour with its splayed skirt of horizontal metal lames, was hastily made for the young and athletic King Henry in the Royal Armoury at Greenwich by his Master Armourer, Martin van Royne. Compare its grey severity with the foot-combat armour made for the Elector Christian I of Saxony by Anton Peffenhauser of Augsburg in 1591, with its etched and gilded fronds and flowers, or to the lion armour

(1545–50), a blaze of golden tooling embossed with snarling lions' heads.

The same richness of display may be found in the museum's collection of Asian armour, which dates from the 17th century: the two armours given to James I by the Shogun of Japan, Tokugawa Ieyasu; the Mughal Indian elephant armour, made up of panels of mail and plate (c. 1600); or the lamellar armour, small plates laced together by leather, of the Mongolian heavy cavalry.

The armourers who made these were great craftsmen who, in the 16th century, worked to the designs of artists such as Albrecht Dürer and Hans Holbein the Younger. Every known technique of metalwork was employed in an armour such as that made by Konrad Sensenhofer of Innsbruck in 1511–14 for the Holy Roman Emperor Maximilian I to present to Henry VIII, its horned helmet, grinning teeth and brass spectacles making it fearsome.

There is simpler artistry in the embossed buffe, signed and dated 1538, made by perhaps the greatest of 16th-century armourers, Filippo Negroli and his brothers, of Milan. With work of such quality it is not surprising that armour was frequently inscribed with dedications: a Turkish 'turban' helmet of 1480 is decorated with the wish that the owner should have 'happiness, health and strength to the length of his life, as long as the dove coos'; a wheellock petronel (c. 1590) has on its walnut stock inlaid with stag horn and mother of pearl, a simple 'Forget me not', painted under a glass panel.

These skills of ornament transferred easily to sporting guns of the 18th and 19th centuries, as demonstrated by an English flintlock gun made by William Simpson of York (c. 1738), its stock inlaid with silver wire in rococo flourishes, or in the garniture made for the Empress Elizabeth of Russia in 1752.

As the collection approaches the present day, decoration and personality are eliminated in mass-produced automatic weapons: Hiram Maxim's first machine gun, a Gatling gun of 1873, a Draganov S.V.D. sniping rifle (c. 1975), the standard sniping rifle of most Eastern-bloc armies, perhaps the last remnant of personal warfare in an age in which the pressing of a button can kill sight unseen.

THACKRAY MEDICAL MUSEUM *

Beckett Street, Leeds, West Yorkshire LS9 7LN
Tel. 0113 244 4343
www.thackraymuseum.org

The history of medicine; recreated slums; created remedies

In 1842 Robert Baker was commissioned to report on the health of Leeds, which had expanded from a population of under 25,000 in 1790 to over 70,000 in 1840 without any thought having been given to health or living conditions. Baker found that only 38 of the 586 streets had sewers and, until 1841, the city's drinking water was drawn from the River Aire, polluted by industry and sewage. Almost half of all deaths were of infants under the age of five. This museum leads you through reconstructions of the homes, shops, slaughterhouses, privies and middens that compounded this ill health and led eventually to legislation and improvements. By 1860, 95 per cent of Leeds had mains water and by 1901 four-fifths of homes had water closets.

The museum also puts before you the remedies and equipment that were available to doctors to cope with disease. Here is a chemist's shop of the 1850s dispensing fuller's earth, marina, boric, and vaseline from ceramic jars. Here are Potter's Kasbah Kidney Remedy, Epp's Glycerine Jujubes and 'the True Aperient', Seidlitz Powders.

Here too are the saws, knives, cutting forceps and chamois leather stump-covers of general surgery in 1830 (half of all amputees died) and a scarificator (twelve hidden blades in a box) and leech jars for bleeding, of the same period.

More sophisticated equipment followed: Morton's ophthalmoscopes (*c.*1885) for looking at the back of the eye; Louis Pasteur's and Robert Koch's microscopes and a litholite

(*c.*1850) to crush stones in the bladder, obviating the need for a lithotomy, the operation which Samuel Pepys survived on 26 March 1658, a date he celebrated for the rest of his life.

The museum, in the former St James's Hospital, has its origins in a small company museum established by Paul Thackray in the 1980s to conserve the archives and equipment associated with his family firm of medical suppliers, Charles F. Thackray & Co. He sold the business in 1990, established a charitable trust and opened the museum in 1997, having attracted a major bequest of the John F. Wilkinson Collection of pharmaceutical ceramics, the largest collection of its kind in existence.

John Wilkinson was a Manchester doctor who spent forty years collecting English and European apothecary jars dating back to the 16th century. It is a ceramics feast. There are Italian jars, richly decorated in blue, yellow and green from Florence (1500), Siena (1525), Castel Durante (1530) and Urbino (1574). There are blue and white tin-glazed earthenware jars made in London, Liverpool and Bristol, pale blue jars from Venice, and jars decorated triumphantly with putti, angels, garlands and trumpets.

In pride of place are the arms of the Society of Apothecaries with the figure of Apollo, the god of medicine, slaying the python at Delphi. The tableau is flanked by two unicorns rampant with the motto 'OPIFERQUE PER ORBEM DICOR' ('I am said to be the maker throughout the world'). The python arose out of the slime and stagnant water that followed the deluge of Deucalion that Jupiter unleashed to destroy the world because of its impiety. This museum follows Robert Baker in proposing less radical remedies.

HAREWOOD HOUSE ****

Leeds, West Yorkshire LS17 9LQ
Tel: 0113 218 1010
www.harewood.org

Old Masters and 20th-century works, furniture by Chippendale; Adam's palace in a Capability Brown landscape

Here is Arcadia, as imagined by Edwin Lascelles, Lord Harewood (1712–95), who commissioned John Carr of York to build the house, Capability Brown to landscape the park, Robert Adam to design the interiors and Thomas Chippendale to make the furniture; and by Edward, Viscount Lascelles (1764–1814), his cousin, who commissioned Turner and Girtin to paint views of the house and of 'one of the most delectable landscapes'.[81]

It is another of those great English houses that you approach quietly from the side, as you do Knole, Chatsworth, Petworth House and Nostell Priory in West Yorkshire. Inside, the Entrance Hall has 'a stern character'[82] that concentrates your attention on one of the glories of the house, the partnership of Adam and Chippendale, and the way in which Chippendale's furniture has a 'great affinity with the Stucco and carved ornaments'[83] designed by Robert Adam and made by Joseph Rose of York and William Collins, whose ceiling has a Greek-key frieze, ribbons, swags and radiating leaves that all reappear as motifs on the chairs.

This was the largest and most magnificent commission that Chippendale undertook. Edwin Lascelles advised Adam, 'I would not exceed the limits of expense that I have always set myself. Let us do everything properly and well, mais pas trop,' but he ended up spending £10,000 on furniture. This compares with the £6,000 spent on Capability Brown's landscaping and the £11,000 that was the entire cost of building and equipping nearby Denton Hall (also designed by John Carr).[84]

Chippendale supplied everything: chairs, beds, glasses, carpets, curtains and wallpapers, in a variety of styles (modern, Chinese, Gothic, neoclassical), from the simple functional steps in the Library to the sumptuous extravagance of the 'very large State Bedstead with a dome canopy decorated on the Inside with Carved Antique Ornaments ... the whole Gilt in Burnished Gold'.[85] For the adjacent Dressing Room he made one of his masterpieces, the Diana and Minerva commode, 'inlaid with various fine woods'[86] with the figures of the goddesses in ebony and ivory.

The settings provided by Adam also covered the gamut of richness and ornamentation, from the functional and less sophisticated decor of the private rooms to the chaste neoclassical ceilings of the Old Library and the Entrance Hall, the grandeur of the State Bedroom and the two Drawing Rooms, to climax in the Gallery with Adam at his most magnificent and expansive. The windows are framed by pillars and pilasters 'painted by Mr Hutchinson, of London, in imitation of the verd antique marble'[87] and the ceiling is a complex design that incorporates all the new 'Antick' motifs, urns and masks, bows, festoons and rosettes, lightened by acanthus leaves and honeysuckle flowers.

Here, in the grandest room in the house, it is as if Adam and Chippendale were pushing one another to ever greater heights. Adam's ceiling incorporates painted panels by Biagio Rebecca[88] and Angelica Kauffmann while Chippendale crowns the achievement of his marble-topped console tables with rams' heads and lions' feet, his torchères and towering mirrors by the windows' pelmets that are carved and painted to imitate heavy swags of silk finished off by gilded fringes and tassels.[89]

The family portraits throughout the house are by some of the best English portrait painters of the past 250 years, of each generation of Lascelles: Reynolds (Edwin Lascelles, and the 1st and 2nd Earls), Hoppner (1st Earl), Lawrence (2nd Earl), Grant (3rd Earl) and Poynter (4th Earl), down to the present 7th Earl painted as a child by McEvoy, but the main collection of paintings is in the Gallery.

The core of this collection originates with Lord Clanricarde, 2nd Marquess of Clanricarde (1832–1916), the brother-in-law of the

4th Earl and grandson of George Canning, who left his collection, plus £2.5 million, to his great-nephew Henry Lascelles, later the 6th Earl, in 1916 as a result of the latter's kindness to him.[90] With this the Earl bought judiciously after the First World War. Here is an outstanding Giovanni Bellini, *Madonna and Child with Donor*, a very good late Lorenzo Lotto, *Portrait of an Old Man*, and an intensely interesting St Jerome by Giovanni Bazzi, called Il Sodoma.[91] The collection also includes works by the other great Venetians – Cima da Conegliano, Titian, Tintoretto and Veronese – an Annibale Carracci and an El Greco, *Allegory*, one of three versions, the others being in the Prado in Madrid and the National Gallery of Scotland (q.v.).

Despite the quality of this collection, which would grace any museum, the greater interest at Harewood is a collection of watercolours by Turner and Girtin because of their excellence and their association with the house and the Lascelles family who commissioned them. These commissions occasioned important developments in both artists' work, particularly that of Turner.

In 1798 Edward Lascelles, the 1st Earl, commissioned two oil paintings by Turner of *Plompton Rocks* to fill spaces created by alterations to the Saloon (now the Library): they remain in their original positions. However it was the patronage of his son, the Regency beau Edward Lascelles, that was more important.

Turner's topographical watercolours were already well established but in each of his two watercolours of Harewood House in 1797 he takes a step away from topography to landscape. The house is moved further into the background and the focus is shifted to the foreground landscape and figures. In the following year his view of *Harewood House from the South East* (from an identical spot to that chosen by Girtin three years later) places the house in the far distance, linked to the beautiful foreground by the light that falls on both.

Girtin's two great watercolours (1801) of the house from the south-west and the south-east take this approach further, secreting the house

in the broad landscape in deep shadow underneath a vast sublime sky that extends above and beyond infinitely. With these landscapes Turner and Girtin closed the book on 18th-century topographical watercolours.

Bizarrely the 4th Earl chose to sell all his watercolours at Christie's in 1858, save only the Turners of Harewood, which he divided between his sisters. The Turners, Girtins and Varleys have subsequently returned to Harewood, leaving a bright train of superb pictures in the Fitzwilliam Museum, the Whitworth Art Gallery, the Cecil Higgins Art Gallery and the Ashmolean Museum (all q.v.). Enough remain here to celebrate the Yorkshire landscape, Harewood and the enlightened patronage of Edward Lascelles.

TEMPLE NEWSAM ✶✶✶✶

Temple Newsam Road, off Selby Road,
Leeds, West Yorkshire LS15 0AE
Tel. 0113 264 7321
www.leeds.gov.uk

Great Jacobean house displaying reacquired Old Masters: the north's best-kept secret

A great Tudor-Jacobean mansion set in a park designed by Capability Brown; family portraits by Reynolds, Hoppner and Russell; early 18th-century paintings acquired on the Grand Tour; furniture by Chippendale and silver by de Lamerie: opened to the public, the resulting museum should be a triumph. So Temple Newsam is, but in a rather more complicated way than the description above might lead you to expect.

The violently various circumstances of the Ingram/Irwin family – 300 years of fortunes made and lost, mortgages contracted, heiresses married – brought Temple Newsam to the Hon. Edward Wood, later Lord Halifax,[92] who finally sold the house and park to the Leeds Corporation in 1922. The collection that had once contained pictures by Rubens, Rembrandt and Claude, and featured Titian's *Portrait of a Man*[93] (invariably chosen by such experts as Waagen as the single most beautiful

The Adoration of the Shepherds *by Matthias Stöm (Temple Newsam)*

painting), was dispersed, leaving the house almost empty.

From that low point, Leeds, guided by a succession of excellent directors of Leeds City Art Gallery with responsibility for Temple Newsam, has rebuilt the collection by means of acquisitions, bequests, gifts and long-term loans. Lord Halifax gave eighty-five of the original pictures back to the house in 1948.

If such iconic paintings of the collection as the Titian are no longer here, there are fine examples of the work of other painters of real quality. Here is an early *Portrait of a Young Man* by Frans Pourbus the Younger, its view cool and penetrating, the head framed by a ruff that reflects light up into the face. Pourbus was painting this in Italy while, in England, Paul

von Somer, Marcus Gheeraerts and Daniel Mytens, all of whom have works in the collection, were continuing to paint portraits of a rich and stiff stylisedness.

Landscape with Sportsmen and Dogs, painted in oil on copper, underlines the influence that Paul Bril (with Adam Elsheimer) had on the development of Italian landscape painting. *The Adoration of the Shepherds* by Matthias Stöm offers an opportunity, of which there are too few in Britain,[94] to see this artist's work. The blaze of light that emanates from the Christ child draws rapt wonder from the shepherds while behind them is a wary Joseph on whose face the shadows form a disturbing second profile. Here too is a Grand Tour portrait of *Horatio Walpole* by Pierre Subleyras, better known for his religious and history pictures, commissioned at a time when most Grand Tourists were settling for the more obvious attractions of Pompeo Batoni.[95]

To them should be added a Stubbs portrait of *Phillis, a Pointer of Lord Clermonts* (1772) and works by painters who are not frequently found in British regional collections: Carlo Maratta, Giovanni Antonio Pellegrini and Giorgio Vasari. Here too is a subtle and seductive Henry Morland (the father of George Morland), of a courtesan as *The Fair Nun Unmasked*, and a curiosity: a landscape by Ebenezer Tull, an amateur who painted in the Dutch-influenced style of the young Gainsborough and whose rather perfunctory composition is more than redeemed by a high sky of calm beauty.

Reassembling the collection of family portraits has required patience and skill. The portrait of Sir Arthur Ingram, who bought and restored Temple Newsam in 1622, by George Geldorp, came back with the help of a government grant. Sir Arthur Ingram, having made a fortune in the City of London as an entrepreneur, bought five houses in Yorkshire, each of which contained startling collections. Sir William Brereton described the contents of Sir Arthur's palace adjacent to York Cathedral in 1634 as 'his store of massive plate, rich organ, and other rich hangings, lively pictures, and statues rich £150 pearle glasses, fayre stately £500 organ, and other rich furniture in every Roome Prince-like'.[96] Sadly none of those treasures has survived at Temple Newsam. Lord Halifax gave the Leonard Knyff of the 3rd Viscount as part of his 1948 gift. The purchase of the Benjamin Wilson of the 9th Viscount Irwin, which shows this Leeds-born artist at his handsome best, was grant-aided and Reynolds's full-length portrait of Isabella, Marchioness of Hertford was given by the National Art Collections Fund.

Of particular charm is a group of portraits and conversation pieces by Philippe Mercier, the French artist whose chief patron was Frederick, Prince of Wales, and who painted portraits of many local families while he was in York between 1738 and 1748 (v. Wakefield Art Gallery).

The two Antonio Jolis are in their original positions as overmantels in the Picture Gallery (for which they were painted to complement the fireplaces made after a design of William Kent by the sculptor Robert Doe), and there are capriccios by Panini, Coccorante and Clerisseau, as well as Guardi's ravishing *S. Giorgio Maggiore*, reflected in the glassy lagoon.[97] An earlier Grand Tour, by the 4th Viscount Irwin, 1704–7, brought to Temple Newsam a group of forty paintings by Antonio Marini, whose romantic melodrama is in sharp contrast to the classic polish of landscapes by Claude or Poussin. Twenty remain, reassembled in the Great Picture Gallery which, like most of the interiors at Temple Newsam, has been recently restored to its historic appearance – in this case in c. 1745.

The pleasures of this unusual collection are increased not just by its being dispersed throughout the house and the Picture Gallery, whose grandeur bears comparison with Harewood House, Wilton House or Petworth House (all q.v.), but by the lighting, or the absence of it. Artificial lighting has been kept to the minimum, so that we see the paintings in a 'natural' state. The experience is quite different from the highly lit, dramatic presentation of contemporary galleries, and makes us see pictures with fresh eyes.

Excellent ceilings complement the paintings (plasterwork by Thomas Perritt and his apprentice Joseph Rose of York) and some exceptional pieces of 18th-century furniture: a coffer by Richard Pigge; the Murray cabinet by John Channon (c. 1750); the Hinton state bed; a Chippendale writing table from Harewood, with marquetry; a pier glass by Chambers (c. 1774) and a suite of chairs made by James Pascall (1745) for the Picture Gallery. There is also silver by de Lamerie, by Pierre Harache and by David Willaume and his daughter, Anne Tanqueray, and silver-gilt by Matthew Boulton.

In case you should forget that great houses were also homes, there is an evocative maid's room appropriately furnished from house sales at Raby Castle, County Durham, and Eaton Hall, Cheshire; and, at the top of the house, a group of portraits of servants and employees of George Lane Fox of Bramham

Park, five of them by George Gallard while he was staying at Bramham painting Lane Fox's family and houses.

In the late 1930s Temple Newsam was empty; in the 1940s its interiors were stripped to allow it to serve as the city's art gallery. Today, restored, it has one of the country's finest small collections of fine and decorative art; it merits wider recognition. Credit for this transformation is due to a succession of directors of Leeds City Art Gallery: Sir Philip Hendy (1934–45); Ernest Musgrave (1946–58), who bought with great flair (Vasari, Subleyras, Morland, Stubbs, Coccorante) and secured the gift of the Guardi by Ernest Cook; Robert Rowe (1958–63), an authority on English silver, who also acquired the Matthias Stöm and the Maratta from the Barberini Collection and arranged the return of the Jolis; and Christopher Gilbert (1983–95), in whose directorship the loan, and promised gift, of the Pier Francesco Mola landscape was made by Sir Denis Mahon. Their taste and judgement, unobtrusive and appropriate, runs through every room of Temple Newsam.

BECK ISLE MUSEUM OF RURAL LIFE **

Bridge Street, Pickering, North Yorkshire
YO18 8DU
Tel. 01751 473653

Pretty building houses exemplary energetic museum; Pickering's past displayed with love

Its location is in its name, a museum which, during occasional floods, has to be emptied; it is on a small island surrounded by the waters of Pickering Beck, which flow round, past and under the four arches of a stone bridge. Its entrance is half-hidden under the canopy of a giant beech tree.

In this building, Beech Grove, William Marshall,[98] the 18th-century agricultural reformer, tried, and failed, to establish the country's first Agricultural Institute, taking his lead from Reynolds's Royal Academy of the Arts.[99] The building had become a doctor's

surgery and tenanted flats when in 1965 a group of enthusiasts led by local historian John Rushton attempted to start a Beck Isle Museum and Arts Centre, beginning with a loan exhibition.

Dr J. L. Kirk, the curator of the Castle Museum in York and a Pickering resident, had offered the town his personal archaeological collection in the 1930s and been rejected,[100] and many local people wrote off the embryonic museum as 'doomed to failure'. Within two years it had run out of funds and was within days of closure, but four members of its board each gave one quarter's rent. Gordon Clitheroe, now the museum's chairman, was elected treasurer and the museum survived and prospered.

John Rushton saved the murals in the Memorial Hall that Rex Whistler had painted when stationed here with the Welsh Guards in 1943–4 and in 1968 the museum acquired the contents of the studio and workshop of Sidney Smith, Pickering's photographer for over forty years.[101] Slowly a delightful mixture of objects and collections came together to give the museum its informal atmosphere and convey something of the changes experienced by this pretty market town on the edge of the North Yorkshire Moors during the 19th and 20th centuries.

The traction engine, even the steam engine, did not make the horse redundant in local farming until the 1940s and the museum's collection of rakes, ploughs, drills and disc harrows illustrates the slow transition. These changes affected the blacksmith, the wheelwright, the cooper, even the cobbler, and their tools here can bear comparison with the great Salaman Collection at the Museum of St Albans (q.v.). There is even a Gunter surveying chain whose 100 links, 7.92 inches each, measure 22 yards.

The changes to trades in the town have been almost as great. A series of rooms richly reconstructs the village shop, gentlemen's outfitter, chemist and pub of the 1920s and '30s.

Sidney Smith was recording these changes from 1902, when he set up a photographic business in a lock-up shop in Park Street, until

1956, when failing eyesight forced him to retire. Later he was joined in the business by his wife Maud. They photographed Pickering's celebrations for the coronation of George V in 1911 and for victory in the First World War in 1919; a ship aground at Whitby in 1914 and the great floods of 1927. Better still are his photographs of daily life: of shearing sheep, scything corn, threshing; of draymen and postmen; of George Smith, the Hartoft shepherd, with his dog, and of an old gypsy woman with a clay pipe clenched between her teeth; sheep on the moors in snow; hens outside the Old Swan Inn at Bilsdale; Captain Vane's hounds; floods and blizzards; haymaking and Sunday School outings. Smith's photographs equal in quality those of Sutcliffe. But with the exception of some moorland landscapes and some essays in heroic socialist realism with men following the plough silhouetted against the sky, these are photographs of record such as every town should have.

What every community does not have is a huge Victorian printing press in full working order, a Columbian press built in 1854,[102] a mighty cast-iron beast decorated with fruit and flowers, serpents and a dolphin topped by an eagle; nor Beck Isle's collection of miniature carts, made by Thomas W. Foster of Riccall, every nut, bolt, angle iron, nail an exact replica, scale 3 inches to 1 foot ('It's just something I do,' said Mr Foster; 'fortunately I had a few friends who were wheelwrights or joiners so they put me on the right track'); nor a Rocket Type Model No. 3 washing machine made of plywood before the First World War by Cropton wheelwright Moses Morley. It cost two guineas. Mr Morley died in 1912, aged seventy-three.

I should declare an interest. My father was stationed in Pickering with the Welsh Guards in the Second World War, an infantry regiment learning to handle tanks on the moors. I was conceived here shortly after the Christmas party for which Rex Whistler painted murals (the museum has his murals of two larger than life, bear-skinned, red-tunicked guardsmen). Searching for the remaining murals I crossed the road to the Memorial Hall, which was throbbing, on a Saturday morning, with the music of a local band. The main hall with the murals was locked up and in darkness but a young lad opened it up.

This is a community in the proper sense, at ease with itself, in whose congenial atmosphere it is no wonder that a museum 'doomed to failure' has survived and thrived. Gordon Clitheroe, the chairman, dedicated his book of Ryedale photographs to all those who had opened his eyes to the beauty and richness of the area. This museum, so considerably his achievement, has the same effect.

MILLENNIUM GALLERIES: METALWORK GALLERY *

Arundel Gate, Sheffield, South Yorkshire
S1 2PP
Tel. 0114 278 2600
www.sheffieldgalleries.org.uk

The history of cutlery in the cutlers' city, from the 18th century to David Mellor today

R. E. Leader, the historian of the Sheffield Company of Cutlers, records the existence of a Sheffield knife in the king's possession in the mid 14th century,[103] fifty years before Chaucer wrote about a Sheffield 'Thwitel' in the *Canterbury Tales*.

This museum, celebrating the making, designing and manufacturing of metalware in Sheffield, has a knife by Thomas Tucker of 1658, one made in the early 16th century with a 'blade broken with intent' and a folding knife, late 17th century, whose blade has the inscription 'My love is fixt. I will not range./My choice so good, I will not change.'

Sheffield metalware is put into a wider historic context: a Bronze Age knife (Staffordshire, *c.* 2500 BC); Celtic silver (75–50 BC); Roman coins from the time of Vitellius (AD 69), Hadrian (AD 134–8) and Gratian (AD 375–83); a delicate 7th-century Anglo-Saxon pendant of gold, garnet and ivory; a 15th-century iron dagger from Maltby. But its particular strengths begin in the 18th century, when metalwork changed from a craft into an industry.

The five rivers of Sheffield were sluiced to provide the water power to drive the machines, such as tilt hammers, that are essential to the hardening of steel. The Sheffield Company of Cutlers flourished,[104] as did subsidiary crafts (shear smiths, scythe smiths, scissor smiths) and techniques (stamping, piercing, beating, grinding, etching, die stamping), a vocabulary of violent, constructive action.

In one large exhibition space inside the new Millennium Galleries designed by architects Pringle Richards Sharratt (2002), is displayed the diversity of the metalware industry: 18th-century plating and ormolu, 19th-century hollowware and electroplating, and silver cutlery of every age.

A cutlery time line extends from 14th-century and 15th-century knives with no handles, through Tudor knives with hammer finials, to knives with hafts in bone, ivory, porcelain, stamped brass, stamped silver, enamel, plastic. 'Even what shall appear to be the most common, small and simple of objects can reveal itself to be on its own terms as complex and grand as a space shuttle or a great suspension bridge.' Henry Petrowski was writing about the pencil[105] but he could as well have been writing about the knife.

Here, as the industry and the market expand in the 19th century, the designer becomes of central importance. The story of Sheffield metalware assumes new personality, pushing aside the master cutlers and manufacturers of the 18th century, Thomas Bolsover, Joseph Hancock, George Cadman.

The roots of this age of design are in the Sheffield School of Art,[106] particularly after Young Mitchell was appointed principal in 1846. Mitchell had trained at the government's School of Design at Somerset House with Alfred Stevens and, when Stevens came to Sheffield in 1850 as a result of the manufacturer H. E. Hoole's search for a designer to create work worthy of a display at the Great Exhibition of 1851, Mitchell's students came as much under Stevens's sway as Mitchell was.

Tea urn by Omar Ramsden (*Millennium Galleries: Metalwork Gallery*)

Here is Stevens's cast-iron fireplace, *The Rape of Proserpine*, which shows his love of the Renaissance, his training in Italy[107] and his work in the studio of the Danish sculptor Bertel Thorvaldsen. Stevens had never worked with metal but there seems to have been no period of research, uncertainty or experiment. His work for Hoole was as immediate in its mastery of technique as of design. Two of Mitchell's students, James Gamble and Godfrey Sykes (represented here by an electro-plated tobacco jar, 1853), went on to work on the interiors of the Victoria and Albert Museum (q.v.), while Charles Green, although at the School of Art after Stevens had left Sheffield in 1852, was wholly influenced by him.

It is to the credit of Sheffield firms that they employed designers of such talent. James Dixon and Sons commissioned Christopher Dresser in 1879–82 and the beautiful tea set in sterling silver (1879), and another in electro-plated nickel silver (1880), that he designed for them are here.

One consequence of this sustained investment in design and designers trained at the School of Art was a genealogy of skill. Omar Ramsden, the Arts and Crafts designer, whose silver communion chalice and paten (1918) are here, trained William E. Bennett,[108] who trained David Mellor, the latest in this blade-true line.

Mellor's work here – cutlery, candlesticks, bowls, tea services – gives only a partial glimpse of the range of his gifts. He has designed telephones, office equipment and kitchenware, street furniture, traffic lights and the typography of the first motorway signs, still in use after more than forty years. The eighteen-light silver candelabra and two brass candlesticks for St Silas's Church, Sheffield (1960), are examples of the ecclesiastical commissions he has received throughout his career.[109] Here too is the Pride range of cutlery designed for Walker and Hall (1953) before Mellor had left the Royal College of Art. The design won one of the first Design Centre Awards in 1957 and is now a modern classic, alongside his other sets of cutlery, Symbol, Savoy and City.

Mellor's Royal College of Art thesis was on 'The Development of the Cutlery Industry'[110] and his designs demonstrate a respect for the past and an acknowledged debt to the elegant restraint of English Georgian cutlery. His work amalgamates the elements of this museum: tradition, skill, craftsmanship, design and, not least, marketing, for Mellor, like Hancock, Hoole, Dixon, Walker and Hall, found new ways to sell his wares, opening shops in Sloane Square, Covent Garden and Butler's Wharf in London, and at his factory in Hathersage[111] outside Sheffield.

That metalwork is a living tradition is clear from the work to be found here of young designers: Nick Munro, Alex Brogden, Keith Tyssen and Brett Payne.

RUSKIN GALLERY *

Millennium Galleries, Arundel Gate, Sheffield, South Yorkshire s1 2PP
Tel. 0114 278 2600
www.sheffieldgalleries.org.uk/coresite/html/ruskin.asp#ruskin1

A pale shadow of Ruskin's great gift to Sheffield of paintings and books

A notice welcomes you: 'This is a gallery about the way we look at things . . . based on the unique collection of the Guild of St George, founded by John Ruskin.'

Ruskin established the Guild of St George on Christmas Day 1871, with a gift of £7,000. He was driven by his rage against the ugliness, poverty and lack of educational opportunity in 19th-century England. The guild was to implement the ideals that he had spelt out in *Fors Clavigera*, his open letters to 'the workmen and labourers of Great Britain', urging them to create a new social order through cultural education. 'The teaching of Art,' he wrote, 'is the teaching of all things.'

To this end Ruskin set up a museum at Walkeley, near Sheffield, to inspire the city's metalworkers, who were, in his view, the finest in Europe. He gave paintings, drawings, medieval manuscripts, casts of architectural details, minerals and a small library of books on art and ornithology, and put Henry Swan, a favourite pupil from his classes at the London Working Men's College, in charge of it.

As Ruskin's reputation waxed and waned so did that of the guild and its museum. In the 1950s Sheffield City Council moved it to Reading University; sold its most valuable painting, the *Madonna Adoring the Child* by Verrocchio,[112] to the National Gallery of Scotland (q.v.) in 1975; then, ten years later, reinstated the collection in a 19th-century building in the centre of the city. In 2001 the collection came here to a unit in the Millennium Galleries, a piece of architecture by Pringle, Richards, Sharratt that lacks detail, texture or the merest sense of nature. One cannot imagine that Ruskin would have approved. His founding passion has been erased and replaced by a generalised, aimless aesthetic. Despite this unsympathetic setting the collection, or what little there is of it exhibited here, refuses to be suppressed.

Ruskin commissioned artists to go to France and Italy to make exact visual records of the cathedrals and palaces he revered. Henry Roderick Newman was sent to paint watercolours of the Duomo at Lucca (1885). John Wharton Bunney had recorded the Palazzo Manzoni on the Grand Canal at Venice and, when Ruskin realised in 1876 that the west front of St Mark's was to be restored by his old adversary, the architect G. B. Meduna, who had already in Ruskin's view prejudiced the beauty of Ca' d'Oro, he commissioned Bunney to paint the whole facade in oils. Bunney spent 600 days doing this between 1877 and his death in 1882 without completing the task.[113]

Ruskin grasped the advantages offered by photography and employed Arthur Burgess to record the *North Door of Rouen Cathedral* (1880), in Ruskin's view 'one of the most beautiful pieces of Gothic work in the world', as can be seen from his own meticulous and numerous drawings of it.

Some of the most memorable drawings and watercolours here are of architectural details, notably by Ruskin's protégé Frank Randal (a study of the stained glass in Bruges Cathedral;

a leaf crocket carved in the choir stalls of Amiens Cathedral).

Here too are watercolours by Ruskin himself (*A Panorama of the Alps from above Brieg*, 1844) and by such pupils as Kate Greenaway, a *Study of Rock, Moss and Ivy* (1885) worthy of Ruskin at his best (see his exquisite *Study of a Peacock's Breast Feather*).

The new gallery offers little space to display the library that Ruskin gave: books of ornithological prints by John Gould, Edward Lear and John James Audubon; J. M. W. Turner's *Rivers of France*; a copy of William Morris's *The Well at the World's End* (Kelmscott Press, 1896) with glorious illustrations by Edward Burne-Jones;[114] or the guild's urtext, Ruskin's *Fors Clavigera* – in short, 'a working man's Bodleian Library'.

This is all fine but you wonder why Sheffield bothered. Shoehorned into this space with no room for reflection, let alone education, this could be the collection of any 19th-century connoisseur with a taste for architecture, ornithology and the Renaissance. There are glimpses of Ruskin's aesthetic here, but none of his politics or passion. Of Ruskin's original Utopian ideals, let alone of the anger against industrial capitalism, short-term profit and the sacrifice of natural resources[115] that drove him to establish the guild, there is no sign. St George has no dragon.[116]

GRAVES ART GALLERY ***

Surrey Street, Sheffield, South Yorkshire
S1 1XZ
Tel. 0114 278 2603
www.sheffieldgalleries.org.uk

Clean hang of British and European artists of the 19th and 20th centuries, Stanley Spencer, Matisse, Cézanne

Although John Rothenstein did not publish the first volume of his *Modern English Painters*,[117] his invaluable overview of the century's painting, until 1952, it was the five years during which he was director of the Graves Art Gallery (1933–8) that gave him the opportunity

to develop and explore his taste and views.

Having fallen out with Leeds City Art Gallery after one year as its director, the 31-year-old Rothenstein was brought to Sheffield by Alderman Dr J. G. Graves, Britain's first mail-order millionnaire and the dominant force on the city council, and given a good budget with which to create a collection of contemporary paintings for the new gallery, designed by W. G. Davies (1929–34), that Graves had financed.

For thirty years the only paintings that Sheffield had seen were those at the Mappin Art Gallery (now the Weston Park Museum and Art Gallery, q.v.), from J. N. and F. T. Mappin's Victorian collections: Landseer and Linnell, landscapes by Clarkson Stanfield and Henry Dawson, genre paintings by Thomas Webster and historical scenes by Ernest Crofts and John Pettie. Using his connections, Rothenstein mounted an opening exhibition at the Graves with loans from the National Gallery, the Tate, the Royal Academy and the Home House trustees. For his permanent collection he threw open the doors of the Graves to the 20th century and exposed Sheffield to the New English Art Club and the Camden Town Group, to Walter Sickert and Lucien Pissarro; Harold Gilman, Charles Ginner and Spencer Gore, as well as the art of the next generation, represented by such artists as Stanley Spencer.

Downstairs the new building housed the Central Library. On the second floor the picture galleries were top-lit and had low ceilings and simple clean proportions, ideal for showing the contemporary paintings that Rothenstein acquired.

The elements of Rothenstein's taste that were to prove damaging limitations at the Tate in the 1940s (a lack of interest in American or European contemporary artists, a resistance to abstraction) did not inhibit him here. There was occasional friction with Alderman Graves, who had forceful opinions about art and whose own collection was as strong in works by Murillo and Anthonus Mor, by Burne-Jones and Millais, as it was in paintings by Roger Fry and Eric Ravilious. However

the local artist and picture restorer George H. Constantine, whom Rothenstein had appointed to establish a conservation studio at the gallery, acted as a buffer between the two egos[118] and the success of Rothenstein's work with schools and the unemployed, and his innovative temporary exhibition programme (which included an exhibition of original drawings for Walt Disney's cartoons, several of which were purchased by Graves for the collection), meant that, by the time Rothenstein left to become Director of the Tate Gallery in 1938, the Graves rivalled the Ferens Art Gallery in Hull (q.v.) as the best gallery in the north in which to see 20th-century painting.

Rothenstein trod a careful line between the traditional and the modern. He did not subscribe to Sickert's view that the more 'advanced' schools of art were 'the biggest racket of the century';[119] nor did he accept Herbert Read's view that 'there is an inherent superiority in revolutionary art'.[120] He remained a staunch believer in representation and later saw, before many others, the quality of Francis Bacon and Lucian Freud.

It took the Graves, and Sheffield, twenty-five years to digest the diet that Rothenstein had prescribed but, in the 1960s and '80s, two directors, Frank Constantine (the son of George H.) and Julian Spalding, extended Rothenstein's legacy by acquiring the next generations of British artists. Constantine in particular bought works such as C. R. W. Nevinson's *Ypres After the Bombardment* (1916) and secured, as a gift from her sister-in-law Dorelia, Gwen John's enchanting interior *A Corner of the Artist's Room in Paris* (1907–8). Such purchases both reflected and extended Rothenstein's original intentions. Buying from Marlborough, from Madeleine Ponsonby and Carol Hubbard at the New Art Centre and from Alec Gregory-Hood at the Rowan Gallery, they added to the collection paintings by John Hoyland, Bridget Riley and Patrick Caulfield; two excellent Frank Auerbachs, *Minuet* by Tess Jaray, a group of St Ives paint-

Stanley Spencer's Helter Skelter, Hampstead Heath *(Graves Art Gallery)*

ings by Patrick Heron and Wilhelmina Barns-Graham, and a fine Keith Vaughan, *Landscape in Belsize Park* (1954).

Since 1989 cuts in local government expenditure have curtailed new acquisitions and the focus has moved from works of art to capital investment with the building of the Millennium Galleries (incorporating the Ruskin Gallery and the Metalwork Gallery) and the redevelopment of the Weston Park Museum and Art Gallery. But, with the establishment of the Sheffield Galleries and Museums Trust and the appointment as chief executive of Nicholas Dodd, who demonstrated at Wolverhampton Museum and Art Gallery (q.v.) an enthusiasm for contemporary art and an ability to forge a partnership with the Contemporary Art Society, art in the 21st century may prove itself, for Sheffield, better than that of the 20th century, of which Rothenstein wrote, despite the many good paintings he acquired for the Graves, that 'It is unlikely, it is hardly indeed imaginable, that the 20th century will be accounted one of the great periods of painting.'[121]

WESTON PARK MUSEUM AND ART GALLERY **

Weston Park, Sheffield, South Yorkshire
S10 2TP
Tel. 0114 278 2600
www.sheffieldgalleries.org.uk

The archaeology of the moors, the social history of Sheffield; pictures, too

The Weston Park Museum looks out across Sheffield's Weston Park in the north of the city. The giant Ionic portico and recessed colonnade of its facade blare Greek Revival but its design by T. J. Flockton & E. M. Gibbs (1886–8) owes as much to mid-19th-century German civic architecture.

This may seem to be a model of Victorian civic philanthropy but such an impression is deceptive. Its history is chequered. Built in 1887 with bequests from the brewer John Newton Mappin and his nephew Sir Frederick

Mappin[122] and named the Mappin Art Gallery, its early popularity and celebrity fell away and by the 1920s it was considered 'an entire failure'.[123] It was largely destroyed by war in 1940 and remained a bombsite for twenty-five years. Rebuilt in the 1960s, it was redesigned yet again in 2004, and renamed the Weston Park Museum. Its art collection was amalgamated with that of the Graves Art Gallery (q.v.) and the building devoted to the city's archaeological and social collections, which previously had been restricted to the extension built on the western end of the museum in 1937.

The Sheffield Literary and Philosophical Society had been collecting antiquities since the 1870s, primarily from the north Derbyshire, north-east Staffordshire and south Yorkshire moorlands, in what is now the Peak District National Park. There had been settlements here since at least the late Neolithic/Early Bronze Age, c. 2500 BC.

Perhaps the most significant site is Arbor Low, where there had been excavations since the late 18th century.[124] In the 19th century Thomas Bateman began a series of excavations that yielded, in the 1840s and '50s, the stoneball (1840), stone axe (1850) and arrowhead (1852) that are exhibited here.

Bateman went on to excavate other local Bronze Age and some Saxon burial mounds that were rich in Bronze Age jet jewellery, but his most notable excavation was a Neolithic burial site at Benty Grove, where he found flint axes, pottery vessels, boars' tusks, a macehead and the superb Benty Grove Saxon helmet.

His writings give us valuable insights into mid-19th-century archaeology.[125] When his collections came to be sold in 1893 the 3,500 objects, which included coins, medals, arms, armour, manuscripts and Greek, Etruscan and Roman antiquities, occupied the auctioneers for six days.

The sites excavated by Bateman cannot match the scale of Avebury (v. Alexander Keiller Museum) or Windmill Hill but, high on the roof of the moors, they are as grand and have continued to draw archaeologists. The British Archaeological Association conducted further excavations of Arbor Low in 1860, as did Harold St George Gray in 1901 and 1902.[126]

In the 1920s and '30s J. C. Heathcote uncovered a series of important sites: the early Bronze Age standing stones and ring cairns on Stanton Moor, and the Romano-British settlement at Harthill. The collection draws from all these sites.

There are objects here from the hillfort at Mam Tor and from burial mounds at Cow Low, Grindlow and Windle Nook, and from Wharncliffe,[127] a quarry north of Sheffield, where stone corn-grinding querns were produced that were widely traded and reoccur at sites all over the region.

In the museum your eye is inevitably drawn to the beauty of the 7th-century bronze shield whose tight concentric rings were hammered out from behind,[128] to the amber buttons and polished jet necklaces from Beaker sites, to the faience and flint arrowheads from Stanton Moor and to the brilliant blue glass beads, 3,000 years old, found at Gardon's Edge. Beside them, from the same site, is a strange curved object, made of lead, also 3,000 years old. It is not clear for what it was made or used. These ancient sites on the moors above Sheffield have more to teach us about the lives of our ancestors.

WAKEFIELD ART GALLERY **

Wentworth Terrace, Wakefield,
West Yorkshire WF1 3QW
Tel. 01924 305796
www.wakefield.gov.uk/culture/galleries

Drawings and sculptures by local artists, Henry Moore and Barbara Hepworth, plus paintings and 20th-century prints

Wentworth Terrace in Wakefield is a street of respectable Edwardian town houses set back behind hedges, suitable homes for solicitors and accountants: an unlikely setting for a gallery that has been committed to modern British art since it opened in 1934.

The gallery had a succession of outstanding directors, starting with Ernest Musgrave,[129]

Reclining Figure *in elmwood by Henry Moore (Wakefield Art Gallery)*

who went on to be director of Leeds City Art Gallery. He was followed by Eric Westbrook (later the Director of the Arts Council Collection and then of the National Gallery of Australia), Frank Atkinson (Director of the Bowes Museum, 1951–70, and Beamish in the 1970s) and perhaps the most brilliant of them all, Helen Kapp. It is not surprising that the quality of the collection here, and of the temporary exhibitions that have maintained the gallery's momentum, outstrip other regional galleries of this size (five small rooms in a domestic dwelling).

Henry Moore was born nine miles away in Castleford and Barbara Hepworth in Wakefield. She was a pupil at Wakefield Girls' High School across the road from the gallery. Both are well represented here: Moore by sculptures and by drawings that were commissioned in 1942 by Kenneth Clark and the War Artists' Advisory Committee to record the work of the

'Bevin Boys' scheme under which young men were sent to work down the pits as an alternative to military service. Moore's father had worked at Wheldale Colliery and these drawings, of which *Pit Boys at the Pithead* (wax crayon, pen, ink and wash, 1942) was Moore's favourite, are heartfelt. Here also are two of the series he drew in the London Underground during the Blitz of 1941. They share with the pit drawings a tenebrous, half-lit world of dream and muffledness, and were among the last drawings he made that sought to create the illusion of sumptuous roundedness. For the rest of his life his drawings were deliberately flat, as if notes to himself.

His sculptures here include the large *Reclining Figure* (1936), in polished elmwood, a crucial work in his development towards a biomorphic abstraction and one of the earliest of the reclining figures to which he would return throughout the rest of his working life. 'There are three fundamental poses of the human figure,' he maintained. 'One is standing, the other is seated and the third is lying down . . . But of the three poses, the reclining figure gives the most freedom, compositionally and spatially . . . It is free and stable at the same time.'

The gallery also has early works by Barbara Hepworth: *Kneeling Figure* (polished rosewood, 1932), *Mother and Child* (pink Ancaster stone, 1934) and one of her first pierced works, *Pierced Hemisphere* (white marble, 1937). She too has drawings here including *Tibia Graft* (*c.*1951) from the series she made after attending medical operations at Princess Elizabeth Orthopaedic Hospital in Exeter, and later in London at the National Orthopaedic Hospital and the London Clinic. 'When I entered the operating theatre I became completely absorbed by two things: first, the extraordinary beauty of purpose and coordination between human beings all dedicated to the saving of human life, and the way that unity of idea and purpose dictated a perfection of concentration, movement and gesture; and secondly by the way this special grace (grace of mind and body) induced a spontaneous space composition, an articulated and animated kind of abstract sculpture very close to what I had been seeking in my own work.'[130]

Moore and Hepworth shared two characteristics: they were Yorkshire-born and they were carvers who responded to natural materials. The sculptures here take from, and absorb, the strong landscapes of their Yorkshire childhoods.

The inaugural exhibition had paintings and sculptures by 270 of the best British artists, including Matthew Smith, Paul Nash and Jacob Epstein. The exhibitions became annual events and from them the gallery acquired works by Pasmore, Roberts, Hitchens and Piper as well as paintings by the earlier Camden Town Group, Harold Gilman, Charles Ginner and Spencer Gore. By the late 1930s the gallery was already too small for its permanent collection.

Helen Kapp's arrival in 1951 brought a European perspective. Marini, Morandi and Severini, almost unknown in Britain at the time, featured in an exhibition of Italian contemporary art in 1954 and Jantal Adler, Josef Herman and Oscar Kokoschka in a 1959 show of Continental Europeans working in Britain. She promoted and purchased the work of the St Ives artists (Patrick Heron, Roger Hilton, Peter Lanyon, Terry Frost, John Wells). A rarity, a bronze by Hepworth's excellent studio assistant Denis Mitchell, was acquired by Antonino Vella, the current keeper of art.

With Kapp's departure in 1961 there was a decline in the pace of acquisitions, and in the purchasing budget, but the gallery's commitment to contemporary artists was re-established in the 1970s and '80s by the development of a collection of prints, allowing such artists as Euan Uglow, Bridget Riley, Richard Hamilton, Leon Kossoff, David Hockney, Paula Rego and Allen Jones[131] to enter the collection.

More recent sculptures by Hepworth and Moore have been acquired. Displayed in the galleries or outside in the small garden, they allow a quieter and more intimate response than is elicited by these artists' major public pieces in the nearby Yorkshire Sculpture Park (q.v.) or the Tate Gallery. In his essay on Henry Moore for the early 1940s series *Penguin Modern Painters* Geoffrey Grigson cites a statement he believes befits the work of Moore: 'Nature is played out as a Beauty, but not as a Mystery . . . I don't want to see the original realities – as optical effects, that is. I want to see the deeper reality underlying the scenic, the expression of what are sometimes called abstract imaginings.'[132] The statement was made by another great artist of the landscape, Thomas Hardy. This gallery helps you to see those deeper realities in the work of Moore and of Hepworth.

NATIONAL COAL MINING MUSEUM FOR ENGLAND **

Caphouse Colliery, New Road, Overton,
Wakefield, West Yorkshire WF4 4RH
Tel. 01924 848806
www.ncm.org.uk

Re-creation of a working mine; visit the face,
see the lamps, sense the danger

The A642 from Wakefield to Huddersfield
passes the village of Flockton. Beside the road,
a mile from the village, in open country, is a
group of 19th-century industrial buildings,
a sixty-foot chimney and the headframe of a
mining shaft. This is Caphouse Colliery,
now the National Coal Mining Museum for
England (NCMME). Its original shafts were
sunk in the 1780s and are now probably the
earliest coal-mining shafts in use in Britain.
Mining ceased here in 1985 and three years
later the Yorkshire Mining Museum opened.[133]

How best to site a museum of coal mining at
a colliery has taxed museum professionals for
thirty years. It is not easy to find the balance
underground between authenticity and health
and safety, between the desire to give visitors
some sense of what life is like in a working
pit (the noise, the smell, the dust, the temperature, the quality of the air) and to make their
visit comfortable. The Big Pit Mining Museum
(q.v.) offers one solution (the underground
experience but no strong tradition of collecting); Chatterley Whitfield in Stoke-on-Trent
(now closed) offered another, concentrated in
the main on surface buildings and displays.
The NCMME reconciles these competing demands thanks to the quality and commitment
of its staff and their understanding of the coal-
mining industry.

The heart of the museum is underground.
You are issued with a pit helmet, a belt,
battery and lamp, and a brass check to record
your presence underground and your return.
Accompanied by a retired miner who worked
in this or a nearby pit, you enter the cage (lift)
and drop over 400 feet into the blackness of
the Yorkshire coalfield.

You are in another world. The sounds,
the smells, even the textures of the air are
different. The roadways to the face are tall
enough to stand in and have electric light.
They contain sections that show the mining
techniques and conditions of the past 200
years: the employment of women and children, the use of pit ponies, the manual hewing
of coal; 20th-century methods of longwall
mining (cutting a face between two parallel
roadways, filling behind as the face moves
forward). In 1915 three 8-hour shifts a day of 10
men would produce 200 tons every 24 hours.
In 1980 the introduction of drum shearers,
hydraulic power supports and conveyor belts
could increase that output to 800 tons a day
from a 218-yard face.

Some aspects cannot be conveyed: the dark
before the introduction of electric lighting; the
dust before modern extraction; the fear of gas;
the danger of collapse; the claustrophobia of
working on faces that were often less than two
and a half feet high and sometimes as low
as eighteen inches,[134] worked lying on your
side, every working day of your life; the speed
of modern man riding-belts that carried men
to faces that were, in some coastal pits, a mile
or more under the sea. The belts move quickly
and never stop, requiring men to jump on and
jump off. You look at the pit-props and wonder at the weight, beyond calculation, of the
mountains of rock that they uphold.

Back on the surface you return your equipment and brass check and pass the pithead
baths, where a notice says flatly 'no money, no
soap, don't ask'.

The NCMME is the collecting museum
for the English coalfields. In the museum's
galleries are displayed the objects essential to
the life of a miner and a colliery: air com-
pressors, capacitators, dumpy levels, theodo-
lites; hammers and mallets; ammeters,
ohmmeters, voltmeters; caulking tools, swag-
ing tools, tongs; props and chocks; picks,
wedges, augers and stools; knee pads and steel
capper boots; every form of light from the
candle holder and tallow torch to handlamps,
midgey lamps, Clanny lamps, Davy lamps and
cap lamps. And what is believed to be the last

corf in Britain, a basket woven from twigs, used to transport coal from the face to the surface.[135]

The collection includes drawings, paintings, watercolours and prints by such artists as W. Heath Robinson and H. A. Freeth, who was commissioned by the Coal Board for the 'Pit Profile' series in *Coal Magazine* in the late 1940s.

Here is also a powerful archive of photographs under the curatorial direction of Rosemary Preece,[136] whose images record every aspect of mining life: sinking, winding, boring, blasting; the housing conditions, the rescue teams, the disasters – Cadeby Colliery where eighty-eight died in 1912; Senghenydd in Wales, where in 1913, 439 men and boys lost their lives as a result of faulty management practices for which the owners were fined £24, setting the value of a miner's life, as one commentator pointed out, at just over one shilling – an archive that informs us about the industry upon which the 19th-century industrial development and wealth of Britain were founded.

YORKSHIRE SCULPTURE PARK ✳✳✳

Bretton Hall, West Bretton, Wakefield, West Yorkshire WF4 4LG
Tel. 01924 830642
www.ysp.co.uk

The country's first permanent sculpture park in an 18th-century landscape amid high moors; Moore, Hepworth, Caro, Gormley and more

Henry Moore maintained that 'Sculpture is an art of the open air. Daylight, sunlight is necessary to it. I would rather have a piece of my sculpture put in a landscape, almost any landscape, than in or on the most beautiful building I know.' Here, it is.

Founded in 1977 by Peter Murray, the Yorkshire Sculpture Park was the first such park in Britain and remains the grandest and most sublime. You drive into the park through pillared gates. The road curves up a rise to the right revealing a rolling valley. On the bend,

to your left, is Moore's *Reclining Figure*, glossy black, head erect, presiding over the view. Friesian cows graze near by, taking their bronze companion for granted, politely ignoring her. This is an open-air art gallery that places figures as interventions in the landscape.

Having no founding bequests or endowments, the sculpture park has developed this collection by means of gifts, loans and occasional commissions. It now has works by most of the finest British sculptors of the past fifty years (Moore, Hepworth; Paolozzi, Turnbull, Chadwick, Frink; Caro and King), excellent contemporary artists (Antony Gormley, Tony Cragg, David Nash) and some rising talents (Dhruva Mistry, Joanna Mowbray, Nigel Hall and Richard Wentworth). There are also sculptures by Americans Sol Le Witt and Richard Serra, by Europeans Anke de Vries and Giò Pomodoro and by the Japanese Kan Yasuda.

The landscapes into which their works have been placed are various: formal gardens, parkland, woods, agricultural fields, an 18th-century, man-made lake, punctuated by terraces, lawns, paths, bridges, ha-has, hillsides, even a disused quarry. Everywhere there are trees, indigenous and exotic. Oak, ash, elm, beech, chestnut, hornbeam and lime are what you might expect to find in an English park. In the gardens are cypress, yew, holly, juniper, cherry, plum, pear, seven varieties of maple, acer and a gingko from Japan.

As you walk round, sculptures reveal themselves. Joel Shapiro's bronze *Untitled* (1987) struggles up on to its three thin legs in a corner shaded by yew and oak. On the wall of the Bothy Garden, once the estate's vegetable garden, the six pieces of Giò Pomodoro's *Heraldry for the Sun* (1974–5) are nailed to the brick beside an espaliered pear tree. A door in this wall leads you to the two massive skewed spinning tops of Tony Cragg's *Untitled 2000*, one in Anrochter dolomite, one in red sandstone, both with a patinated texture that asks to be stroked.

Some pieces are sited conventionally: Antony Gormley's *Rhizome III*, a puzzle of legs, dominates the Formal Terrace; Austin Wright's *Ring 1960*, a hoop of aluminium,

Barbara Hepworth's The Family of Man *at the Yorkshire Sculpture Park*

catches the light against a dark background of hedge; Anke de Vries's *Watchtower 2000* looks out across the sculpture park from an upper slope of the Bothy Gardens.

Others are hidden: Nigel Hall's *Passage* (1995) round the back of a yew, Serge Spitzer's *Untitled* (1994–8) in the corner of the quarry. Richard Wentworth's *Meal* (1990–93) is scattered over a lawn, a set of iron plates thrown with massive apparent petulance down into the turf.

By the lake the breeze-block geometry of Sol Le Witt's *123454321* (1993) looks urban and out of place from the side – an impression that begins to evaporate when it is viewed from the end on, and disappears completely when a child clambers up its stepped form.

That these sculptures are all interventions in the landscape, hidden or blatant, large or small, is demonstrated most clearly by Antony Gormley's *One and Other*. As you cross the west end of the lake on an 18th-

century bridge the path through the wood rises up ahead of you. Beside it is a sycamore tree trunk twenty feet high. Against the dark backdrop of the trees beyond, it is just possible, from the glint of light on head and shoulder, to make out a single sculpture's shape on top of the trunk. When you have passed and climbed the rise and looked back the figure is transformed by the sunlight into a blaze of bright-red rust. It stands in a characteristic Gormley pose, feet together, arms at its sides, but here the mood, unlike the triumph of the *Angel of the North*, is reflective. Its head is to one side in thought. It contemplates the quiet of the surrounding woods.

This is a living gallery whose pieces are in flux, played on by light, by the time of day or year, by the weather. Seen through soft autumn rain, in the long shadows of a summer evening, or in sharp silhouette against snow, the sculptures reveal modulations, new ways of being seen. Released as they are from the controlled environments of indoor galleries, they might have been let out to play.

The master works here are by Moore and

Hepworth. Both were born locally: Hepworth in Wakefield, Moore in Castleford. For both the West Yorkshire landscape was an influence. Hepworth wrote in 1952: 'The whole of this Yorkshire background means more to me as the years have passed; I draw on those experiences not only visually, in texture and contour, but humanly ... The importance of man in the landscape was stressed by the seeming contradiction of the industrial town springing out of the inner beauty of the country.'

The Family of Man consists of nine pieces of sculpture. Hepworth made them in 1970 in the depths of the Cold War. They stand on a slope, upright forms, spaced apart though in a group, facing in the same direction across the valley, watching and waiting. They are figures and yet not figures. Their geometric shapes seem to resist their domestic familial title. They are abstract but their effect on the viewer is wholly human. The silence they emanate compels.

Hepworth made a bronze edition of six. All the other groups have been broken up, except this, and one in the United States.

There are thirteen sculptures by Moore here, spanning the last thirty years of his life from the *Upright Motives No. 1, 2 and 7* of the mid 1950s to *Reclining Figure: Bunched*, made in 1985. 'Perhaps what influenced me most,' he wrote, 'over wanting to do sculpture in the open-air and relate my sculpture to landscape comes from my youth in Yorkshire, seeing the Yorkshire moors, seeing, I remember, a huge natural outcrop of stone ... and also the slag heaps which for me as a boy, as a young child, were like mountains ... perhaps those impressions when you're young are what count.'

These pieces have returned to this landscape across which they are ranged. Their power charges the experience of seeing them in open country. They seem to guard the park; they confirm Moore's belief that 'Sculpture is an art of the open air.'

SUTCLIFFE GALLERY *

1 Flowergate, Whitby, North Yorkshire
YO21 3BA
Tel. 01947 602239
www.sutcliffe-gallery.co.uk

A great photographer's record of lost lives, ships and ways

Although open to the public six days a week, this collection of the photographs of Frank Meadow Sutcliffe (1853–1941) is in a small, busy commercial gallery. Downstairs its walls are hung with prints for sale. Upstairs there are more prints, some labelled, from the Sutcliffe Collection bought in 1959 by the father of the gallery's owner, Michael Shaw. In 1965 the Shaws gave the original plates to Whitby Museum.

All this, far from disqualifying this collection, positively commends it. There could be no more suitable setting. Sutcliffe, too, had a studio and shop in Whitby and throughout his life was a jobbing commercial photographer whose work can stand beside that of Julia Margaret Cameron, Roger Fenton, David Octavius Hill and Robert Adamson. For the last nineteen years of his life he was curator of the Whitby Museum.

What distinguishes Sutcliffe from the droves of photographers inspired by the new medium is his eye. His father was a landscape painter in watercolours. He raised Sutcliffe to revere John Ruskin. Before he died, when Sutcliffe was eighteen, he had suggested that his son should take up photography as a profession and one of Sutcliffe's first commissions was to photograph the great author of *Modern Painters* and *The Stones of Venice* at Brantwood.

Sutcliffe specialised in portraits but to sustain the photographic business that he set up in Whitby in 1876 he took other subjects to sell as postcards, in series. In them it is easy to see quotations from van de Cappelle and Cuyp in his harbour scenes; Turner in the atmospheric treatment of Whitby Abbey; and Cotman in his landscapes. His photographs of men at

Water Rats *by Frank Sutcliffe (Sutcliffe Gallery)*

work owe something to Stanhope Forbes and La Thangue, to Millet and Bastien–Lepage, but the calligraphic play of masts and poles and rigging, and the dark, rich tones are his own.

More striking than his technical assurance and ability to compose a scene is the detailed affection with which he views a subject, whether it is a group of fishermen's wives buying and selling fish on the New Quay or a man hoeing or 'singling' turnips up on the moors at Lealholm, the furrows stretching across the landscape. His photographs of Yorkshire farming (cutting corn, ploughing, harrowing behind a pair of Clydesdales, washing sheep at a ford, steeping straw or 'thack' for thatching) are more than mere records of late Victorian farming: they are the relived memories of a man who described himself as being 'born by the road side . . . I used to roam about hill and dale . . . eating blackberries, climbing trees, catching butterflies, bird-nesting.'

It is for his Whitby photographs that he is best known. *Water Rats* (1888), in which young skinny boys are messing about naked in the harbour, was exhibited in London in 1888. The Prince of Wales bought a print to hang in Marlborough House and the image has sold ever since. Through Sutcliffe's lens the fishermen of Whitby become heroes, figures stepped out of myth with weathered faces and pale eyes. His portrait of *Henry Freeman*, a lifeboatman for forty years and the only survivor of the Whitby lifeboat disaster of 1861 when twelve men drowned, is an edifice constructed of texture, detail and line: the cork of the lifejacket that straddles his chest, the roughness of his oiled sweater and his grizzled beard. Above them all, the creases are etched deep round his eyes and his granite gaze. He brings into the studio the tang of salt and tar and tobacco.

After Sutcliffe retired he continued to lecture and to write articles on photography, leaving us one of the best records of early techniques and the practical problems of working with heavy, cumbersome cameras and, at first, wet plates[137] that had to be sensitised in an improvised dark tent on the spot within half an hour[138] – plates that make him the poet of Whitby.

CAPTAIN COOK MEMORIAL MUSEUM *

Grape Lane, Whitby, North Yorkshire
YO22 4BA
Tel. 01947 601900
www.cookmuseumwhitby.co.uk

Beautifully rescued town house, near the quay, where the great discoverer served his apprenticeship; models and maps

The harbour of Whitby is little changed in the 250 years since James Cook was indentured here to a Quaker master-mariner, John Walker, in 1747. Gulls cry, the tide comes in and goes out, lifting the fishing boats; the ruins of the abbey look down. The Walkers' house is still the corner house of an alley overlooking the sea.

Painted ox-blood red, it now houses the Captain Cook Memorial Museum, its elegantly panelled rooms decorated, perhaps, more to Mrs Walker's taste than to that of a ship's master. The museum sets Cook's career in the context of Whitby and its maritime trade in coal and alum with London; 18th-century navigation; and the Royal Navy in which Cook enlisted in 1775. But the main focus is on Cook's three voyages: in the *Endeavour* (1768–71) and in *Resolution* (1772–5 and 1776–9).

A splendid table-top model[139] of *Resolution*

in a glass case conveys a sense of the size, and individual responsibilities, of the crew. Deployed beside the model ship are: Cook and his five officers; marines; the quartermaster, clerk, surgeon; boatswain, sailmaster, carpenter, etc. The detail is delightful, down to the barrels, pyramids of cannonballs, guns, pikes, tools, sails, ropes, rolled hammocks and oars.

It is not easy to convey the scale of achievements or reality of these men's voyages to the ends of the world: the ice floes of Antarctica, the tropical islands of the Pacific; the dangers and weathers they faced; the fear and exhilaration. They saw the first kangaroo, 'like a greyhound in size and running but had a long tail';[140] charted the Great Barrier Reef; observed the transit of Venus, which was the ostensible purpose of the first voyage; and found thirteen types of banana. Above all it is not easy to convey to the modern visitor the exotic strangeness of what Cook and his crew found and experienced: animals and plants that no European had ever seen; tattooed natives who ate human flesh.

The museum exhibits a shark's tooth from Hawaii, a hafted adze and tattooing needles from Tahiti, an octopus lure from Tonga and some of the shells brought back from the third voyage by William Bligh, master on the *Resolution*'s second voyage and later captain of the *Bounty*. They all sit politely in cases in these measured and proportioned rooms, but to the eyes of 18th-century Whitby or London they must have been bizarre and exotic. It is no surprise that the collecting of such shells became a mania. Mrs Bligh had forty drawers of them.[141] Margaret, Duchess of Portland, employed Dr Daniel Solander, the naturalist who sailed with Banks, to catalogue her shells.

Joseph Banks, who, 'well versed in natural history',[142] was charged by the Admiralty with serving 'the advancement of useful knowledge',[143] had returned with 3,600 specimens, of which 1,400 were new to science: plants, insects, reptiles, mammals (many preserved in glass bottles). These treasures made him a public hero and celebrity. He and Solander had, as the *Westminster Journal* put it, 'the honour of frequently waiting on his Majesty at

Richmond' and they both received honorary doctorates at Oxford, where the great Carl Linnaeus took leave of him with the words 'Vale vir sine pare' – farewell, O unequalled man.[144]

However, shells and plants, no matter how novel, could not convey the worlds through which Cook and his crew had sailed with the immediacy of paintings and drawings. Cook took with him on each voyage a variety of official and unofficial artists. On the first, Banks had invited Alexander Buchan, an artist of landscapes and figures, and Sydney Parkinson, a young Scot expert in painting plants and animals. Parkinson's botanical drawings here are indeed superb, of a *Knightia excelsa* found on the North Island of New Zealand (October/December 1769) and a *Jasminum volubile* from the Thirsty Sound, Australia (May 1770).[145] On the return he was one of twenty-seven members of Cook's crew to die from either the foul fevers of the Canals of Batavia or the dysentery that immediately followed.

For the second voyage Banks persuaded Johann Zoffany to be the artist, promising him £1,000,[146] but Banks himself withdrew[147] when the additional superstructure that he required to be added to its upper decks, to accommodate his group and the working space they needed, made the ship top-heavy and had to be removed. Zoffany was replaced by William Hodges, whose sumptuous paintings of the *Resolution* in Matavai Bay, of Tahitian war galleys and the stone statues on Easter Island, are the most efflorescent records of Cook's achievements.

The Swiss John Webber, the artist on the final voyage, was pedestrian by comparison but the surgeon's second mate, William Ellis, proved to be a competent draughtsman,[148] as did the carpenter James Cleveley. Cleveley produced aquatints of several islands (Moorea, Matavai, Huaheine and Kealakekua Bay, where Cook died).

The corridors here are lined with engravings of the faces of Pacific Islanders, their whorled tattoos covering every inch of skin, incised, not pricked, as in England, and also with the maps that Cook made. He had originally been selected by the Admiralty because of the meticulous surveys he had made of Newfoundland and the St Lawrence River. Here his maps and charts are wonders of delicate precision, emblems of one way in which the European Enlightenment ordered and organised these new worlds.

You can trace the skills of Cook the cartographer back to what he learnt here when indentured to John Walker. He and his fellow young indenturees lived on the attic floor. From its high window they could look out at the grey North Sea and wonder what lay beyond.

CASTLE HOWARD ✸✸✸

York, North Yorkshire YO60 7DA
Tel. 01653 648444
www.castlehoward.co.uk

Thrillingly presented palace in a landscape packed with treasures

No family house, no building even, in Britain has an approach more splendid. Five miles of Roman-straight road switchback across the high moors north of York; up Whitwell Hill; under the Carrmirr Gate; through Vanbrugh's gatehouse, weighed down beneath its huge central pyramid; up the rise between an avenue of trees to Vanbrugh's 100-foot obelisk at the junction of two grand avenues. It is a route, in the words of Charles Saumarez Smith, of 'controlled magnificence',[149] with echoes of the Roman campagna prompted by the classically inspired monuments in its landscape.

The house is a palace built in golden limestone by John Vanbrugh[150] for the 3rd Earl of Carlisle. Its splendour distracts from its architectural oddity. Vanbrugh embellished a symmetrical body with a riot of baroque detail. Fifty years later the 3rd Earl's son-in-law, Sir Thomas Robinson, completed the west wing in a pure, sober Palladian style, but what the visitor sees is a building as theatrical and confident as Vanbrugh's plays.[151]

The Long Gallery, Castle Howard

Over the next 100 years the 3rd Earl, and his son and grandson, set about filling this palace with works of art. All three loved Italy. The 3rd Earl bought to furnish: a portrait of his daughters by Pellegrini, landscapes by Marco Ricci, the four tapestries of *The Seasons* by John Vanderbank in the Octagon.

The 4th Earl bought to collect: such Venetian artists as Marieschi, Zuccarelli, Canaletto and his nephew Bellotto, and, on his second Grand Tour in 1738–9, capriccios commissioned from Giovanni Paolo Panini. He also acquired the busts, statues and urns that are now in the Antique Passage[152] in a 19th-century arrangement.[153]

Joining forces with his father-in-law, Lord Gower, 1st Marquess of Stafford, and the Duke of Bridgewater, the 5th Earl bought paintings by Bassano, Titian, Bellini, Carracci and Rubens from the great Orléans sale in 1798. Many of these have been sold, or given to the nation, but Annibale Carracci's *Self-portrait* remains here in the Music Room, as do Leandro Bassano's *Portrait of his Mother* and Girolamo Bedoli's[154] *Two Dukes of Ferrara*. The 5th Earl also patronised English artists: Gainsborough, Stubbs, Hoppner, Zoffany and Reynolds, to whom he sat three times.[155]

The collection was added to by the 9th Earl, the painter George James Howard, who was a pupil of Alphonse Legros and Giovanni Costa. With Costa and George Hemming Mason, he formed the Etruscan School. Landscapes by Howard and Costa, and portraits of the Earl by Legros and W. B. Richmond, are in the Museum Room. Also from the 1870s is the redecoration of the Chapel with embroidered panels by William Morris[156] and stained glass by Edward Burne-Jones.

Dispersed around the house are fine pieces

of furniture by John Linnell and Christopher Fuhrlohg and side tables (c. 1735) by William Kent in the Crimson Dining Room. There are pieces of ormolu by Matthew Boulton and a pagoda Delft tulip vase in the Museum Room.

More spectacular than any of the objects or paintings in the house is the Great Hall, Vanbrugh's supreme triumph at the heart of the building. You enter a room that, at floor level, is impressive but low lit and austere, empty save a black-and-white marble floor and a massive fireplace with elaborate scagliola surrounds. Your eye is taken up by the capitals in each corner that rise and rise to support four mighty arches, from above which bursts the light from the rotunda, the lantern and the cupola seventy feet overhead. The columns and capitals elaborately carved by Nadauld and Samuel Carpenter are interspaced by Giovanni Antonio Pellegrini's paintings of the *Four Elements*, the *Twelve Figures of the Zodiac*, *Apollo and the Muses* and, swirling around the cupola, *Phaeton*, Apollo's son, surrounded by cloud and his horses' hooves, plunging from the heavens towards you.[157] The *trompe l'œil* sets the head spinning as, in Addison's translation of Ovid's *Metamorphoses*, 'The breathless Phaeton, with flaming hair/Shot from the chariot, like a falling star.' A fire in 1940 destroyed the dome and Pellegrini's murals, which have been repainted by a Canadian artist, Scott Medd.

The Great Hall's rotunda, the first in a private house in England, gives Castle Howard its distinctive profile. It is the classical heart of the house. Outside, as you drive away through the park, the Temple of the Four Winds and the Mausoleum reassert the homage to the classical world that informs Castle Howard and reaffirm its position as one of the most magnificent marriages of collection, building and landscape in Britain.

YORK ART GALLERY ✳✳✳

Exhibition Square, York, North Yorkshire
YO1 7EW
Tel. 01904 551861
www.york.art.museum

Great pictures, few great names, William Etty, the local artist; superb studio ceramics

Everything changed for York in 1947 when Hans Hess was appointed curator. His inheritance was not promising: a run-of-the-mill 19th-century collection and a gallery in a Victorian exhibition hall that had been severely damaged in the Second World War.

Hess was German and Jewish, the son of a successful shoe manufacturer in Erfunt, a patron of the arts. The artists Kandinsky, Klee, Feininger and Pechstein were family friends. This proved valuable when, having fled Germany, Hess worked under Trevor Thomas at the Leicester Art Gallery and Museum in the mid 1940s, helping Thomas to build up that gallery's remarkable collection of German Expressionist paintings.

York Art Gallery had been founded in 1879 with a bequest from a local businessman, John Burton, whose taste was for 19th-century domestic genre and narrative painters such as Frederick Daniel Hardy.[158] The gallery also inherited from the late-18th-century Kirkleatham Museum an unusual collection of 'Bustos and Images', bronzed plaster busts by John Cheere (1749), of Horace, Cicero, Shakespeare, Bacon, Milton, Locke, Newton, Dryden, Pope and others.[159]

Since 1911 the gallery had been collecting paintings and drawings of York-born William Etty, notable not just for his moralistic biblical and historical paintings[160] but also for his landscapes and beautiful studies of the male nude, as it had views of York, mainly on paper, boosted by the 1,200 images of York collected by Dr W. A. Evelyn.

Hess determined that this modest provincial gallery should become of national importance. He redesigned and re-lit the galleries, erected wall-sized screens covered in oatmeal linen, re-hung the collection and began to buy work by artists including Lely and Reynolds. He persuaded the York 1951 Festival of Britain committee to hold an exhibition, *Masterpieces from Yorkshire Houses*, in imitation of Manchester's famous 1857 *Art Treasures* exhibition, but his great chance came in 1954, when F. D. Lycett Green offered his collection of over a hundred Old Masters to the gallery.

Lycett Green came from an old York family. His cousin Frank Green had owned and restored the 16th-century Treasurer's House beside the Minster. During and after the Second World War, although living in South Africa, he set about forming a collection of Old Master paintings that would be representative of Western European art between 1500 and 1800. When he looked for a public gallery to which to give them he was spurned by the National Gallery of South Africa. Impressed by the changes that Hess was effecting at York, he decided to leave them to his native city.

Lycett Green made a virtue of not being able to afford to acquire a Titian, a Rembrandt or a Botticelli by concentrating on the best examples of work by less well-known or less fashionable painters. Working through such dealers as Agnew and Zanetti, he put together a collection that was particularly strong on Dutch painters of the 17th century (Nicolaes Berchem, Karel du Jardin, Jan Victors, Frans Snyders) and Italian of the 15th, 16th and 18th centuries.[161] Its notable rarities include *Interior of the Church of St Bavo, Haarlem* (*c.* 1690) by Isaak van Nickelen, influenced by Pieter Saenredam, and *The Sleeping Soldier* (*c.* 1522), one of four glorious panels by Bernhard Strigel,[162] the only example of his work in an English public collection.

Inevitably there were attributions that have since been reconsidered: is *The Agony in the Garden* (*c.* 1525) by Francesco Ubertini Bacchiacca or Pier Francesco Foschi; is the portrait of *Monsignor Agucchi* (*c.* 1615–20),[163] captured, startled, in a shaft of light, by Domenichino or by Annibale Carracci? Whoever the artists are, there is no doubting the excellence and freshness of Lycett Green's eye, equally apparent in his choice of a panel

depicting *St Clement Striking the Rock* by the Sienese painter Bernardino Fungai, a true Primitive and a delightful one.

Hess and the gallery had a second piece of good fortune. The Very Reverend Eric Milner-White, Dean of York from 1941 to his death,[164] gave his collection of English stoneware pottery, in which the work of those he considered 'the true Master Potters of the Century', (Bernard Leach, Shoji Hamada and William Staite Murray) were particularly well represented. Leach's lyrical vase, *Leaping Salmon* (1931), with its 'creamy-white, big-crackled glaze, which we have never since equalled . . . it was hard and it was soft at the same time',[165] Staite Murray's *Jar: Persian Garden* (1931)[166] and (probably) his last and largest pot, *Very Tall Pot: 'Kwan Yin'* (1937–9),[167] make this the outstanding collection of English contemporary studio pottery.[168] Milner-White also presented some forty early-20th-century British paintings, including several Sickerts, Wilson Steer, Gilman, Gore and Gwen John.

By 1967, when he retired, Hans Hess had, with the help of the Lycett Green bequest and the Milner-White gift, transformed the gallery's collections, but as important was his legacy of high curatorial and scholarly standards. He trained John Jacobs and John Ingamells. The latter wrote the gallery's catalogue (1974) and, after a period at the National Museum and Gallery of Wales, returned to York as curator from 1967 to 1977.

From 1977 to 2002 the gallery was directed by Richard Green who, in times that were far less helpful to collectors than those enjoyed by Lycett Green, continued to acquire Old Masters. Apart from the national galleries, the Ashmolean Museum and the Fitzwilliam Museum, only the Barber Institute of Fine Arts (all q.v.) had had the ambition and the skill to maintain that policy. Green added a catholic range of paintings: a sketch portrait of *Nicolas Poussin* by Bernini; a portrait by Hogarth of *Elizabeth Hoadley* (1741); *The Honourable Lady Stanhope and the Countess of Effingham as Diana and her Companion* (1765) by Francis Cotes, probably his masterpiece; watercolours by Turner; paintings by Ben Nicholson, David Hockney, John Hoyland and John Golding; studio pottery by two of the finest potters of the post-Leach/Staite Murray/Lucie Rie generation, Joanna Constantinidis and Ewen Henderson; and the two panels that complete Bernardino Fungai's altarpiece for the church of Santa Maria dei Servi in Siena, whose first part was given by Lycett Green.

The story of the York Art Gallery under Hess, Ingemells and Green is proof that given high standards of scholarship, a love for good painting and curators who have confidence in their judgement, a gallery can prosper. At York the priorities have been right. The gallery glows with the idiosyncratic excellence of the paintings on its walls.

TREASURER'S HOUSE *

Chapter House Street, York,
North Yorkshire YO1 2JD
www.nationaltrust.org

*Frank Green's triumphant restoration of a
house with a past*

Frank Green, who owned Treasurer's House from 1897 until he gave it to the National Trust in 1930, wrote a letter in 1916 in which he 'expressed a wish that the house may never be considered as a museum or show a museum flavour.'[169] Nevertheless the way in which Treasurer's House celebrates English craftsmanship and design, particularly in furniture, would surely have pleased him, since it is his taste that pervades every room.

The post of Treasurer at the cathedral was a medieval sinecure, created in 1091 and abolished in 1547 at the time of the Reformation. The house, built in local stone in the 16th century, added to and altered by subsequent owners, looks on to the eastern edge of the Cathedral Close in the shadow of the Minster and its soaring buttresses. This history means that, despite its elegant, mainly 17th-century, face, it is a mongrel building whose hybridity was compounded when Green commissioned Temple Moore, a pupil of George

Gilbert Scott Jnr, to restore it in 1897.

The younger son of Sir Edward Green, MP and Wakefield industrialist, whose father had made a fortune from Green's Fuel Economiser, a patented device to heat steam boilers, Frank Green was a collector, even a connoisseur. Treasurer's House was the setting he wanted for his collections, which were primarily of furniture, and with Temple Moore he set about remodelling and redesigning it. 'The main object was to give an idea of the rooms and furniture of the various periods.'[170] In this ambition, to recreate period rooms, he was in advance of his time, anticipating the achievements of the Victoria and Albert Museum (q.v.), Winterthur and the American Museum in Britain (q.v.).

The house presented obstacles as well as opportunities. The continual additions and alterations to it over the previous 300 years, and its subdivision into five separate properties, meant that there was no one, definitive, house that could be recovered. Green and Moore removed most of the 19th-century changes to recreate the 17th- and 18th-century rooms that Green sought.

The Tapestry Dressing Room, whose panelling and Flemish verdure tapestries are 17th century, contains a fine English table (*c.*1695); a joined oak chest (*c.*1670) from Green's parents' house, Heath Old Hall; 17th-century stumpwork telling the Old Testament story of Esther; and, on the table, a 17th-century bead basket, used to carry rosemary for guests at weddings and christenings.

The two main bedrooms, the Queen's Room and Princess Victoria's Room,[171] have early 18th-century interiors and appropriate furniture: in the Queen's Room, a pair of English carved giltwood stools (*c.*1705) at the foot of the bed; a carved giltwood and gesso toilet mirror, and a walnut veneered bidet (both *c.*1730). In Princess Victoria's Room are a walnut and parcel-gilt slab table (*c.*1715); another carved giltwood and gesso pier mirror (*c.*1730); and a beechwood and cane chair (*c.*1715). Both rooms are dominated by tester beds (*c.*1740) from Houghton Hall, Norfolk and both have the incongruous insertion of

19th-century pieces in the manner of André-Charles Boulle: a flamboyant pair of ebony, tortoiseshell and brass inlaid cabinets (c. 1860) in the Queen's Room; a clock in the style of Louis XIV with a movement by Nicolas Fortin of Paris in Princess Victoria's.

This taste for Boulle extends, surprisingly happily, into the most spectacular room in the house, the Blue Drawing Room. The chimney piece and the peacock-blue panelling are 18th century, as are the two pairs of English giltwood pier glasses (c. 1720 and 1730), the set of four walnut chairs with needlework covers (c. 1725) and the carved giltwood torchères (c. 1715), bearing the monogram of John Churchill, 1st Duke of Marlborough, made, presumably for Blenheim, perhaps by James Moore.

Into this Green introduced a pair of Boulle cabinets and a Boulle desk,[172] which stands facing the chimney piece. A suite of carved and gilt seat furniture (c. 1790), English but in the French style, effects a visual link between the two centuries and styles.

Green's most ambitious and least successful intervention is in the centre of the house, where he created a 'medieval great hall', of double height, by removing the upper floor and replacing the 18th-century sash windows with mullions and transoms, and by leaving one wall of exposed beams, bizarrely supported by classical pillars. The result is clumsily theatrical and lifeless. It fails to do justice to the excellent 17th-century English furniture, notably a mighty oak table (c. 1600) made from a single tree; two joined oak great chairs (mid 17th century); a walnut and cane elbow chair (c. 1685); and a pair of upholstered chairs with walnut frames (c. 1700) that came from Rushbrooke Hall, Suffolk. It also contains the one good painting in the house, Joachim Beuckelaer's Kitchen Scene.

Frank Green was, in person and address, confident and stylish. Daphne Fielding recalled him: 'He wore all sorts of elegant waistcoats, charms, fobs, capes, sweeping sombreros, grey top hats, floppy bow ties and frilly shirts. He always smelt delicious and I adored him,'[173] and Lady Diana Cooper remembered, 'He gave my sisters hunters. To me he gave antiques, Battersea snuffboxes and paste brooches . . . He was a big-fortuned eccentric who taught us about furniture, architecture and ornament.'[174] That confidence and thorough knowledge of furniture account for the many and varied pieces throughout the house that are of quality and that were widely disregarded in the late 19th century when he collected them: the 18th-century Venetian glass chandelier in the Staircase Hall, thought to have hung in Lord Burlington's Assembly Rooms in York from 1730 to c. 1840; the 'love-seat' with its original needlework (c. 1730) in the Tapestry Room and the walnut cabinet in the Court Room, illustrated, as are several other pieces, in Percy Macquoid's History of English Furniture[175] (1904–8, 4 vols.). They also account for his boldness in commissioning wallpaper, based on examples from Knole (q.v.) and Hardwick Hall in Derbyshire, from Watts and Co., for the staircase ('Malmesbury') and the Court Room ('Pear'); and for the curiosities of the wax relief portraits (c. 1800) of a lady and a gentleman in the Tapestry Room and the clock on the Landing, whose thirteen-foot pendulum extends into the Great Hall below.

Green always maintained that he made Treasurer's House a house to live in: 'a house as conceived and occupied by a Yorkshire sub-lieutenant of industry with artistic and antiquarian tastes at the beginning of the 20th century.'[176] Green protested, 'I have just given South Kensington[177] all my "museum pieces". Everything is usable and used,' but in practice Treasurer's House was always a showpiece, as the 1920s articles in Country Life and the three guidebooks to its contents that he published in 1906, 1908 and 1919 demonstrate. It may now be the museum he claimed to resist but, home or museum, it is a treasure house of English furniture.

JORVIK VIKING CENTRE *

Coppergate, York, North Yorkshire YO1 1NT
Tel. 01904 643211
www.jorvik-viking-centre.co.uk

An underground ride through York's Viking past, complete with smells

Our history is beneath our feet. When the York Archaeological Trust (YAT) began excavating the foundations of a former sweet factory on Coppergate in 1976, it found, sixteen feet below the level of the present city street, evidence of street life in York in AD 975: the Viking-age city of Jorvik. Here was an opportunity to qualify the image of the Vikings as violent warriors and to show their civic and domestic culture.

The Vikings first came to the coast of Northumbria in 793, when they sacked the monastery at Lindisfarne. They began settling permanently in England in the late 9th century. They attacked and took York in 866 and over the next 100 years developed a city that became a sophisticated commercial centre, with new streets, a new bridge over the River Ouse and numerous new churches, including a minster.

The ground beneath 20th-century Coppergate was wet and peaty. In these conditions objects made of wood, cloth or leather that would normally have decayed had been preserved, as had leaves and insects. The trust had discovered an archaeological treasure trove.

The Jorvik Viking Centre, which the Trust opened in 1984, is not a museum. The artefacts are authentic, but what it offers is an experience that employs film, sound, models, even smells, in an attempt to recreate something of street life in Jorvik in AD 975.

In eight years of excavation the trust retrieved 40,000 objects as its archaeologists sifted down through 36,000 separately identifiable layers of history in those sixteen feet: layers of concrete, bricks, rubble, cobbles, soil of different colours and textures; layers of dust, dirt, mud and ash. In them were not only the

pieces of bone, timber, metal, glass and pottery that might be expected but also woollen socks, leather shoes and cloth.

The visitor enters Jorvik through a modest entrance in the middle of a shopping precinct and descends the sixteen feet to the 10th-century street level where, in a cinema room that seats twenty people, you are shown a short film in which a young couple are transported back, first by decades, then by centuries, to 975. The passing of time is marked by changes of the couple's clothes and in painted backdrops of the city centre.

The visitor is then installed in a simple open capsule on rails, as might be found on a fairground ride. This proceeds at a stately pace through a recreated Jorvik street while a taped commentary is relayed to speakers behind each seat.

In low lighting of a greenish tinge, the capsules pass the houses and workplaces of a blacksmith, a wood turner, a butcher, etc. In front of each are life-sized mannequins, appropriately costumed, some of which move mechanically. A woman leans over a fence and gossips. Some children play games. Another child steals an egg. The woodturner turns wood. A man crouches over a cesspit, hidden from the chest down by a wattle fence.

There is a soundtrack of conversational Old Norse. Ordered blasts of 'authentic' odour issue from kitchen, butcher and cesspit. When the mannequins are motionless, in low light, their faces turned away, it is possible to catch some sense of the intended activity. Full face, fully lit, in motion, they fail sadly, their mechanical movements recalling television animation of the 1950s.

At the end of the ride, the visitor disembarks and can examine the display cases in the Artefact Gallery, where museum staff in costume are available to demonstrate the Viking board game Hnefatafl[178] (the 'l' is pronounced 'p') or show how Viking coins were struck in dies. Lying in the cases is evidence of the crafts and skill of the Viking world that brought to this northern city amber from the Baltic, soapstone from Norway, pottery from the Rhine, gold pins and brooches from Ireland, cowrie shells from the Red Sea, precious metals and silk from Samarkand. In Jorvik Viking crafts-men made rings and beads of glass; combs of bone; bowls, cups and spoons of alder, ash and maple; saw bows, padlocks, bolts and keys from the crucibles and moulds of their metal workers; axes, chisels, wedges, knives and augers; musical instruments, buzz-bones and a glass smoothing iron for pressing material. Here too are the leather boots and shoes, the thongs and scabbards, and the woollen socks that have emerged from 1,000 years in spongy peat.

The same mistrust of human imagination that decided upon the use of mechanical mannequins does not trust the visitor to gaze and wonder at these actual riches. The lighting in the cases comes and goes in twenty-second waves to show these objects now lying in darkness, spotlit on a glass shelf, now in full light, the shelf transformed to a Viking crafts-man's bench over which another mannequin looms; wonders of this great excavation are reduced to accessories in a shadow-puppet show.

In uncovering this site YAT has enriched our knowledge of a period of our history that had previously been caricatured by crude and mistaken myths (there is not a horned helmet here; none has ever been found on any site) and they have brought this knowledge to a wide audience. Regrettably, the experience is apparently pitched at the curiosity and concentration span of someone's idea of a reluctant ten-year-old.

Visitors who want more can go to Jorvik's Archaeological Resource Centre, where it is possible to examine such individual objects as the two coin dies found on the site, the only dies of this period anywhere in the world. They are not a pair, both being 'head' dies. One is the St Peter's penny, first struck in York c. 910–20, showing the cross, hammer and sword of Thor. The other is an Anglo-Saxon penny from the reign of King Athelstan, who drove the Vikings out of Northumbria in 927 and declared himself 'King of All Britain'. They are authentic objects that do justice to a tremendous feat of archaeology.

NATIONAL RAILWAY MUSEUM ∗∗∗

Leeman Road, York, North Yorkshire
YO26 4XJ
Tel. 01904 621261
www.nrm.org.uk

All trains meet here – irresistible even for non-trainspotters

Railways are not new. In 15th-century mines trucks on wheels – 'dogs' – were held in grooved paths by hanging metal pins that slotted between two planks. By the early 17th century wagonways were being built to carry coal in Nottingham, in the Severn Valley and on Tyneside. But all these were constrained by the limited power of muscle, either human or equine.

To move greater weights, iron rails and steam power were necessary. In the 18th cen-tury both were achieved, but the steam power provided was by such fixed engines as the Weatherill winding engine (1833) here, which hauled wagons for the Stanhope and Tyne Railway up two inclines, over a mile long, with maximum gradients of 1½ in 2, to a height of 1,400 feet above sea level.

In 1803 Richard Trevithick invented the first steam locomotive to move on a track but it moved like a snail and consumed bunkers of coal. Finally, in 1829, the directors of the Liverpool and Manchester Railway organised the Rainhill trials, offering £500 to anyone who built an engine that could pull three times its own weight seventy miles at an average speed of ten miles per hour. The *Rocket*, built by George and Robert Stephenson and incor-porating three key innovations (direct cylinder drive, a multitubular boiler and draught created by the pipe for the exhaust steam), was the only one to do so. It averaged 13 mph. Railways and steam locomotion had been born.

The original *Rocket* is in the Science Museum (q.v.), of which this museum is a part. She is here in replica only (1979), in her brilliant yellow livery, her barrel-chested

Mallard, *locomotive No. 4468 (National Railway Museum)*

engine cased in gleaming wood, her twelve-foot-high white funnel, with its black coronet, carried before her. Her first-class carriages were modelled on the stage coach: uphol-stered, button-back seats, a step up and a place for the guard on the roof with the luggage. Second-class carriages were open to the sky, with wooden seats.

The *Rocket* is the Adam and Eve of conventional steam locomotives, her steam-engine progeny numbering 110,000[179] in Britain alone, of which some of the most important, innovative or typical are here in the National Railway Museum, near York station, designed by Thomas Prosser in 1870. Its roof, by the engineer Thomas Cabrey, is 800-foot long on a slow curve. Described by Pevsner as 'of the simplest iron construction with spidery trusses',[180] it makes York one of the most beautiful stations in Britain.

Beside the *Rocket* are the Great Northern

Railway's 4–2–2 No. 1, the first of the elegant Stirling Single class (1870–1907); the London and North Western's 2–4–0 No. 790, *Hardwicke* (1892), which took part in the 540-mile race to Aberdeen (from Euston) in 1895; and *Mallard* (1938), London and North Eastern's 4–6–2 Class A4, No. 4468, which meets you in the entrance to the Great Hall. *Mallard* set the world speed record in 1938, touching 126 mph between Grantham and Peterborough, coal flying from its tender, showering the platform and smashing windows as she blasted through Little Bytham station. The record still stands.

While *Mallard* welcomes visitors with her bright blue livery and black Bugatti-inspired nose, the other locomotives are arranged in a circle, pointing inwards in locomotive convocation, celebrants of some rail rite: the Great Northern Railway's 4–4–2 Passenger Express No. 251 (1902), the Great Western Railway's *Lode Star* No. 4003 (1907), which completed 2 million miles before being withdrawn in 1951, and British Rail's Class 9F No. 92220, *Evening*

Star (1960), the last steam locomotive to be built for mainline operation in Britain, at Swindon.

You stand in their lee, sensing their power, imagining the taste of steam, the smell of oil. Here is romance: the sleeper to Inverness, the boat train to Paris; W. H. Auden's night mail ('This is the Night Mail crossing the border, Bringing the cheque and the postal order,'[181]); the sense of loss as the departing carriage disappears; the pounding blood as the train you are to meet draws into the station.

George Earl's paintings here, *Going North: King's Cross Station* (1893) and *Coming South: Perth Station* (1895), capture the excitement, the tense jostle of dogs, children, porters, racquets, rods, guns, trunks, hampers, hatboxes. Railway advertisements of the 1920s and '30s promote the new freedoms of travel for all: to Torquay on the Riviera Express; to 'East Coast Joys' in Tom Purvis's set of pictures (1931) in praise of the London and North Eastern Railway's services to 'the Drier Side of Britain'.

The locomotives here thundered across Britain on tracks that linked cities. Cuttings, bridges and viaducts reshaped the landscape as nothing had since the Roman roads. This demanded feats of engineering (Isambard Kingdom Brunel's majestic Royal Albert Bridge, spanning the River Tamar between Devon and Cornwall; Benjamin Baker and John Fowler's mile-long Forth Bridge) and of architecture (George Gilbert Scott's Midland Grand Hotel and St Pancras Station, 1876; J. P. Pritchett Snr's classical station at Huddersfield; Phillip Hardwicke's Doric arch at Euston station, 1838, RIP,[182] proclaiming the gateway to the north).

Travel was no longer just for the rich. The Midland Railway's third-class[183] dining car (1914) here offered solid comfort: mahogany-veneered tables, silver-plated holders for wine bottles. This was spartan compared with the 4th Duke of Sutherland's private train, built for him by the London and North Western Railway to designs by C. A. Park in 1899 and in use until 1948. It comprised day saloon, sleeping car, kitchen, electric light, central heating and an 'Adam style' interior with oddly feminine chintz curtains and covers, and carried him to his own station for Dunrobin, his castle in Sutherland. Edward VII was so impressed that he commissioned Park to redesign Queen Victoria's royal train in 1902. The royal train that may be seen here outdid Sutherland with desks, telephones, leather armchairs in the 'smoking room', an iron double bedstead and a bath (originally silver-plated, later ceramic).

This museum is as much about the people who made and used the railways as it is about the majesty of locomotives: the navvies and surveyors who built them; the generations of rail workers who ran them (a fireman on a steam locomotive had to shovel a ton of coal every forty miles); the Sutherlands and the royal family who rode in state; the passengers, *not* customers, who learned to take the railways for granted; the sung heroes (Stephenson, Brunel and George Hudson of York, 'the Railway King' who once owned 1,000 miles of track) and the unsung (Edward Bury, an early rival of Stephenson whose *Coppernob*, 1846, here, worked until 1900; R. E. L. Maunsell, whose *Sir Lamiel*, 1925, is here to show how he responded to the demands for express travel between the wars; Eric Gill, who developed the Gill Sans typeface for the London and North Eastern Railway in 1932 as their company logo on vehicles, station signs, timetables, etc.; and Joe Duddington, the driver of *Mallard*).

Part ode, part elegy, the museum's tone captures the hold that railways have on the imagination of all age groups (as do the minute seductions of Bassett-Lowke No. 0, 1¼-inch-gauge model trains). It alludes to railways' impact for good (a daily postal service, the availability of fresh food) and for ill (the encroachment of town on countryside as commuting became possible), but it does not chart the decline of rail services in the last fifty years as car ownership grew.

It does, however, show an alternative: the pride and confidence of the Japanese, as expressed in the Shinkansen Series 0 Bullet Train (1976–2000) that covered the 163 miles from Tokyo to Osaka every day in two and a half hours, without accident, reliable to within twenty-four seconds of its schedule. Europe's response, the Eurostar, is represented here by the front of its engine, sawn off behind the cab like the head of a dead shark.

The sad decline is marked by a display of signs that is a tribute to stations that have closed since the Beeching Report (1963): Long Houghton, Upper Denton, Little Weighton, Coal Road; Castle Howard, Newton Dale, Belah, Ings Wood; Newington, Gilling and Goathland Summit; Willerby, Sinderby, Robin Hood's Bay.

As you leave you hope, in vain, to catch the smell of oil. Across the tracks trains continue to pull out of York station under Cabrey's sweeping roof, carrying passengers to London in 120 minutes, faster than any motorway.

YORKSHIRE MUSEUM **

Museum Gardens, York, North Yorkshire
YO1 7FR
Tel. 01904 687687
www.york.yorkshire.museum

The remains of Roman York just beneath the city's skin, and great 20th-century studio ceramics

The magnificent marble head of *Constantine the Great*[184] here in the Yorkshire Museum, twice life size, was 'found in excavating for a drain in Stonegate'[185] in 1823. It is 'the earliest portrait of him in the Roman World and certainly the most interesting'[186] and was made AD *c.*306 when Constantine was proclaimed, in York, emperor of the Roman army, in succession to his father Constantius Chlorus, who had died in the city on 25 June. His broad, flat face, set mouth, thick neck all reveal him as a haughty but human Caesar.

Since then the Brigantes, the Romans, the Anglo-Saxons, the Vikings and the Normans all left their mark on this city. It is not surprising that the Yorkshire Museum has some of the richest archaeological collections outside the British Museum.

The museum was built (1827–9) by the Yorkshire Philosophical Society to original designs by Richard Hey Sharp, executed by William Wilkins,[187] who added a classical facade: a portico with four massive Doric columns, an entablature across the full width and a pediment. It is set in the former St Mary's Abbey precincts (13th century), now a botanic garden, beside the River Ouse, and within it are buildings and ruins of buildings that also embody York's history: the foundations of the Roman fortress wall; the 12th-century Gatehall; the ruined lancet arch of the Early English abbey (1270–94); the 14th-century Hospitium, the abbey's guesthouse; St Olave's Church (Perpendicular, 15th century) and the 19th-century observatory built by J. Sweaton, the designer of the Eddystone Lighthouse. In 1912 the museum added an unusual wing, the Tempest Anderson Hall, whose pilasters, frieze and entablature echo Wilkins but within which is an early example of reinforced shuttered concrete.

With Constantine's head in the museum's first catalogue was the Ormside bowl (8th century), whose silver-gilt outer shell is enlivened by *repoussé* decoration. Since then the Anglo-Saxon collection has been enriched by material from the only 7th-century cemetery in the north, at Uncleby; the 9th-century York helmet, its design as elegant as its craftsmanship, bearing the inscription 'In the name of our Lord Christ, the Holy Spirit (and) God and to all we say Amen. Ostere'; and the 9th-century Gilling sword, its grips, guard and pommel of applied silver strips.

The Roman collection differs from those at Colchester, St Albans, Fishbourne and other southern museums, in being mainly from the 3rd and 4th centuries. There are good examples of tombstones, cult objects, mosaics (a nearly complete *Four Seasons*) and blue glass flagons from Cologne in good condition, but there are also less usual objects: pots in the form of heads; pottery face masks (4th century) excavated at Catterick, probably used in religious rituals or performances; a bun of auburn hair preserved by gypsum;[188] much jet and shale jewellery; and fine statuary, notably a full-sized figure of Mars and a woman's head delicately carved in stone, her hair upswept in a chignon.[189]

The medieval collections contain many complete or near-complete ceramic jugs and cooking pots, and some alabaster panels that retain their polychrome decoration, but the centrepieces undoubtedly are the 15th-century Middleham jewel and ring.[190] The jewel is a gold, lozenge-shaped pendant engraved with religious scenes and figures. On the front are a large sapphire, a Latin inscription and an engraving of the Trinity. On the back are the Lamb of God and a Nativity, with the figures of fifteen saints on the frame. The jewel opens by means of a sliding panel and within were found small roundels of silk embroidered with gold thread.

These superb examples of late-15th-century jewellery were found by metal detectors in 1985 and 1990. By contrast the remainder of the museum's collections was excavated by outstanding archaeologists in the 19th century, including, among others, the Revd W. Greenwell, William Hargrove and John Thurman, and in the 20th century by Sir Mortimer Wheeler, Professor John Wacher and Peter Addyman of the York Archaeological Trust. The presiding spirit of the collection is that of the Revd Charles Wellbeloved, the first curator of antiquities and the real founder of the modern study of Roman York. He was ahead of his time in giving a warning to modern archaeology: 'the plough that discloses the rust-eaten javelin and the empty helmet ... levels the rampart and obliterates the causeway, and effaces all the labours of the victorious legions of Rome.'[191]

Beside these archaeological treasures is a somewhat incongruous bequest of an outstanding collection of 20th-century studio ceramics, put together by Mr W.A. Ismay of Wakefield. He started by acquiring the work of Yorkshire potters in the 1950s but quickly the range of his taste widened. Here beside powerful pieces by Bernard Leach and Michael Cardew are the translucent delicacies of Lucie Rie and Mary Rogers and thirty pieces by Hans Coper; the staunch salt glazes of Jane Hamlyn, the cool creamy glazes of Jim Malone, the black tenmoku glazes of David Lloyd Jones and Mick Casson.

Michael Cardew has several pieces, including a fine tall grain jar. More surprising is the work of African potters, made during Cardew's time as pottery officer to the Nigerian government (1950–65), when he set up a training centre at Abuja. Here are a bowl and jar by Ladi Kwali and burnished pots by the Kenyan Magdalene Odundo.

W.A. Ismay put together this collection of more than three hundred pieces on a modest income and latterly on a pension. A tribute to his eye and love of pottery, it took over every space in his terraced house 'save for a tiny corner where Bill wrote and ate ... The floor was a sea of pots with little causeways to allow passage to the doors and stone sink ... Yet Bill always seemed to be able to reach any pot ... balancing like a dancer, with typical stubbornness, refusing all offers of assistance to reach a Hamada above the fireplace.'[192] It is a spirit that connects him with the Revd Charles Wellbeloved.

Scotland

My journeys across these islands began and ended in Scotland. To view Britain from the northern eyrie of Orkney is to see it afresh.

The geological rift that is the Great Glen makes it easier to understand how the tectonic plates of the world have moved and continue to move so that, as the fossils in the Elgin Museum show, the Moray Firth was once part of the Indian subcontinent and may become so again.

From Orkney this slow engagement and disengagement of continents, the emptiness of old hillsides, the cry of birds and the sea that stretches cold and grey across the top of the world, from the Americas to Scandinavia, place what man has made or discovered, the material of these museums and galleries, into another span of time.

Scotland has, in proportion to its population, more and better museums than any other part of Britain. I hope that their richness and diversity is represented by the forty-five that I have chosen. Omitting museums here was harder than anywhere else: the museums that celebrated great Scotsmen (David Livingstone at Blantyre, Andrew Carnegie at Dunfermline, Hugh Miller at Cromarty, Robert Burns at Dumfries); the clan museums (Gunn at Latheron, Grant at Carrbridge); the regimental museums, particularly those of the Black Watch in Perth and the Argyll and Sutherland Highlanders in a high tower above Stirling Castle with its diorama of the Thin Red Line at Balaclava; the museums of golf at St Andrews and of rugby at Murrayfield: all had to be put to one side.

Loving typography, I was sad not to include Robert Smail's Printing Works at Innerleithen with its 19th-century composing and press rooms, and the orderly pleasures of typesetting by hand. Saddest of all was to include so few of the more than twenty museums in the islands: Mull and Skye, Islay and Tiree, North and South Uist, Orkney and Shetland. The Hanseatic Booth on the island of Whalsay, accessible only by ferry from Laxo on the Shetland mainland, may be the most remote museum in Europe. Left as yet unvisited, it is for me a point of hoped-for return.

○GAIRLOCH   A835

Highlands

A

FORT WILLIAM○   A95

A82

A85   A8

A816

Co

○KILMARTIN

COLONSAY &○
ORONSAY

GREENOCK○   M8

PAISLEY
M

40 miles

ARRAN   Stra

ORKNEY
ISLANDS

○STROMNESS

DUNBEATH
A99
A9
○HELMSDALE
A9

○ELGIN
INVERNESS
A96
A96
A95
A9
A939
A95

BANFF
○FRASERBURGH
A90
A947
○TURRIFF
A96
○ABERDEEN

Grampian

A9
A90

Tayside

PERTH
○DUNDEE
A85
A9
○CERES
Fife
STIRLING
A92
○KIRKCALDY
M80
M9
A80
EDINBURGH○
A1
M8
Lothian
GLASGOW
M74

○BERWICK-UPON-TWEED

○NEW LANARK
Borders
A1
M74

ABERDEEN ART GALLERY ∗∗∗∗

Schoolhill, Aberdeen, Aberdeenshire AB10 1FQ
Tel. 01224 523673
www.aagm.co.uk

Important gallery with exhilarating hang and good 18th–20th-century British art: Scottish artists and French Impressionists

Some galleries make it look hard; some easy. Aberdeen achieves excellence by doing the simple things well: a good building; confidence in its collections; consistent, judicious purchasing; respect for the intelligence of visitors.

It is not surprising therefore that people should want to make bequests; or that major galleries around the world should wish to work in partnership on temporary exhibitions; or that Aberdeen should be one of the best liked and most respected regional galleries.

Built to a serious neoclassical design by Matthews and Mackenzie (1885), it has top-lit galleries of fine proportions, leading off a rotunda, as good for exhibiting sculpture as for paintings.

Its founding collection was given in 1900 by Alexander Macdonald (1837–84), a local stonemason whose father, also Alexander Macdonald, had made a fortune from carving headstones out of the intractable Aberdeen granite. He had been impressed by the polished Egyptian granite given to the British Museum (q.v.) by Giovanni Belzoni in 1832. He realised that the new steam engines powering the most

modern Aberdeen manufactories could be used to polish granite. By 1832 he had produced a machine-polished granite headstone for the new Kensal Green Cemetery in London. In the same year the Glasgow Necropolis opened, creating a huge new market for granite headstones as smooth and as durable as marble. His son bequeathed his collection of 19th-century paintings and portraits, and an endowment to buy contemporary works made in the preceding twenty-five years.

His son's art collection included a group of ninety-one portraits and self-portraits of contemporary artists: Leighton, Frith, Alma-Tadema, Sargent, *Du Maurier* by Millais, *Millais* by Sir George Reid, *Briton Rivière* by P. H. Calderon, *P. H. Calderon* by Reid. To ensure uniformity, Macdonald supplied the canvas and the frames. His taste was conventional and sound: landscapes and narrative set pieces (G. F. Watts's *Orpheus and Eurydice*; Orchardson's *A Social Eddy*). There are Scottish artists (Pettie, Chalmers, Hugh Cameron) but also French, Dutch and Spanish, the latter having become very popular after Sir William Stirling-Maxwell (v. Pollok House) published his *Annals of the Artists of Spain* in 1848.

With help from Sir James Murray, the gallery acquired a Monet and Lavery's *The Tennis Party*. Alexander Webster, an advocate, followed Macdonald's example in providing money for future purchases. Webster gave splendid watercolours that, together with a separate gift of five works by Paul Sandby, formed the basis of the gallery's exceptional watercolour collection.

An art gallery committee was set up, of

Train Landscape *by Eric Ravilious*
(Aberdeen Art Gallery)

which Sir James Murray was chairman from
1901 to 1928. It used the Webster bequest
to acquire works by Varley, Girtin, Rooker,
Prout, Cozens, Dayes, Towne, Bonington and
four Turners, early (*The Interior of Ely
Cathedral*, 1796) and late (*Bellinzona from the
Road to Locarno*, 1843). The quality of acquisitions was maintained in subsequent decades
and enhanced by Ian McKenzie Smith, the
Director of the gallery, 1968–89, who was
latterly president of the Royal Scottish Society
of Painters in Watercolours and who added
works by John Piper, Gwen John, William
Gillies, Elizabeth Blackadder and John Bellany.

Successive committees and directors proved
to be equally skilled in buying paintings, usually before reputations were established. In the
1930s Stanley Spencer, Edward Wadsworth,
Ivon Hitchens and Christopher Wood entered
the collections, as did a Léger and a Sickert.
Works by the four leading Scottish Colourists
(Cadell, Peploe, Fergusson and G. L. Hunter)
were bought in the 1940s and early '50s, as
were paintings by Ben Nicholson, Wyndham
Lewis and Matthew Smith. To have sustained
an acquisitions policy of this quality for a
century, despite the currents and tides of
fashion, recessions and wars, is a magnificent
achievement.

The 19th-century French collection takes you through good examples of Daubigny, Harpignies, Lepine, Fantin-Latour, Boudin and Bastien-Lepage to Monet, Renoir, Vuillard, Toulouse-Lautrec and Bonnard, without any one work lifting you to the heights.

The Scottish and English paintings are more uneven. In addition to the predictable Thomas Faed, William McTaggart and David and Joseph Farquharson, there is an arrestingly bad Landseer, a caricature of melodrama, *Flood in the Highlands* (1860): tempest, torrent, staring-eyed children, a biblical old man and, at the centre of this maelstrom, a distraught mother nursing her youngest with not a hair out of place, surrounded by an attentive menagerie of sheep, goats, hens, ducks, dogs and a cat.

There are good examples of the work of J. W. Waterhouse (*The Danaides*) and of William Dyce, the Aberdeen artist favoured by Pugin and the Fine Art Commissions to paint murals for the new Houses of Parliament. His *Beatrice* (1859), illustrating Dante, was commissioned by Gladstone. The model was Miss Maria Summerhayes, a prostitute 'rescued by Gladstone, July 1859'. It compensates for Dyce's inept *Titian's First Essay in Colour* (1857), a pictorial libel on the Venetian.

It is a relief to return to the solid ground of Scottish portraiture: interesting self-portraits by George Jamesone and Andrew Robertson, a cool Allan Ramsay of *Miss Janet Sharp* (1750) and a magnificent Raeburn, *Lady Abercromby* (1816), painted for her wedding. It is an example of Raeburn's ability to make you melt before feminine beauty; here you are lost in Lady Abercromby's eyes.

The gallery has two further strengths: a collection of 20th-century sculpture (Epstein, Hepworth, Butler, Paolozzi, Lijn, Caro) and as good a representation of the Camden Town Group as there is outside the Tate (q.v.), with the possible exception of the Leeds City Art Gallery (q.v.). Good examples of Ginner, Gilman, Gore and Pissarro are here, as you would expect, but so too are Malcolm Drummond, James Dickson Innes, Derwent Lees and William Whitehead Ratcliffe, alongside a masterly Robert Bevan, *Ploughing on the Downs* (1907).

The knowledge and the scholarship of successive curators transmits confidence. This is a gallery whose staff like and know their collections in particular detail, so it is not surprising that there are collections of two neglected Scottish artists: James McBey and Robert Brough.

McBey, self-taught, was that rarity, an artist who made a very remunerative career out of etchings and watercolours. His widow gave his entire archive to Aberdeen, the best-known image in which is his drawing of T. E. Lawrence (1918) in Arab scarf, done on his last day in Palestine when McBey was a war artist with the British Expeditionary Force.

Brough is a stranger and more interesting artist. A contemporary of S. J. Peploe, with whom he went to the Royal Scottish Academy and then to France in 1894, he specialised in portraits, of which Aberdeen has twelve. Brough brimmed with flair and facility. He absorbed influences, notably that of Whistler. In his portrait of *Dolly* (1896) (Theodora Crombie, daughter of an Aberdeen magnate), the blazing red-curtain background, red flowers and red velvet dress are a homage to Velásquez (suiting Dolly's Habsburg chin), while placing *Master Philip Fleming* (1899, private collection) on a prancing horse is a quotation from Van Dyck.

All are carried off with varying degrees of assurance but his great success at such a young age, which led one critic to write 'should he fulfil the expectations he has excited, his success is likely to be as phenomenal as his appearance',[1] led also to work that was hurried and crude, lacking the penetration of his *Mrs Nicol of Rescobie* (1897) or his stern full-length of *Sir James Murray* (1903), in which the benefactor of the gallery emerges calmly from darkness.

There are signs that he was beginning to feel, in the words of John Singer Sargent, who was his friend and mentor, that 'every portrait is an enemy'.[2] Brough could have gone in any direction: become an Orpen or a McEvoy, burnt himself out or given up portraiture altogether. The choice was obviated by his death: he was trapped and burned in a rail accident in 1905.

Although many of his subjects were the magnates of Aberdeen a generation after Alexander Macdonald, his work could scarcely be further from the granite foundation of the Macdonalds' fortune, or of the fortune of the city. Yet, in view of his delight in paint and painting, his work has found the right gallery here.

In recent years the gallery's sustained collecting of contemporary art has been admirable. Charles Saatchi has donated ten works and recent acquisitions include a piece by Jake and Dinos Chapman. Nevertheless its most important late 20th-century painting remains Francis Bacon's *Pope 1 – Study after Velásquez's Portrait of Pope Innocent* (1951) in which the Pope, so authoritative and stern in his certainties in Velásquez's painting, is in despair at the loss of faith. The portrait itself, a 'study after . . .', has something of a provisional nature, as if Bacon, 'an old-fashioned militant atheist',[3] was waiting to make a more definite statement.

These are collections worthy of any major international city but, lest you forget that this is Aberdeen, the gallery has a memorial court in the second rotunda. In its quiet white light, the rolls of honour of the two world wars, and of those who died in the Piper Alpha disaster of 6 July 1988, are looked over by a 6th-century BC bronze Corinthian war helmet. Eyeless, beautiful, it contemplates the hardness of sacrifice.

MARISCHAL **

Marischal College, Broad Street, Aberdeen, Aberdeenshire AB10 1YS
Tel. 01224 274301
www.abdn.ac.uk/marischal_museum/index.htm

Aberdeen exhibited alphabetically, and what her sons and daughters sent back from the ends of the empire.

The Marischal is the museum of the University of Aberdeen, reached through handsome academic courtyards of dark vaulting granite. It consists of two large galleries on either side of a landing. Around the walls of the first are mahogany-framed cases displaying objects: they tell the story of Aberdeen and of the north-east of Scotland, and are arranged alphabetically.

A is for Aberdeen, B is for branks. C is for corbie. D is for dag, a firearm. E is for Elgin and its cathedral, from which here is a keystone. F is for Finnan Haddie, a smoked haddock originally from the village of Findon. G is for Robert Gordon, the first MA of Marischal College in 1597. And on: J is for a Jacobite pincushion embroidered with the names of those who died at Culloden in 1745. K is for a 17th-century kirk communion cup. L is for leister, a pronged spear for catching salmon. M is for the Marischal College mace, late 17th century. And Q is for quaich, a silver drinking cup made in 1700 by Robert Cruickshank. S is for Shore Porters, the Aberdeen removals firm, established 1498. T is for tobacco, a brass 18th-century pipe case. W is for witches and witchstones to guard against them: an amulet of perforated stone; a stone with a hole from Buchan (1887); a cruik from Rayne, marked with three crosses to protect food from witchcraft (late 18th century). Here is the museum as encyclopaedia.

The second gallery has a collection of objects that were sent back to Aberdeen by former students. They chart the rise and fall of the empire as these men and women took their learning, energy, theology and skills to other countries. The university's graduates were missionaries, physicians, traders, soldiers and administrators in every part of the British Empire and beyond.

Here is a cabinet of Egyptian scarabs from Dr James Grant, collected when he was physician at the court of the Khedive of Egypt in the 1840s, and another containing Indian carvings sent by General Sir Alexander Reid from his posting on the North West Frontier.

Margaret Hasluck[4] was an ethnographer who worked in Albania in the 1920s and '30s and collected beadwork, dolls, a saddle bag and love philtres. Captain William Mitchell served in British Columbia in the mid 19th century and donated Haida spirit masks. A brass effigy of the Yoruba god Ogun was acquired by Sir Charles Burnett while serving in Nigeria with the West African frontier force and a dance shield by Sir William McGregor in Papua New Guinea, where he was imperial governor.

Perhaps the most remarkable collection was made by Alexander Thompson of Banchory House, a country gentleman with a restless curiosity and a thirst for knowledge. His interests in geology and agriculture, Scottish history and classical antiquity, science and the social conditions of the poor are reflected in his collection, a true 19th-century cabinet of curiosities: a papoose's cap from Nova Scotia; a carved wooden Hawaiian club; a Gaelic prayer book; a flat bronze Roman coil; a terracotta head from Paestum; and a bracelet presented to his wife by Queen Victoria.

Charles Hunt, the curator of the museum from 1979 to 1998, has formed these objects into a diorama of the motives and ambitions that stirred the graduates of this university to go out and collect the world.

ABERDEEN MARITIME MUSEUM *

Shiprow, Aberdeen, Aberdeenshire AB11 5BY
Tel. 01224 337700
www.aagm.co.uk

Whaling, shipowning, fishing, wrecks and rescues in a modern extension to an 18th-century merchant's house

It is not surprising that there has been a harbour here since 1710. Aberdeen, at the mouth of the River Dee, is *the* northern port, facing the North Sea, Norway and the northern fishing grounds. Its history is the history of every aspect of life related to the sea: fishing; whaling; designing, building and repairing ships; and, today, drilling the sea bed for oil.

The fount of Aberdeen's economy has always been the shoals of herring (the word deriving from the Teutonic 'heer', an army, but known locally as 'silver darlings'), haddock, cod and halibut. In 1894 there were 365 fishing boats out of Aberdeen providing work fishing, curing, gutting, packing and coopering for 5,968 people. Today, following massive decommissioning, fewer than a dozen Aberdeen registered boats land only a few hundred fish boxes each day.

In the mid 18th and 19th centuries Aberdeen's economy depended on the pursuit of the Arctic whale, the Greenland right whale, for its blubber and bone. All that is left of those quests are cabinets here of harpoons, whale's teeth, scrimshaw, models, paintings and a whale's eardrum.

As the whales waned the clippers waxed. Aberdeen shipbuilders Alexander Hall, John, William and Alexander Duthie and Walter Hood competed to build the fastest clippers. In 1868 the White Star Line's *Thermopylae* reached Australia in sixty-one days on her maiden voyage, straining every stay, shroud, halyard, sheave and block to make seventeen knots an hour. Ships sailed from Aberdeen to India, to China across the South Pacific, to Australia, to Costa Rica and South America, carrying passengers, mail and supplies on the way out, and tea, wool and coffee on the return voyage.

The reign of the clippers was poetic, glorious, brief. By the 1870s iron ships were outstripping them as their owners (John T. Rennie, Alexander Nicol, John Cook) kept ahead of the times. Whatever they ordered, the Duthie brothers and the Halls could build. Between 1811 and 1991 2,768 ships were built in Aberdeen: schooners, brigantines, barques, brigs, trawlers, drifters, clippers, cargo steamers and warships, the rise and fall of orders year by year charting booms, recessions and wars: seventy-nine built in 1918, one in 1981.

The modern oil industry experiences the same ebb and flow. For the present there is work witnessed by a model here, the height of the building, of the 1980 Murchison oil production platform named after the 19th-century Scottish geologist Sir Roderick Murchison, and sited 120 miles north-east of the Shetlands. There are core samples from BP's Andrew Field, taken from 2,843 yards below the surface, the oil held in porous sandstone. When trapped in glass phials these samples, laid down millions of years ago, are oddly everyday: Amethyst 47/14A–103 is colourless, Marchar 23/26A–7 is bright orange; Cyrus 16/28–11 dark as blood.

The museum building is up a bank, looking down on the harbour. Its entrance and main galleries are glass faced, designed in 1995 by Aberdeen City Council project architect Trevor Smith. Next door the galleries of whaling are in the 19th-century harbour-master's house. If you stand on the top floor, Aberdeen's harbours past and present are laid before you: the quays, the Upper and Victoria Docks, the fish market, and beyond, the Shore Brae (road) and the fishing villages of Torry, Fittie and Banagask. All are clustered round the Dee and are defended against foe by the Torry Battery (1860) and against the sea by the Gridleness Lighthouse, built in 1833 by Robert Stevenson.

It is a busy but peaceful panorama that tells little of the risks, dangers and deaths, the fortunes and bankruptcies, the will and the courage that these harbours have witnessed. Outside, beyond the harbour, and the grass headland, is the North Sea.

BRODICK CASTLE *

Isle of Arran, KA27 8HY
Tel. 01770 302202
www.nts.org.uk

A fastness for seven centuries; the collections of the Dukes of Hamilton and William Beckford

The stern serenity of Brodick Castle, in the shadow of the 2840-foot-high Goatfell, is an unlikely location to find what remains of the exquisite collection of William Beckford, the wonder of his age.

Brodick Castle, a natural defensive site between bay and hillside, was contested by Vikings, the English and warring factions of Scots until the 17th century. It was sacked three times in the 15th century and twice more by feuding Campbells and MacLeans in the 16th.

Since then it has been owned by the Dukes of Hamilton. Alexander, the 10th Duke, married William Beckford's younger and favourite daughter, Susan Euphemia, in 1810. Put under pressure by his own extravagance and by the collapse of the West Indies slavery and sugar economy on which his family fortune was based, Beckford sold much of his Fonthill Abbey collection in 1822 but he held back many small-scale, superbly crafted works of art and even continued to commission and to collect.

Here in the somewhat domesticated and tamed Brodick Castle, rebuilt by the 10th Duke for his son when he married Princess Mary of Baden in 1843,[5] is a collection, principally of silver and porcelain, that offers a glimpse of Beckford, the connoisseur and collector.

Most of the objects he commissioned were to designs of his own; some were to designs made jointly with his friend and agent Gregorio Franchi. He trusted only the finest craftsmen to make his designs: silver by Paul Storr, James Aldridge, Cato Sharp for Philip Rundell; porcelain from the Sèvres factory or from Barr, Flight and Barr of Worcester, the leading potters for armorial services.

Here is a pair of candlesticks made by John Scofield, from 1760 designs by Robert (or possibly James) Adam, in 1781 when Beckford came of age. That apart, the pieces at Brodick date from the ten years that preceded the Fonthill sale in 1822, years during which even Beckford sometimes surprised himself with his appetite for acquisition. He wrote to Franchi in 1813, 'I see from the buying mania that dominates you that we are well on the way to ruin. Oh, my God, so many things!'[6]

That did not stop him ordering a service of cups, saucers and plates from Barr, Flight and Barr later that year[7] or having a rare Sèvres teapot and cover, glazed in dark prune brown,[8] set in a silver mount of his own design in 1815–20.

Beckford and Franchi fed each other's acquisitiveness. Of a consignment of hardstones shipped from Italy to Britain by Franchi in 1814, Franchi wrote, 'the agates are all cohesion and one in particular is of such quality that I've never seen another.' An agate bowl is here, mounted by Paul Storr (1816–17), as is a gold ladle, set with nephrite and rubies, finished by a jade finial.

Beckford had a raven's glitterstruck eye. The pieces here glint with agate, enamel, jasper, crystal, coral, shell and ivory. Nor could he resist a crest. Most pieces have the Beckford crest (a heron holding a fish in its beak), the Beckford martlets or the Hamilton cinquefoils. Usually the crests are placed prominently. An exception is a cup and cover by James Aldridge on which the heraldic devices are visible only when you handle the pieces, the martlets being under the rim of the cover, the cinquefoils on the band at the top of the base.

Even after the 1822 sale Beckford could not resist acquiring new pieces. When Franchi died his appetite faded somewhat but here is a salt cellar (1843–4) that Beckford designed and had made by the Bristol jeweller Alfred Short.

Beckford's love of objects left its stamp on Susan Euphemia. Her husband too was a collector and connoisseur, mainly of paintings and drawings. Here are paintings of them both

by Willes Maddox, he resplendent in his Garter Star, and a further painting by Maddox of William Beckford on his deathbed, commissioned by his daughter. 'I am almost ashamed of being so old,' Beckford wrote, 'really death seems to have forgotten me.' Maddox depicts him in a narrow truckle bed but in the shadows of this seemingly modest picture are the symbols of William Beckford's vanities: a silver gilt cup and ewer, an open book and heraldic devices woven into the carpet.

DUFF HOUSE COUNTRY GALLERY ✶✶✶

Banff, Aberdeenshire AB45 3SX
Tel. 01261 818181
www.duffhouse.com

Thrilling William Adam house with National Gallery of Scotland collections

Successful museum buildings seek to provide an appropriate and sympathetic setting for their collections. Duff House inverts that ambition. The house comes first; the collection decorates it. This is William Adam's last and most brilliant house. When William Duff (1697–1763), Lord Braco, later the 1st Earl of Fife, commissioned Adam he requested 'a magnificent family seat'. Adam understood and realised the contradiction between these adjectives. He gave Braco a house that achieved grandeur and domestic ease, balanced ebullience and reserve, set in a design of measured symmetry, in each dimension, horizontal and vertical.

The four fronts are of almost equal weight. From a distance all is harmonious ease. Close up the facade, the south front, is an architectural fanfare: arcaded windows, fluted octagonal chimneys on each corner tower, the richly carved heraldic tympanum of the pediment, all held together by giant Corinthian pilasters. Below, the balustrades sweep down like arms to welcome the visitor and carry him up to and into the house where the proportions and details are equally exhilarating.

The house was lived in by the Fifes for

150 years until the 6th Earl/1st Duke gave it to the towns of Banff and Macduff in 1906 and sold some of its contents. The house became an hotel, a sanatorium and a prisoner-of-war camp and billet before being taken back into the care of the government in 1952. Historic Scotland and the National Galleries of Scotland (NGS) and the local authorities combined to restore and furnish its interior. It opened in its present splendid form in 1995.

Almost nothing is left of the Fife collection,[9] so strong on portraits, and Timothy Clifford, director of the National Gallery of Scotland (NGS), has, with flair and good fortune, brought together collections appropriate to the history and the aesthetic demands of the house, guided by two principles: that the work should be 'in period' (generally late 18th/early 19th century) and should relate in some way to the Fifes.

To achieve this he has used the reserve collections of the NGS and two major loans, from the fine Magdalene Sharp Erskine Trust Collection at Dunimarle and from the Marquess of Zetland. The coming together of these collections, and the restoration of the interiors, bring full-blooded life back to Duff House.

The portraits are notable, particularly in the Vestibule, which has works by Daniel Mytens the Elder, George Jamesone, David Scougall, David Martin, Gavin Hamilton and Thomas Campbell, and a – poor – Reynolds.

In the Dining Room, with a Thomas Hudson and another Jamesone, are three works by Allan Ramsay, of which the star is an early full-length portrait of *Elizabeth, Mrs Daniel Cunyngham* (*c.*1740). This is Ramsay at his most cool and poised, where all the elements (the swagged curtain, the cloudscape mural, the still life of a vase on the table, the classical pillar) provide a quiet background to the sumptuous modesty of Mrs Cunyngham's silk dress of palest pearl grey. On the Dining Room table is a pair of magnificent bronze silver-gilt candelabra from the workshop of Paul Storr, originally purchased by the 4th Earl of Fife.

Elsewhere there are works by Tintoretto and El Greco, Cuyp and David Allan; and a huge and splendid Etty; a series of plaster casts by Carlo Albacini and Filippo Albacini; and more portraits by Andres Soldi, William Aikman, John Michael Wright, Sir William Beechey and Sir Daniel Macnee.

More exciting than these individual works is the marriage of house and gallery. The two finest rooms on the first floor, the North Drawing Room and the Great or South Drawing Room, illustrate this. The latter is a room of wonderful simplicity with its plain plasterwork and its original chimney piece, which was tracked down to a storeroom in the University of Aberdeen and restored to the house. It is a sympathetic setting for the Zetland loans. On the walls is a selection from a suite of Gobelins tapestries made in the workshop of Jacques Neilson with designs by François Boucher.[10]

Around the room's edge is one of the finest sets of 18th-century British furniture: armchairs and sofas in gilded beech by Thomas Chippendale to a design by Robert Adam, supplied to Sir Lawrence Dundas for his London house in 1765. Despite their working together at Harewood House, this set is the only one on which Chippendale is definitely known to have executed one of Adam's designs.[11]

The North Drawing Room is William Adam's most splendid room, with a painted frieze of swagged husks and an elaborate rose. It was redecorated by Agnes, wife of the 5th Earl, in 1857, who added the gilded enrichments to the corners of the ceiling and the carved gilt pier glass,[12] and brought the composition chimney piece from London. This has inset tablets from the Roman Meleager sarcophagus and from the Muses' sarcophagus, now in the Louvre. The chandelier installed by the Countess, and sold in 1906, has now been repurchased and hung in the room.

The gilded furniture is from Dunimarle, made by Fratelli Santi in Rome (*c.*1800) for Napoleon's step-uncle, Cardinal Fesch, from whose post-Waterloo sale (in 1816) they were bought by Sir James Erskine.[13]

The room was always a picture gallery and on the walls are a Jacob van Ruisdael landscape, two works by Philips Wouwermans and six by Raeburn, from which stands out his portrait celebrating the delicious beauty of *Elizabeth Forbes, Mrs Colin Mackenzie of Polmore* (*c.*1803), the soft billow of her white dress floating against the background sunset.

Were it not in north Banffshire, 170 miles from Edinburgh, Duff House would be widely recognised as one of the jewels among Britain's galleries and museums, its collections complementing the masterpiece that houses them.

PAXTON HOUSE **

Berwick-upon-Tweed, Northumberland
TD15 1SZ
Tel. 01289 386291
www.paxtonhouse.com

Outstation of the National Gallery of Scotland in elegant Borders mansion

The Picture Gallery at Paxton predates all Scottish public galleries. It was designed, in 1811–13, by Robert Reid, Master of the King's Works in Scotland, for George Home, who inherited the house, aged sixty-one, from his elder brother Ninian in 1795 and the picture collection of his cousin, Patrick, in 1808.

It is a partner gallery of the National Gallery of Scotland in which sound examples of its collections are hung. Paxton's other claim to attention is its witness to the architecture and decorative art of John Adam, who built it for Patrick Home, 1758–63. Its south front is one of the simplest expressions of the principles set out by Palladio,[14] by Colen Campbell[15] and, later, by Isaac Ware.[16] The great flourishes of John Adam's younger brother Robert (Kedleston Hall, q.v., Osterley Park and Syon House in West London, Nostell Priory in Yorkshire) are not here, allowing the sweet bones of symmetry and proportion to reason with the eye.

As Robert Adam had his team of craftsmen, so did his brother John: the master carpenters George Pirrie of Haddington and Sandy Cairns, and the plasterer George Morrison, whose work is as delicate as, and lighter than,

anything that the great Joseph Rose of York could produce at Temple Newsam (q.v.) or for Castle Coole in County Fermanagh. Morrison's chimney breast in the Entrance Hall is a swirl of scrolls, laurels, birds and shell patterns gathered together top and bottom by garlands.

As Paxton was being built, Robert and John Adam were designing another house for Patrick Home near by at Wedderburn, so it is not surprising that they finished Paxton's principal rooms, more metropolitan in feel, and it is appropriate that the house contains the largest documented collection of furniture by Chippendale, Haig and Co., so favoured by the Adams, in Scotland: 106 pieces, of which some fifty remain in the house (dining room chairs, pedestals, urns, a sideboard, four mahogany bergères in the Dining Room; a mahogany serpentine chest of drawers upstairs; painted wheel-back chairs of pale delicacy in the Principal Bedroom).[17]

As beautiful as any of these is John Adam's sliver of a staircase, slipped between the Entrance Hall and the Drawing Room, with its wrought-iron banister rail and its open net of iron pinched at each intersection by small round finials.

Patrick Home undertook two Grand Tours between 1752 and 1780 and collected some 150, mainly Italian, 17th-century, paintings. Alongside the many copies were works by Vasari, Salvatini and Lorenzo Lippi. It was to house these that George Home commissioned Robert Reid, forty-eight years younger than John Adam, to add a picture gallery (and library).[18] Its heaviness is in marked contrast to the Adams' work but is not far removed, on a domestic scale, from Playfair's designs for the National Gallery of Scotland, 'a long top-lit room of an austere and architectural character'.[19]

'I yesterday had the opportunity of long conversation with Mr Raeburn and attended to the effect of the light in his rooms, along with him,' wrote Reid in a letter of 14 September 1811 to Home, and the result is one of the first top-lit galleries in Britain. It opened in the same year as Sir John Soane's picture gallery for Dulwich College (Dulwich Picture Gallery, q.v.). The gallery is 'totally void of what is generally called ornament', he wrote on 28 March, and is 'wholly in imitation of stone' with mouldings that are 'Strong and massy'. It provides a fine setting for William Trotter's suite of specially designed Greek Revival furniture and for paintings from the National Galleries' reserve collection.

The National Gallery of Scotland (NGS) has selected paintings that date approximately to the time that the Picture Gallery of Paxton House was under construction (late 18th/early 19th centuries) and that relate in some way to the history of the Homes who lived here and the house (local views, portraits). Patrick Home had close ties with Germany and there are works here by German artists Wolfgang Dietrich Mayer and John Christian Schetky.

There are Scottish landscapes by Andrew Wilson and Horatio McCulloch and by Elizabeth Nasmyth and Charlotte Nasmyth, two of the six daughters of Alexander Nasmyth, all of whom were trained as artists for practical reasons. In the words of their brother James, 'My father's object was to render each and all of his children – whether boys or girls – independent on their arrival at mature years. Accordingly, he sedulously kept up the attention of his daughters to fine art. By this means he enabled them to assist in the maintenance of the family while at home, and afterwards to maintain themselves by the exercise of their own abilities and industries after they had left.'[20]

Some English landscapes have been included – scenes by Richard Wilson and Peter De Wint, and, unusually, small oil paintings by Anthony Copley Fielding and John Sell Cotman – but it is the portraits that dominate the gallery. Although there are likenesses by Julian Opie, Sir Joshua Reynolds, John Singleton Copley and Sir Thomas Lawrence, the prime positions go to the Scots and particularly to five canvases by Sir Henry Raeburn.

These are, in the main, mature Raeburns dating from the first decade of the 19th century. His skill at bringing some informality and gentle sensuality to grand portraits of women is evident in *Justine Wynne, Mrs Alexander Finley of Glencorse* (*c.*1810), but the pick of them is his portrait of Lord Falconer's German gamekeeper *John Henry Rucklitsch*, described by his employer as 'a most faithful, honest man. He was a great character and a perfect gentleman in his manners'.

For once Raeburn has it over Allan Ramsay, represented here by only one portrait. There is also a good Andrew Geddes, of *Hannah Fry, Mrs Harris Prendergast* (1838) and a David Scott at his most fraught and dramatic, *Philoctetes* abandoned in agony and despair on a rock as the Greek fleet sails off to Troy under an ominous sky.

The quality of these paintings, the hang and the group of Albacini busts, also from the NGS, in the adjoining Library, does honour to Paxton House which, in return, provides a worthy setting for them.

LAIDHAYE CROFT MUSEUM **

Dunbeath, Caithness KW6 6EH
Tel. 01593 731244

Just room to move among the lovingly accumulated gleanings of generations of a crofting family

A croft is not a house: it is the rented land on which a house may be built.

Laidhaye Croft is high above the sea on the empty Caithness coast between Lybster and Dunbeath. The house was built in 1805–10 and was lived in continuously by the Bethune family until William Bethune died in 1951, aged ninety-one. It opened as a museum in 1974, its structure essentially untouched and its contents maintained by a tactful hand. Lamps, china, boots, pans, bills are all in their place, that place not 'reconstructed' but where they might have been put in life, on a convenient surface.

The building is a longhouse, three rooms with a byre at one end and a stable at the other, on a croft of thirty acres. Its roof is supported on bare beams, clad by heather turf cut in six-inch sods, and thatched overall.

To the left is the bedroom/living room, to the right the kitchen, the byre pantry beyond that. A further stable beyond the bedroom was for the horses, and the cows which give off eleven times the heat of a man.

The Bethunes look out from a photograph, taken in 1948: Donald, in uniform, the harbourmaster at Dunbeath (died 1948, aged ninety-one); William (Beil), whose croft this was (died 1951, aged ninety-one); Mary, their sister, in service (died 1951, aged eighty-nine). Behind them stand Christina (Kirstie), (died 1954, aged eighty-six) and their niece, Mary Mackay.

Around them are the bones of the rooms: the boxed double bed, the hearth and the range. There is a clock, an organ, a squeezebox and a fiddle; a Bible, the best bowl and pitcher and a hat box; a packet of Craven A and a box of Barr's birdseed on the mantelpiece. Given no pride of place are a Singer sewing machine and a wind-up gramophone bought by a shepherd at a displenishing sale.

Invoices detail their lives: for 7s. from Mowat Bros., Motor Haulage Contractors, for moving a load of peat in 1930; £1. 4s. 0d. from John A. Mowat, auctioneer and appraiser, for the hire of a tractor to work four acres of land; 11s. from Dr J.R. Kennedy for professional attendance; and a 1902 invoice from Adam Mackay of Caithness for two suits at 15s. 6d. each, and a pair of shoes costing 5s., receipted over a stamp.

In the kitchen are a four-candle mould; a box of Oxydol, 'the complete household soap'; a 3½ pound bag of Spratt's dog food and an advertisement for Erinmore Shag inviting the user to 'Smoke More'. Standing by itself is a Baby Daisy vacuum cleaner like a deflated Cubist hippo. It needed two people to work; it was given to a maid by the 'big house', a token more of status than of utility.

The byre pantry contains a clutter of butter churns, cheese presses and a cream separator; a wringer and a mangle (from the 'big house') and a bath brick for cleaning the doorstep.

Beyond the longhouse the barn also has its original roof with beams of driftwood, among which are recognisable the shapes of oars and masts, pegged not nailed in place. There is a threshing mill, a winnowing machine (a 'fanner') made by W. & A. Geddes of Wick, and harrows; whetting stones, peat tools, like iron dentists' blades, an oil cake grinder and a machine for chopping gorse to feed the horses. Outside there are sheep and views inland to the Scarabens.

There can be few more modest museums. The croft cost £600 to acquire in 1969 and £4,000 to convert. It is run by local people who care a very great deal for the way of life into which they were born and which is now passing.

FIFE FOLK MUSEUM *

High Street, Ceres, nr. Cupar, Fife KY15 5NF
Tel. 01334 828180

Tools of trade and craft for all weathers and all conditions of men, handsomely set out

Above the door is carved a balance and the words 'GOD BLESS THE JUST': a 17th-century visual pun, on the weighing of justice and of trade. The low stone building doubled as 'the Jongs' (courthouse and gaol) and the Weigh House (in which tenants paid their rent and had their produce measured).

Inside, there are old weights and measures for every need. Pints and stones varied from market to market. Even after the 1707 union with England and the imposition of the imperial system, old Scots measures, such as the 'lippy' for weighing potatoes, continued in use to within living memory.

The tools of the trade that kept local communities self-sufficient are here: those of tiler and slater, thatcher and plasterer, tinsmith and blacksmith, cobbler and saddler; the stonemason's mell and 'crooky bar' for setting large stones; the bealer and needle for thatching; the hawk for holding plaster and scatches for rendering lime, sand and cow's hair; the tinsmith's luggie and his planishing hammer for burnishing copper; the cobbler's fudge wheels and sewing awls. The vocabulary of

Sampler at the Fife Folk Museum

skills and the language of crafts are here made to live.

All these tools have come from local sources: from J. C. Forgan, the cobbler in Auchtermuchty in the 1900s; from John Bough, the last thatcher in Fife; from the workshop of Thomas Brett in the Crossgate, Cupar, who paid his apprentice son Robert 3s. 6d. a week in 1902; and from John White & Son, who continue to make machines as they have done since the early 18th century.

Folk and agricultural museums run the risk of courting nostalgia for work that was hard and ill paid. This museum avoids doing so by clear, unemotional presentation and by linking its objects to people.

Here is a plan, painted in bright watercolours, by Mr Eric Ferris, head gardener of the kitchen garden of Dalgairn House, Cupar, in 1939, carefully placing each variety of potato (Kew's Pink, Fenwald Perfection, Edzell Blue) and of gooseberry (Whiteham, Pitmaston, Early Sulphum) beside the rows of Scarlet Queen strawberries and Norfolk Giant raspberries.

Near it, also from the 1930s, is a floral wall hanging made from the flowered-silk tokens that came from each packet of Kensitas cigarettes by Miss Effie Terras of Dairsie.

These are the people and the lives that made this rural community. We should honour them, lest, forgetting how objects are made or food is grown, we lose our own just balance.

ISLANDS OF COLONSAY AND ORONSAY *

Argyll PA61
www.colonsay.org.uk

A do-it-yourself museum of a Scottish island: standing stones, cairns, corncrakes and bloody feuds

The islands of Colonsay and Oronsay, the outermost islands of Argyll, are not a heritage site. They are beautiful, 'a low green place

cradled deep in the sea where one would live as in a ship with the sound of waves always in ears',[21] but they have no museum, no visitor centre. Why then should they be included in this book? The answer is that Colonsay and Oronsay, which are joined at low tide, *are* a museum: of geology and archaeology; of ecclesiastical and natural history.[22]

They lie at the entrance to the Firth of Lorn at the south-west end of the Great Glen fault. On them are Mesolithic and Neolithic sites, Bronze Age cairns, Iron Age forts, standing stones, Viking burial sites, early Christian monuments and a ruined priory. Here the MacFies held the Lordship of the Isles under the MacDonalds until the rebellion of Sir James MacDonald was finally crushed in 1614. Here too is a living natural history museum of birds and flora, and one of the most important rhododendron gardens in Britain at Colonsay House,[23] all within an island eleven miles long and between one and three miles wide.

If the collection, selection and interpretation of objects are what define a museum, Colonsay and Oronsay[24] might reasonably score low. The objects here are in the landscape. Their sites are dispersed, the island's portable treasures removed long since to the Museum of Scotland (q.v.). What is left is not presented to you neatly. You must seek it out and, when you have found it, you must strive to conjure up the past. This is not hard. The landscapes here have changed but little in hundreds of years. With stout boots and a good Ordnance Survey map you can be Prospero and summon up a museum as beautiful as any.

Colonsay is shaped by its geology. The Great Glen fault that runs diagonally across Scotland from the Moray Firth, along Loch Linnhe to Oban, and so to Colonsay, tilts the entire land mass, causing conspicuous ridging across the island and creating raised beaches. There is one to the south of Balnahard, where lies a whale made by the artist Julian Meredith, of thousands of stones; it is over five hundred feet long. There is another such beach at Uragaig and, most notably, a sequence of three at Kilchattan.

The islands are the first landfall from Donegal to the south-west. They guard the route to the Highlands. They benefit from the Gulf Stream. It is not surprising therefore that they have been inhabited since Mesolithic times 7,000 years ago and that every age since has left its mark on the landscape.

Among the oldest marks are the Mesolithic shell mounds excavated by Symington Grieve in the late 19th century. They are not easy to see.[25] The mound at Caistell nan Gillean (OS map reference NR 358879) on Oronsay from which you can look across to the Paps of Jura, is large (86 feet in diameter, 10 feet high) but to the lay eye it is no more than a mound covered in scrub grass. The most visible and striking, Cnoc Sligeach (NR 372890), green and symmetrical, may best be seen from the sea, off Oronsay.

Bronze and Iron Age cairns, cists, duns and standing stones abound.[26] Of these the most dramatic are the two Fingal Limpet Hammers (NR 367949) at Lower Kilchattan, so called because their shape resembles the stone tools used to detach limpets from rocks.

The transition on Colonsay from prehistory to history in the second half of the first millennium is marked by the interweaving of Christian and pagan, Scottish and Viking. St Columba and St Oran are said to have established a religious foundation on Oronsay in the 6th century, though no evidence of it remains, and there are at least eight probable or definite Viking burial sites of the same period. That at the startlingly beautiful white sand beach of Kiloran (NRC 400976) is of a man buried with ceremony, iron sword, axe head, iron pot, seven decorated weights beside him. His grave was covered by an upturned boat, a northern Sutton Hoo. Near by were buried the skeleton of a horse and an elaborate harness with brass mounts.[27]

This Christian and pagan overlap is clear from the most remarkable artefact on the islands, Riasg Buidhe (NR 405954), a cruciform stone (c. 7th–8th centuries), once at the east end of the chapel and removed to the grounds of Colonsay House in about 1870. 'The front is carved in low relief with a Latin cross, terminating at the foot in a fish-like forked tail and at the top in a human face,'[28] bearded. The other side is phallic: so two worlds are set back to back. There is nothing else like it in Scotland but similar carvings exist in Ireland. The fish-like tail, the symbol of Christ, links it with the Mediterranean.

Across the strand to the south is the tidal island of Oronsay and the ruins of the 14th-century Augustinian Oronsay Priory (NR 394889). Its treasure is the freestanding Oronsay Cross, more than ten feet in height. Its crucified Christ is set against incised interlaced patterns of plant stems and foliaceous roundels. At the base are the tails of griffins and, inscribed in Lombardic capitals: 'This is the cross of Colinus, son of Christinus Mac Duffie' (the chief of the clan at the end of the 15th century) and a second inscription 'Mael-Sechlainn Ō Cuinn, mason, made this cross.' He also rebuilt the cloister here.[29]

All around are similarly carved gravestones decorated with quillons, ring knots, oak and holly leaves, birds, hounds, an otter, a fish and two stars, and effigies of men in armour with swords, aventails and basinets.

In the sheltered gardens of Colonsay House are palm trees, giant magnolias and rhododendrons, from the monster 'Polar Bear' to fairy-like miniatures. As you walk past they smell of lemons, cream and honey.

When Thomas Pennant, a fellow of the Royal Society, naturalist and correspondent of Gilbert White, visited Colonsay and Oronsay in 1772 he was struck not by its history but by its flora and fauna, observing 'rockstone formed of glimmer and quartz', 'hills . . . with pretty meandering vales full of grass,' even 'barnacles . . . in vast flocks in September'[30] and peacocks thriving well on the farm at Oronsay as they do today. Now Oronsay is a bird sanctuary.

Pennant might also have seen the machair bursting into life in spring round Ardskenish, embroidered by tormentil, bird's foot trefoil, wild violas, saxifrages and a dozen different speedwells. The bogs hold bog cotton, bog myrtle, bog asphodel. The two Lochs Fada are edged with yellow flag iris and plated with water lilies. Fulmars nest on the high cliff ledges; choughs probe. Wheatears and ringed plovers abound among the dunes of Balnahard, and flocks of eider ('the Colonsay duck'), on the Strand[31] and under the lowering bulk of Dun Cholla (NR 348931). Here Carraig Mhic A'Phi (MacPhee's Stone) marks the spot (NR 348914) where Malcolm, the last chief of the MacPhees, was hunted down and shot on the orders of Coll Ciotach MacDonald[32] in 1623, the final spasm of Sir James MacDonald's rebellion.

In the shores and rocks, beinns and lochs, there is a rough magic here, blasted by the Atlantic weather, circled by sea fowl.

As you leave on the ferry back to Oban the view is as Murdoch McNeill saw it in 1910: 'Huge green seas rise over sunken rocks far out from shore, sometimes passing onwards with white and curling crests, sometimes breaking into masses of snowy foam.'[33] Here every visitor will make a museum for himself.

MCMANUS GALLERIES AND MUSEUM **

Albert Square, Dundee, Tayside DD1 1DA
Tel. 01382 432084
www.dundeecity.gov.uk/mcmanus

Good Scottish paintings in Gilbert Scott building, local industry, shipping and jute

In front of the entrance to these galleries, raised to mark her Diamond Jubilee in 1897, is a large statue of Queen Victoria. Around it is a frieze that recalls scenes from her life and reign: her marriage; the Crimean War; turbanned subjects of her Empire; the industries of Dundee, shipbuilding, textiles, railways; and, always with her, the poor. Victoria is seated, holding the orb and sceptre. On the hem of her skirt are a Scottish thistle and an English rose.

This most Victorian of galleries was founded in 1863 by a group of Dundonian men of commerce, in memory of Prince Albert, as an institute dedicated to science, literature and the arts and crafts. They appointed Sir George Gilbert Scott to design the building, a library

and great hall in what he called 'a thirteenth or fourteenth century secular style with the addition of certain Scottish features'.

You enter through a hall of marble pillars and carved stone capitals beneath a vaulted ceiling. At the top of the staircase hangs a huge painting by John Singleton Copley, *The Victory of Admiral Duncan at the Battle of Camperdown*, a heroic image to inspire the 19th century.[34] The museum and art gallery, designed by David Mackenzie, were added in 1871 and, to mark the Jubilee, the Victorian Galleries in 1887, designed by the town architect William Alexander, financed by the local jam and marmalade magnate John Keiller.[35] Alexander's design was innovative, with a double-skinned glass roof to diffuse daylight and curved walls that angle higher pictures down towards the viewer. It also had electric, rather than gas, lighting.[36]

Keiller's personal art collection included works by Turner, Constable and Millais. To the McManus he gave *The Swineherd* by the Dumfries artist William Ewart Lockhart.

The Victorian Galleries suit the 19th-century Scottish paintings that make up a major part of the collection. Their quality is variable. There are several by William McTaggart at his most sentimental (*Children at the Sea Shore; Two Boys and a Dog in a Boat; Through Mist and Rain*), numerous genre paintings by Thomas Faed, John Philip (*Mitherless*) and Erskine Nichol (*Steady, Johnnie, Steady!*), and a Millais (*Puss in Boots*, 1877) that shows him at his most commercial and unthinking, a miserable example of the ways in which he squandered his great talent.

There is a small but distinguished group of 18th- and 19th-century Scottish portraits that illustrate how the skills of portraiture were passed on: Allan Ramsay to his pupils David Allan and David Martin, and so to Henry Raeburn, taught by Martin. Their successors, Sir Daniel Macnee and the less well-known, Dundee-born John Zephaniah Bell also have less well-observed portraits here.[37] Here too is an excellent landscape, *Broughty Castle During a Storm* (1810), by Alexander Nasmyth, who studied with Martin under Allan Ramsay.

The Visit of the Patron and Patroness to
the Village School *by Thomas Faed (McManus
Galleries and Museum)*

The Glasgow School and the Colourists are
represented, as are some later 20th-century
Scottish artists: William Gillies, William Gear,
Anne Redpath, J. Macintosh Patrick; there
are sculptures by Eduardo Paolozzi and the
Dundee-born William Turnbull, a student at
Dundee's excellent Duncan of Jordonstone
Art School, now a faculty of the University of
Dundee.

The collection is not exclusively Scottish.
There are watercolours by Paul Sandby and
J. S. Cotman, drawings by David Cox,[38] Frank
Brangwyn,[39] David Bomberg and Edward
Burra, and an interesting, late painting by
Dante Gabriel Rossetti, *Dante's Dream on the
Day of the Death of Beatrice* (1880), in which
the figure of Love takes Dante to the bedside of
the dead Beatrice, for whom, unsurprisingly,
Janey Morris was the model.[40]

Along the corridor the cathedral-like
vaulted ceilings of the Great Hall of the Albert
Institute, into which light pours, is a better
setting for sculpture, large paintings (two
Gainsboroughs, two good school of Lely) and
miscellaneous objects: 18th-century spinets
and pianos, a lacquer clock by Alex Smith
of Dundee (*c.* 1720), some Burne-Jones stained
glass[41] and one of the oldest complete mari-
ner's astrolabes, made in Portugal by Lopo
Honem (1555).

DISCOVERY MUSEUM *

Discovery Quay, Dundee, Tayside DD1 4XA
Tel. 01382 201245
www.rrsdiscovery.com

*Scott's expedition to the Antarctic: ice, snow,
huskies and tinned food for a year – phlegm and
endurance in close quarters*

The size of *Discovery* continually shifts. Stand
on the quay and she looks small, capable of
no more than a night's crossing. Stand on the

deck and the masts rise above you like great trees. Go below deck and it is hard to grasp how a ship's company of forty-six men could live here for two and a half years, enduring two Antarctic winters, during which there is total darkness, the sun disappearing below the horizon in April not to reappear until August.

Discovery was built in 1900–01 in Dundee shipyards that had great experience, from the port's whaling past, of building wooden ships that could withstand Arctic conditions. The purpose of the Polar expedition led by Captain Robert Falcon Scott in 1901 was, ostensibly, research, not polar exploration. The company included a meteorologist, a magnetic observer, a marine biologist, a geologist, a botanist, a zoologist who was also an artist and photographer, a physicist, a surveyor and one laboratory assistant. Their research filled ten volumes and twenty-three scientists were required to describe the specimens they found.

On their return Scott was feted at a great meeting of the Royal Geographical Society in the Royal Albert Hall in London and created a CVO.

The museum on the quay here describes the background to the expedition and attempts the task of distinguishing between Scott's expedition on *Discovery*, 1901–4, which he and Shackleton survived, and his subsequent expedition in 1910–13 on *Terra Nova*, when Edgar Evans, L. E. G. Oates, Scott, Edward Wilson and Henry Bowers perished, the last three just eleven miles from a food depot.

The move from the museum's galleries and videos to the ship brings into focus the realities of such expeditions: the bunkers that held 350 tons of coal; the boxes of rock salt to absorb water and so help preserve the ship's timber; the magnetic exclusion zone; the absence of baths (all washing taking place in portable canvas contraptions); the pressure on space for the 'other ranks', the size of the officers' cabins, either single or double; above all, the mountains of food.

In the repetitive boredom of the Arctic winters, food and smoking kept up morale. The ship took forty-five sheep on board when leaving New Zealand and her company fished

and killed seals and penguins for fresh meat. Nevertheless dried and tinned food were staple: Quaker Oats, bottled fruit, suet, sugar, preserved potatoes; tins of mutton cutlets, duck, green peas and Keiller Dundee marmalade.

It is these, and Scott's pipe put to one side in his cabin, that connect the ship, safely berthed, to the expeditions and the Arctic winters.

DEAN GALLERY ✳✳✳

Belford Road, Edinburgh, Lothian EH4 3DS
Tel. 0131 624 6200
www.nationalgalleries.org

Eduardo Paolozzi's studio; Keiller and Penrose's collections: surreal

In 1995 Eduardo Paolozzi offered the Scottish National Gallery of Modern Art (SNGMA, q.v.) the contents of his studios,[42] a Heritage Lottery Fund grant allowed the purchase of twenty-six works from the late Sir Roland Penrose's collection and Mrs Gabrielle Keiller died, leaving her collection to the gallery. Between them the Penrose and Keiller Collections gave the gallery a holding of Dada and Surrealist art rivalled only by the Peggy Guggenheim Collection in Venice.

A new building was needed. In 1999 the Dean Gallery opened on the other side of the road to the SNGMA, in the former Dean Orphan Hospital designed in 1831–3 by Thomas Hamilton. You drive in and park at the back, behind its openwork towers, topped by eight octagonal chimney shafts united by arches, an idea that Colin McWilliam believes 'must have come from Vanbrugh'.[43]

Entering through the pillared portico, you are confronted by Paolozzi's thirty-foot-high sculpture of *Vulcan* (1998–9), the son of Juno, the god of fire, the patron saint of artists, lamed in one foot when he was thrown out of Olympus and fell to earth. Paolozzi has modelled Vulcan on himself.

Even in the double-height space that architect Terry Farrell has made in his conversion of the building, *Vulcan* is trapped by the confines of the room; the viewer is hemmed in by

Vulcan's mass, able only to shuffle round Vulcan's feet, inches away from the welts of welded steel.

Across the corridor is the recreation of Paolozzi's studio: a rummage of objects piled up, shoved under, thrown over, stacked on, spilling off every surface: shelves, tables, desks, a sleeping platform, the floor. There are plaster casts of heads, legs, feet, Pavlov's dog; tools, hammers, files, saws; brushes hung up, cast down, in pots, lying around; string, wire, a can of varnish, a tube of glue. There are boxes of toys (the Return of the Jedi, an Action Man), comics and magazines. There is a bag of piano hammers, an old electric typewriter and rather tidy shelves of books. A clock has stopped at 11.25.

Paolozzi has 'never really believed that there was a special category of figures, objects and situations that were reserved for art'.[44] This view attracted him to Surrealism when he was introduced to it at the Slade School of Art by a fellow student, Nigel Henderson. All objects, all materials were potentially of use in his collages. In the 1950s he started to develop a new style of sculpture that consisted of the casts of random objects yoked and welded together, 'the metamorphosis of rubbish', as he described it in a lecture at the ICA.[45]

The gallery has sculptures from all stages of his career but the works of the late 1950s and early '60s are particularly strong and bring together the machine idols (*The Bishop of Kuban*, 1962) and the painted aluminium pieces (*Four Towers*, 1962, and *Chord*, 1964) that reflect his excitement with American popular culture.[46]

Paolozzi and Gabrielle Keiller met at the 1960 Venice Biennale when his work was shown in the British Pavilion. Keiller was Paolozzi's principal patron throughout the 1960s and '70s. With her third husband Alexander Keiller, an archaeologist,[47] she skied, played golf and collected. Initially their interests were 17th- and 18th-century furniture

The Bishop of Kuban by Eduardo Paolozzi (Dean Gallery)

and embroidery, and 18th-century ceramic cow creamers (v. Potteries Museum and Art Gallery, to whom she subsequently gave 338 of them), each with its own name, provenance and price entered in a Herd Book. After Alexander Keiller died in 1955, Gabrielle Keiller turned to paintings: a small panel by Gerard David, a landscape by Corot, a portrait by Renoir. In 1960 she visited Venice, met Peggy Guggenheim and Eduardo Paolozzi, and was introduced to Surrealism. From then on, with the zeal of the convert, she collected only Dada and Surrealist works.

She became friendly with Roland Penrose, who, like Paolozzi, sometimes advised her. Penrose had studied under André Lhote, was a close friend of Picasso, Ernst, Miró and Paul Eluard, and organised the International Surrealist Exhibition held in London in 1936. His own collection of Cubist and Surrealist art was outstanding.

As well as acquiring pieces by Picasso, Gabrielle Keiller bought Ernst, Tanguy and Picabia in the 1960s; Dalí, Delvaux and more Picabia in the 1970s; photographs by Man Ray, a collage by Schwitters and, in 1987, *Cadavre Exquis (Exquisite Corpse)* (1938) by André Breton, Jacqueline Lamber and Yves Tanguy, a collage based on the Surrealist game of the same name invented by Breton that was described by Marcel Duhamel as 'at last . . . an infallible method of overruling the mind's critical faculties and completely liberating its capacity for metaphor'.[48]

In 1979 she had bought, from Penrose, Magritte's *La Répresentation*[49] (1937), one of the outstanding works in her collection. It is the only shaped work that Magritte painted, a portrait of a woman's genitalia from stomach to thigh, in a curved frame, described by Magritte as 'a rather surprising object, I think'.[50]

In Keiller's view the central work in her collection was Marcel Duchamp's *Bôite-en-Valise* (1935–41). Containing one original work (a collotype of the *Large Glass*, 1939) and sixty-nine miniature reproductions, it is, in Duchamp's words 'a portable museum'[51] that holds the essence of his work, a Surrealist contradiction: Duchamp's anarchic imagination locked up neatly in a cabinet of curiosities to be packed away again.

Crucial to Keiller's collection are the rigorous critical standards she maintained. 'I am certain that one masterpiece is worth all the lesser works by lesser artists,' she wrote to Douglas Hall,[52] and she acted on this belief, selling paintings by Picasso, Braque, Léger, Magritte and Francis Bacon when there was an opportunity to exchange them for better examples, two Magrittes (*La Révolution*, 1935 and *Perspective: Madame Recamier de Gerard*, 1950) being bought and then sold before she acquired *La Répresentation* from Penrose.

Keiller had what Douglas Hall called an 'acerbity of eye' but Penrose was steeped in an understanding of art that was reflected in the twenty-six works from his collection that the gallery acquired, notably Miró's *Maternity* (1924), Henry Moore's *The Helmet* (1939–40) and Picasso's *Guitar, Gas-jet and Bottle* (1913). All the works, in both Keiller's and Penrose's collections, are animated by the libraries they built of sketchbooks, correspondence, reviews and magazines which help us trace the ideas and relationships surrounding Surrealism.

In the 1st Surrealist Manifesto of 1924 in Paris André Breton wrote that 'the aim was to explore the world of psychic experience revealed by Freud and by psychoanalytic research' and to transmute 'those two seemingly contradictory states, dream and reality, into a sort of absolute reality, of surreality'.[53] This collection is the only one in Britain that allows us to see those aims being worked out over the subsequent thirty years and, in doing so, it illustrates the link between art in Europe in the 1920s and '30s and post-war American Abstract Expressionism.

RAYMOND RUSSELL COLLECTION OF EARLY KEYBOARD INSTRUMENTS **

St Cecilia's Hall, Niddry Street, Cowgate, Edinburgh, Lothian EH1 1LJ
Tel. 0131 650 2805

Important early keyboard instruments in Scotland's earliest concert hall

St Cecilia's Hall is the oldest purpose-built concert hall in Scotland, designed by Robert Mylne for the Edinburgh Music Society in 1763. In its brief heyday the society's concerts featured the music of Corelli and Purcell, Handel and Haydn. Its members included Sir John Clerk of Penicuik, advocate, judge, signatory of the 1707 Act of Union and a pupil of Corelli.

The concert hall closed in 1798 and in the following 150 years its stern stone features were successively a Baptist church, the Freemasons' Hall of the Masonic Grand Lodge of Scotland, a school, a bookbinding and printing business and an art deco Palais de Danse before being reconverted into a concert hall by Miss Madeleine Cairns, the owner of the 'Excelsior Ballroom'. She sold it in 1959 to the University of Edinburgh, who recognised that it was the ideal setting for the superb collection of early keyboard instruments that they had been given by the English antiquarian and collector Raymond Russell, FSA, FTCL (1922–64). They commissioned the architect Ian Lindsay to reconstruct its elliptical Concert Room and double staircase.

Russell collected early keyboard instruments in the late 1940s and early '50s and in 1959 published *The Harpsichord and Clavichord – an Introductory Survey*[54] which, though no longer in print, is still a standard work on the subject.

The collection concentrates on the most important schools of harpsichord and clavichord building: the 16th- and 17th-century Italian builders of harpsichords and virginals and the Dutch, German and French builders of harpsichords of the 17th and 18th centuries. At the heart of the collection are four harpsichords by the Ruckers family of Antwerp, two by Pascal Taskin of Paris and a harpsichord and a clavichord by Johann Adolph Hass of Hamburg.

The Ruckers family made harpsichords in Antwerp from 1580 to 1650 and influenced all subsequent builders. Their instruments are prized for the beauty of their tone, said to be at once silvery and clear with a rich, underlying resonance. Regrettably, in a collection in which most of the instruments are playable, there is presently no playable Ruckers.

The two Taskin double-manual harpsichords (1764–84 and 1769) contrast: one has a booming resonance, the other a brighter tone with a deeper bass. Hass's instruments – an unfretted clavichord (1763) and a single-manual harpsichord (1764) – are thinner and brighter, excellent for the contrapuntal music of the Bachs. Their sophisticated and elaborate innovations almost mirror organ techniques. Only six survive.

Music students are encouraged to play and the galleries are alive with the carried tonal voices. Almost as lively are the painted decorations on many of the instruments. The 1608 double-manual Ruckers harpsichord has under its flaplid a painted scene of classical romance by Pieter Codde and, typically for a Ruckers instrument, tempera flower painting on the soundboard.

The 1763 Hass clavichord has unusually sumptuous decoration: its exterior is lacquered in red, black and gold Chinoiserie, while the inside of the lid has an oil painting of a river scene, framed in olive veneer.

Many of the instruments have notable histories: the 1764 single-manual harpsichord appears to have been owned by Mozart.[55]

Around this core, playing out the history of the keyboard instruments, are Italian virginals (a 16th-century pentagonal made by Alessandro Bertolotti in Verona in 1586 and a rectangular enharmonic by Francesco Poggio, c. 1620); 18th-century English bentside spinets; a square piano, a pianino and a grand pianoforte by Americus Backers (1772); and an enharmonic chamber organ by Thomas Parker (c. 1765).

Russell's collection guides you through the evolution of the pianoforte, and elucidates with grace and clarity.

SCOTTISH NATIONAL GALLERY OF MODERN ART ★★★★

Belford Road, Edinburgh, Lothian EH4 3DR
Tel. 0131 624 6200
www.nationalgalleries.org

Airily displayed and unrivalled collection of modern art: Matisse, Giacometti, Picasso and Scottish artists

At the opening ceremony in 1960 Sir Kenneth Clark praised the SNGMA, for being 'the first National Gallery exclusively devoted to modern art in the British Isles'.[56] This was to England's shame, Scotland's pride. It opened with a transfer from the National Gallery of Scotland (NGS) and a purchasing grant of £7,500 a year. Today it has a collection of 5,000 works and spends considerably more each year on acquiring new works.

Having been started so late, its collection can never be representative of 20th-century European art, but it has strong holdings of French late-19th- to early-20th-century paintings, Cubism, German Expressionism and, particularly, Dada and Surrealism. They provide a context for the more fully representative Scottish and English collections.

Campaigners for a gallery of modern art wanted it to be purpose built and the architect Alan Reiach was commissioned to submit designs in 1940, and again in 1956. Neither design was approved and the gallery opened in Inverleith House in the Royal Botanic Garden, moving in 1984 to its present home, the former John Watson's Institution, a stern, neo-classical building designed by William Burn in 1825.[57]

Visitors can drive into the extensive grounds that spread before the gallery and that provide an excellent setting for sculpture. In 2001

Charles Jencks was commissioned to design a large environmental sculpture, *Landform*, whose manicured grass covers and appears to contain a rising coiled spring of earthworks. It is fresh, surprising, pitched on a slight incline; its central position pushes sculpture by Hepworth, Moore and Cragg to the edges of the site.

Inside, twenty-two galleries on two floors display all parts of the permanent collection (and temporary exhibitions) except the Penrose Collection and Keiller Bequest of Dada and Surrealist art and the gift (and recreated studio) of Eduardo Paolozzi that are in the Dean Gallery on the other side of the road (q.v.).

The original thirty-eight paintings (and much 20th-century graphic material) transferred from the NGS were immediately augmented by Sir Alexander Maitland's gift[58] of French paintings that included works by Bonnard, Rouault and Matisse, and an early Picasso, *Mère et Enfant* (1902). Within ten years Mr and Mrs Scott-Hay[59] (in 1967) and Dr R. A. Lillie (in 1971) had given collections of Scottish paintings. Dr Lillie's includes paintings by all the Colourists and 168 landscapes and still lifes in oil and watercolour by William Gillies covering his career from 1916 to 1965.

From that base Douglas Hall, the Keeper from 1961 to 1986, and Richard Calvocoressi, the Keeper (now Director) since, have had to create a gallery of modern art mainly by purchase. In the early years financial restraints caused many artists initially to be represented by prints or drawings. However works by Léger, Braque, Picasso, de Stael, Marini and Morandi were purchased in the 1960s, as were paintings by the Germans Kirchner, Nolde and Jawlensky[60] and an unusual group of paintings by pre-revolutionary Russian artists Natalya Goncharova, Mikhail Larionov and Lyubov Popova – Goncharova figurative, indebted to icons, Popova indebted to Malevich.

By the 1970s even contemporary paintings and sculpture were expensive to buy. Despite

Francis Bacon's Figure Study I *(Scottish National Gallery of Modern Art)*

this, English art was collected in depth and strength: Gwen John, Matthew Smith, David Bomberg, Christopher Wood, Stanley Spencer, and drawings and paintings by Ben Nicholson from the 1920s to the 1960s; sculpture by Reg Butler, Lynn Chadwick, Kenneth Armitage and Eduardo Paolozzi, who had exhibited together at the Venice Biennale. The gallery already had works by Epstein, Moore and Hepworth and went on to purchase pieces by Henri Gaudier-Brzeska and Alexander Calder. Later, an impressive collection was assembled of contemporary British sculpture in the 1980s and '90s: Anthony Caro, Antony Gormley, Richard Long, Tony Cragg, Rachel Whiteread.

In 1989 the substantial gift of her collection by Miss Elizabeth Watt brought a strangely mixed group of work to the collection: Leon Underwood, William Roberts, Roy de Maistre, Osip Zadkine, Victor Pasmore, Paul Nash and Marcello Mascherini.

Richard Calvocoressi's attention to the acquisition of contemporary work, English and Scots, has been impressive. Glasgow School of Art in the late 1980s is represented by Ken Currie, Peter Howson, Steven Campbell and Adrian Wisniewski while, in the 1990s, it is mainly the work of London-based artists that has been acquired: Damien Hirst, Julian Opie, Tracey Emin and Richard Billingham.

If the money is available it is relatively easy to buy Bacon, Freud, Auerbach or Hockney once they have become established names. A national gallery that buys works as they are being made demonstrates real confidence.

This collection, of the past 100 years of European art, collected during a period half as long, cannot but offer a view of what has engaged artists in those more recent years: the tensions between form and line, construction and narrative, representation and abstraction.

A century that starts with the apparent certainties of figurative representation in the paintings of Vuillard, or the Scottish Colourists, ends with very different representation as expressed by Paolozzi's welded steel *Vulcan* (1998–9), a man-machine twenty feet high trapped in the confined space of a 19th-century building,[61] and by Rachel Whiteread's sculpture, *Untitled (Pair)* (1999), cast from the last hard bed a person rests upon, a mortuary slab, its runnels made to drain away the body's fluids.

The apparently straightforward still life of Vuillard's *The Candlestick* (roses in a small vase, books, lace tablecloth, a satchel) is confined to a small central area by encroaching geometric shapes (the door panel, the papered wall, the bedspread). By 1913 Picasso makes his figuratively titled *Head* out of *papiers collés* whose abstract configuration is qualified only by four charcoal lines that give the figurative reference, while in Léger's *Woman and Still Life* (1921) the woman is represented only by machine parts.

Abstraction appears to have thrown off any semblance of the human or organic in Friedrich Vordemberge-Gildewart's *Composition 14* (1925), of which he wrote, 'The spiritual in art does not exist . . . For absolute art, so-called content and object are totally impossible', and in Piet Mondrian's *Composition* (1932), one of the earliest of his 'train line' paintings in which four lines intersect to make six rectangles,[62] but appearance can and will deceive. Mondrian arrived at his grid by studying natural forms, particularly tree branches, and was influenced by the doctrines of theosophy.

For British artists here the engagement between abstraction and representation had scarcely begun by 1930. It was only in 1933 that Ben Nicholson moved from landscapes (*Walton Wood Cottage*, 1928) to his first abstract relief, the *White Relief* of 1935, the earliest of his reliefs in this collection, which does not fully demonstrate his later stylistic oscillations: the representations in the St Ives landscapes of the 1940s, the return to abstract reliefs in the 1950s and '60s (*White Relief, Paros*, 1962), the late still life etchings and *Two and a Half Goblets* (1967).

Representation is sustained, not only in the paintings of Balthus, Francis Bacon (*Figure Study I*, 1945–6) and Stanley Spencer (*Christ Delivered to the People*, 1950) but in the imagination of the Surrealists. At the same time,

on either side of the Atlantic, such Abstract Expressionists as Jackson Pollock (*Untitled*, *c.*1942–4) and William Johnstone (*A Point in Time*, *c.*1929–37) were pursuing a physical form of automatism.

This dialogue between abstraction and representation continues in the gallery's more recent acquisitions: Lichtenstein and Warhol, Freud and Andrews, Currie and Howson, Vasarely and Riley; unresolved and unresolvable. Léger wrote in 1925: 'I have never enjoyed copying a machine. I invent images from machines as others have made landscapes from their imaginations. For me the mechanical element is a means of conveying a feeling of strength and power'; and Henry Moore described one of the gallery's finest sculptures, his own *The Helmet* (1939–40), as 'One form inside another, so you get the mystery of not entirely knowing the form inside'.

For a collection that cannot be comprehensive and is, on its own admission, not fully representative, this one nonetheless constitutes a considerable achievement that more than deserves the praise of Kenneth Clark.

SCOTTISH NATIONAL PORTRAIT GALLERY ✴✴✴✴

1 Queen Street, Edinburgh, Lothian EH2 1JO
Tel. 0131 332 2266
www.natgalscot.ac.uk

A rosy Gothic house of worthies, villains, kings and beauties from Scottish life

'It has always struck me,' wrote Carlyle, 'that Historical Portrait Galleries far transcend in worth all other kinds of National Collections of Pictures whatever.' His determined support was crucial in the establishment of the Scottish National Portrait Gallery (SNPG) as a collection that aims to tell the history of Scotland through the likenesses of its most celebrated men and women.

This intention is confirmed by the statues of monarchs, poets and politicians who look down from their high red sandstone niches on to Queen Street and North St Andrew's Street, and, when one enters the gallery, by the pageant frieze that runs around the walls of the main hall by William Hole, of more than eighty great Scots: from Columba, Macbeth, Mary, Queen of Scots, John Knox, Charles Edward Stuart, David Hume, Robert Adam, James Watt, Walter Scott, David Livingstone to Thomas Carlyle himself, whose seated marble likeness, massively gowned, presides over the hall. It is by Sir Joseph Edgar Boehm (1881) who declared it 'the best thing I ever did'. Here is history as written by Carlyle and Macaulay in which men shape events, and biography and portraiture embody that history.

Despite Carlyle's advocacy, the founding of the National Portrait Gallery in London in 1856 and the grandeur of the Scottish enterprise, the then government refused to commit public funds and only the generosity of the proprietor of *The Scotsman*, John Ritchie Findlay, in creating an endowment and financing the building to the designs of Sir Robert Rowland Anderson, allowed the SNPG to open in 1889.

Anderson's 'Victorian bonus'[63] of a 'Venetian Gothic Palace'[64] in red Dumfriesshire sandstone stands out from the symmetrical elegance of Georgian Queen Street to the west. Within, the proportions of its imposing galleries adapt as well to sculpture as to painting or photography.

The ambition of Hole's pageant frieze, taking Scottish history back fourteen centuries to Columba and even nodding at Hadrian and Agricola, cannot be realised because Scottish portraiture, whether by Scottish or foreign artists, does not start here until the late 16th century with portraits of *Mary, Queen of Scots* (after François Clouet) and her mother, *Mary of Guise*, by Corneille de Lyon.

Then the doors open and all Scottish history floods through: murdered *Lord Darnley*, a beautiful youth as depicted by Hans Eworth, and the murdering *Bothwell*, in a miniature; *James VI and I*, as a child, holding a shrewd-eyed falcon (by Adrian Bronckorst); the devious *1st Marquis of Argyll* (by David Scougall); romantic *Montrose* (attributed to

William Dobson); handsome *'Bonnie Dundee'* (pen and ink by David Paton).

There are several (Jacobite) images of *Charles Edward Stuart*, one of *Flora Macdonald* (by Richard Wilson), and Gainsborough's portrait of their pursuer, the *4th Duke of Argyll*, looking uncertain in old age.

The great figures of the Enlightenment are present: the philosopher *David Hume* by Ramsay; the architect *Sir William Chambers* by Francis Cotes; *James Hutton*, the father of modern geology, by Raeburn; but the only likenesses of *Robert Adam* and *Adam Smith* are in the form of paste medallions, from a set of over two hundred portrait gems by James Tassie.

James Watt, Robert Burns and Walter Scott hang alongside Sir Colin Campbell, hero of Balaclava and the raiser of the second Siege of Lucknow, to make clear Scotland's contribution to engineering, literature and the Empire in the 19th century.

In each gallery, among the likenesses, there are outstanding paintings: Van Dyck's severe portrait of *Alexander Henderson* (c. 1641), the cleric who drafted the Solemn League and Covenant; George Jamesone's canny self-portrait, looking back at the viewer, one eyebrow raised; an early (perhaps the first) depiction of a tartan plaid worn as fashionable national dress by *Lord Mungo Murray*, painted by John Michael Wright (c. 1680s); Allan Ramsay's knowing plain portrait of himself; Raeburn's of *Lord Braxfield*, the model for Robert Louis Stevenson's *Weir of Hermiston*; and *Stevenson* himself by Count Girolamo Nerli.

Hung among these men of history there are glimpses of the less famous (Raeburn's affectionate portrait of the fiddler *Neil Gow*), the infamous (crude engravings of the grave-robbers *Burke and Hare*) and the not famous (Richard Waitt's *The Laird of Grant's Fool* or *A Gardener Holding a Cabbage with a Candle*, 1731). Without more documentation its subject and meaning remain obscure. From the grand, if tattered, waistcoat, he might be not a labourer but a Hallowe'en reveller, a fool.

Photography opened up new possibilities

Part of William Hole's pageant frieze of Scottish history (Scottish National Portrait Gallery)

for portraiture which David Octavius Hill and Robert Adamson were among the first to grasp in their series of calotypes, here of *The Fishermen and Women of the Firth of Forth* (1844). Hill was a painter who initially saw the calotype, invented by Fox Talbot (v. Fox Talbot Museum) and passed from Talbot to Hill by their mutual friend Sir David Brewster, principal of the United College of St Andrew's University, not as a medium in its own right but as a means of recording the faces of the clerics he needed to portray in his panoramic painting of *The Disruption of the General Assembly of the Church of Scotland* (1843–66) at which dissenting ministers, led by the charismatic Dr Thomas Chalmers, split from the Church of Scotland and formed the Free Church. From this fortuitous start the SNPG has built a remarkable collection of photographs which includes portraits (of *R. L. Stevenson* by A. G. Dew Smith, 1885, and *George Mackay Brown with Gypsy* – his cat – by Gunnie Moberg, 1990), the gaunt-faced inhabitants of St Kilda, by Alex Hutchinson (1880), James Cox's clean-eyed picture of poor children *At Auchmithie* (1881), and Humphrey Spender's photograph, for the newly formed *Picture Post*, of *Women in a Public Washhouse, Glasgow* (1939).

Photography has offered portrait galleries the possibility of the collective portrait, the portraits of a nation, grasped here in this collection by Hutchinson and Spender; in the images of children playing in the Gorbals by Bert Hardy, in the 1940s, and by Roger Mayne, in the 1960s; by Chick Chalmers in his photographs of 1970s life in the Orkneys.[65]

You walk from these past a series of bright, emphatic, painted portraits on the walls of the gallery's shop by Alexander Moffat, of 20th-century Scottish writers (Norman McCaig, Edwin Morgan, Robert Garrioch and Muriel Spark), past the numerous portrait busts by such various hands as Sir Francis Chantrey, Joseph Nollekens, Louis-François Roubiliac, Benno Schotz and Eduardo Paolozzi, and through a contemporary gallery where, notwithstanding new technologies, the memorable images are all painted: Oswald Birley's tense, intense *Lord Reith* (1953, copy); the pale tired eyes of *James Maxton*, the Clydeside MP, by Sir John Lavery; the generous, gentle intelligence of the Byzantine scholar *Sir Steven Runciman*; the impatient beauty of the novelist *Naomi Mitchison* by Wyndham Lewis; and, above all, *The Oncologists* by Ken Currie, in which three eminent surgeons, Sir David Lorne, Sir Alfred Cuschieri and Professor Steele, turning to the viewer, in a beam of light, red-eyed, anxious, are caught blood-handed, aghast.

As you walk round these halls of history you return to Hole's pageant frieze of *Scotland's History* and the gaze of Thomas Carlyle.

TALBOT RICE GALLERY **

University of Edinburgh, Old College, South
Bridge, Edinburgh, Lothian EH8 9YL
Tel. 0131 650 2211
www.trg.ed.ac.uk

*Erskine of Torrie collection of mainly Dutch
art in setting by Robert Adam and William
Playfair; and paintings by William Johnstone*

In a deed of settlement dated 10 April 1824, Sir
James Erskine of Torrie left his collection of
paintings and bronzes to the University of
Edinburgh. His intention was 'to lay the foundation of a Gallery for the encouragement of
the Fine Arts'.

His will made no provision for the building
of a gallery, so for the next 148 years the Torrie
Collection was moved between the university's
library, the library stair, the National Gallery
of Scotland and the Senate Room before coming to rest in the present room, designed by
William Playfair to display the university's scientific collections.

The gallery is not easy to find. You enter the
university from South Bridge and cross the
main courtyard, designed by William Playfair
from an original design by Adam, in heavy,
sombre stone. Tucked in the far corner, up two
flights of stairs, is the gallery, intact, much as
Playfair designed it, if a little tired. The neo-
classical proportions remain (if incorrectly
coloured), as do the Ionic pillars, the pilasters,

the central cupola and much of the original
moulding. It is an appropriately quiet and
elegant setting for a collection that has not
grown in the way that Glasgow University's art
gallery has.

Erskine was a soldier, a handsome fellow (as
an oil sketch here by Lawrence confirms) and a
friend of the Prince Regent. He shared the
Prince's liking for Dutch paintings, Italianate
landscapes (Adam Pynacker, Jan Both) and
genre pictures (Jan Steen). Unlike others in
the Prince's circle (Lord Yarmouth, later 3rd
Marquess of Hertford,[66] or Lawrence), Erskine
was not a connoisseur.

His pictures provide a sound overview
of the Dutch School, with the Jan Both *Landscape with Figures* making the link between
those who influenced Both in Rome (Claude,
Paul Bril, Adam Elsheimer) and those he influenced in Holland (Pynacker and Berchem)
and, through them, Berchem's pupil, Karel du
Jardin.

Few of these paintings are of the first rank,
although the early Jacob van Ruisdael, *The
Banks of Aruler*, painted in 1649 when he was
only twenty-one, contains all the elements
developed in his later work: a stillness, the sky
reflecting dark shadows in the water, figures
and distant buildings that are small and
vulnerable in such an open landscape, while
contours twist through the picture. There are
also paintings by Adam Pynacker, Salvator
Rosa and Gaspard Dughet.

The bronzes are better. Two stand out: one

by Adriaen de Vries and one by Giambologna. The de Vries (*Cain and Abel*, 1612) is a powerful piece made in the last years of his life in Augsburg where he was Emperor Rudolph II's official sculptor. The Giambologna (*Anatomical Figure of a Horse*), made in Florence (*c.*1585), is ceremonial, the neck arched, the right foreleg raised. The smaller bronzes, tucked in corner cabinets, include a *Cupid*, now known to be by Francis Duguesnoy, a friend of Poussin's and the best non-Italian 17th-century sculptor working in Rome,[67] and a set of bronze vases, rare models by Zoffoli.

Before the establishment of the Watson Gordon Chair of Fine Art in 1880,[68] the university was uncertain about the purpose of the collection. The first professor, Gerald Baldwin Brown, set out his aims:[69] '1. To bring before students ... the chief ancient and modern works of Architecture, Sculpture, Painting and the Decorative and Industrial Arts. 2. To exhibit the value to human life of these works as things of beauty' – ideals that were shared by his successors, the art historian Sir Herbert Read (1931–3) and the Byzantine scholar David Talbot Rice (1934–1972). The present gallery opened a year after the latter's death in 1972 and has initiated, and maintained, an ambitious programme of temporary exhibitions.

The quality of these exhibitions led to a major bequest, by Mrs Hope Scott, comprising a small number of 20th-century European paintings (by Bonnard, Utrillo and Ernst, and an early Picasso, painted *c.*1900 while he was still in Barcelona), pictures by Scottish artists (Peploe, Gillies) and a major collection of works by William Johnstone.

Since a major retrospective at the Hayward Gallery in 1981, Johnstone has not attracted the critical attention that his unusual career deserves. Like his near-contemporary Christopher Wood (v. Kettle's Yard), Johnstone worked at André Lhote's art school, the Academie Montparnasse, where he too was influenced by the surrealism of André Breton, Louis Aragon and, in particular, the unconscious composition (*décalomanie*) of Max

The Talbot Rice Gallery

Ernst,[70] a quite different experience of 1920/30s Parisian modernism from the architectural minimalism of Le Corbusier that Ben Nicholson and Barbara Hepworth brought back to Unit One in 1938. By that time Johnstone had married the American sculptor Flora Macdonald and gone to California, where he encountered the work of the previous generations of American artists, Georgia O'Keeffe and Thomas Hart Benton. It is these influences (especially Surrealist automation), quite unlike those of any other British artist of his generation, that can be seen in such paintings here as *Ettrick Raining* (1936), *Untitled* (1943–4) and *Red Spring* (1958–9) and that relate so clearly to the paintings of his slightly younger contemporary Jackson Pollock.

For more than twenty years, from 1938 to 1960, Johnstone was, successively, principal of Camberwell School of Art and of the Central School of Arts and Crafts, where he had a profound impact on art education, as well as on such individual students as Alan Davie, Eduardo Paolozzi and William Turnbull. In the last year of his life, 1981, he received an honorary degree from the University of Edinburgh, which led Mrs Hope Scott to give her collection of his paintings, drawings and prints to the Talbot Rice Gallery and the then professor, Giles Robertson. In doing so she made a connection back to Johnstone's time at the Edinburgh College of Art immediately after the First World War when he was influenced by two lectures on Celtic and Anglo-Saxon art by the Watson Gordon professor Gerald Baldwin Brown.

Baldwin Brown's scholarship and Johnstone's paintings are happily conjoined in these two collections. Their unusual qualities, augmented by Talbot Rice's acquisitions of paintings by Joan Eardley, Margaret Mellis, Gillies and Cadell, and gifts from Alan Davie and John Bellany, merit the restoration of Playfair's gallery; a better hang; and more confidence in promoting this gallery so that it can be what Erskine, Baldwin Brown, Talbot Rice, Giles Robertson and William Johnstone wanted it to be, 'a Gallery for the encouragement of the Fine Arts'.

PALACE OF
HOLYROODHOUSE *

Edinburgh, Lothian EH8 8DX
Tel. 0131 556 5100
www.royal.gov.uk

Royal palace of dark deeds around Mary,
Queen of Scots; De Witt's gallery of Scottish
kings, real and imagined

Holyroodhouse evolved into a royal palace
during the 11th and 12th centuries[71] as Edinburgh became accepted as capital of Scotland.
A former Augustinian monastery, it is set in
parkland, outside the city walls, at the bottom
of the Royal Mile, in the shadow of the sleeping lion of Arthur's Seat.

In 1528 James V added a massive tower
and created new royal apartments on the west
front. When he died in 1560 and his daughter
Mary, Queen of Scots, returned from France,
Holyroodhouse became the setting for many
of the central events of her life: her marriage to
Henry Stuart, Lord Darnley; the murder of her
secretary, David Rizzio; Darnley's own death;
her subsequent marriage to James Hepburn,
Earl of Bothwell. A painting by Livinus de
Vogelaare, *The Memorial of Lord Darnley*
(c.1567), in the Queen's Outer Chamber,
depicts the story of Darnley's murder and
indicts Mary.[72]

In 1671 Charles II commissioned the
Scottish architect Sir William Bruce[73] to
remodel the palace, employing around the
chastely elegant inner quadrangle the three
Orders of Architecture – Doric, Ionic and
Corinthian – in ascending order on the
palace's three floors:[74] a design that is careful
and correct rather than uplifting. English
monarchs visiting Scotland have stayed here
ever since in preference to the castle.

Within, Bruce's Palladian designs give way
to a riot of baroque with elaborate plasterwork
ceilings in most of the state rooms, by John
Houlbert and George Dunsterfield, with 'lavish
foliage and cherubs holding the honours of
Scotland ... wreaths and cartouches in the
corners'[75] and carved woodwork by Alexander

Eizat. On the Great Stair are frescoes by
the 16th-century Italian Lattanzio Gambara
(*Mercury, Apollo, Diana,* etc., c.1550), bought
by Prince Albert as exemplars when he was
trying to revive fresco painting in Britain
in order to decorate Barry's new Houses of
Parliament (q.v.).[76]

Holyroodhouse has its share of the Royal
Collection. In 2002 a new Queen's Gallery,
designed by Ben Tindall, was opened to show,
on a temporary, rotating basis, works from
the Royal Collection. Almost all the paintings
in Holyroodhouse itself have links with the
palace or with Scotland: François Clouet's sad
painting of *Mary, Queen of Scots in White*
Mourning (1559–61);[77] Paul van Somer's 1618
portrait of her son, *James VI and I*; Daniel
Mytens's of James's son, *Charles I* (1628), a flat
likeness that shows how penetrating is Van
Dyck; and a stiff portrait, attributed to Hans
Eworth, of *Henry Stuart, Lord Darnley and his*
Brother Charles, 5th Earl of Lennox (c.1562),
a youth and a child about to be swept away
by events.

Most rooms are furnished with late-
17th-century tapestries: four Mortlake panels
of *The Life of Diogenes*, bought by Charles II
(1683), and two Flemish panels, of the same
date, with scenes from *The Aeneid* (the meeting of Dido and Aeneas – a fragment – and the
death of Dido). The Mortlake tapestries show
that, even after the glory days of Sir Francis
Crane as director in the 1620s and the disruption of the Civil War, the Mortlake workshops
could weave wool and silk in a dazzling
number of colour tones as though painting.

Holyroodhouse is also a showcase for the
talents of the Dutch painter Jacob De Witt
(1640–97), brought to Edinburgh in 1675 by
Bruce. Several rooms have overmantels by him
framed, in the Morning Drawing Room, by
Jan de Santwort's exotic carving, with subjects from Greek mythology and the Bible
(Hercules, Galataea, Moses). To decorate the
Great Gallery, in effect a long passage linking
the King's and Queen's Apartments, he was
commissioned to 'compleatly draw, finish and
perfyte' the portraits of 110 real and legendary
kings of Scotland from 'Fergus I' to Charles II

and 'to make them like unto the Originalls which are to be given him'. Fortunately De Witt had 'a fertile imagination and a ready pencil';[78] his imagined kings inherit down their generations long and pronounced noses.[79] Queen Victoria described them in her diary as 'a collection of most frightful portraits of Kings of Scotland, beginning with a full length one of a King 330 years before Christ'.[80]

Later English monarchs favoured Holyroodhouse: George IV came here for a state visit in 1822, recorded in a rare poor painting by David Wilkie (*The Entrance of George IV at Holyroodhouse*, 1822–30), and a theatrical full-length, also by Wilkie, of the King in full Highland dress, socks, sporran, a Glengarry and all (1829).[81]

Queen Victoria took to staying here en route to Balmoral. Her diary records her first visit, 29 August 1850: 'Our living here is quite an epoch in the annals of this old pile which has seen so many deeds more bad, I fear, than good.'[82]

In recognition of these 'many deeds' the Queen purchased from Horace Walpole's collection[83] the Darnley jewel, a bauble of rubies and an emerald (and a large false sapphire) set in gold and enamel whose decoration expresses the hope of the Countess of Lennox that her grandson James, son of Mary, Queen of Scots, would succeed to the throne of England, to be the sixth James of Scotland, the first James of England. It is exhibited in the Queen's Apartment. The great thickness of the walls, small windows, ancient heraldic ceilings and lugged panels on the doors make these rooms heavy with the past. It was here in the Ante-Chamber that Darnley and his co-conspirators met on the night of Rizzio's murder; here that they mounted the spiral turnpike stair to where the Queen and her ladies, and Rizzio, were at supper; here that they dragged him to the door and stabbed him fifty-six times.

George IV recognised the romantic horror of these events and ordered that 'these apartments should be preserved, sacred from every alteration'.

MUSEUM OF SCOTLAND
★★★★

Chambers Street, Edinburgh, Lothian EH1 1JF
Tel. 0131 225 7534
www.nms.ac.uk

Scotland, very past and very present

The Monymusk reliquary, a small silver-mounted wooden box (*c.* 8th century), is a revered repository of Scottish identity and pride.[84] It is presumed to be the Breccbennach of St Columba[85] which was carried into battle at Bannockburn in 1314, an icon of the medieval kingdom of the Scots, an almost hallowed object in a museum that describes Scotland and Scottish identity.

There is no firm evidence that the reliquary was the Breccbennach, nor how it came to be in Monymusk House in the 19th century, but when it was sent to be sold at a London auction house, the public outcry was so great, supported even by the prime minister of the day, Ramsay MacDonald, that it had to be acquired for a museum that seems 'to provide tangible expressions of the qualities that have made Scotland the nation she is'.[86]

On a site high in the middle of the Old Town, two long-established institutions have been brought together to form one national museum: the National Museum of Antiquities, founded in 1780, and the Royal Scottish Museum, which has been here since 1854 in a building designed by the original architect of the South Kensington Museum (later the Victoria and Albert Museum), Francis Fowke. Its Lombardic Renaissance facade is impressive but it is its Great Hall that is memorable, described by Colin McWilliam in the *Buildings of Scotland* as a 'huge elegant birdcage of glass and iron ... with galleried aisles and a lofty nave spanned by stilted timber arches on slender iron columns'.[87] Beside it, to house the collections of antiquities, is a new (1998) building designed by Gordon Benson and Alan Forsyth, a penetrated keep in Clashach stone from whose upper storeys you can look across a panorama of the city from the castle to

Arthur's Seat. There can be no better place to bring together objects that have made Scotland and that Scotland has made during its 8,000-year history. This is the only European country that was neither overrun by barbarian hordes nor conquered by the Romans.[88]

The Tower Entrance of the new building leads you through the Hawthornden Court to the Monymusk reliquary and other objects that illustrate the emergence of the Scottish nation. In proud place is the Declaration of Arbroath (1320), the letter sent by the Barons of Scotland to Pope John XXII in the name of the 'whole community of the Realm' pledging support for King Robert provided that he did not betray them. 'As long as only one hundred of us remain alive we will never under any

The Monymusk reliquary (Museum of Scotland)

conditions be brought under English rule,' they affirmed in Latin. 'It is not for glory or riches or honour that we fight, but only for liberty.' Near by is a flag of faded blue, the Saltire, symbol of an independent Scotland, that was carried into the battle of Dunbar in 1650.

Other objects tell of an historic Scotland that was making things of beauty and sophistication centuries before the Romans or the English threatened: a hinged bronze collar from the 1st century AD; a bronze shield, 700–600 BC, beaten out from a circular ingot and decorated with ribs and bosses; and a bronze lunula (collar) made from sheet gold, edged with delicate geometric incision (c. 2,000 BC). So elegant and simple is the design of this collar that it could have been made last year, as could each individual silver ring of a Pictish chain, were it not for their massive size and length: a giant's necklace, its purpose or meaning lost in the past.

Perversely we can read more fluently the fossils, minerals and rocks here that have been truly buried in time: marble that was laid down 400 million years ago; chlorite mica schist from Loch Lomond (650 million years); striated metamorphic rocks, Lewisian gneiss (2,900 million years).

Beneath the Scottish landscape are worlds of dazzling variety. The collection of Professor Matthew Forster Heddle[89] contains hydrocarbons (bitumen and oil-rich shales), minerals, gems (smoky quartz, pale brown citrine, vibrant red garnets from volcanic rocks at Elie Ness, pearls from the freshwater mussels of the River Tay) and, richest-seeming of all, rocks (the hard crystals of the Highlands, the soft silts of the Clyde Beds and the Carse of Forth).

Regrettably the rocks collected by James Hutton in the 18th century that led him, by deduction and observation, to his *Theory of the Earth*[90] are no longer here, having been 'lost' in the 1830s by the then keeper of the museum, Professor Robert Jameson. (From the archives it appears that Hutton's collection was never deposited at the museum. It most probably went to Edinburgh University, although some, certainly, eventually ended up in the collections of the Hunterian Museum, Glasgow University, q.v.). Jameson continued to resist Hutton's theory that our planet was not 6,000 years old, as maintained by such theologising geologists as Dr William Buckland, but that it went back innumerable aeons. Hutton saw the bens and glens of Scotland not as immutably solid but as endlessly on the move. Continents shifted and collided, in a dance of deep time in which the world turned upside down, with the rocks on the peaks of mountains having been formed on the beds of the oceans. Scotland, once the twin of India at the equator, would be so again. As his biographer John Playfair said of Hutton, 'the mind seemed to grow giddy by looking so far into the abyss of time.'

If Hutton is presiding genius of the museum he shares that accolade with Hugh Miller, the self-educated stonemason from Cromarty who discovered fish fossils in the early 1830s. His 'winged fish', *Pterichthyoides milleri*, are here, held fast in Old Red Sandstone laid down 380 million years ago. A photograph here shows him, sleeves rolled up, chisel in hand, brow furrowed, leaning on a standing stone.[91] His work is being carried forward today by such contemporary fossil collectors as Stan Wood at excavations in Fife (Cowdenbeath) and West Lothian (East Kirkton).

Hutton's *Theory of the Earth*, 'grand, elegant, systematic',[92] is at the heart of the Scottish Enlightenment as surely as are Adam Smith's *The Wealth of Nations*, David Hume's *A Treatise on Human Nature* and the development of modern chemistry by Hutton's friend Joseph Black who, 'in the absence of the author, read the first part of Dr Hutton's *Theory of the Earth*' when it was presented to the Royal Society of Edinburgh on 7 March 1785. These titans of the Enlightenment dominate the museum: here are Black's chemical apparatus (his cucurbit and alembic, his curved retort, employed in his lectures at Edinburgh University to demonstrate how heat changed solids into liquids and liquids into gases – latent heat: the foundations of modern chemistry) and the machines made possible by the work of Black's pupil James Watt, who in May 1765 was on Glasgow Green 'when the idea came into my mind that, as steam was an elastic body it would rush into a vacuum . . . I had not walked further than the Golf-House when the whole thing was arranged in my mind.' Watt devoted himself to improving Newcomen's atmospheric engine for the next thirty-five years, taking out patents in 1769, 1782, 1784 and 1788 and joining Matthew Boulton of Birmingham in 1775 to form one of the most famous engineering partnerships in history, Boulton & Watt. A fine model of the Watt engine built for Boulton's Soho factory in 1788 is on display, as is a Boulton & Watt engine of 1786. But Newcomen's engine continued to be built where fuel was cheap, and the Caprington Colliery pumping engine, built from parts supplied by the Carron ironworks near Falkirk, is here.

These discoveries unleashed the Industrial

Revolution and the brilliant Scottish engineering that applied it: 'Puffing Billy', the oldest surviving locomotive in the world; and the Stevensons' lighthouses with the French Fresnel lenses that spread their light.

Some of the resulting trade and wealth that came back to Scotland from all parts of the world is displayed here: porcelain from China and Japan; bronzes from Benin; sculpture from India; textiles from Persia acquired for the museum on his travels by its director, Robert Murdoch Smith, in the 1880s. These objects express how Scots saw Scotland in the 19th century, a country of worldwide position and influence whose capital was 'the Athens of the North'.

On the opening of the Benson and Forsyth building the museum invited Scots to select objects to represent the 20th century. They chose a fiddle, a mountain bike, football boots, a microphone, a ballot box, a First World War army chaplain's cross; Carmen rollers, Doc Martens, 'Oor Wullie' cartoons, chewing gum, a biro, a MacDonald's hamburger; a duvet, a Roberts radio, the first Penguin paperback.[93]

In the Great Hall there are clocks at either end: a chiming clock made by Jas. Richie & Son in Edinburgh in 1921 and a 28-foot-tall pyramid of a clock made to celebrate the Millennium. Its base is a crypt; its body, a nave and a belfry; it is topped by a spire, a pietà. Within it are wheels, bells, chains, skulls, beasts, saints in chains. At its centre it is an ancient spirit, imprisoned by cogs and wheels, expressing the hopes and fears of the 21st century. It is, in the words of the sculptor and furniture maker Tim Stead, who made the base and the spire,[94] 'full of the past and the past is dark'.

There are more than three million objects in the museum's collections. Together they give a sense of Scotland, its land and its people, but it is inevitable and proper that much will remain unclear and unknown. The Lewis chessmen, found in c. 1831, witnesses of an ancient Scotland, remain an enigma. They sit there, carved from walrus-ivory, wide-eyed: kings and queens; bishops and knights; pawns and warders, each one individual within the hoard, the 'berserker' warder biting into his shield.

James Hutton closed his *Theory of the Earth* with the sentence, 'The result therefore of our present enquiry is that we find no vestige of a beginning – no prospect of an end.' He came to this conclusion by walking the 'small tract of land' that he owned in the Borders. In it, by looking aright, he could see Scotland, and the world, as Scots saw it and Scots as others see them. So, in the rooms of this museum, it is for us.

NATIONAL GALLERY OF SCOTLAND *****

The Mound, Edinburgh, Lothian EH2 2EL
Tel. 0131 624 6200
www.nationalgalleries.org/

Some of the loveliest paintings in the world: Titian's Venus, Poussin's Seven Sacraments, Botticelli's 'Wemyss Madonna', and the national collection of Scottish art, Allan Ramsay to the fore – all in a stylish, dramatic hang

'I can truly say that there is not in the whole of the Florentine collections any one picture for which I would exchange this picture of mine,' wrote Lord Wemyss[95] in 1859 about *The Virgin Adoring the Sleeping Christ Child* by Sandro Botticelli.

Acquired by the National Gallery of Scotland (NGS) in 1999, the Botticelli 'Wemyss Madonna' reinforces the position of the NGS in the first rank of galleries, a position long since established by and added to by the gallery's Scottish collection, its Impressionists and Post-Impressionists, and the Titians, Raphaels and Poussins that have been on loan from the Duke of Sutherland since 1948.

The gallery stands on the Mound between the Old and New Town, behind the Royal Scottish Academy (RSA). William Henry Playfair's neoclassical designs[96] for both buildings look sternly at Princes Street, whose shops grow more lurid yet standardised each year.[97]

Botticelli's The Virgin Adoring the Sleeping Christ Child *(the 'Wemyss Madonna')*
(National Gallery of Scotland)

Within, the ground-floor galleries have been returned to their original decoration[98] (dark-red walls, green carpet) and something of the original hang, with some of the lesser works skied. A skilful compromise has been found between how contemporary visitors expect, and think they want, to see them (close-up, at eye level) and how many of them were painted to be hung: five feet off the ground, viewed from fifteen feet away – hence the non-naturalistic extension of legs, in full-lengths, such as Van Dyck's *The Lomellini Family* or Raeburn's swaggering *Colonel Alastair Ranaldson Macdonell of Glengarry*. There are superb examples of the High Renaissance and it is not surprising that the layout of the galleries gives them priority. Upstairs are the early Italian and Northern collections and 18th- and 19th-century European paintings including those bequeathed by Sir Alexander Maitland in 1960 and 1965. In the basement is the Scottish collection. Distributed around the galleries are 16th–19th-century casts by Filippo Albacini, the pupil of Bartolomeo Cavaceppi,[99] and pieces of 18th-century furniture that, although of high quality,[100] have only tangential relevance to the paintings.

The gallery opened to the public in 1859 with paintings from three sources: the Royal Institution collection, which included three Van Dycks acquired by Andrew Wilson in Genoa in 1830, and a delicious, theatrical Tiepolo, *The Finding of Moses* (c. 1730s); a loan from Edinburgh University of the collection of Sir James Erskine of Torrie;[101] and the Royal Scottish Academy's collection of (mainly) Scottish pictures,[102] also on loan.

For the next fifty years the collection grew solely by gifts and bequests. In contrast to the experience of some galleries, where gifts have diluted or distorted collections, the NGS's were of quality and strengthened its founding collection. Robert Graham of Redgorten bequeathed in 1859 the ravishing *Honourable Mrs Graham* (1775–7) with which Gainsborough triumphed on his return, after an absence of five years, to the Royal Academy in 1777; two years later Lady Murray of Henderland bequeathed Allan Ramsay's delicate portrait of his second wife (1758),[103] and paintings by Watteau and Boucher; and in 1892 the brewer William McEwan gave Rembrandt's *A Woman in Bed*, whose identity is as mysterious as the pose: in bed; half-dressed; half-hidden behind the bed curtain; sensual, anxious, waiting.[104]

The gallery had neither purchasing funds nor a full-time director until the early 20th century and consequently could not develop its collections with the speed and authority that Sir Charles Eastlake and other directors gave to its sister National Gallery in London. At last in 1906 an Act of Parliament gave the gallery access to public finance and the following year Sir James Caw was appointed as director. He and his successor, the artist Sir Stanley Cursiter[105] (Director, 1930–48), enriched and widened the collection greatly: Caw by the purchase of works by Corot, Bastien-Lepage, Monet and Gauguin, and a magical Paul Bril, *Fantastic Landscape*;[106] Cursiter by acquiring a Bernardo Daddi triptych and a Filippino Lippi *Nativity with Two Angels*; and paintings by Constable and Wilkie, Degas and van Gogh.

Despite these, the prize works continued to be provided by gift (Henry Vaughan's collection of thirty-eight Turner watercolours in 1900 with the proviso that they would be exhibited each January and at no other time, to prevent them being exposed to strong daylight) and loan: the Hugo van der Goes *Trinity Altarpiece* lent from the Royal Collection in 1931, and the twenty-seven paintings lent since 1945 by the Duke of Sutherland, a loan more glorious than any other in Britain, comprising the 'Bridgewater Madonna' by Raphael; one of the finest, and most bleak, *Self-portraits* by Rembrandt, painted after his bankruptcy in 1658; Poussin's *Seven Sacraments*, exhibited to stunning effect in a small octagonal gallery; and five Titians that include the delicious, sensual *The Three Ages of Man*; *Diana and Callisto* and *Diana and Actaeon*; and *Venus Anadoymene*.[107] They have a glittering provenance, having been in the collections of Queen Christina of Sweden, until 1662, and of Philippe, Duc d'Orléans and his successors, from 1721 to 1798, before being acquired at the Orléans sale by a syndicate formed by the

Duke of Bridgewater, his nephew (later the 1st Duke of Sutherland) and the Earl of Carlisle.

Nevertheless the NGS's collection of Old Masters is neither comprehensive nor even representative. Rather it is illuminated by flashes of brilliance. Beside these Titians and Poussins, there are a sublimely beautiful Claude, *Landscape with Apollo and the Muses* (1652), an unusual Vermeer, *Christ in the House of Martha and Mary* (c. 1654) and Velásquez's *An Old Woman Cooking Eggs*, painted in 1618 when the artist was aged nineteen.

By contrast the Scottish collection is comprehensive, with paintings by every artist of note from John Scougall and George Jamesone in the 17th century to the Glasgow Boys (Sir James Guthrie, Sir John Lavery, George Henry, E. A. Hornel) at the end of the 19th century. It includes paintings by artists who are currently somewhat overlooked: the bold, expressive paintings of David Scott in whom the debt to William Etty is marked; and portraits by Andrew Geddes who, Cursiter noted in the 1940s, 'seems to have been a revelation to visitors to every great show of Scottish art for the past forty years, only to lapse from the public's memory again each time'.

Despite the pleasures of these and an excellent group of works by Sir David Wilkie,[108] it is Ramsay and Raeburn who bring true distinction to this collection. The fourteen Ramsay portraits tend to support Horace Walpole's comment that '[Ramsay and Raeburn] can scarcely be rivals their manners are so different ... Mr Raeburn seldom succeeds in women, Mr Ramsay is formed to paint them.' His portraits here of *Jean-Jacques Rousseau* and the steely *Sir Peter Halkett Wedderburn* put the counter-case but, faced by *The Artist's Wife* and the exquisite *Mrs Anna Bruce of Arnot*, they would have to concede the argument.

Set beside Ramsay, Raeburn's portraits can look genial, lacking in rigour. Yet this group of thirty-six canvases demonstrates that, if he was no Ramsay nor Gainsborough, yet by how much he excelled such contemporaries as Hoppner in technique (his treatment of material and costume, of skin and texture is subtle and fluent) as well as in his ability to convey the morality and understood proprieties of the day. His portraits are studies in serenity, self-command and good manners, yet they have humour (the dash, and the pink laces binding the skates, of *The Revd Robert Walker*) and, on occasion, breathless sexiness (*Mrs Robert Scott Moncreiff*).

After the Second World War the pace of acquisitions quickened: a lovely Camille Pissarro, *The Marne at Chennevières* in 1947; El Greco's *Christ Blessing* and Reynolds's portrait of Horace Walpole's great-nieces, *The Ladies Waldegrave*, in 1952. In 1958 Keith Andrew was appointed keeper of prints and drawings. This department, founded on the bequests of two Edinburgh antiquarian booksellers, David Laing and William Findlay Watson, at the end of the 19th century, was already strong, with sheets by Jordaens. Andrews now reorganised and enriched it, acquiring drawings by Pietro Testa and Seurat and Poussin's preparatory drawing for *A Dance to the Music of Time*, wilder, more Dionysian than the finished painting in the Wallace Collection (q.v.). Like Caw, Andrews bequeathed to the NGS works from his own collection, notably a *Self-portrait* by Palma Vecchio, once owned by Sir Peter Lely.

In recent years, under the directorship of Timothy Clifford,[109] the NGS has further enriched its collection with a series of brilliant coups, made with the help of the National Art Collections Fund, the National Heritage Memorial Fund (predecessor to the Heritage Lottery Fund) and public donations, at a time when most galleries have despaired of making major acquisitions.

El Greco's enigmatic, sinister *An Allegory* ('Fabula') was bought in 1989; Raphael's ravishing little study for *The Madonna of the Fish*[110] in 1993; Antonio Canova's *The Three Graces* in 1994,[111] and the Botticelli 'Wemyss Madonna' in 1999.

The size of the permanent collection demanded that new temporary exhibition spaces should be provided and in 2000 John Miller and Partners, the architects who designed the extension to Tate Britain, were commissioned to tunnel into the Mound and construct an underground link to the RSA, connecting once again Playfair's two great buildings.

ELGIN MUSEUM *

1 High Street, Elgin, Moray IV30 1EQ
Tel. 01343 543675
www.elginmuseum.demon.co.uk

Geology from when the Moray Firth was in India; mighty fossils

As the continents collided and fragmented many million years ago, land near the equator came to rest in what is today the Moray Firth. Fossil evidence of that life lay concealed in the Old Red Sandstone of the Firth until a group of amateur geologists, all friends, among them the Revd Dr George Gordon and Patrick Duff, the town clerk of Elgin, began to uncover this history. They founded the Elgin and Morayshire Scientific Society (1836), of which Duff was the secretary. In turn the society established the Elgin Museum in 1843, a single classical design in local stone by a local architect, Thomas MacKenzie.

Duff, who believed he had discovered the first Moray fish fossil,[112] stagonolepis, in 1844, was a friend of the celebrated geologist Hugh Miller of Cromarty (v. Stromness Museum). Miller[113] had found fish fossils in Cromarty as early as 1830[114] but he immediately recognised the potential riches of the Moray Firth and alerted geologists throughout Europe, including Louis Agassiz.

Gordon discovered the Triassic period fossil reptile hyderopedon (1850), later recognised by T. H. Huxley as being related to similar creatures found in Warwickshire, Devon and India. The fossil species *Gordonia* was named after him.

A second generation of local geologists, led by William Taylor and Dr William Mackie,[115] made discoveries of equal significance: the *Taylori* species of small fossils and the fossil plant *Asteroxylon mackiei*, 395 million years old, discovered in a chert near Rhymie, Aberdeenshire, in 1912.

Fish fossils from the Devonian period (*c.* 408–360 million years ago) are here: the only known examples of the lung fish (*Rhynchodipterus elginensis*), and of the lobe-finned *Glyptopomus elginensis*, both found at Rosebrae, in Quarrywood.

The region continues to yield up geological treasures. Reptile fossils from two periods have been found at Lossiemouth, Spynie and Findrassie (late Triassic, *c.* 220 million years old) and at Cutties Hillock (late Permian, 250 million years old). In 1997 a stonecutter working at Hopetown, near Elgin, observed an inconsistency, a hole in a rock. He called the museum and Carol Hopkins, the local expert and an Open University student, identified it as the mould of a fossil bone. An MRI scanner revealed it as a fossil three feet in length, with spines and bumps, a relation of the modern turtle. It was a mammal-like reptile, dicynodont, from the Permian period, and is one of the most important fossil discoveries of the late 20th century, proudly named *Elginia mirabilis*.

The museum has other objects of note: a good collection of Pictish stones (AD *c.* 500) carved with animals and geometric symbols; bulls from Burghead, the fort site (Torridun) that is the key to our understanding of the Picts; and Scotland's only extant coracle.

The museum continues to be run by the society, which was also made the custodian of a small but excellent collection of watercolours donated by Miss Etta Sharp of Rothes. She collected, with considerable discretion, works by the finest late-18th-century/early-19th-century watercolourists: Paul Sandby, Edward Dayes, John 'Warwick' Smith, Julius Caesar Ibbetson, Thomas Hearne, J. M. W. Turner, John Constable and David Cox: a collection worthy to share a building with Elgin's marvellous fossils.

WEST HIGHLAND MUSEUM **

Cameron Square, Fort William, Highland
PH33 6AJ
Tel. 01397 702169

Beautifully proportioned small museum, stuffed with Jacobite mementoes, keepsakes, glass and scraps

On the banks of Loch Linnhe, at the end of the Great Glen, Fort William is at the heart of the Highlands, and the point at which geology, history and myth meet.

The Great Glen fault runs south-west to north-east across Scotland, a rift almost from coast to coast. It is a turbulent landscape made by 'cauldron subsidence', surface lava sinking into underlying molten rock, causing outcrops such as Ben Nevis, which looks down on Fort William, and it is still subject to small earth tremors. Its stone is granite, 400 million years old; its minerals mica schist encrusted with particles of garnet (Glen Roy).

The museum was founded, almost single-handedly, by Victor Hodgson, an English architect who came to Appin on holiday, fell in love with the landscape and stayed. He opened it without a collection, indeed without one single object, and moved it to its present building, a former British Linen Bank in the town centre, in 1922.

Victor Hodgson was interested in archaeology and the museum has Mesolithic axes, flints and spearheads from when man first lived here 5,500 years ago. Of particular note is a jadeite axe, ground and polished (a Neolithic innovation), found in the River Spean in the 1890s. It is one of only 104 in Britain. They were imported from Continental Europe, there being no jadeite in these islands. The delicacy and thinness of its stone suggests it was a decorative or ritual axe.

The Gulf Stream brought drift seeds, nick-named 'molucca beans', to Scotland from the West Indies and South America. To find one was lucky and they were valued as charms to cure sterility and ease childbirth. This collection includes the relatively common *Entada gigas* and *Dioclea reflex*, and the rare, pearly *caesalpinia*, and *menemia* with its naturally occurring cross indentation.

In the surrounding glens is evidence of Bronze Age and Celtic communities: burial cists, vitrified forts and crannogs (lake dwellings constructed on platforms of timber and stone). A leather shoe, neatly stitched, survives from a crannog of the 6th or 7th century.

Here is a pair of Irish, late Bronze Age, gold penannular amulets from Kilmallie. They were found in 1871 by a crofter who was guided to the spot in a dream. His laird, and chief, Cameron of Lochiel, remitted his rent for life.

In the charms and incantations displayed here, the past lies in shadow: round stone rings to cure snake bites or nightmares; a 'witch's stone' of smooth, polished brown stone and a clach dubh, a black stone with the knowledge of mischief (both stones held evil at bay); the touchpieces, coins, given by Stuart kings to cure scrofula.

In 1815 Miss Unity Matthews sent a letter wrapped in a tartan silk hussif to her love, Colonel John Cameron of Fassifern, serving in Belgium with Wellington's army. In it she stitched a small square of satin containing pebbles and seeds (germander speedwell) and wrote: 'I trust it will save you from your enemy . . . it will be no great trouble to put it Round your Neck.' He did so, but to no avail, for he fell at Quatre Bras on the eve of Waterloo.

Fort William is heavy with history. The Marquis of Montrose, for Charles I, defeated the Earl of Argyll's Covenanters here in 1645. The old MacIain, chief of the MacDonalds of Glencoe, struggled into Fort William in a snowstorm on 30 December 1691 too late to take the oath of allegiance to William of Orange. His lateness gave Argyll the pretext to massacre the MacDonalds at Glencoe on 13 February 1692. Fifty years later Charles Edward Stuart, the Young Pretender, raised his standard at nearby Glenfinnan on 19 August 1745 and his Jacobite forces besieged the fort for twenty days the following March.

These last events make it appropriate that the largest Jacobite collection in Scotland should be here. At its heart are the archive of Cluny McPherson, bought in 1928, and the collections of Charles Hepburn, and of Alexander Carmichael, donated in 1991.

An embroidered silk waistcoat; a plaited cream silk sash, fringed at both ends; Charles Edward Stuart's blue bonnet, left at Moy Hall with Lady Mackintosh; his embroidered jacket: there is an entire wardrobe here, plus buckles, sleeve links, a peppermill and a fragment of his kilt. Here is an oak chair sent to the Prince by Lochiel when he raised his standard at Glenfinnan and a gnarled stick carried by MacDonald of Kinlochmoidart on that occasion.

As the Young Pretender, he captured the imagination of all Europe and his likeness was painted repeatedly, by Domenico Dupra (in 1739–40), Maurice Quentin de la Tour (1747) and Louis Tocque (1748); there is also a bust by J. B. Lemoyne in 1746 and, the best-known image, the 'Highlander portrait' by Sir Robert Strange in 1748. The West Highland Museum has an anamorphic portrait, whose swirls of colour coalesce into a likeness when a reflective cylinder is placed beside them. It has, too, his death mask.

Anything worn or used at the battle of Culloden has become a relic, sustaining the Jacobite myth for 250 years. Here are plenty.

Culloden was a tactical disaster: a depleted, exhausted and starving Jacobite army cut down by the Duke of Cumberland's forces which outnumbered, outgunned and out-manoeuvred it on ground that could not have been more ill-chosen. The Young Pretender wrote afterwards, 'the fatall field of Culloden has dashed all our hopes to pieces and has left us nothing to deliberate on but the mere safety of our person.'[116]

The myths were compounded by the atrocities committed by Cumberland's troops as they pursued the fugitive rebels. Jacobites in arms were killed outright, their houses burnt and their stock confiscated. In the mountains that overlook Fort William men took to the heather. McPherson of Cluny hid out for nine years in the 'natural caves in Benalder, Mealchnoch and other high

mountains'[117] in the summer months and, in the winter, in artificial caves such as that beneath the floor of Ralia's House owned by a MacPherson relative.

The memorabilia from Culloden here include a targe (shield), broadswords, dirks, hand cannon and powder horns: the arms with which the Highlanders defended themselves against the musket fire from the Hanoverian army. Here too are sporrans, cookpots, razors and medals left on the field of battle.

The most prized objects are those associated with Charles Edward Stuart and with Flora MacDonald (her shawl, quaich, buckles and sandalwood fan). 'The blessed memory' was sustained by Jacobite societies, a selection of whose wine glasses, engraved with thistles and mottoes, are here.

The lines between Jacobite life and literature have become blurred, not least by Walter Scott, R. L. Stevenson and D. K. Broster, but here, displayed on a wall, is the authentic long Spanish gun, called an t-Slinneanach, the 'black gun of misfortune',[118] with which the Appin murder was committed on 14 May 1752. Alan Breck Stewart (later the model for the fictional character in Stevenson's *Kidnapped*) was accused of killing the Crown factor, Colin Campbell of Glenure, on the Appin hillside overlooking Loch Linnhe. Alan Breck escaped to France. James Stewart of the Glen was hanged as an accessory to the crime, reading on the scaffold from Psalm 35, 'For they have privily laid their net to destroy me without charge . . . False witnesses did rise up: they laid to my charge things that I know not.'

In this landscape, memories are long. As you step out of the museum and walk the few yards down to the banks of Loch Linnhe, overlooking you are the great hills and the changing light that have long fostered Jacobite history, Jacobite myth.

MUSEUM OF SCOTTISH LIGHTHOUSES *

Kinnaird Head, Fraserburgh, Aberdeenshire
AB43 9DU
Tel. 01346 511022
www.lighthousemuseum.co.uk/

Collection of great Northern lights

Scotland has more than 7,000 miles of coastline, most of it wild and unforgiving, battered in winter by the North Sea and the Atlantic Ocean. In 1786 the Northern Lighthouse Board was established to build four lighthouses. Thomas Smith was appointed engineer to the board. His first lighthouse was at Kinnaird Head (1787), outside the fishing port of Fraserburgh, looking across the North Sea to Denmark and the Baltic.

Smith built on a point of rock beside Kinnaird Head Castle, designed in the late 16th century by Sir Alexander Fraser, the 8th Laird, who founded the town and built the harbour. When Robert Stevenson, Smith's son-in-law, redesigned the lighthouse in 1824,[119] he had to set the tower within Fraser's castle because Sir Walter Scott had campaigned to stop the old castle keep being demolished.

In 1991 a new, automatic light was erected a few yards away and the redundant lighthouse became this museum. Only half a dozen people can climb the seventy-two narrow spiral steps at any one time, up past the lighthouse keeper's room to the lamp, the optic, set at the pinnacle to which all in the building aspires.

The 1902 light, designed by David A. Stevenson, replaced Smith's 1787 fixed light. It sent its beam twenty-five miles out to sea, an eye through the storm. The highest wind speed recorded at low level anywhere in Britain was here on 13 February 1989 at 123 knots.

The present lamp is set in majesty. Three and a half tons of glass and metal revolve silently on steel rollers. Below it, chains, whose mechanism was adapted from the cuckoo clock, tick away each shift. All around are neat muslin curtains, drawn to protect the lens from reflecting the sun and causing fire, an ever-present danger in a lighthouse.

Each light is an individual with a unique signature, the time gap between beams. Kinnaird Head's is fifteen seconds. Together these signatures make a code of timed and soundless light that all ships' masters can read.

From the gantry outside, the visitor sees a panorama of town, harbour, coast, sea and sky within which the lighthouse itself is set. Lighthouse men too were indeed set apart. Their shifts (three weeks on, three weeks off) were sometimes extended for months if the seas did not allow supplies and relief to reach them. Inside they were locked into a rhythm of routine, centred on the needs of the light, its maintenance, its timing, its power. Concentration was everything, a second's inattention fatal. Their room was spartan; they were forbidden to read or write; their only recreations were handcrafts, in leather or wood.

Back on the ground, where twenty-foot cast-iron buoys are strewn like giants' playthings, there are excellent videos in the former lighthouse keeper's house: *The Northern Lights* made by the BBC in 1968 and narrated by Tom Fleming, and filmed interviews with men who served in lighthouses. For once film and video augment, rather than distract from, experience.

In the reception building are objects and an archive that add helpful detail: a copy of 'the General Order Book, CXIV, regarding the neglect of Duty' by Alex Cunningham, secretary, 1870; uniforms; lifebelts; tables showing the lighting and extinguishing of lights expressed in Greenwich Mean Time; the family tree and brief history of Thomas Smith and four generations of Stevensons from Robert (1772–1850) to David Alan (1891–1971), including Robert's nephew, Robert Louis (1850–94). Each generation added to the technology of lights: Alan (1807–65) the dioptic lens (1851); David (1854–1938) a new lens assembly giving 690,000 candlepower. Jane Stevenson's Bell Rock flag (1820), embroidered with a ship in full sail and a huge Saltire, is here, as are letters between Alan Stevenson and William Wordsworth while Stevenson was building the Skerryvore lighthouse.

A wall of enamel nameplates charts the lighthouses of Scotland: Bell Rock and Bass Rock; Flannan Isle, Fair Isle; Auskerry, Sule Skerry, Skerryvore; Sanda, Stroma, Pladda, Roma; Ailsa Craig, Rhu Vaal, Oronsay, Holy Island.

The optics of several of them have been gathered here, each different in design, the lenses usually horizontal, Fair Isle's dropping vertically – a rigid inverted chandelier. From them the white walls of the building are bathed in a flow of light.

GAIRLOCH HERITAGE MUSEUM *

Achtercairn, Gairloch, Highland IV21 2BP
Tel. 01445 712287

Life in Gairloch from prehistoric times: Pictish stone, agriculture, recreated croft and schoolroom holding a tragedy; a testament to the fortitude of the hardworking poor

From the east the visitor approaches Gairloch on the Destitution Road[120] past Beinn Eighe and along the shores of Loch Maree, finally winding down a wooded defile into Gairloch harbour and beyond to a long beach of pink sand. On the horizon is the Isle of Skye. This is where the road west ends.

People have lived here since the Stone Age, making a precarious living from the sea and from the reluctant pasture. In a modest building, converted from a farm steading, this museum tells of the parish of Gairloch and of rural life. The pipes and drums of Scottish history, of kings, rebellions and governments, sound at a distance.

It is a history that goes back more than four thousand years, marked here by a stone axe head and a carved stone ball, possibly a symbol of power, as is the Gairloch ingot, excavated in 1972 and now in the Museum of Scotland (q.v.). It may have been a blank from which a dagger blade was to have been beaten.[121]

Gairloch has never provided an easy living. An attempt in the 17th century by Sir George Hay to establish an iron smelting works beside Loch Maree failed, but not before over 20,000 acres of forest had been felled to feed the furnaces. The economy returned to fish, wool and whisky, all devastated by the 1846 famine.

The museum has collections that illustrate the foundations upon which parish life was built: the school, the chapel, the village shop, and the croft.

The 1878 logbook for the Sand School (forty pupils in 1899), built following the 1873 Education Act, which made schooling compulsory, notes that the school was closed for twelve weeks in 1882 by an epidemic of diphtheria. The teacher, writing in his lovely, flowing, looped hand, records the deaths of his own three children, aged 7, 3½ and 1½. Eight former pupils were killed in the First World War: four in France, three at sea and one at the Dardanelles, serving with the Australian Infantry Regiment.

There is a photograph of Roddie MacLean in his shop, serving. What he sold is on the shelves of the recreated shop:[122] Linlow's Dundee toffee; Sloan's liniment; tins of Varnene oil varnish and of oatmeal; Zelso grate polish; a case of Bovril, corned beef and a large jar of Zubes which 'Defy Fog and Damp'. Postcards, 'Real photos of Loch Maree and Gairloch' in the 'Best of All' series, were 1s. 6d. for a set of twelve. On the wall is a 1957 timetable for the bus to Ullapool, sixty miles to the north-east. The charge was £1 return.

For a scattered community, distances assume particular importance, as does a postal service. Gairloch and two other communities opened post offices in the 1850s. A further eight opened in the 1890s as literacy grew, until by 1914 there were sixteen in total. In the 1990s the process was reversed, with three of them closing.

The museum records other aspects of parish life. There is a shoe maker's workshop from the early 20th century complete with lasts, hammer, a buffing and grinding machine, a leather palm strap, beeswax and an Armed Services Bible in Gaelic, presented to the shoe maker, Alexander Grant, in 1916. There is a bier for carrying coffins from Alligin, by land or sea, to the burial ground at Annat.

There are the amusements of the lairds, a fishing basket, trout and salmon rods and a stalker's telescope.

The museum also records the schisms and divisions of religious life in Gairloch over the past three hundred years. Nine times have sections of the church split, to form the Free Church, the Free Presbyterian Church and the Free Church Continuing, this last only in 2000. The first Presbyterian minister, sent to Gairloch in 1711, the Revd John Morrison, so offended his parishioners, who still clung to Episcopalianism, that they imprisoned him and his servant for five days in a shed with cattle. Undeterred, he continued to preach, so they stripped him naked and bound him to a tree for the pleasure of the midges. He was transferred to Urray. A travelling pulpit (a shed on wheels with a flap) is a reminder of the years 1892–1920, when the Free Presbyterians held services, in Gaelic, in the open air, on the 'preaching ground' outside the village.

There are three further elements deep-laid in this museum: fish, wool and the land. Wool has been the staple of Gairloch's economy for hundreds of years. Here unroll its many textures and definitions: the shearing, the carding, the spinning, the plying, the dyeing, the winding, the weaving – a dictionary of wool. Herring and saithe, for food and for trade, were important until large-scale commercial fishing destroyed the dependable plenty of the sea. In contrast, the land, a thin skimming over the rocks of Lewisian gneiss, has only grudgingly yielded up a living, save for the wool and peat.

This is a modest museum that well conveys its community, self-reliant, resilient, quietly proud. How lives have been lived here is worth the recording. Sorley MacLean, the Gaelic poet of the highlands and islands, writes of

Smoke of the generations climbing
over peaks of memory of varying value,
the great men and the small
appearing and being lost in the hardship
that squinting fortune gives, or the choice
made by vision and devotion.[123]

BURRELL COLLECTION ★★★★

Pollok Country Park, 2060 Pollokshaws Road, Glasgow, Strathclyde G43 1AT
Tel. 0141 287 2550, fax 0141 287 2597
www.glasgowmuseums.com

Shipowner Sir William Burrell's vast eclectic collection of decorative arts in a highly intelligent building designed to hold and reveal it

The Burrell Collection is on the edge of a wood overlooking Pollok Park. When Sir William Burrell (1861–1958) gave his great collection to the city of Glasgow in 1944 he specified that it should be housed at least sixteen miles from the noise and pollution of the city centre.[124] His trustees in the 1970s settled for this site between woodland and meadow.

The architect of the building, Barry Gasson, celebrates the site by placing the long north wall of glass up against the wood so that chestnuts and sycamores appear to enter the galleries, the light diffused through their branches continually moving through the days and the seasons.

If the distinction between landscape and museum is blurred, so too is that between building and collection. You enter through a 14th-century sandstone arch and great double doors of oak. The arch and the portal beyond (both 16th century) are from Hornby Castle in Yorkshire and were formerly in the collection of the American newspaper magnate William Randolph Hearst. Between them is a covered courtyard flooded with light in which are fig trees, bronzes[125] and, in the centre, the War-wick vase, an 18th-century reconstruction[126] of the 2nd-century original, the torsion of its twisted handles contrasting with the delicacy of its acanthus leaves. The vase was purchased by the trustees in 1979, one of only a small number of objects in the collection that Burrell did not choose himself.

The vase is a noble work of great beauty but it is somewhat misleading, as the collection contains very few classical Greek or Roman pieces and no neoclassical. Burrell's taste was

broad. He loved German armour and English woodwork; Chinese ceramics and 19th-century French painting; Assyrian sculpture and European stained glass; medieval church relics and Eastern carpets. He was drawn to forms, colours and textures that were rich and strong. He admired Egyptian and Mesopotamian antiquities; his Renaissance was robust, northern. The Italy he favoured was Etruscan.

In over sixty-five years of collecting his enthusiasms waxed and waned: the best of his 150 tapestries were bought in the 1920s and '30s; he acquired no carpets after 1940; stained glass and antiquities were the interests of his later years, the 1940s and '50s. But, throughout, his abiding love was for Gothic and early Renaissance northern Europe from the 14th to 17th centuries. It is not surprising that those parts of his collection whose works are surpassed in Britain only by the Victoria and Albert Museum (q.v.) (the tapestries and stained glass) are from this period, nor that they feature in the re-creation of three of the rooms from his home, Hutton Castle.

Gasson groups these rooms round the Courtyard so that there is a source of light to illuminate their panels of stained glass, while the rooms themselves with their linenfold panelling, oak furniture, stone chimney pieces and tapestries remain quietly lit. Indeed all the period rooms, and on the mezzanine level the picture galleries, are clustered in the middle of the building, leaving the full blaze of natural light for the galleries of oriental art, the antiquities, the bronzes and the remainder of the stained glass.

Among the antiquities are works of arresting beauty: a black granite head of the lioness goddess Sekhmet;[127] a chunk of pink-, black- and gold-flecked granite from which the profile of *Rameses II* emerges with its fixed smile;[128] a life-sized head of a snarling lion from the Isin/Larsa period in Babylon;[129] a 7th-century BC bronze bull's head from Urartu,[130] north of Assyria. Burrell bought from dealers for aesthetic rather than archaeological reasons and the artefacts are presented

The Warwick vase in the Burrell Collection

like that, individually, in free-standing elegant glass cases on a plain stone floor.

In the next gallery the Chinese jades and ceramics are in wall cabinets. Buying them throughout his life, Burrell assembled a representative collection from the Neolithic period to the 18th century. In addition to a fine range of Song Dynasty ware (Longqhan celadon, Ru, Jun, cracked Guan, white Ginghai, black Henan) the collection has a fine group of Tang Dynasty[131] grave figures: horses, camels and the less common fangxiang figures in exaggerated, curious human forms.

Upstairs is the most baffling part of the collection, the paintings. In the 1880s and '90s Burrell's taste was for the Hague School[132] (the Maris brothers; Anton Mauve, a cousin of Vincent van Gogh). They were popular precisely because they were bland. He began by buying the French equivalents – Monticelli, Bonvin – but graduated in the 1920s to Daumier, Manet, Degas and, in 1937, one superb Cézanne, *Chateau de Médan*, quite outside his natural taste. The eighteen Degas are the finest collection of his work in Britain, surpassing those at the National Gallery, the Courtauld Collection or the National Museum and Gallery of Wales (all q.v.). *The Rehearsal* (c. 1877); the portrait of Degas's dealer *Edmond Duranty* (1879); a pastel, *Woman in her Bath* (c. 1884), the pentimenti conveying her shifting movement as she reaches for the bottom of her spine; *Jockeys in the Rain* (c. 1886), another pastel whose marks capture the suppressed excitement of the horses – all are supreme.

There are other good paintings here: Lucas Cranach the Elder's *The Stag Hunt* (1529), Hans Memling's *The Annunciation* (c. 1460), an early self-portrait (1632) by Rembrandt, a beautiful Alfred Sisley, *The Bell Tower at Noisy-le-Roi* (1874). But there are too many works that seem to have been bought for the celebrity of the artist rather than the quality of the painting.

Downstairs in the medieval heart of the collection, the tapestries, the stained glass, the ecclesiastical artefacts, there are no such uncertainties. The panels of stained glass include early 12th-century panels commissioned by

Abbot Suger, described by Louis VII as the 'father of his country'; the rich colour of 15th-century German artists; the cooler style of the 16th century with its detail borrowed from engravings; the simplicity of English armorial glass of the 16th century. Here you can see them all, close up, as you cannot in a church, and appreciate their rich variety, as you can the tapestries in the Tapestry Gallery: the beauty of the embroidery on the clothes in the German *Adoration of the Magi* (1471–80), the inter-weaving of figures in *The Camp of the Gypsies* (Franco-Netherlandish, early 16th century), the wit and detail of *Peasants Hunting Rabbits with Ferrets* (Franco-Burgundian, *c.*1450–75, probably from Pasquier Grenier's workshop in Tournai), the interlocking squares, circles and quatrefoils of the Luttrel table carpet (either Ely or the Netherlands, mid 16th century).

In all these it is Burrell's love of objects that is impressive. There is no painting or photo-graph here of either him or his wife, Con-stance, none of the vainglory of an Arthur Gilbert (v. the Gilbert Collection). He loved every aspect of collecting: the choosing, the assessment, the comparison, the valuation, the competition, the bargaining, the decision and the ownership.[133] He was as cautious in his acquisitions, always taking expert advice,[134] as he and his brother were bold in business, building their shipping fortune by the simple but terrifying strategy of ordering large num-bers of new ships in a slump[135] in the (un-certain) knowledge that, come the recovery, the demand for new ships would reward them.

That love of objects is nowhere more appar-ent than in his collection of medieval church figures: the tiny, simple boxwood *Virgin and Christ* (French, 14th century), the swayed, wil-lowy *St John and the Virgin* (Spanish, poly-chrome, late 13th century), three knights of the bronze-gilt *Temple Pyx* (12th century), each a personality, patient behind his shield, and the painted alabaster *Holy Trinity* (English, *c.*1375–85). The Trinity is seldom depicted. Here the Father sits, Christ crucified on the Cross between his knees, a group of human souls hanging from the Father's neck in a sling, the Holy Ghost: a collective mystery appropri-ate to a great collection.

GLASGOW MUSEUM AND ART GALLERY ★★★★

Argyle Street, Glasgow, Strathclyde G3 8AG
Tel. 0141 287 2699
www.glasgowmuseums.com

Bold, energetic collections from extinct birds to French Impressionists and more, in an enormous confident building expressive of Glasgow's presiding nature; vast, never tiring

In a city notable for its 19th-century architec-ture, the Glasgow Museum and Art Gallery at Kelvingrove nonetheless stands out. Staring proudly up at Glasgow University across the River Kelvin and the park, it is a massive building in vivid red sandstone, designed (1891–1910) by the London architects John W. Simpson and E. J. Milner Allen.[136]

The building is a bravura mixture of styles, described by the architects as 'on severely classic lines, but with free Renaissance treat-ment in detail': part Hispanic baroque (the two massive towers derive from the Cathedral of Santiago de Compostela), part northern European Gothic (the steeply pitched roof). Its exterior is decorated with sculptures and reliefs, by George Frampton and others.[137] Within the Centre Hall, arcaded, three storeys high, is a large carved shield of the Scottish lion rampant and the motto 'LET GLASGOW FLOURISH'.

When it opened in 1901, the Glasgow Corporation filled it with its scientific and historical collections, previously housed near by in Kelvingrove House,[138] and with its col-lections of fine and decorative art that since 1856 had been in the McLellan Galleries in Sauchiehall Street.[139] The first entry in the museum register, in March 1870, had been from the Natural History Collection and the second was for 'two Japanese swords,

Raeburn's Mrs William Urquhart *at Glasgow*

presented by Mr Young'.[140] The arms and armour are indeed remarkable, a bequest by Robert Lyons Scott, who gave the remainder of his collection to the McManus Galleries in Greenock (q.v.), where he was chairman of the Scott Shipbuilding and Engineering Company. Here is his European armour, a Gothic Milanese field armour (c.1450), formerly owned by the American newspaper magnate William Randolph Hearst, and the Greenwich armour for man and horse (c.1550–58) that was worn by William Herbert, 1st Earl of Pembroke (1501?–1570) at the battle of St Quentin in 1557 and is the only example of its type to survive.

The Archaeology Collection has material from William Flinders Petrie's excavations in the 1880s and '90s; the Ethnography Collection contains African artefacts with the handwritten tag 'Collected by Dr Livingstone and bequeathed by T. S. Livingstone'. This rich mixture was recalled in 1936 by the first director of Glasgow Museums and Galleries, James Eggleton: 'The objects it contained promoted wonderment within them – the ring of alum, the model of the brougham, the pulpit, Edinburgh castle in cork, the nugget of gold, the stuffed birds and the very much alive fish in the aquarium – all contributed delight in the halcyon days of summer holidays and the brief respite from school of the Saturday forenoons.'

Notwithstanding these delights it is upon the fine and decorative art collections that the museum and gallery's reputation rests.

Archibald McLellan (1797–1854) was a rich carriage builder who collected Italian, Dutch and Flemish paintings for thirty years with the intention of bequeathing them to the city. In doing so he overstretched himself and died deep in debt. The Glasgow Corporation settled the claims against his estate and acquired his collection for £44,500. It included works by Ruisdael, Hobbema and De Heem, but the outstanding painting was *The Adulteress Brought before Christ* (c.1508–10),[141] attributed to Giorgione and subsequently in the Orléans Collection. In 1971 the gallery succeeded in acquiring a fragment from the right-hand side of the picture that had been cut away at some stage (*Head of a Man*).

Around it the gallery assembled a small group of excellent 15th-century Italian paintings: Giovanni Bellini's *The Madonna with the Child Blessing*; and, from further bequests, Botticelli's *The Annunciation* (late 1490s), in which the Angel Gabriel is separated from the Virgin by the severe, sharply receding architecture; his pupil Filippino Lippi's *Madonna and Child with the Infant St John and Two Angels*; and a *Nativity* by Francesco Francia, part of a predella.[142]

One of the museum's most important gifts is *A Man in Armour* (c.1655), once owned by Joshua Reynolds.[143] A Rubens, *Nature Adorned by the Graces* (c.1615), painted on his return to Antwerp jointly with Jan Brueghel the Elder,[144] was bequeathed by John Gilbert-Graham.

There had been enthusiasm in Glasgow for contemporary French painting since Craibe Angus opened a gallery in 1874 selling the works of the Hague[145] and Barbizon Schools, as did Daniel Cottier in his gallery. In the 1890s Alexander Reid, who had worked for the Paris fine art dealers Boussod and Valadon, where Theo van Gogh was also an assistant, began to sell Impressionist paintings.[146] The influence of these pioneering dealers on such collectors as James Donald and William Chrystal, Sir William Burrell and Sir John Richmond, was marked but it was not until these private collections began to be bequeathed that the gallery reflected the influence of these dealers.

Still more significant was the period that T. J. Honeyman spent as a dealer with Alex Reid and Lefèvre in the 1930s. In 1939 he was appointed Director of Glasgow Museums and Galleries. With fine art prices depressed by the war he bought Derain's *Blackfriars* (c.1906) (the brilliant blues of the barges and the London skyline, in Derain's words, 'charges of dynamite') for £142.

With the help of money from the Hamilton Trust (1927) and a windfall from William McInnes, Honeyman transformed the collection. McInnes, another client of Alex Reid, had a superb collection. Its seventy paintings included Monet's *Vétheuil* (1880), van Gogh's

Le Moulin de Blute-Fin, Montmartre (1886), Degas's *Dancers on a Bench* (pastel, *c.* 1898), the Cézanne still life *Overturned Basket of Fruit* (*c.* 1877) and Matisse's *The Pink Table Cloth* (*c.* 1925).

Honeyman was one of the outstanding directors in Britain in the 1940s. His rare combination of scholarship and commercial flair shaped this excellent collection of 19th- and 20th-century French painting. It has its weaknesses (no Impressionist painting from the early years, the 1870s; no early Cubists; no works by Chagall; no late Gauguins) but no other British collection takes you with such authority from Corot, Millet and Rousseau, and the early days of the Barbizon School, to Picasso, Braque and Matisse a century later.

In doing so it demonstrates the influence that French art has had on the late 19th- and early 20th-century Scottish painters represented here, notably on the Glasgow Boys and the Scottish Colourists. Like their English contemporaries the Newlyn School, the Glasgow Boys looked to Bastien-Lepage. Unlike the Newlyn artists, their influences spread widely: Japan on George Henry, and such American landscape artists as Moran on T. Millie Dow and James A. McNeill Whistler on James Guthrie and John Lavery.[147]

Under pressure from the Glasgow Boys, the Glasgow Corporation had bought Whistler's great *Arrangement in Grey and Black No. 2: Portrait of Thomas Carlyle* (1872–3)[148] in which the seated, profile pose is almost identical to that in *Arrangement No. 1* (of Whistler's mother, now in the Musée d'Orsay, Paris). Guthrie's fine *Old Willie – the Village Worthy* (1886) borrows Whistler's sombre palette, penetrating attention to detail, and precision and balance of all elements in the painting (the 'Arrangement'), including the placing of the artist's name (in Whistler's case his signature butterfly).

The influences on the Colourists (S. J. Peploe, J. D. Fergusson, G. L. Hunter and F. C. B. Cadell), a generation younger, were the Fauves, Cézanne and Matisse. Later still William Johnstone and William Gillies studied under André Lhote in Paris and the influ-

ence of Picasso and Braque runs through the work here of Scottish artists as dissimilar as Gillies, Anne Redpath, Robert MacBryde and Robert Colquhoun.

The width of the gallery's collections allows you to see these artists in the context of the history of Scottish, and English, painting since the 17th century: of Ramsay and Raeburn; Reynolds and Gainsborough; Wilson and Constable; Wilkie and Nasmyth. The museum's collection of British paintings from the 17th to 19th centuries is typical rather than exceptional, but there are two of Raeburn's most sympathetic portraits (of the beautiful *Mrs William Urquhart* (*c.* 1813) and the dramatically lit *Mr and Mrs Robert Campbell of Kailzie*). There are also surprises: two landscapes by Jacob More (*Morning* and *Evening,* 1785) that show why More was so admired by Goethe and why Reynolds considered him 'the best painter of air since Claude'. Only his comparatively early death and his residence in Rome have held back his reputation in Britain.

To an extent possible in few other major galleries the collections here provide a wide decorative arts context for the gallery's paintings. James Paton, superintendent from 1876 to 1914, founded the Decorative Arts collections, which are, thanks to major bequests of silver and glass by Victor Cumming (1945) and of jewellery by Mrs Anne Hall Grundy, particularly strong in Scottish and English works of the past 200 years. Furniture by Charles Rennie Mackintosh,[149] George Logan and E. A. Taylor, the most brilliant of Mackintosh's contemporaries, complements the work of the Glasgow Boys. The collection is strong in Scottish metalwork and in the Glasgow style.

This is a treasure house in which you can wander and make connections between geology and ceramics, armour and sculpture, the art of 19th-century Africa and that of Scotland today. A major redesign of the museum will (2003–6) facilitate those wanderings and connections. Within it you may find a museum within the museum, a metaphor for the whole, the Seton Murray Thomson Collection. It comprises 449 representations of the horse, from all over the world. The oldest is Cypriote (15th century BC); the most recent comes from F. W. Woolworth & Co. There are horses here in jade and chalcedony; malachite and ivory; wax and bone; silver, glass and celluloid. They take a variety of forms: a candlestick, a tile, a toy, a buckle, a meerschaum pipe. All that Murray Thomson demanded was that each was a good representation of a horse, just as Kelvingrove is a good representation of a museum.

ST MUNGO MUSEUM OF RELIGIOUS LIFE AND ART *

2 Castle Street, Glasgow, Strathclyde G4 0RH
Tel. 0141 553 2557, fax 0141 552 4744
www.glasgowmuseums.com

Panoptic review of the religions of the world without prejudice

The St Mungo Museum of Religious Life and Art is that rarity: a museum that seeks 'to reflect the central importance of religion in human life'.[150] It is sited a few yards from Glasgow Cathedral in a former visitor centre that was converted in 1990 into three galleries by architects Page and Park Ltd in association with Iain Begg. From the top floor there is a view east across the city past the cathedral to the city's Necropolis on a hill in Fir Park. Against the skyline is the 1825 monument to John Knox in a Geneva gown, holding a Bible. A museum of religious life in Glasgow does not want for material.

The museum is named after the 6th-century patron saint of Glasgow, St Kentigern, better known by his familiar name St Mungo,[151] who is believed to have brought Christianity to the area. Since St Mungo was not written about until the 12th century, by Bishop Jocelyn, stories about how St Mungo's mother St Thenog was raped, thrown from a cliff, set adrift without oars and rescued by monks at Culcross to give birth to St Mungo have to be treated with some caution.

The museum's displays draw on Glasgow's vast collections. They concentrate on religion in Scotland, with artefacts from Neolithic times (a jadeite axe, 2000–3000 BC), from the Bronze Age (a beaker from Kilmartin, v. Kilmartin House Museum), and from the Roman occupation (a 2nd-century altar) before they tackle the trials of Christianity in Scotland (a Roman Catholic Bible in Latin beside a Post-Reformation Bible; a Covenanter's sword; a Catholic rosary; an 18th-century moderator's gown and an Orange drum from the 1940s).

The displays show the Scottish religion exported (by missionaries and by such explorers as David Livingstone, who wrote on 4 December 1857, 'I go back to Africa to try to make an open path for commerce and Christianity') and imported (plaques to commemorate the Muslim and Baha'i faiths, a plaque for the Lascar sailors who worked the Queen's Dock, c. 1900, an image of the Polish Black Madonna; and the songbook from Billy Graham's meeting at Kelvin Hall in 1955).

The collection is rich in works of religious art: an alabaster pietà (c. 1400), by the Rimini Master; a bronze Shiva Nataraja (c. 1800); stained glass by Edward Burne-Jones and William Morris for Woodlands Parish Church (1882), an adaptation of 13th-century grisaille with a delicate palette of rose pinks, blues and greens and a painting by Salvador Dalí, *Christ of St John of the Cross*. It was bought in 1952 at the insistence of the city's director of museums, Dr Tom J. Honeyman, with the last of the fund set up from the profits of the Kelvingrove International Exhibition of 1901.[152]

Inspired by a pen and ink drawing by the Spanish Carmelite friar who was canonised as St John of the Cross, Dalí has depicted Christ, as did St John, from above, looking down, his body precipitously foreshortened. Below him and beneath striations of cloud is the rocky harbour of Dalí's home village of Port Lligat in Spain.

The painting angered many. Lovers of contemporary painting complained that in eschewing Surrealism Dalí was retreating into the past; students at Glasgow School of Art protested that the money should have been spent on encouraging Scottish artists. Honeyman recognised the strange beauty that Dalí creates through an unblemished figure of Christ crucified. In a letter to Glasgow Art Gallery in 1952 Dalí wrote: 'My aesthetic ambition in this picture was completely the opposite of all the Christs painted by most of the modern painters, who have all interpreted him in the expressionistic and contortionistic sense, thus obtaining emotion through ugliness. My principal preoccupation was that my Christ would be as beautiful as the God that He is.'

In a gallery of 'Religious Life' consideration is given to the ways in which different religions approach the mysteries: birth, death, life after death. To attempt this is ambitious and, especially regrettably here, reductive. Glimpses of a 15th-century English alabaster carving, *The Saved Entering Heaven*, or of a 16th/17th-century Ming stoneware figure of *Yenle, King of the Dead*, convey little, particularly when no distinction has been made between different concepts of deity or even between those who may or who may not be permitted to be represented in human form.

Outside, a Zen Garden has been made by Yasutaro Tanaka (1993). The museum informs us that the garden suggests 'the land, sea and mountains in miniature, reflecting the principle of seeing more in less, part of the Zen method of contemplation. There are many ways of interpreting the Garden, and it is part of the tradition that everyone will see different things in it.'[153]

Glasgow is a city of many faiths in which religion is a highly charged issue. The museum, in promoting debate and dialogue about faiths, takes an admirably non-sectarian approach. It is the argument of faith that has priority rather than the awe and passion that may be expressed in ritual, in music or in architecture.

Fifty yards away is Glasgow Cathedral. Built in the 13th century, it has been the focus of every tide of religious belief in the city for the past 700 years. Here in the air between soaring perpendiculars hangs the wonder that the museum lacks, a place in which may be renewed, expressed or even discovered the faith that is of 'central importance', the mystery of religion.

GALLERY OF MODERN ART **

Royal Exchange Square, Glasgow, Strathclyde
G1 3AH
Tel. 0141 229 1996
www.glasgowmuseums.com

Bold, unsnobbish collection housed in the old Royal Exchange; a refreshing openness to modern art of other cultures

For a brief period in the late 1980s and early 1990s Glasgow lit up the sky. The Burrell Collection (q.v.) opened, at last, in 1983, followed by a gang of new galleries for contemporary work including Third Eye. A stream of young artists came out of the Glasgow School of Art: John Byrne, Ken Currie, Steven Campbell, Peter Howson, Jock MacFadyen, Bruce McLean, Alison Watt. In 1990 the city was chosen as the European City of Culture.

A new confidence ran through the city council. In 1988 Pat Lally, leader of the council, appointed the then director of Manchester City Art Galleries, Julian Spalding, to oversee Glasgow's museums and, the following year, made available to Spalding a £3 million fund to buy contemporary art. To house the new collection the council converted the old Royal Exchange, designed in 1827 by David Hamilton as the mansion of a Glasgow tobacco magnate, William Cunninghame. The pillars, marble walls and splendid ceilings of the main hall make a surprisingly effective setting for contemporary art.

Few British cities in the 20th century have created a museum of modern art from scratch. With the agreement of the council Spalding imposed on himself and on his senior curator of art, Stefan van Raay,[154] two conditions: that only the work of living artists would be acquired and that the collection would not be confined to Scottish or British artists. In

creating such a collection Spalding was determined 'to remain open-minded and responsive to the art that is actually being produced today' and 'to look particularly for art that seems to spring naturally . . . from a society and people's lives of which it is part. Such art had more chance of being truly modern, because it will be a real product of its age, of what it has been like to experience life today.'[155]

The original displays featuring Scottish, English and international artists were hugely controversial both with the public and with art critics. The public were surprised, and engaged, by the works of such artists as Niki de Saint-Phalle and by paintings by Aboriginal artists (Lindsay Bird Mpetyane, Robert Campbell); the art critics less so by the gallery's inclusive view that mixed such popular artists as Beryl Cook, generally scorned by public collections, and the playful sculptures of Eduard Bersudsky with sculptures and paintings by established artists (Sir Anthony Caro, Bridget Riley, David Hockney, Alan Davie) and those who were relatively unknown (Nick Waplington).

Scottish artists are well represented in the founding collection, not only by those from the Glasgow School of Art but by those of an earlier generation, William Gear and Sir Robin Philipson. In the delicate, painterly studies of flowers and cats of Elizabeth Blackadder, in William Gear's abstractions, in Craigie Aitchison's *Crucifixion* and in Peter Howson's violent, muscular study of yobs, bone and bull terriers, *Patriots* (1991), the breadth is as obvious as it is in the English artists chosen: David Hockney, Andy Goldsworthy and Jenny Saville. There are relatively few photographers but those that are here are of the highest quality, including Henri Cartier-Bresson and the Brazilian Magnum photographer Sebastião Salgado.

But it is the work of the artists Spalding found from Mexico, Australia, New Guinea and Hong Kong that is unlike painting in any other British public gallery. The Aboriginal

The Night Sky Dreaming *by Paddy Japaljarri Sims (Gallery of Modern Art)*

The Night Sky Dreaming (1993) by Paddy Japaljarri Sims appears at first sight to be a richly coloured painting of myriad dots that calls to mind the work of Chris Ofili. In fact it is a collective, ceremonial painting, made over three weeks as part of the storytelling associated with the night sky ceremony, re-enacted approximately every twenty years: a map of the skies of shimmering luminescence.

Spalding's successor, Victoria Hollows, is continuing to develop the gallery with new acquisitions and temporary exhibitions by such major artists as David Mach, Anthony Gormley, Peter Howson, Nancy Spero and Bill Viola, justifying Julian Spalding's assertion, in 1996, that '[This] is only a beginning.'

HUNTERIAN ART GALLERY
★★★★

University of Glasgow, Glasgow, Strathclyde G12 8QQ
Tel. 0141 330 4221
www.gla.ac.uk/Museum

The best of Whistler; and Stubbs, Ramsay, Rembrandt too, beside Charles Rennie Mackintosh's house, transported here

In the same way that the Courtauld Collection is associated with the French Impressionists and Post-Impressionists so is the Hunterian Art Gallery with James McNeill Whistler and Charles Rennie Mackintosh. In each case the association is misleading, as the collections of both galleries go considerably wider.

The gallery's founding collection is that of Dr William Hunter (1718–83), anatomist and pioneer in obstetrics. He wrote in 1768, 'I am pretty much acquainted with most of our best artists and live in friendship with them.' Allan Ramsay was a friend from the 1730s when they were students at Edinburgh University and his portrait of Hunter, aged about forty-five, shows a canny eye and resolute mouth. He began collecting in his mid-thirties with a *Panoramic Landscape* by Philips de Koninck, which he mistook for 'a capital work by Rembrandt' and for which he gave sixteen

guineas. Scholars have subsequently shown that he was similarly mistaken about a 'Titian' and a 'Correggio' but he bought three outstanding Chardins and, in 1771, a tiny oil sketch, *The Entombment of Christ*,[156] that is indeed by Rembrandt.

However it is the work of his contemporaries (Reynolds's fine stern portrait of *Lady Maynard*, and three superb paintings of a *Bull Moose*, 1783, a *Blackbuck*, c. 1770–80, and *The Nylghai*, 1769, which he commissioned[157] from Stubbs as illustrations for lectures on natural history), that distinguish his collection.

There are other 18th-century portraits here by Hudson, Ramsay, Romney and Raeburn. The portrait by Reynolds of the beautiful actress and courtesan *Nelly O'Brien* (c. 1763–7) is a different pose from that in his portrait of her in the Wallace Collection (q.v.). Both Hudson (*Barbara Bagot*, 1749) and Ramsay (*Lady Ann Campbell*, 1743) employed that expert in drapery Joseph van Aken for Lady Ann's ermine and Barbara Bagot's lovely lace collar.

The quality of these collections has attracted gifts and bequests, notably from William Cargill in 1970 (a Corot, a Camille Pissarro, the Reynolds of *Nelly O'Brien*) and two important collections of prints from Dr W. R. Scott (1940) and from Dr James A. McCallum (gifts from 1939 and a bequest in 1948). Dr McCallum's 4,000 prints include works by Dürer, Rembrandt, Goya[158] and Picasso. They augment the overall collection of almost 20,000 prints, the most comprehensive in Scotland, necessitating a separate gallery upstairs.

In 1936 the university received a gift from Miss Rosalind Birnie Philip, Whistler's sister-in-law, of thirty-nine of his oil paintings and over two hundred etchings, watercolours and lithographs.[159] This turned the Hunterian into the most important centre for Whistler studies and made the case for a new gallery imperative. It took forty-four years to achieve.

The London architect William Whitfield, who had designed the new university library,

Red and Black: the Fan *by James McNeill Whistler*

was commissioned. His 1973 design incorporated Charles Rennie Mackintosh's original (now demolished) home at 78 Southpark Avenue (seventy-five yards away), a sculpture courtyard, print gallery and six other galleries in a building of cast and hammered concrete, elegant and unyielding.

The new gallery is set on the other side of University Avenue from the Hunterian Museum and the main university buildings. You approach it up a slow, steep slope. You enter through four cast-aluminium doors, by Eduardo Paolozzi, into galleries bathed in top light. You progress through the 16th, 17th, 18th and 19th centuries to the Whistler Collection, whose central area is given over to the huge portraits of the 1890s: *Red and Black: the Fan* (c. 1891–94);[160] *Harmony in Brown: the Felt Hat* (1890s);[161] and *Brown and Gold* (1895–1900), a self-portrait in which he adopted the pose of Velásquez's *Pablo de Valladolid* in the Prado in Madrid. Beside them is a miniature version of his late full-length portrait-style *Miss Rosalind Birnie Philip Standing* (c. 1879) and several studies of young children. In his studies of Lizzie Willis and Lillie Parmington, Whistler employs a form of the head that he took from Hogarth's *The Shrimp Girl* (National Gallery, q.v.).

Although by the 1890s Whistler was inundated with portrait commissions, he worked and reworked these private portraits, writing to his wife on 11 November 1895, 'The one *great* truth that has impressed me is that time *is* an element in the making of pictures!! And *waste* is their undoing.' With his health failing he wrote to her, 'Do you think all this suffering and this persistence *can* be for nothing? . . . And then one can walk upright – and outrun the fleetest! And failure will be no more. And the past will be forgiven – and time will be as nothing!' This is in marked contrast to the ebullient Whistler who, when asked by the opposing counsel, the Attorney-General Sir John Holker, in the libel case he brought against Ruskin in 1878, 'The labour of two days is that for which you ask 200 guineas?' replied: 'No. I ask it for the knowledge I gained in the work of a lifetime.'[162]

If Whistler was poised on the brink of the 20th century, Charles Rennie Mackintosh and his contemporaries the Scottish Colourists (Cadell, Fergusson, Peploe and Hunter) were plunged into it, experiencing a very different Paris (that of Matisse, Cézanne) from Whistler's (Pissarro, Vuillard, Puvis de Chavannes). The good selection of the work here of the Colourists makes it clear how influenced they were by France. In particular, Fergusson's *Les Eus* (1910–13), a circle of Dionysian, dancing nudes, owes much to the Fauves and Matisse.

In recent years the Hunterian has collected sculpture (Eduardo Paolozzi; Anthony Caro, William Turnbull, Dhruva Mistry, Gavin Scobie) alongside the works of Scottish and English painters: Joan Eardley, William Gear, Alan Davie, Robin Philipson; John Golding, John Hoyland. The cramped, rather joyless Sculpture Court does not do justice to the sculpture in the way that the galleries do to the paintings. Nevertheless the sculptures embody the spirit of an outstanding collection that has been developing and reinventing itself for over 200 years.

HUNTERIAN MUSEUM ✳✳✳

University Avenue, University of Glasgow, Glasgow, Strathclyde G12 8QQ
Tel. 0141 339 8855
www.gla.ac.uk/Museum/

The collected hoards of Dr William Hunter: geology, coins and Pacific treasures from Cook's voyages

Look up from where the River Kelvin rushes through a gorge in Kelvingrove Park and the University of Glasgow appears lofty and remote. Approach from University Avenue and you can walk into its halls and quadrangles, part Gothic, part Baronial, designed by Sir George Gilbert Scott. The Hunterian Stair with its 'magnificent scrolled wrought iron balustrade'[163] leads to the Bute Hall and so to the Hunterian Museum through an arcaded and apsed entrance hall. You pass statues of

Adam Smith by Hans Gasser (1867) and James Watt[164] by Francis Chantrey (1823) and turn right into the main galleried exhibition hall. It is a stately progress into the academic heart of the university.

The museum's founding benefactor William Hunter (1718–83) was a great anatomist and obstetrician, and friend of Adam Smith, Edmund Burke and Edward Gibbon, all of whom attended his lectures. He assembled celebrated collections of anatomical and zoological specimens, coins and medals, books, manuscripts and paintings,[165] with which he wanted to found a museum in London, but successive Whig administrations, first Grenville's, then Shelburne's, procrastinated and when Hunter died, his heir Matthew Baillie[166] brought the collections to Glasgow in 1807 and surrendered them to the university.

They were joined by the university's other collections (Roman antiquities, archaeology, ceremonial silver) but in the 20th century the collections, growing too large, were split between the Graham Kerr building (zoology), the university library and the Hunterian Art Gallery (q.v.). Those that remain are riches enough.

The Roman antiquities, the only collection that predates Hunter's, extend our knowledge of how the Antonine Wall (AD 142) between the Clyde and Forth Estuaries was built and by whom. Inscribed distance slabs marked the completion of each section of the wall. Of the original 42, 19 survive, of which 17 are here. On the slab from Hutcheson Hill, Bearsden, is carved a triumphal archway. In the centre, flanked by kneeling, naked captives, a wreath is being offered to the eagle of the Twentieth Legion.

Hunter's own collecting was omnivorous. His income from his medical practice, lecturing and his position as doctor-in-waiting to the Queen rose to £10,000 a year in the 1760s. His younger brother John Hunter,[167] with whom he enjoyed conspicuously bad, competitive, relations, called him 'in the strictest sense, a miser'. Yet it is estimated that he spent more than £100,000 on acquisitions.[168] He paid only twelve guineas of that for Rembrandt's

The Entombment of Christ in 1771, £21 for a gold noble, the first ever Scottish gold coin, struck in the reign of King David II and £8,000 for the coins of Matthew Duane.

Some of his collecting was of direct relevance to his medical work, some of it was for enjoyment, some of it has not survived: his herbarium has been absorbed into Edinburgh's Royal Botanic Garden. He would occasionally buy individual coins, instruments or artefacts but his preferred method of collecting was to purchase existing collections. Duane's collection of coins included the collection that he in turn had acquired from Robert Harley, the Earl of Oxford. James Douglas's was an outstanding anatomical collection.

That method could not be employed in building his ethnographic collection. That had to be acquired piecemeal from sailors returning to London's docks, though a significant proportion of the 200 artefacts in his collection were brought from the expeditions commanded by Captain Cook that arrived back in Britain in 1771, 1775 and 1780. The botanical

Imperial Roman gold coins illustrate the career of Nero at the Hunterian Museum

specimens were promised to the Royal Botanic Gardens at Kew and to the British Museum (both q.v.)[169] but there remained substantial pickings: a Maori knife, decorated with shells, whose cutting edge was made from sharks' teeth; a Tongan bag woven from coconut fibre from Cook's first voyage; a Nootka Indian bird rattle from what is now Alaska, and a model Eskimo kayak from Cook's third and most northerly voyage.

Hunter's collection has a remarkable geographic scope (North America, Tierra del Fuego, the Pacific, Australasia) but its greater importance is that these are objects of 'first contact' from communities that had not previously encountered Europeans and which consequently can yield untainted evidence of other cultures. The collection was further strengthened in 1860 by the addition of much 19th-century Melanesian and Polynesian material originally acquired by a Scots missionary, the Revd Dr George Turner.

Hunter's coin collection, after those of the British Museum and the Ashmolean Museum (both q.v.), is the third most important in Britain. It consists of more than 30,000[170] coins and when it was moved from London to

Glasgow in 1807 six armed guards were needed to accompany it.

Hunter's particular interests were Roman, Greek and British coins, although he also acquired medallions, medals and tokens of various kinds, including a group of Roman brothel tokens (spintria)[171] from the time of Tiberius.

His imperial Roman coins are outstanding. One sequence of gold coins from the 1st century shows the changing faces of Nero from the pretty, innocent boy adopted by Claudius to the double image of his profile facing that of his mother, Agrippina, when she was politically dominant; and to a later double image with her when his profile overlays hers. The coins from his final years record his decline into corpulence and coarseness.

These coins are, as ever, historical records. The English silver penny of 790 from the reign of Offa, King of Mercia, is the only British coin to depict a consort (Queen Cynethryth, wife of Offa). The Ryal (dollar) of Mary, Queen of Scots was inscribed during her brief marriage to Lord Darnley, 'Mary and Henry, Queen and King of Scots'.

This museum well expresses the intellectual curiosity and distinction that have for centuries kept Scots and Scotland at the edge of discovery and the heart of scholarship.

MUSEUM OF TRANSPORT *

1 Bunhouse Road, Glasgow, Strathclyde
G3 8DP
Tel. 0141 287 2720, fax: 0141 287 2692
www.glasgowmuseums.com

Carriages, trams, and models of the warships and liners of the old Clyde, in the former tramway works

Cities are defined and shaped by their systems of transport; this is particularly true of Glasgow. The River Clyde has made the city, the city the Clyde. The west coast line from Glasgow Central used to be the fastest rail link to England.

On its streets Glasgow remained faithful to its green and orange trams, 'the caurs', from their introduction in 1895 until the withdrawal of the last tram on 2 September 1962. This withdrawal coincided with, and gave impetus to, the development of the Museum of Transport, which from 1964 to 1987 was housed in the Coplawhill Works in which the trams were originally built.

Today you approach the museum down Bunhouse Road, beside the River Kelvin, and enter an unprepossessing side door of Kelvin Hall, whose main entrance on Argyle Street, opposite the Glasgow Museum and Art Gallery, leads into an indoor sports and recreation centre.

Inside, the cavernous hall is jammed with every form of transport: buses and trolleys; lorries, locomotives and fire engines; cars, cabs and coaches; bicycles and tricycles, with and without motors; and trams.

You may walk beside, between and behind the trams, get close to them, size them up, admire the detail of their furniture, their coachwork and their finish. You can gaze at every generation of tram: the horse-drawn No. 543 (1895), the (converted) No. 779 (1908) and the Standard No. 1088 (1924), still in service in the early 1960s. You can inspect the experimental single-decker, the Baillie Burt, No. 1089 (1926), the last Coplawhill-built tram No. 1173 (1938) and the last double-decker built in Britain, the stately Cunarder, No. 1392 (1952).

Beside them the Ardrishaig Belle (1890), in service until 1950, and Lawson's omnibus plying from Glasgow to Kirkintilloch, both horse drawn, are jostled by the mighty presence of the locomotives, immaculate in their company liveries: the pale yellow and green of the Highland Railways whose 4–6–0 Loco No. 103 (1894) tackled the gradients of the route to Perth, Inverness and the far north; the bright green of the Glasgow and South Western Railway's 0–6–0 Loco MG (1917) which shunted in the docks. Across from them, gleaming black, is the 1931 Rolls Royce Phantom II with a landaulette body by Hooper, a gift to Sir William Burrell from his wife, parked next to a tiny Lipton's delivery van, an Austin 7, advertising on its side 'Lipton's for Bacon'.

Along one side of the wall a car showroom has been recreated, its models ranging from the American Stanley Steam Car 735 of 1917 to a Lagonda Tourer (1953) and a white Jaguar Mk 2 saloon (1961). Despite the glamour of these exotics, it is the mass-produced models that intrigue, Austins and Morrises of every decade from the 1920s to the 1960s, and the car my mother owned, the Ford Popular 1955, whose indicators rise, politely as gloved fingers, from external cases.

Museums rightly eschew mentioning the price or value of the objects they exhibit but here an intelligent exception is made and each car displays its original, showroom cost. An Austin Saloon of 1928 (£325), a Talbot Saloon of 1938, (£398), the 1955 Ford Popular (£413. 17s.), and a 1959 Morris Mini Minor (£497) demonstrate the price benefits created by mass production and competition in a growing post-war market.

Pre- and post-war, that market was dominated by Austin and Morris, but the museum provides a reminder that Scotland had an indigenous motor-manufacturing industry in the early 20th century with such firms as Albion, Arroll-Johnson and Argyll. A parked line of Argylls demonstrates the swift rise and fall of Scottish motor design and engineering.

Their 2¾ h.p. Voiturette (1900) has a rudder, not a wheel. By 1906 the wheel had arrived, in the Model 6, and the lamp. The following year the 10/11 h.p. Tourer had a windscreen, mudguards and upholstered seats, front and back. By 1908 their improved Tourers boasted 14/16 h.p. engines but, with the gathering speed of these annual innovations, Argyll's expanded too fast and went into liquidation in 1914.

A mezzanine floor displays the history of the bicycle from the Rudge Rotary of 1885 to the Singer de Luxe (1905), with diamond frame, clamp brakes and Dunlop pneumatic tyres, and the daring drop-handlebars of the 1935 racing bike. Here too is a copy of 'the world's oldest bicycle' made by Kirkpatrick Macmillan. He designed and constructed,

from blocks of solid wood, an improved hobbyhorse with handlebars, front-wheel steering and iron-spoked back wheels, with metal rims, that were connected by rods to the pedals. To prove that it worked, he rode it to Glasgow in June 1842. On arrival he was arrested for running over a child. He never rode again and never made another bicycle, although this copy, by Gavin Dalzell in 1845, was exhibited at the Glasgow Exhibition of 1888.

In the Clyde Room are model ships from the museum's collection of over seven hundred: sloops and ketches, battleships and merchantmen; ferries and liners; dredgers and harbour craft; steamers, with paddles and without, that worked the Clyde or toured the islands. There are Admiralty models from the late 17th century when Samuel Pepys, as Secretary to the Admiralty, required that all new ships for the navy should be submitted as models, scale 1:48, before a decision to commission was made.

There are delicate, intricate models made from bone, hair, straw, threads and shell by French prisoners in the Napoleonic Wars, 1775–1815. Here too are models of the great liners built in the Clydeside shipyards in the early 20th century by John Brown and Co.: the *Empress of Russia* for Canadian Pacific Steamships in 1913, and its sisters, the *Empress of Scotland* (1930) and the *Empress of Britain* (1931); the *Queen Mary* (1936), and the *Queen Elizabeth II* (1967), the last great transatlantic liner from the Clyde.

The skills that powered Glasgow's economy for over a hundred years have been rendered redundant. All that remains are these models: funerary objects for a dead industry.

PEOPLE'S PALACE *

Glasgow Green, Glasgow, Strathclyde G40 1AT
Tel. 0141 554 0223, fax 0141 550 0892
www.glasgowmuseums.com

Red French Renaissance building with winter gardens attached; a people's history of Glasgow

It is a palace, a huge red sandstone palace, opened in 1898, designed by A. B. Macdonald, the city engineer, in French Renaissance style, with a giant rotunda topped by a cupola, the whole pretending it is St Paul's Cathedral. Behind it are Winter Gardens with seating for up to 500, a glasshouse Paxton might have admired, a bleached upturned keel. It is by, with, of and for the people.

Within is a rattlebag of Glasgow history, humour and style, celebrating work, play, health, housing, songs, jokes and people, gossipily plural: John McLean, Jimmy Maxton; Edwin Morgan, Liz Lochhead; John Byrne, Benny Lynch; Billy Connolly, Jimmy Boyle; Rab C. Nesbitt, Elaine C. Smith; Sir Alex Ferguson; Albert Pierrepoint, the famous executioner at Barlinnie. The memories are here of every man, woman and reluctant child who has used a steamie, kicked a footie, had a bevy, gone 'doon the watter' and smelt the Clyde.

The People's Palace is ideally situated, on its own, surrounded by Glasgow Green, a place that stands for something. This has always been common land. Cattle grazed it, the Clyde flooded it, clothes were dried on it and Bonnie Prince Charlie reviewed his troops on it in 1746, which did not amuse this non-Jacobite city. It has been a place for marches, protests and public executions (until 1865). The people of Glasgow have defended it against exploitation, whether by open-cast mining or a railway viaduct. It is the people's place for the People's Palace.

Inside, its galleries, on two floors, focus on aspects of Glasgow life: housing, crime, the Second World War. On the top floor are eight panels painted by Ken Currie that present the struggles of the working people of Glasgow, from the Calton weavers in the 1790s to John McLean in 1920s Red Clydeside and through to the Upper Clyde Shipbuilders' work-in in 1971.

The poor quality of Glasgow's 19th-century housing schemes and the ill health that arose as a result need no tricks of presentation to move you. Single objects are eloquent enough: an Improved Earthenware Inhaler by S. Maw, Son and Sons, as the damp caused every sort of bronchial problem from asthma to tuberculosis; Lavapine Spraying Fluid, to attack bed bugs; a tin bath; a slop pail, for the cludgie.

To cheer you up there's a chip pan, a skipping rope, an old leather football, a peever and a 1950s television flickering old programmes from its veneered cabinet. Looped tapes of people's memories are matter of fact in tone.

Throughout, good use is made of paintings from the city's art collections. *The Barras* by Avril Paton (1984) shows the outdoor market that has sold cheap goods, new and used, since the 1850s. John Byrne's portrait of *Billy Connolly* (1973) gives hope of one kind of escape.

The sound of the past is important: loops of trains, trams, factory hooters, clogs on setts, songs. 'I am the Means Test Man' says it all.

In the most successful galleries, sounds and objects and texts tumble over each other. Banners of trade and unions, the 1915 rent strike, the Spanish Civil War, the poll tax protests of 1987 and the welcome to Nelson Mandela in 1993, when he was given the freedom of the city, jostle for attention. Beneath them the desk of John McLean, revolutionary socialist and nationalist, has lying on it some of his books and papers, including Pierre Kropotkin's *L'Anarchie*, the manifesto of the Socialist Workers' Republican Party.

You are not allowed to forget that this is a city of work, 'the workshop of the Empire', making its living from tobacco, sugar, cotton and slaves in the 18th century; from iron and steel, ship-building and engineering in the 19th; from publishing and the media in the 20th. In 1928 the publishers William Collins (now owned by Rupert Murdoch's News International) printed and sold 10 million books.

For all its heat and charm, Glasgow offers its sons and daughters incentives to get on and, sometimes, out. Here are Connolly's banana shoes and Lulu's startling green trouser suit. Here is the typewriter on which Ian Patterson wrote *Rab C. Nesbitt* with his diet of booze, fags and deep fried Mars bars. Near them are Alasdair Gray's sober pictures of successful contemporary Glaswegian writers: Liz Lochhead, Edwin Morgan, James Kelman.

If you can't get on or out, you can laugh, and the humour of Stanley Baxter and Billy Connolly is palpable in the museum.

This is a museum and a city whose energy is manifest in its comics, its politicians, its football and its life. It is one aspect of the fierce spirit of Scotland. The People's Palace explains why.

POLLOK HOUSE ***

Pollok Country Park, 2060 Pollokshaws Road, Glasgow, Strathclyde G43 1AT
Tel. 0141 616 6410
www.glasgowmuseums.com

Fine Spanish art (Murillo, Goya and an El Greco) in a handsome, austere Scottish house

The route of the Grand Tour, through France and Italy to Rome, determined the development of the taste of collectors and connoisseurs in Britain in the 18th century. Spain was largely ignored until after the Peninsular War, its painters little known and rarely collected.[172] Ever since, British public galleries have not much favoured Spanish art. Pollok House is an exception. It has one of the best and most comprehensive collections in Britain of paintings from the golden age of Spanish painting, the 16th and 17th centuries.

The collection was made between 1852 and 1859 by Sir William Stirling Maxwell, whose books *Annals of the Artists of Spain* (1848, 3 vols.) and *Velásquez and his Works* (1865) were the major studies of Spanish painting in English in the 19th century.[173] His collection is particularly strong on the painters of the reign of Philip II: the court painters Juan Fernandez de Navarette (called 'El Mudo' because he was deaf and mute) and Alonso Sánchez Coello, who were employed to make paintings for the Escorial, and El Greco,[174] who, having failed to win Philip II's favour, worked in Toledo for the rest of his life.

At first sight Pollok House might appear to be an unlikely setting in which to display 17th-century Spanish painting. Sir John Maxwell, who built it in the late 1740s, had commissioned designs from William Adam ten years earlier. It has a narrow, neoclassical facade, 'three storeys above a tall basement',[175] that owes much to Adam. Certainly by the time Sir William's son, Sir John Stirling Maxwell, came to enlarge the house in 1890, he had convinced himself that William Adam had been the designer and commissioned Sir Robert Rowland Anderson to work 'in increasing sympathy with Adam's style'.[176] The resulting austerity of the design, its sombre ashlar and, especially, the quietly elegant proportions of the rooms, suit the sobriety of the paintings well.

Within, the entrance hall is hung with family portraits and around the house are others by English artists: a portrait of *Lady Stirling Maxwell* by William Etty, portraits by Hogarth and Romney,[177] by Michael Dahl, Cornelius Johnson and Isaac Oliver. There are also landscapes by Guardi, Jan Both and Jan Hackaert. However these are side dishes: the feast is Spanish and its centrepiece is an El Greco of sublime beauty, *Lady in a Fur Wrap* (c. 1577–9).

This is not the El Greco of flame-like distortions and tortured expressions, his idiosyncratic version of Mannerism depicting spirits rather than bodies. The identity of the sitter is unknown but it has been suggested that she was El Greco's mistress and the mother of his son. He describes the texture of her white skin, her dark eyes and the softness of the fur with tender attention. She is caught in the light, as it were of the moon, a silvered light, set against the deepest shadow, her right hand fingering the edge of the fur. It is a picture of, literally, wrapt love.[178]

In his lifetime El Greco enjoyed neither the celebrity nor the fortune of Navarette or

Alonso Sánchez Coello. Navarette's *Christ Carrying the Cross* is a copy of a Titian. The monks of the Hieronymite Convent of La Estrella, where Navarette was educated, paid for him to go to study in Venice, in the words of his biographer, Father José de Sigüenza, 'the dark tones of his teacher Titian and the light, gay tones of Correggio'.[179] In taking Titian and the Venetians as his models Navarette was breaking with the Spanish Habsburg traditions of sombre formality (in Alonso Sánchez Coello's portrait here of *Archduke Rudolf of Austria* the decoration is more animated than the rigid pose) and the religious emotionalism of Luis de Morales's *Pietá*, in which the boneless body of Christ hangs limp in his mother's arms.

Although there is no work here by Velásquez, the collection shows the diversity of Spanish artists of his generation and the different ways in which they were influenced by Dutch art. The impeccable realism of an *Allegory of Repentance* by Antonio de Pereda derives from Dutch *vanitas* paintings, while the later portrait of *Charles II, King of Spain* by Juan Carreño de Miranda owes as much to Van Dyck as to Velásquez.

These were turbulent years for Spain: financial volatility and unemployment at home, the Thirty Years War in her empire in the Low Countries (1618–48, extending in reality until 1659). The legacy of such traumas is apparent in the next century, in the violence depicted in Goya's work. Here he is represented by a set of his etchings, *Los Proverbios*, and two small oils, *Boys Playing at Seesaw* and *Boys Playing at Soldiers*.

Sir Kenneth Clark[180] omitted Spain from his view of *Civilisation* on the grounds that it is not clear 'what Spain has done to enlarge the human mind'. In his view Spain 'has simply remained Spain'.[181] In this he reflects the priority implicit in British public galleries and their modest holdings of Spanish art. This collection should make us reconsider Clark's apophthegm and attempt to grasp some of Spain's rich intractable Spanishness.

Lady in a Fur Wrap *by El Greco (Pollok House)*

MCLEAN ART GALLERY AND MUSEUM ***

15 Kelly Street, Greenock, Renfrewshire
PA16 8JX
Tel. 01475 715624

Models of ships and boats in this Clyde port, birthplace of James Watt; paintings, big game trophies and Japanese armour

The McLean is that rarity, a museum and art gallery whose elements are of a piece. In it community and industry, bequests and collections, lock shipshape together under one roof.

Greenock, with neighbouring Gourock and Port Glasgow, is among the first ports of the Firth of Clyde. There has been a fishing harbour here since the 17th century and docks and shipyards have operated since the early 18th century. Around them grew industries (timber, ropeworks, sugar refining) that developed out of the cargoes brought back from overseas and from the engineering skills needed to build and repair the ships that carried them.

James McLean (1802–77) was a local timber merchant who helped the Greenock Philosophical Society, of which he was a member, found the museum. Its solid stone building, set back from the street, was designed by Adamson with the clarity of an early, rather than a late, Victorian eye, and opened in 1876. It has a splendid top-lit main hall, around which runs a gallery. Although it was renovated in 1990 with money from the Scottish Museums Council, its 19th-century atmosphere has been retained.

At ground level the main hall is given over to models of ships and engines. As Greenock was the birthplace of James Watt, steam engines abound, unobtrusive in their smooth running: the fine half-model of PS *Windsor Castle*, her white funnel raking back between her spoon bow and graceful stern; Henry Bell's stolid PS *Comet* (1812),[182] the first steamship to carry passengers, driven by a 4 h.p. engine; the magnificent model of PS *Mona's Isle*, raised on four turned chocks in her carved mahogany case.

Here too is an exquisite model of a revenue cutter[183] something like fully rigged, her jib extended at the end of a long bowsprit, her stay, gaff and upper and lower topsails making a full wardrobe of sail, and a model of the 1863 paddle boat PS *Iona II*. An observer described her steaming into Ardrishaig Pier: 'Who shall say that paddlers are prosaic, and that there is no poetry in a steam boat? . . . on a brilliant day in August, we have watched the Iona steam in, a thing of life and beauty, crowded with animation, graceful in her lines and motions, with her every span and plank white like snow . . . a very epic, in short of swiftness and steam.' To describe the work of James & George Thomson (*Iona II*), or James D. Rennie (the revenue cutter) or A. M. Paterson (a paddle-steamer engine), as 'models' is perhaps to belittle the immaculate craftsmanship, the precision and the loving attention with which they have been made. Only their scale is Lilliputian. Their grace and presence carry weight.

Around these models are objects illustrating other aspects of Greenock's maritime and industrial past: a low-swivel harpoon gun;[184] the fierce steel of a harpoon from SS *Hope*;[185] ropes, cables, cordage and chains from ropeworks and sailmakers;[186] a model of a sugar-cube-making machine; and memorabilia of James Watt, including his chemical balance, poised in a case.

The hall has something of the chandler's and shipwright's: tar and varnish; polish and paint. The brass fittings of its mahogany cases gleam.

In the next gallery is a picture collection based on the bequests of Peter H. Mackellar, a local merchant, and of Stuart Anderson Caird.[187]

As with other galleries set up in Scotland in the late 19th century, the collections feature a familiar cast: Courbet, Corot and Boudin; Orchardson; a Ramsay and a Raeburn (of a young *Sir Francis Chantrey*, the benefactor of the Tate); McTaggart; examples of the Glasgow School and the Colourists; and a curiosity: a portrait by Leighton, *Yasmeenah*, an oriental sweetmeat.

But the interest and flavour are in the careful collections that the gallery has built up of the work of local artists. Caird owned several small canvases by Robert Herdman, a pupil of Scott Lauder at the Trustees' Academy, and works by Greenock artists, John Fleming, Thomas Carsell and William Clark. There are no masterpieces here, no 'Greenock School', but there are works of charm that provide a record of Greenock, whether civic and ceremonial (Clark's *The Queen's Visit to the Clyde*; Robert Knox's *The Royal Squadron Passing Greenock*), topographical (Carsell's *Greenock, 1854*, a curious stiff view of the docks with a passing train, the railway having come to the town in 1841) or marine (Steele's *Great Tea Race*, 1866, between the clippers *Ariel* and *Taiping*, which ended, after ninety-nine days, with them separated by ten minutes).[188]

Caird specified, when setting up a trust of £6,000 to purchase works of art to be added to his collection, that it should be 'for the promotion of Art in the town of Greenock'. The views of the docks, ships and the coast by Robert Salmon and by Patrick Downie, and the more recent etchings of ships and shipbuilding by William Niven and Muirhead Bone, achieve this. Outstanding here is John Fleming. His small landscapes of a Greenock before the grip of industry tightened have a gentle grace and his *Self-portrait*, surprised and open-eyed, is the work of an artist whose work deserves to be more widely known.

In a museum whose more strictly indigenous riches have been collected, and are exhibited, with such care and affection, the somewhat surprising glories are the Japanese collection made by George Rodgers Macdougall (1910–14), objects from the Egypt Exploration Society expeditions between 1880 and 1914, and the natural history collections of Robert Lyons Scott.

Macdougall went to New York to become head of the sugar firm Czarnikow & Co., on whose behalf he visited Japan. His collection covers the Edo period of the Tokugawa Shogunate (1603–1867) and the subsequent Meiji period (1868–1912), during which time the role of the Samurai evolved from that of feudal warrior to estate administrator. The helmets, kura (saddles) and stirrups of the 18th century are very fine, the latter lacquered and luminously decorated with images of trees, leaves and fishes; but it is the detailed beauty of the metalwork in the iron scales, greaves and the gauntlets of the swords, the tsuba (sword guards) and the kosuka (sword handles) that most impress, intricately cut, chased and hammered before being inlaid with gold, silver, agate and ivory.

The religious and hierarchical values that underpinned this culture are explained simply for the layman. This is also true of the Egyptological Collection, whose curator's exegesis of the symbolism of Egyptian colours ('the mountain of gold' for the sun, eternal life; the ambivalence of red, being fire, blood and regeneration, as well as the descent into the realm of the god of chaos, Seth) and the animal images on Canopic jars used for storing the internal organs of the dead – hapi (baboon) for lungs; duamutef (jackal) for stomachs; qebhsenuef (falcon) for intestines – is exemplary. These labels are a model of how interpretation can be simply expressed and intellectually illuminating without insulting the inexpert visitor's intelligence.

Robert Lyons Scott's interests, and gifts to the museum, return us to the way in which collections and community so satisfactorily conjoin here. Scott was chairman of his family's shipyard, the largest in Greenock, from 1915 until his death in 1939.

He was also a hunter of big game for over twenty-five years and here his bag, all stuffed, includes a leopard from Sudan, a lion and lioness from Kenya, a tiger from India, tiger sharks from the West Indies, a crocodile from the White Nile and a giant sloth bear, rearing on its hind legs, from the central provinces of India. Like Macdougall, he also collected Japanese arms and armour, a collection he gave to the Glasgow Museum and Art Gallery (q.v.).

Many less confident museums would consider Scott's enthusiasms politically incorrect. The McLean, rightly, does not, and his quarry makes a rare and thrilling display. It is pleasing that collectors as diverse as Scott and

Macdougall, and craftsmen of the quality of Rennie and the Thomsons have found, in the McLean, a museum worthy of them.

TIMESPAN, HELMSDALE *

Dunrobin Street, Helmsdale, Sutherland
KW8 6JX
Tel. 01431 821327, fax 01431 821058
e-mail:admin@timespan.org.uk

From very old rocks indeed to Barbara Cartland, via the Highland Clearances

The name of this museum tells you nothing and is likely to be outdated betimes but the stories the museum tells of Helmsdale and its coast are old and alive.

Helmsdale is at the head of the Strath of Kildonan, one of several straths draining the interior of Sutherland. Man has been here since Neolithic times. Near by are Bronze Age cairns and hut circles (4,000 years old); brochs – small defensive towers (2,000 years); and medieval byres. In more recent centuries, gold and oil have played their parts, products of the region's geology, which is well demonstrated here by massive rock samples.

Sutherland lies on black Lewisian gneiss, the oldest surface rock in Britain, laid down 2,900–1,400 million years ago. It heads a gallery of pink, marbled pegmatite (2,500–1,500 million years old), grey limestone (500 million), old red sandstone (410–355 million), red granite (400 million), whose colour comes from quartz, mica and crystals of red feldspar, and glossy black flagstone, the mudstone from the bed of Lake Orcadie, which cleaves easily along its bedding planes and whose slabs paved the streets of London, New York and Amsterdam.

In 1869 Robert Gilchrist found traces of gold, which led to the Kildonan goldrush and for a few months Sutherland became California, although most of the panners found iron pyrites (fool's gold) rather than their fortunes. Oil came in the 1960s from the Beatrice oilfield in the Moray Firth.

As elsewhere in the Highlands, fishing,

crofting and digging peat provided a subsistence living for generations. To get surplus cattle to Falkirk involved a four-week drove, which enabled the cattle to find a market but halved the value of each beast (£14 at home, £7 at Falkirk). So cut off was the coastline with its 'narrow tracks on the edges of precipices' and 'rude and inconvenient ferries'[189] that in 1740 it took Lord Lovat's coach eleven days to travel from Inverness to Edinburgh and the journey cost him three broken axles.

To increase the return from the land it seemed clear to landowners that the inefficient crofts had to give way to the greater productivity of larger units with significantly fewer tenants, and that the interior of the Highlands had to be opened up by roads and bridges.

The Sutherlands owned most of Caithness. Elizabeth, Countess of Sutherland, of Dunrobin Castle, and of Cleveland House in London, instructed her factor, Patrick Sellar, to clear her land of surplus tenanted crofters. He did so with unprecedented ruthlessness, driving families to work in the factories of the new industrial cities or to emigrate to North America. Some who went to Canada founded Kildonan on the Red River, near Winnipeg.

The clearances severed the ancient bonds of kinship which had underpinned Gaelic life and culture for centuries by which the Cean Cinnidh, the clan chieftain, was the leader, the father of his clan (from the Gaelic *clanna* meaning children).

The scars caused by the Sutherland Clearances were not healed by the huge investment of £60,000 in her estates that Lady Sutherland made between 1811 and 1833, although it was enough to secure a dukedom for her husband in 1833. Helmsdale benefited from the fine double-span stone bridge that crosses the Donan beside the museum. This bridge was built by Thomas Telford, who was employed by Lady Sutherland to bring modern communications to Caithness. Heretofore there were no maps, no roads, no bridges and no skills. The most northerly bridge was at Inverness, built by General Wade as a means of more effectively suppressing the Jacobites in 1745. In sixteen years Telford built 150 miles of road and 134 bridges.

For Helmsdale his roads, and the harbour, pier and ice house, built in 1820, meant an immediate expansion of the village's fishing industry. Within twenty years herring was being cured, gutted and packed in thirty-nine sheds and 46,000 barrels were being exported each year. Only the decline of drifters in the 1920s and the introduction of Seine nets in the 1930s brought long-line fishing to an end.

These stories are well told by means of graphics, objects and documents, but less happily by tableaux whose manikins (of Patrick Sellar and others) have a stiff gaucheness which is so much less vivid than the pictures in the mind that well-chosen objects provoke.

There is one further landowner who has had an impact on Helmsdale and who is celebrated here: Barbara Cartland, whose McCorquodale family estate is near by. A display, in which the manikin is animated by Miss Cartland's pink flounces and frills and by her immaculate white hair, a miracle of backcombing, conveys something of her style, even if it fails to capture her unique qualities. She is surrounded by a few of her 700-plus books: *The Duke and the Priest's Daughter*; *Who Can Deny Love?*; *A Princess in Distress*; *The Irresistible Force* and *Paradise Found*.

The museum is designed by Edinburgh-based architect John Hope, who has faced the simple structure with harling and enhanced its position, beside the river and below the bridge, with a garden. Through it, on door handles, on floors, on walls he has run a Helmsdale motif: the silver herring which does span time.

INVERNESS MUSEUM **

Castle Wynd, Inverness, Highland IV2 3EB
Tel. 01463 237114
inverness.museum@highland.gov.uk

*Clan display, Scottish paintings, fine
Highland silver, extensive dioramas;
fascinating taxidermy and a reconstructed
taxidermist's shop*

Inverness is the capital of the Highlands. South
of the city on Drummossie Moor, Prince
Charles Edward Stuart's Highland army was
cut down by the Duke of Cumberland's forces
on 16 April 1746 at Culloden – what the Prince
called 'the fatall field'.[190]

In this museum, built in 1963 in the shadow
of Inverness Castle, are the symbols of the
Highlands: arms, bagpipes, fiddles.

To look at the simplicity of the 17th-century,
ribbon-hilted broadsword made by the great
Spanish armourer Andrea Ferrara,[191] the
several powder horns or the studded targe
(shield), scant protection in the face of
Hanoverian rifle fire, is to see again the inevitable fate of the Highlanders' charge at
Culloden.

Memorabilia from the battle are displayed
as relics: a Jacobite cap found buried under
three feet of peat bog; the sporran said to
have been worn by Duncan McGillivray of
Dunlichity that day; a plait of Charles Edward
Stuart's hair, his pocket knife and a fragment
of Mackintosh tartan plaid worn by him the
previous day with this, contemporary, note
affixed: 'He left it at Moy Hall and this piece
was cut off and given me by Lady Mackintosh.'
Other, presumed, fragments of this Moy
Hall plaid can be found at the West Highland
Museum and at Duff House Country Gallery
(both q.v.).

Beside such memorabilia a broadsheet dated
21 September 1745 is displayed, which describes
the high point of the Jacobite Rising, the
victory at Prestonpans. Published immediately
after the battle, it tells how the Highlanders
slipped past Sir John Cope's advance guard
before dawn and 'in about seven or eight

minutes were absolute masters of the field'. An
alternative, Hanoverian, report by one of
Cope's officers describes it thus: 'the Artillery
Guard and Gardner's Dragoons were in confusion. He [Cope] endeavoured to get them in to
order but it would not do, away they Run. The
General then attempted to keep the Foot
together, but they having their Right Flank
exposed by the Flight of the Dragoons, were
likewise seized with a Pannick ... the Retreat
was made with Decency.'[192]

These days were remembered, and Charles
Edward Stuart toasted, whenever Jacobites met
together for decades afterwards, and the number, beauty and ingenuity of Jacobite glasses
bear witness to the depth of support. The
collection here includes a baluster glass with
an airtwist stem, made in Newcastle (*c.* 1750), a
glass engraved 'FIAT' (May it come to pass)
and one on which the Prince is set within a
wreath of roses and buds, a petal or bud for
each member of the House of Stuart since his
grandfather James II of England and VII of
Scotland was deposed in 1688.

Reports of Culloden describe the playing of
the pipes before the fatal charge and here are
an early-17th-century bellow pipe and a 19th-
century ebony chanter known as the Black
Chanter of Kintail.

There are few, if any, extant examples of
17th-century Highland fiddles but the collection here includes some 20th-century instruments, by the fiddler and piper Torquil
McLeod of Tain (1935) and by Alistair Grant
of Inverness (1926) and Alexander Grant's
strange experiment, a round fiddle or rondello
(1934).

Inverness has been a centre for silver since
the 17th century and the museum's collection is
strong on the work of the silversmiths who
passed down their skills: Robert Innes; John
Baillie; his brother-in-law Robert Anderson;
James Dallas, whose pewter communion plates
are here. There are spoons and sugar tongs
by Charles Jameson, William Mason and his
partner Robert Naughton, through to the work
of such contemporary silversmiths as John
Fraser and Lucy Woodley, and Alan Baillie.
Every smith made quaichs – finely starred

Jacobite relic at Inverness Museum

wooden bowls with silver panels – and the earliest, by Robert Innes, is particularly fine.

One further trade has flourished in Inverness since the early 19th century: taxidermy. At one time there was work for as many as seven firms in the city. The workshop of John Wilson MacDonald is recreated. He trained at W. Malloch & Co., Perth, and moved to Inverness in 1910, working at MacPherson's Sporting Stores on Inglis Street for fifty-nine years. His records show that in 1935 he worked on 162 stags' heads, 13 birds and 116 animals for skins. Examples of taxidermy here include black cock, ptarmigan, snipe, grey hen and a huge capercaillie with full fan tail, by N.A. MacLeay & Co. (1909) of Church Street.

The star of the taxidermy collection here is a huge set piece, *The Combat*, also by MacLeay's, depicting two fierce stags, their antlers locked, with a painted backcloth of a Highland landscape by John Guille Millais, son of J. E. Millais and his wife Euphemia (v. Perth Museum and Art Gallery).

These collections, intimate in their detail, contain emblems of an idea of the Highlands which can encourage memory to slip into myth. Here are objects that predate the legends that have grown up around them and root us in our past.

KILMARTIN HOUSE
MUSEUM ***

Kilmartin, Argyll PA31 8RQ
Tel. 01546 510278

Exemplary interpretation of landscape and time in fine, modest Scots house

Kilmartin Valley is shallow-scoured by a glacier. Along it the River Add finds its slow way through the Móine Mhór (or Moss) to Loch Crinan, the Sound of Jura and the sea. This is the route in reverse that nearly 8,000 years ago brought men from the west, from Oronsay and Colonsay, from Islay and Jura, to this silt-rich valley, which yielded crops; to the

woods of hazel, birch, oak and elm, which sheltered red deer; to the shoreline, which gave up oysters and mussels, limpets and whelks.

For thousands of years the descendants of these men prospered here. When Marion Campbell mapped prehistoric Mid-Argyll in the 1950s she identified 640 sites and, in Kilmartin Valley, a landscape marked by cairns, standing stones, rock carvings (petroglyphs), cists, a henge and a barrow. It is a landscape that wears its history.

Kilmartin House Museum interprets that landscape both in the landscape and in its galleries, in a manner that is its own. The museum is the valley, the valley the museum.

It has grown out of the work of Marion Campbell in the 1950s, who was untrained and worked 'with a notebook, a six-foot steel tape and a 33-foot surveyor's tape the largest we could handle on a windy hillside'[193] and the imagination of David Clough, who played among these cairns as a child and who determined in the early 1990s that others would only be able to share his love for the valley and its history if that was interpreted in a centre. He founded a charitable trust in 1992 and the museum opened in 1997.

The museum peels away layers of memories and generations of actions and voices that were buried before history began. Some of the means employed are familiar enough: display cases of polished stone axes and carved balls; a bronze blade; shards of earthenware; a jet spacer-plate necklace; food vessels, elaborately incised, from the cairn (Glebe Cairn) that can be seen from the museum's windows; a crucible and brooch mould; inscribed stones; three bronze swords (*c.* 800 BC) from the Isle of Shuna, left in a bog, points down.

There are, too, quieter, more insistent messages from the past: charred hazelnuts from a midden on Colonsay; pearly cockle shells; pollen preserved in the peat of the Móire Mhór, from barley, plantain, purslane. They lie here as if dormant, to be called back to life, the barley to be sown.

Outside the galleries is the landscape, waiting, as if untouched. This is not so. We catch only glimpses and whispers from a landscape that has changed and is changing continuously from natural processes and human actions and interventions. Some were planned (the building of cairns, a linear cemetery down the valley; the draining of Móire Mhór); some were unplanned (the destruction of heather and native trees by intensive sheep grazing; the effect of commercial forestry planting of Sitka spruce and other non-native trees).

The line of cairns makes the strongest mark on the valley. The Glebe Cairn was excavated in 1864 by the eminent Dr Greenwell, pioneer of British domestic archaeology in the mid 19th century. Under it he found two rings of stone and two burial cists containing fine pottery and a jet necklace. He also excavated the central cairn, Nether Largie South. It had already been robbed to provide building material for walls and drains but in an inner cist he found 'shards of Beaker pottery and unburnt bones [that were] found scattered around [and] probably represented the original interment'[194] alongside cremated bones, 'three perfect and two broken barbed-and-tanged arrowheads, several other flint implements, great numbers of broken quartz pebbles and a bronze tooth'.[195]

Further down the valley to the south in an arable field are the standing stones at Ballymeanoch. Of the original seven stones, six remain, of which two are decorated with plain cupmarks, and cups and rings. It is not known what these decorations signify. They were made, probably, in the 3rd century BC. The confidence and intensity of the carvings, and the repetition of grooves and shapes, makes it clear that they were of importance.

There are fragments of more recent valley history that are transparent: a portion of the Blaeu map, 1649, depicting Argyll torn by civil war; the minutes of the Argyll Synod, describing the parish of Glassary 'desolat of people and altogether destitute of maintenance';[196] the 6th-century psalter, whose illuminations were coloured by pigments of orpiment, red lead and malachite.[197]

The tactful intelligence of this museum leads us to look more closely at this landscape and perhaps to a better ignorance of the processes that shaped it. It does so by taking a further step in archaeological method. Pitt Rivers in the 1870s understood that the context in which objects were excavated was as important as the objects themselves. Professor Barry Cunliffe, at Fishbourne Roman Palace (q.v.), showed that the context (the site itself) could encompass a museum. Now Kilmartin shows that the landscape that contains sites can itself be a living museum. It is not a totally original perception. Sir Neil Cossons created a museum in the 1970s from the dispersed industrial landscape at Ironbridge (q.v.).

Our knowledge, whether of the carved walls or the cup-and-ring decorations, is fragile. To borrow words attributed to St Columba in the *Auditor Laborantium*, describing himself as

... a little man
Trembling and most wretched,
rowing through the infinite storm of this age,

if we find ourselves 'rowing through the infinite storm' of our history, Kilmartin offers us a course to set.

KIRKCALDY GALLERY ***

War Memorial Gardens, Kirkcaldy, Fife
KY1 1YG
Tel. 01592 412860

The Scottish Colourists at their best, plus Wemyss ware and the smell of linoleum

Kirkcaldy, gallery and town, exhales the clean smell of linoleum, the sweet smell of linseed.

The fortunes of both were made by Nairn and Son, linoleum manufacturers. John Nairn gave the building in 1925 as a memorial to those, including his own son, who died in the First World War. The gallery, by architects Heiton and McKay, of Perth and Glasgow, is long-fronted, plain and restrained in local grey sandstone. Inside, the collection is shown in a series of small, top-lit galleries on the first floor.

At its heart are forty-four works by S. J. Peploe and thirty-one by William McTaggart. Most of these were bought from the estate

S. J. Peploe's Blue and White Teapot
(Kirkcaldy Gallery)

of John W. Blyth, a linen manufacturer and contemporary of Nairn. What links both men to the third main benefactor, the engineer A. Harley, is their passion for paint and colour and their preference for contemporary, mainly Scottish artists, working between 1900 and 1930.

Harley gave paintings by Boudin and Fantin-Latour, but otherwise the collection is mainly of the Camden Town Group, (Sickert, Gore and Gilman), the New English Art Club (Wilson Steer, Sir William Nicholson) and the Glasgow School (Guthrie, Lavery, Arthur Melville, E. A. Hornel, George Henry).

Paintings by the Colourists J. D. Fergusson, F. C. B. Cadell and G. L. Hunter provide a context for Peploe. It is a coherent, painterly collection.

The gallery was fortunate in its first curator, Thomas Corsan Morton, a painter of the Glasgow School. He shared Blyth's passion for Peploe. 'We must push Peploe down their throats whether they like it or not,' he wrote. With advice from the Glasgow dealer Alexander Reid and Peter McOmish Dott of the Scottish Gallery in Edinburgh (both of whom had regularly exhibited his work), Blyth and Morton built up the largest collection of Peploe's work in any gallery.

The gallery has as strong a representative selection of his early work, pre 1913 (landscapes of Comrie, North Berwick, Northern France; still lifes; a portrait of *Peggy Macrae*, 1909,) as it does of his painting after he returned from France in 1913 and established his studio in Edinburgh. This allows you to explore the influences he absorbed: Chardin in the early still lifes (*Pear, Plums and Knives*, 1900, with its solid shapes and dark palette); a passing flirtation with Impressionist brushwork in *Spring, Comrie* (1902); the lightness of Monet in *Plage Scene* (1907).

After 1913 he gradually settled into his own style with its several debts to Cézanne, which are apparent in one of his finest still lifes, *Blue and White Teapot* (*c.*1917). Its subject and composition were developed in *Still Life* (1931) and in the massive solidity of the foreground tree in *Palm Trees, Antibes* (*c.*1928), with its fronds obscuring an almost-Mont St Victoire in the far distance.

These works offer an opportunity to study Peploe's technique: the paint, thick and creamy on panel, not canvas; the strength of colours, especially in the still lifes, after his encounter with the Fauves in 1910–13; the tangible density and weight of objects.

Beside him the other artists in the gallery pale, not least Blyth's second great enthusiasm, William McTaggart. There is a place for McTaggart in the hearts of many lovers of 19th-century Scottish painting. Kirkcaldy, and the National Gallery of Scotland (q.v.) are the places to examine this attachment.

There is no doubt that after a fallow period in the 1850s and '60s (the Faeds, Horatio McCulloch, Joseph Noel Paton, James Drummond) the talented pupils of Robert Scott Lauder at the Trustees' Academy (Orchardson, Pettie, McTaggart) raised spirits. Orchardson and Pettie went to seek their fortunes in London and became 'the London Scottish'. McTaggart remained in Scotland, painting stirring nationalistic subjects (*The Sailing of the Emigrant Ship* and *The Coming of St Columba*, both 1895), but his reputation is built on more than the sentiment of national loyalty. Hugh Cameron and George Paul Chalmers also stayed in Scotland. Chalmers was as interested as McTaggart in the natural

effects of light, both of them hovering on the edge of Impressionism.

What is it then about McTaggart that places him apart? Stanley Cursiter believed that 'No one has translated better the quality of Scottish atmosphere, the subtle distinctions between the East and West coasts, the sparkle of the Atlantic shores, the grey mists of the North Sea. McTaggart remains the great interpreter of the Scottish scene . . .'[198] J. D. Fergusson maintained that no one painted the sea better than McTaggart.[199]

There is no doubt that his brushwork in waves and skies is full of movement, but it is repetitive. All waves are the same wave for McTaggart. He does them prettily but they are not observed. The light that flickers off their crests is the same light. There is little sense of the depth, or danger, of the sea. He is not Turner. Perhaps this is a consequence of his working in his studio. It was only in his last few years (from which there are few paintings at Kirkcaldy) that he painted *en plein air*. His work from this final period is notably darker.

He has a love of children. It is a feature[200] of almost all his pastoral works and many of his seascapes, but it is a love that slips into sentimentality. Even in *The Storm* (1883) here, a strong study for a larger work in the National Gallery of Scotland, he cannot resist having the not-very-wild sea overlooked by two boys lying exchanging confidences on the cliff in the foreground.

Too often the composition of the larger sea scenes is loose, the image petering out towards the edges of the canvas. Nevertheless, there is no better gallery outside the National Gallery of Scotland in which to consider McTaggart than Kirkcaldy.

Blyth, Nairn and Harley were united by their love of painting. Blyth died owning 237 paintings which filled every corner of his house, were hung in the office at his factory and were loaned, 116 of them, to the gallery.

Nairn's relish of paint can be seen in his gift of two large watercolours by Arthur Melville. In *Bullring Crowd* the left half of the paper is a blank white haze out of which the image of the bull and matador can be glimpsed. To the right the crowd is dense, highlit by dots of brilliant red and blue which are then partially sponged out: an inversion of Alexander Cozens's blot technique 100 years earlier. Painting this good suggests that Melville's work merits reassessment.

The many qualities of Kirkcaldy inspire confidence and have encouraged people to make bequests in the knowledge that their gifts would be hung in good company. George Henry's executors donated one of his finest paintings, *Lady with a Goldfish*. The rich brown depth of the palette, the model's vivid red lips and languid left hand, the gleam of light on the bowl and the ambiguity of the fish make this a triumph of silent sensuality.

That quality has been sustained by a policy of acquisition of works by contemporary Scottish artists: William Gillies, William Gear, Anne Redpath, Joan Eardley, John Houston, John Bellany and Elizabeth Blackadder.

Nairn's and Blyth's taste could only be expressed as a result of their management of major Kirkcaldy manufacturing companies, some of whose products can be seen in the museum downstairs: a large black-and-white Wemyss-ware pig from the Fife Pottery; two mid-19th-century chairs and a mirror carved by Thomas Williamson out of local coal;[201] linoleum printing blocks; and a chunk of 'Stevie beef', spongy rubber made by beating air into a mixture of resin and linseed oil. This admirable museum encourages visitors to handle and smell the Stevie beef and so inhale the idiosyncratic smell of Kirkcaldy.

NEW LANARK *

New Lanark, South Lanarkshire ML11 9DB
Tel. 01555 661345, fax 01555 665738
www.newlanark.org

Robert Owen's ideal community, perched on the banks of the falls of the Clyde

The placid River Clyde, flowing west to the sea, plunges suddenly through a deep gorge over the falls of Corra Linn, down and down 100 feet to Stonebyres. Here in 1785 David Dale built cotton mills to be powered by this torrent of water.

You approach New Lanark by winding down a zigzag road to its mills and terraced cottages built of pale sandstone. At once the architecture informs you that this is no ordinary manufactory. Colin McWilliam, in *Scottish Townscape*, describes it: 'There are four mills, of which the earliest have Venetian windowed stairs. Slightly above them, tenement housing is strung out along the lower contours of the densely wooded hill down which you have come. In the middle, opposite the mills, are the new buildings, a four-storey block the same size as the north side of Charlotte Square, but at no pains to disguise the repetitive pattern of the windows. A plain pediment marks the centre of the frontage and is also (helped by the little bell-house overhead) a sufficient focus for the whole composition.'[202]

In 1799 Dale sold New Lanark to his son-in-law Robert Owen, who used it to put into practice what he called 'the most important experiment for the happiness of the human race that has yet been instituted in any part of the world', commencing on 1 January 1800. Owen believed that men and women would work better if they were educated and well treated. A notice in the Institution for the Formation of Character reads 'The object of human existence, as of all that has life, is happiness.' For Owen that could be achieved 'only by nurturing and inspiring young minds'.

It is hard for industrial museums to convey anything of the heat, dust, smell and unremitting noise of a 19th-century factory. New Lanark shows you working machinery on one floor of a mill but elsewhere concentrates on the social aspect of Owen's experiment: housing and education.

The school is a hall, flooded with light. Today's children are encouraged to put on the white cotton tunics that Owen designed for his pupils and to use the forms, slates and mathematical models he provided. Here is the huge terrestrial globe (a replica) used until 1884 and the 'Stream of Time' oil cloths on which were laid out the chronology of world history, ancient and modern. Pupils were taught to dance and sing and learnt about nature out in the valley and by handling objects (here are cowrie shells, fossils, an ammonite, a palm tree section, coconuts).

To Owen this was all common sense but some aspects of it are still radical today. There were no punishments or rewards in school. The teaching ratio was twenty children to one teacher,[203] 30 per cent better than the government's target today. School hours were 7.30–9 a.m., 10 a.m.–12 p.m., and 3–5 p.m. In winter this was changed to 7.30–9 a.m., then 10 a.m.–2 p.m. with a half-hour interval. There were night classes for those over twelve, a nursery and an infant school, the first in the world.

The housing conditions are easier to show and two homes in a tenement have been reconstructed. A single room from 1820 has a set-in (a bed built into the wall); a hurlie (a bed to be tucked away beneath the set-in when not in use); a kist (chest); a creepie (stool); and an open fire. The 1933 room has electricity and cold running water, and the use of a cludgie, an indoor toilet, at the top of each stairhead. The objects in the room (dolly pegs, Shredded Wheat, a stone hot-water bottle) provide the triggers for nostalgia, direct or vicarious.

New Lanark avoids nostalgia because Owen avoided it. His ideals were utopian, a mixture of philanthropic humanism, paternalism and self-interest, but he was a businessman and New Lanark had to succeed financially. In the early years Owen increased the hours worked each day from thirteen to fourteen without any increase in pay, at the wish of his partners, but these were later reduced to ten and a half; watchmen were employed to keep order; and individual output was strictly monitored. The museum shop does a brisk trade in replicas of the Robert Owen silent monitor, painted white (good), yellow (fair), blue (not good), black (bad), that hung by each worker's place, but the monitors were for discipline and control, not for amusement.

A visitor in 1807 noted that 'Mr Owen is said to be a very strict man and is not popular in the neighbourhood.' He gained a measure of popularity after he maintained the workforce on full wages when, in 1806, an American embargo made spinning uneconomical and the mills stopped for six months. He was a competent capitalist, twice raising capital to buy back the company when his partners lost faith in it.[204]

His 'most important experiment' was indeed ahead of its time, ending child labour, providing free education, allowing labour to organise and questioning the profit motive, but it failed at New Harmony when he took it to America in 1824, as it failed at Orbiston 'World Town' in 1827. For the rest of his life, Owen concentrated on promoting his ideas in campaigns, speeches and essays (*A New View of Society or the Formation of Character*, 1813 and *Report to the County of Lanark*, 1820).

Owen had no interest in political organisation, believing that his ideas would prevail by the force of reason, a view of which such radicals as William Hazlitt and Francis Place despaired. Hazlitt shrewdly observed: 'His schemes, thus far are tolerated, because they are remote, visionary, inapplicable.'[205]

The extent to which Owen's ideals have been tolerated, been ignored or prospered is raised here in a pod-ride-cum-video-show. The hologram of a young girl called Harmony (gentle Edinburgh accent, short skirt, bobbed hair, silver make-up) comes back from the future to assess the impact of Owen's work and his writings. Her intervention sits strangely beside the authentic palpable objects elsewhere in New Lanark: the 1891 Platt spinning mule, the carding machine, the waterwheel, the buildings. Their authority better conveys the enduring, practical good sense of Robert Owen's *New View*.

STROMNESS MUSEUM ✳✳✳

52 Alfred Street, Stromness, Orkney Islands
KW16 3DF
Tel. 01856 850025
www.orkney.org/museums/stromness.htm

Brilliantly ordered small museum of Orkney life, model boats and scrimshaw

The Orkney Islands are about the sea and rock and the sky. Wherever you go – past the Old Man of Hoy or the Knap of Howar, round Tor Ness or Grim Ness, past Skara Brae, in Scapa Flow – the sea is there, giving and taking away, to be relied on only to change. It is fitting that at this museum there is the tang of salt within and the cry of gulls without.

In the main room, wherever you look there are ships and tackle: ships in cases, ships in bottles, fore-rigged schooners, inshore trawlers; herring drifters, tugs and traders; barques and brigs and stocky seiners; octants and logs, long-line fishing baskets, moulds for fish hooks, 'auskerries' for baling, a poke net for sillock fishing, a sea chest with a painted lid.

This may not be, as the museum's original notice claimed, 'the largest collection of Curios and Rare and Interesting Exhibits to be seen in the North of Scotland' (displayed when the museum moved to its present building in 1858) but few museums have more savour or sense of self.

The Orkney Natural History Society was founded on 18 December 1837, 'in Mrs Flett's large room' in the Commercial Hotel. Its purpose was declared to be: 'the promoting of natural Science by the support of a museum'. Its first president was the Revd Dr Charles Clouston, a contributor to the *Encyclopaedia Britannica* on meteorology.

By 1858 the society's collection had outgrown Mrs Flett's room, so it was moved to the upper floor of its present building, the lower becoming, for a time, the new town hall. The building is straightforward, double-fronted, stone-faced and slate-roofed, on a corner where the narrow passage-like streets meet and open out. On its gable end, looking out blankly

over the harbour, is a single-storey pilot's house. The poet George Mackay Brown lived across from the museum.

Inside the door there is no standing on ceremony. You plunge into the collection of objects that the sea brings in or takes away. Among the flotsam is a billet of dyewood from the forests of Coromandel, washed up after the Swedish East Indiaman the *Svecia* sank in 1740, having lain broken-backed on the North Ronaldsay rocks for three days. Sixty men died, forty-four survived. Here too are beans, carried from the West Indies on the Gulf Stream: molucca beans, sea-sword beans, horse-eyed beans from Jamaica.

The jetsam includes objects retrieved when the fifty-two ships of the German fleet, scuttled at Scapa Flow in June 1919, were raised in 1932: uniforms, binoculars, compasses, life-belts, pottery, silver, a ship's bell. Admiral van Reuter had thought, wrongly, that peace talks had failed and scuttled his fleet rather than let it fall into Allied hands.

Stromness is the last port for taking in provisions and water before the long leg west into the north Atlantic. Captain Cook docked here in 1780 before beginning his voyage to the south Pacific. A lantern clock is displayed that was owned by Alexander Stewart, who entertained Lieutenant Bligh at his home. His son, George, later sailed as midshipman on the *Bounty* and was the model for Torquil in Byron's *Don Juan*.

Its position made Stromness the ideal base for the Hudson's Bay Company, which had its main offices here for 200 years. By the late 18th century more than three-quarters of the company's workforce was Orcadian. The museum has many objects that attest to the company's links with North America: Cree beadwork from Fort Chipewyan; 'point' blankets on which the number of stripes indicate the number of beaver skins traded in exchange; moccasins; decorated sheaths for knives and combs, many donated by the company's chief factor, W. H. Watt, in the late 19th century.

Dr John Rae, on behalf of the Hudson's Bay Company, led three arctic expeditions to map Canada's Arctic coastline. He discovered the fate of the Franklin expedition, and the Rae Strait, the final link in a navigable North West Passage.

Here is the powder horn belonging to Franklin, which Rae recovered from Eskimos at Pelly Bay in 1854. Here, too, are Rae's octant, fiddle and the Inuit snow goggles that he used as he covered 13,000 miles between 1846 and 1854, while mapping 1,800 miles of coast.

Stranded beside the (later named) Richardson River, Rae got his colleagues and equipment over by crossing fourteen times in an inflatable cloth boat using two tin plates as paddles. The boat had been invented by Lieutenant Peter Halkett RN and Rae's boat, one of two known to exist, is displayed here.

Here too are objects brought back by another Orcadian explorer, Dr William Balfour Baillie RN, the surgeon on the 1854 expedition to the Niger, who had to take command when his superior officers died. Baillie spent more than a decade in the area, establishing trading posts and good relations with the native people.

Not all Orcadian sailors had such virtuous lives. John Gow, the son of a Stromness merchant, turned pirate. He and his crew were captured in 1725 and he was hanged at Execution Dock in London. Daniel Defoe wrote an account of his trial, a copy of which is here in its original edition: 'An Account of the Conduct and Proceedings of the late John Gow, alias Smith, Captain of the late PIRATES, Executed for Murther and Piracy ... with a Relation of all the horrid Murthers they committed in cold blood.'[206]

In whatever corner you peer there are curiosities: a copy of Stromness's newspaper, the *Stromness News and Weekly Advertiser*, of Friday, 16 May 1884, printed by W. R. Rendall, whose company remains the island's printer and who published the 1963 guide to the museum; a photograph of a young Robert Louis Stevenson, with his father, Thomas, on a visit that took in the eleven lighthouses that the Stevensons built in the Orkney Islands between 1788 and 1915.

Next door, in the Pilot's House, are sailmaking tools (thimbles and needles, marlin-spike and stitch mallet, beeswax for the sewing line, a punch and block to make metal grommets)[207] and objects that record the days when whaling was a major source of employment in the islands (harpoons and harpoon guns, walrus tusks, whalebones and scrimshaw).

On the first floor, above the swirl and eddies of these maritime collections, are those that record the natural history of the islands. The core of these collections is geology: granite, sandstone and flagstone from the Devonian period, 360 million years ago, when Lake Orcadie was south of the Equator. On the shore west of Stromness, the geologist Hugh Miller discovered the fossil fish *Homosteus Milleri* and the *Gyraptchius milleri*, as described in his book *Footprints of the Creator or the Asterolepis of Stromness*,[208] a book that contributed to, and amplified, Darwin's theses on evolution.

Miller was an honorary member of the Orkney Natural History Society, which has had a succession of distinguished scientists among its members: Magnus Spence, a dominie and author of the first compete *Flora Orcadensis*, whose herbarium is here in a handsome case; Robert Rendall, specialist in seashells; and James Sinclair, the curator of the Botanic Gardens in Singapore (1948–65).

Rendall's shells (molluscs, crustacea and echinoderms) make a display as rich as a brittle garden. To the expert, they are an outstanding collection. To the layman, they are objects of beauty: the pearl-pink thin tellin; the yellow dwarf winkle; the delicate beige, pink and blue, microscopic tiger scallop; the encrusted great scallop.

Around the walls are case after case of birds, stuffed by Victorian taxidermists, recording the remarkable number of varieties that live, or winter, in the islands: cliff birds; sea birds; perching birds; marsh birds. Here are crakes and shanks; plovers and fulmars; skuas and petrels; the little auk with its fluffed white breast, the puffin with its perky outsized beak and red shoes. There are guillemots and cormorants and an elegant black shag topped by its surprised tuft. Ospreys and kestrels, marlins and goshawks and a Greenland falcon with fierce eyes and commanding beak; gadwalls and whimbrels and velvet scoters; mergansers and gooseanders; pipits, winchats, waxwings, a tiny dunlin, a bartailed godwit with its long, fine beak, and every variety of gull – glaucous, Iceland, herring, ivory and the minatory great black-beaked.

Overhead there flies, suspended from the ceiling, not only the last great auk to be shot in Britain (outside St Kilda) at Papa Westray in 1813,[209] but the cast of a giant leathery turtle, six feet in length, caught by a Westray fisherman, Edwin Groat, in 1996.

These are ancient islands, inhabited since the Stone Age, their landscapes punctuated by cists and quoits and standing stones. Half a mile along the coast from the museum is the Warbeth cemetery. Its stones record in orderly rows the islands' families: Rendalls, Baillies, Cloustons, Mackays, Browns. The museum is a witness to their lives and to this land.

PIER ART CENTRE ***

Victoria Street, Orkney Islands KW16 3AA
Tel. 01856 850209

The St Ives painters' far northern fastness; yet an anomalous and perfect gem

Barbara Hepworth's *Figure in Sycamore* (1931) has a quiet authority. The set of the head and the facial expression, suggested by minimal detail, are aloof and dignified. The form flows under the eye. Hepworth demonstrates here her sympathy with materials as she discovers the figure in the grain of the wood. She stretches that grain sheer over the thighs and collarbone, and draws it through the figure's hair. It is a fine illustration of the conversation between eye and hands, between tools and material, that she and Henry Moore were exploring, and a work of achieved beauty.

Near by in Ben Nicholson's *Still Life with Pear* (c. 1931) the jugs, mugs, table and baroque legs are beginning to disappear into abstraction.

Both capture the quality and qualities of this collection, comprised of works by Hepworth and Nicholson and those St Ives artists who were influenced by them.

It is a personal collection put together slowly over more than thirty years by Margaret Gardiner, who was a friend of all these artists. She bought them because she liked them, to live with them and to enjoy them, in her house in Hampstead, near the Heath. They exude that delight and easy affection. They also make a collection of considerable importance.

The twenty-four works by Nicholson and Hepworth chart the ways in which in the early 1930s they were influenced by new friendships with Picasso, Arp, Calder and Mondrian, and how they, in turn, influenced almost all the artists Margaret Gardiner collected: Terry Frost, Peter Lanyon, Roger Hilton, Margaret Mellis, John Wells, Patrick Heron.

There is no neat thesis here. Almost all these artists moved between representation and abstraction. Nicholson himself returned to representation in works such as *St Ives, Cornwall* (1943–5) (in the Tate) and in his architectural etchings in the 1960s and '70s. This was the last time in the 20th century that British artists were influenced by European work before Jackson Pollock and the tide of American Abstract Expressionism swept through the 1950s.

Nicholson's and Hepworth's influence on these works is less easy to identify. Those working in St Ives were a close but not coherent group. Lanyon and Frost, Mellis and Wells, Heron and Hilton are not a school.

Peter Lanyon's *Box Construction* (1939–40) shows the pull of Nicholson and Naum Gabo, his *Heather Coast* (1963) that of the landscape. Terry Frost has not deviated from exploring pure abstractions of line and colour, in such worked as *Collage* (1950) and *Black and Orange* (1959).

There are works here that have tenuous, or no, links with St Ives: a small, early Paolozzi figure, and works by Alan Davie, Keith Vaughan and the lesser-known Julius Bissier and Italo Valenti.

All these are on a domestic scale, well suited to a gallery that, from the unpavemented

*Hepworth and Nicholson at the Pier
Art Centre*

corridor of the street outside, appears to be a
house. Behind it is a slate pier jutting out into
the harbour and the movement of fishing
boats, as if seen by Alfred Wallis.

The collection is well served by this gallery,
on the pier, designed in 1976 by Kate Heron
and Axel Burroughs of Levitt, Bernstein
Associates.[210] Orkney, like St Ives, has a salt,
alert quality of light found only beside northern seas. To have caught that light has been the
great achievement of the architects. It is let in
on one side through the pitch of the roof and
on the other by windows below waist height.
Perspectives, glimpses of Nicholson and Gabo,
are cut through the length of the building,
opening up the small galleries with new angles.
This quality of light goes some way to explaining why this collection of mostly St Ives work
is here, and is so comfortable.

Margaret Gardiner came to Orkney in the
1950s, looking for a remote place in which she
and her National Serviceman son could spend
his periods of leave. They loved the islands,
which became their adopted home – hence her
gift to the Pier.

It was an appropriate choice. Although
Cornwall and Orkney are 1,000 miles and two
nations apart, both have strong landscapes
surrounded by sea. Both are ancient places,
marked by standing stones, quoits and crom-
lechs. Both are swept treeless by ocean gales.
Both have this light that refreshes the eye and
sifts through these works.

With the nearby Stromness Museum (q.v.),
the Pier Art Centre provides a compelling
reason to visit Orkney if the beauty of these
islands made of rock and God were not reason
enough.

PAISLEY MUSEUM AND ART GALLERY **

High Street, Paisley, Renfrewshire PA1 2BA
Tel. 0141 889 3151
www.renfrewshire.gov.uk

The Paisley shawl reflects a history of utopian socialism, of boom and bust; good studio pottery, and Scottish and French paintings

The shawl that bears its name is woven into the fabric of Paisley. In its patterns are the stories of the town in the 19th century: the rise and fall of its industry; its social and political development; and the founding of this museum.

Paisley and its weavers have long traditions, radical and literary. By the early 1800s the town had three subscription libraries, several reading clubs, and literary and philosophical societies at which Owen and Paine, Burns and Scott, Shakespeare and Sterne were read and discussed. Out of them came the Weaver Poets, Robert Tannahill, remembered today for the song, 'Will Ye Go, Lassie, Go?', and Alexander Wilson; the *Weavers' Magazine* (1818–19); and an informed and articulate trade union, the General Association of Operative Weavers, which led a twelve-week strike in 1812–13. A working community with such an appetite for knowledge and self-improvement provided a strong base of support for a museum as soon as one could be afforded.

The depression of 1841–3 devastated Paisley: 67 of the town's 112 manufacturers went out of business; 15,000 weavers and their families were on relief; and the town itself went bankrupt, unable to repay until 1870 the money it was forced to borrow.

In 1871 the new museum opened. It was designed by John Honeyman and funded by Sir Peter Coats, chairman of J. & P. Coats, the great threadmakers. It is a Greek Revival building faced with four Ionic columns, two pilasters and a plain pediment. It may lack the majesty of Alexander 'Greek' Thompson's work but it is a clean, handsome building on an elevated site in the middle of the town.

Its premier collection concerns the Paisley shawl, flag of the town's economy through recessions and booms for over seventy years. Shawls whose patterns were based on 17th-century Kashmiri designs were made fashionable first by the trading activities of the British East India Company and later by the Empress Josephine, following Napoleon's campaigns in the Near East.[211] The all-over patterns associated today with Paisley did not emerge until the 1850s. The patterns at the edges and ends gradually encroached on the originally white centres, as shown on the Kirking shawl in soft grey, pink and blue (1840s).

Here are all the swirls of pattern and plumage colours – shapes of mango and almond, that kept Paisley ahead of the competition from Edinburgh and Norwich; and the looms, at first hand looms in traditional but-an-ben cottage loom shops, then in the 1830s in factories where as many as 6,000 Jacquard looms were installed. Here too are displays about the designers (James Foote, Thomas Holdway and, for three years in the 1840s, the young J. Noel Paton). There is evidence of the radicalism that grew with the industry, sharpened by five depressions between 1816 and 1843 in the wake of the Napoleonic Wars.

Coats also provided money to build a collection. Its catalogue of 19th-century French, Scottish and English paintings makes fine reading: Corot, Courbet, Boudin, Fantin-Latour; Troyon, Rousseau, Daubigny from the Barbizon School; Ramsay, Raeburn; Paton, Orchardson, McTaggart the elder; the Glasgow School and the Colourists – although none of these artists is represented by his best work.

Twentieth-century Scottish painters with work here include Joan Eardley and Robin Philipson, head of drawing and painting at Edinburgh College of Art, whose pupils included John Bellany, Alexander Moffat and the Paisley-born John Byrne. (He is well represented in such other Scottish galleries as GOMA, the Hunterian Museum and Art Gallery, Glasgow Museum and Art Gallery, the People's Palace and the Scottish National Portrait Gallery, all q.v.). Paisley has eleven of his works. Byrne stopped exhibiting

John Byrne's Paisley Sunset

for seventeen years (1975–1992) but here are paintings from before and after the gap that shed interesting light on and into it: the early *Church Interior* (1963–4) and *Alexander Wilson and Friends* (1969) and the recent *Paisley Sunset* (1997), a near-Vorticist townscape of Paisley's factories as they face the clouds and the violent, dying sun. Before studying painting at Glasgow School of Art (1958–63), Byrne worked as a slab boy at the A. F. Stoddard carpet factory in Paisley, in the days when Paisley's mills still employed 10,000 workers.

Since 2003 Paisley has been one of six Scottish museums to benefit from the Contemporary Art Society's Collecting Scheme for Scotland. The gallery has chosen works that move across the traditional divide between fine and decorative art: a dress by Emily Bates knitted from laboriously spun human hair, a portrait by Enrico David in the craft skill of embroidery.

The museum has the work of one other Paisley artist, now almost forgotten: the sculptor John Henning. His work, if not regarded, is seen in London every day on the friezes on Decimus Burton's Athenaeum Club and on the same architect's screen at Hyde Park Corner. Both were made with his son, John Henning Jnr, in 1828 and in both they employed motifs from the Parthenon frieze.

Like his father, Henning was a building craftsman. At the age of twenty-nine he risked turning his enjoyment in making portrait medallions of friends and acquaintances into his full-time work and moved to Glasgow when his portraits of James Watt, Sir Walter Scott and others had some success. Around the time Henning arrived in London in 1811, Lord Elgin returned with the Parthenon marbles and displayed them in his Park Lane House.

Henning was so moved that he applied to Elgin for permission to draw and model from the marbles, much to the fury of the President of the Royal Academy, Benjamin West, who wished himself to retain exclusive rights and who saw Henning as an untrained commercial outsider. Henning worked on the marbles and those from the Temple of Apollo at Bassae[212] for twelve years and translated them into exquisite plaster casts.[213]

This was the peak of his career. George IV was among the first subscribers. Princess Charlotte sat to him. Josiah Wedgwood commissioned a set of medallions. But the panels were pirated by French and Italian firms, who flooded the market with inferior copies, selling over 12,000.

Throughout his life Henning remained a radical, selling the *Weavers' Magazine* in London, and even persuading Princess Charlotte to read it while she was sitting to him. She later remarked, 'Mr Henning, I am not indulged with that kind of reading.'[214] The Royal Academy, with the exception of Henry Fuseli, continued to ignore him and he died in poverty.

It was not the full-frontal assault of radical trade unionism, or world recession, or new technology that brought down Paisley's shawl industry: it was an assault from the rear. The introduction of the bustle in 1870 meant that no shawl could be worn by a woman of fashion. Within ten years production had dwindled dramatically. The sun had begun to set on Paisley 100 years before John Byrne's townscape.

FERGUSSON GALLERY **

Marshall Place, Perth, Tayside PH2 8NU
Tel. 01738 441944
www.pkc.gov.uk/ah/fergussongallery.htm

*Low round waterworks strangely suitable for
J. D. Fergusson's light-celebrating art*

The Round House stands on the corner of
Marshall Place beside the River Tay, at the
outer edge of the city centre. It was built in
1832, as the Perth Water Works, to the designs
of the engineer and architect Adam Anderson,
its style and strength drawn directly from its
function. The only indication that this is an art
gallery is provided in front of the building by
a polished bronze statue, *Torse de Femme*, an
ecstatic nude, stretching, that owes something
to Boccioni and to Wyndham Lewis, and is
based on a small sculpture by Fergusson.

The Fergusson Gallery opened here in 1992
to house the large collection of John Duncan
Fergusson's work (oil paintings, watercolours,
drawings, sketchbooks, sculptures, letters,
photographs, catalogues, memorabilia) that he
left to the dancer and choreographer Margaret
Morris, his lover from 1913 until his death
in 1961.[215]

The confined space of the round galleries
intensifies the impact of Fergusson's paintings:
their energy and sensuality, the visceral love of
paint and its thick, creamy texture; and above
all, his colours – pinks, red, greens, yellows,
blues that leap at you.

Fergusson's work, like that of the other
Colourists[216] (Samuel John Peploe, Francis
Campbell Boileau Cadell and George Leslie
Hunter), can be seen in all the major Scottish
galleries,[217] and in the Tate, but only here do
you have a collection that spans the whole of
his working life and allows you to consider the
early influences on him, and his development.

Apart from a few weeks at the Trustees'
Academy *c.*1895, Fergusson was self-taught.
His early watercolours and oil paintings
declare his influences: the Glasgow Boy Arthur
Melville and Edouard Manet. More striking
still is his debt to James Abbott McNeill

Whistler. His watercolour *The Trocadero, Paris*
(*c.*1902) is a direct homage to Whistler's *Noc-
turnes* of the 1870s, his portraits (*The White
Dress*, 1904, *The White Ruff*, 1907, and *The
Hat with the Pink Scarf*, 1907) to Whistler's
portraits of the early 1890s. Fergusson wrote
later of Whistler in his book *Modern Scottish
Painters*, 'Here was a man … a man with
real sense of design, a real sense of colour and
quality of paint.'[218] Already Fergusson's work
shows the depth of his own colours (the blues
of the sky and the river at night in *The
Trocadero, Paris*), the richness of his brushwork (the hat and hair in *Jean: the Cock
Feather*, 1903) and the idiosyncratic thickness
of the way he handles paint (*Packet of Matches
and Match Box, c.*1898).

Almost one third of the 143 oil paintings in
the collection date from these early years, up to
1910, and a further third cover his work in the
1920s and '30s, but the crucial years 1910–14 are
less well represented by only twelve canvases.

Fergusson had been visiting France to paint,
often with Peploe, since 1897 but it was only
after he moved permanently to Paris in
1907 that he experienced the combined impact
of the forms and colour of the Fauves;[219]
the movement and rhythms introduced by
Diaghilev and the Ballet Russe;[220] the theories
of Henri-Louis Bergson in his book *Creative
Evolution* (1906) concerning 'abundant Nature'
and 'the life-force'; and the Nude.[221] The effect
of these was dramatic and dominated his
painting for the rest of his working life.

Fergusson's work exploded. What had been
tactile became sensual, even sexual; what had
been static leapt into rhythmic movement;
all this came together in nudes that exuded
confidence and *joie de vivre*. The critic John
Middleton Murry wrote that, 'for Fergusson it
[rhythm] was the essential quality in a painting
or sculpture' and that 'the real purpose of "this
modern movement" – a phrase frequently on
Fergusson's lips – was to reassert the pre-
eminence of rhythm.'[222] Of the three key paintings of this period (*At my Studio Window*, 1910,
Rhythm, 1910, and *Les Eus*, 1911–13) only the
first is here.[223]

Soon after this Fergusson met Margaret

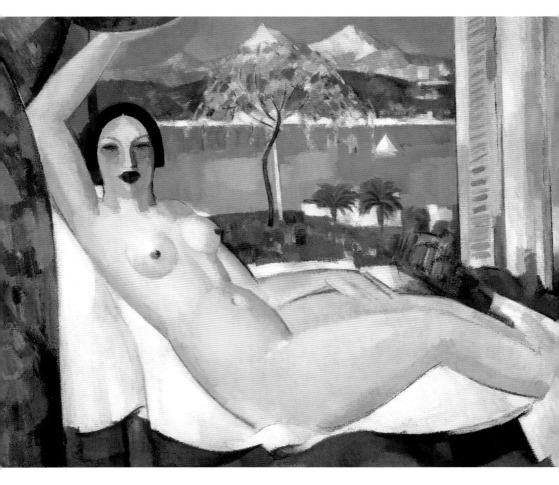

J. D. Fergusson: Spring in the South
(Fergusson Gallery)

Morris, a dancer and a leading proponent, with Isadora Duncan, of the idea of health and beauty. Fergusson had always delighted in painting handsome women but now, and throughout the 1920s and '30s, statuesque beauties (often Morris herself) and their full breasts and wide hips became the main subjects for his drawing, painting and sculpture. The doors to the life of the body, once flung open, could not be closed.

This sensuality set him apart from the other Colourists but did not stop him from continuing to see himself as Scottish, Celtic. 'To go to Paris was the natural thing for the Scot,'

he insisted. 'It doesn't seem to have occurred to the modern Scot that the Scottish Celt, when in France, was among his own people, the French Celts . . . The "Esprit Gaulois" [the Celtic Spirit] still exists.'[224]

He and Morris returned to Glasgow to help promote a Scottish artistic renaissance after the Second World War through the New Art Club. He continued to paint until his death in 1961. The colour, even the enjoyment, are there but they are becoming generalised, lacking in detail or surprise. When he attempted a huge Celtic painting, *Danu, Mother of the Gods* (1952), the result was embarrassing, neither symbolic nor Celtic.

It is his fluent and decisive drawing, his sense of colour and speed, and such painting as *At my Studio Window* that will maintain his reputation. 'They express the rebellion against the grey life, with an almost soapbox show that the human body deserves the right of health and beauty,' wrote the critic Robin Millar. 'It is the pagan exultancy a normal northerner feels in the Southern sun.'[225]

PERTH MUSEUM AND ART GALLERY **

George Street, Perth, Tayside PH1 5LB
Tel. 01738 632488

Antiquities, natural sciences, very good silver, art with a Perthshire connection, weapons and armour

Perth Museum and Art Gallery is one of the oldest museums in Britain, still in its original building. You enter to the left of the colonnaded portico of David Morison's museum and mount the steps into the top-lit entrance hall, from which opens the classical inner rotunda. Around its walls are three full-length portraits, larger than life. Two are by Lawrence at his most grand: *John Murray, 4th Duke of Atholl* (c.1826) and his best friend, *Thomas Graham, Lord Lynedoch of Balgowan* (c.1815). Each married a daughter of Lord Cathcart at a joint ceremony on 26 December 1774. Lynedoch's wife died. He enlisted, raised the 90th Regiment in 1794, joined Wellesley in Spain and retired after the battle of Waterloo, at which he was Wellington's second-in-command. He never remarried. Atholl became the patron of Landseer, host to Robert Burns and builder of the fine stone bridge across the Tay at Dunkeld a few miles upriver from the museum. Lawrence scatters the bridge's plans at the Duke's feet.

Among the museum's paintings is a sketch by Landseer painted on his first visit to Scotland in 1824, *John Crerar and his Pony*. He worked this up for Atholl into *Death of a Stag in Glen Tilt*, which still hangs in Blair Castle. Landseer helped create the 19th-century image of the Highlands, as did Millais in his painting of *John Ruskin* (1854) with the falls of

Glenfinlas cascading behind him. While he painted, Millais fell in love with Ruskin's beautiful young wife, Effie Gray, whom he married in 1855 after the scandal of the Ruskins' divorce on the grounds of non-consummation. Millais's portrait of Effie, *Euphemia Chalmers Millais* (1873), is here. The matronly mother of eight children looks down, buttressed by cushions, her hands in her lap, her eyes on the brink of narrowing. She has become a severe, elderly woman at the age of forty-five, all passion spent.

The fine art collection, based largely on bequests from Robert Hay Robertson and Robert Brough, two local merchants who died in 1925 and left money for the extension to the gallery by Smart, Stewart and Mitchell (1935), has the not-unfamiliar mixture of 19th-century French, English and Scottish paintings: Boudin, Dyce, Scott Lauder, David Octavius Hill, McTaggart, D.Y. Cameron. Horatio McCulloch's romantic *Loch Katrine* (1866) portrays an unblemished landscape twenty years after the first railways opened up the Highlands to tourism.

The landowners of Perthshire were still going on the Grand Tour in the early 19th century and the museum has some of the booty that they brought home. Francis, 15th Lord Gray, of Kinfauns Castle bought a huge marble urn, made for the Empress Josephine, decorated with rams' heads, grasshoppers, birds and vines, on whose base is the imperial eagle. John Campbell, Baron Breadalbane, Earl of Ormelie, 4th Earl and 1st Marquess of Breadalbane, returned in 1831 with a collection of Neapolitan paintings, including two works ascribed to Luca Giordano, of which one is *Esau Selling his Birthright*. Here too are paintings by Jacob More, a Scottish artist who emigrated to Rome in 1771 to paint and deal, producing landscapes with a Claudean light which show how radiant was Claude's own skill.

The nucleus of the musem's collections was the objects collected by the Literary and Antiquarian Society of Perth from as early as 1784. In 1914, they were augmented by a large and distinctly local natural history collection

Loch Katrine *by Horatio McCulloch (Perth Museum and Art Gallery)*

from the Perthshire Society of Natural Science, which had run its own sizeable museum elsewhere in the town.

The collections make it clear that the prosperity of the city of Perth predated the great lairds. Excavations between 1975 and 1977 on the site of Marks and Spencer's store opposite the museum found a 13/14th-century gold brooch. These excavations revealed Perth's rigs, or backlands, whose middens provide rich evidence of the quotidian: food, pots, leather shoes. For the people of Perth, their survival was in commerce. In the 15th century Perth had nine guilds: baxters (bakers), glovers, shoe makers, fleshers, tailors, wrights, weavers, fullers and hammermen (metal workers, both practical and precious); and, in time, the city had notable silversmiths. The museum has a strong collection of silver, including a tumbler cup and chalice by Robert Gairdine, flatware by John Cornfute and much early-19th-century work by the Roberts Keays (uncle and nephew) as well as contemporary pieces by local silversmiths, including Malcolm Appleby.

Curiosities of the collection are the silver balls of Rattray. Probably made by Thomas Ramsay, these balls were the trophy played for by teams of men from the parish of Rattray near Blairgowrie, eighteen miles north of Perth, in all but ten years between 1639 and 1766. The winners' names were engraved on shields, fifteen of which survive, but there is no record of how to play the sport that formed the competition.

On display in the Upper Rotunda is the D. L. Edwards Collection of communion tokens, stamped and issued by the Reformed church and its seceders, to be handed in at communion. Their variety illustrates the extent to which the post-Reformation church in Scotland was split: the United Free Church, the United Presbyterian Church and the Reformed Presbyterian Church; the Original Seceders and the United Seceders; the Associate

Congregation and the United Associate Congregation. In the established Church of Scotland, attended by Atholl, Lynedoch and Breadalbane, no tokens were required.

STIRLING SMITH ART GALLERY AND MUSEUM *

Dumbarton Road, Stirling FK8 2RQ
Tel. 01786 471917
www.smithartgallery.demon.co.uk

Local Scottish life over millennia, and the oldest football in Britain; a favourite of Robert Louis Stevenson

The Stirling Smith is the only art gallery and museum in Britain to have its guide[226] in the form of seventeen sonnets that introduce the visitor to its history, its objects, its dreams, its ghosts.

Thomas Stuart Smith (1814–69), collector, social reformer and artist, left money to build a museum that opened in 1874. He bequeathed it his fine art collection, which included a portrait, entitled *The Pipe of Freedom*, of a former African slave, painted to celebrate the abolition of slavery in America in 1863. It depicts the former slave leaning back as he lights a long clay pipe.

The museum, designed by John Lessels of Edinburgh, has a neoclassical facade. Its four Doric pillars support a pediment that bears the arms of the city, a royal burgh, and the alleged arms of Thomas Stuart Smith.[227]

Stirling is an historic city on a crossing point over the River Forth. This is the site of a Roman fort on the Antonine Wall and of famous battles: the victory of William Wallace over the English at the battle of Stirling Bridge (1297) and of Robert the Bruce near by at the battle of Bannockburn (1314). John Duncan's painting here, to mark the 600th anniversary of the battle, depicts the Bruce slaying De Bohun.

The museum's first curator, Alexander Croall, was an eminent botanist and an expert on seaweed whose four-volume work on the subject is still a standard and whose seaweed collection remains here. Robert Louis Stevenson visited the museum with his parents in its opening year and may well have taken the plot for *Kidnapped* from the circumstances under which Thomas Stuart Smith, like David Balfour, came into his inheritance. Smith's father and uncle loved the same woman. Smith's father won her and emigrated, leaving his brother the family estate, Glassingall. When both father and uncle were dead, in 1849, Smith had great difficulty proving his title to their estate.

The museum has no defining collections but is rich in artefacts of significance in the history of Stirling and of Scotland: Bronze Age funerary urns; Roman ceramics and building materials; the Stirling jug, holding three imperial pints, a pint being by Act of Parliament the standard liquid measure in Scotland from 1457; 'the world's oldest football', dated from 1540, found in the roof space at Stirling Castle and 'the world's oldest curling stone' (1511); the cloak and axe of the headsman, a twenty-year-old medical student, Thomas Moore, who executed the radical weavers Andrew Hardie and John Baird after the insurrection of 1820.

In addition there is a collection of paintings: views of Stirling by Johannes Vosterman and by Alexander Nasmyth, as well as a fine Claude-like landscape by this pupil of Allan Ramsay; the Stirling portrait of Prince Charles Edward Stuart (c. 1750–51) by Cosmo Alexander; a portrait of *Mrs Callendar of Craigforth* (1750–73) by Reynolds; and assorted 19th-century paintings by Sir George Harvey PRSA, Joseph Denovan Adam and John Duncan.

James Robertson in his *Stirling Sonnets* calls the museum 'this breathing ground of buried lives, slow-seeping energy. Agnostic, I believe again – almost – in more to come, a second time around. Can this be all there is? How can it be?' He is answered by Robert Louis Stevenson: 'I always believe we can never be so well employed as in endeavouring to understand as well as we can the original meaning of that system of things in whose ruins we live.'

FYVIE CASTLE *

Fyvie, nr. Turriff, Aberdeenshire AB53 8JS
Tel. 01651 891266
www.nts.org.uk

*Radiant portraits by Raeburn alleviate an
impressive yet oppressive castle*

'The chief attractions of Fyvie Castle are
archaeological, historical, legendary and
romantic,' declared *The Times* of 5 February
1885. The newspaper was trying to sell it for Sir
Maurice Duff-Gordon. It is assuredly a mighty
fortress palace, surrounded by the River Ythan
and buttressed by towers and turrets with
cylindrical bartizans[228] at each corner.

Despite this it did not sell for four years
until it was bought by Alexander Leith, later
Lord Leith of Fyvie, who filled it with his
collection of armour, tapestries and paintings.
These quite fail to dispel its forbidding appearance. Fyvie was a castle in which William the
Lyon (1214), Alexander II (1222) and Robert
the Bruce (1308) held court. Its great wheel
stair, beneath the red crescent of the Setons
who built it,[229] establishes ceremony.

On acquiring Fyvie, Leith began to expand
his collections, purchasing portraits by Scougall and Jamesone, and paintings by Michael
Dahl, Nicolaes Maes, Lawrence, Hoppner,
Reynolds and Romney. In particular he
acquired Gordon family portraits associated
with Fyvie, and portraits of the Forbeses and
Gregorys, from whom he was descended.
It is a collection of British portraiture that
keeps to the established mainstream (Hudson,
Gainsborough, Beechey, Cotes, Millais) but
which contains some paintings that stand out,
notably Pompeo Batoni's grand portrait of
Col. the Hon. William Gordon (1766).

Batoni paints Gordon swathed with tartan,
sword in hand, receiving the victor's laurels
from the figure of Roma against a backdrop of
the Colosseum. From the early 1750s Batoni
and his studio assistants churned out Grand
Tour portraits to young British milords to a
formula: head and shoulders or three-quarter
length; against a pillar or a plinth; a reference

to Rome in the background.[230] It would seem
that Gordon had more money and more time,
and Batoni, let off the leash, shows how good
he could be. It is a full-length on a canvas that
is wider than usual and Batoni spreads the
swagger of the pose to fill, indeed command,
it. The tartan spills around Gordon's manly
chest and cascades to the floor behind, the left
wrist is cocked on the hip, the hair is swept
back, the chin is raised, the nose and lip are
curled, statuary is literally broken at his feet. It
is a proud trophy of Scots glamour to bring
home from a Grand Tour.

Notwithstanding Batoni's *Gordon* the chief
reason to visit Fyvie is the largest and best
collection of portraits by Sir Henry Raeburn
outside the National Gallery of Scotland
(NGS) or the Scottish National Portrait
Gallery (both q.v.). Here, principally in the
Regency-decorated Back Morning Room,
you can see paintings that span his career
from the early *John Forbes of Blackford* (1777)
(at the time when Raeburn, hitherto un-
tutored, was involved in evening classes at the
Theatre Royal, Edinburgh, supervised by the
master of the Trustees' Academy, Alexander
Runciman),[231] to his low-angle, romantic
head and shoulders of *Charles, 5th Duke of
Gordon* (*c.*1819), painted four years before his
death.

Raeburn described himself in 1784 as 'Portrait Painter in Edinburgh'.[232] By not following
Allan Ramsay or his contemporary David
Wilkie to London Raeburn has left an unrivalled record of Scotland in the dimming
years of its Enlightenment. His facility, and his
empathy for sitters, enabled him to paint, with
equal success, men and women, young and
old, children, the vain, the quiet, the grand, the
reclusive. His finest portraits are of women,
and among these there is none finer than his
portrait here of *Isabella Macleod, Mrs James
Gregory* (*c.*1798).

A portrait artist who likes and attends to
women is comparatively rare, but one who
displays as much sympathy with elderly or
plain women[233] as with beauties is to be
cherished especially. *Isabella Macleod* does not
have the immediate sensuality of his portrait

of *Margaret Macdonald, Mrs Robert Scott Moncrieff* (NGS) in which, a decade later than the Fyvie portrait, Raeburn heightens the viewer's emotions by playing the almost saintly simplicity of the face against the blatant sexuality of the body and dress. In contrast *Isabella Macleod* is all modesty and calm intelligence. Raeburn sets her to one side, her weight on her right arm, her gaze to the left, against a background of softly mottled greys, greens and silver. This sets off the creams and whites of her skin and her dress and, at the centre, the black fruit of her eyes.

This painting has passages of Raeburn's most brilliant painting: her hair and the turban are a soft confection of grey/brown (her hair) and strokes of gentle white (the turban); the drifts of material in her dress and scarf are tinged by the faintest grey picked up from the velvet ribbon tied under her bust. This portrait alone is worth the journey.

It is curious to find it here within the stern masculinity of this castle, a place of stone and wood, where stories fester of 17th-century ghosts and the 13th-century curse of Tammas the Rhymer, a seer. It is a place of dark weather in which the sunlight is provided by Raeburn.

Wales

The reasons why there are relatively few museums and galleries in Wales are not easy to discern. Its culture is rich and ancient; its geology fascinating; its archaeology still considerably untapped.

Welsh industrial magnates made as much money in the 19th century as those in Lancashire and Yorkshire, or in Scotland. Yet Wales's museums do not entirely reflect all this. There are comparatively few large towns and cities in which to found major museums; some of the great Welsh industrial fortunes were made by such men as Lord Bute (mining in South Wales and Cardiff's docks) and Richard Pennant (slate quarries at Llanberis) who invested in their estates (Bute in Cardiff Castle and Castell Coch; Pennant in Penrhyn Castle) rather then in civic philanthropy in the form of museums.

Richard Glynn Vivian in Swansea was an exception, as were Gwendoline and Margaret Davies, the daughters of the timber king 'Sawyer' Davies, whose collection of French 19th-century paintings enriches the National Museum and Gallery of Wales.

The local authority museums that exist are good, Swansea being one of the oldest in Britain (founded 1835) and Oriel Yns Môn that rarity, a new civic art gallery.

The National Museums and Galleries of Wales, whose outstations at Caerleon, Llanberis and St Fagan's are described here, and the excellent National Library of Wales, by drawing to themselves so much of the best material in the country (particularly natural history, geology and archaeology to the National Museum, and works on paper to the National Library), may inadvertently have inhibited the growth of other collections.

I have included the delightful local museum at Brecon but been unable to find space for several others that have collections with as much local savour: the Castle Museum at Haverfordwest, whose collections of armour, heraldry and all things military are housed, appropriately, in its 13th-century castle; Llandrindod Wells Museum, which records the life of this spa town and has material from the excavations of the Roman fort at Castell Collen; and Plas Newydd at Llangollen, the 18th-century black-and-white house that was once home to the 'Ladies of Llangollen', Lady Eleanor Butler and Miss Sarah

LLANGEFNI○   ○BEAUMAR

A5

BANGOR○   A55

A487

○
LLANBERIS

Gwynedd

A487

A470   A4

A487

ABERYSTWYTH○

A487

Dyfed

A487

A40   A40

A48

West
Glamorgan
○
SWANSEA   M4

20 miles

Ponsonby, a celebrated couple in Regency Wales whose friends included Sheridan and Burke, Castlereagh and Canning, Wordsworth and Scott, and, perhaps strangely, the Duke of Wellington. Although Plas Newydd is overlooked by the ruined castle of Dinas Bran, it is a far distance from the ancient world of Cadwallader, Llywelyn the Great, Owen Glyn Dwr and the great deeds of the *Mabinogion* that echo through the culture of Wales.

NATIONAL LIBRARY OF WALES ✳✳✳

The University of Wales, Buarth Mawr,
Aberystwyth, Ceredigion SY23 3BU
Tel. 01970 632800
www.llgc.org.uk

The great texts and manuscripts; maps and music

The library is set on a high place overlooking Aberystwyth, far enough back from the sea to command the broad sweep of the bay. Designed by Sidney Kyffin Greenslade, the building is serious and grand, as befits a copyright library (since 1911) that is the custodian of all written knowledge in Wales and in Welsh. Here are 4 million volumes that tell how England and the world have viewed Wales and how Wales has viewed itself.

This is a library of libraries, in which prime place must go to Robert Vaughan of Hengwrt (1592–1666). He wrote of his lifelong research into the five royal tribes of Cambria, which led to his one published work, *British Antiquities Revived*, 'My love and zeal to know the truth and certainty of things past moves me sometimes to a passion, when I call to mind the idle and slothful life of my countrymen, who, in the revolution of a thousand years almost, afford but only Caradoc of Lancarvan … to register anything … of the acts of the Princes of Wales, … some piece-meals excepted.'

That zeal resulted in a library that contained 200 manuscripts, most of them annotated by Vaughan, some transcribed by him, including the *Hendregadredd Manuscript*, the earliest witness of the works of the Gogynfeirdd, the Welsh court poets of the 12th–14th centuries.[1] It was probably copied by the Cistercian monks of the Abbey of Strata Florida in Ceredigion.

Of greater value still is *The Book of Taliesin*, a manuscript that contains some of the oldest poems in Welsh, many attributed to the 6th-century poet Taliesin. It is evidence of the sophistication of Celtic literature and learning, having roots as firmly in Latin and Greek texts as in Welsh, with allusions to Hercules and Alexander as well as to King Arthur[2] and Dylan eil Ton.

Welsh medieval scholars prized English texts and the library has a mid-15th-century copy of Lydgate's *Life of Our Lady* and several texts by Chaucer, including his *Treatyse on the Astrolabe* and his translation of Boethius's *De Consolatione Philosophiae* and the Hengwrt Chaucer, an early manuscript of *The Canterbury Tales* that reached Wales by the mid 16th century and found its way into the library of Robert Vaughan. These, like the rest of Vaughan's library, came here via the mid-19th-century library of W. W. E. Wynne, Conservative MP for Merionethshire, who sold them to Sir John Williams, one of the founders of the National Library.

Sir John also collected watercolours and drawings. These include landscape studies (mainly Welsh) by Thomas Rowlandson from his tour through Wales in 1797 and by J. M. W. Turner, whose oil paintings of *Aberdulais* and *Dolbadarn* (both 1795) are here. *Dolbadarn* is an earlier and smaller version of the landscape he presented to the Royal Academy. Also here are works by the Cozens (father and son), Sandby and Gainsborough, and by Welsh artists from Richard Wilson and Thomas Jones to contemporaries (Will Roberts and Sir Kyffin Williams).

The scope of the National Library is wide, encompassing ecclesiastical and legal archives, maps and surveys, photographs and letters. Among the latter are those written by David Lloyd George to his brother, William George, and to his first wife, Dame Margaret. Such a far fling nets oddities, including a Welsh prayer book of 1770 that belonged to David Samwell, the surgeon who sailed with Captain Cook. Samwell has left us his autograph account of the execution of Louis XVI in 1792.

This is a library in which Robert Vaughan, with his 'love and zeal to know the truth and certainty of things past', might find himself at home.

'Breuddwyd a welwyn neithiwr . . .' from the Black Book of Carmarthen (*National Library of Wales*)

ABERYSTWYTH SCHOOL OF ART COLLECTION **

The University of Wales, Buarth Mawr, Aberystwyth, Ceredigion SY23 1NE
Tel. 01970 622460

Printing as a fine art and as a teaching tool

The School of Art at the University of Wales in Aberystwyth offers one of the few remaining print-making courses. As a teaching resource for the course it has a unique collection of (mainly) 20th-century prints, etchings, engravings and posters, open to the public.

The collection spans six centuries from engravings by Albrecht Dürer to lithographs by Glyn Boyd Harte, from etchings by Francisco Jose Goya to photographs by David Bailey. It is housed appropriately in the Edward Davies Building, named after the brother of Gwendoline and Margaret Davies, who paid for its construction and were early benefactors of the School of Art,[3] though this location is a happy and belated coincidence since the building was originally chemistry laboratories for the university and only passed to the School of Art in 1993.

It is an impressive building, designed by Alfred William Stephens Cross in dark local stone with architrave, parapet and central cupola, set on a hillside overlooking the centre of town.

In an age of mass production it is curious that, in the visual arts, there is so little interest in reproduction. Few public art galleries value or collect posters or prints, or even photographs. It is the unique object that is prized. There is much talk of 'art for the many, not the few' but little enthusiasm for the techniques that could make that a present reality. This collection is an exception. Here all techniques of reproduction are valued and appreciated for their craftsmanship as for their aesthetic content.

The university collections developed erratically until 1918 when an Arts and Crafts Department and Museum was established, partly in response to a *Report on the Teaching of Art in the Intermediate Schools of Wales*[4] that stated that 'in our universities from among 641 degrees there is not one degree in Fine Art' and partly encouraged by a £5,000 endowment given by the Davies sisters 'to provide income for the museum's needs'.

The sisters invited architect Sidney Kyffin Greenslade to become 'Consulting Curator' to the museum. He was still working in Aberystwyth on the building of the National Library of Wales (q.v.), the competition for which he had won in 1909, and he was a collector and acknowledged expert on ceramics. With a budget of £250 a year, Greenslade set about acquiring ceramics and glass, calligraphy, prints and fine books.

He bought from artists, art schools, dealers, publishers and galleries, never paying more than five guineas[5] for a print. What he sought was 'very simple and unaffected work by acknowledged masters of their Art' from which students could learn the techniques of printmaking by 'careful study of the good influence of the collections'.[6]

Neither the celebrity of the artist nor the likely investment value of a work concerned him. Nevertheless he bought prints by Graham Sutherland, when he was still a student at Goldsmiths' College of Art in 1924, and by Edgar Holloway, when he was only seventeen.

It was a good time to be acquiring prints. The work of James Abbot McNeill Whistler and Augustus John was inspiring a young group of etchers: Gerald Brockhurst, John Minton, Rex Whistler, Edward Bawden, Charles Tunnicliffe and Eric Ravilious, the latter two taught by Robert Austin at the Royal College of Art.

In the late 1930s the newly established Contemporary Art Society for Wales gave the collection an oil painting by Cedric Morris, to which was added after the war works by Kyffin Williams and Thomas Rathmell, and the Davies sisters gave their collection in 1952, including work by Dürer and Rembrandt, Whistler's *Thames Set* (1859) and eighty-four etchings by Augustus John. Despite this the museum struggled to survive as a teaching resource until 1962 when a new keeper and

senior lecturer, David Tinker, developed the Gulbenkian Loan Scheme with the artist Arthur Giardelli and started to collect contemporary prints: Henry Moore, Sidney Nolan, William Scott, Ceri Richards; Terry Frost, Victor Pasmore, David Hockney, Zoran Music.

In recent years Tinker's successor, Robert Meyrick, has encouraged the acquisition of an outstanding collection, by Alistair Crawford, of post-war Italian photographs and has himself begun to acquire artists' collections whose drawings, studies, cartoons, sketchbooks are a rich resource for teaching and research. Collections acquired include those of Keith Vaughan, Edgar Holloway and, appropriately, Hugh Blaker, the etcher, printer, collector and curator[7] whose advice was crucial in the formation of the Davies sisters' collection of Impressionist paintings.

CERAMICS GALLERY **

School of Art, University of Wales, Buarth Mawr, Aberystwyth, Ceredigion SY23 1NE
Tel. 01970 622460

Twentieth-century studio ceramics: Leach, Rie, Coper et al.

In 1919 Sidney Greenslade, the architect and 'Consulting Curator' at the Aberystwyth School of Art Collection (q.v.), began to acquire ceramics. In the same year Bernard Leach and Shoji Hamada were setting up the St Ives Pottery, William Staite Murray was starting to produce pots in Rotherhithe, and Charles and Nell Vyse were experimenting with glazes along the river at Chelsea. Studio pottery in Britain was being born.

Greenslade's collecting over the next sixteen years tracks the infant movement. The first pots he bought were by William Staite Murray. His budget of £250 a year did not allow him to acquire large pieces like the ones the collec-

Fragment as a Complete Form *and* Bowl with Graphics *by George Baldwin at the Ceramics Gallery*

tor the Very Revd Eric Milner-White was buying (*Ra*; *Tall Pot*: now in the York Art Gallery, q.v.), but he could afford smaller pieces by Leach, Michael Cardew and Katherine Pleydell-Bouverie.

By 1935 the museum's collection comprised over four hundred pieces, one of the largest collections of earthenware and stoneware in Britain. It is exhibited here in a small gallery in a corner of the lower level of the university's Art Centre. The display cases are elegant and well lit; pieces are given reasonable breathing space; but the information and labelling are cursory. The present gallery is not adequate to show the beauties of studio pottery in the 20th century or the ways in which Leach, or the Vyses, or Cardew, or Rie, absorbed themselves in British and Japanese traditions and developed new ways of combining clay and water and fire, oxides and pigments and wood ash, to produce new pieces, with the power of slabs and the delicacy of wafers, that are chalk, slippery, every shade of black and white, and red and purple, variegated and feathered. Nevertheless Greenslade's achievement cannot be denied.

His interest in ceramics had its origins in the works of the Martin brothers, whom he met in 1898. In their salt-glaze stoneware, produced in multiples, the dividing line between handmade studio pottery and art pottery, made by a team of potters, is blurred, as it is in Derby ware (J. Bourne & Sons) or in the work of Seymour and Sidney Wately of the Upchurch Pottery. They were friends of Edward Martin and of Reginald Fairfax Wells, who had been experimenting with the methods and materials of medieval potters and with oriental glazes at his pottery in the King's Road, Chelsea, since the end of the First World War, several years before Bernard Leach.

More mass-produced still was the work of Alfred and Louise Powell who produced for Wedgwood at the studio in Red Lion Square, Holborn, decorating Wedgwood ware with glazes and motifs that drew on Arts and Crafts designs and on Islamic calligraphic tradition.

At the same time (1971) as David Tinker

was reviving the Arts and Crafts museum at the School of Art lower down the hill, Moira Vincentelli was beginning to add to the ceramics collection, which had lain dormant since Greenslade's last acquisition in 1935. Her first purchases were works by Gordon Baldwin, Alan Caiger-Smith and Michael Casson, who was introducing studio pottery to a new audience on BBC television.

The budget available to her did not allow the gaps that had developed since 1935 to be filled. Instead, advised by Michael Casson, she concentrated on exploring the new directions that studio pottery had taken after the war. Beside the 'ethical pots' of Bernard Leach, Shoji Hamada and Ray Finch (utilitarian, crafted, direct) had developed a 'second strand' of modernist pottery that was non-functional, conceptual, experimental, tending to sculpture rather than use: the work of Lucie Rie, Hans Coper, Mary Rogers, Katherine Pleydell-Bouverie.

New pieces by Bernard Leach and Denise Wren were purchased,[8] as were pieces made by Michael Cardew in the 1960s when he was the Nigerian government's ceramics officer, as well as work by the most talented pupil at his training centre at Abuja, Ladi Kwali, but the emphasis was on modernist pieces and, with the help of the Welsh Arts Council, the National Art Collections Fund and loans from Henry Rothschild, examples of the work of this new generation have been acquired. Pieces by Joanna Constantinidis, Janice Tchalenko, Alison Britton and Sophie MacCarthy have entered the collection. All they need now is a good catalogue and a new gallery worthy of their work.

BEAUMARIS GAOL *

Bunkers Hill, Beaumaris, Isle of Anglesey
LL58 8PE
Tel. 01248 810921

Nineteenth-century penal life: the last treadmill, and a gallows

Beaumaris Gaol is in the centre of the town, hemmed in by tight narrow streets. Its massive grey stone walls loom above. It was built[9] in 1829 as part of a response to John Howard's survey,[10] which described the filth and disease rife in the country's prisons. Beaumaris, replacing the old gaol by the sea in which neither water nor straw was supplied, was a new model prison. Nevertheless there is no question but that this is a place of punishment. 'The main elements of prison discipline are hard work, hard fare and a hard bed,' was the view of a House of Commons Select Committee.

New prisoners were scrubbed clean. 'The Bath admirably fulfils its two-fold function. It ensures a thorough wash and removes the last trace of one's former self,' recalled one inmate, though it is hard to see how when he goes on to describe the water as 'curious dark greasy slime . . . not unlike mutton broth'.

Prisoners were named by the number of their cell: 'that little box, 8 foot 6 inches in length, 7 foot in height, 5 foot in width, with its floor and roof of stone, would be my only home. Would be, must be – and no power could avert my fate.' The regime in place was the Separate System. Prisoners worked, ate and slept in isolation. Even in the exercise yard they were fastened at intervals along a chain to prevent contact, which was considered corrupting. Later, in 1862, Henry Mayhew condemned this as 'unwarrantably severe . . . Instead of reforming it utterly overwhelms and destroys.'[11]

Old prisoners became 'past masters in the art of ventriloquism. The words appear to be formed at the back of their throats and are so low in tone that unless you have a remarkably keen ear, they speak to you in vain.'

The work was hard, breaking stones[12] or picking oakum, pieces of old rope to be reused in caulking the hulls of wooden sailing ships. Punishments were severe: the whipping post or the darkness and isolation of the punishment cell, both of which are here. The post is a frame, nine feet high, to which the miscreant was strapped at wrists, calves and thighs to receive the lashes of the cat. The punishment cell, in which prisoners usually spent three days with only bread and water, is a cell of total blackness: 'not one luminous chink or crack could the sight detect. Indeed the very air seemed as impervious to vision as so much black marble and the body seems to be positively encompassed with the blackness, as if it were buried alive, deep down in the earth itself.'

Eventually in the 1860s Beaumaris Gaol received running water. The price paid was a treadmill on which prisoners had to walk, ten minutes on, ten minutes off. 'They move their legs as if they were mounting a flight of stairs, but with this difference – that instead of their ascending, the steps pass from under them, and . . . it is this that is so particularly tiring, owing to the want of a firm tread.' It is the last working treadmill in its original position. A government reorganisation in 1878 led to the closure of Beaumaris, with prisoners being moved to the county gaol at Caernarfon.

Surprisingly in those fifty years only two prisoners were executed here: William Griffiths, a bigamist who murdered one of his wives in 1830, and Richard Rowlands, sentenced to death for killing his father-in-law in 1862. Rowlands went to the scaffold that hangs out into the side street insisting, 'I tell you I am totally innocent of the blood of the old man.' Both were dispatched by the Newgate executioner William Calcraft.[13]

There have been reforms. W. E. Gladstone's *Report on Prisons* (1895) introduced books, some education, more visits and a reduction in the initial term of solitary confinement. The 1948 Criminal Justice Act ended penal servitude and labour, but overcrowding and poor conditions led to the prison riots of the 1960s and '70s and the Strangeways riot of 1990 when prisoners took control of the Manchester Prison for twenty-five days. A subsequent report by Lord Woolf recommended the end of slopping out and a new prison-building programme which may result in prisons that are as new and 'model' in their turn as Beaumaris was in 1829. It is yet not heartening.

ORIEL YNS MÔN *

Rhosmeirch, Llangefni, Isle of Anglesey
LL77 7TQ
Tel. 01248 724444, fax 01248 750282
www.anglesey.gov.uk/english/culture/index.htm

Museum of Anglesey: natural history and fine art; the watercolours of Tunnicliffe

'You will find much on Anglesey which is worthy of your attention,' wrote Gerald of Wales in his *Journey Through Wales* in 1188.[14] It is remarkable that Anglesey, Môn mam Cymru, Mona the Mother of Wales, should have had to wait for more than eight hundred years for its first museum, founded in 1991 as Oriel Yns Môn.

Even then it took a threat to the work of an English artist to startle the gallery into existence. Charles Tunnicliffe had lived and worked at Malltraeth on Anglesey for thirty-two years, painting the wildlife, particularly the birdlife, of the island he loved. After his death in 1979 his work was put to auction at Christie's and bought by the local borough council only at the last minute.

Once founded, the gallery attracted other gifts and in 1991 opened in a new building designed by the Cardiff-based architects Alex Gordon & Partnership. The main gallery tells the island's story geographically in a circular progress of fifteen steps. A decorated, incised urn from Bedd Branwell provides evidence from a Bronze Age burial site; a Celtic sandstone carving from Llanfairpwll of a human head shows the sophistication of Celtic culture several hundred years before Christ. But, having started late, the museum collection cannot do justice to the riches of

Charles Tunnicliffe watercolour at
Oriel Yns Môn

the island, not least because archaeological artefacts and geological specimens are already in the National Museum and Gallery of Wales (q.v.).

What the gallery can do is show the beauty of the island, its landscape and wildlife through the eyes of artists. It has recently acquired six books of botanical drawings done in and around Beaumaris in the 1930s and '40s by two sisters, Edith and Gwendolen Massey of Llangoed; and the artist Sir Kyffin Williams, who lives on the island and played a central role in securing the Tunnicliffe studio and archive, has given work. However it is principally through Tunnicliffe's work that the island is interpreted here.

Charles Tunnicliffe was born near Macclesfield in Cheshire and trained at the Royal College of Art, where he was a contemporary of, and shared a room with, Eric Ravilious. He stayed on at the RCA to study engraving, his first exercise being to copy a small Rembrandt self-portrait. His second was a scene of farmers and carthorses leaving a field.

He had no difficulty finding work as an engraver, illustrating catalogues, advertisements[15] and books, and drawing on diverse influences from Bewick to Millet. In 1932 he illustrated a new edition of Henry Williamson's *Tarka the Otter*[16] but failing eyesight forced him to concentrate on drawing and watercolours and, after the Second World War, to settle permanently on Anglesey.

'Looking south-east,' he wrote, 'is the mile-wide estuary. Beyond, filling the middle distance is a long ridge of high ground, crisscrossed by hedges and dotted about with farms, which at its seaward end deteriorates into rock and sand dune, and above this ridge loom the great mountains of Caernarvonshire, the Kingdom of Eryri, with Snowdon lording it over all – a stupendous panorama.' The variety of landscape (coves, dunes; woods, forest; marshland, saltmarsh and estuary) ensured a diversity of birdlife: razorbill, curlew, ringed plover; Greenland wheatear, Wilson's phalarope; puffin, gull; whimbrel and cock stonechat; the last glimpole.

In addition to drawing from life he wrote that 'for some years I have been in the habit of making careful measured drawings, in colour, of any dead bird which has come into my hands.' Kyffin Williams observed that 'the [measured] drawings are important because they show the art student what real hard work and dedication mean; they are important because of their scientific value; but above all they are important because quite unintentionally they are works of art.'

The gallery now has fifty of Tunnicliffe's sketchbooks and the contents of his studio. They make a strong case that he can be compared with Audubon or Gould and that, in his words, 'Nature is lavish with her riches for those who have eyes to see.'

PENRHYN CASTLE **

Bangor, Gwynedd LL57 4HN
Tel. 01248 353084
www.nationaltrust.org.uk

Neo-Norman extravaganza: castle and furniture by Thomas Hopper

When you think of Gothic it is Ruskin, Pugin's Houses of Parliament (q.v.), Butterfield's churches and Waterhouse's Natural History Museum (q.v.) that come to mind: all these looked back to 14th- and 15th-century Italy and France.

At Penrhyn, Thomas Hopper, the architect chosen by George Dawkins-Pennant, looked to Inigo Jones's refacing of the Tower of London (1637–8) for Charles I, and to Hugh May's redesign of Windsor Castle (1671) for Charles II, and to the round-arched Norman style of the 11th century. He was not alone.

Robert Adam at Culzean in Ayrshire (begun 1777) and Robert Smirke at Eastnor in Herefordshire (begun 1812) employed versions of neo-Norman, but no one plunged in with the enthusiasm of Hopper, armed only with a copy of John Carter's *The Ancient Architecture of England* (1795–1814), rich in Norman detail.

Dawkins-Pennant had chosen a dramatic ancient site on a spur of land east of Bangor looking back along the north Wales coast and across to Snowdonia. He was immensely rich from the Pennant slate quarries in north Wales and sugar plantations in Jamaica. While he lived in 'a humble cottage in the neighbourhood, with a small establishment',[17] the castle grew and grew to exemplify Uvedale Price's description of medieval architecture: 'the outline of the summit presents such a variety of forms, of turrets and pinnacles . . . it is often disguised by an appearance of splendid confusion and irregularity.' Hopper added tower after tower, each topped by battlements and, to the south, a keep 115 feet high. The exterior, severe in dark Penmon limestone, is restrained when compared with the interiors, where Hopper, unleashed, created what Christopher Hussey described as 'the baroque of romantic revival architecture' as a setting for tables, chairs, bookcases, beds, chimney pieces, stained glass and ornament that are dense with Norman detail.

As you enter, your eye is allowed to attune itself in the Entrance Hall, where Hopper has designed carved oak tables, desks and chairs, topped with cherubs' heads and double-headed eagles. Nothing, however, prepares you for the vast volume of the three-storey-high Grand Hall, huge stained-glass windows by Thomas Willement, oak chairs whose backs are carved into what seem to be marine fossils with pointed hooves, and fantastical composition-stone luminaries. The Grand Hall is restrained compared with the Library's vast stone arches, four chimney pieces of polished Penmon limestone, all carved as exhaustively as the ceiling bosses, and square 'Norman' tables with cluster-column legs.

These rooms are mere rehearsal for the Grand Staircase, which rises through the house in a salmagundi of carving in which geometric details, Norman and Arab, give way to Celtic interlacing, mournful gargoyles, grotesque masks, writhing serpents and finally an arch made up of carved human hands.

The scale and drama of these interiors is not sympathetic to the hanging of pictures. Dawkins-Pennant's son-in-law and heir, Edward Gordon Douglas-Pennant, 1st Baron Penrhyn, favoured 17th-century Dutch and 18th-century Venetian paintings, which he bought on the advice of the London-based Belgian dealer C. J. Nieuwenhuis. With the exception of a good School of Dieric Bouts, *St Luke Painting the Madonna and Child*, much restored, in the low-ceilinged Ebony Room, Henry Hawkins's vertiginous, populous view of *The Penrhyn Slate Quarry*, and a Clarkson Stanfield seascape that is now a ruin, destroyed by its own bitumen, the oil paintings are almost exclusively confined to the Dining Room and the Breakfast Room (upstairs there are two unusual sets of watercolours, of the Jamaican estates from which the Pennants' fortune came, by George Robertson, and of the Douglas-Pennants' Welsh lands, by G. F. Robson). There are works here by Wouwermans, van der Neer, and van der Velde; by Guardi and Canaletto; by Gainsborough, Richard Wilson and Allan Ramsay; a severe, late Rembrandt of *Catrina Hooghsaet* (1657); and an excellent Bellotto. But they are almost incidental: Penrhyn is all about Hopper.

There is in Britain no other set of neo-Norman furniture that can match this. If exhibited in a gallery it would be almost devoid of meaning. Here it is the expression of a remarkable, fevered mind.

BIG PIT: NATIONAL MINING MUSEUM **

Blaenafon, Gwent NP4 9XP
Tel. 01495 790311
www.nmgw.ac.uk/bigpit

Surface and coal face

Come over the top from the heads of the valleys and the road drops down towards Blaenafon. There, on the far side of the valley on a hillside barren of trees, is Big Pit, a cluster of nondescript buildings around a small pit-head. The buildings themselves tell you little about life underground, to provide a glimpse of which is the purpose of this museum.

Big Pit is on the eastern edge of the South Wales coalfield, whose seams of coal run from Pontypool in the east to Ammanford in the west, an area of 1,000 square miles.[18]

Mining is all about geology. An arch or anticlinal ridge in the strata brings seams of high-quality steam coal near the surface. The nature of the seams determined how they were worked. Coal in the South Wales fields is loose-jointed and friable, so as a face was worked it needed immediate support. This made the coal somewhat easier to extract. As a result, coal continued to be hewn by hand for longer, and machine cutting was introduced more slowly than in other coalfields. By 1938 54 per cent of all UK coal was being cut by machine. The South Wales figure was 26 per cent. At Big Pit the last, lowest and best seam, Garw, was not mechanised until the 1970s.

Big Pit opened in 1880, an amalgamation of three smaller pits: Forge (sunk in 1835), Coity (1840) and Kearsley's (1860). Their seams were near the surface, the deepest being only 366 feet. The opening of new drifts meant that coal could be taken more easily to the surface and that men could walk down to the face.

By 1970 only the Garw face was working. Big Pit closed as a working colliery in 1980 and opened as a museum with underground tours in 1983, employing former miners to interpret the pit to visitors.

For an underground tour, collect your

The Big Pit

helmet and light, give up your lamp check, step into the cage and drop 366 feet into darkness. Underground you are able to see three different types of coalface: a 19th-century pillar-and-stall face, supported by timber; an early-20th-century 'longwall' face, and a face mechanised in the 1960s, supported by rigid steel posts and served by a belt conveyor.

You will see mechanical conveyors on which both men and coal rode; ventilation systems; various coal-cutting machines (a cutter-loader, shearers). You will see the darkness itself and glimpse something of what conditions were like in the 19th century, when children as young as six or seven worked in the pits (until 1842), six days a week.

As with all industrial museums, the setting and the experience are all, and are the things that are impossible to recreate and convey, thanks to modern health and safety regulations. When you return to the surface you are clean, not begrimed; there is no black dust in your lungs that will give you pneumoconiosis before you are fifty and kill you before you reach sixty;[19] you will not walk home dirty, and often wet, and scrub yourself in a tub before the fire. Big Pit did not install showers until 1939.[20]

On the surface you will see the baths and the winding house and the blacksmith's shop and the stables for the pit horses. The museum centre allows you to learn more about coal and examine some of the details of colliery life: how coal formed 300 million years ago; how it is surveyed, by theodolite and a plumb bob; how you can see underground (a Davy lamp, a Stephenson lamp, a Channy lamp and a Marsant lamp, the first electric hand lamp, not introduced at Big Pit until the 1920s); the lamp checks; the dangers; the trade union, the 'Fed'; the coal reserves buried; what is made from coal; and the tools of the pit (mandrels and shovels; sledges and wedges; a churn for boring, a hatchet for cutting; a pair of clamps, a measuring rod and a bucket).

What these cannot adequately convey is

the filth and the danger; the comradeship; the sensation of being there every day of your working life. 'The hewer is down in the mine away from the sunlight and fresh air, and sometimes in a temperature of up to 90°, every moment of the day inhaling coal and shale dust ... liable always to wounds and death from falls of roofs or sides; and ever and over all the sickening dread of the awful explosion.'[21]

Or the anger felt by many miners. 'All the dangers I had passed through and the dust I had swallowed, had gained me this much: that I had to go and beg for parish relief.'[22]

For many the pit was a way of life, sons following fathers for generations. For others it was not, and parents would do anything to prevent their sons going into those dark seams.

BODELWYDDAN CASTLE *

Rhyl, Bodelwyddan, Denbighshire LL18 5YA
Tel. 01745 584060
www.bodelwyddan-castle.co.uk

The National Portrait Gallery's Welsh outpost; the rest of G. F. Watts's Hall of Fame

Bodelwyddan is a mock castle, its grey limestone towers, parapets and battlements designed in the 1830s by Joseph Aloysius Hansom, the inventor of the Hansom cab, and Edward Welch,[23] as if for the set of a stage play. It has an unrestricted view of the dual carriageway A55 and of Rhuddlan beyond.

The Williams family gave up the struggle to maintain it in the 1890s and, when the girls' school that occupied it from 1920 to 1982 closed, it was taken on by Clwyd County Council, who opened it as the Victorian outstation of the National Portrait Gallery (NPG) in 1988. The designer Roderick Gradidge was commissioned to redesign its interior as a sequence of rooms ranging in period from early to late 19th century with furniture loaned by the Victoria and Albert Museum (q.v.).[24]

You enter down the Apostles' Corridor, a long narrow hallway with William Morris wallpaper, in which is hung one half of George Frederic Watts's *Hall of Fame*,[25] his sequence of more than fifty portraits of eminent Victorians, which preoccupied him from the 1850s until he died.

Watts gained early fame when he exhibited at the Royal Academy at the age of twenty and then won two of the competitions organised by Prince Albert's Fine Art Commission to select artists for the new Houses of Parliament (for fresco in 1843 and for oil painting in 1847). A succession of commissions to paint frescoes followed, notably in the Great Hall of Lincoln's Inn (1853–9). Like Reynolds and Gainsborough before him, he saw portraiture as tainted, but financially necessary. However he convinced himself that to create a 'house of fame', in which would be depicted the politicians, soldiers, poets, artists, academics, scientists, philanthropists and social reformers who were shaping Victorian England, would be a public service.

Watts painted to a standard size (approximately 25 by 21 inches), format and type of frame: wide, butt-jointed, flat and gilded, with mouldings of husks around the inside, and bead-and-bobbin alternating with acanthus on the outside. Double hung along the hallway they make a handsome show, *Tennyson* (c. 1863–4), *Browning* (1866), *Millais* (1871); *Lord Salisbury*, the Prime Minister, *Field Marshal Lord Roberts* (1898). Swinburne wrote, 'Of course it is a great honour for one to be asked to sit to him, now especially that he accepts no commissions and paints portraits only for three reasons – friendship, beauty and celebrity; having the "world" at his feet begging to be painted.'[26]

Watts's view of eminence was conventional and moralistic. In his view artists should 'condemn in the most trenchant manner prevalent vices' and 'utter warning in deep tones against lapses from morals and duties'[27] – hence the inclusion of the ship owner and writer of social questions, *Charles Booth* (1901) and the philanthropist *John Passmore Edwards* (1894). Some slipped through his moral mesh.

The Hall of Fame: G. F. Watts by Watts at *Bodelwyddan*

He painted *Sir Charles Dilke* in 1873, twelve years before the notorious divorce that ended his political career.

All his sitters are seen against a dark, neutral background; head and shoulders. The lighting concentrates attention on the sitter's face, but surprisingly few are viewed full on and the half- or full-profiles (including his self-portrait) offer scant opportunities for the ambiguity or penetration of character that he achieves in his depiction of his then wife, the actress Ellen Terry, in *Choosing* (1863–4). Tentatively she stretches to smell one of the camellias that surround her head while holding a small, vulnerable bunch of violets in her hand. Watts was forty-seven and she sixteen when they married, in his view (and words) 'to remove an impulsive young girl from the dangers and temptations of the stage'.[28] The marriage lasted a year.

Too many of the other paintings here reveal the problems inherent in the NPG's founding criterion, set out by Gladstone, the then Chancellor of the Exchequer, that 'the authenticity of a portrait, and the celebrity of the person represented, will be the grounds for the admission of a picture, and not its excellence as a work of art.'[29] Celebrity fades faster than good painting. How many recall Stephen Lushington, MP and reformer, Sir Henry William Lucy, journalist, or John Allen, historian?[30]

After the glories of 18th-century portraiture the work of John Partridge, Field Talfourd, Stephen Pearle, Sir Hubert von Herkomer, does not clamour for exhibition. Even the paintings here by Thomas Phillips (*Matthew Arnold*), Lawrence Alma-Tadema (*Arthur Balfour*) or Ford Madox Brown (*Henry Fawcett and his Wife Millicent Garrett*) are workaday, and John Singer Sargent's full-length of *Joseph Chamberlain* (1896) lacks any of the swagger of his portrait of *Arthur Balfour*, acquired by the NPG in 2003.

There are interesting curiosities (*George Henry Lewes and his Wife, Agnes Jervis, with Thornton Leigh Hunt*, drawn by Thackeray, before Lewes lived with George Eliot; *Frederick Sandys*, drawn by his father Anthony Sandys in 1848, as young, handsome and hopeful, before his rapid success and his long decline). And there is a room, the Sculpture Gallery, high vaulted, that houses sculptures by John Gibson on loan from the Royal Academy (q.v.): *Hebe, Bacchus*; and portrait busts of Sir Charles Lock Eastlake, director of the National Gallery, and of Mrs Anna Jameson, whose *Companion to Public Picture Galleries in London* (published in 1842) provides the best view of the state of galleries in the early years of the National Gallery (q.v.) and the Dulwich Picture Gallery (q.v.) – the observer observed.

BRECKNOCK MUSEUM ∗

Captain's Walk, Brecon, Powys LD3 7DS
Tel. 01874 624121

Local history in a handsome shire hall

Brecon was a county town, the seat of the county assizes. In the political turbulence of the 1840s a huge shire hall was built,[31] on the rise of the main street, set to dominate town and county. Four grand fluted Doric columns hold high a weighty pediment that declares 'VICTORIA REGINA MDCCCXLII'.

When first the assize courts and quarter sessions, and then the County Council, were abolished in 1971, the building was handed over to the Brecknock Museum, which was at the time squeezed into a former chapel. If the collections were too large for the chapel, they are too small for the shire hall, in which they rattle like loose teeth.

The collections have their features: a scattering of Roman material from Sir Mortimer Wheeler's excavation of the Roman fort Y Gaer in the 1920s; early medieval stones inscribed in both Latin and Ogam; a 9th-century canoe from Llangors Lake, associated with an artificial lake settlement or crannog, identified in the 1860s and excavated in 1987 – the only known crannog in Wales or England. The logboat canoe has recently been dramatically re-displayed with help from the National Museums and Galleries of Wales.

In the comprehensively arranged Brecknock

Town Life Gallery there is a carved-oak four-poster bed, yet another that Charles I is said to have slept in when he passed through Brecon after the battle of Naseby in 1645, and a lovely example of 17th-century raised stumpwork embroidery depicting Pyramus and Thisbe. Pyramus appears twice, Thisbe once (angry). There is a lion, and moon (full-face), and a mulberry tree whose fruit stains the second Pyramus (dead). It is the genuine article and needs no dubious association with Charles I to beef it up.

But this is a big building. The museum has filled the old assize court with a life-sized tableau, recreating a court case of the 1880s. It is more elaborate, but no more successful, than the Court Room at Beaumaris Gaol and Courthouse (q.v.) (computerised lighting, a taped re-enactment of a trial in which Joe Grundy from *The Archers* plays both judge and counsel for the prosecution).

The second ruse is the Art Gallery, which has an ambitious exhibition programme strongly featuring contemporary art from Wales. After only a handful of years there is already the beginning of a collection: watercolours by Josef Herman, Edgar Holloway, David Jones, John Piper and Graham Sutherland; paintings by local artists Ivor Davies, Shirley Jones, Laurie Williams, Roy Powell. Here too is a small landscape of *Llangors Lake* (1770), somewhat optimistically attributed to Thomas Jones, who seems in this to have forgotten all he learnt in Italy. But there is a finer oil, *The Wye Valley*, certainly by Jones. There are few enough small public art galleries in rural Wales and this, supported by the Arts Council of Wales, the V&A Purchase Grant Fund, the National Art Collections Fund, the Brecknock Museum Art Trust and the Contemporary Art Society for Wales, deserves to succeed.

ROMAN LEGIONARY MUSEUM, CAERLEON **

High Street, Caerleon, Newport, Gwent
NP18 1AE
Tel. 01633 423134
www.nmgw.ac.uk/rlm/rlmhome.html

The Welsh edge of a Roman Empire: a hoard of gemstones

Relics from the Roman legionary fortress at Caerleon had been turning up by chance since before 1602, but it was not until an amateur archaeologist from Yorkshire, John Edward Lee,[32] came to Caerleon to take up a position with a firm of iron manufacturers in Newport that systematic excavations took place.

In 1847 Lee and Sir Digby Mackworth founded the Caerleon Antiquarian Association. The following year Sir Digby, the association's president, made land available for a museum of antiquities to house the artefacts that had been discovered. The Caerleon Antiquarian Association set about raising the necessary funds and the museum opened in 1850.

The museum, at the very centre of the legionary fortress, has 'a handsome and scholarly four-column Greek Doric portico of Bath stone ashlar' (1850)[33] that was retained when the original museum was rebuilt in 1987, being one of the sites of the National Museum and Gallery of Wales since 1930.

Caerleon (City of the Legion; Isca, to the Romans) was one of only three permanent legionary bases in Britain, the other being Chester (Deva) and York (Eboracum). Since John Lee's dig in 1849–50 it has been excavated: briefly in 1908; in 1926 by Mortimer and Tessa Wheeler; and then continuously until his death by Dr Vincent Nash-Williams, Keeper of Archaeology at the National Museum.

Wheeler, then Director of the National Museum, persuaded the *Daily Mail* to sponsor the excavation of the amphitheatre, which had been popularly supposed to be the location of King Arthur's Round Table since Geoffrey of Monmouth identified it as such in his *History of the Kings of Britain.* Gerald of Wales also notes its 'lofty tower, and . . . remarkable hot baths' on his *Journey Through Wales* (1188).[34] To justify its investment, the *Daily Mail* carried regular reports, that of 10 July 1926 announcing: 'Yesterday's excavations in the occupation level below the four successive roads round the amphitheatre revealed a pair of deer's antlers. This suggests that deer were used in arena sports.' Excavation revealed that the arena walls had been capped by a project-ing course of bathstone blocks to prevent beasts climbing into the auditorium.

The legionary fortress had considerable strategic significance. The Romans had failed to subjugate the local tribe, the Silures, losing part of a legion in a battle against them in A D 52. In A D 74 Emperor Vespasian chose Sextus Julius Frontinus (governor, A D 74–8) to pacify Wales. He moved the II Augusta Legion into Silurian territory at Caerleon on well-chosen ground, at a point of the River Usk that could be bridged, on raised ground, easily suppliable by sea. Tacitus reports that 'he conquered the warlike tribe of the Silures, overcoming not only a fierce and stubborn enemy, but the difficulties of the terrain.' In the historian's view he was a 'truly great man', who later wrote books on military tactics and on Rome's water supply, for which he became responsible.

Caerleon's fifty-acre site, much of it under the modern village, also contains the excavated foundations of several important buildings: the Fortress Baths, the Prysg Field Barracks (Nash-Williams's most significant excavation, in 1927–9) and the Amphitheatre. These have been consolidated for public display.

The baths covered two and a half acres, of which only a small part is visible, and included a 117-foot open-air swimming pool and a 186-foot exercise hall. Part of the baths com-plex is now displayed under a cover building. A fragment of mosaic, from the second heated changing room, is displayed on the wall of the interior and a glass bath flask for oil and a copper strigil inlaid with silver and gold are in the museum, as are gaming counters and dice and, Caerleon's most remarkable find, eighty-eight gemstones excavated in 1979 from a drain beneath the cold bath hall.

These delicate stones – jasper, cornelian, citrine, green amethyst, yellow sard, blue nicolo – are likely to have been dropped from rings, signets, charms or talismans, singly, over a period of 150 years (A D 80–230) and washed down into the drain. Many are engraved with deities (Mars, Minerva, Diana, Mercury, and Bonus Eventus as a huntsman); with symbols of prosperity (corn, scales and a raven); or with scenes (an eagle devouring a hare; Silenus, Bacchus and an eagle). They comprise one of the largest single deposits to have been found anywhere in the Roman Empire.

The museum also has fine collections of jewellery (jet, amber, bronze, silver), funerary sculpture and tombstones, and monumental inscriptions, including one, unusually, carved in Tuscan marble[35] that records the rebuild-ing in stone of one of the major buildings or gates in A D 100.[36]

All the buildings here are remarkably well documented, with bricks and tiles stamped by the legionary authorities to regulate their use and prevent theft,[37] and inscribed stones that named the centurion responsible for a par-ticular section of walling, discovered by the Wheelers in 1926–7 in the foundations of the amphitheatre. The amphitheatre is one of the best preserved in Roman Britain, designed for military ceremonies and parades and for entertainment. It was constructed in A D 90 almost on top of the fortress rampart, a position that is so incorrect from a military viewpoint that it has been used to support the theory that the Silures had been thoroughly pacified by Sextus Julius Frontinus, confirm-ing Tacitus's estimation of him as a 'truly great man'.

CARDIFF CASTLE **

Castle Street, Cardiff CF10 2RB
Tel. 029 2022 9367, fax 029 2023 1417
www.rrw.org.uk

William Burges realises his, and Lord Bute's, fantasies

The medievalism that gripped 19th-century design took many forms: A. W. N. Pugin's English Gothic in the Houses of Parliament (q.v.); Thomas Hopper's Norman Gothic at Penrhyn Castle (q.v.); Ruskin's Italian Gothic. None was as elaborate, exotic or extravagant as the French Gothic that William Burges employed at Cardiff Castle.

Burges was an architect and designer steeped in medieval scholarship, particularly that of his contemporary Eugène Viollet-le-Duc,[38] the architect who restored the medieval fortress of Carcassone and the chateau at Pierrefonds.[39] Both were in thrall to the 13th-century master builder Villard de Honnecourt, whose architectural sketchbook they studied for construction, carving and decoration.

The two buildings that Burges created for the 3rd Marquess of Bute, Cardiff Castle and Castell Coch, were his masterpieces. In Cardiff Castle each room is a gallery of craftsmanship and witness to the ideas and scholarship that he shared with Lord Bute. The 3rd Marquess (1847–1900) was, by common consent, the richest man in Britain. He had estates in Scotland and in Wales, including much of the land on which Cardiff was built. His father completed Cardiff's Bute West Dock in order that he might export the coal excavated from his South Wales coalfields. He himself was reclusive and scholarly, an antiquarian with a passion for Celtic history.[40] At Oxford he encountered the future Cardinal Henry Manning, John Henry Newman and the shadowy Monsignor T. W. Capel[41] and in 1868 converted to Catholicism.

Initially Bute employed Burges to repair the south wall of the castle in 1865. Burges's 'repair' involved building the splendid Clock Tower, in which he designed bachelor apartments for the eighteen-year-old Marquess, the Winter and Summer Smoking Rooms, and the Bachelor Bedroom. They contain every element of Burges's wizardry in little: a delight in materials (alabaster columns, gilded bronze, encaustic tiles, inlaid precious stones, stained glass), brilliant craftsmanship (his mason Thomas Nicholls carved the gilded chimney piece in the Winter Smoking Room that declares 'OMNIA VINCIT AMOR'),[42] jokes (marquetry beasts and grotesques inlaid into panelling; metal fish inset into the sides of the bath so that, when it was filled, they appeared to swim) and a theme for each room (time for the Winter Smoking Room, the cosmos in the Summer Smoking Room, in whose dome are the heavens and the elements, and from which is suspended a chandelier in the form of the sun god on a golden chariot wheel). It is not surprising that Bute commissioned Burges to redesign and extend the rest of the castle that Henry Holland had rebuilt in the 1770s.

For Burges, Bute was the dream client. He responded by tailoring his designs to Bute's passions. Bute's Bedroom (1873) has a biblical theme with Bute's name saint, St John the Evangelist, depicted in a gilded bronze statue over the chimney piece by the sculptor Ceccardo Fucigna, and with stained-glass windows that illuminate the seven churches of Asia referred to by St John in the Book of Revelation.

The Library has the themes of literature and language. Ancient languages (Runic, Assyrian, Aramaic, Egyptian and Greek) are sculpted over the fireplace to designs by Horatio Walter Lonsdale,[43] the bookcases have marquetry panels that depict the Greek dramatists; there are birds, insects and animals, carved and painted, flocking everywhere.

The last room that Burges designed before his death in 1881 was the Arab Room, inspired by the Islamic architecture of La Ziza, Palermo. The walls and floor are of Carrara marble; there are Iznik tiles, a mosaic mantelpiece with the Bute coat of arms and a ceiling of stalactites or muqarnas glowing with gold leaf. Small polychrome effigies of parrots look down with beaky regard from the cornice.

Burges was well served by his craftsmen Nicholls and Lonsdale, his chief draughtsman and clerk of works John Starling Chapple, and all those who worked on the castle, and on Castell Coch, from Bute's workshops off North Road in Cardiff. This glorious extravaganza is a more fitting memorial to Burges than his recreated bedroom at the Cecil Higgins Art Gallery (q.v.) or the Yatman cabinet (1858) at the Victoria and Albert Museum (q.v.). No wonder that when he died from spinal myelitis after three weeks of semi-paralysis Lady Bute mourned the passing of 'ugly Burges who designs lovely things. Isn't he a duck?'.

NATIONAL MUSEUM AND GALLERY OF WALES *****

Cathays Park, Cardiff CF1 3NP
Tel. 029 2039 7951
www.nmgw.ac.uk

Good collections of everything; French Impressionist and Post-Impressionist paintings, collected by the Misses Davies twenty years before Samuel Courtauld; fine works on paper

The National Museums and Galleries of Wales are on several sites: the National Museum and Gallery in Cardiff (1927); the Museum of Welsh Life, St Fagans (q.v.) (1947); the Welsh Slate Museum, Llanberis (q.v.) (1972); the Roman Legionary Museum, Caerleon (q.v.) (1930); the National Woollen Museum, Drefach Felindre (1976); the Big Pit: National Mining Museum (q.v.); the Welsh Industrial and Maritime Museum (1971); the Turner House Gallery, Penarth. In 2005 the National Waterfront Museum will open at Swansea.

A slow start was made at the originally envisaged Cardiff Museum and Art Gallery. A building was not found for it until 1882, just in time to receive the first bequest, thirty-six paintings collected by a Dowlais steelmaster, William Menelaus. The National Gallery of Scotland had opened in 1850 and the National Gallery of Ireland in 1854.

The right to house Wales's national mu-

seum was granted to Cardiff by Royal Charter in 1907. A design for a new building, by A. Dunbar Smith and Cecil C. Brewer, was not commissioned until 1912. The building has the confident solidity of a national museum but not the élan, being without architectural features beyond utility.

You approach it through Cathays Park, across which the museum faces tired regiments of tulips, geraniums or begonias in their allotted seasons.

Inside, the main hall extends across the width of the building: a fine, generous space that has the style the facade lacks. It was completed, and officially opened, in 1927. By then the collections of the museum and of the gallery were well developed.

Having little more than Menelaus's modest founding collection, to which was added in 1898 149 watercolours, the bequest of Unitarian corn merchant James Pyke Thompson, the gallery had no option but to develop by means of purchase.

The acquisitions policy to be pursued was a matter of prolonged debate. Should they collect the best? Or should they give priority to objects made in, or connected with Wales? A report in 1895 by Pyke Thompson advocated that 'local artists, and Welsh artists whether living or deceased, should be represented more or less fully, according to their position in the world of art.' The gallery's first art adviser, Sir Frederick Wedmore, art critic of the *London Standard*, added in 1906, 'provided always that it attains to a standard of excellence'. The gallery existed, in his view, not only to show what good art Wales might have produced, but also to represent art generally. In 1913 the Welsh sculptor, writer, photographer and founder member of the museum's Court of Governors Sir William Goscombe John sought to readjust the policy, urging that it 'should concentrate upon the purchase of works by artists connected with Wales ... and buy occasionally, for the purposes of comparison and study, works of art of various kinds by distinguished modern artists of other nations, both British and foreign'.[44] This question of balance has

Renoir's La Parisienne *(National Museum and Gallery of Wales)*

exercised curators and directors ever since.

Two gifts, by the banker Wilfred De Winton of porcelain, and by the Misses Gwendoline and Margaret Davies of 19th-century French paintings and sculpture, changed everything. They remain the most celebrated collections in the gallery.

The De Winton Collection was, in the opinion of Bernard Rackham, keeper of ceramics at the Victoria and Albert Museum (q.v.), 'the best public collection in this Kingdom of Continental porcelain, other than figures'. It is as strong on early Meissen porcelain of *c.* 1715, when the factory was managed by Johann Friedrich Böttger, who developed the first true European porcelain paste, as it is on the post-1720 Chinoiserie decoration of Johann Gregorius Höroldt. Winton's collection, numbering over two thousand pieces by 1917 when he gave it to the gallery, included examples from all the major German, French and English factories (Höchst, Berlin, Vienna, Sèvres, Chelsea, Bow) with, at its centre, the 368-piece Sèvres service made for the Duc de Rohan, French Ambassador to Vienna in 1771. It also included examples of William Billingsley's work at Pinxton and Swansea, and the exceptionally translucent porcelain he produced at Nantgarw in 1818–20 (v. Derby Museum and Art Gallery and the Usher Gallery, Lincoln). A further gift of Welsh ceramics from the bequests of Ernest Morton Nance[45] consolidated the gallery's position in the collecting of ceramics.

The collections of the Davies sisters were first shown in the museum's Loan Exhibition of Paintings in 1913. The sixty-one paintings included canvases by Wilson, Turner, Constable, Raeburn and Romney but most were French. For five years since 1908, advised by Hugh Blaker (the brother of their governess, Jane), the curator of the Holburne Museum in Bath[46] from 1906–13, they had been collecting the work of French Realist and Impressionist painters (Daumier, Millet, Corot and Boudin; Monet and Manet) and sculptures by Rodin. They continued to buy through the First World War. By 1920 they had added works by Pissarro, van Gogh and Cézanne.

Since they never married and lived together all their lives, their paintings were hung together but the two collections were distinct. They did not buy together and each left her collection separately to the gallery.

They both bought Corot, Boudin, Manet and Monet, but it was Gwendoline who bought the Daumiers, Millets and Rodins; the Vlamincks and the van Gogh; perhaps surprisingly, the six canvases by the now largely forgotten symbolist Eugene Carrière; the two watercolours and three oil paintings by Cézanne, which include the *Still Life with a Teapot* (1902–6) and the important landscape *Mountains at L'Estaque*, which, when loaned to the Tate Gallery in 1922, became the first painting by Cézanne to be exhibited in a public gallery in Britain.

Margaret's taste was less defined, perhaps more decorative: Pissarro, Morisot, Sisley, Lhermitte, Meisonnier, Puvis de Chavannes. After 1920 they collected little, but, when Gwendoline died in 1951, Margaret began to buy again, acquiring landscapes by Utrillo, Bonnard and Marguet, and the romantic near-abstracts of Yves Rouvre and Pierre Hauret.

Their courage and the originality of their taste should not be underestimated. When they began collecting before the First World War there was little interest in, or knowledge of, these artists in Britain. Samuel Courtauld, who saw Gwendoline's Cézannes in Cardiff in 1922, did not start his collection until the following year (v. the Courtauld Collection) and the National Gallery (q.v.) had only single examples of Daumier,[47] Millet, Monet and Cézanne and three Manets, and those thanks only to the Lane and Salting bequests.[48] With the De Winton porcelain, the Daviese's French paintings established Cardiff as a gallery of major importance.

Although the gallery bought a superb Richard Wilson in 1913, *Carnaervon Castle*, in which he catches the light of an Italian evening and casts it over Wales, the picture collections were thin and funds were limited. The gallery concentrated on works on paper. In 1928 the gallery's first assistant keeper of art, David Baxandall, was appointed, becoming keeper in 1940. He was a friend of H. S. ('Jim') Ede (of Kettle's Yard, q.v.) and shared his enthusiasm for the artists of Unit One and of the Seven and Five Society[49] – Ben Nicholson, Henry Moore, Barbara Hepworth, John Piper, Christopher Wood, Ivon Hitchens and David Jones, whose work (particularly that of David Jones) the gallery began to acquire.

In the early 1950s more paintings by Richard Wilson (*Landscape with Banditti: the Murder* and the ravishing homage to Claude, *Rome and the Ponte Mollo*, 1754, and paintings by his pupil Thomas Jones were bought, as was Pompeo Batoni's only known triple portrait, *Sir Watkin Williams Wynn, 4th Bt, Thomas Apperley and Captain Edward Hamilton* (1768–72), in 1947. But it was not until the Welsh Office grant was raised in 1972–3 to £100,000 a year that the obvious gaps in the Old Masters collection could begin to be filled by the acquisition of a Cima da Conegliano (*Virgin and Child*), an Andrea Sacchi (*Hagar and the Angel*) and an Amico Aspertini (*Virgin and Child between St Helena and St Francis*). Also purchased was a trophy from the Grand Tour, the Jenkins vase, probably brought in 1796 from the Caraffa Collection in Naples by the Rome-based dealer Thomas Jenkins, who turned it into a vase by adding a foot and stem, and sold it to James Hugh Smith Barry of Cheshire for the fabulous sum of £500.

At the same time the collection of Welsh artists, which by now included paintings by Augustus John, Gwen John, Frank Brangwyn and J. D. Innes, and by the next generation – Ceri Richards, Evan Walters, Merlyn Evans and Kyffin Williams – had been strengthened by the long-term loan of the collection of a local surveyor, Derrick Williams,[50] and by access to a trust fund he established that allowed the gallery to purchase works by such contemporary artists as Frank Auerbach, Bridget Riley, Leon Kossoff, Lucian Freud and David Hockney.

These are fine and varied collections, further distinguished by the 30,000 works on paper and the outstanding silverware, much of it loaned since 1922 by Sir Charles Jackson, and acquired in 2001.[51] The late start, and the occa-sional periods of torpor and of inadequate resources, have not prevented the creation of a national gallery that has fulfilled the dual aims of its foundation charters of 1907 and 1911 to illustrate the 'art history . . . of Wales' and of 'all works of fine art of any kind'.

The museum tells of the evolution of the Welsh landscape from the volcanic eruptions of 465–450 million years ago and, with the help of video, places this flicker of time into the 4,600 million years of the earth's development, with explanations of the importance of the sun (and its effect on weather systems), of gravity (and its effect on the oceans) and of the drift of continents (with Europe and North America moving apart at the rate of an inch a year, the speed at which your nails grow).

Using every available means (television, video; live action, animation; sound, lighting; models, taxidermy) and authentic objects, much the best means, the geology of Wales beneath our feet is brought alive. The visitor is whisked through those 450 million years in a graphic whirr of Cambrian, Ordovician, Silurian, Carboniferous, Cretaceous, Permian, Triassic, Jurassic and Pleistocene ages, but it is only when one sees a lump of moon rock (brought back from the *Apollo* space mission in 1969), or the oldest rock in Wales (from Stanner-Hanter in Powys, 702 million years old), or a trilobite (540 million), or an ammo-nite (210-million-year-old forerunner of the octopus, cuttlefish and squid), or the treasures of jewel-like minerals (cubed pyrites, pink gypsum, fluorite), anorthosite (a fragment of ancient crust from Harris in Scotland) or the family of Pre-Cambrian rocks (mylomite, basalt brecchia, jasper) that the non-scientist can attempt to relate the rest of the display to the world as it feels to inhabit it.

Compared with the ancient rocks and minerals that make up our landscape, the archaeological evidence here of man's recent past appears remarkably remote. The National Museum has been the Centre for Welsh Archaeology since its formation. Sir Mortimer Wheeler was Director here, briefly, in the 1920s and there are artefacts on show from digs at Caernarfon, Caerleon (v. Roman Legionary

Museum) and elsewhere, including the Caergwrle bowl (1200–1000 BC), in gold leaf, shaped like a boat with maritime motifs (oars, shields, waves), excavated near Mold in Flintshire; an Iron Age bronze plaque from Llyn Cerrig Bach, near Holyhead; and bronze statuettes and other Roman artefacts from Caerwent, near Chepstow.

There is a small, circular inner gallery in which Christian stones keep vigil and there are a 14th-century Oxwich brooch and a 15th-century processional cross, which could as well, conjoining the museum's two paths, be upstairs in the art gallery.

WELSH SLATE MUSEUM *

Gilfach Ddn, Parc Pardarn, Llanberis,
Gwynedd LL55 4TY
Tel. 01286 870630
www.nmgw.ac.uk/wsm

Galleries of slate

You are led by the landscape. As you drive across the mountains from Betws-y-Coed to Llanberis, first trees then grass are steadily stripped away, leaving stone and shale. As you enter Llanberis, the face of Elidir rises up to your right, its walls of slate sliced back by galleries that have been won by the daring of quarrymen. The museum is a building of slate, slate walls, slate roofs, approached across a forecourt of slate paths. It will teach you slate, and respect for slate and those who worked it.

Slate is rock formed 500 million years ago as continents shifted and compressed the muddy sediment on the sea floor. The immense heat and pressure three miles beneath the earth's surface realigned the minerals in the mudstone into parallel layers known as planes of cleavage, along which the rock splits easily under a skilled hand.

Slate has been quarried in North Wales for nearly 2,000 years. The Roman fort at Segontium, near Caernarfon, had roofs of slate. In 1788 Assheton Smith evicted the handful of local slate workers and opened this, the Dinorwic Quarry, which, with nearby Penrhyn

Quarry, made North Wales into one of the largest slate areas in the world, with 17,000 men producing 485,000 tons of slate a year.

Winning the slate from the mountain by blasting and by turning the blocks of slate into pillars, each weighing 220–440 pounds, was only the start of the process. The pillars had to be brought down to the valley floor, moved to the works, sawn, split into slates and transported to the coast by steam railway for shipment. Each stage required equipment that had to be designed, cast, forged, welded, maintained, repaired and powered. The foundry, forges, machine shops and cropping sheds, all powered by the largest waterwheel in mainland Britain, form the museum.

Here in the museum, former slate workers demonstrate the speed and precision with which each slate was split and split again into roofing tiles as thin as a quarter of an inch – the sizes of slates being named Ladies (16 by 12 inches), Countesses (20 by 12 inches) and up through the aristocracy to Queens (42 by 27 inches) – at the rate of sixty an hour.

When the quarry was in production the machine shops shuddered to the noise of boring, drilling, turning, cutting and pounding of the power hammers. The air in each shed was so thick with dust that the farther end could not be seen. It filled the men's lungs as surely and fatally as coal dust the miners', yet as late as 1922 the medical officer was insisting, 'we have no case of Silicosis in this quarry of which I am aware . . . Slate dust is not merely harmless, but beneficial.'[52]

The museum has transported and re-erected a row of quarry workers' houses from Fron Haul, near Blaenau Festiniog. They have been fitted out to show living conditions at the time of the great age of slate (1860–70s); at the time of the Penrhyn strike (1901) (when 2,800 men walked out and stayed out for three years); and in 1969 when Dinorwic Quarry closed.

By the time you leave your eye has adjusted to the many shades of grey, caused by variations in the mineral content: sevicite mica, quartz, chlorite, occasional haematite and rutile. Nine layers of slate run through Elidir mountain, green and wrinkled, old

The Welsh Slate Museum at Llanberis

quarry blue, new quarry blue, grey mottled, sage green, bronze, purple red: the declensions of slate.

PLAS NEWYDD *

Llanfairpwll, Isle of Anglesey LL61 6DQ
Tel. 01248 714795

James Wyatt house overlooking the Menai Straits; huge mural by Rex Whistler

Small sailing boats work their way up the Menai Straits past Plas Newydd towards Robert Stephenson's masterpiece of engineering, the Britannia Bridge.[53] Across the water the summits of Snowdonia rise to the clouds. It is a fine setting for this 18th-century house remodelled by James Wyatt and Joseph Potter (1793–9) in a cool, delicate Gothic style, topped by parapets and small turrets wearing Tudor caps.

As you walk through the park towards the house you pass a cromlech, a Neolithic burial chamber of four or five mighty boulders, a reminder that this is old land: Anglesey; Môn Mam Cymru, Mona the Mother of Wales.

Attractive and interesting though site, house and cromlech are, they cannot commend Plas Newydd for inclusion in this book. What do are Rex Whistler's last and finest mural and the small military museum dedicated to the 1st Marquess of Anglesey, who, when riding from the field of Waterloo beside the Duke of Wellington as his Commander of Cavalry, lost his leg, blown off by grapeshot.

Although none of his ancestors or descendants was a serious collector, there are some

*Rex Whistler's mural in the Dining Room at
Plas Newydd*

good paintings here: a still life, *A Butcher's
Stall*, by Frans Snyders in the Gothick Hall;
eight small sketches by or after Louis Laguerre
of episodes from Marlborough's victories at
Blenheim, Ramillies and Malplaquet;[54] and
four huge pastoral scenes (1789) by the Flemish
Balthasar Paul Ommeganck, whose endless,
soft evening skies dominate the walls of the
Saloon.

There are seven watercolours of views of,
and around, the house by John 'Warwick'
Smith and a small collection of family portraits
that includes a Romney, a Lawrence and several Hoppners. Hoppner's painting of *Henry,*

Lord Paget, later the 1st Marquess of Anglesey
(1798) as Lieutenant-Colonel of the Hussars
confirms the contemporary view that he was
'*le plus beau garçon d'Angleterre*'; he is depicted
with improbably long legs crossed, leaning
against a proud, nervous stallion (painted by
Sawrey Gilpin, while Hoppner painted Paget).

Paget abandoned his beautiful first wife,
Lady Caroline Villiers ('Car'), also painted
here by Hoppner, to elope with Lady Charlotte
Wellesley, Wellington's sister.[55] It was a very
public scandal. Car's brother challenged him
to a duel (he shot and missed; Paget discharged his pistol into the air), and Wellington
refused to employ him despite his brilliance
as a cavalry commander (he had covered with
courage and flair the retreat of Sir John Moore

to Corunna). When Napoleon escaped from Elba, Wellington recalled him as his second-in-command.

On the morning of the battle of Waterloo Paget, by then Lord Uxbridge, observed, 'We shall have sharp work today.' He did, and he had his leg shot away, which led to this exchange: Uxbridge: 'By God, Sir, I've lost my leg.' Wellington: 'By God, Sir, so you have.' Here is the wooden artificial leg that was made for him, on which he is said to have walked seven miles a day for the rest of his life. In a cabinet, surrounded by uniforms, medals, sables and shakoes, it draws the eye. Later that year he was created Marquess of Anglesey. In 1935–6 his great-grandson, the 6th Marquess, remodelled the north wing of Plas Newydd,

creating a long rectangular dining room that looked across the Straits to Snowdonia. He invited Rex Whistler to decorate the room with murals.

Whistler's first commission on leaving the Slade was the mural in the new restaurant at the Tate Gallery (now Tate Britain, q.v.). The Whistler gallery here demonstrates the range and fluency of his work in the 1930s: more murals, book illustrations, designs for theatre sets and costumes, toiles de Jouy, ceramics for Wedgwood, bookplates, portraits.

Here on a wall fifty feet long he created a vast capriccio of a port, the sea, ships, two coastlines. It is an Arcadian confection of real and imagined buildings, of family references and jokes (their pug dog, Lady Anglesey's spectacles, a lit cigarette) that shows he was as elegant and fluent a pre-war artist as Noël Coward was a writer of plays and songs.

On the outbreak of war he enlisted in the 2nd Battalion Welsh Guards but, in a letter to Lord Anglesey written in 1940, he promised to return to 'dot the anchors and cross the masts', having painted himself into the scene as a gardener sweeping up leaves in a side arcade. He was killed in Normandy in 1944.

This room, the Tate restaurant and the murals at Mottisfont Abbey in Hampshire and at Port Lympne in Kent for Sir Philip Sassoon, are his contributions to a mural tradition that was out of tune with post-war Britain and has not yet been fully revived. Nevertheless Whistler was one of a generation of artists – alongside Ravilious, Bawden, Minton, Farleigh, Tunnicliffe and even, for most of his career, Piper – who maintained a graphic, figurative line that has its roots in the 17th and 18th centuries and embodies a distinctive Englishness.

CYFARTHFA CASTLE MUSEUM AND ART GALLERY *

Brecon Road, Merthyr Tydfil,
Mid Glamorgan CF47 8RE
Tel. 01685 723112

In a mock Gothic iron master's castle, the history of Merthyr, complete with brass band

William Crawshay the Second built Cyfarthfa Castle in 1825 on a hillside on the edge of Merthyr Tydfil looking down into the valley of the River Taff at his Cyfarthfa Ironworks. His father, Richard Crawshay,[56] had built the company until, by 1803, it was 'by far the largest in this Kingdom; probably, indeed, the largest in Europe; and, in that case, as far as we know, the world'.[57]

Before the coming of ironworks, Daniel Defoe had described this site as 'a most agreeable vale opening to the South, with a pleasant river running through it called the Taffe'.[58] A century later W. and S. Sandys wrote: 'About

five miles from Merthyr we saw . . . a faint glimmering redness . . . everything in utter darkness heightened by a thick red fog . . . we could see men moving among the blazing fires, and hear the noise of huge hammers, clanking of chains, whiz of wheels, blast of bellows . . . the effect was almost terrific when contrasted with the pitchy darkness of the night.'[59]

Cyfarthfa made the Crawshays hugely rich, as its nearby rival, the Dowlais Ironworks, made its owner, John Josiah Guest.

The industrial competition from Dowlais intensified and though Cyfarthfa struggled, turning to steel-making in 1879, it could not compete. The Crawshays left the castle in 1890 and the Borough Council took the building on, opening the museum in 1909, in the absence of a founding permanent collection, with an exhibition of loans from the Victoria and Albert Museum and others.

Just as Cyfarthfa built on the works and skills of the iron and steel industries, so the museum today begins, in its basement, with Merthyr Tydfil's social, industrial and political history, in galleries created in the 1980s by its then curator Nick Mansfield.[60] The rise and the fall of these industries, once the greatest in Wales (in the mid 19th century Merthyr Tydfil was larger than Cardiff and Newport combined), is an epic story. The town's expansion brought employment but it made living conditions hellish. The town had no public water supply until 1860. The Rammel Report of 1849 noted that 'when this water is kept 24 hours it is impossible to drink it, on account of its offensive smell which I can compare to nothing else than that arising from decayed animal matter . . . communicated to the water for it being surface water passing through the burial ground.'

These conditions made Merthyr Tydfil a breeding ground for radicalism and a Chartist riot in 1831 ended with twenty people being killed, seventy imprisoned and the troops being forced to retreat. Twelve were transported and one, Dic Penderyn, the local Chartist leader, hanged in Cardiff protesting his innocence.

Radicalism took root and in 1900 Keir

Interior of Cyfartha Castle Ironworks at Night
*by Penry Williams (Cyfartha Castle Museum
and Art Gallery)*

Hardie was elected as the town's Member of Parliament, the first Labour Party MP, but no amount of political protest, within Parliament or without, could prevent the fall of a town dependent on a single industry, and in 1939 a Royal Commission recommended that the town be abandoned and relocated on the coast, a fate that was averted only by the outbreak of war.

Upstairs the museum has redecorated, in period, the ground-floor rooms of the Crawshays' castle and crammed them full of pictures, ceramics, sculptures and an allsorts assortment of objects about the family, the town, the ironworks and more: oriental curios, Victorian bodices, marble fireplaces, a dappled rocking horse, marble busts, Nantgarw pottery and crashing crystal chandeliers. In short it is a museum tombola, for

in whichever direction you dip you will find something to please and amuse. This is true, too, of the paintings.

There is a core of local paintings; some, by Penry Williams, that go back to the original 1909 Loan Exhibition; views of Cyfarthfa and valley landscapes. There are works by Julius Caesar Ibbetson, invited to Merthyr by the Crawshays, and a J. F. Herring, a Frank Brangwyn, drawings by Burne-Jones and Augustus John, an unusually good John Collier and a Mary Beale (attributed but unlikely). Mixed in with these are paintings donated by the Welsh Contemporary Arts Society, of which Geoffrey Crawshay was a founder member: a Mary Potter still life, Jack Yeats's *The Hackney Car* (1925), Harold Knight's portrait of W. H. Davies, the author of *Diary of a Supertramp*, and Welsh paintings by Allan Gwynne-Jones, Kyffin Williams and Cedric Morris.

It is not easy to reconcile the infectious high spirits and good humour upstairs with the galleries below. Cabinets of brass musical instruments achieve balm if not reconciliation. Robert Thompson Crawshay founded the Cyfarthfa brass band in 1838, determined to make it the best in Wales. He trawled Britain for the best players, many poached from Wombwell's Menagerie, a celebrated band who played in Lancashire and Yorkshire. Their instruments, buffed and polished, are here: flugelhorn, euphonium, slide trumpet, slide drum (steel), a keyed bugle and an ophicleide. Places in the band were passed from father to son. John England, a patriarch of the band, bred three generations of brass players. One of his sons, Joseph, played for fifty-four years. 'Heredity was important,' wrote Huw Williams, an historian of brass bands, 'the same way that sons of miners followed their fathers down the pit. Brass Band playing relatives tended to stick together.'[61]

NEWPORT MUSEUM AND ART GALLERY **

John Frost Square, Newport NP9 1PA
Tel. 01633 840064

Roman walks, Chartist riots, pottery and pictures

John Frost Square, named after the great Newport Chartist leader, is a sad example of 1970s municipal architecture. John Newman, in *The Buildings of Wales*, is generous when he admonishes 'the anonymous and un-memorable work of the Newport Borough Council's Architect's Department.[62] Stretches of grey, caramel and brown facing brick'.[63] Hiding within it behind a facade of PVC panels is the combined library, art gallery and museum above a tourist information office. Three emblematic mosaics announce this triple function without enhancing it.

Neither this, nor the automaton clock in the centre of the square, a dwarfish, deliberate parody of the Euston arch in polished steel, should deter the visitor from going up to the first floor where, without ceremony or entrance, the museum waits.

It is a museum and gallery of parts: part collections, part record, in which for once the records are the stronger and richer. There are two collectors' collections of ceramics: John Wait's 18th- and 19th-century teapots and the Wemyss ware of Iris and John Fox.

Teapots are barometers of manners and history, rising and falling with trade, taxes and territories. John Wait brought together examples from all the leading 18th-century manufacturers (Minton, Derby, Worcester), including tea bowls as well as pots. His 19th-century collection (Doulton, Copeland) features a Pontypool, Japanese ware tea urn.

Iris[64] and John Fox were omnivorous collectors, akin to Charles Paget Wade of Snowshill Manor (q.v.). At Craigievar, their Victorian house on the edge of Edinburgh, they accumulated pottery, porcelain, furniture, glassware, dolls, toys, enamel baths and Burnsiana, tucked into every crevice. Among the Staffordshire figures, the German porcelain, the pieces of Clarice Cliff pottery and the cabinet of pepper pots, like small Toby jugs, it is the Wemyss ware that the eye fastens upon.

Wemyss ware pigs and cats are forever optimistic, smiling, wide-eyed, determined to ignore the garlands of garish flowers that decorate their backs. An affronted bulldog here disowns the roses that bedizen him.

Newport, the Roman Novus Burgus, on the Usk, the largest town in the county, is the obvious guardian of Gwent's history. As well as Caerleon (v. Roman Legionary Museum), three miles north of Newport, the Romans established a settlement at Caerwent,[65] ten miles to the east. Excavations in 1903 brought to light a Four Seasons mosaic floor of which only Summer and Winter survive, and fragments other than the usual combs, jewellery and Samian ware. Here are a table top, leg and chair foot, carved from Dorset shale; a pewter jug and dish; fragments of finials and columns; the lead panel of a sarcophagus decorated with a frieze of myrtle leaves; a rich haul of domestic ware.

The Norman marcher lords who built castles at Chepstow and Monmouth also founded priories and the Cistercians followed with abbeys, carved fragments of whose ruins are here from remote Llanthony, buried in the Black Mountains in the Vale of Enyas; Llantharnam with its eleven-bay stone barn, roofless and ivy-stifled; and Tintern, the earliest Cistercian abbey in Wales (1131), colonised by monks from L'Aumône and built in local old red sandstone, its colours shifting from purple to mauve, from buff to grey. The 18th-century collector and connoisseur Sir Richard Colt Hoare of Stourhead wrote of it, 'No ruin I have seen in England has so striking effect on the mind and sense as that of Tintern when the door first opens and presents the whole extent of this most beautiful Gothic aisle, overhung with ivy in the most picturesque manner.'

Less picturesque was the fate of John Frost (of the square), Zephaniah Williams and William Jones, the leaders of the Newport Chartists' rising in 1839, who were transported to Australia, having had their death sentences commuted. The museum maps their march by means of contemporary posters, etchings and portraits of the main participants, from Tredegar, Ebbw Vale and Pontypool, and the clash at the Westgate Hotel between the marchers and soldiers of the 45th Regiment in which twenty Chartists were killed. Despite its growing population Newport had been ignored by the 1832 Reform Act and still shared one Member of Parliament with Monmouth and Usk.

John Frost (1784–1877), draper, borough councillor, Justice of the Peace and Mayor of Newport (1836), was one of those who, moved by the campaign of the London Working Men's Association, the writings of William Cobbett (*The Political Register*) and the publications of Richard Carlile, 'preferred to be known as Chartists and Republicans rather than as special constables'.[66]

In 1838 the House of Commons rejected, without debate, the People's Charter, supported by 1.28 million signatures, and the imprisonment of Henry Vincent for making 'seditious speeches' brought matters to a head: the rising, the march, the clash, the deaths. It was the most militant event in the essentially constitutional campaign of the Chartists. Five of the six demands of the charter were eventually met but not until well into the 20th century.[67]

If the museum building is a design failure, the Newport Transporter Bridge is not. Designed in 1906 by the French engineer Ferdinand Arnodin, it spans the River Usk, a roadway suspended from its towers of latticed steelwork, as handsome a 20th-century bridge as any in Britain, as its model here bears witness.

MUSEUM OF WELSH LIFE **

St Fagans, Cardiff CF5 6XB
Tel. 029 2057 3500
www.nmgw.ac.uk/mwl/

The folk life of Wales: hats, harps, transported buildings and eisteddfods

In 1836 Lady Llanover, whose bardic name was Gwenynen Gwent, the Bee of Gwent, published an essay on the 'presentation of the Welsh language and national costume of Wales'[68] as part of her campaign to revive the Welsh culture. She brought Welsh-speaking servants from the north to her mansion near anglicised Abergavenny and dressed them in red cloaks, flannel petticoats and tall black hats, turning 'farm servants' working clothes into a conscious, or rather self-conscious, national costume'.[69] This national costume was no more Welsh than Lady Llanover, née Augusta Waddington, whose husband Benjamin was a Gwent iron master and the Commissioner for Works in London. He gave his name to Big Ben. However her 'national costume' survives as a symbol of Welshness in dolls, tea cloths and tourist souvenirs.

In doing so it poses the questions that lie at the heart of this, the first open-air museum in Britain, and every other museum of national folk life: what constitutes a national identity and how is it expressed? The museum's response, that it 'shows how the people of Wales lived, worked and spent their leisure time over the last five hundred years', is somewhat generalised.

Lady Llanover constructed a notional national dress out of Welsh flannel and working clothes, much as the kilt and 19th-century Highland dress were conceived around the plaid in Scotland. Materials can be metaphors, and the Costume and Textile Collection here has fine displays of quilts and patchwork, cloth and lace, embroidery and samples, but their particular Welshness is muted.

Questions of identity are particularly hard to answer in relation to Wales, which is a country,

Rhyd Y Car: 200 years of miners' cottages at the Museum of Welsh Life

but not a state; which has a capital, but no government enacting primary legislation; 'a flag, but no embassies; an indigenous language, but no indigenous laws'.[70] Even without the trappings of a state to carry and sustain identity, Welsh pride burns fiercely. This is a country whose roots are Celtic, Roman and Christian, untouched by the invasions of Angles, Saxons, Jutes and Franks that shaped England. This museum offers an opportunity to consider the nature of Welshness.

'Two arts have changed the surface of the world, Agriculture and Architecture,' wrote W. R. Lethaby.[71] This museum rests heavily on both. Spread across over over 100 acres of woodland and pastures, the museum has a fine setting for its collection of more than forty original buildings. They have been moved from all over Wales and re-created here to show the development of Welsh vernacular architecture over the past 600 years.

The site is not organised chronologically. You wander from century to century, from a 1760 Powys woollen mill to an 1880 summerhouse from the grounds of Cardiff Castle.

There are examples of cruck-frame buildings in which the ridge trees in the roof are supported by curved timbers (the crucks) that reach from the ground to the roof apex: Hendre'r-ywydd Uchaf farmhouse, Denbighshire, built in 1508; Hendre-Wen barn, Gwynedd, built a century later.

Nant Wallter and Llainfadyn cottages are later, both built in the 1760s–70s, but both use older techniques. The walls of Nant Wallter, from Taliaris in Carmarthenshire, are made of clom – clay or mud, mixed with straw and stone dust; its thatch and wattle of gorse and straw. Llainfadyn, a one-room cottage, is built of mountain boulders with a roof of slate from local quarries.

From a distance, the buildings appear to be clustered together like a village, an impression strengthened by the wisps of smoke that rise from chimneys. Such a view is historically misleading, since Wales has little urban tradition before the 19th century. Gerald of Wales, writing in 1188, observed that the Welsh 'do not dwell together in either town or village or fort but, like hermits, live in the woods. And their custom on the edge of forests is not to build large mansions or fine costly buildings of stone or brick, but to build huts of wattled rods to serve for a year.'[72] The reliance on agriculture and the marginal nature of much land sustained that pattern of living for the next 500 years, with smallholdings supporting single houses.

At the centre of the site is a group of 19th-century buildings (a terrace of 19th-century ironworkers' houses from Merthyr Tydfil, c. 1800, a school and a village store, both 1880) and others from the early 20th century, a bake-house, a tailor's shop, a post office and a huge workmen's institute (1916), built by the Tredegar Iron and Coal Company for their model village at Oakdale, Caerphilly.

Most affecting is the youngest building in the museum, an aluminium prefabricated bungalow, a Type B2, erected in 1948 as part of the building boom to replace houses destroyed by bombing in the war. It was delivered on site in four sections, complete with wiring, plumbing, gas, water and cupboards, and was bolted together, ready for occupation. Made to last ten years, many such bungalows are still being lived in today.

As an anthology of vernacular building techniques the collection is fine. It conveys the scale of dwellings. But there is an absence of detail, of the sense of lives being lived. Even the ghosts are absent; except perhaps in the tiny Unitarian chapel. Devoid of any decoration, with a beaten-earth floor, its pews faced each other rather than God.

Like the Weald and Downland Open Air Museum (q.v.) that it resembles, the Museum of Welsh Life maintains traditional livestock breeds on site (Welsh black cattle, Hill Radnor sheep, Welsh pigs) and historically accurate crops are grown, using original techniques. There is a wide range of agricultural buildings – corn mill, gorse mill, tannery, smithy, hayshed – but the collection of agricultural equipment (wagons, haywains, ploughs, post-Second-World-War Fordson and Ferguson tractors) is kept indoors in the museum's galleries.

In the Cart and Agricultural Vehicle Gallery, specific Welshness remains elusive. In the music sections of the Gallery of Material Culture it is pervasive. Gerald of Wales writes that the Welsh 'make use of three instruments, the harp, the pipes and the crwth'.[73] All are well represented here.

The crwth is a six-stringed instrument, with a flat back and sound board, played with a bow: a rectangular, ungainly instrument with a plangent voice. The pipes are not bagpipes but a pighorn or hornpipe with six finger holes, a thumb hole and a reed, as in a clarinet. The harps are several: a pedal harp; a single string; and the earliest, the triple. Although this last is, by tradition, the Welsh harp, that tradition is only 200 years old and it probably originated in Italy in the 16th or 17th centuries.[74] Here, too, is a rococo gilt harp made by Bassett Jones of Cardiff in 1843 for Lady Llanover to present to Albert, Prince of Wales (later Edward VII): a Welsh instrument that could not function.

The search for the quiddity of Welshness comes to rest at the eisteddfod, its history traced by means of the medals won by famous bards. Yet even here, at the heart of the Welsh language, we are not free of issues of authenticity. Beside the eisteddfod memorabilia is a cabinet that records the gorsedd, the ceremony of conferring orders on druids, bards and ovates.

But the gorsedd is a fiction. It was invented by Iolo Morganwg, pacifist, Unitarian, opponent of slavery, Welsh nationalist, poet, antiquarian and literary forger. He convened the first gorsedd in 1791 in that sanctum of Welshness, Primrose Hill (London), validating its rituals with forged manuscript evidence,[75] which purported to show that the old Druidic traditions had survived intact in his native Glamorgan. He then grafted his gorsedd on to the established eisteddfod tradition by holding a gorsedd ceremony at the 1819 Cambrian Society of Dyfed in Carmarthen. His scholarship and his talent for poetry and pastiche are not doubted, even by those scholars who have unmasked him and reattributed his 'medieval' poems (G. J. Williams and Dr Thomas Parry). Parry, the greatest living authority on the poems of Dafydd ap Gwilym, included in *The Oxford Book of Welsh Verse* a poem by Morganwg that hitherto had been attributed to ap Gwilym for nearly two centuries.

Morganwg's bardic motto was 'The Truth against the world' but his name was not Morganwg, it was Edward Williams, a stonemason.

Here there are many pieces of the broken mirror and several that are missing. Music and landscape present problems for any museum. There is little sense here of the poverty and harshness, or of the sea that surrounds Wales on three sides and that provided fishing,

trading and the means of emigration. There are remarkable collections here that evoke well many aspects of Welsh life but the history of Wales that they present skips over social unrest, political tension, ideology and nationalism, all of which are parts of 'how the people of Wales lived [and] worked . . . over the last five hundred years'.

GLYNN VIVIAN ART GALLERY ***

Alexandra Road, Swansea SA1 5DZ
Tel. 01792 516900
Website www.swansea.gov.uk/glynnvivian/

Swansea ceramics and Welsh painting: Augustus and Gwen John, Evan Walters and supreme Ceri Richards

Richard Glynn Vivian[76] died in 1911, the year before the gallery he gave to Swansea was opened. His gift of £10,000 made the gallery possible. His collection of fine and decorative art gave it life.

Glynn Vivian was the youngest son of a copper magnate. With his three older brothers running the family company he was free to live on the Continent and build a collection of paintings and ceramics. In his sixties, with rapidly failing eyesight, he returned to Swansea and devoted himself to good works, founding a mission for miners at Hafod, a home for the blind, and this gallery.

Glynn Vivian loved Italy and wanted his gallery to resemble an Italian palazzo. In the entrance hall are two plaster figures of 15th-century Medici princes[77] cast from Michelangelo's originals in the New Sacristy within the Church of San Lorenzo in Florence, but the overall effect of Glendinning Moxham's building is more Edwardian baroque than Italian.

Glynn Vivian's founding bequest was eclectic in its taste, a mix of Old Masters (thought at the time to include a Reni, a Correggio and a Veronese,[78] each now re-attributed to 'School of'), some 19th-century French paintings (Harpignies, Boudin, a small Monet), eighteen works by Gustave Doré,[79] a friend; and an assortment of 19th-century English paintings: a portrait of Sir Robert Peel by Lawrence, a good David Cox (*Carreg Cennan Castle*) and a small Monet, acquired in 1975.

His ceramics included pieces from Worcester and Derby,[80] Swansea and Nantgarw,[81] some rare Meissen (Jaspice ware, the first hard paste porcelain made in Western Europe by Johann Böttger in 1708) and a series of Nymphenburg figures (*c.* 1747) by F. A. Bustelli.

Both collections have been built upon. There were major bequests and purchases of Thomas Pardoe's magnificent Cambrian cream ware and botanical supper set (*c.* 1800)[82] and of Cambrian porcelain from the period 1814–17, during which Lewis Weston Dillwyn had William Billingsley[83] working for him. Here too are oddities: Glamorgan and Cambrian cow creamers and early Toby jugs (*c.* 1770s) made by Ralph Wood in Stoke-on-Trent, and a female Prattware Toby of Martha Gunn.

For some years progress in developing the painting collection was modest. In the twenty years before the Second World War the sixty-two preliminary studies for the British Empire panels in Swansea's Guildhall by Sir Frank Brangwyn were acquired, as were paintings by Dod Procter and Patricia Preece, Stanley Spencer's second wife. A start was made on collecting the work of Welsh artists, in particular of Evan Walters and Ceri Richards, both of whom were pupils of Grant Murray at Swansea School of Art.

After the war paintings by Augustus and Gwen John were acquired, as were works by Ivon Hitchens, Alfred Janes and David Jones, and over 120 by Evan Walters. The work of 20th-century British artists (Wyndham Lewis, Matthew Smith, John Piper, Paul Nash, Jacob Epstein) strengthened the collection, and an important gift was made in 1988 by the Swansea architect Sir Alex Gordon, whose collection included Ben Nicholson, Barbara Hepworth, Henry Moore and Elisabeth Frink. Here too is one of Mark Gertler's best paintings, *The Artist's Mother*, a solid portrait of a solid woman sitting on a solid chair, her large hands on her lap. Her chins are thick, her lips

heavy; a red-spotted handkerchief holds back her hair. She watches with wary eyes the process of being painted by her son.

A bequest of prints and drawings from John Deffett Francis, made at intervals between 1876 and 1901, was transferred belatedly from the School of Art to the gallery. It included a print by Albrecht Dürer, *The Knight, Death and the Devil*, and drawings by Richard Wilson, Thomas Gainsborough and John Sell Cotman.

The gallery's strongest holding is of the work of Ceri Richards, comprising paintings, drawings and constructions from the late 1920s to the 1960s. There is an early portrait of his wife, the artist and designer Frances Richards,[84] *Portrait of the Artist's Wife*. The details are sketched in: sensual lips and nose, wide face, a pink blouse edged with a folkloric pattern. Her hands are folded meekly in her lap, her face is lost in sadness, the eyes look down, past and beyond the painter. It contrasts disturbingly with her own small self-portrait, *On Being Alone*, in which the several small images of herself, each confined within a rectangle (bare feet, lank hair, hands again clasped in front of her) become ever smaller until all the features and identity are lost in the slightness.

There are paintings from Ceri Richards's *Hammerklavier* series of the 1950s and from the *Lion Hunt* series (variations on Delacroix's *Lion Hunt*). There are paintings of great poignancy provoked by the death of his friend, the poet Vernon Watkins, calling up the beauty of Watkins' Gower Peninsula: flowers, blossom, clear colours, geometric shapes and the shadow of a black swan.

It is *La Cathédrale Engloutie III* which most clearly shows Richards' strengths. One of a series inspired by Debussy's piano prelude with the same title (1910), its subject is the legend of the cathedral of Ys, sunk off the coast of Brittany, which is said to rise towards the surface at moments of profound calm, its bells tolling slow beneath the water.

The architectural features of the cathedral (pillars, arches, masonry) appear and disappear, and swoon in and out of focus beneath the water; there is a sense of immense depth, disturbed. The stone shapes are set at different angles to one another like Debussy's sonorous whole-tone scales. The painting is an allusive haunting work that shifts as you look through its blues, now translucent, now opaque, rising and falling with a tide.

Richards is suggesting that the cathedrals we make, however beautiful their architecture, however resonant their music, will be subsumed by the elements. The ambition of the work, its power, its assurance, make it easy to see why Richards was so admired, particularly by other painters, in his lifetime; conversely it is hard to see why his reputation is presently muffled. In the landscape of post-war Welsh poetry and painting, he stands on a summit with the best of Dylan Thomas and Vernon Watkins, dark and fierce. Yet he is always a European and his work is steeped in Delacroix, Debussy, Matisse, Picasso, squarely in the spirit of Richard Glynn Vivian.

SWANSEA MUSEUM **

Victoria Road, Maritime Quarter,
Swansea SA1 1SN
Tel. 01792 653763

The oldest museum in Wales: Welsh pottery, 19th-century photographs and an Egyptian mummy

The Royal Institution of South Wales founded this museum in 1841. Designed by Frederick Long of Liverpool with a full flourish, it has four orders of Ionic columns and a splendid pediment in Bath stone:[85] it is a building that proclaims the institution's royal status conferred three years before.

The Royal Institution evolved out of the Swansea Philosophical and Literary Society, formed in 1835, whose museum was 'for the advancement of Science, Literature and the Arts'.[86] Its first accessioned object was a Roman milestone[87] presented by George Grant Francis in 1835 but its key early collections were scientific, notably the collection of shells given by John Gwyn Jeffreys on which he was to base his *British Conchology* (5 vols., 1862–9),

the standard work in the 19th century, and the material from Dr William Buckland's excavations in 1823 at Paviland and other caves on the Gower coast, at which Buckland was assisted by Jeffreys and Lewis Weston Dillwyn.

At the time Wales had only six towns with populations of over 8,000. Compared with Merthyr Tydfil, the largest, Swansea had no significant industrial base and, in order to grow, promoted itself as the 'new Welsh metropolis' and bathing resort by building assembly rooms, libraries, etc. A Philosophical and Literary Society sat well with that and was supported by the town's intellectual elite. Among its founders were four Fellows of the Royal Society: Dillwyn, and his elder son Dillwyn Llewellyn, Jeffreys, Sir William Logan and John Henry Vivian, who worked with Humphrey Davy and Michael Faraday on the development of new copper alloys. William Grove was elected FRS in 1840 at the age of twenty-nine for his work in combining oxygen and hydrogen by an electric current.[88]

All were men of parts. John Dillwyn Llewellyn's wife, Emma, was a cousin of William Henry Fox Talbot. Within a year of Fox Talbot's first successful photographic image in 1838, Dillwyn was experimenting in Swansea. The ten volumes of his photographs here include portraits (James Brooke, the white rajah of Sarawak, in his Indian finery when visiting Britain in 1858–61; Hormuzd Rassam, who assisted Layland in excavating Nineveh), 'scenes' (one here entitled *The Gypsies* features his two sons and one of his daughters in costume, picnicking) and sea and cloudscapes, with one of which he won the Silver Medal at the Paris Exhibition of 1855.

John Llewellyn Dillwyn's brother Lewis managed the family business, Cambrian Pottery, bought by their grandfather in 1802. That the origins of Swansea Pottery go back to the mid 18th century is shown here by the Morgan John flask, made by William Coles & Sons in 1768, its incised decoration filled with blue; but it was the work of such designers as Thomas Rothwell, and Cambrian's Thomas Pardoe and William Billingsley, that made a local industry national.

Lewis Llewellyn Dillwyn and his father, Lewis Weston Dillwyn, were keen botanists,the latter giving Pardoe *Curtis's Botanical Magazine* from which to copy the flowers that grace his ware: yellow day lilies, scarlet ipomoea, cranesbill with its delicately kidney-shaped leaves. It is not surprising that Billingsley, the master of the rose, came here from Derby.

As in Staffordshire, a wide range of ware was produced in Swansea: armorial (plates for Lord Nelson, 1802), oriental (Imari designs), local views (engraved on black and green ware by Rothwell), even Etruscan (1847–50), in imitation of Wedgwood.

Everywhere the origins of the museum are apparent: geology, archaeology, natural history. On the wall at the bottom of the stairs are Jurassic fossils, a plesiosaur and an ichthyosaur. Upstairs are the finds from Buckland's 1823 cave excavations, the bones of mammoths, a woolly rhino and a sabre-toothed tiger, and of the Red Lady of Paviland, with tools of bone and chert, and scrapers, blades, burins, ivory beads and pierced shells.[89] There are carved stones from the 10th century from Gellionen and from Gnoll,[90] the latter part of a wheel-cross, depicting a Celtic priest in a pleated kilt, a rare example of a human figure on a Celtic cross (v. Islands of Colonsay and Oronsay).

The museum's leading curiosity is the 2,000-year-old Mummy of Hor, an Egyptian priest. General Sir Francis Grenfell, whose family owned a copper smelting works in Swansea, was Commander-in-Chief of the British Army in Egypt in 1885 and, assisted by the archaeologist Wallis Budge, brought this mummy, in its coffin, back to Swansea in 1888. In the coffin is a picture of the goddess Sekhmet.

Downstairs in a room to the right of the entrance is the library of the Swansea Philosophical and Literary Society, still in existence after 175 years, still furnished by the original tables, bookshelves, cabinets. In them is the complete sequence of editions of the *Cambrian Newspaper*, Wales's first weekly publication, from 1804 to its closure in 1918, recording the lives of the Dillwyns, John Gwyn Jeffries and Sir Francis Grenfell, and of this museum.

POWIS CASTLE *

Welshpool, Powys SY21 8RF
Tel. 01938 551920/551944
www.nationaltrust.org.uk

A red castle on a rock, ringed by huge yew hedges, guarding Clive of India's treasures

Powis is the reddest of red castles, each stone gaining depth of colour from the whole and from the red mortar that binds them.[91] From a ridge it looks down on the River Severn and the Montgomery Canal and across to the Long Mountain and the Welsh Marches. For centuries this was the border fortress of the Princes of Powys until Owain ap Gruffydd ap Gwenwynwyn was forced to pay homage to Edward I in 1286.

Retaining the fortress walls and the drum towers that guard the entrance, Sir Edward Herbert converted it into a great house in 1587. All that remains of his work is the Long Gallery, one of the most romantic 16th-century rooms in Britain, comparable to the Great Hall at Knole (q.v.) and with a cornice that is lighter and more delicate, with fronds of leaves that circle and sweep around central rosettes. The cornices boast Herbert arms, lions rampant argent and a wyvern vert, and those of all Sir Edward's other ancestors, which are also brought together in the quarterings of his heraldic achievement over the fireplace. Around the overmantel is plasterwork that depicts Adam and Eve and the Tree of Knowledge.

In the 1660s Sir Edward's grandson, the 1st Marquess of Powis, remade the State Bedroom (1667–70; the only one to retain a balustrade separating the bed alcove from the room, in imitation of Louis XIVs levée rooms at Versailles) and the Grand Staircase, whose stately construction (wide, with shallow treads) is attributed to William Winde, and its ceiling painted in the 1670s to Antonio Verrio.[92]

The 2nd Marquess completed the Grand Staircase by commissioning Verrio's pupil Gerard Lanscroon to do wall paintings depicting *The Triumph of Neptune and Amphitrite* (1705) and *Vulcan Forging the Arms of Achilles*, above which more deities carry the Powis monogram and coronet to the heavens.

In 1902 the 4th Earl of Powis commissioned the Victorian ecclesiastical architect G. F. Bodley to transform the Dining Room and the Oak Drawing Room.[93] It was a curious choice. Bodley was at the end of his career. His Liverpool masterpiece, St John's, Tue Brook, had been built thirty-five years before. Indeed this was, with Holy Trinity, Liverpool, his last major work.[94] Bodley was a friend of William Morris but here he creates two rooms in an atypical, richly Jacobean style in keeping with the ancient fortress, with elaborate ceiling plasterwork and woodwork that nod to the armorial frieze in the Long Gallery.[95] Powis's collections of paintings and sculpture are distinguished by a fine *View of Verona* (*c.* 1745–7) by Bernardo Bellotto and one of Isaac Oliver's most beautiful miniatures. He depicts *Edward, 1st Lord Herbert of Cherbury*, lover, philosopher, poet and diplomat, lying, resting on his right elbow, in an idyllic setting. Behind him in the distance are his knightly charger and armour. The horizontal pose and sylvan setting were copied by Joseph Wright of Derby for his portrait of *Sir Brook Boothby, Bart* (1781).

The later Herberts were not notable connoisseurs. There are portraits by Hudson, Gainsborough, Reynolds and Sir Francis Grant, and Brussels tapestries, but only the 2nd Earl appears to have been interested in the arts, going on the Grand Tour (1772–6), being painted by Batoni and returning with a *pietra dura* table, said to have come from the Borghese Collection in Rome.

One further exception is Robert Clive, 'Clive of India', whose elder son Edward married into the Herberts in 1784. This brought to Powis Clive's collection of Roman statuary (now in the Long Gallery but originally bought for Claremont, Surrey, where he lived, just before his death) and his collection of paintings, which once filled the Ballroom, but of which only a handful now remain (others being in the National Gallery, the National Museum and Gallery of Wales, and the Barber Institute of Fine Arts, all q.v.).

In the (separate) Clive Museum, in vitrines, are the Indian textiles, weapons, ivories and jewellery, trophies from his campaigns between 1744 and 1753 (the battles of Pondicherry and Trinchinopoly, the lifting of the siege at Arcot) and between 1755 and 1760 (the battle of Plassey). Beside them are the treasures brought back by his son, Edward, 2nd Lord Clive, from his period as Governor of Madras (1798–1803) when Arthur Wellesley, later Duke of Wellington, and General Harris finally defeated Tipu Sultan at Seringapatam. Here are Deccan swords of watered steel, hilts inlaid with gold; quilted and studded velvet armour from Hyderabad; a Mughal dagger with a pale grey nephrite jade hilt. Here too are huqqas of silver gilt and enamel set with diamonds and rubies; patkas (sashes) of immense length, their blazing orange silk woven with silver and silver thread; and elephant saddlecloths in red velvet encrusted with massive zardozi work.[96] The trophy of trophies is the sword of Tipu Sultan with its tiger-head pommel, the quillons of crouching tiger and curving, single-edged steel blade within a scabbard of dark green velvet. Out of the mouth of the tiger that grips the blade proceeds Persian poetry: 'My blade that lays down the foundations of victory is the lightning that flashes through the lives of the infidels.'[97]

Clive of India looks down from his portrait by Nathaniel Dance (*c.* 1770) on these Mughal treasures shipped across the world to the Marches of Wales. Outside the fierce face of the castle is framed by the line of ancient yews clipped into huge, heaving shapes.

ERDDIG **

Wrexham LL13 0YT
Tel. 01978 355314

Portraits of all the staff in a Victorian house seen from the servants' entrance

Erddig is buried in the country outside Wrexham. You reach it along long lanes and up a drive that is more like a track, from which you catch no more than a glimpse of the handsome front of the house. It was built by the architect Thomas Webb in 1684 for Joshua Edisbury, the High Sheriff of Denbighshire, and refaced in stone in 1772.

You enter through the estate yards, past workshops and stores: the blacksmith's shop, the joiner's shop, the wagon shed, the sawpit and sawmill; into the stableyard, past the carriage house, the bakehouse, the dairy, the wet and dry laundries and, at last, into Erddig by the servants' entrance.

Within is the New Kitchen, one of the grandest rooms in the house, with a large Venetian window and great rusticated arches. Beyond is the Servants' Passage, and the Servants' Hall, which looks directly into the main entrance.

A plain scrubbed table runs the length of the hall, and around the walls are portraits of the servants who worked here in the late 18th and early 19th centuries: the 'housemaid and

Erddig: call bells in the Servants' Passage

spider-brusher' Jane Ebbrell, aged 83; Jack Nicholas, 'the kitchen man', 71; Edward Prince, the estate carpenter, 73; Jack Henshaw, the gamekeeper, a mere boy of 59; William Williams, the blacksmith, 70; and Thomas Jones, 36, the publican of the Royal Oak at Wrexham and a butcher, the only person not directly employed in the house. All were painted between 1791 and 1793 by the Denbigh artist John Walters, who depicts them with their familiar tools (axe; inn sign; butcher's stall). All have an attendant cat or dog, and all have a descriptive verse on a scroll or plinth: Jane Ebbrell, 'the Mother, of us all', 'from room to room/She drove the dust, with brush and broom,/And by the virtues of her mop,/To all uncleanliness put a stop.' These affectionate verses were written by their employer, Philip Yorke I, who published them as 'Crude-ditties' in 1802. The following generation of servants was painted in 1830 by William Jones of Chester. The odd man out of the series, a young black man in uniform carrying a splendid horn, purports to be the earliest, but was actually painted in the late 18th century over another portrait.

These portraits of servants are far from being unique. The Royal Collection has *Bridget Holmes*, 'a necessary woman', and Christ Church Picture Gallery (q.v.) has *A Scullion*, both painted by John Riley. There are portraits of servants at Knole (q.v.) and George Garrard was commissioned by George Lane Fox to paint eleven portraits of servants at Bramham Park, Yorkshire, in the early 1820s.[98] But none matches these at Erddig.

The portraits continued in daguerreotypes and photographs, hung along the Servants' Passage, completed with doggerel, the final one being a photograph taken by *Picture Post* in 1943 of the last two remaining servants, one in livery.[99]

Joshua Edisbury was declared bankrupt in 1709, having been found guilty of stealing Chancery fees with his brother, a Master in Chancery, and Erddig was bought, in 1714, by John Meller, an unmarried barrister who left the house and estate to his nephew Simon Yorke I in 1733. Five generations of Yorkes, all named Philip or Simon, lived here until Philip Yorke III passed the property to the National Trust in 1973.

After the Servants' Hall, the main rooms. The Dining Room was remodelled by Thomas Hopper (1826–7) in a heavy-handed neoclassical style (Greek coffered ceiling, Doric scagliola columns and pilasters) that has none of the flair he displayed at Penrhyn Castle (q.v.). Although the Drawing Room is hung with minor Old Masters, the Yorkes were not connoisseurs. Philip Yorke I had himself painted by Gainsborough at Bath in the 1770s and his first wife by Francis Cotes (1726–70). There is a curious portrait of John Meller by Charles Jervas that Philip Yorke had repainted by Gainsborough in 1780. The unusual transversal gallery contains a group of 17th-century portraits, some of protagonists of the Thirty Years War, and some extraordinary models, made of mother of pearl, mica and glass, by Betty Radcliffe, lady's maid to Mrs Yorke.

These apart, Erddig is distinguished only by its furniture, bought by Meller in the 1720s from John Belchier, the London cabinet maker: a pair of splendid gilded sconces or girandoles, two giltwood pier glasses, a scarlet japanned bureau cabinet and side chairs, stools japanned, unusually, in green and a spectacular state bed. It is one of the best sets of documented early Georgian furniture in Britain.

There is a Boulle bureau, veneered with brass and tortoiseshell (*c.*1695) and, in the Tapestry Room, a silvered gesso pier table beneath a set of Soho tapestries (1720s) depicting the story of Solomon and Sheba. But the pièce de résistance is the *lit à la duchesse* made by John Hutt in 1720, upholstered with beautifully muted Chinese embroidered silk, painstakingly restored by the Victoria and Albert Museum in the 1960s and placed, sadly, for its own protection, behind glass, in the State Bedroom, which is hung with 18th-century hand-painted Chinese wallpaper. It is incredible to think that water used once to pour directly on to the bed from the leaking roof.

The estate was sustained by the income from mining (copper, lead, iron ore and, especially, coal). After the First World War that income began to decline and it collapsed following nationalisation in 1947, as did the fabric of the house, undermined by shafts from the nearby Belsham colliery. Simon Yorke IV refused to accept any government compensation 'as much of government money had been subscribed by people worse off than himself'. The house had no electricity.

Around the Chapel walls, cut out by Philip Yorke II in 1909, is the text, 'Lord, thou hast been our Refuge, from one generation to another. Save, Lord, and hear us, O King, when we call upon thee.' Their call was heard by the National Trust.

Northern Ireland

The layers of event that make the history of Ireland, north and south, so rich as well as so painful should be teased out and revealed in the museums and galleries of the country. The flowering of the Celtic culture; the lighting of the torch of Christianity in these islands by Columba and Oran; the golden age of the Gaels, of princes and poets; conquest and conflict; oppression, famine and migration; religious hatred – all should reverberate through the nation's museums. But that reverberation is muted, in part as a consequence of partition, with so many of Ireland's greatest treasures being in the National Museum of Ireland in Dublin.

Despite this, the Ulster Museum has assembled fine collections. Indeed, in drawing to itself so much of Northern Ireland's industry, natural history, vernacular architecture, geology, decorative arts and more, it has presented a challenge to other museums, which have responded, in the main, by creating niches, as have the Somme Heritage Centre in Newtownards and the Royal Inniskilling Fusiliers Regimental Museum in Enniskillen, and, not included here, the Ulster American Folk Park in Omagh and the Royal Ulster Constabulary Museum in Belfast.

Almost all Northern Irish museums struggle to represent any aspect of Northern Ireland's history, which since 1688 has been torn by sectarian differences. The Linen Hall Library in Belfast is an exception in facing these frontally and collecting all published documents that relate to the Troubles. Ballymena Museum and Derry Museum, not included here, also address directly aspects of the events of the past thirty-five years.

River Finn

River Foyle

A5

A5

Tyrone

A32

River Mourne

A5

A4

Fermanagh

ENNISKILLEN○

A509

EIRE

SCOTLAND

A37

Londonderry

River Bann

A26

Antrim

A6

M2

A26

A505

A26

M2

A8

Lough Neagh

HOLYWOOD

BELFAST

NEWTOWNARDS

A4

M1

LISBURN

A2

M1

Down

A24

Armagh

N2

50 miles

LINEN HALL LIBRARY ***

17 Donegall Square North, Belfast, Antrim
BT1 5GB
Tel. 028 9032 1707

A radical library for troubled times; its first librarian was executed for treason

The Linen Hall Library is a child of the Enlightenment. It was founded in 1788 as a subscription library by the members of the Belfast Reading Society, 'intelligent artisans' and 'sans culottes', in a Belfast whose population was overwhelmingly Presbyterian.[1]

By the early 1790s they were joined by leading merchants who were as committed to a radical agenda as the 'sans culottes': free, universal education, the rights of women, Catholic emancipation, the history and language of Ireland. They looked to what was happening in France and to the recently successful War of Independence in America, so it is not altogether surprising that in September 1796 Lord Castlereagh arrived in Belfast with warrants for the arrest, on charges of high treason, of leading members of the Society of United Irishmen, including Samuel Neilson, a library committee member, and Thomas Russell, the Linen Hall librarian.[2] Both were arrested in the library's rooms. Russell was interned until 1802. On his release he was involved in Robert Emmet's revolt of 1803, tried and executed. Another one-time committee member, Henry Joy McCracken, was executed in 1798 for his role as United Irish General at the Battle of Antrim.[3] The library was spared from closure in the aftermath of the 1798 rebellion by the advocacy of its president, the Revd Dr William Bruce, and others who were as strongly opposed to rebellion as Russell and McCracken were supportive.

In the early 19th century, with the defeat of France, the library's radical liberalism gave way to tolerant conservatism, but its determination to 'promote knowledge' was uncompromised and it maintained its roots in the Enlightenment in a city that had no university and few schools. Many of its members were either autodidacts or had garnered an education from itinerant teachers in so-called 'hedgerow schools'.

By the 1870s cotton, linen and shipbuilding[4] had made Belfast a rich city. Men of wealth and leisure enabled the library to return to one of its founding tenets, 'to collect such materials as will illustrate the antiquities, the natural, civil, commercial and ecclesiastical history' of Ireland. In 1892 the library moved to new premises and resolved 'that a new class of Irish books be formed'[5] and re-catalogued.

The library has been in the new premises in a former linen warehouse on the corner of Donegall Square ever since. Above its handsome door is the Red Hand of Ulster at the centre of swags of linen carved in stone. Inside a generous, freestanding wooden staircase takes you up in its spiral to the second floor.

The collection provided a strong base on which to build: Corry's *History of Ireland*, given in 1791 by the library's first librarian, Robert Cary; a complete set of the *Belfast Newsletter*, 1738–1838; and the manuscript and 'scattered materials' of Henry Joy's four-volume *Annals of Ireland*. There are fine maps (*Hyberniae Novissima Descriptio*, 1591, by Jodocus Hondius; a manuscript map of Belfast on vellum by John Maclanachan, 1715); the first book printed in the city in 1697; and Edward Bunting's *Ancient Irish Music* (1796), which arose out of the Belfast Harpers' Festival in 1792,[6] promoted by the library, the urtext of all contemporary Irish folk music. Not everyone was rapt. Wolfe Tone recorded in his diary: 'July 13 (the third day of the festival) . . . The Harpers again. Strum. Strum and be hanged . . .'

The old front door at the Linen Hall Library

LINEN HALL LIBRARY

The twentieth century was difficult. Following Partition in 1922 John Hewitt described the lot of the writer in Northern Ireland as being that of 'the bitter gourd'.[7] So too for the library.

The Troubles in 1968 might have sealed the library's fate. The city centre became deserted. Membership fell. Direct rule led to a considerable improvement in the public library service (following the Hawnt Report of 1966), accelerating the decline. The library's ability to provide 'a breathing hole in the ice cap that is closing over us'[8] was threatened. By 1980 it seemed that there was no alternative to a 'permanent loan' to, or amalgamation with, either Queen's University or the public library service. The board at one point actually voted for closure.

A remarkable fight-back ensued, led by a governor, Brian Trainor. That the library was able to mobilise unprecedented public support was due both to the historic importance of its collections and the significance of new interventions and, notably, to the growing importance of its controversial Political Collection. This had begun in 1968 when, it is reported (possibly apocryphally), the then librarian, Jimmy Vitty, was handed a civil rights leaflet in a city centre bar. He kept it, saw its significance and sent his staff out to gather every sort of material published about the Troubles. By 1972, at the height of the Troubles, this was a truly controversial role, and on one occasion the police threatened both to seize the collection and to arrest the deputy librarian. Wiser counsel prevailed and the archive survived. By 1981 the collection had 10,000 items; by 1998 135,000. Today it has 250,000: the Troubles are the most comprehensively documented conflict in the world.

The collection was celebrated in *Troubled Images*, the catalogue of an exhibition in 2001 which has subsequently toured internationally.[9] It expressed, in the words of the librarian John Gray, 'the Library's commitment to openness in an often-censorious society'.

Its posters spanned the political spectrum: 'FOR GOD AND ULSTER' (1960s), 'SMASH UNIONIST JUNTA STORMONT' (1969);

'DUBLIN IS JUST A SUNNINGDALE AWAY, VOTE UNIONIST' (1974), 'REMEMBER DERRY' (1976); 'VOTE D.U.P., SMASH SINN FEIN' (1985), 'DISBAND THE R.U.C.' (1995); 'STOP THE WAR: BETTY WILLIAMS'S PEACE PEOPLE' (1976), 'ACCOMMODATION, NOT SEGREGATION' (1998).

From its founding commitment in 1788 'to excite a spirit of enquiry' the library has been committed to an 'involved neutrality' in a community often riven by prejudice and hatred. In the dark night the library has held steady a light by which people could read the eternal truths: of free speech, free education; of the freedom to tolerate others, the freedom to imagine a better future. As the Nobel Laureate Seamus Heaney has written, 'No institution in Northern Ireland has done more to promote enlightenment and represent a better future for all our citizens.'

NAUGHTON GALLERY *

1st floor, The Lanyon Building, University Road, Belfast, Antrim BNT INN
Tel. 028 9097 5380
e-mail: art@qub.ac.uk.

A brave new art gallery in Queen's University

Until 1968 Queen's was the only university in Northern Ireland, its long west facade by Charles Lanyon embodying the Victorian virtues of confidence and continuity, pomp and circumstance. 'A temple of concord rising in symmetrical and harmonious form' was how the university's first president described it in his speech at its opening in 1849.

Lanyon was an architect of great talent who would be more widely admired had he not worked exclusively in Northern Ireland and had Nikolaus Pevsner written a volume on the buildings of Ulster. Lanyon designed Queen's west front ten years after Charles Barry's Palace of Westminster. Despite its differences in scale and material (red brick), Lanyon's building, like Barry's, imposes Tudor Gothic detail on a symmetrical classical structure with similar success.

Despite this architectural achievement Queen's made its reputation not in the arts but in medicine, mathematics, science, engineering and law. Professor Sir George Bain was appointed vice chancellor in 1998 and resolved to fill this artistic vacuum. The university appointed a curator, commissioned architects, Consarc, to redesign the interior of the long narrow room that runs half the length of the west front and created an art gallery, the Naughton. Opened in September 2001, it hosts a rolling programme of temporary exhibitions.

As yet the university's permanent collection is small, comprising mostly 20th-century portraits of academics which are hung in the Great Hall, overlooked by James Atkins's copy of Titian's huge *St Peter the Martyr* (the original was destroyed by fire in Italy in 1867) and by a portrait of the young *Queen Victoria* (1838) by Sir George Hayter.

The portraits are functional, concerned more with likeness than character. There are works by Philip de Laszlo (1934), Sir James Gunn (1942), Ruskin Spear (1960) and William Conor's portrait of the 2nd Chancellor, the 7th Marquess of Londonderry, in his university robes, standing awkwardly, hands on hips, at Mount Stewart: a pose that defeats Conor's usual fluency.

Conor has two drawings in a collection that includes works by Thomas Faed (a genre subject, *The Doctor's Visit*, 1889) and a self-portrait by Sir John Lavery, subtitled *The Silver Casket* (1935), in the robe of a doctor of laws, which must be one of his most inept paintings. He is somewhat redeemed by *A Moorish Landscape in Winter* (1912). John Luke, described by the poet John Hewitt as the 'craftsman painter', has a painting, *Connswater Bridge* (1934), a view of factories that is an early example of his graphic stylisation, its meticulous, minute brushwork and primary palette moving towards the surreal. Outside, in the quadrangle, is an impressive bronze *Reclining Figure* (1963) by the Ulster-born sculptor F. E. McWilliam.

The collection is moving cautiously into the contemporary, purchasing the landscapes of Richard Croft, Terry Flannagan and Ross

Wilson. Recent acquisitions include works by John Keane, Tai-Shan Schierenberg, Colin Middleton, Basil Blackshaw, Simon McWilliams, Rita Duffy, Paul Bell, Brian Ferran and Keith Wilson.

ULSTER MUSEUM ***

Botanic Gardens, Belfast, Antrim BT9 5AB
Tel. 028 9038 3000
www.ulstermuseum.org.uk

The national museum: everything from fossils to fashion, minerals to modern art, and sunken treasure from the Spanish Armada

All national museums present problems. Whose country? Whose history? For Ulster, with over three hundred years of sectarian division, those difficulties are more acute, even dangerous. Everyday curatorial decisions (purchasing, labelling, even loans) can be loaded with the weight of the past, of beliefs and perceptions.

Even the name of the museum can be seen as contentious. The origins of this museum lie in Belfast's first public museum, opened in 1831 by the Belfast National History Society. An art gallery was founded by the corporation in 1890 and, early in the 20th century, designs for a new combined art gallery and museum were commissioned from James Cumming Wynne. The First World War intervened and the depressed state of the post-war economy allowed the building of only one quarter of the planned museum. It opened in 1929 as the Belfast Museum and Art Gallery, and became the National Museum for Ulster in 1961 when new galleries were added, and the Ulster Museum in 1962. Since 1998 it has been officially a part of the Museums and Galleries of Northern Ireland (MAGNI), but it continues to answer to the Ulster Museum.

There are some departments of the museum, such as geology, in whose galleries it is not difficult to avoid sectarian contentions. The granite of the Mountains of Mourne (50 million years old), the igneous rock of the Giant's Causeway (60 million), the white limestone of the Antrim coast (80 million) and the schists and gneisses of the Sperrins (400 million) are all indifferent to human schism. So too are the megalithic tombs at Newgrange or the Giant's Ring Henge outside Belfast, the Malone hoard (sixteen stone axes, deep speckled black, polished smooth) and the crescent of a gold lunula excavated at Cooltrain, Co. Fermanagh, which are the context (in graphics and photographs) of the megalithic collections here.

The presence of the Mummy of Tjesmut-peret (*c.* 650 BC), whose hieroglyphics the self-taught Revd Edward Hincks deciphered in the late 1840s, and the fragment (a giant fist of fingers) from the monumental red granite statue of *Rameses II*, is contentious, if at all, only in Egypt. Hincks was unique in his time, being able to translate Mesopotamian cuneiform writing as fluently as Egyptian hieroglyphics. He has never received the acclaim in Britain he deserves. The British Museum declined to publish the result of the translations he made for them, of a Persian cuneiform prism. By contrast the Cairo Museum commissioned a marble bust of Hincks, erected in its entrance hall in 1906.[10]

If antiquities are usually beyond controversy, other than scholarly, so too, strangely, are the galleries here of Belfast's industrial past. The vast vertical or horizontal steam engines, built by Victor Coates & Co., that powered the linen mills of Belfast, cared not whether their operators were Catholic or Protestant. The managers and shareholders of the textile, rope, shipbuilding, tobacco and brick-making companies that transformed Belfast into a city of great wealth, whose products are displayed here as 'MADE IN BELFAST', were interested in the cheapness of labour, not the colour of its beliefs.

The treasures from the Spanish Armada galleass[11] *Girona*, wrecked off the Antrim coast in 1588 and recovered by Robert Sténuit,[12] 1967–9, in an amazing feat of marine excavation, are also beyond controversy.[13] The piles of gold and silver coins, the lapis lazuli cameos, the sumptuous jewellery, notable amongst which is a gold brooch encrusted with rubies in the form of a winged salamander, are witness to the riches and sophistication of the 16th-century Spanish nobility; the simple artefacts of everyday use (an olive jar, comb, bellows; buttons, a velvet collar, a sock, miraculously preserved and conserved) to the poignant human story of the Armada.

If you search here for evidence of Ireland in the 17th, 18th, or early 19th centuries, you encounter silence, disturbed only by the collections of fine and decorative art. Here the museum has adopted a forthright policy of collecting on merit. There is a handful of Old Masters: a finely painted *St Cecilia* by Giovanni Francesco Romanelli; the large handsome *St Christopher Carrying the Christ Child* in which Jacob Jordaens is vying with Honthorst and Terbrugghen to create dramatic lighting effects to outshine and outglower Caravaggio. There are 18th-century English paintings, mainly portraits by Gainsborough, Reynolds, Beechey and Lawrence: a small but representative group of English watercolours (Sandby, Dayes, Cotman, Palmer, Cox) and a group of intimate, attentive drawings by John Henry Fuseli, more impressive by far than his fevered Apotheoses.[14]

In 1927 the museum was bequeathed the art collection of Sir Robert Lloyd Patterson. The art critic and sometime director of Leeds City Art Gallery Frank Rutter was asked to assess the 135 paintings. He reported that they 'would bring discredit on the Art Gallery . . . [and] . . . do actual harm . . . since these pictures would give false standards of taste to the uninformed and ignorant'.[15] The museum gained permission to sell the collection, raising only £425. 15s. 6d., but with that they laid the foundations of a collection of 20th-century English paintings: Sickert, Gertler, Gore; John and Paul Nash; William Roberts, Matthew Smith and an outstanding Stanley Spencer, *The Betrayal* (1922).

In the 1960s the keeper of modern art, Ann Cruickshank, assembled as strong a collection of 1960s artists as there is in any regional gallery: Bridget Riley, John Hoyland, Mark Boyle, Gillian Ayres; the now less fashionable Mark Lancaster and Jeremy Moon; Heron, Frost, Hilton and Lanyon from St Ives; and, the outstanding work here, a brilliant painting by the American Morris Louis, *Golden Age* (1958), the equal of any of his in Tate Modern (q.v.).

Rightly the collection of Irish painting here is strong: historically (a good 1820 landscape by James Arthur O'Connor, portraits by Hugh Douglas Hamilton) and in the 20th century, oils and drawings by William O'Connor, the Synge or O'Casey of Irish painting, and oils by Jack Butler Yeats. The surprises are painters who are not immediately thought of as Irish. Sir John Lavery, often claimed by Scotland, was born in Belfast. He bequeathed a large group of his work, including the stunning, Whistler-like *Lady in Black (Mrs Trevor)* (*c.*1908); Dublin-born Francis Bacon and William Scott also have works here. The revelation to English eyes is Mainie Jellett, a fine draughtswoman and an unheralded painter of real quality.

In recent years, with financial restraints, the museum has collected fashion and contemporary craft works. Here are dresses by Pierre Balmain and Coco Chanel, Paco Rabanne and Courrèges, but the curators, each year, have also bought works from the high street (from Dolly Rockers, Miss Cutts, etc.), making a collection that is as interesting to social historians as to designers.

The Ulster Museum may give a somewhat cautious view of Ireland to the Irish. A visitor seeking evidence of Ulster in the 17th, 18th or 19th centuries will find galleries of silence, but the museum's treasures throw light on many corners of life in Ulster.

CASTLE COOLE **

Enniskillen, Co. Fermanagh BT74 6JY
Tel. 028 6632 2690
www.nationaltrust.org

Neoclassical house (James Wyatt); rich Regency interiors (John Preston, a star waiting to be seen)

In the late 1780s Armar Lowry-Corry, newly created Baron Belmore (1781) and later 1st Earl (1797), determined to surpass his brother-in-law, the Earl of Enniskillen, who had recently remodelled Florence Court (q.v.). He appointed a good Irish architect, Richard Johnston,[16] but within months replaced him with the brilliant James Wyatt, the designer of William Beckford's Gothic Fonthill Abbey and of the neoclassical Pantheon in Oxford Street, London.[17] Intent on outdazzling Robert Adam, Wyatt designed for Belmore the greatest, most aloof country house in Ireland. The scale is grand, the facade confident, radiantly stripped of all detail. The Ionic columns of the portico, the Doric of the colonnaded wings, the mighty central pediment need no ornament to ravish the eye. The house stands impassively commanding the view down to Lough Coole.

Wyatt chose Joseph Rose for the plaster-work and Richard Westmacott for the principal chimney pieces. Like him they did their work from a distance, sending designs to be made up in Dublin or on site (Wyatt came to Ireland only once), but together they created the finest neo-classical interior since Adam.

This is Wyatt at his simplest and best. The Entrance Hall, repainted the original dull ointment pink, is bare but for scagliola columns (by Domenico di Bartolo, to resemble porphyry), two fireplaces, two delicate fanlights over the inner doors and low, wide mahogany armchairs by Wyatt. Its clarity and simplicity are matched by his oval Saloon, his double-return staircase and his sublime top-lit Lobby, which stops you and holds you.

In the Entrance Hall and throughout the house Rose demonstrates the varieties of his skills: feather-light in the Dining Room, closely worked in the Lobby and Saloon. Even when, on the Staircase Hall, Belmore insisted, for the sake of economy, that Rose should tone down Wyatt's original designs, the result puts other plasterwork of the period into very low relief.[18]

Just as you are savouring the achievements of Wyatt/Rose/Westmacott, Castle Coole pulls a surprise. By 1795 the building had cost £54,000, excluding Wyatt's 5 per cent fee and some of Westmacott's fireplaces. Belmore was spent. Work slowed to a halt and in 1802 he

died. However his son, Somerset Lowry-Corry, 2nd Earl of Belmore, depicted here in the Morning Breakfast Room in a full-length portrait by Hugh Douglas Hamilton, resolved to build new stables and complete the house, and, in 1807, employed the Dublin upholsterer and decorator John Preston to do so. Preston was as lavish as Wyatt was restrained. His designs were heavier, more elaborate, looking back to William Kent in his use of rich materials and deeply carved giltwood, and they were superbly executed.

Curtains and bed-hangings are trimmed and tasselled. Couches and chairs are plumply stuffed and covered with rich satins or, in the Drawing Room, with salmon pink watered silk so expensive that Preston felt it desirable to supply two extra sets of protective covers. The tables in the Saloon are edged with Boulle borders, whose hunting theme of leaping deer and hounds is taken from a German print. On the borders of the drop tables in the Drawing Room Preston employs the reverse of the pattern.

Surprisingly, so strong are Wyatt's designs that Preston's exuberances are absorbed within the architectural discipline of the house. Upstairs, in the family's private Sitting Room, which looks out to the Lough, Preston shows that he is not simply an addict of *luxe* and conjures up a room that is all light and fresh air: Chinese wallpaper, fresh chintz, faux-bamboo furniture and two small side tables supported on carved leopards' heads that are as pretty as any pieces in the house.

Neoclassical Wyatt and Regency Preston make an unlikely pairing. The result confirms Wyatt's brilliance. That it did not turn Preston into a household name can only be accounted for by geography.

Couch designed and upholstered by John Preston (Castle Coole)

FERMANAGH COUNTY MUSEUM *

Enniskillen Castle, Castle Barracks, Enniskillen, Co. Fermanagh BT74 7HL
Tel. 028 6632 5000

Medieval castle of the Maguires housing the history of Fermanagh: natural and feudal

Fermanagh is a county of precipitous limestone cliffs and gentle ash woodland, of peat bog and wetland. It is split in two by the River Erne, between the Upper Lough Erne and Lower Lough Erne. Within them an archipelago of more than three hundred islands lies scattered. Stretching out to the west coast of Ireland and the Atlantic, remote from Belfast, it is a place conducive to myth and story. It is not surprising that its county museum should guard its archaeology and its history, Neolithic, Bronze Age and Christian.

The Fermanagh County Museum was founded in 1976 and sited in Enniskillen Castle, built in the early 15th century by Hugh 'the Hospitable' Maguire. The castle keep is an impressive fortification, on a bend of the river, with stone walls four feet thick, and with an attractive two-towered outer structure built in the early 17th century. By the time the museum was founded the artefacts from the many local excavations[19] conducted since the late 19th century had been deposited in the National Museum of Ireland in Dublin or, more recently, in the Ulster Museum (q.v.).[20]

Some objects have been loaned back and there is enough here to give a good impression of Fermanagh's past. There are Neolithic flintheads, a saddle quern and funerary pots from court tombs at Aghanaglack and Ballyreagh. From the Bronze Age there is a copper halberd found in the River Erne at Portora Ford, a delicate gold fastener, amber beads and a beautiful gold bracelet with trumpet-shaped ends from Cleenaghan.

Since the coming of Christianity there has been a pilgrimage route of European importance to the Caves of St Patrick on Lough Derg.[21] A monastery, founded by and dedicated to St Molaise, was established on Devenish Island on Lower Lough Erne and the museum displays a good 19th-century copy of St Molaise's book shrine, the original of which is in the National Museum of Ireland in Dublin. Known as the Soiscel Molaise it is a fine 8th-century bronze box (redecorated with silver and gold in the 11th century) inscribed with the name of Cennefaeled, Abbot of Devenish. An 8th–10th-century horn of yew bound with bronze, with a copper mouthpiece, is here, cured and preserved in the waters of the River Erne.

Fermanagh's economy has remained rural and a display of 19th- and 20th-century farm implements, alongside the usual scythes, bill-hooks and reaping rakes, contains a loy[22] and a graip.[23]

To create employment in the decades of famine and depression in the 19th century, John Caldwell Bloomfield founded the Belleek Pottery after he discovered china clay and feldspar on his estate. With assistance from potters from Stoke-on-Trent and a manager from Worcester, the company prospered, and remains in production. The museum has a good selection of its varied products, the most characteristic of which is its Parian ware, represented here by the biscuit figure of a *Crouching Venus* and a glazed *Gypsy Bather*, both 1863–90.

What are not here, regrettably, are any of the Maguire chalices. The Maguires dominated Fermanagh from the 13th to the 16th centuries, eventually making Enniskillen Castle their stronghold. They were devout as well as warlike (described by Paedar Livingstone as 'great benefactors of the Church'[24]) and commissioned some beautiful silver chalices and patens, of which five are known to survive.[25] The chief of the clan, the Maguire, has tracked down at least three of them and it is likely that some will return to Fermanagh, and to this museum, in due course.

FLORENCE COURT **

Enniskillen, Co. Fermanagh BT92 1DB
Tel. 028 6634 8249

Elegant 18th-century Irish furniture in elegant 18th-century Irish house

John Cole, later Lord Mount Florence, built Florence Court in the shadow of brooding Ben Aughlin and the Chilagh Mountains in the 1740s.

The architect is not known, but when Mount Florence's son, the 1st Earl of Enniskillen, added two elegant arcaded wings and pavilions, it is likely that he employed the Sardinian-born Davis Ducart, who had added similar wings to Castletown Cox in Co. Kilkenny in about 1767. Ducart drew together the building phases by running a stone balustrade the length of the facade.

The interiors are notable for their exuberant plasterwork and for the Irish furniture, some of which is original to the house, some of which has been acquired subsequently.

Like much about the house, the plasterwork presents a mystery. In the Entrance Hall it is severe and architectural: a Doric frieze and a pilastered alcove. However the ceilings over the Stairwell, in the Dining Room, the first-floor Lobby (and the frieze in the Dining Room) are pure rococo, presumably by another hand. The Dining Room ceiling is an extravaganza. In its central panel is Zeus in the form of an eagle, surrounded by the Four Winds. The delicate garland that borders the panel is decorated with six small birds, in flight. The rest of the ceiling has intricate swirls of acanthus leaves, twisting, turning and flowing over the edges of the border frieze. The stuccadores either were French or had studied French rococo designs.

A serious fire in 1955 gutted the house. Thanks to photographs taken in 1911 the ceilings over the Stairwell and in the Dining Room could be restored by Professor Sir Albert Richardson, but those on the attic floor, which had not been photographed, were lost for ever. The house was damaged more severely when the 6th Earl fell out with the National Trust (to whom it had been given) and left, removing most of the contents, the furniture and the family portraits.

The trust, with the help of the Knight of Glin, put together a collection of 18th-century Irish furniture that includes a matching armchair and sidechair, a mahogany writing table and a delightful bureau-bookcase, made in Dublin in about 1750, with a marquetry broken pediment. The outstanding piece is a bed (c. 1760s), also in mahogany, its four posts, already slim at their bases, tapering to capitals of the utmost delicacy. The bed head has, at its centre, a beautifully carved scallop shell.

In 1997 the Dowager Countess, following the death of her husband, offered to return the original family furniture and portraits, in accordance with his dying wishes. The furniture has nothing to match the marquetry bureau or the four-poster bed but it has, nevertheless, interesting pieces, more curious than beautiful: two studded chests that belonged to William III and Mary II; a circular table in the Entrance Hall; a handsome dining table and set of ladder-back chairs; and an ugly, clumsy sideboard carved from the timbers of HMS *Royal George*. There is also an Italian specimen table, its top set with concentric, interlocking circles of marble and other stones, acquired by the 1st Earl on his Grand Tour of 1756.

Only one of the Enniskillens was a collector: the 3rd Earl, who was a geologist and palaeontologist of distinction. His collection of 10,000 fish fossils was sold to the British Museum in 1885 and is now in the Natural History Museum (q.v.). The best of his distinguished scientific library was also sold, though its remnants are here. He also commissioned a fine set of wax portrait reliefs of himself and his relatives from Richard Cockle Lucas, later notorious for forging a wax bust of *Flora*, acquired by the Berlin Museum as by Leonardo da Vinci.

The Enniskillens commissioned portraits by local artists, of the family and of their horses, but only the 2nd Earl bought pictures of any quality. When in Italy he acquired twelve sepia drawings of Italian views by Franz Keiserman and three watercolours by Abraham-Louis Ducros that are the equal of those at Stourhead (q.v.). One, of the remnants of the ancient stables at the *Villa of Maecenas, Tivoli*, is a fellow to Colt Hoare's; another, of the *Arch of Vespasian*, nods to Piranesi.[26]

It is likely that it was the 1st Earl who bought or commissioned the three huge Irish landscapes depicting *Enniskillen, Belleek Falls* and *Devenish Island* on Lower Lough Erne. The fourth in the series, of *Castle Crom*, was given by the Enniskillens to the Earl of Erne in the 1860s and is now at Crom.

ROYAL INNISKILLING FUSILIERS REGIMENTAL MUSEUM *

The Castle, Enniskillen, Co. Fermanagh
BT74 7HL
Tel. 028 6632 3142

The regiment from 1688: medals, maps and military glory

In the centre of Enniskillen is the castle, in the centre of the castle is the keep, in the keep is the Inniskilling museum. It chronicles the deeds of the Infantry and Dragoon Regiments raised by the people of Enniskillen in 1688 to defend their town against the forces of the deposed King James II. Enniskillen is the only town in the British Isles to have given its name to two regular army regiments.

The stone walls of the keep are four feet deep, destroyed and rebuilt continually in the 15th and 16th centuries by generations of Maguires as they fought the O'Donnells, the O'Neills and the English. There is a hand-painted map dated 1593, 'made and drawn by John Thomas, soldier' (it is a copy, the original being in the British Museum, q.v.), of 'CAPTAIN GEORGE BINGHAM'S BATTLE PLAN' depicting how Captain Bingham defeated the Maguires. Captain William Cole, whose descendants built Florence Court in the 18th century, was, in 1607, appointed constable of the royal fort of Enniskillen. The castle was developed and remained as a military barracks until 1926.

Within, the Queen's and Regimental Colours and the Battle Honours of the Royal Inniskilling Fusiliers record their service in the Peninsular and Napoleonic Wars (Vittoria, Salamanca, Badajoz, Waterloo), and in the two world wars (the Somme, Ypres, Gallipoli, Monte Cassino). They fought in the American War of Independence, the Indian Mutiny, the Boer Wars; in Turkey and Palestine; Sicily, Burma and at Anzio; in Kenya, containing the Mau-Mau, in Cyprus, Eoka. Napoleon called these 'hard-biting fellows of long standing' the most obstinate mules he had ever seen when they held the centre of the Allied line against the pounding of the French artillery at Waterloo.

In the museum are the mementoes of these battles and campaigns: the Guidons of the Inniskilling Dragoons, carried at Waterloo; the regimental Brian Bow pipes; buttons, badges, crossbelt and shako plates going back to 1776; and, a bequest from Colonel Salvin-Bowlby, a collection of 3,000 badges and insignia from regiments through the British Army (the West Surrey, Leinster, Durham, Herefordshire Rifle Volunteers, etc.).

There are regimental silver, uniforms that go back to 1778, a photographic archive of their service in the 20th century and, their ark, relics from the Boyne (lead musket shot; a Boyne medal that may be the first awarded for gallantry, to a Major Roberts by King William; and the remnants of the flag carried in the battle, all colour faded).

The Inniskillings have been awarded eight Victoria Crosses. Pride of place is given here to the medals and stick of Lance-Corporal Edward 'Dutchy' Pearce, who served with the regiment for 56 years 11 months, from 1866–1923 (longer than any other soldier in the army's history) in Afghanistan, the North West Frontier and the Boer Wars; he was frustrated to be confined to a staff job in the First World War.

A photograph records his retirement, sitting in the middle of the front row surrounded by bemedalled officers. Another records the last ceremony of the regiment, at midnight on 30 June 1968, when the regiment was merged with others to form the Royal Irish Rangers, its regimental flag was lowered and the guard marched off in slow time to 'Fare thee well, Enniskillen'.

ULSTER FOLK AND TRANSPORT MUSEUM ***

Cultra, Holywood, Co. Down BT18 0EU
Tel. 028 9042 8428
www.nidex.com/uftm

Every vehicle that moves, and houses moved here from all over Ulster

The groundwork for the Ulster Folk Museum was laid in the 1930s, when Professor Emyr Estyn Evans began to establish Irish folk life (its housing, work, field patterns, traditions, customs, superstitions) as a subject worthy for serious study.[27] His work culminated in his *Irish Heritage* (1942), the standard text.[28]

However it was not until 1958, nine years after the Welsh National Folk Museum, St Fagan's, was established, that the Ulster Folk Museum Act created this museum, sited on 180 acres of the Cultra estate on hillsides that look over Belfast Loch and across to County Antrim. It is a fine wooded and undulating estate on which to try to make the Ulster landscape in epitome.

The idea of an Ulster folk museum had a long germination in the minds of Evans, and of the young academics he inspired. The politicians were slow to be convinced, and slower still to realise that their first choice of site, five acres of grounds around Belfast Castle, was wholly inadequate. This allowed time for planning and for the new keeper of antiquities and ethnography at the Ulster Museum (G. B. Thompson, later to be the first director of the Ulster Folk Museum), to visit Stockholm to study the Skansen Folk Museum established by Artur Hazelius in 1891.

Evans and Thompson were clear that the Skansen heritage approach, 'to create old traditions in a living environment',[29] resulted in, at best, 'architectural zoos' (Thompson's excellent phrase), authentic but not realistic, and avoided addressing the troubled history of Northern Ireland. The Linen Hall Library (q.v.) and the Ulster Museum were the guardians of the urban and industrial history of Belfast; here was an opportunity to consider the history of the rural poor.

The thirty-two buildings re-erected here cover the social and economic spectrum. The Meenagarragh Cottier's House is a mid-19th-century, stone-built version of the sodhouse consisting of one room, about nine feet square, lived in by a family of eleven during the famine, and by a family of six in the 1950s. Opposite it, here and on its original site at Plumbridge, Co. Tyrone in the Sperrin Mountains, is the Cruckaclady Farmhouse, more substantial, with a bedroom over the byre for the livestock. Cruckaclady's last owner, Patrick MacBryde, farmed ten acres in the early 1950s.

The Corradreenan Farmhouse (late 18th century, from near Florence Court, Co. Fermanagh) was on a 100-acre farm and the Patterson family who owned Drumnahushin Farmhouse, built in the 1820s and enlarged twice, ran, as well as a farm, a flax-scutching mill and could afford the luxury of two downstairs living rooms.

In contrast to St Fagan's the cottages and farms are positioned half-hidden by copses, in the hollows and corners of the estate, giving, as far as possible, the settled sense that they belong in the landscape.

The re-created town has the bleak severity of many small Ulster towns, with a register of grey stone, grey harling. Unlike them it has both a Church of Ireland parish church, from Kilmore, Crossgan, Co. Down (1762) and the Roman Catholic church of St John the Baptist, from Dumcree near Portadown. The latter, built in 1783, is a simple 'barn' structure, a spartan and undecorated place of worship.

The poverty of rural Northern Ireland took no account of religious faith and there is no attempt to avoid the problems of sectarianism here. The museum gallery has items that relate to Francis Joseph Biggar, the passionate republican promoter of Irish culture and the

Irish language. In a speech in 1909 he insisted: 'I cannot see a solitary reason why we should love the English nation. She is and has always been our most bitter enemy.'[30]

For its first thirty-eight years the folk museum had only two directors, G. B. Thompson and Alan Gailey, both pupils of Estyn Evans. This gives the museum an inherent coherence. Being yoked to a transport museum inevitably challenges that coherence.

This is an excellent transport museum, housed in impressive purpose-built hangars. The collections cover transport by land, by sea and in the sky: the Belfast-built vertical-take-off Short's SC1, the 120-ton steel schooner *Result* and a photograph of the building, in the Harland and Wolff shipyard, of the RMS *Titanic*, launched in Belfast on 31 May 1911.

Less dramatically there are bicycles from the 1818 Denis Johnson 'hobby horse' to modern mountain bikes, and motor cars, from an old model T Ford to the Belfast-built De Lorean. The hangar's central stage is taken by the mighty locomotive *Maedhbh* (Maeve), one of the largest to be built or operated in Ireland, used to pull the Dublin-to-Cork express.

These handsome machines relate hardly at all to the issues of history, conflict and famine that are faced at Cultra by Evans, Thompson, Gailey and their successors. Thompson wrote in 1961 that the true purpose of a folk museum is based not only in the past but in a vision of the changes that await us in the future.[31]

IRISH LINEN CENTRE AND LISBURN MUSEUM **

Market Square, Lisburn BT28 1AG
Tel. 028 9266 3377
www.lisburncity.gov.uk/

The story of linen from fibre to fine fabric

Tucked away in this museum is a map entitled *The Lagan Navigation in the Estate of the Most Noble Marquess of Hertford*. It was drawn by Thomas Pattison in 1842, to a scale of '20 Irish Perches to the inch'. Within it are the determining elements of 19th-century Lisburn, a town of barely 6,000 people:[32] the ownership of its land, the dominance of the linen industry, the importance of the River Lagan as a source of power and the Lagan Navigation Canal as the means of transporting its finished products.[33]

The Conways (raised to the Marquisate of Hertford in 1793) owned Lisburn and the surrounding 60,000 acres. The 4th Marquess (1800–70) lived in Paris and used the fabulous wealth[34] he had derived from his estate to acquire works of art that now comprise the Wallace Collection (q.v.). His illegitimate son and heir Richard Wallace was a more attentive and popular landlord. As MP for the town he visited his estate at least five times. He is commemorated by a limestone Gothic memorial in Castle Gardens, Lisburn's central park.

He left no works of art to Lisburn and, although the town had a historical society that collected artefacts, a local authority museum was not established until 1979. It opened in the Assembly Rooms in the centre of Market Square, formerly the old market house with a surviving 18th-century assembly room. In the early 1990s the buildings adjoining Lisburn Museum were rebuilt by Hall, Black & Douglas Architects as the Irish Linen Centre.

Upstairs in the assembly room are casts of busts of Sir Richard and Lady Wallace[35] and portraits of such town worthies as William Barbour, a thread manufacturer, but the story of Lisburn's linen industry is that of the men and women who grew the flax, spun the yarn, wove and bleached the cloth, and of the companies who employed them.

Flax has been grown, and linen woven, in Ireland since at least the 11th century, but an export trade in cloth only began to develop in the latter half of the 17th century. One of the best-known efforts to promote the industry was William III's appointment in 1698 of the Huguenot refugee Louis Crommelin as Overseer of the Royal Linen Manufacture in Ireland and his establishment of weaving premises in Lisburn. Crommelin's *An Essay Towards the Improving of the Hempen and Flaxen Manufactures in the Kingdom of Ireland* (published by Andrew Crook, Dublin, 1705) is here, as is Joseph Beaumont's first technical treatise on weaving.[36]

Here are many of the tools needed to produce linen: scutching blades; spinning wheels, bobbins, click reels, weaving looms (broad and narrow; hand and jacquard);[37] shuttles; and, for use after bleaching, a beetling engine. Here too are the seals with which each man stamped his cloth. James Christy, a bleacher at Moyallon in the late 18th century, used his seal as a book plate.

Craftsmen and women are on hand to demonstrate the stages of production. The end product is also here. Spotlit in cabinets in a darkened room, the creamy surfaces of linen, damask and fine cambric glow: the napkin woven by J. W. and W. Coulson & Co. to commemorate the battle of Trafalgar; a 19th-century woven underskirt of gossamer delicacy; a silk dress with a linen underskirt that Jane Austen might have discussed with her sister Cassandra; and a 1965 wedding dress by the Irish designer Sybil Connolly, heavy with intricate pleating and double ruffles at cuffs and hem.

The linen in Queen Mary's dolls' house at Windsor Castle (q.v.) was woven by the Old Bleach Linen Company: perfect Lilliputian sheets, pillowcases, damask table cloths, and napkins with a monogrammed 'GR'. Many linens here are from a collection given by Robinson and Cleaver. They opened a store in Donegall Square, Belfast, in 1885, solely 'to retail linen goods at wholesale prices' on five floors. Only in 1894 did they open in Regent Street, London, as a department store.

Lisburn means linen but the museum has other artefacts: a collection of photographs[38] that record the town and its hinterland over the past 150 years – from an image of the Very Revd James Stannus, rector of the cathedral and the autocratic agent for the Hertfords from 1817 to 1853, to one of Bow Street devastated by a terrorist car bomb in the Troubles. It also has some good furniture: a mahogany dining table by George Gillington of Dublin (c.1815), a handsome prayer chair made from Irish bog oak, carved with roses, thistles, shamrocks and berries, by Curran &

Son of Lisburn (1852)[39] and a rosewood veneered cabinet, containing 'musical glasses' (c. 1813), played by wetting your fingers.[40]

There is a small collection of paintings of local views by Irish artists (Samuel McCloy, William Conor, Joseph W. Carey, John Luke). Many are of the River Lagan and the Navigation Canal that, as is right in Lisburn, return the thread to the linen.

SOMME HERITAGE CENTRE *

233 Bangor Road, Newtownards, Co. Down
BT23 7PH
Tel. 028 9182 3202

Slaughter at the Somme

On 1 July 1916 5,553 men of the 36th (Ulster) Division were killed or wounded on the opening day of the battle of the Somme. Two months later, on 3 and 9 September, a further 4,314 men of the 16th (Irish) Division fell. The Somme Heritage Centre is a memorial to those men and to all who served in Irish regiments in the First World War.

The centre is on rising ground looking east. On the hill behind it is Helen's Tower on the Clandeboye estate where the men of the 108th Brigade of the 36th did their training before leaving for France. It is in a nondescript, single-storey building that opened in 1994, without collections. It now has more than 3,000 items: diaries, medals, uniforms, equipment. They tell the story not of the action, or the calculations and miscalculations of generals and politicians, but of those soldiers of the 16th and 36th.

Three volunteer divisions were raised in Ireland at the outbreak of the war: the 10th (Irish), which fought at Gallipoli, losing 3,114 men in two months on the peninsula; the 16th, a Roman Catholic, Nationalist division, raised principally in Cork, Tipperary and West Belfast, which captured the villages of Guillemont and Guichy; and the 36th, formed largely from the Protestant Unionist Ulster Volunteer Force, who stormed the supposedly

impregnable Schwaben Redoubt at Thiepval.

One recruiting poster, printed in green, reads: 'ENROL UNDER THE GREEN FLAG. Secure your Rights and Liberties (the few left to you). Help your country to a place among the nations. Give her a National Army to keep her there. Get a gun and do your part.' It is signed by Eoin MacNeill. The other reads: 'GOD SAVE THE KING!' Signed by Lt. General Geo. Richardson, GOC, UVF, it carries an additional message from Edward Carson, 'Quit yourselves like men and comply with your country's demand.'

What befell those who responded to these calls is told in two ways: an 'experience' that walks the visitor through enlistment, training, embarkation, the trenches, no-man's-land. As such experiences go this one is cool and clear, the detail telling: the cans of Merry Monk English Peas, Arnold's Corned Beef and bottles of Mason's OK Sauce in the trenches; the size and weight of the standard issue Lee Enfield Short Magazine Mk III, range 2,000 yards, capable of penetrating 18 inches of oak at 200 yards.

But inevitably the letters, notebooks, paybooks and postcards are the most affecting. Ronald Waterman, an eighteen-year-old lance corporal, writes to his mother: 'Tell her to keep up her heart till I come home, a brave man doing my bit for my country' (12 December 1915). 'I have landed safe here and it seems to be a nice place. It is just like Ireland here only the people do not talk the same' (25 November 1915). 'I had a dream last night that the war was over and I was home again but when I woke up this morning I found out it had all been a dream.' He was killed on the first day of the Somme.

Four Victoria Crosses were awarded to the 36th Ulster Division on the first day at the Somme; two more were awarded to the 16th Irish for the whole battle. Rifleman William Frederick McFadzean, aged twenty-one, threw himself on a grenade that was about to explode in his trench. Men of great ability were lost, including the professor of law, poet and former Nationalist MP Tom Kettle, and the Nationalist MP Willie Redmond, retrieved from no-man's-land by Protestant comrades.

Back in the Memorial Hall there are rolls of honour that reiterate the unhelpful verities, 'Unconquerable Except by Death'.

For reasons that are hard to discern, interest is growing in the First World War. In the terraced streets of Belfast new murals are being painted. One, on Clonduff Drive, is a huge reproduction of the telegram received by McFadzean's parents: 'Lord Kitchener expresses his sympathy.'

London

'Two cities divided by a river' is how Angela Carter described London in her novel *Wise Children*. Almost all London's museums are north of the river; some are on its banks: Tates Britain and Modern, linked by a ferry; the Houses of Parliament, Somerset House (the Courtauld and Gilbert Collections), the Design Museum on Butler's Wharf and the Museum of the Port of London, part of the Museum of London.

London draws so much, too much, of British life into its maw, and museums and galleries are not exceptions to this. There are more than 140 museums here: museums of windmills (Wimbledon) and clocks (Guildhall); of rugby (Twickenham) and tea (Bramah, near the Design Museum); of money (the Bank of England) and the Salvation Army (near King's Cross). Here is perhaps the greatest concentration of museums and galleries in the world, or the concentration of the greatest, with the British Museum, the National Gallery, the Victoria and Albert Museum and Tate Britain clustered in the centre of the city.

I have included sixty, but choosing those has involved leaving out the museums dedicated to Dr Johnson, Hogarth, Keats, Dickens and Carlyle and the two great Robert Adam houses, Osterley and Syon, as well as Lord Burlington's austere homage to Palladio, Chiswick House. Such delights as the Chelsea Physic Garden, founded in 1673, whose calm soothes as effectively as its medicinal plants, have been omitted, as has the Museum of Garden History, beside Lambeth Palace, with its knot garden, cast-iron Victorian lawnmowers and its tributes to the Tradescants and to Gertrude Jekyll.

In no other city is it easier, more enjoyable or more instructive to test Simon Jenkins's thesis that churches are 'the museum of England'. Those built by Jones, Hawksmoor, Wren, Gibbs, Bodley and Butterfield will yield as rich a collection as the museums in this book. Less happily, there is a growing number of 'leisure destinations' masquerading as museums (the Sherlock Holmes Museum, the London Dungeons) that debase the name.

This is not true of the Tower of London, a real castle and a genuine tourist attraction, but not included here since much of its collection has moved to the Royal Armouries in Leeds (q.v.) in 1990. The Beefeaters, the Crown jewels and the presiding ravens remain.

Royal Air Force Museum ⊙

Jewish Museum Finchley ⊙

A406

M1

Kenwood House ⊙

A41

Freud Museum ⊙

Ben Uri Gallery ⊙

Jewish Museum ⊙

1 British Museum
2 Cabinet War Rooms
3 Courtauld Collection
4 Fleming Collection
5 Gilbert Collection
6 Houses of Parliament
7 London transport Museum
8 Michael Faraday Museum
9 National Gallery
10 National Museum of the Performing Arts
11 National Portrait Gallery
12 Percival David Foundation of Chinese Art
13 Petrie Museum of Egyptian Archaeology
14 Pollock's Toy Museum
15 Queen's Gallery
16 Royal Academy
17 Sir John Soane's Museum
18 UCL Art Collection
19 Westminster Abbey Chapter House

A40(M)

Wallace Collection ⊙

M41

4 ⊙
8 ⊙

Apsley House Wellington Museum ⊙   16 ⊙

15 ⊙

Leighton House Museum ⊙

Science Museum
⊙ ⊙ Victoria and
National History Museum ⊙   Albert Museum

A4

A4

National Army Museum ⊙   A3212

River Thames

Royal Botanical Gardens, Kew ⊙

A316

A205

De Morgan Centre ⊙

A3

⊙ Marble Hill House

William Morris Gallery

A10

Estorick Collection of Modern Italian Art

A501

Geffrye Museum

Bethnal Green Museum of Childhood

British Library

13 Foundling Museum
8 12
14 1
7 17 Hunterian Museum
11 10 5 3
9

Museum of London
Guildhall Art Gallery

Tate Modern

Saatchi Gallery

2 6
19

Imperial War Museum

Tate Britain

Cuming Museum

Type Museum

A3

Design Museum

Old Operating Theatre

Fashion and Textile Museum
(Zandra Rhodes)

River Thames

National Maritime
Queen's House Museum

Royal Observatory, Greenwich
Fan Museum Ranger's House

1 mile

Dulwich Picture Gallery

Horniman Museum

A205

APSLEY HOUSE
WELLINGTON MUSEUM ✶✶

Hyde Park Corner, London W1J 7NT
Tel. 020 7499 5676
www.londonvisions.com/main_museums.htm

Adam and Wyatt made the house, Wellington fills it

In 1798 Napoleon marched his army through Italy, scooping up great works of art. The *Laocoön* and the *Apollo Belvedere* were shipped back to the Louvre and exhibited as 'Monuments of Ancient Sculpture. Greece gave them up. Rome lost them. Their fate has changed twice. It will not change again.'[1] The contents of Apsley House go some way to giving the lie to that boast, being in large part the loot and trophies from the Duke of Wellington's campaigns against the French Emperor.

After Wellington's victory at Salamanca in 1812, the Intendant of Segovia wrote to him offering him 'such trifles in the Royal Palace of San Ildefonso as might have been most agreeable to you' and presenting him with 'the twelve best and most artistic pictures which I have been able to find'.[2]

When, on 21 June 1813, Wellington defeated the army of Napoleon's brother, Joseph Bonaparte, at Vittoria, he captured Joseph's coach, which contained over two hundred paintings. Wellington discovered that they had been expropriated from the Spanish Royal Collection: he attempted to return them, only to be resisted by the Spanish Minister in England, Count Nunez, who assured him that 'his Majesty, touched by your delicacy, does not wish to deprive you of that which has come in to your possession by means as just as they are honourable.'[3] The result of this decorous exchange was that eighty-three paintings came to London, among them Correggio's *Agony in the Garden* and Elsheimer's *Judith and Holofernes*. With them were works by Ribera and Murillo, two very early Velásquez (*Two Young Men Eating at a Humble Table*, c.1618–20, and *The Waterseller of Seville*, 1623, the most famous of the 'bodegones', or scenes from everyday life, that he painted before he left Seville for Madrid aged twenty-three), and the ecstatic *Saint Catherine of Alexandra* by Coello.

They comprised on an instant the first, if not the finest, collection of 17th-century Spanish paintings in England. It was only after the Peninsular War when travellers and connoisseurs such as Sir William Stirling-Maxwell[4] visited Spain that the taste for Spanish paintings began to be developed. The National Gallery acquired its first Murillo in 1826, its first Zurbaran and Velásquez not until 1853. Here were glimpses of the Palacio Real and the Escorial.

In 1816 Wellington bought from his elder brother, the Marquis Wellesley, the house that Robert Adam had built in the 1770s for Lord Apsley. Wellington employed Benjamin Dean Wyatt, the son of James Wyatt,[5] to face Adam's red brick with Bath stone and to enlarge the house, adding a great picture gallery to show these paintings.

To furnish his new home Wellington began to buy: French 18th-century furniture, Sèvres porcelain and Dutch paintings. His taste was for 17th-century genre paintings: Nicolaes Maes, Adriaen Brouwer, Adriaen van Ostade and above all Jan Steen (*The Wedding Party: the Egg Dance*). He added these to the Teniers, Brueghels and de Hoochs that he acquired from Spain. They make a good collection, though not comparable with that of George IV or of Sir Robert Peel, much of which is now in the National Gallery.

At the same time Wellington was acquiring English narrative paintings: John Burnet's *The Greenwich Pensioners Commemorating*

Trafalgar, and Sir William Allen's panoramic *Battle of Waterloo*, which the Duke judged 'Good – very good. Not too much smoke.'[6]

More interesting are the paintings he commissioned. His friend and second in command at Waterloo, Lord Lynedoch,[7] introduced him to David Wilkie, who painted *Chelsea Pensioners Reading the Waterloo Dispatch* for him in 1816. It was not finished until 1822 but when it was finally exhibited at the Royal Academy it had changed from being a genre painting of old soldiers to being a history painting of a dramatic and emotional moment. The change made the painting, and Wilkie, famous. Wellington proceeded to commission Sir Thomas Lawrence, George Dawe and the Dutch Willem Pieneman to execute portraits of his own generals, the heads of state of Britain's Allies and Napoleon and his family. These were to hang in the Yellow Striped Drawing Room, replicating on a smaller scale the Waterloo Chamber at Windsor Castle.

Downstairs in the basement are Wellington's uniforms, decorations and trophies, his Orders of the Garter and of the Bath, the Orders from every Allied country and presentation services of Meissen and Sèvres. Here too are more personal mementoes: a lock of hair from his stallion, Copenhagen, orders written at Waterloo on prepared pieces of vellum.

Upstairs is the Waterloo vase in silver gilt, and the Waterloo shield, both designed by Thomas Stothard, the Deacon service (125 pieces of silver parcel gilt given to him by his officers in the Indian campaigns of 1803) and the swords of vanquished generals, including Napoleon's court sword by Martin Guillaume Biennais, c.1809, and Tippoo Sultan's sword and dagger, taken from his body after the capture of Seringapatam in 1799.

Dwarfing all these in its triumphal display is the Portuguese service, in silver parcel gilt, designed by D. A. de Sequiera, its monumental centrepiece showing the Four Continents paying tribute to the armies of Britain, Portugal and Spain. The service sits, twenty-six feet long, dominating the Dining Room, a sumptuous reminder to those who attended the annual Waterloo dinner of Wellington's greatest victory.

There is a second presence in the house, bound perpetually to Wellington: Napoleon. At the bottom of the staircase, addressing those who come and those who go, is a huge statue by Antonio Canova of the French Emperor, classically nude, a toga draped over his left arm, a winged victory in his right hand, a spear in his left. Napoleon hated it. Its position in Apsley House represents a double triumph for Wellington.

Wellington was no connoisseur. Apart from the Spanish spoils, his collection consists of the solid pictures that any rich military man of the early 19th century might favour: straightforward pictures that brook no nonsense, depictions of the virtues exemplified throughout Wellington's career.

BEN URI GALLERY, THE LONDON JEWISH MUSEUM OF ART **

108a Boundary Road, London NW8 0RH
Tel. 020 7604 3991
www.benuri.org.uk

Great Jewish artists: Gertler, Bomberg, Kramer, Kossoff and Auerbach

The Ben Uri Gallery arose out of a Jewish art society whose purpose was to 'enrich and ennoble the Jewish population',[8] whether achieved by Jewish art, made for a Jewish purpose, or by artists who were Jewish.

Formed in 1915 by the Polish decorative artist Lazar Berson, the Ben Uri Art Society derived its name from the craftsman-builder of the Tabernacle, mentioned in Exodus chapter 31, verse 2: 'Bezaleel the son of (Ben) Uri, the son of Hur, of the tribe of Judah.'

The Ben Uri moved its collection six times around central London, from one temporary home to another, before coming to rest here in a parade of shops in Boundary Road behind a plate-glass window that, from the street, appears to belong to a commercial gallery.

Jewish artists have worked successfully in London since at least the 18th century, when Johann Zoffany was elected as a foundation member of the Royal Academy, but the collection goes back only to the mid 19th century. Its first acquisition was a group of drawings by Simeon Solomon, a member of the Pre-Raphaelite Brotherhood.

Solomon was untypical of his generation in having been to art school in England, at the Royal Academy Schools. Jozef Israels, who has a fine Rembrandt-like etching here, and Max Liebermann, the German Impressionist and friend of Israels, were trained abroad, Israels at the Academy of Fine Arts in Paris, Liebermann at the Kunstakademie, Weimar.

The generation that followed was trained here: Bomberg, Gertler, Kramer and Meninsky at the Slade, taught by Henry Tonks; and it is with them that this collection comes into fuller flower. At the time of the First World War there were no more confident or exciting painters in England than Mark Gertler and David Bomberg. The works here by each of them show why.

Gertler's *Still Life with a Bottle of Benedictine* (1908) is a chamber masterpiece in which he turns down the source of light to a gleam that he directs through glass and bottle so that they glow, bringing their contours to life, the curve of the rim of the glass, the straight set of the knife on the table. In the magnificent large drawing *Rabbi and Rabbitzin* (1914), he sits the couple, looking straight ahead, arms stiffly linked, as solid and set as the teapot and loaf on the table cloth. Bomberg has three superb paintings here: *At the Window* (1919), *Englishwoman* (1920) and *Ghetto Theatre* (1920). They were painted just before the disappointment of the Canadian War Memorial commission, which punctured his confidence and left him, in David Sylvester's words, the 'humble servant [of nature], content to alternate between conscientious topography[9] and the charming sketch.'[10] These three paintings reveal, in their grappling with structure, Bomberg's debt to Cézanne. Among his papers, found after his death, were the phrases, 'Drawing is sculpturally conceived in the full like architecture ... Drawing ... reveals the

Nude by Mark Gertler (Ben Uri Gallery)

unknown things . . . Style is ephemeral – Form is eternal.'[11]

The Ben Uri collection is distinguished by the work of two other painters: Bomberg's pupil Leon Kossoff and Frank Auerbach. Their qualities can only be glimpsed here. Auerbach has two early (1954) drawings and seven etchings (1985–90), Kossoff a drawing and two etchings, none of which can convey what David Cohen has described as their 'pigment loaded expressiveness',[12] heavy impasto worked and reworked to seek 'real penetration into clearly defined areas of reality'.[13]

The visitor who comes here looking to enquire into the nature of 'Jewish art' since the 18th-century Jewish Enlightenment, Haskalah,

will find evidence to support the view that it is rooted in subject matter (Samuel Hirszenberg's *The Sabbath Rest*, 1894; Gertler's *Ghetto Theatre*; Jacob Kramer's drawing *The Day of Atonement*, 1919[14]) and/or that it is dependent on qualities of Jewishness that are easier to identify than to define. Jewish artists are seldom decorative or playful (the drawings of Léon Bakst and Sonia Delaunay[15] are exceptions not unconnected with their works being in the ephemeral world of theatrical costume and design). Rather, there is here a serious, even sombre, moral weight, a baritone or bass register, that runs through the collection, from Jozef Israels and Simeon Solomon to Alfred Wolmark and Josef Herman. The peripatetic history of the collection, exhibited, since 1925, in seven galleries before this one, echoes the wider Jewish experience.

The collection has no easy answer to the question whether Jewishness in art is intrinsic or extrinsic. What it does have is good paintings by artists whose work is seldom seen in other public galleries (Amy Drucker, Bernard Meninsky), and the opportunity to see the work of three of the outstanding British artists of the 20th century (Bomberg, Auerbach and Kossoff) together.

To survive the financial instabilities that have dogged the Ben Uri Gallery, Gertler's masterpiece *Merry-Go-Round* had to be sold in 1984 to the Tate Gallery. It was a loss worth sustaining if it has secured the long-term future of this collection, whose quality and involvement with English art is caught in Leon Kossoff's recently (1993) acquired etching *Christ Church, Spitalfields, Spring* (1989–92), one of a series in which Kossoff engages intimately with Nicholas Hawksmoor's most English church.

BETHNAL GREEN MUSEUM OF CHILDHOOD **

Cambridge Heath Road, London E2 9PA
Tel. 020 8980 2415
www.museumofchildhood.org.uk

A world of childhood, its history, dress, pastimes and companions

Beneath its red-brick skin the Bethnal Green Museum of Childhood is an historic museum building. Its wrought-iron skeleton began life in 1856 as a hastily designed and erected structure[16] to house temporarily in Brompton the Museum of Ornamental Art, formed from elements of the 1851 Great Exhibition.

As the museum, which became the South Kensington Museum, developed, the temporary 'Brompton Boilers' became redundant and the director, Henry Cole, proposed that the building be dismantled and used to found new museums in London's north, south and east suburbs. Only Bethnal Green took up the offer and, encouraged by the Prime Minister, W. E. Gladstone, received two-thirds of the

original building, which was re-erected in 1872 beside the Green, clad in its brick skin designed by General Henry Scott and J. W. Wild. The outside walls have twenty-six decorative panels by F. W. Moody, representing, on the north side, subjects that include mowing, fishing, shearing sheep, haymaking; on the south, architecture, poetry, science, astronomy. Inside is a magnificent black-and-white mosaic floor.[17]

As the all-inclusiveness of the mosaics' subjects suggest, South Kensington was never sure what collections should be exhibited at Bethnal Green. Initially 'Food' and 'Animal Products' were favoured on the ground floor, with the art collection of Sir Richard Wallace upstairs.[18] A *National Portraits* exhibition here in 1885 led to the creation of the National Portrait Gallery (q.v.). In 1896 an exhibition of the Royal Academy's (q.v.) Chantrey Bequest furthered the case for establishing the Tate Gallery (v. Tate Britain). The Pitt Rivers Collection (v. Pitt Rivers Museum) was here before finding a permanent home in Oxford. It was not until after the First World War that a new curator, Andrew Sabin, began to give some emphasis to those parts of the collections of what was by now the Victoria and Albert Museum that concerned, and might be of interest to, children, following a special children's exhibition at the V&A in 1915, and set up a 'Children's Section' in 1923. Even then this was pursued with some caution, with Sir Trenchard Cox (director of the V&A 1956–66) designating Bethnal Green a museum of English costume. In 1974, Roy Strong (director 1973–87) committed Bethnal Green to being a museum of childhood.

Its collections range widely over childhood (costume, education, child-care equipment) and children's play (rocking horses, puppets, theatres, games) but its strengths are doll's houses and teddy bears.

Although the collection is predominantly English, the oldest doll's house here is German, an apothecary's house from Nuremberg. Its date, 1673, is inscribed on the chimney. It has a doorbell that still rings when pulled and a portrait of Martin Luther pasted inside the door. Its purpose, shared with many pre-19th-century doll's houses, was to teach young girls how to manage a household.

Some houses, particularly those that are models of real buildings, are so elaborate that they were intended both as adults' and children's playthings. The Kaleidoscope House (2000),[19] made by the American company Bozart, contains artworks and furniture in miniature (1:12 scale): chairs by Ron Arad and Dakota Jackson, art by Cindy Sherman and Laurie Simmons. Some houses were simply for play. Amy Miles helped to make hers as a child

The Nuremburg House, Bethnal Green

in the 1890s, a classic Victorian house with stairs and nine rooms including a nursery and a billiard room. Its detail, all to scale, is mesmerising: paintings, carpets, food, china, books, a Lilliputian world complete with a dozing dog, and billiard balls and cues.

The collection of dolls, one of the largest and finest in the world, contains dolls made from every material: wood, wax, cloth, plastic; from many countries; in national costume and in everyday clothes; by famous makers (Piarotti, Jumeau, Bru) and by modern manufacturers (Effanbee, Mattel, Pedigree). The nubile Barbie, Sindy and Whatserface sidle in literally plastic poses beside the dignified female doll that James III of Scotland (the Old Pretender) is said to have given to a family of loyal Jacobites.

The teddy bears come from every decade since 1902, when the President of the United States, Theodore Roosevelt, associated himself with a bear and, like Brer Rabbit, found himself stuck to the honey of teddydom. All the leading British, German and American manufacturers have bears here: Bing, Merrythought, Pedigree, Chad Valley and the most famous, and the maker of the handsomest of all, Steiff.[20]

The collection's richness summons a de-lighted response in the memory. Prams, cradles, high chairs, push chairs; baby Nikes and tiny Doc Martens; a child's rasta hat; Corgi and Matchbox cars; Action Man; bears (Rupert, Paddington, Pudsey); skipping ropes, yo-yos, marbles; butchers' shops, bakers', chemists'; an 1850 leather cricket ball, an 1875 badminton set with shuttlecocks made with real feathers; Jokari (the craze of the 1950s), a 1970 orange Space Hopper; and serious educational toys to aid learning.[21]

My childhood in the 1940s and early 1950s was brought back to me by seeing Dinky cars, Meccano, Hornby 00; Pelham puppets, a Pollock's theatre and Monopoly; quoits and bagatelle; and a farmyard that for me, a child brought up in London, was the symbol of all that was orderly and safe, each cow in its field, each duck by its pond.

Childhood is what we all share. Here is its world. Each visit, a return in itself to a part of life, will determine your return to the museum.

BRITISH LIBRARY ✶✶✶✶✶

96 Euston Road, London NW1 2DB
Tel. 020 7412 7332
e-mail: visitor-services@bl.uk

All ideas – set down, bound and set free – are here

Where would you expect to find the *Diamond Sutra*, the earliest dated printed book in the world, produced in China in AD 868; the *Codex Sinaiticus*, the earliest manuscript of the complete New Testament, written in Greek in the middle of the 4th century; the only sur-viving medieval manuscript of *Beowulf*; the First Folio of the plays of William Shakespeare; the Gutenberg Bible, the book from which all printed books are descended, produced in Mainz in 1455 by Johann Gutenberg and Johann Fust?

Where but here in the British Library, the ark of the English language and its literature, the custodian of the world's books and manu-scripts.

The library was founded in 1753 as part of the British Museum (q.v.). An Act of Parlia-ment voted money to purchase the manuscript collections of Robert and Edward Harley, the 1st and 2nd Earls of Oxford, for the library and collections of Sir Hans Sloane, and to house them in a new 'British Museum' with the library of Sir Robert Cotton, the 17th-century antiquary, acquired by the Crown in 1700. The trustees were charged to preserve the collec-tions 'for Public Use, to all Posterity' and to provide access to 'all studious and curious Persons', so establishing the basis of all future public libraries.

Many of the library's most precious works came in these three foundation collections: the Lindisfarne Gospels, the *Anglo-Saxon Chron-icle*, Bede's *History of the English Church and People*, Magna Carta, the Harley Latin Gospels. To these were added, in 1757, the Royal Library, a gift from George II that contained books and manuscripts going back to the library of Edward IV and, in 1823, George III's collection, the Royal Library, which became known as the King's Library.

Despite this the library expanded slowly. In 1777 John Wilkes complained that 'the British Museum is rich in manuscripts . . . but it is wretchedly poor in printed books'.[22] It was not until Antonio Panizzi was appointed first keeper of printed books and then principal librarian that the library had an effective political advocate. To a Parliamentary Com-mittee he declared, 'I want a poor student to have the same means of indulging his learned curiosity, of following his rational pursuits, of consulting the same authorities, of fathoming

The new (model) British Library

the most intimate inquiry, as the richest man in the Kingdom, as far as books go, and I contend that government is bound to give him the most liberal and unlimited assistance in this respect.'[23] Panizzi was impelled by an ambition that the British Library should be, and be seen to be, the greatest library in the world. The Bibliothèque Nationale in Paris had more books, 80,000 in 1848. 'Paris must be surpassed,' Panizzi declared. In his 1845 report he drove forward that ambition and vision with a determination that would brook no obstacle: 'The expense will no doubt be great, but so is the nation which is to bear it.'[24] The library's annual grant was raised to £10,000 a year and a new power of attorney secured which, by allowing the Trustees to threaten legal action, effectively implemented the provision of the 1842 Imperial Copyright Act, under which publishers were obliged to lodge copies, free of charge, of all books published but which, until then, had widely been ignored.

The resulting growth in the library's book stock necessitated a new Reading Room, the obvious site for which was the redundant quadrangle in the middle of Robert Smirke's British Museum. Sydney Smirke, his younger brother, was commissioned and designed a great dome in cast iron, 140 feet wide, the largest in the world after the Pantheon at Rome.[25] Thackeray wrote, 'It seems to me one cannot sit down in that place without a heart full of grateful reverence.'[26] Among those who have held readers' tickets to work there are Karl Marx, George Bernard Shaw, Virginia Woolf and Seamus Heaney.

By the middle of the 20th century the library had outgrown the Reading Room and Sir Leslie Martin and the architect Colin St John Wilson were selected to draw up new plans. Wilson's proposals were not finally approved until 1978, work did not begin until 1984 and the building did not open until 1998, on account of a miserable saga of havering and cowardice by successive governments. Edmund Burke warned that 'those that would carry on great public schemes must be proof against the most fatiguing delays, the most mortifying disappointments, the most shocking insults and, worst of all, the presumptuous judgements of the ignorant on their designs.' Wilson endured all these, as had Robert Smirke nearly two hundred years before him.

Fortunately, the library had in Wilson an architect of Fabian patience with a real understanding of the building. 'The Library, and what it houses,' he wrote, 'embodies and protects the freedom and diversity of the human spirit in a way that borders on the sacred.'[27] Responding to the site that adjoins Sir George Gilbert Scott's St Pancras Chambers (1868) he designed a building whose form, profile and materials follow the library's function, human and mechanical. He manages to combine a symbolic rhetoric that declares the central importance of language within a restrained exterior whose mass and height, colour and texture stand happily beside Gilbert Scott.

Set back from the Euston Road, in the forecourt is a monumental statue by Eduardo Paolozzi of *Newton*, after a painting by William Blake. Within, the great concourse of its entrance hall rises to the glory of the King's Library whose books, with spines of tooled leather, red, gold and ochre, and the ivory of vellum, are set in a glass building at the symbolic heart of the library. Stand at the foot of this face of sheer learning and you look down into a moat of black marble of apparently unplumbable depth.

The concourse is a space of calm grandeur, given solidity by its materials: marble floors, a red-brick wall, brass rails bound with soft leather, doors of oak, a balcony of carved travertine. Off the concourse are the Reading Rooms for scholars, the Education Department for schoolchildren and the Gallery in which is exhibited a selection of the library's treasures – manuscripts, maps, illuminated books: a secret place of near-darkness, to conserve the works on ancient paper, displayed in cases that glow with pools of light.

Here is the *Codex Sinaiticus*,[28] its lettering whispering the word of God in writing so bleached that it barely raises itself off the page; the memoirs of the Emperor Babur, founder of the Mughal Dynasty, their images brilliant with colour, their script set in gold; and a Koran[29] of AD 1304, copied by the calligrapher Muhammed Ibn al-Wahîd in the cursive hand known as Thuluth, its frontispiece illuminated by geometric patterns and the counter rhythms, right to left, of the ornamental Eastern Kufic script.

With it, in this library of the religions of the world, are the oldest surviving Buddhist scrolls, from ancient Gandhara, written on fragments of birch bark (*c.*100 BC–AD 200);[30] the palm-leaf manuscript of the *Devimahatmya* (*c.*1549), which glorifies the Hindu goddess Devi; a richly decorated 14th-century copy[31] of the Haggadah, the Jewish prayerbook that tells the story of the Passover; and fragments of the Gospel according to St John, written in Greek on papyrus in Egypt in the 3rd century and found in the early 20th century on a midden in the Egyptian city of Oxyrhynchus. On them are Christ's words to the disciples at the Last Supper: 'A little while, and ye shall not see me; and again, a little while, and ye shall see me, because I go to the Father.'[32]

Beside these sacred texts are secular documents, some mighty, some of historical importance (the Magna Carta; the Charter of the East India Company on which the British Empire was founded, illuminated by a wealth of contemporary documents, British and Indian),[33] some displaying man's invention (one of Leonardo da Vinci's notebooks),[34] others recording the mere thumbprint of great artists (Beethoven's note in the score of the Ninth 'Choral' Symphony which he gave to the Philharmonic Society in London).

If the Gutenberg Bible is the parent of the printed books here, the King James Bible is considered by many to be the ur-text of modern English. Here is the first edition, 1611, of the 'one uniform translation' of the Authorised Version. Beside the Bible as translated by William Tyndale[35] it can be seen to have achieved its aim, as set out at the Conference at Hampton Court in 1604, 'not to make a new translation but to make a good one better, or out of many good ones, one principal good one'.[36]

In recent years the library has responded to new technology by embracing the digital world and to new demands on its stock by decentralising to Boston Spa. It continues meanwhile to acquire great historic texts and documents. One such is the *Luttrell Psalter*, written and illuminated in the early 14th century in Lincolnshire, illustrating the Psalms with scenes of everyday life in medieval England, purchased in 1929;[37] another the Sherborne *Missal*[38] (1400–1407), which is as richly illustrated with images of kings, nobles, monks, saints, angels and the birds of Britain as the Luttrell Psalter is with the daily tasks of farming.

The library's shelves hold worlds, and the world. As Macaulay wrote, 'if everything else in our language should perish, [this] alone would suffice to show the whole extent of its beauty and power.'

BRITISH MUSEUM *****

Great Russell Street, London WC1B 3DG
Tel. 020 7323 8299
www.thebritishmuseum.ac.uk

The museum of the Enlightenment and of the great civilisations: the world in one room

This is where Britain's museums begin, in the King's Library. The British Museum is not the oldest, but it is the template, 'the Mother of Museums'. Here, in one room, is the world as it was known when the British Museum was founded in 1753, in the morning of the Enlightenment.

Diderot and D'Alembert had published the first volume of their *Encyclopédie*[39] in 1751 in the belief that all knowledge could be described in words upon the page. The ambition of the British Museum was to bring together in one building, in one room, from the sciences and the arts, from the civilisations of the world, not words but objects that embodied that knowledge, in order that the general public might learn and that scholars might gain understanding.

That ambition is a conceit that represents the development of man's understanding in the course of the 18th century. In 1700 knowledge was bound by the text: the Bible, the classics. By 1800 empirical evidence had taken its place beside textual exegesis. The British Museum was founded at the mid-point of that revolution.

Here, in the King's Library, designed by Robert Smirke to house the library of George III and the grandest interior of the period in London, are the parameters of that knowledge, divided into 'Natural and Artificial Rarities', objects found in nature and objects made by man: natural history, archaeology, antiquities, *objects de vertu* (gems, coins, medals, seals, bronzes). These objects charted new beliefs, new disciplines, new plants, new continents, new ways of living. Here, in the King's Library, was the essence of the 'universal museum', what John Ruskin called 'the grandest concentration of the means of human knowledge in the world', the Orders of Knowledge arranged: books above, around the gallery; cases of objects below.

When the museum collections outgrew the original building, Smirke expanded the building, describing the Ionic order[40] of his mighty new facade as 'simple, grand, magnificent, without ostentation'.[41] Above the eight bays of its portico is a huge sculptural pediment by Sir Richard Westmacott, on the theme of *The Progress of Civilisation*. 'Man is represented as emerging from a rude savage state through the influence of religion and progressing by means of the study of Astronomy to Mathematics, the Fine Arts, terminating with Natural History.'[42] Building and pediment express the scale and ambition of the enterprise.

Although the scale is grand its purpose was not to symbolise power nor to inspire awe, but to express and further democracy. This was a museum founded not on a royal collection but by the will of the people in an Act of Parliament. If its overt ambition was the advance of scholarship and learning, its underlying motives were to promote order and tolerance. Memories were still fresh of the panic in the streets eight years before at the approach of Charles Edward Stuart's Jacobite

The King's Library: the world in one room at the British Museum

army. 'The rebels having got to Derby in their intended march to London,' wrote Sir John Clerk of Penicuik, 'this put the Citty of London in the utmost consternation. Stocks fell but the King declared he would live and dye the King of England and a considerable army of old and new raised troops were immediately ordered to assemble on Finchly common.'[43]

Parliament passed 'An Act to incorporate the British Museum' by which 'one general repository shall be erected . . . for public use to all posterity.' Into that repository were placed Sir Hans Sloane's collection of natural history specimens,[44] many of which were brought back from the West Indies in 1689, and to which he added throughout his long career as the most distinguished physician in London,[45] and his collection of coins, medals, antiquities and paintings;[46] the library of medieval manuscripts of the 17th-century antiquarian Sir Robert Cotton, which included the Lindisfarne Gospels, the *Anglo-Saxon Chronicle* and the Magna Carta; and the library of Robert and Edward Harley, 1st and 2nd Earls of Oxford,

the greatest private archive of English history: 6,000 volumes of manuscripts, 14,500 charters and rolls, 400,000 pamphlets.

The founding collections, augmented by George II's gift of the old Royal Library[47] in 1757, set high standards of scholarship and quality, but it was the next wave of bequests and acquisitions of antiquities that exerted a decisive influence on how the museum was to develop and how its collections appear today.[48]

In 1802 the defeat of Napoleon in Egypt brought to England, and thus to the museum, the Rosetta Stone, the sarcophagus of Nectanebo II (30th Dynasty, 360–43 BC) and other antiquities. Even more significant perhaps were the Roman treasures received from Thomas Hollis[49] in 1757, Sir William Hamilton in 1772, Charles Townley in 1824 and Richard Payne Knight in 1825.[50] Unlike the *milordi*, most of whom throughout the 18th century bought antiquities as fashionable souvenirs, these four were connoisseurs whose collections were worthy of the scholarly scrutiny of the great Johann Joachim Winckelmann.[51] Instead they were subjected to the charm and enthusiasm of Baron d'Hancarville, whose scholarly standards[52] were markedly less rigorous.

Nevertheless what Hamilton described to Palmerston as his 'good little bronzes',[53] and Townley's marbles (the *Discobolus*; the *Cannibal* from the Barberini Palace; and, his favourite, the *Clytie*, a beautiful girl arising, deliciously, from a lotus flower)[54] make these the best collections outside Italy of what was excavated in the 18th century. They include few original Greek pieces, but the museum soon received the Elgin Marbles (1816) and, in 1815, the friezes of the battle between the Centaurs, Lapiths, and Amazons from the Temple of Apollo at Bassae.

By now the British Consul-General in Egypt, Henry Salt, assisted by his agent, the prodigious 'Paddington Samson' Giovanni Belzoni, was assembling a collection of Egyptian antiquities that included the colossal head of Rameses II, a head and arm of Tuthmosis III and six seated statues of the goddess Sekhmet from the Temple of Mut.[55]

In the course of little more then twenty-five years the museum had acquired the basis of a collection of antiquities that described the great civilisations of the Mediterranean and Middle East from which Europe has evolved. What it gained next was at least as valuable: scholarship of the highest order.

Edward Hawkins, a numismatist, became keeper of antiquities in 1826 and held that post for thirty-four years, transforming the department and establishing its international reputation. He was helped by the work that was taking place in the field on behalf of the museum by such archaeologists as Claudius James Rich, who correctly deduced the site of the ancient city of Nineveh, and Sir Henry Layard, who went on to excavate it. It is indicative of how rudimentary was archaeological knowledge at this time that when, in May 1825, the trustees ordered that 'Mr Rich's smaller Babylonian antiquities'[56] be exhibited, one table case, scarcely three feet square, was able to enclose all the known evidence not only of Nineveh but of Babylon itself (a carved stone, fragments of glass furnace waste, small bronze figures of animals).[57]

It is the golden links of scholarship that bind tight a museum and its objects and invest

a collection of curiosities with meaning. In Britain the discovery and recording of antiquities, particularly of ancient monuments, have been pursued at least since the 16th century (William Camden's *Britannia*, 1586; William Stukeley's field work at Stonehenge and the Alexander Keiller Museum, q.v.). When William Cunnington and his patron Sir Richard Colt Hoare published the report of their excavations in *The Ancient History of Wiltshire* (1812–19) they prefaced it with the quintessentially Enlightenment dictum, 'we speak from facts not theories'.

The British antiquities that were accumulating in the museum were greatly enhanced by the appointment of Augustus Wollaston Franks, who became keeper of medieval antiquities in 1866. Franks was the very model of the gentleman scholar: aristocratic, rich, brilliant. Not only did he transform the Medieval Department with a dazzling succession of acquisitions (over 4,000 in the late 1860s, many of them financed out of his own pocket) but he laid the foundations of the ethnographic collections.

In doing so he brought into focus material in the founding collection that Sloane had brought back from the West Indies, and the rich haul from Captain Cook's Pacific voyages. To these had been added material from the Chartered Companies and from the expeditions that Banks sponsored as President of the Royal Society (Archibald Menzies's to Vancouver in the 1780s and Mungo Park's to Africa in 1795). Franks's coup was to secure the bequest of Henry Christy[58] in 1865. That collection of over 10,000 objects (from the Esquimaux of North America; from the Aztecs in Mexico) widened the scope of the museum from the great classical civilisations to those of the whole world.

Before Hawkins and Franks, the scientist Sir Humphry Davy had, in the 1830s, despaired of what he saw as 'this ancient, misapplied and, one might almost say, useless Museum'.[59] Now it was the museum of world civilisations, each department, each gallery distinguished by objects of significance, wonder and beauty.

Walk up Smirke's Great Staircase, past the

Townley *Discobolus*,[60] and consider the Medieval and Romano-British Galleries, which hold the *Mildenhall Treasure* (4th century AD), the silver-flanged bowls and great dish a dull grey; the helmet and gold buckle from Sutton Hoo; the Lewis Chessmen and the silver-gilt 13th-century reliquary from Basle Cathedral. Go through the Roman Gallery and consider the Portland vase (1st century BC/AD), its cameo-glass a miracle of skill, its repair, when it was smashed in 1845 into more than two hundred pieces, a miracle of restoration. Go into the Babylonian Room and see the gaudy statuette, *The Ram in the Thicket* (ur, *c.* 2,500 BC), a symbol of fertility gods, vibrant with power.

Return down the North Stairs lined by mosaic pavements from Carthage and Utica, and wherever you turn there are objects of great age (the marble figure of a woman from Amorgos, *c.* 2,800–2,000 BC) and of no age (a man's coat – Ghana, 1998 – made by El Anatsui, *b.* 1944, shimmering with recycled foil wrappers and bottletops); objects of simplicity (a carved hand from Rapa Nui on Easter Island, from Cook's second voyage) and of complexity (the Godefroid de Huy cross, late 12th century, a masterpiece of Romanesque gilt copper and champlevé enamel); of beauty (the 2nd-century Roman marble *Aphrodite Bathing*), of vanity (the royal gold cup, late 14th century, made for Charles V)[61] and of quietus (Napoleon's death mask, 1821, by Francesco Antommarchi, the former Emperor's doctor).

Downstairs the miracle of Phidias's carving on the Parthenon friezes (447–438 BC), seen in the quiet and pale, cool lighting of the Duveen Gallery, is matched by the detail of the reliefs from the palaces of Nineveh, the crabs and fishes in the rippling water of the river that runs before Sennacherib's army as subtly observed as Phidias's rearing and prancing processional horses. At the end of the Nineveh Gallery are the monumental and mysterious human-headed winged bulls from the palace of Khorsabad (721–705 BC), smiling enigmatically, their plaited beards as precise as their hooves are delicate.

The wonders of the museum brought here to Bloomsbury from all the round world's imagined corners are numberless. How can they be named? As well tally each leaf of a tree. They come here out of the living minds of generations of men and women now dead – Greek and Assyrian, Aztec and Inuit, Chinese and Indian – who have conceived and carved and hammered and tempered and cast these objects to represent the worlds around them, visible and invisible.

Wonders though they are, the great objects, the friezes from Bassae and the Parthenon or the remains of the Mausoleum at Halicarnassus, are somewhat misleading. What distinguishes the British Museum is not only its iconic objects but the series of more mundane objects that speak with patience, consequence and detail of these civilisations. Of Rome and medieval Europe we learn more from the coins and medals here (the greatest collection in the world) than from the gold cup of France or the Warren Cup. The thousands upon thousands of sheets of prints and drawings are eloquent of the felt life of Renaissance Europe.

The building could no longer contain the profusion of these treasures. In 1883 the Natural History collections moved to South Kensington. New galleries were built in the 20th century. In 2000 the British Library, the custodian of the founding Cotton and Harley collections, had to vacate the Reading Room at the heart of the museum and move to a new building at St Pancras. The axes of the museum shifted. Not only was space for display gained but so too was the possibility of peace for visitors, appreciated by Prosper Merimée when he visited in 1858, 'Vous ne pouvez vous faire une idée de la beauté du British Museum un dimanche, quand il n'y a absolument personne que M. Panizzi et moi.'[62]

With the removal of the library the conceit of the universal museum of the Enlightenment was no longer possible, but the founding values of the museum could be reasserted: democracy, liberty, tolerance and, above all, humility, inspired by the contemplation and study of these civilisations, their achievements and their passing.

The Great Court, redesigned by Sir Norman Foster in 2000, has become the architectural hub of the museum, the King's Library the heart of its being.

CABINET WAR ROOMS *

Clive Steps, King Charles Street,
London SW1A 2AQ
Tel. 020 7766 0120
www.iwm.org.uk

The bunker from where Winston Spencer Churchill directed the Second World War

After the Munich crisis of 1938, war gradually became inevitable and preparations accelerated to protect the government, its cabinet and its officials from the anticipated German bombing. Sites were considered at Dollis Hill, the north-west London suburb, and, later, in Worcestershire, for what Churchill referred to 'with repugnance as the "Black Move" '.[63] Some secure accommodation was provided by the London Passenger Transport Board in a disused Underground station on the corner of Down Street and Piccadilly. Sir John Colville, Churchill's private secretary, records a dinner there on 19 November 1940: 'I went with the P.M. to Down Street for the night and dined excellently, far beneath the level of the street . . . The L. P. T. B. do themselves well: caviar (almost unobtainable in these days of restricted imports), Perrier Jouet 1928, 1865 brandy and excellent cigars'.[64]

The working areas of the Cabinet War Rooms, which comprise this museum, were more spartan. The Cabinet Room here is functional, containing simply a few maps, a wall clock and tables covered in blue baize, arranged in a square. In the centre of the table, directly in front of his distinctive wooden chair, sits Churchill's red box for his official papers.

A room, complete with desk and bed, was provided for Churchill, but he preferred to live and work above ground until late 1940 when the Blitz became too intense. Even then he was reluctant to take refuge. 'His favourite occupation during air raids was to climb onto the nearest roof or turret and watch the action.'[65]

His room here has a desk with an ashtray, a blotting pad, two telephones (one with a green receiver for scrambled conversations), a carafe of water, two inkwells with red and black ink, and two microphones. It was from here that he made four of the broadcasts that rallied the nation in 1940–41. On his pillow is a folded nightshirt, on the bedside table a green shaded lamp and a candle in a candlestick. On the wall behind is a map of Western Europe.

The accommodation for Churchill's most senior officials, Sir Edward Bridges, Secretary to the Cabinet, and General Sir Hastings Ismay, Churchill's personal Chief of Staff, is subtly, but distinctly, different: an iron bed, no eiderdown, no bedside table. Other, junior, staff had to rough it in 'the dock', where the rooms and dormitories had concrete floors, bare brick walls and chemical WCs. Betty Green, Ismay's personal secretary, wrote, 'Sometimes I was there for about three nights running, because I just couldn't get home, so in some ways I was fortunate that even in this revolting place called "the dock" one could get a good night's sleep, because you didn't hear the bombs raining down, which is just as well, because we'd all have been buried alive in the Cabinet War Rooms.'

The heart of the war rooms was the Map Room. News of the war's progress across the world came here first to the bank of white, black, red, green or ivory phones. The changes, casualties and losses of ships, aircraft and men were all logged and then plotted on to the many wall maps. Access was rigidly controlled. The King and Queen visited only once, in May 1942, as did General Eisenhower some weeks later.

The exclusivity of working here was palpable. Churchill's wartime secretary, Elizabeth Nel, wrote in her memoirs of the 'Map Room boys': 'they didn't work particularly hard. They oozed glamour and success and they managed to be in on every damn thing that was going.'[66]

In these dank, low-lit corridors there is no

shortage of atmosphere. Hidden speakers bring sound effects from the past: a telephone ringing, footsteps echoing on concrete floors, a distant air-raid siren and silences at the centre of world war.

COURTAULD COLLECTION
****

Somerset House, Strand, London WC2R 0RN
Tel. 020 7848 2526
www.courtauld.ac.uk

The finest lesson in art history, showing man – and God – to man

It is generally accepted that the Courtauld Collection, given by Samuel Courtauld, the former chairman of the great textile company, comprises one of the finest collections of Impressionist and Post-Impressionist paintings in Britain. Each part of that statement is true, but the story is more complicated.

The idea of the Courtauld was conceived by Arthur Lee, later Viscount Lee of Fareham, in 1917. He had given to the nation his home, Chequers, in Buckinghamshire, as an official country residence for future prime ministers, and with it his first collection. He wanted his second collection to form the basis of a British equivalent to the Fogg Art Museum at Harvard: a collection that would support the undergraduate and post-graduate teaching of the history of art.

To establish this he looked to his friends for help. Financial support and the beginnings of a collection were forthcoming[67] but no building, until one of the benefactors, Samuel Courtauld, offered his home in Portman Square, the magnificent Robert Adam-designed Home House (1774). In recognition of this generosity, Lee insisted that the new body should be called the Courtauld Institute of Art. A gallery exhibiting the institute's collection opened to the public in Woburn Square in 1957.

By then Lee and Courtauld had died (both in 1947) and the Courtauld had been bequeathed the collection of Sir Robert Witt. It comprised 4,000 Old Master drawings,

approximately 20,000 prints and the library of photographs of paintings so familiar to researchers. The collections were further extended in 1966 by the addition of trecento and quattrocento paintings collected by Thomas Gambier Parry and bequeathed by his grandson, Mark; classic English watercolours from Mr and Mrs William Wycliffe Spooner in 1967; two collections of 20th-century paintings from the dealer Lillian Browse and from Dr Alistair Hunter;[68] and, in 1978, an outstanding collection of Old Master paintings and drawings, called the Princes Gate Collection in order to preserve, initially, the anonymity of the benefactor, Count Antoine Seilern.

With these gifts and bequests the collection outgrew Woburn Square and, in 1989, the gallery was moved to Somerset House, where it was reunited with the Institute. The home until 1837 of the Royal Academy, Somerset House is a setting worthy of the collection, the finest building of George III's architect Sir William Chambers, a masterpiece of classical architecture.[69]

From the Strand you enter a three-arched vestibule, beyond which is the magnificent courtyard of Somerset House, presided over by John Bacon's statue of George III. To your left is the Institute; to your right is the door to the Courtauld Galleries. You go from the shade of the vestibule to the airy light of a hall dominated by a Doric screen and, once more in shade, a staircase whose stone steps sweep unsupported around curved walls to the galleries on the two upper floors. The staircase gets steeper and more narrow, the *gradus ad Parnassum*, until you gain the top storey, whose Corinthian screen is flooded with light. You have climbed one of the most beautiful and exciting staircases in London through what is a metaphor for the gallery: Doric to Corinthian, darkness to light, ignorance to enlightenment; the past (13th- and 14th-century paintings on the ground floor) to the near-present (20th-century works in the Great Room at the top of the building).

Lee had wanted to establish a great teaching collection that would bind the gallery and the Institute together. A succession of

fine directors, from Anthony Blunt to John Murdoch, furthered that ambition. The most recent director, James Cuno, has looked afresh at how the gallery expresses those aims and has rearranged the rooms to express the distinct identities of the individual collections and to emphasise the Courtauld's overall identity as a collection of collections.[70] The Gambier Parry Italian Primitives are now on the ground floor; the Lee, Courtauld and Seilern Collections in the parade of first floor rooms; and the 20th-century works (and a temporary exhibition space) on the second floor.

The small ground-floor gallery's low ceiling and absence of natural light suit the detailed intensity of the mainly 14th-century works in Gambier Parry's collection, chief amongst which is a polyptych altarpiece by the Florentine Bernardo Daddi, his last signed and dated work: *The Crucifixion with Saints*, painted in 1348 for the church of S. Giorgio a Ruballa. Also here are Lorenzo Monaco's richly patterned *The Coronation of the Virgin* (*c.* 1394–5) and a set of predella panels depicting the story of *St Julitta and St Quiricus* by Borghese di Piero.

The gallery's proportions are particularly sympathetic to the long, horizontal panel on which Mariotto Albertinelli painted *The Creation* (*c.* 1513–15). The scenes, from the Book of Genesis, chapters 2 and 3, are laid out from left to right: the creation of the animals; the creation of man (God pulls Adam to his feet); the creation of Eve (she is emerging from the rib of a sleeping Adam); and the temptation and fall, in which an exotic serpent with a beautiful human head offers Eve not an apple but a succulent split fig. In the background is a gentle, idyllic landscape. It is a work whose disturbing spell is akin to that of Piero di Cosimo's slightly earlier *A Forest Fire* in the Ashmolean Museum (q.v.).

On the first floor is a parade of rooms originally designed for the Royal Society, the Royal Academy and the Society of Antiquities. They are magnificent, but their decorative details (plasterwork by Thomas Collins, fire-

The Courtauld: Renoir's La Loge

places by Joseph Wilton, and ceiling paintings by Giovanni Battista Cipriani, and Biagio Rebecca) are not totally sympathetic to Samuel Courtauld's collection of the finest Impressionist and Post-Impressionist paintings in Britain.

Samuel Courtauld did not start his collection until he was in his forties. He was unmoved by Roger Fry's two Grafton Gallery exhibitions (1910 and 1912), which brought the work of Cézanne and others to London, and it was not until he saw paintings by Manet, Degas and Renoir at Sir Hugh Lane's exhibition at the Tate Gallery in 1917 that he began to see their qualities.

In 1922 he went to an exhibition of French art loaned by Gwendoline Davies[71] at the Burlington Fine Arts Club, saw Cézanne's *Provençal Landscape* and recognised 'the magic [that] I have felt in Cézanne's work ever since'.[72] It is not surprising that so many of the artists who featured in that 1922 exhibition are represented here. What is remarkable is that, guided often by Percy Moore Turner, of the Independent Gallery, Courtauld's eye was so good. Almost every painting here illustrates an important moment or development in its artist's work. One of the first that Courtauld bought, in 1922, was the late (*c.* 1910) Renoir *Woman Tying her Shoe*, in which Renoir's rich, sensual impasto and sweeps of colour fill the canvas with the physicality of the model. Three years later Courtauld bought an early Renoir, the beautiful *La Loge* (1874). Both paintings express Renoir's love of women, and of Rubens, an influence also apparent in Manet's poignant masterpiece *A Bar at the Folies-Bergère*.

Manet's painting is flanked by two groups by Cézanne: landscapes from the 1880s (*La Montagne Sainte-Victoire*, *c.* 1887 and *Le Lac d'Annecy*, 1896, in both of which the scene is framed by a massive, overhanging tree) and interiors from the 1890s (*The Card Players* and *Man with a Pipe*, both *c.* 1892–5, their figures as solid as mountains). Opposite them are the great Tahitian Gauguins *Nevermore* and *Te Rerioa* (*The Dream*) (both 1897), sensuous, watchful.

Courtauld loved the art, and the act, of painting. He was a traditionalist who saw Manet, Cézanne and Gauguin not as revolutionaries but as continuing and renewing, in France, the great tradition of European painting that reached back to the Italian Renaissance. The paintings in this room are a summation of that tradition at the close of the 19th century.

Of the two other rooms dedicated to Courtauld's collection, the first has paintings from the early years of Impressionism: canvases by Manet and Monet painted in 1873 and 1874 at Argenteuil, where Monet was living; and Renoir's *La Loge* (1874), which was exhibited that year at the first Impressionist exhibition. Here it is hung near Gainsborough's touching *Portrait of Mrs Gainsborough* (c. 1778–9), painted a century earlier, underlining Courtauld's belief in the continuity of the European tradition.

The third room is presided over by Renoir's portrait of *Ambroise Vollard* (1908), the Paris dealer for many of the Impressionists, who commissioned portraits of himself from Cézanne, Bonnard and, later, Picasso. The room is small and can only show a selection of the rest of Courtauld's collection: Toulouse-Lautrec, Bonnard, Vuillard, Rousseau, Signac and Georges Seurat, whom Courtauld admired almost as much as Cézanne.

In this company the strength of Seurat's painting is striking. The portrait of his mistress, Madeleine Knobloch, *Young Woman Powdering Herself* (c. 1880–90), has the calm detachment of a Vermeer.[73] Within an internal, asymmetrical border (echoed by the small, framed picture of flowers high on the wall behind the woman) Seurat moves the viewer's eye across passages of paint that shimmer and shift like sand beneath water. The chromatic *pointillisme* of *The Bridge at Courbevoie* (c. 1886–7) is contained within a geometry as distinct as that created by Cézanne with flat planes of colour. Here it is held in place by Seurat's scaffolding of repeated verticals, all parallel, but not quite at ninety degrees.

Lord Lee's collection is confined to a single room in which it is difficult to do justice to the breadth and quality of this, his second collection. His first collection was particularly strong on English portraiture and on the works of Constable. This collection, too, has fine portraits (by Dobson and Lely; Goya; Romney and Raeburn), but Lee here assembles paintings that range across the European tradition: Botticelli's altarpiece *The Trinity with St Mary Magdalen and St John the Baptist, the Archangel Raphael and Tobias* (c. 1491–4); a delightful, decorative Cranach, *Adam and Eve* (1526), and Hans Eworth's strange *Allegorical Portrait of Sir John Luttrell* (1550) in which Sir John's powerful, naked torso arises out of a stormy sea like that of a Neptune to reach for the olive branch held by the figure of Peace.[74]

Lee was a determined and decisive collector who had little time for the dealers or the art world, preferring to trust his own taste, manifested here by a superb pair of *cassoni*, richly carved by Zanobi di Domenico for the Morelli–Nerli marriage in Florence in 1472.[75]

In forming this great teaching collection Courtauld and Lee shared a lofty aim. 'Today we need teachers and leaders for the great host of laymen whose interest in art might be awakened, or further stimulated,' wrote Courtauld. 'It is obvious that we must train enough scholars and experts to teach these more popular teachers of tomorrow.'[76] Their collections contribute to that purpose, but it is the third founding collection, of Count Seilern, that truly sets the Courtauld apart.

Seilern's collection is informed not just by his taste and his wealth but by his scholarship, developed as a student at Vienna University, where he wrote his doctoral thesis on the Venetian origins of Rubens's ceiling paintings. While at the university he met Johannes Wilde, who, after the Second World War, became deputy director at the Courtauld, where his presence was, perhaps, a contributory factor in Seilern's decision to bequeath his collection to the gallery.

Seilern's taste was catholic. His collection goes back to the 15th century and the Master of Flémalle (Robert Campin), whose triptych (c. 1420) is one of the great works of Early Netherlandish painting, and forward to Oscar

Kokoschka, a friend of Seilern, who commissioned the huge triptych here, *The Myth of Prometheus* (1950).

Here too are a dreamy *Landscape with the Flight into Egypt* (1563) by Pieter Brueghel the Elder and his startling grisaille *Christ and the Woman Taken in Adultery* (1565); a Van Dyck; and the tender, delicate *Virgin and Child* (c. 1524–7) by Parmigianino. It is a remarkable collection that can afford to tuck away the exquisite Claude *Landscape with an Imaginary View of Tivoli* (1642) and Quinten Massys's *The Madonna Standing with the Child and Angels* (c. 1500–9).

At the heart of the Seilern Collection are the thirty-two paintings and twenty drawings by Peter Paul Rubens, which include the oil sketches for the side panels of the powerful Crucifixion triptych[77] painted in 1612 for the high altarpiece in Antwerp Cathedral, a portrait of *The Family of Jan Breugel The Elder* (c. 1613–15) and one of Rubens's masterpieces, *Landscape by Moonlight* (c. 1637–8).

Rubens had returned to Antwerp from Italy, famous, rich and married (to Isabella Brant, in 1609). *Cain Slaying Abel* (c. 1608–9) and *Moses and the Brazen Serpent* (c. 1609–10) are good examples of the style that had established his reputation: huge in conception, heroic in manner, magnificent in colour. The oil sketches for the Antwerp Cathedral triptych, a commission of considerable prestige, show a greater subtlety: the contrasts are more smooth, the compositions strong but more fluid, the lighting and colours more tender, though no less dramatic.

Finally there is *Landscape by Moonlight*, a supreme example of the painting he did for his own enjoyment in the 1630s, the final ten years of his life. Isabella had died, he had remarried in 1630 (Hélène Fourment, aged sixteen; he was fifty-three), he had abandoned court politics and diplomacy and retired to his house, Het Steen. In his 8th Discourse Reynolds said of *Landscape by Moonlight*, 'Rubens has not only diffused more light over the picture than is in nature, but has bestowed on it those warm glowing colours by which his works are so much distinguished. It is so unlike what any other painters have given us of Moon-light, that it might be easily mistaken, if he had not likewise added the stars, for a fainter setting sun.'[78] The moon is phosphorescent. Around it dance stars like sparks.[79] The light glows as if buried in the water; its reflection infiltrates the branches of the trees and the crevices of the riverbank. It is a painting that has to be seen and studied close up to appreciate its thrall.

Courtauld, Lee and Seilern were all outstanding collectors who trusted their own judgement and bought, in Seilern's words, 'for the enjoyment of it', but the way in which Seilern slowly accumulated the sketches, by Rubens and Giovanni Battista Tiepolo, that deepen our understanding of major paintings is the hallmark of a true scholarly connoisseur.

These collections follow the European painting tradition from the 14th century to the beginning of the 20th century. Although Samuel Courtauld acquired a Modigliani, and paintings by Edouard Vuillard, Pierre Bonnard and Maurice Utrillo, his real interests ended with Cézanne, Gauguin and van Gogh. However, their influence on the next generation of Henri Matisse, André Derain, Raoul Dufy, Maurice de Vlaminck and the Fauves is crucial and on the top floor of the Courtauld loans from the Fridart Foundation and from some anonymous private collectors explore that influence.

In particular a group of canvases painted in the summer of 1905 at Collioure, and in the following summer, by Henri Matisse and André Derain record the moment of innovation with colour that was the birth of Fauvism. Matisse wrote of *The Red Beach* (1905) that 'what characterised fauvism was that we rejected imitative colours and that with pure colours we obtained stronger reactions – more striking simultaneous reactions; and there was also the *luminosity* of our colours.'

Paintings here by Maurice de Vlaminck (*Reclining Nude*, 1905), Georges Braque (*Port of L'Estaque* (1906), Raoul Dufy (*14 July at Le Havre*, 1906) and Alexei Jawlensky (*The Blue Cap*, 1912) show how these ideas spread. These loan collections also bring to London fine examples of the work of the German *Blaue*

Reiter group (Heinrich Camperdonck, August Macke) and of Max Pechstein, closely involved with Die Brucke. They bridge the gap between Courtauld's collection and those of Roger Fry, Dr Alistair Hunter and Lillian Browse, and show Courtauld and Lee's European tradition sailing deep into the 20th century. In doing so they demonstrate that this collection continues to grow and evolve.

CUMING MUSEUM *

155–157 Walworth Road, London SE17 1RS
Tel. 020 7701 1342
www.southwark.gov.uk/CultureHeritage/
MuseumsAndArtGalleries/
TheCumingMuseum

An affecting museum of life in the city from prehistory to post-industry

Three pieces of fossil and a Moghul coin started Richard Cuming collecting. He and his son, Henry Syer Cuming, built a collection of over 100,000 objects, an unruly mix of social history, geology, archaeology and frivolity; of coins, textiles and stuffed animals, advertisements, statuettes and fakes.

Richard Cuming's father was a tin plater from Totnes in Devon who came to London in 1760, did well in the City and married a rich woman, allowing his son and grandson to devote themselves to collecting. Richard's prime interests were natural history, science and art. There is a watercolour here of irises, and a cardboard cabinet that he made at the age of fourteen to hold his collection of larvae, bitumens and metals. Here too is the pectoral fin of a great white shark; the stuffed head of a polecat; a microscope he made when he was fifteen from mahogany, card and flakes of mica; and a whalebone bracelet from Prince William Sound, Alaska – echoes of John Tradescant's Cabinet of Curiosities at the Ashmolean Museum (q.v.).

Cuming kept his collection at home but he had a passion for museums. At this one are advertisements for the Temple of the Muses at Finsbury Square and for the Calonnian Museum at Savile House, Leicester Square, where for 1s. you could see birds, fishes, insects, shells and 'quadrupeds', collected by the French Statesman, Charles Alexandre de Calonne, 'to which have been recently added a Perpetual Motion, a Hail Storm, elegant Performances in Shellwork, glass temples and other Artificial Curiosities' along with objects from the Friendly Islands, the Solomon Islands, Nootea Sound 'and other newly discovered countries in the Southern Hemisphere'.

When Sir Ashton Lever's Leverian Museum in the Rotunda Building on Blackfriars Road closed in 1806, Cuming bought much of its stock, including a stuffed bear, objects brought back from Captain Cook's voyages and a malformed pig with eight legs and two tails. More conventionally he acquired an Egyptian collection: the lower part of an ushabti from the tomb of Amenhotep II in the Valley of the Kings, the lid of a canopic jar made to hold the internal organs of mummified bodies, a statue of the god Osiris and the gilt head from a coffin, both dating from the New Kingdom, c. 1200 BC.

These were significant Egyptian artefacts. Cuming had bought them at auction from the collection of Henry Salt, British Consul in Egypt in the 1830s. The Salt Collection, much of it now in the British Museum (q.v.), could stand beside Drovetti's in Turin or Anastasy's in the Louvre. All three owed much to Belzoni, the Titan of Padua, the discoverer of seven new tombs in the Valley of the Kings.

Henry Syer Cuming maintained his father's interest in antiquities. There is a Roman glass jar here, probably made in Germany and imported to Britain between AD 50 and 450. However his passion was for the archaeology of London and the social history of the communities that lived south of the river. Mid-19th-century London was a building site. The creation of the canals, the docks and the railways necessitated building on a scale never before seen. The city and its river yielded a trove of objects which shed light on the past lives of Londoners. He recorded the life of contemporary London by collecting theatre tickets, playbills, rail tickets, toys.

As vice president of the British Archaeological Association, he published papers on Celtic and Roman remains in the Thames (1858), the history of mistletoe (1878), the superstitions surrounding fingernails (1884) and the history of slings (1889). He also wrote articles on archaeological fraud.

The booming market in historic objects threw up people such as William Smith and Charles Eaton ('Billy and Charley') and Flint Jack, who worked the Thames at low tide searching for antiques. Since demand outstripped supply they began, in 1857, to fake 14th-century 'antiques': figurines, pilgrim badges, small shrines, Roman coins, even a Roman urn. Cuming exposed them in an article, causing some controversy until several of their moulds were stolen and displayed in public.

The Cumings' butterfly enthusiasms are now crammed into one room above the Walworth Road public library. The confined space makes the collections' variety appear yet more random. The hand of Tlaloc; a Colombian idol of the god of Rain, made of volcanic stone; Persian playing cards; an ivory comb from Bengal; the sculpture of an African sailor by George Tinworth, a Walworth-born sculptor who designed for Doultons; a single page from Shakespeare's First Folio (1623); an Etruscan bronze ladle (*c.* 600–500 BC) – all jostle each other.

DE MORGAN CENTRE *

38 West Hill, Wandsworth, London sw18 1rz
Tel. 020 8871 1144
www.demorgan.org.uk

William De Morgan's exotic tiles, Evelyn De Morgan's paintings

Towards the end of his life the *Times Literary Supplement* wrote, 'Mr De Morgan is a national institution; and one would as soon think of criticising the Bank of England as of criticising one of his . . .' The missing word is not 'tiles' or 'pots' but 'novels'. After thirty-five years of designing pottery to great acclaim

he stopped in 1907, his business a financial failure. His first novel, *Joseph Vance*, published in 1906, was an instant success in Britain and the United States, with eight editions being published in eighteen months. Six more novels followed before he died in 1917, giving him and his wife Evelyn a financial security that they had never previously enjoyed.

Yet it is his pottery that has endured and this museum shows why. Housed in what was the West Hill reference library, in Wandsworth, it brings together the collection that his sister-in-law Mrs Wilhelmena Stirling made of his pottery and of Evelyn De Morgan's paintings and drawings.

Evelyn De Morgan was taught by Edward Poynter at the Slade School of Art, where she was one of the first female students in 1873. Her student drawings, accurate and meticulous, won her prizes and a Slade scholarship. Her drawings here demonstrate her understanding of anatomy and her ability to capture the softness of skin and the solidity of form. Among her models were *Janey Morris*, still handsome in old age, and the Pre-Raphaelite-featured *Jane Hales*, nursemaid to her younger sister Wilhelmina, who returned to the family and lived with William and Evelyn De Morgan as their maid after they married in 1887.

The De Morgans were part of a circle including William Morris, Edward Coley Burne-Jones, Simeon Solomon and Henry Holiday, who were fellow students at the Royal Academy Schools where William studied to become a painter. Holiday introduced De Morgan to Morris[80] who commissioned first stained glass and subsequently tiles.

At first his designs based on flowers and foliage showed the close influence of Morris but even in these De Morgan was beginning to develop a striking depth in his glazes, particularly in the rich blues and turquoises of 'Bedford Park Daisy' and 'Bedford Park Anemone' (1862–3).

When the South Kensington Museum (later the Victoria and Albert Museum) began to buy and exhibit Turkish and Persian tiles, textiles and carpets, De Morgan found in

16th-century Iznik tiles the inspiration and ceramic tradition through which he could marry the low-key Englishness of Morris's floral motifs with his own bursting colours. Later, in 1882, Morris said, 'To us pattern-designers, Persia has become a Holy Land.'[81]

De Morgan always, incorrectly, called his Iznik-inspired designs 'Persian' but, whatever their name, their colours (cobalt-blue, pink, green, turquoise) capture the eye wherever you look in this gallery, animating the De Morgan repertoire of flowers (carnations, roses, water lilies, sunflowers), animals (antelopes, snakes, fishes, peacocks) and shapes, particularly the continuous double S-shaped curve of the oriental ogee.[82]

De Morgan inherited from his father, a philosopher and astronomer who was the first to hold the Chair of Mathematics at University College London, an interest in chemistry and experimentation. Initially he bought in blank tiles to decorate, and later the tiles he made in his own works also allowed him to work in relief. Painted in underglaze colours, often inspired by the Middle East, they included his rediscovery of the long-forgotten art of lustre, first seen in Persia in the 13th century, brought to Europe by the Moors and lost in Italy some two hundred years earlier. De Morgan described in a lecture to the Society of Arts (1892) how 'the pigment consists simply of white clay, mixed with copper scale or oxide of silver' which released a fine metallic film on to the ceramic body when flammable material was added to the kiln during firing. De Morgan's great achievement was to extend this to polychrome lustre, seen at its most beautiful and sophisticated here in the silvery, smoky tones of the *Moonlight Suite*.

The gallery glows with the silken lustres: pink, silver, golden, green. They slide softly on the eye, a film around De Morgan's pots and bowls and jars. There are examples here of lustre glazes that did not work, whose colours bled. In their imperfect beauty they show how fragile a skill this is.

The large, handsome space was built as a reading room in 1887. Its current use as a gallery was designed with confidence and clarity by Michael Davies Exhibitions (2001). The fine barrel-vaulted ceiling of dark stained wood and its architectural features (pilasters, dados and pediments) have been retained. Simple, modern-glass cabinets, sparklingly lit, hold the pottery; Evelyn's paintings are hung, packed close and skied to the ceiling. The two styles co-exist happily.

Evelyn De Morgan's paintings and William De Morgan's ceramics draw together Islamic and Arts and Crafts elements with 19th-century social concerns and demonstrate a quietly eccentric sort of Englishness. Together they were, in the opinion of Sir Edward Poynter, President of the Royal Academy, 'two of the rarest spirits of the Age'.

DESIGN MUSEUM **

28 Shad Thames, London SE1 2YD
Tel. 020 7403 6933
www.designmuseum.org

First museum of industrial design, featuring the chair

The Design Museum is on the south bank of the Thames, downstream from Tower Bridge. Across the river you can see design changing the skyline of London as office blocks and apartments by Norman Foster, Piers Gough, Broadway Maylan and Richard Rogers replace the 19th-century docks and warehouses of Wapping.

The Design Museum arose out of the Victoria and Albert Museum's Boilerhouse Project in the 1980s. When that ended the designer and entrepreneur Terence Conran and the historian of design Stephen Bayley recognised the need for a museum dedicated to design and established this in a former banana warehouse in 1989. Architects Conran Roche converted it.

To attempt to collect examples of design (good and bad) would be to collect the whole world. The museum mounts temporary exhibitions that explore different aspects of design and limits its permanent collection to objects that are typical of, or metaphors for, manufactured design. There are small sub-collections of domestic equipment, office furniture, tableware, textiles and graphics, but the core collection concentrates on the chair, starting with the Bentwood chair that the Austrian designer Michael Thonet designed *c.*1860, in bent, solid and laminated beech with a moulded plywood seat. It became the chair of choice of bars and restaurants all over the world and by 1930 was achieving sales of fifty million.

From then to the present day the museum has examples of chairs by almost all the great designers: Marcel Breuer, Mies van der Rohe and Alvar Aalto in the 1920s and '30s; Charles and Ray Eames, Harry Bertoia, Arne Jacobsen and Eero Saarinen in the 1950s; Gae Aulenti and Joe Colombo in the 1960s; and Philippe Starck and Frank O. Gehry in the 1990s. It is striking, although not surprising, how many of the designers are architects.

There are here chairs functional and chairs playful; chairs for comfort, chairs for elegance; cheap chairs, practical chairs; chairs designed for an occasion (the Barcelona International Exhibition 1929)[83] and chairs designed to ease the breathing of tubercular patients.[84]

There are chairs here in oak, ash, beech and ply; in fibreglass and plastic, aluminium and foam rubber; chrome steel and tubular steel; polypropylene, polyethylene and polyurethane. There is a chair, by Frank O. Gehry, in corrugated cardboard. Gerrit Thomas Reitveld's *Red Blue Chair* (1918), made for mass production from standard lengths of wood is, as it were, a three-dimensional Mondrian painting. Some designs are classical: van der Rohe's Barcelona chair was inspired by the *sella curulis*, the stool used by Roman magistrates. Of his Series 7, Model 3017 chair (1955), compact and stackable, Arne Jacobsen wrote, 'The fundamental factor is proportion. Proportion is precisely what makes the old Greek temples beautiful . . . and the most admired buildings of the Renaissance or the Baroque . . . are all well proportioned. That is the essential thing.' For Saarinen the starting point for his *Tulip Chair* (1955–6) was his conviction that 'the undercarriage of chairs and tables in a typical interior creates an ugly, confusing and restless world. I wanted to clear up the sum of legs,' he said. 'I wanted to make the chair all one thing again.'

Not surprisingly, in a collection of mass-produced objects, the role of the manufacturer is manifest. The Italian company Kertell has worked with designers (Joe Colombo, Anna Castelli-Ferrieri, Gae Aulenti, Philippe Starck) since the 1960s to explore the potential of plastics and of chairs that stack. Knoll International, US, have tended to work in steel, from van der Rohe and Breuer in the 1920s to Saarinen and Bertoia in the '50s, until Gehry designed *Crosscheck* for them in 1992, using bent and woven laminated wood.

There are chairs here that inhabit a place between play and art. The brothers Castiglioni (Achille and Pier Giacomo), made a series whose use of ready-made industrial objects – a tractor seat (*Mezzadro*, 1954–7), a racing bicycle saddle (*Sella*, 1957) – borrows from Marcel Duchamp; Philippe Starck's W.W. stool (a homage to the film director Wim Wenders, 1990) is a Dadaist object that barely provides a surface to be sat on.

Of his *Diamond Chairs* (1952–3) Harry Bertoia said, 'You will see that they are mainly made of air, just like light sculptures. Space goes clean through them.' They have become classics, in production for Knoll for more than fifty years. The characteristic that they have in common with the chairs here by the truly great designers Aalto, van der Rohe and above all Ray and Charles Eames, is simplicity.

For the Eameses that simplicity was the result of continual refinement and experiment. From their first LCW (lounge chair wood) (1945), designed in plywood, smuggled out of the Metro-Goldwyn-Mayer production lot where Charles Eames worked, to their 1956 lounge chair, their version of the club chairs of Adolf Loos and Le Corbusier, inviting and reassuring in rich veneer and opulent black leather, the Eameses produced a succession of ground-breaking designs: the DKR-2 (1951), its legs inspired by the Eiffel Tower, dubbed 'the bikini' for its two-piece leather upholstery; the low-cost DAR (1948), originally in aluminium

as the LAR, then in fibreglass, the first mass-produced chair made from an unlined fibreglass shell; *La Chaise* (also 1948), named after the French sculptor Gaston Lachaise and resembling a reclining figure by Henry Moore.

Outside, beside the river, is a sculpture by Eduardo Paolozzi, *Invenzioni* (1989). Around its massy metal bulk Paolozzi incorporates the words of Leonardo da Vinci, 'though human genius in its various inventions with various instruments may answer the same end, it will never find an invention more beautiful or more simple or direct than nature because in her inventions nothing is lacking and nothing superfluous.'

DULWICH PICTURE
GALLERY *****

Gallery Road, Dulwich, London SE21 7AD
Tel. 020 8693 5254
www.dulwichpicturegallery.org.uk

A gallery of art, perfected by Soane, perfectly filled

Quietly set back from the road beyond an apron of lawn, Sir John Soane's building was the first purpose-built public picture gallery. Ever since, architects designing picture galleries have struggled to improve on the simple symmetry of its facade and the uncluttered proportions of its galleries, top-lit by lanterns and gracefully linked by Soane's high arches: the ideal balance of light, space and calm in which to enjoy pictures.[85]

In 1790 Stanislaus Augustus, King of Poland, commissioned the London art dealer Noel Desenfans and his friend and lover the Swiss painter Sir Francis Bourgeois to form a royal collection 'to encourage the progress of the fine arts in Poland'.[86] As the collection grew, Stanislaus's regime crumbled, Poland was partitioned and in 1795 the King was forced to abdicate. The fall of the monarchy in France, and the turmoil across Western Europe that followed the rise of Napoleon, made it diffi-

Celestial Soane at the Dulwich Picture Gallery

cult for Desenfans and Bourgeois to find a purchaser for the collection. First the Tsar of Russia and then the British government declined the opportunity to buy. The trustees of the British Museum vacillated and made conditions. When Bourgeois died four years after Desenfans he left the collection to Dulwich College, subject to two conditions: the paintings should be available for the 'inspection of the public' and the architect of the picture gallery that would house them should be Bourgeois's friend Sir John Soane. Soane's design had to incorporate almshouses and a mausoleum for Mr and Mrs Desenfans and Bourgeois, and was originally more elaborate, its final simplicity being as much the result of the demands of thrift as of architectural restraint.

As you enter at once all is peaceful and ordered. The galleries are laid out along a north-south axis by country and period: Dutch and English paintings to the left, French, Italian and Spanish to the right. All are from the 17th and 18th centuries.

The collection is small and thus representative rather than comprehensive. Its authority derives from its quality. There are pre-eminent works, of course: by Rembrandt, Rubens, Van Dyck, Cuyp and Canaletto. There are seven Poussins and one wonderful Claude. There is scarcely a poor or dull picture. Those by the less celebrated (Adam Pynacker or Aert de Gelder; Charles le Brun or Gerrit Dou) hold their own in this company.

Landscapes and portraits predominate: Bourgeois was landscape painter to George III and a pupil of Philip de Loutherbourg. From the Dutch Golden Age, there are works by Nicolaes Berchem, Jan Both, Philips Wouwermans, Jan Wijnants, Jacob van Ruisdael and Bartholomeus Breenbergh. All convey a sense of wonder at the skies and the detailed domestic landscapes of the Netherlands, and the moral lesson drawn from them. 'Whatever may be said, from trees one learns; Whatever green is blooming is honour to the creator . . . Who in the fields combines his vision with reason will find many a thing to edify his morals.'[87]

The portraits left to Dulwich College by Edward Alleyn[88] and a later actor-manager William Cartwright have augmented Bourgeois's founding bequest, as has a gift in 1911 of forty-six portraits that included works by Gainsborough, Hogarth, Lely and Van Dyck, from Charles Fairfax Murray, artist, collector and friend of William Morris and Burne-Jones. Fairfax Murray had been won over by the offer of the chairman of the gallery's trustees Henry Yates-Thompson to build a separate wing to house the collection. The portraits provide an unusual view of the development of Stuart and Georgian portraiture, whose inspiration was Van Dyck. That main stream is refreshed by glimpses of its tributaries: William Dobson and Cornelius Johnson; Isaac Fuller and his pupil John Riley; John Greenhill and Mary Beale, taught by Lely; Kneller, Hudson and Highmore.[89] It culminates in Reynolds and Gainsborough.

Gainsborough has seven paintings here of his great friends, the Linley family, who dominated music in Bath,[90] and even in London, in the 1760s and '70s. They were all handsome. Elizabeth, seen here seated with her sister Mary (*The Linley Sisters*, 1772), married Richard Brinsley Sheridan. Gainsborough's affection for them is palpable, and the family's good looks are confirmed independently by Lawrence's portrait here of the son, *Thomas Linley*,[91] a painting entirely without the huff, puff and spurious glamour of Lawrence's later portraits of 'great men'.

There is only one portrait here by Reynolds but it is a mighty and moving one, of *Mrs Siddons as the Tragic Muse*.[92] In it Reynolds reveals more of himself than he does in any other of his portraits. Setting his subject against the rich brown of her dress and the shadows behind, he concentrates all light on the grace of her arms, her neck, her face.[93] The ghostly shadow of the Muse behind exalts her beauty. Reynolds is in thrall to her, and to his fantasy of her beauty.

There is one further surprise held by the English collection here: Lely. *Nymphs by a Fountain*[94] does not depict his familiar, voluptuous court beauties. Its nudity is more innocent and erotic. The nymphs tumble over each other, asleep. Lely's silky application of paint whispers, and delights in the softness of their slumber.

Despite the claims of Claude and Cuyp; of Rubens's triumph of love over war, *Venus, Mars and Cupid*; of Guercino's *The Woman Taken in Adultery*, the inclinations of the heads of the men standing behind Christ satirising the caustic arguments of the Pharisee; of the sublime light behind Aert de Gelder's descending angels in *Jacob's Dream*; of *Old Walton Bridge*, its 21st-century high-tech architecture placed among Canaletto's Lilliputian people by a Gulliver – pride of place must be given here to the paintings of Poussin and Rembrandt.

Poussin's *Rinaldo and Armida* (*c.* 1628–9) and *The Triumph of David* command the eye with their certainty and economy of composition, and their clarity of colour. Whether in the chubby fingers of the putto at Armida's shoulder, or the crowd welcoming David, every one of whose gestures and reactions are fresh and distinct, Poussin demonstrates how a master, without strain, builds detail into composition. In this finest collection of 17th-century French classical painting in Britain, *Rinaldo and Armida* stands out. Painted early in Poussin's career, it shows his debt to Titian. It takes a scene from Tasso's epic *Gerusalemme Liberata*.[95] In the act of killing the Christian Rinaldo, Armida's hand is stayed by his beauty. Poussin's brilliant handling of paint is apparent in Rinaldo's helmet, armour and hair, and in the delicacy of the receding landscape.

There are no examples of Rembrandt's heroic manner here (no *Night Watch*, or *Three Crosses*) but *Jacob III de Gheyn*[96] (1632) and *A Girl at a Window* (1645) show Rembrandt's genius in a quieter key. The lines on the eyelids and under the eyes of de Gheyn, the creases in the still childlike fingers of the girl, show his mastery of suggestive detail. The painting of light, glowing behind de Gheyn, pulling the girl forward and seeming to emanate from her, is spellbinding.

Among the pictures at Dulwich there may

be no great visions of God to compare with the Barber's *Ecce Homo* by Van Dyck but, as at the Barber Institute of Fine Arts (q.v.), there are pictures of the very highest quality. The similarities between the two galleries are striking: both are small; both are packed with examples of the work of the finest artists; both are in outstanding, purpose-built galleries that put the paintings first; above all, both collections were formed by people of remarkable flair and taste (Bourgeois and Desenfans here, Thomas Bodmer at the Barber). It is from seeing paintings through their eyes that you walk out into the now-suburban greenness of Dulwich enriched and refreshed.

ESTORICK COLLECTION OF MODERN ITALIAN ART
***

39a Canonbury Square, London N1 2AN
Tel. 020 7704 9522, fax 020 7704 9531
e-mail: info@estorickcollection.com

A Georgian English home for the Italian Futurists

Northumberland Lodge is an elegant, Grade II listed house, set back on a corner of Canonbury Square, shaded by a plane tree, separated from the traffic that grinds round Highbury Corner and down Upper Street. It is a deceptive setting for a collection of Italian modern art[97] containing works by artists who backed Tommaso Marinetti in 1909 when, in *The Founding and Manifesto of Futurism*, he declared, 'We will destroy the museums, libraries, academies of every kind,'[98] and who the following year published their own *Futurist Painting: Technical Manifesto*, in which they maintained 'that all forms of imitation must be despised, all forms of originality glorified' and said, as a postscript, 'We demand, for ten years, the total suppression of the nude in painting.'[99]

All five artists – Umberto Boccioni, Carlo Carrà, Luigi Russolo, Giacomo Balla and Gino Severini – have works in the Estorick Collection that, despite the bombast of the manifestoes, are generally small in scale, figurative and well painted – qualities that are shown to advantage by the calm, well-proportioned rooms, two to a floor, that are the collection's galleries.

The collection was formed by Eric and Salome Estorick in the late 1940s and 1950s. Eric Estorick had been inspired before the war by Albert Eugène Gallatin's Gallery of Living Art in New York, which contained works by Léger, Miró, Picasso, Arp, Brancusi, Braque, Matisse and Mondrian. On the Estoricks' honeymoon in 1947, he was introduced by the art therapist Arturo Bryks to Boccioni's book *Pittura Scultura Futuriste* (1914) and to the artist Mario Sironi. He bought most of the contents of Sironi's studio, 'hundreds and hundreds of drawings and as many pictures as I could get into my Packard Convertible Roadster'.[100] Twenty of those drawings (1915–42) remain in the collection. Over the next three years he acquired paintings by Massimo Campigli, Severini and Boccioni.

The contents of and even the intention behind the collection are complicated. Eric Estorick was as much dealer as collector. Indeed he saw that the two could complement one another. The exhibitions to which he contributed in 1953 and 1954, organised with Helen Kapp, director of the Wakefield Art Gallery (q.v.), and the exhibition at the Tate Gallery in 1956, were public-spirited in that they brought these artists before a public that was largely unaware of contemporary Italian art. At the same time they increased the market value of these artists.

Estorick bought and sold on behalf of Hollywood clients[101] and in 1961 opened the Grosvenor Gallery in London, from where he also dealt in Russian, Czech and South African paintings and the works of the designer Erté.

The collector Estorick did not like to part with paintings. The dealer loved to turn a deal. In the mid 1950s and early 1960s he sold paintings by Balla, Carrà, de Chirico, Soffici, Severini. Some such deals were to finance the purchase of better works by the same artists (he found Balla's *The Hands of the Violinist*, 1912, in a backroom at the Alex Reid and

The Estorick Collection: Modern Idol *by*
Umberto Boccioni

Lefèvre Gallery in 1954 and bought Boccioni's *Modern Idol*, 1911, the following year); some were to explore new interests (Russian artists); some were simply a matter of business.

Estorick's love for these paintings is clear. He never considered selling the masterpieces, once bought, the Balla or the Boccioni, or de Chirico's *Melanconia* (1912), Carrà's *Leaving the Theatre* (1910–11) or Campigli's *Il Belvedere* (1930). Many of the artists, especially Campigli and Sironi, became close friends of the Estoricks. Severini drew a *Portrait of Eric Estorick* (1956) which is here.

It is a courageous collection. When Estorick first showed these artists in Britain there were some enthusiastic reviews, by Robert Melville in *The Studio*, and Marini and de Chirico were praised, but Quentin Bell called Boccioni 'unpleasant' and 'inept'[102] and *The Times* deplored his 'laughable crudity'.[103]

Even today the collection is misunderstood, being dubbed 'Futurist', a catch-all description that ignores the Divisionist influence on Balla, the Metaphysical works of de Chirico and his influence on Surrealists, the adoption of classical and archaic motifs by Campigli, de Chirico and Marino Marini, the later social realism of Renato Guttuso, and the participation of Morandi, Carrà and Severini in the *Novecento Italiano* exhibitions of 1926 and 1929. All left the callowness of Marinetti's Futurist sloganising far behind.

What is clear is the quality of the painting. Carrà's diagonal brushwork and slurs of colour give *Leaving the Theatre* perpetual motion. Balla's trapeze-like frame within a frame, the repeated twist of the wrist, the sharply combed paint surface, the blur of speed capture *The Hands of the Violinist* in a depicted instant and make it long endure.

This is a figurative collection. Its presence is metropolitan, knowing: the wind that sweeps through Severini's bright winter *Boulevard* (1910–11); the circus-like poise of the horses in Marini's relief *Quadriga* (1942); the sheets becoming shrouds in Guttuso's *Death of a Hero* (1953); even the patient nudes who watch from their doll's house windows in Campigli's *Il Belvedere* (1930). That the collection is

figurative is surely true of the two portraits: Boccioni's *Modern Idol*'s eyes are as blazing fierce as the eyes of Modigliani's *Dr Francois Brabander* (1918) are distant and aqueous.

They bring into this most English, calmly proportioned house not the light of the Italian Renaissance, nor of Rome, Venice, Tuscany or Puglia, but the new light of urban Italy.

The Tate Gallery, having had key works from the Estorick Collection on long-term loan for nearly ten years, wished to keep them;[104] the Italian government showed interest in purchasing the collection entire in 1979. Remembering the Gallatin Collection, Eric Estorick resisted and before he died in 1993 donated his Italian works to a trust administered by his children, Michael and Isobel Estorick, who brought them to their present home in Canonbury Square, within earshot of the 'mighty noise'[105] of the city's traffic that was the starting point of Marinetti's manifesto a century before.

FAN MUSEUM

12 Grooms Hill, Greenwich, London SE10 8ER
Tel. 020 8305 1441
www.fan-museum.org

A flock of fans at rest; fashion's animation holding its breath

Useful, decorative, provocative, protective, fans have been used for at least four thousand years, the earliest known fan, made of ivory and ostrich feathers, having been found in Tutankhamun's tomb. Hélène Alexander has collected more than two thousand. They come from China and Japan, Macao and India, but the main emphasis is on European fans of the 18th and 19th centuries. Through them this museum tells the history of fans.

The elements of the folding fan are few – leaf, rib, guards, sticks, head – but the range of materials is considerable. Here are sticks and handles of ivory, mother-of-pearl, bone, tortoiseshell. Here are leaves of vellum, lace, silk, cotton and paper-thin kid.

On them are galleries of paintings: a

landscape in Martinique by Gauguin (1887); a fine copy of *Bacchus and Ariadne* by Guido Reni, of particular interest since the original, once owned by Charles I, was destroyed by a subsequent owner on the grounds that it was too lascivious; a copy of Raphael's *Diana and Endymion.*

Fans depicting topographical subjects sold well to those on the Grand Tour: scenes of the Piazza San Marco (*c.* 1750–60), the eruption of Mount Vesuvius (1767), the Parthenon (1785). The detail of historical and mythological subjects (the siege of St Omer, *c.* 1678, the Grand Dauphin's twentieth birthday, *c.* 1681) provided reading material to while away bored hours. There are fans to commemorate weddings and births, fans as mementoes, fans as love tokens. There are fans of cool simplicity (the Japanese *Waterfall of Wisteria*, Edo Period, *c.* 1860), fans with two faces, Chinese fans with poems backed by landscapes and jewelled fans such as that painted by Cesare Dell'Acqua, a wedding present to Stephanie of Belgium in 1881, from her relations, encased in solid gold and encrusted with 1,500 rose diamonds.

The ultimate fan in the collection is a confection of mother-of-pearl and bird-of-paradise feathers, complete with head and beak, a fan that could be straight out of a portrait by Sargent or Boldini: extravagance, beauty and utility in a single pass.

FASHION AND TEXTILE MUSEUM *

83 Bermondsey Street, Bermondsey, London SE1 3XF
Tel. 020 7403 0222
www.ftmlondon.org

Moving display of how our dreams today are clothed, in a building of many colours

There are not many buildings in London that are rendered and painted raspberry pink and sherbet yellow, as is this museum. But then there are not many women in the world like Zandra Rhodes, who founded it.

This designer has been outfacing peacocks for thirty-five years with hair, make-up and clothes of turquoise, mauve, violet and fuchsia.

She opened her museum in 2003, in a former cash-and-carry warehouse in Bermondsey. To convert it she commissioned Ricardo Legorreta, one of Mexico's most exciting architects. He shared her love of exotic and dramatic colour and has created the perfect stage for this collection of the best of European and American fashion and textile design, by designers from Emanuel Ungaro, Paco Rabanne and Mary Quant in the 1960s, to Issey Miyake, Alexander McQueen and John Galliano today, at the centre of which are 3,000 of Zandra Rhodes's designs, and an archive of her drawings and materials with their characteristic use of nearly typographical line, reminiscent of a kind of gigantic, Miró-like Pitman's shorthand, and wonderful petal-like cutting.

From the moment you go through the bright pink arch of the entrance, Legorreta and Rhodes dazzle you, just as they intend. Above your head is a deep indigo barrelled ceiling; beneath your feet is a terrazzo floor inlaid with scattered gemmy stars.[106] Ahead of you is a canary yellow ramp that leads up and into the cavern of the main gallery and the museum's *coup de théâtre*: dresses, spot-lit, suspended several feet above the ground on wires that gently rotate.[107]

Heretofore even the best fashion collections (the Victoria and Albert Museum, the Museum of Costume, the Ulster Museum, all q.v.) have exhibited their clothes on solid, static mannequins. These may be adequate for displaying uniforms and other tailored costumes but they do nothing for clothes that have been designed to move on and with a body, and to suggest shape rather than confine it.

Much of women's fashion in the late 20th century, away from the office, has stressed simplicity and movement, and has sought to complement, and delight in, the grace of the body. For such designers as Christian Lacroix, Guy Laroche, Amanda Wakeley and Zandra Rhodes herself, these delicate, rotating mannequins are a magical way to exhibit dresses.

Zandra Rhodes and Ricardo Legorreta:
outfacing peacocks at the Fashion and Textile
Museum

The green chiffon of Rhodes's favourite dress, owned by Jackie Kennedy and her sister Lee Radziwill, is sheer as a waterfall; Vera Wang's silk tulle wedding dress is a momentarily held and captured breath; John Galliano's romantic shift of mousseline, bias cut, is, in his words, 'light as air, as pale as snow'. There are famous dresses here (Mary Quant's black-and-white Daisy Dress, which was the emblem of Swinging London in the 1960s); crazy dresses (Paco Rabanne's mini, decorated with mother-of-pearl discs); ugly dresses (a vast silver duvet in which you could lose the ugliest sister); and a dress of supreme elegance (Valentino's 1966 ostrich-feather coat over an azalea pink empire-cut dress).

Christian Lacroix has written that the aim of couture is to reveal the body by changing its silhouette, by cutting, by line, by texture, in effect making a dress 'a moving sculpture'. In an exhibition of this range and variety there are designs not entirely suited to these mannequins. The more architectural lines of Courrèges, Hardy Amies or Balmain and the severities of Nicole Farhi or Giorgio Armani stand aloof. But dresses like Zac Posen's *Circe*, that hark back to classical sculpture, and James Galanos's, that drift over a leotard, convey the glamour of couture and of this museum.

The museum has a serious intent: to provide a research collection and archive for the next generation of designers, and a textile studio in which the design process, from materials to cutting and finishing, can be studied. It is a worthy enterprise but one that does not forswear the playful high spirits of the burst of colour that Legorreta's building brings to Bermondsey, or of the flamingo pink and tortilla orange that Rhodes herself brings to couture.

FLEMING COLLECTION *

13 Berkeley Street, London w1j 8du
Tel. 020 7409 5730
www.flemingcollection.co.uk/

Scottish art at its bright best

Scottish art is not well represented in English public galleries. The Fleming Collection, with its strong coverage of the work of Scottish artists from Ramsay, Raeburn and Alexander Nasmyth to the present day, begins to fill that gap.

Its provenance is unusual: it is a collection put together by a bank for the enjoyment of its employees that is now a public collection for the enjoyment of all; a collection formed by the tastes and enthusiasms of three individuals[108] untrammelled by trustees or purchasing committees.

In the 1970s and '80s corporations started to collect works of art. Their motives for doing so varied. Some, like British Rail, considered that paintings were assets whose capital appreciation would outperform the Stock Market. The origins of Flemings's collection were less calculated.

In 1968 David Donald, a director of Flemings, had suggested that some paintings would relieve the starkness of their new City offices. In view of the bank's roots in Dundee it was agreed that the paintings should be by Scottish artists or of Scottish scenes. At first David Donald bought cautiously: Victorian landscapes and seascapes by William McTaggart, John Knox and Walter Hugh Paton, and Thomas Faed's elegy to the Highland Clearances, *The Last of the Clan*. Gaining confidence, he started to suit himself. He bought paintings by the Glasgow Boys (E. A. Walton, E. A. Hornel, Sir John Lavery, Arthur Melville, Joseph Crawhall, a lovely pastel by George Henry). He assembled a solid collection of the Colourists: paintings by Peploe from his years in France (1907–12) and still lifes from the 1920s; Iona landscapes by Cadell; and early portraits and still lifes by J. D. Fergusson that do him scant justice.

When Donald retired in 1984 the collection comprised over a thousand paintings. For the next twelve years it was the responsibility of another of Fleming's executives, Bill Smith, who concentrated on acquiring the work of 20th-century artists, notably those who made up the loose Edinburgh School (Anne Redpath, William Gillies, John Maxwell in the 1930s and '40s, and their successors Robin Philipson, William Baillie, Elizabeth Blackadder and Anne Redpath's son, David Michie) and those trained at Glasgow School of Art in the early 1980s, Ken Currie, Peter Howson, Steven Campbell (known as the New Glasgow Boys). As the collection grew and more of it was exhibited in the public spaces at Fleming's new offices in Copthall Avenue it gradually evolved into a public collection. Bill Smith began consciously to fill gaps, adding a landscape by Alexander Nasmyth from the early 19th century, and a characteristically dark and theatrical scene by James Pryde.

In 2002, with Fleming's having been taken over by the Chase Manhattan Corporation and the collection bought back by the Fleming-Wyford Art Foundation, the collection was moved to a new gallery in Berkeley Street in Mayfair. Its plate-glass frontage and location give the misleading impression that here might be another commercial gallery. It consists of two small spaces, ground floor and basement, able to show only a fraction of the multifaceted collection at any one time in its changing exhibitions. Here is a Raeburn, of *Dr Alexander Lindsay of Pinkieburn*, from his prime years in the 1790s, with that glowing back lighting that raises the heart. Here too is a Ramsay of *An Officer* (unnamed), in uniform. Ramsay was, as Walpole noted, 'formed to paint women'. His studies of men were penetrating when their subjects were men of affairs or men of the Enlightenment purple (*Jean-Jacques Rousseau* or *David Hume*, both 1766).[109] This young man exhibits neither beauty nor intellect but the picture demonstrates Ramsay's mastery of cross-hatching, learnt from the pastels of Maurice de la Tour, giving a dense, velvet texture to his skin tones.

The collection gives an opportunity to study

in some detail the work of three Scottish artists: Sir David Wilkie, Sir David Young Cameron and Anne Redpath.

As with Romney's, Wilkie's sketches and drawings change the way in which you look at his finished oils. He was a fluid, fast draughtsman who could catch, in a line, the curve of an arm, the weight of an elbow, the turn of a neck. This fluency is clear in the small still-lifes that are tucked into his major narrative oils, of plates and pans, jars, hats, furniture, books and papers.

The Camerons are distinguished by architectural clarity whether in the townscapes (*Old Paris*, *c.*1911) or the landscapes (*The Hills of Ross*, *c.*1934, or the magnificent, moody *Boddin*, *Angus*, *c.*1911).

The twenty-six Redpaths emphasise the artist's mastery of white. It glows, phosphorescent, through her richer colours; it holds within it all her familiar tones (blues, pinks, greys). In *House on a Hill* she weaves it through the tumble of colours and brushstrokes that convey the hill. We are reminded that her father was a designer of tweeds.

This is not a Scottish national collection in miniature. There are few abstract works here; none by William Gear; few portraits; no work by Robert Scott Lauder, which is surprising since it was his teaching as co-director of the Trustees' Academy in Edinburgh in the 1850s that influenced Scottish painting for the next generations. Those of his pupils who stayed in Scotland (William McTaggart, George Paul Chalmers, John McWhirter) are here; those who sought their fortunes in London, the 'London Scottish' (William Quiller Orchardson, John Pettie, Thomas Graham), are not.

The collection reaffirms the qualities of reputations that may have dimmed: those of William Johnstone and William McCance. It confirms certain strengths in Scottish painting: landscapes (disparate views of Arran by John Knox, *c.*1820, and John McWhirter, 1891, and a watercolour, *A Stormy Day on the Fife Coast*, 1889, by James Watterston Herald in which wind and wet sheet across the scene); decorative painting (Elizabeth Blackadder,

Craigie Aitchison, John Maxwell and John Bellany); and a rich use of colour (John Houston, Robin Philipson, Joan Eardley, Barbara Rae).

This is a collection that should lead non-Scottish visitors back to the great galleries of Edinburgh and Glasgow and to the fine collections of Scottish painting in Aberdeen, Perth and Kirkcaldy; or, indeed, Scottish visitors, unaware of what they had missed.

FOUNDLING MUSEUM *

40 Brunswick Square, London WC1N 1AZ
Tel. 020 7841 3600
www.coram.org.uk/heritage/museum.htm

London's first public art gallery, founded to raise money for an 18th-century orphanage, with the help of Hogarth and Gainsborough and Handel's Messiah

In mid-18th-century London three-quarters of all children died before they were five years old. In workhouses the rate of child mortality was nearer 90 per cent. There was only one orphanage, Christ's Hospital, and that did not accept illegitimate children.[110] When Thomas Coram, a shipwright, retired to London in 1719 after twenty-six years working in Massachusetts, he was horrified by the sight of infants abandoned in the streets.[111] In the twenty years that followed the passing of the Poor Law in 1722, he lobbied and petitioned for the establishment of a foundling hospital, assisted by William Hogarth, the physician Dr Richard Mead and others, until in 1739 George II yielded and granted a royal charter. Fifty-six acres of Bloomsbury Fields were purchased and a hospital designed by Theodore Jacobsen was built, opening in 1745.

At once the demand for places exceeded the supply, despite the introduction of a system of entry by means of a random ballot. By 1752 the hospital housed 600 children. Four years later Parliament voted £10,000 for the hospital but attached a condition: that all children offered should be accepted. The hospital was overwhelmed. The condition was lifted in

1760, but not before the mortality rate had risen to 70 per cent and the hospital had acquired a reputation for encouraging loose morals.

Following Coram's death in 1751, the burden of raising money for the hospital was taken up by the most energetic governors, notably Hogarth and George Frederick Handel. Handel conducted a benefit concert in 1749, for which he composed the *Foundling Hospital Anthem* ('Blessed are they that considereth the poor'). The following year he conducted the first benefit performance of his *Messiah*, playing the organ[112] that he had given to the hospital. Performances of the *Messiah* became an annual tradition and by his death had raised over £8,000.[113]

Hogarth's initiative proved even more significant. By persuading leading artists to follow his lead and donate paintings, he turned the hospital into a hugely successful public art gallery. Francis Hayman, Joseph Highmore and James Wills joined him in painting biblical scenes that illustrated aspects of 'the foundling'.[114] These were exhibited in the hospital's Court Room, in which meetings of the Governors were held. Hung between them, within gilded plaster roundels, a further eight, smaller, paintings of London's other hospitals were donated by Thomas Gainsborough, Samuel Wale, Edward Haytley and Richard Wilson.[115] John Michael Rysbrack presented a marble relief of *Charity*, set into the chimneypiece, and Allan Ramsay gave a superb portrait of *Dr Richard Mead*. In return, all (with the exceptions of the 21-year-old Gainsborough, Wale and Wills) were elected Governors of the hospital. The rich and the fashionable came to see the paintings in what was the first public picture gallery in London, and stayed to make donations.[116]

The original hospital was demolished in 1926 and the children moved, first to Surrey and then to Hertfordshire, but in 1937 a new building was erected in Brunswick Square. In it the Court Room and Picture Gallery, with their original ceilings, were remade and this unusual collection of 18th-century paintings rehung. In addition to the above there are works by Benjamin West and John Singleton Copley; a *Landscape with Figures* by George Lambert; an altarpiece, depicting *The Adoration of the Magi*, originally in the hospital chapel, by Andrea Casali; and a collection of portraits of people connected with the hospital. It includes works by Francis Cotes, Thomas Hudson, Thomas Phillips and Sir Joshua Reynolds, the latter being an indifferent portrait of the *2nd Earl of Dartmouth*, vice-president of the hospital 1755–1801.

To see Gainsborough's first major commission (and Hayman and Highmore atypically tackling biblical narrative subjects) would be interesting enough, but here also are two outstanding Hogarths. In *The March of the Guards to Finchley* (1749) he packs into one canvas as much social, political and religious satire as are in the six paintings of *Marriage à la Mode* (1743). In it Hogarth contrasts the upstanding Protestant Guards marching to defend London with the drunken, debauched Jacobites who sympathised with the Young Pretender. Hogarth's anti-Jacobite, anti-Catholic prejudices are displayed with vigour.

His painting of *Moses Brought Before Pharaoh's Daughter* (1746) has running through it a sinuous line that connects the whispering servant, the handmaiden, Pharaoh's daughter – her arm outstretched to the uncertain child Moses, clutching his mother's skirt – and, through her inclined head, the smoke from the burning pyre, a warning of the destruction that the revelation of the secret of Moses's true identity could bring. It is a line of beauty and of grace that exemplifies the aesthetic theory that Hogarth describes in *The Analysis of Beauty* (1753).

The contrast between Ramsay's portrait of *Dr Mead* and Hogarth's of *Thomas Coram* is even more memorable. In them, both artists are at their best, but they take very different approaches to the grand full-length baroque portrait. Ramsay, recently returned from his first visit to Italy at the start of his career,

Founder of the Foundling Hospital: Captain Thomas Coram *by William Hogarth*

The Royal Charter

Painted and given by W. Hogarth. 1740.

puts everything into the magisterial pose; the classical allusions (the alcove, the statue of Hygeia, goddess of health); the depth of colour in the scarlet drapery and tablecloth; and Mead's dark brown robe, which sets off the white lace at his neck and wrist and his finely powdered wig. At the centre is Ramsay's depiction of the doctor's imposing face, his skin rendered matt, as if in pastel, by Ramsay's cross-hatching brushwork,[117] his gaze penetrating. It is a portrait that challenges the popular view, for which much evidence exists, that Ramsay was primarily a portraitist of women.

Hogarth subverts these conventions in his portrait of Coram. All the elements with which Reynolds habitually constructed his portraits are here: the classical pillar, the draped curtain, the distant seascape, the still life of documents and seal on the table, the symbolism of the globe and the hat.[118] But Hogarth turns them on their heads, deploying them not to describe dignity and hauteur but to capture Coram's character which, in the opinion of his friend Dr John Brocklesby, was full of 'cheerfulness, frankness, warmth, affection and great simplicity of manners'. Hogarth paints him sitting solidly in his chair, his bandy legs wide apart. His face is ruddy; he has no wig, just a tumble of white hair. His strong, veined hand grasps a pair of gloves. His scarlet coat is fustian, serviceable, cut not for fashion but to protect him from the weather. The whole captures the straightforward and generous nature of the man.

The museum also honours the contribution of Handel, whose terracotta bust by Louis-François Roubiliac is here,[119] as are important Handel memorabilia from the Gerald Coke Handel Collection: early printed editions and manuscript copies of his music, libretti of his operas and oratorios, his will and a score of the *Foundling Hospital Anthem*, written by his principal music copyist with numerous amendments and revisions in Handel's hand.

The museum does not lose sight of the motive behind the efforts of Coram, Hogarth, Handel and many others since: to provide shelter, care and education for orphaned and abandoned children. As well as an archive of documents, photographs and, recently, the beginnings of an oral history in the form of interviews with children brought up in the hospital, there are many of the original petitions submitted by mothers desperate to gain admission for their children. More poignant still are the tokens left by mothers as a means of identification in case they were ever in a position to return and reclaim their children. The modesty of these buttons, metal name tags, lockets, crucifixes, coins, corners of embroidery (none reclaimed) will catch the breath of any parent.

Beside the museum, which was redesigned and reopened in 2004, is the Coram Community Campus. This centre provides help, care and support for the hundreds of deprived or traumatised children who continue to be referred to the Coram Family nearly three hundred years after Thomas Coram first looked in horror upon the condition of the children on London's streets.

FREUD MUSEUM **

20 Maresfield Gardens, London NW3 5SX
Tel. 020 7435 2002
www.freud.org.uk/

The home and possessions of the founder of psychoanalysis and his daughter Anna

Twenty Maresfield Gardens is a house of solid Hampstead respectability, one of three built for sale by James Tomblin and described in the auctioneer's brochure as 'A very fine and well planned modern freehold residence . . . enjoying a delightful sunny aspect with splendidly proportioned lofty rooms'.

This was Sigmund Freud's final home, to which he came in 1938 when he and his family had to flee Austria after the Anschluss[120] in 1938. After his death the following year his widow Martha and Anna his daughter continued to live here and kept the house, and Freud's study and consulting room, exactly as he had left them: the same furniture, the same books on the shelves, the same objects on the desk.

The house is red brick, designed in a mock Queen Anne style then fashionable in Hampstead. Inside there are oriental rugs on the polished wooden floors, bookshelves, glass cabinets, curtains of velvet and chenille, and good clocks and mirrors.

As you enter, you are confronted by a print of Moses holding the sacred tablets of the Commandments[121] above his head. Freud, having given the world a (scientific) law, identified with Moses. He completed his book *Moses and Monotheism*[122] at Maresfield Gardens.

Freud's surroundings were of the utmost importance to him. Before the family left Vienna the position of every object in his study was recorded so that his maid, Paula Fichtl, could recreate it exactly in London. On arrival he wrote to his friend and analysand Jeanne Lampl de Groot, 'All the Egyptians, Chinese and Greeks have arrived, have stood up to the journey with very little damage, and look more impressive here than in Berggasse.'[123] These were the objects from his collection of antiquities which he kept lined up on his desk in front of him and that he used as aids and inspiration during sessions with his patients.

Although he sold many[124] of his books before he left Vienna he was determined to save his collection of rings, scarabs and statuettes, his friend Princess Marie Bonaparte paying the Nazi authorities a 25 per cent 'tax' to do so. He had been collecting for forty years, since his father's death in 1896. For him objects were 'a source of exceptional renewal and comfort'.[125] He was a knowledgeable but not systematic collector, acquiring objects for their symbolic and aesthetic value rather than for reasons of archaeological rarity or mint condition. For him, they were a metaphor, and a central part of the psychoanalytical process: 'The psychoanalyst, like the archaeologist in his excavations, must uncover layer after layer of the patient's psyche, before coming to the deepest, most valuable treasures.'[126]

On his desk, in addition to several ashtrays, a cigar box and an inkstand, are two rows of more than forty figures from his collection. In the centre is the small bronze *Pallas Athena* (4½ inches high, Roman, 1st or 2nd century AD after a Greek original, 5th century BC), the goddess of wisdom and war. On her breastplate is an image of the 'decapitated, serpent-tressed head of Medusa'. To Freud decapitation signified castration. This was his talisman, the only piece he was determined not to lose, and so he arranged for Princess Marie Bonaparte to smuggle it out of Austria via Paris.

The poet Hilda Doolittle was a patient of Freud's in 1933 and 1934. She recalled being handed Pallas Athena by him with the words '"This is my favourite" . . . He held the object toward me . . . One hand was extended as if holding a staff or rod. "She is perfect," he said, "only she has lost her spear." I did not say anything. He knew I loved Greece.'[127]

Beside Pallas Athena was a figure of the Baboon of Thoth, the god of intellectual pursuits who conflates instinct and intellect, whom Freud would frequently stroke; a two-headed balsamarium[128] (3rd century bronze, Etruscan) with the head of a male satyr and the body of a female maenad; and a figure of Imhotep, the Egyptian architect and sage who had the healing power of dreams – in sum, a patron of intellect, a figure who can see both ways, a dualist.

Before the desk is Freud's chair, a strange design by architect Felix Augenfeld. It has a narrow, straight back and an upright pin-headrest as if sculpted by Henry Moore. On the far side of the desk is the couch, one of the most resonant pieces of furniture in the world, locus of something that has become part science, part religion, part medicine, part psychiatry, part confessional. On it is a rug of rich blues and reds, woven by one of the tribes of the Qashqa'i Confederacy in western Iran, its deep pile making it into a flying carpet for the retelling of dreams. On the desk are Freud's spectacles, set down as if waiting for his return.

This is the theatre in which Freud worked, listening to his last four patients in 1938–9. Around it are ranged the books that shaped him: by Flinders Petrie and Heinrich

Schliemann; Lord Macaulay and H. G. Wells; Goethe and Shakespeare; Dante and Dostoevsky; Stefan Zweig and Thomas Mann. From their shelves all face the desk and the couch.

Freud's life spans modern archaeology. When he was born in 1856 Troy was a myth.[129] By the time he died in 1939 archaeology had become a science.

This is a shrine, a site at which the ley lines of the 20th-century's psyche cross and let loose our dreams, fears, desires and nightmares, in a red-brick house of solid respectability.

GEFFRYE MUSEUM ***

136 Kingsland Road, Shoreditch,
London E2 8EA
Tel. 020 7739 9893
www.geffrye-museum.org.uk

Fine rhythmic setting for a history of domestic design arranged through room sets

The collector Henry Francis du Pont, founder of Winterthur in Connecticut, maintained that you could 'only understand furniture in its setting'. Among British museums that view has been adopted by the Victoria and Albert Museum (q.v.), the American Museum in Britain (q.v.) and at the Geffrye Museum.

In twelve period rooms here is a chronology of English furniture design, and of interior decoration, over the past 400 years, from the oak panelling and furniture of 1600 to the London loft conversions of today.

The museum buildings are former almshouses, built in 1714 with a bequest from Sir Robert Geffrye, a former master of the Ironmongers' Company and Lord Mayor of London. They are set back from the traffic that grinds along Kingsland Road between Dalston and Shoreditch, around three sides of a garden, shaded by tall plane trees. When the London County Council bought the houses and the land from the Ironmongers' Company in 1910, such leading members of the Arts and Crafts movement as C. R. Ashbee, C. F. A. Voysey and M. H. Baillie Scott lobbied the council to create in them a woodwork and furniture museum that would educate and inspire the craftsmen of the furniture industry, then centred on the surrounding area. When the industry declined and largely moved out of the area in the 1930s, the focus of the museum was redirected from craft to general education.

The museum's rooms are typical of the taste of the urban middle class of each period. The furniture and objects in them are authentic, but this is not a collection of pieces by the great furniture makers or designers. You will look in vain for signature works by John Channon, Thomas Chippendale, James Moore, Robert Adam, William Ince and Thomas Mayhew. For these you should visit, respectively, Temple Newsam, Harewood House, Chatsworth and Soho House (all q.v.), and Nostell Priory, West Yorkshire. Instead here is quotidian furniture that demonstrates the qualities, and sometimes the limitations, of English furniture making.

In the early 17th century Britain lagged behind the Dutch and the French. An Antwerp merchant, Van Meteren, Consul in London, observed that the English did not have 'so much furniture or unnecessary house ornaments' as Dutch people.[130]

The development of parquetry and marquetry, imported from the Continent, in which such contrasting woods as holly and sycamore were inlaid into oak, as in the *c.*1620 livery cupboard in the misnamed Elizabethan and Jacobean Room, was staunched by the puritan taste of the Commonwealth but, with the Restoration in 1660, Britain entered a golden age of furniture design and architecture that extended until the 1830s.

Town houses became smaller; furniture lighter and more compact, veneered and decorated with ivory and mother of pearl, and with woods imported from America, the Far East and, in the early 18th century, from the West Indies. The 1710 staircase here, with its fine handrail, panelling and spiral-turned balusters, shows how the influence of Grinling Gibbons, Master Carver to Charles II (introduced to him by the diarist John Evelyn),[131]

The Regency Room at the Geffrye Museum

spread. The middle classes could not aspire to carving of the lightness and delicacy that Gibbons achieved in such soft, close-grained woods as lime or pear, or to the ornamentation of William Kent in the early 18th century, but they could imitate fashions and did so with the help of books and directories (such as *Treasury of Designs*, Batty and Thomas Langley, 1740; *The Gentleman and Cabinet-maker's Director*, Thomas Chippendale, 1754; *One Hundred and Fifty New Designs*, Thomas Johnson (1755); and *The Cabinet-maker and Upholsterer's Guide*, George Hepplewhite, 1788), as these rooms bear witness, with ladder-back chairs in the style of Chippendale (1760), and a pair of mahogany shield-back chairs in the style of Hepplewhite.

The museum has some fine pieces (the 1652 veneered and engraved cabinet that belonged to John Evelyn; the walnut writing cabinet, *c.*1690, made by the Huguenot John Guillbaud, who worked at Long Acre at the sign of 'The Crown and Looking Glasse' and, like his father-in-law Jean Pelletier, supplied furniture to the royal palaces of William and Mary)[132] but its strengths are in the unexceptional, and the opportunity offered here to observe the flux of fashion and the rise of the cabinet maker, the upholsterer and the cane-chair maker. An Introductory Gallery on the Chair allows you to see the techniques, processes and materials, from the carving of oak (1620) to the beech-veneered plywood of Jasper Morrison (1989).

Whereas the Victoria and Albert Museum traces the development of furniture, in its English Galleries, through the bed, the Geffrye's focus is on the chair. The simplicity of the ebonised beech chair upholstered in red leather (1877), by the Art and Crafts designer E. W. Godwin, and of the armchair designed by Philip Webb for Morris, Marshall, Faulkner and Company (1866) leads into the museum's 20th-century rooms which, with the 18th-century rooms, are its strongest. Here are pieces by the finest 20th-century British designers (C. F. A. Voysey, Ambrose Heal, Trevor Chinn) and the best design companies (Gordon Russell, Heal, Conran), set in the context of the European designers who influenced them (Vico Magistretti, Giancarlo Piretti, Arne Jacobsen). Context is provided by the ceramics of Susie Cooper and Keith Murray, as it is in earlier rooms by portraits and paintings by Cornelius Johnson, Mary Beale, Arthur Devis, Frank Holl, C. R. Leslie.

Outside, a herb garden, opened in 1992, and a series of period garden rooms (1998), like the museum itself, arise out of the history of the surrounding area. Nicholas Culpeper had a nursery in Spitalfields in which he grew herbs for medicines in the 17th century and Thomas Fairchild, author of *The City Gardener* (1772), had a nursery on the far side of Kingsland Road, in Hoxton.

George Hepplewhite, in the preface to *The Cabinet-maker and Upholsterer's Guide*, wrote that 'To unite elegance and utility, and blend the useful with the agreeable, has ever been considered a difficult, but an honourable task' – a motto admirably suited to the Geffrye.

GILBERT COLLECTION **

Somerset House, Strand, London WC2R 1LA
Tel. 020 7420 9400
www.gilbert-collection.org.uk

Highly finished decoration in precious metals and stones; boxes of delight

Today museums do not value silver and jewellery as greatly as painting and sculpture. It was not always thus. John Evelyn records in his diary being allowed to handle cameos, brooches, miniatures and small sculptures the better to appreciate them when visiting Charles II's 'cabinet and closet of rarities' in the King's Privy Lodgings at Whitehall.[133]

Evelyn records 'an ancient woman, who made these lodgings cleane, and had all the keyes, let me in at pleasure, for a small reward, by the means of a friend' so that he could examine 'divers curious clocks, Watches and Pendulo of exquisite work, and other Curiosities'. Now, thanks to Sir Arthur Gilbert, access to the treasure chest that is the Gilbert

Collection at Somerset House is somewhat easier. Nevertheless the silver, gold, miniatures, gold boxes, *pietra dura* and micromosaics would please any monarch.

Sir Arthur, then plain Mr, a British émigré real estate entrepreneur in California, began to collect English 18th- and 19th-century silver and Italian micromosaics in the 1960s with a jackdaw's eye. He scorned understatement. Enchanted to discover Roman micromosaics (a term he coined as snappier than *mosaico in piccolo*), he acquired more than two hundred examples: large pictures, tables, urns, jewellery, snuffboxes.

He was dazzled by the technique of the Vatican mosaic workshops in the early 19th century and of masters such as Giacomo Raffaeli[134] and Benedetto Boschetti, who could concentrate 1,400 tesserae to the square inch. Michelangelo Barberi's *The Flora of the Two Sicilies* for Tsar Nicholas I (*c.* 1850) is beautiful, but whether anything is gained by translating into stone Stubbs's *Tigress Lying Below Rocks* (the original is at Blenheim Palace, q.v.) is doubtful.

In theory the same criticism could be made of the *pietra dura* pieces in which hard stones (marble, agate, chalcedony, alabaster, amethyst, jasper, lapis lazuli) are manipulated to depict petals, leaves or birds' wings. The textures and colours of the stones, mottled, smoky, speckled, offer strange, non-naturalistic effects of light, shade and perspective that, at best, result in the glorious floral still lifes of the panels in the clock cabinet by Giovanni Battista Foggini (Florence), at worst the sentimental kitsch of *Two Little Tykes* (a boy and a dog) by Mario Montelatici.

The flamboyance of Gilbert's taste is most happily expressed in his 18th-century English silver collection. Ignoring the more chaste delights of Robert Adam, Gilbert put together a dazzling display of the work of Paul de Lamerie, Paul Storr, Digby Scott and Benjamin Smith in the tradition that stemmed from the Huguenot refugee silversmiths who came to London after the St Bartholomew Day Massacre of 1666 and the Edict of Nantes in 1685: David Willaume, Pierre Harache, Pierre

Platel. The latter was de Lamerie's master.

The Gilbert Collection has examples of de Lamerie's work from all stages of his career: the relatively plain early work (a pair of sconces, 1717, and a tureen, 1722–3); increasingly elaborate commissions for Robert Walpole (a pair of candelabra, 1722–3) and for Sir John Brownlow at Belton (a dress table mirror, *c.* 1732); and the majesty of his ewer and dish for the 6th Earl of Monmouth (1742–3) and the cup and ewer in silver gilt, of the same year, a climax of swirling vines around two figures of the infant Bacchus, rising to a mound of grapes topped by a salamander.

Fifty years later Paul Storr was making pieces for equally illustrious collectors: a ewer and basin, and a basket, for William Beckford at Fonthill (1790–98), a fourteen-piece dinner service for the 12th Duke of Norfolk (1816–18) and a silver-gilt tankard representing *The Drunkenness of Silenus*, with another infant Bacchus on the cover.

George IV was a major patron, buying from Rundell, Bridge and Rundell 'at the sign of the golden salmon' in Ludgate Hill. Philip Rundell and John Bridge were salesmen rather than designers and subcontracted modelling to Edward Farrell, John Flaxman and others to recreate the designs of Piranesi. In 1811, the year after he became Prince Regent, George ordered a grand service from Rundell's in honour of the birthday of his father George III. The cost was £70,000.

Whichever way you turn in this collection you are dazzled, by the pierced and gilded silver of the iconostasis gates presented by Catherine the Great to the Pechersk monastery in Kiev in 1784, the only such gates outside Russia or the Ukraine, or the portrait miniatures in enamel, copper and gesso by Henry Bowe,[135] or the 18th-century snuffboxes, 220 of them. One group, of Meissen porcelain, was designed by Johann Friedrich Böttger and Christian Friedrich Herolt. There is a box in gold and tortoiseshell, given by Philip V of Spain to his wife, Isabella Farnese of Parma, and a group of six boxes designed by Jean Guillaume Kruger for Frederick the

Great, c.1775. The simple ones are in gold, agate and diamonds, or gold, black marble and hard stones. The most elaborate is in gold, hard stones, diamonds, rubies, emeralds, glass and foil, a fantasy of flowers – though whether it is an exhausting virtuosic gem or a thing of beauty is moot.

The architects Inskip and Jenkins, who converted this wing of Somerset House in 2000, have brought life to Sir William Chambers's great courtyard. In the Gilbert galleries they have attempted to offset the blaze of its treasures by exposing the brickwork of the walls. This attempted austerity is not helped by the exclusion of any daylight, making the displays as exhausting on the eye as they are oversweet on the teeth.

A hoard of precious metal and jewellery cannot be self-effacing, but less of the collection might have been more. The oldest object here suggests this. It is a ewer from Bronze Age Anatolia, c. 2500 BC, raised from a single sheet of gold, embossed with a simple, regular pattern, chased and chaste with, on its base, a swastika, the ancient symbol of good fortune.

GUILDHALL ART GALLERY
**

Guildhall Yard, London EC2P 2EJ
Tel. 020 7332 3700
www.guildhall-art-gallery.org.uk

The London Corporation's own collection: civic portraits, Victorian painting and Matthew Smith

You might expect a fine art collection assembled by a body as conscious of its own history and dignity as the Corporation of the City of London to be long on custom and ceremony. The Guildhall does not disappoint, with its formidable array of portraits of monarchs – by Charles Jervas (George II), Allan Ramsay (George III[136] and Queen Charlotte) and Sir George Hayter (a young Queen Victoria) – of representations of London and of its Lord Mayors in their fig and pomp.

This is the seed of the collection. After

the Great Fire of London in 1666 twenty-two judges settled the disputes and claims that arose. To thank them the Corporation commissioned John Michael Wright to paint their portraits, which were hung in their Guildhall. Less predictable, perhaps, is its comprehensive selection of Victorian paintings and sculpture and its studio collection of Matthew Smith, a painter who is now somewhat overlooked but who was described by Roger Fry as 'pushing to the farthest limits the essentially modern view of the functional as opposed to the ornamental role played by colour in pictorial design'[137] and, more simply, by Augustus John as 'one of the most brilliant and individual figures in modern English painting'.[138] Smith's images of nudes and flowers are delightfully incongruous here. They provide a corrective to the well-intentioned, public-spirited pomposity of Alderman John Boydell, who gave the City his art collection, 'First, to show my respect for the Corporation and my fellow citizens. Secondly, to give pleasure to the public, and Foreigners in general. Thirdly, to be of service to the Artists, by shewing their works to the greatest advantage, and Fourthly, for the mere purpose of pleasing myself.'[139]

John Boydell[140] (1719–1804) was an engraver who made a fortune publishing and exporting prints of London and of scenes from British history, being elected Lord Mayor in 1790. He proceeded to open a Shakespeare Gallery in Pall Mall exhibiting the paintings he commissioned from, among others, Reynolds, Romney, Fuseli, Wright of Derby and Angelica Kauffmann. The collection here features the large historical paintings he favoured: Richard Paton's *The Relief of Gibraltar*; Robert Dodd's *Rodney's Victory at La Grasse, off Dominica*; John Opie's *The Murder of Rizzio* and John Singleton Copley's monumental *The Siege of Gibraltar*.

The paintings of London, from the 17th century to the present day, complement the large collection in the Museum of London (q.v.). There are 18th-century views by Samuel Scott and William Marlow; an unusual *Allegory of London* by Sir James Thornhill (1725–7), the central panel in the Aldermen's Court Room;

and a moving portrait of London in pain, *The Demolition Squad* (1941) by William Roberts. The pick of these is a series of engravings by Wenceslaus Hollar showing London before and after the Great Fire: Whitehall in 1647 with Inigo Jones's Banqueting Hall rising; the Piazza in Covent Garden *c.*1650; and an aerial map of central London 'and the suburbs thereof . . . since the last sad accident of fire'.[141]

The collection charms most when it departs from its core brief. Much of the Victorian collection was bequeathed in 1902 by Charles Gassiot, a City importer of port and sherry. It offers a compressed survey of Victorian genre painting: scenes from history (Richard Burchett's *Sanctuary*, a priest begging mercy of Edward IV in the sanctuary of Tewkesbury Abbey); scenes from the Bible (Sir Edward Poynter's *Israel in Egypt*, the Bible as epic); scenes from classical mythology (G. F. Watts's *Ariadne at Naxos*, John Collier's *Clytemnestra*); sentimental scenes (A. E. Mulready's painting of two poor children in a snowstorm, J. J. Tissot's *The Last Evening* in which five people avoid each other's eyes); and scenes from literature and drama – by Augustus Leopold Egg (*The Winter's Tale*), Daniel Maclise (*Macbeth*) and Thomas Webster (*The Deserted Village*, after the work by Oliver Goldsmith), and Lawrence's bravura depiction of *John Philip Kemble as Coriolanus*. Only a few paintings rise above any genre: Rossetti's *La Ghirlandata*, Constable's *Fording the River – Showery Weather with Salisbury Cathedral in the Background* and William Holman Hunt's first submission to the Royal Academy when aged only twenty, *The Flight of Madeline and Porphyro* (1848). Finished with the help of his friend John Everett Millais, it can be seen as the first painting produced by the Pre-Raphaelite Brotherhood, founded a few months later. It may lack the voluptuous quality of Keats's poem 'The Eve of St Agnes', whose penultimate stanza it illustrates, but it does express Holman Hunt's high sense of vocation in contrast to most of this Victorian collection, which confirms the view of William Blake Richmond (expressed in Holman Hunt's book *Pre-Raphaelitism and the Pre-Raphaelite Brotherhood*) that the Victorian public 'want what they can take in at a glance, without expenditure of time or trouble'.[142]

All this is handsomely displayed in a new purpose-built gallery. Its predecessor (1886) was burnt down in an air raid in 1941 and not replaced until 1999 with this design by Richard Gilbert Scott,[143] which forms one side of the public square in which stands the 15th-century Guildhall. The gallery has something of the corporate headquarters or hotel about it: pile carpet, foyer, all sound discreetly muffled. While this may suit the royal and civic portraits, it provides a strange setting for Matthew Smith, a proportion of whose 175 oils and 1,000 plus drawings, easily the biggest collection of his work, are exhibited in small galleries on the lower floor. He bequeathed them to his model Mary Keene, who lived in the Barbican.

Alone among his contemporaries he employed colour to express not just form but light. Those colours (pink, orange, crimson; turquoise, green, ultramarine; magenta and peacock) may appear loud or inharmonious but Smith worked them hard, brushstroke by brushstroke. Sometimes they are solid; sometimes they flow round, never into, one another.

The only English Fauve, Smith's colours are forever on the brink of freeing themselves from form. They never describe or illustrate an object. They are that object. Yet there is no abstraction here. Each painting has a subject: still lifes, with a fish, with a plaster cast; fruit in a dish; portraits of Henry Yorke;[144] Madame Monay with a mouth organ; Mary Keene; and nudes, kneeling, reclining, holding a fan, in an arm chair, exuberant; back to the Fitzroy nudes of 1913 that marked his breakthrough from provincial Yorkshire painter to colourist. These are paintings of passion, sumptuous with colour, the paint rich and thick.

When Boydell presented his somewhat different collection in 1794, he concluded his pamphlet by saying, 'The poor, and all in the inferior stations of life, may profit by the advice which many of the subjects in this collection may impart to them . . . When the whole is completed and arranged, I hope and trust, it will convince my Fellow-Citizens of the utility of the Arts' – a grand ambition somewhat beyond the scope of a collection of this size.

HORNIMAN MUSEUM ★★★★

100 London Road, Forest Hill,
London SE23 3PQ
Tel. 020 8699 1872
www.horniman.ac.uk

The world, its people and their cultures, and its environments

Trade and tourism feature continually in the early years of ethnographic collections. John Horniman (1803–93) was a tea trader. As he travelled, in Africa and the Near East, he collected.

Horniman was also a Quaker, a supporter of temperance and a man of probity. The ending of the East India Company's monopoly in 1834[145] led to malpractices in the tea trade – short measures, leaf mixed with grass or dust. Horniman sold his tea in sealed, airtight, tinfoil packets, a guarantee of freshness and quality. Virtue was rewarded. He made a fortune.

His sons, William Henry and Frederick John, inherited the fortune and the business. Frederick John also inherited his father's taste for collecting. He began with natural history (birds and butterflies) and moved on to armour and coins, porcelain, ceramics and glass. After visits to India and Ceylon (1844–5) and Japan, China, Burma, India and Egypt (1895–6) his collecting took on an Eastern bias.

He opened his house to the public, turned it into a museum in 1890 and in 1896 commissioned C. Harrison Townsend to design a new museum[146] which he gave to the London County Council following its opening in 1901.

It has an asymmetrical facade in stone and brick, its long horizontal lines stopped abruptly by a high clock tower. Pevsner called it 'one of the boldest public buildings of its date in Britain'.[147] Across its entire width is a huge allegorical mosaic panel by R. Anning Bell.

By 1901 Horniman's collection was extensive: about 8,000 objects were recorded in the register. The eclectic collection covered oriental and European armour; Egyptian mummies; and over two hundred musical instruments, among them a Chinese temple bell made of meteoric iron and silver, from the Buddhist temple at Kuhlan. He acquired the Chinese collection of the Revd Robert Davidson, the former Resident in Szechwan, and some good pieces, notably a carved arch bought from Sir Somers Vine, but the museum archives suggest that acquisitions were driven more by enthusiasm than knowledge. Horniman's two visits to India and the Far East yielded a mort of tourist curios: kimonos, dolls, toys, sake cups and the Jaipur heads that depicted different castes in India. At home he and his curator, Richard Quick, bought from a wide variety of auction rooms and dealers. Both Quick and Horniman were early members of the Japan Society.

In 1902 the London County Council invited the distinguished Cambridge University anthropologist Alfred Cort Haddon to become the adviser to the museum. As Sir Edward Tylor had been the *éminence grise* to the Pitt Rivers Museum (q.v.), so Cort Haddon became here.

He set about bringing order and some academic discipline to this mass of material. 'The day has passed,' he wrote in 1901, 'when we can consider a collection of "curios" as a museum. If properly arranged a museum is an educational institution of the greatest value.' Drawing on his own experience in the field as an anthropologist (v. Cambridge University Museum of Archaeology and Anthropology), he collected with a purpose: in his words, 'to illustrate the evolution of culture'.

In particular he concentrated on the cultures of the Pacific, as he had done at Cambridge, acquiring ancestor figures from Papua New Guinea, spears from the Torres Straits, pubic shields from North Western Australia, tatauna masks from New Ireland. By the 1930s the delightful muddle that he had inherited had become an important and significant

Sri Lankan mask at the Horniman Museum

ethnographic collection, without ceasing to be enjoyable or surprising. Horniman's original natural history specimens, such as the walrus brought to England in 1886 for the Great Colonial Exhibition by J. H. Hubbard, were augmented by Rowland Ward's diorama cases featuring musquash and polecats, foxes and badgers.

For eighteen years after the Second World War, the museum's curator was a German émigré, Otto Samson, who, while continuing the museum's 'orientalist' fascination, extended its interest to, for instance, European (particularly Balkan) folklore and popular culture, acquiring carnival masks and costumes from Switzerland and Cyprus, a hobby-horse, or *Mari Lwyd*, from Wales, a hobby-goat from Romania. During his term, Samson managed to acquire more than ten thousand objects of high aesthetic quality. He also enhanced the museum's African collection, through purchases, fieldwork and the transfer of collections from other museums.

Building on Horniman and Quick's collection of sub-Saharan African, European, Indian, Chinese and Japanese musical instruments, and objects subsequently acquired during the course of fieldwork by anthropologists such as E. Evans Pritchard, Samson established a musicology department. He secured the donation of over three hundred historic European wind instruments from Adam Carse (1947), which included such jewels as the earliest French horn known to have been built in England. Samson negotiated the first of many transfers of objects from other museums to the Horniman; this was a collection of Asian and African instruments from the Victoria and Albert Museum (1956), among them a Zande harp described as '*un chef-d'oeuvre de la lutherie zandé du début du XIXe siècle*'.[148] This collection also features the earliest-known kamanche (Iranian spike fiddle) in a public collection, and an 18th-century Provençal drum, considered by the authors of a recent survey to be the most important of all the surviving examples on account of its 'equilibrium and sobriety'.[149] The collection of historic European instruments belonging to

the pioneer of early music and re-inventor of the recorder Arnold Dolmetsch (1981–3), the Wayne collection of over 600 concertinas and related free reed instruments (1996) and, most recently, the collection of historic wind instruments, factory ledgers and technical drawings from the firm of Boosey & Hawkes (2003) have attracted generous grants from the Heritage Lottery and National Art Collections Funds, facilitating their purchase by the museum. The Horniman Museum's musical instrument collection is now one of the largest in the UK and is widely considered to be the most comprehensive.[150]

Around 1,500 of the musical instruments in the collection are now displayed in the Horniman Museum's Music Gallery, designed by Ralph Applebaum Associates. There is provision for the visitor, at the press of a button, to hear dozens being played, some of them in recordings made by the museum's musical instrument curators.

In the extraordinary treasure house of fossils, insects, models of extinct birds (the dodo, the great auk, passenger pigeons, the curved-billed huia birds), primate skeletons and casts of the skulls of early man (both Neanderthal and *Homo erectus*)[151] it is the ethnographic collection, estimated to comprise over eighty thousand items from most parts of the world, that gives the Horniman an international reputation.

Among the outstanding objects in the African ethnographic collection there are figures and models that celebrate maternity (Eloi and Yoruba); items linked to initiation of girls and boys, such as the Sande masks and the Kikuyu boys' initiation shields; items that depict etiquette and beauty, such as the elegant Pende greeting cups; Kudaru dung bowls (given as part of a girl's dowry in the Sudan) and shrines that show different types of African and diaspora religious systems. However the full diversity of the collection is captured by the masks and the figurative sculptures: animal masks (an antelope, a bush cow) from Mali and Burkina Faso;[152] attractive, narrow-eyed masks from the Gola in Liberia; Chokwe Akishi masks from

Zambia, wide-eyed, open-mouthed, painted, that represent Cikunza, the 'father of masks', 'the father of initiation'.

Overlooking this collection, which in one room summons up the people of Africa and their histories, are the bronze plaques of Benin. In 1897 a British military expedition took Benin city, burnt the Royal Palace of the Oba and removed its treasures (ivories, bronze statuettes and these plaques)[153] which depict the history of the Benin civilisation since the rule of Oba Orhogbna, divine monarch of the 16th century, military and political commander, ritual king. These plaques, as detailed and finished as Renaissance bronzes, show Benin war chiefs, impassive, in elaborate armour. Everywhere the Oba is depicted laden with ornaments made of coral, the symbol that links the King to the sea and the wealth it brought to the people.

Benin is only one of the African civilisations that have been damaged or destroyed by the slave trade and European colonisation, their people becoming part of an African diaspora, scattered across the world. The Kemet (Ancient Egypt), Zimbabwe, Mali and Songhai are also remembered here. Talking of the recent looting of Nigerian antiquities guest curator Joseph Eboreime said, 'We . . . appeal to the conscience of the world for a meaningful dialogue for a peaceful resolution of this history of shame.' The beauty, craftsmanship and resonance of these objects should give us pause for thought as 21st-century international capital and development aid continue to shape the future of Africa with merely cosmetic regard for the history of these nations and their civilisations.

The museum's Horniman origins, in tea trade and Far Eastern tourism, are still apparent but have been reshaped by a succession of outstanding curators, so that its curiosities continue to make visiting it a delight for people of all ages and interests,[154] while it is one of the most impressive and respected ethnographical collections in Europe.

HOUSES OF PARLIAMENT **

Westminster, London SW1A 0AA
Tel. 020 7219 3000

Barry and Pugin's fantastically realised romance of parliamentary democracy in stone and pattern and a museum of the history of that great ideal in these islands

Sir Charles Barry's son wrote of his father's concept for the rebuilding of the Palace of Westminster, 'His great idea was, by the aid of the sister arts, to make the New Palace a monumental history of England. Sculpture without, sculpture, painting and stained glass within, were to preserve the memorials of the past, and declare the date and object of the building.'[155]

Barry's 'sister arts' were the design and making of metalwork, furniture, stained glass, tiles, textiles and wallpapers. All were made to designs by A. W. N. Pugin, and executed by John Hardman (metalwork and stained glass), Herbert Minton (tiles), J. R. Crace (wallpapers and carpets) and John Webb (furniture). Together, they helped to realise Barry's 'great idea', the celebration of Britain's constitution and the place of Parliamentary democracy and the monarchy within it. The result is a résumé of British fine and decorative art in the middle of the 19th century, in a building whose architecture and decorative detail are everywhere consistent, of a piece.

In the crowd that watched the old Palace's warren of buildings burn on 16 October 1834 were J. M. W. Turner, who recorded the fire in a series of sketches and watercolours, Charles Barry himself and the 22-year-old Augustus Pugin who wrote, 'There is nothing much to regret and a great deal to rejoice in.'[156]

In 1836 Pugin's drawings helped Barry win the competition to design the new palace. The design brief was for a building in the Gothic or Elizabethan style. Balancing symmetry and asymmetry in the elevations, Barry gave, in Pugin's words, 'an Italian outline to Gothic details'. Of the river front his judgement was:

'All Grecian, Sir; Tudor details on a classic body'.[157]

Pugin's (anonymous) mastery of the Gothic style convinced the judges, but there is no doubt that, in concept and execution, the building is Barry's. Pugin did a further five months' work on designs and then was not involved until 1844 when, under pressure from the Royal Fine Arts Commission's increasing interference, Barry asked him to work on the interiors. 'Dear Pugin, I am in a regular fix respecting the working drawings for the fittings and decorations for the House of Lords, which it is of vital importance should now be finished with the utmost despatch.'[158]

Pugin's decorative exuberance is seen at its best in the Chamber of the House of Lords and in the design of the throne, the centre of what Bagehot called the 'dignified'[159] part of the British constitution. This is Pugin's masterpiece, a blaze of gold, a fanfare of detail and symbol. He took as his model the coronation chair in Westminster Abbey, first used by Edward II in 1308, and embellished it with quatrefoil carving, with pinnacles surmounted by royal beasts, with enamels decorated with heraldic lions on the back and crystals with trefoil patterns on the arms.

The mighty pierced brass doors that Hardman made for the entrance to the Lords' Chamber match it for splendour, as does the ceiling, carved by Crace, each gilded compartment of which contains four cartouches. In the Peers' Lobby Minton translated Pugin's rich patterns of blue and brown, beige and gold, into tiles. In the centre of the floor is a Tudor rose in Derbyshire marbles, set within two interlocking squares of brass.

The Royal Fine Arts Commission, chaired by Prince Albert,[160] had been set up in 1841 to commission murals with which to decorate the palace.[161] Following a competition, William Dyce and Daniel Maclise were chosen to paint frescoes in the Lords' Chamber. Maclise later (1861 and 1865) painted two huge murals, in waterglass, in the Royal Gallery of *The Meeting of Wellington and Blücher after Waterloo* and *The Death of Nelson*. Later still the walls of St Stephen's Hall and the corridors leading into the Central Lobby were painted by, among others, John Byam Shaw and Henry A. Payne (East Corridor, 1910) and Glyn Philpot and Sir George Clausen (St Stephen's Hall, 1925–7). The first corridors, painted by E. M. Ward and C.W. Cope (1858), had subjects chosen by the historian Lord Macaulay,[162] the last by the poet Sir Henry Newbolt. All presented a picture of an heroic, decent England (there are no scenes from Welsh or Scottish history) in which the King and Commons are equally courageous and honourable. The subjects were intended, in Newbolt's words, 'to awake us to the greatness and wonder of our growth as a nation, our evolution from a group of tribal states to a world-wide Commonwealth'.[163]

This somewhat selective celebration of the nation's history extends through the corridors, stairways and Committee Rooms of the palace.

On the Committee Stairs is Solomon J. Solomon's richly decorative *The Commons Petitioning Queen Elizabeth to Marry* (1911); upstairs in a Committee Room is *Alfred Inciting the Saxons to Prevent the Landing of the Danes* by G. F. Watts, described by Ruskin as 'the only real painter of history or thought we have in England'.[164] Watts dedicated it 'to patriotism and posterity' and declared, 'I have endeavoured to cast my figure in the most heroic mould – simple, grand and elegant. Pheidias, my adored Pheidias, shall reign throughout'.[165]

From the four sides of the Central Lobby, mosaics of the patron saints of the nations of the United Kingdom look down: *St George and St David* by Sir Edward Poynter (1869) and *St Andrew* and *St Patrick* by Robert Anning Bell (1923 and 1924).

Statuary is everywhere: *Benjamin Disraeli* (by Count Gleichen) in the Members' Lobby, *William Ewart Gladstone* (by F.W. Pomeroy, 1900) in the Central Lobby; *David Lloyd George* (by Uli Nimptsch), *Clement Attlee* (by Ivor Robert-Jones) and *Sir Winston Spencer Churchill* (by Oscar Nemon) in bronze, in the Members' Lobby. Elsewhere are bronze heads of *Keir Hardie* (by Benno Schotz, 1939), *Ramsay Macdonald* (by Sir Jacob Epstein, 1926) and *R. A. Butler* (by Angela Conner, 1991).

It is hard to think of another institution that has depicted itself and its purpose in this way, in a building that is (through its works of art, decoration and architecture), an extended exegesis of a certain 19th-century view of the British Constitution and monarchy.

Postscript
One work stands defiantly outside this coherent exposition: an equestrian statue of *Richard, Coeur de Lion* (cast 1856) by Carlo, Baron Marochetti. The clay model for it was exhibited at the 1851 Great Exhibition and then here, in New Palace Yard. Charles Barry considered it inappropriate and had it removed.

The Fine Arts Commission placed it in its present position in the middle of what is now the car park of the House of Lords. There is no finer equestrian statue in London. Monarch and steed are magnificent: his right arm holds a broadsword effortlessly aloft; the stallion's left hoof is raised. Man and beast are proud and poised. It is a work that can stand comparison with the great equestrian statues of Europe: Andreas Schlüter's of *Frederick William I*, the Great Elector of Brandenburg, in Berlin; Etienne Falconet's *Peter the Great* (1782) in the Square of the Decembrists in St Petersburg, the Tsar's horse rearing from a vast block of white granite to leap the River Neva.

Historiographically Barry might have been right: Richard I has no connection with Parliament. Artistically, he was wrong: this is a work that gloriously defies political conformity however manifested.

HUNTERIAN MUSEUM, LONDON (THE ROYAL COLLEGE OF SURGEONS) ***

35–43 Lincoln's Inn Fields, London WC2A 3PN
Tel. 020 7869 6560
www.rcseng.ac.uk

The advance of medical science

The Royal College of Surgeons, in which is housed the Hunterian Museum, looks across from the south side of Lincoln's Inn Fields to Sir John Soane's Museum on the north. Its building is as grandly institutional as Sir John Soane's house is domestic. Together their collections describe the condition of medical science and the arts 200 years ago.

John Hunter (1728–93) displayed his collection in a private museum at his house in Leicester Square. It comprised initially over five hundred species of plants and animals, to which were added medical specimens from his experiments in comparative and human anatomy and pathology, conducted at the Anatomy School he started in the 1760s.

These are not curiosities. They illustrate Hunter's ideas on adaptation and evolution. He used them to teach, and to demonstrate, in his words, 'by example rather than precept', and are arranged by function (Growth, Locomotion, Digestion, Circulation, etc.).

He was more tactful, and better connected, than his brilliant elder brother William[166] (whose pupil and assistant he had been when he first came down to London from Glasgow in 1748) and, after his death, his executors and friends succeeded in persuading Parliament to purchase the collection for the nation. It was passed to the Company of Surgeons (which became a Royal College in 1800) and opened as a museum in 1813 in a handsome new building in Lincoln's Inn Fields, designed by George Dance and James Lewis, and curated by Hunter's last assistant and amanuensis, William Clift.

You enter the museum today, on the first floor of the Royal College, into a dazzling room whose walls consist of free-standing illuminated vitrines, from the floor to the ceiling, containing Hunter's specimens. It is as if you are in a reliquary or have entered into the whole of Hunter's life's work and bright consciousness.

Here are some of his greatest specimens: the two-tailed lizard he collected when a young army surgeon in Portugal in 1762; a Surinam toad shown at the moment that the young toads are emerging and crawling over her back; a human spinal cord ending, unravelling like the strands of a horse's tail. Being encased in these walls of glass emphasises the

specimens' vulnerability. You gaze in wonder at these pieces of bone and tissue miraculously suspended in liquid.

To Hunter's specimens and his collection of fossils,[167] probably the largest assembled in Britain in the 18th century, have been added the eye speculum (*c.* 1730) of William Chesleden,[168] to whom Hunter was apprenticed at the Royal Hospital, Chelsea; an aneurysm needle (*c.* 1795) devised by Hunter's pupil Astley Cooper, and used for over a century; and such early 19th-century instruments as Lister's linear bone-cutting forceps with curved blades (*c.* 1820), still in use today.

Here too is the skeleton of Hunter's famous patient the Irish giant Charles Byrne,[169] and the skeleton of the didine Moa. In 1839 Richard Owen, conservator of the Hunterian, was given a six-inch length of bone that resembled an ox's marrow bone. He deduced that it was part of the femur of a flightless bird, unknown to science, and drew a sketch of the whole bone. In 1843 the discovery of more bones proved Owen's deductions correct.[170]

Near by are the brain of the mathematician Charles Babbage, wax models of brains made by Joseph Towne and the surgical instruments and research equipment of Joseph Lister, the pioneer of antisepsis: his microscope made by his cousins, the Becks, *c.* 1865; the carbolic acid steam spray, introduced in 1870; and catgut prepared in phenol that Lister researched, the first safe ligature material.

Most celebrated of all are John Evelyn's anatomical tables. Three of these four wooden boards, 5 feet by 2 ½ feet, had laid out on them the veins, arteries and nerves of the human body, not as a diagram but in real tissue. Made in Padua and bought by Evelyn in 1646, they are the oldest anatomical preparation in Europe. Only two sets survive: one here and one at the Royal College of Physicians in London.

William Clift was succeeded as conservator by Richard Owen, Clift's son-in-law and assistant, and Owen, after a gap of four years,[171] by William Henry Flower who, like Hunter, had

Specimen at the Hunterian Museum

begun his medical career as an army surgeon.[172] Both Owen and Flower went on to be superintendent of the British Museum (Natural History), Owen 1856–84, Flower 1884–98.

Richard Owen was undoubtedly a brilliant scientist,[173] if misguided. His religious faith led him implacably to oppose Darwin's theories of evolution, and to obstruct and discredit the work of Gideon Mantell, whose dating of dinosaur skeletons undermined Creationism. Flower outstripped him. He had 'the temper of a saint, the manners of an ambassador, the inspiration of a genius and the patience of a philosopher': he was the finest conservator the Hunterian had ever had, the finest director of the Natural History Museum and, possibly, the most innovative museum director of the 19th century.

As remarkable as this line of conservators is the succession of members of the Pearson family. William Clift appointed Edward Pearson as a porter in 1804. He learnt the technique of preparing specimens that Hunter had taught Clift and passed them on first to his son and then to his grandson, William Pearson, who was prosector to the college for sixty years until his retirement in 1957, ending 153 years of family service.

The museum and three-quarters of the collections were destroyed by the bombing of 10 May 1941. The 3,500 of Hunter's original specimens that remain are enough to ensure that his principles of medical research and teaching 'by example rather than precept' are carried into a fourth century.

IMPERIAL WAR MUSEUM, LONDON ✴✴✴

Lambeth Road, London SE1 6HZ
Tel. 020 7416 5320
www.iwm.org.uk

All Britain's wars gathered and memorialised in the old Bedlam

Britain has always hymned the glories of war. We celebrate past victories, troop battle colours, ennoble our heroes. So it is not surprising that our war museum, our Imperial War Museum,[174] is in a grand building fronted with a huge Ionic portico topped by a dome.[175] Before it two 15-inch guns from HMS *Ramillies* and HMS *Resolution* stand guard. The badge on the muzzle of the gun from HMS *Ramillies* reads 'Faithful, though unfortunate'.

In the entrance hall there are objects of comparable grandeur – a Royal Horse Artillery battery (1914), a 9.2-inch howitzer, a Churchill tank – but all this militaristic defiance is misleading. This is a museum planned in 1917 as men were dying in their thousands in the mud of Ypres.

In the remit of the museum are wars that have involved Britain or the Commonwealth since 1914. It bears witness to a century in which there were wars more devastating and total than those experienced by any previous age, culminating in a succession of terrible genocides. The horror and the pity are more eloquent than the glory.

The museum was opened in 1920 in the Crystal Palace. It moved first to South Kensington and then, in 1936, came here to the Bethlem Royal Hospital, or Bedlam, once 14th-century London's madhouse.

The First and Second World Wars are evoked in displays that draw on the experiences of both sides: an equality of warfare. A Heinkel He162 carries its jet on its back beside a battle of Britain Spitfire 1A. A German Biber one-man submarine lurks near the *Tamzine*, the smallest civilian vessel, a wooden fishing dinghy, from Dunkirk. The casing of a Little Boy atomic bomb of the type dropped on Hiroshima in 1945 lies near a V1 and V2, the Vergeltungswaffen (reprisal weapons) with which Germany targeted London and southeast England.[176]

The wars in Spain, Korea, Malaya, Cyprus, the Falklands and the Gulf are all remembered, no doubt soon to be joined by Iraq. All aspects and artefacts are covered: spying, imprisonment, escape; badges and medals, helmets and gas masks, uniforms and weapons; the front and home front; rationing, coupons, a reconstructed air-raid shelter; posters exhorting people to 'DIG FOR VICTORY' or 'COME INTO THE FACTORIES', 'WOMEN COME AND HELP!' 'MORE AEROPLANES ARE NEEDED'; and letters to and from the front, some returned undelivered, marked 'Killed in Action'. Since 1916 conflicts involving British armed forces have been recorded by official war artists. Their paintings here trace a line through 20th-century British art: Sir William Orpen, Sir John Lavery, Sir George Clausen and Muirhead Bone in the First World War; then Paul and John Nash, Wyndham Lewis, Eric Kennington, Stanley Spencer and C. R. W. Nevinson, who was that rarity, an artist who welcomed the war. A Futurist, he shared with his mentor Marinetti a fierce excited engagement with the technology of war. In his view artists 'were in love with the glory of violence . . . they were all ready for the great machine that is modern war.'[177] In the Second World War, Henry Moore, Graham Sutherland, John Piper, Eric Ravilious, Edward Ardizzone and Edward Bawden were commissioned as, again, were Stanley Spencer and Paul and John Nash.[178]

In the First World War the most memorable and moving images are from the battlefield: John Singer Sargent's huge *Gassed* (1918) in which a line of men blinded by gas stumbles across a landscape strewn with dead or wounded soldiers; Paul Nash's *The Menin Road* (1919) and *We are Making a New World*, from whose landscape of blasted trees and cratered soil all human life has been erased. Twenty years later the best images are not of events on stage but of those in the wings: Moore's drawings of civilians sleeping in the Underground during the Blitz, Ravilious's of North Sea patrols and of training aircraft. It was left to the poignant drawings of Ronald Searle to evoke the half-life and death-in-life of the Japanese camps.

It is so that some artists found inspiration in war. Of *Travoys with Wounded Soldiers Arriving at a Dressing Station at Smol, Macedonia* (1919) Spencer wrote, 'One would have thought that the scene was a sordid one, a terrible scene . . . but I felt there was a grandeur . . . a spiritual ascendancy over everything.'[179] Max Beckmann insisted, 'For me, the war is a miracle. My art can gorge itself here.'[180] For Nevinson the harsh tone of his war paintings – *After a Push* (1916) – was a high point to which he never rose again.

It is not surprising that in an age of film and photography there should be some startling images here: the advance of the 16th (the Queen's) Lancers from the Marne in September 1914, the officers on horseback; Neville Chamberlain waving the text of the Munich Agreement, 30 September 1938; the signing of the Instrument of Surrender in a tent on Lüneburg Heath, 4 May 1945; the atom bomb at Nagasaki, 9 August 1945, a perfect mushroom above the clouds backlit by the sun and the blast. Such images are reinforced by the museum's archives of oral history, film and broadcasts.

To the weight of these warnings against war has been added the museum's latest gallery on the Holocaust. There has been a proliferation of Holocaust museums in recent years, employing some of the world's great architects to erect buildings costing millions: Daniel Libeskind in Berlin,[181] James Ingo Freed of Pei, Cobb and Freed at Washington.[182] In both, as in Libeskind's Imperial War Museum North (q.v.), the buildings are metaphors for the collections. Here in London is one of the simplest and smallest, a handful of galleries within the museum that tell the story with a calm and clarity that make their own impact.

You are led inexorably from the photographs of pre-war Jewish families facing the studio camera in their best clothes to the burning of books (May 1933) and the first images of men lined up in Dachau (1933), from copies of *Die Sturmer* preaching hatred of Jews to its 500,000 readers, to copies of the 1935 Nuremberg laws that made Jews outcasts, non-people, defined by their ancestry not their religion;[183] from the instruments used by 'race scientists' to determine the racial classification of eyes, skull dimensions, bone structure, hair colour, to the dissecting tables of the doctors who operated in the 'mental health assessment clinics'.

As you proceed, the gallery spaces become smaller, the lighting lower, the soundtrack of Nazi chants and Goebbels's shouted words more insistent, until you arrive at the opening of the death camps (Chelmo, 1941, Treblinka, 1942) and at a can of Zyklon B.[184] You go from near darkness to blazing light, white floor, black walls, a huge white model of Auschwitz that fills the room, grey chairs against the wall facing it. Behind glass, on shelves, there are the possessions of the dead, and terrible mounds of shoes.

By the end you are dismantled but the museum neither flinches nor emotes; that vulgar mercy is commendably withheld. One survivor, Roman Halter, was told by his grandfather at the outset of the war: 'When you survive, you must speak clearly of what happened.' The last survivors of the Holocaust and the Russian purges are growing old, those of subsequent genocides in Cambodia and Rwanda not yet so. This museum in Bedlam does speak, clearly, of other madnesses.

JEWISH MUSEUM *

Raymond Burton House, 129–131 Albert Street, Camden Town, London NW1 7NB
Tel. 020 7284 1997
www.jewishmuseum.org.uk

Jewish life in Britain from the conquest to today

At the centre of every act of Jewish worship, within the mantle of the Torah, is the Pentateuch, the five books of the law of Moses in which are told the origins and destiny of the Jewish people, the children of Israel,[185] from the Creation. 'In the beginning God created the heaven and the earth.'[186] For the Jewish people history and religion are woven together. In this museum in a quiet side street of Camden Town, the troubled history of the Jews in England is addressed on the ground floor; upstairs are the treasures of Jewish religious ceremony.

Jews were invited by William I, the Conqueror, to come from Rouen in Normandy to Britain. They prospered under Henry II but, with the start of the Crusades against the Infidels in 1099, persecution commenced. A

group of Jews were ejected from Richard I's coronation in 1189. Edward I imprisoned 600 Jews in the Tower of London, hanging 270 of them. By the end of the 13th century Edward had expelled every Jew from England, and seized their property. Works of art and libraries are the privilege of settled prosperity, passed from generation to generation in confidence of a future. In view of this troubled history it is not surprising that the medieval period is marked in the museum by no more than a 13th-century brass signet ring, inscribed 'AARON' in Hebrew, and a wooden tally stick of 1241, the notches on which record that Isaac Carnifex, a butcher of Gloucester, paid 1s. towards the tax of 60,000 marks levied on the Jewish community.

It was not until Cromwell's Commonwealth that Jews were allowed to live here openly. Immigration was slow and understandably cautious. By 1700 only 1,000 Sephardic Jews lived in London, working as merchants, brokers, physicians, notaries. By the end of the 18th century this had risen to 3,000.

In the 17th century Ashkenazi Jews came to London from Holland and Germany. A small painting here by Benjamin Senior Godines of Amsterdam, commissioned by his patron Isaac Aboab, of *Charity*, shows, in crude but direct imagery, the Scales of Justice with two hands, one giving, one receiving, and a palm tree above words from Psalm 92, verse 12: 'the righteous shall flourish like the palm tree.'

Slowly the London Jewish community did flourish, its progress assisted by the small annual offerings of silver plate that were presented to the Lord Mayor (a dish by John Ruslen in 1702; a cup by George Boothby in 1745). Portraits mark this slow ascent within London society. By the 1760s Napthali Franks, a merchant and warden of the Great Synagogue, had the money and connections to have himself and his wife painted by the society portraitist Thomas Hudson. Another East India merchant, Daniel de Castro, had Tilly Kettle paint him and his 'wife and niece'

Rimmonim at the Jewish Museum

Sarah in India in 1770. By the mid 19th century Henry Ezekiel, an engraver and silversmith, and Nathaniel Levy, known as 'Turnpike Levy' as he had a monopoly on all turnpikes into London, had their portraits done by the distinguished painter Abraham Solomon. Others, including the pedlars and second-hand clothes salesmen, remained much lower in the social heap.

From the 1820s, Jewish progress in the City of London was quickening. Permission to open shops there, in 1830, was followed by Daniel Salomon being made a sheriff in 1835 and (by now Sir Daniel), being elected Lord Mayor in 1855. A fine Torah mantle bears the Salomon coat of arms. Within sixty years the Jewish community had produced Members of Parliament (Lionel de Rothschild in 1858), peers (Sir Nathaniel de Rothschild, created Baron in 1885), cabinet ministers (Herbert Samuel in the Liberal cabinet of 1908), a Lord Chief Justice (Sir Rufus Isaacs in 1913) and a Viceroy of India (Rufus Isaacs, now Viscount Reading, in 1920). These worldly successes are not reflected in the history collections on display here. Intent on assimilation, the many Jewish patrons of the 19th and 20th centuries – Mayer, Leverhulme, Wernher, the Samuels, the Rothschilds – have left what they collected elsewhere.[187]

Upstairs, you enter small, low-lit rooms, in which are the sacred objects of ritual: Sabbath lamps, menorahs (Hanukah lamps), a circumcision chair and rimmonims, pomegranate-shaped ornaments which adorn Torah scrolls. There is a simple, silver Kiddush cup used every Sabbath in the ceremony of prayer and blessing over wine; a silver filigree Torah scroll and mantles made of brocaded silver taffeta richly embroidered with panels of raised work.

In pride of place is a magnificent synagogue ark which, in use, would contain the Sefer Torah, the Scrolls of the Law. On it is the inscription 'Know Before Whom You Stand'. It was made of Italian walnut, probably in Venice in the 17th century, and probably acquired on his Grand Tour by the Earl of Tankerville.

A Shofar, the ram's horn used as an ancient musical instrument, the 'crooked trumpet', takes you from grand ceremony back to early struggle. It was excavated in 1855 in Leadenhall Street, and may have been buried or hidden before the expulsion of the Jews in 1290.

JEWISH MUSEUM FINCHLEY *

The Sternberg Centre, 80 East End Road, Finchley, London N3 2SY
Tel. 020 8349 1143
www.jewishmuseum.org.uk

Complementary to Jewish Museum Camden; social history of 20th-century Judaism

The Jewish Museum is on two sites. The objects here at Finchley are as plain and humble as the Torahs and the synagogue ark at the Camden site (Jewish Museum, q.v.) are grand and beautiful. This collection comes not from such successful City merchants as the Salomons, but has been given by working people to preserve the memory of the lives of Jewish immigrants in the East End of London in the late 19th and 20th centuries.

The 150,000 Yiddish-speaking Ashkenazi Jews who fled the pogroms in Russia, Poland and Romania between 1881 and 1914 arrived in London and settled around the docks. They were tailors and bakers, barbers and cabinet makers. Collected here, in reconstructed workshops, are the tools of their trades: there are thimbles, tapes, boxes of buttons; irons, scissors, sewing machines and tailors' dummies; combs and razors.

They struggled to make a living. A woman making cigarettes on piecework in the late 19th century was paid 2s. 6d. for 1,000. With that she could buy three and a half loaves of bread.

They formed trade unions. There is a splendid banner here from the Bakers' Union, in English on one side, in Yiddish on the other; a plaited Chola loaf is shown proudly beside the figure of the baker. They assimilated, not by leaving Jewishness behind but by joining the British Army in both world wars.

Most affecting is the small gallery in which is told the story of Leon Greenman, a British survivor of Auschwitz. Born in England with Dutch grandparents, he, his wife and small son found themselves trapped in Holland in 1940. His British papers were destroyed by a nervous Dutch official and, unable to prove British nationality, the Greenmans were sent to Auschwitz, where mother and son were killed. Leon Greenman's striped camp uniform and beret, from Buchenwald, hang here, small and limp, in a cabinet. Near by are the few mementoes he could save, or trace after the war: his son's tiny boots, his baby car, a wooden toy, his money box, still containing Dutch *halfjes*. They are exhibited plainly and unrhetorically. 'I only ask that I am not forgotten,' Leon Greenman said in an interview.[188] To ensure that he is not, he has come to the museum every Sunday since the 1960s to talk to visitors.

These two Jewish museums spring from different roots. They merged in 1995 and there are plans for them to come together on a Camden site in a former piano factory.

KENWOOD HOUSE ***

Hampstead Lane, London NW3 7JR
Tel. 020 8348 1286
www.english-heritage.org.uk

Iveagh bequest of fine art housed in a mansion built, decorated and furnished by Robert Adam; crowned by Vermeer's ravishing Guitar Player

The 1929 Act of Parliament that established Kenwood as a museum described it as seeking to present 'a fine example of the artistic home of a gentleman of the 18th century'.

Between 1887 and 1891 Edward Guinness, 1st Earl of Iveagh, collected what would have been popular in Georgian society of the 1770s and '80s: contemporary English portraiture (Reynolds, Gainsborough, Romney) and the 17th-century Dutch painting (Rembrandt, Vermeer, Hals, Cuyp, van der Velde, van de

Mary, Countess Howe *by Thomas Gainsborough (Kenwood House)*

Cappelle) that was just coming into fashion. Finally he collected an Adam villa, Kenwood, in which to show them, surrounded by an estate that is itself a living museum of English landscape design in the 18th century, from the early formal garden, through the mid-century picturesque (lakes, a *trompe l'œil* bridge) to Humphry Repton's landscaping of the 1790s.

You enter the house from the north through a pretty but surprisingly restrained Ionic portico into an similarly modest hall (a ceiling roundel of *Bacchus and Ceres*, 1773, by Antonio Zucchi and two low Adam stools).[189] None of this prepares you for the riches of the collection within, or for the Great Library designed by Adam in 1767.

The Music Room provides an unusual opportunity to compare the three great portrait painters of the 18th century, Reynolds, Gainsborough and Romney.

Romney offers a full-length of *Anne, Countess of Albemarle and her Son* (1777–9), a major work that took him thirty-five sittings. He gives it all he has: a studio landscape and sky; a Grecian urn; Cavalier King Charles spaniels; a tender pose that teeters on the brink of sentimentality – son, dogs and recently widowed mother.

Reynolds may not be at his peak either with *Lady Louisa Manners* (1779) or with *Mrs Musters as 'Hebe'* (1782), but in both he manages to rise above the limitations of his own formulae (antiquity, theatricality, allegory). The beautiful Sophia Musters's hair and diaphanous scarf stream in the wind; Lady Louisa's dress cascades to the bottom corner of the picture.

It is Gainsborough who carries the room with *Mary, Countess Howe* (c.1763–4), one of his last Bath portraits, in which landscape and figure are in close correspondence, the faint stormy pink of the sky with the smoky pink of her dress. Gainsborough draws the faintest chiffon over the neck and breast, a layer of shivering delicacy over the certainties of the five ropes of choker pearls at her throat and the black ribbon at her wrist. His handling of colour, materials and skin is as demure and provocative as Lady Howe's pose, and

contains some of the most exquisite passages of painting he accomplished, as brilliant as in his portrait of *Mrs Graham* (1777) with which he re-entered the Academy five years later.[190]

In the Dining Room and its Lobby are Lord Iveagh's Dutch paintings: a Wijnants, a van Ostade, a Cuyp, a Snyders, early works by van der Velde and by Hals, and *A Portrait of a Lady* by Ferdinand Bol, a pupil of Rembrandt, that shows why his work has often been mistaken for that of his master. It is however *The Guitar Player* by Jan Vermeer that takes the eye with its odd, asymmetrical composition, the figure and guitar in the bottom left quarter being balanced by the empty wall that occupies the entire upper right quarter of the painting.

Despite Vermeer's immaculate brushwork and control of light, the room is dominated by Rembrandt's *Portrait of the Artist* (c.1665), which has a genuinely tragic weight and majesty. It is set two octaves deeper than anything else here, a portrait of Time.

There is much else: wonderful Georgian furniture, although none, other than an Adam pedestal and sideboard in the entrance hall, that has associations with the house, the other Adam pieces (pier tables and a suite of seat furniture) being from the Dundas house, Moor Park;[191] more paintings, by Turner and Crome; and in the Library, or 'Great Room', one of Adam's masterpieces, with vast pier glasses,[192] three carved curtain cornices and a ceiling with plasterwork by Joseph Rose and painted panels by Antonio Zucchi.

On the other side of the marble chimney-piece are mirrored recesses with 'French plate glass, in London Silver'd' by Thomas Chippendale in 1769.[193] We are fortunate that the room, and Kenwood as a whole, are so well documented in Adam's *Works* (1774) and in designs that are now in Sir John Soane's Museum (q.v.). The room, now stripped of its contents, does not distract you from consideration of the detail of Adam's work or from the views through the windows, the grounds falling away from the terrace to the lake, the false bridge and the 'Caen Wood' beyond. 'The whole scene is amazingly gay, magnificent, beautiful and picturesque,' wrote Adam in 1774. 'The hill and the dale are finely diversified, nor is it easy to imagine a situation more striking without, or more agreeably retired and peaceful within.'

Ever inept in matters artistic, Parliament got it wrong in describing Kenwood as seeking to present 'the artistic home of a gentleman of the 18th century'. The contents do not comprise an 18th-century collection; the bringing together of Rembrandt, Gainsborough, Reynolds, Adam and Chippendale in such a setting would do credit to anyone in any century.

LEIGHTON HOUSE MUSEUM **

12 Holland Park, London W14 8LZ
Tel. 020 7602 3316
www.rbkc.gov.uk/LeightonHouseMuseum

Leighton's love of the exotic, summed up in the Arab Hall

The year 1864 was decisive for Frederic Leighton. *Dante in Exile*, his exhibit at that summer's Royal Academy, was bought for 1,000 guineas by the dealer Ernest Gambart and secured his election as an associate academian. The *Art Journal* called it 'one of the most remarkable pictures of the year'.[194] Young, handsome and accomplished, with this success he could at last build himself a house.

The architect was his friend and fellow Royal Academian George Aitchison.[195] Together they created a house that described his life: both home and studio, it expressed his interests and his tastes. Every room was filled with oriental carpets, tapestries, pictures, objects, hot-house flowers. In it he displays his collections of Venetian Renaissance artists – Titian, Tintoretto, Giorgione, Bassano – and of 19th-century French artists – Corot, Delacroix, Daubigny, Harpignies. Here too were Constable's sketch for *The Haywain* and Reynolds's double portrait of *Lord Rockingham and Edward Burke*.

Today the house is emptier, his possessions having been sold after his death to establish a trust for Royal Academy students, but there is still enough here of his work and taste to enrich our enjoyment of his paintings.

The house is focused upon two rooms, the Arab Hall and the Studio. The hall is an Eastern fantasy, inspired by the banqueting room of La Zisa, a Sicilio-Norman palace at Palermo. The walls are covered with 16th- and 17th-century Islamic tiles, around which Walter Crane designed a gilt mosaic frieze. Edgar Boehm and Randolph Caldecott both made capitals for the alabaster columns. In the centre is a fountain and pool carved from a single block of black marble and lit by a magnificent gasolier of beaten copper and gilded wrought iron. Overlooking the hall is a balcony or zenana, brought from Cairo. The panels and tiles set pattern beside pattern, orchids, carnations, parrots, peacocks, Arabic script, turquoise and gold, the colours of Mediterranean luxury.

Upstairs the Studio is the heart of the house. Here Leighton worked, and each summer held parties attended by, among others, Millais, Burne-Jones, Alma-Tadema, Robert Browning, the beautiful Countess of Brownlow, Walter Crane and Clara Schumann. It is now stripped bare. Stripped bare too was his reputation in the 20th century, until Richard and Leonée Ormond began to revive it, their efforts culminating in an exhibition at the Royal Academy in 1996, the centenary of his death.

His major works are in Tate Britain (q.v.), the Lady Lever (q.v.), the Uffizi in Florence, in Philadelphia and in Puerto Rico. Leighton House has a handful of his paintings, including *The Death of Brunelleschi* (1852), which marked the end of his student days, and the stupendously entitled *Clytemnestra from the Battlements of Argos Watches for the Beacon Fires which are to Announce the Return of Agamemnon* (1874), showing a grim, implacable caryatid.

More interesting are the works from the margins of his career: landscapes, architectural paintings, oil sketches and drawings. His oil sketch for Robert Browning of the entrance hallway of the Palazzo Rezzonico in Venice, where Browning lived, recedes through seven or eight planes of soft greys to a distant

enalcoved cartouche. Sketches for major works such as his portrait of *Lady Brownlow* (at Belton House, Lincolnshire) and for *Electra at the Tomb of Agamemnon* (in the Ferens Art Gallery, q.v.), show him working with composition and figures, adjusting setting, pose, perspective. Two small landscapes (*Pasture, Egypt*, 1868, and *Mullenmore Island*) suggest that had he not lived at a time when both the Royal Academy and the market little valued landscape painting he might have excelled as a painter of landscapes. The bruised purple and violet of the sky over Mullenmore Island are as threatening as the massing clouds and fierce sunlight in his *Clytie* (Fitzwilliam Museum, q.v.) as Apollo deserts Clytie.

Most impressive are his studies, for *Helios and Rhodos* (1868–9), executed in soft pencil with fine *hachure* in the Paris style, and for *And the Sea Gave up the Dead Which Were in It* (*c.*1891–2) (Tate Britain) in chalk. These rude studies have the speed and fluency of Michelangelo. Leighton wrote to Henry Tate about the finished roundel of *And the Sea Gave up the Dead Which Were in It*, 'This is the work I should like to be remembered by in our National Gallery.'[196] However his studies are warmer and more fluent than the finished work.

Compared with these, the paintings around the house, by friends such as Millais, J. W. Waterhouse, Frederick Sandys and Alma-Tadema, appear make-weights. Leighton's work, in which idealism and realism, romanticism and naturalism, are held in tension by the discipline of his classical training, gives Leighton House its heart as well as its personality.

Apart from the Arab Hall, and staircase with tiles by William De Morgan, the house may lack the living *Arabian Nights* exoticism that it had in Leighton's own time, but the works of his that remain here confirm his belief that 'art is the utterance of our delight in the phenomena of nature and an endeavour to communicate to others and perpetuate that delight.'[197]

The Arab Hall at Leighton House

LONDON TRANSPORT MUSEUM **

Covent Garden Piazza, London WC2E 7BB
Tel. 020 7565 7299
www.ltmuseum.co.uk

Museum of moving London: transport, above and underground, in former flower market

Any city works only as well as its transport. It is 'the maker and breaker of cities'.[198] Of no city is this more true than of London.

This is not a museum about transport in London. It is the story of London Transport, the public company responsible for buses and the Underground in the city since 1933. There is little here about bicycles, boats, helicopters or even motor cars. It nods at the history of transportation in the city: a Thomas rowing skiff (1800), borrowed from the National Maritime Museum (q.v.); an 1820s stage coach; a mid-19th-century cabriolet, designed by Joseph Hansom in 1834 and improved by John Chapman (1839), with the driver at the back. It has an 1829 omnibus with brilliant yellow wheels and one from 1875 that carried fourteen on top and had knife-board seats. But it is not until it displays its splendid collection of scarlet double-decker buses, from the 1911 open-top K-type to the 1954 RT-type and the 1956 Routemaster (RM), that masterpiece of design by Douglas Scott that is recognised all over the world, that the museum picks up speed.

The parked lines of buses dominate the museum, which is in what was the Flower Market of Covent Garden before the market was moved to Nine Elms. The airy, elegant glass and cast-iron building designed by William Rogers and built by William Cubitt and Co. is reminiscent of a 19th-century railway station. It is a fine setting for buses, and for the similarly scarlet vehicles that engaged in the battle at the turn of the 20th century between trams (south of the river) and trolley-buses (north).

The museum finds its heart, and its central archive, with the formation of London Transport, a public company legislated into life in

1933 by the Labour leader of the Greater London Council, Herbert Morrison. Of London Transport's two blood lines, buses and the Underground, there is no doubt which is this museum's favourite. Although the double-decker buses are rightly loved it is the Underground, the 'tube', with its stations and signs, its architecture and advertisements, whose stamp is on the city, and in whose stations Londoners sought refuge every night during the Blitz, recorded in ghostly drawings by Henry Moore.

From the building of the first underground railway in 1863[199] when the 'cut and cover' method of construction gouged giant trenches across the city, the underground has been anything but hidden. So strong has been its personality and so cohesive its symbol, the London Transport roundel, that it is easy to forget that it serves little more than half the capital, only 37 of its 269 stations being south of the river.

That sense of unity gathered strength with the formation of London Transport in 1933 and the appointment of Frank Pick as its first chief executive. Here are the coordinated designs he developed for signage and posters, lights and furniture, maps and upholstery. He commissioned Edward Johnston to design a new typeface, Johnston Sans;[200] brought together some of the finest artists (Graham Sutherland, Man Ray, Frederick Herrick, E. McKnight Kauffer) to design advertisements; and worked with Harry Beck to develop his diagrammatic map of the Underground, which uses only vertical, horizontal and 45° diagonals. It bears no relation to the real geography of London, yet is a design classic recognised, and imitated, around the world. Beck was trained as an electrical engineering draughtsman: hence the map's similarities to an electrical circuit. This museum's archive shows how the map began in 1931 with solid blobs for stations and developed in subsequent drafts the present small rectangular ticks that give greater prominence to station names.

The architects whose stations feature so strongly across the city are honoured here, from T. G. Figgis's stations for the City and South London Railway (1890–1910), Leslie Green's and Charles W. Clark's for the Metropolitan Line (1910–30) with their ox-blood glazed tiles, Harry Ford's for the District Line, the suburban-classical stations of Stanley Heaps and those designed by the greatest transport architect of the 20th century, Charles Holden. Amazingly Holden was exactly the same age as Green and Harry Ford, and five years older than Stanley Heaps, yet his stations appear to originate in another, later century.

Here are drawings and photographs of his early stations on the Northern Line (Clapham South, Morden, early 1930s), the severe brick stations that ran through the suburbs (Sudbury Town, Arnos Grove, mid 1930s) and his masterpieces, Piccadilly Circus, 'the hub of the Empire', and London Transport's headquarters at St James's Broadway.[201] At the latter he and Pick gave the sculptors Jacob Epstein and Henry Moore their first major public commissions for sculptures, which dominate the exterior of the building.[202] As Nikolaus Pevsner has said, for Pick every detail was 'visual propaganda'.

The museum records the present with the new Victoria and Jubilee Lines (which feature the architecture of Norman Foster, Will Alsop, Michael Hopkins, Richard MacCormac and Ian Ritchie) and looks to a future of monorails, cable cars and sustainable transport. Yet it is the red double decker and the designs of Beck and Holden that stay in the mind of the visitor, and the fibre of the city.

MARBLE HILL HOUSE *

Richmond Road, Twickenham, Middlesex
TW1 2NL
Tel. 020 8892 5115
www.english-heritage.org.uk

Lord Burlington's chaste Palladian villa built for a chaste Hanoverian love

If you seek a romantic view of aristocratic and literary life in the early 18th century, Marble Hill, the house of Henrietta Howard, Countess of Suffolk, would be a good choice. Designed by Colen Campbell and built by Roger Morris under the supervision of its architect Henry Herbert, 9th Earl of Pembroke,[203] it is a perfect example of a small Palladian villa. Here Henrietta Howard entertained the leading figures of the Augustan age: Alexander Pope, Jonathan Swift, John Gay and Horace Walpole.

Its setting is a Thames-side Arcadia with its garden, designed by Charles Bridgeman and Pope, leading down through groves of trees to the river: the perfect retreat for a royal mistress, although there is considerable evidence that her long affair with the Prince was based more on intimate friendship than on passion. James Lees-Milne describes her as 'the indispensable companion of the Prince of Wales, the confidante of the Old King'.[204] Marble Hill was the setting for royal passions when George II's grandson, the Prince Regent, rented it for his morganatic wife, Mrs Fitzherbert, in 1795. Today it is more decorously the setting for a collection of early-18th-century furniture and paintings, many of which have associations with the house. Some are original: the stone chimney piece in the Hall; the magnificent mahogany staircase; the piers and the overmantel in the Great Room on which gilded putti recline; and an elaborately carved table in the same room, with its milky marble top and central motif of a peacock, the attribute of the goddess Juno, protector of women. This had been removed in 1817 and was found in a private collection in Australia in 1987. Happier still has been the rediscovery of the five Panini capricci which were removed *c.* 1900, scattered, and rediscovered throughout the 1990s. The four overdoors and one overmantel, *Statues in a Ruined Arcade*,[205] were probably commissioned for the room and are examples of what Oliver Millar describes as Panini's ability to create 'an airy classical temple in which to display classical remains and his own views of classical buildings and ruins'.[206]

Associated with the house are a bust of Pope in the Hall by John Cheere; Hogarth's portrait of *Sir Robert Pye, Bart* (1731), a half cousin of Henrietta Howard; and Kneller's oval portrait of the handsome *Charles Mordaunt*, 3rd Earl of Peterborough (*c.* 1695), whom she called her 'knight-errant' and with whom she conducted a bizarre correspondence – love letters lacking the spark of love. Peterborough, a soldier, diplomat, socialite and rake, was, at sixty-five, forty years older than she, but among his elaborate, dry compliments, he did manage one poem to her which concludes: 'O wonderful creature! A woman of reason! Never grave out of pride, never gay out of season; when so easy to guess who this angel should be, would one think Mrs Howard ne'er dreamt it was she?'[207]

The work that most closely stitches the current collection to her life at Marble Hill is a portrait of her by Charles Jervas, to whom she sat at about the time that the house was built. The portrait was owned by Pope, who left it in his will to Martha Blount,[208] at whose sale Henrietta Howard bought it and gave it to Horace Walpole. It confirms that Jervas had scant talent for depicting women but it shows too that Walpole's description of her was just: he said she was 'well-made, extremely fair, with the finest light hair; well dressed always and simply: her face regular rather than beautiful'.[209]

Using the first inventory of the house of 1767 as its source, English Heritage has assembled a collection that reflects the likely tastes and preoccupations of Henrietta Howard and her friends, and the fact that, being inspired by Andrea Palladio, Marble Hill was utterly modern.

In the 1720s it was becoming commonplace to concentrate the Grand Tour on France and Italy. Accordingly the house has been given two paintings by Francesco Baltaglioni, along with the rediscovered Paninis, and works by the rake Marcellus Laroon, whose *A Lady and a Gentleman with a Page* displays what Wilenski calls his 'French daintiness',[210] and by Philippe Mercier, friend of Watteau. There is also a rare oil by the engraver Hubert François Gravelot, Gainsborough's master, and two paintings by Francis Hayman, who taught with Gravelot at the St Martin's Lane Academy, and hell-raised with Gainsborough.

The most interesting painting in the house is a landscape by Richard Wilson. *The Thames near Marble Hill, Twickenham* (*c.*1762) was known to Walpole, who noted it at the Society of Artists exhibition that year. Wilson shows that he has learnt much from studying Poussin and, particularly, Claude, in Rome, but whereas Dutch artists such as Adam Pynacker transported the clear light of Italy to Dutch landscapes, Wilson's light here has a thoroughly English feel. The air is still, so too the reflections in the river, but the light is less celestial, more palpable. The composition too is more direct and engaged than that in a Claude, showing why Reynolds thought that Wilson's pictures were 'near common nature'.

This landscape has considerable charm, even beauty, but it is possible to see why, nevertheless, Wilson had such difficulty selling his work in a market that revered Claude and Poussin. An English artist painting English scenes 'near common nature' was valued less highly by English connoisseurs. By 1777 fifty English art collectors owned over a quarter of Claude's total output, but only three owned paintings by Wilson.[211] Wilson was too good simply to supply pastiche Claudes for this market, but was not sufficiently original to produce something entirely new.

Outside, in the real landscape that Bridgeman and Pope created, the view of the house from the river and the river from the house are largely unchanged. Marble Hill offers a delicious, if sanitised, glimpse of 18th-century life. Jonathan Swift was more acerbic in his poem, 'Pastoral Dialogue between Richmond Lodge and Marble Hill' (1727), satirising Henrietta Howard's fading influence at court. In it Richmond Lodge, larger, grander and being built with more lavish expenditure by George II, says:

I pity you dear Marble Hill,
But hope to see you flourish still.
All happiness – and so adieu.

To which Marble Hill replies (with equable condescension):

Kind Richmond Lodge; the same to you.

MICHAEL FARADAY MUSEUM AT THE ROYAL INSTITUTION *

21 Albermarle Street, London W1X 4BS
Tel. 020 7409 2992
www.rigb.org

Faraday's laboratory, the birthplace of electricity, within the Royal Institution

'All this is a dream. Still, examine it by a few experiments. Nothing is too wonderful to be true if it be consistent with the laws of nature.' Michael Faraday wrote these words on the eve of the experiments, in 1849, by which he hoped to establish the connection between gravity, electricity and magnetism. They describe his romance with science. He defined the process by which that romance should be pursued in the concluding sentence of these notes: 'in such things as these, experiment is the best test of such consistency.' His experiments, all conducted here in his laboratory in the basement of the Royal Institution, laid the foundations of modern chemistry and physics.

The museum recreates his laboratory, set up for an experiment on demagnetism. The room's simplicity is startling. Shelves of bottles and wooden tables make it appear more kitchen than laboratory, yet it was here that he first liquefied gases (1823), isolated and described new organic compounds, among them benzene (1825), and investigated steel alloys, establishing the basis of scientific metallurgy.

Here too he conducted the now historic series of experiments in August 1831 from which he discovered electro-magnetic induction and made the first transformer and generator capable of producing electric current (October 1831). The originals of both devices are displayed here. They revolutionised physics and established the principles on which all power stations have generated electricity ever since.

The origins of those experiments go back to his first enquiries into the possibility of an electric motor in September 1821. Such a thing is reconstructed here in its original simplicity: a wire carrying a current being caused to rotate continuously around a magnetic pole producing streams of electricity on the conjunction of its two ends. These revelations did not occur in an intellectual vacuum. They built on the discovery of electro-magnetism the previous year by Hans Christian Oersted and on papers by André-Marie Ampère demonstrating the implications of Oersted's work by showing that the magnetic force was circular. Both owed much to Alessandro Volta's invention of the electric pile, or battery, an original of which is here, given to the 22-year-old Faraday by Volta when Faraday toured Europe as assistant, secretary and valet to his mentor, Sir Humphry Davy. It sits here, a stacked sandwich, made up of discs of copper, felt soaked in brine, zinc, copper, felt, zinc, etc.

The innocence of the materials used cuts to the core of scientific thought and process and incidentally reflects the personal simplicity of Faraday himself. His father was a blacksmith. The family was poor. Faraday's education was basic. At fourteen he was apprenticed to a bookbinder and began to educate himself from the books he bound, including the third edition of the *Encyclopaedia Britannica*, which contained an entry on electricity. Given a ticket to a lecture by Sir Humphry Davy at the Royal Institution (founded only in 1799), he sent his notes to Davy and eventually secured a job as his laboratory assistant in 1812.

The Faraday family were Sandemanians, members of a small literalist Christian sect to which he was committed all his life. He saw his scientific work as a search for the laws of nature established by God in the Creation. For him the purpose of science was to bear witness to the glory of God and to better the lot of Man. His Bible is displayed here beside his slide rule, his portable microscope and his penknife.

He refused almost all honours, including a knighthood and the presidency of the Royal Institution, whose servant, rather than master, he wished to be. His memorial is in the objects held in this museum, in the Faraday Evening Discourses and Christmas Lectures for young people that he was instrumental in founding, and in the mighty issue of his work on electricity and magnetism, that 'dream' which illuminated the laws of nature by experiment.

MUSEUM OF LONDON ✱✱✱

London Wall, London EC2Y 5HN
Tel. 0870 444 3852
www.museumoflondon.org.uk

Chronological collection of London life since before history

London from Southwark (c. 1630), a painting by an unknown Dutch artist, is probably the earliest panoramic view of the city. It lacks the scale of the panorama by Wenceslaus Hollar, published in 1647, which gave more of this view. With the *Rhinebeck Panorama* (c. 1807) (so called because it was discovered in 1941 lining a barrel full of pistols in Rhinebeck, New York) it gives some sense of the city's size.

This is a city that has been for 2,000 years a centre of commerce, culture and power. It has been the capital of Roman Britain, of England, of the United Kingdom, of an empire; the home of Thomas Becket, Thomas More, Shakespeare's theatre, Wren, Pepys, Dr Johnson, Hogarth, Dickens. It has been so built over, written about, painted and photographed that it ought to provide a great hoard to furnish a museum, a Treasury of London Past.[212]

It is perhaps too rich a source. No museum can hope to tell the centuries of stories, the lives and deaths, brave hopes, chill failures, silken wealth, grating poverty of such a city, or capture its smell: the fog from the river, acrid tanneries, sweet breweries, coal dust and smoke. It would require an encyclopaedia of a museum.

The constraints imposed by circumstance help. The Museum of London, founded in 1976, was an amalgamation of the Guildhall Museum, strong on London's archaeology and the City of London's history, and the London Museum, reliant since its foundation in 1910 on eclectic collecting to determine its character. Other museums and galleries chart the city's varied lives: in transport, the theatre, the sea, medicine, science, the fine arts. Here is an archaeology of London and the daily life of its past, illuminated by the insights objects can bring.

Urban development facilitates archaeological excavation, and in the past thirty years Roman London has been revealed as never before. The Roman waterfront and port at such sites as Regis House and Pudding Lane, the amphitheatre at Guildhall Yard, the public baths at Huggin Hill, the forum and basilica near Leadenhall and Gracechurch Street, cemeteries outside the original city walls at Southwark, Spitalfields and Aldgate and the excavations at No. 1 Poultry and over a hundred other sites have led to our discovering much about both the public and the private life of Londinium.

The museum displays a wealth of Roman material, from everyday personal effects of Roman Londoners to public buildings; a large 2nd-century wall painting (Southwark); a 3rd-century limestone relief depicting four mother-goddesses (Blackfriars) to augment the 3rd-century room where the mosaic was excavated in 1869 at Bucklersbury, and the glories of the Temple of Mithras discovered in 1954 by Professor W. F. Grimes at Walbrook.

A Carraran marble head of Mithras (c. AD 180–220) depicts him as a beautiful young man, wearing his usual Phrygian cap. When the temple was rededicated to Bacchus in AD 350, a sculpture of the god supported by a satyr and a maenad was made, under which was written 'HOMINIBUS VAGIS VITAM' – 'you give life to wandering mortals.'

The Spitalfields cemetery has yielded a limestone sarcophagus and an inner lead coffin, finely decorated with a scallop-shell motif, which tells us much about the life of the 4th-century Roman elite. The woman within was wrapped in a gold shot-silk damask robe, her head on a pillow of bay leaves, surrounded by grave-goods including a phial of embalming unguent.

To create a context for these treasures there are tableaux of models: *Bridging the Thames*, *The Public Baths* and *The Forum and Basilica*, all in immaculate and hypnotic detail. Sacks, tiles, kindling, barrels, stall, waterpipes – all are held in miniature perfection.

A thousand years on, in the 12th century, there are more artefacts: the seal of the first Mayor of London, Henry FitzAilwyn; 14th-century badges from pilgrimages to Canterbury; 15th-century statues of the Four Virtues from niches in the porch of the Guildhall; later still, Cromwell's death mask (competing for authenticity with another, sans beard, in the Ashmolean Museum, q.v.); the arms of the Hanseatic League carved by Caius Cibber (1670); a silver-gilt cup from the South Sea Bubble (1720); and the chair in which Dickens wrote *A Tale of Two Cities*.

The beauty of the Venetian glass from Henry VIII's Nonsuch Palace is *sans pareil*: pink, turquoise, ivory, it plays the light. The modest splendour of John Baker's carving from the Mercers' Chapel, its features folding in a gilded frond, contrasts with the gaudy of the Lord Mayor's state coach *c.* 1757, with panels by the Florentine artist Battista Cipriani.

Two set pieces throw a more personal light on London life. Panelling from Wellclose Square prison, made up into a cell, bears the names of inmates: the fine calligraphy of Edward Ray is incised beside crude outlines of houses, and 'John Dewar, 1790', laboriously carved out. The Cheapside hoard reveals a 16th-century jeweller's stock-in-trade. Here are cameos, intaglios, emeralds and amethysts; garnets from India, turquoises from Persia; a pair of rock-crystal tankards, a Swiss astronomical calendar watch and a scent bottle set in opaline chalcedony plaques with rubies, spinel and diamonds. Peridot, a sliver of palest green from St John's Island in the Red Sea, a bowl of agalmatolite the colour of cool mustard and a knife handle of nephrite jade from Turkestan all trace the flow of trade through the hands of 17th-century London.

The collection of paintings and photographs shows daily life. Gustave Doré painted *A Poor House* (*c.* 1869), a hell of darkness and hollow faces. George William Joy's *The Bayswater Omnibus* (1895) is a novella of class attitudes and distinctions. Henry Moore's watercolours of Londoners sleeping in air-raid shelters in 1944 record the war even more starkly than the work of Arthur Cross and Fred Tibbs, City of London policemen who photographed bomb damage as part of their duties.

No museum could hope to convey the full diversity. The city shown here is not a city of music, of Handel, Haydn, Mozart; it is not seen through the eyes of Whistler, Monet, Hogarth, Constable (though views by William Marlow, Canaletto, Samuel Scott, Spencer Gore, Sickert and David Bomberg are here). The god of money, given pride of place in the person of Mercury by Hollar, sleeps. The Thames, the river of death and dreams, does not flow.

Nevertheless this is a remarkable collection that conveys much of the vitality, spirit and generosity of the city. Its roots are strong and its diversity does justice to the words of the old London alchemist: 'It is the city of gold, it is the city of fire, it is the city of death.'

NATIONAL ARMY MUSEUM **

Royal Hospital Road, London SW3 4HT
Tel. 020 7730 0717
www.national-army-museum.ac.uk

Five centuries of army life: heroes, heroics and battle honours

Armies march through the history of these islands. They have been raised by kings and barons, pretenders and rebels since memory began, but the idea of a standing national army dates only from 1660, when, after the Restoration, Charles II established the nucleus of the first standing army England had possessed, consisting of the troops of the cavalry now known as the First and Second Regiments of Life Guards.

This comparatively short history presents a challenge to a museum. That this national museum was established only in 1960 and moved here into a plain, functional building[213] makes that task more daunting.

The museum concentrates on the past 200 years. There are objects here that predate the mid 19th century (an emphatic portrait by Louis Laguerre depicting Marlborough's victory at the battle of Malplaquet on 11 September 1707 in the style of his master, Charles le Brun)[214] but it is with the Napoleonic Wars that the collection comes to life: the blood-stained glove of the aide who staunched Lord Uxbridge's leg, shattered by a cannonball as he rode beside Wellington at Waterloo; the French Eagle standard of the 105th Regiment captured on the battlefield; Captain William Sibourne's fifty-square-foot model of the battle that shows 75,000 model soldiers in position.

The museum brings together some memorable painted images of events and soldiers, heroes and heroism. Here is Godfrey Douglas Giles's painting of *The Charge of the Heavy Brigade* at Balaclava on 25 October 1854, owing much to the composition and style of Elizabeth, Lady Butler, whose own *Painted Heroes* (1885) shows the Royal Horse Artillery gun team in the snow. Giles, a major who served in the Sudan and South Africa, also has a painting of *The Battle of Tamai*, in the Sudan campaign.

Giles records soldiers straight on, without irony or subtext, indeed without fear, cold or hunger. It is an approach shared by other artists here even when recording, as Charles Edwin Fripp has, a defeat as devastating as *The Battle of Isandhlwana* (c. 1885), when 858 British troops were killed on 22 January 1879, or *The Battle of Ulundi* (1879) by Adolphe Yvon, or *The Capitulation of Kars* (1859), painted by Thomas Jones Barker.

Commanders sit to artists more easily than do battlefields and there are some fine ones here: *John Churchill*, 1st Duke of Marlborough, attributed to Michael Dahl (c. 1702); *Robert Clive* (c. 1764), by Gainsborough; and three by Reynolds, including the *Marquess of Granby*, whose demobilised troops showed their gratitude for his largesse by naming public houses all over southern England in his memory.

There is only one self-portrait, by Rex Whistler (1940), wearing the uniform of the

The Zulu victory at The Battle of Isandhlwana *by Edwin Fripp (National Army Museum)*

Welsh Guards. He stands, casually elegant, rummer in hand, a bottle of Dubonnet and a soda siphon on a tray, his 2nd Lieutenant's cap and gloves on a chair, his paintbrushes on the balcony. He was killed on his first day in action, 18 July 1944, near Caen (v. Beck Isle Museum of Rural Life).

The galleries that cover the 20th century are more sombre. Television screens show original footage of conflicts; there are reconstructions of a First World War trench and a Burmese prisoner-of-war camp. These wars had their heroes but they were clothed in workaday khaki not in the scarlet of the 93rd Highland Regiment at Balaclava or the flowing dark cavalry cloak worn by Captain L. E. Nolan, Aide-de-Camp to General Airey, when he carried the fateful message to the Light Brigade.

As you leave, in the shop are eight cases of toy soldiers made by William Britain & Co. Manufactured for over a hundred years, once hollowcast lead, now mostly plastic, these are the soldiers of childhood dreams playing out war.

NATIONAL GALLERY *****

Trafalgar Square, London WC2N 5DN
Tel. 020 7747 2885
www.nationalgallery.org.uk

Masterpiece after masterpiece: Western European painting from 1200

It has long been axiomatic that the National Gallery is a great gallery. Hans Tietze in his book on 'the famous museums of the Western World' believes that 'it is scarcely possible to imagine it ever being displaced from the position of the greatest of the great galleries'.[215] Is that the case? If so, why? Wherein lies its excellence?

Of the great galleries it is one of the smallest, containing 2,300 paintings, almost all on view. It was the last to be established, in 1824 – the Louvre opened in 1793, the Kunsthistorische Museum in Vienna in 1781.[216] Like the Rijksmuseum, but unlike the Louvre, the Prado or the Kunsthistorische Museum, the National Gallery had no founding royal collection. Here, under one roof, are some of the finest Italian, French and Dutch paintings from 1200 to 1900, the bloodlines of Western European painting.

Its start was faltering. Throughout the final decades of the 18th century, calls for the establishment of a national art gallery were ignored, whether they came from Dr Johnson, Sir Joshua Reynolds or such connoisseurs as Sir George Beaumont. Opportunities were lost: the government declined to acquire Sir Horace Walpole's famous Houghton Collection in 1777; the Empress Catherine of Russia bought it for her palace in St Petersburg, L'Hermitage. Beaumont offered to leave his own paintings to the nation, as did the Revd Howell Carr, both making the same condition that the government provide a suitable gallery: all in vain.

It was the news that, following the death of John Julius Angerstein, his celebrated collection was to be sold and was on offer to the Prince of Orange that finally stirred Lord Liverpool's government into action. Parliament voted £60,000 and on 10 May 1824 the embryonic National Gallery opened in Angerstein's house at 100 Pall Mall, with thirty-eight paintings, the first of which, No. 1 in the catalogue, appropriately, was Sebastiano del Piombo's landscape *The Raising of Lazarus*, a metaphor.

The founding thirty-eight included Raphael's reflective portrait of *Pope Julius II*; two Rembrandts, *The Woman Taken in Adultery* and *The Adoration of the Shepherds*; a late Rubens, *The Rape of the Sabine Women*; and five Claudes, among which, from the Bouillon Collection, were *The Marriage of Isaac and Rebekah* and *The Embarkation of the Queen of Sheba*.

No gallery could have had a more glitter-ing beginning, and Beaumont and Howell Carr soon made good their earlier offers: Beaumont with works from his collection at Coleorton that included Rubens's landscape *The Chateau of Steen*[217] (*c.*1636) and Claude's *Angel Appearing to Hagar and the Angel, Ishmael*;[218] Howell Carr with Titian's *Saint George and the Dragon* and Rembrandt's ravishing *A Woman Bathing in a Stream*.

The collection grew and in 1838 moved to a new building designed by William Wilkins on a superb site looking south across Trafalgar Square down Whitehall. However problems soon arose. The gallery had a Keeper but no proper management. The trustees had determinedly conservative tastes. Some good paintings were bought (van Eyck's *Arnolfini Marriage*) but important opportunities were missed (Titian's *Rape of Europa*, Mantegna's *Agony in the Garden*, Cima's *Madonna with a Goldfinch*).[219] Eventually a very critical House of Commons Report in 1851 established a new beginning. There was to be a professional, qualified Director with independence and authority and an acquisition fund.

Over the next fifty years the gallery had three outstanding Directors, Eastlake, Sir William Boxall and Sir William Burton, who between them established the collection you see today. Study it or sip it; walk through it or wander; as you look, slowly and carefully, so will you be rewarded.

Stand in the new piazza that was Trafalgar Square and consider Wilkins's facade. It is drawn out in repetitive sections with, in the words of the architectural historian Sir John Summerson, 'a dome over the portico and turrets over the terminal pavilions, like the clock and vases on a mantelpiece, only less useful,'[220] but the steps leading up to the central portico are impressive and the sense of occasion is maintained as you enter. More steps take you up to the Central Hall, designed by E. M. Barry. Above and behind you is Lord Leighton's *Cimabue's Celebrated Madonna Carried in Procession Through the Streets of Florence* (1854–5),[221] a celebration of the triumph of Florentine painting described by Vasari in *The Lives of the Artists*.[222] In the

The Nativity *by Piero della Francesca*
(National Gallery)

Central Hall, to the left, to the right and before you, lie the galleries. Through their doorways, at the far end of each axis, can be seen Cima's *The Incredulity of St Thomas* (left), Stubbs's *Whistlejacket* (right), Van Dyck's *Charles I on Horseback* (ahead): dramatic and noble prospects that anticipate the riches within and describe at a glance the chronological layout of the gallery: 1260–1600 to the left; 1600–1700 ahead; 1700–1900 to the right.

In whichever direction you go you walk into a history of art. To your left is a room of paintings from late 15th-century Florence in which are Leonardo's *Virgin of the Rocks* (*c.*1405), Michelangelo's 'Manchester Madonna' (1497), Filippino Lippi's *Virgin and Child with Ss. Jerome and Dominic* (*c.*1485), Ghirlandaio's *Portrait of a Young Man in Red* (*c.*1480). Near by is Duccio's triptych *The Virgin and Child with Saints*, a trophy of Eastlake's campaign to introduce into the gallery the works of the 14th century, the so-called Italian Primitives, previously dismissed by such powerful trustees as the former Prime Minister and collector of Dutch paintings Sir Robert Peel, with the comment 'I think we should not collect curiosities.'

Near by are works by Robert Campin, by his pupil Rogier van der Weyden and by Jan van Eyck and, next door, Uccello's *The Battle of San Romano*, bought by Eastlake as part of the Lombardo-Baldi Collection.

In the furthest corner of the Sainsbury Wing[223] in which these early treasures are displayed is a small room that epitomises the scholarship and taste that Eastlake and Burton contributed to the gallery. It contains only five paintings: Piero della Francesca's *The Nativity*, *The Baptism of Christ* and *St Michael*, and two works (heavily repainted) by his master, Domenico Veneziano. In the 1850s the work of Piero della Francesca, and the praise given to him by Vasari in *The Lives of the Artists*, were scarcely remembered. Eastlake found *The Baptism of Christ* in the Sacristy of the Duomo in Sansepolcro 'almost ruined by sun and damp' in 1861 when he, his wife and their friend John Charles Robinson, an agent for the South Kensington Museum, were on one of their annual tours of Italy in search of works

of art for their galleries. Later the Eastlakes bought *St Michael* and in 1874 Burton purchased *The Nativity*. Here, in this still, quiet room, in the depiction of the two events at the heart of the Christian faith, is the kernel of the National Gallery.

Return to the Central Hall and there, ahead, are rooms of Dutch paintings that the gallery acquired while Burton was Director, in part from Sir Robert Peel's collection in 1871 and in part from the Wynn Ellis bequest in 1876. Here is a room devoted to Rembrandt, mainly from the 1650s and 1660s, the years of mounting financial difficulties that culminated in his bankruptcy in 1656. In these paintings he looks with ruthless clarity into his own face and the faces of those who sat to him (*Jacob Trip* and his wife *Margaretta de Geer*). Next door is a room of paintings by Rubens (portraits, narratives, landscapes) and, beyond, the landscapes of Hobbema and Ruisdael, and the seascapes of van der Velde and van de Cappelle.

By the time of Burton's retirement in 1894, the character and shape of the gallery's collections were established and its strengths and weaknesses apparent. It is predominantly a collection of Italian and Dutch painting. Its holdings of German and Spanish artists are of high quality but are limited. Despite shrewd purchases of works by Ingres, Delacroix and Manet at the Degas sale in 1918 and gifts by Sir Hugh Lane and Samuel Courtauld, the French collection here cannot compare with the 18th- and early 19th-century collection at the Wallace, or the Impressionists and Post-Impressionists at the Courtauld Institute (v. Wallace Collection and Courtauld Collection).

There remains a small number of fine paintings by Reynolds, Gainsborough, Turner and Constable in the National Gallery, but it has not housed the national collection of British art since the building of the Tate Gallery (now Tate Britain, q.v.) in 1897, and the final transfer of paintings from Trafalgar Square to Millbank in 1954.[224]

The 20th century saw the embellishment of the National Gallery's collections by bequests of paintings from George Salting in 1920 and of forty-three Italian paintings of the 15th and 16th centuries from Dr Ludwig Mond in 1924. The gallery was also enriched by purchases: the *Wilton Diptych* in 1929, the Leonardo cartoon *Madonna and Child with St Anne and John the Baptist* (purchased 1965), Bartolomé Bemejo's *St Michael Triumphant over the Devil* (1995), Cimabue's *The Madonna and Child Enthroned with Two Angels* (2000) and Raeburn's *The Archers* (2000). In 2004 the gallery acquired Raphael's *Madonna of the Pinks*, further strengthening its exceptional group of Raphaels.

To have achieved all this without a founding royal collection is remarkable. The Prado brought together the collection of Charles V from the Alhambra and those of Philip II and Philip IV from the Escorial. The collections of Francis I and Louis XIV, advised by Richelieu and Mazarin, merged with the trophies of Napoleon Bonaparte to enrich the Louvre. The Kunsthistorische Museum in Vienna combines the collections of the Emperor Maximilian I, patron of Dürer, with what was left of Rudolph II's collection after Prague fell to the Swedes in 1648. The National Gallery turned the disadvantage of having no princely provenance into the advantage of being able to build a collection from scratch, subject only and always to the availability of paintings coming on to the market and to the money, whether from public taxation or gift, to afford them.[225]

If this is not a national collection of British art it is a collection for the nation, in Eastlake's words, for 'instructing the public in the history of art' or, more precisely, in the history of Western European painting.

That education can take many forms: directly, by the ways in which curators hang and interpret works, drawing our attention to the correspondences and dialogues between paintings; indirectly, by the way in which each visitor approaches the collection differently: wandering at random from one great work to another, from Botticelli's *Mystic Nativity* to Velásquez's *The Toilet of Venus* (the 'Rokeby' Venus) or seeking out the less well known, Pisanello's *St Eustace*, Gaspard Dughet's *A Road near Albano* or Jan van Eyck's tiny *Man in a Turban*, possibly a self-portrait with its inscription round the frame 'ALS ICH CAN' – 'As I can [but not as I would]'.

We can find here an education about what art has been most concerned with (Greek myth, Christian faith, the beauty of the world around us); and about art itself, about perspective, about light, about colour. We can come up close to great paintings and inspect the quality of the paint. We can come within an inch of the artist's mind at the moment at which he made a brushstroke, fast or slow, light or heavy, tentative or confident. All this is beyond the grasp of reproduction or any new technology. Above all we can learn here about life, and how to look at it.

Every emotion is here. The grief of satyr and dog in Piero di Cosimo's *The Death of Procris*; the wonder of Gainsborough's daughters chasing butterflies; vulnerability in Piero della Francesca's *Baptism of Christ*; belief in Michelangelo's *The Entombment*; sublime love in Bellini's *Madonna and Child*. These paintings are evidence enough, if it is needed, of Bernard Berenson's judgement of the efficacy of art: 'A good rough test is whether we feel that it is reconciling us with life.'[226] At the National Gallery we do.

NATIONAL MARITIME MUSEUM ✱✱✱✱

Greenwich, London SE10 9NF
Tel. 020 8858 4422
e-mail www.nmm.ac.uk

Wren's great fleet of buildings, full of Britain's sea-girt history

Where should the nation's maritime museum be but Greenwich? Who at its centre but Nelson? This is the site of a royal palace, a royal park, and the Old Royal Naval College (originally the Royal Naval Hospital for Seamen). From here Drake set sail to circumnavigate the world and Frobisher to find the North-West Passage.

Here, among the Nelson relics, is the undress uniform coat he wore at Trafalgar, its

Arthur William Devis's Death of Nelson
(National Maritime Museum)

four glittering orders pinned over the heart, inviting and defying French snipers aloft, the fatal bullet hole in the left shoulder.

It was purchased by Prince Albert and presented to the hospital in 1845 for the 'national Naval Gallery' in the Painted Hall – an idea of the hospital's Lieutenant Governor, William Locker, who served as young Nelson's captain in the *Lowestoffe*.

In 1936 the contents of the 'Naval Gallery' passed into the care of the new National Maritime Museum, over the road, becoming part of a collection, now comprising nearly 2.5 million items, that charts how this small island has sent men over the seas to explore, trade

or conquer for over four centuries. Here are the instruments and sea charts that gave them direction, here the drawings, paintings and photographs that record their deeds.

The museum itself (opened in 1937) was founded by Act of Parliament in 1934, after a long campaign led by the Society for Nautical Research and on the generosity of the Scottish shipowner Sir James Caird: from 1927 to his death in 1954 he put more than £1.25 million into collections, purchase and building works. The magnificent buildings (1807–76) were originally developed round the Queen's House (q.v.) as the 'jewel in the crown' to accommodate what became the Royal Hospital School, which moved to Suffolk in 1933.

Caird also donated his own collection of maritime art, rare books, manuscripts, models and instruments, including an Iberian astrolabe of 1588; an astronomical regulator (1725) made for the Astronomer Royal, Edmund Halley, by George Graham; and an astronomer's alarm clock (Grimalde and Johnson, 1827).

There are thematic displays about Maritime London, the Ship of War, Passengers, Trade and Empire, Oceans of Discovery, and a lively hands-on interactive gallery for children called All Hands. Aspects of the Future of the Sea are also tackled, as well as its history.

Most of the museum's collection of over a hundred boats has now left Greenwich for its associated 'branch', the award-winning National Maritime Museum, Cornwall (q.v.), but highlights remain. These include the gilded barge designed for Frederick, Prince of Wales, by William Kent in 1732, built by John Hall and carved in a rococo riot of mermaids, shells, fishes and 'sea-lion' heads by James Richards, who succeeded Grinling Gibbons as Royal Carver.

The Art and the Sea gallery displays some of the 4,000 oil paintings and 70,000 prints and drawings in its collection. Greenwich saw the birth of 'maritime art' in England in the 1670s, when the great Dutch marine painters, the Willem van de Veldes, arrived at the invitation of Charles II, who provided them with a studio to work for him in the Queen's House.

The marine tradition in which they were trained is displayed here in works by Jan Porcellis, Jan van Goyen, Andries van Eertvelt and Bonaventura Peeters the Elder. They recorded with exactitude every aspect of maritime life: merchant ships and men-of-war, convoys and battles, dockings, embarkation and manoeuvres. The van de Veldes had their own yacht which sailed with the fleet and from which they gathered the material for the paintings, notably the Younger's masterwork here, The Battle of the Texel, fought in 1673, based on drawings by his father, also exhibited. The museum in fact has the finest single collection of Dutch 17th-century marine art in existence and its influence is clear in the equally impressive works of English followers of the 18th century, such as Peter Monamy,

Charles Brooking, Samuel Scott, Dominic Serres (a French émigré) and Nicholas Pocock – both the last two being ex sea-captains. The adjacent Nelson gallery is dominated by Turner's mighty Battle of Trafalgar, the largest canvas he ever painted, which brings to a head the balance that the collection tries to maintain between paintings of record and works of art. It was commissioned by George IV in 1822, as a pendant to Philip de Loutherbourg's Battle of the First of June 1794 (also in the museum), as part of a royal 're-hang' commemorating British victories in St James's Palace.

Butlin and Joll tell us that 'Turner as usual took immense pains to get the details right,'[227] obtaining sketches of all the ships involved. Thornbury recounts in his biography that Turner was 'instructed daily by the naval men about the Court. During eleven days he altered the rigging to suit the fancy of every fresh critic.'[228] Despite this, the review in the Literary Gazette attacked it as 'full of glaring falsehoods and palpable inconsistencies'.[229] Sir Thomas Hardy, Nelson's flag-captain at Trafalgar, considered that it was like 'a street scene, as the ships had more the effect of houses than men of war'. Such criticisms provoked Ruskin to defend Turner by claiming that the picture 'at a moderate estimate, is simply worth all the rest of the [Greenwich] hospital-grounds-walls-pictures and models put together.'

It isn't. It cannot compare with Turner's greatest marine paintings, The Slave Ship (Slavers)[230] (1840) and Burial at Sea[231] (1838); nor is his attempt wholly successful to reconcile the fear and pain of the sailors struggling in the water for their lives in the foreground, with the stately triumph of the Victory, with the motto 'England expects' visible beneath the waves.

A comparable gap to that between 'Nelson the man' and 'Nelson the hero' runs through this collection. The personal relics (the dirk and sword given to him by Captain Suckling, c.1790; his writing box; his walking stick) contrast with the bloodstained stockings and breeches cut from the legs in death; the shy young captain depicted by John Francis Rigaud in his portrait of 1781 contrasts with

Lemuel Abbott's famous portrait, and with the Christ-like figure, bathed in light, in Arthur William Devis's historically inaccurate *Death of Nelson*, 1807.

There are glimpses of the man – his vanity (the chelengk[232] given to him by the Sultan of Turkey after the battle of the Nile, seen in the Abbott portrait), his love for Emma Hamilton (painted here as a young woman by Romney, before Nelson knew her), her neglect by the British government after Nelson's death – but it is 'Nelson the icon' that appears to dominate, until you are confronted by the battle plan of Trafalgar. On the back of a yellowing scrap of paper, Nelson fleetingly sketched the idea that, when he revealed it to his admirals, gave them 'an electric shock'.[233] Where the British fleet, in three divisions, cuts the enemy line in two places, Nelson's pen digs into the paper.

This is a collection packed with virtues, in the ideal location from which to explore Britain's glorious naval and maritime history. The collection, the museum's cargo, is, like all ships' cargoes, mostly stored below decks, out of sight. With its origins in Prince Albert's 'national Naval Gallery', the collection is weighted towards the naval and so too, until the 1960s and '70s, was the museum, which had a tendency to list towards the heroic.

Neither the darker corners of naval life (the press gangs, the work of ships' surgeons, life below decks) nor the many aspects of Britain's non-maritime history were very prominent. A visitor could leave little wiser about how and why two of Europe's smaller nations (Britain and Holland) should have dominated the oceans in the 17th and 18th centuries, or about the contribution of naval power to our island's wider history, its trade and its science; the importation of ideas and, indeed, people.

In recent years the museum's curators and directors, led first by Basil Greenhill and now by Roy Clare, have worked to present a wider picture, most evident in the Neptune Court. Exploration, navigation, trade, passengers and 'the Future of the Sea' are now tackled clearly and well, and it is inevitable and right

that future acquisitions will tend to favour the maritime (and its environment) over the naval.

It is equally inevitable and right that visitors will continue to be drawn here by the resonance of 'Greenwich' and by the hero who remains at the centre of the museum, Horatio Nelson.

NATIONAL MUSEUM OF THE PERFORMING ARTS **

Russell Street, Covent Garden, London
WC2E 7PR
Tel. 020 7943 4700
www.theatremuseum.org.

Star turns in Covent Garden

After thirty-six years in storage, in 2004 the largest Picasso canvas in the world was rolled out by the curators of the National Museum of the Performing Arts.[234] No wall in the museum was large enough to exhibit it: for that a redesign and redevelopment of the museum will be necessary.

The museum, an outstation of the Victoria and Albert Museum on the edge of Covent Garden, is not short of exciting artefacts and collections from 400 years of British theatre: programmes and playbills, sets and costumes; posters, puppets; and Somerset Maugham's collection of paintings. These include David Garrick as Jaffier in Thomas Otway's *Venice Preserved*, by Johann Zoffany; Garrick and Kean as Richard III, by, respectively, Francis Hayman and George Clint; and, two centuries later, Richard Burton as Henry V by Frank Salisbury.

Star names jostle for top billing throughout the collection. It contains the Sir Henry Irving Archive; the designs of Edward Gordon Craig; the letters of Sir Michael Redgrave; and videos of some of the most praised productions of recent years (Tom Stoppard's *Arcadia*, directed by Trevor Nunn; Declan Donnellan's production of *As You Like It* for Cheek by Jowl, 1995; Jocelyn Herbert's set for the Royal Shakespeare Company's production of Samuel

Beckett's *Endgame*, 1958; and Sally Jacobs's for Peter Brook's 1964 *Marat/Sade* at the Aldwych.

The collections are equally strong in material from opera and dance: Léon Bakst's costumes for Michel Fokine are here (for *Sheherazade*, 1910, *Le Dieu Bleu*, 1912 and *Papillons*, 1914); as are William Chappell's costume for Alicia Markova in Ashton's *Les Rendezvous* (1933), and John Piper's models for Britten's *Rape of Lucretia* at Glyndebourne (1946).

Despite these star turns, and the museum's location in the centre of the West End, the museum has struggled to establish a public profile since opening here in 1987. The building has not helped. Its galleries are underground, a warren of ramps, corridors and small galleries, poorly designed and poorly lit.

The V&A knows all about the distinctions between study collections, for experts and research, and secondary collections, for the enjoyment and education of the general public. The study collections here are of the greatest importance: about 100,000 playbills, programmes and playtexts given to the V&A by Gabrielle Enthoven in 1924 (continuously updated),[235] Harry R. Beard's collection of theatrical and operatic prints and texts; and material that came from the British Theatre Museum Association and from Richard Buckle's Friends of the Museum of Performing Arts which contributed much Ballets Russes material. To these have been added books[236] (as published and 'graingerised', with interleavings and additions), prompt books, diaries and manuscripts.[237] The English Stage and the D'Oyly Carte Companies have given their archives. These, and the administrative papers of the Contemporary Dance School, are likely to be of interest principally to researchers, but much else is immediately attractive and intriguing: Noël Coward's dressing gown, the Victorian Tiller Clowes marionettes, the sets and props of the National Theatre's production of *The Wind in the Willows*.

Edward Gordon Craig's set model for Konstantin Stanislavsky's *Hamlet* at the Moscow Arts Theatre in 1911[238] carries you across the theatrical history of Europe in the 20th century, while 19th-century photographs (such as Ellen Terry as Juliet in Irving's 1882 production) give us an illusion, for an instant, that we can stretch out to the theatre of the past. Meanwhile the National Video Archive allows you to retrieve the performance of a contemporary star such as Robert Stephens in Adrian Noble's RSC production of *King Lear* and compare it with Yvonne Brewster's production for Talawa Theatre the following year, with Ben Thomas as Lear. All that is needed is the redesign that will allow these collections, and Picasso's canvas, the space they deserve.

NATIONAL PORTRAIT GALLERY ★★★★

St Martin's Place, London WC2H 0HE
Tel. 020 7312 2463
www.npg.org.uk

Great British men and women, taken from the life

Curiously the National Portrait Gallery (NPG) offers only the slightest of faces to the outside world. While the National Gallery looks down on Trafalgar Square and its new piazza, the National Portrait Gallery is wrapped around its side, in Henry James's view, 'like a bustle attached to the cladding of the National's posterior'.

It was founded in 1856 after a prolonged campaign that culminated in a debate in Parliament on a motion that 'a Gallery of the Portraits of the most eminent Persons in British History' should be formed. Lord Palmerston, the Prime Minister, spoke in support; the government voted a sum of £2,000 and proceeded to appoint Lord Macaulay to the Board of Trustees.[239] He was joined the following year by Thomas Carlyle.[240]

Initially the gallery had no permanent home and its collection, whose first picture was Lord Ellesmere's gift of the so-called Chandos Shakespeare,[241] moved from Great George Street, Westminster, to South Kensington, and then to Bethnal Green before a philanthropist, Mr W. H. Alexander, offered to pay for a new building. Designed by Ewan Christian, it is an undistinguished piece of architecture (a half-hearted pastiche of an Italian palazzo, with Early English round-headed windows) on an inauspicious site. You enter, without ceremony, off St Martin's Place. Neither in the sombre entrance nor in the new foyer, a blazing white space three storeys high designed by Jeremy Dixon and Edward Jones (2000), is there any indication that this is a portrait gallery.

Yet the NPG is not short of confidence. It has no doubt that the past is interesting and important. It is aware that the public is drawn to its temporary exhibitions and to contemporary images of celebrities but it also knows that the worth lies in its historic collection, which can fascinate and excite, if only the visitor can be persuaded to look beyond the present.

From the white clarity of the foyer you are carried, by escalator, up to the top floor and plunged into the darkness and intrigue of the 16th century, from which you will descend, through 500 years, to the celebrities of today on the ground floor.

The criteria for inclusion in this pantheon were quickly established. In a letter to Lord Ellesmere after the debate, thanking him for the gift of the Chandos Shakespeare, the then Chancellor of the Exchequer W. E. Gladstone wrote, 'the authenticity of a portrait, and the celebrity of the person represented, will be the grounds for the admission of a picture, and not its excellence as a work of art.'[242] Draft rules, adopted at the trustees' first meeting, add that 'no portrait of any person still living ... [or] deceased less than ten years shall be admitted' and 'no portrait admitted by donation' nor any 'modern copy of an original portrait'.[243]

Such criteria beg questions for a national portrait gallery. What nation? Mainly England. Whose history? The history of men and events, heroic, not Marxist. How you define 'eminent Persons' and celebrity, or what constitutes a portrait, are more difficult questions to answer. What constitutes 'eminence' varies from age to age. The portraits of monarchs and

courtiers, soldiers and statesmen of the 16th and 17th centuries are succeeded by those of the writers, connoisseurs and architects of the 18th century and those who mapped and claimed the Empire, and by the scientists and engineers, novelists and reformers, philanthropists and magnates of the 19th century. It is easy to see why Wellington and Nelson, Dr Johnson and Dickens, Captain Cook or Sir Walter Raleigh, are here just as it is hard not to feel that Sir Robert Vyner, Lord Mayor of London in 1674,[244] or Captain Frederick Gustavus Burnaby, elegant soldier and balloonist though he was (and elegant though his portrait, by J. J. Tissot, is) have had eminence thrust upon them.

Some of the portraits here are also magnificent paintings: Rubens gives us the shrewd and worldly *Thomas Howard*, 2nd Earl of Arundel, the remains of whose collection of antique sculptures are in the Ashmolean Museum (q.v.); Reynolds catches the novelist Laurence Sterne, aquiline of beak and eye.

Other paintings are barely competent, although the least skilled can sometimes be the most revealing. The timid drawing of *Jane Austen* by her sister Cassandra captures the Jane Austen whom her brother Henry described as being 'so refined, unmarked by contemporary notoriety'. The canvas on which Branwell Brontë painted his sisters Anne, Emily and Charlotte lay folded and creased on the top of a cupboard for more than a hundred years, yet the sisters' eyes burn and the set of Charlotte's chin and mouth are as stubborn as Jane Eyre's.

Ideally, eminent sitters merit the consideration of eminent painters but some portraits here fall short. Sickert's treatment of *Winston Churchill* (1929), painted in his years in the political wilderness, captures little of his charm or the complexity of his character. Churchill disliked it and gave it away soon after it was presented to him. Karsh's later photographs give us the war leader but without conveying any of the personal insecurities. Kneller's oil sketch of Churchill's ancestor, the 1st Duke of Marlborough (*c.*1706), is a delightful pastiche of Rubens, with the victor of Blenheim and

A long perspective in the National Portrait Gallery

Ramillies being crowned with laurels, watched over by Justice, while Discord falls beneath the hooves of his prancing steed, but it tells us nothing of the man.

Conversely, in his portrait of a lonely, exhausted *Charles Darwin* (1881), in the year before he died, John Collier captures the calm patience with which Darwin regarded the world.[245] Helmut Newton's photograph of a desolated *Margaret Thatcher* (1991), taken after she was removed from office, is eloquent on the subject of power and the loss of power.

Despite Gladstone's insistence on the primacy of the sitter over the artist, the gallery cannot but hold up a unique mirror to British portraiture. Until the early 18th century artists from the Low Countries and Germany dominate. Holbein, Eworth, Flicke; Mytens,

Oliver, Van Dyck, Rubens, van Honthorst; Lely, Kneller, Wissing and Dahl continually reinvent the portrait while Walker, Dobson, Hawker, Jervas and John Michael Wright work in the shadow of their talents. It is only in the 18th century that the portrait in Britain emerges: Richardson and Hogarth, Devis and Highmore, Hudson and Joseph Wright, and the high summer of Reynolds and Gainsborough, Ramsay, Raeburn and Romney.

Of these last only Reynolds is shown to full advantage, in his portraits of *Dr Johnson*, *Garrick*, *Sterne* (above) and *Horace Walpole* (1757). The author of *The Castle of Otranto* is depicted (in the opinion of one contemporary observer) as having a 'most unhealthy paleness'.[246]

In the 18th century, portraiture was commonly referred to as 'face painting' and portraits as 'likenesses'. Gainsborough maintained that 'Likeness is the principal beauty and intention of a Portrait' but, in a post-Freudian age, we expect a portrait to go beyond a mere attempt to produce a likeness and most admire those artists who can, in Graham Sutherland's words, tease off 'layer upon layer of wrapping [that] cover personality'.

To read the portraits here demands a wider vocabulary than 'representations and likeness' or 'psychological insight'. Allegory or symbolism are frequently employed to augment the evidence of a face. Many are not what they seem. In *Edward VI and the Pope: an Allegory of the Reformation*, it would appear that Henry VIII, on his deathbed, is passing on responsibility for the reform of the Church to his son, Edward VI. At his feet is a downcast Pope, across whose chest is written 'ALL FLESHE IS GRASSE'. Beside him are monks evicted from their monasteries. A picture on the wall behind the members of the Council of Regency shows a building, representing the old church order of Rome, collapsing: a straightforward narrative. But this wall picture, and the position in which Henry VIII is lying, are taken from a print after the Flemish painter, Marten van Heemskerk, that was published in 1564, more than ten years after Edward VI's death.[247] This portrait is a piece of propaganda to sustain the Reformation in the reign of Queen Elizabeth I. Most portraits of the 19th century, by such worthies as Frank Holl, Daniel Maclise, Edward Matthew Ward and William Strang, are untroubled by such complexities, tending to be more literal works. They feature markedly fewer still lifes, background landscapes or symbolic props that add meaning to the central image. The portraits painted by G. F. Watts for his 'Hall of Fame' (of *William Morris, Thomas Carlyle, Matthew Arnold, Cecil Rhodes, Cardinal Manning*, etc.) and by Frederick Richard Say for Sir Robert Peel's 'Statesmen's Gallery'[248] are little more than records with singular exceptions (Watts's sensuous portrait of his wife, Ellen Terry, smelling a camellia, while holding a simple bunch of violets, and entitled *Choosing*. She chose to divorce Watts, thirty years her senior, a year later). At the end of the century there

are portraits by John Singer Sargent (of *Arthur Balfour*) and Giovanni Boldini (of the provocative beauty *Lady Colin Campbell*), which introduce a new swagger, not least by stretching the rules of anatomy by giving their sitters gloriously, exaggeratedly, long legs.

The invention of photography twenty years before the National Portrait Gallery was founded should have offered new possibilities. David Octavius Hill and Robert Adamson had grasped these in Edinburgh in the 1840s (v. Scottish National Portrait Gallery); Roger Fenton had brought back portraits of those fighting in the Crimea in 1885[249] and by 1860 commercial photographic studios were opening in both Paris and London. No longer was portraiture the preserve of those who could commission painters; nor were the settings for portraits limited to the studio. The NPG has fine photographs by Julia Margaret Cameron of *Tennyson, Carlyle*, and *Darwin*; Napoleon Sarony's portrait of *Oscar Wilde* (1882) as a dreaming dandy at the start of his American tour, in cravat, quilted smoking jacket and knee breeches; and Robert Howlett's monumental image of *Isambard Kingdom Brunel* (1857), stovepipe hat on head, cheroot in mouth, in front of the anchor chains of his ship the *Great Eastern* just before it was launched.

There are fine 20th-century photographs (George Charles Beresford's of *Virginia Woolf*, 1902, Richard Avedon's of *W. H. Auden*, 1960, in a snow storm) but the memorable images are drawings (*T. E. Lawrence* by Augustus John, 1919, completed in two minutes at Lawrence's St John's Wood flat) and paintings: Laura Knight's *Self-portrait* (1913) as she paints her friend, Ella Naper, whose pale naked back is set against the clash of oranges and reds; Ruskin Spear's *Harold Wilson* (c. 1974) in a cloud of obfuscation and pipe smoke; Patrick Heron's Cubist analysis of *T. S. Eliot* (1949), overlaying his full face with his profile; Ben Nicholson's ravishing double portrait of himself and *Barbara Hepworth* (1933), their profiles rippling over each other, in the year that they married and in which he (later) abandoned representation; and Tom Phillips's view of

Dame Iris Murdoch (1986) in front of Titian's *Flaying of Marsyas*, beside a sprig from the world's most ancient tree, the gingko, in a portrait whose clean Holbein-like lines belie the complexity of her novels.

Since 1967, under the directorship of Sir Roy Strong (1967–74), John Hayes (1974–94) Charles Saumarez Smith (1994–2002) and Sandy Nairne (appt. 2002), the ten-year rule has been abandoned (1969). Portraits of contemporary celebrities are continually commissioned and new media embraced. Tom Phillips's portrait of *Professor Susan Greenfield* (1999–2000), the director of the Royal Institution, combines computer-processed drawings and video: 169 drawings on paper and 22,500 frames in computer, whose sequence changes and decomposes Professor Greenfield's face. Marc Quinn has depicted *Sir John Sulston*, the director of the Sanger Centre and principal participant in the Human Genome Project, by framing a sample of Sir John's own DNA set between a photograph of the artist and one of the subject.

Having descended from the Tudor monarchs to Sir John's DNA, it is hard to say what picture the National Portrait Gallery gives us of the nation. Is there an English face? Each gallery gives a different answer.

The England shown here is predominantly male, metropolitan, effective. Rural, marine and industrial Britain are largely absent. Children peer from the edges of some paintings. There are few references to work, poverty or ill health. Nevertheless the human diversity of images and characters sweeps aside most reservations. Here are lust, authority and pride; foresight and wisdom; arrogance and kindness. When you come across uncertainty, irony and humour, they wink at you across the generations. Recognition is one of the many social pleasures this hugely entertaining gallery offers.

There are few objects more fascinating, beautiful, revealing or enigmatic for us than the human face; the National Portrait Gallery will always be a gallery that the visitor returns to time and again to look into faces not his own and catch a glimpse of an otherness and of himself. Carlyle called the portrait 'a small lighted candle' by which we could read biographies. Here is a celebratory procession of such candles.

NATURAL HISTORY MUSEUM *****

Cromwell Road, London SW7 5BD
Tel. 020 7942 5000
www.nhm.ac.uk/

Waterhouse's magnificent creation shelters and documents all creation

'It is indeed wonderful to consider that there should be a sort of learned men who are wholly employed in gathering together the refuse of nature . . . and so hoarding up in the chests and cabinets such creatures as others industriously avoid the sight of.' Joseph Addison was writing in *The Spectator* on 26 August 1710, more than forty years before Sir Hans Sloane's 'universal collection'[250] of plants, insects, shells, corals and other curiosities became one of the founding collections of the British Museum (q.v.) in 1753.

Since then the 'hoarding up in the chests and cabinets' of this museum amounts to over 70 million specimens,[251] probably the greatest natural history museum in the world. Here is evidence of what man has learnt about fossils and minerals, mammals and reptiles, birds and fishes, insects and plants, in the past 250 years.

To the layman, the diversity and curiosity of these specimens might appear to dazzle and bewilder. 'I wish I was as good a Natural Historian, that I might give you some idea of our entertainment in seeing birds, beasts, shells, fossils, etc,' wrote Susan Burney to her sister, the novelist Fanny Burney, 'but I can scarce remember a dozen names of the thousand I heard that were new to me. The birds of paradise and the humming birds were, I think, among the most beautiful.' Susan Burney was describing a visit to Sir Ashton Lever's museum in Leicester House, but although a visitor today to the Natural History Museum

(NHM) might recognise her response, the method and effect of the NHM is precisely other: to order and to inform.

These galleries describe the development of natural history from when, in the 17th century, specimens were classified by their degrees of usefulness to man (edible or not; wild or tame) to the taxonomy of Sloane which, with ponderous accuracy, needed a sentence to describe a plant: *nerium arboreum* (a tree), *folio maximo obtussiore* (blunt leaf shape), *flore incarnatus* (colour: flesh pink) – in other words, the frangipani. The genius of the Swedish botanist Carl von Linné, aka Linnaeus, reduced such descriptions to two words, genus and species; and, in the last fifty years, the identification of genes, composed of DNA molecules, has allowed further simplification.

The museum's collections have provided the evidence cited in the great debates that divided public and academic opinion in the late 18th and 19th centuries about the age of our planet and the evolution of life, and of man. Sloane collected in a world that believed the word of the Bible that God created the world in six days, 4,500 years ago. Fossil and geological specimens were arranged to fit into that frame. William Buckland's discovery in 1821 of animal bones in the Kirkdale Cave indicated that Yorkshire must once, tens of thousands of years ago, have been a subtropical land where elephants and rhinoceros roamed. He was supported by the findings of Sir Charles Lyell, Mary Anning, Roderick Murchison, Gideon Mantell and others. Their conclusions, and those of Charles Darwin in *On the Origin of Species*,[252] were dismissed by Sir Richard Owen, superintendent of the natural history departments of the British Museum.[253] Owen had coined the term 'dinosaur' ('terrible lizard'), at a meeting of the British Association of the Advancement of Science in 1841. Only when he retired in 1884 and was succeeded by William Henry Flower did the Natural History Museum fully reassess the evidence of its own collections.

Flower has a good claim to be the most original and influential British museum director of the 19th century. Not only did he, by

putting aside Owen's reactionary views, bring the museum into the light of the emerging sciences; he did so by rethinking the way in which museums were organised and how they should relate to the public.

In his presidential address to the British Association in 1889, Flower described his 'new museum idea'. The museum should serve equally the public (through exhibitions of its 'primary collections') and the scholar/expert (through research and access to 'study secondary collections'). An 'Index Museum'[254] in the main hall would explain the nature of the collections; labels and graphic commentaries would accompany objects; dioramas and tableaux would show animals in their habitats. The museum would have five departments: botany, zoology, mineralogy, entomology[255] and palaeontology. Instead of the jumble of objects, inadequately labelled and comprehensible only to the expert, that Owen had favoured, the public were going to be welcomed and the objects used to educate them.

Flower was fortunate to have a new, purpose-built museum in which to develop his revolutionary approach. It became clear in the early 1860s that the natural history collections could no longer be adequately exhibited at the British Museum in Bloomsbury. Francis Fowke, the architect of the Royal Albert Hall and the South Kensington Museum (later rebuilt as the Victoria and Albert Museum, q.v.), won the competition to design it in a Renaissance style inspired by the Uffizi in Florence. He died in 1865 before the work could begin and Alfred Waterhouse was chosen to redesign it on Romanesque lines.[256] Following Deane and Woodward's design for the Oxford University Museum of Natural History (q.v.) in 1860, it marked a decisive step away from the neoclassicism of Robert Smirke that had dominated museum building and museum thinking for more than fifty years.

As at Oxford the ornamentation, within and without, reflected the collections: carvings of leaves and flowers; of pigeons, rheas, raccoons; and a gecko.[257] The entrance hall soars up to a glass and iron roof and is dominated by a monumental staircase at the

Origins and evolution at the Natural History Museum

far end. It is a building that speaks of confidence, utility, technology and scholarship. From the apex of the central gable, Adam looked down.[258] It opened on Easter Monday 1881, when 16,000 people 'of a most orderly and respectable class' visited.

The museum is a collection of collections: the plants that Sloane brought back from Jamaica in 1689, including the type specimen for cacao from which he made a fortune by selling his recipe for milk chocolate[259] to Cadbury Bros; the plants that Sir Joseph Banks brought from Australasia on Captain Cook's HMS *Endeavour* (1768–71); the finches from the Galapagos Islands, said to have led Charles Darwin to his theory of evolution; Henry Walter Bates's 14,000 insects collected in Amazonia in the 1850s; and the rare 'living specimen of the pearly nautilus' from HMS *Challenger*'s exploration (1872–6) of ocean depths, which had previously been thought to be lifeless.

Here too are the collections of those who were less fortunate, of John Lawson, the Surveyor-General of North Carolina, killed by Tuscarora Indians who 'stuck him full of fine splinters of torchwood, like hoggs' bristles, and so set them gradually on fire'. Or Wallace Bates's friend Alfred Russel Wallace, who developed a theory of evolution independently of Charles Darwin but has never received equal recognition. His library and his collection of personal papers and tropical species honour him here.

These collections combine the rare (the first example of parrotfish, collected by Darwin; the emperor penguin eggs found by Bowers and Wilson on Captain Scott's ill-fated Antarctic expedition, 1911), the curious (Sloane's glove made from the 'beard' of the mussel; the water buffalo horns given by Mr D'Oyley, whose name is immortalised in paper mats) and the beautiful (the vermilion cinnabar and the cranberry-red bixbite gleaming in the dark of the minerals gallery); the paintings[260] by Ferdinand Bauer of flying fish and weedy seadragons and by Albertus Seba of puffer fish and giant squid; and the museum's wonderful taxidermy, among which are many animals prepared by the great 19th-century taxidermist James Rowland Ward.

It is a testament to the remarkable diversity of the collections here that, until now, no mention has been made of the museum's meteorites (over half the meteorites that have hit this planet are here) or the collection of the skeletons of the 'terrible lizards', the naming of which made Owen's reputation: the tyranno-saurus, the camarasaurus and the small, running dromaeosaurus; the iguanodon and the triceratops; the club-tailed euplocephalus and the 150-million-year-old, 75-feet metre long, plant-eating diplodocus, a replica given to the museum in 1905 by the Carnegie Museum in Pittsburgh.

Today, Phase 1 of the Darwin Centre, opened behind the Waterhouse building in 2002, designed by architects H.O.K. International, is developing a new type of museum, as revolutionary as was W.H. Flower's 120 years ago. In it visitors will not only see (more of) the NHM's collections but will be brought into contact with the research work that the museum's 350 scientists are doing behind the scenes.

The latest technology will allow visitors to talk with scientists around the world, whether in the tropical forests of Central America or the icy wastes of Antarctica. Visitors will be able to debate with scientists such con-temporary topics as genetically modified food, global warming or pollution. Phase 2, designed by Swedish architects C.F. Møller and Partners,[261] will open in 2008, in which the

full wonders of the collections of plants will be exhibited.[262]

These centres, and their technology, will be the new face of the museum, but its work will continue, in the field, around the world: on new types of edible seaweed in Japan, on monitoring dolphins, porpoises and whales – work that reflects back to the museum's first dedicated Whale Room, opened by Flower in 1897.

OLD OPERATING THEATRE MUSEUM AND HERB GARRET **

9A St Thomas Street, London SE1 9RY
Tel. 020 7955 4791
www.thegarret.org.uk

A secret space full of the pity and terror of mortality, and advances in our struggle against it

The Church of St Thomas Apostle in South-wark was the parish church of St Thomas's Hospital from 1215 to 1862.[263] In its roof space is this small museum. You reach it by climbing thirty-two steps up a tight wooden wheel-stair to the museum's entrance and then up again to the garret, a ship of a space, all wooden beams and boards.

From every beam bunches and festoons of dried herbs are swagged and hung. The air is sweet with borage, fennel, cloves, camomile, lady's mantle, marjoram ('joy of the mountain') and self-heal, of which John Gerard wrote 'there is no better wounde herb in the world than that of Self-Heal . . . the decoction of Prunell made with wine and water doth join together and make whole and sound all wounds, both inward and outward.'

Within this roof space is London's oldest operating theatre (1821–62). It is a little wooden drum of a room, around which are five rows of steeply raked, arc-shaped benches, so that students and assistants could observe the skill of the surgeon and, before the introduction of anaesthetics, the screaming pain and/or courage of the patient, who was held down on the small wooden operating table, below which was placed a box of sawdust to absorb the blood. Outside the theatre, the rest of the garret is a museum whose exhibits show the advances in medical thinking and practice between 1700 and 1900.

The garret was a 'Herb Garrett' from which the apothecary, the hospital's chief medical officer, dispensed prescriptions. On every surface are pestles and mortars for grinding herbs, bowls and jars in which they should be steeped or stored, scales, pots and in the corner a Boschian alembic for distilling medicines. A python skin uncurls itself across the rafters; a skeleton stands in the corner. This is a place in which alchemy, custom and superstition give way gradually to experiment and knowledge, itself often confirming the 'punitive' nostrums.

Exhibits here tell us that the 10th-century *Leech Book of Bald* recommended a medicine that might cure a 'Fiend Sick Man; to be drunk out of a Church Bell'. In the 12th century the Pope forbade trained physicians to spill blood, so giving rise to the distinction, still in use today, between physicians being addressed as 'Doctor' and surgeons as 'Mister'. Dr Richard Mead, the physician of his generation who worked at St Thomas's from 1703 to 1715,[264] advocated Snail Water, a treatment for venereal disease (committed to paper in 1718 in *Pharmacopoeia Pauperum*, edited by Henry Bayer) made up of six gallons of snails, three gallons of earthworms, eight gallons of cloves, plus ivy, wormwood, pennyroyal, juniper and fennel.

As you progress round the garret, 18th-century medicines give way to 19th-century surgery and its instruments. Black metal forceps are arranged neatly in cabinets beside a vaginal speculum and an eight-pronged cervical dilator that resembles an instrument of torture. Seeing these, it is not surprising that Florence Nightingale estimated that 33 in every 1,000 women died in childbirth. Beside them are a vectis (a half forceps), a membrane perforator, a 'blunt hook and crochet' and, finally, a decapitating hook for saving the life of the mother of a child that had died within.

The displays lead you round to the Operating Theatre by way of saws, bone shears, amputation knives and a late 18th-century trepanning set for operating on the brain, without anaesthetic or antiseptic. There was a 30 per cent mortality rate after amputations before Humphry Davy (with nitrous oxide) and Michael Faraday (with ether) developed anaesthetic, and John Lister (with carbolic) antiseptics.

In the Theatre the 1822 regulations are painted on a board. 'Apprentices and the Dressers of the Surgeon who operates are to stand round the Table. The Dressers of the Surgeons are to occupy the 3 front Rows, The Surgeon's pupils are to take their Places on the Rows above.'

Although medicine has come far from the days of quacks, mountebanks and 'cunning men', from snailwater and python skins, it is a relief for the squeamish to return from the Operating Theatre to the sweet-smelling garret and to recall the hospital's motto: 'MISERATIONE NON MERCEDE' – for compassion not for gain.

PERCIVAL DAVID FOUNDATION OF CHINESE ART ★★★★

53 Gordon Square, Bloomsbury, London WC1H 0PD
Tel. 020 7387 3909

Glowing beauty of the greatest 20th-century collection of Chinese ceramics outside China

'The colour of ashes after burning' is how a Chinese archaeologist described the Ru ware excavated at Qingliangsi in Henan province in the late twentieth century.

Ru ware[265] is rare. It was made only between 1086 and 1127 in the years before the Song court was forced to flee south to Hangzhou. Most Ru pieces are undecorated, relying for their appeal on the simple elegance of their forms and the beauty of their glazes, grey blue, clear blue, purple. Here there are twelve Ru pieces, more than in any other collection outside China. It is said that Sir Percival David was allowed to bring them out of China in 1927 as an acknowledgement of the help he had given three years earlier, with the re-exhibition of the treasures of the Imperial Collection, much of which had lain in boxes since the departure of the last empress from the Forbidden City in 1907.

To further the understanding of Chinese art among European scholars and collectors Percival David established a chair at the Courtauld Institute and then in 1935 curated[266] the first International Exhibition of Chinese Art at the Royal Academy. The piece chosen as the most beautiful ceramic object at the exhibition was one of the first batch he brought to Europe in 1927–8: an exquisite pear-shaped Guan ware bottle vase whose ice-pale blue-green glaze is broken by a wide irregular golden-brown crackle. R. L. Hobson described it as realising

'all our most extravagant ideas of what Kuan [Guan] ware should be'.

By 1952 the collection had grown to over 1,700 pieces, including a gift of 150 18th-century monochrome porcelains given by the Hon. Mountstuart Elphinstone. Sir Percival established a foundation, donated the collection to the University of London and opened this museum in a house on the corner of Gordon Square in Bloomsbury. Its cool, calm rooms have pale grey walls and dove grey carpets. The ware is displayed in elegant glass cases; the light filters through the plane trees outside.

The first floor is given over to monochrome ware: Ru, Guan, Yuan (13th–14th centuries), Ming (15th–16th centuries), Qing (17th–18th centuries). Here are pieces whose glazes shift subtly from white to cream to yellow to green to blue to startling purple; the greenish lime glaze of Yue ware (3rd–4th centuries, the oldest in the collection, from Zhejiang province in the east); gently incised Yue bowls of the 9th–10th centuries; northern Song white ware (9th century);[267] cream (and black) Ding ware (11th century), its mouth rims bound with copper alloy; a spinach green Yaozhou cylindrical box (11th–12th centuries); creamy green Longquan funerary urns (12th–13th centuries) – all arranged not chronologically but chromatically according to the colour of their glaze.

On the second floor the restraint of monochrome gives way to colour: luminous lime greens, brilliant turquoises, deep berry purples, prune browns, made possible by the importation in the 14th century of cobalt and by the introduction of underglaze painting in south China. The David Vases (1351) combine these two innovations. Around these temple vases, in brilliant blue, writhe dragons and phoenixes. Into a band of plantain leaves circling each neck is set an inscription 'as a prayer for the protection of the whole family and for the peace and prosperity of his descendants'.

New techniques such as doucai (dovetailing colours) made possible polychrome designs while, in the 15th and 16th centuries, the development of low firing glazes, both lead-fluxed and alkaline, produced colours of depth and brilliance.

After Beijing fell to the Manchu armies in 1644, the great porcelain-producing town of Jingdezhen was razed to the ground in the ensuing civil wars, but the industry was rebuilt on the orders of the Kangxi Emperor. A large bowl here, c. 1700, recaptures the rich copper red glaze of the 15th century and adds to it subtle fluctuations of colour.

The Kangxi period also saw the development of delicate painting in overglaze enamels that characterises the *famille verte* ware (and its subgroups the *famille noire* and the *famille rose*) that are a feature of the collection.

Roger Fry observed that Chinese art presents 'relatively few obstacles to our appreciation'.[268] He believed that in Chinese art 'the balance between geometric regularity and sensibility is of an almost unique kind.'[269] Certainly it is easy to be soothed and ravished by this collection, but these pieces are also barometers of Chinese history and civilisation. Their designs reflect the shifting circumstances in Chinese trade and prosperity while their use, and basic shapes, have remained unchanged for centuries. 'Exquisite tea requires bowls from the Yue kilns,' wrote Zheng Gu.[270] Unchanged too, lest we sentimentalise their beauty, is the reality that these pieces were made for practical use. Lu You, in the 13th century, wrote, 'The green wares of Yaozhou are called Yue because they resemble the secret colour of Yuyao [kilns]. Yet they are extremely coarse and are used only in restaurants because they are durable.'[271]

The David Vases (Percival David)

PETRIE MUSEUM OF EGYPTIAN ARCHAEOLOGY **

University College London, Malet Place,
London WC1E 6BT
Tel. 020 7679 2884
www.petrie.ucl.ac.uk/

*Prehistory to Roman Egypt; archaeological
material in what was a stable for drayhorses*

The Petrie Museum holds finds from the
numerous Egyptian excavations of Sir William
Flinders Petrie (1853–1942), at the Great
Pyramid at Giza (1880); the Roman Period
cemeteries at Hawara (1888); Amarna, city of
Akhenaten (1891); Abydos (1899–1901); the
first true pyramid, Meydum, where he uncovered some of the earliest evidence of
mummification; and in Palestine in the 1930s.

The museum would not exist but for the
bequest of the popular novelist Amelia
Edwards, who spent the last twenty years of
her life campaigning to protect monuments
and antiquities in Egypt. She left her collection
to University College London, and a sum to
establish a chair of Egyptology, the first at
any British university. Petrie, her favourite
archaeologist, was appointed to that chair.

In his introductory lecture[272] on 14 January
1893 he set out what he wanted to achieve:
a recognition of the 'historical sense, the reali-
sation that everything is in continual flow and
change'; a concern with 'the whole history of
a great civilisation'. Citing Brugsch Pasha's
Die Aegyptologie he addressed the 'history and
geography of Egypt' – dynastic, political, constitutional, spiritual, philosophical, aesthetic,
material and personal. In 1890 these last three
had 'scarcely been looked at'.

Amelia Edwards's bequest gave the university a standard late 19th-century collection that
contained some objects of particular importance: a head of a small statue of Amenemhat
III, wooden stela of Neskhons, a fragment
from a coffin of Amenemipet. This emphasis
on art objects was typical of the period. They
were what museums and collectors craved,

the beautiful, the sensational, the unique, but
for Petrie they were only a part of Egypt.
His Egyptian workmen nicknamed him Abu
Bagousheh, 'father of pots', and this museum
contains cabinets of humble objects: shards
of pottery, beads, scarabs, metals; such small
objects as toys, tools, jewellery, amulets. It is a
collection for teaching and research, arranged
in lines of cabinets, every object hand numbered. It may initially be somewhat baffling to
the lay person, but from it emerges gradually a
picture of everyday life.

Petrie was also a populariser, a tireless
lecturer and writer of books and articles
for non-specialist journals.[273] After each dig
the best pieces were, by law, lodged with the
Museum of Cairo. What he could export
abroad was distributed to museums and
universities. Petrie material is in 120 museums
worldwide (notably in Brussels and Copenhagen) of which sixty are in Britain (including
the British Museum, the Ashmolean Museum
and the Manchester Museum, all q.v.).

Even after such wide distribution, there
are objects here of great beauty: a lovely black
ceramic bird from Qurneh, Dynasty XIII,
tomb B23; a bronze figurine of Isis as the
Mother of the Apis bull with a bovine head,
Ptolemaic Dynasty XXX; and curiosities (jars
with the faces of the African god Bes from
Dynasty XXXI).

And there are treasures: the Gurob sleeves,
Dynasty XVIII–XIX, excavated by Petrie in
1889; the Roman period funerary portraits
from Hawara (1888–1911);[274] the torso of
Akhenaten's daughter, a triumph of delicate
modelling that flows silkily over her belly and
hips, unlike any other Egyptian sculpture.

Petrie excavated on such a scale that some of
the museum's most remarkable objects have
only come recently to light. Two Desh Asheh
dresses, Dynasty V, that he excavated at Fayum
in 1897, were discovered in 1979 wrapped up
in a page of newsprint from the *Athenaeum*
of 26 December 1898. The Tarkhan dress,
dated to the middle of Dynasty I (*c.* 2,800 BC),
may be the oldest dress in the world. Petrie

Shabti at the Petrie Museum

excavated it in 1912 but it was rediscovered by staff at the Victoria and Albert Museum in a packet of dirty, scrumpled funerary linen, turned inside out, creased at the elbow and stained by perspiration.[275]

Petrie's influence has been very considerable. He trained Howard Carter, the discoverer of Tutankhamun's tomb. Sir Mortimer Wheeler and Sir Leonard Woolley both won the Petrie Medal and his students at UCL and at the British School of Archaeology in Egypt constitute a roll-call of 20th-century British archaeology: Margaret Murray, Stephen Glanville (his successor at UCL), John Garstang and Eric Peet of Liverpool, Guy Brunton.

The museum's collection continues to grow with major gifts from the Wellcome Foundation, and from the excavation, by Guy Brunton, of two of the museum's outstanding exhibits, both from Qau: a Predynastic figurine, *c.* 5020–2835 BC (excavated 1927), and a bead net dress (excavated 1923–4), Dynasty V, *c.* 2400 BC. Its size suggests that it was made for a girl aged nine or ten but its mesh of beads (turquoise, blue, green, brown, black, cream) and its fringe of 127 Mitra shells, which would have clicked and chinked as the child moved, give it an erotic charge that is reinforced by the small metal breast caps with darker nipples which, like the shells, were fertility symbols.

These finds, indeed the whole museum, confirm Petrie's belief that 'Every fragment of the products of the past is concrete history . . . We raise from the dust the body of material facts of history, and the written word gives life and speech to it.'[276]

POLLOCK'S TOY MUSEUM *

1 Scala Street, London W1P 1LT
Tel. 020 7636 3452

A toy cupboard of toy theatres, toys, teddies, games and lost childhood

Childhood, as we know it, is largely a 19th-century concept, described by Frances Hodgson Burnett, Charles Kingsley and Charles Dickens and made possible by the Shaftesbury

Acts[277] which, by restricting child labour, made the lives of children distinct from those of adults.

So say social scientists. Toys deny this simplistic view. The Egyptian mouse with moveable head and tail you see here dates from around 2000 BC and suggests that toys have a long history and come in many guises and disguises.

That Egyptian mouse is joined here by Japanese teddy bears, Felix the Cat (American, 1924) and a Noah's ark, c. 1910, that because of its Biblical origins was a 'Sunday toy' that might be played with only on the Sabbath. There are dolls from India, puppets from Indonesia, whistles from Bulgaria, Bavarian wax figures and a wax 'Jesus' made by French nuns. But at the centre of the museum are the toy theatres made by Benjamin Pollock and sold from his shop at 73 Hoxton Street.

Pollock inherited the business in 1876 from his father-in-law, John Redington. Each theatre came complete with a proscenium arch stage,[278] wings, sets, scripts and a cast of actors poised on the edge of rods. The titles of the plays (*King Pippin*; *The Maid and the Magpie*,[279] *Othello*, *Old Dame Trott*, *Whittington and his Cat*, *The Rover's Bride*, *Robinson Crusoe*) go back to the theatre of Edmund Kean and the great clown Joseph Grimaldi, to a theatre of high drama and magic, of heroes and villains, pirates and corsairs, fairies and demons.

Toy theatres have inspired generations of actors, directors and lovers of theatre. As a child Robert Louis Stevenson bought scripts from a shop in Leith Walk, Edinburgh.[280] The designer Edward Gordon Craig bought Pollock theatres and called them 'the Best Theatre in London', and Peggy Ashcroft and Peter Brook each trace their passion for theatre to a Pollock's set.

Benjamin Pollock died in 1937. The business went bankrupt in the early 1950s and was saved by a French actress, Marguerite Fawdry, who re-opened it as a museum in 1956, first in Monmouth Street and, since 1969, here in Soho on the corner of Scala Street and Charlotte Street.

Pollock's theatres were her inspiration, but she assembled a collection that extends into every area of play, and offers each visitor a route back to childhood. For me, the toys here that made me feel five years old again were the Hornby oo trainsets, William Britain's lead soldiers, building bricks, the boards of Battleship and L'Attaque, and the bears (mine was a panda that I named, imaginatively, Panda).

It feels as though every type of toy made in the last 200 years is crammed into these two small adjoining terraced houses in which all surfaces bar the ceilings are covered with toys. As you climb the narrow, rickety stairs the walls are hung with games: Ludo and, appropriately, Snakes and Ladders, both of Indian origin. Ludo, introduced into Britain in 1896, derives from Pachisi (meaning twenty-five, the highest possible score). It was played by the Moghul Emperor Akbar with slave girls as pieces. In playing Snakes and Ladders (Hindi Moksha-patamu) you are imitating the journey of the soul on its way to heaven: ascending ladders as reward for virtue and good deeds, descending snakes as punishment for evil and vice. The timeless (if unspoken) metaphysics of Snakes and Ladders has proved extremely popular, rivalled only perhaps by the game devised by an unemployed engineer, Charles Darcow, in 1932 in Atlantic City, Monopoly, that has sold more than 80 million sets.

Play is a serious business, in both senses, certainly for the adults who make, sell and buy these toys. For the idealists among them, toys are not simply entertainment or amusement; they are a preparation for life, providing 'play' that teaches children: to build (Anker Bricks, first made in Germany in the 1870s; Bakelite Bayko, c. 1938, whose suburban designs never changed; the French Urbania); to be a mother (dolls of every size, shape and nationality; their clothes; their houses); to wage war (guns, forts, lead soldiers, Action Man); to compete and win; to make things; and, of course, to perform.

To its credit and our enjoyment this museum has little time for such theorising. It is a Christmas stocking, a lucky dip, a crammed magical toy cupboard that will not fail to amuse, whatever age your outer self.

QUEEN'S GALLERY *****

Buckingham Palace, London SW1A 1AA
Tel. 020 7321 2233
www.royal.gov.uk

Royal treasures

In 1629 Rubens wrote, 'I must admit that when it comes to pictures by the hands of first-class masters, I have never seen such a large number in one place as in the royal palace in England and in the gallery of the late Duke of Buckingham.'[281]

Charles I's collection was indeed stupendous. He had been given Titians by Philip IV when he and Buckingham visited Madrid in 1623 to seek the hand of the Infanta Maria; he had acquired the Raphael cartoons in Genoa[282] and, in 1626, the famous Gonzaga Collection in Mantua, en bloc, which included Mantegna's *The Triumphs of Caesar*[283] (*c.*1485–94) and Annibale Carracci's *The Butcher's Shop.*[284] Only the Spanish Royal Collection of Philip II and that of Rudolf II of Austria at the Hradschin Palace in Prague could compare.

After the execution of the King in 1649, the collection was put up for sale by Commissioners appointed by Cromwell.[285] Paintings from it are now in national galleries across Europe,[286] although Charles II managed to piece a good part of it together after the Restoration.

It is a collection that is older and larger than any other described in this book. It comprises paintings and drawings, sculpture and ceramics, books and manuscripts, jewellery and furniture, acquired both for private use and public show. With few exceptions, each piece, whether purchased or commissioned, reflects the personal taste of the royal family.

These collections are dispersed across the royal palaces and residences that remain. Those at Windsor Castle, Hampton Court Palace and the Palace of Holyroodhouse are described separately. The new Queen's Gallery (2002) at Buckingham Palace, by means of temporary exhibitions, shows works[287] from all parts of the Royal Collection.

You enter the old Queen's Gallery through a door in the wall on Buckingham Palace Road. The new gallery, designed by John Simpson, has an imposing portico of Doric columns in Portland stone that leads to three decorated galleries and a number of cabinet rooms. Simpson's response to the complicated, 300-year architectural history of the palace (Sir William Chambers, John Nash, Sir James Pennethorne, Sir Aston Webb) has been classical, respecting, as advocated by Leon Battista Alberti, the great architectural theorist of the Renaissance, 'the original intentions of the author'.[288] Within are sculptures and friezes by Alexander Stoddart, and rich ornament throughout.

Charles I created a sumptuous foundation for the collection with his taste for Italian artists generally and for those from Venice in particular. He was as judicious when commissioning, favouring first Rubens and then, from 1632 until 1641, Van Dyck, who produced portraits that managed simultaneously to convey regal power and human frailty. In his first portrait, *Charles I and Henrietta Maria with their Two Eldest Children* ('The Great Peece', 1632), the crown, orb and sceptre rest by the King's right hand but his child presses at his knee, a small dog moves under his feet and the Queen holds their second child. Even in the great equestrian portraits such as *Charles I with Monsieur de St Antoine* (1633), the King's expression is uncertain, almost weary.

Some of Charles I's successors handle the obligatory official portraits less successfully. Although they liked one another, Gainsborough's of *George III* is one of his rare failures, the background landscape as dull as the likeness; although Queen Victoria sat sixty-one times to fifteen artists in her coronation year, only Thomas Sully dared to capture her bold prettiness and rosebud mouth. The present Queen has gone from the polite stiffness of Sir James Gunn (1954–6) to Lucian Freud's tiny portrait (2000–01) in which the artist's penetrating gaze into the face of an elderly woman contrasts with the unwithering diamond diadem (1820) perched on her head.

It is generally accepted that, after Charles I,

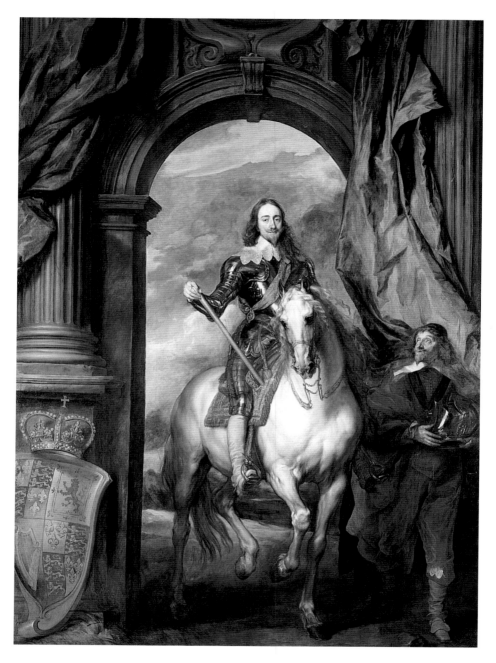

Charles I with Monsieur de St Antoine *by*
Van Dyck (Queen's Gallery)

the great royal collectors were George IV and Queen Victoria, with Prince Albert. Taking advantage of the weakness in the art market after the French Revolution, George IV did indeed buy superb Dutch paintings (Rubens, Rembrandt, Cuyp, Hobbema) and a dazzling array of Sèvres, silver (Paul Storr), French furniture (Riesener) and sculpture (two untouchable, marmoreal nymphs by Canova; a delicious de Vries bronze, *Theseus and Antiope*, c. 1600–01), but the collection also owes much to his father George III and grandfather Frederick, Prince of Wales. Without George III there would be no Canalettos[289] here. Frederick, Prince of Wales, favoured Claude, Poussin and the artists loved by Charles I: Rubens and Van Dyck. After the death of Prince Albert, his widow reverted from her husband's severe taste for the Italian Primitives to 'good likenesses' by Winterhalter, Landseer and Tuxen.

In each century portraits and historical paintings predominate, followed closely by landscape and sporting subjects,[290] mainly of horses. The relative absence of religious paintings is noticeable, an exception being Hans Holbein the Younger's intimate *Noli me Tangere* (c. 1524), which unusually gives a side glance into the tomb, where two angels are seated in blazing light.

Throughout the 20th century the Royal Collection has loaned works so widely (W. P. Frith's *Ramsgate Sands*; *Life at the Seaside*; Vermeer's *A Lady at the Virginal with a Gentleman*; the Van Dycks) that they are lodged in the national (collective) memory. Others, reproduced less often, come as a surprise: Annibale Carracci's *Allegory of Truth and Time* (c. 1584–5); de la Tour's intense *St Jerome* (c. 1621–3); the two Canovas, *Circe* (1820–24) and *Fountain Nymph* (1815–17).

With this new gallery, the Queen has opened up the Royal Collection to the public, continuing what she started with the renovation and reopening of Osborne House in 1954 and the Queen's Gallery at the Palace of Holyroodhouse in 2000. It will bring to public attention hitherto unknown corners of the Royal Collection, such as the Danish paintings,

rare in British collections, bought by Edward VII for Queen Alexandra, and Prince Philip's admiration for the paintings of Sidney Nolan and Ivon Hitchens and the ceramics of Lucie Rie.

The art historian Francis Haskell has observed the several constraints on royal collectors: 'certain obligations – to the expectations of their courtiers and subjects, to the traditions of their ancestors, to the Church, even to the cause of ostentation itself – which may stand in the way of expressing a more personal discrimination.'[291] Nevertheless although monarchs have always taken advice (Charles I from Arundel and Buckingham, George III from Lord Bute, Queen Victoria and Prince Albert from Ludwig Gruner)[292] this is a collection that expresses the personal taste of a small number of English men and women over a period of 500 years. In that one or two of them were enthusiasts, and a few had little interest,[293] they form a randomly chosen, atypical, group. Their motives for acquiring works have been various: glorious (Charles I and Rubens), vainglorious (Charles I and Van Dyck), notorious (Charles II and his mistresses, Lely's *Windsor Beauties*); perhaps, in that case, lascivious. Their collection brings together some curiosities, a few vulgarities and many stunning masterpieces: a supremely English collection.

QUEEN'S HOUSE **

Romney Road, Greenwich, London SE10 9NF
Tel. 020 8293 9618
www.gmt2000.co.uk/meridian/place/
plcqoal.htm

Sublime flower of Inigo Jones's architectural genius, built for James I's wife; severe without, an exquisite revelation within

The Queen's House, designed by Inigo Jones, is the first purely classical villa built in England. Having been commissioned by James I's wife, Queen Anne of Denmark, in 1616 and completed by her daughter-in-law, Queen Henrietta Maria, the wife of Charles I, between 1629 and about 1638, its name distinguishes it from the former 'King's house', the old Tudor palace of Greenwich, to which it was the last addition as a 'secret' garden villa.

When Inigo Jones revisited Italy in 1613–14 he admired and was influenced by what he called the 'solid, proportionable . . . and unaffected' style of Palladio with its chaste symmetry and clarity of line. However the specific model for the facade of the Queen's House was the villa at Poggio a Caiano built for Lorenzo di Medici by Giuliano da Sangallo with its open staircase curving down to a north terrace.

Intended by both Queens as a smaller, more private alternative to the rambling Tudor palace demolished in the 1660s, it makes a fine setting for picture collections that relate to the Tudor and Stuart royal families, to naval heroes of the 17th–20th centuries and to Greenwich.

Here are portraits of *James I* and *Anne of Denmark* by John de Critz; of *Elizabeth I*; and of *Princess Elizabeth, the Winter Queen*, as a child in 1603, by Robert Peake the Elder.

There is a room of Lelys, including the early *Peter Pett and the Sovereign of the Seas*, with his famous 'Flagmen' series, and works by Mytens, Dobson and Kneller (including Samuel Pepys). Hogarth, Gainsborough and Reynolds follow, the last in profusion from early to late, including the great full-length of his friend *Augustus Keppel* which made his name in the 1750s. All, including 20th-century painters (McEvoy, Orpen, Monnington among others) are interspersed with marine works from the van de Veldes and before, in the 17th century, up to war artists of recent memory – though changing displays always bring something new.

However it is Inigo Jones's building that is the signal work of art. A portrait here of *Inigo Jones* by William Dobson, *c.* 1644, about four years after the completion of the Queen's House, shows him ageing. It is a small work in which Dobson comes close up to explore Jones's tired, wry eyes.

Their caution contrasts with the exuberance of the building and particularly of the Tulip Stairs, the first centrally unsupported spiral stair in Britain, which swirls with apparently effortless poise around an open well, a 'vacuum in ye middle' as Jones describes it. The idea is from Palladio's staircase in the Villa Capra, Vicenza. The inspiration and the engineering are entirely Inigo Jones's, a sparklingly achieved elevation of spirit over gravity, befitting a queen.

RANGER'S HOUSE ***

Chesterfield Walk, Blackheath, London
SE10 8QX
Tel. 020 8853 0035
www.english-heritage.org.uk

Official residence of the Ranger of Greenwich Park, now holding the Northern Renaissance treasury of Julius Wernher: ivories, bronzes, intaglios

Ranger's House is a handsome red-brick villa, *c.* 1700, at the top of Croom's Hill, with views across Blackheath. In front of it are high wrought-iron railings and gates decorated with gilded leaves. Between 1748 and 1773 it was the house of the Earl of Chesterfield after he retired from politics, where he could 'hide myself at Blackheath and converse with my vegetables'.[294] He is best known for his letters to his illegitimate son, Philip Stanhope,[295] which Dr Johnson maintained 'taught the morals of a whore and the manners of a dancing master', a judgement not unconnected to Chesterfield's refusal to admire Dr Johnson's *Dictionary*.

It is a house of 18th-century symmetry and order but upstairs, with the main collection, you enter the world of the 15th and 16th centuries. This could be the treasury, the Wunderkammer, of a Renaissance prince: ivory altarpieces, Venetian jewellery, Brussels tapestries, Limoges enamels, Italian maiolica, bronzes from Bologna. It is in fact the collection was made between 1880 and 1912 by Sir Julius Wernher (1850–1912), one of the 'Randlords' who developed the diamond and gold mines of South Africa and who was, in the 1890s, one of the two richest men in England.

Although Wernher was advised by one of the finest scholars and connoisseurs in Europe, Dr Wilhelm Bode, curator of paintings and sculpture at the Prussian Royal Picture Gallery in Berlin,[296] he relied to a great extent on his eye, trained by years of scrutinising the qualities of diamonds when 'every stone has to be judged individually'.[297] The collection he created is comparable in quality to the Wallace Collection (q.v.) and to those established by Baron Ferdinand de Rothschild at Waddesdon Manor (q.v.) and by J. P. Morgan in the United States. Its jewellery is good, as are its 16th-century bronzes and 16th-century religious tapestries, but its ivories, maiolica and Limoges are matched only by the British Museum and the Victoria and Albert Museum (both q.v.).

Although Wernher's collection of maiolica is small (only twenty-seven pieces, many fewer than Beit's collection) they are, in the opinion of Timothy Wilson,[298] of 'stellar quality',[299] four of the plates coming from the most celebrated workshop in Italy. Of the two from the Gubbio workshop of Maestro Giorgio Andreoli (c.1526), one has a border of foliate scrollwork with putto heads and masks; the other depicts a scene from the *Aeneid*, of Neptune driving his chariot through the waves, drawn by four rearing horses. Two more plates by Nicola da Urbino (1524) were probably a gift to Isabella d'Este[300] from her daughter and show scenes from Ovid's *Metamorphoses* (*Apollo and Marsyas* and *Meleager and Atalanta*).

Of the Limoges enamels the most celebrated is the polychromed ewer by Martial Courtois, the son of Pierre Courtois, admired by two generations of British Museum experts: A.W. Franks, in the 19th century, found it 'remarkable for the brilliancy of [its] colouring'; for Dora Thornton, curator of Renaissance collections, it is 'the most exceptional enamel in the collection'.[301]

The ivories are displayed here, as they were in Wernher's London home, Bath House in Piccadilly, in purpose-built vitrines, some single, others mixing ivory panels, pendants and figures (such as *St Catherine*), with box-wood carvings, bronzes and small pieces of maiolica. Around the walls of the Red Room recreated here are carved wooden relief panels. *The Nativity* (c.1500) is hung precipitously over the doorway, with startling foreshortening of the figures and faces. The curtains are drawn; the lights are low so that the objects in the vitrines gleam and glow. 'Every vitrine must be like a picture,' Wernher insisted.

Only the pictures on the walls are spotlit: a Hans Memling *Virgin and Child*, a tondo by Filippino Lippi and a beautiful Lorenzo Marini Da Cattano, *The Annunciation*.

In parallel to this collection of Medieval and Renaissance treasures Wernher was acquiring other works with which his wife could decorate Bath House and Luton Hoo, their home in Bedfordshire. Here too they are separated, in the ground-floor rooms: 18th-century tapestries from the Gobelins and Beauvais factories; paintings by Jean-Antoine Watteau, Gabriel Metsu and Sir Joshua Reynolds; a 17th-century bronze, after Bernini, of *Apollo and Daphne*, and a huge, melodramatic and sentimental sculpture, *The Love of Angels*, by Guilio Bergonzoli (1864), which loomed at the base of the Grand Staircase at Luton Hoo.

Wernher was a compulsive accumulator. He wrote, 'it is difficult to make people understand that for the merchant his rise in material prosperity, therefore acquisition, is his aim, just as for the scholar his science and for an artist, his ideal. It is only human not to stop and even a measure of success does not give full satisfaction.' He collected for himself, not to endow a public museum. Much of his taste was at odds with that of his contemporaries and of his wife. He favoured the harsh angularity of German woodcarving, the discreet beauty of ivories, the grotesqueries of the ceramics of Bernard Palissy, even, as he confessed to his friend and fellow collector Lord Carmichael, the 'splendidly ugly'. His taste makes it a most un-English collection, despite being housed in this most English of houses.

ROYAL ACADEMY **

Burlington House, Piccadilly,
London W1J OBD
Tel. 020 7300 8000
www.royal academy.org.uk/

*The diploma work of every Royal Academician
since Reynolds, in Burlington House*

Around the courtyard of Burlington House
are grouped Britain's learned societies: the
Royal Society of Chemistry, the Royal Astronomical Society, the Geological Society, the
Linnaean Society and the Society of Antiquaries. At their centre is the Royal Academy
of Arts. Steps lead up to its entrance, august
and grand in keeping with the Royal Charter it
was granted in 1768.

The facade of Burlington House was remodelled by Colen Campbell for the 3rd Earl.
In 1872–3 Sydney Smirke added a third storey
in what Pevsner calls an act of 'High Victorian
cruelty'.[302] The courtyard incorporates the
work of many architects, chiefly Banks and
E. M. Barry.[303]

The Royal Academy has been here since
1868, holding from 1870 temporary exhibitions in the galleries on the garden side of
Burlington House and teaching young artists
in the Royal Academy Schools. It has, too, a
permanent collection of painting and sculpture, made up in part by gifts, in part by the
diploma works of academicians.

Among the gifts are Thomas Gainsborough's *Romantic Landscape* (*c.*1780), John
Constable's *The Leaping Horse* (1825), an early
16th-century copy of Leonardo da Vinci's *The
Last Supper* (one of the finest extant copies of
his fresco, and possibly made from original
cartoons),[304] and the *Taddei Tondo* by Michelangelo, the only marble sculpture by him in
England.[305]

The diploma works arise out of a council
minute of 1771 that states: 'No Academician . . .
should receive his Letter of Admission' until
he 'hath deposited . . . a Picture, Bas-relief, or
other Specimen of his abilities'[306] for which, in
return, a diploma should be issued, entitling

him to full academician status. Among the
foundation members were its first President
Sir Joshua Reynolds, Thomas Gainsborough,
Benjamin West, Richard Wilson, Angelica
Kauffmann and the watercolourist Paul
Sandby.

You might expect that the diploma requirement would produce a collection that gave
what Reynolds hoped would be 'a repository
. . . of great examples of art',[307] offering as
comprehensive a view of British art since the
mid 18th century as does Tate Britain (q.v.).
Despite the excellence of its foundation members, it does not consistently do so. After
Paul Sandby and his brother Thomas it did not
welcome watercolourists, apart from those,
such as J. M. W. Turner, who also painted in
oils. Mary Moser and Anglica Kauffmann were
elected as foundation members but no other
woman artist was elected until 1922 (Annie
Swynnerton). Provincial artists were ignored,
so neither Cotman nor Crome is here. The
only Scottish academicians are those who, like
Raeburn and Wilkie, moved their studios to
London.

By the mid 19th century the Academy had
become so cautious and conservative that
the young Pre-Raphaelite artists rejected it
altogether, Burne-Jones only being persuaded
against his better judgement to join following
a personal plea from the then President,
Frederic, Lord Leighton.

In the 20th century the Academy failed
to support Jacob Epstein in 1935 when his
sculptures on the British Medical Association
building on the Strand were attacked; and in
1949 the then President, Sir Alfred Munnings,
in his annual dinner speech made a bitter
attack on all art since Matisse.[308] As a result the
list of those who have not been members,
particularly in the early 20th century, is sober-
ing – Jacob Epstein, Wyndham Lewis, Henry
Moore, Barbara Hepworth, Ben Nicholson and
Francis Bacon – confirming the view of the
critic Frank Rutter that 'you did not speak
of the Royal Academy if you pretended
to be interested in modern art.'[309] Nevertheless the collection contains some fine paintings: Turner's brooding, romantic *Dolbardarn*

Castle (1800); intriguing self-portraits by Benjamin West, Reynolds and Lawrence. The last has a quiet, modest scrutiny quite unlike his stylish public and royal portraits.

The Academy's record in architecture and sculpture is stronger. Almost all the great British architects since Sir William Chambers and Sir John Soane have been members and many have given architectural drawings.[310] John Gibson, Prince Albert's favourite neo-classical sculptor, pupil of Canova and Thorvaldsen, bequeathed a number of plaster originals, and the work of the late Victorian sculptors (Brock, Gilbert, Leighton, Theed, Pomeroy) is well represented.

In the last twenty years attitudes have changed considerably under the presidencies of Sir Roger de Grey (1984–93), Sir Philip Dowson (1993–2002) and Professor Philip King (since 2002). The class of honorary academicians that brings distinguished foreign artists into the Academy has been expanded and now includes I. M. Pei, Jorn Utzon, Daniel Liebeskind, Jasper Johns, Frank Stella, Cy Twombly and Ellsworth Kelly, while contemporary British academicians are being elected when they are still in early or mid career: Antony Gormley, Will Alsop, Alison Wilding, Fiona Rae. They bring a vigour to the diploma collection that has, for the past fifteen years, been a feature of the Academy's temporary exhibition programme.

Passing below the painted ceilings by Benjamin West and Angelica Kauffmann, which you may not have seen on entering,[311] you leave a collection that does not fulfil Reynolds's ambition that it should be 'a repository ... of great examples of art'[312] but is one from which may be learned 'the principles which many Artists have spent their whole lives in ascertaining'.[313]

ROYAL AIR FORCE MUSEUM *

Grahame Park Way, Hendon,
London NW9 5LL
Tel. 020 8205 2266
www.rafmuseum.org

Biplanes to fighters in early aerodrome

For man, flight is the latest, perhaps the greatest, mechanical achievement. The dreams of Daedalus and the conjectures of Leonardo finally became reality when the Wright Brothers' aeroplane flew through the air for twelve seconds at Kitty Hawk, North Carolina, USA, on 17 December 1903.[314]

In 1909 Louis Blériot flew the English Channel. Inspired by Blériot, Claude Grahame-White set up an aerodrome and training school here at Hendon in 1910. Within five years Europe was at war, and the miracle and beauty of flight were requisitioned by politicians and military commanders. The developments of civilian and military aircraft have been enmeshed ever since.

War accelerated that development. The earliest biplane here, the Caudron G III (1915–18), has fragile wings and wheels spoked like a pram's. Its top speed was 65 mph. By the end of the war the Sopwith Camel could fly at 115 mph and its machine gun was ratcheted in order to shoot between revolutions of the propeller.

After the war, the Royal Air Force's pilots and engineers transferred to the civil industry. Geoffrey De Havilland, the son of a clergyman, set up the De Havilland Aircraft Company in 1920, making the Moth series of light aircraft. Alliot Vernon Roe's Manchester construction firm recruited Roy Chadwick to design the Avro 504 and later the Avro Vulcan. Reginald Mitchell designed flying boats for the Supermarine Aviation Works. His S5 formed the basis of the Supermarine Schneider that went on to win the Schneider Trophy in 1927, 1929 and 1931. Briefly, flying was an elegant and daring sport. Competitions like the Schneider Trophy, and air shows at Farnborough, Paris

and here at Hendon, drew enormous crowds. Mitchell's huge silver flying boat, the Supermarine Stranraer, as beautiful and as ungainly as a thrashing swan as it rises from the water before eventually assuming grace in flight, was ordered by the RAF in 1935 and was in service by 1937. The following year they commissioned a small fighter from Mitchell, the Spitfire, delivered just months before Mitchell died of cancer in 1938. Its stocky, simple shape is almost domestic in scale.

To display aeroplanes in the confines of a hangar is to remove them from their element. The utilitarian shape of the Spitfire cries out for the exaltation of flight. But this confinement is, curiously, of benefit to the visitor.

It is when their wings tower darkly above you that you experience the power and weight of the bombers, the Lancaster and the American B-17 Flying Fortress. Their only frailty was human: the average age of Lancaster pilots was twenty-two. They survived, on average, twenty missions.

More massive still is the Vickers Valiant, which dropped Britain's first hydrogen bomb, its fuselage painted white to reflect the explosion's flash.

In the Pitt Rivers Museum (q.v.) you can see how, a hundred years earlier, it was Pitt Rivers's study of the evolution of the rifle that established the principles that informed the development of anthropology.[315] Here, at Hendon, this collection takes you, within five hangars and within a span of 100 years, in sequence from the fragility of a wooden biplane to a nuclear bomber, beyond even the imaginings of Leonardo or the hopes of the Wright Brothers.

The Royal Air Force Museum, Hendon

ROYAL BOTANIC GARDENS, KEW *****

Kew, Richmond, Surrey TW9 3AB
Tel. 020 8332 5655
www.rbgkew.org.uk

The world's botanical life classified and maintained, including the Palm House in the great Glass Palace, masterpiece of Decimus Burton.

The white iron ribs of the Palm House at Kew soar up, holding in suspension this great house of glass. At sunset, seen against tall trees, it appears to float, a work of solemn lightness, the masterpiece of the architect, Decimus Burton.[316] It is also 'one of the boldest pieces of 19th century functionalism', in the opinion of Nikolaus Pevsner and Bridget Cherry,[317] owing as much to the engineer Richard Turner[318] as to Burton. It is the symbol of Kew across the world and, by combining beauty and science with enjoyment, a metaphor for this working museum of plants.[319]

You enter the main gates and see at once a great processional path ahead, the Broad Walk, designed, as were the gates, by Burton. This leads you into the gardens, 330 acres of them. They are not the largest botanical gardens in the world, or the oldest (the Orto Botanico in Pisa was founded in 1545 and Padua, Zurich, Lyons, Rome, Bologna and Montpelier all created gardens in the 16th century)[320] but it is the greatest and the most influential in the world of plants. There are trees here from its earliest days; a few yards to the south of the Broad Walk is a *Sophora japonica*, its ancient branches supported on metal crutches. It was planted here in Princess Augusta's garden in 1753, introduced from France by one of the leading 18th-century nurserymen, James Gordon of the Mile End Nursery.

It is with Princess Augusta[321] and her adviser Lord Bute[322] that the present gardens originate. She began with nine acres but, by 1775, 110 acres had been walled in or fenced and Bute was supervising the planting of trees, flower beds and the creation of pleasure grounds,

The Palm House (Royal Botanic Gardens, Kew)

which included a classical orangery and a pagoda (both 1761), designed by Sir William Chambers.[323]

It was Joseph Banks who transformed the botanical role of the gardens. At the age of twenty-three, rich, well connected and a fellow of the Royal Society, he had sailed on Captain James Cook's HMS *Endeavour* to Tahiti, New Zealand and Australia, returning in 1771 with 3,600 species of plants, of which 1,400 were new to science. With the friendship of the King and Princess Augusta, Banks soon created a role for himself at Kew. This was a period in which knowledge of botany was advancing apace. Carl Linnaeus was transforming the nature of plant description and classification at Uppsala University. Advised by Linnaeus's 'beloved pupil', the botanist Daniel Solander, and working with the head gardeners at Kew (John Haverfield until 1784; William Aiton and his son thereafter), Banks inspired the sending of collectors around the world in search of new plants, not simply as beautiful curiosities, exotics or botanical novelties but for their potential economic value, the new products

and processes, indeed new industries, that might derive from them. Between 1772 and 1798 Francis Masson, a gardener at Kew who was the first of these collectors, made expeditions to the Cape of Good Hope, the Azores, the West Indies, Tangiers and North America, returning with proteas, crassulas, ericas, pelargoniums and gladioli.

Banks was ambitious and competitive, and had a genius for what is now called promotion. He was determined that 'as many of the new plants as possible should make their first appearance at the Royal Gardens'.[324] The gardens' first catalogue, *Hortus Kewensis* (1768), compiled by Bute's protegé John Hill, was updated by Aiton's *Hortus Kewensis* in 1789 and the gardens' reputation was further enhanced by the work of such botanical painters as Sydney Parkinson, the artist with Banks on Cook's first voyage, and the Austrian Franz Bauer, engaged by Banks to paint new introductions at Kew.[325]

With the gardens' success and growing fame in the early 19th century came tensions. The public, having gained access, wanted to enjoy them as pleasure gardens. Aiton's successor, Sir William Hooker, responded by 'making the garden gay and ornamental; I admire the effect, and believe that in thus gratifying the public is the surest way of making the estimates palatable.'[326] Sir Joseph Paxton, designer of the Crystal Palace and head gardener at Chatsworth (q.v.), believed that the gardens were being reduced to 'a gaudy flower show' to the detriment of their scientific work. Despite that, Paxton was happy to take back to Chatsworth one of the seeds of the *Victoria amazonica*, the giant water lily that had been introduced from South America and that had been successfully propagated and exhibited in the Water Lily House built by Richard Turner in 1852.

The gardens today bear witness to the successes of those years: the glorious Caspian Sea chestnut-leaved oak (*Quercus castaneifolia*), planted in 1846 near the Water Lily House, now 110 feet tall; the towering Corsican pine (*Pinus nigra* var. *maritima*); and such succulents as the Mexican *Echinocactus platyacanthus*, 4½ feet high and weighing one ton.

Come in spring and walk among the bluebells by the Water Lily Pond or the hummock of daffodils beside Burton's replica of Chambers's Temple of Eolus;[327] or in deep winter and see the rimed statuary and the ponds thick with ice. To go from the Rhododendron Dell, to the Bamboo Garden, to the high technology of the electronically controlled environment of the Princess of Wales Conservatory (1987), the largest botanical glasshouse in the world, is to walk through a Flora Mundi.

Today the gardens, which already have the world's largest seed bank, containing more than 4,000 species, are engaged on a Millennium Seed Bank project.[328] Its influence across the globe is remarkable and offers practical promise of conservation and change.

Yet the visitor is always drawn back to the Palm House and its profusion of sugar cane, rubber trees and palms. The palms are beautiful but many of the 2,600 species are at risk. In the Maya Forest, which spreads across Mexico, Guatemala and Belize, 75 per cent of the species of the genus *Chamadorea* are threatened. To help in the conservation of such palms is the modern triumph of Burton and Turner's climate contained in metal and glass.

ROYAL OBSERVATORY, GREENWICH **

Greenwich Park, Greenwich, London
SE10 9NF
Tel. 020 8312 6565 (recorded information)
and 020 8858 4422 (administration)
www.rog.nmm.ac.uk/

The home of Greenwich Mean Time

Time and space are measured in relation to longitude zero (000° 00′ 00″). It runs through the Meridian Building of the Royal Observatory. This is the dead centre of the world. To identify where in the world you are, on land or at sea, a knowledge of time is essential, because one hour's difference in time is the same as 15° of longitude. So the concerns of the Royal Observatory are the stars and the seas, place and time.

A digital clock at the entrance flickers through one-hundredths of a second. Wherever you go there are timepieces. There are machines for measuring sidereal time, that is by the stars; an astrolabe dated *c.* 1360; a Persian astrolabe (1659–60) made by Ibn Muhammed Amin, inscribed with a line from the Koran, 'the world is decorated with the stars'; armillary spheres, Ptolemaic and Copernican, from the 18th century, and a 16th-century pocket compendium which can gauge the phases of the moon, determine the tides, calculate the latitude of major cities and tell the time.[329]

There are clocks, ranging from that made by John Harrison between 1730 and 1735, part of whose mechanism is made of wood, to John Arnold's 'No. 36' (1778), which was so accurate that the word 'chronometer' was coined to describe it, to the Junghans Mega wristwatch, the most accurate in the world today.

Outside is the red time ball (1833) on Flamsteed's House, which rises and then falls at 1 p.m. every day, originally a signal from which ships could calibrate their marine chronometers. Indoors there are quadrants and sextants of all sizes, instruments of intrinsic beauty with which man through the ages has sought to place himself in the infinity of time and space.

From the 15th century, when explorers took to the seas in search of new worlds and wealth, that search assumed an urgency. The limitations of astronomy became apparent. It was competent to measure the size of the earth or to calculate latitude, the north–south co-ordinates in relation to the equator, but without fixed points it could not ascertain the east–west axes of longitude.

To gain the political and economic prizes that awaited the nation first to solve these problems, Charles II appointed an Astronomer Royal, John Flamsteed, 'To apply himself with the utmost care and diligence to the rectifying the tables of the motions of the heavens, and the places of the fixed stars, so as to find out the so much desired longitude of places for the perfecting the act of navigation',[330] and commissioned an observatory, to be designed by Christopher Wren (1675–6). It was constructed quickly and cheaply, using old bricks from Tilbury Fort and wood and lead from the recently demolished gatehouse of the Tower of London, but its architectural features were, in Wren's words, 'a little for pompe'.[331]

On taking up residence, Flamsteed found it destitute of instruments. The Surveyor-General to the Ordnance, Sir Jonas Moore, gave him a seven-foot iron sextant,[332] two telescopes and two clocks by Thomas Tompion. With these he set about the creation of a sure basis for astronomy, establishing first the latitude of the Observatory and, from that, the obliquity of the ecliptic and the position of the equinox. He ascertained this last by means of making simultaneous observations of the sun and a star near both equinoxes. It is on this wholly original solution that modern astronomy is founded.

To accommodate the long telescopes needed for this work, Wren designed the Octagon Room from which the movements of the heavens could be observed. It has a telescope tube, and three replica clocks, based on those originally supplied by Tompion, built into the wall,[333] each having a thirteen-foot pendulum which ran behind the wainscoting,

The Octagon Room at the Royal Observatory

above the clock movements, inside the wall, on which are portraits of Charles II and James II. Their length, and the Dead Beat Escapement which Flamsteed and Tompion devised to prevent the wheels, and therefore the second hands, recoiling backwards at each swing of the pendulum, provided the accuracy needed. The clocks were sold by Flamsteed's wife after his death, but one, which had been converted into a long-case clock, was bought in 1994 and returned to the Octagon Room.

The Octagon Room is glorious, but it was useless for measuring star positions. Built on the foundations of an earlier tower, the Observatory did not run true to the meridian so, for the next forty-three years, Flamsteed made his observations from a small shed at the bottom of his garden.

The progress of his work proved contentious. Flamsteed was unwilling to publish his great catalogue of stellar maps until it was perfect. The King and the government were impatient to put them to use. Sir Isaac Newton needed them to further research of his own. Using his influence at court, Newton prevailed and 400 copies were printed in 1712, 300 of which were burnt by Flamsteed 'as a sacrifice to heavenly truth' when they fell into his hands. Flamsteed's work, *Historia Cælestis Britannica*, was finally published six years after his death, having been revised by his assistants, Abraham Sharp and Joseph Crosthwait. A copy of this 1725 first edition is in the museum.

By this time the Royal Observatory's second great controversy was gathering pace. In 1714 Parliament offered a prize of £20,000 to anyone who could discover a way to determine longitude at sea to within half a degree. John Harrison, the son of a Lincolnshire joiner, proposed a solution whose elegance delighted both Edmund Halley, Flamsteed's successor as

Astronomer Royal, and George Graham, the greatest clockmaker of the day.

Harrison's clock, H1, reckoned to within a degree and a half. Further models, H2 and H3, narrowed the gap. But the Board of Longitude was losing patience and refused to help him develop H4, which Harrison at last saw should be in the form of a large watch. It came well within the half degree but the board refused to pay and it was only after ten years, and the intervention, finally, of George III, that Harrison, now aged eighty-one, was paid, having grappled with the problem for over fifty years.

Here, lined up in four cases, are his time-keepers: H1, an elaborate web of rods and levers behind four elaborate faces; H2, topped by two brass balls; H3, with its roller bearing; and the triumphant H4. It appears to be an ordinary pocket watch but it has a balance that oscillates five times per second, a bi-metallic strip to compensate for temperature changes and a miniature remontoir which rewinds eight times a minute in order to keep constant power.

The museum contains evidence of further battles and triumphs: the establishment of a new meridian and longitude 0°, the basis for all Ordnance Survey maps across the world; the primacy of Greenwich Mean Time, a necessity once railways and telegraph communications moved faster than the sun; its adoption as a world standard at the 1884 International Meridian Conference in Washington, DC; the development of larger and more accurate telescopes and clocks until in 1948 the Astronomer Royal was forced to relocate to a new observatory at Herstmonceaux in Sussex, and then to Cambridge in 1990. The working Observatory was closed down in 1998.

Before you leave, stand on Airy's meridian. Orient yourself at latitude 51° 21′ 38″, longitude 000° 00′ 00″, and take one step over the base line, under the flickering watch of the digital clocks. You will have moved from West to East.

SAATCHI GALLERY **

County Hall, South Bank, London SE1 7PB
Tel. 020 7823 2363
www.saatchi-gallery.co.uk

A remarkable use for the old GLC building: Hirst's cow, Emin's bed, in offices

'It's not that *Freeze*,[334] the 1988 exhibition that Damien Hirst organised with his fellow Goldsmiths' College students, was particularly good,' recalls Charles Saatchi.[335] 'Much of the art was fairly so-so, and Hirst himself hadn't made anything much ... What really stood out was the hopeful swagger of it all.'

Saatchi maintained his confidence in that hopeful swagger by mounting six *Young British Artists* exhibitions at his gallery in Boundary Road between 1992 and 1996, following them with the *Sensation* exhibition at the Royal Academy in 1997, and by purchasing and commissioning works. In 2003 he transferred the entire collection from Boundary Road to the new gallery he made at County Hall. Fifteen years on, what does this collection say about the artists he favours?

Since the first show he put on at Boundary Road in 1985,[336] it has been clear that Saatchi is an outstanding curator. It was a masterstroke to commission Max Gordon to convert an old paint factory into one of the most memorable contemporary art spaces in the city, the original and best 'white cube'. The artists he chose to show there over the next five years (Cy Twombly, Andy Warhol, Carl Andre, Dan Flavin, Richard Stella, Jeff Koons, Bruce Nauman) confirm the quality and consistency of Saatchi's eye. All benefited from being exhibited in a space that had superb proportions and fine light, both natural and artificial.

To move his collection into the formal Edwardian architecture of County Hall appeared to be a risk. How would Hirst's shark or Wilson's tank of oil transfer from the white cube of Boundary Road to the brown boxes of narrow corridors, parquet floors, the sequence of small, oak-panelled offices that Ralph Knott had designed in 1911 to house the administrative bureaucracy of the London County Council? Was it not a building haunted by minutes, agendas, tea trolleys and scuttles of coal for each office's fireplace? The filing cabinets and desks had gone but no door or wall could be removed in what was, rightly, a heavily listed building.

Saatchi has confounded the doubters and turned these constraints to advantage. Against dark-panelled walls that seem to ask for a watercolour, a drawing, a well-observed landscape, he has placed Hirst's vitrines and Mueck's super-real sculptures in rubber and resin, and made you look at them again, afresh. From the moment that you enter and are confronted by Hirst's *Spot-Mini* (2002) careering towards you, nose first, down the wide marble staircase, Saatchi ambushes you with jokes and surprises. At the end of a corridor Gavin Turk's *Pop* (1993), a life-sized Sid

Vicious, revolver in hand, defies you. Another, low-lit, panelled corridor is lined with Hiroshi Sugimoto's photographic portraits of *Henry VIII* and his wives, their waxen skins and staring eyes glistening from the gilded frames.

Each small office is home to a single work. You open a door on Ian Munroe's *Cumulus* (2003) or Hirst's room lined with medicine cabinets of drug bottles, *Holidays/No Feelings* (1998). The most startling new identity is that assumed by Richard Wilson's *20:50* (1987), the single most memorable and beautiful work at the Boundary Road gallery where the perfect mirror of its lake of black sump oil reflected the skylights above and the blank walls that encased it. Here it turns the panelled room, its windows and the sky outside on their heads, subverting your sense of perspective and scale. As Wilson says, 'your mind tells you one thing, but you perceive something else.'[337] It is a work of timeless beauty and fascination.

There are some larger spaces. The twelve vitrines of Hirst's dissected cow, *Some Comfort*

Tracey Emin: My Bed *(Saatchi Gallery)*

Gained from the Acceptance of the Inherent Lies in Everything (1996), are lined up to grand effect in a long slow diagonal sequence. In the central rotunda it is surprising that the open space is unkind to some works, Sarah Lucas's *Au Naturel* (1994) (mattress with womanly melons, oranges, bucket and a penile cucumber) being lost close by the skirting board; Chris Ofili's paintings looking pallid and slight. More successful are Hirst's monumental *Hymn* (1996) and Ron Mueck's superlative diminutive *Dead Dad* (1997), shrunk, abandoned, on the rotunda's parquet floor.

Seventy-five years before Saatchi, the collector Edward Marsh offered to support Mark Gertler with £10 a month, in the belief that buying the work of established artists was too easy: 'How much more exciting to back what might roughly be called one's own judgement . . . to go to the studios and the little galleries, and purchase, wet from the brush, the possible masterpieces of the possible Masters of the future.'[338] Saatchi, alone in his generation, has had that confidence and courage, has trusted his instincts and bought works that he liked 'wet from the brush', indeed in many cases, straight from the art school.

It is not easy to deduce why someone who exhibited excellent, but established, American artists in the early 1980s should switch exclusively to collecting and exhibiting young British artists but it was a high-risk strategy. Some of the artists he has backed have fallen away, but it is remarkable how many of his artists from *Freeze* have survived, not only Hirst, Hume and Lucas, but Fiona Rae, Anya Gallacio and Ian Davenport.

They form no coherent 'school'. In an age supposedly in thrall to Conceptual Art, it is notable how the work of so many of them (Hirst, the Chapmans, Mueck, Marc Quinn) is led by content, by explorations of death, memory, loss, time; how frequent and clear are references to past masters (the Chapmans to Goya and Bosch, Hirst and Mark Wallinger to Stubbs, Sugimoto to Holbein); and how many are painters (Rae, Davenport, Hume, Ofili, Marcus Harvey, Glenn Brown and Jenny Saville). Saville is perhaps the finest artist in the collection. Her monumental nudes are painted with a physical appetite that glories in flesh, that dissolves the borders between paint and skin, while observing the secret details of a welt or a nipple with compassion and tenderness – painterly qualities that go well beyond 'hopeful swagger'.

SCIENCE MUSEUM ✳✳✳

Exhibition Road, London SW7 2DD
Tel. 020 7942 4000
www.sciencemuseum.org.uk

The collated understanding of how things work and why things happen, from Stephenson's Rocket to space flight

Prince Albert believed that Britain 'would recede as an industrial nation unless her industrial population became much more conversant with science than they are now'. With a fall in the proportion of students taking science A-levels and doing science degrees in recent years, his words have a fresh urgency. It is by no means certain that society in the early 21st century is interested in becoming more conversant with science than it was 150 years ago.

The Science Museum's response to this challenge is embodied in the new Wellcome Wing (2000) and in a new statement of its purpose (2002): 'We engage people in a dialogue to create meanings from the past, present and future of human ingenuity.'[339] The fields in which this engagement is to take place remain as before: science, technology, medicine, transport and the media.[340] The museum 'is not there to tell you what to think. It is there to enable you to think.'[341] Its role is to pose questions, to 'provoke a personal response'.[342]

In the Wellcome Wing Richard MacCormac has designed, in his words, 'a theatre of science'. A wall of blue glass the height of the building immerses everything in whatever it is that you think blue represents: sea, sky,

Templates from Crick and Watson's DNA molecular model (Science Museum)

universe, past, future, hope? In a museum that is standing back from any didactic role, it is a suitably open-ended design.

The new galleries seek to engage the visitor. On the ground floor there are temporary exhibitions that address current scientific issues: AIDS, drugs in sport, the human genome, climate change, GM crops. The content is concise and informative. As a sign of 'involvement', you are invited to cast a vote, although it is not clear on what basis or to what end.

The floor above is concerned with individual identity and brain science. The theme 'Who am I?' is explored with the help of computer programmes. Iron Age genetics, DNA, the distribution of surnames in Britain now and in the past, fingerprints, the central nervous system are variously explored.

As you rise through the building on escalators that go only up (to descend you must take the stairs), the stack of floors or 'trays' gets smaller and each has less on it: the top floor, The Future, is almost an empty space.

The Wellcome Wing is grappling simultaneously with the problems of how to involve the general public in scientific ideas and issues and of how to use new technologies to widen the experience of visiting a museum. Some of its successes are notable: A Pattern Pod explores patterns in nature and in science (the structure of snowflakes, insect wings, computer pixels) in ways that are intellectually challenging and aesthetically beautiful, but the central paradox of an object-light museum that works through computers remains: why visit when you can log on at home? MacCormac is right. The museum should be theatre. The new technologies are not even cinema, although there is an IMAX screen here.

The Wellcome Wing is an exciting barn of a building plugged on to the back of one of the blandest museum buildings in Britain, designed by Sir Robert Allison of the Office of Works between 1913 and 1928.[343] Its collections, mainly of industrial technology rather than pure sciences, have their origins in the South Kensington Museum (later the Victoria and Albert Museum, q.v.) which opened in 1857 in the wake of the Great Exhibition.[344]

You enter the main hall, the full height of the building, in which are exhibited the machines that powered the Industrial Revolution: from Boulton and Watt's rotative steam engine (4–100 h.p.) (1788) and its 1797 successor, whose vast bored cylinders Watt described in a letter to John Smeaton as being 'not farther distant from absolute truth than the thickness of a thin sixpence at the worst point'. Their thumping and hissing gave way to the slow, oiled, silent movement of the 1903 mill engine built for the Harle Syke Mill in Burnley. This engine is symbolic of the period when steam was still king in manufacture, thirty years before the development of the electrical grid brought this phase of our manufacturing history slowly to a close.

'I sell here, Sir, what all the world desires to have ... Power,' wrote Boulton in 1776. This hall displays it as a new religion, a question of faith. 'The velocity, violence, magnitude, and horrible noise of the engine give universal satisfaction to all beholders, believers or not,' wrote Watt in 1777.

Linking this to the Wellcome Wing is a gallery entitled Making the Modern World, which contains seminal objects: George Stephenson's *Rocket* (1829) and the 1814 *Puffing Billy*,[345] the oldest railway locomotive in the world, an encrusted black beast whose metal flanks are held by huge rivets and whose chassis comprises massive wooden beams.

Near them, sitting neatly in a display case, is Babbage's Difference Engine No. 1 (1832), the first known automatic analytical engine and calculator, the parent of the computer. Babbage's project collapsed in 1834 when his partner Joseph Clement refused to continue work on the machine. From the 20th century is Crick and Watson's model for DNA (1953), a delicate yet solid pointillistic spiral that looks somehow practical and very much of its time, and Dorothy Hodgkin's 1967 model of insulin.

On upper floors there is a gallery of Flight, with aircraft from the early pterodactyls of the flying age, constructs of canvas and wooden bones in which men first launched themselves into the air no more than a hundred years ago, through Reginald Mitchell's planes (the seaplane winner of the Schneider Trophy and the Spitfire) to the huge silver jet engines of Rolls Royce and Pratt and Whitney in the 1960s.

Here too a gallery of medicine (an earlier Wellcome gift) manages to explain the influence that patients, doctors, campaigners and politicians have had on the development of medicine in recent generations.

Finally the oldest, most traditional gallery in the museum contains the collection of 18th-century scientific instruments of George III: Thomas Wright's Grand Orrery (*c.* 1731), made for Frederick, Prince of Wales; and the ornate, grandiose silver microscope made in 1763 for George III himself by George Adams, an edifice of pillars and pediments enshrining the magnified image.

The Science Museum has coined an adage to describe its role, 'inspire, educate, involve', echoing the Reithian mission of the BBC. It is grappling with the problems of exhibiting and explaining technologies that are complex and often intangible. At the same time it is attempting to ask questions about the role of the museum in an age of mass entertainment.

Science and museums have mutual needs and the museum ought to be, in the words of a 1909 Board of Education report, 'of incalculable benefit alike to intellectual progress and to industrial development'.

SIR JOHN SOANE'S MUSEUM ★★★★

13 Lincoln's Inn Fields, London WC2A 3BP
Tel. 020 7405 2107
www.soane.org

A great mind displayed, unfolded, crammed in two London houses

Behind the modest facades of the two houses that Sir John Soane rebuilt as his home, overlooking Lincoln's Inn Fields, is a museum which broke the mould of museums before that mould was ever made. In it Soane surrounded himself with the paintings, antiquities, sculptures, books and drawings that

he collected in a lifetime given to art and to architecture.

The front door to No. 13 is kept locked. You seek entry by ringing the bell and are admitted not just into the rooms and passages of Soane's home but into the maze of his mind.

This is the house of a classicist, an architect, an obsessive collector. It is as full of perceptions, opinions, enthusiasms and visual jokes as it is of objects. It is a labyrinth of surprise vistas, of reflections in mirrors, of changes of level and perspective, of darkness and light. Look up and the heavens are above you, in skylights and canopies. Look down and you glimpse the depths of catacombs and vaults, as it were encrypted.

Wherever you go, John Soane is at your shoulder, nudging you to notice, in his own words, 'a succession of those fanciful effects which constitute the poetry of architecture', looking down on you with the quizzical smile caught by Sir Thomas Lawrence in his 1828 portrait hanging over the fireplace in the Dining Room.

John Soane was the youngest son of a Berkshire builder-bricklayer, born in 1753. A chance meeting with George Dance, the architect of Newgate Prison (1770–80) (the contemporary building Soane most admired), secured him a position in Dance's office as his pupil. He entered the Royal Academy school and won its gold medal (presented to him by its president, Sir Joshua Reynolds), and with it a travelling scholarship which he spent in Italy. There he met Piranesi, who became and remained the definer of his taste, his love of Roman classicism. Piranesi gave him the four engravings from the *Vedute di Roma* series (the Pantheon, the Arches of Constantine and of Septimus Severus, and the tomb of Cecilia Metella) that hang in the Picture Room.

Back in London, his confident classicism won for him the commission to design the Bank of England (1788–1833). He married and bought, in 1792, No. 12 Lincoln's Inn Fields as a home (the front) and as an office for his architectural practice (at the back).

In 1806, now Professor of Architecture at the Royal Academy, he 'began to arrange the

Books, casts and models in order that the students might have benefit of easy access to them' (as he said in his sixth lecture to the Royal Academy) and in 1813 he opened his recently acquired house next door, No. 13, to his students at the Royal Academy. In 1833 he negotiated a private Act of Parliament which left his museum to the nation for the benefit of 'Amateurs and Students in Painting, Architecture and Sculpture ... intended to benefit the artists of future generations, but ... chiefly for the advancement of the architect' with the proviso, printed on the tickets, that there would be 'no admission in wet or dirty weather'.

The museum has four basic collections: antiquities and architectural fragments; paintings (Turner, Canaletto, Hogarth); some 30,000 architectural drawings including Piranesi, Robert Adam, George Dance, Wren and Hawksmoor; and Soane's own architectural models and drawings.

Once you leave the Entrance Hall there is no right way to proceed. Let your eye lead you to discover the museum for yourself. Every visit is different. There are highlights: the original paintings of Hogarth's two series, sold as engravings, *A Rake's Progress* (1733) and *An Election* (1754); the sarcophagus of Pharaoh Seti I (died 1279 BC), discovered in the Valley of the Kings, and purchased by Soane in 1824 after the British Museum jibbed at the asking price of £2,000. Soane celebrated this by giving three evenings of parties, for 300 people each night. But it is the collection itself, and the way that Soane presented it, that is remarkable, rather than any individual object. Every room is crammed with delights, apparently at random, actually with knowing artifice, to surprise and to catch the corner of your eye with strange juxtapositions. You are invited to look again at the past, through glass, in glimpses, edgeways, close to, far off, first hidden, then revealed.

Although there is order, there is no hierarchy of objects. Ancient sits beside modern, priceless by worthless, casts beside models, real beside fake. Soane was scholarly but there are few signs here of scholarship and objects are not labelled.

To the right of the Entrance Hall, the Pompeian red Dining Room and Library introduce you at once to Soane's use of mirrors to stretch the dimensions of rooms, and reflect at night the flickering candle and lamplight. The mirrors are framed to turn reflections into compositions, as if in a 'Claude glass'.

The niches which hold antique busts are lined with mirrors, an idea he adapted from the Villa Albani in Rome, to pile reflection upon progressive reflection. Don't overlook, among the many vases in the two rooms, two remarkable Apulian vases (4th century BC): the Cawdor vase, in the windowsill, and the Englefield vase, on the pier, with what Soane called its 'extraordinary design and presentation'. Before exploring the inner recesses of the museum, go through the narrow door, to the left of the North Window, into the Breakfast Parlour and marvel at Soane's ability to transform a small space with planes, mirrors and light. The dominant feature of the room is its domed ceiling, painted in Turner's patent yellow, and pierced by a central oculus through which light streams. The domed billow of the canopy appears to be held down by convex mirrors at each of its four corners, while being buoyed up by the planes of light beyond it. The result is an illusion of weightlessness which holds the canopy over us without apparent support, a flourish of design and artifice.

Return to the Dining Room and go through the Study and the Dressing Room, looking out of the window to your left into Monument Court and on your right the Monk's Yard with its architectural fragments and mock ruins. You now enter the Picture Room, the most remarkable space in the museum.

At first sight it seems impossible that this small room, measuring twelve by thirteen feet, could contain over a hundred pictures, including the two Hogarth series. This expansion of space is achieved by a series of hinged screens which will be opened out for you by an attendant, if you ask.

Behind the north screens are a Turner watercolour of *Kirkstall Abbey* and fifteen drawings of the temples at Paestum by Piranesi. Behind the south screens are glorious watercolours of Soane's designs by his pupil Joseph Gandy. Then these screens open yet again to reveal in the Picture Room Recess the statue of a *Nymph* by Sir Richard Westmacott, lit as if on a tiny stage. Over the edge of a balcony you are given a further view which drops down through the height of the house to the Monk's Parlour in the basement.

Down there, in the cellars of the house, you pick your way through dark passages and catacombs as you encounter Soane's fascination with death. In the central space, the Sepulchral Chamber, is the sarcophagus of Seti I, Soane's most treasured possession. Here among the funerary urns and grave ornaments, the Roman antiquities, the altar dedicated to Hercules (2nd century AD), the fragments and ruins, even the jokes are about death. The Parlour of Padre Giovanni (the Monk's Parlour) is not just a simple play on his own name but a tease of the fashion for Gothic antiquarianism. Above the Monk's mock grave in the Monk's Yard outside are the words 'Alas, Poor Fanny!' Fanny, who really is buried here, was Mrs Soane's dog.

To bring your eye back to the present, end by going into the new Soane Gallery in No. 12. Here all is as orderly as the rest of the house is random. The architect Eva Jiricna has designed the gallery in what was the dining room of No. 12. She has not been afraid to test her line against Soane's and has made four fine cabinets in glass, pinned by thin steel, to display his architectural drawings.

So what story does this museum tell? Soane in his Fifth Lecture to the Royal Academy in 1819 said, 'Every building, great or small, simple or elegant, must, like the picture, speak intelligibly to the beholder. Each must have a positive character peculiar to itself, sufficient to point out the purposes and uses for which it was erected. This cannot be attained if the work is deficient in character. The Athenian orator being asked what were the great requisites in his art, replied, action, action, action. So if it were asked what constituted the distinctive beauties in architectural compositions, the answer would be, character, character, character.'

This museum expresses the character of Soane in all its moods: his love of architecture and the Corinthian order; his steady gaze on death and mourning; his admiration for Piranesi, whose drawings of great buildings in decay combine both these; his compulsion to teach and to try to ensure that the echoes of architecture are carried over the centuries.

It does what every good museum should do: make you look and see and think afresh. If you want to hear the voice of collecting, it is here, in the Soane, the museum of museums.

TATE BRITAIN *****

Millbank, London SW1P 4RG
Tel. 020 7887 8000
www.tate.org.uk

Four hundred years of painting in England, and the bequest of J. M. W. Turner

If you seek the story of English art it is to be found here in the galleries of Tate Britain.

You will find its chronology, from the Tudor portraitist John Bettes[346] to the latest shortlistee for the Turner Prize; its range, every subject, every genre, every medium from oils to prints; the work of the great (the line from Van Dyck through Hogarth, Reynolds, Gainsborough, Turner and on) and of the good.

What you will not see are the roots of English art. The Tate's story starts mid chapter. To find what preceded the collection here, you must seek out the works, made before the Reformation, that are in the churches and cathedrals of England;[347] the illuminations in such manuscripts in the British Library as the Lindisfarne Gospels or the Sherborne missal; or the medieval treasures in the Victoria and Albert Museum. To find what influenced the artists here, attend to the European Old Masters in the National Gallery or the Celtic and classical masterpieces in the British Museum (all q.v.).

What is here is the best of art made in Britain or, to be precise, made in England, since the work of Scottish, Welsh and Irish artists can be seen to better advantage in the

The Decline of the Carthaginian Empire *by
J. M. W. Turner (Tate Britain)*

national galleries of those countries. Here,
under one roof, is how artists in England have
seen themselves, their world, the world.

It has taken more than a hundred years to
achieve this unity of location for these works.
As the National Gallery grew in the second
half of the 19th century, it became clear that,
even after the gallery's extension in 1876, it
could not adequately accommodate the growing British School.[348] Robert Vernon, a patron
of Turner, had given 157 pictures in 1847, of
which 70 were by English artists. In 1856 these
were joined by 34 works from the Turner
Bequest. Henry Tate, the Liverpool-born sugar
magnate, had written to the National Gallery
in 1889 offering to donate his collection of
modern British art. The following year the

landscape painter James Orrock[349] provoked
a campaign, taken up by *The Times*, for 'the
creation of a great British gallery'.[350]

With popular support a site was eventually
secured from the government in 1893, the grim
Millbank Penitentiary,[351] which was demolished. Tate's favourite architect, Sidney R. J.
Smith, was chosen to design the new building.

Smith laboured to produce what he saw as
his masterpiece, borrowing ideas and details
from the design of art galleries all over Europe.
The result was a derivative building, in
Pevsner's view 'with neither discretion nor
with originality',[352] a somewhat garbled collection of domes, cupolas and columns. It exudes
civic dignity but it is not pretentious and its
architectural imperfections make it a human,
rather friendly, building, with galleries that are
spacious and adaptable for the display of both
paintings and sculptures.

The development of the permanent collection was constrained by the gallery's status as an annexe of the National Gallery. In 1915 a government report by Lord Curzon[353] concluded that the Tate should develop two national collections, historic British art and modern foreign painting, but without making 'rash purchases in the occasionally ill-disciplined productions of some contemporaneous continental schools, whose work might exercise a disturbing and even deleterious influence upon our younger painters'.[354] At the same time 200 English paintings were transferred from the National Gallery.

The main source of funding for new acquisitions came from the Chantrey Bequest[355] whose trustees purchased exclusively from the annual Royal Academy exhibition. Their choices,[356] which at this time filled seven of the galleries, were resolutely cautious.

The early keepers struggled: D. S. MacColl, one of the founders of the National Art Collections Fund in 1903, with determination but all too briefly (1906–11); Charles Aitken, a painter (mainly of flowers) and member of the Camden Town Group, kindly but feebly (1911–30); James Bolivar Manson (1930–35) in a haze of sickness, depression and alcohol. Progress came mainly from bequests and gifts (a Whistler, *Miss Cecily Alexander: Harmony in Grey and Green*, 1872; John Singer Sargent's swagger portrait of *Lord Ribblesdale* in 1916; Samuel Courtauld's gift of superb French Impressionists and Post-Impressionists).[357] William Blake's illustrations to Dante's *Divine Comedy* were purchased. With the help of the NACF and others, in 1918 the art dealer Joseph Duveen financed the building of a new gallery designed by W. H. Romaine-Walker and Gilbert Jenkins in which to show modern foreign paintings (1923).[358]

In 1938 Manson had a nervous breakdown and retired, to paint: 'The roses are dying, and so am I.'[359] His successor, the 36-year-old John Rothenstein,[360] fresh from his successes galvanising the Leeds City Art Gallery and the Graves Art Gallery, began transforming the Tate, devoting three rooms to modern British art. 'For the first time the modern English school (Whistler to Wadsworth) is treated seriously and hung with taste and discrimination,' wrote Herbert Read.[361]

Rothenstein's love for, and knowledge of, the work of the Camden Town Group artists[362] resulted, in time, in the formation of the gallery's immensely strong collection of early 20th-century English figurative painting.

At last it was becoming possible to see the gallery's superb holding of 18th- and 19th-century paintings in a context that embraced the (near) contemporary: Gainsborough, Reynolds, Whistler and Sargent; William Blake, Richard Dadd, Samuel Palmer, Edward Calvert, Stanley Spencer and (soon) Cecil Collins; the English landscape as seen by George Lambert and Spencer Gore. The masterpieces (des Granges's *The Saltonhall Family*, c. 1636–7; Dobson's *Endymion Porter*, c. 1642–5; Stubbs's *The Reapers*, 1785; Gainsborough's *Lady Bate-Dudley*, 1787, or his only – unfinished – nude, *Musidora*, c. 1780–88; Millais's *Ophelia*, 1851–2; Sickert's *Ennui*, 1914) could be viewed beside the works of their contemporaries.

And, of course, there is J. M. W. Turner, of whose work Tate Britain has the definitive collection: oils, watercolours, prints, sketchbooks, all the work that remained in his studio at his death and was given to the nation in the 1856 Turner Bequest.[363] In 1987 it was moved from the Duveen Galleries to the new Clore Wing designed by James Stirling. The wing's facade is a piece of toy-town post-modernism, scarcely worthy of the architect of the Stuttgart Statsgalerie, but inside the nine galleries,[364] spacious, calm, well lit, allow the visitor to explore all aspects and periods of Turner's work. There are surprises. His debts to Claude (*Aeneas and the Sibyl, Lake Avernus*, c. 1798, *The Decline of the Carthaginian Empire*, 1817) and to Poussin (*The Tenth Plague of Egypt*, 1802)[365] are well known; less so his homage to Watteau (*Boccaccio Relating the Tale of the Birdcage*, 1828).

This concentration of so many of his works provides a unique opportunity to consider the ways in which he expressed his mastery of light: dissolving it in water (*Norham Castle*,

1845, or *Venice: the Giudecca from the Lagoon*, 1840); making it a beam (on the sail in *The Shipwreck*, 1805); or producing pyrotechnics (as the rainbow lights the valley in *Buttermere Lake, with Part of Cromackwater, Cumberland, a Shower*, 1798). In this last the passage at the rainbow's end is as free and impressionistic as any in his late works (*Rough Sea*, c. 1840–45). It was painted in 1798, when Turner was twenty-three years old, the same year as his ravishing, rare *Moonlight, a Study at Millbank*, which anticipates Whistler. It is a collection that will convince many of the justness of Ruskin's view that Turner was 'the man who beyond all doubt is the greatest of the age; greatest in every faculty of the imagination, in every branch of scenic knowledge; at once the painter and poet of the day'.[366]

Turner's watercolours were augmented in 1996 by the bequest of Paul Oppé, whose collection of more than three thousand watercolours and drawings, from William Hogarth, Richard Wilson and Alexander Cozens in the mid 18th century to John William Inchbold and Frederic, Lord Leighton[367] a hundred years later, bears witness to Oppé's 'humour, humanity and generous width of sympathy', in the opinion of Sir Kenneth Clark.[368]

Rothenstein's enthusiasm 'to show the development of the national school'[369] was offset by his scepticism about abstraction in general and Cubism in particular. Foreign art was confined to the lower galleries and, in the years after the Second World War when the art market was weak, no Cubist paintings were acquired. After some dithering, and in response to encouragement and pressure from H. S. Ede and Douglas Cooper, works by Matisse and Edvard Munch did enter the collection but the opportunity to receive Dr Rosa Schapire's outstanding collection of German Expressionists was needlessly lost.[370]

Rothenstein's successors as Director, Sir Norman Reid (1964–79), Sir Alan Bowness (1980–88) and Sir Nicholas Serota (appointed 1988), had much ground to recover. All three had excellent personal links with contemporary artists in Britain, the US and Europe. Reid secured, among many other works, the

Seagram set of paintings by Mark Rothko; Bowness (son-in-law of Barbara Hepworth) greatly strengthened the representation of paintings and sculptures by the St Ives School; and Serota's promotion of the Turner Prize ensured that many British artists born in the 1950s, '60s and '70s now have works in the Tate.

While enriching the collection, these acquisitions made desirable, even necessary, the creation first of two regional outstations, Tate Liverpool (q.v.) and Tate St Ives (q.v.), and then, in 2000, Tate Modern (q.v.) on Bankside, which finally divided the collection as the Curzon Report of 1915 had hinted, into English School and modern (and foreign) works.

This division created breathing space for the collection, as did the addition of new galleries designed by John Miller and Partners in 2001 in which the full glories of the historic and English collection may be seen: truly as 'incredible [a] quantity of pictures' as that praised by Rubens nearly four hundred years ago.

Tate Britain's collection raises the question: is there a school of English art? John Rothenstein was convinced 'that it is unlikely, it is hardly indeed imaginable, that the twentieth century will be accounted one of the great periods of painting.'[371] By the highest critical standards (comparison with the Italian Renaissance, Dutch painting in the 16th and 17th centuries, French in the late 19th century) that could be said to apply generally to English art, although I would want to enter pleas for the flowering of English painting, architecture and the decorative arts in the 18th century and for the development of the English School of watercolourists, 1750–1850.

Tate Britain's collection provides evidence for both prosecution and defence in the consideration of that question. What is clear is that there is a distinct Englishness in English art. Britain's history as a nation dependent on trade and expansion has always opened us to outside influences and our artists have usually absorbed foreign influences, although this was less apparent at the height of the British Empire in the late 19th century when those such as Whistler (and later Roger Fry) who brought news of what was happening in France, were largely ignored.

On the walls of these galleries is the evidence of the Englishness of English art that Nikolaus Pevsner explored in his 1956 Reith Lectures:[372] the roast beef and full blood of Hogarth, the 'gentle curves of Gainsborough, Reynolds and Adam',[373] the insularity (Constable never went to Italy, nor to Paris; neither did Gainsborough nor Hogarth); those whom Pevsner called 'the Contraries' (Blake, Fuseli).

Here, in the landscapes and the seascapes, are the vagaries of English light. It can be no accident that the quintessential English School (watercolourists, 1750–1850) recorded the horizontals of the rivers and plains of the English landscape. Even when they took to the wilds of the Lake District or North Wales it was the water in the light, the rain and the mist that was evident.

Tate Britain shows that Englishness in art comes in many forms and guises, and celebrates those curious varieties.

TATE MODERN ***

Bankside, London SE1 4RG
Tel. 020 7887 8888
www.tate.org.uk

A power station for international modern art

It is the Cyclopean scale of the building that makes Tate Modern remarkable. It was remarkable when Sir Giles Gilbert Scott designed it, having worked on the Anglican Cathedral in Liverpool. It was remarkable when it stood empty: a diplodocus, redundant after only thirty-five years, the last of the brick power stations built to burn oil not coke.[374] It is remarkable now that the Swiss architects de Meuron & Herzog have stripped out the Turbine Hall and redesigned the shell of the Boiler House into eighty-two galleries.

London has wanted, in both senses, a museum of modern art for at least forty years. Douglas Cooper, the pre-eminent art historian of Cubism, had made a case for such a place in a letter to *The Times* in April 1964.[375] Nicholas

Serota, the director, and his chairman Dennis Stevenson, made it a reality by persuading the Heritage Lottery Fund to support the conversion.

Most of the museum and gallery buildings in this book are classical. Its scale and impassive profile make this one Egyptian. On entering, you go down, the better to be dwarfed and awed by the cavernous Turbine Hall that reduces the visitor, and most works of art that are sited within it, to insignificance. It invites immediate comparisons with a cathedral, but cathedrals make the spirit soar towards heaven; the mighty work of the Turbine Hall, while cheaply thrilling, is an architectural Ozymandias, edging awe with despair.

By contrast the galleries are flooded with natural light, are human in scale and offer occasional snatched views across the river to the City and St Paul's.

Converting a power station provided space, in the centre of the capital, that no new museum could have afforded to have built, and a pleasing neutrality, as had the conversion of the Musée d'Orsay in Paris. The drama of the building makes a visit into an event. It also turns the gallery from being the servant of its collection into being its own prime exhibit. In this Tate Modern follows the path charted by the Pompidou Centre in 1977 and the Bilbao Guggenheim Museum twenty years later, in each of which the architecture (by Richard Rogers and Renzo Piano, and by Frank Gehry, respectively) is more memorable than the collection it houses. It is a path that leads to the museum as performance, even fun house, and the curator as impresario and, soon, showman.

The collection here suffers from the lamentable failures between 1897 and 1956 of successive Tate Gallery directors to build a collection of the contemporary art of the 20th century. The mistakes and missed opportunities are too numerous and too painful to more than glance at: no paintings by French Impressionists or Post-Impressionists (despite Roger Fry's Grafton Gallery exhibitions in 1910 and 1911) until Samuel Courtauld's Fund provided the money to make acquisitions in the 1920s;[376] the general resistance to Abstraction, summed up by the trustees in 1945, 'in view of the vitality of so-called abstract art . . . a small room at the Tate should be devoted to its representation';[377] the (repeated) failure to buy Matisse's *The Red Studio* in the late 1940s;[378] Rothenstein's refusal in 1955 of the offer by the artist's widow of three Moholy-Nagy sculptures;[379] no Soutine until the late 1940s; no Brancusi until the 1970s. While the Tate turned its face away from what was happening in Paris and New York, other galleries across Europe and the United States made acquisitions. After 1956 all that Norman Reid, Alan Bowness and Nicholas Serota could do was to try to recover some of the ground lost. With the help of gifts and bequests[380] and, at last, some government money for acquisitions,[381] gaps were filled but the collection still has poor representation of the German Expressionists and Italian Metaphysicals and Futurists, and is weak on Russian art, and on photography in general; 20th-century painting in China is unrepresented.

In his 1996 Walter Neurath Lecture Nicholas Serota made a determined case for rethinking how museums could and should hang their collections, by theme rather than chronology. Tate Modern adopts that approach with themed galleries. Here such a hang is inevitable, rather than desirable, if the gaps are not to be more eloquent than the works.

There are good arguments for a thematic hang. Few people hang pictures in their homes by period. Our minds do not work simply on a linear timescale. But these are personal arguments and galleries are public spaces with public responsibilities. Nikolaus Pevsner said 'most intelligent visitors after a time find that they need history to understand and even to appreciate art'.[382] More sternly, the art critic David Sylvester wrote, 'It is all very well for curators to want to ignore chronology. But chronology is not a tool of art-historical interpretation which can be used at one moment, discarded at another. It's all objective reality, built into the fabric of the work. And into the

Tate Modern

artist's awareness.'[383] Bizarrely the themes chosen here are not reimagined but borrowed from the French Academy of the 17th century: Landscape, Still Life, the Nude, History. The works in the collection suggest that, in the century after Freud, racked by world wars and holocaust, artists worked less clearly in these established areas but were more concerned with exploring pain (Francis Bacon, Max Beckmann, Willem De Kooning), or perception (the Surrealists, the Italian Metaphysicals) or with reordering the world (Piet Mondrian, Donald Judd, Barnett Newman).

Despite the gaps there are fine works here: Francis Bacon's *Three Studies for Figures at the Base of a Crucifixion* (1944), of which he said later, 'I began'; Henri Matisse's *The Snail* (1953); Morris Louis's *Alpha-phi* (1961); Frank Stella's *Six Mile Bottom* (1960). The title refers to a village near Cambridge where Byron's half-sister Augusta Leigh lived. Stella commented, 'I felt that it [the aluminium surface of the painting] had the character of being slightly more abstract.'

Some artists command a single room, alone, effortlessly: Bridget Riley, Joseph Beuys, Mark Rothko, who bequeathed the Tate Gallery nine 'darkly glowing' paintings in 1968 on condition that they should not be shown in a room shared with any other artist. Apart from his friendship with Norman Reid, his decision to give works to the Tate was reinforced by his love for J. M. W. Turner and his desire to have his work hang in the same building; now two miles of river separate them.

Some artists are combined to good effect: Francis Picabia and Marcel Duchamp; Barnett Newman and Alberto Giacometti, whose figures, as emaciated as Etruscan bronzes, can command voids. Hanging Pierre Bonnard beside Howard Hodgkin says something surprising about each of them. Placing Monet beside Richard Long is facile and wrong-headed.

For a collection that has excellent sculpture from every period of the past hundred years, and good spaces in which to show it, Tate Modern is failing to do justice to Gaudier-Brzeska and Moholy-Nagy; Moore and Hepworth; Paolozzi and Chadwick; André and Le Witt; Gormley and Whiteread. The uncertainty about how and where to show their work to best effect is less pressing than what to show in the Turbine Room.

Exhibiting work by Louise Bourgeois at the opening cruelly exposed her limitations. To command this space calls for work of great presence and resonance. Anish Kapoor's *Marsyas* was more successful; Olafur Eliason's elemental use of light (*The Weather Project*) more so again.

The challenge to make this canyon of a hall work mimics the challenge of building a collection worthy of this building which will make us look past the architectural drama to individual works and beyond.

TYPE MUSEUM *

100–100A Hackford Road, London, SW9 0QU
Tel. 020 7735 0055

Literally, the story of words made legible, in a south London stable

'This is the Type Museum. Refuge of All Man's Achievements in Recording his Long History with Metal Type on Paper. This Collection remains to witness 500 years of transferring the written word to a machine . . . fixed in time having been cast in lead or cut in wood. Friend, you stand on sacred ground. This is the Type Museum.' So writes Anthony Ray of the British Printing Society.[384]

The sacred ground is at the end of a quiet side street in Stockwell in a building that was a Horse Hospital, home in 1912 to two elephants.

For five centuries the printed word has communicated all human knowledge; ideas and news; fact and fiction; truth and the lie. The writ of type has run. 'With twenty five soldiers of lead I have conquered the world,' wrote one anonymous 17th-century printer. Such power is ruthless, each technological improvement condemning its predecessor to oblivion and bankruptcy.

In recent years computers have brought

printing and publishing on to the top of desks, as Susan Shaw, printer, publisher and typographer, recognised in the 1980s. In 1992 she established the Type Museum Trust to acquire the archive, manufacturing plant and stock-in-trade of the Monotype Corporation, which had throughout the twentieth century swept all before it and established a virtual monopoly of hot metals for bookwork, in all languages and alphabets, but which went into receivership in 1991.

The corporation's 390 tons of type history were moved to Hackford Road, where they were joined by the machinery of Robert De Little & Co., York, the last surviving manufacturers of woodletter type in Britain, used for printing all type over one inch high (72 pt) for posters, playbills, etc., and the archive and plant of Stephenson Blake and Co. Ltd, Sheffield, the last surviving commercial type foundry in the country. Stephenson Blake had itself absorbed Sir Charles Reed and Sons Ltd in 1905 and with it the old fonts of such former famous letter foundries as Thorowgood, Fry, James and Glover. Their fonts went back to the 16th century: Caslon's Egyptian (the first sans serif type), Fry's Sans Serif Shaded, Thorowgood's Italic, Jackson's Bengalee (the first Bengali type, 1773) and Joseph Moxon's Irish (c. 1669).[385]

In the forecourt of the museum the visitor climbs the outside iron steps and enters a room that is filled with machinery: an 1890 wood letter router for carving typeface on to seasoned Canadian maple; an 1897 prototype Monotype composition keyboard and caster, patented by Tolbert Lanston, that united the two processes of type founding and printing; the 1960 Monotype caster; machines for punch cutting and for matrix making; drawers of patterns, punches and matrices representing every major alphabet (Latin, Greek, Cyrillic, Arabic, Hebrew, Amharic, Armenian, Hindi) made by Monotype in types designed by some of the greatest 20th-century designers: Stanley Morison, Eric Gill, Jan van Krimpen. Everywhere there is the smell of oil and iron, and hot metal. This is a living museum continuing to secure and fulfil orders for Monotype

matrices and spare parts from wherever hot metal is still in everyday use (Ethiopia, Bangladesh) and from fine art printers.

Across the yard in a separate building is the museum's gallery. In cases are Sumerian imprinted cuneiform, made in 2000 BC; ancient Roman 'stereotypes'; examples of woodcut Sinhalese type; and the last major commercial order in the world, cancelled for political reasons and never delivered, each letter curling and twisting, an alphabet of tendrilled beauty.

A collection of books demonstrates the excellence of 18th-century English printing and paper. Here are the three volumes (1702, 1703 and 1704) of Clarendon's *History of the Rebellion*, printed at the Oxford University Press, with engravings by Michael Burghers;[386] Virgil, printed by John Baskerville (1757), credited with starting the revolution in type design; Somerville's poem *The Chase*, printed in 1796 by Thomas Bewick and W. Bulmer.[387] Here too is a cabinet devoted to the work of Berthold Wolpe,[388] the German Jewish émigré who came to London in 1936 and designed for Faber and Faber from 1943 to 1975.

As you leave, with your lay eye attuned to typeface, you notice that the sign for the museum and for all the nearby Stockwell streets are in the face that Wolpe designed, Albertus Titling.

Type is important. Beatrice Warde warned that 'the misplaced comma might start a riot, or a suit for libel'.[389] It is also beautiful, an art akin to architecture, whose employment, in printing, 'conveys thought, ideas, images from one mind to other minds'.[390]

The work of generations of great designers of type is celebrated here, from Johann Gutenberg, Christopher Plantin and John Baskerville to Eric Gill and Berthold Wolpe.

UCL ART COLLECTION *

The Strang Print Room, University College London, Gower Street, London WC1E 6BT
Tel. 020 7679 2540
http://collections.ucl.ac.uk

The collection of the Slade School of Art

The origin of the UCL Art Collection lies in the group of sculptures and reliefs by John Flaxman that were bequeathed by his sister-in-law Miss Maria Denman in 1847.[391] These are exhibited in a magnificent top-lit rotunda, designed, within William Wilkins's university building, by T. L. Donaldson.[392] At its centre is *St Michael Overcoming Satan* (1819–24), a full-scale model for the marble at Petworth House (q.v.), commissioned by the 1st Earl of Egremont. An heroic St Michael spears an already cast-down Satan, attended by a huge, writhing serpent.

Around the eight walls of the rotunda are thirty-nine models for reliefs, monuments to early 19th-century clerics, politicians and philanthropists whose finished marbles are in churches all over the empire, from Madras to Barbados, and all over Britain, from Yorkshire to Devon. Notable among them is a monument to the Baring family,[393] *The Lord's Prayer: Deliver Us from Evil* (1809–13) in Micheldever Church, Hampshire. With them were bequeathed Flaxman's drawings and tracings of designs for prints. These were subsequently augmented by three further bequests of Old Master prints and drawings. They include a drawing by Hans Burgkmair the Elder, an Augsburg master and contemporary of Hans Holbein the Elder (given by George Grote, MP and classicist); an engraving by Andrea Mantegna of an allegorical Bacchanalian group (the gift of publisher and printer Charles Davies Sherborn,[394] as were a woodcut and engraving by Albrecht Dürer and an etching by Anthony Van Dyck); and several by the collector, and friend of J. M. W. Turner, Henry Vaughan. This latter group comprised a Turner watercolour and eight rare trial proofs for the 'Liber Studiorum Sequel' or 'Little Liber';[395] two De Wint watercolours; two etchings by Rembrandt and two of the seven prints of Mantegna's *The Triumphs of Caesar* (1480s).[396]

This Old Master collection became a model and inspiration for pupils and staff at the Slade School, founded as part of University College in 1871. The efficacy of this can be considered in the two final parts of the UCL collection: the gift of Henry Tonks, who taught at the Slade as professional assistant and then professor from 1892 to 1930, and the examples of the work of Slade students, primarily of those who have won the annual summer prizes for drawing and painting.

In the history of the Slade two periods were particularly distinguished: the 1950s when William Coldstream was professor, with pupils who included Michael Andrews, Paula Rego, Euan Uglow and Craigie Aitchison; and the generations taught by Tonks, which stretched from Augustus and Gwen John to Rex Whistler by way of Wyndham Lewis, David Bomberg and Stanley Spencer.

Certain paintings stand out: Augustus John's *Moses and the Brazen Serpent* (Prize, 1898) which owes much to Rubens, Dora Carrington's sculptural *Standing Nude* (1913)[397] and David Bomberg's *The Tragedians* (1919). The painting that rises above all others, however, is Stanley Spencer's *The Nativity* (1912), which must rank as one of the most remarkable student paintings of the 20th century. A further picture by Spencer, *The Apple Gatherers* (1912–13), won another prize and was bought by Sir Edward Marsh.[398]

Spencer spent four years at the Slade. When he arrived there, his experience was limited to the reproductions that he had seen at his Cookham home and at Maidenhead Technical School, one of the provincial art schools founded after the 1851 Great Exhibition. The Slade, and particularly Tonks, introduced him to Giotto, Masaccio, Fra Angelico, Duccio, to the disciplines of drawing from life and to rigorous standards: to Tonks, 'to do a bad drawing was like living with a lie'.[399] Spencer's brother Gilbert noted that 'The Slade held a mirror in front of him, the like of which did not exist at home, and he saw himself among the forebears of his art in all their glory.'[400]

Although Tonks disapproved of neo-primitivism and of Gauguin (two clear influences on Spencer in *The Nativity*), he was not dogmatic. Paul Nash, a student contemporary, described the Slade as 'seething under the influence of Post-Impressionism'[401] following Roger Fry's two exhibitions at the Grafton Gallery in 1910 and 1912, at which he introduced British artists to Cézanne, van Gogh and Gauguin. Despite this Tonks could see that 'Spencer has shown signs of having the most original mind of anyone we have at the Slade and he combines it with great powers of draughtsmanship.'[402]

Tonks himself was a fine draughtsman, as witnessed by his *Study of a Girl in a Loincloth*, which he included in his bequest, along with a riotous Rowlandson and Rubens's *Two Studies of a Female Nude from Behind* (*c.* 1630s), which was his joy. He loved to entertain, with evenings that featured 'For his friends – the very best – the Chateau Lafite, 1870, and afterwards the drawing, the wonderful drawing by Rubens . . .'[403] His work, his teaching, his love of Old Masters and, above all, his faith in the primacy of drawing from life mark out Henry Tonks as the presiding spirit of the UCL collection.

VICTORIA AND ALBERT MUSEUM *****

Cromwell Road, South Kensington, London sw7 2RL
Tel. 020 7942 2000
www.vam.ac.uk

The decorative arts gathered in Imperial profusion, nowhere greater

The Victoria and Albert Museum (V&A) is a place so freighted with masterworks that one might walk its galleries every week of a long life and still come across a new beauty: the *Two Angels* carved in limewood by Tilman Riemenschneider (*c.* 1505), or the terracotta model by Michael Rysbrack for his marble figure of *Sir Isaac Newton* (*c.* 1730), in Westminster Abbey;[404] the Florentine porcelain oil and vinegar flask (*c.* 1580), made as an experiment for Francesco Maria de'Medici more than a century before Böttger perfected hardpaste porcelain in Saxony,[405] or the tiny ivory relief *The Entombment* (*c.* 1677–80), carved by Balthasar Permoser, its figures swooping and swaying deep within the actually shallow surface of the ivory.

Its collection of Italian Renaissance sculpture is the finest in the world outside Italy; its medieval collection, a treasury that gathers together the work of the greatest craftsmen in Europe. It houses one of the last remaining 19th-century collections of casts and its English furniture is an encyclopaedia of the craft. Notwithstanding the collections' origins as teaching collections intended to demonstrate the exemplary rather than the exceptional,[406] the V&A is crammed with objects that are supreme: the sculpture of *Neptune and Triton* by Gianlorenzo Bernini, all power and godly rage, acquired by John Pope-Hennessy, the museum's director 1967–74; the Hereford Cathedral screen, designed by Sir George Gilbert Scott; Michelangelo's tiny model of a *Young Slave* (*c.* 1513)[407] that is emerging from its thumb-soft red wax as if from mortal clay.

These objects are here as a result of the excellence of the museum's curators, there being a direct link between the generations of their scholarship and the quality, for instance, of the Renaissance sculpture collection. Robinson's catalogue of 1862,[408] definitive in its time, was succeeded by that of Eric Maclagan and Margaret Longhurst in 1932, which was, in turn, updated by the 1964 publication of John Pope-Hennessy and Ronald Lightbown, all establishing and maintaining the collection's pedigree.

The presence of eminent scholars gives confidence to collectors and the museum has been shaped to a considerable extent by gifts and bequests of outstanding quality: the French furniture and decorative arts collected by the reclusive John Jones, which reflected his passion for anything associated with Marie-Antoinette (furniture by Carlin and Riesener, Sèvres porcelain, the miniature models in lapis lazuli of the *Five Orders of Architecture*)[409] and, best of all, the collection of George Salting, described by *The Times* in its obituary of 14 December 1909 as 'the greatest English art collector of this age', its bronzes and reliefs, enamels, maiolica, ivories, miniatures and medals transforming many areas of the museum.

Charm, tenacity, wit and nerve of the highest order are needed by directors and curators if a museum is to acquire collections of the quality of Jones's and Salting's; Ralph Bernal's decorative art,[410] maiolica, armour; or Jules Soulages' French Renaissance ceramics, furniture, metalwork. The V&A has had a succession of outstanding Directors, Henry Cole (1852–73), Philip Cunliffe-Owen (1874–93), Eric Maclagan (1924–45), John Pope-Hennessy (1967–74) and Roy Strong (1974–88), who have shaped, and re-shaped, the museum.

Each has with skill and passion added to the whole. Today the museum has over four million objects. The visitor is dazzled but is also in danger of being overwhelmed, even confused: a sense that is exacerbated by the building's different wings and levels.

At times this sense of confusion has been shared by the museum itself. As bequests and acquisitions were made, curators have had to ask themselves: what is the purpose of the museum? Education, training; commerce, manufacture; university or treasure house? Is it for the artisan or the artist; the expert or the public; the manufacturer or the customer?

This dichotomy between training and art, between model and masterpiece, is more apparent than actual. The greatest single work in the museum, the Raphael *Sistine Chapel Tapestry Cartoons*, reinforces the point. Originally made as practical patterns for the tapestries in the Sistine Chapel in Rome and subsequently used at the Mortlake tapestry works set up by James I in 1619, they came to be seen as consummate works of art.[411]

In 1908, to coincide with the imminent completion of the new Aston Webb building

(1909) and in response to the prospect of the museum sinking under the weight of the Sheepshanks, Salting, Jones, Soulages and Bernal bequests, a Committee of Re-arrangement was established. Its secretary, the senior civil servant Sir Robert Morant, concluded that the museum should be organised on craft lines with galleries of glass, ceramics, metalwork, etc. Across Europe, museum directors, led by Wilhelm Bode, the Director of the Kaiser Friedrich Museum in Berlin, were introducing galleries organised by period, a change that was not introduced here until 1948 by the then Director, Leigh Ashton. The debate continues and the museum today incorporates both approaches: British, European, Asian galleries; galleries of jewellery, tapestry, silver, etc.

The building offers a metaphor for the playing out of these debates. From the Cromwell Road you enter the Aston Webb building of 1909. Its facade is impressive rather than beautiful, particularly striking when floodlit. Behind it is the original South Kensington Museum built by Captain Francis Fowke of the Royal Engineers[412] in an Italian Renaissance style, around an elegant courtyard. Inside are rooms that are showcases for the new industrial arts (ceramics, metal and glass work) that the Schools of Design[413] were set up to develop: tiles by Doulton and Minton; enamelled iron, a technique that Cole had seen at the 1851 Great Exhibition and used throughout the building.[414] The designers involved form a roll-call of the best: Godfrey Sykes, James Gamble and Reuben Townroe, trained by the sculptor Alfred Stevens at the School of Design in Sheffield; William Morris, Philip Webb and Edward Burne-Jones. The West Dining Room (Morris and Webb) and the Refreshment Room (Gamble and Sykes) remain two of the most enjoyable mid-19th-century interiors in London.

The galleries match them for effect: two huge Architectural Courts (1868–73), vaulted and polychrome, predominantly red and green, superb spaces in which to display the museum's cast collection. Here are Ghiberti's bronze doors from the Baptistry in Florence;[415] and, at the centre, the massive pillars of

The Healing of the Lame Man: *Raphael's cartoon at the V&A*

Trajan's column, cut in two for purposes of accommodation, so enormous it is.

Near by are sculptures large (Giambologna's *Samson Smiting the Philistine, c.* 1565, 6 feet 10 inches; the *Virgin and Child* from the Scuola della Misericordia in Venice, 1441–51, 8 feet 3 inches); and small (Donatello's bronze *Lamentation over the Dead Christ,* c. 1458, 12⅝ inches); and a medal inscribed 'NOW IS THE TIME', a quotation from Robinson's letter to the museum's trustees, 6 September 1866, from Madrid, which announced the beginning of this great collection of sculpture.

The urgency that leaps from Robinson's letter runs through so much of the museum. These are collections formed in the middle of a century of unprecedented upheaval: new industries, new sciences; the undermining of religious beliefs held for 2,000 years by the publication of Darwin's *On the Origin of Species*; the emergence of democracy and organised philanthropy; the gradual development of democracy; and new visual techniques, electroplating and photography, which go to the heart of this museum. Here is the first collection of photography, started as the plates were still wet with the acquisition in 1865 of Julia Margaret Cameron's *St Agnes*[416] (1864), one of twenty of her photographs bought that year.

Cole's enthusiasms for photography and electroplating[417] spilled over into other aspects of the museum. The V&A was the first museum to provide refreshment rooms and the first to stay open in the evenings. Cole took parts of the collection to East London by setting up the Bethnal Green Museum (q.v.) and lobbied the government for public transport so that all Londoners who lacked private carriages could come to the (then) green fields of South Kensington.

It was these green fields surrounding the museum that persuaded the collector John

Sheepshanks to give his collection of paintings, watercolours and drawings to the V&A, rather than to the National Gallery, so that they could be, in his words, 'in an open and airy situation, possessing the quiet necessary to the study and enjoyment of works of art, and free from the inconveniences and dirt of the main thoroughfare of the metropolis'. His collection included paintings by Wilkie, Landseer, Frith, Mulready and his friend John Constable – six works, of which the finest is *Salisbury Cathedral* (1823). The watercolours were the first in a now enormous collection in which are represented all the major English watercolourists, from Paul Sandby and Alexander Cozens to the present day. Sheepshanks's Constables were followed, in 1888, by the artist's daughter's gift of the contents of Constable's studio (95 paintings, 297 drawings and 3 sketchbooks), the definitive collection of his work.

The Constables and the Prints and Drawings[418] galleries are tucked away in the back of the building in the five floors of the Henry Cole wing, unlike the Asian and Near Eastern galleries[419] that greet you on the ground floor as you enter from Cromwell Road. Each of these might, incorrectly, be seen to be at a slight remove from the European/Renaissance bloodstream of the museum. Closer examination of these collections will quickly persuade the visitor of the influence that the architecture, ceramics, sculpture, metalwork, textiles and painting of these great civilisations have had on Europe, particularly since the 18th century; the Islamic Collection since much earlier. Each collection is of sufficient size and quality to furnish a dedicated museum.

There are objects in these collections that will remain in the mind and the eye of any visitor: a *Head of the Buddha* from Gandhara, Afghanistan (4–5th centuries) as strongly modelled as Benvenuto Cellini's *Head of Medusa* (*c.*1545–50); the sandstone *Torso* from Sanchi, central India (*c.*800–850), swaying supplely to the right; the Han dynasty *Head and Partial Torso of a Horse* (*c.*200 BC) in cloudy jade; the Iznik porcelain bowl (*c.*1550–55), from a period whose glazes and

design so influenced Morris, De Morgan and the Arts and Crafts Movement.

The same is true of many 20th-century objects: the Rodin sculptures;[420] the complete suite of office furniture that Frank Lloyd Wright made for Edgar J. Kaufmann's office in 1937; dresses by Christian Dior, Issey Miyake and Christian Lacroix; the opaque blue glass sculpture *Arcus 1* by the Czech husband-and-wife artists Stanislav Libenský and Jaraslove Brychtóva, cast in a plaster mould from molten glass.

Nevertheless for most visitors it will be earlier works to which they will continually return: the Bernini marble bust of *Thomas Baker* (*c.*1620–30); the boxwood *Madonna and Child* (*c.*1520) by Veit Stoss; the *Christ Crucified* (*c.*1300) by Giovanni Pisano; and the mighty bronze portrait relief by Adriaen De Vries of the *Emperor Rudolph II* (*c.*1609), whose paintings, by way of the collections of Queen Christina of Sweden and the Duc d'Orleáns, make appearances throughout the pages of this book:[421] Rudolph II, a collector, collected in this museum of great collections.

WALLACE COLLECTION
★★★★

Hertford House, Manchester Square, London W1N 3BN
Tel. 020 7563 9500
www.wallacecollection.org

Unparalleled gift of French painting, porcelain and furniture to the nation from an illegitimate son

As you step into the forecourt of Hertford House you feel that you are stepping from London into the late-19th-century Paris of the Goncourts and Proust. The house was built in 1776 for the Duke of Manchester but the steep roof and the porte cochère with which the architect Thomas Ambler refaced it gives it the appearance of an *hôtel de ville*.

Within, there arises a magnificent staircase with a balustrade of forged iron and chased and gilded bronze made in the 1730s for the

Bibliothèque Royale, later the Bibliothèque Nationale.[422] To your left is a French chimney piece of Carrara marble (*c.*1785) on which is a mantle clock by André-Charles Boulle.[423] Beside it are two marble busts by Charles-Henri-Joseph Cordier.[424] The animals in the large Landseer on the opposite wall look down on this French elegance with a certain English sang-froid.

If you want to see the paintings of Watteau, Fragonard and Boucher, Gobelins tapestries, Sèvres porcelain, French bronzes, statues by Houdon and Clodion, and furniture by Riesener, Caffiéri or Carlin, this is the museum. But there is much else besides: paintings by Van Dyck and Rubens, Claude and Poussin, three Rembrandts and a major Titian; portraits by Reynolds and Gainsborough, watercolours by Richard Parkes Bonington and one of the finest collections of armour in Europe. And this is only half of the combined collections of the Marquesses of Hertford and Sir Richard Wallace. Much was left in Lady Wallace's house in Paris in 1890, some pieces were lost in a fire and more were sold after Wallace's heir, Sir John Murray Scott, died in 1912.

The major part of the collections grew over three generations. The 3rd Marquess (1777–1842)[425] was a connoisseur who bought the Titian, *Perseus and Andromeda* (1553–62), painted for Philip II of Spain and owned in the 17th century by Van Dyck. Vasari, in his *Life of Titian,* said 'a more beautiful painting than this could not be imagined'.[426] He bought some of the Dutch genre paintings in the collection (Steen, Metsu, van Ostade). His advice to his friend the Prince Regent influenced the choice of Dutch paintings now at Windsor Castle (q.v.) and Buckingham Palace.

The 4th Marquess (1800–70), the greatest collector of his generation, was a recluse who visited only once the estates in Northern Ireland from which he derived much of his wealth. It was said of him that he would not look out of the window even if there was a revolution in the streets outside. For the last

Fragonard's The Swing *at the Wallace Collection*

thirty years of his life he lived in Paris, interested only in collecting, which he did through the agents he employed in London (S. M. Mawson) and in Paris.

He collected obsessively, often leaving unseen what he had bought. He was brought up in Paris by his French mother and his love of France shaped the collection. What he favoured were paintings that were romantic, sentimental and unchallenging (Watteau and Fragonard, Murillo). Baudelaire damned his Delaroche paintings of Cardinals[427] as '*des oeuvres charmantes dans les regions moyennes du talent et du bon goût*'.

Neither German paintings nor the Italian Primitives interested him. He wrote in 1857, 'My collection is the result of my life.' He served briefly in the 10th Hussars and travelled in the Middle East; military and oriental subjects occur frequently among the French contemporary paintings he bought, for example by Vernet and Descamps.

Many of his favourites were pupils or disciples of Baron Gros, notably Delaroche, Delacroix and Richard Parkes Bonington, whose literary and historical subjects were greatly to his taste.

Although he employed Richard Wallace as his secretary, he never told him that he was his illegitimate son. Wallace learned of his paternity, and his inheritance, only when the Marquess's will was read. He inherited during the Franco-Prussian War. He remained in Paris throughout the siege and when it ended spent a reputed 2½ million francs on a British hospital and 100 drinking fountains across Paris. For his philanthropic activities on behalf of British citizens in the city Queen Victoria made him a baronet.

His taste in painting and porcelain was similar to his father's, although his love of Sèvres did not prevent him valuing 16th-century maiolica; he collected both Derutà and Urbino. In the aftermath of war, major collections became available and he acquired the vast hoard of armour owned by the Comte de Nieuwerkerke[428] and that originally formed by Sir Samuel Meyrick.[429] When put together with the oriental armour that his father had collected towards the end of his life, they comprised a collection that contained pieces of the highest quality going back to the 10th century, and armour and swords from every European country.

Soon after he inherited he brought the collection to London, to Hertford House, and started the negotiations that led to the house and the collection being left to the nation on the condition, in Lady Wallace's will, that the collection 'shall be kept together, unmixed with other works of art'. Such a proviso, preventing any development by means of acquisition, would normally deter the best curators, but the Wallace is an exception. In 1970 Sir Kenneth Clark called its Great Gallery 'the greatest picture gallery in Europe' and, even if that is an overestimation, its diversity and riches have attracted the finest scholars. Sir Claude Philips, one of the four founders of the National Art Collections Fund, was its first keeper in 1900. It was he who spotted the Titian hanging in a bathroom at Hertford House, Waagen having 'dismissed' it as a Veronese. Philips was succeeded by D. S. MacColl, who came to the Wallace after five years as keeper of the Tate Gallery. James Mann, subsequently keeper of armour in the Royal Collection and at the Tower of London, catalogued the collection here and, after the Second World War, Trenchard Cox was assistant keeper before becoming Director at the Victoria and Albert Museum, and John Ingemells before running York City Art Gallery and the National Museum and Gallery of Wales. Today the Sèvres scholar Rosalind Savill is Director.

What attracts and holds them is the quality of each of the collections. The Wallace Collection is a rococo paradise of the decorative arts that demonstrates that the style 'invented' by Robert de Cotte and Gilles-Marie Oppenord (pupils of the architect of Versailles, Jules Hardouin-Mansart) can soar without restraint and in any material: in stucco, wood, ormolu, metal and, perhaps most freely, porcelain. Antoine-Robert Gaudreau's and Jacques Caffiéri's masterpiece here, the commode they made for Louis XV's bedroom at Versailles, is the apogee of the rococo style. Every line,

every surface, curves and curls. Its gilt-bronze mounts, including disguised drawer handles, set up sinuous rhythms that scroll over the curvaceous lines of the main body. Hanging above it is Caffiéri's huge, twelve-light chandelier in gilt bronze. Only pieces of this brilliance could outdazzle such furniture as the secretaire that Jean-Henri Riesener made for Marie-Antoinette for the Petit Trianon or the profusion of work by André-Charles Boulle: pier glasses, a wardrobe and a cabinet-on-stand that show off his marquetry, in wood and turtleshell, and mantel clocks that are set at marginally different times so that midday is marked by a ripple of chimes through the house.

The porcelain collection does not contain any dazzling complete service such as the one at Waddesdon Manor (q.v.); nonetheless, many of the pieces have proved to have royal provenance and none surpasses the inkstand (1758) designed by Jean-Claude Duplessis, which was bought by the 4th Marquess. The French royal crown at the centre is flanked by an inkwell in a terrestrial globe. On the other side is a celestial globe painted with the signs of the zodiac. It holds a silver-gilt sand shaker that, when the globe is closed, shines through the pierced stars and causes them to twinkle in candlelight. It is as beautiful as it is ingenious, but it was only recently, in 1922, that William King established its true provenance: the 'M. A.' stands not for Marie-Antoinette but for Marie-Adélaide, Louis XV's daughter, who was given this gorgeous instructive bauble by her father.

There is nowhere in Britain that can match the 18th-century French paintings collected by the 4th Marquess, not only by Boucher, Watteau and Fragonard, but Oudry, Nattier, Lancret and Greuze.[430]

The pair of huge Bouchers on the landing, *The Rising of the Sun* (1753) and *The Setting of the Sun* (1752), in which he was said to have employed, amid the swirling clouds, waves and nudity, the face of Madame de Pompadour as Tethys (though he stopped short of casting Louis XV as Apollo), demonstrate that his excellence as an illustrator of designs that were adapted for use on porcelain and tapestries emphasises his emptiness as a painter. He is not as simply joyous as Tiepolo. Beside Rubens he is trite. The rococo and Olympus mix unhappily.

Watteau is more skilled (the patches of sunlight in *The Champs Elysées*,[431] the trees as elegant as the women, the vitality of colour in the dresses) and Fragonard more subtle (the contrast in *The Swing* between the eyes of the lovers; the shoe, indeed the whole scene, in mid air, with the ambiguous role of the elderly husband in the shadow of the tree).

Although the 4th Marquess was enchanted by 18th-century France, his tastes ranged more widely. Poussin's *A Dance to the Music of Time* (c. 1640), painted for the future Pope Clement X, had been acquired at the Cardinal Fesch sale in 1845 and Hals's *The Laughing Cavalier* (1624), neither laughing nor probably a cavalier, in 1865 from the Comte de Pourtalès, who died in 1853. He also purchased landscapes by Cuyp, Ruisdael and Hobbema and the sublime Rubens, *The Rainbow Landscape*,[432] despite his own misgivings. 'I do not much like Rubens's landscapes, and, besides, I have a good one,' he wrote to Mawson on 31 April 1856 two months before Mawson bought it at Christie's for 4,550 guineas. As Hertford admitted, 'our Collection . . . owes a great deal of its splendour to the interest you [Mawson] have always taken in it.'[433]

In addition to the portraits by Reynolds and Gainsborough, given to or bought by the 4th Marquess, his father and grandfather, there are outstanding portraits by Velásquez, of his daughter, *The Lady With a Fan*, and by Rembrandt, of his son *Titus*. A lesser-known portrait by one of Rembrandt's most gifted pupils, Willem Drost, *A Young Woman in a Brocade Gown* (c. 1654), should not be overlooked.

This is not an entirely coherent or comprehensive collection of paintings. Its beauty is that it brings together a group of some masterpieces, some great paintings, in a handful of rooms, to make a collection of which many national galleries would be proud.[434]

From these rooms on the first floor you pass the Bouchers, descend the stairs and step out from 19th-century Paris into the everyday world of the London street.

WESTMINSTER ABBEY CHAPTER HOUSE, PYX CHAMBER AND ABBEY MUSEUM **

Chapter House, East Cloisters, Westminster Abbey, London SW1P 3PE
Tel. 020 7654 4832
www.westminster-abbey.org

Treasures of the abbey, including effigies of monarchs since the 14th century, held in its undercroft

The undercroft, in which is the museum, is the oldest part of Westminster Abbey, built in about 1070, quoin-vaulted in bays, without ribs, from massive central piers.

In this ancient abbey, beloved of monarchs, where they have for almost a thousand years been crowned, you might expect to find a dazzling array of plate and regalia, not least because the abbey, protected by royalty, has survived intact, its monuments to Roman Catholic kings touched neither by the Reformation nor by Cromwell's Commonwealth.

This museum has no such ecclesiastical treasures. It has other curiosities: Queen Mary II's coronation chair (the original chair of Edward II is in the abbey); replica coronation regalia; a Roman sarcophagus (3rd century AD); a cope chest; the Essex ring, given by Elizabeth I to Robert Devereux, Earl of Essex;[435] and, most gloriously, the Achievements of Henry V carried at his funeral in 1422, the helm, the limewood shield on whose padding are embroidered fleurs-de-lys in yellow silk, on whose crimson velvet armband are worked the arms of Navarre.[436] The prized treasures of the museum are the royal effigies of (most) kings and (some) queens, from Edward III (1312) to Charles II (1660). Effigies of dead monarchs were carried in the funeral procession, generally dressed in coronation robes, and exhibited for some weeks after the burial as a focus for prayers and mourning, and a reassurance of the monarch's death. Effigies, life-sized, resembling the dead monarchs, were carved in wood, with heads of plaster or gesso.[437]

The earliest effigy here is of Edward III, 5 feet 10½ inches high, carved from one piece of walnut, hollowed at the back to reduce the weight. The stern head would have had a beard, eyebrows, wig and crown.[438] It was a death mask (the earliest that survives in Europe). The King suffered a stroke before death that paralysed his face. The mouth of the effigy droops to the left and the left cheek is flattened.

The head of the 1374 effigy of Richard II's beloved wife, Anne of Bohemia, broken from its body, is of painted wood, its carved almond eyes shown open. That of Katherine de Valois, the wife of Henry V, has a groove where sat her crown.

The effigies of Henry VII (1509) and his wife, Elizabeth of York (1503), were of a new design: plaster heads and feet round a wooden scaffolding, the remainder of their bodies being formed on skeletons of hoops stuffed with hay[439] and covered with leather. Henry VII was 6 feet 1 inch, Elizabeth, 5 feet 11 inches. Their funerals were the first to be fully described[440] and their effigies can be compared with their gilt-bronze tomb effigies in the abbey by the Florentine sculptor Pietro Torrigiano.

These effigies are not generalised images. They bring us face to face with distant monarchs and render them palpable: Anne of Bohemia's soft double chin, Anne of Denmark's Roman nose, Henry VII's clear forehead and set mouth.

Called variously 'ymages', 'casts', 'pyctures' and 'personages',[441] they provide ready evidence of the development of sculpted portraiture. The 1619 effigy of James I's wife, Anne of Denmark, made by Maximilian Colt,[442] Master Sculptor to the Crown from 1608, is as delicate in colour and texture as in detail, her pale blue veins showing at her temple, around her eyes and on her breast. On her left cheek Colt records a pimple. Neither Charles I nor Cromwell had funerals at the abbey and Charles II's funeral was devoid of pomp, an imperial crown of tin gilt being placed on the coffin, but this life-sized and life-like effigy was placed above the vault in Henry VII's chapel and remained there in a wooden display case until the 1830s,[443] confirming the accuracy of Marvell's description of Charles II as 'of tall stature and sable hue'.[444] With Charles II the funeral effigies ceased.

To come out of the low-lit undercroft into the octagonal Chapter House next door is to step from night into day; sunlight pours through its six great forty-foot-high windows. It was part of Henry III's magnificent rebuilding of the abbey in 1257. This is where the monks met each day to hear a chapter read from the Rule of St Benedict (hence its designation as Chapter House) and, from 1352 to 1395, where the House of Commons met.

It is a room of the greatest beauty and a gallery in miniature of 13th-century art. Inside its entrance is a sublime life-sized sculptural group of the *Annunciation*, overseen by two pairs of winged angels. Its floor is of encaustic tiles depicting the royal coat of arms and a rose window pattern, separated by narrow tiles on which pike swim; on its walls, within arches, are 14th-century paintings representing *The Last Judgement*, *The Apocalypse* and a series of *Beasts* from the visions of the end of the world in the Book of Revelation.[445]

Westminster Abbey itself is the greatest museum of sculpture and decorative art from the 13th to 19th centuries. This Chapter House embodies in a single room its virtues and delights.

WILLIAM MORRIS GALLERY *

Lloyd Park, Forest Road, London E17 4PP
Tel. 020 8527 3782
www.lbwf.gov.uk/wmg

What William Morris believed to be useful and knew to be beautiful; his life and his work

Articulated lorries lumber past, grinding their way north out of London, heading for the M11, Stansted airport and Cambridge. Water

William Morris's satchel and Socialist pamphlets (William Morris Gallery)

House, where William Morris lived from the age of fourteen, a plain, double-bow-fronted, 18th-century building, is set back from this traffic behind shrubs, an apron of grass and a circular tarmacked drive. At its rear is a small municipal park with civic flower beds of straight tulips edged with alyssum, a bowling green and an aviary. There is nothing of Morris here, save a small section of the medieval moat that gave the house its name.

Change here is nothing new. Morris described the surrounding area, Walthamstow, as 'a suburban village on the edge of Epping Forest and once a pleasant enough place, but now terribly cockneyfied and choked up by the jerry builder'. The Morris family sold the house in 1856 to Edward Lloyd, the publisher of the *Daily Chronicle*. He left it to the local council. The only surviving house of the three that Morris lived in as a child, it was opened as the William Morris Museum

by the Prime Minister, Clement Attlee, in 1950.

When Morris asked himself the rhetorical question 'what was the thing most to be longed for?' his immediate answer was 'A beautiful house'.[446] He was thinking not of this house but its predecessor, Woodford Hall, where he lived six years from the age of eight, a Palladian mansion in fifty acres of parkland, bought at the height of the family's financial fortunes when his father was a director of a city discount house and had the income from a successful speculation in Devon Great Consols. It was on the edge of Epping Forest and from here Morris discovered not only the ancient forest lands, little changed over centuries, but Queen Elizabeth I's hunting lodge, from where Henry VIII would watch the hunt on Chingford Plain. Morris remembered it, and its tapestries, as being 'hung with faded greenery'.[447] It made an 'impression of romance' that provided a source of ideal images he drew on throughout his life.

The interior of Water House is little changed from the time when he knew it and the carved oak staircase remains, but the museum is decorated throughout with William Morris wallpapers and materials. The Entrance Hall and stairs are carpeted with 'Lily' (c. 1875), a pattern he produced for Wilton.

Images recollected from his early life recur throughout the museum: the 'Sleeping Beauty' tiles, designed by Edward Burne-Jones and painted by Lucy Faulkner (1863–4); the 'Peacock and Dragon' fabric (1878), described in Morris & Co.'s catalogue as 'the perfect hanging for a medieval castle or mansion'; the 'Trellis' wallpaper (1862), Morris's first attempt at designing a wallpaper pattern; the oak chair and settle (c. 1856), made for his house in Red Lion Square; and the hanging of *Verdure, Armorials, Birds and Animals*, embroidered in silk by May Morris. Here too is the *Woodpecker* tapestry.[448] Burne-Jones described tapestry as being 'half-way between painting and ornament' and in its 'richness of detail . . . [and] overtones of chivalry' it recalls the Hunting Lodge.[449]

As moving as these are the large blocks from which the wallpapers were printed. These were designed by Morris and cut in pearwood by Alfred and James Barrett with a delicacy that delights.

Morris's second answer to his what-was-most-longed-for question was 'A Beautiful Book' and here are first editions of Kelmscott Press books, including *The Works of Geoffrey Chaucer* (1896), its title page designed by Morris during his final illness. This is one of the finest volumes of 19th-century English book production and the crowning achievement of the Kelmscott Press. Burne-Jones described it as 'a little like a pocket cathedral.

My share in it is that of the carver of images at Amiens, and Morris's that of Architect and Magister Lapidica.'

The museum also represents the work of those artists-craftsmen who worked with or were inspired by Morris. Here are tiles by Philip Webb, ceramics by De Morgan, a silver bowl by C. R. Ashbee, copper dishes by W. A. S. Benson, wallpapers by C. F. A. Voysey, furniture by William Burges, Arthur Heygate, Mackmurdo, Sidney Barnsley and Ernest Gimson.[450] Here too are paintings by Ford Madox Brown, Dante Gabriel Rossetti, Edward Burne-Jones, Arthur Hughes and Walter Crane and a portrait of Morris by his erstwhile assistant, the collector Charles Fairfax Murray.[451] A more distant influence is here in the drawings, paintings and furniture of Frank Brangwyn, who revered Morris, collected his work and donated it to the museum. The debt may have been clear to Brangwyn but it is hard to detect, particularly in his *Study of Nude Bathers* (c. 1907), which appears to owe more to Lovis Corinth.

For Morris his designs were not simply beautiful objects: they manifested his spiritual life, his philosophy, his aesthetic. The Red House,[452] built for him by Philip Webb, was a 'Morris environment'. Here at Water House the rooms are galleries, the objects displayed in isolation or in cabinets of like objects. The museum well demonstrates the beauty, craftsmanship and influence of Morris's work but to feel the spirit of Morris and the mixture of medievalism and socialist outrage that inspired him, read Fiona MacCarthy's biography, *William Morris: a Life for Our Times.*

Appendix
Additional Museums

NT = National Trust

INTRODUCTION

Bakelite Museum
East Dulwich, London SE22 0NQ

Bankside Gallery
48 Hopton Street, London SE1 9JH
Tel. 020 7928 7521

Dog Collar Museum
Leeds Castle, Maidstone, Kent ME17 1PL
Tel. 01622 765400
www.leeds-castle.com

J. Paul Getty Museum
1200 Getty Center Drive, Suite 1000,
Los Angeles, CA 90049-1687, USA

Musée du Louvre
75058 Paris Cedex 01, France
Tel. (+33) 01 40 20 50 50,
fax (+33) 01 40 20 54 42
e-mail: info@louvre.fr

Museum of Witchcraft
The Harbour, Boscastle, Cornwall
PL35 0AE
Tel. 01840 250111
www.museumofwitchcraft.com

Skansen
PO Box 27807, S-115 93 Stockholm, Sweden
Tel. +46 8 442 80 00, fax +46 8 442 82 80,
information +46 8 578 900 05
www.skansen.se
e-mail: info@skansen.se

Tower of London
London EC3N 4AB
Tel. 0870 756 6060
www.hrp.org.uk

Vasa Museum
PO Box 27131, S-102 52 Stockholm, Sweden
Tel. +46 8 519 548 00, fax +46 8 519 548 88
e-mail: vasamuseet@smm.se
Booking office: bokningen.vasa@smm.se

THE SOUTH-WEST

Antony House (NT)
Torpoint, Cornwall PL11 2QA
Tel. 01752 812191

Bath Postal Museum
8 Broad Street, Bath, Somerset BA1 5LJ
Tel. 01225 460333
www.bathpostalmuseum.org

Building of Bath Museum
The Countess of Huntingdon's Chapel,
The Vineyards, Bath, Somerset BA1 5NA
Tel. 01225 333895
www.bath-preservation-
trust.org.uk/museums/bath/

Cotehele House (NT)
St Dominick, Saltash, Cornwall PL12 6TA
Tel. 01579 351346

Kingston Lacy House (NT)
Wimborne, Dorset BH21 4EA
Tel. 01202 883402

Saltram (NT)
Plympton, Plymouth, Devon PL7 1UH
Tel. 01752 333500

William Herschel Museum
19 New King Street, Bath, Somerset BA1 2BL
Tel. 01225 311342
www.bath-preservation-trust.org.uk

THE SOUTH-EAST

Canterbury Museum
Hastings Museum and Art Gallery, Johns
Place, Bohemia Road, Hastings, East Sussex
TN34 1ET
Tel. 01424 781155

Millennium Seed Bank
Wakehurst Place, Ardingly, West Sussex
RH17 6TN
Tel. 01444 894066

Museum of Canterbury
Stour Street, Canterbury, Kent
Tel. 01227 452747
www.canterbury-museum.co.uk

Osborne House
Royal Apartments, East Cowes, Isle of Wight
PO32 6JY
Tel. 01983 200022
www.english-heritage.org.uk

Polesden Lacey (NT)
Nr. Great Bookham, Dorking, Surrey RH5 6BD
Tel. 01372 452048

Royal Holloway Picture Gallery
University of London, Egham Hill, Egham,
Surrey TW20 0EX
Tel. 01784 434455

Seaford Museum and Heritage Society
c/o Tourist Information Centre, 25 Clinton
Place, Seaford, East Sussex BN25 1NP
Tel. 01323 898222
www.seafordmuseum.org

Turner Contemporary Visitor Centre
Droit House, Margate Harbour, Margate,
Kent CT9 1HB
Tel. 01843 294208
e-mail: info@turnercontemporary.org

Uppark (NT)
South Harting, Petersfield, Surrey GU31 5QR
Tel. 01730 825415

The Vyne (NT)
Sherborne St John, Basingstoke, Hampshire
RG24 9HL
Tel. 01256 881337

Winchester Museum
The Square, Winchester, Hampshire SO23 7DW
Tel. 01962 848269
www.winchester.gov.uk

EAST ANGLIA

Anglesey Abbey (NT)
Lode, Cambridge, Cambridgeshire CB5 9EJ
Tel. 01223 811200
www.nationaltrust.org.uk/angleseyabbey

Blickling Hall (NT)
Blickling, nr. Aylsham, Norwich, Norfolk
NR11 6NF
Tel. 01263 738030
www.nationaltrust.co.uk

Cambridge University Museum of Zoology
Downing Street, Cambridge, Cambridgeshire
CB2 3EJ
Tel. 01223 336650
www.zoo.cam.ac.uk/museum

Chelmsford and Essex Museum
Oaklands Park, Moulsham Street,
Chelmsford, Essex CM2 9AQ
Tel. 01245 615100
www.chelmsfordbc.gov.uk/leisure/museums

Ickworth House (NT)
The Rotunda, Horringer, Bury St Edmunds,
Suffolk IP29 5QE
Tel. 01284 735270

Time and Tide Museum of
Great Yarmouth Life
Great Yarmouth, Norfolk

Wisbech and Fenland Museum
Museum Square, Wisbech, Cambridgeshire
PE13 1ES
Tel. 01945 583817

THE EAST MIDLANDS

Belton House (NT)
Belton, nr. Grantham, Lincolnshire
NG32 2LS
Tel. 01476 566116

Boston Guildhall Museum
South Street, Boston, Lincolnshire PE21 6HT
Tel. 01205 365954

Burghley House
Stamford, Lincolnshire PE9 3JY
Tel. 01780 752451
www.burghley.co.uk

Grantham Museum
St Peters Hill, Grantham, Lincolnshire
NG31 6PY
Tel. 01476 568783

Hardwick Hall (NT)
Doe Lea, Chesterfield, Derbyshire S44 6QJ
Tel. 01246 850430
www.english-heritage.org.uk

Newark Museum
Appletongate, Newark, Nottinghamshire
NG24 1JY
Tel. 01636 655740
www.newark-sherwooddc.gov.uk

Newstead Abbey
Ravenshead, Nottingham, Nottinghamshire
NG15 8GE
Tel. 01623 455900

North Lincolnshire Museum
Oswald Road, Scunthorpe, Lincolnshire
DN15 7BD
Tel. 01724 853433
www.northlincs.gov.uk

Watford Museum
194 High Street, Watford, Hertfordshire
WD1 2HG
Tel. 01923 232297

THE WEST MIDLANDS

Black Country Living Museum
Tipton Road, Dudley, West Midlands
DY1 4SQ
Tel. 0121 557 9643
www.bclm.co.uk

Chastleton House (NT)
Chastleton, Moreton-in-Marsh,
Gloucestershire GL56 0SU
Tel. 01608 674355

Cheddleton Flint Mill and Museum
Leek Road, Cheddleton, nr. Leek,
Staffordshire ST13 7HL
Tel. 01782 502907

Compton Verney Art Museum
Compton Verney, Warwick, West Midlands
CV35 9HZ
Tel. 01926 645500
www.comptonverney.org.uk

Shugborough Hall (NT)
Shugborough Estate, Milford, Stafford,
Staffordshire ST17 0XB
Tel. 01889 881388
www.staffordshire.gov.uk/sams

Wedgwood Visitor Centre
Barlaston, Stoke-on-Trent, Staffordshire
ST12 9ES
Tel. 01782 204218
www.wedgwood.co.uk

THE NORTH-WEST

Grosvenor Museum
27 Grosvenor Street, Chester, Cheshire
CH1 2DD
Tel. 01244 402008
www.chestercc.gov.uk

Nantwich Museum
Pillory Street, Nantwich, Cheshire, CW5 5BQ
Tel. 01270 627104
www.nantwichmuseum.org.uk

Peter Scott Gallery Lancaster University
Lancaster, Lancashire LA1 4YW
Tel. 01524 593057
www.lancs.ac.uk/users/peterscott/Scott.htm

Rochdale Art Gallery
Arts and Heritage Centre, Esplanade,
Rochdale, Greater Manchester OL16 1AQ
Tel. 01706 342154
e-mail: artgallery@rochdale.gov.uk

Silk Museum
Park Lane, Macclesfield, Cheshire SK11 6TJ
Tel. 01625 612045
www.silk-macclesfield.org

Tabley House
Knutsford, Cheshire WA16 0JR
Tel. 01565 750151
www.tableyhouse.co.uk

Tatton Park (NT)
Knutsford, Cheshire WA16 6QN
Tel. 01625 534400
www.tattonpark.org.uk

Williamson Art Gallery and Museum
Slatey Road, Birkenhead, Merseyside CH43 4UE
Tel. 0151 652 4177
www.wirral.gov.uk/ed/williamson.htm

World of Glass
Chalon Way East, St Helens, Merseyside
WA10 1BX
Tel. 08700 114466
www.worldofglass.com

THE NORTH-EAST

Berwick-upon-Tweed Borough Museum and
Art Gallery
The Clock Block, Berwick Barracks,
Ravensdowne, Berwick-upon-Tweed,
Northumberland TD15 1DQ
Tel. 01289 330044 ext. 430

Binchester Roman Fort
Bishop Auckland, Durham DL14 8DJ
Tel. 01388 663089
www.durham.gov.uk/binchester

Chesterholm Museum
Bardon Mill, Hexham, Northumberland
NE47 7JN
Tel. 01434 344277
www.vindolanda.com

Chesters Museum
Chesters Roman Fort, Chollerford,
Humshaugh, Hexham, Northumberland
NE46 4EP
Tel. 01434 681379

Corbridge Roman Fort Museum
Corbridge, Northumberland NE45 5NT
Tel. 01434 632349
www.english-heritage.org.uk

Hartlepool Art Gallery
Church Square, Hartlepool TS24 7EQ
Tel. 01429 869706
www.thisishartlepool.com/gallery/index

YORKSHIRE AND HUMBERSIDE

Fisheries Museum
National Fishing Heritage Centre, Alexandra
Dock, Great Grimsby, Humberside DN31 1UZ
Tel. 01472 323345

Kelham Island Museum
Alma Street, off Corporation Street, Sheffield,
South Yorkshire S3 8RY
Tel. 0114 272 2106
www.simt.co.uk

Kirkleatham Old Hall Museum
Kirkleatham, Redcar TS10 5NW
Tel. 01642 479500

Leeds Industrial Museum
Armley Mills, Canal Road, Armley, Leeds,
West Yorkshire LS12 2QF
Tel. 0113 263 7861
www.leeds.gov.uk/armleymills

Magna Science Adventure Centre
Sheffield Road, Templeborough, Rotherham,
South Yorkshire S60 1DX
Tel. 01709 720002
www.visitmagna.co.uk

Nostell Priory (NT)
Doncaster Road, Nostell, nr. Wakefield,
West Yorkshire WF4 1QE
Tel. 01924 863892

Rotunda Museum
Vernon Road, Scarborough, North Yorkshire
YO11 2NN
Tel. 01723 232323

SCOTLAND

Andrew Carnegie Birthplace Museum
Moodie Street, Dunfermline, Fife KY12 7PL
Tel. 01383 724302
www.carnegiemuseum.co.uk

Black Watch Regimental Museum
Balhousie Castle, Hay Street, Perth PH1 5HR
Tel. 0131 310 8530
www.theblackwatch.co.uk

British Golf Museum
Bruce Embankment, St Andrews, Fife
KY16 9AB
Tel. 01334 460046
www.britishgolfmuseum.co.uk

Clan Grant Museum
Duthil, by Carrbridge, Inverness-shire
PH23 3ND
Tel. 01467 651333

Clan Gunn Heritage Centre and Museum
Old Parish Church, Latheron, Highland
KW5 6DG
Tel. 01593 721325

David Livingstone Centre
165 Station Road, Blantyre, South Lanarkshire
G72 9BT
Tel. 01698 823140

Hanseatic Booth
Symbister Harbour, Whalsay, Shetland

Hugh Miller's Cottage
Church Street, Cromarty IV11 8XA
Tel. 01381 600245

Mull Museum
Clumba Buildings, Main Street, Tobermory,
Isle of Mull PA75 6NY
Tel. 01688 302208

Museum of Islay Life
Port Charlotte, Isle of Islay, Argyll and Bute
PA48 7UA
Tel. 01496 850358

Orkney Museum
c/o Broad Street, Kirkwall, Orkney KW15 1DH
Tel. 01856 3191
www.orkney.org/museums/tankhouse.htm

Regimental Museum of the Argyll and
Sutherland Highlanders
The Castle, Stirling FK8 1EH
Tel. 01786 475165
www.argylls.co.uk

Robert Burns House
Burns Street, Dumfries, Dumfries and
Galloway DG1 2PS
Tel. 01387 255297
www.dumgal.gov.uk/museums

Robert Smail's Printing Works
7–9 High Street, Innerleithen, Borders
EH44 6HA
Tel. 01896 810206

Scottish Rugby Union Library and Museum
Murrayfield, Edinburgh, Midlothian
EH12 5PJ
Tel. 0131 346 5073

Shetland Museum
Lower Hillhead, Lerwick, Shetland ZE1 0EL
Tel. 01595 695057
www.shetland-museum.org.uk

Skerryvore Museum
Upper Square, Hynish, Isle of Tiree, Argyll
and Bute PA77 6UQ

Taigh Chearsabhagh
Lochmaddy, Isle of North Uist, Western Isles
HS6 5AA
Tel. 01876 500293
www.taigh-chearsabhagh.org

WALES

Castell Coch
Castle Hill, Tongwynlais, Cardiff CF15 7JS
Tel. 02920 810101

Castell Collen
between Llandrindod and Rhayader, Powys
Tel. 01597 824513

Haverfordwest Town Museum
Castle House, Haverfordwest, Pembrokeshire
SA61 2EF
Tel. 01437 763087
www.haverfordwest-town-museum.org.uk

Radnorshire Museum
Temple Street, Llandrindod Wells, Powys
LD1 5DL
Tel. 01597 824513
www.powysmuseums.powys.gov.uk/English/
radnorone.htm

NORTHERN IRELAND

Ballymena Museum
3 Wellington Court, Ballymena, Antrim
BT43 6EG
Tel. 028 25 642166
www.ballymena.gov.uk

National Museum of Ireland
Collins Barracks, Benburg Street, Dublin 7
Tel. (+353) 1 6777444
www.museum.ie

Royal Ulster Constabulary Museum
Constabulary Headquarters, Brooklyn,
Knock Road, Belfast BT5 6LE
Tel. 01232 650222 ext. 22499
www.ruc.police.uk

Ulster American Folk Park
Mellon Road, Castletown, Omagh, Tyrone
BT78 5QY
Tel. 02882 243292
www.folkpark.com

LONDON

Bank of England Museum
Bartholomew Lane, London EC2R 8AH
Tel. 020 7601 5491
www.bankofengland.co.uk/museum

Bramah Museum of Tea and Coffee
40 Southwark Street, London SE1 1UN
Tel. 020 7403 5650
www.bramahmuseum.co.uk

Carlyle's House
24 Cheyne Row, Chelsea, London SW3 5HL
Tel. 020 7352 7087
www.nationaltrust.org.uk/places/carlyleshouse

Charles Dickens Museum
48 Doughty Street, London WC1N 2LX
Tel. 020 7405 2127
www.dickensmuseum.com

Chelsea Physic Garden
66 Royal Hospital Road, London SW3 4HS
Tel. 020 7352 5646
www.chelseaphysicgarden.co.uk

Chiswick House
Burlington Lane, London W4 2RP
Tel. 020 8995 0508
www.english-heritage.org.uk

Dr Johnson's House
17 Gough Square, London EC4A 3DE
Tel. 020 7353 3745
www.drjh.dircon.co.uk

Florence Nightingale Museum
St Thomas' Hospital, 2 Lambeth Palace Road,
London SE1 7EW
Tel. 020 7620 0374
www.florence-nightingale.co.uk

Hogarth's House
Hogarth Lane, Great West Road, Hounslow,
London W4 2QN
Tel. 020 8994 6757
www.cip.org.uk

Keats House
Keats Grove, Hampstead, London NW3 2RR
Tel. 020 7435 2062
www.cityoflondon.gov.uk/keats

Museum of Garden History
Lambeth Palace Road, London SE1 7LB
Tel. 020 7401 8865
www.museumgardenhistory.org

Osterley Park House (NT)
Osterley, Middlesex TW7 4RB
Tel. 020 8568 7714

Sherlock Holmes Museum
221B Baker Street, London NW1 6XE
Tel. 020 8374 0053
www.sherlock-holmes.co.uk

Twickenham Museum
25 The Embankment, Twickenham, Middlesex
TW1 3DU
Tel. 020 8408 0070
www.twickenham-museum.org.uk

Wimbledon Lawn Tennis Museum
The All England Lawn Tennis and Croquet
Club, Church Road, Wimbledon, London
SW19 5AE
Tel. 020 8946 6131
www.year-round.wimbledon.org/en_
GB/about/museum/museum.html

Tourists *by Duane Hanson (Scottish National Gallery of Modern Art)*

Bibliography

BOOKS

Ablett, Noah, *What We Want and Why*, pamphlet, 1922

Abse, Joan, *The Art Galleries of Britain and Ireland*, Sidgwick and Jackson, 1975

Adam, *Ruins of Spalato*, 1764

Adams, Dart, *Barbara Hepworth: a Pictorial Autobiography*, Tate Gallery, 1970

Adams, Len and Yvonne, *Meissen Portrait Figures*, Magna, 1987

Agnew, Geoffrey, *Agnew's 1817–1967*, Agnew's, 1967

Agnew, Julian (introduction), *A Dealer's Record: Agnew's 1967–81*, Barrie and Jenkins, 1981

Alexander, Boyd (transl. and ed.), *Life at Fonthill, 1807–22, With Interludes in Paris and London from the Correspondence of William Beckford*, R. Hart-Davies, 1957

Allardyce, Keith, and Hood, Evelyn M., *At Scotland's Edge*, HarperCollins, 1996 (first published 1986)

Appleton, Josie, *Museums for 'The People'? Conversations in Print*, Academy of Ideas, 2001

Archer, Mildred, Rowell, Christopher, and Skelton, Robert, *Treasures from India*, The Herbert Press in association with the National Trust, 1987

Arnold, Matthew, *Culture and Anarchy*, 1882

Atterbury, Paul, and Wainwright, Clive, *Pugin: A Gothic Passion*, Yale University Press in association with the Victoria and Albert Museum, 1994

Aubrey, John, *Brief Lives* (ed. Dick, O. L.), Secker and Warburg, 1949

Auden, W. H., *Night Mail*, Faber and Faber, 1936

Axten, Janet, and Orchard, Colin, *Gasworks to Gallery: the Story of St Ives*, privately published, 1995

Bacharach, A. L. (ed.), *Lives of the Great Composers*, vol. 1, Penguin, 1935

Bagehot, Walter, *The English Constitution*, 1867

Baily, J. T. Herbert, *George Morland*, Otto, 1906

Bain, Iain, *The Workshop of Thomas Bewick*, Thomas Bewick Birthplace Trust, 1989 (first published 1979)

Baker, Malcolm, and Richardson, Brenda (eds.), *A Grand Design: the Art of the Victoria and Albert Museum*, Harry N. Abrams, Inc. with the Baltimore Museum of Art, 1997

Ball, Philip, *Bright Earth: the Invention of Colour*, Penguin, 2002

Barker, David, *William Greatbach: a Staffordshire Potter*, Jonathan Home, 1991

Barrington Haynes, Edward, *Glass through the Ages*, Penguin, 1970 (first published 1948)

Barrington, E. I. R., *G. F. Watts: Reminiscences*, 1905

Barrington, Russell (ed.), *Life, Letters and Work of Frederic Leighton*, 2 vols., AMS Press, George Allen, 1906

Barry, A., *The Life and Works of Sir Charles Barry*, 1867

—, *The Architect of the New Palace of Westminster: a Reply to a Pamphlet by E. W. Pugin Esq.*, 1868

Bateman, Thomas, *Vestiges of the Antiquities of Derbyshire*, John Russell Smith, 1848

Bathurst, Bella, *The Lighthouse Stevensons*, HarperCollins, 1999

Beanland, W., *The History of the Royal Institution of South Wales*, Swansea, 1935

Beaumont, Joseph, *Mathematical Sleasing – Tables: or, the Great and Only Mystery of*

Beaumont, Joseph – *cont.*
    Weaving Linnen-Cloth Explained, Dublin,
    1712
Beckett, R. B. (ed.), *John Constable's
    Correspondence*, IV Suffolk, HMSO, 1962
Bede, *A History of the English Church and
    People* (transl. L. Sherley-Price), Penguin,
    1968
Bennett, J. A., Johnston, S. A., and Simcock,
    A.V., *Solomon's House in Oxford: New Finds
    from the First Museum*, Museum of the
    History of Science, 2000
Berenson, Bernard, *The Italian Painters of the
    Renaissance*, Phaidon, 1952
Bernrose, W., *The Life and Works of Joseph
    Wright ARA Commonly Called "Wright Of
    Derby"*, 1885
Bewick, Thomas, *Memoir*, Longman, Green &
    Co., 1822–8
Bidwell, P. T., and Speak, S. C., *Excavations at
    South Shields Roman Fort*, Society of
    Antiquaries of Newcastle upon Tyne with
    Tyne and Wear Museums, 1994
Billcliffe, Roger, *The Glasgow Boys: the
    Glasgow School of Painting 1875–1895*, John
    Murray, 1985
Bills, Mark (ed.), *Art in the Age of Queen
    Victoria: a Wealth of Depictions*, Russell-
    Cotes Art Gallery and Museum, 2001
Binyon, Laurence, *English Watercolours*,
    A. & C. Black, 1944 (first published 1933)
Bishop, Phillippa, Sloman, Susan, and Wright,
    Amina, *Pickpocketing the Rich*, Holburne
    Museum of Art, Bath, 2002
Blackie, Sebastian, *Ceramics in Society*, Oxford
    University Press, 1933, reprinted 1970
Blake Roberts, Gaye (ed.), *True Blue: Transfer
    Printed Earthenware*, Friends of Blue, 1998
Blayney Brown, David, *Turner in the Tate
    Collection*, Tate Publishers, 2002
Blom, Philipp, *To Have and to Hold: an
    Intimate History of Collections and
    Collecting*, Allen Lane, 2002
Blunt, Sir Anthony, *Artistic Theory in Italy
    1450–1600*, Oxford University Press, 1996
    (first published 1940)
Blunt, Wilfred, *England's Michelangelo: a
    Biography of George Frederick Watts*,
    Columbus Books, 1975

Blurton, T. Richard, *The Enduring Image:
    Treasures of the British Museum*, British
    Council, 1997
Boase, T. S. R., *English Art 1100–1216*, Oxford at
    the Clarendon Press, 1953
—, *English Art 1800–1870*, Oxford at the
    Clarendon Press, 1959
Bodkin, Thomas, *The Approach to Painting*,
    Collins, 1945
Boswell, David, and Miller, Corinne,
    Cotmania and Mr Kitson, Leeds City Art
    Gallery, 1992
Bowness, Alan, *British Contemporary Art
    1910–1990: Eighty Years of Collecting by the
    Contemporary Art Society*, Herbet Press,
    1993
Brears, Peter, and Davies, Stuart, *Treasures for
    the People: the Story of Museums and
    Galleries in Yorkshire and Humberside*,
    Yorkshire and Humberside Museums
    Council, 1989
Brears, P., *Of Curiosities and Rare Things: the
    Story of Leeds City Museum*, Friends of the
    City Museums, 1989
Brocklesby, Dr John, *Private Virtue and
    Publick Spirit Display'd in a Succinct Essay
    on the Character of Captain Thomas Coram*,
    1751
Brookner, Anita, *Soundings*, Harvill Press, 1997
Brown, Beverley Louise (ed.), *The Genius of
    Rome, 1592–1623*, Royal Academy of Arts,
    2001
Browne, Sir Thomas, *The Works of Sir Thomas
    Browne* (ed. Geoffrey Keynes), 4 vols.,
    Faber, 1964
Bruce-Mitford, R. L. S., *The Sutton Hoo Ship
    Burial*, 3 vols., British Museum Press, 1975,
    1978 and 1983
Buchan, James, *Capital of the Mind*, John
    Murray, 2003
Buchan, John, *The Island of Sheep*, Nelson,
    1936
Buchanan, R. Angus, *Industrial Archaeology in
    Britain*, Penguin, 1972
Buckman, David, *James Bolivar Manson: an
    English Impressionist, 1879–1945*, Maltzahn
    Gallery, 1973
Bull, Revd Josiah, *Life of John Newton*,
    Religious Tract Society, 1868

Butlin, Martin, and Joll, Evelyn, *The Paintings of J. M. W. Turner*, 2 vols., Tate Gallery and Yale University Press, 1984

Butter, Rachel, *Kilmartin: an Introduction and Guide*, Kilmartin House Trust, 1999

Buzas, Stefan, *Sir John Soane's Museum*, Ernst Wasmuth Verlag GmbH and Co., 1994

Cadbury, Deborah, *The Dinosaur Hunters*, Fourth Estate, 2000 (first published 1987)

Calder, Jenni (ed.), *The Wealth of a Nation*, National Museums of Scotland and David Drew Publishing Ltd, 1989

Cambridge, Matt, *Richard Parkes Bonington, Young and Romantic*, Nottingham Castle, 2002

Camden, John, *Britannicus*, 1586

Campbell, Colen, *Vitruvius Britannicus*, 1756

Carle, Donald de, *Clocks and their Value*, National Art Gallery Press, 1979 (first published 1968)

Carline, Richard, *Stanley Spencer at War*, Faber and Faber, 1987

Carver, Martin, *Sutton Hoo: Burial Ground of Kings?*, British Museum Press, 1998

Castleugh, Jon, *William de Morgan Tiles*, Richard Dennis, 1991 (first published 1983)

Caygill, Marjorie, *The Story of the British Museum*, British Museum, 1981

—, *The British Museum A–Z Companion*, British Museum, 1999

—, *The British Museum Reading Room*, British Museum, 2000

Cecil, Lord David, *The Stricken Deer*, Crown Constables, 1933

Chadwick, Nora, *The Celts*, Penguin, 1970

Chalmers, Chick, *Life in the Orkney Islands*, Harris, 1979

Chapel, Jeannie, and Gere, Charlotte, *The Fine and Decorative Art Collections of Britain and Ireland*, Weidenfeld and Nicolson, 1985

Childe, Gordon, *What Happened in History*, Penguin, reprinted and revised 1954

Chippendale, Thomas, *The Gentleman and Cabinet-Maker's Director*, 1754

Churchill, Winston S., *A History of the English-Speaking Peoples*, vol. iii, Cassell, 1957

Clark, Kenneth, *Civilisation*, Penguin, 1987 (first published 1969)

—, *Landscape into Air*, Penguin, 1949 (republished 1956)

—, *Leonardo da Vinci*, Penguin, 1967 (first published 1939)

—, *Looking at Pictures*, John Murray, 1972 (first published 1960)

Clitheroe, Gordon, *Pickering*, Tempus Publishing, 1999

—, *Ryedale*, Tempus Publishing, 2000

—, *Pickering, the Second Selection*, Tempus Publishing, 2002

Close-Brooks, Joanna, *Notes on Museums' Acquisitions*, Museum of Scotland, 1972–4

Collins Baker, C. H., *Lely and the Stuart Portrait Painters*, 1912

Collis, Maurice, *Stanley Spencer*, Harvill Press, 1962

Colville, J., *Fringes of Power: Downing Street Diaries, 1939–55*, Orion, 1985

Cooke, E. T., and Wedderburn, A. (eds.), *The Works of John Ruskin*, The Library Edition, 1903–12

Coombes, B. L., *These Poor Hands: a Miner's Story*, Gollancz, 1974

Coombes, Trevor, *Watercolours: the Charles Lees Collection*, Oldham Art Gallery, 1992

Cooper, Diana, *The Rainbow Comes and Goes*, Houghton Mifflin, 1958

Cooper, Douglas, *The Courtauld Collection: a Catalogue and Introduction*, University of London, Athlone Press, 1954

Corlett, Dr Euan, *The Iron Ship*, Chrysalis Books, 1990

Cormack, Malcolm, *The Paintings of Thomas Gainsborough*, Cambridge University Press, 1991

Cossons, N., and Trinder, B., *The Iron Bridge: Symbol of the Industrial Revolution*, Phillimore, 2002

Cowling, Elizabeth, and Mundy, Jennifer, *On Classic Ground: Picasso, Léger, de Chirico and the New Classicism 1910–1930*, Tate Gallery, 1990

Cowling, Elizabeth, with Richard Calvocoressi, Patrick Elliot and Ann Simpson, *Surrealism and After*, Scottish National Museum of Modern Art, 1997

Cox, Ian (ed.), *The Scallop*, Shell T & T Co. Ltd, 1957

Craig, Gordon, *Towards a New Theatre*, 1913

Cumberland, R., *Anecdotes of Eminent Painters in Spain*, 2 vols., C. Dilly, 1987

Cuno, James (ed.), *Whose Muse?: Art Museums and the Public Trust*, Princeton University Press and Harvard University Art Museums, 2004

Cursiter, Stanley, *Scottish Art*, George G. Harrap, 1949

Cust, Lionel (ed.), *Notes on Pictures in the Royal Collection*, Chatto and Windus, 1911

Cuzin, Jean-Pierre, Rosenberg, Pierre, and Thullier, Jacques, *Georges de la Tour*, Réunion des Musées Nationals, 1997

Dampierre, É. de, *Harpes Zandé*, Klincksieck, 1991

Daniel, Glyn, *A Hundred Years of Archaeology*, Duckworth, 1950

Darwin, Charles, *The Origin of Species*, 1859

Davey, N., and Ling, R., *Wall Painting in Roman Britain*, Society of Promotion of Roman Studies, Britannia, 1982

Davidson, E. F., *Edward Hincks*, Oxford University Press, 1933

Davies, D. Gareth, and Davies, Dr Kath, *A Burning Issue: a Survey of Welsh Coalmining Collections*, Council of Museums in Wales, 1996

Davies, David (ed.), *El Greco*, National Gallery, 2003

Davy, John, *Life of Humphrey Davy*, Henry Coburn and Richard Bently, 1831

De Beer, E. S. (ed.), *The Diary of John Evelyn*, 6 vols., Oxford University Press, 1955

Defoe, Daniel, *A Tour through England and Wales*, J. M. Dent, 1948

—, *An Account of the Conduct and Proceedings of the Late John Gow, Alias Smith, Captain of the Late Pirates, Executed for Murther and Piracy, Committed on Board the George Galley, Afterwards Called the Revenge; with a Relation of all the Horrid Murthers They Committed in Cold Blood: as also of Their Being Taken at the Islands of Orkney, and Sent up Prisoners to London*, John Applebee, c. 1725

Dektanel, Frederick B., *Edvard Munch*, Max Parrish & Co., 1950

Desmond, Ray, *Kew: the History of the Royal Botanic Gardens*, Harvill, 1995

Diderot, Denis, and D'Alembert, Jean le Rond, *Encyclopédie ou Dictionnaire Universel des Arts et des Sciences*, 28 vols., 1751

Doolittle, Hilda, *Tribute to Freud*, Pantheon Books, 1952

Dorment, Richard, and Macdonald, Margaret F., *Whistler*, Tate Gallery Publications, 1994

Downes, Professor Kerry, *Vanbrugh*, Zwemmer, 1977

Drage, C., with additional material by T. Foulds, *Nottingham Castle: a Place Full Royal*, Thoroton Society, 1989

Duboisson, A., *Richard Parkes Bonington: His Life and Work* (ed. and transl. C. E. Hughes), Bodley Head, 1924

Dunwich by the Stormy Sea, Trustees of Dunwich Museum, 1988

Ebin, V., and Swallow, D. A., *The Proper Study of Mankind: Great Anthropological Collections in Cambridge*, University Museum of Archaeology and Anthropology, Cambridge, 1984

Ede, H. S., *A Way of Life*, Cambridge University Press, 1984

Edwardians and After: the Royal Academy 1900–1950, The, Royal Academy of Arts in association with Weidenfeld and Nicolson, 1990

Edwards, George, *A Natural History of Unknown Birds*, 7 vols., 1802

—, *Gleanings of Natural History*, 1758–64

Edwards, Ralph, and Jourdain, Margaret, *Georgian Cabinet-Makers*, Country Life, 1946 (first published 1944)

Eglon Shaw, Bill, *Frank Meadow Sutcliffe, Photographer*, Sutcliffe Gallery, 1998 (first published 1974)

Elderfield, John, *Kurt Schwitters*, Thames and Hudson, 1985

Elliot, David B., *Charles Fairfax Murray: the Unknown Pre-Raphaelite*, Book Guild, 2000

Elliot, Patrick, *A Companion Guide to the Scottish National Gallery of Modern Art*, National Gallery of Scotland, 1999

Ellis, Patricia, *100: the Work that Changed British Art*, Jonathan Cape, 2003

Evans, Mark, and Fairclough, Oliver, *A Companion Guide to the National Art Gallery*, National Museums and Galleries of Wales, 1993

Evans, Richard J., *The Coming of the Third Reich*, Penguin, 2003

Evelyn, John, *Numismata, Or A Discourse Of Medals*, 1676

—, *Memoirs* (ed. E. S. de Beer), Oxford University Press, 1955

Exploring Colonsay: The West Highlands Series No. 11, House of Lochar

Farington, Joseph, *The Diary* (eds. Kenneth Garlick and Angus Macintyre), 17 vols., Yale University Press, 1978

Fastnedge, Ralph, *Last Lectures*, Cambridge University Press, 1939

Fedden, Robin, *Treasures of the National Trust*, Jonathan Cape, 1976

Fenton, James, *Leonardo's Nephew: Essays on Art and Artists*, Viking, 1998

Fergusson, J. D., *Contemporary Scottish Painting*, Hazlitt Gallery, 1952

Ferry, B., *Recollections of A. N. Welby Pugin and his Father, Augustus Pugin*, 1861

Fielding, Daphne, *Memory Presides*, Harcourt, Brace, 1955

Finaldi, Gabriele, and Kitson, Michael, *Discovering the Italian Baroque: the Denis Mahon Collection*, National Gallery, 1997

Fleming, John, *Robert Adam and his Circle in Edinburgh and Rome*, John Murray, 1962

Fleming, John, and Honour, Hugh, *Penguin Dictionary of Decorative Arts*, Viking, 1979 (first published 1977)

Foister, Susan, Gibson, Robin, Rogers, Malcolm, Simon, Jacob, *The National Portrait Gallery Collection*, National Portrait Gallery, 1988

Ford, Brinsley, *The Drawings of Richard Wilson*, Faber and Faber, 1951

Foster, Norman, Sudjic, Deyan, and de Grey, Spencer, *Norman Foster and the British Museum*, Prestel, 2001

Fox Talbot, William, *The Pencil of Nature*, 1844–46

Fraser Jenkins, David, and Pullen, Derek, *The Lipchitz Gift: Models for Sculpture*, Tate Gallery, 1986

Frayling, Christopher (introduced by), *David Mellor: Master Metalworker*, Sheffield Galleries and Museums Trust, 1998

Frizot, Michel, *A New History of Photography*, Könemann, 1998

Fry, Roger, *Last Lectures*, Cambridge University Press, 1939

—, *Vision and Design*, Penguin, 1961 (first published 1920)

Galinou, Mireille, and Hayes, John, *London in Paint: Oil Paintings in the Collection at the Museum of London*, Museum of London, 1996

Games, Stephen, *Nikolaus Pevsner on Art and Architecture: the Radio Talks*, Methuen, 2002

Gardner, Muriel (ed.), *The Wolf Man by the Wolf Man*, Hogarth Press, 1971

Gardner, Thomas, *An Historical Account of Dunwich, Blythburgh and Southwold*, 1754

Gay, P. (ed.), *Sigmund Freud and his Art: his Personal Collection of Antiquities*, Freud Museum, London, 1989

Gerald of Wales, *The Journey Through Wales*, Penguin, 1978

Gifford, John, McWilliam, Colin, and Walker, David, *The Buildings of Scotland: Edinburgh*, Penguin, 1984

Gilbert, Christopher, *The Life and Work of Thomas Chippendale*, Studio Vista, 1978

Gombrich, E. H., *The Preference for the Primitive: Episodes in the History of Western Taste and Art*, Phaidon, 2002

Gooding, Mel (ed.), *Painters as Critic, Patrick Heron: Selected Writings*, Tate, 2001

Gordon Craig, E., *Towards a New Theatre*, B. Blom, 1969 (first published 1913)

Gordon, Catherine (ed.), *Evelyn de Morgan: Oil Paintings*, De Morgan Foundation, 1996

Gore, John (ed.), *The Creevey Papers*, Macmillan, 1963

Gorman, John, *Images of Labour*, Scorpion, 1985

—, *Banner Bright*, Penguin, 1986 (first published 1973)

Gouk, Penelope, *The Ivory Sundials of Nuremberg 1500–1700*, Whipple Museum of the History of Science, 1988

Gould, Brian, *Two Van Gogh Contacts: E. J. Wisselingh and Daniel Cottier*, Naples Press, 1969

Graham-Dixon, Andrew, *Howard Hodgkin*, Thames and Hudson, 2000 (first published 1994)

Grahame, Kenneth, *The Wind in the Willows*, Methuen, 1908

Grape, Wolfgang, *The Bayeux Tapestry*, Pristel, 1994

Graves, Robert, *The Greek Myths*, vols. 1 and 2, Penguin, 1964 (first published 1955)

Greenhill, Basil, and Allington, Peter, *The First Atlantic Liners*, Conway Maritime Press, 1997

Grieve, Alastair, Martin, Kenneth, and Sears, Sarah, *The University of East Anglia Collection of Abstract and Constructivist Art, Architecture and Design*, University of East Anglia, 1994

Grieve, Symington, *The Book of Colonsay and Oronsay*, 2 vols., House of Lochar, 1923

Grigson, Geoffrey, *Henry Moore*, Penguin, 1943

Grigson, Jane, *Fish Cookery*, Penguin, 1975

Guide to the Antiquities of Roman Britain, A, Oxford University Press, 1922

Guerin, Marcel, *Edgar Germain Hilaire Degas: Letters*, Bruno Cassiter, 1947

Guis, M., Le François, T., and Venture, R., *Le Galoubet-Tambourin: Instrument Traditionnel de Provence*, Charly-Yves Chaudoreille, 1993

Halén, Widar, *Christopher Dresser*, Phaidon/Christie's, 1990

Hall, J., *The Life and Correspondence of Henry Salt*.

Hall, Mr and Mrs S. C., *The Book of the Thames*, Charlotte James Publishers, 1976 (first published 1859)

Hardie, Martin, *Peter De Wint*, The Studio, 1929

Harris, John, *James Gibbs: Eminence Grise at Houghton*, Georgian Group Annual Symposium, 1998

Harrison, Colin, *Samuel Palmer*, Ashmolean Museum, 1997

Harrison, Michael, *Kettle's Yard and its Artists*, Kettle's Yard, Kettle's Yard Publishing, 1995

Hartrick, A. S., *A Painter's Pilgrimage through Fifty Years*, Cambridge University Press, 1939

Harvey, A., and Mortimer, R., *Funeral Effigies in Westminster Abbey*, Boydell, 1994

Haskell, Francis, *History and its Images*, Yale University Press, 1993

—, *The Ephemeral Museum*, Yale University Press, 2000

Haskell, Francis, with Penny, Nicholas, *Taste and the Antique*, Yale University Press, 1998 (first published 1981)

Hassell, Christopher, *Edward Marsh, Patron of the Arts*, Longman, 1959

Hawkes, Christopher and Jacquetta, *Prehistoric Britain*, Penguin, 1949 (first published 1943)

Hayes, John, *The Letters of Thomas Gainsborough*, Yale University Press, 2001

Hayley, William, *Life of Cowper*, 2nd edition, 1806

Hendy, Philip, *Piero della Francesca and the Early Renaissance*, Weidenfeld and Nicolson, 1968

Hendy, Philip, *Spanish Painting*, Avalon Press, 1946

Hewison, Robert, *Ruskin and Venice*, Thames and Hudson, 1978

—, *The Heritage Industry*, Methuen, 1987

Hewison, Robert, with Warrell, Ian, and Wildman, Stephen, *Ruskin, Turner and the Pre-Raphaelites*, Tate, 2000

Hill, David, *Turner's Birds*, Phaidon, 1988

— *Thomas Girtin, Genius in the North*, Harewood House Trust, 1999

—, *Harewood Masterpieces: English Watercolours and Drawings*, Harewood House Trust, 1995

History of Collection, A (ed. Steven Hooper), Yale/University of East Anglia, 1997

Hoare, Sir Richard Colt, *Ancient History of Wiltshire*, 1812

Hoffman, Paul, *Wings of Madness*, Fourth Estate, 2003

Hogarth, William, *The Analysis of Beauty* (ed. Robert Paulson), Yale University Press, 1997

Holman Hunt, William, *Pre-Raphaelitism and the Pre-Raphaelite Brotherhood*, 2 vols., 1905

Holme, Charles (ed.), *The Genius of J. M. W. Turner, R. A.*, The Studio, 1903

Holmes, George, *Renaissance*, Weidenfeld and Nicolson, 1996

Holmes, Sir Charles, *Pictures and Picture Collecting*, 1903

Holroyd, C., *Michael Angelo Buonarroti, with Translations of the Life of the Master by his Scholar Ascanio Condivi, and Three Dialogues from the Portuguese by Francisco D'Ollanda*, 2nd edition, 1911

Hone, Joseph (ed.), *The Life of Henry Tonks*, Heinemann, 1939

Honour, Hugh, *Neo-Classicism, Style and Civilisation*, Penguin, 1968

Honour, Hugh, and Fleming, John, *A World History of Art*, Lawrence King, 1984

Horn, Pamela, *William Marshall (1745–1818) and the Georgian Countryside*, Beacon Publications, 1982

Horsley, Juliet (ed.), *L. S. Lowry in the North East*, Tyne and Wear Museums Service, 1989

Howard, John, *The State of the Prisons in England and Wales with an Account of Some Foreign Prisons*, 1777

Howard, Maurice, *The Tudor Image*, Tate, 1995

Howard, Michael, *A Guide to Manchester Picture Gallery*, Scala Publishers Ltd, 2002

Hudson, Kenneth, *Shell Guide to Country Museums*, Heinemann, 1980

—, *Museums for the 1980s: a Survey of World Trends*, Blackwell, 1977

—, *Museums of Influence*, Cambridge University Press, 1987

Hudson, Kenneth, and Nicholls, Ann, *The Cambridge Guide to the Museums of Britain and Ireland*, Cambridge University Press, 1987

Hughes, Peter, *French Art from the Dawes Bequest*, National Museum of Wales, 1982

Hughes, Robert (introduction), *Patrick Heron on Art and Education*, University College, Bretton Hall, 1996

Hutton, James, *Theory of the Earth*, 3 vols., 1785–99

Hyman, Timothy, and Wright, Patrick, *Stanley Spencer*, Tate, 2001

Impey, Oliver and Macgregor, Arthur, *The Origins of Museums*, House of Stratus, 2001 (first published 1985)

Ingamells, John, *The Davies Collection of French Art*, National Gallery and Museum of Wales, 1967

Ingleby, Richard, *Christopher Wood: an English Painter*, Allison and Busby, 1995

Irwin, Francina, *Brush to Paper: Three Centuries of British Watercolours from Aberdeen Art Gallery*, Aberdeen City Arts Department, 1991

Jackson, Sir Charles J., *English Goldsmith and their Marks*, 1905

—, *History of English Plate*, 2 vols., Country Life and Batsford, 1911

Janssen, Rosalind, M., *The First Hundred Years: Egyptology at University College London 1892–1992*, UCL, 1992

Jardine, D.C., *The Birds of Colonsay and Oronsay*, The House of Lochar, 2002

Jenkins, I., and Sloan, K., *Vases and Volcanoes*, British Museum, 1996

Jenkins, Roy, *Churchill*, Macmillan, 2002

Jenkins, Simon, *England's Thousand Best Parish Churches*, Penguin, 2000

—, *England's Thousand Best Houses*, Penguin, 2003

Jervis, Thomas, *The Energy of Talent and the Reward of Active Virtue ... An Address Delivered at the Interment of Joseph Dawson*, 1814

Jewell, John, *The History and Antiquities of Harewood in Yorkshire*, 1819

Joannides, Paul, *Michelangelo and his Influence: Drawing for Windsor Castle*, Fitzwilliam Museum, 1996

John, Sir William Goscombe, *The Method of Purchasing Works of Art*, 1913

John, Augustus, *Finishing Touches* (ed. and introduced by David George), Readers Union/Jonathan Cape, 1966

Joll, Evelyn, *Watercolours and Drawings*, Cecil Higgins Art Gallery, 2002

Joll, Evelyn, Butlin, Martin, and Hermann, Luke, *The Oxford Companion to J. M. W. Turner*, Oxford University Press, 2001

Jones, Huw, and Wickham, Annette, *Francis Skidmore: a Coventry Craftsman*, Coventry Arts and Heritage, 2003

Jones, Thomas, *Geralltgymro*, University of Wales Press, 1947

Kaplan, Wendy, *Charles Rennie Mackintosh*, Glasgow Museums and Abbeville Press, 1996

Kauffman, C. M., *Catalogue of Paintings in the Wellington Museum*, HMSO, 1982

Kent, Sarah, *Shark Infested Waters*, Zwemmer, 1994

Keynes, Geoffrey (ed.), *The Works of Sir Thomas Browne*, 4 vols., Faber and Gwyer, 1994

Keynes, Geoffrey, *William Blake, Poet, Printer, Prophet*, Methuen & Co., 1965

Khoroche, Peter, *Ben Nicholson, Drawings and Painted Reliefs*, Lund Humphries, 2002

Kidson, Alex, *George Romney 1734–1802*, National Portrait Gallery, 2002

Killen, John, *The History of the Linen Hall Library, 1788–1988*, Linen Hall Library, 1990

Lanyon, Peter, *Coastal Journey*, Tate St Ives broadsheet, 2000.

Late King's Goods: Collections, Possessions and Patronage of Charles I in the Light of the Commonwealth Sale Inventories, The, 1909

Laver, James, *Paintings by Michael Ayrton*, Grey Walls, 1948

—, *Fashions and Fashion Plates 1800–1900*, King Penguin, 1943

Leader, R. E., and Bradbury, Frederick, *The History of Old Sheffield Plate*, Macmillan, 1912

Leader, R. E., *History of the Company of Cutlers in Hallamshire in the County of York*, 2 vols., printed by the authority of the Company of Cutlers, by Pawson and Brailsford, 1905–6

Leber, Michael, and Standing, Judith, *L. S. Lowry*, Phaidon Press and Salford Art Gallery, 1987

Lees-Milne, James, *The Earls of Creation: Five Great Patrons of Eighteenth Century Art*, Penguin, 2001 (first published 1963)

—, *National Trust Guide: Buildings*, Batsford, 1940

—, *The Age of Adam*, Batsford, 1947

Legeza, Irerieus Laszlo, *Malcolm Macdonald*, Oxford University Press, 1972

Leidtke, Walter, with Plomp, Michiel C., and Rüger, Axel, *Vermeer and the Delft School*, Metropolitan Museum of Art, New York, and Yale University Press, 2001

Lemprière, John, *Bibliotheca Classica/Classical Dictionary*, 1788

Leslie, C. R., *Memorials of the Life of John Constable Esq.*, Longman's Brown, Green and Longman's, 1845

Lethaby, W. R., *Architecture* (2nd revised edition), 1939

Levell, Nicky, *Oriental Visions: Exhibitions, Travel, and Collecting in the Victorian Age*, Horniman Museum and Gardens, 2000

Levey, Michael, *Early Renaissance: Style and Civilisation*, Penguin, 1967

—, *The Burlington Magazine: a Centenary Anthology*, Yale University Press, 2003

Lewison, Jeremy, *Ben Nicholson*, Tate Gallery, 1993

Lindsay, Jack, *Turner*, Panther Books, 1973 (first published 1966)

Livingstone, Paedar, *Fermanagh Story*, Cumann Seanchais Chlochair, 1969

Lloyd, Christopher, *The Paintings in the Royal Collection*, Royal Collection, 1999

Loder, John de Vere, *Colonsay and Oronsay in the Isles of Argyll: their History, Flora, Fauna and Topography*, Colonsay Press, 1995 (first published 1935)

Lodwick, Marcus, *The Gallery Companion*, Thames and Hudson, 2002

Lyles, Anne, and Hamlyn, Robin, *British Watercolours from the Oppé Collection*, Tate Gallery Publishing, 1997

Lynton, Norbert, *Ben Nicholson*, Phaidon, 2000 (first published 1993)

Lyster, Grania, *A Guide to the Wallace Collection*, Wallace Collection, 2000

MacCarthy, Fiona, *Stanley Spencer, English Visionary*, Yale University Press, 1977

—, *William Morris: a Life for our Times*, Faber and Faber, 1994

Macdonald, Murdo, *Scottish Art*, Thames and Hudson, 2000

MacGregor, A. (ed.), *The Late King's Goods: Collections, Possessions and Patronage of Charles I in the Light of the Commonwealth Sale Inventories*, 1909

Mackey, Brian, *Lisburn: the Town and its People 1873–1973*, Black Staff Press, 2000

Maclagan, Eric, and Longhurst, Margaret H., *Catalogue of Italian Sculpture*, 2 vols., Oxford University Press, 1932

Maclean, Sorley, *Poems 1932–82*, Columban Celtic Series, vol. 2, Iona Foundation, 1987

Maguire of Fermanagh, The, *Historic Maguire Chalices*, The Maguire of Fermanagh, 1993

Malden, John, *John Henning*, Paisley Museums, 1977

Mallalieu, Huon, *The Norwich School: Crome, Cotman and their Followers*, Academy Editions, 1974

Markham, S. F., *The Museums and Art Galleries of the British Isles*, Carnegie United Kingdom Trust, 1938

Marks, Richard, and Williamson, Paul, *Gothic: Art for England 1400–1547*, Victoria & Albert Publishing, 2003

Marshall, William, *Proposals for a Rural Institute or College of Agriculture and the other Branches of Rural Economy*, 1799

Martineau, Jane, and Hope, Charles, *The Genius of Venice 1500–1600*, Royal Academy of Arts, 1983

Marwick. E. W. (introduced by), *Life on the Orkney Islands*, P. Harris, 1979

Maurois, André, *Shelley: a Biography*, Penguin, 1935

Mayer, Luigi, *Views in Egypt, Palestine and the Ottoman Empire*, 3 vols., 1801

Mayhew, Henry, *London Labour and the London Poor*, 4 vols., 1861

McGirr, Nicola, *Nature's Connections: an Exploration of Natural History*, Natural History Museum, 2000

McGrail, Sean, *Ancient Boats in North West Europe*, Longman, 1983

McLaughlin, Robert, *Gifted*, Mainstream, 1990

McNeill, Murdoch, *Colonsay: One of the Hebrides*, House of Lochar, 2001 (first published 1910)

McNeillie, Andrew (ed.), *The Essays: 1904–13, vol. I* (Virginia Woolf), Harcourt, Brace, Jovanovich, 1986

McWilliam, Colin, *Scottish Townscape*, Collins, 1975

Mellars, Dr Paul, *Excavations on Oronsay: Prehistoric Human Ecology on a Small Island*, Royal Commission on the Ancient and Historical Monuments of Scotland, 1984

Merimée, Prosper, *Lettres à une Inconnue*, 2 vols., Calmann-Lévy Editions, 1871

Merthyr Teachers Centre Group (ed.), *Merthyr Tydfil, a Valley Community*, Cowbridge, 1981

Meteyard, Eliza, *The Life of Josiah Wedgwood*, 2 vols., Hurst and Blackett, 1866

Millar, Oliver, *Zoffany and his Tribuna*, Paul Mellon Foundation of Art, 1967

Miller, Edward, *That Noble Cabinet*, Deutsch, 1973

Miller, Hugh, *My Schools and School Masters*, Band W. Publishing, 1993

—, *The Old Red Sandstone*, John Johnstone, 1841

—, *The Testimony of the Rocks*, Thomas Constable & Co., 1857

Milner, Frank, *The Pre-Raphaelites*, Bluecoat Press, 1995

Monkhouse, Cosmo, *The Earlier English Water-Colour Painters*, Seeley & Co., 1897

Mordaunt Crook, J., *The British Museum*, Allen Lane, 1972

—, *The Rise of the Nouveaux Riches*, John Murray, 1999

Morris, Edward, *Public Art Collections in North-West England*, Liverpool University Press, 2001

Morris, Jan, *Wales: Epic View of a Small Country*, Viking, 1998

Moxham, Ray, *Tea, Addiction, Exploitation and Empire*, Constable, 2003

Mundy, Jennifer (ed.), *Surrealism: Desire Unbound*, Tate Publishing, 2001

Mundy, Peter, *The Travels of Peter Mundy, in Europe and Asia 1608–1667*, 1914

Murdoch, John, *Courtauld Collections Catalogue*, Thames and Hudson, 1998

Murdoch, John, and Twitchett, John, *Painters and the Derby China Works*, Trefoil, 1987

Murphy, Yvonne, Leonard, Alan, Gillespie, Gordon, and Brown, Kris, *Troubled Images: Posters and Images of the Northern Ireland Conflict*, Linen Hall Library, 2001

Murray, Lynda J., *A Zest for Life*, Morven Books, 1999

Murry, John Middleton, *Between Two Worlds*, Jonathan Cape, 1935

Myrone, Martin David, *George Vertue (1683–1756) and the Graphic Arts in Eighteenth-century Britain* (dissertation), University of London (Courtauld Institute of Art), 1994

Nash, Paul, *Outline of an Autobiography and Other Writings*, Faber and Faber, London, 1949

Naylor, Gillian (ed.), *Bloomsbury: its Artists, Authors and Designers*, Little, Brown & Co., 1990

Neal, Elizabeth, *Churchill's Secretary*, Hodder & Stoughton, 1958

Newall, Christopher, *The Etruscans: Painters of the Italian Landscape 1850–1900*, Stoke-on-Trent City Art Gallery and Museum, 1989

Newbolt, H. J., *Admirals All, and Other Verses*, Elkin Mathews, 1897

Newby, Evelyn, *William Hoare of Bath, R. A. 1707–1792*, Bath Museum Service and Alan Sutton, 1990

Newman, John, *The Buildings of Wales: Glamorgan*, Penguin, 1995

—, *The Buildings of Wales: Gwent/Monmouthshire*, Yale University Press, 2000

Nicolson, Adam, *The Power and the Glory*, HarperCollins, 2003

O'Brian, Patrick, *Joseph Banks*, Harvill, 1997 (first published 1989)

O'Brien, R., *The Autobiography of Wolfe Tone 1763–1798*, London, 1893

O'Dwyer, Frederick, *The Architecture of Deane and Woodward*, Cork University Press, 1997

—, *Oxford Museum: Deane and Woodward*, Phaidon, 1992

O'Neill, A., *A Dictionary of Spanish Painters*, 1833–4

Orchard, Karin, *Kurt Schwitters: His Life and Work*, Baltic Centre for Contemporary Art, No. 4, 1999

Orpen, Sir William (ed.), *The Outline of Art*, revised edition by Horace Shipp, G.P. Putnam's Sons, 1924

Ostergard, Derek E. (ed.), *William Beckford 1760–1844: an Eye for the Magnificent*, Yale University Press, 2001

Ovid, *Metamorphoses* (transl. A.D. Melville), Oxford University Press, 1998

Owen, Trefor M. (ed.), *From Corrib to Cultra: Essays in Honour of Alan Gailey*, Institute of Irish Studies, Queens University, Belfast, in association with the Ulster Folk and Transport Museum, 2000

Oxford Dictionary of National Biography (ed. Brian Harrison), Oxford University Press, 2004

Palladio, A., *Quattro Libri dell Architettura*, 1507

Parris, Leslie, Fleming-Williams, Ian, and Shields, Conal, *Constable: Paintings, Watercolours and Drawings*, Tate Publishing, 1976

Pater, Walter, *The Renaissance: Studies in Art and Poetry*, Penguin, 1961 (first published 1873)

Payne, Ffrancis G., *Welsh Peasant Costume Folk Life II*, Welsh Folk Museum, 1964

Pears, Iain, *The Discovery of Painting: the Growth of Interest in the Arts in England 1680–1768*, Yale University Press, 1988

Pearson, Fiona, *Paolozzi*, National Galleries of Scotland, 1999

Peate, Ior Werth C., *Tradition and Folklore: a Welsh View*, Faber and Faber, 1972

Pennant, Thomas, *A Tour in Scotland and Voyage to the Hebrides*, 1772 (2nd edition 1776)

Penny, Nicholas, *Ruskin's Drawings*, Ashmolean Museum, 1997

Perl, Jed, *Eye Witness: Reports from an Art World in Crisis*, Basic Books, 2000

Petrowski, Henry, *The Pencil*, Knopf, 1990

Pevsner, Nikolaus, *The Buildings of England* published:
Bath, 2003
Bedfordshire, Huntingdon and Peterborough, 1968
Berkshire, 1966
Buckinghamshire 1960, 1994
Cambridgeshire, 1954, 1970
Cheshire, 1971
Cornwall, 1951, 1970
County Durham, 1953, 1983
Cumberland and Westmorland, 1967

Derbyshire, 1953, 1978
Devon, 1952, 1989
Dorset, 1972
Essex, 1954, 1965
Gloucestershire: the Cotswolds, 1970, 1999
Gloucestershire: the Vale and Forest of Dean, 2002
Hampshire, 1967
Herefordshire, 1963
Hertfordshire, 1953, 1977
Kent: North East and East, 1969, 1983
Kent: West and the Weald, 1969, 1976
North Lancashire, 1969
South Lancashire, 1969
Leicestershire and Rutland, 1960, 1984
Lincolnshire, 1964, 1989
London 1: the City of London, 1997
London 2: South, 1983
London 3: North-West, 1991
London 4: North, 1998
London City Churches, 1998
Manchester, 2001
Norfolk 1: Norwich and North East, 1962, 1997
Norfolk 2: South and West, 1962, 1999
Northamptonshire, 1961, 1973
Northumberland, 1957, 1992
Nottinghamshire, 1951, 1979
Oxfordshire, 1974
Shropshire, 1958
Somerset: North and Bristol, 1958
Somerset: South and West, 1958
Staffordshire, 1974
Suffolk, 1961, 1974
Surrey, 1962, 1971
Sussex, 1965
Warwickshire, 1966
Wiltshire, 1963, 1971
Worcestershire, 1968
Yorkshire: the North Riding, 1966
Yorkshire: the West Riding, 1959, 1967
Yorkshire: York and East Riding, 1972, 1995
Pevsner, Nikolaus, *Pevsner on Art and Architecture*, Methuen, 2002
Pevsner, Nikolaus, and Arneil Walker, Frank, *Argyll and Bute*, Penguin, 2000
Pevsner, Nikolaus, and Bradley, Simon, *The Buildings of England: London 6: Westminster*, Yale University Press, 2003

Pevsner, Nikolaus, and Sherwood, Jennifer, *The Buildings of England: Oxfordshire*, 2002
Pevsner, Nikolaus, Williamson, Elizabeth, Riches, Anne, and Higgs, Malcolm, *The Buildings of Scotland: Glasgow*, Penguin, 1990.
Philips, *In the Geology of Oxford and the Valley of the Thames*, 1871
Phillips, Barty, *Tapestry*, Phaidon, 1994
Phillips, Tom, *Aspects of Art: a Painter's Alphabet*, Bellew, 1997
Pickvance, Ronald, *A Man of Influence: Alex Reid*, Scottish Arts Council, 1967
Piggott, Professor Stuart (foreword), *Guide Catalogue to the Neolithic and Bronze Age Collections in Devizes Museum*, Wiltshire Archaeological and Natural History Society, 1964
Piggott, Stuart, *Approach to Archaeology*, Penguin, 1959
Piper, David, *Painting in England 1500–1880*, Penguin, 1965 (first published 1960)
—, *The Treasures of Oxford*, Paddington Press, 1977
Pitt Rivers, A. H. Lane Fox, *Excavations at Cranborne Chase*, 1887
—, *The Evolution of Culture and Other Essays*, Clarendon Press, 1906
—, *On the Improvement of the Rifle as a Weapon of General Use*, Clowes & Son, 1857
—, *Principles of Classification*, 1874
Pope-Hennessy, John, *Renaissance Bronzes from the Samuel H. Kress Collection*, Phaidon, 1965
Prather, Marla, *Willem De Kooning: Paintings*, Yale University Press, 1994
Prior, E. S., and Gardiner, A., *An Account of English Medieval Figure Sculpture in England*, Cambridge University Press, 1912
Puyvelde, Leo van, Rubens, Peter Paul, *The Letters of Bruxelles*, Editions de *La Connaissance*, c. 1939
Rajnai, Miklos, and Allthorpe-Guyton, Marjorie, *John Sell Cotman 1782–1842: Early Drawings 1782–1812 in Norwich Castle Museum*, Norfolk Museum Services, 1979
Rathbone, F., *Old Wedgwood Acquired from the Cabinets of Arthur Sanderson*, 1907

Rawson, Jessica (ed.), *The British Museum Book of Chinese Art*, British Museum Press, 1992

Read, Sir Herbert, *The Meaning of Art*, Penguin, 1956 (first published 1931)

Redgrave, Samuel and Richard, *A Century of British Painters*, Phaidon, 1947 (first published 1866)

Rewald, John (ed.), *Paul Cézanne: Letters*, Bruno Cassiver, 1946 (first published 1941)

Reynolds, Graham, *Thomas Bewick, London: Art and Technics*, Art and Technics 1949

—, *An Introduction to English Watercolour Painting*, Country Life and Charles Scribner and Sons, 1950

Reynolds, Sir Joshua, *Discourses on Art*, with introduction and notes by Roger Fry, Seeley and Co., 1905

—, *Discourses on Art* (ed. Robert R. Wark), Yale University Press, 1997

Richards, J. M., *Spencer, Stanley, Sermons by Artists*, Country Life, 1938

—, *High Street*, Country Life, 1938

Richardson, John, *Sacred Monsters, Sacred Masters*, Jonathan Cape, 2001

Richardson, Margaret, and Stevens, Mary Anne, *John Soane: Architect*, Royal Academy of Arts, 1999

Riddick, Sarah, *Pioneer Studio Pottery: The Milner-White Collection*, Lund Humphries in association with York City Art Gallery, 1990

Riding, Christine, and Riding, Jacqueline, *The Houses of Parliament: History, Art and Architecture*, Merrell, 2000

Roberts, Jane (ed.), *Royal Treasures: a Golden Jubilee Celebration*, Royal Collection, W.W. Norton and Co. Inc., 2002

Roberts Jane, *Master Drawings in the Royal Collection: from Leonardo da Vinci to the Present Day*, Collins Harvill, 1986

Roberts, Pam, *The Royal Photographic Society Collection*, Royal Photographic Society, 1999 (first published 1994)

Robertson, James, *Stirling Sonnets*, Keltilonia, 2001

Robinson, Duncan, *Stanley Spencer*, Phaidon, 1990

Robinson, John Charles, *Italian Sculpture of the Middle Ages: a Period of the Revival in Art: a Descriptive Catalogue of the Works Forming the Above Section of the Museum*, Chapman and Hall, 1862

Roscoe William, *The Life of Lorenzo De' Medici, Called "The Magnificent"*, 2 vols., 1795, and Henry G. Bohn, 1936

Rose, Walter, *The Village Carpenter*, Stobart Davies, 1937

Rosenthal, Michael, *The Art of Thomas Gainsborough*, Yale University Press, 1999

Rothenstein, John, *An Introduction to English Painting*, Cassell, 1933

—, *Modern English Painters*, 2 vols., Arrow Books, 1962 (first published 1952–56)

—, *Summer's Lease: Autobiography 1901–38*, vol. 1, Hamish Hamilton, 1965

—, *Time's Thievish Progress: Autobiography*, vol. 3, Cassell, 1970

Rothenstein, John, and Butlin, Martin, *Turner*, Heinemann, 1964

Rothenstein, William, *Goya, At The Sign of the Unicorn*, 1900

Rouquet, André, *The Present Stage of the Arts in England*, 1755, reprinted by the Cornhill Press, 1970

Ruskin, John, *By Time and Tide*, J. M. Dent & Sons Ltd, 1921 (first published 1867)

—, *Letters on a Museum*, 1880

—, *Modern Painters* (eds. E. T. Cook and A. Wedderburn), 39 vols., Library Edition 1903–12

—, *Praeterita*, Library Edition, Oxford University Press, 1978

Russell-Cotes, Sir Merton, *Home and Abroad*, 2 vols., privately printed, Bournemouth, 1921

Rutter, Frank, *Art in my Time*, Rich and Lowan, 1933

Rye, W. B., *England as Seen by Foreigners in the Days of Elizabeth and James I*, 1856

Sackville-West, Vita, *Knole and the Sackvilles*, George H. Doran, 1922

Sadie, Stanley, *New Grove Dictionary of Musical Instruments*, 3 vols., Oxford University Press, 1935

Salaman, R. A., *Dictionary of Tools: used in the woodworking and allied trades c. 1700–1970*, George Allen and Unwin, 1975

Sanouillet, M., and Peterson, E. (eds.), *The Essential Writings of Marcel Duchamp*, Thames and Hudson, 1975

Saumarez Smith, Charles, *The National Portrait Gallery*, National Portrait Gallery Publishing, 1997

—, *The Rise of Design: Design and the Domestic Interior in Eighteenth Century England*, Pimlico, 1993

—, *The Building of Castle Howard*, Pimlico, 1997

Savage, George, *Porcelain through the Ages*, Penguin, 1954

Schwab, Walter, and Weiner, Julia, *Jewish Artists: The Ben Uri Collection*, Ben Uri Art Society in association with Lund Humphries, 1994

Scott, Jonathan, *The Pleasures of Antiquity*, Yale University Press, 2003

Scott, Rosemary E., *Percival David Foundation of Chinese Art*, SOAS, University of London, 1989

Sellars, Jane, *Women Works*, National Museums and Galleries Merseyside, 1988

—, *The Art of Thomas Chippendale, Master Furniture Maker*, Harewood House Trust, Tanner and Nevinson, 2000

Serota, Sir Nicholas, *Experience or Interpretation: the Dilemma of Museums of Modern Art*, Thames and Hudson, 2000

Shanes, Eric (with essays by Evelyn Joll, Ian Warrell and Andrew Wilton), *Turner: the Great Watercolours*, Royal Academy of Arts, 2000

Shanes, Eric, *The Genius of the Royal Academy*, Royal Academy/John Murray, 1981

—, *The Golden Age of Watercolours: the Hickman Bacon Collection*, Dulwich Picture Gallery in association with Merrell, 2001

Shaw, Simeon, *History of the Staffordshire Potteries*, 1829

Shelton, Anthony (ed.), *Collectors: Individuals and Institutions*, The Horniman Museum and Gardens, 2001

Sheppard, Francis, *Book of Maritime*, HMSO, 1999

Shone, Richard, *The Art of Bloomsbury: Roger Fry, Vanessa Bell and Duncan Grant*, Tate Gallery Publishing, 1999

Sickert, Sir Walter Richard, *A Free House*, AMS Publishing, 1922

Siegel, Dr Ronald K., *Intoxication*, E. P. Dutton, 1989

Sigüenza, Father Jose de, *Historia de la Orden de San Jeronima*, 3 vols., 1595, 1600, 1605

Simcock, A.V. (ed.), *Robert T. Gunther and the Old Ashmolean*, History of Science Museum, Oxford, 1985

Simister, Kirsten, *Living Paint: J. D. Fergusson, 1874–1961*, Mainstream, 2001

Simpson, Colin, *The Partnership*, Bodley Head, 1987

Sitwell, O., *Left Hand, Right Hand*, Macmillan, 1948

Sloan, Kim, *Enlightenment: Discovering the World in the Eighteenth Century*, British Museum Press, 2003

Smiles, Samuel, *Men of Invention and Industry*, 1884

Smith, George, *Dictionary of National Biography*, 63 vols., 1882–1900

Smith, Greg, *Thomas Girtin: the Art of the Watercolour*, Tate Publishing, 2002

Smith, Reginald Allender, *A Guide to the Antiquities of Roman Britain in the Department of British and Mediaeval Antiquities*, British Museum, 1922

Smith, William (ed.), *Old Yorkshire*, 1884

Snodin, Michael, and Styles, John, *Design and the Decorative Arts: Britain 1500–1900*, V&A Publications, 2001

Somers Cocks, Anna, *The Victoria and Albert Museum: the Making of the Collection*, Windward, 1980

Southey, Robert, *Life of Cowper*, 1835–7

Spalding, Frances, *The Tate: a History*, Tate Publications, 1998

Spalding, Julian, *Gallery of Modern Art Glasgow: The First Years: 'Art For People'*, Scala Books, 1996

—, *The Poetic Museum*, Prestel, 2002

— (introduced by), *St Mungo Museum of Religious Life and Art*, Chambers, 1995

Spencer, Gilbert, *Stanley Spencer by his Brother*, Victor Gollancz, 1961

Spencer-Longhurst, Paul (ed.), *Robert Atkinson 1883–1952*, Scala Books with the Barber Institute of Fine Arts, 2000

Spencer-Longhurst, Paul, and Brooke, Janet M., *Thomas Gainsborough: the Harvest Wagon*, Birmingham Museums and Art Gallery/Trustees of the Barber Institute of Fine Arts, 1995

Spencer-Longhurst, Paul, *The Blue Bower: Rossetti in the 1860s*, Scala Books with the Barber Institute of Fine Arts, 2000

Stevenson, Michael, *Art and Aspirations: the Randlords of South Africa and their Collections*, Fernwood Press, 2002

Stevenson, R. A. M., *Rubens: Paintings and Drawings*, Phaidon Press, 1939

Stevenson, Sara, and Forbes, Duncan, *A Companion Guide to Photography in the National Galleries of Scotland*, National Gallery of Scotland, 2001

Stevenson, Sara, *Facing the Light: the Photography of Hill and Adamson*, Scottish National Portrait Gallery, 2002

Storey, Caroline, *Harewood House 1767–1797, Chippendale's Most Magnificent Commission: the Art of Thomas Chippendale*, Harewood House Trust, 2000

Strong, Roy, *The Spirit of Britain: a Narrative History of the Arts*, Hutchinson, 1999

Stroud, Dorothy, *Capability Brown*, Faber and Faber, 1975

—, *Sir John Soane: Architect*, de la Mare, 1996 (first published 1984)

Sugden and Edmondson, *History of English Wallpaper 1509–1916*, Batsford, 1926

Summerson, John, *Georgian London*, Penguin, 1962

Sumner, Ann, and Smith, Greg, *Thomas Jones 1742–1803: an Artist Rediscovered*, Yale University Press in association with National Museums and Galleries of Wales, 2003

Supple, Barry, *A History of the British Coal Industry*, 4 vols., Clarendon Press, 1913–46

Sykes, Christopher, and Montgomery-Massingberd, Hugh, *Great Houses of England and Wales*, Rizzoli, 1994

Sylvester, David, *About Modern Art: Critical Essays 1948–97*, updated edition, Pimlico, 1997 (first published 1996)

—, *Francis Bacon: the Human Body*, Hayward Gallery and University of California Press, 1998

Sylvester, David, *Magritte*, Arts Council of Great Britain, 1969

—, *Interviews with American Artists*, Pimlico, 2002

—, (ed.), *Patrick Heron*, Tate Gallery Publishing, 1998

Talbot Rice, D., *English Art 871–1100*, Oxford at the Clarendon Press, 1952

Tanner and Nevinson, *On the Funeral Effigies of the Kings and Queens of England with Special Reference to those in the Abby Church of Westminister*, Archaeologia, 1906

Tasso, *Gerusalemme Liberata*, 1581

Taylor, Basil, *Cézanne*, Hamlyn, 1970 (first published 1961)

Taylor, Gerald, *Silver*, Penguin, 1970 (first published 1956)

Taylor, Michael R., *Giorgio de Chirico and the Myth of Ariadne*, Philadelphia Museum of Art, 2003

Teague, Ken, *Nomads: Nomadic Material Culture in the Asian Collections of the Horniman Museum*, Horniman Museum and Gardens, 2000

Thackeray, W. M., *Roundabout Paper*, 1862

Thackray, John, and Press, Bob, *The Natural History Museum: Nature's Treasurehouse*, Natural History Museum, 2001

Thetze, Dr Hans, *Treasures of the Great National Galleries*, Phaidon, 1955

Thomas, Keith, *Man and the Natural World: Changing Attitudes in England 1500–1800*, Allen Lane, 1983

Thompson, E. P., *The Making of the English Working Class*, Penguin, 1963

Thompson, Thomas, *A System of Chemistry*, 1802

Thomson, Duncan, *Raeburn: the Art of Sir Henry Raeburn 1756–1823*, Scottish National Portrait Galleries, 1997

Thomson, Keith, *Treasures on Earth: Museums, Collections and Paradoxes*, Faber and Faber, 2002

Thornbury, Walter, *The Life of J. M. W. Turner R. A.*, 2 vols., 1862

Thorpe, W. A., *English Glass*, The Library of English Art, 1934

Tibbles, Anthony, *Transatlantic Slavery: Against Human Dignity*, National Museums and Galleries on Merseyside/HMSO, 1994

Tong, Jiaoying (ed.), *Tong Shuye Meishu Lunji*, 1989

Tooby, Michael (ed.), *In Perpetuity and Without Charge: A History of the Mappin, 1887–1987*, Sheffield Museums and Galleries, 1987

—, *Tate St Ives: an Illustrated Companion*, Tate Gallery Publications, 1993

Treuherz, Julian (introduction), *Pre-Raphaelite Paintings*, Manchester City Art Gallery, 1993

Trollope, C. (transl.), *Sigmund Freud: His Life in Words and Pictures, with a Biographical Sketch by K.R. Eissler*, Norton 1978

Tuckwell, W., *Reminiscences of Oxford*, Cassell & Co., 1901

Turner, W. J., (ed.), *Aspects of British Art*, Collins, 1947

Uglow, Jenny, *The Lunar Men*, Faber and Faber, 2002

Vainker, Shelagh, *Chinese Pottery and Porcelain: from Pre-History to the Present*, British Museum Press, 1991

Valentine, Helen (ed.), *Art in the Age of Queen Victoria: Treasures from the Royal Academy of Arts Permanent Collection*, Royal Academy of Arts, 1999

Vasari, Giorgio, *The Lives of the Artists*, World Classics, 1991

Verdi, Richard, *Anthony Van Dyck 1599–1641, Ecce Homo and the Mocking of Christ*, Birmingham Museums and Art Gallery/ the Trustees of the Barber Institute of Fine Arts, 2002

—, *Apocalypse Then: Graphic Art and the Great War*, Birmingham Museums and Art Gallery/the Trustees of the Barber Institute of Fine Arts, 2001

—, *Matthias Stom: Isaac Blessing Jacob*, Birmingham Museums and Art Gallery/ the Trustees of the Barber Institute of Fine Arts, 1999

—, *Nicolas Poussin, Tancred and Erminia*, Birmingham Museums and Art Gallery/ the Trustees of the Barber Institute of Fine Arts, 1992

Vertue, George, *The Notebooks of George Vertue*, 5 vols., Walpole Society, 1934

Wade, Charles Paget, *Days Far Away*, National Trust Enterprises, 1996

Wainwright, Clive, *George Bullock: Cabinet Maker*, John Murray, 1988

Wallace, J., *The History of Liverpool*, 1795

Walpole, Horace, *Anecdotes of Painting in England* (ed. Ralph H. Wornum), 1876 (first published 1761)

Ward Usher, James, *An Art Collector's Treasures*, Chiswick Press, 1916

Warde, Beatrice, *Some Words by Beatrice Warde and Types by Varied Hands*, privately published, reprinted 1953

Ware, Isaac, *The Complete Body of Architecture*, 1756

Warner, Malcolm, *The Victorians: British Painting 1837–1901*, National Gallery of Art, Washington, DC and Abrams, 1997

Waterfield, Giles, *A Nest of Nightingales: Thomas Gainsborough and the Linley Sisters*, Dulwich Picture Gallery, 1988

Waterhouse, Ellis, *Gainsborough*, Spring Books, 1958

Watkin, David, *The Life and Work of C.R. Cockerell*, Zwemmer, 1974

—, *The Making of the Ashmolean*, Ashmolean Museum, 1974

Watson, Vera, *The British Museum*, Quartet Books, 1973

Watts, M. S., *George Frederick Watts: the Annals of an Artist's Life*, 3 vols., 1912

Wellbeloved, Charles, *A Descriptive Account of the Antiquities in the Grounds and in the Museum of the Yorkshire Philosophical Society*, 1852

Wheeler, Sir Mortimer, *Rome Beyond the Imperial Frontiers*, Penguin, 1955

Whinney, Margaret, and Millar, Oliver, *English Art 1625–1714*, Oxford at the Clarendon Press, 1957

Who Was Who, A. & C. Black, 1929

Wilenski, R. H., *English Painting*, Faber and Faber, 1946 (first published 1933)

—, *Dutch Painting*, Faber and Faber, 1945 (first published 1939)

—, *French Painting*, Medici Society, 1949 (first published 1931)

Wilenski, R. H. – *cont.*
—, *The Modern Movement in Art*, Faber and Gwyer, 1927
—, *Modern French Painters*, Faber and Faber, 1947 (first published 1940)
Williams, Brian, and Gormley, Sarah, *Archaeological Objects from County Fermanagh*, Black Staff Press, 2002
Williamson, Elizabeth, et al, *Buildings of Scotland: Glasgow*, Penguin, 1990
Wilson, Colin St John, *Design and Construction of the British Library*, British Library, 1998
Wilson, David M., *The British Museum: Purpose and Politics*, British Museum Publications, 1989
Wilson, Michael, *The National Gallery, London*, Book Club Associates, 1977
Wilton, Andrew, and Bignamini, Ilaria (eds.), *Grand Tour: the Line of Italy in the Eighteenth Century*, Tate Gallery Publishing, 1996
Winckelmann, Johann, *Briefe*, 4 vols., Wide Gruyter, 1952–7
Wittkower, Rudolf, *Gian Lorenzo Bernini*, Phaidon Press, 1955
Wolff Purcell, Rosamund, and Gould, Stephen Jay, *Finders, Keepers: Eight Collectors*, W. W. Norton and Co., 1992
Woodward, John, *Essay Towards a Natural History of the World*, 1695
Wooley, Sir Leonard, *Digging up the Past*, Penguin, 1937 (first published 1930)
Woolf, Virginia, *Walter Sickert: a Conversation*, Bloomsbury Workshop, 1992
Wright, Christopher (ed.), *Catalogue of Foreign Paintings from the de Ferrières Collection and other Sources*, Cheltenham Art Gallery and Museums, 1988
Wright, F. A., *Lemprière's Classical Dictionary of Proper Names Mentioned in Ancient Authors: a New Edition*, Routledge and Kegan Paul, reprinted 1963
Wright, Karen (ed.), *Writers on Artists*, Dorling Kindersley in association with Modern Painters, 2002
Young, Eric, *Catalogue of Spanish Paintings*, 2nd edition, Bowes Museum, 1988

CATALOGUES AND GUIDE BOOKS

Allan Ramsay (1713–1784): his Masters and Rivals, National Galleries of Scotland, 1963
Allan, Rosemary, *Beamish: the Making of a Museum*, Beamish, 1991
Annable, F. K., and Simpson, D. D. A., *Guide Catalogue of the Neolithic and Bronze Age Antiquities*, Devizes Museum, 1964
Art in Britain 1890–1940, catalogue, University of Hull, 1967
Art in Seventeenth Century Holland, National Gallery, 1976
Art of Drawing and Painting, The, catalogue of Pallant House Gallery exhibition, 1999/2000
Art of Thomas Chippendale, The, catalogue of Harewood House exhibition, 2000
Art Treasures of England: The Regional Collections, Royal Academy of Arts in association with Merrell Holberton, exhibition catalogue, 1998
Arthur William Devis, Harris Museum and Art Gallery, 2000
Arts of Asia, catalogue of the Macdonald Collection, 1983
Beaulieu guide, Beaulieu, 2002
Ben Uri Catalogue, 1930
Bickle, Richard, *Harewood: a Guide Book*, 1959 and 1962
Birmingham Museums and Art Gallery, 1999
Blazwick, Iwona, and Weston, Simon (eds.), *Tate Modern: the Handbook*, 2000
British Museum Guide (introduction by Sir John Pope-Hennessy), British Museum Publications, 1976
Catalogue of the Collection of Drawings in the Ashmolean Museum, Italian Schools, Clarendon Press, 1956
Catalogue of the Galpin Society's 21st Anniversary Exhibition in Edinburgh, 1968
Catalogue of the Tate Gallery's Collections of Modern Art, Tate Gallery, 1981
Catalogue to the Barbara Hepworth retrospective exhibition, Whitechapel Gallery, London, 1954
Catalogue to the British Council Spencer exhibition at the Hirshhorn Museum and

Sculpture Garden, Smithsonian Institution, Washington, DC, 1997

Century of Collecting, 1882–1982, A, a guide to Manchester Art Galleries, Manchester, 1983

Companion Guide to the National Gallery of Scotland, A, National Galleries of Scotland, 2000

Companion Guide to the Scottish National Portrait Gallery, National Galleries of Scotland, 1999

Ede, Jim (introduction), *Kettle's Yard: an Illustrated Guide*, University of Cambridge, 3rd reprint, 1991

Eden Project: the Guide, 2003–4

Elliott, Patrick (compiled by), *The Concise Catalogue of the Scottish National Gallery of Modern Art*, National Galleries of Scotland, 1993

Exhibition of Works by Italian Futurist Painters, Sackville Gallery, London, 1912

Exhibition of Works from the Paul Oppé Collection, Royal Academy of Arts, 1958

Fleming-Williams, Ian (introduction), *The Barkers at Bath*, Victoria Art Gallery 1986

Francis Bacon, Louisiana Museum for Modern Art, 1998

Frederic Leighton 1830–96 (essays by Stephen Jones, Christopher Newall, Leonée Ormond, Richard Ormond, Benedict Read), Royal Academy of Arts, 1996

French Paintings and Drawings, Art Gallery and Museum Glasgow (introduction by Anne Donald), Collins in association with Glasgow Museum and Art Galleries, 1985

From London, catalogue of the Arts Council exhibition, 1995

From Reynolds to Lawrence: the First Sixty Years of the Royal Academy of Arts and its Collection, ed. Mary Anne Stevens, Royal Academy of Arts, 1992

From View to Vision: British Watercolours from Sandby to Turner in the Whitworth Art Gallery, Whitworth Art Gallery, 1993

Gallery of Modern Art, Glasgow (introduction by Julian Spalding), Scala Books, 1996

Genius of Venice, catalogue of Royal Academy exhibition 1983, Royal Academy of Arts and Weidenfeld and Nicolson

Glasgow Art Gallery and Museum, foreword by Julian Spalding, HarperCollins in association with Glasgow Museums, 1987

Golden Age of Spanish Painting, exhibition catalogue, Royal Academy of Arts, 1976

Grand Design, A, V&A exhibition catalogue, 1998

Hay, Malcolm (compiled with Jacqueline Riding), *Art in Parliament: the Permanent Collection of the House of Commons*, Jarrold Publishing, 1996

History of the Collection, A., University of East Anglia/Yale University Press, 1997

Holloway, James, *Catalogue of the Picture Gallery at Paxton House*, NGS, 2003

Hooper, Steven (introduction), *Catalogue of the Sainsbury Centre for the Visual Arts*

Hyman, Timothy and Wright, Patrick (eds.), *Stanley Spencer: Catalogue to Retrospective Exhibition at the Tate Gallery*, 2001

James McNeill Whistler, catalogue to exhibition at the Arts Council Gallery, 4 St James's Square, London, 1960

Kauffmann, C. M., *Catalogue of Paintings in the Wellington Museum*, HMSO, 1982

Kilmartin: Prehistoric and Early Historic Monuments (extracted from Royal Commission of the Ancient and Historical Monuments of Scotland, *Argyll*, vol. 6, 1999)

Lady Lever Art Gallery, Bluecoat Press, 1996

London Museum's Costume Collection (introduction by R. E. M. Wheeler), 1933

National Galleries of Scotland (introduction by Timothy Clifford), Scala Books, 1989

National Gallery: Illustrated General Catalogue, 1980

Objects with Visual Ambitions: a Report on Decorative Arts Collections in Museums and Galleries in Yorkshire and Lancashire, Yorkshire and Humberside Museums Council, 1997

Peter De Wint 1784–1849, Usher Gallery, Lincoln, 1998

Pier Gallery, Stromness, Orkney, Pier Centre Trust, 1978

Pope-Hennessy, John, assisted by Ronald Lightbown, *Catalogue of Italian Sculpture in the Victoria and Albert Museum*, 3 vols., HMSO, 1964

Raphael Cartoons, The (introduction by John Pope-Hennessy), Victoria and Albert Museum/HMSO, 1950

Rococo: Art and Design in Hogarth's England, Trefoil Books and Victoria and Albert Museum, 1984

Roger Fenton, Photographer of the 1850s, catalogue of exhibition at the Hayward Gallery, London, South Bank Board, 1968

Rowan, Alastair, *The Paxton Picture Gallery*, NGS, 2003

Royal Collection, The, The Royal Collection, 2002

Royal Commission on the Ancient and Historical Monuments of Scotland, *Argyll*: vol. 6, 1999

Sackville-West, Vita, *National Trust Guide Book to Knole*, 1947

Sekules, Veronica, *University of East Anglia Collection of Abstract and Constructivist Art, Architecture and Design*, catalogue, edited by University of East Anglia, 1994

Sensation: Young British Artists from the Saatchi Collection, Royal Academy of Arts exhibition, Thames and Hudson, 1997

Shawe-Taylor, Desmond, *Dulwich Picture Gallery: a Visitor's Guide*, Dulwich Picture Gallery, 2000

Slowe, V. A. J., catalogue to *Treasures from Abbot Hall, Kendal*, an exhibition at the Leger Galleries, Old Bond Street, London, 1989

Stainton, Lindsay, *Images of the Grand Tour: Louis Ducros 1748–1810*, catalogue of exhibition, Whitworth Art Gallery, 1985

Stanley Spencer at Burghclere, National Trust guide

Stanley Spencer: an English Vision, touring exhibition, the British Council and Yale University Press, 1997

Stonehenge and Avebury, Pitkin guide, 2002

Stourhead, National Trust guide

Swindon Collection of Twentieth Century British Art, Thamesdown Borough Council, 1991

Sylvester, D., and Whitfield, S., *René Magritte, Catalogue Raisonné*, Merrill Foundation, 1992

Tate Gallery's Collections of Modern Art, The, Tate Gallery, 1981

Tate St Ives, an Illustrated Companion, Tate Gallery Publications, 1994

The Draughtsman's Art: Master Drawings from the National Gallery of Scotland, National Galleries of Scotland, 1999

Treasures of St Cuthbert, The, Dean and Chapter of Durham Cathedral, 2000

Treasures of the British Museum, Collins, 1971

Turner 1775–1851 (essays by Martin Butlin and Andrew Wilton), Tate Gallery and Royal Academy, Tate Publications, 1974

Upton House, National Trust, 1996

Verdi, Richard, *Saved!: 100 Years of the National Arts Collections Fund*, catalogue of exhibition at Hayward Gallery, 2003–2004, Hayward Gallery, 2003

Verdi, Richard, *Art Treasures of England*, Royal Academy, 1999

Walker Art Gallery, The, Scala Books, 1994

Walking the Landscape, with Cotman and Turner in Teesdale, Durham County Council, 1996

Wallace Collection Catalogue: Pictures and Drawings, 15th edition, HMSO, 1928

World Art, from Birmingham Museums and Art Gallery, Merrell Holberton, Birmingham Museums and Art Gallery, 1999

Notes

INTRODUCTION

1. The *David*, 18 feet high, was taken from the marble original by Michelangelo in the Accademia di Belle Arte, Florence, and installed in the South Kensington Museum (now the V&A) in 1857, having been presented to Queen Victoria by the Grand Duke of Tuscany as a gesture of goodwill after he had refused to permit the export to Britain of a painting by Ghirlandaio that the National Gallery had wanted to buy.

2. The cast of Michelangelo's *Madonna and Child* (1504–8) from the Church of Notre-Dame in Bruges (hence, known as the Bruges Madonna) was secured by Henry Cole in 1872 following an agreement, the International Convention, signed by fifteen crowned princes of Europe at the 1867 Paris Exhibition. The Convention promoted exchanges between museums across Europe. John Charles Robinson, the Superintendent of the Art Collections at the museum, called the Madonna 'one of the most highly finished, complete and most beautiful works of the great master'.

3. The portico of the west front of Santiago Cathedral, the Portico de la Gloria, was cast by D. Brucciani and Co. in 1865 on the insistent advice of Robinson, who declared it 'incomparably the most important monument of sculpture and ornamental detail of its epoch', 'a masterpiece for all time'. I am indebted here to Diane Bilbey's notes (26 and 27, pp. 131–2) in the V&A's exhibition catalogue *A Grand Design* (1998).

4. I now realise that this, the taste of anchovy, appropriately goes back to the Greeks and Romans who 'relied heavily on a sauce called *garum* or *liquamen*' (Grigson, J., p. 369).

5. I was chair of Staffordshire County Council's Arts, Museums and Libraries Committee, 1981–3.

6. *Christ Washing the Disciples' Feet*, in the Shipley Art Gallery, Gateshead.

7. The Ulster Museum, Belfast.

8. *One and Another* by Antony Gormley, in the Yorkshire Sculpture Park, Wakefield.

9. *Christ on the Cross* by Salvador Dalí in the St Mungo Art Gallery, Glasgow.

10. The Manchester Museum.

11. *Spong Man*, in the Norwich Castle Museum.

12. Now renamed ICOMOS (International Council on Monuments and Sites).

13. The space that museums allocate to temporary exhibitions, and the additional pressure that this puts on the display of their permanent collections, means, inevitably, that objects mentioned in this book may not always be on display.

14. Hudson and Nicholls.

15. I am particularly indebted to Hudson's *Museums of Influence*, his *Shell Guide to Country Museums* and his *Museums for the 1980s*. He founded the European Museum of the Year Award and was museum consultant to UNESCO.

16. Hudson, *Museums of Influence*, p. viii.

17. A bezoar was a calculus or stone found in the stomach of such ruminants as goats. It was believed to be an antidote or counter-poison. The original *lapis bezoar orientale* was found in the wild goats of Persia; the *lapis bezoar occidentale* in llamas of Peru; the *German bezoar* in chamois.

18. 'Francis Bacon, Gesta Grayorum' (1594) in Browne, vol. VIII (1862), pp. 335.

19. Mundy, Peter. I am indebted to Blom, p. 55, for bringing Peter Mundy's account to my attention.

20. The catalogue that Edmund Howard, one of Sloane's assistants, made in 1742 runs to forty volumes in folio. By the time of Sloane's death in 1753 his collection comprised around 200,000 objects.

21. Sir John Soane, Royal Academy, Lecture VI.

22. A letter from Susan Burney to her sister, Fanny Burney.

23. *A Companion to the London Museum and*

Pantheirion, printed by Whittingham and Rowland, Goswell St, London (British Library, 1044.a.31 and B.677 (10)).

24. *Hansard*, Select Committee Minutes, 1836, paragraph 4795.

25. The Museum of Witchcraft in Boscastle, Cornwall.

26. The Dog Collar Museum, Leeds Castle, Maidstone, Kent ME17 1PL.

27. The Bakelite Museum, East Dulwich, London SE22 0NQ.

28. Jenkins, p. viii. He insists, correctly, that 'A church is a museum and should be proud of the fact.'

29. There are two Jewish Museums, in Finchley and Camden.

30. The National Museum of Labour History, Manchester.

31. The Passmore Edwards was a museum of the archaeology and social history of Essex.

32. Typescript account made by Edith Mary Fawkes, quoted by Joll, Butlin and Hermann, p. 109. The typescript is now in the library of the National Gallery.

33. Colin St John Wilson.

34. Browne (ed. Keynes) vol. III, p. 73.

THE SOUTH-WEST

1. Hoare.

2. This landscape also contains the unchambered Beckhampton Road Long Barrow (3250 BC); Windmill Hill (3300 BC); the Sanctuary, a temple on Overton Hill (3000–2500 BC); the double avenues of standing stones that link the Sanctuary and Beckhampton (2400 BC); and various round barrows (*c.* 1800 BC).

3. President of the Ski Club of Great Britain.

4. Keiller collected Ushabti and Egyptian antiquities, and manuscripts by William Stukeley, which he gave to the Bodleian Library, Oxford.

5. He was married four times, latterly to Gabrielle Styles, the collector and benefactor of the Potteries Museum and the Scottish National Gallery of Modern Art.

6. His library of 240 books on witchcraft and demonology were given by his widow, Gabrielle Keiller, to the National Library of Scotland in 1966.

7. Alexander Keiller letter, 12 April 1937, in the archive of the museum. *The Times*, on 6 July 1938, wrote: 'No archaeologist had ever fought a giant with the grim single-minded thoroughness with which Keiller was then wrestling with Avebury . . . Although he might not know it, [he] had attained the position of the foremost field archaeologist in Britain.'

8. In addition Keiller led excavations at Thickthorn Down, East Dorset (1933), Badshot Lees, Farnham, Surrey (1936), Lanhill, Chippenham (1936) and over two hundred surveys of archaeological sites in Scotland in the 1920s (including stone circles in Aberdeenshire and Kincardineshire).

9. From Windmill Hill, Ditch III.

10. *Stonehenge and Avebury*, p. 26.

11. Murray, p. 86.

12. Ibid. p. 88.

13. Wyatville (originally Wyatt) was apprenticed to his uncle Samuel Wyatt and in the 1790s worked in the office of James Wyatt (v. Castle Coole).

14. The description of the museum by its two founders Dallas Pratt and John Judkin.

15. On 26 July 1897, a speech to members of the Primrose League on the recent strike by railworkers.

16. Stockwell later became a trustee of the museum, in 1963. He sold only one piece to the museum, a ladder-back chair attributed to Daniel Trotter (*c.* 1785), but he and his wife gave several pieces including a Boston block-front desk (*c.* 1770).

17. Letter from Dallas Pratt to Electra Havemayer Webb, founder of the Shelburne Museum, Vermont, 1958.

18. Blomfield was the architect who redesigned Buckingham Palace, giving it its present facade.

19. Pevsner, *North West and Somerset*, p. 137.

20. Langley Moore, an expert on Byron, also designed the costumes for the film *The African Queen*.

21. Laver, *Fashions and Fashion Plates*, p. 7.

22. Each year in a Dress of the Year scheme, the museum invites a fashion expert to choose from the international collections. Their choice is then added to the collection.

23. Lemprière, pp. 381–2.

24. v. Fishbourne Roman Palace.

25. v. Victoria Art Gallery.

26. Fleming-Williams and Farington, 10 November 1807.

27. Vertue, p. 149.

28. The pose is copied, in reverse, from Van Dyck's *Lord John and Lord Bernard Stuart.*

29. His *Self-portrait* (1742) in the Royal National Hospital for Rheumatic Diseases, Bath; *Sarah Lethieviller, Lady Featherstonhaugh* (*c.*1746–9) in Uppark, Sussex; and *Lady from the Camden Family* (*c.*1745), private collection.

30. The gallery has attractive views of the city by Thomas Malton, but they fall somewhat short of the Bellotto that the city would merit.

31. Brydon was also architect of the side wings of the Guildhall, and of the Concert Room extension to the Pump Room next to the site of Gainsborough's first Bath house.

32. It was discovered in a private museum in Lichfield belonging to Dr Greene.

33. *Who Was Who*, pp. 177–8.

34. Russell-Cotes, p. 688.

35. Matthew Arnold, 'Barbarians, Philistines, Populace' in *Culture and Anarchy*, 1869.

36. Russell-Cotes had discovered that the Prince of Wales had stayed there in 1856.

37. Russell-Cotes, p. 469.

38. Pevsner, *Hampshire*, p. 127.

39. These panels were made by William Scott Morton in 1893 at his Albert Works in Edinburgh. Scott Morton also made the canvas wall coverings throughout the house, embossed to imitate tooled leather.

40. I am indebted to Shaun Garner's article 'Sir Merton Russell-Cotes and his Japanese Collection: The Importance and Impact of an Unplanned Trip to Japan in 1885' in Shelton.

41. Russell-Cotes owned several works by Moore. These were purchased by the gallery in 1936.

42. Now in the Royal Collection.

43. Sickert.

44. *Art Journal*, 1895: 342.

45. Schwanthaler was the favourite sculptor of King Ludwig I.

46. Hubert von Herkomer, in his speech at the opening of the gallery. Although born in Bavaria he was brought up first in America and then in England. He was Slade Professor of Art (1885–95), and was knighted in 1907.

47. Pevsner, *Somerset*, describes it as being 'a kind of moderate Baroque typical of English architecture about 1900'.

48. William J. Müller was a pupil of the Bristol artist James Baker Pyne, who also has works in the collection.

49. Redgrave, p. 400.

50. Théodore Géricault painted *The Raft of the Medusa* in 1819. The American Washington Allston had exhibited *Rising of a Thunderstorm* in Bristol in 1814, which seems to have influenced Danby.

51. *Diana and Callisto* (*c.*1765), one of four classical subjects painted for Henry Blundell of Ince Hall, Lancashire (v. Blundell's classical sculpture in the Walker Art Gallery).

52. Lawrence's rather crude portrait of *Portland* was commissioned by the City of Bristol for the Mansion House in Queen Square. Lawrence is shown to better effect by a lovely, unfinished oil sketch, *Head of a Young Woman* (*c.*1805).

53. Mount-Edgecumbe was a particular friend of Reynolds who, when the painter returned from Italy in 1753 and established his first London studio in St Martin's Lane, recommended sitters, mostly from the political opposition. During 1755, 125 people sat to him.

54. Another version is in the Watts Gallery, Compton.

55. The painting's subject derives from Goethe's poem, 'Der Fischer', whose final couplet is 'Half drew she him,/Half Sunk he in,/And never more was seen.' Leighton described it as 'as little naturalistic as anything could be,' Barrington, p. 62.

56. A carnivore found in Africa, related to the skunk and weasel.

57. Belzoni left Egypt in 1820. He was a celebrity throughout Europe, billed when he appeared at Sadler's Wells as 'the Patagonian Samson', dubbed also 'The Titan of Padua'.

58. Verdi, *Saved!*, p. 193.

59. Richard Verdi, in the catalogue of the 1999 *Art Treasures of England*, p. 350, believes it was formerly at Longleat. It was sold at Christie's in 1958.

60. At 322 feet in length, 3,443 tons and with a cargo capacity of 1,200 tons, 252 passengers and 120 crew, she was a third larger than any previous ship.

61. Corlett, p. 203. Corlett, a distinguished naval architect, surveyed the ship in the Falklands in 1968, prior to her recovery and return to Britain in 1970.

62. Greenhill and Allington.

63. In her prime she had six masts.

64. *Bristol Mirror*, 20 July, 1843.

65. Ibid., footnote 2.

66. Prime benefactor of another Bristol museum, the British Empire and Commonwealth Museum.

67. A new scheme designed to conserve the ship for the next 125 years and including a new museum, recreating the Victorian dockyard, new interpretation on board and creating access for the disabled is due for completion in April 2005.

68. Now in the British Museum (q.v.) and the Horniman Museum (q.v.).

69. Fox Talbot.

70. 'The Art of Photographic Drawing', a paper given by William Fox Talbot to the Royal Society on 31 January 1839.

71. Novalis: Frederick Leopold von Hardenberg.

72. Hoare.

73. Daniel.

74. Letter from Colt Hoare to Cunnington. Annable and Simpson, p. 4.

75. Annable and Simpson, items DM1629 and 1781, p. 35.

76. Hawkes, p. 49.

77. Camden.

78. Hawkes, p. 69.

79. Guide Catalogue to Wiltshire Heritage Museum, foreword by Stuart Piggott.

80. Ibid.

81. M. J. Long had worked for thirty years with her husband, Colin St John Wilson, on the new British Library. Her partner is Rolfe Kentish.

82. 'Pilchards! Whose bodies yield the fragrant oil and make the London lamps at midnight smile.' Peter Pindar, 1783. The oil from the pressing of pilchards, 18–45 litres per hogshead (called 'train oil'), was sold for lamps, paint and treating leather.

83. The canoe, in MacGregor's words, was 'built around me lying as the others had been built about me sitting'. MacGregor did a lecture tour in costume, with a primus stove and lamp, and ended his lectures by going to bed in his canoe in a nightdress and nightcap. In 1866 he founded the Royal Canoe Club and wrote, not surprisingly, 'canoodling mania has set in'.

84. Stanhope Forbes, 'A Newlyn Retrospective', *Cornish Magazine*, vol. 1, 1898, p. 53.

85. Stanhope Forbes, typescript of a paper read at the Passmore Edwards Gallery.

86. Letter from Forbes to Elizabeth Armstrong (later his wife), 31 March 1888.

87. Ibid.

88. Published by W. Clowes, London.

89. Darwin.

90. Pitt Rivers, *Principles of Classification*.

91. Canon William Greenwell, 'Ancient Gravel in the North Riding of York', *The Archaeological Journal*, 1865.

92. An Iron Age hillfort and an Anglo-Saxon cemetery at Winklebury Hill (1881–2), two Romano-British villages at Woodcuts (1884–5) and at Rotherley (1886), a Neolithic long barrow at Handley Down (1893–5) and a Roman villa at Inverne (1897).

93. Professor Christopher Hawkes and Stuart Piggott, 'Britons, Romans and Saxons', *The Archaeological Journal*, 1947.

94. *A Short Guide to the Larmer Grounds*, 1894.

95. Larmer Grounds, 'A Notice To All Visitors', 1930.

96. James Lees-Milne, *Earls of Creation*, p. 68.

97. According to the diarist John Aubrey, who attributes the 1632–3 design first to Isaac de Caus and then, following a fire in 1647–8, the rebuilding to Inigo Jones's nephew John Webb, using Jones's designs.

98. Chambers designed the arch in 1758–9 on top of the hill to the south of the house. It was moved to the forecourt by James Wyatt when he rebuilt the north front entrance in 1801.

99. Designed for the 17th Earl by David Vickery in 1971. The Cloister Garden, a modern knot garden, was designed by Xa Tollemache in 1996.

100. A biographical note on Wilson first printed in the catalogue of an exhibition of his paintings at the Ferens Art Gallery, 1936, p. 14.

101. The provenance of Holbein's portrait is discussed in an article by Elizabeth Goldring in the *Burlington Magazine*. It was commissioned by Henry VIII during brief marriage negotiations in 1538 with the widowed Duchess and was in the inventory of the 1st Earl's pictures at Barnard Castle and Wilton House in 1561.

102. *Architecture Today*, 19 June 2001.

103. *Eden Project: Guide 2003–4*, p. 11.

104. The architects of the International Terminus at Waterloo Station (1994).

105. Structural engineers on Richard Rogers's Lloyd's Building; the Millennium Dome; Norman Foster's Great Court, British Museum;

and numerous other late-20th-century buildings.

106. Michael Wigginton, 'Eden Regained', *Architectural Review*, No. 119, June 2001, p. 46. I am indebted to Michael Wigginton for all the architectural and technical detail in this entry.

107. This material, whose technology was twenty years old, had been used in the atrium of Sheppard and Robson's Chelsea and Westminster Hospital in London.

108. This and the following quotations are all from *Eden Project: Guide, 2003–4*.

109. Adams and Dart.

110. Catalogue to Barbara Hepworth Retrospective Exhibition, Whitechapel Gallery, London, 1954.

111. Adams and Dart.

112. Sir Richard Carew Pole, foreword to *Tate St Ives, an Illustrated Companion*, Tate Gallery Publications, 1993, p. 6.

113. Ibid, p. 7.

114. Sir Norman Reid, Director, 1964–80, and Sir Alan Bowness, Director 1980–88.

115. Shalev and Evans had previously designed the award-winning Crown Court at Truro.

116. In an interview with the film maker Tony Mangion quoted in Axten and Orchard, p. 111.

117. Frances Hodgkins, the New Zealand-born artist, came to St Ives in 1914 and remained here throughout the First World War, leaving in 1920. Other artists who visited include Charles Ginner, Matthew Smith and Cedric Morris.

118. This painting pieces together motifs and images seen from the window of the St Ives Studio lent to him by Denis Mitchell, the sculptor and assistant to Barbara Hepworth. Heron wrote, 'While I work away, there in London, I cannot think – with my conscious mind – of anything but my St Ives room, with its window. While I paint, I am in St Ives.'

119. *Spectator*, 2 December 2000, p. 54, quoted by Laura Gascoigne, 'Responding to Landscape', in Peter Lanyon, *Coastal Journey*, Tate St Ives.

120. Quoted by Laura Gascoigne, *Spectator*, 6 October 2001, p. 77, in a review of Bryan Wynter: a Selected Retrospective, 1948–75.

121. Made by Studio Devix of Wiesbaden, Germany, its coloured glass cut and laminated on to Pilkington's 'float' glass without the aid or intrusion of leading.

122. An Act of Parliament was necessary to break the trusts set up under Richard Colt Hoare's will.

Its preamble explains that the decline in agricultural rents from the estate's 5,000 acres was so severe that their income was not sufficient to maintain the house and land. The proceeds paid off a mortgage that Colt Hoare's executors had taken. (*Stourhead*, National Trust guide, p. 43, notes on the family by Kenneth Woodbridge.)

123. Colt Hoare went to Italy after the death of his wife Hester and stayed there until the French Revolution. He returned to England once, briefly, in 1787.

124. The east front is illustrated in Campbell.

125. Palladio, book 2.

126. Sylvio Belli, a member of the Academia Olimpica and friend of Palladio.

127. Maratta's painting is a *Self-portrait of the Artist, with the Marchese Nicolò Pallavicini led by Apollo to the Temple of Virtù* (1705). The Marchese was a great collector, remnants of whose collection were acquired by the dealer William Kent in Florence for Sir Nathaniel Curzon, 1st Baron Scarsdale (v. Kedleston).

128. v. Florence Court.

129. Lindsay Stainton, 'Ducros and the British', *Images of the Grand Tour: Louis Ducros 1748–1810*, pp. 26–30.

130. Henry Thomson was a pupil of John Opie and, later, the Keeper of the Royal Academy.

131. Apart from the torchères and the curtain cornices in the Picture Gallery, Chippendale's furniture for Stourhead is restrained and ungilded, relying on the beauty of the line rather than on ornament: see John Kenworthy-Browne, 'Notes on the Furniture of Thomas Chippendale the Younger at Stourhead', National Trust Year Book 1975–76, pp. 93–102.

132. To keep abreast of the progress of work at different points on the track Brunel employed a fast, horse-drawn carriage, dubbed 'the Flying Hearse'.

133. Appointed Deputy Director of the Arts Council in 1984.

134. Crucial to this was the strategic policy of Thamesdown Borough Council that was operating a groundbreaking 'Public Art Percentage for Art' scheme.

135. Buckland's excavations feature in the collections of the University of Oxford Museum (q.v.) and of Adam Sedgwick in the Museum of Geology named after him at Cambridge.

136. Philip Sambell Jnr was deaf and dumb at

birth but nevertheless had a successful architectural practice in Devon and Cornwall. He specialised in chapel design, lecturing, writing essays and designing many chapels in the region. He also stood for Parliament in 1835.

137. The portrait is possibly the work of James Northcote, but no authentication has been made.

THE SOUTH-EAST

1. A magnificent, snarling tiger, shot by George V in 1911.
2. The only African mammal species not in the collection are those that were already extinct (for example, the Quagga; the Bluebuck antelope) and those (such as the Bonobo pygmy chimpanzee) not discovered until the 1950s.
3. Inspired by, and named after, the German film director Wim Wenders.
4. Designed by Dalí and Edward James who collaborated with him on other designs including the *Lobster Telephone*.
5. *Open Landscape at the Edge of a Wood*, (c. 1744–5), when Gainsborough was seventeen or eighteen.
6. Along with *Walton Wood Cottage, Cumbrian Landscapes* (1928) and *Banks Head* (1925).
7. Berenson.
8. The Electors of Saxony, Frederick III ('The Wise') and John I ('The Constant').
9. Henry George Hine, J. Morgan Rendle, Ernest Sallis Benny, Dorothy Coke.
10. The Behrends commissioned Stanley Spencer's paintings in the Sandham Memoral Chapel (q.v.).
11. Both were officials: Alldridge, a civilian administrator in Sierra Leone; Green, serving with the British Army in Burma, where he mapped the north of the country in 1926. They became engrossed by, respectively, the Sande and the Kachin people.
12. Henry Holland, a relative of Lancelot 'Capability' Brown, was the designer of Carlton House, Pall Mall (1788), the Sculpture Court at Woburn (1789), the original Drury Lane Theatre for R. B. Sheridan (1791) and Albany Chambers, Piccadilly (1804).
13. Indian designs were popularised by William Hodges's *Views of India* 1786 and Thomas and

William Daniell's *Views of the Oriental Scenery*, 4 vols., 1795.
14. Pevsner, *Sussex*, p. 439.
15. Ibid,. p. 440.
16. Robert Jones worked on the Pavilion between 1815 and 1823.
17. It finished third in the Transit Class.
18. John, 2nd Baron Montagu, 1906, quoted in *Beaulieu Guide*, p. 44.
19. Benz and Daimler sold a 23 h.p., four-cylinder car to Emile Jellinek, the Consul General of the Austro-Hungarian Empire in Nice. Jellinek called it after his daughter, Mercedes, and sold Daimler's cars to his friends: Mercedes Benz was born.
20. William Tucker & Sons, West End Garage, Wedmore, north Somerset, and Reginald Sibley's garage in Southampton.
21. As was not uncommon in the early 18th century, it was built to a 'model' of a London house by a local mason, Henry Smart.
22. Henry Moore's *Madonna and Child* (1944) whose maquette is in Northampton Museum and Art Gallery (q.v.).
23. Graham Sutherland's *Christ Appearing to St Mary Magdalen* (1961) for the Chapel of St Mary Magdalen in Chichester Cathedral.
24. Hussey's first commission at Chichester was for the design of six copes by Richards.
25. M. J. Long is the architect of Falmouth Boat Museum (2001).
26. Hussey bought Moore's *A Child Suckling* (1930) and *Helmet Head* (1952) from the artist in 1947 and 1952 respectively.
27. Designed by Maxwell Fry and Raymond Myerscough-Walker.
28. This house is now the offices and library of Sculpture at Goodwood (q.v.).
29. v. the Estorick Collection.
30. Colin St John Wilson, 'A Certain Addiction', introduction to the catalogue of Pallant House Gallery Exhibition, *The Art of Drawing and Painting*, 1999/2000, p. 6.
31. Colin St John Wilson, 'Art for All: the Print from Sickert to the Sixties', introduction to catalogue of an exhibition at Pallant House, 2001/2002.
32. Ibid.
33. Long & Kentish Architects in association with Colin St John Wilson.
34. Designed by Alex Welch.
35. Designed by Daniel Weil of Pentagram.

36. 'Sculpture at Goodwood', *British Contemporary Sculptures*, February 2003, p. 22.
37. *Stanley Spencer: a Retrospective Exhibition*, Tate Gallery, 1955.
38. Spencer, p. 37.
39. Rothenstein, *Summer's Lease*, p. 133.
40. Both on loan from private owners.
41. v. Sandham Memorial Chapel.
42. Quoted in the catalogue to Retrospective Exhibition at the Tate Gallery, March 2001, edited by Timothy Hyman and Patrick Wright, p. 167.
43. Ibid.
44. Richards.
45. Quoted by MacCarthy, *Stanley Spencer*, p. 8, and from Rothenstein, *Time's Thievish Progress*, p. 51.
46. Fountain Court and the east and south fronts, designed for William and Mary.
47. Rooms for George II and his children.
48. Vasari.
49. Since then the gallery has acquired, with the help of the Heritage Lottery Fund and the V&A Purchase Grant Fund, a number of Ravilious's paintings including *The Stork at Hammersmith*.
50. Richards.
51. G. F. Watts, a letter to his friends Andrew and Mary Hitchens, who lived at Compton, 1890.
52. There is a later (1879) self-portrait here in which Watts, in profile, wears the skullcap that became his trademark.
53. The *Hall of Fame* is split between the National Portrait Gallery in London and its Welsh out-station, Bodelwyddan Castle (both q.v.).
54. Lord and Lady Holland befriended Watts when he went to Italy in 1842 with the money he had received for winning the competition for a history painting for the new Houses of Parliament. Lord Holland was British Minister at the court of Tuscany in Florence. The Hollands had Watts to stay at the Casa Feroni in the city and at the Villa Careggi in the country, providing studios for him in both. His five years in Italy gave him a lifelong love of Michelangelo and Titian, and of Dante, evident here in *Paolo and Francesca* (1872–84).
55. *Dictionary of National Biography*, p. 618.
56. Watts, vol. 2, p. 245.
57. Rossetti and the Pre-Raphaelites have been the subjects of major shows in the 1990s at the Tate, the Walker and the Royal Academy.

58. Douglas Cooper, 'The Tate Gallery', *Burlington Magazine 90*, 1948, p. 28.
59. Kenneth Grahame, *The Wind in the Willows*.
60. Hall, p. 1.
61. T. S. Eliot.
62. Grahame.
63. V. Woolf, 'Haworth. Nov 1904' in McNeillie, p. 5.
64. Vanessa Bell lived here with her lover, Duncan Grant; her husband, Clive Bell; and her children, Julian, Quentin and Angelica.
65. Roger Fry, letter to Vanessa Bell, quoted in Naylor, p. 151.
66. A portrait of the family's lurcher, Henry.
67. In the Dining Room.
68. In the Library.
69. In Duncan Grant's Studio.
70. In the Garden Room.
71. In the Garden Room.
72. In Clive Bell's Study.
73. In the Spare Bedroom.
74. In Duncan Grant's Bedroom.
75. He married the Russian ballerina Lydia Lopokova.
76. Now the home of Keynes's biographer, Robert Skidelsky.
77. Published by Penguin Books.
78. Published by Cambridge University Press.
79. Volume One is in Lambeth Palace.
80. Brenchley's motto, inscribed here on the stone doorway of the County Room, was 'VAGOR, MIROR ET ADORO' (I wander, I wonder and I adore).
81. Here is also a portrait of his sister, Margaret Hazlett.
82. v. Russell-Cotes Museum.
83. Carline, p. 185.
84. Wilenski, p. 282.
85. *Stanley Spencer at Burghclere*, p. 15.
86. MacCarthy, 'Stanley Spencer, English Visionary', in the catalogue to the British Council exhibition at the Hirshhorn Museum and Sculpture Garden, Smithsonian Institution, Washington, DC, 9 October 1997–11 January 1998, p. 30.
87. Gilbert Spencer, quoted by P. J. Kavanagh in *The Spectator*, 11 July 1998, pp. 38–40.
88. Designed and built for the 1st Earl of Leicester in his collaboration with Lord Burlington and William Kent.
89. v. Segedunum and Arbeia, Roman Fort and Museum.

90. The Claude was acquired by the 6th Duke of Somerset.

91. Acquired by the Earl of Northumberland.

92. Gore, p. 277.

93. Joll et al, p. 86 and p. 226.

94. Now in Tate Britain (q.v.).

95. Pevsner, *Sussex*, p. 305.

96. There are twenty paintings by Van Dyck at Petworth including *The 10th Earl of Northumberland and his Family* in the Square Dining Room and *Lady Dorothy Percy (or the Countess of Newport)* in the Little Dining Room.

97. Christopher Rowell, 'Turner at Petworth', *Apollo*, June 2002, p. 43.

98. Ibid., p. 46, and G. Storey, 'The Painter', quoted in Thornbury, vol II, p. 11.

99. Acquired in 1980 with help from the V&A Purchase Grant Fund and the Art Fund.

100. May had been concerned with the building of St George's Chapel at Windsor and of Henry VII's Chapel at Westminster Abbey.

101. Bentham, the brother of the social reformer Jeremy Bentham, was a man of prodigious energy and resource. For Catherine the Great he built the dockyards used by Prince Potemkin; he invented the recoil-less gun, caisson dock gates and the first steam dredger (1803).

102. Father of Isambard Kingdom Brunel, and architect of the Woolwich Tunnel.

103. The report of the Ambassador of the Holy Roman Emperor, Francis van der Delft. Other sources identify different causes: the refitting and uprating that increased her original 500 tons to 700 tons, possibly making her top heavy; the large number of seamen on board who had been masters of other ships and were not prepared to take orders with which they disagreed.

104. The crew of the *Mary Rose* is listed on the Anthony Roll as 200 mariners, 185 soldiers and 30 gunners, but some witnesses report as many as 700 people on board. The remains of 200 people were found.

105. It is embroidery, not tapestry, 70 metres long, 50 centimetres in height.

106. Grape, pp. 62–3.

107. George Beaumont, letter to William Wordsworth, 25 February 1808, Wordsworth Library, Grasmere.

108. Sackville-West, *Knole and the Sackvilles*.

109. She was a famous ballerina whose painting by Gainsborough (formerly at Knole) is in Tate Britain (q.v.). She was the Duke's mistress of twenty years and bore him a son, John Frederick Sackville.

110. Sackville-West, *National Trust Guide Book to Knole*.

111. This conference, chaired by J. R. Armstrong, reflected a growing interest in vernacular architecture across Britain. The Vernacular Architecture Group was founded in 1954, inspired by the work of Professor R. A. Cordingly at the School of Architecture in the University of Manchester.

112. Dendrochronology (tree-ring dating) has established that the trees out of which this barn was made were felled in 1536.

113. Designed by Barry Weber.

114. Simpson.

115. Letter from Kenneth Clark to G. L. Conran, 4 July 1939.

116. The other part, comprising 170 pieces, was given to York Art Gallery (q.v.), where Milner-White was Dean (1941–63).

117. Arthur Jeffress left his collection of 17th-century portraits by Mary Beale to the Manor House Museum (q.v.).

118. The University of Sheffield holds the private collection of Mr Ken Hawley, which is probably larger and more comprehensive, including industrial tools and tool-making tools. By contrast with the Salaman Collection, Mr Hawley, collecting in the 1970s–90s, recorded many of these tradesmen on film.

119. Salaman always used the terms 'trades' and 'tradesman' 'because this is what they call themselves. The term "craftsman", though often used by writers, is seldom heard in the workshop' (Salaman).

120. Salaman.

121. Ibid., p. 154, figure 232.

122. *Oxford Dictionary of National Biography*: 'Raphael Anthony Salaman' by Chris Green, director of the St Albans Museum.

123. Salaman, p. 296, figure 443. 'Pincher Jack' was Jack Millet. The pincers were made for John M. Kaye of Staincliffe, near Dewsbury, Yorkshire.

124. Ibid.

125. Rose.

126. Ibid.

127. v. Salisbury and South Wiltshire Museum and the Pitt Rivers Museum, Oxford.

128. Exhibited here, in Merston Hall.

129. Recalling Noël Coward's lines, 'Lie in the dark and listen./It's clear tonight so they're flying high.'

130. Only three of Verrio's thirteen ceilings survive, the most extravagant being in the Queen's Audience Chamber, in which Charles II's wife, Catherine of Braganza, is drawn in a chariot by a swan. There are cornices by Gibbons in the King's Dressing Room and carving round the alcoves and the chimney piece of the King's Dining Room.

131. The Rembrandt is not currently hanging. It has been moved to the Palace of Holyroodhouse (q.v.).

132. The St Leger is often replaced in the Bedroom by a Canaletto Venetian view.

133. Such drawings as Leonardo's *A Political Allegory* (*c.*1495) had been bought in Spain for Thomas Howard, Earl of Arundel, and were acquired later (by 1690) by Charles II.

134. The Royal Collection contains around 40,000 drawings and watercolours and 150,000 prints, housed here in the Royal Library.

135. Holroyd, p. 275.

136. Lawrence's portraits are in two sizes: full-lengths for the sovereigns and the Pope (a canny likeness of the subtle, political Pope Pius VII), half-lengths for the minor players. This elaborate conceit had been initiated after the battle of Leipzig and Napoleon's subsequent abdication and had to be abandoned when he escaped from Elba. Lawrence did not complete several of them until the early 1820s, and *Charles X of France* and the *Duke of Angoulême* not until 1825.

EAST ANGLIA

1. Lees-Milne, *National Trust Guide: Buildings,* p. 99.

2. Belmont at Faversham in Kent has a good collection of over three hundred pieces including clocks by Joseph Knibb, George Graham and Thomas Tompion. The Wallace Collection (q.v.) has fine French 18th century clocks, with examples by Andre-Charles Boulle.

3. George Graham was born in Cumberland and apprenticed to a London watchmaker. After his apprenticeship he went into partnership with Thomas Tompion, married his niece and eventually succeeded to Tompion's business (left to him

in Tompion's will). As well as perfecting the deadbeat escapement (1315) he developed an 'equation of time' device (1721) which calculated the difference between solar time and mean time , i.e. between sunset and sunrise each day. In an age in which most people kept track of time by means of sundials, this was an important innovation.

4. *Cambridge University Reporter,* 29 May 1883.

5. Ibid.

6. *Cambridge University Reporter,* 27 November 1883.

7. Cook had given these to his patron, the Earl of Sandwich, who subsequently gave them to his college, Trinity.

8. Tietze, pp. 11–13.

9. J. C. Bach gave Lord Fitzwilliam a copy of his Opus 5 (sonatas for the keyboard).

10. The *Fitzwilliam Virginal Book* contains the most important contemporary collection of 16th and 17th-century keyboard music in existence (over 300 works by some thirty composers). It was given to Fitzwilliam by the Edinburgh bookseller Robert Bremner.

11. Charles Robert Cockerell, designer of the Ashmolean Museum, Oxford; St George's Hall, Liverpool; Bowood House, Wiltshire; the Cockerell Library, Cambridge University. See Watkin.

12. Pevsner, *Cambridgeshire*, pp. 210–11.

13. Told to his biographer, Wilfred Blunt.

14. Director of the Fitzwilliam Museum, 1893–1908, James was Provost of Eton College and of King's College, and the author of ghost stories.

15. McClean's manuscripts almost doubled the existing collection. The links forged with the museum led one of his sons to give more than 10,000 Greek coins and another to pay for the building of the Manuscript Room and the Coin Room. A descendant, Philip McClean, gave a group of paintings in 1996.

16. Elliott, p. 190.

17. Elliott, p. 187.

18. Cima da Conegliano. This was painted for the church of Sta Maria dei Crociferi, Venice.

19. The Marlay Gallery opened in 1924.

20. Carl Winter, Director, 1946–66.

21. Michael Jaffe, Director 1973 to 1990.

22. Gayer-Anderson's Islamic Collection is now in the Beitel-Kretliya Museum.

23. These casts had been collected by Sir George Wombwell, whose widow offered to sell them

to the university. Kirkpatrick bought them and presented them to the Fitzwilliam Museum.

24. Colvin's Slade Lecture of 1873 was entitled 'On the Study of Greek Art'. In 1875 he applied to the Syndics of the Fitzwilliam for 'a sum not exceeding £100' for the purchase of 'illustrations', presumably casts, for that year's Slade lectures. The request was refused, but the next year the Syndics approved the purchase of the *Demeter of Cnidos* when Colvin's lectures were on the theme of 'Demeter and Persephone' (see Mary Beard, 'Casts and Cast-offs: the Origins of the Museum of Archeology', *The Proceedings of the Cambridge Philological Society*, 1993–4).

25. Beard, op. cit. pp. 2–5.

26. Designed by the Casson Conder Partnership.

27. Honour and Fleming, p. 149.

28. Beard, op. cit. p. 22.

29. Darwin was also taught principles of geology by Hope and Jameson while at Edinburgh University.

30. Other early collections include Sir Andrew Balfour's in Edinburgh, and those of Robert Woodrow of Eastwood, and John Beaumont and William Cole of Bristol.

31. Among those from whom Woodward obtained specimens were Sir Thomas Browne, Sir Isaac Newton, John Locke, Sir Christopher Wren and John Flamsteed and Sir Edmund Halley, successive Astronomers Royal (v. the Royal Observatory), (David Price, 'John Woodward and a Surviving British Geological Collection from the Early Eighteenth Century', *Journal of the History of Collections*, 1, Oxford University Press, 1989, p. 91).

32. Price, op. cit. p. 79.

33. Whewell was later appointed Master of Trinity College, Cambridge. He coined the words 'Scientist', 'Electron', 'Anode' and 'Cathode'. Among his pupils was Alfred, Lord Tennyson.

34. Most of the specimens on display entered the collection after Whewell's spell in the chair – in fact probably after his death. There were mineral specimens available to Sedgwick but they were not part of his Woodwardian Museum. When Miller succeeded Whewell the collection would probably have gone 'over the wall' from Trinity to St John's, into the museum Miller established on the New Museums Site.

35. The Miller Indices were originally devised by Whewell.

36. Designers Will Daykin and Clare Gresswell.

37. Babbage was professor of mathematics here and developer of the calculators that became the computer.

38. Aubrey, p. xxxiii.

39. 'After he had tried to sell a painting for a year or so he would tell me I could have it for the price of the canvas and frame, usually one to three pounds', (Ede, *Introduction to Kettle's Yard*).

40. In 1970 an extension was designed by Sir Leslie Martin and David Owers.

41. Ede broadcast on the BBC Third Programme on 28 November 1931, describing his ideal living space: 'First I would empty it . . . having nothing there but the bare floor and the bare walls.'

42. He was describing how he designed his house in Tangiers (*Kettle's Yard and its Artists, an anthology*, 1995, p. 8).

43. This was found on a beach, not by Ede but by his grandson. Although placed in different rooms it relates to the carved *Radar II* by Ovidiu Maiteo.

44. Henri Gaudier and Sophie Brzeska never married; she was twenty years older than he was. 'I am too old for you really, but I will be a mother to you, if you agree,' she told him. Their relationship was passionate and devoted, but chaste. To mark his love for her he added her name to his, becoming Gaudier-Brzeska.

45. 19 sculptures, 13 oils and pastels and 1,595 drawings, for which Ede paid the Treasury Solicitor £60, on the valuation of the art critic R. H. Wilenski. Ede subsequently gave many of these to the Musée d'Orleans, the Musée d'Art Moderne in Paris, the University of Essex and the Tate Gallery.

46. With the notable exception of Douglas Cooper.

47. Ede, *A Way of Life*, p. 50.

48. Camulodunum is the only place in Britain where it is certain that Samian pottery was produced.

49. The figures are named: Valentinus, Secundus, Memnon, Marius. The vase was found in 1848.

50. The Grubbe Collection, found on Dunwich beach, late 19th/early 20th century. Donated to Southwold Museum in 1937.

51. Now in the Anglo-Saxon collection of the British Museum.

52. Marine archaeological excavations took place in 1971, 1979, 1981 and 1983.

53. His father, also Sir George, began the building of Downing Street in the mid 17th century. He founded Downing College, Cambridge, in 1717.
54. Gardner.
55. Mrs D. Jay.
56. *Dunwich by the Stormy Sea*, the Trustees of Dunwich Museum, 1988.
57. Created Lord Foster in 1999.
58. The Concorde here is the pre-production prototype for this Franco-British project.
59. The case for Gibbs has been persuasively made by John Harris in 'James Gibbs, Eminence Grise at Houghton', *Georgian Group Annual Symposium*, 1988, pp. 5–9, and in his article in *Country Life*, 2 March 1989, pp. 92–4, 'Who Designed Houghton?' The arguments are summarised in Pevsner, *Norfolk 2*, pp. 428–9.
60. Ripley later succeeded Grinling Gibbons as Master Carpenter to the Crown.
61. Most of his collection was sold to the British Museum (q.v.) in 1951.
62. The collection of Margaret Fountaine and her companion Khalil Neimry, who bred and collected 22,000 butterflies between 1892 and 1940.
63. The British Museum has an earlier version of *Greta Bridge* (1807).
64. Until the St Ives School, 1930–80 (v. Tate St Ives and the Pier Art Centre).
65. Sir Robert Sainsbury, 'My Criterion for Acquiring – my Purpose in Disposing', *Architectural Review*, vol. CLXIV, number 982, December 1978, p. 347.
66. Marina Vaizey (1989) in the introduction to the catalogue of the Sainsbury Centre for the Visual Arts, *A History of the Collection*, p. xxvii.
67. Alistair Grieve, 'A Retrospective View of the University Art Collection', in Sekules, p. 7.
68. The Anderson Collection, formed by Colin Anderson, a co-trustee with Sir Robert Sainsbury of the Tate Gallery.
69. Norman Foster, 'Architects' Note', *Architectural Review*, vol. CLXIV, number 982, December 1978, p. 353.
70. Ibid.
71. Pevsner, *Norfolk 1*, p. 353.
72. Spalding, F., p. 65.
73. Sekules, p. X/iii.
74. The limit of £1,000 per year lasted from 1946 to 1952. They raised it to £2,000 in 1953–6 and to £3,000 in 1957.
75. Sir Robert Sainsbury, op. cit. p. 347.

76. Sekules, p. X/ix.
77. This was the Sainsburys' last major Giacometti acquisition, in 1974. The model and sitter was Isabel Rawsthorne.
78. Fry, *Last Lectures*, p. 76.
79. Honour and Fleming, p. 832, Moore writing in 1934.
80. *Kunstlerschriften I: Manifeste Manifeste 1905–1933*, Dresden, 1964, p. 48, quoted by Gombrich, p. 224.
81. A left tibia found in 1975 by John J. Reydon (750,000 years old); part of the base of a skull (1.5 million years old) found in 1931 by Mrs Ida Gittens.
82. The Grubbe Collection, found on Dunwich beach in the late 19th/early 20th century. Donated in 1937.
83. Reynolds, 14th Discourse.
84. If watercolours were included, the list would include Sandby and Cozens.
85. Pevsner, *Suffolk*, p. 454.
86. *Mr and Mrs Robert Andrews* (c. 1748–50) in the National Gallery; *Heneage Lloyd and his Sister, Lucy* (c. 1750–2), in the Fitzwilliam Museum; and *John Pamplin* (c. 1753–5) in the National Gallery (all q.v.).
87. The works 'on which Gainsborough's fame chiefly rests', in the flawed opinion of William Hazlitt, 1814.
88. He developed these transparencies from the Eidophusikon of his friend, de Loutherbourg. Placed in a box with a lighted candle behind them they cast diffused shadows over a scene. They are now in the Victoria and Albert Museum (q.v.).
89. Other studies are in the Cecil Higgins Art Gallery (q.v.) and the Huntington Library and Art Collections, San Marino, California.
90. Gainsborough made this from memory, three years after his father's death.
91. Hayes.
92. An enlarged version of Burlington's Gallery at Chiswick House.
93. Coke's agent, Matthew Brettingham the Younger, brought home eleven statues, eight busts and a relief in 1754.
94. The fluted columns were copied from Antoine Desgodetz's plates of the Temple of Fortuna Vivilis in *Les Edifices Antiques de Rome* (published 1682); see Pevsner, *Norfolk 1*, p. 415.
95. Lees-Milne, *Earls of Creation*, p. 255.

96. The original was destroyed and this is the only copy, a *tour de force* of male anatomy.

97. Bede.

98. He was originally identified by the great Anglo-Saxon scholar Hector Munro Chadwick of Clare College, Cambridge, who drove post-haste at 20 mph from his home in Herefordshire to examine the find.

99. Bede, II, p. 5.

100. The Sutton Hoo ship is the earliest, most complete and largest Anglo-Saxon ship yet found. Only the largest Viking ships, made some 300 years later, were larger.

101. The 1939 excavation found a purse containing thirty-seven coins, one from each of the Frankish mints. It is not clear what their significance was.

102. *c.* AD 698.

103. Described by an archaeological colleague, Richard Dumbreck, in the Sutton Hoo Archive, X2/3.4.

104. Carver, p. 5.

105. They were assisted by John Ward Perkins, later Director of the British School at Rome, and Grahame Clark, later Disney Professor of Archaeology at Cambridge University.

106. R. L. S. Bruce-Mitford was author of the definitive *Sutton Hoo Ship Burial*, 3 vols., British Museum Press, 1975, 1978 and 1983.

107. Martin Carver, Professor of Archaeology at York University and Director of Research at Sutton Hoo since 1983. The report of his excavations will be published by the British Museum in 2004.

EAST MIDLANDS

1. Daniel Defoe and the travel writer Celia Fiennes visited Chatsworth in 1702, before and after the Great Fountain was built.

2. Thomas Archer designed the north facade.

3. The Dome Room that links the 1st Duke's house to the 6th Duke's north wing has columns of palest pavonazza and giallastro and two vases of occhio di pavone. In his new Great Dining Room are a pair of vases of Blue John, mined locally.

4. Samuel Watson came to Chatsworth in 1689 and worked here, in stone and wood, until his death in 1715.

5. Carved from one piece of stone quarried on nearby Sheldon Moor.

6. Allegorical figures representing Faith and Justice.

7. Pevsner, *Derbyshire*, p. 134.

8. This is the traditional attribution but it is likely that much of the carving throughout the house (notably in the State Dining Room and Drawing Room) was done by Lobb, Young & Davis of London, and by Samuel Watson, possibly to Gibbons's designs.

9. Codicil to Cecil Higgins's will, Clause 5 (I) (e).

10. Graham Reynolds was the leading art historian of his day on engraving (Thomas Bewick) and watercolours. He gave the collection a superb start, acquiring in 1952 (its first year) works by Alexander Cozens, J. R. Cozens, Peter De Wint, Edward Dayes, David Cox, Thomas Girtin, Thomas Gainsborough and J. M. W. Turner. In 1954 he acquired for the gallery Turner's *The Great Falls of Reichenbach*.

11. Codicil to Cecil Higgins's will, Clause 5 (1) (c).

12. Only about twenty-five pieces bearing Ravenscroft's seal survive.

13. Ravenscroft was a wealthy merchant trading with Venice who set up a glass factory in London, in the Savoy area, to make glass with a high lead oxide content that was heavy, slow-cooling and impossible to decorate with fine pulled threads, but which could be engraved. His patent ran from 1674 to 1681.

14. Augustus II stands on a base, beside a plinth, all of whose panels are painted with architectural views by J. G. Herold, Meissen's chief decorator.

15. Augustus the Strong, so called because he was said to have fathered 350 children (Augustus II being the only one who was legitimate), established the first Meissen factory in 1710, having effectively kept Johann Freidrich Böttger imprisoned while he conducted the experiments that rediscovered the secret of hard-paste porcelain. Augustus was so obsessed by porcelain that in 1717 he exchanged 600 soldiers from his army for 127 pieces of Chinese porcelain owned by King Frederick William of Prussia. Adams, p. 9.

16. Modelled by Chelsea's chief modeller, Joseph Willems.

17. A curiosity of a later refurbishment in 1970 is the installation of a fishpond, on the first floor; this is the only art gallery in the country to have this amenity. The plashing of its fountain is

refreshing; the problems of condensation less so.

18. Although the pieces that Burges and William Morris exhibited at the 1862 International Exhibition met with acclaim, Burges's painted furniture was never a commercial success, except with his patron the 3rd Marquis of Bute, whose acquisitions can be seen at Cardiff Castle (q.v.) and Castell Coch.

19. The V&A has a near-identical decanter, also made in 1865, designed by Burges, made by Josiah Mendelson for James Nicholson (see *A Grand Design*, p. 332).

20. In an article in *The Gentleman's Magazine* (September 1862, p. 224) entitled 'The Japanese Court in the International Exhibition', Burges wrote: 'I hope I have said enough to show the student of our reviving arts of the thirteenth century that . . . these hitherto unknown barbarians appear not only to know all that the Middle Ages knew, but in some respects are beyond them and us as well.'

21. The V&A (q.v.) has good examples of his work, as does Cardiff Castle (q.v.) and Castell Coch.

22. The watercolour was owned by William Beckford, who sold it in 1805. This is the description in the catalogue of the Beckford sale.

23. This was probably the first 'Samuel Palmer' that Keating forged. Keating's deception was exposed by Geraldine Norman in *The Times* (16 July and 10 August 1976).

24. With Martin Butlin and Luke Hermann, Evelyn Joll wrote *The Oxford Companion to J. M. W. Turner*.

25. See Eric Shanes, 'Turner and the Creation of his First Rate in A Few Hours', *Apollo*, March 2001, pp. 13–15.

26. Pevsner, *Staffordshire*.

27. v. Tate Britain, the National Gallery, the Fitzwilliam, Temple Newsam and the Walker Art Gallery.

28. Myrone.

29. Scarsdale sent the dealer William Kent to Italy in 1758–9 to acquire pictures for him. Several came from the famous Roman collection of the Marchese Nicolò Pallavicini (v. Stourhead) which had passed to the Marchesi Arnaldi in Florence.

30. On his return to Britain Curzon was appointed Foreign Secretary (1919–24) and rented Montacute House, where he lived with the novelist Mrs Elinor Glyn, of whom it was asked

'Would you like to sin/with Elinor Glyn/on a tiger skin?/Or would you prefer/to err with her/on some other fur?' He was made Marquis in 1921.

31. This may well have been inspired by James Paine's bridge at Chatsworth (1762). Indeed Curzon, and Adam, were striving to create a house and park that would compete with Chatsworth.

32. A Gothic temple (1759–60), the North Lodge, a bathhouse on the Middle Lake (1759–61), an orangery, the designs for the Stables (1767–9), (executed by Samuel Wyatt), the three-arched Bridge, and a fishing-room-cum-cold-bath-and-boathouse (*c.*1770–2) in which the Curzons could fish from the arched window on the storey above the Bathhouse and Boathouse. Roundels of putti riding sea monsters, carved by George Moneypenny, adorn the exterior, while fine still lifes of fish in landscape settings attributed to Arthur Devis, and a fishing scene in the manner of Zuccarelli, decorate the interior. Sadly the Adam/Rose plasterwork ceiling had to be taken down in 1909.

33. Pevsner, *Derbyshire*, p.255. 5a – medallions, of *Vintage*, *Pasturage*, *Ploughing* and *Bear Hunting* by William Collins (1769); lead statuary by John Cheere. See Paine's engraving, *Works*, vol. ii, 1783.

34. Paintings by Zucchi and Zuccarelli are only in the Dining Room.

35. The alabaster for the columns was quarried on the estate of Sir Nathaniel's brother, Assheton, 1st Viscount Curzon, at Ratcliffe-on-Soar. Amazingly the fluting was carried out *in situ* after the columns had been installed. The alabaster for the capitals was from Chaddesdon, Derby.

36. There is no firm evidence that these are by Adam – they could be by Adam, or Adam's office, or by Richardson.

37. As Adam explains in his book *Ruins of Spalato* (1764).

38. The Wedgwood Museum at Barlaston closed in 1999 and has yet to reopen. Royal Doulton, the owners of Minton, sold most of its collection piecemeal in 2002. Some important pieces were bought by the Potteries Museum (q.v.).

39. Obtained by mixing ground glass and clay, the glass giving translucency and sharpness, the clay plasticity.

40. By 1890 50 per cent of the formula was made up of bone.

41. I am indebted to Murdoch and Twitchett, p. 62, for this and for much in this entry (John

Twitchett was former curator of the Royal Crown Derby Museum).

42. Designed by Trevor Dannatt, 1960–2.

43. Pevsner, *Leicestershire*, p. 227.

44. Having been discovered in 1830, it was built over and incorporated into a chamber of the railway viaduct in the 1890s and re-excavated in 1977.

45. The Norfolk Street Roman Villa was in the countryside, half a mile outside Roman Leicester's west gate.

46. N. Davey and R. Ling, 'Wall Painting in Roman Britain', Society of Promotion of Roman Studies, *Britannia*, Monogr. Series 3, 1982.

47. E. E. Lowe, 'Romance in the Museum', presidential address to the Museums Association Annual Conference, 1922, held in Leicester.

48. Federico Zeri, 'Investigations into the Early Period of Lorenzo Monaco-II', *Burlington Magazine*, CVII, 742, 1965, pp. 3–11.

49. Purchased from Hans Hess's mother, Mrs T. Hess.

50. Ward Usher, preface. The book contains eighty illustrations in colour, reproduced from the author's own watercolours.

51. £59,125. 1s. 4d.

52. Ward Usher.

53. Nikolaus Pevsner and John Harris, *Lincolnshire*, p. 152.

54. Given to the gallery in 1930.

55. v. the Royal Observatory. Harrison lived and worked at Barrow, near Lincoln. Sutton was called on to repair a Harrison wooden clock and was inspired to make two of his own, both now in the Usher Gallery, Lincoln.

56. Found in 1851 near the foundations of the Scartho windmill, near Grimsby; eventually acquired by Mr L. W. Pye and bequeathed by him in 1954.

57. Found at 82/4, Bargate, Grimsby, in 1954.

58. For *Picturesque Views of England and Wales* (1825–38).

59. *Peter De Wint*, introduction by Martin Hardie, The Studio Ltd, 1929, p. 5. His pigments were: Indian red, purple lake, yellow ochre, gamboges, brown, pink, burnt sienna, Prussian blue and indigo.

60. A larger version of this painting is in the National Gallery of Scotland and a sepia drawing in the Fitzwilliam Museum (both q.v.).

61. In the mid 19th century Melton had stabling for 500 horses.

62. *Sporting Art in Britain*, catalogue of a loan exhibition by the British Sporting Art Trust at Christie's, 2003, p. 26.

63. Born in Antwerp, Jan Siberechts came to England between 1672 and 1674 at the invitation of the 2nd Duke of Buckingham. He specialised in landscapes and portraits of country houses.

64. For the medieval castle, see Drage. For the 17th-century ducal palace, see T. Foulds, '"This Greate House, so lately begun, and all of Freestone": William Cavendish's Italianate Palazzo called Nottingham Castle', *Transactions of the Thoroton Society 106*, 2002, pp. 81–102, and T. Foulds, '"The Warmest I have": Henry, second Duke of Newcastle and Nottingham Castle', in J. Beckett (ed.), *Nottinghamshire Past*, 2003, pp. 99–115.

65. Pamela Wood, 'A Passion for "Old Wedgwood": the Felix Joseph Collection of Wedgwood', *Ars Ceramica*, 1995, Number 12.

66. Ibid. Pamela Wood notes that the dealer Frederick Rathbone lists 'thirty well known Wedgwood collections' in the 19th century. These collectors included W. E. Gladstone and Sir Richard Tangye, whose gift helped to found the Birmingham Art Gallery and Museum.

67. It bears the mark 'WEDGWOOD & BENTLEY'.

68. Numbered '29' just inside the lip with a manganese pencil.

69. See Prior and Gardiner, and A. Gardiner, 'Alabaster Tombs of the Gothic Period', *Architectural Journal*, lxi (1904) and lxxx (1923).

70. A. Cozens (1717–86).

71. Apart from the British Museum and the V&A, the Royal Collection has fine Sandbys. His elder brother, Thomas Sandby, was Deputy Ranger of Windsor Great Park, and Paul Sandby was commissioned by the King to do a series of views of Windsor Castle and the Great Park. There are watercolours by Thomas Sandby in Nottingham's collection.

72. Beckett, p. 140; quoted in Patrick Noon's essay 'Collecting Bonington' in Cambridge.

73. Given in 1901 by S. W. Oscroft.

74. Rothenstein, *Modern English Painters*, p. 153.

75. Duboisson, p. 102.

76. This was the last public hanging, public execution being made illegal in 1868. Those hanged were buried beneath the Exercise Yard in unconsecrated ground.

77. The music to which they are commonly sung

is, in each case, of a later date. 'Amazing Grace' is set to an American folk tune, imported to the American colonies and reimported to Britain in the 18th century. The music of 'Glorious Things of Thee are Spoken', 'Austria', was written by Frans Josef Haydn for the birthday of the Habsburg Emperor, Francis II, in 1797 and first used as a hymn tune in England in 1805. Alexander Robert Reinagle's tune used for 'How Sweet the Name of Jesus Sounds' was published first in 1830 and Charles Hutchenson's tune 'Caithness' was not used for 'O for a Closer Walk with God' until the 1840s.

78. *Dictionary of National Biography*, p. 1320.

79. He was painted by Lawrence and Lemuel Abbott and twice by Romney, one of whose paintings is in the National Portrait Gallery (q.v.).

80. Hayley.

81. 4 June 1791.

82. Both translations sold well. Cowper received £1,000 for the first edition from his publisher, Joseph Johnson, who also published Mary Wollstonecraft.

83. *Dictionary of National Biography*, p. 397.

84. Letter of John Constable to Miss Bicknel, 15 June 1812 (Leslie, *Life of Constable*). Leslie records that Constable was reading Southey's life 'little more than an hour before his death'.

85. Robert Southey's *Life of Cowper*, Lord David Cecil's *The Stricken Deer* and the Revd William Bull's *Life of John Newton*.

86. This site is now part of the National Museum and Gallery of Wales (q.v.).

87. See his work at Salisbury and South Wiltshire Museum.

88. The British Museum (q.v.) has portrait busts of two men (*c.* 125–135) from Lullingstone.

89. Davey was a fine engineer who later designed the acoustic reflector system inside the dome of the Royal Albert Hall.

90. Pevsner, *Derbyshire*, p. 76.

91. His son Richard predeceased his father in 1921. The estate eventually passed to Sir Vauncey's grandson Charles Jenney, who changed his name to Harpur-Crewe, as did his brother Henry Harpur-Crewe. Sir Henry Harpur, 7th Baronet, changed his name to Crewe in 1808 in a vain attempt to revive the dormant barony of Crewe of Steane. His grandson, Sir John, 9th Baronet, re-incorporated Harpur, as did his son, Sir Vauncey, 10th Baronet.

92. Until the death of Charles Harpur-Crewe in 1981, admittance to the house was rigorously barred to all strangers.

WEST MIDLANDS

1. Marcus Samuel and his brother Samuel Samuel adopted a shell as their trademark as a mark of respect to their father, Marcus Samuel the Elder, who made boxes decorated with exotic shells brought back from the East by sailors. The scallop shell was not adopted until May 1904. See Cox.

2. Walter Samuel built this collection with the Hon. Henry Marsham, a son of Lord Romney, who also had business interests in the Far East. The collection comprised of inro, netsuke, swords, armour and lacquerware from the Edo period (*c.* 1600–1868).

3. An original, 15th-century set of seven, formerly at Hardwick Hall, is now in the V&A. The other two Upton tapestries are elsewhere in the house.

4. These are not the only versions: variants of *Haymakers* and *Reapers*, painted in 1785, are in Tate Britain (q.v.) and an earlier version of *Labourers*, painted on Wedgwood's ceramic plaques (1767), partially repainted, is in the Philadelphia Museum of Art. Oval versions of *Labourers* (1781) and *Reapers* (1795) are also in the Paul Mellon Collection in the Yale Center for British Art, New Haven. An oval version of *Haymakers* (1795), along with a variant (1794), are in the Lady Lever Art Gallery (q.v.).

5. His grandson-in-law, Robert Waley-Cohen, in 'The Bearsteds at Upton' *Upton House*, National Trust, 1996, p. 10.

6. Van der Weyden, like his master Robert Campin, painted the refinement of hands, their fingers slivers of cool ivory: Campin's *Salting Madonna* (National Gallery); van der Weyden's *Columba Triptych* (Alte Pinakothek, Munich) and *Descent from the Cross* (Prado, Madrid).

7. See the related, but much more ambitious, *Purification of the Virgin*, in the Metropolitan Museum of Modern Art, New York.

8. Hogarth. The two other paintings, *Noon* and *Evening*, are in the Ancaster Collection at Grimsthorpe Castle.

9. This 800-piece service, one of the most splendid produced at Sèvres, is in the Hermitage Museum, St Petersburg. In 1837 160 pieces were looted following a fire in the palace. They were bought by Lord Lowther and eventually some were returned to St Petersburg.

10. The Burrell Collection, the Cecil Higgins Art Gallery, and the Ascott Collection (all q.v.).

11. Rothschild properties extend across Bedfordshire and Buckinghamshire: Baron Meyer de Rothschild's Mentmore Estate, of which Ascott was originally part; Waddesdon Manor, built by Baron Ferdinand de Rothschild (1877); and Tring Manor which houses the Rothschild Zoological Museum.

12. The collection was given to the National Trust by Mr and Mrs Anthony de Rothschild in 1950. The house is open to the public for more than a hundred days a year.

13. Pevsner, *Buckinghamshire*, p. 51.

14. Until recently this was considered to be by Bronzino.

15. This painting has attracted a variety of attributions. In the Milan collection of Achillito Chiesa it was attributed to Alvise Vivarini.

16. This painting was acquired in the late 1780s by Count Josef Fries, a friend of Goethe, who wrote that the count had paid 600 zecchini for it and that its sale was much regretted by Angelica Kauffmann. It was brought to England by Lord Stewart, the British Ambassador in Vienna (1814–22), and acquired by Baron Lionel de Rothschild in 1870.

17. Buckinghamshire is Rothschild country. Baron Mayer de Rothschild, who sold Ascott to Leopold de Rothschild, bought Mentmore in 1852–4; Lionel Walter, 2nd Lord Rothschild, moved to Tring Park in 1872. Baron Ferdinand acquired the land for Waddesdon c. 1875–80; Alice de Rothschild, Eyethrope in 1883, and Baron Alfred, Halton in 1884.

18. Baumhauer was 'ébéniste privilégé du Roi', thanks to the patronage of the Duc d'Aumont.

19. His work at Ascott is restrained when compared to the 'very French fountain with nudes and a huge cockleshell' that he made for Lord Astor at Cliveden (Pevsner, *Buckinghamshire*, p. 99).

20. A catalogue of the collections, with detailed notes on the paintings by F. St John Gore, was published in 1963 and revised in 1978. There is a full, scholarly catalogue of the Chinese porcelain by Regina Krahl and a new catalogue of the paintings is in preparation.

21. Bodkin, pp. 81 and 82.

22. Holmes.

23. Bodkin, p. 82.

24. From the note he sent to William Wiltshire when giving him *The Harvest Wagon* in 1774, to thank him for his gift to Gainsborough of his grey horse (shown in the painting).

25. Bodkin, p. 78.

26. Ibid.

27. One of the four marble busts made from this is at Temple Newsam (q.v.), Leeds, dated 1738.

28. The other is his *Neapolitan Coast with Vesuvius in Eruption* (1820), purchased by the Fitzwilliam Museum (q.v.) in 1986.

29. Thomas Collier Barnes, secretary of the Flint Glass Makers' Friendly Society, whose gift of glass prompted the museum's glass collection.

30. Richard (later Sir Richard) Tangye, managing director of R. & T. Tangye Co. Ltd.

31. Martin Ellis, 'Introduction: World Art', from *Birmingham Museums and Art Gallery*, p. 16.

32. Feeney gave from his collection of Asian and Far Eastern metalwork. In 1905 he bequeathed £50,000, for the building of a new art gallery.

33. Osler gave £3,000 as an endowment for the purchase of works of art.

34. Ellis, op. cit., p. 14.

35. The executor of Holliday's will was Sidney Cockerell, the then Director of the Fitzwilliam Museum.

36. The loan includes paintings by Francesco Albani, Salvator Rosa and Pier Francesco Mola and Guido Reni's *A Lady with a Lazuli Bowl*.

37. Also designed by H. Yeoville Thomason for Birmingham Water Department, now converted by Associate Architects. These were originally designed for the Birmingham Gas Department, but taken over by the Water Department when the gas offices moved across the road to the new Council House Extension (housing the new Feeney Art Galleries at second-floor level) when it was built in 1911–12.

38. I am indebted to Jenny Uglow's book for her research into the Lunar Society's workings and its members. Other members included the Irish inventor Richard Lovell Edgeworth, and Thomas Day, both followers of Rousseau; James Keir; and the Derby clockmaker John Whitehurst.

39. The architectural practice was Herbert, Son and Sawday.

40. Pevsner, *Warwickshire*, p. 265. 'Brown stone & brick. Of varied grouping.'

41. Introduced into Coventry in 1820.

42. Thompson, E. P., p. 287.

43. v. Cecil Higgins Art Gallery for examples of Burges's woodwork.

44. The committee's acquisition policy was 'Social History, Life and Leisure'.

45. Sylvester, *About Modern Art*, p. 295, a quotation from Sylvester's 1995 text 'Against the Odds', in the catalogue of an exhibition, co-curated by Sylvester and Andrea Rose, of *Leon Kossoff: Recent Paintings 1987–94*, Venice Biennale 1995.

46. Sylvester, *About Modern Art*, p. 296. A phrase found among his papers.

47. Ibid. Leon Kossoff is describing Bomberg's style of teaching to the art critic Richard Cork.

48. Rent is still paid annually to Magdalen College.

49. The thorn apple has powerful hallucinogenic properties. In the event of there having been a 'Garden of Eden' and in the event of there having been an 'Apple', this (according to Dr Ronald K. Siegel's book *Intoxication*) may well have been it.

50. The 1648 bed originated in 1992 when the late Henry Scholick bequeathed his copy of the catalogue to the garden.

51. Brought back from the New World by John Tradescant the Elder.

52. The post of superintendent was brought to an end in October 2003 and the responsibilities divided between a director and a curator.

53. The inaugural meeting of the Galpin Society was on 17 May 1947 in Trinity College of Music. Among the founders were Eric Halfpenny, Edgar Hunt and Thurston Dart (see Hélène La Rue, 'Anthony Cuthbert Baines (1912–1997)', *Proceedings of the British Academy*, I. 115, p. 63.

54. The *Galpin Society Journal*, edited by Anthony Baines for twenty-one years, was the first ever dedicated to musical instruments.

55. Baines was a bassoonist and contrabassoonist. He had been assistant conductor of the London Philharmonic Orchestra in 1949 and had been a teacher and writer (see his *Woodwind Instruments and their History*, 1957, *European and American Musical Instruments*, 1967, and *The Oxford Companion to Musical Instruments*, 1992).

56. Kemp's pipe and tabor made him a one-man band, the precursor of modern buskers. This instrument was lent by Anthony Baines.

57. Psalm 150, verses 3–6.

58. Beale played the trumpet at Cromwell's accession and at his funeral, and was then appointed Trumpeter in Ordinary to Charles II.

59. Illustrated in the *New Grove Dictionary of Musical Instruments*, figure 1c, and in the catalogue of the Galpin Society's 21st Anniversary Exhibition in Edinburgh, 1968, no. 422.

60. National Portrait Gallery (q.v.). Martin Sonter has recorded the first five Handel suites on the instrument. Given to the Bate by Mrs Audrey Blackman, it was restrung and requilled with crow.

61. Woodward's original design was for a freestanding building that could be viewed from three sides. The expansion of the university's science departments had encroached on two of these sides.

62. The son of Sir Charles Barry, the architect of the Houses of Parliament. His design was classical in the style of his father's Treasury Buildings, Whitehall (1845).

63. Ruskin's *Stones of Venice* had been published in 1851. The competition for the museum was held in 1853.

64. Particularly Ypres Cloth Hall and Brussels Town Hall.

65. Not surprisingly Ruskin's opinion was muted. 'I think ND [Nisi Dominus – Deane and Woodward's motto for their submission] though by no means a first-rate design, yet quite as good as is likely to be got these days and on the whole good.'

66. Francis Skidmore was the designer of the Albert Memorial in Kensington Gardens and the choir screen in Hereford Cathedral (1862), now in the V&A (q.v.). The University Museum was his first large-scale project, won because of the work he had done in the 1851 Great Exhibition and his screen at Cubbington Church, Warwickshire (1852).

67. Each rock was selected by Professor John Philips, the geologist and the museum's first keeper.

68. Letter from James O'Shea to Acland, 14 October 1859.

69. Ms Acland, D95, f. 38, Bodleian Library.

70. They responded by carving parrots and owls, monkeys and cats, taken to be satirical references to members of Convocation. Their work on the windows of the facade was left uncut and has never been completed.

71. I am indebted to O'Dwyer.

72. Described by Philips in *The Geology of Oxford and the Valley of the Thames* (1871), found by Mr Chapman, a nightwatchman at Kirtlington station. The quadruped herbivore is an estimated 168 million years old.

73. Tuckwell.

74. Both Tradescants were Keepers of the Gardens, Vines and Silkworms of King's Gardens at Oatlands Palace, John the Younger inheriting the position from his father in 1638. A portrait of Queen Henrietta Maria, by Van Dyck, is here.

75. *The Museum Tradescentianum*: the second catalogue of their collection, published by John Tradescant the Younger in 1656.

76. I am indebted to Michael Hunter's essay 'The Cabinet Institutionalized: the Royal Society's "Repository" and its Background' in Impey and Macgregor, pp. 226–7. Hunter notes that the Latin usage of the word 'museum' in the 17th century is commonly 'a place for learned occupations' (see the Museum of the College of Physicians, 1654). The Royal Society used 'repository' to describe the location of their collection.

77. The full story is less happy. Tradescant made his museum over to Ashmole in 1659 by a deed of gift. In 1661 his will left it to his wife, Hester, 'during her naturall life, and after her decease I give and bequeath the same to the Universities of Oxford or Cambridge, to which of them she shall think fit'. When Tradescant died the following year his widow challenged the deed of gift in the courts. The Lord Chancellor found in favour of Ashmole who, in 1674, moved into the house next door to her in Lambeth and began to transfer the collection, much against her will. On 4 April 1678 Ashmole's diary records, 'Mrs Tradescant was found drowned in her pond . . . as appeared by some circumstances'.

78. Watkin.

79. Ibid.

80. The gold chains and medals presented to Ashmole by Christian V of Denmark, the Elector of Brandenburg and Elector Palatine.

81. At the top of the stairs is a bust of Arundel by François Dieussart, presented in memory of the art historian Ellis Waterhouse.

82. Before he retired Parker wrote the definitive *Catalogue of the Collection of Drawings in the Ashmolean Museum, II, Italian Schools*, to which H. MacAndrew added a supplement in 1980.

83. The one exception is the Cast Gallery in a separate building behind the museum in St John's Lane.

84. West Saxon version of Pope Gregory's 'Pastoral Care', *Early English Text Society*, 1871–2, edited by Henry Sweet, pp. 7–8.

85. It was bequeathed to the museum by Nathaniel Palmer in 1718.

86. Evelyn, *Numismata*.

87. I am indebted for this, and for much else in this entry, to *The Treasures of Oxford* by (Sir) David Piper, Director of the museum 1973–85. This quotation is from p. 77.

88. Ibid., p. 27.

89. Designed by George Clarke, Fellow of All Souls 1717–72.

90. Sherwood and Pevsner, *Oxfordshire*, p. 126.

91. v. the Walker Art Gallery.

92. Eastlake had been appointed to the senior curatorial post (keeper) at the National Gallery in 1843 by the Prime Minister, Sir Robert Peel, whose taste, reflected in his own excellent collection, was for Dutch painting. They soon fell out over the purchase of what Lord Aberdeen, President of the Society of Antiquaries, called 'antiquarian and medieval pictures'. Peel agreed. 'I think we should not collect curiosities', he told Eastlake, who finally resigned when his decision to reduce the heavy, dark varnish with which his predecessor, William Seguier, had attempted to combat the effects of the London atmosphere. In 1850 Eastlake was elected President of the Royal Academy and in 1854 he returned to the newly created post of Director of the National Gallery with a new brief to create a national collection that represented the whole field of Western European painting.

93. It is based on *Vitae Patrum*, a compilation of legends by Palladius. Originally there were twenty scenes. Nine are in Zurich, one in Yale and one in the National Gallery of Scotland (q.v.).

94. Brother of the archaeologist Sir Arthur Evans, ex-curator of Knossos.

95. For this history I am indebted to Simcock.

96. Pevsner, *Oxfordshire*, p. 254.

97. Evans was a successful paper manufacturer with a degree in science. His half-sister, Dame Joan Evans, noted that he 'could not spell, but liked blowing himself up with chemicals'.

98. Ascribed to Charles Whitewell (died 1611) and based on a map of England and Wales engraved by Augustine Ryther.

99. While giving a public lecture on general relativity at Rhodes House.

100. This drawing measures five feet across. A smaller version (23 by 18 inches) is in Soho House (q.v.). It shows a different phase but is still of a gibbous (or more than half-full) moon.

101. First in a lecture to the Anthropological Institute, entitled 'The Evolution of Culture' (1874), later collected in *The Evolution of Culture and Other Essays*.

102. Pitt Rivers, *On the Principles of Classification*, p. 300.

103. Pitt Rivers, *The Evolution of Culture*, p. 46.

104. Pitt Rivers papers, Salisbury Museum, L846.

105. Pitt Rivers, *On the Principles of Classification*.

106. Pitt Rivers, 'Typological Museums as Exemplified by the Pitt Rivers Museum at Oxford and his Provincial Museum at Farnham, Dorset, *Journal of the Society of Arts*, 1891, pp. 115–22.

107. v. the Salisbury and South Wiltshire Museum.

108. Pitt Rivers, *Excavations at Cranborne Chase*, p. xix.

109. W. Chapman, 'Ethnology in the Museum', unpublished D. Phil. thesis, vols. I and II, quoted by Alison Petch, 'Assembling and Arranging' in Shelton, p. 242.

110. Pitt Rivers regretted his choice of Oxford. 'I should never had given it there if I had not been ill at the time and anxious to find a resting place for [it],' he wrote to F.W. Rudler on 23 May 1898 (South Wiltshire Museum Pitt Rivers Papers, Correspondence).

111. Exceptions include the display of North American clothing in the court of the museum and Cook and Benin material on the Lower Gallery.

112. Wade.

113. Ibid.

114. The 'works with meadow adjoining', as they were in about 1785, is a scene painted on a Spode bone china dessert plate of about 1805: four bottle kilns, trees, meadows and, in the foreground, the River Trent or an arm of the new Grand Trunk Canal, completed in 1787.

115. The museum became a charitable trust in 1987 and the present museum opened in 1996 in the same buildings, as part of the Spode Visitor Centre.

116. Spode benefited in two ways from this cut in the tax on tea introduced in the Commutation Act (1784). Tea drinking became widespread, increasing the market for chinaware, and the Honourable East India Company found that it made greater profits from importing tea than from importing chinaware, so left that market open to Spode and other potteries. Tea consumption rose from 8 million pounds (weight) in 1780 to 50 million in 1840. Between those years the population of Stoke-on-Trent rose from 8,000 to 60,000, of whom 24,724 worked in the pottery industry.

117. Willow was not adapted from any one Chinese design but was an amalgamation of motifs put together and developed, probably, by Spode.

118. Named after the port from which Japanese wares were originally exported.

119. *Tower* of the Bridge of Salaro, near Rome (1814); *Castle*, the Gate of St Sebastian leading to the Appian Way (1806); *Rome* depicts St Peter's Basilica and the Castel Sant' Angelo from the Tiber (1811).

120. Mayer, pp. 3 and 4.

121. Spode made several services and pieces for the Prince of Wales, including eight three-foot-tall torchères, transfer printed twice in royal blue, for the Banqueting Room of the Royal Pavilion, Brighton (q.v.).

122. Such pieces as dog bowls, ladles, unhandled teacups and ladies' travelling toilet pots that were made less frequently.

123. The most significant of these were John Hendley Sheridan, tenant, then owner, from 1815 to 1857; Thomas Cooper, who was responsible for much of the present appearance of the pot-bank; various members of the Proctor family (1885–1939); and the family of Thomas Poole, related by marriage to the Proctors.

124. An 1890s machine made by Marshall & Sons, Gainsborough, Lincolnshire.

125. Jollying: making a bowl by hand.

126. Saggars: large ceramic containers in which ware is put before being fired. The saggars are placed on top of each other until they reach the top of the bottle oven.

127. Encaustic tiles have differently coloured clays inlaid. The first 19th-century tile was designed by William Chamberlain of Worcester in the 1830s. Both Chamberlain and Minton bought rights to make encaustic tiles from Samuel Wright, a

Staffordshire potter and trader in cobalt, who had taken out a patent for making encaustic tiles in 1830.

128. Pugin adapted these designs from medieval tiles discovered in Westminster Abbey. Timber flooring was taken up for replacement and these tiles, hidden for centuries, were revealed.

129. When the Minton tiles began to wear thin in the late 1970s/early 1980s, Parliament approached Minton & Co., now owned by Royal Doulton, to replace them. Doulton's had not made encaustic tiles for at least a generation and declined to tender. The contract went to H. & R. Johnson of Tunstall, as did similar contracts with other buildings across the world.

130. Maud & Co. made Burges's tiles for Cardiff Castle (q.v.), 1872–4; Arnoux was art director at Minton & Co., 1849–92, where he pioneered brightly coloured maiolica tiles. John Moyr Smith designed tiles for the architect Sir Gilbert Scott.

131. Pottery had been made here since Roman times. The Stoke-on-Trent Roman pots are in the archaeology galleries downstairs.

132. I am indebted to David Barker's several publications, especially *William Greatbach*, pp. 1–25, and his 'Unearthing Staffordshire – Towards a New Understanding of Eighteenth Century Ceramics', *International Ceramics Fair Catalogue*, 1990 (with Pat Halfpenny).

133. Shaw, the definitive, if not always accurate, 19th-century history.

134. The W. G. may refer to a client, rather than the maker (Enoch Booth).

135. The British Museum (q.v.) has a bowl of cream-coloured earthenware inscribed 'E.B.1743' in which are set panels painted in blue that depict flowers and animals: an even finer piece.

136. Wedgwood's Experiment Book, 23 March 1759, p. 71, Wedgwood MSS: E. 19115–26.

137. Ibid. E. 18073–25.

138. Ibid. E. 18080–25.

139. *Aris's Birmingham Gazette*, 9 June 1766.

140. Ralph Wood I, (1715–72), Ralph Wood II (1748–95), Enoch Wood (1781–1807).

141. The Wedgwood Museum, with its outstanding collection, is currently closed. The Spode Museum (q.v.) is open, on the site of Josiah Spode's original potbank in Stoke.

142. Thomas Whieldon was also master to Josiah Spode I and William Greatbach at Whieldon's Fenton Vivian potbank.

143. One who makes saggars or safeguards, fire-clay containers on to which pottery is placed to protect it during firing in stacks the height of the bottle kilns. His 'bottom-knocker' is his assistant.

144. Gabrielle Keiller, widow of Alexander Keiller, archaeologist of Avebury, went on to collect Surrealist painting and sculpture, which she bequeathed to the Scottish National Gallery of Modern Art (q.v.).

145. The Revd E. Milner White's collection at York Art Gallery (q.v.) and at Southampton City Art Gallery (q.v.); W. A. Ismay's collection at the Yorkshire Museum (q.v.); the Ballantynes' at Nottingham City Art Gallery; and Lisa Sainsbury's collection at the Sainsbury Centre for Visual Arts (q.v.).

146. In the 1930s Victor Stellern, head of design at Wedgwood, employed the young artist he had known at the Royal College of Art. See Ravilious's *Coronation Mug* (1936), *Alphabet* (1937) and *Barlaston Mug* (1939).

147. Currie worked under the French designer Camille Solon.

148. Hassell.

149. As a 2002 exhibition, arranged jointly by the Potteries Museum and Tate Britain, demonstrates.

150. See P. J. de Loutherbourg's oil painting *Coalbrookdale by Night* (1801), now in the Science Museum in London (q.v.), which shows the Bedlam furnaces further down the valley below the Iron Bridge.

151. Wilkinson was an iron fanatic. He insisted on being buried in an iron coffin and caused a cast-iron obelisk to be raised to him in Lindale, where he is buried.

152. Steam-engine cylinders of the type designed by Thomas Newcomen in 1712. They were later improved by Wilkinson at his Bersham works in Wrexham and employed by Watt and Boulton at Soho (1775).

153. The iron wheels were cast for use on a colliery line.

154. The iron boat, a barge, designed by John Wilkinson to carry Coalbrookdale castings down the Severn to Bristol. 'It answers all my expectations,' wrote Wilkinson, 'and it has convinced the unbelievers, who were 999 in a thousand' (*Dictionary of National Biography*, p. 273 and Smiles, p. 52).

155. The aqueduct built by Thomas Telford and William Reynolds at Longdon on Tern.

156. At Ditherington, Shrewsbury.

157. His statues of *Africa* and *Europe* are now in the museum's tearoom.

158. Sir Neil Cossons, Director of Ironbridge Gorge Museum 1971–83, Director of Science Museum 1983–2000, Chairman of English Heritage since 2000.

159. 'The Museum of the Valley, Ironbridge Gorge', *Museum*, vol. XXXII, No. 3, 1980, p. 142.

160. At the time of nomination it was the only industrial World Heritage Site.

161. Pevsner, *Shropshire*, p. 157. He adds: 'See the minute books at the Shrewsbury public library, and A. Raistrick, Dynasty of Iron Founders, 1953.'

162. Cossons and Trinder.

163. Pevsner, *Buckinghamshire*. Pevsner describes it as 'a gabled, tilehung house, dated 1889' with 'utilitarian additions' by G. D. Hamilton of the Property Services Agency, *c.* 1972.

164. Hartert and Jordan devoted their working lives to the museum, working here from 1892 to, respectively, 1930 and 1958.

165. The museum in Tring still houses most of his collection of mounted animals. However the majority of his study collection is now at the Natural History Museum (q.v.).

166. *The Red Book*, introduction by Baron Ferdinand de Rothschild, Waddesdon Manor Archives, p. 3.

167. The Rothschilds were great builders, building more than sixty houses across Europe in the 19th and 20th centuries, including Ascott (q.v.).

168. The carved oak panelling in the Breakfast Room and in the Green Boudoir from the house of a Parisian banker Pierre Dodun at 21 rue de Richelieu; the 1730 rococo panelling for the Grey Drawing Room from the home of the Duc de Biron in the rue de Varennes (now the Musée Rodin); the neoclassical panelling for the Tower Drawing Room (1770–75) from the country house of the financier Nicolas Beaujon, designed by the architect E. - L. Boullée.

169. The Savonnerie carpet in the Red Drawing Room, one of fourteen in the collection, was made for Louis XIV in 1683 for the Long Gallery of the Louvre.

170. The Beauvais tapestry in the Small Library, by Boucher, is *Le Déjeuner* and is, like the two in the Dining Room, part of a series, *La Noble Pas-*

torale by Boucher, woven for the first time in 1755.

171. One of a set of five blue vases, dated 1769, in the Tower Drawing Room.

172. From George Edwards, *A Natural History of Unknown Birds* (1743–64) and *Gleanings of Natural History* (1758–64).

173. French Ambassador in Vienna, 1771–4. More of this service is in the Bowes Museum (q.v.).

174. A delicious sepia drawing by Fragonard, *L'Education Fait Tout*, in the Baron's Room.

175. This is the beautiful singer, Elizabeth Linley, daughter of Thomas Linley, the composer. She eloped with Richard Brinsley Sheridan, the playwright. Gainsborough, who was a close friend of the whole Linley family in Bath, where Thomas Linley ran the music at the Pump Rooms, painted Elizabeth with her sister Mary as *The Linley Sisters* (1772) (Dulwich Picture Gallery, q.v.) and by herself (*c.* 1783–5) (National Gallery, Washington, Mellon Collection): Mellon bought this portrait from Victor, 3rd Lord Rothschild in *c.* 1936/7.

176. Her grandfather was the Irish-American millionaire and collector Thomas Fortune Ryan. His portrait bust by Rodin is in Tate Britain (q.v.).

177. The largest collection of his work in a public gallery.

178. This was Epstein's first major public commission, at the invitation of the architect Charles Holden. The building is now Zimbabwe House. The sculptures were attacked, particularly in the London *Evening Standard*, in whose pages (19 June 1908) they were described as 'a form of statuary which no careful father would wish his daughter, and no discriminating young man his fiancé [sic] to see.'

179. Inspired by Assyrian carving of winged bulls in the British Museum (q.v.), the male genitalia of the sphinx-like angel caused offence and had to be covered, against Epstein's will, by a bronze fig leaf.

180. Influenced by Futurism and Vorticism. Epstein said of it, 'Here is the armed, sinister figure of today and tomorrow. No humanity, only the terrible Frankenstein's monster we have made ourselves into.'

181. The Tate *Rock Drill* is a cut-down version of the original, which has been reconstructed in polyester resin, metal and wood, and can be seen in the Birmingham Museum and Art Gallery (q.v.).

182. 300 objects were sold to the collector Carlo

Monzino; others to museums that included the British Museum (q.v.) and the Metropolitan Museum of Art in New York.

183. Pevsner, *Staffordshire*, p. 317.

184. David Rodgers, the Director from 1969 to 1981, was responsible for the 1976 catalogue of British and US Pop Art. He directed Exeter Museum and Art Gallery, 1981–6, and the Geffrye Museum, 1986–90.

185. Quoted by Nikolaus Pevsner, 'Victorian Architecture', BBC Third Programme, 25 July 1951, published in *Games*, p. 119.

186. Morris, Marshall, Faulkner & Co. was founded in 1861 by William Morris, D. G. Rossetti, Philip Webb, Ford Madox Brown, Charles Faulkner and Peter Paul Marshall. It was referred to colloquially as 'The Firm'. It was dissolved, with considerable acrimony, by Morris in 1875, after which it continued trading under Morris's sole ownership as Morris & Co.

187. Watts-Dunton painted them to Rossetti's designs.

188. Jane Nassau Senior, to whom Watts was devoted, was the sister of Thomas Hughes (*Tom Brown's Schooldays*) and a talented amateur soprano who first tested the acoustics in the Royal Albert Hall. She was the first woman to be appointed an Inspector of Workhouses and Prisons.

189. Maria Zambaco was one of three Greek beauties dubbed The Three Graces. The others were Marie Spartali, Janey Morris's great friend, and Aglaia Coronio.

190. MacCarthy, *William Morris*, p. 228.

191. These are on long-term loan to Wightwick by Mrs Katherine Macdonald, the granddaughter of Alexander Munro.

192. Letter from John Vanbrugh to Lord Poulet, 1710.

193. In 1712, when it was only part built.

194. Churchill, p. 42.

195. Vanbrugh to Lord Poulet.

196. Sherwood and Pevsner, *Oxfordshire*, p. 463.

197. Ibid.

198. The Duke was also painted by Kneller, on horseback. This is now in the National Portrait Gallery (q.v.).

199. A further bust of the 9th Duke by Sir Jacob Epstein is in the Entrance Hall.

200. Laguerre charged £500 for the whole room.

201. Townesend and Peisley were also the masons who built the Grand Bridge.

202. Sherwood and Pevsner, *Oxfordshire*, p. 471.

203. Marches Nos. 1–4, 1901–07, and No. 5, 1930.

THE NORTH-WEST

1. William Feaver, *The Observer*, 10 March 1963. The one wall that survives is now in the Hatton Gallery (q.v.), moved there in 1965–6 under the supervision of the artist Richard Hamilton.

2. Examples of which can be seen in the collection at Abbot Hall (q.v.).

3. In a letter (1925), unpublished but cited by Klaus Hinrichsen in 'Schwitters' Portraits of Internees on the Isle of Man' (unpublished, 1987), Schwitters writes that he had painted 'continuously and with honest endeavours both landscapes and portraits coincidental with purely artistic work', by which he meant his abstracts and collages.

4. Elderfield, p. 386, n. 8.

5. With help from the NACF and the V&A Purchase Grant Fund, the gallery acquired in 2003 Schwitters's Ambleside assemblage, *Wood on Wood*.

6. Pevsner, *Lancashire*.

7. Searle is also responsible for the mosaic murals in the entrance and the Parthenon-derived friezes in the Art Gallery.

8. She represents a princess of the Amarna period (*c.* 1350–1334 BC), possibly a daughter of the Pharaoh Akhenaten and his queen, Nefertiti.

9. Hindley Smith made other substantial bequests to the Ashmolean Museum, the Fitzwilliam, the Tate Gallery, the British Museum, and locally to the Atkinson Art Gallery and Oldham Art Gallery.

10. This Expressionist sculpture depicts slavery breaking its chains. Epstein said, 'There is nowhere I would rather think of it going than to Bolton . . . I think the people of Bolton behaved admirably during the difficult years of the cotton famine and the fight against slavery.' Morris, E., p. 40.

11. *Nearing Camp, Evening on the Upper Colorado River* cost £1,343,000.

12. A letter from John Ruskin to Thomas Moran among Moran's papers. Nevertheless Ruskin purchased several etchings by Moran when he, Moran, visited England in 1882.

13. M. H. Baillie Scott, *The Studio*, 15 November 1895.

14. Ruskin was appointed Slade Professor of Art at Oxford University in 1869.

15. See Roscoe's crucial role in creating the collection that became the Walker Art Gallery, (q.v.).

16. Now in the National Gallery (q.v.).

17. Ruskin, *Praeterita*, vol. I, IV.

18. Ruskin, *Unto This Last*, vol. III, p. 54.

19. The *Discobolos* was Townley's last major purchase from the excavations (1790–91), led by Gavin Hamilton and Piranesi, at Latium. The *Lansdowne Hercules* in the Getty Museum was excavated at the same time.

20. With Gavin Hamilton and James Byres, Thomas Jenkins was one of the major antiquarian dealers in Rome for fifty years in the late 18th century.

21. His collection included the Townley caryatid, the 2nd-century AD group of dogs from Monte Cagnolo and the cabinet of engraved sealstones from the collection of Christian Dehn.

22. Townley visited Italy in 1767–8, 1771–4 and 1776–7. He planned a fourth tour in 1779 but was prevented from travelling by the outbreak of war with France.

23. Pevsner, *South Lancashire*, pp. 82–3.

24. A dalmatic from this set of vestments is in the Burrell Collection (q.v.).

25. Ten of these were engraved for Whitaker's *History of the Parish of Whalley* (published 1800–01).

26. Pevsner, *South Lancashire*, p. 98.

27. Later raised to £200 a year.

28. Augustus John said that Rothenstein 'was among the first to acclaim the satirical genius of Wyndham Lewis'.

29. In all Rothenstein bought over eighty-three works including a Paul Nash watercolour from the First World War, and watercolours by Eric Ravilious and Edward Bawden.

30. Quoted in John Rothenstein, *Summer's Lease*, p. 133.

31. Bottomley edited Rosenberg's *Poems*, 1922.

32. 'King Lear's Wife' (1915) was published in *Georgian Poetry*, Penguin, 1913–15, edited by Sir Edward Marsh, who was also a friend of Bottomley.

33. Bottomley wrote to Paul Nash that, in his view 'Lizzie was the catalyst who made possible all Rossetti's finest conceptions. I think he knew it, too.'

34. See George Howard's paintings at Castle Howard (q.v.).

35. Bottomley also admired 'the Ancients'. His collection includes an oil by Edward Calvert and, by Samuel Palmer, a watercolour, engravings and drawings of designs for an illustrated edition of Virgil's *Eclogues*, undertaken at the end of his life. His drawing of *Pan* for the Tenth Eclogue is probably Palmer's penultimate drawing.

36. Letter, 31 December, 1828.

37. Ruskin, *Modern Painters*, Vol. III.

38. Ibid.

39. Grill Dockray, Architects, Kendal.

40. Ruskin, *Letters on a Museum*.

41. William Hazlitt's essay 'My First Acquaintance with Poets', 1823. I am much indebted to Dr Robert Woof, the Director of the Wordsworth Trust, for drawing this, and much else, to my attention.

42. *The Prelude*, I, 1805, lines 372–426.

43. Letter to John Leigh Phillips, 29 May 1795, quoted in Bernrose, p. 95.

44. Reynolds (ed. Wark), p. 258.

45. Rebuilt by John Carr of York in 1759.

46. *The Lonsdale Magazine* of 1821 (Vol II, p. 3) says, 'This hall was rebuilt in 1759 under the superintendence of Mr Carr of York by the late Colonel George Wilson, at a reputed cost of £8,000.'

47. V. A. J. Slowe (Abbot Hall's then Director), catalogue to *Treasures from Abbot Hall, Kendal*, an exhibition at the Leger Galleries, Old Bond Street, 1989, p. 3.

48. Ben Nicholson's painting here, *Crowned Head: The Queen* (1932), is of Barbara Hepworth, in profile framed in a window, painted just as they were falling in love. He made several portraits of Hepworth, all in profile, at about this time. One, a linocut (1933) is in the V&A (q.v.).

49. Schwitters described *Merz* as 'the combination, for artistic purposes, of all conceivable materials', assemblages brought together for their formal, sometimes literary, references. His last, and greatest, Merz work, *Merzbarn*, is now at the Hatton Art Gallery (q.v.).

50. Richard MacCormac of MacCormac Jamieson Prichard (see the Wellcome Wing of the Science Museum, London).

51. *Architects' Journal*, 18 December 1997.
52. This was probably taken by John Hobbs, 1849–50, under Ruskin's direction.
53. Ibid (2).
54. In particular the curator, the Ruskin scholar Stephen Wildman.
55. Ruskin, *Modern Painters*.
56. Ibid (2).
57. Peter Hall & Son of Staveley, Kendal.
58. In addition to a complete holding of Ruskin's published works and all books about Ruskin, it contains 29 volumes of his diaries (1835–88); 7,400 letters (including correspondence with Carlyle and Browning), largely unpublished; and 1,500 drawings and 500 prints, 950 of which are by Ruskin.
59. Letter 54, June 1875.
60. Ruskin, *Praeterita*, vol. 35, pp. 35–75.
61. Ruskin, *The Stones of Venice*, vol. 10, p. 365.
62. *Notes by Mr Ruskin*, Fine Art Society catalogue, 1878, library edition, vol. 13, p. 507.
63. Wallace.
64. However, material evidence of the slave trade is scant in itself, not only in this museum.
65. Liverpool's trade grew dramatically in the 19th century and was not only dependent on emigration. The port was the centre of the British cotton trade, both importing the raw material and exporting finished products.
66. Pevsner, *North Lancashire*, p. 164.
67. Herbaria originating with Dr J. R. Forster, the surgeon on Cook's second voyage; J. F. Royle; and Sir J. E. Smith. William Roscoe had purchased the Forster herbarium from Forster's widow in Halle in 1799.
68. Stanley is the Derby family name.
69. The museum kept those that were mainly original. The art gallery received the casts.
70. Drawings prepared by Indian artists for John Forbes Royle (whose herbarium was deposited here by the University of Liverpool in 1952) at the Saharanpur Botanic Garden.
71. The Museum's Department of Archaeology has conducted excavations at Mesolithic sites (Greasby, Croxleth); Iron Age sites at Lathom and Irby; a Romano-British farmstead at Irby; Meol's harbour; and Port Louis and Port Egmont in the Falkland Islands. HMS *Beagle* stopped at Port Louis in 1833 on its way to the Galapagos.
72. In 1806 he published the classic children's verse, 'The Butterfly's Ball and the Grasshopper's Feast' (*The Gentleman's Magazine*, November 1806).
73. Roscoe.
74. When the Liverpool Royal Institution was wound up in 1948 the loan was converted into a gift.
75. Statues by Warrington Wood.
76. The Liverpool Academy had promoted the annual exhibitions from 1822 to 1867; the City Council from 1871.
77. A moodily atmospheric, moonlit *The Ruins of Holyrood Chapel* (*c.*1824) by the inventor of the daguerreotype (1839).
78. Roscoe bought it at Christie's, London, on 12 May 1804, for five guineas.
79. Hogarth's aesthetic theory expounded in *The Analysis of Beauty* (1753).
80. Its pendant, *Landscape with the Body of Phocion Carried out of Athens*, is in the National Museum and Gallery of Wales (q.v.).
81. *Dictionary of National Biography*, p. 224.
82. The National Museum and Gallery of Wales also has a fine collection of sculpture by Gibson.
83. The architect is not known but it may have been Thomas Harrison, who designed similar houses for Liverpool merchants between 1811 and 1815.
84. Robinson was Mayor of Liverpool, 1828–9. A portrait of him in his mayoral robes, by T. C. Thompson, hangs over the stairs.
85. John Philip, *Gypsy Sisters of Seville*, two dark-eyed beauties.
86. *Margate Harbour* (1835–40) may have been one of those paintings owned by Mrs Booth. Luke Hermann considers it too weak to be by Turner.
87. Gillott's collection is now dispersed among public galleries: *Cilgerren Castle* (1798), Leicester Art Gallery and Museum (q.v.); *Calais Sands, Low Water* (1830), Bury Art Centre; *Cicero at his Villa* (1839), Ascott Collection (q.v.); *Van Trump Going About to Please his Masters* (1844), Getty Museum, California.
88. I am indebted to Lucy Wood, Keeper of Furniture at the Lady Lever art gallery (q.v.) until 2003, and to Clive Wainwright's introduction to *George Bullock, Cabinet Maker*, John Murray, 1988.
89. See Gandy's watercolours of Sir John Soane's house in Lincoln's Inn Fields in Sir John Soane's Museum (q.v.).

90. Pevsner, *South Lancashire*, p. 164. Pevsner is quoting Picton.

91. Spalding, F., p. 223.

92. After the riots in the Toxteth district of Liverpool in 1981, Mrs Thatcher appointed the then Secretary of State for the Environment, Michael Heseltine, to regenerate the city. He set up the Merseyside Development Corporation, which chose as its first project the renovation of Liverpool's docks.

93. James Stirling, Michael Wilford and Associates had designed the Staatsgalerie in Stuttgart (1977–83). The Clore Gallery was under construction. In the 1990s the firm designed the Lowry Centre.

94. The Steenson, Varming, Mulcahy Partnership.

95. Minutes of trustees' board meeting, 21 June 1973.

96. *A Century of Collecting 1882–1982: a Guide to Manchester Art Galleries*, Manchester, 1983, p. 30.

97. *Astarte Syriaca* (1877), purchased 1891. His beautiful chalk drawing *La Donna Della Fiamma* (1870) was purchased 1900.

98. Collins's composition follows Raphael's cartoon for the tapestry *The Death of Ananais* (1515), as Julian Treuherz explains in his introduction to *Pre-Raphaelite Paintings*, Manchester City Art Gallery, 2nd edition, 1993, p. 9.

99. They were joined by William Michael Rossetti, Frederic George Stephens, James Collinson (who has two paintings here) and the sculptor Thomas Woolner.

100. Landseer painted this ten years before his sculptures of lions for Trafalgar Square. The painting was used, after 1885, as the image of the lion on Tate and Lyle's tins of Golden Syrup.

101. Mengin, a French Leighton, exhibited this at the Paris Salon of 1877, the year of the third Impressionist exhibition. It was given to the gallery by Thomas Lloyd.

102. He painted *Au Chat Botté* (literally 'Puss in Boots', the name of a shoe shop in La Grand Rue, Dieppe) in 1932 and wrote about it in Cyril Connolly's magazine *Horizon* in 1941.

103. Commissioned by the Roman patrician Carlo Cardelli, who also commissioned Claude's *Landscape with Jacob, Laban and his Daughters* at Petworth House (q.v.).

104. In collections in London and Melbourne.

105. Rutherford moved to Cambridge the following year and published his experiment in 1919.

106. Charter of the Whitworth Institute, sealed on 2 October 1889.

107. Proverbs, chapter 7, verse 27, and John Milton, *Paradise lost*, Bk VII, 224–8:

Then staid the ferrid wheels, and in his hand
He took the golden compasses, prepared
In God's eternal store, to circumscribe
The Universe, and all created things.

108. I am indebted to David Morris of the Whitworth Gallery and his article in *Printmaking Today*, winter 2001, that describes the collection.

109. The collection was made by Margaret Pilkington, Director of the Whitworth in the 1940s and '50s, herself a wood-engraver.

110. I am indebted to Christine Woods of the Whitworth and her essay 'An Object Lesson to a Philistine Age' in *Journal of Design History*, vol. 12. no. 2, the Design History Society, pp. 159–71.

111. Joseph Dufour established the firm Dufour and Leroy in Paris in 1820. It continued in production until 1860.

112. Christine Woods (op. cit., p. 159) estimates that the WPM Ltd controlled 98 per cent of British manufacturing.

113. The decorator John Gregory Crace, the grandson of John C. Crace, decorator for the Prince Regent, lamented that by the 1830s French manufacturers were the acknowledged masters of wallpaper design ('The Crace Papers'; two lectures to RIBA, 4 and 18 February 1839, eds. A.V. Sugden and E. A. Entwhistle, Birmingham, 1939).

114. Purchased at Sotheby's Monaco auction, 1982.

115. Sugden and Edmondson.

116. Ibid.

117. The rest was acquired by the V&A, and by the Royal Museum of Scotland.

118. Isaiah, chapter 2, verse 1.

119. The archive contains some of his notebooks, diaries and designs for book illustrations.

120. C. Willet Cunnington, 'The Scientific Approach to Period Costumes', *Museums Journal*, vol. 147, no. 7, October 1947, p.125.

121. Ibid, p. 126.

122. Anthea Jarvis, 'An Agreeable Change from Ordinary Medical Diagnosis: the costume collection of Drs C. Willet and Phillis Cunnington', *Journal of the Costume Society*, no. 3, 1999.

123. Ibid., p. 5, letter from Dr Willet Cunnington to Anne Buck, 29 February 1948.

124. A year later Lightoler supplanted John Carr in precisely the same way at Burton Constable in Yorkshire.

125. Jarvis, op. cit.: letter, Cunnington to Buck, 6 February 1948.

126. The library contains 17,000 items.

127. R. E. M. Wheeler, introduction to the catalogue of the London Museum's Costume Collection, 1933.

128. Thompson, E. P.

129. Ibid., p. 9.

130. The pumping station, opened in 1909, provided power for the hydraulic presses used in the cotton industry for baling and packing. As well as providing power for industry, the pump raised the curtain at the Opera House and wound the Town Hall clock.

131. I am indebted to the two Directors of the museum, Terry McCarthy (1975–89) and Nick Mansfield (since 1989); over the years to Bill Fishman, Stan Newens and Michael Foot; and, above all, to John Gorman, who wrote *Images of Labour* and *Banner Bright*, the ur-texts on the museum's collections.

132. The oldest banner in the collection.

133. Made by the Poplar Labour Party as part of the opposition to the Chamberlain Government's 'non-intervention' in 1936 that prevented the elected Spanish government from buying arms on the open market in order to defend itself against the Fascist insurrection on 18 July 1936.

134. On the banner a London dockworker clasps the hand of his Australian brother. The strike brought together the previously disparate groups of dock workers (stevedores, boiler makers, porters, carpenters, lightermen, casual unskilled labourers) to get wages raised from four to six pence an hour. Ben Tillett's tiny Tea Operatives and General Labourers' Association led the struggle and, helped by the Australian trade unions, who contributed a staggering £25,000 to the strike fund, they closed the docks and brought London to a halt when 50,000 men marched through the East End.

135. Crane designed all the banners for Tom Mann's militant Workers Union, formed on May Day 1898, and subsequently for numerous trade unions. Many of them were made by George

Tuthill and Co. Tuthill had started life as a fairground showman painting fascias to booths and roundabouts. He exhibited at the Royal Academy in 1847 and started the company that, by the end of the century, dominated the making of banners, producing more banners than any company in the world.

136. The banner was designed by Winifred Horrabin. The embroidery was done by the novelist Rebecca West and Winifred Blatchford, the daughter of the socialist writer and editor Robert Blatchford.

137. That Yeomanry (Manchester merchants, shopkeepers on horseback) did more damage than the regular Hussars became clear in evidence at the subsequent inquests into the death of John Lees (1820). See Thompson, E. P., pp. 752–3.

138. Labour won forty seats in the January election and forty-two in December.

139. Ramsay MacDonald led the Labour Party to its first general election victory.

140. Armstrong, with the help of the *Daily Mirror* cartoonist Donald Zec, designed eight posters for the campaign and the election manifesto 'Let Us Face the Future'.

141. The Combinations Acts of 1799 and 1800 made trade unions illegal.

142. Note that this is a Workers' Society, of skilled tradesmen, as anxious to protect its trade's interests against those less skilled as to resist exploitation by their employers.

143. Before him on the table, when he removed the blindfold he was required to wear before he was accepted into the society, was the image of a skeleton.

144. 136 oil paintings were bought at the Spring Exhibitions between 1888 and 1935.

145. The gallery subsequently bought fourteen of the seventeen prints that Frank Short made from the unfinished engravings that Turner left when he abandoned the project in the early 1820s.

146. Unusually these were bought not from Agnew's but from Christie's on 11 July 1887.

147. Pevsner, *North Lancashire*, p. 196.

148. The gallery continues to collect work by the Devis family, including acquiring the only known triptych by Arthur Devis in 2002.

149. Tate Britain.

150. Tate Britain.

151. Holburne Museum and Gallery (q.v.).

152. Leber and Sandling, p. 131.

153. Ibid., p. 133.

154. Ibid., p. 131.

155. *Ashton Herald*, 6 September 1890, p. 6.

156. Cheetham was also a guarantor against the exhibition's losses to £10,000. Report of the Executive Committee, 'Exhibitions of Art Treasures of the United Kingdom Collected at Manchester in 1857', Manchester, 1859, appendix 20, p. 39.

157. John Cheetham, the father, is known to have travelled extensively in Italy, so it is possible that the Florentine works originate with him.

158. By Jonathan Alexander in *Presents from the Past*, exhibition catalogue, 1978.

159. By Richard Offner, who named the artist after a *Virgin and Child*, now in the Museum of Fine Arts, Houston, that once belonged to Percy C. Straus, New York.

160. See *Small Altarpiece: the Crucifixion* (1468), *Seraphim, Cherubim and Angels Adoring* (571 and 572) and *Altarpiece: the Coronation of the Virgin with Adoring Saints* (569). The latter three are the principal remains of the Altarpiece of S. Pier Maggiore at Florence, now destroyed.

161. Edward Morris believes it is possible that Cheetham, or his father, might have known the similar early Italian collection of the Revd Walter Bromley Davenport at Capesthorne.

162. The Masaccio, Luini, Bonington, Clarkson Stanfield and three works by G. F. Watts were sold by Christie's in London in 1823 when Cheetham's wife Beatrice died.

163. The Tameside Museum Service covers both Ashton-under-Lyme and Stalybridge, at either of which parts of the collection may be exhibited.

164. Bridgewater's canal brought cotton from India and the Americas via Liverpool and Manchester and, within ten years (1783), Thomas Bell had patented his roller printing machine. Samuel Crompton patented his spinning mule in 1779, Cartwright his power loom in 1785.

165. Turner sketched at the Falls of Clyde in 1802 and again in 1834. They are the subject of Plate 18 (1809) in the *Liber Studiorum*.

166. The Wedgwood Museum, the best collection of Wedgwood ware in the world, closed in 1998, and the collection is presently in store. It is the company's intention to reopen it as soon as a new museum can be built at Barlaston. A few pieces are on view at the visitors' centre there.

THE NORTH-EAST

1. The National Gallery has only one painting by El Greco, *Christ Driving the Traders from the Temple*, and a sketch (*The Adoration of the Name of Jesus*) of a larger painting by El Greco in the Escorial, *The Dream of Philip II*.

2. In addition to the 'Rokeby Venus', the National Gallery has seven paintings by Velásquez and an example of the work of his principal pupil Juan Bautista del Mazo. It holds five Murillos, three Zurbaráns, including two of *St Francis in Meditation* (c. 1639, when Zurbarán first came to Madrid), and two outstanding paintings by Goya, *Dona Isabel de Porcel* (c. 1806) and *Don Andres del Peral*, known as 'Dr Peral' (1798).

3. Francisco Xavier, Conde de Quinto, had been Director of the National Museum of paintings in Madrid.

4. Her full name was Benoit-Josephine Coffin-Chevalier. An actress, she and Bowes married in 1852.

5. Louis XV had given the château to his mistress, the Comtesse du Barry.

6. Josephine Bowes, the driving force behind the museum, died in 1874 and her husband soon gave up collecting.

7. Begun by Bishop Walcher, before the cathedral nave. Pevsner, *County Durham*, pp. 110–11.

8. *The Treasures of St Cuthbert*, p. 4. The right to sanctuary was abolished in 1623.

9. 'A small room or chapel attached to an abbey or a church in which shrines were deposited', *Oxford English Dictionary*, vol. IV, F–G, p. 161.

10. *Treasures of St Cuthbert*, p. 24. The Golden Seal made for Henry IV in 1401 was used, unaltered, by Henry V and Henry VI. These seals are considered as the high point of English seal engraving.

11. Ibid., p. 25. Its decoration displays stylistic similarities to the Lindisfarne Gospels. It may have come from the monastery at Jarrow, home of the Venerable Bede.

12. Ibid. This two-volume Bible was given to the monks of Durham by Bishop St Calais and was probably made in Normandy during the Bishop's exile there.

13. Ibid., p. 12. Printed by E. Cervicorus and Jo Soter at either Cologne or Marburg.

14. Ibid. Printed in London by Robert Barker and John Bill.

15. Ibid., pp. 8–9. Made by F. Butty and N. Dumee, London.

16. Ignatius Bonomi was the elder brother of Joseph Bonomi, sculptor and Egyptologist.

17. Northumberland admired Champollion's work on hieroglyphs. Between 1862 and 1885 he financed Edward Lane's work in preparing an Arabic lexicon. For this and for all the information on the Egyptian and Mesopotamian collections I am indebted to John Ruffle's paper 'The Provenance and Resources of the Ancient Egyptian, Islamic and Arabic Collections of the Oriental Museum of Durham University'.

18. Henry Salt was the British Consul in Egypt. After the Duke's death in 1865 his collection was catalogued by Samuel Birch, keeper of the Egyptian and Oriental antiquities at the British Museum. It was published in 1880 by the 6th Duke, illustrated with drawings by Joseph Bonomi.

19. The sphinx was the model for the two at the base of Cleopatra's Needle on the Embankment.

20. Probably excavated by Sir A. H. Layard 1846–51.

21. *The Catalogue of the MacDonald Collection, Arts of Asia*, November–December 1983. See also Laszlo Legeza.

22. Spink's valuation of £12,000 was accepted by the Duke, with half being provided by the University Grants Committee and half by Professor Spalding.

23. A wooden chest for holy books. Decorated in gilt gesso and mirror glass, and with scenes from the funeral rites of the Buddha: somewhat wasted on a dairy herd.

24. *Policy for a Regional Open Air Museum.* Report of a working party set up on 4 October 1966.

25. Hudson, *Museums of Influence*, p. 128.

26. v. Natural History Museum. Flower was the first person to distinguish between a museum's duty to provide research facilities for scholars and its duty to interest, instruct and entertain the general public.

27. Atkinson had previously directed museums in Wakefield and Halifax.

28. The first drift mine had opened here in 1763 and at least three deep mines had been sunk: Beamish Air Pit (1849), the Chophill (1855) and

the Beamish Mary (1883). It is Chophill that is represented in the museum.

29. *Beamish: the Making of a Museum*, introduction.

30. A cracket is a heart-shaped piece of wood with three short legs against which a miner would rest his thigh or shoulder when cutting coal.

31. Made by Lever Brothers of Port Sunlight, the Wirral, whose profits for William Henry Lever allowed him to found the Lady Lever art gallery (q.v.).

32. v. Salisbury and South Wiltshire Museum, which has the remains of the museum that Pitt Rivers founded on his Dorset estate.

33. Bulwer called him 'more original, more self-dependent than Raphael or Michelangelo'.

34. Robinson's master was the Newcastle furniture maker Thomas H. Tweedy.

35. R. Pallucchini, 'Il Tintoretto di Newcastle-upon-Tyne', *Arte Veneta*, XXX, 1976, pp. 81–97.

36. Purchased with help from the V&A, the Pilgrim Trust and Sir James Knolt.

37. *Free Form Dish* (1982), slabbed stoneware.

38. Much of the Pease Collection was later transferred to the Sunderland Museum.

39. The prospectus of the Art Furnishers' Alliance, 15 June 1880.

40. Karin Orchard, 'Kurt Schwitters: his Life and Work', *Baltic Centre for Contemporary Art*, No. 4, 1999.

41. The *Hanover Merzbau* was destroyed by Allied bombing in 1943.

42. The *Lysaker Merzbau* was accidentally burnt down by children in 1951.

43. A letter he wrote to Ludwig Hilbersheimer in October.

44. Donated to the Hatton by Henry Pierce in 1965.

45. 103 feet 9 inches long, 9 feet wide.

46. Newcastle's population more than doubled between 1871 and 1911, from 128,000 to 267,000, as shipbuilding and engineering boomed.

47. The new lecture theatre at the Mining Institute (1902); Barclays Bank, Collingwood Street (1903), the Bridge Hotel (c. 1899, Clackett by himself); the Magistrates Court at Berwick (1899–1901) (Burns Dick). Later they designed Cross Home, Westgate Road (1911) and the Northern Conservative Club, Pilgrim Street (1909)

48. The Margaret and Winneford bowl (1767),

enamelled by Beilby for Henry Foster of Alnwick, depicts his sailing ship the *Margaret and Winneford*, named after his two daughters. Beilby ran an engraving workshop in Newcastle with Thomas Berwick.

49. A 1748 coffee pot by James Kirkup is a piece of rococo silver that can be put beside work by Paul de Lamerie or Nicholas Sprimont, working in London.

50. Rothenstein, *Modern English Painters*, p. 15.

51. At Blackwell Grange, a public museum bought by a solicitor, George Allen, for £700.

52. The Natural History Society still exists, has 800 members and meets regularly. Since 1957 it has leased the Hancock Museum to the University of Newcastle upon Tyne.

53. The other is at Liverpool Museum (q.v.).

54. Found before 1757 at Hotbank Milecastle on Hadrian's Wall.

55. Before the discovery of this inscription it was presumed that Hadrian had built the Vallum and Emperor Septimius Severus the Wall.

56. The Second Legion Augusta also built the Roman Antonine Wall in Scotland, AD *c.* 138–161. The original inscription, of which a cast is here, is in the National Museum of Scotland.

57. Two altars to Antenociticus, found at Benwell, between Mile Castle and Newcastle.

58. Carrawburgh, Rudchester and Housesteads.

59. The Textoverdi are thought to be a division of the Brigantes tribe.

60. The triad is Celtic. Naming supernatural beings was frequently taboo among the Celts.

61. The oldest person known in Roman Britain is a centurion who died aged 100 at Caerleon (q.v.) in Roman Wales.

62. The site of such a port has yet to be identified.

63. Excavated in 1893.

64. The protective tip at the end of a scabbard.

65. The shipwreck has yielded military equipment, coins and paterae. The ringmail shirt was found during excavations of a barrack block that burnt down in the late 3rd or 4th century. The shirt has approximately 50,000 links, half of them riveted.

66. Pevsner identifies the different stones used to construct each of these buildings: magnesium limestone for the earliest; pink micaceous sandstone from the local Dean quarries for the second; and harder yellow sandstone from Gates-head Fell for the 4th-century buildings. Pevsner, *County Durham*, 1953, p. 214.

67. See Bidwell and Speak.

68. Bewick.

69. A prospectus for *A General History of Quadrupeds*, dated 2 April 1788, two years before the publication commenced.

70. He drew many of the birds from stuffed specimens in the private museum of Marmaduke Tunstall at Wycliffe, North Yorkshire. Tunstall's collection is now in the Hancock Museum (q.v.).

71. In 1826 Bewick announced a *History of British Birds* but engraved only sixteen subjects before he died.

72. He was a religious, God-fearing man and, in politics, a radical, strongly supporting the Americans in the War of Independence.

73. During his stay in London, his biographer, Graham Reynolds (Graham Reynolds, pp. 17 and 18) recounts, he was taken up by Isaac Taylor, one of the leading engravers and illustrators of the day, who had worked for Gravelot, Gainsborough's master, and Wade. He rejected Taylor's help. Of Taylor's masterwork, his illustrations to Samuel Richardson's *Sir Charles Grandison*, Bewick wrote: 'Not many plates have been engraved superior to these, though as a designer he has . . . attended too much to fashion and the change of mode'.

74. Ruskin, *Time and Tide*, p. 3.

75. Ibid.

76. Colchester, Essex, also did so in 1846 but its museum did not open to the public until 27 September 1860.

77. The sketches were of Janey Morris, in preparation for Rossetti's oil painting *Astarte Syriaca* (Manchester City Art Gallery, q.v.).

78. Some collecting had been started in the 19th century.

79. Barrie Stuart-Penrose, 'L. S. Lowry: A Man of his People', *Nova*, August 1966, p. 32.

80. In a rare slip, Pevsner ascribes this building to 'Tiltman' (Pevsner, *County Durham*, 1953, p. 228; Edward Pinnington, 'Robert Brough, Painter', *Art Journal*, 1898, p. 147).

YORKSHIRE AND HUMBERSIDE

1. I am greatly indebted to the work of Peter Brears whose several publications – *Treasures for the People*, with Stuart Davies; *Of Curiosities and Rare Things*; 'Temples of the Muses' *Museums Journal 84*, pp. 3–19, 1984 – record much of the history of museums in Yorkshire. Every region would benefit from the scholarship of a Peter Brears.

2. There is no documentary proof that the design is by Thornton. But Pevsner was convinced by the discovery of evidence in the Metropolitan Museum in New York (Pevsner, *Yorkshire, the North Riding*, p. 78) that refers to him as the architect of John Bourchier, the hall's owner (*The Building Dictionary*, 1734).

3. The window's design is based on an engraving of Bernini's Palazzo Chigi in Rome (Domenico de' Rossi's *Studio d'Architettura Civile*, 1702).

4. 120 portraits from the NPG were moved here in 1979 by the then Director, John Hayes.

5. Fluted pilasters, topped by Corinthian capitals, probably by John Bagnall of York.

6. The rich carving (friezes, plinths, overmantels, door surrounds) would not disgrace Gibbons or Selden, with its profusion of shells, palm fronds, acanthus brackets and monograms.

7. Wrought-iron work (also on internal balconies in the hall) attributed to the Derbyshire blacksmith Robert Bakewell.

8. Giovanni Boldoni's 1897 portrait of Lady Colin Campbell is in the National Portrait Gallery (q.v.), all black eyes, white skin and electrifying eyebrows.

9. A dining club of Whig grandees, politicians and writers who met at the Temple Bar tavern of Christopher Cat. His mutton pies were called Kit-cats.

10. *Vanbrugh*, attributed to Thomas Murray (*c.* 1718); *James Gibbs* by John Michael Williams (*c.* 1752); *Burlington* after Kneller; *John Carr* by Sir William Beechey (*c.* 1791); *Sir William Chambers* by Reynolds (*c.* 1755).

11. Fox Talbot's negative of the *Latticed Window* at Lacock Abbey measures only 28 by 36 millimetres. It is mounted on a piece of black paper, itself mounted on a sheet of writing paper on which is written 'Latticed Window (with the

Camera Obscura). August 1835. When first made, the squares of glass about 200 in number could be counted with the help of a lens.'

12. Lady Eastlake, 'Photography', *Quarterly Review*, 1857.

13. Blazwick and Weston, p. 104.

14. A plaque on it declares 'No camera is guaranteed if it does not carry the signature of M. Daguerre and the seal of M. Giroux.' (Alphonse Giroux was the Paris manufacturer of Daguerre's cameras.)

15. Johnston was president of the society, 1923–5 and 1929–31, and honorary curator 1924–55.

16. v. the National Portrait Gallery of Scotland.

17. v. the Sutcliffe Gallery.

18. In 1870 Cunliffe-Lister sold his family home, Manningham Hall, and fifty acres, to the Bradford Corporation. Lister Park was landscaped on the fifty acres. By 1898 the hall was to be demolished and the art gallery was built on the site.

19. Cunliffe-Lister's claim to have perfected the Square Motion Comb from Cartwright's original woolcombing machine was contested by his erstwhile partner Isaac Holden. After their partnership was dissolved in 1858 they quarrelled publicly and continually about their respective claims to the patent. Naming the gallery after Cartwright was Cunliffe-Lister's compromise.

20. *Bradford Observer*, 29 May 1879.

21. *A Rake's Progress* (1961–3), *The Poems of C. F. Cavafy* (1966), *Six Fairy Tales from the Brothers Grimm* (1969) and *The Blue Guitar* (1977) as well as the diptych *Le Plongueur* (1978).

22. St Matthew, chapter 23, verse 10.

23. A note here explains that the canvas of the picture is creased because, after Charlotte died, her husband Mr Nicholls folded it and took it to Ireland where he lived for the rest of his life, and where it remained in a cupboard until discovered in the 1930s.

24. Codicil to Cecil Higgins's will, clause 5 (1) (c).

25. The borough council approved the acquisition after an hour's debate by twenty-nine votes to fifteen. Ken Aldridge, interview in a BBC Home Service programme, *Arts Magazine*, 26 November 1958.

26. When Ken Aldridge died he bequeathed to the gallery the drawing on which Lowry based this painting: a rare record, since Lowry seldom retained such sketches and very few are in public collections.

27. In the former Philosophical Museum in Albion Street.

28. H. T. Schaffer's *Needle and Thread*.

29. £5,000 in five tranches of £1,000 over five years, in 1905; £35,000 for a new building, in 1917; and a further endowment of £20,000 in 1928 to form a purchase fund.

30. See his paintings of a trial in the Old Bailey in the University of Hull Art Collection (q.v.).

31. Major Kay was a collector whose paintings (including Monets, Tintorettos, Rembrandts and Sickerts) were sold in the 1970s.

32. A total of fifty logboats have been found in Europe, of which only twenty date from the 1st century A D or earlier (McGrail).

33. I am indebted to Martin Millett and Sean McGrail, 'The Archaeology of the Hasholme Longboat', *Archaeology Journal*, 144, 1987, pp. 69–155.

34. Originally called the Museum of Fisheries and Shipping.

35. The ice age coastline was ten to twelve miles offshore from its current line.

36. Timber from the Baltic has always been a major import into Hull.

37. In 1299 it received a Royal Charter, from Edward I, and became Kingston-upon-Hull. In the 18th and 19th centuries trade expanded in the Mediterranean and North America.

38. It was Scoresby who alerted Sir Joseph Banks and the Royal Society, in 1817, to ice-free seas in northern Greenland. This information led to the 1818 expedition led by John Ross during which the polar Inuit people were first encountered. Artefacts brought back from Ross's expedition, including a sled lashed together with bone and ivory pieces, are in the British Museum (q.v.).

39. See also Whitby Museum for Scoresby memorabilia, including the home-made electromagnetic instruments he made.

40. v. Ferens Art Gallery.

41. *Art in Britain 1890–1940*, catalogue, 1967, p. 6.

42. Further gifts by the V&A Museum, the Gulbenkian Foundation and the National Art Collections Fund.

43. v. Ferens Art Gallery, Hull.

44. Sitwell described Moat's voice as 'like some foghorn endowed with splendour' in his autobiography, *Left Hand, Right Hand*.

45. This piece is only on loan.

46. *Hull Museums Publication*, No. 34, 1906, p. 8 (Malet Lambert History Reprints, No. 50. 1983).

47. The collection was bought by the council from Jessie Miller for £100 in 1886, even before the old Keighley museum was founded. The specimens were arranged by the old museum's first curator, Seth Lister Morley, 1904–10.

48. Lees's *Flora of West Yorkshire*, 1888, remains the standard work. His collection contains important voucher specimens.

49. Hebden lichens are in the Leeds Museum (q.v.). He also collected for the Royal Botanic Gardens, Edinburgh, and for the Ulster Museum (q.v.).

50. I am indebted to Alison Armstrong, curator of the museum from 1975 to 2003, for all the background information on these collections.

51. Miall went on to be curator of Leeds Museum 1871–91.

52. I am indebted to A. J. Pacey and his paper, 'Emerging From the Museum: Joseph Dawson, Mineralogist, 1740–1813', *British Journal of the History of Science*, 36 (3), September 2003, p. 8, for information on Joseph Dawson, his collection and his catalogue.

53. The fossil was scientifically described in 'On a new Labyrinthodent from Bradford', *Quarterly Journal of the Geological Society*, vol. xxv, 1869.

54. Ibid.

55. Ibid. Thomas Thompson (the 'p' was a 19th-century form), in *A System of Chemistry*, Edinburgh, 1802, set out a system of classifying chemicals suggested by Abraham Gottlob Werner, of the Freiberg Mining Academy in Saxony, that took account of the chemical composition of minerals. It differed in its view of how rocks had been formed from that of the Scottish geologist James Hutton.

56. Entomology collections include that of C. R. Haxley, a British lepidoptera collection, one of the best visually in the north of England. It includes voucher specimens.

57. Thomas Jervis, '*The Energy of Talent and the Reward of Active Virtue* . . . an Address Delivered at the Interment of Joseph Dawson', pamphlet, Bradford, 1814.

58. The magazine *Blast* was published by Lewis in 1914.

59. The Vorticists held their only exhibition in June 1915 at the Doré Gallery, organised by Wyndham Lewis, with work by William Roberts and Edward Wadsworth, among others.

60. Of Iris Barry, later the curator of film at the Museum of Modern Art, New York.

61. This is the preliminary painting for a life-sized version in the Museum of Modern Art, New York.

62. Rothenstein, *Modern English Painters*, p. 15.

63. John Cheere. Cheere made a profitable business out of reproducing antique marbles (and the work of contemporary sculptors such as Michael Rysbrack, Peter Scheemakers and Roubiliac), in ceramic and plaster, painted to pass as bronze at a distance, in alcoves or on top of bookshelves.

64. Joseph Nollekens was trained by Scheemakers, worked in Rome 1760–70 and returned to England, where he established a career as a portraitist.

65. v. Marble Hill House, where there is a plaster version.

66. Joseph Gott has more than twenty pieces here: busts in marble of local worthies and patrons, classical mythological subjects, reliefs, medallions and a fine marble of *A Greyhound* (1827), made three years after he moved to Rome. His *Dying Spartacus* (1820) is in Sir John Soane's Museum (q.v.).

67. Entitled *A Dream of Joy after a Sleep of Sorrow* (c. 1908–14) and adapted from the work by Rafael Monti (*A Sleep of Sorrow and a Dream of Joy* in the V&A, q.v.), it was, for Gilbert, an auto-biographical work and perhaps his major achievement. It was made for Wilson's house in Leeds, Rutland Lodge. A plaster wax maquette for it is also in the collection.

68. Gill's design was executed by David Kindersley.

69. *Maternity* (1929) in Hopton Wood stone; and the enigmatic *Mask* (1929) in cast concrete.

70. The maquette and working model for this, both in plaster, are also in the collection. The bronze itself is on loan from the Henry Moore Foundation at Perry Green, Hertfordshire.

71. Rothenstein, *Modern English Painters*, p. 321.

72. The manuscript, 1929, has original drawings by Gaudier-Brzeska, and photographs by Walter Benington. The first edition, 1930, was published by William Heinemann, London.

73. The maquettes are exhibited in the art gallery.

74. At the time of writing the Leeds Museum building has been reclaimed by the City Library. A new building is under construction.

75. I am indebted for this and much else about Leeds Museum to Brears, and Brears and Davies.

76. *Victoria Museum Almanac*, Leeds, 1870. Admission to the Victoria Museum cost one penny.

77. Chantrell served his articles with Sir John Soane, 1807–14.

78. Augustus Woolaston Franks, when Keeper of the Department of British and Medieval Antiquities and Ethnography at the British Museum, regularly visited regional museums, filling notebooks with drawings and notes. He describes it as a 'chief's cap from New Guinea'.

79. See Beowulf.

80. Freyr, son of Njord, was the old Norse god of fruitfulness, the giver of sun and rain, the font of all prosperity.

81. Stroud, *Capability Brown*.

82. Richard Bickle, *Harewood: A Guide Book*, 1959 and 1962.

83. Forrest's *Tour of Derbyshire*, c. 1769–70 ff. 32–34, British Library Additional Manuscript 42, 232, noted by Storey, pp. 35–6.

84. Storey, p. 23.

85. Chippendale's invoice for £250. See Gilbert, pp. 296–307.

86. Chippendale's invoice for £86 for, in his words, 'A Very Large rich Commode with exceedingly fine Antique Ornaments . . .', Storey, p. 31.

87. Jewell.

88. See his work at Windsor Castle (q.v.) and Kedleston.

89. These tables, part of the same commission, may have been made by Thomas Chippendale Jnr, after his father's death.

90. Sykes and Montgomery-Massingberd, p. 352, tell how when Lord Clanricarde, a notorious miser who dressed like a tramp and frequently 'Stank to high heaven', was lunching alone in his club, Lascelles, out of courtesy, sat with him for half an hour, a rare occurrence. A rather less charitable interpretation of Clanricarde's motives is that he changed his will to spite the 5th Earl.

91. This was at one time attributed to Leonardo da Vinci. The rocky landscape, the saint's hand against a page of the Bible, the deployment of colour and texture in the cloak: all are evidence of a great talent.

92. Later Foreign Secretary and British Ambassador in Washington.

93. On loan to the National Gallery (q.v.).

94. See also the Barber Institute of Fine Art, (q.v.).

95. See Batoni's portrait of Sir Thomas Gascoigne at nearby Lotherton Hall (q.v.).

96. Smith, W., p. 255.

97. Guardi painted this at least eight times, probably in the 1770s. Other examples can be seen in the Wallace Collection (q.v.) and Penrhyn Castle (q.v.).

98. William Marshall was at the forefront of the 18th-century agricultural revolution, alongside his bitter rival, Arthur Young. Young was a skilful worker of the London establishment and was appointed to be the first Secretary of the Board of Agriculture (1790), but Marshall's surveys of the rural economy of Britain, county by county, 1787–1815, were informed by a greater practical knowledge of agriculture than Young possessed and, probably, had more influence on the development of agriculture. See Horn.

99. William Marshall, *Proposals for A Rural Institute*. A copy is in the museum.

100. The collection, including material from Kirk's excavation of the Roman Villa at Rudston, went to the Castle Museum, York.

101. Sidney Smith's widow, Maud, telephoned John Rushton and donated everything to the museum on condition that Rushton and Clitheroe removed it during the course of one Sunday: cameras, glass negative plates, and over two thousand photographs, later collected by Gordon Clitheroe in *Pickering* (1999), *Ryedale* (2000) and *Pickering, the Second Selection* (2002).

102. Invented in 1813 by George Chymer of Philadelphia.

103. Leader.

104. Leader and Bradbury.

105. Petrowski.

106. School of Design until 1855.

107. Alfred Stevens studied in Italy and was particularly influenced by High Renaissance art, employing architectural motifs, with which to decorate his cast-iron stoves and fireplaces, which have a Renaissance flavour. Some of his designs for the interior of Dorchester House, London (demolished 1929), are now in the Walker Art Gallery (q.v.).

108. Freyling, p. 7.

109. See also the Silver Crucifix and Candlesticks for the Lady Chapel of the Roman Catholic Metropolitan Cathedral in Liverpool (1969),

with the figure of Christ by Elisabeth Frink, and the large nave altar cross and candlesticks for Southwell Minster (1963).

110. 1952, unpublished, Royal College of Art Archive.

111. The Round Building, Hathersage, designed by Michael Hopkins and Partners (1990).

112. The guild commissioned a reconstruction of it by Philippa Abrahams (2000), in tempera on panel, which is here.

113. The painting, 57 by 89 inches, is too large to exhibit in the space allotted to Ruskin in the Millennium Gallery. Bunney was paid £500 for it.

114. Notably the black-and-white illustration in chapter 1, 'Help is to hand in the world perilous'.

115. Hurled against Victorian values in *Unto This Last*, four short essays published in 1860.

116. Outside the gallery, the Guild of St George continues to do good work, notably in its Campaign for Drawing, launched in 2001, which has reasserted the importance of drawing as a means of teaching people how to see.

117. Rothenstein, *Modern English Painters*.

118. Spalding, F., p. 296.

119. Rothenstein, *Modern English Painters*, p. 18.

120. Ibid.

121. Rothenstein, *Modern English Painters*.

122. A further bequest by J. Y. Cowlishaw, another nephew of J. N. Mappin, financed the landscaping of Weston Park.

123. Tooby, *In Perpetuity*.

124. J. Pilkington had led an excavation at Arbor Low in 1789.

125. Bateman.

126. St George Gray was trained by General Pitt Rivers, whose assistant he was on the excavation of the Romano-British villa at Iwerne in 1897.

127. Wharncliffe is a corruption of Quern-cliffe.

128. Excavated at Carleton-on-Trent, Nottinghamshire.

129. When Musgrave succeeded Philip Hendy, Leeds's main remit was to support modern art. At Leeds Musgrave managed to maintain that remit while developing Temple Newsam and making some superb acquisitions: Vasari, Subleyras, Stubbs, Morland.

130. Tooby, *Tate St Ives*, p. 44.

131. The collection includes etchings by sculptors: Jacob Epstein, Elisabeth Frink and Eduardo Paolozzi.

132. Grigson, G., p. 16.

133. It became the NCMM, opened by the National Heritage Minister, Iain Sproat MP, on 28 June 1995.

134. In some pits, such as the Victoria Colliery, Biddulph, shafts were not only lower than two feet in height but cut at an angle of forty-five degrees.

135. This corf, made of willow, was used at the abandoned William Pit, c. 1875, and brought to the surface in 1947.

136. Curator of the NCMM from September 1988 to October 1996, the daughter of a miner at Houghton Main Colliery.

137. Dry plates were not introduced until the 1880s.

138. *The Photographic Journal*, June 1931, p. 255.

139. The model made by R. A. Lightly.

140. Joseph Banks's diary, 26 June 1770, quoted in O'Brian, p. 135.

141. Many of which are now in the British Museum (q.v.).

142. Letter from the Royal Society to the Admiralty, 9 June 1768, quoted by O'Brian, p. 64.

143. Ibid.

144. Banks's diary, MS 8094 33. The Banks MS is in the Mitchen and Dixson collections at the State Library of New South Wales, Sydney, Australia.

145. Both were painted, from Parkinson's drawings, by J. F. Miller, the draughtsman on the voyage.

146. O'Brian, p. 154, but he also quotes the *Endeavour* Journal, 1 73, on which page a footnote reports Banks's list as 'Resolution, Zoffany, J.F. Miller and James Miller (draughtsmen) £100 per year each'. It seems unlikely that Zoffany, already a Royal Academian, would accept £100 per year, or the same remuneration as two draughtsmen.

147. Banks was replaced by the 'unscrupulous and disagreeable' (O'Brian, p. 156) Johann Reinhold Foster.

148. Ellis flouted Royal Navy regulations by publishing his account of the voyage before the official one, thus ending his naval career.

149. Saumarez Smith, *The Building of Castle Howard*, p. 130.

150. Vanbrugh was assisted by Nicholas Hawksmoor.

151. *The Relapse* and *The Provok'd Wife* brought Vanbrugh instant success and celebrity. Just as he had never designed a building before Castle Howard, he had never written a play before *The Relapse*.

152. The 4th Earl went on two tours of Italy: 1714–15, when he was aged twenty; and 1738–9, by which time he had become an experienced collector. On the second visit he took his son with him.

153. Jonathan Scott (pp. 68–71) chronicles Carlisle's dealings with his agents in Italy, particularly Belisario Amadei, Antonio Maria Zanetti (in Venice) and the ubiquitous Francesco de' Ficoroni.

154. The 5th Earl bought this from the Orléans sale as a Tintoretto. It was later reattributed to Parmigianino and it is now thought to be by Bedoli.

155. He first sat to Reynolds as a nine-year-old, dressed in Van Dyck costume, in 1757–8. The portrait is in the Long Gallery.

156. The three panels, from an original set of eight depicting figures from Chaucer's *The Legend of Good Women*, were originally in the Red House.

157. Downes (p. 33) notes that Vanbrugh was not alone in depicting Apollo and Phaeton. It had served Antonio Verrio on the Queen's Staircase at Windsor Castle (q.v.) and Sir James Thornhill at Chatsworth (west front staircase) (q.v.).

158. See *The Volunteers* (1860), a painting that is saved from being sentimental and stereotyped by Hardy's observation and attention to detail: see the still life of fruit on the table, the mother rolling out pastry.

159. This is the earliest extant group of such bronzed casts, made soon after the introduction of this process. See Brears and Davies, p. 6.

160. See *Benaiah* (c. 1829), a smaller version of the National Gallery of Scotland's painting of the same subject. 'My aim in all my great pictures,' wrote Etty, 'has been to paint some great moral on the heart.'

161. The Sienese Gerolamo Di Benvenuto and Bernardino Fungai; Giovanni Di Niccolo Mansueti, a pupil of Gentile Bellini; Giulio Cesare Procaccini, the Venetian Giovanni Battista Pittone and Bernardo Bellotto, the nephew of Canaletto.

162. The other panels are in Munich at the Alte Pinakothek.

163. Giovanni Battista Agucchi was secretary to Cardinal Pietro Aldobrandini, the patron who

brought so many Bolognese painters to Rome in the early 17th century and so shaped the development of Baroque painting. He was a friend of both Domenichino and Annibale Carracci.

164. Milner-White was chaplain (1912–18) and then dean (1918–41) of King's College, Cambridge, where he instigated the Service of Nine Lessons and Carols on Christmas Eve (1928).

165. Bernard Leach, *Beyond East and West: Memoirs, Portraits and Essays*, Faber and Faber 1978, p. 175, quoted by Riddick, p. 64.

166. In Milner-White's view, 'Probably Murray's masterpiece – he so considers it', although his *Cow and Trellis* (in the Fitzwilliam Museum, q.v.) has strong claims to that accolade.

167. Soon after Murray made this he resigned his post as head of department at the Royal College of Art and emigrated to Rhodesia. He lived a further twenty-three years but made no more pots. Maurice Collis, in his introduction to the catalogue of the 1958 Leicester Galleries exhibition, wrote of this and the small group of other tall, slender pots, that they were 'quite unique, for no other potter of today, to my knowledge, has attempted such a difficult task' (Riddick, p. 100).

168. Other collections of quality include Ernest Marsh's (now at the National Museums and Galleries on Merseyside); Henry Bergen's (the Potteries Museum); Bernard Rackham's (V&A); Sydney Greenslade's (National Museums and Galleries of Wales) and George Eumorphopoulos (Sainsbury Centre for Visual Arts), and the forty-seven pieces that Milner-White gave to Southampton City Art Gallery (his home town) in 1939 (all q.v.).

169. Jeremy Musson, *Country Life*, 8 June 2000.

170. Christopher Hussey, *Country Life*, 29 July 1922.

171. Their names derive from a visit by Edward VII and Queen Alexandra (and their second daughter, Princess Victoria) in June 1900 when they were Prince and Princess of Wales.

172. Green bought the Boulle, which was originally part of the Hertford Collection (now The Wallace Collection, q.v.) from the sale that followed Lady Wallace's death in 1897.

173. Fielding.

174. Cooper.

175. Macquoid was a friend of Green, who may well have encouraged Macquoid to undertake his *History*.

176. Jeremy Musson, *Country Life*, 8 June 2000.

177. By which he meant the V&A.

178. This is still played in Scandinavian countries.

179. 650,000 steam locomotives have been built worldwide.

180. Pevsner, *Yorkshire*, p. 138.

181. Auden.

182. Designed by Philip Hardwick and built in 1838 for the London to Birmingham Railway. Euston was for many years the only northbound railway exit from London. The most notable feature was the massive Doric arch entrance. The London to Birmingham was the first trunk railway in the world and Hardwick's arch represented a monument to railway achievement. Either side of the arch were stone lodges; each had a grand Doric central door, linked together by ornamental gates. This cast-iron screen was designed by the locksmith and inventor J. J. Bramah. At the time of completion, the Euston arch was higher than any other building in London. In 1846 Sir Philip Hardwick, along with his son Philip C. Hardwick, designed the Great Hall at Euston, one of the finest public rooms in London. The station was extended again in 1873. Between 1963 and 1968, every trace of the old station was destroyed by British Railways. The construction of a new station building was carried out in conjunction with the electrification of the West Coast mainline. The new station was opened by HM The Queen in 1968. To the front of the station are reminders of the old station. Beside the Euston Road stand two Portland stone lodges that once guarded the entrance to the old station. The war memorial, another survivor, is set a little further back.

183. Midland Railways abolished second-class travel in 1875 and brought third-class up to the standard of second, notionally.

184. Flavius Valerius Constantinus, Roman Emperor AD 306–37.

185. Charles Wellbeloved, *A Descriptive Account of the Antiquities in the Grounds and in the Museum of the Yorkshire Philosophical Society*, 1852: the museum's first catalogue.

186. *Yorkshire Philosophical Society Record*, 1958, p. 4.

187. Architect of the National Gallery.

188. Excavated in 1875 on the site of the railway

station, this perfectly preserved switch of a young girl's hair was held in place by two cantharus-headed pins.

189. Excavated at Fishgate. Chignons were fashionable in the middle of the 3rd century.

190. The jewel was found by Mr Ted Seaton in 1985 and the ring by Mr Robert Angus in 1990.

191. *Yorkshire Philosophical Society Record*, 1829, p. 5.

192. Blackie.

SCOTLAND

1. Edward Pinnington, 'Robert Brough, Painter', *Art Journal*, 1898, p. 147.

2. Hartrick, p. 206.

3. Sylvester, *About Modern Art*, p. 457.

4. Margaret Hasluck settled in Albania, the country she loved, until forced to flee in 1943 when the Germans invaded.

5. Designed by James Gillespie Graham.

6. Letter from William Beckford to Gregorio Franchi, 18 September 1813, quoted in Alexander, pp. 136–7.

7. The last year of Barr, Flight and Barr's partnership (1804–13).

8. This was wrongly catalogued as Meissen by the great connoisseur A.W. Franks, Keeper of Medieval Antiquities at the British Museum, in 1896.

9. Catalogued by the 2nd Earl in 1807 with a dedication by Sir Benjamin West, president of the Royal Academy. In it he wrote: 'Being possessed of several good portraits which belonged to my family, I began many years since to make additions to them. I have lately had an opportunity of increasing my Collection, so that I believe, there are few more numerous.' Apart from Duff family portraits, it included works by Cornelius Johnson, Van Dyck and numerous portraits by Reynolds bought at his studio sale (1792). Fife also had works by Raphael, Titian and Rubens at Fife House in London.

10. Other, similar, sets are in the Metropolitan Museum, New York; Weston Park, Shropshire; and Osterley Park, Middlesex.

11. Chippendale's invoice of 9 July 1765 for eight large armchairs and four large sofas totalled £510. 4s. od., almost twice as much as Chippendale charged for any other commission in his long career.

12. This is the only piece of furniture that survived in place from the pre-1904 house.

13. Other pieces from the Fesch Sale are in the Royal Pavilion (q.v.) and the Lady Lever (q.v.).

14. Palladio.

15. Campbell.

16. Ware.

17. Most of the Chippendale furniture arrived in 1774 and had nothing to do with John or Robert Adam.

18. On the Grand Tour Patrick Home amassed a significant library of some 4,000 volumes.

19. Essay by Professor Alistair Rowan, *Paxton Picture Gallery*, p. 8.

20. James Nasmyth, quoted in Holloway, p. 17.

21. Buchan, *The Island of Sheep*, p. 241.

22. Throughout I am indebted to John de Vere Loder.

23. The rhododendron gardens were inspired by the 3rd Lord Strathcona's father-in-law, Sir Gerald Loder, later Lord Wakehurst, whose Wakehurst Place Gardens are now a Sussex outstation of the Royal Botanic Gardens, Kew. Seeing how ponticum thrived, he proposed the introduction in the late 1920s first of popular hybrid rhododendrons and then of over a hundred species in a designated Rhododendron Dell. I am indebted to Patrick M. Synge's 'Rhododendrons at Colonsay', *RHS Rhododendron and Camellia Yearbook*, 1955, and to an unpublished paper outlining the history of the garden by Tim Longville of Mayport, Cumbria (2003), quoted by kind permission of Lord Strathcona.

24. The derivations of the names Colonsay and Oronsay are disputed, although there is agreement that the 'ay' is the Norse for island, *ey*. Col may come from Gaelic for hazel (*coll*) or the Norse for hilltop (*kollr*), although some authorities argue for Colbhansiagh (Kolbein's or Colvin's island). Oronsay is accepted as the Norse *Orfiris-ey*, ebb-tide island (Loder, p. xliv).

25. Between 1879 and 1882 Symington Grieve excavated limpet shells and barbed bone and shell implements from Caistellnan Gillean (Grieve), as did Dr Paul Mellars in the 1980s (Mellars).

26. There are fine standing stones at Garvard and Balnahard, and one half-fallen at Ardskenish, north of the Strand at Garvard. There is a stone circle on Beinn Earrnigil, south-east of the summit, 98 feet east to west, 108 feet north to south.

27. These artefacts, and the iron rivets of the

boat, are exhibited at the Museum of Scotland (q.v.).

28. 'Colonsay and Oronsay', *An Inventory of the Monuments Extracted from Argyll*, vol. 5, Royal Commission on the Ancient and Historical Monuments of Scotland, 1994.

29. Pevsner and Arneil Walker, pp. 590–94. 'Colonsay and Oronsay', op. cit., pp. 55–63.

30. Pennant.

31. I am indebted to Jardine and *Exploring Colonsay* for details of plants and birds.

32. a.k.a. left-handed Coll.

33. McNeill.

34. The Duncans were a local family. A three-quarter-length oil sketch of the figure of Admiral Duncan is in Yale University Art Gallery, New Haven. Three chalk studies for *The Victory* are in the Metropolitan Museum of Art, New York.

35. James Keiller & Son had been established by his grandfather in 1797 and a century later was an international company with factories and outlets around the world.

36. Electric lighting had only become available ten years before. The McManus was one of the first galleries to install it.

37. Bell's portrait of the Dundee surgeon *John Crichton* owes much to Raeburn and would be worthy of him.

38. The sixty-one Coxes and the Cotman were part of a large bequest by William G. Shiell (1954–5).

39. The McManus is yet another gallery to which Brangwyn presented paintings and drawings (more than fifty). Mr Frank Lewis left his collection of more than 250 drawings, purchased in 1965 with a grant from the NACF.

40. Unlike the larger version of this in the Walker Art Gallery (q.v.), this has two predelle in the same frame. The subject is taken from Dante's *La Vita Nuova*.

41. Burne-Jones designed the stained glass for St Giles's, Dundee, and while he was in the city the corporation commissioned six stained-glass portraits of Scottish heroes: *William Wallace, Robert the Bruce, Mary Stuart*, etc.

42. Paolozzi's studios contained 'some five thousand sculptures (mainly plaster), fragments, and works on paper, the studio effects (home-made furniture, tools), rummage boxes of small plaster casts, toys, boxes of tearsheets and manuscripts, an archive of photographs and slides (both of the

artist's own works and of things that have interested him throughout his career) and a library of nearly three thousand books and catalogues'. Pearson, p. 7.

43. Gifford, McWilliam and Walker, *Edinburgh*.

44. Ibid., p. 9.

45. On 30 April 1958.

46. He explored these ideas in 'Bunk', an illustrated lecture at the ICA, April 1952.

47. In the early 1930s he excavated the Stone Circle and West Kennett Avenue at Windmill Hill, Avebury, Wiltshire, with Professor Stuart Piggott. The Alexander Keiller Museum (q.v.) is described by English Heritage as 'one of the most important prehistoric archaeological collections in Britain'.

48. Cowling et al., p. 84. It is a game like Poetry Consequences or Head, Body and Legs. Each player writes a random line, or draws part of a figure, folds the paper over, passes it on to the next player, and so the game continues. When the bottom of the page is reached it is opened and read aloud.

49. It was painted by Magritte in 1937. Magritte exchanged it with Paul Eluard for a painting by Max Ernst and Penrose acquired it in 1938 as part of his block purchase of Eluard's collection.

50. Sylvester and Whitfield, vol. II, Oil Paintings and Object, 1931–1948, no. 434.

51. Sanouillet and Peterson, p. 136.

52. Cowling et al., p. 16.

53. Honour and Fleming, p. 809.

54. *The Harpsichord and Clavichord – an Introductory Survey*, Oxford, 1959, second edition, 1973. Russell also wrote the catalogue for the collection of keyboard instruments in the Victoria and Albert Museum.

55. As evidenced by a letter from C. J. Rheinhold, Amsterdam, 1867.

56. 10 August 1960.

57. It was converted by architects Robert Matthew, Johnson-Marshall and Partners, in 1981.

58. The remainder of Sir Alexander Maitland's gift of paintings by all the major Impressionists and Post-Impressionists is exhibited in the National Gallery of Scotland (q.v.).

59. The Scott-Hay collection contains notable paintings by Joan Eardley and Robin Philipson.

60. This group was strengthened by purchases of Grosz, Dix, Beckmann, Barlach and Feininger in the 1980s.

61. The Dean Gallery of the SNGMA, see below. Another version has been installed near Newcastle upon Tyne railway station.

62. Mondrian was a Theosophist. Theosophists saw existence in terms of polarities (male/female, positive/negative, black/white, horizontal/vertical). Mondrian's grids exemplify such opposites, in balance. This painting was acquired by Winifred Nicholson from Mondrian in the 1930s.

63. Gifford, McWilliam and Walker, *Edinburgh*, p. 318.

64. Ibid., p. 283.

65. Chalmers.

66. Yarmouth's pictures formed the basis of the Wallace Collection (q.v.).

67. The *Cupid* is part of a group, *Apollo and Cupid*, from which it has been detached. Only two versions are known: in the Royal Palace in Madrid and in the Liechtenstein.

68. Professor Watson Gordon, 1880–1930.

69. In an undated syllabus, Duncan Macmillan, *The Torrie College Catalogue*, p. 13.

70. See Ernst's *Antediluvian Landscape* (c. 1967) in the Torrie Collection.

71. By the reign of Malcolm Canmore (1057–93) Edinburgh Castle had become the residence of the king.

72. These inscriptions are partially obliterated – presumably an attempt by those close to her son, James I of England, to clear her name.

73. The Scottish National Portrait Gallery (q.v.) has a painting (c. 1664) by John Michael Wright of the handsome Bruce, quill in hand.

74. Bruce was the King's Surveyor of Royal Works. His builder was the King's Master Mason, Robert Mylne, who did the original designs for St Cecilia's Hall, Cowgate, which now houses the Russell Collection (q.v.).

75. Gifford, McWilliam and Walker, *Edinburgh*, pp. 144–5.

76. After Prince Albert's death Gambara's original frescoes were transferred on to canvas and moved to the Palace of Holyroodhouse (q.v.) in 1881.

77. In eighteen months her father-in-law, her mother and her husband, Francis II of France, died.

78. Cursiter, p. 22.

79. De Witt remained in Edinburgh when his work on the palace was completed and painted still lifes and genre scenes for, among others, Sir John Clerk of Penicuik (v. the Russell Collection).

80. The journal of Queen Victoria, the Palace of Holyroodhouse, 29 August 1850.

81. Regrettably the pink tights that the King was said to have worn under his kilt are not in evidence.

82. Queen Victoria's journal, op. cit.

83. The jewel belonged to Lady Waldegrave at the time of purchase.

84. The reliquary is one of only nine such Irish/ Scottish shrines, shaped like houses, that survive in Europe. It, like the comparable reliquary at the Abbey of San Salvatore in Tuscany, probably contained saintly relics, perhaps fragments of the bones of saints.

85. It was identified as the Breccbennach by Joseph Anderson in 1880 (J. Anderson, 'Notice of an Ancient Celtic Reliquary Exhibited by Sir Archibald Grant, Bart, of Monymusk', *Proceedings of the Society of Antiquaries of Scotland 14*, 1879–80, pp. 431–5). Recent research by David H. Caldwell, Keeper of History and Applied Art at the National Museums of Scotland, casts doubt on that identification. His paper in *Proceedings of the Society of Antiquaries of Scotland 131*, 2001, pp. 267–82, describes the history of the reliquary, and the arguments for and against it being the Breccbennach.

86. Calder, p. vii.

87. Gifford, McWilliam and Walker, *Edinburgh*, p. 187.

88. Scotland shares this distinction with Ireland, which, too, was not conquered by Rome.

89. The museum's collection of minerals is based on those of Patrick Dudgeon (1878) and of Professor Forster Heddle (1894), the largest collection in existence, acquired by the museum for £1,000.

90. Hutton.

91. Miller documented his discoveries in *The Old Red Sandstone* and his life in *My Schools and School Masters*. He moved to Edinburgh in 1840 to edit *The Witness*, a periodical at the centre of the controversy between Church and people about Congregationalists' right to choose their ministers. Miller passionately opposed the Highland Clearances. He shot himself in 1856, his masterwork *The Testimony of the Rocks* being published posthumously in 1857.

92. James Buchan, p. 296.

93. Maurois.

94. The mechanics and carved figures were made by Eduard Bersudsky; the artistic director was Tatiana Jakovskaya.

95. Lord Wemyss, *Memoirs*, vol. 1, 1912, pp. 26–7, quoted by Timothy Clifford in 'Botticelli's Wemyss Madonna', *Burlington Magazine*, 1999.

96. The RSA was built 1822–6 and 1831–6; the NGS, 1850–57.

97. With the exception of William Hamilton Beattie's department store Jenner's (1893–5).

98. An anonymous painting here, *c.* 1865–70, shows the original Playfair scheme designed by David Ramsay-Hay who also designed the interiors of the Palace of Holyroodhouse. His claret walls, geranium-pink pedestals, Dutch-weave green carpet and grained oak skirtings grow out of his colour theories, described in his book *The Laws of Harmonious Colour* (1828). Timothy Clifford's 1980s redesign replaces the sombre designs, 1937–8, of Stanley Cursiter, also seen here in a Cursiter watercolour.

99. Purchased for the Trustees' Academy in Genoa (1839) by Andrew Wilson, its former master. Albacini's casts, of which there are more than two hundred, were taken from originals in the Villa Borghese (viz. a bust of *Lucius Verus*, AD 130–169, co-Emperor with Marcus Aurelius).

100. A pair of English tables designed by Robert Adam, carved by Sefferin Alken (*c.* 1775) for Sir Watkin Williams Wynn; a pair of Italian rococo giltwood sofas from the collection of Marchese Sacchetti.

101. These have, with the exception of Jacob van Ruisdael's *The Banks of a River* (1649), been returned to Edinburgh University and now form the main part of the collection of the Talbot Rice Gallery (q.v.).

102. The RSA's collection also included Veronese's late *Mars, Venus and Cupid* (*c.* 1580) and Guercino's early *Virgin and Child with the Infant St John the Baptist* (*c.* 1615).

103. Lady Murray also gave a drawing in which Ramsay observes his wife, looking down, with great tenderness, one of a portfolio of preparatory studies for portraits.

104. The model may have been Geertje Dircx.

105. The Orcadian artist Stanley Cursiter was educated at the Edinburgh College of Art. His own early painting shows the influence of Futurism, particularly of Severini, and reinforced his enthusiasm for a Scottish national gallery of modern art, for which he made a proposal in 1930. After retiring from the directorship of the NGS he was appointed His Majesty's Painter and Limner in Scotland in 1948.

106. Sir James Caw gave to the gallery, from his own collection of Scottish paintings, works by Sir James Guthrie, Arthur Melville and William McTaggart.

107. In 2002 this entered the gallery's permanent collection, being purchased under the government's acceptance-in-lieu scheme, with help from the NACF, the Heritage Lottery Fund and the Scottish Executive.

108. The NGS owns twenty-three paintings by Wilkie. In addition to the narrative, genre paintings (*The Letter of Introduction; The Irish Whiskey Still; Distraining for Rent*) there are portraits that make you wish Wilkie had given more time to portraiture (the early *Artist's Sister* and that of *William Chalmers Bethune and his Wife and Daughter*, 1804, which owes much to Raeburn, and matches the best of that master). The NGS also has drawings by Wilkie that show that his skills as a draughtsman match those as a painter.

109. Sir Timothy Clifford was appointed Director of the NGS in 1984 and Director-General of the National Galleries of Scotland in 2001. Previously he had been Director of the Manchester City Art Gallery, 1978–84.

110. A preparatory study for the altarpiece known as *The Madonna of the Fish* in the Prado, Madrid, painted by Raphael (*c.* 1512–14) for the chapel of the Del Doce family in San Domenico, Naples.

111. This is the second version of the sculpture that Canova originally made for the Empress Josephine in 1813 (now in the Hermitage Museum, St Petersburg). The 6th Duke of Bedford commissioned a second, slightly changed, version in 1815–17 for the specially built Temple of the Graces at Woburn Abbey. When the Duke of Bedford offered it for sale in 1994, the NGS acquired it jointly with the Victoria and Albert Museum. It will be on display alternately for periods of seven years.

112. Both Duff and the Swiss geologist Louis Agassiz believed the fossil to be that of a fish. Later T. H. Huxley realised it was that of a reptile, stagonolepsis.

113. The main collection of Miller's work is in the Museum of Scotland (q.v.).

114. Miller, *The Old Red Sandstone*.

115. Elgin's medical officer of health.

116. The National Archives of Scotland, Miscellaneous collections, GD 1/53/7: Charles Edward Stuart's letter to the remaining Jacobite forces a few days after Culloden, thanking them for their support and ordering them to disband and save themselves.

117. Ibid. GD 1/53/93.

118. Even this is not clear. Three other guns lay claim to this 'authenticity'.

119. Bathurst.

120. The building of the Destitution Road was financed by the government's Destitution Committee in 1848 to provide work after the devastation caused by the potato famine of 1846.

121. Close-Brooks.

122. The recreated shop is Farquhar Macrae's shop. Roddie Maclean's shop was at Badachro, but the shops are similar.

123. 'A Poem made when the Gaelic Society of Inverness was a hundred years old', MacLean, p. 255.

124. The Deed of Gift specified that the building should be within four miles of Killearn in Stirlingshire and not less than sixteen miles from the Royal Exchange in Glasgow.

125. Four by Rodin (*The Age of Bronze*, 1875, *Eve After the Fall*, 1887, *The Thinker*, 1880 and *The Call to Arms*, *c.*1878) and an Epstein (*Lilian Shelly*, 1920). The collection contains fourteen Rodin bronzes in total.

126. Fragments of the original vase were found in Hadrian's Villa at Tivoli and were reconstructed, probably by Giovanni Battista Piranesi and the sculptor Bartolomeo Cavaceppi. The reconstruction was financed by Sir William Hamilton, who presented the vase to his nephew, the 2nd Earl of Warwick.

127. Sekhmet, 18th Dynasty, 1560–1304 BC.

128. Rameses II, King of Egypt, *c.*1290–24, 19th Dynasty: the builder of the rock temple of Abu Simnel.

129. Isin and Larsa were two of the city states that grew early in the 2nd millennium (*c.*2020–1600 BC).

130. Urartu was north of Assyria, in modern Turkey, between the Black and Caspian Seas.

131. Tang Dynasty, AD 618–907. These figures

stood guard at the entrance to tombs against evil spirits – hence their fierce or grotesque appearance.

132. Dutch painters who in the 1870s and 1880s emulated the Barbizon School with great caution and commercial success. Burrell bought more than fifty paintings by Mattijs Maris through the Glasgow gallery owned by Craibe Angus.

133. He kept the records of his dealings after 1911 in twenty-eight exercise books.

134. Wilfred Drake (glass), Frank Partridge (furniture), John Hunt (medieval), John Sparks (Chinese ceramics) and Alexander Reid (paintings).

135. In 1893–4 they ordered twelve new ships at the bottom of the market. In 1905, they built a further twenty-nine, and eight more in 1909–10, selling the lot in the first two years of the First World War.

136. Simpson and Milner Allen also designed the Cartwright Hall Art Gallery, Bradford. The competition for Glasgow was judged by a committee chaired by Sir Alfred Waterhouse, the architect of the Natural History Museum, London. The decision to appoint London architects was greeted with anger and derision, just as, twenty years earlier, had been the appointment of Sir George Gilbert Scott to design the new University of Glasgow in preference to a Scottish architect such as Alexander 'Greek' Thompson.

137. Frampton was commissioned in 1897 to oversee all the external sculpture. He completed *St Mungo*, the city's patron saint, but other sculptures are by F. Derwent Wood, W. Birnie Rhind, Johann Keller, Edward George Bramwell and Aristide Fabbrucci.

138. Kelvingrove House, designed in Adam style in 1782, was demolished to make way for the Glasgow International Exhibition of 1901 with which the city celebrated the new century and the opening of the art gallery and museum.

139. Built in 1855–6 by Archibald McLellan to display his collection of paintings in a purpose-built gallery designed by James Smith.

140. James 'Paraffin' Young, a pioneer in the oil industry, was a voracious collector. In addition to these swords, he acquired African material from the expeditions of Dr David Livingstone. These were given to the museum by Young's son, as were a number of paintings including two large landscapes by Salvator Rosa.

141. Attribution has been keenly contested for more than a hundred years. I am indebted to Francis Richardson, whose entry in the catalogue of the Royal Academy 1983 exhibition, *The Genius of Venice* (p. 170), chronicles the history of disagreements over its attribution, variously to Caviani in 1871, his pupils Sebastiano del Piombo (1913) and Titian (1927, by Longhi), or a collaboration between Giorgione and Titian. Berenson at various times gives it to all the above.

142. The altarpiece of the *Madonna Enthroned* is in the Bologna Gallery; another panel, *Baptism of Christ*, is in the Keller Collection in New York.

143. Reynolds wrote comparing *A Man in Armour* with Rubens's *Moonlit Landscape* (v. the Courtauld Collection): 'Rembrandt, who thought it of more consequence to paint light than the objects that are seen by it, has done this in a picture of Achilles which I have. The head is kept down to a very low tint, in order to preserve this due gradation and distinction between the armour and the face; the consequence of which is that upon the whole the picture is too black.' (Reynolds, ed. Wark, p. 162.) It, and Rembrandt's *The Carcase of an Ox*, were given in 1877 by Mrs Graham-Gilbert, the widow of the Scottish Academician John Graham-Gilbert. John Graham-Gilbert married one of his sisters, a rich heiress, Miss Gilbert of Yorkhill. He added her name to his and together they employed her fortune to acquire works of art.

144. It was originally in the collection of the Duke of Buckingham, who probably purchased it from Rubens, when sitting to him. Later it was in the collection of Sir James Thornhill, who painted the ceilings and walls of, among others, St Paul's (1717) and the Painted Hall at Greenwich, in each of which the debt to Rubens is clear. He was appointed History Painter in Ordinary to George I in 1718. He may have bought this Rubens when in Holland and Flanders in 1711, it having returned to Antwerp on Buckingham's death in 1628. Like the two Rembrandts (above), it was bequeathed by John Graham-Gilbert.

145. Angus's father-in-law was the Dutch dealer Elbert van Wisselingh. See Gould.

146. Theo and Vincent van Gogh shared a flat in Paris with Alex Reid (see Pickvance). Van Gogh painted Reid in 1887, a portrait that the gallery acquired in 1974 with the help from the NACF and a public appeal.

147. Lavery was born in Belfast (v. Ulster Museum and Art Gallery) but studied at Glasgow School of Art.

148. Although he was elected president of the Society of British Artists in 1885, Whistler was ignored by the London art establishment. This was the first of his paintings to enter a British public collection.

149. Mackintosh is strongly represented by his furniture for Miss Cranston's Tea Rooms in Ingram Street (1900–11) and by work produced by 'The Four': Mackintosh; his wife, Margaret Macdonald Mackintosh; her sister, Frances Macdonald MacNair; and Frances's husband, Herbert MacNair.

150. Spalding, J., *St Mungo*, p. 5.

151. Given to him by St Serf, on account of their close friendship. St Serf trained Kentigern as a priest.

152. The price of £8,200, reduced from £12,000 included copyright, the exploitation of which has returned a profit to the ratepayers of Glasgow.

153. Spalding, J., p. 71.

154. Van Raay was appointed Director of Pallant House Gallery, Chichester, in 1997.

155. Spalding, J., *Gallery of Modern Art Glasgow*, p. 24.

156. Hunter paid twelve guineas for this at Sir Robert Strange's sale.

157. Hunter gave a paper on *The Nylghai*, the Indian antelope, to the Royal Society on 28 February 1771.

158. The forty-three prints by Goya include first editions of *Los Caprichos* (1799) and *The Disasters of War* (1810–20).

159. Subsequent acquisitions have increased this to 80 oils, 100 pastels, 120 drawings and watercolours, over 390 etchings, 150 lithographs and 16 sketchbooks, in addition to his painting equipment and his collection of furniture, silver and ceramics.

160. Whose model is Ethel Birnie Philip, one of his three sisters-in-law.

161. Also of Ethel Birnie Philip, but unfinished and never exhibited in his lifetime.

162. Whistler was awarded a farthing's damages. The costs of the case, and the spiteful behaviour of a former patron Frederick Leyland, made Whistler bankrupt and homeless.

163. Williamson et al, p. 339.

164. Both Adam Smith and James Watt are former pupils of the university.

165. His picture collection included works by Rembrandt, Reynolds and Stubbs. It forms the basis of the Hunterian Art Gallery, opposite (q.v.).

166. William Hunter bequeathed the collection to Glasgow University, but with the stipulation that they were available for use for thirty years by his heir, Matthew Baille, who surrendered them in 1807 when they came from London to Glasgow.

167. The founder of the Hunterian Museum in London.

168. McLaughlan, pp. 29, 33 and 37.

169. O'Brian.

170. It is now twice this size.

171. Each token has an erotic or pornographic image on the obverse and a number on the reverse.

172. El Greco, Murillo, Velásquez and Goya are well represented in the National Gallery (q.v.) and the National Gallery of Scotland (q.v.); Murillo in the Dulwich Picture Gallery (q.v.); Velásquez, Ribera, Murillo in Apsley House (q.v.), which also has single examples of the work of Claudio Coello, Francisco de Zurbarán and Jusepe Martinez; and El Greco, Juan Batista Mazo, Antonio de Pereda and Goya at the Bowes Museum (q.v.) in the collection of John and Josephine Bowes.

173. R. Cumberland had published *Anecdotes of Eminent Painters in Spain* in 1787 (two vols.).

174. Domenikos Theotokopoulos, known as 'El Greco' (The Greek) when he moved to Spain in 1576.

175. Williamson et al, p. 612.

176. Ibid., p. 612.

177. Romney's portrait is of *Richard Cumberland*, who wrote the pioneering *Anecdotes of Eminent Painters in Spain* (two vols., 1787), on which Stirling Maxwell leant for his *Annals of the Artists of Spain* sixty years later, as he did on A. O'Neill's *A Dictionary of Spanish Painters* (1833–4).

178. This, and El Greco's *Portrait of a Man* (*c.* 1590), were bought from the sale at Christie's of King Louis Philippe's collection (previously in the Spanish Room at the Louvre). At the same time Queen Victoria purchased several Spanish portraits, including two by Antonio Moro of *King Philip II* and *Queen Juana of Austria*, now in the Royal Collection.

179. Sigüenza.

180. During his directorship of the National Gallery (1932–45), he was unable to add to the gallery's modest holdings of one El Greco, five Murillos and five Goyas.

181. Clark, *Civilisation*, pp. 13–14. Although he accepted that 'had [he] been talking about the history of art, it would not have been possible to leave out Spain'.

182. Built by Messrs John Wood & Sons, Port Glasgow, its engine is in the Science Museum (q.v.).

183. Model built by James D. Rennie, 1877.

184. By D. Neave & Son, Dundee, 1868.

185. Built by Alexander Hall, Dundee, 1873 (v. Aberdeen Maritime Museum).

186. Gourock Ropeworks, *c.* 1770s.

187. Mackellar's bequest was made in 1911, Caird's in 1918.

188. This is a reproduction, not an original.

189. Thomas Telford, 1808 survey.

190. The National Archives of Scotland, Scottish Record Office, miscellaneous collections. A message from Charles Edward Stuart to his remaining supporters. 'The fatall field of Culloden has dashed all our hopes to pieces and has left us nothing to deliberate upon but the mere safety of our person,' GD 1/53/7.

191. Ferrara was probably Spanish originally. There was also a Ferrara working in Venice in the 16th century; the name itself began to be adopted as a sign of quality by the German workshops; the majority of 18th-century blades are indeed German; the steel flintlock pistols are by J. Murdoch of Doune.

192. Scottish Record Office, Lord Forbes Papers: GD 52/139.

193. Marion Campbell of Kilberry, FSA Scot (Iton), Butter.

194. 'Kilmartin', *An Inventory of the Monuments Extracted from Argyll*, vol. 6, Royal Commission on the Ancient and Historical Monuments of Scotland, 1999, p. 22.

195. Ibid. The finds are now in the British Museum (q.v.).

196. Minutes of the Argyll Synod, 1946 and 1650.

197. From Italy, Hungary and Turkey (orpiment), Romania (red lead), Cornwall, France or Siberia (malachite).

198. Cursiter, p. 125.

199. Macdonald, p. 122.
200. He had fourteen children, from two marriages. His earliest biographer, James Caw, wrote that McTaggart 'loved to wreath the beauty of nature with the charm and innocence of childhood'.
201. They are carved from cannel, or parrot coal, so called because of the clicking noise it emits when burnt.
202. McWilliam, p. 106.
203. 274 pupils to 14 teachers.
204. In 1810 he had to raise £84,000 to take over the village as a separate concern. Four years later he bought the company at public auction for £114,100.
205. William Hazlitt, *Examiner*, 4 August 1816. See Hazlitt's *Works*, VII, p. 97.
206. Defoe, *An Account of the Conduct and Proceedings of the Late John Gow.*
207. The tools of Peter Peace Hercus of Kirkwall, Master of the *Narcissus*, 1913.
208. Published by William Nimmo, 1869.
209. The great auk became extinct in 1844.
210. Kate Heron is the architect daughter of the painter Patrick Heron.
211. John Irwin, 'Le Cachemirien', *John Morgan & Co. and the Kashmir Shawl*, Victoria & Albert Museum/HMSO, 1974.
212. The Phygaleian marbles, now in the British Museum, bought by the Prince Regent in 1814 for £15,000.
213. At a scale of 1:20, each of the forty-eight moulds was 2½ inches high and 6 inches long. They sold, framed, for thirty guineas a set.
214. Malding, p. 3.
215. Fergusson and Morris maintained separate addresses from 1913 to 1939. When they returned to Glasgow they lived together, from 1939 until his death, at 4 Clouston Street.
216. The description 'Colourists' was coined by Dr T. J. Honeyman, the Glasgow art curator and later Director of the Kelvingrove Art Gallery.
217. The National Galleries of Scotland: Glasgow Art Gallery and Museum, Kelvingrove; the Hunterian Art Gallery; the McManus Galleries, Dundee; the University of Stirling; Kirkcaldy Art Gallery; Paisley Art Gallery; the Aberdeen Art Gallery.
218. Fergusson, p. 49.
219. The Fauves, led by Matisse, exhibited for the first time at the Salon d'Automne in 1905.

220. The premieres of Diaghilev's production of Mussorgsky's *Boris Godunov* and the Ballets Russes were in 1909.
221. Matisse's *Blue Nude* and Derain's *Three Bathers* were both painted in 1909.
222. Murry, p. 155.
223. *Rhythm* is owned by the University of Stirling and *Les Eus* by the Hunterian Art Gallery, University of Glasgow.
224. Fergusson, p. 69.
225. Robin Millar, 'The Man Who Found the Rainbow', *Glasgow Evening Citizen*, 5 May 1948.
226. *Stirling Sonnets* by James Robertson.
227. The arms are not matriculated in any known heraldic register and must have been made up by the masons.
228. A battlement, overhanging parapet: a 'modern antique' word first used by Sir Walter Scott in *Heart of Midlothian*, chapter 26.
229. The wheel stair has a radius of ten feet.
230. See Batoni's portrait of *Caulfield*, later 1st Earl of Charlemont, now in the Yale Center for British Art, Paul Mellon Collection.
231. He shared these classes with the minimalist Archibald Robertson and the portrait painter George Watson (Thomson, D., p. 12).
232. Ibid., p. 7.
233. *Mrs Colin Campbell of Park c.*1808 (Glasgow Museum and Art Gallery, q.v.) or *Lady Clerk* (painted with her husband, Sir John Clerk), *c.*1792 (National Gallery of Ireland, Dublin).

WALES

1. In it is a poem that is possibly in the autograph of Dafydd ap Gwilym, the most celebrated Welsh poet of the 14th century.
2. The *Preiddeu Annwfn* refers to Arthur and his knights sailing in search of a spear and a cauldron.
3. The Davies sisters used part of the fortune they inherited from their industrialist grandfather David Davies, 'Top Sawyer', to create a collection of French Impressionists (now in the National Museum and Gallery of Wales) and to open a rural centre for Arts and Crafts at Gregynog Hall, near Newtown.
4. The 1918 report was written by painter and art educationalist Frederick Charles Richards. He was secretary of the Royal Society of

Painter-Etchers and Engravers, 1918–19. Fifteen of his etchings are in the collection.

5. He broke this by paying six guineas for F. L. Griggs's *Minsden Episcopi* in 1922 and seven guineas for Joseph Webb's *Chepstow from the Cliff* at Colnaghi's in 1933.

6. Annual Reports, 1925.

7. Blaker was appointed curator of the Holburne Museum of Art (q.v.) in 1905, where he had a studio and etching press. Several of his etchings and drawings are in the Aberystwyth Collection, including *Tête Farouche.*

8. Leach's *Pilgrim Plate* (*c.* 1973), bought in 1976; a vase by Denise Wren at Christie's auction in 1988.

9. Designed and built by Hansom & Welch of York. Hansom designed the carriage that bears his name.

10. Howard, *The State of the Prisons in England and Wales.*

11. Mayhew.

12. Stones had to be smashed into chippings, small enough to pass through the holes of a basin.

13. William Calcraft, chief hangman at Newgate Prison 1828–74. He oversaw 700 executions, of which he conducted 200 himself.

14. Gerald of Wales, p. 187.

15. For ICI, Spillers, Bob Martin's Biscuits, Brooke Bond, Cusson's Imperial Leather.

16. This was followed by Williamson's *The Lone Swallows* (1933), *The Old Stag* (1933) and *The Peregrine Saga* (1934) (all Putnam's) and books by Alison Uttley and Negley Farson.

17. As described by Hermann von Pückler-Muskau after a visit in 1828.

18. I am indebted to Davies and Davies.

19. 40.7 per cent of Welsh miners aged between 55 and 59 had pneumoconiosis in 1962 (Supple, p. 570).

20. I am indebted to Ceri Thompson and all at Big Pit for the information in this entry.

21. Ablett.

22. Coombes, p. 142, referring to the 1921 strike.

23. Hansom & Welch had won the competition in 1830 to design Birmingham Town Hall, a commission that ultimately forced their partnership into bankruptcy.

24. The furniture here includes pieces by William Morris, E. W. Godwin and Alfred Waterhouse.

25. The rest are at the NPG in London: William Morris, Algernon Swinburne, John Stuart Mill, Matthew Arnold et al.

26. Quoted in Orpen, p. 522.

27. Swinburne, in a letter dated 22 May 1867, written at the time that Watts was painting him.

28. David Loshak, 'G. F. Watts and Ellen Terry', *Burlington Magazine 105*, November 1963, pp. 476–85.

29. W. E. Gladstone in a letter to Lord Ellesmere dated 10 June 1856. Ellesmere had just offered his so-called Chandos portrait of Shakespeare, the first painting to be accessioned.

30. Their portraits here by William Holman Hunt, J. S. Sargent and Sir Edwin Landseer respectively.

31. Designed by T. H. Wyatt and P. Brandon, in Bath stone.

32. Lee published *Delineations of Roman Antiquities Found at Caerleon and the Neighbourhood* (1845) and *Isca Silurum; or an Illustrated Catalogue of the Museum of Antiquities at Caerleon* (1862). Both were illustrated by Lee.

33. Newman, *Gwent/Monmouthshire*, p. 144. The 1850 portico is by H. F. Lockwood of Hull.

34. Gerald of Wales.

35. Very few Roman British inscriptions were cut on marble. This may have been made in Italy in AD 99. This would account for the rather crude alteration to the number of Trajan's consulship from II to III, as by AD 100 Trajan had begun his third period as consul.

36. The fortress was originally constructed in timber with earth ramparts.

37. This practice was introduced at Caerleon about AD 100.

38. Viollet-le-Duc's ten-volume *Dictionnaire Raisonné de l'Architecture Française* (1854–68).

39. Viollet-le-Duc restored Pierrefonds for the Emperor Napoleon III.

40. He purchased and preserved St Andrew's Cathedral and Rothesay Castle and studied the Welsh language, supporting the National Eisteddfod.

41. Manning and Capel officiated at Bute's wedding in 1872 to Lady Gwendoline Fitzalan Howard, the daughter of the Duke of Norfolk, at the Brompton Oratory.

42. Designed while Bute was courting his future wife.

43. Lonsdale won a Royal Academy travelling scholarship in 1871 but gave it up to work with Burges, designing stained glass, murals, metal work and sculpture in all the buildings of Burges's last ten years.

44. John, W. G.

45. E. M. Nance, author of *Pottery and Porcelain of Swansea and Nantgarw*, 1942.

46. Then called the Holburne of Menstrie Museum.

47. In May 1914 the trustees of the National Gallery in London initially declined a loan of Sir Hugh Lane's oil sketch of Daumier's *Don Quixote Charging a Flock of Sheep*. Gwendoline Davies bought *Don Quixote Reading* (1865–7) in 1918. It had previously belonged to Degas (Aviva Burnstock and Mark Evans, *Burlington Magazine*, 14 June 2000, p. 281).

48. Sir Hugh Lane began collecting the work of Honoré Daumier in 1904, Sir William Burrell (v. the British Collection, Glasgow Museum and Art Gallery) in 1901 and Constantine Ionides in the artist's lifetime.

49. The Seven and Five Society was formed in 1919 as a conscious reaction to Roger Fry. In the 1930s, influenced by Ben Nicholson, it changed direction in favour of non-representational art. It held its last exhibition, at the Zwemmer Gallery, in 1935.

50. Mainly consisting of works on paper.

51. Sir Charles J. Jackson's *English Goldsmiths and their Marks* (1905) remains the standard work on British hallmarks, as is his *History of English Plate* (two vols) on plate in general.

52. Letter from J. Bradley Hughes, Medical Officer, Penrhyn Quarry Hospital, Bethesda, N. Wales, 6 January 1922.

53. Built between 1845 and 1850, and rebuilt in the 1970s after a fire, with steel arches between the towers in place of the original, revolutionary tubular tunnels that carried the Holyhead railway.

54. Related to the series that Laguerre painted for the Duke of Marlborough in the hall and on the stairs at Marlborough House, St James's (1713).

55. He had eight children with Car, and a further ten with Char. Between them his children gave him seventy-three grandchildren.

56. Richard Crawshay altered the spelling from Crawshaw in an effort to sound more distinguished.

57. B. Malkin, 1803, quoted in Merthyr Teachers Centre Group, p. 289. At the rival Dowlais Steelworks an engineer, Adrian Stephens, invented the world's first steam whistle in 1835, a safety device to warn when the boilers ran dry.

58. Defoe, *A Tour*.

59. W. and S. Sandys.

60. Now Director of the National Museum of Labour History, Manchester.

61. Huw Williams, 'Brass Bands, Jazz Bands, Choirs: Aspects of Music in Merthyr Tydfil', *Merthyr Historian*, vol. III, 1980.

62. The building was in fact designed by the London architects Schullheiffer and Burley. Apocryphy has it that one was deaf and the other was blind. They are no longer in business. The borough architects had produced plans but were disappointed when the contract went outside.

63. Newman, *Gwent/Monmouthshire*, p. 453.

64. Iris Fox bequeathed more than five hundred items of pottery and porcelain to the museum.

65. Caerwent (Venta Silurum) was built in the 4th century AD on the site of the former capital of the now vanquished Silures tribe.

66. Thompson, E. P., p. 902.

67. The right of all men over the age of twenty-one to vote; the secret ballot; 300 constituencies of equal size; abolition of property requirement for a Member of Parliament; salaries for MPs. Only annual parliamentary elections remain outstanding. It is noticeable that the charter did not include women's suffrage, although this was supported by Henry Vincent.

68. Peate, p. 65.

69. Payne, pp. 42–57.

70. Morris, Jan, p. 1.

71. Lethaby, p. 7.

72. Translated from Jones, T., p. 202.

73. The players of these instruments, the harpist, the crythor and the piper, are all mentioned in *The Books of Taliesin* (c. 1275).

74. Joan Rimmer, 'The Morphology of the Triple Harp', *The Galpin Society Journal*, XVIII, pp. 90–103.

75. Peate, pp. 66–7.

76. Richard Glynn Vivian, 1835–1911.

77. Lorenzo, Duke of Urbino, born 1492, and his uncle, Giuliano, Duke of Nemours, born 1479. The images of both are idealised, having the features of young men. In reality Lorenzo had a short beard and bulging eyes. Both are dressed as Roman emperors. On Lorenzo's helmet is a lion head, the symbol of power or fortitude.

78. The 'Guido Reni' (*Suzanna and the Elders*) is probably by his follower, Simone Cantarini; the 'Correggio' (*Madonna Della Scodella*) is now

attributed to Anton Raphael Mengs; and 'Veronese's' *A Holy Family* is by one of his school.

79. Bought from Doré's studio sale in Paris in 1885.

80. Bequeathed by Herbert Eccles, 1919, and by Trevor Jones, 1972.

81. Bequeathed by Leonard Rudolphe Warrens in 1947.

82. The set was formerly owned by Sir Leslie Joseph (v. Nottingham Castle Museum).

83. After his departure from Derby (v. Derby Museum and Art Gallery) and the failure of his company in Mansfield, Billingsley needed finance in order to experiment further with porcelain pastes. The pieces he produced for Cambrian Pottery, alongside Thomas Baxter, particularly those decorated with flower painting, are among the finest pieces of British porcelain.

84. Frances Richards had been a designer for Doulton in Stoke-on-Trent before winning a scholarship to the Royal College of Art, where she met Ceri Richards in 1926.

85. Newman, *Glamorgan*, p. 593.

86. Ibid.

87. Erected in 268/270 A D by the Roman legion stationed at Bovium, mid-Glamorgan, in honour of the Emperor Marcus Piavonius Victorinus Augustus; discovered as part of a stone wall in 1835.

88. Beanland, pp. 14–17.

89. The skeleton was found wearing a necklace; hence its name, the Red Lady. Subsequent tests revealed it to be male.

90. Named after the home of Sir Humphrey Mackworth, who found it in the 18th century.

91. The red gritstone was quarried from the park surrounding the castle.

92. See Verrio's ceilings in the Queen's Presence Chamber at Windsor Castle (q.v.) and the later King's Staircase at Hampton Court Palace (q.v.) (c. 1700). Very unusually, this one celebrates Catherine of Braganza, in a composition taken from an engraving of Paolo Veronese's *Apotheosis of Venice* in the Doge's Palace.

93. Lord Powis required Bodley to design two elaborately carved chimney pieces for the room.

94. G. F. Bodley died in 1907.

95. Bodley based the Drawing Room ceiling design on the Long Gallery at Aston Hall, Birmingham (c. 1615–18).

96. Mughal zardozi work is embroidery of silver-gilt thread raised on a core of thick yellow tussore silk. The embroiderers of zardozi were invariably Muslim and male.

97. Translation by Robert Skelton in 'An Introduction to the Collection', in Archer, Rowell and Skelton, p. 47.

98. Now at Temple Newsam (q.v.). See the catalogue of the exhibition at the National Portrait Gallery in London and the Scottish National Portrait Gallery in Edinburgh in 2003–4, *Below Stairs*, for a representative showing of such portraits.

99. These portraits are celebrated in *The Servants' Hall* by Merlin Waterson, who was responsible for the restoration of the by then dilapidated house for the National Trust in 1973.

NORTHERN IRELAND

1. In the 1790s only 10 per cent of Belfast's population were Roman Catholic.

2. Neilson was the editor of the United Ireland newspaper *Northern Star*; McCracken had been a member of the committee of the Belfast Society for Promoting Knowledge; Russell had served in the army in India, where he met and became a close friend of Wolfe Tone. Having had to sell his commission to redeem the bail of a friend who defaulted, he was elected librarian in 1794.

3. I am indebted to John Killen.

4. Belfast's shipyards were the largest in the world.

5. Minutes of the Committee of the Belfast Library and Society for Promoting Knowledge, 16 November 1893.

6. Ten harpers (including one woman) attended, aged between 15 and 91. Six were blind. They performed on four consecutive days. Tone wrote, 'seven execrable, three good, one of them, Fawning, far the best. No new musical discovery. Believe all the good Irish airs are already written' (O'Brien, I, p. 96).

7. From 'A Library and a City in Conflict', a paper presented by the Linen Hall's librarian, John Gray, to the French Libraries' Conference, 1992. I am greatly indebted to Mr Gray for so much in this entry.

8. Sam Hanna Bell, *Linen Hall Review 1*, summer 1984.

9. Murphy, et al., p. 7.

10. See Davidson.

11. A galleass is 'a heavy, low-built vessel, larger than a galley, impelled both by sail and oars, chiefly employed in war' (*Oxford English Dictionary*): small wonder that the Spanish galleasses could not cope with the storms they encountered off the coasts of Scotland and Ireland.

12. I am indebted to Robert Sténuit's 'The Girona Treasure' in Verdi, *Saved!*, pp. 180–83.

13. The excavated remains here are from three Spanish ships: the *Girona*, wrecked at Lacada Point, Co. Antrim; *La Trinidad Valencera*, which ran aground in Kinnagoe Bay, Co. Donegal; and the *Santa Maria de la Rosa*, which sank in Basket Sound, Co. Kerry.

14. Fuseli painted a number of canvases entitled *The Apotheosis of . . .* The ones here were given, as a group, by Mr James F. Johnston in 1896. One is in Wolverhampton Museum and Art Gallery (q.v.), *The Apotheosis of Penelope Boothby*.

15. Frank Rutter, *Report on the Lloyd Patterson Collection, to the Chairman and Committee of the Belfast Art Gallery*, 13 December 1927.

16. Johnston designed the Assembly Rooms in Dublin, now the Gate Theatre.

17. The Pantheon, designed by Wyatt in 1772, made his reputation. It was converted into an opera house, which burnt down in 1792. A painting of its interior by William Hodges is at Temple Newsam (q.v.).

18. Belmore considered Wyatt's designs too expensive and ordered a plain ceiling with only a frieze. Rose obliged, though he warned Belmore that 'it will amount to more than half the first design'. Belmore compromised.

19. I am indebted to Brian Williams and Sarah Gormley's *Archaeological Objects from County Fermanagh*, in which are catalogued more than a hundred objects excavated since 1897, when the local amateur archaeologist Thomas Plunkett, assisted by George Coffey, excavated the cairn on Topped Mountain, Mullyknock, up to the excavations by Dudley Waterman and Pat Collins in the 1950s.

20. Archaeological treasures from Fermanagh are in the collections of more than a dozen museums worldwide, including the British Museum (q.v.); the Ashmolean (q.v.); the Royal Ontario Museum; the National Museums of Denmark and Scotland; the National Museum of Ireland; and the Ulster Museum.

21. The pilgrimage probably did not begin until the late 12th century, although there almost certainly was an Early Christian foundation on St Patrick's Island before the 12th-century Augustinian foundation; references to European pilgrims are from 1411 to 1517.

22. A narrow Irish spade.

23. Dung fork.

24. Livingstone.

25. The Maguire of Fermanagh.

26. Ducros made etched outlines for his water-colours, to facilitate repetition. There is a further version of the *Villa of Maecenas* in the Musée Cantonal des Beaux-Arts, Lausanne.

27. Estyn Evans had been appointed the first lecturer in geography at Queen's University in 1928, having studied at Aberystwyth under Professor H. J. Fleure, the first chair of the study of Geography and Anthropology together, established in 1917.

28. I am indebted to G. B. Thompson's article 'Estyn Evans and the Development of the Ulster Folk Museum', in *Ulster Folklife*, vol. 15/16, 1970, and to Owen.

29. Nils Erik Bachrendtz, Arne Biömstad, Ingmar Liornan and Per Olof Palm, 'Skansen – a Stocktaking at Ninety', *Museum*, vol. XXXIV, no. 3, 1982, p. 173.

30. The Biggar Archive, Biggar Scrapbook No. 3, Ulster Folk and Transport Museum.

31. A paraphrase of his remarks in the Annual Report of the Ulster Folk Museum, 1958–60 and 1960–61.

32. In 1852 the population was only 6,500, of whom only 230 had the right to vote (Mackey, p. 10).

33. The railway from Lisburn to Belfast opened on 12 August 1839: Ulster's first stretch of railway (ibid., p. 11).

34. In 1863 Hertford received £55,000 in net rental from his estate. He visited Lisburn only once, in 1845, hosted a party for his tenants and departed for Paris (ibid. pp. 10–11).

35. *Sir Richard* by E. Hannaux of Metz (1899); *Lady Wallace* (1872) by Charles-Auguste Lebourg – the originals of which are in the Wallace Collection (q.v.).

36. Beaumont.

37. The Jacquard loom was invented in the early 19th century by Joseph Marie Jacquard of Lyons. It was a mechanical apparatus whose pattern

dictated the opening and closing of a loom's shuttles in the weaving of figured fabrics.

38. Mackey, Director of the museum since 1979.

39. Made for the Countess of Eglinton, the wife of the then Lord Lieutenant of Ireland.

40. Invented by Richard Pockrich, Co. Monaghan.

LONDON

1. Spalding, J., *The Poetic Museum*, p. 15.

2. Letter from Ramon Luis Escovedo, the Intendant of Segovia, to Wellington, 15 August 1812. Only two of these pictures are identifiable: a *Head of St Joseph*, attributed to Guido Reni, and a *Sainted Nun*, possibly School of, or an imitation of, Bronzino.

3. Letter from Count Ternan Nunez to Wellington, September 1816.

4. v. Pollok House.

5. v. Soho House.

6. Kauffmann, p. 12.

7. See his portrait by Lawrence in the Perth Museum and Art Gallery (q.v.).

8. Judah Beach, one of the founders of the Ben Uri Art Society, writing in the *Ben Uri Catalogue*, 1930.

9. The Ben Uri has a good example of his topographical painting in Palestine in the 1920s, *Mount Zion with the Church of the Dormition: Moonlight* (1923).

10. Essay by David Bomberg originally in catalogue of a Tate Gallery exhibition, March/April 1967, Sylvester, *About Modern Art*, p. 167.

11. Sylvester, ibid., p. 296.

12. David Cohen, 'Grand, Living and Quirky Forms: Six Painters of the School of London', catalogue of the 1995 Arts Council Exhibition, *From London*, featuring Francis Bacon, Lucian Freud, Leon Kossoff, Michael Andrews, Frank Auerbach and R. B. Kitaj, p. 17.

13. Sylvester, *About Modern Art*, p. 173.

14. The powerful oil painting that Kramer developed from his drawing (also 1919) is in the Leeds City Art Gallery (q.v.).

15. Sonia Delaunay was the wife of the French painter Robert Delaunay, whose work is in the collection of Pallant House (q.v.).

16. It was designed by Charles Young & Co., who were influenced, as were Isambard Kingdom Brunel (Temple Meads Station, Bristol), Decimus Burton (Palm House, Kew Gardens, q.v.), and Sir Joseph Paxton (the Crystal Palace), by the utilitarian thinking of Jean-Nicholas-Louis Durand, professor of architecture at the École Polytechnique in Paris (1795).

17. To the fish-scale design used beneath the Sheepshanks Gallery at the V&A, laid by E. F. du Cane's female prisoners from Woking Gaol (designs in the V&A Department of Prints and Drawings).

18. Now the Wallace Collection at Hertford House in Manchester Square.

19. The Kaleidoscope House was designed by the architect Peter Wheelwright and the artist Laurie Simmons.

20. German toy maker Margarete Steiff started to produce stuffed toy animals in 1880; the first was a little elephant. Her nephew Richard Steiff convinced her to produce a toy bear cub in 1902, to his own design; he remained the chief designer.

21. The museum has the Paul and Marjorie Abbatt Archive and contains designs by Friedrich Froebel, Maria Montessori, and Rachael and Margaret Macmillan, and those for nursery school furniture and toys by the architect Erno Goldfinger for the Abbatts.

22. *Hansard*, 1777.

23. Report to the Select Committee on the British Museum, 12 June 1835.

24. Antonio Panizzi, *Report to the Commons*, 1845.

25. It was widely copied: the US Library of Congress (1897), Manchester Central Library (1930–34).

26. W. M. Thackeray, *Roundabout Paper*, 1862.

27. Wilson, Colin St John, introduction.

28. The Codex Sinaiticus was found in 1859 in the Monastery of St Catherine at the foot of Mount Sinai by Constantine Tischendorf, a German biblical scholar. He gave it to Tsar Alexander II of Russia. Further leaves were discovered in the monastery in 1975 and remain there.

29. The library holds a number of important Korans. The word Koran means 'to read'.

30. The kingdom of Gandhara straddled modern Pakistan and Afghanistan, the gateway through which Buddhism reached India and China.

31. Written and illuminated in Northern Spain, AD c. 1320.

32. Gospel according to St John, chapter 16, verse 16.

33. Four copies of the Magna Carta survive. Two are held at the British Library while the others can be seen in the cathedral archives at Lincoln and Salisbury.

34. This notebook is not a bound volume used by Leonardo, but was put together after his death from loose papers of various types and sizes. The first section was begun at Florence on 22 March 1508, but the remainder comes from different periods in Leonardo's life, covering practically the whole of his career. The text is written in Italian, and in Leonardo's characteristic 'mirror-writing', left-handed and moving from right to left. This manuscript, frequently referred to as 'The Codex Arundel', was probably acquired in Italy by Thomas Howard, Earl of Arundel, the greatest English collector of art of his day. In 1681 it was presented to the Royal Society by Henry Howard (his grandson) and transferred to the British Museum in 1831.

35. William Tyndale's translation was solely his, unlike the 1539 Great Bible produced for Henry VIII, translated by 'dyverse excellent learned men'; or the Geneva Bible, translated by a small team of three or four English divines; or the Bishops' Bible, translated by a team of fourteen bishops, appointed by the Archbishop of Canterbury; or the Bibles of English Roman Catholics who employed men at the colleges of Rheims and Douai (see Nicolson, p. 68). Remarkably Tyndale made his translation while on the run and in hiding across Germany and the Netherlands.

36. The team of forty-eight translators, plus the directors of the six companies, included Lancelot Andrewes, Bishop of Chichester (1605) and of Ely (1609), chief translator; John Overall, Bishop of Norwich; James Montagu, Bishop of Bath and Wells; Sir Henry Savile, the only lay translator; all under the supervision of Richard Bancroft, Archbishop of Canterbury.

37. The Luttrell Psalter, c.1320–40, was written and illuminated for Sir Geoffrey Luttrell of Irnham, Lincolnshire. Having been on loan to the British Library since 1896, it was put up for sale in 1929 by Mr Herbert Weld of Lulworth Castle and seemed destined to be exported to the US until the American financier John Pierpoint Morgan made an interest-free loan that allowed a public subscription to be raised, supported by the National Art Collections Fund, and the book was secured for £31,500.

38. The Sherborne Missal, written and illuminated at the Benedictine Abbey of Sherborne in Dorset (1400–07), is the only medieval service book to have survived intact. It contains the texts and music to be used in service throughout the year. It was bought, in France, by the Duke of Northumberland in 1703 and offered by the 12th Duke to the government in lieu of inheritance tax in 1998, valued at £5.5 million.

39. Diderot and D'Alembert.

40. Smirke based the order on that of the temple of Athena Polias at Priene in Asia Minor that had been illustrated in the Dilettanti Society's *Ionian Architecture* (1769).

41. This is how Smirke described the Grecian style that he considered superior to what he considered the 'corrupt taste' of Roman architecture, admired by Palladio, Piranesi and, in the previous generation, Sir John Soane. His words here are taken from manuscript fragments now in the Library of the Royal Institute of British Architects. I am indebted here to Mordaunt Crook, *The British Museum*, chapters 3 and 4 (this quotation, p. 97) and throughout to the several publications of Marjorie Caygill, former keeper and assistant to the director of the museum, and its definitive contemporary historian.

42. Described by Sir Henry Ellis, principal librarian, 1827–56.

43. Clerk of Penicuik muniments, GD 18/3284/2.

44. A fuller description of this collection is in the entry for the Natural History Museum.

45. Queen Anne consulted him; he was appointed physician to George II in 1727 and was elected President of the Royal Society (1727–41).

46. And Sloane's *Herbarium* comprising 337 folio volumes, now in the library of the Natural History Museum (q.v.).

47. Founded in 1471 by Edward IV and including Queen Mary's Psalter and a 5th-century manuscript of the Bible, the *Codex Alexandrinus*.

48. For consideration of the contributions made by the collections of natural history of Joseph Banks, Charles Greville's minerals and others, v. Natural History Museum; for further bequests and acquisitions of books and manuscripts, v. the British Library.

49. Hollis was a republican and strong supporter of the American Revolution. He gave Harvard

University his collection of Milton, inscribed 'People of Massachusetts . . . ware your liberties!' (J. L. Abbott, 'Thomas Hollis and the Society 1756–1774', *Royal Society of Arts Journal 119*, 1971 p. 713.

50. I am indebted here, as elsewhere, to J. Scott, pp. 169–219.

51. Papal antiquary, librarian to Cardinal Albani, the abbé Winckelmann's *Briefe*, 4 vols., Berlin 1952–7, is the most serious study of the period.

52. Pierre-François Hugues, Baron d'Hancarville, 'Catalogue of Sculptures in Park Street, Westminster, Towneley', MS, British Museum, undated.

53. Hamilton's letter to Lord Palmerston, June 1765: see Jenkins and Sloan, p. 50.

54. When Townley's house was threatened during the 1780 anti-Catholic Gordon riots this was the piece he was determined to save, smuggling it away in his coach. It was copied several times by Nollekens.

55. Salt had been asked to collect for the museum by Sir Joseph Banks in 1815. By the time he delivered, opinion had shifted and many, including Banks, saw Egyptian antiquities as inferior to Greek or Roman and not fit to be placed beside 'the grand works of the Towneley Gallery' (Banks's letter to Salt, 14 February 1819 in Hall, p. 313).

56. Trustees' Committee Minutes, vol. 10, p. 296, 14 May 1825, quoted in Miller, E., p. 203.

57. The case is recreated in the King's Library. When it was originally displayed in the museum's Grand Central Saloon it inspired the French to mount serious excavations by Paolo Emilio Botta. Further excavations by Layard, and by archaeologists from America, Germany and Turkey, led to a wide public interest in Assyrian antiquities.

58. Henry Christy was a hatter who began to travel, and to collect, at the age of forty. Franks was a close friend and a trustee of his estate.

59. Davy, vol. II, p. 342.

60. Excavated at Hadrian's Villa, Tivoli; a copy of Myron's original, 470–440 BC.

61. Bought by A.W. Franks for £8,000 in 1891 when the museum was unable to raise the asking price.

62. Merimée.

63. Jenkins, R., p. 636.

64. Colville, p. 280

65. Jenkins, R., p. 636.

66. Neal.

67. Apart from Lee and Courtauld, several of those who provided the initial financial support, later gave works of art, including Sir Robert Witt and Sir Martin Conway. The art critic Roger Fry, who curated the exhibitions at the Grafton Gallery in 1910 and 1912 that introduced Cézanne and the Post-Impressionists to Britain, gave his collection in 1932. It included works by Bonnard, Derain, Seurat, Sickert, Matthew Smith and himself; a small ethnographic collection; and furniture and ceramics made by the Omega Workshop that he founded in 1913 with Vanessa Bell and Duncan Grant (v. Charleston).

68. Dr Hunter gave other 20th-century paintings from his collection to the Fitzwilliam Museum (q.v.).

69. In the proportions, symmetry and composition of Somerset House, Chambers was working out the aesthetic theories of Edmund Burke, described in Burke's *A Philosophical Enquiry into the Origin of our Ideas of the Sublime and Beautiful* 1757. Chambers told Burke that Somerset House was 'a child of your own'.

70. Cuno's view in his book of essays (Cuno, p. 52) is that 'the museum is not just a treasure house, it is also a centre of a very special kind of research and education'.

71. These paintings are those that Gwendoline Davies and her sister later gave to the National Museum and Gallery of Wales (q.v.).

72. Cooper, *The Courtauld Collection*, pp. 3–4.

73. In this painting of his mistress, Madeleine Knobloch, Seurat initially painted his own face looking down at her before eventually replacing it with this vase of flowers.

74. I am indebted here, and throughout, to John Murdoch and his introduction and notes to the collection's 1998 catalogue.

75. These giant chests, set on gilded claw feet (a later addition), have scenes from Livy's *Histories*, painted on panels by Jacopo del Sellaio and Biagio d'Antonio. They were commissioned to celebrate the marriage of Lorenzo di Matteo Morelli to Viaggia di Tanai di Francesco Nerli.

76. Cooper, *The Courtauld Collection*, pp. 6–7.

77. The central panel was acquired by Lord Lee and is now, happily, reunited with the two Seilern side panels.

78. Reynolds, (ed. Wark), p. 161. Reynolds owned, and loved, this painting. It was sold, with the rest of his collection, on 14 March 1795.

79. These stars owe something to the sparks in

Adam Elsheimer's *Apollo and Coronis* (Walker Art Gallery q.v.). Rubens knew and admired Elsheimer and owned several of his paintings.

80. Morris had founded his company Morris, Marshall, Faulkner & Co. two years earlier in 1861.

81. William Morris, 'The History of Pattern Making', lecture, published 1882.

82. De Morgan's inventions included a system of gears for a bicycle and an anti-submarine device, offered to the Admiralty but ignored. For the full impact of De Morgan's Iznik-inspired tiles, see his commission for Frederick Leighton in the Arab Hall, Leighton House Museum (q.v.), designed by George Aitchison.

83. By Mies van der Rohe, for the German Pavilion.

84. Alvar Aalto's Paimio lounge chair 41 (1930–31) for the Paimio Sanitorium in Finland: the first pliant chair to be built without a rigid framework.

85. Soane's design here inspired Richard Maier when planning the Getty Museum in California, Louis Kalm at the Kimball Art Museum, Fort Knox and the internal galleries at Frank Gehry's Guggenheim, Bilbao.

86. Desenfans was Polish Consul-General in London.

87. Jacob Cats.

88. Alleyn's bequest includes a full-length of Alleyn and a likeness of Richard Burbage, Shakespeare's favourite actor and Alleyn's rival.

89. It is, in effect, an illustrated commentary on C. H. Collins Baker's *Lely and the Stuart Portrait Painters*, 1912.

90. Fanny Burney wrote of Elizabeth Linley that the 'applause and admiration she has met with can only be compared to what is given to Mr Garrick' (G. Beechey, 'The Linleys and their Music', in Waterfield, p. 10).

91. Lawrence too was a family friend of the Linleys. He left this portrait to the Dulwich in his will.

92. The original (1784), in the Huntington Art Gallery, San Marino, impressed Desenfans and she commissioned this replica (1789).

93. Gainsborough's portrait of *Mrs Siddons* (1785) in the National Gallery (q.v.) lacks any sense of how she appeared on stage.

94. Walpole wrote of Lely: 'His nymphs trail fringes and embroidery through meadows and purling streams.' They don't here.

95. Tasso, Canto xiv.

96. Inspiring the couplet by Mauriys Huygens's brother, 'This is Rembrandt's hand and Gheyn's face. Marvel, reader, this is but is not Gheyn.'

97. I must declare an interest: I am a trustee of the Estorick Foundation.

98. Marinetti, 'The Founding and Manifesto of Futurism', *Le Figaro*, 20 February 1909.

99. Published as a leaflet by Poesia (Milan), 11 April 1910. This translation is from the catalogue of the *Exhibition of Works by Italian Futurist Painters*, Sackville Gallery, London, March 1912.

100. Eric Estorick, unpublished memoir, 1985, p. 30.

101. His American clients included Lauren Bacall, Jack Lemmon, Burt Lancaster, Billy Wilder and Anthony Quinn.

102. Quentin Bell, *The Listener*, December 1956.

103. *The Times*, 21 November 1956.

104. The Tate had them on loan 1966–75 to augment the small number of 20th-century Italian works that it owned: De Chirico's *The Understanding of the Poet* (1913), Modigliani's *Head* (1911–12), Boccioni's bronze sculpture *Unique Forms of Continuity in Space* (1913) and Guttuso's *The Discussion* (1959–60). In recent years it has bought Luciano Fabro's *Ovaries* (1988) and Guiseppe Penone's *Tree of 12 Metres* (198?–82).

105. Marinetti, op. cit., p. 1.

106. Designed by the Australian artist David Humphries.

107. Mannequins designed by Adel Rootstein, the revolutionary doyenne of this mirrored world of always changing life-sized dolls.

108. Its three keepers: David Donald (1968–1984), Bill Smith (1984–1996) and Selina Skipworth (since 1996).

109. Now separated: *Hume* (Scottish National Portrait Gallery, q.v.), *Rousseau* (National Gallery of Scotland, q.v.).

110. Other European cities made better provision. Florence had the Spedale degli Innocenti, designed by Filippo Brunelleschi in 1421; Rome, the 13th-century Conservatorio della Ruota; Venice, the 14th-century La Pietà orphanage for girls; and Paris, L'Hôpital des Enfants-Trouvés (1670).

111. 1,000 children were abandoned in London every year, out of a population in 1750 of 679,000.

112. Bacharach, p. 98.

113. Handel's biographer, Newman Flower

(*George Frederick Handel*, Cassell, 1922), estimated the proceeds at £11,000.

114. a) William Hogarth's *Moses Brought Before Pharaoh's Daughter* (1746). The inscription on the frame, from Exodus, chapter 2, verse 10, reads: 'She brought him unto Pharaoh's daughter and he became her son. And she called his name Moses.'
b) Francis Hayman's *The Finding of the Infant Moses in the Bullrushes* (1746). Exodus, chapter 2, verse 9: 'And Pharaoh's daughter said unto her, Take this child away, and nurse it for me and I will give thee thy wages.'
c) Joseph Highmore's *Hagar and Ishmael* (1746). Genesis, chapter 21, verse 17: 'Fear not; for God hath heard the voice of the Lord where he is.'
d) The Revd James Wills's *Little Children Brought to Christ* (1746): St Mark, chapter 10, verse 14: 'Suffer the little children to come unto me, and forbid them not.'

115. a) Thomas Gainsborough, *The Charterhouse* (*c.*1748).
b) Edward Haytley, *Bethlem Hospital* (*c.*1747).
c) Edward Haytley, *Chelsea Hospital* (*c.*1747).
d) Samuel Wale, *Christ's Hospital* (*c.*1748).
e) Samuel Wale, *Greenwich Hospital* (*c.*1748).
f) Samuel Wale, *St Thomas's Hospital* (*c.*1748).
g) Richard Wilson, *St George's Hospital* (*c.*1746–50).
h) Richard Wilson, *The Foundling Hospital* (*c.*1746–50).

116. Heretofore there had been no public place in London in which artists could exhibit their work. Artists exhibited at their own studios. The novelty provided by the Court Room at the Foundling Hospital was as successful in promoting British art as it was in promoting the hospital. The Swiss miniaturist and writer André Rouquet wrote in 1755 that the hospital's 'exhibition of skills, equally commendable and new, has afforded the public an opportunity of judging whether the English are such indifferent artists, as foreigners, and even the English themselves, pretend' (Martin Postle, 'The St Martin's Lane Academy: True and False Records', *Apollo*, July 1991, pp. 33–8, and Rouquet). The hospital held a dinner on 1 April 1747, and subsequently each year on 5 November, attended by leading artists, connoisseurs, benefactors and the hospital's governors. From these exhibitions and dinners may be traced the founding of the Society of Arts,

Manufactures and Commerce (1754) and, finally in 1768, the securing by Sir Joshua Reynolds of the Royal Charter for the Royal Academy.

117. A technique he learnt from studying under Solimena in Italy and which became such a feature of his later portraits.

118. The globe is turned to show the Atlantic, on both sides of which Coram traded. The hat honours Coram's intervention which preserved the vital and profitable trade that the London Hat Manufacturers enjoyed with the American Colonies. Coram refused to take any financial reward but accepted the present of a hat 'as often as he had Occasion, and which in its Size spoke the good wishes of the Makers in a very legible Character' (Brocklesby, p. 11).

119. This is the terracotta study of the marble bust of Handel (also 1763) in the Royal Collection at Windsor Castle (q.v.).

120. The house was found for Freud by his youngest son, Ernst, an architect, and purchased for £6,500, of which Barclays Bank provided a £4,000 loan.

121. The engraving is by Kruger (1770) from the original by Rembrandt (1659).

122. This 'historical novel' had been started at Berggasse. Freud's contention that Moses was not a Jew but an Egyptian aristocrat gave offence to Jews and Christians. Both disputed the biblical scholarship that informed this thesis.

123. Sigmund Freud to Jeanne Lampl de Groot, 8 October 1938, quoted in Trollope, p. 313.

124. About 800 out of 2,400. They were bought by the New York Psychiatric Institute and taken to America, and are now in the Library of Columbia University, New York.

125. Gay, *Sigmund Freud and Art*, p. 24.

126. Gardiner, p. 139.

127. Doolittle, pp. 102–4.

128. A balsamarium held perfumed oil, incense or ointments.

129. Heinrich Schliemann first excavated Troy in 1873. Evans excavated Minos in 1900 and Carter the Valley of the Kings in 1922.

130. Van Meteren, *History of the Netherlands*, edition of 1614, translated from the Dutch and quoted in Rye.

131. On 18 June 1671, Evelyn, *Memoirs*, vol. 1, pp. 433–4.

132. Queen Mary's accounts for 1690 show that Guillbaud was paid £30 for two 'scriptors [writing

desks] inlaid with flowers' (Tessa Murdoch, 'Doors Open on the Capital's Cabinets', *Country Life*, 6 December 2001).

133. Evelyn, *Memoirs*, vol. iv, pp. 216–17.

134. To whom the invention of 'smalti filati' is attributed, a mix of silica, oxide of tin (for opacity) and metal oxide (for colour).

135. Of Charles I (after Van Dyck), George IV and George Washington (after Gilbert Shaw). A further set by Denis Brownell Murphy depicts the whole royal house of Stuart from Mary, Queen of Scots, to Prince Charles Edward Stuart.

136. Ramsay was Painter-in-Ordinary to George III.

137. Roger Fry, 'Plastic Colour', essay published in *Transformations*, 1926.

138. Augustus John, *Vogue*, 5 October 1928.

139. From a pamphlet, 1794, written by Boydell on the presentation of his collection.

140. Depicted here, in oils, by Sir William Beechey (1801).

141. These prints are not part of the Guildhall Art Gallery collection, but are in the Guildhall Library (Prints and Maps).

142. Hunt.

143. Richard Gilbert Scott, the son of Sir Giles Gilbert Scott, who designed the Battersea and Bankside Power Station (now Tate Modern, q.v.).

144. The novelist Henry Green.

145. See Moxham.

146. Harrison Townsend had made his name with the Whitechapel Art Gallery.

147. Pevsner, *London: South*, p. 418.

148. De Dampierre, p. 92.

149. 'Aussi est-ce volontairement que nous plaçons en tête de cette évocation naturellement sélective un instrument tout à fait remarquable par la qualité de sa sculpture, son équilibre et sa sobriété acquis en 1885 par le Victoria and Albert Museum et transféré en 1956 au Horniman Museum de Londres.' Guis, Le François and Venture, p. 30.

150. The quality of the musical instrument collection owes much to Jean Jenkins, its curator from 1953 to 1978.

151. This is an amazing array: Swanscombe Man; Steinheim Man; Combe-Capelle Man; Cro-Magnon Man; Tabun Man from Mount Carmel.

152. Samson maintained a particular interest in French-speaking Africa: Mali; the Ivory Coast, Burkino Faso.

153. The haul was divided between British museums. There are Benin bronzes in the British Museum, Bristol City Museum and Art Gallery and the Fitzwilliam (all q.v.).

154. Made yet more enjoyable by the redesign and development of the museum by architects Allies, Morrison in 2003, which opens up the back of the building to the gardens and so restates F. W. Horniman's original vision.

155. Barry, p. 258.

156. A. W. N. Pugin to E. J. Wilson, letter, 6 November 1834, in the Fowler Collection, John Hopkins University, Baltimore.

157. Ferry, p. 248.

158. Barry, p. 39.

159. Bagehot, pp. 4–5.

160. The secretary was Sir Charles Eastlake, President of the Royal Academy and the first Director of the National Gallery.

161. I am indebted to Malcolm Hay, curator of works of art, Houses of Parliament, and his catalogue *Art in Parliament*.

162. Thomas Babington Macaulay, author of *The History of England* (1848, 1st two volumes), was at the time Member of Parliament for Edinburgh.

163. Newbolt, p. 4.

164. Letter by John Ruskin, 1849.

165. Blunt, W., p. 45. Watts frequently referred to Pheidias as though he was a painter, not a sculptor.

166. William Hunter, founder of the Hunterian Museum, University of Glasgow (q.v.). He too wished the nation to purchase his collections of paintings, specimens, coins, medals, etc. John and William had the same executors, Matthew Baillie and Edward Hone. Although both brothers were equally brilliant, their collections equally glittering, the greater personal popularity of John was probably the factor that led his collection to be bought by the nation and William's to be given to the University of Glasgow.

167. Hunter's 'Observations and Reflections on Geology', written in the last years of his life, was published posthumously, in 1859, as an introduction to the Royal College's *Catalogue of Fossils*.

168. Chesleden was a patron of the arts, a connoisseur and a friend of Pope.

169. Byrne was 7 feet 7 inches tall. People paid 2s. 6d. to see him at the height of his celebrity. In

April 1783 he lost his life savings (two bank notes to the value of £770) when drunk. He died two months later.

170. The moa here was presented to the museum in 1873 by Dr Julius von Haast.

171. Owen's immediate successor was his assistant conservator, John Thomas Quekett.

172. Flower was Assistant Surgeon to the 63rd Regiment in the Crimea, 1854–5. Hunter was with the army in France and Portugal, 1760–63.

173. While conservator at the Hunterian, he published more than 300 learned papers.

174. The museum records the contributions and experience of the peoples of the Empire and Commonwealth in the two world wars and later conflicts.

175. Designed by James Lewis in 1815. The dome, by Sidney Smirke, was added in 1846.

176. 6,500 'V' weapons fell on London and the south-east, killing 8,938 people.

177. Interview in the *New York Times*, 25 May 1919.

178. All Second World War artists were selected by a committee, chaired by Sir Kenneth Clark, Director of the National Gallery.

179. Carline, p. 112.

180. Max Beckmann to Minna Beckmann, 18 April 1915, quoted in the catalogue of the 1992 Tate Gallery exhibition, *Otto Dix 1891–1969*, Tate Gallery Publications, 1992.

181. The Jewish Museum, Berlin (1989).

182. The United States Holocaust Memorial Museum, Washington, DC.

183. The chronology of the rise of Nazism, the strength of Hitler's appeal and the failure of the Weimar Republic to resist him are well described, but the phenomena of Hitler and Nazism arise here fully formed, without an historic context. There is no sense of the atavistic yearning and hunger felt by many for the Reich, the revival of the Holy Roman Empire broken up by Napoleon in 1806 and the consequent shame that such Germans had for the Weimar Republic, a contemptible substitute in their view, nor for the proliferation of anti-Semitic organisations that arose in the late 19th century, nor even for the humiliation and loss of territory in 1919. All these prepared the soft seed-bed of Nazism. This case is made with brilliant clarity by Richard J. Evans in his *The Coming of the Third Reich*.

184. Hideously, a commercial pesticide. It was first used to kill Jews in August 1941 in an imprisoned gas chamber at Auschwitz I.

185. Genesis, Exodus, Leviticus, Numbers and Deuteronomy.

186. Genesis, chapter 1, verse 1.

187. To the World Museum Liverpool (Mayer), the Lady Lever art gallery (Leverhulme), the Rangers House (Wernher), Upton and Maidstone (the Samuels), Waddesdon and Ascott and Tring (various Rothschilds).

188. *Night and Day*, 10 June 2001.

189. After a design by Adam for the Earl of Shelburne, *c.*1768. Other stools from the same set are in the mausoleum at Bowood.

190. *Mrs Graham* (1777) in the National Galleries of Scotland.

191. The pier tables were probably supplied by Laurence Tell and William Tutton. The pedestals, for Dundas's London house, 19 Arlington Street, were probably by Chippendale.

192. Originally installed by William France, the King's cabinet maker. It took eight men three days to hang them.

193. The recesses were lined with bookshelves in 1815. The present mirrors and decoration are modern reproductions of Adam's and Chippendale's original designs.

194. *Art Journal*, 1 June 1864, p. 157.

195. Aitchison did not join the Royal Academy until 1881.

196. Letter to Henry Tate, the Tate Archive, Tate letter book, 7811.2.28.

197. Sketchbook note, Royal Academy collection, LE 1/21, quoted by Christopher Mewall in his essay 'Leighton and the Art of Landscape', catalogue of the Royal Academy 1996 exhibition.

198. Colin Clark, 'Transport: Maker and Breaker of Cities', *Town Planning Review*, 28, 1957, pp. 237–50.

199. The Metropolitan Railway line from Paddington to Farringdon Street, via King's Cross, three miles long, with trains pulled by steam engines.

200. Replaced in 1979 by New Johnston.

201. Twenty-six of Holden's stations are listed, Grade II.

202. *Day and Night*, by Epstein; the *West Wind* by Moore. Commissions for the other seven winds were given to Eric Gill, Eric Anmonier, A. H. Gerald, Allan Wyon and Samuel Rabinovitch.

203. Campbell drew designs for Marble Hill in

1723, and an engraving of 'A house in Twickenham', identical to Marble Hill, save for an order of pillars, appeared in his *Vitruvius Britannicus*, vol. iii, in 1725. Campbell played no part in the building, which was undertaken by Roger Morris, who went on to build Inveraray Castle for the 3rd Duke of Argyll.

204. Lees-Milne, *The Earls of Creation*, p. 71.

205. Panini painted these architectural fantasies all his life, culminating in the huge composite *Views of Ancient Rome* (*c.* 1755), owned in the mid-19th century by the 1st Earl of Egerton, and now in the Staatsgalerie, Stuttgart.

206. Millar, p. 10.

207. Lees-Milne, op. cit., p. 79.

208. Lees-Milne, ibid., p. 74.

209. Lees-Milne, ibid., pp. 74–5.

210. Wilenski, *English Painting*.

211. Evans and Fairclough, p. 38.

212. Sheppard.

213. The first part was designed by William Holford & Partners in 1971; the second part by Carl Fisher & Partners in 1980.

214. Laguerre was the godson of Louis XIV. He was commissioned by Sarah, Duchess of Marlborough, to decorate Marlborough House.

215. Tietze, p. 106.

216. The Rijksmuseum, Amsterdam, opened in 1808; the Prado, Madrid, 1809; and the Kaiser Friedrich, Berlin, 1823.

217. Rubens bought the fief of Steen in 1635 and painted views of it several times in the last five years of his life. There is a fine, closer view in the Kunsthistorische Museum, Vienna.

218. Beaumont loved this painting so much that he arranged for it to be loaned back to him for life, leaving the other Claudes (*Narcissus*, 1644, and *Landscape with a Goatherd and Goats*) with the gallery, together with *The Death of Procris*, a copy corresponding to No. 100 in Claude's *Liber Veritatis*, the original painting of which has not survived.

219. Titian's *Rape of Europa* was bought by the Isabella Stewart Gardner Museum in Boston. Cima's *Madonna with a Goldfinch* was eventually acquired with the Beaucousin Collection in 1860.

220. Summerson, p. 209.

221. On loan from the collection of HM The Queen.

222. Vasari, p. 11.

223. Venturi, Scott, Brown, Associates won an international invited competition for design of the new Sainsbury Wing of the National Gallery after a previous design was abandoned at the urging of the Prince of Wales. Built on the last open space on Trafalgar Square, the Sainsbury Wing houses one of the world's greatest and most visited collections of early Italian and Northern Renaissance paintings. Stylistically, the wing is designed to connect to and reflect the original National Gallery building (designed by William Wilkins in 1838) while maintaining its own identity as a work of contemporary architecture. Elements from the Wilkins facade are replicated on the new building.

224. The National Gallery and Tate Gallery Act, which ended the National Gallery's claim to the British paintings previously in its collection.

225. In 1985, Sir Paul Getty or Mr J. Paul Getty Jnr, as he then was, pledged £50 million to the National Gallery as an endowment in an attempt to enable it to continue to acquire great paintings in conditions of ever-rising prices.

226. Berenson, p. xiii.

227. Butlin and Joll, pp. 155–7.

228. Thornbury.

229. 'James's Naval History from 1793–1820', *Literary Gazette*, 1826, pp. 389–90.

230. Museum of Fine Arts, Boston, Massachusetts.

231. Tate Britain.

232. The Imperial Order of the Ottoman Crescent, instituted in August 1799, the chelengk, or plume of triumph.

233. Nelson's description.

234. It was painted for *Le Train Bleu* (1924), a Diaghilev ballet for Les Ballets Russes, scenario by Jean Cocteau, costumes by Coco Chanel, music by Darius Milhaud. Picasso signed the cloth, scaled up and painted by the Russian émigré Prince Alexander Shervashdze, and dedicated it to Diaghilev. The original Picasso painting (*Deux Femmes Courantes sur le Plage*, or *La Course*, painted in Dinard in 1922), is in the Musée Picasso in Paris. *Le Train Bleu* was only performed on thirty occasions but Diaghilev's ballet adopted the painting as its permanent front-cloth.

235. The museum has over one million programmes and playbills, dating from 1704.

236. In the 1990s the museum acquired the collection of the actor Robert Eddison.

237. Including the manuscript for R. B. Sheridan's *The School for Scandal*: the house receipts for the 1776–7 production are here, over £200 being taken each night.

238. The set illustrating Gordon Craig's dictum 'Once upon a time, stage scenery was architecture.' (Craig, p. 6).

239. Thomas Babington Macaulay, author of *The History of England* (1848).

240. v. the Scottish National Portrait Gallery, which Carlyle helped to found in 1889.

241. Attributed to John Taylor (*c.*1610), by the 18th-century antiquarian George Vertue, who said it was 'by one Taylor a player and painter contemporary with Shakespeare and his intimate friend'.

242. W. E. Gladstone, letter to Lord Ellesmere, 10 June 1856.

243. Minutes of trustees' meeting, 9 February 1857.

244. Vyner was also banker to Charles II, which perhaps accounts for the portrait and his inclusion here.

245. Despite the NPG's rule only to accept original paintings, this is a copy by Collier of the portrait he did for the Linnaean Society. In a letter to Lionel Chat in 1896, Darwin's elder son, William Erasmus Darwin, believed that 'as a likeness it is an improvement on the original'.

246. Reynolds painted three versions of this. The others are in the Art Gallery of Ontario in Toronto and in the collection of the Marquess of Hertford at Ragley Hall.

247. Howard, *The Tudor Image*, pp. 16 and 19.

248. See too the three tiers of black busts (*Bright, Darwin*, etc.), which look down in judgement on the visitor. The majority of them are by Sir Joseph Edgar Boehm.

249. His portrait of Lord Raglan is in the NPG.

250. The diarist John Evelyn's description of what Sloane brought back from Jamaica, in 1691.

251. Of these, 60 million are of biological origin and 6 million botanical. There are 28 million insects and 95 per cent of all known birds.

252. Darwin.

253. Owen was never Director, always Superintendent. Flower gained the title of Director following pressure by the Trustees.

254. Owen had already approved some of these ideas, and they informed Waterhouse's design for the main hall of the new South Kensington museum and for the narrow reference galleries for study that alternated with the public galleries.

255. Although formation of a separate department of entomology was recommended in 1906 this did not happen until 1913. Until that date entomology was part of zoology.

256. Waterhouse also designed the neo-Gothic Manchester Town Hall.

257. The modelling was carried out by Dujardin of Farmer and Brindley.

258. The statue of Adam was damaged by enemy action in 1940 and never replaced.

259. 'DIRECTIONS: Put one Ounce of Chocolate (which is two Squares) to a pint of boiling Milk, or a pint of Milk and Water; add Sugar and Milk as other Chocolate.'

260. There are also paintings on vellum of Newfoundland plants by George Dionysius Ehret. Ehret, a friend of Linnaeus and one of the greatest botanical artists, was employed by Joseph Banks. He had been brought to England by Sloane (O'Brian, p. 60).

261. Architects of the new extension to Copenhagen's National Museum of Fine Arts.

262. Phase One of the Darwin Centre exhibits the zoological specimens preserved in alcohol: 22 million of them.

263. In 1703 the church was rebuilt by Thomas Cartwright, Master Mason to Sir Christopher Wren.

264. v. the Foundling Museum for his involvement in the founding of the Foundling Hospital.

265. Ru ware (also spelt Ju in the Wade–Giles system of Romanisation used in the early 20th century) is discussed in Percival David's 'A Commentary on Ju Ware', published in the *Transactions of the Oriental Ceramic Society*, 1937.

266. The exhibition was curated jointly by Percival David, R. L. Hobson, George Eumorfopoulos and Oscar Raphael.

267. These bowls have usually been referred to as Samara since bowls of this type were excavated from an early Islamic site at Samara on the Euphrates, in Iraq.

268. Fry, *Last Lectures*, p. 98.

269. Ibid., p. 100.

270. From Zheng Gu, 'Song Li Bu Cao Lang Zhong Mian Guan Nan Gui', in Tong Jiaoying, p. 751.

271. 'Lu You (Song) Lao Xue An Istji', cited in Vainker, p. 112.

272. Janssen, Appendix 2, pp. 98–102.

273. His book *A Digger's Life*, full of anecdotes and opinions, was first published in *The English Illustrated Magazine* (1886) and describes his excavations at Naukratis and Tanis (the biblical Zoan).

274. Petrie assumed these were portraits of middle-class people, but the woods of the 146 panels (yew and lime) were imported, available only to an elite. The panels were secured over the face by linen wrappings. Some portraits were individually named.

275. It was conserved by Sheila Landi, who succeeded in turning the dress and re-pleated the fine knife pleats on the yoke and sleeves.

276. Introductory lecture, 14 January 1893.

277. The government's 1833 Factory Act was passed by Parliament on 29 August. Under the terms of the new act, it became illegal for children under nine to work in textile factories, and children aged between nine and thirteen could not be employed for more than eight hours a day. In 1840 Lord Ashley helped set up the Children's Employment Commission. Its first report on mines and collieries was published in 1842. Lord Ashley piloted the Coal Mines Act through the House of Commons. Women and children were prohibited from working underground. In 1851 Anthony Ashley Cooper became the 7th Earl of Shaftesbury.

278. Each theatre is a replica of a real theatre: the Regency; the Adelphi (1829); the Princess Theatre (1852); the Theatre Royal, New York.

279. *The Maid and the Magpie* is the oldest set on display, made by William West in 1820.

280. R. L. Stevenson, 'A Penny Plain and Two Pence Coloured', *The Magazine of Art*, 1884.

281. Letter to Nicolas-Claude Fabli de Peiresc, 9 August 1629, Puyvelde, pp. 320 and 322.

282. Now on loan from HM The Queen in the Victoria and Albert Museum (q.v.).

283. Its nine canvases are now at Hampton Court Palace (q.v.).

284. In the Christ Church Picture Gallery, Oxford (q.v.).

285. 1,570 pictures were listed in a sale that extended from October 1649 to the mid 1650s.

286. Namely Raphael's *Madonna Della Perla* (the Prado); Leonardo da Vinci's *St John the Baptist* (the Louvre); Van Dyck's *Portrait of Nicholas Lanier* (Kunsthistorisches Museum, Vienna).

Lanier, with Charles I's agent Daniel Nys, had conducted the negotiations for the Gonzaga Collection.

287. Approximately fifty at a time.

288. I am indebted to Sir Hugh Roberts's 'The Royal Collection', and to David Watkin's 'The Queen's Gallery Rebuilt (pp. 63–6), both in Roberts, *Royal Treasures: A Golden Jubilee Celebration*.

289. In addition to Canaletto's well-known views of Venice, painted between 1725 and 1735, the collection has five less familiar paintings of Rome (*c.*1742).

290. George III favoured Stubbs, and also collected Sawrey Gilpin and Ben Marshall.

291. Francis Haskell, 'Charles I's Collection of Pictures', *The Late King's Goods; Collections, Possessions and Patronage of Charles I in the Light of the Commonwealth Sale Inventories*, pp. 202–3.

292. George V and George VI from Sir Kenneth Clark (1934–45) and Sir Anthony Blunt (1945–78).

293. Thomas Unwins, Surveyor of the Royal Pictures 1844–57, recorded that William IV 'did not know a picture from a window shutter'.

294. Lord Chesterfield, April 1753.

295. Philip Stanhope succeeded his natural father and became the 5th Earl. His portrait as a boy, by John Russell, is here.

296. Bode also advised Wernher's friend and partner, Alfred Beit, and J. P. Morgan.

297. Stevenson, M., p. 19.

298. Keeper at the Ashmolean Museum (q.v.).

299. Timothy Wilson, 'Italian Maiolica in the Wernher Collection', *Apollo*, June 2002.

300. Isabella d'Este, known as 'The Tenth Muse', was given these by her daughter, Eleonora Gonzaga, Duchess of Urbino, as a gift for her villa at Porto.

301. Dora Thornton, 'Painted Enamels of Limoges in the Wernher Collection', *Apollo*, June 2002.

302. Bradley and Pevsner, *London 6: Westminster*, p. 488.

303. Other architects who have worked on the site include Samuel Ware, James Gibbs, Sir James Pennethorne, William Kent, John Carr of York, Sidney Smirke, Sir T. G. Jackson, Norman Shaw and J. Cadbury-Brown.

304. The artist of this copy is not known. Suggested attributions include Marco d'Oggiono or Boltraffino, pupils of Leonardo, or Giampietrino, a follower.

305. The Tondo (*c.*1504–5) was commissioned by Taddeo Taddei for his palace in Florence, where it remained until bought by Sir George Beaumont in 1822. In accordance with his wishes, his widow bequeathed it to the Royal Academy in 1830.
306. Council minutes, 9 February 1771.
307. Reynolds (ed. Wark), p. 15.
308. Mary Anne Stevens, 'A Quiet Revolution: the Royal Academy 1900–1950', *The Edwardians and After*, p. 15.
309. Rutter, p. 53.
310. Twentieth-century diploma works include Sir Edwin Lutyens's New Delhi monument and Colin St John Wilson's cross-section drawings of the new British Library.
311. West's *The Graces Unveiling Nature* and Kauffmann's *Design, Invention, Composition, Colour* (*c.*1780), both moved from the Assembly Room at Somerset House.
312. Reynolds (ed. Wark), p. 15.
313. Ibid.
314. The Brazilian Alberto Santos-Dumont had invented powered, heavier-than-air balloons, and flown them successfully, in 1901 (see Hoffman).
315. Lane Fox.
316. Burton, who designed the triple screen at Hyde Park Corner and the Athenaeum Club, Lower Regent Street, had been the super-intending architect for the great conservatories at Chatsworth, 1836–41.
317. Pevsner, *London 2: South*, p. 510.
318. Turner was the leading designer and builder of glasshouses in Ireland. Kew's director Sir William Hooker said, 'He knows more about hothouses and greenhouses and the best principles of heating them than any man I ever met with' (Hooker's letter to Lord Lincoln, 1st February 1844, Nottingham University archive). Turner devised a means to span fifty feet using lighter wrought iron, thus obviating the need for pillars.
319. Throughout this entry I am deeply indebted to Ray Desmond, *Kew*, the definitive history by the former chief librarian at the Gardens.
320. England's oldest botanical garden, at Oxford (v. University of Oxford Botanic Garden), was founded in 1621, followed by Edinburgh in 1670.
321. Princess Augusta married George II's oldest son, Frederick Prince of Wales.

322. John Stuart, 3rd Earl of Bute. He created gardens at Luton Hoo and Highcliffe.
323. Sir William Chambers, architect of Somerset House, of the Courtauld Collection.
324. Letter by Banks to Clarke Abel, 10 February 1816, in the archives of the Botany Library of the Natural History Museum (the Davison Turner copies of Banks's letters, vol. 19, f. 240).
325. Bauer's drawings are in the Natural History Museum (q.v.), as are twelve paintings by Parkinson, watercolour on vellum.
326. Natural History Museum, Robert Brown Letters, vol. 1, f. 214.
327. Aeolus, son of Hippotas, was the king of storms and winds; the god of the wind who gave Ulysses all the winds of the world, tied up in a bag, to blow him back to Ithaca.
328. The Millennium Seed Bank is located at Wakehurst Place in Sussex as part of the Royal Botanic Gardens.
329. Made by Humphrey Cole in 1569.
330. Royal Warrant, dated 4 March 1675.
331. Improvised in this way, with a limited budget and time, it is Wren at his most informal.
332. This was only a loan from the Royal Society and was reclaimed on Moore's death in 1679. After fruitless applications to government for a replacement, Flamsteed built his own, a mural quadrant with a radius of fifty inches, in 1683.
333. One of these originals is in the British Museum (q.v.).
334. *Freeze* was an exhibition in the Port of London Authority building, London SE1, curated by Damien Hirst, with works by Hirst, Ian Davenport, Fiona Rae, Anya Gallaccio, Sarah Lucas, Stephen Park, Angela Bullock and Gary Hume.
335. Charles Saatchi, introduction to Ellis, p. 11.
336. The show featured Donald Judd, Brice Marden, Cy Twombly and Andy Warhol, March–October 1985.
337. Kent, p. 109.
338. Bowness, pp. 28–9.
339. 'In the 21st Century What Role Should a Museum Play?', NMSI brochure, July 2002, p. 3.
340. Ibid.
341. Ibid., p. 5.
342. Ibid.
343. Pevsner, *London*, p. 495.
344. v. Victoria and Albert Museum for the history of these collections.

345. Inherited from the Patent Museum.

346. John Bettes's portrait of *A Man in a Black Cap* (1545) is the earliest painting in the collection.

347. See the Chichester roundel (in the Chapel of the Bishop's Palace, Chichester), the Eton College frescoes (grisaille paintings by William Baker), the paintings in the Chapter House, West-minister, and such paintings as the screen in St Mary's, Silchester, Hampshire, and All Saint's, Croughton, Northamptonshire, whose wall paintings have figures whose 'swaying poses' are praised by Simon Jenkins (p. 489) and compared by the historian on medieval art Professor E. W. Tristram with Giotto. See too the Wilton diptych (*c.* 1395) in the National Gallery (q.v.).

348. I am greatly indebted throughout this entry to Frances Spalding.

349. Orrock advised, and bought for, Henry Lever as he built the collection with which he founded the Lady Lever art gallery (q.v.). His paper to the Society of Arts led to the article in *The Times* (below).

350. *The Times*, 13 March 1890. The article demanded to know 'Why cannot we have in London . . . a gallery that shall do for English art what the Luxembourg does for the French?'

351. Millbank Penitentiary was notorious for its employment of Jeremy Bentham's 'panoptic' design. Every one of its 1,500 cells could be seen from an 'inspection-station' at its core.

352. Pevsner, *London*, 1957, p. 518.

353. The report into 'the Retention of Important Pictures in This Country and other matters connected with National Collections', HMSO.

354. The Curzon Report, quoted by Ronald Alley in *Catalogue of the Tate Gallery's Collections of Modern Art*, pp. viii–xix.

355. A bequest established by the sculptor Sir Francis Chantrey.

356. Sir George Clausen (1905), Sir Lawrence Alma-Tadema (1909), Charles Shannon (1916). In 1883 they had bought *The Joyless Winter Day* by Joseph Farquharson, Laird of Finzean. Farquharson sent a (very skilled) snowy land-scape to the Royal Academy every year from 1894 to 1925 (with the exception of 1914). He painted these scenes of shepherds and sheep struggling in blizzard conditions from within a wooden hut, specially constructed with a large glass window and heated by a paraffin stove.

357. With the help of the Courtauld Fund (a trust set up in 1923), the Tate acquired paintings by Manet, Monet, Degas, Renoir and Cézanne, Seurat's *Bathers, Asnières* and van Gogh's *Chair and Pipe*.

358. In 1915 Duveen had paid for Romaine-Walker and Jenkins to redecorate the lower ground-floor galleries.

359. Buckman.

360. John Rothenstein was the son of the painter Sir William Rothenstein and brother of the Manchester Art Gallery benefactor Charles Rutherston.

361. Herbert Read, *The Listener*, 27 October 1938.

362. Rothenstein's two volumes of *Modern English Painters* demonstrate his understanding of these artists, all thirty-four of whom he (and/or his father) knew well, from W. R. Sickert and P. W. Wilson Steer to David Jones and Henry Moore.

363. It covered 100 finished oils, 182 unfinished and over 19,000 watercolours and drawings (Joll, Butlin and Hermann, p. 382).

364. One reserved for watercolours; one a study room.

365. Overlooked perhaps in recent years, Joseph Farington considered it one of his 'five favourite pictures'. (Farington, 3 May 1802).

366. John Ruskin, diary, 22 June 1840 (Cook and Wedderburn, p. 305).

367. One surprising omission is Samuel Palmer.

368. Sir Kenneth Clark in the foreword to the catalogue *Exhibition of Works from the Paul Oppé Collection*, Royal Academy of Arts, 1958.

369. Sir Lawrence Gowing in a taped conver-sation with Corinne Bellow, Tate Gallery Archive.

370. As a result her executors gave this collection to Leicester City Art Gallery, where Trevor Thomas and Hans Hess had mounted an exhibi-tion of German 20th-century painting in 1994.

371. Rothenstein, *Modern English Painters*, p. 15.

372. Nikolaus Pevsner, Reith Lectures, BBC Third Programme, October to November 1955. Extracts published in Games, pp. 174–240.

373. Games, p. 217.

374. Engineers, Mott, Hay and Anderson.

375. As the 1946 report, chaired by Vincent Massey, had recommended, splitting the Tate into two departments (British and Modern). Norman Reid, Director (1964–79), finally achieved this in 1964, appointing Ronald Alley as keeper of the Modern Department.

376. Charles Aitken refused the loan of two of Cézanne's *Portrait of Madame Cézanne*, in 1922, even though Duveen offered the money for it. No Cézanne entered the collection until 1929.

377. Minutes of the board meeting, 15 February 1945: Tate Gallery Archive.

378. The Redfern Gallery was prepared to sell it for less then £1,000. It went to the Museum of Modern Art in New York.

379. This resistance to contemporary sculpture was a continuation of J. B. Manson's attitude. In 1932 he vowed that no sculpture by Henry Moore would enter the collection while he was Director (tape of a conversation between Sir Robert Sainsbury and Corinne Bellow, Tate Gallery Archive).

380. Janet de Botton's gift in the 1990s of fifty-six works, including Andy Warhol's self-portrait (1956), Gilbert and George's *Red Money Trouble* (1977), one of Cindy Sherman's *Film Stills* (1978–80) and works by Gary Hume and Nancy Spero.

381. A grant of £50,000 over three years in 1955.

382. Nikolaus Pevsner, Reith Lectures, BBC Third Programme, Sunday 16 October 1955. Extracts published in Games, p. 174.

383. David Sylvester, 'Mayhem at Millbank', *London Review of Books*, 18 May 2000, p. 20.

384. This is a rather laboured reworking of Beatrice Warde's monumental 'THIS IS A PRINTING OFFICE' inscription at the Government Printing Office in Washington, DC. Mrs Warde, writing as Paul Beaujon (in *The Fleuron*, Number V, 1926), showed the true origin of the Garamond types.

385. Stephenson Blake had taken over more than forty type foundries.

386. Oxford University Press still has the original drawings.

387. *The Chase* was printed in the shop of William Bulmer with exquisite wood engravings by Bewick. They were childhood friends in Newcastle.

388. The Type Museum is shortly to launch an appeal to acquire the whole working library of Berthold Wolpe.

389. From a paper, 'Typography in Art Education', by Beatrice Warde, quoted in *Concealing Some Words by Beatrice Warde and Types by Varied Hands*, reprinted in May 1953 to commemorate a visit to the United States by Mrs Warde.

390. Beatrice Warde, ibid., from an address to the British Guild, London.

391. Flaxman had his models cast in plaster rather than clay as was more normal. He rarely worked the finished marble himself so these plaster casts are where his work can be most readily seen at first hand.

392. T. L. Donaldson, the college's professor of architecture, remodelled Wilkins's interiors in 1848–9, building a main staircase and, with C. R. Cockerell and Sir Charles Eastlake, adapting the rotunda to take Flaxman's work.

393. Sir Francis Baring (d.1810) was founder of the finance house Baring Brothers & Co., and director and chairman of the East India Company.

394. Sherborn's major work was the *Index Animalium*, published over thirty years in thirty-three parts – the zoological equivalent of the *Dictionary of National Biography*. For this he was awarded a D.Sc. (honoris causa) from Oxford University in 1931, the same year as Albert Einstein.

395. Turner prepared these proofs himself.

396. Prints were made of seven of the nine canvases that comprise *The Triumphs of Caesar* at Hampton Court Palace (q.v.). *The Elephants* and *The Trophies* correspond to the fifth and sixth canvases.

397. Other students taught by Tonks included Edward Wadsworth, C. R. W. Nevinson, Mark Gertler, John Currie, Jacques Raverat, Gwen Darwin, Paul Nash, William Roberts and (earlier) Dora Carrington, William and Isaac Rosenberg, William Orpen, Albert Rutherson and Ambrose McEvoy. Wyndham Lewis has no oil painting in the collection since he won the prize for drawing but not for painting.

398. It is now in the Tate.

399. Spencer, p. 104.

400. Ibid., p. 103.

401. Nash, pp. 92–3.

402. Henry Tonks in a letter to Spencer's parents, 1912, quoted by Collis, p. 39.

403. Mary Hutchinson, introduction to Hone.

404. The Mermaid was designed by William Kent. The V&A has Kent's preparatory drawing for this, acquired eight years after the model, in 1946.

405. Only sixty pieces of Medici Porcelain survive, of which the V&A has nine. Sir Charles

Robinson described their discovery, in 1860, as unearthing 'a new feature in the history of the art' (*Art Journal*, October 1860).

406. The Schools of Design (1837) were set up to raise the standard of British manufacturers by training good designers, in response to the report of a House of Commons Committee that concluded that British manufacturing lagged behind its continental competitors. The schools' collections were for instruction and, although the schools were replaced by the National Course of Art Instruction (1853), their supporting collections in the Museum of Manufactures remained pedagogical. The first exhibition in Marlborough House in 1852 had a room to show 'Examples of False Principles in Decoration', which enraged Charles Dickens.

407. A preparatory study for the sculpture on the tomb of Pope Julius II.

408. Robinson, J.; Maclagan and Longhurst; Pope-Hennessy and Lightbrown. Robinson was, in the words of Anna Somers Cocks, 'like an explorer in virgin territory' (p. 61). All he had to guide him were Vasari and one book on Italian sculpture by Count Cicognara.

409. Perhaps made by Robert Arnould Drais *c.* 1780. Its association with Marie-Antoinette, believed by Jones, has since been questioned.

410. The sale of Bernal's collection at Christie's, in 4,294 lots, lasted thirty-two days.

411. Referring to the finished tapestry, Vasari wrote, 'This work was executed so marvellously that it arouses astonishment in whoever beholds it.'

412. Fowke also built the Royal Albert Hall and the Royal Scottish Museum (v. the Museum of Scotland) and was the architect originally chosen for the Natural History Museum. He died before work here could begin.

413. In 1835 the House of Commons Select Committe on Arts and Manufactures recommended the setting up of Schools of Design in several cities. The first of these, the London School of Design, from which the V&A evolved, was founded in 1837, in Somerset House, with a small library, a group of plaster casts and a budget for acquiring examples of well designed manufactures, old and new, initially purchased from the Great Exhibition. The London School's first Headmaster was the painter, William Dyce. By the 1850s most of the schools had closed.

414. It had been revived in 1843 at the Sèvres factory, who showed it at the 1851 Great Exhibition.

415. Here too is the cast made by Domenico Brucciani in 1873 of the Portico de la Gloria from the west front of Santiago Cathedral, in J. Robinson's view 'incomparably the most important monument of sculpture and ornamental detail of its epoch'. A photograph (1866) of it by Thurston Thompson is in the Photographic Collection.

416. Cole had already bought, in 1856, a large group of photographs from an exhibition at the Photographic Society of London. He set up a dark room in the museum and employed Charles Thurston Thompson as the museum's photographer.

417. Cole had numerous objects copied in electrotype, for example a silver-gilt Flemish standing cup and cover (1611–12) copied in electrotype in 1863.

418. Now on the ground floor between the temporary exhibition galleries.

419. The Chinese, Japanese, Korean, Islamic and Indian Collections.

420. Donated by Auguste Rodin in 1914 to commemorate Anglo-French brotherhood.

421. In the Fitzwilliam Museum, National Gallery, the National Gallery of Scotland, the Ashmolean, etc. (all q.v.).

422. It was sold as scrap iron when the Palais Mazarin, later the Banque Nationale and then the Bibliothèque Nationale, was reconstructed (1855–62).

423. Its movement by C. Martinot (1726).

424. Bought at the Cordier sale in 1861.

425. He was the model for the Marquess of Steyne in Thackeray's *Vanity Fair* and for Lord Monmouth in Disraeli's *Coningsby*.

426. *Perseus and Andromeda* is one of six paintings for Philip II that Titian based on scenes from Ovid's *Metamorphoses*. Two are in the Prado in Madrid (*Venus and Adonis*, and *Danaë and the Shower of Gold*), two are in the Scottish National Gallery (q.v.) (*Diana and Actaeon*, and *Diana and Callisto*) and one, *The Rape of Europa*, is in the Isabella Stewart Gardner Museum in Boston, Massachusetts.

427. Delaroche's historical tableaux: *Cardinal Mazarin's Last Sickness* and *The State Barge of Cardinal Richelieu on the Rhône*. There are only two of the Delaroche historical tableaux in the collection and they are fine paintings.

428. Nieuwerkerke was Napoleon III's Surintendant des Beaux-Arts and Director of the Louvre. He fled Paris during the siege.

429. Meyrick was the pioneer of the study of arms and armour in England.

430. In comparison the National Gallery (q.v.) has one painting by Watteau, two each by Boucher and Nattier, three by Greuze, one by Fragonard and none by Oudry. Only with the two Lancret series, *The Four Ages of Man* and *The Four Times of the Day*, can it attempt to match the Wallace. Lancret is better represented at the Wallace Collection than at the National Gallery.

431. The 4th Marquess bought this from the Comte de Morny's sale in 1848 for what the *Art Union* called an 'outrageous price'. It, and Watteau's *Fête in the Park* (also here) anticipate Manet's *Déjeuner Sur L'Herbe* and the less peaceful *Music in the Tuileries Gardens* (National Gallery, q.v.).

432. Certainly a pendant to the *Chateau de Steen* in the National Gallery (q.v.) and painted at the same time as the *Landscape by Moonlight* (1636–7), as Rubens revelled in the light and countryside around Vilvored and Mechliw where he had bought the Chateau de Steen in 1635.

433. *Wallace Collection Catalogue*, p. xv.

434. The 4th Marquess lent forty-four paintings to the famous 1857 Art Treasures exhibition at Manchester, where they filled a wall of the gallery. When asked whether he would miss them he replied 'Au fait, je ne suis pas faché d'envoyer mes tableaux à Manchester; ce sera pour moi une occasion de les voir' (*Gazette des Beaux Arts*, IV, 1859, p. 53, and Chapter Blanc, quoted in the *Wallace Collection Catalogue*, p. xvi). The paintings lent included the Poussin, Rembrandt and Rubens referred to above, and Reynolds's *Nelly O'Brien* and *The Strawberry Girl*, Gainsborough's *Mrs Robinson* ('Perdita'), five paintings by Murillo, and Andrea del Sarto's *The Virgin and Child, with St John the Baptist and Two Angels*, but not, surprisingly, Titian's *Perseus and Andromeda*.

435. The ring was given to the Dean of Westminster in 1927 by Ernest Makowen.

436. Henry V's stepmother was Joan of Navarre.

437. The correct procedures to be followed 'when that a king annoynted is deceased' are laid out in a paper delivered to the Society of Antiquaries in London in January 1769 by Sir Thomas Aster: 'Ceremonial of the Burial of King Edward IV, from a MS of the Late Mr Anstis', *Archaelogia 1*, 1779, pp. 350–57, followed until the funeral of James I in 1625.

438. Traces of eyebrow hairs remain. Analysed by Dr H. S. Holden of the Metropolitan Police Laboratory, they proved to be those of a small dog. For this and for much else I am indebted to Harvey and Mortimer, p. 32.

439. Twelve different grass seeds were identified in the hay.

440. College of Arms MS 1.11, f. 85. The manuscript describes her image and identifies the man who carved the effigy, 'Mr Laurence' (Laurence Elm) 'and Frederick his mate'. The funeral of Elizabeth is also described in the Wriothesley manuscripts in the British Library (q.v), BL Add. 45131 ff. 41v–47, from the collection of Sir Thomas Wriothesley, Garter King of Arms, 1505–34.

441. Julian Litten, 'The Funeral Effigy: Its function and Purpose', in Harvey and Mortimer, p.3. All from terms in use between 1413 and 1553.

442. Colt came to England from Arras as a religious refugee in the mid 1590s. His tomb effigies of Elizabeth I, and of James I's two infant children, are in the abbey; his tomb of the first Earl of Salisbury (1614) is at Hatfield House.

443. Tanner and Nevinson.

444. *Dictionary of National Biography*. Charles II was six feet two inches tall.

445. Revelation, chapter 5, verses 7–8: 'The Lamb … took the scroll … the twenty-four elders fell down before the Lamb.'

446. MacCarthy, *William Morris*, p. 267.

447. William Morris, 'The Lesser Arts of Life', lecture.

448. The *Woodpecker* tapestry was designed by Morris and woven at his Merton Abbey workshops in 1885.

449. MacCarthy, *William Morris*, p. 16.

450. See their work at Cheltenham Art Gallery and Museum (q.v.).

451. See his benefactions to Fitzwilliam Museum (q.v.) and Dulwich Picture Gallery (q.v.).

452. National Trust.

Photographic Acknowledgements

p. ii Sir John Soane's Museum, London: the Dome Area with R. W. Siever's bust of Sir Thomas Lawrence (by courtesy of the Trustees of Sir John Soane's Museum; photographer Martin Charles)

p. vi Charles Rennie Mackintosh furniture, Hunterian Art Gallery (© Hunterian Art Gallery, University of Glasgow)

THE SOUTH-WEST

p. 8 *Rosamund Sargent*, 1749, Allan Ramsay, oil on canvas 76.2 × 63.5 cm (© Holburne Museum of Art)

p. 12 Cocktail dress of cream silk gauze with applied diamanté and ostrich feathers, designed by Yves St Laurent, 1967–8, Museum of Costume (© Bath and North East Somerset Museums Council)

p. 14 The Roman Baths, Bath (Heritage Services, Bath and North East Somerset Museums Council)

p. 16 *The Canal Bridge, Sydney Gardens, Bath*, John Nash (© Victoria Art Gallery, Bath and North East Somerset Museums Council)

p. 24 *The State Entry Procession at the 1903 Delhi Durbar*, 1903, Roderick Mackenzie (© British Empire and Commonwealth Museum)

p. 26 Silverware (© Cheltenham Art Gallery and Museum)

p. 33 Tahitian mourner's costume (© Exeter City Museums and Art Gallery, Royal Albert Memorial Museum and Art Gallery, Exeter City Council)

p. 35 Falmouth flotilla (© The National Maritime Museum, Cornwall)

p. 39 *The Rain it Raineth Every Day*, Norman Garstin (© Penlee House Gallery and Museum)

p. 40 Portrait of Charles Rogers FRS FSA (1711–84), 1777, oil on canvas, Sir Joshua Reynolds PRA (1723–92) (© Cottonian Collection: Plymouth City Museum and Art Gallery)

p. 42 A plate from the Frog Service, Wedgwood (© Salisbury and South Wiltshire Museum)

p. 47 *Spring*, 1966, Barbara Hepworth, Barbara Hepworth Museum and Sculpture Garden (© Bowness, the Hepworth Estate)

p. 50 *Window for St Ives*, 1992, Patrick Heron, coloured glass laminated on to safety glass by Dercx and Co. (© Tate St Ives; photographer Bob Berry)

p. 55 *Dido and Aeneas*, AD 350, mosaic (© Somerset County Museums Service)

p. 59 Fleet Air Arm Museum (photography © David O'Brien)

THE SOUTH-EAST

p. 66 Diorama (© The Powell-Cotton Museum Trust, Quex House and Gardens)

p. 70 Bird of paradise roller, Raggi: image courtesy of the Booth Museum of Natural History, Brighton

p. 72 The Music Room, Frederick Crace, Royal Pavilion, Brighton (© Brighton and Hove Museums Service)

p. 77 *Swingeing London '67*, 1967–8, Richard Hamilton, mixed media, Wilson gift through the NACF (Pallant House Gallery)

p. 82 Chapel Royal, Hampton Court Palace, Sir Christopher Wren (© Historic Royal Palaces)

p. 234 Courtesy of the Spode Museum Trust (© Spode)

p. 240 (© The Potteries Museum and Art Gallery, City of Stoke-on-Trent)

p. 244 Walter Rothschild Collection (© The Natural History Museum, London)

p. 246 *Mrs Sheridan as St Cecilia,* Sir Joshua Reynolds, Waddesdon Manor, The Rothschild Collection (The National Trust)

p. 251 *Adonis in Y-fronts,* Richard Hamilton, courtesy of The Wolverhampton Museum and Art Gallery (© ARS)

p. 255 Willis organ (© Blenheim Palace)

p. 257 Manuscript, Edward Elgar (courtesy of the Elgar Birthplace Museum)

THE NORTH-WEST

p. 264 *Dr George Ainslie Johnson,* Kurt Schwitters (© The Armitt Trust)

p. 269 (© Blackwell Arts and Craft House, Cumbria)

p. 274 *An Episode in the Happier Days of Charles I,* Frederick Goodall, Bury Art Gallery and Museum (© The Bridgeman Art Library)

p. 277 *Waterfall and Silver Birches at Brantwood,* John Ruskin, The Ruskin Museum, Coniston

p. 282 *The Leveson-Gower Children,* George Romney, reproduced by courtesy of Abbot Hall Art Gallery, Kendal, Cumbria

p. 287 Benin *Head of Queen Mother,* World Museum Liverpool (© National Museums, Liverpool)

p. 289 The Sculpture Gallery, Walker Art Gallery (© National Museums, Liverpool)

p. 292 Cabinet, Sudley House (© National Museums, Liverpool)

p. 296 *The Light at the End of the World,* Holman Hunt (© Manchester Art Callery, Manchester City Galleries)

p. 302 'The living splendid leaf frog, *Agalychnis calcarifer*' (Manchester Museum, University of Manchester)

p. 304 *Got a Girl,* Peter Blake (© The Whitworth Art Gallery, University of Manchester, and the Artist)

p. 312 *Circe Offering the Cup to Ulysses,* J. W. Waterhouse (© Gallery Oldham)

p. 316 *Seascape,* L. S. Lowry, Lowry Centre (© The Lowry Collection, Salford)

p. 320 *Madonna and Child with Angels,* Di Cione (© Astley Cheetham Art Collection, Thameside Museums and Galleries Service)

p. 322 (© Quarry Bank Mill)

p. 324 Lady Lever art gallery (© National Museums, Liverpool)

THE NORTH-EAST

p. 333 *Crucifixion,* The Master of the Virgin Inter Virgines (© The Bowes Museum; photograph Sid Nevill)

p. 335 Statuette (© Oriental Museum, University of Durham)

p. 338 The Carriage House (© Beamish, The North of England Open Air Museum)

p. 342 *Merzbarn* (1947–8) Kurt Schwitters 36.45 × 57 mm, stone, plaster, mixed media (© The Bridgeman Art Library) Hatton Gallery

p. 347 *Hancock in his Studio,* Henry Hetherington Emmerson (© The Natural History Society of Northumbria)

p. 351 'Close view of the fireplace wall at Cherryburn' (© National Trust Photographic Library)

p. 353 Sunderland Museum and Art Gallery (© Tyne and Wear Museums)

YORKSHIRE AND HUMBERSIDE

p. 365 *La Madonna Riposata,* Julia Margaret Cameron, National Museum of Photography, Film and Television (© Science Museum/Science and Society Picture Library)

p. 368 *Mughal ,* Sarbjit Natt, Cartwright Hall (© The Bridgeman Art Library)

p. 370 Brontë Parsonage (© The Brontë Society)

WALES

p. 520 National Library of Wales (© Llyfrgell Genedlaethol Cymru)
p. 522 *Fragment as a Complete Form* and *Bowl with Graphics*, 1972, George Baldwin, porcelain (© The School of Art Museum and Gallery, The University of Wales, Aberystwyth)
p. 526 Charles Tunnicliffe watercolour (© Anglesey Museums and Culture)
p. 529 Big Pit: used by permission of the National Museums and Galleries of Wales
p. 531 George Frederick Watts, self-portrait, *c.* 1879, Bodelwyddan Castle (© National Portrait Gallery, London)
p. 537 *La Parisienne*, Renoir (© National Museums and Galleries of Wales)
p. 541 Welsh Slate Museum (© National Museums and Galleries of Wales)
p. 542–3 Mural, Rex Whistler, Plas Newydd (© National Trust Photographic Library)
p. 545 *Interior of Cyfarthfa Castle Ironworks at Night*, Penry Williams, Cyfarthfa Castle (© Cyfarthfa Castle Museum and Art Gallery, Merthyr Tydfil)
p. 548 Museum of Welsh Life, St Fagans (© National Museums and Galleries of Wales)
p. 555 'Close up of servant call bells', Erddig (© National Trust Photographic Library)

NORTHERN IRELAND

p. 561 Linen Hall: courtesy of the Linen Hall Library
p. 566 Castle Coole (© National Trust Photographic Library)

LONDON

p. 582 *Nude*, 1938, Mark Gertler (1891–1939), oil on canvas, Ben Uri Gallery, The London Jewish Museum of Art
p. 584 (© Bethnal Green Museum of Childhood)
p. 586 (© The British Library)
p. 589 (© The British Museum)
p. 594 *La Loge*, Renoir (The Samuel Courtauld Trust, Courtauld Institute of Art Gallery, London)
p. 602 By permission of the Trustees of Dulwich Picture Gallery
p. 606 *Modern Idol*, Umberto Boccioni (© Estorick Foundation © DACS)
p. 609 (© The Fashion and Textile Museum)
p. 613 *Captain Thomas Coram*, William Hogarth (© The Foundling Museum Trust)
p. 617 (© The Geffrye Museum, London)
p. 623 Sri Lankan mask, Centenary Gallery, Horniman Museum, photography Heini Schneebeli
p. 628 Hunterian Museum (© The Royal College of Surgeons of England)
p. 632 Rimmonim, Jewish Museum (© Jewish Museum, London)
p. 635 *Mary, Countess Howe*, Thomas Gainsborough, Kenwood House, English Heritage Photographic Library
p. 638 Detail of the Arab Hall, Leighton House, 1870s, Aitchison (© The Bridgeman Art Library)
p. 646 *The Battle of Isandhlwana*, oil on canvas, *c.* 1885, Charles Edwin Fripp (© National Army Museum)
p. 648 *The Nativity,* Piero della Francesca, National Gallery (© National Gallery Picture Library)
p. 651 *Death of Nelson*, Arthur William Devis (© National Maritime Museum)
p. 656 The Ondaatje Wing, National Portrait Gallery, Jeremy Dixon (© Dennis Gilbert/VIEW; photographer Edward Jones)
pp. 660–1 Natural history (© The Natural History Museum, London)
p. 662 *Old Operating Theatre*, William Hogarth (© Old Operating Theatre Museum)
p. 664 'Temple Vases', 1351 (© Percival David Foundation of Chinese Art)
p. 667 Shabti (© The Petrie Museum, University College London)
p. 670 *Charles I with Monsieur de St Antoine*, Van Dyck (The Royal Collection © 2004, Her Majesty Queen Elizabeth II)

p. 676 (© Royal Air Force Museum)

pp. 678–9 The Palm House (© Royal Botanic Gardens)

p. 681 The Royal Observatory (© National Maritime Museums)

p. 683 *My Bed,* Tracey Emin, reproduced by kind permission of the Saatchi Gallery

p. 685 Templates from Crick and Watson's DNA molecular model (© Science Museum/Science and Society Picture Library)

p. 690 *The Decline of the Carthaginian Empire,* exhibited 1817, J. M. W. Turner, oil on canvas, bequeathed by the artist 1856 (© Tate Britain Collection)

p. 694 Tate Modern (© Tate Picture Library)

p. 700 *The Healing of the Lame Man,* Raphael, cartoon, The Victoria & Albert Museum/Royal Collection

p. 702 *The Swing,* Fragonard, reproduced by kind permission of the Trustees of The Wallace Collection, London

p. 707 William Morris's satchel and Socialist pamphlets (© William Morris Gallery, London)

APPENDIX

p. 718 *Tourists,* Duane Hanson, Scottish National Gallery of Modern Art (© National Galleries of Scotland Picture Library)

Every effort has been made to trace copyright holders. The author and publisher will be happy to correct any error of omission or commission at the earliest opportunity.

Name Index

Included are names of those involved in the design and maintenance of the museums and galleries: architects and designers; founders, collectors, benefactors and patrons; directors and curators; also commentators. Individual artists and works are not listed unless subject to significant notice.

excavations at Kahun and Amarna, 302
1880s and 1890s finds, 474
his book, *Tools and Weapons*, inspires Raphael Salaman, 109
life's work at University College, London, 666–7
popularises archaeology, xix
Petty, Revd William, 224
Pevsner, Sir Nikolaus
on Ascott, 202
on Bass malthouses, 167
on Blackburn Museum, 265
on Blomfield, 7, 180
on Burlington House, 674
on Calke Abbey, 193
on English art, 693–4
on Ironbridge, 242
on Kew Palm House, 677
on Liverpool docks, 286
on National Railway Museum, 419
omits Northern Ireland from comment, 562
on Russell-Cotes Gallery, 18
silence on Herbert Art Gallery, Coventry, 213
on Sunderland Museum, 354
on Tate Britain building, 690
on Wolverhampton Museum, 250
Phelips family, 38
Philip, Rosalind Birnie, 481
Philips, Sir Claude, 704
Philips, John, 221
Phillip, Charles, 154
Phillips, Henry, 112
Phillips, Tom, 54, 78, 342, 657–8
Phillpotts, Lt. George, 32
Philpot, Glyn, 68, 375
Piano, Renzo, 693
Pick, Frank, 640
Pickford, Joseph, 151, 169
Pierce, Harry, 269
Piggott, Peggy, 154
Piggott, Stuart, 5–6, 31, 43, 154
Pinchen, Robert T., 239
'Pincher Jack', 109
Pineau, Nicolas, 332
Pirrie, George, 436
Pitt Rivers, Lt. Gen. Augustus Henry Lane Fox
archaeology, xviii-xix
background and interests, 230–2
on context of excavated objects, 496

on evolution of rifle, 677
Salisbury collection, 41–3
scholarship, 32
scientific excavation, 57
on trade and tools, 109
Planché, André, 169, 170, 275
Playfair, John, 459
Playfair, William Henry, 453, 460
Plenty, William, 89
Plura, Giuseppe, 10
Pollock, Benjamin, 668
Ponsonby, Madeleine, 410
Ponsonby, Sarah, 515–16
Pope, Alexander, 641
Pope-Hennessy, Sir John, xxv, 699–700
Porden, William, 71
Porta, Battista, 28
Porter, Enid, 123
Portington, William, 103–4
Potter, Beatrix, 263, 265
Potter, Joseph, 542
Poussin, Nicolas, 112, 126, 151, 206, 288, 462, 604, 703
Powell Brothers and Whittaker, 199
Powell and Moya (architects), 226, 228
Powell-Cotton, Major Percy Horace Gordon, 65
Powis, William Herbert, 1st Marquess of, 553
Powis, William Herbert, 2nd Marquess of, 553
Poynter, Sir Edward, 599, 600
Pratt, Dallas, 6–7
Pratt and Sons (taxidermists), 69
Preece, Rosemary, 406
Preston, John, 567
Pretty, Edith May, 153–4
Price, Uvedale, 527
Priestley, Joseph, 195, 210
Pringle Richards Sharratt (architects), 311, 398
Prior, Melton, 69
Pritchard, E. Evans, 624
Pritchard, Thomas Farnolls, 242
Procter, Dod, 1, 38–9, 41, 241, 345, 375, 551
Prosser, Thomas, 419
Prout, Samuel, 271
Prunier, Madame (restaurateur), 142
Pryce, Gerald Spencer, 310
Pugin, Augustus Welby Northmore, xx, 99, 214, 237, 362, 535, 625–6
Pye, William, 354
Pye-Smith, Dr, 372
Pyke Thompson, James, 536

General Index

Subject headings (e.g. animals; ethnography) are not comprehensive, and show only the more significant collections.

PENGUIN ARCHITECTURE

THE EDIFICE COMPLEX:
HOW THE RICH AND POWERFUL SHAPE THE WORLD
DEYAN SUDJIC

Why have presidents, prime ministers, mayors, millionaires and despots come to share such a fascination with grand designs? What makes the rich and powerful want to leave their mark on the world?

In *The Edifice Complex* renowned writer and critic Deyan Sudjic explores the intimate relationship between buildings, power, money and politics in society. Architecture, he shows, has a unique place in the wielding of authority. It can be used to impress, glorify or intimidate; as an instrument of nation-building and statecraft, an expression of ego or a bid for immortality. From Blair to Mitterrand, from Hitler to Stalin to Saddam Hussein, architecture has become an end in itself, as well as a means to an end.

Drawing on twenty years' thinking about and looking at buildings, on constant travels around the globe, and an unsurpassed knowledge of the major figures in contemporary architecture, Sudjic examines the greatest and most disastrous edifices that humankind has produced, and why they were built: from Winston Churchill's theatrical reconstruction of the House of Commons to the new structure on the twin towers' site, from Mussolini's marble-floored gym to the Mother of All Battles Mosque in Baghdad, from the telling contents of US presidential libraries to Tony Blair's championing of the doomed Millennium Dome. And he looks at the architects themselves – among others Albert Speer, Le Corbusier, Norman Foster and Leon Krier – and their role in the political arena.

This is a book of genuine vision and timeliness, throwing new light on the motivations of those who govern us, and on our profound relationship with the contemporary man made world. It is essential reading for anyone interested in the power of architecture – or the architecture of power.

PENGUIN BIOGRAPHY

MATISSE THE MASTER: THE CONQUEST OF COLOUR, 1909–1954
HILARY SPURLING

'If my story were ever to be written down truthfully from start to finish, it would amaze everyone,' wrote Henri Matisse.

It is hard to believe today that Matisse, whose exhibitions draw huge crowds world-wide, was once almost universally reviled and ridiculed. His response was neither to protest nor to retreat. He simply pushed on from one innovation to the next, and left the world to draw its own conclusions. Unfortunately, these were generally false and often damaging. Throughout his life and afterwards, people fantasised about his models and circulated fabrications about his private life.

Fifty years after his death, *Matisse the Master* shows us the painter as he saw himself. With unprecedented and unrestricted access to his voluminous family correspondence, and other new material in private archives, Hilary Spurling documents a lifetime of desperation and self-doubt, exacerbated by Matisse's attempts to counteract the violence and disruption of the twentieth century in paintings that seem now effortlessly serene, radiant and stable.

If you have ever wondered how anyone with such a tame, dull public image as Matisse could have painted such rich, mysteriously moving pictures, let alone produced the radical cut-paper and stained-glass inventions of his last years, here is the answer. They were made by the real Matisse, whose true story has been written down at last from start to finish by his first biographer, Hilary Spurling.

Praise for *The Unknown Matisse: The Early Years, 1869–1908*:

'A marvellous sunburst of a biography... Shows Hilary Spurling at her brilliant best as passionate scholar, traveller and storyteller'
Richard Holmes, *Daily Telegraph*

'A superlative achievement ... Outstanding as an interpreter of his art and life alike, Spurling provides fresh illumination on every page' Richard Cork, *The Times*

read more

PENGUIN BIOGRAPHY

LEONARDO DA VINCI: THE FLIGHTS OF THE MIND
CHARLES NICHOLL

'Gripping, beguiling ... brings a genius down from his lonely pedestal and into the world' *Daily Telegraph*

'Charles Nicholl, in this bright, cunning, intrepidly intelligent biographical study, has startlingly demystified his enigmatic subject' Peter Conrad, *Observer*

Leonardo da Vinci is the most mysterious of all the great artists, continuing to inspire and intrigue centuries after his death. Who lies beneath the legend of the 'Renaissance genius'? What is the real story behind his elusive masterpieces and tantalizing notebooks?

Charles Nicholl's compelling, lyrical biography explores Leonardo's life – from his beginnings as an illegitimate child in Tuscany to the creation of his great works and his final days – as never before. Delving into hidden corners of his manuscripts and unravelling years of myth and mystery, he brilliantly illuminates the man behind the enigma.

'A splendid and encompassing biography' Peter Ackroyd, *The Times*

'*Leonardo da Vinci* isn't merely a lovely book, it's Leonardesque ... At its best, it glows' David Gelernter, *The New York Times*

'A masterpiece of imaginative reconstruction' Richard Holmes, *Daily Telegraph*, Books of the Year

'Fresh ... vivid ... the most fully human Leonardo we have' Adam Gopnik, *New Yorker*

PENGUIN TRAVEL/ARCHITECTURE

ENGLAND'S THOUSAND BEST CHURCHES
SIMON JENKINS

'Think of Simon Jenkins's book as a hip flask and carry it always' *Daily Mail*

'Marvellous ... this is a book to be kept by the bed or, better still, in the car. A constant excuse to leave the bold highway and let the imagination, body and soul, wander a little' Anna Ford, *Sunday Telegraph*

England's Thousand Best Churches is a celebration of our most glorious and lasting national monuments. Simon Jenkins has travelled England to select the finest churches of all periods and styles, revealing not only an unparalleled collection of English art, but the history of a people.

• With churches from all periods and denominations

• Organized county-by-county for easy use

• Features a star ratings system for each church

• Highlights the very best 100

'Every house in England should have a copy of this book' Auberon Waugh, *Literary Review* Book of the Century

'So excellent are Paul Barker's pictures ... so mouthwatering are Jenkins's descriptions of the buildings he loves, that you want to visit the churches instantly' Andrew Lloyd Webber, *Daily Telegraph*

'In his journeys through the English counties, greater knowledge has deepened his sense that so many of our churches are celebrations in wood and stone of the spirit of the people of England, and they continue to be doors into mystery' Richard Chartres, *The Times*

Penguin Travel/Architecture

ENGLAND'S THOUSAND BEST HOUSES
SIMON JENKINS

'The perfect guide to England's best houses' *Country Life*

'Buy, beg, borrow or steal a copy to keep in the car' *Daily Mail*

'This wonderful book will be in everyone's car pocket for decades …
It makes me want to take a year off … and plunge off into what Jenkins has
memorably described as "the theatre of our shared memory"'
Adam Nicolson, *Evening Standard*

England's houses are a treasure trove of riches and a unique, living record of
the nation's history. Simon Jenkins's lavishly illustrated guide selects the finest
homes throughout the land, from Cornwall to Cumbria, in a glorious
celebration of English life.

• Ranges from famous stately homes and palaces to humble cottages and huts

• Organized county-by-county for easy use

• Features a star ratings system for each house

• Highlights the very best 100 of all the properties in the country

'A heritage enthusiast's *Ode To Joy* … Any passably cultured inhabitant of the
British Isles should ask for, say, three or four copies of this book'
Max Hastings, *Sunday Telegraph*

'This is the perfect book to have beside your bed or on the back seat of your car
… Jenkins's zeal is infectious. He quite rightly sees England's greatest houses as
collectively nothing less than a wonder of the world' Geordie Greig,
Literary Review

'A great book … a feast, enlivened by the sort of tasty snippets that only a
master journalist can produce' Hugh Massingberd, *Daily Telegraph*